BRADLEY

BERLIN ◉

POL.

•LEIPZIG

CZECH.

RNBERG

•MUNICH

AUS.

YUGO.

EISENHOWER

Eisenhower's Lieutenants

RUSSELL F. WEIGLEY

Eisenhower's LIEUTENANTS

*The Campaign of France
and Germany 1944–1945*

BLOOMINGTON

Indiana University Press

Photos courtesy of National Archives, Office of War Information.

Scattered quotations from *The Patton Papers 1940–1945* by Martin Blumenson, © 1974 by Martin Blumenson, reprinted by permission of the publisher, Houghton Mifflin Company.

Quotations from *The Papers of Dwight David Eisenhower: The War Years*, edited by Alfred D. Chandler, Jr., © 1970 by the Johns Hopkins Press, reprinted by permission of Johns Hopkins University Press.

Library of Congress Cataloging in Publication Data

Weigley, Russell Frank.
    Eisenhower's lieutenants.

    Includes bibliographical references and index.
    1. World War, 1939–1945—Campaigns—France (1944–1945) 2. World War, 1939–1945—Campaigns—Germany. 3. World War, 1939–1945—United States. 4. France—History—German occupation, 1940–1945. 5. Germany—History—1933–1945. 6. United States. Army—Biography. 7. Generals—United States—Biography. I. Title.
    D761.W4   940.54′21   80-8175
ISBN 0-253-13333-5   1 2 3 4 5 85 84 83 82 81

for Jared and Catherine

CONTENTS

PART TWO: NORMANDY

PART THREE: FRANCE

Maps

Preface

I have long been troubled by the tendency of the "new" military history of the post-1945 era, the history of armies and soldiers in their social and political context, to avoid venturing into the heat of battle. This avoidance is in part an effort to generate supposed academic and intellectual respectability for modern military history by creating a sizable distance between it and the traditional "drum-and-trumpet" school of military writing. It stems also from the sound recognition that peacetime developments have often more strongly influenced the impact of armies upon the societies they serve, and of the societies upon the armies, than have the relatively brief cataclysms of war. My own work, as well as that of other military historians, has reflected this tendency. Nevertheless, it is to prepare for and to wage war that armies primarily exist, and for the military historian to fail to carry his studies from the political and social evolution of peace to the test of war is to leave his work grotesquely incomplete. A day's trial by battle often reveals more of the essential nature of an army than a generation of peace.

Therefore, having written books about the U.S. Army in institutional, organizational terms and in terms of American military thought, I believe it is appropriate to turn to a study of those military institutions and thought as applied to battle, and specifically to a history of the American army's greatest campaign, told from the perspective of its commanders.

The U.S. army's campaign in France, the Low Countries, and Germany in World War II was its greatest, both in numbers engaged and in geographic sweep, and so it seemed the most appropriate subject through which to apply my earlier conclusions about American military history at the cutting edge of combat. That campaign was also significant as the climactic test of whether an army first nurtured as a constabulary force for the North American Indian frontier could successfully transform itself into a serious competitor of European armies long accustomed to international contests on a grand scale. In the European campaign of 1944–1945, the American army's past clashed with this other, very different, kind of military past, giving the campaign a special additional interest and savor.

At the same time that the American army was preparing itself for this crucial test in European warfare, during the months of World War II preceding the 6th of June 1944, one of America's leading military historians was engaged in writing a history similar to the present work, but concerned with an American army of the nineteenth century. He was also feeling troubled by the difficulties and possibly the disasters that his knowledge of history warned him might lie ahead in Europe. Still, that historian's knowledge of the

American military past afforded him an ultimate confidence in our military capacities as well. In the foreword to the first volume of his *Lee's Lieutenants: A Study in Command*, published in 1942, Douglas Southall Freeman wrote in this regard:

> . . . something, perhaps, may be gained by printing in the first year of this nation's greatest war, the story of the difficulties that had to be overcome in an earlier struggle before the command of the army became measurably qualified for the task assigned to it. If the recount of the change of officers in the first fifteen months of the [Civil] war in Virginia seems discouraging, the events that followed the reorganization [of the Army of Northern Virginia] of July, 1862, are assurance that where the supreme command is capable, fair-minded and diligent, the search for competent executive officers is not in vain. The Lee and the "Stonewall" Jackson of this war will emerge. A Second Manassas will follow the blundering of backward-looking commanders and of inexperienced staff officers during any Seven Days' Battle the new army must fight.[1]

For D. S. Freeman, then, the critical determinative factors in the success or failure of an army are, first, the capability, fair-mindedness, and diligence of the supreme command, and second, dependent on the first, the search for competent executive officers at the level just below the supreme command. This judgment came from a historian whose Civil War histories are permeated by his admiration for the rank-and-file soldiers of the army he chronicled, the Army of Northern Virginia, and indeed for the soldiers of the rival Army of the Potomac; the judgment does not detract from the importance of resolution and bravery among the army's rank and file. Sharing Freeman's belief in the pivotal importance of the characteristics he listed among an army's highest commanders, I considered it proper to focus a study of the American army put to the test of European battle upon the supreme command and the highest executive officers of the army. Freeman looked at R. E. Lee and at Lee's corps, division, and brigade commanders. In the larger American army in Europe in World War II, the analogous focus is upon Dwight D. Eisenhower and his army group, field army, and corps commanders. I have dealt proportionately less with Eisenhower than Freeman did with Lee, because excellent military studies of Eisenhower and his headquarters have already been written.[2] For Eisenhower's lieutenants, however, we have a relative paucity of biographies, especially of studies of generalship, as distinguished from character studies like those about Patton. In choosing a title evocative of Freeman's *Lee's Lieutenants* I do not mean to imply that my abilities as a military historian are comparable to Freeman's, but simply to signify that the supreme commander, his executive officers, and the relationships among them provide the best subject matter through which to assess the merits and deficiencies of an army at war.

In one important regard, a history of Eisenhower's lieutenants cannot parallel the history of Lee's lieutenants. Command in the Civil War was much more personal than command in World War II; the responsibility for command decisions centered more directly upon the individual general and was less diffused through military staffs. The documentation available to the historian reflects this fact and still further blurs the boundaries of responsibility and the identity of the maker or makers of a given decision. The quantity of documentation for World War II is much larger than for the Civil War; modern military staffs generate mountains of paperwork, and many of the mountains originating during World War II remain to be explored. But this staff-generated paper-work tends to obfuscate rather than reveal the decision-making process.

To aggravate the problems of locating the source of decision and tracing the process whereby decision took form, twentieth-century transportation and communication made it possible for World War II commanders to work out their most critical designs in face-to-face conferences or telephone conversations, neither of which were necessarily recorded in full. Commanders of the Civil War era when separated by any considerable distance would telegraph or write; either way, the deliberations they shared were recorded. In one of the very rare letters, in contrast, in which General Omar N. Bradley of the American 12th Army Group discussed strategic and operational issues in detail and explored choices with General Eisenhower, the Allied Supreme Commander, Bradley concluded by saying: "I am asking [Brigadier General Arthur S.] Nevins [chief of the operations section of the G-3 (Operations) Division of Eisenhower's headquarters] to bring this to you when he returns tomorrow as I think it covers the situation better than I could on a regular TWX message."[3] That is, Bradley would ordinarily have sent a simpler teletype message, less useful to the historian; to discuss issues in detail, he would usually have traveled by airplane or car to visit Eisenhower instead of writing.

Since I quote from so many of these documents, a point about those who wrote them should perhaps be made here. They were not stylists attempting to produce elegant literary works, but military men busy fighting a war. For me to correct their grammar, misspellings, and erratic punctuation would be fundamentally an act of disrespect for the integrity of those documents, as well as patronizing to their authors. And scattering *sic*'s among them would be tiresome for all concerned. I have therefore limited my tampering to the occasional use of bracketed insertions where absolutely necessary for the sake of clarity.

For their assistance in my efforts to draw from the peculiarities of modern military decision-making and the records thereof a historian's study in command, certain individuals merit particular acknowledgment amidst the usual heavy claims of gratitude developed in preparing a large book. Richard Sommers, archivist of the United States Army Military History Institute, Carlisle Barracks, Pennsylvania, offered detailed and superbly well informed guidance to a manuscript collection whose diaries and letters offer something of a vantage point from which to perceive personalities and personal responsibilities obscured by the official documentation. The numerous interviews with retired generals kept on tape or transcripts by the Military History Institute-Army War College Oral History Program helped form my overall impressions but did not contribute as I once hoped they might to my specific conclusions about particular issues—suggesting, I think, something of the fundamental problems of oral history. Nevertheless, for access to these materials and many other services, I owe gratitude to a series of directors of the U.S. Army Military History Research Collection, which has become the U.S. Army Military History Institute: Colonels George S. Pappas, James B. Agnew, and Donald P. Shaw. The beginnings of this book lie in a year of full and leisurely access to the collection as Visiting Professor of Military History Research during the directorship of Colonel Pappas. At that time Major (now Lieutenant Colonel) Charles K. Hanson was in charge of the Oral History Program, and I benefited much from the impressions growing out of the interviews that were directed from the office next door to mine.

Among the official documents in the custody of the National Archives and Records Service, I received special help in the Military Archives Division from John Taylor and C. A. Shaughnessy of the Modern Army Branch and—invaluably helpful beyond the call of his formal responsibilities—Timothy K. Nenninger of the Navy and Old Army Branch. Jim Trimble of the Still Pictures Branch helped find the illustrations I wanted. At the Department of the Army Center of Military History, Hannah Zeidlik was my guide to the documents, but many others contributed ideas, information, and encouragement over a long period of time, especially Brigadier General James L. Collins, Jr., the Chief of Military History, Maurice Matloff, and Robert W. Coakley.

Stephen E. Ambrose, biographer of Eisenhower, offered much encouragement at various stages of the project.

Temple University granted me a leave of absence for research. The maps were brought from my sketches to final form by Mark Mattson, staff cartographer of Temple University.

An unusual debt is related to the maps. Knowing my love of travel and materials associated with it, a much esteemed professor of my graduate school days at the University of Pennsylvania, and subsequently my friend, the late Wallace E. Davies, left as his bequest to me his collection of maps and guidebooks. They helped, Wally—even though you'd have disapproved of so much concern with war.

RUSSELL F. WEIGLEY

Philadelphia
July 14, 1980

Eisenhower's Lieutenants

He who has not fought the Germans does not know war.

—British military aphorism

PART ONE : THE ARMIES

★ ★ ★

1: The American Army

THEIR KETTLE-SHAPED HELMETS lent a medieval aspect to the horse soldiers clattering out of the twilight. The year was 1940, the occasion a preparedness parade, the helmets actually those of the 1917–1918 style. Yet to a small boy catching his first glimpse of America's army as it readied itself for the new war, the pennantlike guidons drooping in the chill, damp evening as well as the metallic headgear seemed to represent old wars rather than new, a military past yet more remote than the Mexican border skirmishes for which the troopers in fact were outfitted.

In the early part of that year of the German Blitzkrieg, the American army was antique enough. There were only two Regular divisions in the continental United States that amounted to more than the barest of skeletons and could be said to be reasonably ready for combat. One was traditional cavalry, the 1st Cavalry Division, and the other was the 2nd Infantry. Both were under VIII Corps headquarters at Fort Sam Houston, Texas, to guard against trouble spilling across the Rio Grande from restless postrevolutionary Mexico. The 2nd Infantry was mostly in garrison at the corps headquarters, the 1st Cavalry stretched out along the frontier.

There was a mystique about the horse in the American army in those days. An artilleryman who distinguished himself later while commanding armor remembered fondly: "There was nothing more delightful than to move out at the head of my battalion of 75's in the cool of a frosty morning, guns and caissons rolling, horses snorting, and trace-chains rattling as we trotted along the sandy roads. . . ."[1]

In August 1940, two months after the completion of the German army's mechanized conquest of France, the final phase of the American army's large-scale maneuvers in Louisiana between the IV and VIII Corps opened by pitting the latter's 1st Cavalry Division, horse cavalry, against the 23rd Cavalry Division, more horse cavalry. The 23rd, National Guardsmen from Wisconsin, Illinois, Michigan, Louisiana, Georgia, and Tennessee, unfortunately had to rent horses for the occasion. The only animals they could obtain turned out to be unsuited for the rigors of military life and had to be removed by truck to rest areas at the end of the second day. But American war was still a war of cavalry horses, artillery horses, and infantry pack mules.

Horses were not merely the symbol of a conservatism suspicious of new military technology. Nor was the American army's fondness for the horse at all as resonant with a social significance involving the class status of the officer corps as were equine passions in the British army. Rather, in the American army the importance of the cavalry was yet more fundamental, a representation of all that the army was or ever had been. Historically, the American army was not an army in the European fashion, but a border constabulary for policing unruly Indians and Mexicans. The United States Army of 1940 had not yet completed the transition that would make it an appropriate instrument of its country's claims to world power.

Mobility and Power

The American army's capacity to transform itself during the next few years was as impressive an achievement as any in military history. The achievement was possible in large part because the immense material resources of the United States were available to support it. It was possible also because the 12,000–13,000 officers of the old army had succeeded in preparing themselves mentally for the transition to a greater extent than the observer of mounted parades and maneuvers—and polo matches—might have suspected. The officers did so thanks largely to an excellent military school system modeled on European examples and long embedded, somewhat incongruously, within the frontier constabulary. But the limitations of the Indian-fighting past could not be entirely transcended so soon.

The American officer corps had been able to prepare itself mentally for the transition in part, too, because along with the legacies of the Western frontier, the army had inherited the traditions and the institutional memory of one great, European-style war of its own: the American Civil War of 1861–1865. The Civil War had molded the American army's conceptions of the nature of full-scale war in ways that would profoundly affect its conduct of the Second World War.

Yet the American army's two principal inheritances from its past were also conflicting legacies, which might put the army at cross-purposes with itself as it began in 1940 to prepare for European war. The memory of the Western border wars suggested that the primary military virtue is mobility: the history of the frontier was that of the horse soldier in blue or khaki forever challenged by the quicksilver elusiveness of Mexican irregulars or the Indian light cavalry of the Plains. The memory of the Civil War suggested that the primary military value is sheer power: General U.S. Grant's great blue army corps smothering the gray legions of R.E. Lee under the weight of their weapons and numbers. To reconcile mobility and power, to arrive at the appropriate military compound of the two, proved the central problem of the transformation of the old American army of the frontier to the new army of European war.

The Strategy of Power

The triumph of the United States over the Southern Confederacy in the Civil War had been preeminently a triumph of sheer power. Under General Lee, the Confederacy opposed the superior manpower and resources of the Union with strategic methods derived from Napoleon and applied by Lee with brilliance equalled by no other general since Napoleon: most especially the Napoleonic manoeuvre sur les derrières, the turning maneuver to fall on the enemy's flank and rear and unhinge him psychologically while also inflicting crippling physical damage, masterfully executed by Lee at Second Manassas and Chancellorsville. The reply of the United States to Lee's Napoleonic brilliance was the unsubtle strategy of Grant, who deprived Lee's Army of Northern Virginia of its capacity to maneuver by exploiting superior numbers and resources to lock it in continuous battle, and then traded battle casualties until the Confederate army was bled to death. It was another feature of Grant's strategy that while his Army of the Potomac locked the enemy Army of Northern Virginia in the continuous battle of annihilation, along the whole broad war front from the James River to the Gulf of Mexico all the other armies of the Union attacked simultaneously, so no other Confederate force could go to the assistance of the Army of Northern Virginia. Both the trading of casualty for casualty to bleed the enemy white and the simultaneous offensives on every part of the front were applications of the superior raw power of the United States. General Grant and his lieutenants defeated the Confederacy by drowning its armies in a flood of overwhelming power.

Against a rival general of Lee's genius, the Union's superior manpower and material resources and its war aim of the unconditional surrender of the Confederacy made Grant's strategy altogether appropriate. Because it worked so well, achieving the desired total submission, American soldiers thereafter tended to generalize the United States strategy of the Civil War into the appropriate strategy for all major, full-scale wars.

American participation in the First World War was too brief to make over the American army, and particularly to effect much change in conceptions of war and strategy developed during the Civil War and nurtured by military study of Civil War campaigns thereafter. An image of war rooted in the final campaigns and the outcome of the Civil War surfaced in 1918 when American soldiers grumbled about the incompleteness of the defeat and destruction of the German army and thus of the Allied victory. In the years between the two world wars, the military school system instituted by the United States Army in emulation of European military professionalism, and the instructors and publications that spoke for the American schools, still cultivated as a design for large-scale war the Civil War inheritance with its flexing of sheer power. The appropriate means to victory in a major war was the Union army's method of applying overwhelmingly superior power to destroy the enemy's armed forces, as Grant had done, and the enemy's economic resources and will to fight, as William Tecumseh Sherman and Philip Sheridan had done, to the end that a victorious America might completely impose its political aims upon the vanquished.

The immense resources of the twentieth-century United States continued to reinforce the appropriateness of such means to this nation's warmaking. With American resources so vast that they were the envy of every other nation, an enemy could all the better be attacked everywhere, all along his lines of defense, as Grant had coordinated attacks around the entire circumference of the Confederacy. In the end, overwhelming American power would assure the annihilation of the enemy's strength.

American military men after the First World War were enough in touch with European military thought that they quickly followed the lead of Colonel J. F. C. Fuller of Great Britain in compiling lists of the "principles of war," which were supposed to offer concise guidance in the fundamentals of successful military command. In American formulations, however, the principle of the objective not only appeared consistently first, but it had a special significance. The principle of the objective basically states the truism that every military operation should be directed toward a decisive and attainable objective. With the Americans, the objective became peculiarly clear-cut: it was the destruction of the enemy's warmaking capacity, particularly his armed forces.

The first American codification of the principles of war was published in War Department Training Regulation 10–5 of December 23, 1921. In one of the earliest American exegetical dissections of the principles, Colonel W.K. Naylor told an Army War College audience on January 5, 1922: "The real objective in every war is the destruction of the *enemy's main forces*. And every operation, no matter how insignificant, should be carried out with that end in view."[2] This theme received continual restatement. In 1928, Lieutenant Colonel Oliver Prescott Robinson published *The Principles of Military Strategy* as he had taught them at the Command and General Staff School at Fort Leavenworth. "There is no arguing the question," he said, "—the first objective should be the hostile main force."[3] In 1939, the latest revision of the basic army field manual FM 100–5 reiterated: "The *ultimate objective* of all military operations is the destruction of the enemy's armed forces in battle. Decisive defeat breaks the enemy's will to war and forces him to sue for peace which is the national aim."[4]

The military schools and thinkers of other great powers, to be sure, also called for the destruction of the enemy armed forces as a primary objective of war. The idea permeates Carl von Clausewitz's *Vom Kriege*. Clausewitz's countrymen, the Germans, vied with the Americans in the degree of primacy they accorded this objective. (Military powers less able to assume superior strength over their enemies, such as the British, tended to talk less about annihilation.) But the Americans differed from those in the mainstream of European military thought in the extent to which they expected overwhelming power alone, without subtleties of maneuver, to achieve the objective. Despite the veneration of R. E. Lee in American military hagiography, it was U. S. Grant whose theories of strategy actually prevailed.

In Germany, by contrast, destruction of the enemy armed forces was expected to be accomplished not merely by application of overweening power but primarily through the envelopment and isolation of the enemy, and through maneuver united with power to the achievement of that end. From the elder Helmuth von Moltke onward into the Second World War, the Kesselschlacht, the cauldron battle, the battle of envelopment, persisted as the Germans' preferred means of achieving the object of annihilation. The Austro-Prussian War of 1866 convinced Moltke that rifled and breach-loading muskets and artillery had made most frontal assaults futile, and that accordingly his troops should whenever possible encircle or at least outflank the enemy. Moltke wrote this conclusion into his *Regulations for the Higher Troop Commanders* in 1869, and he demonstrated the efficacy of the battle of envelopment twice the next year against the French, at Metz and Sedan.

Moltke's successor Alfred von Schlieffen glorified Hannibal's double envelopment of the Romans at Cannae in 216 B.C. as the classic historical example of the Kesselschlacht. Schlieffen hoped like Moltke to proceed from theory to application of envelopment as the means to the destruction of the enemy army, and he enshrined his hope in the famous Schlieffen Plan for the rapid elimination of France from the ranks of Germany's adversaries. Schlieffen's admirers could contend after 1914 that the plan had not worked because Schlieffen himself had not lived to execute it, and lesser generals, charged with its execution, failed to follow the original specifications.

Certainly the Germans returned to the successful application of the Moltkean Kesselschlacht in World War II. It was by means of Erich von Manstein's revision and modernization of Schlieffen's scheme for the envelopment of the French armies that Germany defeated France in 1940. Superbly executed cauldron battles permitted Germany to destroy one Soviet army after another in the summer and autumn of 1941.

The American strategy of annihilation approached the Second World War with no such inheritance of the combination of mobility and maneuver with power to achieve battles of envelopment. Grant had persistently attempted to turn Lee's flank—and persistently failed—but his destruction of the Army of Northern Virginia was accomplished by head-on grappling with it. America's confidence in its own unparalleled physical power permitted its army in the twentieth century to contemplate the destruction of the enemy armed forces not by envelopment or similar maneuver but by the head-on application of overwhelming power. In tactics, the First World War experience affected the American army enough that, like most armies, in the 1920s and 1930s it developed a tactical doctrine of fire and maneuver. The doctrine aimed at reducing the casualty toll by substituting for direct tactical assaults a system of pinning down the defenders with firepower to permit the attackers to maneuver into an advantageous position on the enemy's flanks or rear. In the strategic realm, in contrast, American strategists concluded that the First World War demonstrated the impossibility of a similar, strategic application of fire and maneuver, of power and mobility, because mass armies had grown too big to have vulnerable flanks. In strategy, most American soldiers believed, the modern mass army left the frontal assault as the only recourse.

General Tasker H. Bliss, for example, army Chief of Staff for a time in 1917 and then American military member of the Allied Supreme War Council, noted: "The paucity of scientific strategical combinations in the military operations of the World War has often been commented upon." But he argued that this paucity was inherent in the circumstances of twentieth-century war. He believed strategy could no longer be as imaginatively effective as in the past. If in modern war neither belligerent's initial war plan succeeds in producing a strategic surprise,

> these huge masses [of modern armies] cannot be readily manoeuvred into new strategical combinations. The tendency then is for the two sides to take offensive-defensive positions which from the magnitude of the forces engaged, may extend across the entire theatre of war. This theatre, which is the field of strategy, then becomes one great battle-ground, which is the field of grand tactics. . . .
>
> [The pattern of the World War then follows.] And thus the remaining struggle for four years became rather a test of the courage and endurance of the soldier and of the suffering civil population behind him than of the strategical skill of the general. . . .[5]

Commander H. H. Frost of the navy, author of an impressive study of *The Battle of Jutland* and until his death from meningitis in 1935 at the age of forty-four one of the most prolific of American military critics, similarly argued that the old-fashioned strategy of maneuver was bankrupt. There remained possible only the death grapple to be resolved ultimately by superior resources and endurance. "While it may have been possible," Frost said, "for the Germans to have gained a decisive military success in the French campaigns of 1914, this is now beginning to appear more and more doubtful. Two great armies, when their morale is unbroken, tend to reach a state of equilibrium. . . . It was only where a lesser power, Belgium, Serbia, or Rumania, was attacked that a purely military decision could be won, although even here brilliant leadership was usually necessary to supplement superior resources." Unless with the help of surprise an offensive nourished by superior force won a rapid victory, modern war offered no route to decision except the gradual destruction of the enemy forces in the manner of U. S. Grant.[6]

If mass armies made strategic maneuver futile, Colonel Naylor stated the appropriate conclusions to the Army War College in his early analysis of the principles of war:

> I wish to stress this point; that warfare means fighting and that war is never won by maneuvering. . . .
>
> Disabuse your mind of the idea that you can place an army in a district so vital to the enemy that he will say "What's the use" and sue for peace. History shows that the surest way to take the fighting spirit out of a country is to defeat its main army. All other means calculated to bring the enemy to his knees are contributory to the main proposition, which is now, as it ever has been, namely[:] the defeat of his main forces.[7]

Captain George J. Meyers of the navy offered the same conclusion in a 1928 book on *Strategy*: "Maneuvering in itself will not gain victories. . . . Its greatest value is in the making of dispositions [for the battle] in time. . . . The combat is the scene of the greatest violence in war. As it is the only act in war from which victory flows, we should be prepared to achieve victory at a cost no less than the price of blood. All preparation for war and in war must aim at victory in battle."[8]

While thus stressing the principle of the objective, in the form of a focus upon the destruction of the enemy armed forces as the singleminded objective in war, American military thought gave no corresponding emphasis to another of the recently codified principles of war, the principle of mass or, as the British more revealingly tended to call it, the principle of concentration. The historic American means of applying overwhelming power did not favor concentration. Grant had broken through the defenses of the Confederacy not by concentrating force at a few critical places but by attacking all along the battle lines, on the theory that if the United States applied its superior power everywhere it must be able to rupture the defenses somewhere. The example of Grant's campaigns combined with confidence in American ability to exert power everywhere to put concentration at a discount. As an Army War College committee put it in 1926–1927 while analyzing the strategy of the World War: "A superior combatant operating on exterior lines can by a coordinated offensive on all fronts prevent his enemy from using interior lines to gain superiority on one front, and can thus break down the enemy and win victory."[9]

Deprecating the value of both strategic maneuver and concentration, the Americans envisioned frontal assaults all along the line. They concluded that the price of victory must be high in blood, and the resources applied had to be overwhelming, because the climactic battles would be frontal. As Colonel Robinson put the matter in his disquisition on strategy: "War means fighting; it has only one aim, to crush the enemy and destroy his will to resist." He continued:

> The objective for military forces is the defeat or destruction of the hostile main forces, and all the operations of war are indirectly, or directly, directed to that end.

. . . .

. . . So let it be understood that, when war comes, there should be only one question that will ever be asked of a commander as to a battle, and that one is, not what flank did he attack, not how did he use his reserves, not how did he protect his flanks, but did he fight?[10]

The 1939 revision of FM 100–5 again summed it up authoritatively: "An objective may sometimes be gained through maneuver alone; ordinarily, it must be gained through battle." Captain Reuben E. Jenkins's commentary on the revised field manual in the Command and General Staff School journal *Military Review* added: "It should be remembered that the price of victory is hard fighting and that no matter what maneuver is employed, ultimately the fighting is frontal. . . . Blood is the price of victory. One must accept the formula or not wage war."[11]

Notwithstanding the limitations of American experience in war, the American army had developed a clear and confident strategic credo: war is won by destroying the enemy's warmaking ability, particularly his armed forces; mere maneuver will not accomplish this destruction; the destruction is to be accomplished by confronting the enemy's main armed forces directly and overwhelming them with superior power.

Early in 1941, almost a year before the Japanese attack on Pearl Harbor drew the United States into the Second World War, American strategists discussed in Washington with representatives of the British Chiefs of Staff the appropriate strategy to be pursued in the likely contingency that the United States might enter the war. This was the ABC–1 (American-British Conversations 1) meeting. From these discussions onward until the spring of 1944, the American strategists took an undeviating position. To defeat the German-Italian-Japanese Axis, the Anglo-Americans ought to assail the main armed strength of the main enemy directly, to destroy that strength. Thus the Anglo-American forces ought, as soon as possible, to cross the English Channel to do battle with the main German forces in the West, in France. In the Victory Program drawn up in the War Department later in 1941, Major Albert C. Wedemeyer, the principal author, said succinctly: "We must prepare to fight Germany by actually coming to grips with and defeating her ground forces and definitely breaking her will to combat." Just after Pearl Harbor, Brigadier General Dwight D. Eisenhower of the War Plans Division of the General Staff stated more succinctly: "We've got to go to Europe and fight."[12]

In the Anglo-American strategic discussions, British strategists took a different view, arguing for a less direct approach, which would aim first at German positions of relative weakness—in the Mediterranean, for instance—and would wait until the enemy's Fortress Europe was substantially eroded before striking where the Germans were strongest. But, referring to one of the principal works by B. H. Liddell Hart, the principal literary exponent of this British strategy of the indirect approach, the American General Service Schools' *Review of Current Military Literature* had commented significantly in 1925: "Of negative value to the instructors at these schools."[13]

On the other hand, in contrast to the strategy of direct application of overwhelming power, the actual American army that began in 1940 and 1941 to prepare for World War II remained the border constabulary, designed not for the generation and sustained application of power but for mobility, and for the mobility of the horse at that.

2: Weapons and Divisions

DURING THE American army's brief adventure in European war before World War II, in 1917–1918, American officers had betrayed hypersensitive awareness that they were embarked on their first contest in the military major leagues. Not the least of their sources of embarrassment was American dependence on foreign weapons for everything beyond shoulder arms and machine guns.

This awkward dependence provoked a postwar shakeup in the Ordnance Department, the army's designer and in peacetime principal manufacturer of weapons, to try to ensure that henceforth American weapons would adequately serve the combat branches' requirements. One of the changes was a determination that the users of weapons must be able to decide what sorts of weapons Ordnance should provide; previously, the Ordnance Department blandly imposed its own decisions upon the users. This change proved less helpful, however, than might be assumed from the apparent common sense of letting the soldiers who had to face enemy fire indicate what they needed to survive and overcome the fire. The Ordnance Department was more closely in touch than the combat arms with European weapons developments. It was consequently aware of and receptive to European tendencies in the late 1930s toward rapid enhancement of firepower through bringing increasingly heavier weapons closer and closer to the front. These European tendencies might have accorded with American strategic predilections about applying overwhelming power, but they conflicted with the attitudes and practices grown habitual in a frontier constabulary charged with patrolling vast distances and needing above all to be mobile.

The Tanks

In the post–World War I U.S. Army, the tank was an infantry weapon. It was officially proclaimed an infantry weapon, and its use was restricted to the infantry, by the basic organizational statute governing the army, the National Defense Act of 1920. This law had terminated the wartime Tank Corps, which had begun to cultivate the notion that tanks were not mere supplements to the traditional combat arms but the foundation of a new mode of war. Rejecting such a view, both the legislation and postwar army doctrine, which each of the traditional combat arms—infantry, cavalry, coast artillery, and field artillery—prepared for itself, regarded tanks as aids to the foot soldier in his efforts to break enemy defenses and occupy ground.

Attaching tanks to the infantry might conceivably have encouraged the development of powerful, heavily armed tanks, to enhance the impact of the infantry assault as much as possible. The effect ran in the opposite direction. If tanks were to assist the infantry, they must be able to move wherever a rifleman might go. Therefore they must be light and agile. Defining principles to guide tank development in 1922, the Adjutant General's Office declared: "The primary mission of the tank is to facilitate the uninterrupted advance of the riflemen in the attack. Its size, armament, speed and all the accessories for making it an independent force must be approached with above mission as the final objective to be obtained in development." Specifically, the Adjuntant General translated this dictum into a requirement for two basic tank types, both of them small and of necessity lightly armed: a five-ton tank that could be transported from rear areas to the front in trucks along with the infantry, and a "medium" tank that would not exceed the fifteen-ton weight limit of average highway bridges or of the army's medium pontoon bridge. Any tank over twenty-five tons would be too heavy as well for Corps of Engineers emergency bridges.[1]

American tanks thus became machine gun carriers designed to move with the infantry, and armored only against enemy machine guns. As late as 1935, this conception of the tank led to calls upon the Ordnance Department to develop a tank limited to three tons. The arbitary weight limit of twenty-five tons at most, and preferably fifteen, governed the design of medium tanks until 1940 and influenced it thereafter. The Ordnance Department warned repeatedly in the late thirties that American tanks were falling behind their European counterparts in both guns and armor, but the users persisted in demanding lightness and maneuverability.

In 1935, some ordnance officers urged the mounting of a 75mm. pack howitzer in a tank turret, but not until 1938 were they permitted to do so in one experimental tank. By that time, the Germans were experimenting with an 88mm. gun in a tank turret, but the American Chief of Infantry still pronounced a 75mm. a useless weapon for a tank. When the rival European armies fought the Battle of France in the spring of 1940 with 75mm. guns in both sides' main battle tanks—the German Panzerkampfwagen IV and the French Char B—the heaviest gun in an American tank was a 37mm. The War Department's approval to design a tank mounting a 75mm. howitzer came in July 1940. In the spring of 1944, when Anglo-American armies prepared for the invasion of northwest Europe in accordance with the American strategy of direct application of power, Germany's Panther tanks carried long-barrelled, high-muzzle-velocity 75s and her Tigers fired 88s, but the largest gun on an operational American tank was still a short-barrelled, low-muzzle-velocity 75, the standard armament of the then-standard M4 Sherman tank.

Tank Killers

Mobility rather than power similarly shaped the search for weapons with which the traditional American combat arms might protect themselves against enemy tanks. Just after the Armistice of 1918, and as a result of concern about the deficiencies of American ordnance in the World War, the army Chief of Staff, General Peyton C. March, appointed a board of ordnance and artillery officers to convene in France, study existing American and foreign weapons, and draw up recommendations for the American artillery of the future. Headed by Brigadier General William I. Westervelt of the Ordnance Department, the Westervelt Board or "Caliber Board" included among its recommendations an antitank gun of about 75mm., based on the board's projections of the strengthening of tank armor. If this recommendation had been heeded, it would have been just about right for World War II. But the War Department actually chose a 37mm. antitank gun that served the infantry into the 1930s. When reports of thickening tank armor and new antitank guns in Europe led in 1936 to an effort to modernize the American weapon, the result was merely the adoption the next year of a new model 37mm. gun. By this time the Russians had achieved good results in the battle testing of a 45mm. antitank gun in Spain, and the Germans were adopting antitank guns of from 50 to 80mm. Nevertheless, in response to questions about the small American gun raised by officers in touch with European progress, the infantry insisted on mobility and lightness and thus on retaining the 37mm. gun. In 1938 the War Department explicitly instructed the Ordnance Department to expend no funds in fiscal 1939 or 1940 on antitank guns larger than 37mm.

The European war that began in 1939 swiftly demonstrated the shortsightedness of this decision and the emphasis on mobility alone that underlay it. The 37mm. gun could not kill modern tanks, and mobility and lightness were irrelevant if the gun could not do the job it was intended to do. By 1939 and 1940, however, it was late for American gun designers to start catching up. In the spring of 1944, on the eve of the invasion of northwest Europe, the standard American antitank gun had grown only to 57mm., and it remained a weapon that could kill tanks only at short ranges and only by finding their lightly armored flanks or their undersides and treads. By that time, the standard German antitank gun was a mobile 75mm. piece, to say nothing of the Germans' famous dual-purpose 88mm. antiaircraft gun that had become the terror of British (and American-made) tanks in the Western Desert.

If American tanks were undergunned against enemy tanks, and the American army also lacked suitably powerful weapons with which the ground forces in general might take on enemy armor, an attempted solution consistent with the army's habitual attitudes and practice developed in the form of the so-called tank destroyer. The tank destroyer was a special pet of the most influential single architect of the American ground forces in preparation for the European war, Major General (from June 1941 Lieutenant General) Lesley J. NcNair. Chief of staff of General Headquarters, the potential command of the army in the field, from the activation of the headquarters in 1940, and then from March 1942 commander of the Army Ground Forces, McNair was a bantam, efficient, decisive, even opinionated artilleryman whose career as a staff officer and instructor and lack of field and combat experience did not temper his assurance that he knew what was good for the troops in combat. McNair's passion was to keep the American army lean and mobile. Believing that existing tank design was satisfactory because tanks should not fight tanks anyway, he characteristically preferred in a tank killer a bigger gun mounted on a tank chassis but with the vehicle stripped of heavy armor protection and its turret open to save weight and afford rapid mobility. By 1942, the M10 tank destroyer had become standard, a 3-inch high-muzzle-velocity flat-trajectory gun mounted on a Sherman chassis. By 1944, the need for still more gun power to cope with German tanks brought into service the M18, with a 76mm. gun in a shallow open turret on the new M24 light tank chassis, and the M36, an M10 redesigned to accommodate a 90mm. gun. The troubles implicit in this effort to unite mobility and gun power at the expense of a thin skin might have been apparent long before the final report of the First United States Army assessed them in retrospect:

> The tank destroyer was created for the primary mission of destroying the hostile armor. Its initial superiority for this mission lay in its superior gun power. With the development of more adequate tank cannon and due to the offensive

nature of operations the need for this special-mission type of unit has ceased. During operations tank destroyers were required to assume tank missions for which they were not equipped or trained adequately and to perform secondary missions as roving batteries, direct fire assault gun action and augmentation of the fire of armored units. The tank destroyer mission as originally conceived has been superseded by the requirements for a killer tank. Tank destroyers should be replaced by a tank which can equal or outgun enemy tanks and which has sufficient armor to protect itself and its crew from normal anti-tank and tank weapons.[2]

The tank destroyer did not have such armor.

In any event, the tank destroyer was no more able than the newer, more heavily armored tanks, to go everywhere the infantry went, and so there remained the need for tank protection that the soldier on the ground could take with him—preferably an antitank weapon the infantryman could carry and fire from his shoulder. In the late 1930s, the Ordnance Department had developed an interest in an antitank grenade designed by a Swiss inventor, Henri Mohaupt. The Mohaupt grenade drew its special effectiveness from the shaped- or hollow-charge principle discovered by the American physicist Charles E. Munroe in 1880: shaping high explosive with a hollow cone at the forward end focuses the explosive to yield greater penetration per unit weight. Initially the Mohaupt grenade was fired from a spigot launcher resembling a mortar, which did not permit accurate aiming. As early as 1918, Robert H. Goddard of Clark University, the father of modern rocketry, had offered the Ordnance Department his "recoilless gun" or "rocket gun," a portable tube rocket launcher. After the Armistice the army's interest in Goddard's work languished, but it never altogether died, and in 1941 the Ordnance Department returned to the recoilless gun as an instrument for launching the Mohaupt grenade. At the first test firing of the rocket grenade at Aberdeen Proving Ground in May 1942, the firing tube was dubbed the bazooka, because it resembled a curious gas-pipe musical instrument of that name favored by the comedian Bob Burns.

The next month the Ordnance Department standardized a 2.36-inch model of the rocket and launcher. Introduced into battle in Tunisia, the bazooka was troublesome enough to German tanks that the enemy soon began fitting Pzkw IVs with wire mesh antirocket screens and eventually put solid metal covering skirts over the vulnerable bogey wheels. But the bazooka, like American antitank guns, was too small. It could not penetrate the heavy front armor of the German tanks. It demanded careful aim against soft spots, which was no easy chore for an exposed, nervous infantryman when a massive German tank came looming up so close upon him that he could hear the pulsating squeak of the bogies. While the Germans promptly adopted the bazooka principles, their 88mm. Panzerfaust was about twice as powerful. James M. Gavin was colonel of the 505th Parachute Infantry of the 82nd Airborne Division when his troops first used bazookas in Sicily in 1943. He expressed the men's disappointment by writing: "As for the 82nd Airborne Division, it did not get adequate antitank weapons until it began to capture the first German panzerfausts. By the fall of '44 we had truckloads of them. We also captured German instructions for their use, made translations, and conducted our own training with them. They were the best hand-carried antitank weapon of the war."[3] The United States did not initiate a project for a more powerful, 3.5-inch rocket until August 1944.

Some of the weapons with which the American army entered the Second World War were excellent. The Western border constabulary had always cultivated expert marksmanship, utilizing superb rifles from the time when rifles first entered general military service. The Garand .30-caliber M1 semi-automatic rifle was the best standard infantry shoulder arm of the Second World War. No other rifle of the war matched its combination of accuracy, rate of fire, and reliability. The standard American medium artillery weapon, the 105mm. howitzer, was at least the equal of its German counterpart of the same caliber. The effectiveness of this weapon and every other type of American artillery was multiplied by the best equipment and techniques of any army for fire direction, observation, and coordination. By 1944, the U.S. Army Air Forces had more than caught up with the early lead of the German Luftwaffe in quality of airplanes and tactics for direct support of the ground battle, though air–ground teamwork still left something to be desired.

Nevertheless, while American strategy relied not on maneuver or even on concentration but on overwhelming the enemy with the exertion of superior power, American weapons had been designed first for mobility, and the weapons could not be counted on for power appropriate to the strategy.

The Limits of American Manpower

Yet the American army had to be able to count on superior quality and quantity in its equipment to compensate for its inability to mobilize for European war the margins of manpower superiority on which U.S. Grant had relied against the Confederacy.

The limitations upon America's ability to mobilize a mass army were not immediately apparent when the United States first began to plan for entry into the Second World War. On the day before Pearl Harbor, General McNair estimated that to win a war against the Axis, the United States would need an army of 200 divisions. At that time, he felt little doubt that such an army could be created. Soon afterward, the Joint Chiefs of Staff projected a U.S. Army of 334 divisions, to effect the strategy of overwhelming power.

For 1942, the first year of American participation in the war, the army concentrated its efforts on mobilizing new divisions. By the time of Pearl Harbor, more than a year had passed since the beginning of the federalization of the National Guard and of conscription under the Selective Service Act of 1940. The 1939 army of 190,000 officers and men had swelled to 1,600,000, the number of divisions on active service to thirty-six. During 1942, thirty-seven more divisions were formed, and by the end of the year the army numbered over 5,000,000, of whom 1,940,000 were in the Army Ground Forces. In the same year, the Army Air Forces swelled from 270,000 to 1,270,000, while the Services of Supply (later the Army Service Forces) grew to 1,857,000.

The expansion of the Army Ground Forces and the creation of new divisions abruptly ended, however, in the winter of 1942–1943. The War Department, and in particular General George C. Marshall, Jr., the army Chief of Staff, had begun the rapid 1942 expansion of ground combat forces and multiplication of divisions expecting to invade northwest Europe across the English Channel no later than the spring of 1943. By the end of 1942 this expectation had to be abandoned. The cross-Channel invasion obviously depended on British cooperation, not least because England must be its base; but the British did not believe the Anglo-American Alliance could yet muster adequate power to challenge the German army in its defenses along the coast of France. British strategy contrived to divert the main Allied offensives for 1942 and 1943 into the Mediterranean. There would be no cross-Channel invasion until 1944 at the earliest. In these circumstances, and with the specifics of the coming 1943 and 1944 campaigns uncertain, the seventy-three American army divisions created by the close of 1942 were moving overseas much more slowly than anticipated, and those remaining at home were overcrowding facilities to house them. Thus the War Department decided to postpone the mobilization of many of the divisions yet to be formed.

The postponements largely changed into permanent cancellations. By the middle of 1943, the army had to rethink its total manpower projections. Planning to reach a strength of 7,000,000 enlisted men by the end of the year, the army was approaching the limit of the numbers it could remove from the economy without endangering a basic conception of the Allied war effort, that America was to be the industrial arsenal for all the Allied powers. In addition, the American military actions already under way were largely naval. The war against Japan in the Pacific Ocean was preeminently a naval war. The United States needed naval strength in the Atlantic to carry men and munitions to Europe and eventually to mount the desired cross-Channel invasion. In the middle of 1943, the battle against German submarines in the North Atlantic was just beginning to turn in the Allies' favor. Thus the army had to share with a large navy, eventually some 4,000,000 strong, the portion of American manpower not needed in industry and on the farms. Furthermore, by the summer of 1943 the Soviet Union had turned back Germany's eastward assaults, and the Japanese tide had not only been contained but was being reversed in the Pacific. The United States could probably get along with considerably fewer than the 334 divisions projected in early 1942.

On July 1, 1943, in consequence, the War Department issued an approved new Troop Basis calling for the expansion of the army only to 7,004,000 enlisted men and eighty-eight divisions. Two provisional divisions authorized temporarily soon received permanent status, to make an army of ninety divisions.

This mid-1943 Troop Basis shaped the army that henceforth planned for the supreme military effort of the war, the cross-Channel invasion. The new Troop Basis persisted with little change to the end of the war. Early in 1944, the projected enlisted strength was revised slightly downward, to 6,955,000, but officers were incorporated into the Troop Basis to project an army aggregating 7,700,000. The army actually grew in time to some 8,300,000; but the increase over the Troop Basis did not alter the organization of the force, because the added numbers developed mainly in men unassigned to specific units, in replacement centers and depots, reassignment centers and hospitals—"the invisible horde of people," as General McNair described them, "going here and there but seemingly never arriving."[4]

When the 1943 Troop Basis appeared on July 1, the Army Ground Forces had grown only from 1,917,000 enlisted men at the end of 1942 to 2,471,000. Thereafter, their expansion virtually halted. The Ground Forces numbered 2,502,000 on March 31, 1945, at the end of the European war. The additional divisions from seventy-three to ninety could be created despite this slowing and halting of manpower growth because various nondivisional combat units were dissolved, especially antiaircraft battalions made superfluous by the rise of Allied air power. Nevertheless, the last new division was formed in August 1943, and the division ceiling remained at ninety. When the 2nd Cavalry Division was inactivated between February and May 1944, the number of divisions stabilized at eighty-nine.

The Red Army commanded about 400 divisions at the end of the Second World War. Germany raised about 300 divisions for the war. Japan had about 100 divisions. With all due allowances for the variations between different nations' divisions and for the further complexities that make comparing numbers of divisions a misleading exercise, it remains true that mobilizing a ninety-division army for the Second World War was not an altogether impressive performance for a superpower.

The limited number of American combat divisions posed obvious problems for an American strategy built upon a power drive across the English Channel to hit the German Army in the West where it was strongest. Even before a single soldier of the Western Allies put his foot ashore in France with the intention of openly and defiantly staying there, and despite the demands of the Eastern Front upon the German army, the Germans in early 1944 maintained about sixty divisions in France. They would have the advantage against the Anglo-Americans of fighting on the defensive; the offensive almost always requires a numerical preponderance.

The limited numbers of American ground combat troops also raised the question whether the United States would be able to maintain its divisions once they began to suffer casualties. Of the fifty-eight American divisions raised for the First World War, one-third were hollow shells by the time of the Armistice, because they had to be cannibalized to replenish casualties in the other divisions. The campaigns in North Africa and Italy into which British strategy dragged Americans as preludes to the cross-Channel invasion generally put no more than six American divisions into action simultaneously; but the casualties of such limited-scale fighting nevertheless came close to destroying a number of divisions scheduled for late shipment overseas, because these divisions were so badly stripped to provide replacements.

If divisions were few, furthermore, it would become difficult or impossible once the battle for France was launched to rotate them out of the line for rest and refitting. If the divisions could not be rotated, their soldiers would have to fight on knowing that, short of victory, their wounding or death would provide the only relief. If the divisions remained indefinitely in the line, fatigue and anxiety would surely curtail efficiency and produce still more casualties, to aggravate further the problems created by the limited numbers of ground combat troops.

The overriding question, of course, was the most obvious one of all, whether the ninety-division American army would have enough of that sustained combat power on which American strategy depended, and which the cross-Channel confrontation with German military power would most especially demand.

Mobility and Power in Armor

Of the ninety American divisions, sixteen were armored divisions. Like the total number of divisions, the roster of armored divisions fell drastically, from 1942 projections that envisaged as many as sixty of them, in armored corps and perhaps armored armies.

The German Blitzkrieg in Poland in 1939 and France in 1940 and the spectacular German victories in Russia in 1941 established the armored division as the heart of a modern army. The essence of the German armored division was its unification of power and mobility. Before the Germans created their panzer divisions, post–World War I writers on the potentiality of the tank, notably the British strategist J.F.C. Fuller, called for mighty divisions, corps, and even armies whose whole striking power would be concentrated in tanks. Predictions of virtually all-tank forces overlooked, however, the limitations of the striking power of the tank, the tank's difficulties against well-designed obstacles, roadblocks, minefields, fortifications, and stout lines of antitank guns. Here the tanks would need the help of infantry, to infiltrate among the obstacles and defenses, to cover the engineers who were removing mines and traps, and to keep the momentum of the attack going until the tanks could move forward freely again. Against strong defenses, the bigger guns of the artillery would also be useful to assist the tanks. The genius of Heinz Guderian as the German army's Inspector of Mobile Troops who created the panzer division was to unite its tanks with motorized infantry and artillery that could approximate the mobility of the tanks while affording the division a well-rounded power capable of dealing with nearly any defenses or obstacles. In addition, Guderian's panzer divisions could call on Luftwaffe aircraft designed for close support of the ground troops—especially the Junkers Ju87 Stuka based on the American navy's invention of the dive bomber—for further enhancement of their tanks' power.

Other soldiers in other countries of course shared Guderian's insight that armored divisions should combine tanks with mobile infantry and artillery. In 1934, a year before the formation of the Germans' first three panzer divisions, the French army fashioned the Division Légère Mechanique. The D.L.M. combined tanks, mobile infantry, and artillery in proportions similar to those of the panzer division. But the D.L.M. stressed mobility at the expense of power. It was built around light tanks and light weapons and was designed primarily to inherit the reconnaissance and exploitation roles of traditional calvary. The French neglected the potential of the armored division to unite power with mobility as the cavalry had never done in modern times. In fact, in 1939 the French created a second type of armored division, the Division Cuirassée. The D.C. was built around their heavy tank, the Char B, for the purpose of concentrating breakthrough power. The French packaged mobility and power separately, while the panzer division combined both.

In the British army, the bias of an aristocratic officer corps against anything mechanized, greasy, and dirty so isolated the Royal Tank Corps that a promising 1927 experiment in combined arms, the Experimental Mechanised Force, was aborted. British tankers, all the more enthusiasts for their ponderous weapons because the rest of the army scorned them, never altogether escaped Fuller's early notion that tanks could do almost anything for themselves. In North Africa in 1940–1943, any cooperation between British tanks and other arms was so lamentably deficient that the more successful commanders of the British Eighth Army, including the ultimately victorious General Bernard Law Montgomery, habitually tried to make a virtue of weakness by concentrating the armored divisions in a separate corps operating more or less apart from the rest of the army.

By then, another stream of history besides that of the Royal Tank Corps had entered into British armored divisions. The first such British formation, the Mobile Division of 1938, had brought together elements of the Royal Tank Corps with some of the old cavalry regiments, now mechanized. Not only did this arrangement try to marry partners of utterly different social inheritance in an army where such considerations were peculiarly important, but the union also assured that the purpose of the British armored division, like the D.L.M., was primarily reconnaissance and exploitation, cavalry style, without the striking power of the panzer division, for cavalrymen became ascendant in the new mobile formations. The British built fast "cruiser" tanks for their armored divisions, while keeping heavy tanks slow and ungainly, not for service in the armored divisions, but to plod along with the infantry.

In 1936, the Germans hoped to have sixty-three panzer divisions by the end of 1939, but their rearmament program struck so many snags that in 1938 they lowered their sights for the end of the following year to twelve. With the need to replace losses suffered in Poland, they actually had ten of Guderian's combined-arms armored formations when they invaded France in May 1940. This number proved ample, because the French and British had no units that sufficiently combined mobility with power to match them. There were slight variations among the panzer divisions, but in general each of them had an equal number of tank and infantry companies and a total tank complement of 320. To increase the number of panzer divisions to twenty for the invasion of Russia the next year, the allotment of tanks per division fell considerably. A 1941 panzer division had about 150 to 200 tanks and from six to nine tank companies compared with fifteen rifle companies.

The panzer divisions contributed to the German triumph in France and to the early victories in Russia a share utterly disproportionate to the ratio of total German strength they embodied. In France, the panzer divisions befuddled, enveloped, and ruined the French army while the German infantry divisions of marching men and horse-drawn transport were still tramping along far behind them. The panzer divisions' victory, as has so often been said, was not so much a victory of superior tanks as of superior armored organization and doctrine, Guderian's unification of mobility and power.

In the United States Army, where organization and doctrine for mechanized war had languished as much as tank development, the demonstration of the might of the panzer divisions in France was followed immediately by the creation of an Armored Force on July 10, 1940. Fortunately, the first chief of the Armored Force was a strong believer in the combined-arms principle, Brigadier General Adna R. Chaffee, Jr. Chaffee had been striving to create American armored divisions since 1928 when Chief of Staff Charles P. Summerall ordered the General Staff to organize a mechanized force on the model of the British experiment of 1927 and Chaffee became the G-3 (Operations) officer principally involved. For a time he was second in command of the Experimental Mechanized Force at Fort Eustis, but in 1931 Chief of Staff Douglas MacArthur aborted this project by transferring it to the cavalry and turning it into another effort simply to mechanize cavalry exploitation. (In deference to the National Defense Act's assignment of tanks to the infantry, the cavalry's armored vehicles became "combat cars.") Chaffee nevertheless persisted in trying to develop American armor, and in 1939 he acquired command of the principal survivor of the combined-arms experiment, the 7th Cavalry Brigade (Mechanized).

Five days after the establishment of the Armored Force, this brigade became the 1st Armored Brigade and the tank nucleus of the 1st Armored Division. Along with artillery and service units, the brigade had brought together the 1st Cavalry Regiment (Mechanized)—the successor to the United States Regiment of Dragoons formed in 1833—and the 13th Cavalry Regiment (Mechanized); the 1st Cavalry Regiment now became the 1st Armored Regiment, Light, the 13th Cavalry the 13th Armored Regiment, Medium. The 2nd Armored Division was created the same day as the 1st, the 2nd being built upon the old infantry tank regiments. The 66th Infantry Regiment (Light Tanks), which until 1932 had been the 1st Tank Regiment, and the 67th Infantry Regiment (Medium Tanks), which had been the 2nd Tank Regiment, were redesignated the 66th and 67th Armored

Regiments to form the 2nd Armored Division's main tank force, the 2nd Armored Brigade.

In 1941, three additional armored divisions grew up around cadres drawn from the 1st and 2nd Armored Divisions. The five armored divisions were the only completely new divisions formed in the American army before Pearl Harbor; all the others were built upon some semblance of existing Regular Army divisional structures or were National Guard divisions.

Initially, the American armored divisions were exceptionally strong in numbers of tanks. They were patterned in fact on pre-1940 German panzer divisions, in which the proportion of tank strength had been even greater than during the invasion of France, tank companies predominating over infantry companies by about two to one. As the American organization had shaken down upon the issuance of tables of organization on March 1, 1942, an armored division consisted of 14,620 officers and men, with 252 medium tanks and 158 light tanks. The tanks were organized into two regiments with 4,848 officers and men between them, each regiment by now consisting of one light and two medium tank battalions. The "armored infantry" formed a three-battalion regiment 2,389 strong. The "armored artillery" was in three battalions with an aggregate strength of 2,127. Engineers, headquarters, and service troops made up the remainder of the division.

Retaining the high ratio of tank strength of the earliest panzer divisions, the new American armored divisions improved upon their German antecedents in mobility and flexibility. The panzer divisions had only a fraction of their rifle battalions equipped with tracked armored personnel carriers, while the rest were simply carried in wheeled vehicles, and only a fraction of the panzers' artillery had self-propelled guns. From 1943 onward, the Germans' official ratios called for one "panzer grenadier" infantry battalion in four to be mounted in half-tracked armored personnel carriers, one armored artillery battalion in three to be self-propelled. The Americans, in contrast, mounted all their armored infantry in half-tracked APCs, and all their armored artillery consisted of self-propelled 105mm. howitzers, the division's three artillery battalions totaling fifty-four pieces. As for flexibility, the German experience had demonstrated a frequent demand for improvised "Kampfgruppen" tailored in size and in mixture of tanks, infantry, and artillery to perform specific missions. The American armored division prepared for the creation of such flexible task forces by providing in division headquarters two "combat commands," each a subheadquarters under a brigadier general, to which the division commander could delegate missions and assign divisional components as he chose.

Under the first impact of the Blitzkrieg, the American Armored Force enjoyed an autonomy so full that some of its friends hoped and its rivals feared it might go on toward an independence from the rest of the army rivaling the Army Air Corps's. General Chaffee was free to gather like-minded officers around him at Armored Force headquarters and to design the armored divisions for the mobile application of concentrated power. Poor health soon obliged Chaffee to step aside—he died before Pearl Harbor, on August 22, 1941—but his successor, Major General Charles L. Scott, former commander of the 13th Cavalry Regiment and then the 2nd Armored Division, was an old associate of similar views. As time went on, however, the shock of the Blitzkrieg faded, the panzer divisions no longer prevailed in every battle, accustomed habits reasserted themselves in the American army, and General McNair at the Army Ground Forces was able to bring the Armored Force more closely under his direction. Whether dealing with armor or any other ground combat arm, McNair always encouraged mobility; but he was much less sure about the virtues of concentrated power embodied in an armored division strong in tanks.

The Germans reduced the numbers of tanks per panzer division in the Russian campaign of 1941 and thereafter simply because their tank production did not keep pace with the demand for panzer divisions. After 1942, in fact, the tank strength of a panzer division became not uncommonly a matter of how many the division commander could scrounge. General McNair misconstrued these German developments. He misread the tank reductions as expressions of doctrinal change in response to combat experience that had devalued tanks and restored much of the importance of infantry and artillery. In 1943, McNair was able to reorganize the American armored division along the lines of the 1941 panzer division. Behind the new armored division lay a very different conception of armored warfare from the one with which Heinz Guderian had designed the original panzer divisions. From Guderian's and Chaffee's unification of power and mobility, McNair swung the organizational balance back toward mobility above power.

The 2nd and 3rd Armored Divisions were allowed to retain essentially the old organization; but following September 15, 1943, all fourteen other American armored divisions were realigned according to new tables of organization published on that date. The tank, infantry, and artillery components of the armored division were equalized, at three battalions of each. Regiments disappeared from the new-model armored divisions. (Thus in the 1st Armored Division, the 1st Tank Battalion was formed from part of the 1st Armored Regiment, and the 4th and 13th Tank Battalions from the 13th Armored Regiment; but the 2nd Armored Division retained its 66th and 67th Armored Regiments.) Each of the three tank battalions had 729 officers and men, each of the armored infantry battalions 1,001, each of the armored artillery battalions 534. Total strength of the armored division became 10,937. Separate medium and light tank battalions were abolished; each tank battalion now had three companies of medium tanks plus one company of light tanks for reconnaissance and similar purposes. A tank company had seventeen tanks, five tanks in each of three platoons and two at company headquarters. With additional headquarters and reconnaissance tanks, the division had a total of 186 mediums and 77 lights, making 263 tanks in the new armored division compared with 390 in the old.

In order not to exaggerate McNair's changes, it should be noted that the greater reduction was in light rather than medium tanks. In addition, part of the effect of the changes was to enhance the already admirable flexibility of American armored units. Each tank, armored infantry, and armored artillery battalion was administratively self-contained, so the battalions could be assigned with complete flexibility to either of the division's two principal combat commands (one of which, somewhat anomalously, would now be headed by a colonel) or to a newly created third, reserve combat command. Furthermore, every tank, armored infantry, or armored artillery battalion in the army was organizationally identical to every other of its kind, whether or not the battalion was attached to a division. Thus McNair intended that nondivisional battalions might be freely attached to armored divisions, or divisional battalions might be detached, to make the armored forces almost indefinitely variable to adjust to almost any situation. In theory, there was nothing to prevent an armored division from temporarily absorbing any number of battalions in any combination of tanks, infantry, and artillery, as long as its headquarters could manage them.

In practice, however, such possibilities were almost never applied. Another result of the armored reorganization came much closer to the heart of General McNair's conception of a properly organized army. It happened that the freeing of many tank battalions from the armored divisions made the number of nondivisional tank battalions in the army almost identical to the number of infantry divisions. Thus a tank battalion could be, and was, more or less permanently attached to almost every infantry division. The reorganization provided more tanks to assist infantry. McNair did not propose to build the army around masses of armor concentrating together both mobility and power.

The 1943 armored structure reverted toward older conceptions of tanks as less the instruments of a new mode of war than as extensions of the infantry and cavalry traditions—to assist the infantry, henceforth through the tank battalions attached to infantry divisions, or to reconnoiter and exploit in the manner of cavalry, henceforth through the redesigned armored divisions, with their sacrifice of power while retaining an emphasis on mobility. For the armored divisions, McNair stated his purpose plainly. The "general concept of an armored force," he said, is "that it is an instrument of exploitation, not very different in principle from horse cavalry of old." "An armored division," McNair believed, "is of value only in pursuit or exploitation."[5]

To justify the reversion to the past, McNair offered as specific evidence the British experience in North Africa. "The battle of El Alamein," he argued, "demonstrated the correct employment of the British armor, which was held in reserve until the infantry, artillery, and air had opened a hole. The British armor then exploited the success and destroyed the German force."[6] But this explanation of El Alamein was most dubious. In fact, British armor cast in the cavalry exploitation role failed to destroy the German force. Generalfeldmarschall Erwin Rommel had approached closer to the classic ideal of destroying the enemy forces when it was the Germans who were winning the desert battles, before the British attained preponderances of two to one or better in men and tanks, and Rommel's principal means was the panzer division as a weapon of assault as well as exploitation, the combination of pulverizing armored power plus mobility. Furthermore, General Montgomery himself would have used his armored divisions at El Alamein not in the fashion that McNair commended but as Rommel had used the panzers, to spearhead the main attack, had he not concluded unhappily that British armored divisions and particularly British tank-infantry coordination were not good enough to essay the role of the German panzers.

Still, McNair's rejection of armor as concentrated power was firm. To the commander of the 1st Armored Division campaigning in Italy he wrote on April 3, 1944: "The big question in my mind is the relative merit of tank battalions attached to infantry divisions vs. infantry attached to armored divisions. I lean toward employing armored divisions for exploitation and tank battalions attached to infantry divisions for your present job of infighting."[7]

For the strategy of overpowering the German army in the West, then, the American army would rely mainly on the infantry, with attached tanks, to supply the power, while the armored divisions were redesigned to serve as a cavalry of exploitation.

Tanks for European Battle

The design and quality of American tanks became directly linked to the revised conception of the armored division. On May 1, 1940, a month before the creation of the American Armored Force, the U.S. Army had 464 tanks, mainly light tanks of nine to eleven tons armed with .50-caliber machine guns. There were a few M2A4 lights and M2A1 mediums armed with a 37mm. gun. In response to the German Pzkw IV and its 75mm. gun, the Ordnance Department and the Armored Force agreed in August that the United States must produce a new medium tank equipped both with a 75 and with heavier armor than the 25mm. of the M2A1.

Because a 75mm. gun would require a larger turret than any previously used in the United States, development of which would take time, the Ordnance Department chose to hurry a new tank into production by mounting a 75mm. gun in a sponson in the right front hull of the T5E2 medium, which was a prototype tank that Ordnance had developed on its own initiative in 1938 to carry a 75mm. howitzer. The turret would still have only a 37mm. gun. This tank became the M3 General Grant, of twenty-nine tons and 57mm. armor. Despite the obvious defect of limited traverse of the 75mm. gun in the sponson, accentuated by the Grant's high silhouette while the main gun was placed awkwardly low, the British Eighth Army welcomed the Grant as a godsend when it began to arrive in quantity in the late spring of 1941. The Eighth Army gave every tank regiment one or two Grant squadrons as rapidly as possible, because the Grant was the first tank in North Africa to compete with the Pzkw IV on approximately equal terms.

With the Grant as a stopgap, the Americans proceeded to develop their 75mm. turret tank, with armor up to 81mm. on the turret front. The prototype, called the T6, was completed in September 1941, and quantity production began in July 1942. In its production model this was the thirty-three-ton M4 General Sherman. American industry produced 21,000 Shermans in 1943, more than German and British tank production combined. Turned out in such numbers, the Sherman was sure to be the standard American tank for the strategic power drive into France and Germany.

This latter fact was unfortunate, because by 1943 the Sherman had fallen behind in the race for tank supremacy. It remained a good match for the Pzkw IV, which the Germans still used in large numbers. But as the Anglo-Americans planned at last for a cross-Channel invasion in the spring of 1944, a German panzer division usually had not only a battalion of Pzkw IVs but also a battalion of Pzkw Vs, the Panther. The forty-three-ton Panther excelled the Sherman slightly in speed—43.5 to 41 kilometers, or 27 to 25 miles, per hour; considerably in armor—with 120mm. front armor; and almost decisively in the superior muzzle velocity and range of its long—seventy calibers—75 over the Sherman's short 75mm. gun. The Sherman had better mechanical endurance, not only in its engine but in a rubber-block track with about five times the life expectancy of the Germans' steel track; but endurance became irrelevant if the superior Panther knocked the Sherman out early. On solid ground, the Sherman had slightly better maneuverability, but the Panther with wider treads and superior flotation reversed this advantage whenever the ground was at all soft. The Sherman had greater rapidity of fire because it was equipped with a gyrostabilizer and a powered traverse. Nevertheless, the usual dependence of the Sherman in combat against the Panther had to be upon greater numbers of tanks, unless the Sherman's crew were exceptionally skillful tank tacticians.

With numbers, Shermans could surround a Panther and hit its vulnerable flanks and rear. As General Omar N. Bradley was to comment, "this willingness to expend Shermans offered little comfort to the crews who were forced to expend themselves as well."[8]

To make matters worse, from late 1942 onward American and British armor had to cope with the stiffening of the panzers by detachments of fifty-six-ton, and eventually larger, Pzkw VIs, the Tiger, ungainly but frightening vehicles with an 88mm. gun.

If armored divisions were intended primarily to generate mobility, not mobility and power combined, then the lightly armed but mechanically durable and reliable Sherman might be just right. This was the ascendant conviction when the Sherman was standardized and put into production. The Ordnance Department nevertheless believed the United States should not only match but excel the Germans' strengthening of tank armor and armament; but as in the question of heavier antitank guns, Ordnance could not persuade the Army Ground Forces. As early as December 1941, Ordnance had produced a pilot model of a sixty-ton tank whose long 76mm. gun made it the most powerful tank in the world at the time. During 1942, this vehicle went into limited production as the M6; but it was cancelled in December 1942 because the Ground Forces and even the Armored Force perceived no requirement for it. Stubbornly, the Ordnance Department had begun in May 1942 a project for a somewhat lighter but similarly armed tank, the T20, T22, and T23 series. With bad luck, the T23 fell afoul of the gremlins in an excessively innovative electrical transmission, as well as suffering the indifference of the Ground Forces.

Only in February 1944 did Ground Forces headquarters abruptly recognize the obsolescence of the Sherman, whereupon they insisted on a hasty project to mount the turret and the long 76mm. gun of the T20 series on Sherman hulls. It was now too late to put more than a handful of this compromise design into action before the end of the year. The T20 series itself was now redesigned for a 90mm. gun, but its arrival on the battlefield lay still further in the future.

In the spring of 1944, the only tank in the Anglo-American armies capable of jousting with the Panther on terms approaching equality was the Firefly, a Sherman that the British modified to take a 17-pounder (76.2mm.) long gun. First proposed in 1942, this design had been put off by the British Ministry of Supply until 1943 on the pretext that it was impossible to achieve the necessary changes in the Sherman turret. Consequently, only a fourth of the British armored regiments would have the Firefly for the cross-Channel invasion—but at that they were better off than the Americans.

Among the motives causing this newest lag in American tank design there was also General McNair's conviction, widely shared, that tanks should not fight other tanks, but should go after more vulnerable targets, particularly infantry. Defense against enemy tanks should be left to the antitank weapons of the infantry and artillery and to the tank destroyers. Indeed, approximately this same conception had prevailed among the German originators of the panzer divisions during the early years of the war. In North Africa, the deadliest enemies of British tanks were not German tanks but the Germans' skillfully deployed and handled antitank guns, most conspicuously but by no means solely the dreaded 88s. Thus the Germans kept the panzers themselves free for offensive roles. But as the Germans lost control of the war and passed to the defensive, it became their new custom to use the power of the panzer divisions as their principal instrument of counterattack against Allied offensives. Confronting this German habit, the Allies could not escape the result that, it they used their own tanks in the offensive, they could not help but tangle with counterattacking German tanks. Tank-versus-tank battles were implicit in the strategy of the cross-Channel invasion. Inferior or not, the Shermans must take on Panthers and Tigers.

The Infantry

When the Civil War and the First World War had demanded that the mobile, frontier-constabulary American army convert itself into a force of overwhelming power, the power came to reside primarily in Grant's and Pershing's infantry divisions. In the years following the World War, American soldiers mainly believed that if the call came to apply a strategy of overwhelming power again, once more they would muster big, strong, resilient infantry divisions. In October 1938 the War Department General Staff restated that: "the Infantry Division continues to be the basic combat element by which battles are won, the necessary enemy field forces destroyed, and captured territory held."[9]

The American infantry division of 1917–1918 was big, strong, and resilient to the extent of employing about twice the manpower of other nations' divisions. This was the "square" division of four regiments organized into two brigades, the whole some 22,000 strong. From 1935 to 1941, the threat of a new war led the United States Army to conduct the largest sequence of maneuvers in its history. Consistently, the active American senior officer who boasted the most extensive command experience in the World War, Major General (from August 1939 Lieutenant General) Hugh A. Drum, commander of the First Army, affirmed that the maneuvers proved the necessity to retain the combat endurance, the sustained power, of the square division of 1917–1918.[10]

Increasingly, Drum's colleagues thought otherwise. From its origins in 1917, many officers had objected that the square division was too hard to maneuver and supply to be fit for anything except static trench warfare. General McNair, who despite his doubts about the Germans' newfangled panzer divisions was by no means simply a conservative, faulted the square division because it obstructed his passion for mobility. In the late 1930s, McNair was commanding general of a division testing a "triangular," three-regiment structure dispensing with brigade headquarters and altogether tailored for lightness and mobility. General Pershing had recommended such a triangular division as early as 1920 as more suitable than the square division for the open, mobile warfare likely to return in the future, and the War Department had tentatively endorsed the design in 1935. As chief of staff of General Headquarters from 1940 to 1942 and commanding general of Army Ground Forces, McNair could be the principal architect translating the principle of the triangular division into practical detail.

Under tables of organization drawn up in 1940, the Regular Army divisions shifted from square to triangular form by the time of Pearl Harbor. National Guard divisions were converted only after the United States went to war. In contrast to the square division, the triangular division had 15,514 officers and men under tables of organization of June 1, 1941. By July 15, 1943, General McNair had taken the lead in further paring the American infantry division to 14,253.

McNair's special contribution was to enhance the mobility and flexibility of the new division through consistent application of "the sound fundamental," as he put it, "that the division or other unit should be provided organically with only those means which it needs practically always. Peak loads, and unusual and infrequent demands obviously should be met from a pool—ordinarily in the army or separate corps."[11] A combat infantry division should consist of combat infantry and the essential supporting arms and the barest necessities of supporting services, with nothing else. There should be no frills; anything beyond basic combat forces that might be required occasionally should be attached only on occasion, coming when needed from an army or corps pool and then returning to the pool. Nothing unessential should hinder the division's movement. McNair liked his fighting units lean and tough.

The more fully the infantry division adhered to McNair's "sound fundamental" and carried as part of its table-of-organization strength only the men and equipment it would need under practically all conditions, the lighter and more mobile the division became. The more faithfully the whole army observed the fundamental, putting nothing into a division unless the division practically always required it in combat, the more effectively the army could use its limited manpower and resources. Men and equipment would be wasted if they were placed where they were not constantly used. The military principle of economy of force does not mean getting along with little, but making maximum use of available resources, without waste.

It was within the logic of McNair's "sound fundamental" that the infantry division would ordinarily do its own antitank fighting. It should not rely on armored divisions for this purpose, nor should tank destroyer battalions be assigned organically to infantry divisions. McNair believed that the usual complement of antitank guns and bazookas would permit an infantry division to turn back limited numbers of enemy tanks. If enemy tanks should attack not in limited numbers but in mass, then one or more tank destroyer battalions would have to be called on. But the enemy could not mount mass tank attacks against all divisions simultaneously, and a tank destroyer battalion assigned to a division not experiencing such an attack would be wasted. Here was the reason why it was better to pool tank destroyer battalions, so they could readily be concentrated against a mass tank attack, or, if it should become advisable, so they could just as readily be dispersed across a wide front. The same reasoning applied to antiaircraft battalions. Furthermore, McNair regarded both tank destroyers and antiaircraft guns as primarily defensive weapons, and he did not wish to burden the infantry division with logistical strains for the sake of defense. The lean, tough division was supposed to be an offensive weapon.

The mobility of a particular arm was another principal criterion for determining whether the unit handling it should be assigned to the infantry division or pooled. Tanks fight offensively, but they share with tank destroyers and antiaircraft guns the characteristic of high mobility; they can range easily beyond the front of a single division, and this fact helped McNair decide that tank battalions should also be pooled and shared by several divisions rather than assigned permanently to a single division (even though practice eventually led toward virtual permanent assignment).

The range of a weapon also helped determine where it should be assigned. Because 60mm. mortars had a range greater than the frontage of a rifle platoon, they did not go into a rifle platoon but were pooled in a weapons platoon of a rifle company, whence they could assist all of the company's rifle platoons. According to the same thinking, 81mm. mortars and heavy machine guns were not assigned to the rifle company but pooled in a battalion. Field artillery was not assigned to an infantry regiment but pooled in divisional artillery, with additional and especially the larger guns pooled under corps or army control.

The smallest infantry unit was the rifle squad of twelve men, armed with ten M1 Garand semiautomatic rifles, one automatic rifle, and one M1903 bolt-action Springfield rifle. Three squads formed a rifle platoon. In the July 1943 infantry division, a rifle company consisted of three rifle platoons plus a weapons platoon armed with two .30-caliber and one .50-caliber machine guns, three 60mm. mortars, and three bazookas. With headquarters personnel, the rifle company had six officers and 187 enlisted men. The 5,211 officers and men of its twenty-seven rifle companies formed the fighting core of an infantry division.

An organizational feature of the First World War not discarded with the square division was the necessity, even within General McNair's desire for extreme leanness and toughness, to back up the riflemen with heavier weapons as close to the front as possible; otherwise the riflemen would not be able to suppress the heavier weapons of the defense. An infantry battalion united three rifle companies with a heavy weapons company armed with eight .30-caliber and three .50-caliber machine guns, six 81mm. mortars, and seven bazookas. The battalion also had a headquarters company equipped with three 57mm. antitank guns, three .30-caliber and one .50-caliber machine guns, and eight bazookas. The infantry battalion numbered 871. An infantry regiment was made up of three infantry battalions plus a headquarters company, a service company, an antitank company (six 57mm. antitank guns), a cannon company (six 105mm. howitzers and three .50-caliber machine guns), and a medical detachment.

Organic to the division besides its three infantry regiments were division artillery, a headquarters company, a reconnaissance troop, a combat engineer battalion, a medical battalion, a quartermaster company, an ordnance company, a signal company, and a military police platoon. The divisional artillery had three twelve-piece 105mm. howitzer battalions and one twelve-piece 155mm. howitzer battalion. An additional eighty-nine .50-caliber machine guns were scattered through the artillery. Total principal armament of an infantry division was 6,518 rifles, 243 automatic rifles, 157 .30-caliber machine guns, 236 .50-caliber machine guns, ninety 60mm. mortars, fifty-four 81mm. mortars, 557 bazookas, fifty-seven 57mm. antitank guns, fifty-four 105mm. howitzers, and twelve 155mm. howitzers.

An apparently formidable armament; yet throughout, mobility rather than power had also become the outstanding characteristic of the American infantry division. All elements of the division except the infantry were motorized. With the attachment of only six quartermaster truck companies, the infantry could be motorized as well. Or, as the infantrymen promptly demonstrated in combat, the appropriation of enemy transport and the mounting of infantry everywhere conceivable on the division's trucks and artillery vehicles and the attached tanks motorized the division still more easily. In pursuit, an American infantry division readily moved on wheels and tracked vehicles. No other army in the world was so mobile.

German infantry divisions depended on marching and on horse transport for tactical movement, railroads for strategic movement, to the end. To supplement the motorized infantry of the panzer divisions, the Germans created a small number of motorized infantry divisions. In June 1943 these units received the same designation as the infantry of the panzer divisions and became panzer grenadier divisions. Having gone through a phase in 1942–1943 during which one of the original three motorized infantry regiments was replaced by a motorcycle rifle battalion, these divisions now in turn replaced the motorcycle battalion with either a tank battalion or a battalion of assault guns—that is, turretless but otherwise tanklike vehicles intended for infantry support or antitank work, increasingly common in the German army as tank production failed to keep pace with demand. Not only were the panzer grenadier divisions few in number, however; the ordinary American infantry division with its customary attached tank battalion and the ease of its complete motorization was the equivalent in mobility of one of these elite German formations.

Whether the 1943 infantry division could prove to be a satisfactory reservoir of power was another matter. In combat power, the triangular division no longer heavily outweighed a German infantry division as the old square division had done, but instead mustered merely comparable strength. When the German army was on the offensive in 1939–1942, however, its infantry divisions played second fiddle to the panzer divisions in exerting the power to achieve breakthroughs. But American armored divisions were not designed with the power to do what panzer divisions had done. Whether the American infantry divisions could suitably carry the burden of a strategy of head-on assault against German strength across the English Channel was the question raised by their remaining the principal locus of the American army's power, yet being deprived of any impressive amplitude of power.

The Americans had scarcely begun to experience those painful lessons of the First World War in the limitations of infantry's offensive power that had driven the Europeans to the search for substitutes, culminating in the panzer division. In 1921, George C. Marshall, Jr., then a major, writing in the *Infantry Journal*, had warned American officers against generalizing about modern warfare from their 1918 experiences against a German army already stumbling into exhaustion. American infantry had scored offensive accomplishments against a crippled and weary enemy that it could not expect to repeat against a fresh and first-rate foe.[12] The generalizing proceeded nevertheless, not least in unfaltering reliance on the infantry division as "the basic combat element by which battles are won."

American infantry tactics had to bend to the 1918 experience; what was missing was a larger searching to probe how badly the infantryman's vulnerability to modern firepower and the consequent tactical adjustments vitiated the breakthrough capacity of an army whose main offensive reliance was upon its infantry. Like the tactics of all armies influenced by the 1914–1918 display of firepower, those of the American infantry came to be based on a combination of fire and maneuver: fire must neutralize the enemy's fire and cover the American infantry so the riflemen could advance to close combat; in combat, there should be no maneuver without fire and no fire without meneuver. So far so good; but the specific tactical application of fire and maneuver tended to dilute still further the infantry offensive power whose devastation by defensive weaponry was already the source of the fire-and-maneuver philosophy.

An American twelve-man rifle squad had a two-man scout section (ABLE), a four-man fire section (BAKER), which included the squad's automatic rifle, and a five-man maneuver-and-assault section (CHARLIE). Customarily, the squad leader would advance with ABLE to locate the enemy. He would then signal his assistant leader in BAKER to fire, according to whatever plan the situation suggested. Thereupon he would join CHARLIE for the maneuver to exploit the cover laid down by BAKER's fire. In practice, the squad leader tended to get pinned down with ABLE. At best, CHARLIE was likely to have to drive home the final assault alone. At worst, a few casualties to any section could wreck the whole design.

To be sure, enlarging the attack to platoon strength rendered the enterprise less fragile and increased the possibilities for maneuver—such as a pincers movement by two squads while the third squad provided covering fire. Nevertheless, the standard tactics yielded so dull a cutting edge that various substitute systems came out of experience in the field. The most notable and successful was the marching fire attack. In it, the infantry went forward in a thick skirmish line firing everything they had, including automatic rifles and light machine guns, at anything that might harbor an enemy who could fire back. Every available larger weapon laid down supporting fire. The marching fire attack could offer concentration and momentum. It put many more men into the first wave than the standard fire-and-maneuver tactics. It afforded the attackers the assurance of each others' company in considerable numbers, and it multiplied the shock effect upon the defenders. The attack was supposed to keep moving, with no one going to ground, unless superior enemy strength compelled abandoning the whole effort. But the marching fire attack was also more dangerous than the standard fire and movement, less able to take advantage of shelter and concealment, more exposed to enemy fire and counterattack. The troops were not overly fond of it. General Bradley, according to one of his aides, "wonders why American troops will seldom advance with marching fire from their rifles. Says he has been trying to get them doing it since the last world war but they simply do not take to it. 'They seem to need something to shoot at.' "[13]

From the first battles in North Africa, American officers planning for the power drive into northwestern Europe had to note that the infantry on which they would rely as their main combat resource was not particularly aggressive. The enemy did not rate American infantry highly; American officers had to concede a lack of aggressive zeal. By 1943, the army also knew something of the findings of the combat historian S.L.A. Marshall about American riflemen in the Pacific which, further developed, and incorporating observations of the European war, would form the basis of his postwar book *Men against Fire: The Problem of Combat Command in Future War*.[14] The volume of rifle fire laid down by American infantry, Marshall found, consistently left much to be desired. At most, 25 to 30 percent of the riflemen fired their weapons in battle. Well-led, well-trained, crack units such as the paratroopers achieved such levels. In many regiments, only 15 percent of the riflemen ever fired a shot at the enemy. Nor did these figures mean that 15 to 30 percent of the riflemen fired continually throughout a battle. They indicated only the number who tried to shoot at the enemy at least once.

When Marshall's findings became widely known in the army after the war, training methods were revised to stimulate infantry firing, and in Korea and Vietnam the infantry rate of fire became more impressive. Meanwhile, the limitations should not have been surprising. Almost all American soldiers were conditioned from infancy not to kill. On the battlefields of the Second World War, their civilized abhorrence of killing converged with the battlefield's apparent loneliness and the individual soldier's sense of isolation. With the sergeant no longer watching closely as he had in earlier wars and as he had in training, and with the act of firing now deadly serious as it had not been in training, most soldiers could not bring themselves to fire.

In artillery gun crews, or in airplanes, where killing became impersonal, or somehow with heavier infantry weapons than the rifle—even with the Browning Automatic

Rifle—the remoteness of the enemy, the proximity of comrades, or the soldier's conspic-uousness broke the taboo, and men shot to kill despite their nurturing. Among the riflemen, however, it was the relative few who fired who also proved to be the soldiers who maneuvered most aggressively. Thus infantry fire and infantry maneuver both had to depend on a much smaller number of men than the tactical system implied, when the power envisaged by the tactical system was already small enough. It did not help that the American army of World War II habitually filled the ranks of its combat infantry with its least promising recruits, the uneducated, the unskilled, the unenthusiastic. Those left over after the Army Air Forces, the marines, the navy, the paratroops, and the technical branches had skimmed off the best of the nation's military manpower were then expected to bear the main burden of sustained battle.

The inadequacy of the battlefield power generated by the standard infantry division accounted for the custom of attaching one of the separate tank battalions to almost every infantry division. The attached tank battalions were to prove themselves essential to the forward advance of the infantry against recalcitrant opposition, and often on defense against enemy armor as well. Yet the attachment of the tank battalion to a division also underlined the defects of the design of the army. If an attached tank battalion was essential to the effectiveness of the infantry division under most combat circumstances, as it proved to be, then by the logic of McNair's system the battalion should have been organic to the division. The number of separate battalions and the number of divisions did not quite match up; occasionally, in the campaign of France and Germany, an infantry division was to find itself without an available tank battalion, and then some-times substitute armor had to be detached from an armored division, to the detriment of that force, to supply the deficiency. More important, if the infantry division needed tanks consistently, infantry and tanks should have been able to train together and work together permanently, to learn thoroughly each other's ways. Deficiencies in infantry-tank teamwork were to prove a severe problem in Europe at the outset and a persisting problem even as the campaign wore on. Moreover, because the infantry division required consistent tank support, one tank battalion was scarcely enough. The infantry regiments might rotate and rest their battalions, but the infantry division's single attached tank battalion had to fight on, and wear out men and equipment, as long as the division was in action. Finally, the infantry-tank team especially suffered the deficiencies of the Sherman tank. Heavy firepower and protection, gunnery and armor comparable to the panzers', were more valuable than mobility in a tank working with infantry.

Mobile as the American infantry division was, moreover, its designers omitted an artillery weapon both mobile and powerful enough to work up close with the riflemen. The towed 105mm. gun-howitzer was too cumbersome for this role, as any towed gun would have been. With this weapon, divisional artillery too often had to remain well behind the infantry, working with corps and army artillery rather than contributing uniquely and more directly to the division. The need was for a self-propelled gun able to keep pace with infantry movement, at least comparable to the 75mm. self-propelled gun that the Germans used both to support the infantry platoon close at hand in the attack and to assist in repelling enemy tanks. By 1944, the German army no longer had enough of these guns, to the great good fortune of the Allies; but losses of the guns had been high partly because they served so well and were therefore so much in demand on the Eastern Front. In general, relying principally on towed, roadbound guns meant that the artillery detracted from the mobility that was the primary characteristic of the American army. This limitation of the artillery, its difficulties in displacing rapidly either forward or toward the rear, would become conspicuous especially when the American army had to go into retreat.

Nevertheless, an American officer observed that "We let the arty fight the war as much as possible."[15] For the sustained power that its other components lacked, the American army had to look to its artillery. From the time American divisions first entered the Second World War against Germany in 1942, the same Germans who disparaged American infantry consistently praised American artillery. Part of the reason for a good artillery showing from the beginning was that battlefield experience counts less among the guns than in infantry or armor. Artillerymen largely do the same thing in combat that they have done all through their training—laying down fire on targets they do not see. In addition, exceptional communications equipment permitted American artillery to excel in the ability of a single forward observer—often flying in a Piper or Stinson liaison plane—to request and receive the fires of all the batteries within range of a target in a single concentrated barrage. The American guns specialized in "TOT"—time on target—concentrations of multiple batteries, or even of numerous battalions, upon designated targets for designated periods of time. To the catastrophic effects of a TOT, German prisoners gave universal testimony. On all fronts, artillery caused more than half the casualties of World War II battles; but the artillery was the American army's special strong suit.

For all the deadliness of American guns, there remained enough inconsistencies between the American strategy of overwhelming power and the actual design of the American army less to generate power than to exercise mobility, that the strategy could have struck deep trouble against an alert, well-disciplined, well-equipped, battlewise foe. Fortunately for the Americans, the German army in 1944 as in 1918 would not be the German army at the peak of its own power. Yet this foe still had to be respected and feared.

The Germans

The panzer divisions no longer wielded the power of 1940, the Eastern Front demanded the German army's principal resources, and the wounds inflicted by the Russians had already drawn blood from its main arteries, but the German army in 1944 still could claim to be qualitatively the best army in the world. It had held the title in unbroken continuity since 1870. Its quality lay in firepower enhanced by superior professional skill among the officers and superior combat savvy and unexcelled courage among the ranks.

Since its creation in the same wars that unified Germany, the German army with unvarying consistency had surpassed all other armies in the casualty rates it imposed upon its enemies in proportion to its own losses. With unvarying consistency it had achieved proportionately greater results than any other army for the numbers of men and divisions it employed.[16] In the First World War, nearly the whole world had to join in arms against it to bring down this army. In 1944, the German army once again was fending off the blows of nearly all the world. If by the spring of 1944 the tides of war on the Eastern Front seemed to have turned irrevocably against the Germans, nevertheless the Soviets required favorable odds ranging from five to one to fifteen to one to defeat them. In North Africa, the British had never matched the combat effectiveness of the Germans division for division—to say nothing of infantry-tank coordination. The eventual British success from El Alamein to Tunis was founded upon odds of two to one in men and higher in tanks against the Panzerarmee Afrika and its various coadjutors. In North Africa and Italy, the American army also was consistently unable to match the military skill of the Germans division for division. Though by 1944 American strategists had grown impatient to apply their power strategy of an invasion of northwest Europe, it must remain forever doubtful whether at any earlier time their inexperienced divisions could have challenged the German concentrations across the English Channel.

The sources of the German army's fighting capacity lay in large part in the rigorous professional educational system that continually prodded forward and tested the officer corps, in the scarcely less rigorous school system through which the noncommissioned officers had to pass, and in the remarkable abilities of both commissioned and noncommissioned officers to transmit combat skills to their men. German divisions displayed an awesome ability to survive shattering casualties and yet to rebound within weeks, as long as a reasonable remnant of the officer cadre escaped to train the replacement troops. So high were the professional attainments of the German army that a handful of German officers sufficed to accomplish apparent miracles of training and leadership. The officer corps comprised only 2.86 percent of the German army's total strength at the beginning of the Second World War and declined in relative strength as the war went on. In contrast, officers represented 7 percent of the overall strength of the American army (and were to grow to 15 percent of the army during the Vietnam War). Yet so capable were German officers in transforming individual soldiers into cohesive units that in the German army the company developed a sufficient sense of comradeship and solidarity to constitute a primary group, whereas in the American army the usual primary group was the squad, or at the largest, the platoon. It is not dedication to a cause but such unit consciousness and solidarity that makes an army an effective fighting force.

Except in mobility, the structure of the German infantry division resembled the American. From 1939 to 1943, the German infantry division was organized like the American triangular division around nine rifle battalions in three infantry regiments. Its artillery was also comparable to the American division's, comprising one regiment of one medium battalion (150mm. howitzers) and three light battalions (105mm. howitzers or guns), with a total of forty-eight pieces. Additional organic units, principally reconnaissance and antitank, made the German division of the early years of the war somewhat larger than its American counterpart, aggregating almost 17,200.

By 1944, however, the Germans could no longer find enough manpower to keep up such relatively large divisions, and in October 1943 and again in early 1944 they pared their tables of organization. The 1944 German infantry division had only six rifle battalions, in three two-battalion regiments. The loss was partly compensated for by the substitution of a Füsilier battalion for the reconnaissance battalion, an army habitually on the defensive not requiring so much reconnaissance. The Füsilier battalion had the same organization as a rifle battalion, except that one company used bicycles, and the battalion as a whole had some motor transport was well as more horse-drawn vehicles than its contemporaries. With this relative wealth of transport, the Füsilier battalion usually became the divisional reserve; former reconnaissance men complained they had been converted into firemen. Otherwise, to reduce the total strength of the division to 12,769, the Germans mainly cut supply and administrative elements, not combat power. Though they reduced the rifle company to two officers and 140 enlisted men, they increased the proportion of automatic weapons—especially 9mm. Schmeisser MP38 and MP40 submachine guns—to the standard Mauser 7.92mm. bolt-action rifle. The increase in automatic weapons gave the German infantry division superior firepower over its American rival despite its having about 1,200 fewer combat infantrymen.

Many of the German divisions along the coast of France were static, garrison divisions. These formations retained the triangular organization of nine rifle battalions, but they lacked a Füsilier or reconnaissance battalion and had only three artillery battalions. By early 1944, they had been combed out repeatedly to find replacements for the Eastern Front. In this process many had had an entire regiment stricken from their rolls, and all were considerably understrength.

The German army of 1944 also had a variety of divisions not conforming to standard tables of organization. Two of the divisions stationed in Normandy early in the year and potentially participants in a battle for France, the 77th and 91st, had their six rifle battalions formed into two instead of three regiments, lacked Füsilier battalions, and had three instead of four artillery battalions. But the 77th added a rifle battalion and an artillery battery of Osttruppen—soldiers from the subject territories of the East—and the 91st had an attached parachute regiment.

More important variations were those of the ss and Luftwaffe divisions, which were not administered by the principal German defense organization, the Wehrmacht, but rather were elements of the semiautonomous satrapies of Reichsführer ss Heinrich Himmler and Reichsmarschall Hermann Göring, respectively. The ss—the Schutz Staffel, the "protective squadron" first for Hitler and then for the whole Nazi party—and Luftwaffe formations were Nazi elites made up of zealous, even fanatical volunteers and favored in training and equipment. Paratroopers were part of the Luftwaffe. The Luftwaffe divisions, such as the 3rd and 5th Parachute Divisions awaiting the Allies across the English Channel, retained three regiments of three battalions each at approximately full strength. In addition, each regiment had a thirteenth, mortar company; a fourteenth, antitank company; and a fifteenth, engineer company. The rifle companies enjoyed exceptionally high allotments of light machine guns, and the weapons companies of heavy machine guns and mortars. In May 1944, the 3rd Parachute Division, for example, still carried a ration strength of 17,420.

The heart of the German army remained in the panzer divisions. By 1944, however, these varied from one to another still more than the infantry divisions. Six Wehrmacht and three ss panzer divisions waited in France for the Western Allies. Among these nine, the army panzer divisions ranged in strength from 12,768 (9th Panzer) to 16,466 (2nd Panzer), the favored ss panzer divisions from 17,590 (9th ss Panzer) to 21,386 (1st ss Panzer). The ss panzer divisions had three rifle battalions in each panzer grenadier regiment instead of the two of their army counterparts. All the panzer divisions in the West had more men than their American counterparts, but they retained fewer—though generally more powerful—tanks. The 130th Panzer Lehr Division, an exceptionally well equipped Wehrmacht demonstration formation, resembled an American armored division in mobility, because all four of its panzer grenadier battalions and its engineer battalion rode in half-tracks, and all of its artillery was self-propelled. Nevertheless, like most of the 1944 panzer divisions, Panzer Lehr had only two tank battalions, one of

Panthers and one of Pzkw IVs; its tank strength was 190, supplemented by forty assault guns. The big 1st ss Panzer Division had most of its strength in panzer grenadiers; its armor consisted of its full complement of forty-five assault guns but only thirty-eight Panthers and fifty Pzkw IVs of an assigned tank complement of 203. A German tank company was supposed to have twenty-two Panthers or Pzkw IVs, or ten Tigers; it almost always had fewer. There were four or fewer tank companies to a tank battalion.

In preparation for the anticipated Allied cross-Channel invasion, the Germans accelerated deliveries of armor to the West in the early months of 1944. By the end of April, their Western command had 1,608 German-made tanks and assault guns, of which 674 were Pzkw IVs and 514 were Panthers. To oppose an Allied army that must come out of the sea, and whose armored buildup must necessarily consume time, this was no mean force, especially in the hands of the inventors of the panzer Blitzkrieg, and backed by the most professionally skillful army of modern times.

From the beginning of Anglo-American contemplation of a cross-Channel invasion, the power of the German army posed the consistent central problem of all invasion planning, as expressed by Lieutenant General F.E. Morgan: "The essential discrepancy in value between the enemy's troops, highly organised, armed and battle-trained, who await us in their much vaunted impregnable defences, and our troops, who must of necessity launch their assault at the end of a cross-Channel voyage with all its attendant risks, must be reduced to the narrowest possible margin."[17]

The German army of 1944 had long since passed the peak of its power. Yet no American or British soldier who had fought in North Africa or Italy would be inclined to take any part of that army lightly, not even the static divisions. Those Americans already scarred by battle against Hitler's legions would have found nothing surprising in an anecdote circulated soon after the invasion occurred. According to the story, Major General Raymond O. Barton of the American 4th Infantry Division visited one of his battalions to spur them on with assurances that the German formation in front of them was only second rate and not much of an opponent. A young S-2 (Intelligence) lieutenant remarked: "General, I think you'd better put the Germans on the distribution list. They don't seem to realize that."[18]

3: The View of the Far Shore

THE INVASION of northwest Europe was preeminently an American military design. It was rooted in the strategic tradition of U.S. Grant and the Civil War, of the application of overwhelming power. Notwithstanding the inconsistencies that hindered development of an American army as uncompromisingly powerful as the tradition implied, the design was characteristically American in other ways. To carry powerful armies from England to the Far Shore of the Channel and there afford them a solid lodgment required a combination of maritime might and great land forces that only the United States could muster. All other military great powers of the modern era either had been primarily sea powers and only secondarily land powers, such as Britain, or primarily continental powers and very secondarily sea powers, such as France, Germany, and Russia. The United States was the first modern great power capable of grasping primacy on both land and sea simultaneously. Only such a power could embrace with its whole heart the combination of naval and military challenges posed by the cross-Channel invasion. Against the obstacles to thrusting great armies across the Channel, Germany had faltered because she lacked sea power, Britain because she lacked strong enough armies. But America, from even before her entry into the Second World War, had foreseen the cross-Channel invasion as the climax of her military efforts.

Because the eventual invasion had to be an Allied, Anglo-American effort, however, rather than exclusively American, it proved to be shaped by the caution and hesitations of a power of less military breadth than the United States. Since the expulsion of their army from the Continent at Dunkirk in 1940, the British had looked forward to an eventual military return to France. By a twist of fate, it was on the 6th of June, 1940, two days after the Dunkirk evacuation and precisely four years before the eventual date of return, that Prime Minister Winston Churchill addressed to General Sir Hastings Ismay, his chief of staff in his capacity as Minister of Defence, the first of a series of memos urging development of craft *"for transporting and landing troops on the beach,"* to resume offensive operations.[1] The next month, Churchill appointed Admiral of the Fleet Sir Roger Keyes as Director of Combined Operations, to study and command exercises in amphibious assault. Later the direction of Combined Operations fell into the abler hands of Commodore (eventually Vice Admiral, with equivalent rank in the army and RAF) Lord Louis Mountbatten. As early as June 23, 1940, the day after the surrender of France, two boats—the only suitable craft Britain could find—landed 120 men on the French coast near Boulogne in the first of the Commando raids. Eventually the Commandos were to return again and again, in mounting force, to gather information and to harry the Germans.

In a series of conferences with the British Chiefs of Staff and their principal subordinates at Claridge's in London in April 1942, General Marshall arranged for an American section to be attached to Combined Operations. Brigadier General Lucian K. Truscott, Jr., headed the section and began organizing the 1st Ranger Battalion, volunteers chosen mostly from the 34th Infantry Division, to train with the British Commandos, keep abreast of their experiments and techniques, and eventually join in their raids on the coast of Europe. Distributed among Number 3 and 4 Commando Groups, the 1st Ranger Battalion sent fifty of its men into the Dieppe raid on August 18, 1942.

Before the end of 1941, the British Joint Planners had prepared ROUNDUP, a plan for a cross-Channel invasion on a front from Deauville to Dieppe. Still, nothing like a large-scale invasion prepared to come to grips with strong German armies could be initiated by Britain alone. The 1941 ROUNDUP was, as its codename implied, a plan to exploit German disintegration. Though Winston Churchill breathed fiery defiance and vengeance as soon as the British army had returned from Dunkirk, his design for invasion was always one that would be applied only after a combination of aerial bombardment, nourishment of anti-Nazi resistance within Europe, and closing a ring of peripheral attacks around Hitler's empire had so undermined the enemy's strength that the invasion would be simply the coup de grace.

It was not only that Britain was too exclusively a sea power, rather than a truly amphibious military organism like America, to close alone in battle with German land power on the Far Shore. Even after the United States entered the Second World War and promised all the men and matériel required for the cross-Channel invasion, Winston Churchill's government still resisted the importunities of the Americans to hasten into the climactic effort of the war. Churchill blanched at any prospect of a European tournament of mass armies, even with the might of America at Britain's side. In this he sensed the fears and feelings of the people he led; for, as his friend and scientific adviser Professor F.A. Lindemann said to General Marshall, "You must remember you are fighting our losses on the Somme."[2] Against the ghosts of 1916, against Churchill's hope to vindicate his earlier preference for a peripheral strategy all through the 1914–1918 war, against Churchill's perception also that only as long as the Second World War was waged in narrow land areas like those of the Mediterranean without mass armies could Britain best retain equal weight in her partnership with America—against a complexity of British motives, the United States struggled without success for agreement to mount an invasion of northwest Europe in 1942 or 1943.

Under Soviet as well as American pressure to cease at last postponing what the Russians and Americans regarded as the only decisive stroke possible against Germany in the West, the British government promised at the TRIDENT Conference of Anglo-American leaders in Washington in May 1943 to aim for a major invasion of France on May 1, 1944. At the QUADRANT Conference at Quebec in August 1943, Churchill conceded that the cross-Channel invasion should receive the highest priority of the Anglo-American alliance in 1944—but he also inserted into the minutes of the conference a requirement for a staff study of an invasion of Norway as a possible alternative. At nearly the end of 1943, at his Tehran meeting with President Roosevelt and Generalissimo Stalin in November, Churchill strained his skill in debate to postpone the cross-Channel invasion once again until the next autumn, to afford time for further Mediterranean operations. He might have succeeded had not Stalin come down firmly on the American side in behalf of the great invasion now codenamed OVERLORD.

Amphibious Assault

There was also a very specific reason, over and above the general limitations of British power, why British leaders—and in fact some Americans as well—drew back from the thought of a cross-Channel invasion. By 1943, Hitler claimed to have transformed Europe into a vast fortress, with the coast of France battlemented as Festung Europa's sturdy and bristling Atlantic Wall. If German claims for the strength of the fortress and the Atlantic Wall were surely inflated, the German army nevertheless managed to spare formidable strength from the Russian front to garrison France and particularly her coast: for if the Anglo-Americans should gain a foothold in northern France, they would imperil the Reich itself, and especially the industrial center of the Ruhr, more directly than any immediate Russian threat. In the East, the broad buffers of the Baltic states, Poland, and the Balkans still separated Germany from the enemy; in the West, the Channel Coast was much too near.

Against the Germans' consequent defensive preparations in France, the cross-Channel invasion would be the most difficult of amphibious assaults. And any amphibious assault against a defended shore was an operation to compel the most sober of second thoughts. In the face of modern armaments, much of the world's most respected military opinion had long considered amphibious assault impossible. As late as 1943, such opinion had by no means been discarded where a hostile shore as strongly defended as that of conquered France was concerned. The Allies of course had mounted a number of successful amphibious invasions by that time. But those against Guadalcanal and North Africa in 1942—like those of the Japanese earlier—had been against almost undefended beaches; and where the defender had been able to achieve respectable troop concentrations or to prepare reasonably strong fortifications, as at Salerno in September 1943 or Tarawa in November, he had turned amphibious assaults into bloodbaths and come within sight of hurling them back into the sea. What more might the Germans accomplish with the military resources and coastal defenses they had long been accumulating in France?

Gallipoli and the Western Front of 1914–1918 provided the keys to military thought about amphibious operations after the First World War and until the Second. They were the root sources of the dread with which the necessity for such operations remained invested as late as the turn of 1943 into 1944. The failure of the Anglo-French amphibious expedition against Gallipoli was much studied between the wars, and the predominant conclusion was that, conceding all the errors that had plagued the expedition, the fundamental causes of its defeat nevertheless remained inherent in amphibious assault. The problems of an assault from out of the sea against a defended shore, after all, were those of frontal attack on the Western Front, only worse, because the attacker had to struggle up out of the water and his equipment and agility were limited accordingly. If despite having to execute a direct assault under multiplied handicaps the attacker grasped a foothold, as the British indeed had contrived to do at Gallipoli, his buildup over the beaches could not keep pace with the defender's much easier overland buildup. Eventually the defender could concentrate overwhelming strength to drive the assailant into the sea. Because Winston Churchill had been the most conspicuous champion of Gallipoli, the American naval critic W. D. Puleston, biographer of Admiral Mahan, expressed his warning of the futility of amphibious assault by observing that Britain might be able to survive another world war, but not another Winston Churchill. B.H. Liddell Hart also concluded after Gallipoli that the amphibious assault had become foredoomed. So did other prestigious military critics in all armies and navies.[3]

Fortunately, between the wars the military world contained a few who disagreed, notably the leaders of the United States Marine Corps. The marines perceived in amphibious assaults against Japanese islands in a likely Pacific Ocean war a long-sought raison d'être for their service, and they thus developed through study and exercises a doctrine of amphibious war. But so much in late 1943 did the shadow of Gallipoli still darken the prospects of amphibious assault against defenses as strong as those believed to await the Anglo-Americans across the English Channel—so much did Salerno and Tarawa still further becloud the prospect—that virtually all Allied planning for the cross-Channel invasion concentrated on the immediate problem of getting and staying ashore, to the neglect of subsequent movements.

Writing of high command in war, one of the principal planners of the cross-Channel invasion, Montgomery, said of one of his most illustrious predecessors at the head of British armies that the Duke of Wellington always planned with

> foresight, industry, patience and meticulous care. Yet he sometimes lost part of the fruits of victory through an inability to soar from the known to seize the unknown. Napoleon never surpassed Wellington's flawless handling of his command at Salamanca and Vittoria, but the defeated French after Vittoria would never have escaped to fight another day had Napoleon—or Cromwell—been in command.[4]

Their vision gripped by the dangers of amphibious assault, the British and Americans undertook to plan for their invasion of the Far Shore with "foresight, industry, patience and meticulous care." They studied the problems of the assault painstakingly to make them known problems, foreseeable problems, whose perplexities could be thoroughly prepared for in advance. Under the shadow of Gallipoli, and of the more general perils of the invasion in view of the limitations of British power, it was perhaps inevitable that OVERLORD planning should assume this kind of focus. The further danger, however, was to leave a great deal of OVERLORD beyond the assault and the immediately following buildup an unknown, so that "part of the fruits of victory" of a successful amphibious assault might yet be lost "through an inability to soar from the known to seize the unknown."

It does not unduly minimize the trials that lay ahead on that beach in Normandy codenamed OMAHA to say that the amphibious assault across the Channel was to prove much easier than recollections of Gallipoli, Salerno, and Tarawa and the military thought between the wars led the OVERLORD planners to expect. But by concentrating almost all their planning effort on the assault and the immediately following buildup, the planners neglected a maze of troubles awaiting behind the French shore. The greatest trials of OVERLORD, and especially of the American army participating in it, were to appear when the invaders plunged inland into the all too literally unknown—because unstudied and unplanned-for—adversities of waging offensive war in the region of Normandy called the Bocage. There the limitations of the American army in generating sustained combat power were further to cripple the drive into the unknown, on battlefields sorely lacking in appropriate ground to apply mobility.

The High Command

The British Isles must necessarily provide the base for the Anglo-American invasion of France. If there had been no other relevant considerations, this alone would have made British willingness to participate in the venture indispensable. Among the other considerations, the necessity to nourish mutual goodwill in maintaining the Anglo-American alliance, plus British seniority in the alliance—at least in duration of service against the common foe, and for a long time in strength immediately available in the European theater of war—led both Americans and British to concede in 1942 that when the cross-Channel invasion came, the supreme commander would be British. By the time OVERLORD finally received Britain's reasonably firm commitment, however, American military strength mobilized in Europe had already expanded so much, and the American contribution to the ground campaign in Europe would soon outweigh the British by so wide a margin, that the Anglo-American governments changed their minds and agreed the supreme commander must be American.

After President Roosevelt painfully balanced his desire to meet the wishes of General Marshall for field command against his own fear that he could not rest easily at night without Marshall's presence in Washington to share in directing global strategy, the European command went to General Dwight D. Eisenhower. The amiably diplomatic Eisenhower, fifty-three years old and a West Point graduate of 1915, had been Allied chieftain in North Africa, Sicily, and Italy, and had made a notable success in maintaining Anglo-American harmony. His ability to foster friendly Allied teamwork, through a thoroughly internationalized supreme headquarters, principally commended him to Allied civilian leaders and to the senior Allied military agency charged with overall direction of the war, the Anglo-American Combined Chiefs of Staff. Because Eisenhower boasted no combat experience in the First World War, had served largely in staff capacities between the wars, and acted more conspicuously on political-diplomatic than on military issues in the Mediterranean, his claims in the traditional sphere of generalship seemed less well established, especially in British eyes.

With an American designated Supreme Commander, Allied Expeditionary Force, to lead all ground, sea, and air forces in OVERLORD, Anglo-American balance decreed that the immediate commander of ground forces in the invasion be British. The consideration that no American, neither Eisenhower nor anyone else, could claim the experience and renown of several British officers in combat command pointed at least as imperatively to the same conclusion. From among such British officers, Eisenhower desired General Sir Harold Alexander, already his ground commander since the North African compaign, to head the ground forces in the OVERLORD assault. Alexander shared something of Eisenhower's own talent for harmonizing difficult relationships between British and American soldiers. But the choice of a British officer was Prime Minister Churchill's to make, and in response to the spirited urgings of the Chief of the Imperial General Staff, Field Marshal Sir Alan Brooke, Churchill selected Brooke's favorite subordinate, the hero of the Battle of El Alamein and commander of the British Eighth Army, General Sir Bernard Montgomery.

It was an almost inevitable decision. Montgomery had not a trace of Alexander's conciliatory talents, which was too bad for the alliance; but the man who had turned back Rommel and the Panzerarmee Afrika from the gates of Alexandria, the winner of the only major all-British ground victory of the war, could hardly be denied. Besides, there is every reason to believe in retrospect, as Brooke believed then, that Montgomery not only surpassed Alexander as an operational commander but was altogether Britain's ablest general of the war.

President Roosevelt chose Eisenhower as Supreme Commander on December 6, 1943, after the Tehran Conference and following another meeting with Churchill at Cairo. Eisenhower received the news directly from the President when Roosevelt stopped over at Tunis the next day. On December 24 the President and the Prime Minister announced the Eisenhower and Montgomery appointments to the world.

To serve both commanders, headquarters already existed. The early American importunings for a cross-Channel invasion had produced at least the appointment on March 13, 1943, of Lieutenant General F. E. Morgan as "Chief of Staff to the Supreme Allied Commander (designate)." Morgan was chosen out of considerations similar to those that advanced Eisenhower. A veteran of the Indian army, commander of the British 1st Armoured Divison in France early in the war, then head of the 1 Corps District Command in Lincolnshire and Yorkshire, Morgan had served enough with Canadians to have picked up the North American idiom and, more than that, had developed a strong admiration for the hearty, vigorous soldiers he found reinforcing Britain from across the Atlantic. He got along so well with those allies that some of his countrymen thought him more American than the Americans.

Morgan received a directive of April 23, 1943, requiring COSSAC—as Morgan called himself—and his staff to draft plans for the cross-Channel invasion. Upon Eisenhower's appointment to the Supreme Command, the COSSAC staff became the nucleus of Supreme Headquarters, Allied Expeditionary Force (SHAEF). Although Eisenhower brought with him his own American chief of staff from the Mediterranean, Lieutenant General Walter Bedell Smith, General Morgan stayed on as deputy chief of staff. Meanwhile, by the summer of 1943 the British had established 21 Army Group, a headquarters that took over from Home Defence Command all planning and preparations for British expeditionary forces. In November 1943, on COSSAC's recommendation, the commander of 21 Army Group became jointly responsible with the Commander, Allied Naval Expeditionary Force, and the Commander, Allied Expeditionary Air Force, for planning the amphibious assault against France. In December, it was specifically to the command of 21 Army Group that Montgomery was assigned.

Eisenhower had already seen an outline of COSSAC's preliminary plan for OVERLORD. Because General Morgan labored under severe restrictions upon the resources he could anticipate—a reflection of the stepchild status of OVERLORD until December 1943, as opposed to more immediate projects—the plan called for only a three-division assault on a narrow front. Eisenhower immediately thought the front too narrow, the force too small. Because on General Marshall's urging the new Supreme Commander was to return to America briefly at the beginning of 1944, to discuss allocations of men and matériel for OVERLORD and to enjoy a last opportunity for a rest, Eisenhower designated Montgomery to represent him in London in the meantime. Montgomery and Eisenhower conferred in North Africa and agreed that the initial assault must land a minimum of five divisions from the sea, supplemented by a strong airborne force, and that there must also be a more rapid buildup of reinforcements than COSSAC had been able to project.

Other leaders, too, had already insisted that a three-division landing was not enough to assure the success of an assault carrying with it the fate of the war in the West. Churchill was among them, provided the invasion had to take place at all. Montgomery most assuredly would apply himself with alacrity to mustering a larger initial force, for it was already evident as the hallmark of his generalship, consistently apparent from El Alamein to his most recent Italian battles on the River Sangro, that he would not attack without as sure a margin of superior force as he could assemble.

The Cotentin and the Calvados

The 1941 ROUNDUP plan had looked toward amphibious landings on both sides of the mouth of the River Seine. The COSSAC planners early abandoned this design. The first American cross-Channel invasion plans and the 1942 Anglo-American version of ROUNDUP called for the amphibious assault to strike the Pas de Calais, interpreted by the planners as meaning not simply the department of that name but the coast between Dunkirk and the Somme. An invasion of the Pas de Calais would take the assault force as close as it could go to the boundaries of Germany while remaining within the short range of Britain's Spitfire fighters for air cover. But such an invasion consequently would also strike where the Germans most expected it, and where German defenses were heaviest. So the COSSAC planners also rejected the Pas de Calais.

A yet more important deterrent against the Pas de Calais was the question of ports. If the invaders got ashore, there would remain an interval especially fearful to those who dreaded amphibious assault, when the Germans would be able to concentrate strength from all over western Europe against the lodgment, while the Allies raced to match the enemy's buildup of men and matériel against the disadvantage of unloading from ships in the Channel. Against the approximately sixty German divisions in France in the spring of 1944, the Allies would require seven weeks after D-Day before they could commit the thirty-seven divisions they had gathered in Britain. Only if they could win good seaports rapidly, including at least one large port, did the Allied planners believe they could hope to hold their own in the race of the buildup. Yet Britain's disastrously expensive Dieppe raid of August 1942 apparently proved the inadvisability of attempting to invade directly against a port. The defenses would be too strong, and even a successful lodgment would probably cost intolerable casualties. In any event, the ports of the Pas de Calais are small, and the beaches of the Pas de Calais lie unsheltered against the fury of Channel storms.

Just to the West, the area of the mouth of the Seine also had few and unsheltered beaches. The further, critical problem that led to the early abandonment of this target was the considertion that using Le Havre and Rouen would require Allied control of both banks of the Seine, with all the difficulties of operations by troops separated by a major river obstacle.

An area much richer in seaports and sheltered anchorages than the Pas de Calais is the Brittany peninsula, which thus had to receive COSSAC's scrutiny. Yet the crucial disadvantage of Brittany is obvious: its distance from the invasion's eventual objectives in Germany.

In October 1941, General Charles de Gaulle's Free French forces in exile had suggested to the British an invasion plan aimed at the historic Breton redoubt, but also at the Cotentin Peninsula and its port of Cherbourg. The necessity to win early as much port capacity as possible drew the planners back to the latter area, and to the whole shore of the Bay of the Seine, the Calvados coast of Normandy as well as the Cotentin. Before the war,

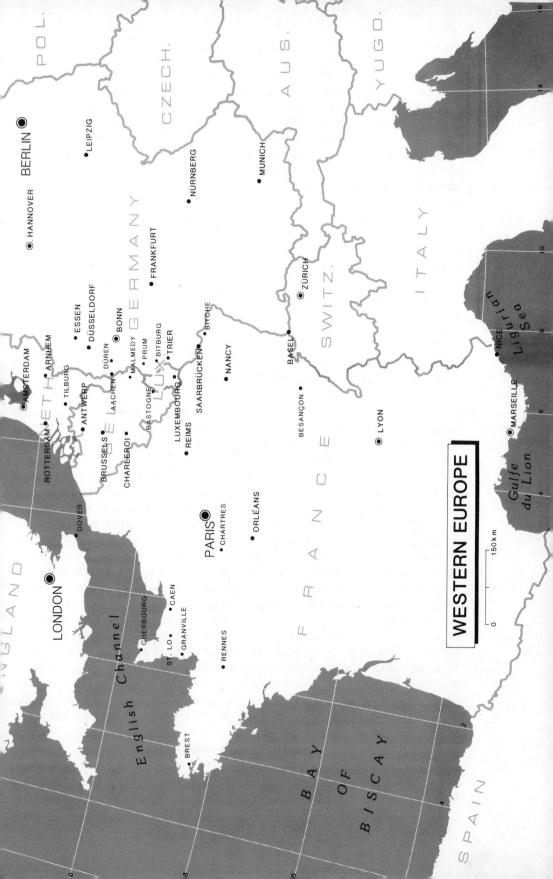

WESTERN EUROPE

Cherbourg had been mainly a harbor for transoceanic passenger liners and naval shipping, and it was not equipped for cargo handling on the scale that would be required by the invasion. But it was the largest port on the north coast of Europe that was readily assailable. Furthermore, the Cotentin affords the beaches of the Côte du Calvados at least a measure of shelter against the weather. The Calvados beaches were wide and firm enough to accommodate adequate quantities of vehicles and supplies at the outset of the invasion. There were also adequate vehicle exits from the beaches and adequate road nets behind them. Because Normandy is separated from the Pas de Calais by the Seine, Allied air power might curtail German reinforcement by attacking the bridges over the river. Finally, from the Normandy coast the invaders might turn right or left to take either the Breton ports or Le Havre as might prove more convenient. No other landing area offered so ample an access to seaports. Once all elements of the decision had been weighed, the Bay of the Seine from the southwest coast of the Cotentin to Caen seemed so obviously the right place to land that no doubts ever developed, and the wonder was that the enemy was to prove incapable of perceiving its obviousness—a failure abetted by Allied schemes of deception, but still a wonder.

Some God-Damned Things Called LSTs

General Montgomery arrived in London from North Africa the day after New Year's, 1944—with unfortunate fanfare that threatened to call undue attention to the invasion planners' location at Norfolk House in St. James's Square, the headquarters of COSSAC and subsequently of SHAEF. COSSAC gave Montgomery and Bedell Smith a formal briefing on the OVERLORD plan on January 3. Immediately, Montgomery voiced his criticism of the narrow, three-division assault. In the next few days he refined the criticism to propose extending the assault from a forty- to a sixty-five-kilometer front, employing five divisions initially, and reaching not from somewhere near the base of the Cotentin but from les Dunes de Varreville, on the Cotentin's east coast, all the way to Cabourg east of the Orne River. The eastward extension would help assure the early capture of Caen, a road junction city beyond which lay open, relatively level countryside inviting tank maneuver and further penetration southeastward. Around Caen, too, were numerous sites suitable for airfields. Thus Montgomery showed he could begin to think beyond the immediate problems of the amphibious assault toward the exploitation that would be necessary to draw from mere lodgment a larger victory—the soaring into the unknown that marks the great commander.

To the west, Montgomery with his characteristic concern for a buildup of superior force emphasized even more than did COSSAC the importance of Cherbourg. The central purpose of landing on the Cotentin was to secure the port's early capture. The wider frontage would also permit several corps and armies to penetrate inland through beachheads won by their constituent divisions, thus minimizing administrative and supply confusion. It would give the invaders a larger number of vehicle exits from the beaches, and thus hasten both penetration inland and the buildup of troops and supplies from the initial landing places. Here again, Montgomery's thinking escaped a constricting focus on the amphibious assault alone and began to look toward exploitation.

The COSSAC planners themselves had long experienced misgivings over the weakness of the three-division assault to which their instructions limited them. Some of these planners nevertheless doubted the wisdom of Montgomery's widening of the front, lest the indispensable success of the first assault be jeopardized by dissipation of its spear-head. Some of the naval and air staffs felt similar concern about dissipating their preparatory and support fire. Such was the fixation of much of the planning staff upon the immediate problem of the amphibious assault. Still, Montgomery won the bulk of staff opinion to his side, applying to his advocacy a confident, even cocksure, earnestness and an importunate, even acerbic, zeal that would prove to be standard expressions of his personality. His American comrades were to have more than ample experience of these characteristics in time to come. In effect, Montgomery at this early moment demanded that he would have his way on the breadth and exploitability of the amphibious lodgment or he would depart, and he had his way.

At least he won in principle. The chief restriction cramping the earlier planning was a shortage not of troops but of landing craft. On January 5, Bedell Smith cabled Eisenhower in Washington to inform him of Montgomery's insistence on an enlarged assault, stating that the obvious precondition was more landing craft, and that enough craft could be procured only be abandoning ANVIL, a projected amphibious assault on the south coast of France simultaneous with the OVERLORD invasion. American strategists, including Eisenhower—and for that matter, the Russians and Generalissimo Stalin when Stalin applied his decisive weight in support of OVERLORD at Tehran—had strongly favored ANVIL to make the Allied return to France a gigantic double envelopment, the nearest possible approach to the assault all along the enemy circumference favored by Grant in the Civil War. OVERLORD and ANVIL together would deny the Germans a full concentration on either the northern or the southern coast and deprive them of secure flanks or rear. But the statistics concerning available landing craft seconded Smith's warning that an ANVIL simultaneous with OVERLORD had to be forsworn. During the following weeks Eisenhower reluctantly let the original ANVIL plan slip away, while at the levels of heads of government and chiefs of staff, the design to invade southern France at some date following the cross-Channel invasion created new cause for tedious debate between American and British strategists just when their old debate about when to invade northwest Europe had expired.

The interwar conviction that amphibious assaults could not succeed had led both Americans and British, not unnaturally, to neglect the development of landing vessels for such assaults. The American marines sponsored prototypes of relatively small armored landing craft with bow ramps, notably Andrew Higgins's shallow-draft boats that evolved into the "landing craft—vehicle, personnel" (LCVP). The controversial American tank designer J. Walter Christie essayed construction of an amphibious tank. But these efforts accomplished so little that in the spring of 1941, Marine Corps landing exercises were still going ashore over the bows of conventional ships' boats. Furthermore, much less was done between the wars about larger craft to transport the small assault vessels to somewhere near the beaches and to carry tanks, artillery, and other heavy equipment.

After Dunkirk, the first British thinking about an eventual return to the Continent occurred when British industry was far too strained with the pressing demands of survival to build such gear for that distant prospect. So in 1941 Captain T. A. Hussey, Royal Navy, carried to America sketches of a "landing ship, tank" (LST), a "landing ship, dock" (LSD), and a somewhat smaller "landing craft, tank" (LCT), to ask the Americans to build them under Lend-Lease. The Navy Department rejected the request because American yards were also overworked with vessels for Britain's transatlantic lifeline. Through informal channels, Captain Hussey then persuaded Justice Felix Frankfurter to interest Harry Hopkins and General Marshall in the project. Pearl Harbor helped by fixing American attention upon amphibious assaults to recapture from Japan the islands of the Pacific. Even in 1942, however, the escalation of Germany's submarine campaign in the Atlantic, a menace not brought under control until at least midway through 1943, demanded that cargo shipping and antisubmarine vessels retain shipyard priority over landing craft.

So it was that continually in the Second World War, "The destinies of two great empires," as Winston Churchill put it, ". . . seem to be tied up in some god-damned things called LSTs."[5] Montgomery's expansion of the OVERLORD assault envisaged an increase in hard-to-find landing vessels amounting to 72 landing craft, infantry (LCIs), 47 LSTs, and 144 LCTs (along with still additional categories of which there was, fortunately, no shortage: one headquarters ship [LSH], six attack transports [LSIs or APAs], with their complements of landing craft, assault [LCAs] and of LCVPs, and 64 motor vehicle cargo ships). To meet these new requirements, not only would ANVIL have to be abandoned or postponed, but OVERLORD itself would have to be pushed back from May 1 to June 1, to obtain another month's American production.

At that, the requirements further aggravated the ANVIL issue's renewal of Anglo-American controversy. The British thought the Americans overestimated the carrying capacity of the vessels under assault conditions, and that still more landing vessels would be required than the Americans were scheduling. More acrimoniously, the British suggested that the root of the persistent shortage at this late date was the American navy's hoarding of the vessels in its favored theater, the Pacific. The Americans rejoined that hundreds of damaged British landing vessels, many of them built in the United States, were scattered about England, unrepaired because the Admiralty would not pay for overtime work in British shipyards. There was an unhappy measure of truth in the charges on both sides, and the solution finally worked out by a high-level "Landing Craft Conference" at Norfolk House on February 15 was a compromise. The British agreed to attempt heavier loading of the vessels according to American scales and to seek increased serviceability. The Americans promised a large diversion of vessels from the Mediterranean—another nail in ANVIL's coffin—and shipment of seven more big LSTs from the United States. (The LST, it might be noted, was indeed no small boat; it was a ship of about 4,000 tons some 328 feet long, capable of lifting 2,000 deadweight tons, including twenty medium tanks on the tank deck.)

In the end, the Americans were to deliver more than they had felt able to pledge. On D-Day, the invasion fleet included 168 United States Navy and 61 Royal Navy LSTs, 245 LCIs about equally divided between the two navies, and more than 900 LCTs of which 664 were British. But the planning, meanwhile, had to proceed against the prospect of a bare minimum of lift for a five-division seaborne assault. However much General Montgomery insisted that there should be no cross-Channel invasion without assured superior strength, however much the American strategy underlying the whole enterprise was one of applying overwhelming power, the sealift was not available to deliver an encouraging margin of strength. The effect upon planning was to reinforce caution, and particularly to rivet attention once again upon the lodgment and whether it could be made secure, not upon exploitation.

NEPTUNE

General Eisenhower returned to Europe on Saturday, January 14, via the Azores and Prestwick, Scotland. He reached London by rail on Sunday morning, without the fanfare earlier accorded the British hero Montgomery. The security of Eisenhower's arrival was assured, in fact, both by the day of the week, when working crowds were at home, and by a fog so thick that two men had to guide the way for the general's car. At that, his party got lost between the curb and the front door of headquarters, European Theater of Operations, United States Army (ETOUSA), at 20 Grosvenor Square.

Assuming command of SHAEF—though he did not receive a formal directive until the next month—Eisenhower promptly conferred with Montgomery and approved the changes Montgomery had begun to effect in COSSAC's planning. A revised invasion plan was now completed under Montgomery's direction by "syndicates" representing the army group, the American and British field armies scheduled to participate, and navies, air forces, SHAEF, and other interested commands. The new plan was published on February 1 as the NEPTUNE Initial Joint Plan, NEPTUNE being now the code name for the assault itself; the word had been used since September on all documents bearing the place and target date of the invasion. The plan was initialed by General Montgomery for 21 Army Group, and by Admiral Sir Bertram Ramsay as Allied Naval Commander Expeditionary Force and Air Chief Marshal Sir Trafford Leigh-Mallory as Commander in Chief, Allied Expeditionary Air Force.

The NEPTUNE plan depicted the invasion in outline, while requiring the armies that were to participate to submit detailed plans for ground operations, to include regimental frontage and objectives, airborne and Ranger or Commando tasks, provisional lists of beach defense targets to be hit by naval and air support with timing for the support, and the approximate number of men and vehicles to be landed in each regiment on the first four tides, with the number and types of landing vessels required. The army plans were also to forecast operations and buildup priorities from D-Day plus 1 to D plus 14. The First United States Army issued its plan on February 25, the Second British Army on March 20. On April 7, General Montgomery assembled all senior ground, air, and naval officers at his headquarters at St. Paul's School in West Kensington for a detailed presentation and review of the planning to date.

Bernard Law Montgomery, the introverted product of his mother's perfectionist discipline in the Victorian household of his father the Bishop of Tasmania, had himself gone to school at St. Paul's. Though he became a school prefect, as a boy he was never allowed to venture into the office of the High Master. Now as England's most famous general he occupied that sanctum as his own. In a large Gothic schoolroom nearby, tiers of hard, narrow benches and a gallery supported by black pillars overlooked a relief map of Normandy the width of a city street, where Montgomery "tramped about like a giant through Lilliputian France."[6] In ordinary circumstances, Montgomery was notoriously secretive about his plans, even with his own staff and senior subordinates. But before a suitably appreciative and prestigious audience, he could be a most lucid and compelling speaker. For the April 7 meeting he produced a crisp, precise, albeit necessarily lengthy review and analysis of the NEPTUNE plan, commanding attention and stilling any restlessness in his audience throughout a day's discussion—even though as usual he strictly prohibited smoking, at least until Churchill and Eisenhower arrived late in the afternoon to hear the final summation.

Montgomery's opponent on the Far Shore would once again be Rommel, his old antagonist of the Western Desert. Late in 1943, Hitler had assigned Rommel to inspect the coastal defenses of France and to prepare recommendations for strengthening them. On January 15, 1944, Rommel received command of Army Group B, to conduct the defense of northern France and implement many of his recommendations. His troops would be those of the German Armed Forces in the Netherlands, of the Fifteenth Army in the Pas de Calais, and of the Seventh Army in Normandy and Brittany. In the German chain of command, Rommel's Army Group B was subordinate to the veteran campaigner whose army group had spearheaded the invasion of France in 1940, Generalfeldmarschall Gerd von Rundstedt, who was Oberbefehlshaber West—Commander in Chief West. As a field marshal himself, however, Rommel had the right of direct access to Hitler. In addition, he remained coastal defense inspector for the whole of the West without clear subordination in this role to Rundstedt. Rundstedt was growing old and lethargic, while Rommel's consuming energy had returned after his recent illnessess. Rommel was the dominant enemy military figure with whom NEPTUNE must contend, whatever his formal position in the German hierarchy.

The ascendancy of the Desert Fox had already produced changes in the German defenses apparent to Allied intelligence and important for the invasion planning. These changes yet again increased the Allied planners' concentration on the immediate problem of gaining a foothold, because they imparted a considerably enhanced reality to the menace of Hitler's Atlantic Wall. As OB West since March 1942—just after his departure from command of Army Group South on the Russian front—Rundstedt had labored to strengthen the French coastal defenses from his arrival onward. But Rundstedt believed that however strong the defensive crust on the coast might become, the Anglo-Americans would break it, because they could choose to concentrate upon the point of assault while the Germans had to defend the whole coast. In an accurate appraisal of Rundstedt's strategy in the summer of 1943, COSSAC had stated:

> 33. The German policy is based normally on counter-attack of the beaches by panzer divisions held in reserve close behind the coast, and coastal divisions are only expected to hold on for eight to twelve hours until these panzer divisions arrive. . . .
>
> 34. The crux of the operation is likely to be our ability to drive off the German reserves rather than the initial breaking of the coastal crust.[7]

Rundstedt's strategy of reliance on counterattack was the classic one for the defender of an extended front. OB West acknowledged the force of an objection offered by many other German officers, including many at Oberkommando der Wehrmacht (OKW), Hitler's supreme headquarters, that the ripostes of German reserves would be curtailed by Allied air superiority and the limited mobility of much of the German army and, because of fuel shortages, even of the critical panzer divisions. Rundstedt believed nevertheless that with impenetrable defense of the beaches impossible, somehow the problem of moving reserves had to be mastered.

Rundstedt had never fought against an enemy who possessed overwhelming air superiority. Rommel had. Remembering Allied air power in North Africa, Rommel believed that it was the movement of large reserves, especially of massed armor, that would be truly impossible in the face of enemy air superiority over France. Furthermore, because the Eastern Front had consumed too many of the best troops and too much of the best equipment of the German army, the German forces in France would not be able to compete in maneuver with the Anglo-Americans, even apart from Allied aerial predominance. Therefore Rommel concluded that the decisive battle for France must be fought directly on the beaches, when the Anglo-Americans came ashore, and that the outcome would be determined within the first forty-eight hours.

He set out accordingly to build a defensive belt five to six kilometers deep all around the French coast, heavily armed with all types of guns, and within which all infantry, artillery, headquarters staffs, and reserves up to division level would be positioned in a network of resistance nests. Between the resistance nests, mines and other obstacles were to block enemy penetration. Behind the coastal zone, all fields suitable for glider landings were to be mined and covered with stakes placed close enough together that gliders could not come down between them, to guard against airborne assault. In front of the resistance nests, the beaches were to be strewn with underwater obstacles to wreck landing craft. At Rommel's direction, tetrahedra and hedgehogs consisting of three iron bars intersecting at right angles like giant jackstraws, previously placed inland as tank obstacles, were moved to potential invasion beaches. They were supplemented by "Belgian gates" or "Belgian barn doors," gatelike obstacles over two meters high. Steel piles and wooden stakes, slanted seaward from out of the beaches, were fitted with mines. Rommel's intention was to install four belts of beach obstacles extending from one fathom under the high-water mark to two fathoms under the low-water mark on all possible landing beaches. Beyond were sixteen mine fields, each about eight kilometers long, laid down in the English Channel between Boulogne and Cherbourg between August 1943 and January 1944, to be kept renewed and supplemented with further minelaying, including shallow-water mines to be set down immediately along the coast when invasion appeared imminent.

All the engineer and labor battalions and French labor that Rommel could get, and all the work that he could commandeer from combat troops, went into strengthening the beach defenses of the Atlantic Wall. Like almost all German commanders, Rommel expected the invasion to fall upon the Pas de Calais, so that area received first priority for strengthening; but Rommel also felt a growing uneasiness about Normandy, and work proceeded rapidly there. At Quinéville on the east coast of the Cotentin, for example, a double row of tetrahedra or hedgehogs 2,100 meters long appeared within four days in April. Leigh-Mallory of the Allied Expeditionary Air Force wanted to strafe the beaches while workmen were installing the obstacles, but Eisenhower vetoed the proposal lest the effort betray the intended invasion targets.

The Germans first emplaced their beach obstacles near the high-water mark and then thickened them seaward. On February 20, Allied aerial photographs for the first time showed obstacles below the high-water mark. This discovery complicated the Allies' problem of adjusting their landings to the tides. If the troops came ashore at low tide, on the Normandy beaches they would have to cross tidal flats averaging almost 300 meters in width, altogether exposed to enemy fire, and they might also have to wade across deep runnels before reaching dry land. They could not, however, land at high tide, because the tide had to be rising to permit the landing craft to ground, unload, and withdraw without waiting for the next rising tide. Furthermore, the new obstacles also decreed that the tide would have to be low enough that the landings would come to ground short of the main belts of obstructions thus far completed, to avoid wrecking the landing craft as they went in. Landing at low tide would now actually offer an advantage, that of maximum time for engineer demolition teams following close behind the first infantry to clear away obstacles before the next tide.

Montgomery decided on a compromise among these considerations. The landings should occur at half-tide or somewhat earlier, three hours before high water, affording adequate time for the engineers to create paths through the obstacles, while limiting the distance of the infantry assault across the tidal flats. During the final weeks before the invasion, a close watch would have to be kept on the seaward progress of the German obstacles, to determine whether the timing of the landings would have to be changed. Like most compromises, this one relating landing time to tides was not altogether satisfactory. One of the American corps headquarters earmarked for the assault commented quietly but aptly that the tasks posed would probably be "expensive."

Recognizing the point, and to cut the expense, Montgomery further decided to employ armor along with the infantry in the first wave. Their caution and their inability to afford heavy casualties often tempted the British into an entanglement with military gadgetry of varying utility. To help bring tanks into the amphibious assault, they had the duplex-drive (DD) tank, invented by the Hungarian-born Nicholas Straussler. Duplex or dual drive permitted hooking up the engine to turn a propeller when the tank was at sea. More ingenious was Straussler's means of getting a tank to float, which involved sealing a collapsible screen to the hull. When erect the screen displaced a sufficient volume of water to produce flotation, but with the difficulties that the tank lumbered along low in the water, could not use its armament, and was exceedingly vulnerable to rough seas as well as enemy fire. To go into action, the tank had to drop the front of its screen when it landed, though it could keep the rear screen erect to prevent following seas from swamping the engine. The Admiralty had rejected the DD as too vulnerable to be practical; but the War Office and particularly Sir Alan Brooke liked it, so 650 old Valentine tanks were converted to DD, and then in July 1943 Brooke ordered the conversion of 900 Shermans. British industry was slow to fill this order because of the usual competing demands, but as soon as Eisenhower saw the DD on January 27, he set Washington to work. Three hundred DD Shermans were on their way from America within two months. It remained to be seen whether the War Office or the Admiralty was right about them; Eisenhower notwithstanding, the Americans were more skeptical of their utility than the British and equipped only three D-Day tank battalions with them, as compared with seven British DD battalions.

The awkward fragility of the DDs worried an American officer of considerable amphibious experience, but so did the relative indifference with which most of his fellow Americans viewed any such means of meeting the peculiar problems of amphibious assault. This officer was Major General Charles H. "Pete" Corlett, recently assigned to England to command one of the early followup corps to go ashore soon after the invasion, the XIX Corps. Corlett had fought in the Aleutians and commanded the 7th Infantry Division in its invasion of Kwajalein Islet, and General Marshall sent him to Europe anticipating that his knowledge of Pacific theater amphibious methods would be of value to the NEPTUNE planners. Corlett early told Eisenhower, Bedell Smith, and anyone who would listen that he thought the DDs too dangerous, proposing instead the Pacific practice of mounting tanks in firing position in landing craft, to fire on shore targets as they ran in. He suggested generous use of amphibious tractors, tracked vehicles which could swim from their mother ships to the beaches and then climb directly over reefs and rough ground; not having enough of these at Tarawa had helped make that landing a brush with disaster, but a plenitude of them had been a godsend in subsequent Pacific landings. Indeed, Corlett urged that with enough such rugged amphibious equipment, an amphibious assault could go ashore almost anywhere and need not hit the smooth, sandy beaches where the Germans most expected it. But even on smooth beaches, an amphibious assault ought to have more specialized supporting equipment than Corlett found the Americans in England allotting it. It should also have more of that very basic commodity, ammunition. The ammunition allowances planned for NEPTUNE were proportionately one-fifteenth those of Kwajalein.

Montgomery's chief of staff, Major General Sir Francis de Guingand, welcomed Corlett and his amphibious experience, arranging an address on the amphibious training and techniques of Kwajalein for an appreciative audience of senior British commanders and their staffs. But Corlett did not find the Americans receptive in the way Marshall had intended. Instead, they seemed to dismiss the Pacific as the bush leagues, and "I felt like an expert according to the Naval definition, 'A son-of-a-bitch from out of town.'"[8] The NEPTUNE planning went forward with remarkably little reference to anything that had happened during amphibious invasions in the Pacific. On the matter of ammunition, in particular, events would apply a direct test to Corlett's warnings, and the test results were not to be happy.

The navies wanted to ferry the invasion force across the Channel under cover of darkness, as a shield against whatever aerial and naval harassment of the convoys the enemy might be able to muster. All the Anglo-American landings in the Mediterranean had occurred at night. The COSSAC planners had not decided on night or day landings for the cross-Channel invasion, but Montgomery's NEPTUNE planners concluded that Mediterranean practice should be reversed, and the invaders should go ashore by daylight. The Montgomery team believed that German radar would surely pick up the coming of the invasion fleet whether by day or night. They also believed that the handicaps imposed by darkness on the enemy's guns would be more than counterbalanced by the Allies' inability in darkness to lay down as heavy as possible an aerial and naval bombardment in preparation for the landings. One of the lessons of Dieppe, as well as of the relatively neglected American experience in the Pacific, appeared to be the need for overwhelming fire support of an assault on a fortified coast, if the specter of Gallipoli was to be exorcised. To provide suitable fire support for the final stages of the approach and to cover the beaches against Rommel's artillery, daylight would be required.

At least forty-five minutes of daylight were judged necessary for adequate observation and fire support. Consequently, a night approach and a daylight landing were reconciled by planning for H-Hour within one hour of first light, with local variations to assure the right tidal conditions on each of the various beaches.

While the navies desired a night approach, the planners wanted to precede the seaborne landings with airborne attacks, and to assure accurate drops would require moonlight. The right combination of a full moon with low tides timed shortly before first light occurred only three days each month. The first possible D-Days after the target date of June 1 were June 5, 6, and 7. Monday, June 5 consequently became the date chosen for D-Day, with the possibility of postponement to one of the two following days in case of bad weather.

The enlargement of the COSSAC plan called for five assault divisions to attack five beaches. Each assault division was to receive fire support as well as transportation from its own naval force. The British Second Army, Lieutenant General Sir Miles Dempsey, would assail three beaches between the mouth of the Orne River and Arromanches. The beaches eventually were designated, from east to west, SWORD, JUNO, and GOLD. Within the GOLD area off Arromanches was the cape where the galleon *Salvador* of the Spanish Armada struck and broke up in 1588, to become the source of the name Côte du Calvados. To shield Dempsey's left flank, the British 6th Airborne Division was to be dropped just east of the Orne during the night before the seaborne landings.

The American First Army, commanded by Lieutenant General Omar N. Bradley, was to assault west of the British, on both sides of the Carentan estuary. The American beaches were initially designated X and Y, but Rear Admiral Alan G. Kirk, commanding the Western Naval Task Force composed of the two naval forces supporting them, suggested they be called OMAHA and OREGON, names familiar to Americans and not easily confused in voice transmission. Somehow, OREGON became transmuted into UTAH.

OMAHA, between the British and the Cotentin, would be assaulted under the First Army plan by the V Corps of Major General Leonard T. Gerow. OMAHA Beach would have been the American target in the original, limited COSSAC plan, and the V Corps and its commander had merited selection to hit this target from the beginning, by virtue of seniority in length of service in the British Isles. The neat, precise Gerow—Virginia Military Institute, 1911—was an experienced planner, a former head of the War Plans Division of the General Staff. His corps headquarters had been established in the United Kingdom in August 1943 as the only American tactical ground command in what was then otherwise an administrative and logistical theater for the United States Army. At that time, the V Corps had commanded only one division, the 29th Infantry.

On D-Day, the V Corps assault would be spearheaded by the 1st Infantry Division, the "Big Red One," formed in May 1917 just a month after American entry into the First World War, and in that war the first American division to land, fight, and suffer casualties in France. Never deactivated between the wars, the 1st Division had landed at Oran to be again among the first American forces in the field in the Second World War. Under the inspirational leadership of Major General Terry Allen and Brigadier General Theodore Roosevelt, Jr., it had reestablished in Africa and Sicily much of its old renown as first among American divisions in more than name. The 29th Division, with its blue-and-gray shoulder patch signifying mixed Union and Confederate antecedents in the Maryland and Virginia National Guard, would have a regimental combat team attached to the 1st in the assault and would become the V Corps's initial followup division.

UTAH Beach, added to the COSSAC plan by Montgomery's expansion, appeared likely to prove more troublesome than OMAHA but was essential to the rapid capture of Cherbourg. The VII Corps, Major General J. Lawton Collins, would comand the UTAH assault, spearheaded by the 4th Infantry Division. The 4th had been reactivated in June 1940, but like the 1st it was a Regular Army formation with a proud World War I record: Pershing had chosen it to march through Paris on the 4th of July, 1918, to display to the French the soldierly improvement of his doughboys since the parade of part of the 1st Division the year before.

UTAH was the best landing beach on the east coast of the Cotentin, but just inside the beach was low-lying pastureland. Rommel's preparations included building upon ancient French plans to meet a hostile invasion by flooding all such lowlands west of Dieppe. Across some three kilometers of flooded pasture, only four causeways led out from the proposed American beach to firmer ground. To protect the UTAH assault force against blockage or blowing up of these causeways, the NEPTUNE planners decided to drop the 101st Airborne Division behind UTAH Beach to secure the western ends of the causeways. Because the low-lying mouths of the Taute and Vire Rivers between Carentan and Isigny presented an additional marshy obstacle to troop and vehicle movement, and because this obstacle would hinder the eventual linkup between UTAH and OMAHA Beaches, the 101st was also to seize crossings of the Taute and its attendant canal north and northeast of Carentan to reach out toward OMAHA Beach. Airborne divisions had lower table-of-organization strengths than standard American infantry divisions, including smaller constituent regiments; for NEPTUNE, however, the 101st would be a reinforced division of four regiments, with the 501st, 502nd, and 506th Parachute Infantry to make its airborne drops and the 327th Glider Infantry to come in from the sea through UTAH Beach after the initial landings.

The marshes and Rommel's inundations might conceivably aid more than they inhibited the Allied design upon Cherbourg. The marshy bottomlands of the Douve River, a tributary of the Taute, had also received the flooding treatment in the Carentan area, and they extended about five-sixths of the way westward across the base of the Cotentin Peninsula. Only three main roads crossed this marshland, and the only dry corridor connecting the Cotentin with the rest of France was a strip some 5,000 meters wide on the west coast between St. Lô-d'Ourville and St. Sauveur de Pierre-Pont. Bradley's First Army therefore asked for another airborne division, to land around St. Sauveur-le Vicomte and block this corridor. The 505th Parachute Infantry of the 82nd Airborne Division, veterans of drops in Sicily and Italy, had arrived in Northern Ireland in December 1943 (the division's 504th Parachute Infantry could not yet be extricated from the Anzio beachhead), and in Britain the 82nd Airborne was reconstituted with the addition of the 507th and 508th Regiments. With the 325th Glider Infantry as well, the 82nd could thus be committed to NEPTUNE as another reinforced airborne division of four regiments, for the blocking role at the base of the Cotentin.

Thus protected on the south and with its exits from UTAH Beach secured, the VII Corps was to clear the southern part of the Cotentin to the Douve River and then turn north into firmer and higher ground toward Cherbourg. The 90th Infantry Division and, if necessary, the 9th were to reinforce the 4th, and despite fortified hills in the north Cotentin and heavy fortification of the port itself, the final First Army plan before D-Day projected the capture of Cherbourg on D plus 15. Although German demolitions would surely have to be cleared away before the port could go into service, anything near D plus 15 should be early enough to keep the lodgment alive.

Beyond the Beaches

On Monday, May 15, Montgomery again strode across his relief map at St. Paul's School, to advise all concerned of the latest modifications of the NEPTUNE plan, and to assure that on the eve of the invasion all commanders knew their assigned tasks. This time Montgomery was drawn from his customary taciturnity by an audience including the King, the entire British War Cabinet, and the British Chiefs of Staff, as well as Churchill, Eisenhower, and all the principal NEPTUNE officers. The eminence and, at least among many of its British members, the confident sympathy of this audience for the commander of 21 Army Group stimulated Montgomery to warmth and enthusiasm beyond his earlier performance. He permitted himself not only uncommon openness but an almost breathtaking optimism about the prospects of the grand assault so long dreaded. His interest in exploitation beyond the landing, a subject so often submerged in caution when others were planning, burst forth in full flower.

Indicating that he expected to capture Caen the first day, Montgomery said he would thrust strong armored columns into that vital road junction and then immediately "knock about a bit down there"—pointing beyond Caen to Falaise, fifty-two kilometers inland by road from the beach, but with good, rolling, open tank country all along the way. According to Montgomery's own notes for the occasion, he urged, "Every officer and man must have only one idea, and that is to peg out claims inland, and to penetrate quickly and deeply into enemy territory." "I consider that once the beaches are in our possession, success will depend largely on our ability to concentrate our armour and push fairly strong armoured columns rapidly inland to secure important ground or communication centres."[9]

In fact, despite Montgomery's expansiveness before the assemblage of dignitaries, the detailed NEPTUNE plans projected no such rapid advance inland. The British planned to take Caen the first day, but not to push quickly farther. Dempsey's Second Army was assigned a considerably larger share of armor than Bradley's First Army to the west, as though to take advantage of the inviting tank country of the Caen-Falaise plain. But it was not at all clear that the weight of British armor would be sufficient to match the likely German armored opposition.

The Second Army intended to put an armored brigade ashore on D-Day on each of its three beaches. In addition, the 7th Armoured Division, the famous Desert Rats of North Africa, would land as an immediate followup to the infantry assault division on GOLD Beach, and a second armored brigade would be part of the immediate followup on SWORD. (All this was in addition to specially equipped amphibious assault teams of the 79th Armoured Division that would participate in the initial landings.)

At the beginning of May, however, the enemy had moved his 21st Panzer Division—also veterans of the Western Desert, successors to the old 5th Light Division of the earliest North African campaigns—from Rennes in Brittany to precisely the Caen-Falaise area about which Montgomery spoke so buoyantly. The Panzer Lehr Division, briefly shifted toward the Eastern Front earlier in the spring, had returned to France, and rather than going back to its former bivouac area around Verdun, it proceeded in May to the area of Chartres-le Mans-Châteaudun, only a day's march from Caen. The movements of the 21st Panzer Division and Panzer Lehr naturally alarmed the Allies: had the Germans discovered the target of the coming invasion? Between the two newly arrived panzer divisions, furthermore, there stood the 12th SS Panzer Division, long since stationed between the Orne and the Seine around Bernay-Evreux-Dreux-Gacé; while just slightly to the east, astride the Seine and also within a day's march of Caen, was the 116th Panzer Division. These four armored formations would overmatch British armor on the Allied left for a considerable time to come, even if fear for the Pas de Calais held the additional three panzer divisions in that sector and the Low Countries in place. And any hard Allied push southeast from Caen would surely alarm the Germans quickly, because only 195 kilometers lay between Caen and Paris, and only 480 kilometers between Caen and the West Wall on the Franco-German frontier.

A yet more fundamental fact should have cast doubt on Montgomery's forecast of a tank knockabout toward Falaise, and had in fact deeply influenced the COSSAC and NEPTUNE planners. General Dempsey's British Second Army would take to the Continent almost the final uncommitted military manpower and material reserves of the British Empire. In time this army would be joined in Europe by another Commonwealth army, the First Canadian. The approach of the bottom of Britain's manpower barrel was signalized in the First Canadian Army's mixed Canadian, British, and Polish composition. After it, there would be no more British armies. American divisions would continue arriving in France throughout 1944; British divisions would not. General Montgomery surely hoped that his British troops might execute a decisive breakout from the beaches to lead the Allies across the Seine and into Germany. He could expect them to do so, however, only if German resistance dramatically crumbled. Otherwise, the glory of achieving the decisive victory of the invasion was too likely to be purchased with casualties that would ruin the last British armies. To risk such casualties would be to risk Great Britain's very stature as a great power. The two Commonwealth armies, and particularly the British Second Army, had to be hoarded to preserve British influence in the peacemaking, to protect nothing less than the purposes behind Britain's waging war at all.

If the American First Army got firmly ashore, its initial priority would have to be the capture of Cherbourg. But if that objective could be achieved by D plus 15 as planned, American strength might early turn southward. According to General Bradley, Montgomery followed the May 15 meeting and his prediction of a rapid drive inland from Caen by urging Bradley "to explore the possibility of a similar tank knockabout behind Omaha Beach." Bradley of course agreed to the exploration; but he had less reason to feel confident of rapid American exploitation of a successful landing than Montgomery did to anticipate a swift British penetration inland. "In contrast to Monty," Bradley said, "I had foreseen a hard enemy crust on the Normandy coast."[10] More to the point, however, behind the Atlantic Wall on the Americans' front lay the Bocage country.

Immediately inland from OMAHA Beach, between Bayeux and Isigny, is a coastal strip known as the Bessin. Through it and parallel to the coast flows the Aure River, whose course turns from north to west at Bayeux and continues westward to join the Vire at Isigny. From Trévières to Isigny, Rommel's flooding operations had widened the Aure to inundate the flat plain adjacent to it, making of the coastal strip a peninsula two to eight kilometers wide. Along this peninsula ran the lateral road that was intended to connect the five invasion beachheads, a portion of Route Nationale 13, the main Paris-to-Cherbourg highway. The Bessin would pose difficulties for the Americans even before they tried to cross the flooded valley of the Aure, because little of the higher ground along the highway is open. Rather, it is divided according to the Norman custom into fields and orchards bordered by hedgerows, earthen dikes that would badly impede tank movement and much restrict observation.

Once across the Aure into the Bocage, however, the Americans would find a still worse tangle of hedgerows. The Bocage is a hilly region extending south almost as far as the base of the Brittany Peninsula. In the Bocage the hedgerows are ubiquitous. They have evolved over centuries, first planted by the Norman farmers as boundary markers, then retained out of custom, to protect fields and flocks from the cold winds off the ocean and the Channel, and as a source of firewood. Their earthen parapets are from a meter to four meters high, on the average somewhat over a meter, and from about a third of a meter to more than a meter in thickness. Growing out of the walls are hedges of hawthorn, brambles, vines, and trees from a meter to five meters high, also adding an additional meter or so to the thickness. The hedgerows divide the whole Bocage into innumerable enclosures, some larger than a football field but most much smaller. Each hedgerow provided the Germans with a natural earthwork, the bushes on top offering a wealth of concealment for small-arms and machine-gun positions. Apart from the few main roads, passage among the hedgerows was by wagon trails, in effect sunken lanes, often overarched by the hedges and thus transformed into a labyrinth of covered ways, to conceal the defender and befuddle the attacker. Each hedgerow-bounded field of the Bocage would tend to become a separate battleground, subject to conquest only by slow advances with rifles and grenades by infantrymen hugging the walls, with tank support useful but the overall situation a nightmare for mechanized forces, a dream for a defending army with the limited mobility of the Germans' ordinary infantry and garrison divisions.

The Bocage behind OMAHA Beach was no place for the tank knockabout that Montgomery suggested to Bradley. It was instead so unpromising a countryside for attack, so much favoring the German defenders while penalizing the Americans' strong suit, their mobility, that it might well have caused second thoughts about the very choice of invasion beaches, whatever their merits in access to harbors. At the least, the wide belt of the Bocage warranted a considerable share of the invasion planners' forethought, to anticipate the problems the hedgerows would pose and to seek solutions for them in advance. Especially did the Bocage warrant forethought if British caution over casualties compelled the Americans to bear the Allies' principal offensive efforts. But so complete was the preoccupation of the NEPTUNE planners with the difficulties merely of grasping the beachheads, so pervasive was the doubt and caution shadowing the whole planning effort, and so much did Montgomery's effort to rescue NEPTUNE from excesses of prudence and to prepare for the great general's leap into the unknown focus upon the Caen-Falaise plain, that no such preparation for the Bocage occurred.

As early as August 1943, the British Chiefs of Staff had responded to COSSAC's initial OVERLORD plan by warning that German defenders were likely to make all too good use of such defensive advantages as the Bocage afforded, and urging that assumptions about a fighting advance through the Bocage be reexamined. The warning made little or no difference; the special dangers and tactical problems of the Bocage received little attention. Montgomery's 21 Army Group headquarters acknowledged after almost a month of fighting ashore: "Experience gained to date in Normandy"—experience since the invasion, not forethought—"has shown that the 'bocage' country is most unsuitable for large scale armoured action and, further, that it would offer the enemy limitless opportunities for delaying action during a withdrawal." Bradley's aide Major Chester B. Hansen, whose diary often reflected his commander's thoughts, recorded after almost two months ashore: "Far behind our original schedule but that schedule did not take into consideration the great difficulty of fighting in this bocage country with its thick hedge rows."[11]

In sum, the limits of British manpower reserves suggested that the major Allied offensive out of the beaches must be American. Bradley's First Army could risk large casualties; Dempsey's Second Army could not. But the terrain beyond the Normandy beaches heavily favored an offensive out of the British beaches, not the American. This combination of factors might seem to have suggested an invasion design bringing the Americans rather than the British into Normandy on the Allied eastern flank, so American mobility as well as the comparatively large American capacity to absorb losses might be put to good advantage. But the COSSAC and NEPTUNE planners never felt able to give this possibility serious consideration. Logistics restrained them. Naturally, from the beginning of the American reinforcement, when plans to invade Europe had barely begun to be formulated, the Americans entered Britain from the west and erected their cantonments mainly in western Britain. Lines of supply and reinforcement would most conveniently run to the western flank in Normandy. Furthermore, as the first OVERLORD plan stated: "Lines of communication will be simplified if the British-Canadian forces are based on ports nearest the United Kingdom. In consequence, United States forces should normally be on the right of the line, British-Canadian forces on the left."[12]

Despite the strategic implications for breaking out from the Normandy beaches, the planners in fact took the placement of British on the left and Americans on the right for granted. The issue rose to conscious scrutiny only in connection with a problem much more remote than that of victory in Normandy, when late in 1943 President Roosevelt sought to assure postwar American occupation of industrial northwest Germany—which would have put the British to the south, or on the right of the Americans. With the COSSAC invasion plan thus challenged on grounds of only indirect relevance to the planners' preoccupations, Major General Ray W. Barker, an American, responded for General Morgan:

> I am sure that the Chiefs of Staff will agree that no change in the alignment of the forces (U.S. on the right; British on the left) for Operation "OVERLORD" can be accepted at this stage. Such a change would involve a complete recasting of the "OVERLORD" plan, and would cut across the unalterable fact that U.S. forces, depots and training areas are in the West and South-West of England and British forces, depots and training areas in the East, South-East, and in Scotland.[13]

Treating the conclusion as though it were as unalterable as the established location of the bases and depots, the planners reduced the chances for any tank knockabout from the beaches to the unlikely ones of a German collapse in front of Montgomery's British. Perhaps it would ask too much of planners to suggest that, like Montgomery's great generals, they should look beyond the known, to the unknown and to the exploitation of victory. The NEPTUNE planners, at any rate, kept their gaze firmly fixed upon the beaches and the ports of the Far Shore, venturing little beyond. Given the history of the perils of amphibious assault, that seemed enough.

ULTRA

The Allies possessed a thorough knowledge of the German formations and defensive preparations they must confront across the Channel, including the ominous gathering of panzers, from a variety of intelligence sources, but particularly thanks to the ULTRA secret. This, their most carefully concealed intelligence triumph of the war, was their ability to read the Germans' most confidential wireless communications, encrypted by the enemy's Enigma machines whose codes the Poles, British, and French had gradually broken.

The Resistance inside occupied Europe, Allied agents on the Continent, and aerial reconnaissance would in any event have told the Allies much about the German order of battle. For these conventional intelligence sources, ULTRA was a complementary and confirmatory source of incalculable value, most especially as a control indicating the varying degrees of reliability of all other sources and kinds of information. Through ULTRA, the enemy passed on to the Allies some of the most basic information about his strength and even his intentions and motives, in his own supposedly well-guarded words.

As the day for launching NEPTUNE approached, ULTRA had already enjoyed its finest hour of the war, and its value for the Anglo-American ground forces had somewhat waned. The finest hour had come in North Africa. When the Germans fought across the Mediterranean, their most urgent communications necessarily traveled by wireless and were therefore subject to interception and to decoding by the ULTRA machines and staff at Bletchley Park in Buckinghamshire. Within the European Continent, in contrast, the Germans conducted much of their military communication by land-line telephone and telex. Such communication was not penetrated by ULTRA. The Germans' own considerable success, especially early in the war, in eavesdropping on Allied radio communications made them wary enough of radio security to prefer land lines when they had them. For precision as well as security, moreover, their headquarters submitted detailed instructions by land-line telex printouts. Nevertheless, the various German headquarters found enough need to talk among each other by radio that ULTRA's special forte was identifying those headquarters and the units they commanded, that is, revealing the enemy order of battle.

Under instructions issued by Marshall to Eisenhower on March 15, 1944, ULTRA intelligence reached Eisenhower's American forces by methods based on British procedure. Special Liaison Units, largely American in personnel for the American commands but attached to MI6, the British Secret Intelligence Service, were attached to each army group, army, air force, and tactical air command headquarters and received ULTRA information from Bletchley Park. Each Special Liaison Unit consisted of a carefully selected officer or officers plus a small section of enlisted cipher and signal specialists. The SLU customarily received ULTRA information four times daily; but during operations, the most urgent material—designated ZZZZ or ZZZZZ on a scale of Z to ZZZZZ—went immediately to pertinent commands. Bletchley decided which information was pertinent to which command, a cause of some complaint by SLUs that did not always feel they had a suitably complete picture. The transmission was often by "one-time pad" cipher to safeguard the ULTRA secret itself; but because this method, though highly secure, is relatively slow and cumbersome, in time increasing use was made of enciphering machines not unlike the Germans' Enigmas, but whose codes fortunately were not broken by the enemy.

The SLU at any field headquarters was, according to Marshall's orders, to "work under the control of the G-2 or A-2 (Intelligence officer) of the command as part of his staff."[14] Beyond constant exchanges with the G-2 or A-2, the SLU customarily delivered a daily briefing to the army group, army, or air commander and the few senior staff officers who would have been authorized recipients of ULTRA information; this latter group varied from command to command but was always small.

The SLU was to make ULTRA useful to the command to which it was assigned, but one of its primary responsibilities under Marshall's directive was also to keep the ULTRA secret secure. Maintaining security could be difficult. The very presence of the SLU detachment attracted curiosity. The SLU officer had to be camouflaged, with some commands employing such titles as Russian Liaison or German Air Force Specialist. Often the SLU shared cramped quarters with other staff sections that were not in on the secret, separated only by the thinnest of partitions and obliged to converse in whispers.

Attached to a British agency, the SLU detachments were also controlled by SLU 8, the detachment at SHAEF, and were at the same time "subject to the administration and discipline of the command to which they are detailed."[15] So anomalous a place in the military hierarchy was bound to create difficulties, but it also gave the head of each detachment a valuable measure of independence from the field commander, to help the SLU resist possible compromises of security. The temptation to compromise could beckon the field commander strongly whenever ULTRA brought information of immediate pertinence to operations—which would no longer be very frequently on the Continent, but would sometimes occur at critical junctures. The rule was to make no operational use of ULTRA intelligence without first assuring that doing so would not tend to give away the secret. The Germans must not be afforded the opportunity to conclude that the Allies possessed information that could have come only from reading coded wireless traffic. The Allies' information must always seem to have derived from some other source. Thus, when in the Mediterranean ULTRA had revealed the sailing dates and other details of shipments of reinforcements or supplies from Italy to Rommel and the British wanted to sink the ships, it had to be arranged that patrolling aircraft would seemingly and conspicuously chance to discover the ships before the sinking. American field commands would have to cover ULTRA with similar ruses.

For whatever the decrease in its value as the war shifted to the European continent, ULTRA remained a pearl beyond price. The secret had to be kept. Yet the eve of NEPTUNE also revealed the most fundamental limitation of ULTRA: it could not do the Allies' fighting for them. It could apprise Eisenhower, Montgomery, Bradley, and their principal staff officers of the German panzer concentration on the very ground where Montgomery desired his own tank knockabout. But ULTRA could not defeat the panzers. It could not solve the problems raised by confronting the panzers with a British army that dared not suffer high casualties, or by landing the Allies' most mobile formations into the narrow mazes of the hedgerows where sustained combat power, not mobility, would be the highest military virtue.

4: By Air and by Sea

THE SENIOR American airman in Europe in 1944 possessed none of the flamboyance or the thirst for applause that we have come to expect in those magnificient young men of the early flying machines. Yet Lieutenant General Carl A. Spaatz had already been flying for twenty-eight years, and few experiences in early aviation had been more risky than his piloting through the winds of the Sierras the canvas-and-bamboo contraptions that the 1st Aero Squadron took with the Pershing Punitive Expedition to Mexico in 1916. By American standards, Spaatz was a veteran aviator by the time the United States entered the First World War, and so as a major he commanded the AEF's 3rd Aviation Instruction Center at Issoudon. His pleas for a chance at the gladiatorial combat of the airmen of the Western Front won him a three-week tour with the 13th Aero Squadron over St. Mihiel in September 1918, enough time for three kills and a near brush with death when two Fokkers got onto his tail; the squadron commander, Major Charles J. Biddle, scored his sixth victory in rescuing Spaatz.

Between January 1 and 7, 1927, Major Spaatz commanded the *Question Mark* when it set an endurance record by remaining aloft over Los Angeles for almost 151 hours. This achievement was a better reflection of his character than his derring-do in flimsy scout and pursuit machines. He was patient, persistent, determined—a sturdy, taciturn Pennsylvania Dutchman. In the 1920s and 1930s he became one of the authors of American air doctrine and a trainer of pilots and evaluator of proposed aircraft to serve the doctrine: Chief of Training and Operations, Chief of Plans, eventually Assistant Chief of the Army Air Corps. Like the other creators of American aerial warfare, he was a friend and champion of Brigadier General Billy Mitchell, and in time he absorbed the ideas of the Italian prophet of independent air power, Giulio Douhet, as brought within the American purview via French translation and made the basis of instruction in Air Corps schools where Spaatz studied and taught.

But Spaatz's and other later American ideas of strategic bombing were honed to a precision absent in Mitchell, Douhet, or the strategic bombing theories of any other nation. Not only were targets to be hit with precision, bombing by daylight with the accurate Norden bombsight, rather than resorting to the British method of indiscriminate bombing of whole cities at night. The American air planners insisted that the very selection of targets to be bombed must be based on a careful study of the enemy's economy. According to American air doctrine, it was through the destruction of the few critical, properly chosen targets around which all the rest of the enemy economy revolved that strategic bombing would win wars. In August 1941, in a document designated AWPD/1, the newly created Air War Plans Division specified the enemy's electric power, transportation, and petroleum as the vital targets, the touchstones of his economy.

In the spring of 1944, General Spaatz commanded the United States Strategic Air Forces in Europe (USSTAF). From this command post, he sought to persist in aiming American air power at those carefully selected vital targets, and in particular at Germany's petroleum. Spaatz was an officer who consistently thought in strategic terms, not only in the air force sense of "strategic" bombing—the use of independent air power to assail targets beyond the tactical battles fought by armies and navies—but in the classic sense: strategy as the combining of the individual elements of war to achieve the purpose of war. As a strategist in the American strategic tradition, furthermore, Spaatz aimed to exploit American material power to overwhelm the enemy's principal warmaking capacity; as an airman in that tradition, he believed air power should leap beyond the traditional army and navy objective, the enemy armed forces, to destroy the very source of the armed forces' power: the economy that sustained them, and in the German instance, the petroleum that moved the tanks and assault guns, the panzers and panzer grenadiers.

When Spaatz took command of USSTAF early in the third year of American participation in the war, the American war effort in Europe thus far had been more aerial than anything else, yet the German war economy still survived and even grew despite its years under Anglo-American strategic bombing. Nevertheless, Spaatz's confidence in the fatal effects of aerial assault against the critical economic targets remained undiminished. In his view, there had as yet been no satisfactory test of American strategic bombing. Too many American warplanes had been diverted for too long into the Mediterranean, where Spaatz himself had served as American air commander under Eisenhower. Operation POINTBLANK, the Anglo-American Combined Bomber Offensive against Germany agreed upon by Roosevelt, Churchill, and their advisers at Casablanca early in 1943, had itself diverted much of its effort from the critical economic targets to submarine yards and launching bases, to assist in the battle for the Atlantic. The Royal Air Force also played its part in POINTBLANK, using night bombing attacks aimed more at German morale than at the critical economic targets favored by the Americans. When the American Eighth Air Force based in England and the Fifteenth Air Force based in Italy at last became able to concentrate large formations of heavy bombers over Germany late in 1943, a preliminary battle against the Luftwaffe's fighter interceptors proved a not altogether foreseen, but a completely necessary preliminary to the trial of American bombing doctrine.

The American heavy bombers, the Boeing B-17 Flying Fortress and the Consolidated B-24 Liberator, were more strongly gunned and armored than any other strategic bombers. Nevertheless, flying over Europe by daylight, without fighter escort, they took unacceptable losses at the hands of German interceptors. In December 1943, however, the North American P-51 Mustang fighter went into escort service, with enough range to accompany the bombers from England to virtually any target in Germany, and with the firepower, speed, and maneuverability to master the enemy's Focke-Wulf Fw 190s and Messerschmitt Bf 109s; untrammeled by a long accumulation of tactical preconceptions, American airplane design was more successful than American tank design. By March 1944, the P-51 was available in quantity, and swarms of Mustangs guarded the B-17s on the first American raids to Berlin. The Mustangs plus intensive bombing of German fighter production facilities, which had culminated during "Big Week" in February, broke the back of the enemy's fighter defenses and gave Spaatz sufficient command of the air to hit any German targets he chose.

Spaatz chose petroleum. On March 5, 1944, he presented to Eisenhower a Plan for the Completion of the Combined Bomber Offensive, and for the maximum contribution of air power to OVERLORD. In the plan, Spaatz warned that the Germans were achieving growing success in the production of synthetic oil, such that during the next six months the enemy might obtain 8,600,000 tons of liquid fuels and lubricants and thus rescue himself from any crippling oil shortages. But a mere fourteen plants produced 80 percent of Germany's synthetic petroleum. Within six months, Spaatz calculated, a campaign of aerial bombing concentrated against synthetic oil production, while the Fifteenth Air Force also went on hitting the crude oil refineries in Rumania and elsewhere in southern and central Europe, would cut German gasoline supplies by 50 percent at the most conservative estimate. Along with the oil campaign, Spaatz proposed a continuing attack on the German air force as a second aerial priority, and attacks on rubber and tire centers as a third priority. After fifteen days of visual bombing by the Eighth Air Force and ten by the Fifteenth—necessarily spread out over a period of weeks, because clear weather for full visual bombing was a rarity in Europe—the heavy bombers could turn to direct support of the cross-Channel invasion. To nail down the benefits of the oil campaign for OVERLORD, Spaatz believed like most ground commanders that the Allies' air power should turn just before the invasion to an interdiction campaign, especially a bridge-busting campaign, designed to isolate the invasion battleground. Meanwhile, the Oil Plan promised the most rapid and effective curtailment of the mobility the Germans would need to turn back the invasion.

OVERLORD and Air Power: Questions Strategic and Moral

Spaatz rejoiced that the triumph of the Mustangs and Fortresses over the Luftwaffe interceptors had opened the way at last to fulfillment of air power's promise to be a weapon that could independently win wars. But he had to draw up his Oil Plan against the threat of still another diversion of his bombers away from this promise, a diversion greater than the simple tactical support of OVERLORD which according to his Douhetian convictions was unnecessary but to which he was reconciled. The Oil Plan was in part a rejoinder to a rival plan for employing the air forces in support of OVERLORD, the Transportation Plan offered by the commander of the Allied Expeditionary Air Force, Air Chief Marshal Leigh-Mallory.

To find a Briton to head the AEAF had not been easy. Obviously, air support of the invasion would not be solely, or even primarily, a task for strategic bombing. Yet the Royal Air Force even more completely than the American Army Air Corps had become committed in the years before the war to strategic bombing by an air force independent of the other armed services as the key to rapid victory in war without prohibitive expense. To Britain, this idea could offer a special appeal. The RAF could present strategic bombing as the appropriate twentieth-century embodiment of the historic British aversion to large-scale ground combat, and thus as a guarantor against repeating the 1914–1918 aberration that had dispatched mass British armies to the Western Front at so terrible a cost. The RAF's best officers were almost all strategic bombing men. Leigh-Mallory, however, had come out of Fighter Command.

In that relatively neglected branch of the RAF, his record had been less than consistently impressive. During the Battle of Britain he was air vice-marshal commanding No. 12 Group to the north and east of London. As such he embroiled himself in controversy with Air Vice-Marshal Keith Park, commander of No. 11 Group south of the Thames. Leigh-Mallory's favored defensive tactic was to build up a heavy weight of interceptors to try for knockout blows against the German raiders. This method unfortunately tended to leave Park's squadrons badly outnumbered while Leigh-Mallory's took their time to assemble. The raiders often dropped their bombs before No. 12 Group arrived. Air Chief Marshal Sir Hugh Dowding, Commander-in-Chief Fighter Command during the Battle of Britain and the command's one supremely capable leader, eventually resolved to relieve Leigh-Mallory. Before Dowding got around to it, however, he himself lost his post for lack of sufficiently charismatic qualities in the approved Churchillian mode. Instead of being sacked, the jowly, ambitious Leigh-Mallory rode an assertive temperament to the top of Fighter Command.

He also went on, as an RAF officer not exclusively committed to strategic bombing, to become chief air planner for COSSAC and thence, on November 25, 1943, head of AEAF. But Leigh-Mallory was not universally respected even as a leader of fighters, and bombing men looked with deep unease upon any prospect that his headquarters might control the whole aerial support of OVERLORD. Too few Americans respected him to permit his American deputy, Major General William O. Butler, to bring enough AAF officers into AEAF to give it a genuinely Allied appearance; AEAF headquarters remained always a preponderantly British organization, and therefore all the more distrusted by the Americans. After their hard fight for ascendancy over the Luftwaffe in German skies, and their recent escape from losing the fight thanks to the arrival of the Mustangs, American airmen in particular raised their eyebrows over Leigh-Mallory's bland and often-announced opinion that complete control of the air was not a prerequisite to OVERLORD. General Spaatz now found Leigh-Mallory prepared to expend Allied air power on a plan that Spaatz regarded as impracticable, dangerous to continued Allied mastery of the air, and—for Spaatz was an airman genuinely troubled over the moral questions raised by aerial bombardment—inhumane in the threat it posed to thousands of civilians.

This was the Transportation Plan. The initial conception was not that of Leigh-Mallory but of some of the host of civilian scientific advisers in the wartime service of the Air Ministry, notably Solly Zuckerman, former professor of anatomy. The COSSAC planners as a matter of course had expected to employ air power to isolate the invasion battlefield as much as possible from German reinforcement, especially by using the accepted aerial interdiction methods of the time to disrupt the railroads—breaking bridges, strafing, destroying critical junction points. Zuckerman thought a much more complete halting of rail traffic could be achieved. He had suggested and then carefully assessed the Allied bombing of the marshaling yards around Rome in July 1943, and he concluded that a properly planned attack on a relatively few key rail centers—a sustained bombing attack, strategic rather than tactical, not merely strafing and bombing for several days before the invasion—could virtually knock out a whole railway system. The consistent attacks on the key centers would destroy the marshaling yards themselves, the repair shops, sheds, stations, switches, roundhouses, turntables, signal systems, locomotives, and rolling stock. Zuckerman the anatomist told the OVERLORD air planners that a railway network is like a nervous system, no part of which can suffer damage without effects upon the whole.

Leigh-Mallory accepted this scheme, and he, Zuckerman, and AEAF headquarters worked out the details. Many of those details added encouragement. AEAF reported on February 12, 1944, that German military traffic occupied two-thirds of the rail capacity of western Europe, so that there was not much excess capacity devoted to civilian activity that the enemy could absorb, and damage would hurt him promptly. The rail centers in

France and the Low Countries were not only accessible to fighters and Allied ground radar search as well as to bombers, but they were small and vulnerable. Between February and D-Day, it ought to be possible for Allied aircraft to drop 108,000 tons of bombs, while the rail targets should require only 45,000 tons, leaving a surplus for other targets.

On the other hand, continued study disconcertingly elevated the number of key rail centers in France and Belgium from 40 to 79 to 101. It was a change in definitions that subsequently rolled the total back to seventy, which supposedly could be disposed of by the 45,000 tons of bombs. A French agent employed by SHAEF contended that the Transportation Plan would injure French civilian traffic more than it would hurt the German military, and a committee of British rail experts hired by the American Embassy in London supported him by arguing that only one-fifth, not two-thirds, of French railway traffic served the enemy armed forces. According to this committee, further-more, as many as 500 rail centers would have to be attacked to inflict significant damage on German military capabilities. At least half these centers were large and difficult to cripple; damage to them could be rapidly repaired. As the required number of targets rose, even by AEAF's reckoning, so did the likelihood of a destructive spillover against French civilian property and lives. Finally, to the extent that the Transportation Plan achieved what it was supposed to, it would later impede Allied movement through France—another aspect of the planners' tendency to look so much toward the first lodgment that they neglected subsequent exploitation.

Churchill himself accepted these arguments against the Transportation Plan. So did his Chief of Air Staff, Air Chief Marshal Sir Charles Portal; the CIGS, Marshal Brooke; and the Ministry of Economic Warfare. Most emphatic among the opponents, however, were the strategic bomber commanders, Air Chief Marshal Sir Arthur Harris of RAF Bomber Command and General Spaatz. Leigh-Mallory wanted their bombers to come under his direction on March 1 to begin the Transportation Plan, diverting Spaatz's force once more from the enemy's strategic vital centers and particularly from its campaign to ruin the Luftwaffe just as the P-51 squadrons were becoming numerous and the battle for control of the air seemed about to reach its climax. When Spaatz raised this latter objection, however, Leigh-Mallory reiterated his view that air supremacy was not essential to OVERLORD.

General Eisenhower very much desired air supremacy, and his desire assured that Leigh-Mallory failed to get the strategic bombers as quickly as he wanted. But Spaatz's counterproposal, the Oil Plan of March 5, did not carry the day either. Eisenhower wanted the isolation of the Normandy battlefield as well as control of the air above it, and he feared that the Oil Plan would not bring results quickly enough to help achieve the lodgment. He placed great trust in the judgments of his Deputy Supreme Commander, the slight, unassuming, logically-minded aviator who had been his air commander in the Mediterranean, Air Chief Marshal Sir Arthur Tedder—and Tedder supported the Transportation Plan. In fact, Tedder's air operations in Italy had provided the inspira-tion for it.

On March 25, all the principal military protagonists conferred at Eisenhower's new suburban headquarters at Bushy Park, Teddington, in the southern outskirts of London. Portal and Harris still expressed doubts about Leigh-Mallory's plan, but the problem of attaining results rapidly enough for direct utility on the invasion beaches left them in so acquiescent a mood that Spaatz had to carry the opposition arguments practically alone. He insisted that the number of key rail centers in France and Belgium was so large, and the proportion of total rail capacity needed by the German military so small, that the Transportation Plan could not achieve decisive effects as rapidly as attacks on the fourteen synthetic oil plants. Destruction of one of those oil plants would require no more bombing than the wrecking of a rail center, and the loss of fourteen oil plants would cripple the enemy infinitely worse than the loss of fourteen rail centers. The Luftwaffe would surely fight to defend the oil plants, so the Oil Plan would also assure completion of Allied control of the air.

Still, German stocks of oil at hand in France extended Spaatz's timetable for decisive results to six months; and while he argued that the Transportation Plan would require a longer, in fact indefinite period before it could achieve decision, here appeared the rub. Spaatz's Oil Plan could not produce decisive effects by D-Day; for all its shortcomings, the Transportation Plan might yield such effects. At least it might hamper German movement into the invasion area enough to provide the margin of success. Just as much to the point, the strategic bomber commanders had all been trumpeting their confidence in victory through air power too long, and yet had also bombed German targets without producing victory too long, for much credibility to remain with them. It happened, as we know now, that in his Oil Plan Spaatz had indeed struck the touchstone of victory through air power. But no one could be sure of this in early 1944, when the airmen had already offered so many unkept promises. The day after the conference, Eisenhower decided on the Transportation Plan.

At the same time, Eisenhower found Spaatz's arguments for a major test of strategic bombing doctrine through the Oil Plan so persuasive that he pledged to free the heavy bombers for an oil campaign as soon as possible. Meanwhile he also accepted Spaatz's insistence on air supremacy as a prerequisite for D-Day, and he cited the destruction of the Luftwaffe as in his view the continuing first priority of Spaatz's USSTAF.

The Supreme Commander's respect for Spaatz, if not complete acceptance of his judgments, was reflected also in the command arrangements for air support of OVERLORD agreed upon on March 26 by Eisenhower, Portal, and Spaatz. The American Joint Chiefs of Staff had long demanded that because the cross-Channel invasion would be the climax of the war, the Allied Supreme Commander must control the air forces during the critical period of the invasion. General Spaatz agreed. SHAEF would have to command the air forces particularly for the interdiction campaign that Spaatz believed must strike enemy transportation immediately before D-Day, a separate matter from Leigh-Mallory's Transportation Plan, as well as for direct support of the troops going ashore. The British government, in contrast, wished to exclude RAF Bomber Command from Eisenhower's jurisdiction, so Harris's strategic area bombing might persist as at least one distinctively British effort unamalgamated into Allied and therefore increasingly American direction. There were also the misgivings of the bomber men, British as well as American, about working under the AEAF commander.

The Eisenhower-Portal-Spaatz agreement of March 26 was, predictably, a compromise. It provided that the strategic air forces should come under Eisenhower's "direction"; the British had wanted to give him merely "responsibility for supervising," while the Americans wanted him to "command." Hitherto the Combined Chiefs of Staff, overseeing their countries' whole military efforts, had conducted the strategic air war against Germany with Portal as their agent; now direction would pass from Portal to Eisenhower as soon as a specific plan of heavy bomber support for OVERLORD could be agreed upon between the two countries. Tedder, however, and not Leigh-Mallory, would serve as Eisenhower's "Executive for the overall supervision and complete coordination of the entire air effort." USSTAF and RAF Bomber Command were to function parallel to AEAF under Eisenhower and Tedder, not subordinate to AEAF. Tedder had conceded at the March 25 conference that destroying the Luftwaffe should continue to have the air forces' first priority even over the Transportation Plan; and while he favored the Transportation Plan, he could be counted on to support many more missions into Germany to goad the Luftwaffe into combat than could Leigh-Mallory. The arrangements would be reviewed, all agreed, once the Allied armies were lodged on the Continent, to assure a return of the heavy bombers to their favored campaigns. The British were also assured that any threat to the security of their islands would take priority over all other air operations.

On April 11, Eisenhower learned from Spaatz that SHAEF's direction of the strategic bombers thus agreed upon was not yet in effect, though the Supreme Commander had thought it was. Spaatz was still getting instructions from Chief of Air Staff Portal as agent of the CCS for the Combined Bomber Offensive. The reason, Eisenhower learned when he questioned Portal and Tedder, was that the British War Cabinet had not yet approved the Transportation Plan, while general acceptance of a plan for the strategic bombers was a prerequisite for carrying out the Eisenhower-Portal-Spaatz agreement. In the War Cabinet had occurred an event rare at this stage of the war, a consideration of morality: like Spaatz, Churchill and his ministers were troubled by the Transportation Plan's implicit inhumanity.

The enlarged number of French and Belgian rail centers that would have to be bombed under the Transportation Plan had by now produced estimates that a byproduct of the plan would be as many as 160,000 French and Belgian casualties, including 40,000 deaths. Even laying the humanity issue aside, the Cabinet had to contemplate the political implications. Foreign Secretary Anthony Eden dwelt upon the postwar necessity for Britain to live in harmony with a Europe that was already looking toward Russia more than might be wished.

The Supreme Commander nevertheless responded to different imperatives, those of assuring a successful lodgment in Normandy; and, having made up his mind that the Transportation Plan might contribute the margin of success where success was likely to be a near thing, "I protested bitterly," he said, "at allowing details of a few targets to interfere with the operation of a whole plan, and the CAS [Portal] agreed to say to Spaatz that he would get his instructions from Tedder."[1]

So the bombers at length entered into Eisenhower's direction, and the Transportation Plan proceeded, as indeed its first operations had already done. But Churchill, though his moral sensitivities had not proven remarkably acute where area bombing of enemy populations was concerned, was not yet ready to dismiss "details of a few targets" when so many innocent and friendly lives and so much high policy might be involved. The Prime Minister still demanded that specific targets of the Transportation Plan be cleared one by one with the War Cabinet. Initially, the War Cabinet approved only fourteen of the first twenty-seven targets presented to it, with only five of the fourteen approved for unrestricted bombing. Churchill persisted in debating the subject with the military commanders, and on April 29 the War Cabinet suggested that the air forces should plan to restrict themselves to transportation targets that would not cost more than 100 lives per target. Churchill forwarded this suggestion to President Roosevelt as well as to General Eisenhower. But Eisenhower's mind was still made up, and he remained firm for the Transportation Plan despite all entreaties, while Roosevelt stood with him. In May, Churchill acquiesced to the limited extent of giving his government's approval to railway bombings as long as civilian casualties did not exceed a total of 10,000. He continued to watch anxiously over the Transportation Plan to the end.

At least, civilian casualties proved far fewer than the pessimists anticipated. The total probably came close to Churchill's maximum tolerable figure. Whatever the civilian casualty level, however, waging war against a peculiarly barbaric regime had eroded old values so that moral issues got short shrift when they were noticed at all, and Allied statesmen and soldiers had left far behind them the traditional principle of war that noncombatants may not be attacked at any time. The American strategic predilection for employing overwhelming power to destroy the enemy's warmaking capacity, further-more, having been extended beyond enemy armies to the civilian economy and the civilian will to support war as early as Sherman's marches and Sheridan's raids in the Civil War, did not offer firm footing for General Spaatz's moral objections to the Transporta-tion Plan.

Even under the traditional principle of war that noncombatants are not to be attacked, deviations might be permitted if a legitimate act of war just happened to harm civilians but achieved military effects large enough to compensate for the incidental evil effects. The Transportation Plan, unhappily, did not stand up well under this test of compensation or proportionality. Carrying out the plan, Allied aircraft dropped 71,000 tons of bombs on rail centers by D-Day, 26,000 tons more than the plan had projected. The index of rail traffic in France dropped from a base figure of 100 in January and February 1944 to 69 on May 19 and 38 on June 9. Postwar surveys confirmed that a greater proportion of French railway traffic than the one-fifth estimated by the American Embassy's experts served German military needs, though on the other hand the truth was also well below the two-thirds estimate of the authors of the Transportation Plan. In fact, German military requirements accounted for one-third of French railway activity. Thus, by cutting rail traffic some 62 percent between February and D-Day, the Tranportation Plan principally eliminated the civilian rail traffic of occupied France that to the German military represented excess capacity.

Those who had devised and adopted the Transportation Plan, Zuckerman, Leigh-Mallory, Tedder, and Eisenhower among them, insisted nevertheless that the plan fulfilled their expectations and made the invasion possible. General Eisenhower always believed that OVERLORD operated against so narrow a margin of success that no single factor contributing to the margin could have been dispensed with. After D-Day, Allied strategists were sufficiently impressed by the results of the Transportation Plan that they went on bombing rail centers through the rest of the war.

The enemy was less sure that the Transportation Plan had decisively injured him. Field Marshal von Rundstedt testified after the war that strategic bombing of rail centers had little or no effect on his communications before July. Not all German authorities agreed with Rundstedt, but an AAF evaluation board that studied the French railroad records concluded from this direct evidence of rail traffic volume that "The pre-D-day attacks against French rail centers were not necessary, and the 70,000 tons involved could have been devoted to alternative targets."[2] A 21 Army Group expert referred disparagingly to the AEAF's "pin-pricking on rail communications." A week before D-Day, SHAEF intelligence reported that the Germans still had three times the rail capacity needed for military traffic, four times the required number of cars, eight times the required locomotives, and ten times the required servicing facilities.[3]

The postwar United States Strategic Bombing Survey reached similar conclusions. Along with General Spaatz, these postwar investigators maintained that the decisive blow against enemy communications in support of OVERLORD was the interdiction campaign, particularly against bridges, which Spaatz had favored all along.

The Vengeance Weapons

The reason for incorporating into the Eisenhower-Portal-Spaatz agreement on aerial command a provision assuring that the air forces would protect the British home islands lay in the recent multiplication along the Channel and North Sea coasts of German launching sites for robot aircraft and rocket-fired bombs. Hitler called these menaces his Vergeltungswaffe, or vengeance weapons. No V-weapons had yet been launched. British intelligence had long known of the preparation of the V-weapons from agents on the Continent, from ULTRA intercepts, and finally from aerial reconnaissance of the testing sites and launching site construction. The potential of the weapons, especially of the V-2 rocket, to elude conventional interception and to wreak destruction on British cities or the concentrations of troops, equipment, and ships assembling for the invasion was frighteningly immeasurable—even omitting the possibility of their carrying atomic warheads. From December 1943, Operation CROSSBOW, the effort to counter the V-weapons, had been sending the heavy bombers of the Eighth Air Force on repeated raids against the launching sites, upon the urgent appeals of the British government that this mission must have the American precision bombers' "over-riding priority."[4]

Here was urgency indeed, but here also was yet another diversion of the American heavy bombers from their desired targets in Germany, and yet another reason, as events developed, for the Americans' misgivings about Leigh-Mallory. The British waited until December 1943, when they wanted the Eighth Air Force to begin immediately to hit the V-weapons sites with overwhelming force, to share with the Americans a reasonably full measure of their knowledge about the sites. The AAF in response not only launched its B-17s but took the trouble to build in the pine barrens of the Florida panhandle full-scale reproductions of the structures observed at the launching sites, and to conduct tests of how best to destroy them from the air. Trials of every available weapon and method of attack proved to the Americans' satisfaction that the most accurate and economical aerial assault on the launching sites would be not high-level bombing by the B-17s but medium-altitude attack by fighter-bombers. The launching sites required so precise an attack and were so well camouflaged that they practically defied attempts by B-17 bombardiers using the Norden bombsight to pick them up at the necessary distance of six miles. Bringing in fighter-bombers instead of the heavies would offer the additional advantage of returning the Fortresses to their campaign in Germany. But the British, and in particular their air officer principally concerned, Leigh-Mallory, insisted "that the best weapon for the rocket sites is the high altitude bomber." Elsewhere, he noted: "I feel certain we must continue to rely on the Heavies."[5]

Britain's perilous exposure to the weapons that might eventually be launched from the ski-shaped installations along Hitler's coast naturally rendered the Americans sensitive to British views. The Americans thus yielded to Leigh-Mallory, and CCS directives continued to instruct USSTAF to accord high priority to CROSSBOW. By D-Day, Allied aircraft dropped 36,200 tons of bombs in 25,150 bombing sorties against the V-weapon sites, of which the VIII Bomber Command of the Eighth Air Force accounted for 17,600 tons and 5,950 sorties. The rest of the raiding utilized the medium bombers and fighter-bombers of Leigh-Mallory's AEAF, with American aircraft again carrying a large share. Withal, the assorted demands on the Eighth Air Force heavies caused Spaatz to worry in May whether he would be able to meet the multitude of direct charges on him that would come upon the eve of OVERLORD.

D-Day was to arrive with the V-weapons still unlaunched. The Allies could congratulate themselves, despite their disputes, on the apparent success of the CROSSBOW attacks. Just how much those attacks contributed to delaying Hitler's V-weapon offensive nevertheless remains uncertain. The United States Strategic Bombing Survey was to estimate after the war that Allied aerial attacks probably forced a delay of three to four months.

Bridge-Busting

The Second World War had already carried Major General Lewis H. Brereton, USAAF, almost completely around the globe. An Annapolis graduate of 1911 who early switched to the army and the next year to army aviation, Brereton had commanded the second American observation squadron to operate in France in World War I and had risen to lead the I Corps Observation Group by the time of Château-Thierry. He later commanded American attack aviation at Soissons, training operations of First Army's air support for St. Mihiel, and the I Corps Air Observation Wing in that battle. He emerged from the war as Chief of Staff Air Service for the American Group of Armies. By 1941 and the coming of another war, Brereton was Commanding General, Far East Air Force in the Philippines, but his title was more impressive than the substance of his command. The core of his little air force was destroyed on December 8, 1941, in the Japanese attack that notoriously found the planes drawn up in neat lines on Clark and Iba Fields and knocked out eighteen of thirty-five B-17s, fifty-six pursuit planes, and twenty-five miscellaneous aircraft. Ever after, Brereton was in the center of the controversy over why the planes had not taken off to attack Formosa after the Philippines received news of the Japanese raid on Pearl Harbor, as Brereton claimed he had advocated.

Perhaps there is little wonder that by the time he reached England, Brereton's colleagues found him perpetually discontented and querulous. From disaster in the Philippines, he had the misfortune to go on to participation in further disaster as commander of United States tactical forces in Field Marshal Sir Archibald Wavell's American-British-Dutch-Australian (ABDA) command for the defense of Indonesia. From this hopeless task he was evacuated out of Java just before its fall to organize an American air force in India for the support of that country and China. During the spring and early summer of 1942, he at last enjoyed a measure of satisfaction in building up the Tenth Air Force; but in June, Rommel's advance to El Alamein led the CCS to order Brereton with all his bombers to the Middle East to help the British save Alexandria.

Success returned to Brereton as his Middle East Air Force, later the Ninth Air

Force, contributed conspicuously to the reversal of Allied fortunes in the eastern Mediterranean. When by late 1943 Allied triumphs in that theater had grown so complete that an American air force was no longer needed, the AAF decided that Brereton should go to England with his Ninth Air Force headquarters to form a new air force for tactical support of OVERLORD. Brereton's Middle East combat units were reassigned to the Twelfth Air Force in Italy, so he began again with only a staff. But it was not long before this smallish, sad-faced general possessed a great deal of power. With transfers of logistical units and of limited tactical forces from the Eighth Air Force, and with much greater infusions of strength direct from the United States, by D-Day his Ninth Air Force had eleven B-26 and A-20 medium bomber groups (each group with four squadrons of sixteen planes each, for a total of sixty-four planes and 1,591 officers and men in the group) and eighteen P-47, P-38, and P-51 fighter groups (each group with three squadrons of twenty-five planes each, for a total of seventy-five planes and 950 to 1,017 officers and men in the group). Altogether, Brereton led about 60,000 men.

The Ninth's size was in proportion to its job; it had to carry the heaviest burden of any single air organization in preparation for OVERLORD. Until March, furthermore, its bombers were also primarily involved in the strategic bombing offensive and the Eighth Air Force continued to have first call on its fighters as escorts. Its place in the chain of command somewhat reflected its diverse responsibilities, for Spaatz's USSTAF headquarters retained administrative and training jurisdiction over the Ninth, while in the OVERLORD operations Brereton's air force was part of Leigh-Mallory's AEAF.

Under Leigh-Mallory, the Ninth naturally found itself in the midst of the Transportation Plan. As early as March 10, its assignments included thirty of the rail-center targets, and while Churchill's Cabinet debated accepting many of the targets, the Ninth went ahead with strikes at Creil, Hirsons, Amiens, and Charleroi. By April, with the list of accepted targets growing, Brereton had worked out a standard operating procedure, in which four or five groups of B-26s would bomb a single rail center, not working in big formations following the signals of a lead airplane as had previously been customary, but breaking up into four- or six-plane sections for improved accuracy and reduced danger to civilians. Frequently, P-47s would follow up with dive-bombing and strafing attacks, so much impressing Leigh-Mallory that he ordered as many Spitfires as possible into bomber escort service to free the big P-47s with their eight .50-caliber machine guns and two 1,000- or three 500-lb. bombs for ground attack.

Nevertheless, Brereton was among the Americans skeptical about the Transportation Plan, and like Spaatz he pressed for a bridge-breaking campaign for direct interdiction of the rail lines into the invasion area. While AEAF closely directed Ninth Air Force OVERLORD operations to coordinate them with Leigh-Mallory's other principal command, Air Marshal Sir Arthur Coningham's RAF Second Tactical Air Force, the directives were thrashed out in conferences among Tedder, Spaatz, Harris, Leigh-Mallory, Coningham, and Brereton. The Americans thus had a forum for discussion. Furthermore, though the Transportation Plan had grown out of the bombing of the Rome marshaling yards, Spaatz and Brereton could point to more recent experience in Italy with Operation STRANGLE, a campaign against German lines of communication beginning in February. According to Lieutenant General Ira C. Eaker of the Fifteenth Air Force, STRANGLE showed that bridge-breaking was the single most effective method of interdiction. Disappointed with the Transportation Plan, 21 Army Group meanwhile urged the air forces to have a go at the bridges. Once more debate flared up among the airmen in Britain. Devotees of the Transportation Plan called forth a British railway expert who estimated that 1,200 tons of bombs would have to be expended on each of the bridges across the Seine. Leigh-Mallory remarked that if Spaatz so much wanted to hit the bridges, he should have his Eighth Air Force heavies do it. Spaatz rejected the idea because the high level bombers could not strike with enough precision. Leigh-Mallory on May 6 thereupon walked away from the argument, calling further discussion a waste of time.

He was right about further discussion. The next day, Brereton chose to send P-47s and B-26s against bridges across the Seine near Vernon, Oissel, Orival, and Mantes-Gassicourt. Eight of the P-47 Thunderbolts dropped two 1,000-lb. bombs each on a 200-meter steel railroad bridge near Vernon and destroyed it. The other strikes succeeded less spectacularly but assured that the bridges could soon be put out of use. This initiative of Brereton's abruptly created debating points that Leigh-Mallory could scarcely resist. The AEAF commander had made mistakes before, however, and had a fine capacity for blandly reversing himself. On May 10, the AEAF ordered a bridge-busting campaign.

With opportune timing, SHAEF itself now acceded to its intelligence section's conclusion that the Transportation Plan was causing only slight delay in enemy rail movements. Eisenhower's headquarters accordingly presented the airmen with a bridge-breaking plan to cut all the bridges up the Seine as far as Mantes, just below Paris, and up the Loire to Blois, along with critical stream crossings in the Paris-Orléans gap between the two rivers. Fortunately, the Seine bridges served the Pas de Calais as well as Normandy, so cutting them would not reveal which stretch of coast the Allies intended to invade. In addition, SHAEF drew a second line of bridge-breaking, which would contribute to isolating the Normandy battlefield but would also encourage deception, along a series of rivers farther east from Étaples to Fismes to Clamecy and thence along the upper Loire to Orléans. Also to continue deception, the Allied command decided that the strikes against the Loire would have to wait until after D-Day, and the attacks on the Seine crossings should not begin until just before D-Day.

When let loose, these attacks amply fulfilled the promise of Brereton's May 7 experiment. The campaign against the Seine bridges commenced on May 24 and received the AEAF's first priority on May 26. The Germans had been repairing their rail centers from the ravages of the Transportation Plan with remarkable efficiency, and on May 24 there was nothing to prevent Rundstedt and Rommel from shifting their big Fifteenth Army across the Seine from the Pas de Calais to Normandy once they learned where the Allies were coming ashore. By D-Day, the B-26s and P-47s, abetted by P-38s and by Hawker Typhoons from the Second Tactical Air Force, had knocked out all nine Seine railroad crossings from Maisons-Lafitte on the western outskirts of Paris to Rouen. They had also destroyed a dozen highway bridges from Conflans-Ste. Honoré to Rouen.

They did so with an expenditure of only 4,400 tons of bombs, averaging some 220 tons to a bridge. Early in the war, bridges had often defied efforts to fell them from the air. They offered pinlike targets even to dive bombers, and the Luftwaffe did not knock out a single crossing of the Thames during the Battle of Britian. The Ninth Air Force's Thunderbolts continued to attack bridges as the German Stukas had done, by dive bombing; but much more effective was low-level bombing, especially by the B-26

Marauders, skipping bombs across the water against the bridge abutments. The Allied raiders also kept the bridges out of service, by returning as often as necessary as soon as reconnaissance showed a bridge about to become usable again, sometimes until the superstructures fell into the river and the Germans had to abandon their rebuilding efforts. When the enemy tried to unload trains at the broken crossings to ferry cargoes across the Seine, Allied fighters came roaring down in strafing attacks. Rundstedt and Rommel were going to have a hard time moving reinforcements into the NEPTUNE lodgment area.

NEPTUNE Takes to the Air

Early in the war, the swarming air fleets of the Luftwaffe seemed to crowd all the skies of Europe. The Germans could build their swarms of planes because they fixed production models early. By 1944, the German air force had long been paying a price for this early numerical preponderance, as the Allies came to enjoy compensation for their initial lack of mass production in the improved quality of designs standardized later. To concentrate as the Luftwaffe did on dive bombing when aerial support of the ground troops demanded pinpoint accuracy proved in time to be another mistake, especially when the weapon at hand was as slow and as lightly armed against fighters as the Junkers Ju 87 Sturzkampfflugzeug, or Stuka. The Allies found that low-level flying "on the deck" was often more effective against tactical ground targets than dive bombing, and in any event the well-armed but fast and maneuverable Allied fighter-bombers could do many more different kinds of jobs better than the Stukas.

When fighter faced fighter, the Supermarine Spitfire Mark I held a slight advantage over the Messerschmitt Bf 109E as early as the Battle of Britain, particularly in speed and maneuverability at low and medium altitudes. The Germans' improved Bf 109F, which appeared in action in January 1941, achieved a similar marginal edge over the Mark I Spitfire; but the Germans thereafter found in the Bf 109 design a most constricted capacity for further improvement, while the later marks of the Spitfire forged steadily into superiority—to say nothing of the designs brought along still later by the Americans, the Lockheed P-38 Lightning, the Republic P-47 Thunderbolt, and the North American P-51 Mustang.

A partial exception to the general rule that the Luftwaffe fell behind because it had failed to prepare a second generation of World War II warplanes was the Focke-Wulf Fw 190. In the summer of 1941, the Germans threw this machine into battle to trump the current Spitfires. The Fw 190's maneuverability at high speeds staggered the imagination. But while it had been under development since 1937, the Germans fumbled too long in tooling up for mass production to permit turning out numbers rivaling the Bf 109. And the later Allied fighters at least equaled the Fw 190 in combat performance.

Still, the sleek Messerschmitts and the Focke-Wulfs in either their snub-nosed air-cooled or long-nosed liquid-cooled engine variations remained most dangerous adversaries. They went on proving it in the battles over Germany through the spring of 1944 to the very eve of D-Day. On May 12, General Spaatz was able to break Major General James H. Doolittle's Eighth Air Force free from direct OVERLORD preparations for a beginning of the oil offensive. Nine hundred thirty-five heavy bombers flew against oil plants at Brüx, Böhlen, Merseburg-Leuna, and Zeitz. They hit their targets, but they lost forty-six of the bombers and ten of their escorts to the Bf 109s, Fw 190s, and Messerschmitt Bf 110s, a twin-engine design that had failed against rival fighters but with heavy armament became a menace to the bombers. On May 28 and 29 the Eighth Air Force sent over 600 heavies against further synthetic oil targets. The Americans lost forty-one heavies in the two days.

Within 500 kilometers of the NEPTUNE beaches there lay about 100 airfields from which German planes might rise to strafe and bomb the invasion forces. Part of the AEAF's preinvasion program was to hit these airfields enough to leave them useless. Another part was to destroy the enemy's radar installations between Ostend and the Channel islands, to deny their assistance to Luftwaffe night fighters as well as to German ships and coastal guns. But while the AEAF, the Eighth Air Force, and RAF Bomber Command dropped 6,717 tons merely on the airfields within 200 kilometers of Caen, and while the campaign against radar stations was one of the most successful AEAF operations, reducing German radar to 18 percent effectiveness according to Allied intelligence, the critical campaign to free the Normandy skies of the Luftwaffe was fought over Germany. Spaatz's attacks on oil production hurt the enemy more than their most enthusiastic proponents knew. The German war production chief, Albert Speer, later said that it was the oil raids of May 1944 that decided the war.[6] To resist the threat to the Reich's entire ability to move vehicles, the Luftwaffe had to remain in Germany and not go to France. Against the threat, the Bf 109s and Fw 190s had to risk themselves in combat—some 150 to 200 of them against the Eighth Air Force's May 12 raid, for example. In May, Luftwaffe pilot losses exceeded replacements at a rate the Germans judged with alarm to be potentially disastrous; according to later American appraisals of German records, the May losses amounted to 2,461 pilots, following an April peak of 2,540.

The NEPTUNE planners could thus with assurance assign to Allied aircraft mainly offensive tasks in support of the invasion, rather than defensive air cover against German resistance. On D-Day minus 3 or D minus 2 as weather permitted, the Eighth Air Force was to shift some 40 percent of its effort from Germany to the Pas de Calais as part of the deception plan. On D minus 1, the Eighth was to rest half its forces, while one-fourth again hit the Pas de Calais and one-fourth struck Normandy. During the last nighttime hours before the invasion, the RAF would plaster the NEPTUNE beaches with some 6,000 tons of bombs. Bomber Command's area bombings were targeted especially against the enemy's coastal batteries. In first daylight the Eighth Air Force would assemble an unprecedented 1,200 of its Fortresses and Liberators to bomb JUNO, SWORD, GOLD, and OMAHA Beaches for half an hour each before the troops came ashore, dropping 4,800 tons, while Ninth Air Force bombers similarly drenched UTAH Beach with 500 tons. To guard against cratering the beaches and thus assisting the enemy, the AAF ran tests of bomb types and substituted for the usual 500- and 1,000-lb. bombs 100-lb. demolition and fragmentation bombs, except at strongpoints. To guard against hitting friendly troops, the bombing was to cease five minutes before the troops went ashore if skies were clear, ten minutes if skies were overcast, allowing a safety zone of about 1,000 yards between the bombs and the first invaders—a compromise between the 1,500-yard safety zone desired by Tedder, Spaatz, and Leigh-Mallory, and the closer, final saturation of the beach defenses desired by the SHAEF ground officers.

The eleven B-26 and A-20 medium bomber groups of the Ninth Air Force's IX Bomber Command would complete their preparatory operations for the invasion just before H-Hour on D-Day by attacking six heavy gun batteries located where they could fire on the invasion fleet in the Channel. Four P-38 groups from the Eighth Air Force and two from the Ninth were to patrol the skies over the fleet. The Ninth Air Force's IX Tactical Air Command would also provide two other P-38 groups and four P-47 groups to hit the enemy's gun batteries again about H-Hour and to give direct support to the ground forces as requested. Another five P-47 groups of IX TAC would provide high cover over the beaches; RAF Spitfires and Typhoons would give low cover.

After the Eighth Air Force heavies had returned to England from their dawn bombing of the beaches and refueled, under Leigh-Mallory's instructions they were to go again to France and hit bridges and towns such as Carentan and Caen just behind the beaches. This assignment provoked Spaatz and Doolittle to a final preinvasion controversy with Leigh-Mallory, because the USSTAF and Eighth Air Force commanders regarded the town bombings as inhumane and unlikely to have a compensating effect on German reinforcement. SHAEF once more supported its AEAF commander, but it offered Spaatz and Doolittle the concession of permitting them to drop warning leaflets about impending bombings on French coastal towns.

Air and the Strategy of the Ground Armies

All the elements of aerial planning and preparation, the Transportation Plan, the Oil Plan, and the final pre-D-Day bridge-busting, might seem to have led directly toward a design for the annihilation of the German army in Normandy. The principles of American strategy of course also led in that direction. If the air forces could isolate the enemy troops in Normandy completely enough to assure the NEPTUNE lodgment, their isolation might open the way to their destruction. If the enemy could be substantially cut off from reinforcement and supply, he might also be cut off from retreat, and thus ruined altogether in Normandy and denied the opportunity to resist the Allies on other days on other battlegrounds.

General Montgomery's briefings sometimes hinted at an intention to fight such a battle of annihilation. After the war, influenced by events that followed D-Day, Montgomery and other participants in the invasion planning claimed to have foreseen a possible Normandy battle of annihilation. But the specifics of the OVERLORD planning did not contemplate it. Instead, the design was merely to push the enemy forces out of the OVERLORD lodgment area, not to destroy them but to compel them to withdraw. The lodgment area was defined broadly for the logistical purposes of remaining ashore as the whole area between the Seine and Loire. In accordance with a British custom of forecasting the progress of operations by drawing projected phase lines on the planning maps—a custom acceded to reluctantly by the Americans—the invasion forces were expected to occupy the entire lodgment area by D plus ninety. By that time, the Germans were expected to have withdrawn to a new defensive line behind the Seine. Once the Allies had consolidated themselves in the lodgment area, assembling supplies and troops and developing airfields, they would assault the enemy on the Seine to drive toward Germany.

Military planners need to be cautious, to be prepared to cope with the bad as well as the good that might develop. The risks of amphibious assault accentuated caution. If, however, the central purpose of strategy is to destroy the enemy armed forces, as American strategic tradition consistently emphasized, then at least the planning should include preparation to seize an opportunity for annihilation if the opportunity should arise. The CCS directive to General Eisenhower as Supreme Commander, issued on February 12, charged him, furthermore: "*Task.* You will enter the continent of Europe, and, in conjunction with the other United Nations, undertake operations aimed at the heart of Germany and the destruction of her armed forces."[7] Again, the call upon the planners was at least to contemplate the possibility of a battle of annihilation. In the stress of combat, and with the cumbersomeness and relative inflexibility of modern mass armies, opportunities not prepared for are opportunities likely to pass unexploited. Yet the NEPTUNE and OVERLORD plans allowed the logical conclusion of the air campaigns as well as of American strategic tradition to trail off into vague hints. The planners' gaze remained focused simply on getting ashore. The opportunities as well as the problems that lay behind the beaches—even the opportunities for a battle of annihilation—seemed too remote to be thought through as they deserved.

To Cross the Channel

Since December, the troops had been training intensively for their roles in the invasion. In April there were full-scale dress rehearsals, including assaults upon Slapton Sands, on the Devon coast southwest of Dartmouth, where the beaches resembled those of the Calvados. Exercise TIGER, the rehearsal of Force "U" that was to land at UTAH, produced a tragedy when nine German E-boats out of Cherbourg, motor torpedo boats displacing about 100 tons and armed with two torpedo tubes and two light guns each, got in among the landing craft in Lyme Bay and sank two LSTs while damaging another. Five other LSTs and two British destroyers engaged the E-boats, but the Germans escaped, and the action cost the Allies about 700 lives.

Force "U," Rear Admiral Don P. Moon, USN, would sortie from eight ports between Plymouth and Poole, organize itself into twelve convoys, and steam for UTAH Beach. Force "O," Rear Admiral John L. Hall, USN, would assemble at Poole and in the ample waters of Portland Harbour, an artificial harbor on the northeast side of Portland Bill, form nine convoys, and head for OMAHA Beach. Commodore C. D. Edgar, USN, would assemble a followup Force "B" at Fowey and Falmouth with reinforcements, the bulk of the 29th Division, to reach OMAHA on the afternoon of D-Day. Those elements made up Admiral Kirk's Western Naval Task Force. Admiral Ramsay, in 1940 organizer and hero of the Dunkirk evacuation when he was Flag Officer Commanding, Dover, now as Allied Naval Commander Expeditionary Force exercised general control over both Kirk's fleet and a similar Eastern Naval Task Force under Rear Admiral Sir Philip Vian, RN. Vian's three assault forces were to sail from the Solent, Spithead, and Portsmouth for JUNO, GOLD, and SWORD. Altogether, the invasion fleets would number some 5,000 ships, 702 of them warships, crossing the English Channel in a phalanx ten lanes and thirty kilometers wide.

If June 5 remained as D-Day, minesweeping groups would precede the main fleets out of the Channel ports at noon on June 3. That same day the gunfire support and bombardment ships of the Western Naval Task Force would set out from Belfast Lough far to the north, and the similar vessels of the Eastern Naval Task Force from the Clyde.

The British had staged the Dieppe raid of 1942 without benefit of preliminary naval bombardment, and one of the apparent lessons of Dieppe's prohibitively high casualties was to confirm the need for overwhelming naval gunfire support to neutralize if not destroy the enemy's batteries before landing on a fortified coast. At that, American experience at Tarawa in the Pacific indicated to Admiral Ramsay that naval bombardment was effective only against open gun emplacements, not against concrete. The low trajectories of big naval guns made it difficult for them to hit shore fortifications anywhere except where their protection was thickest. A planning study in January 1944 suggested that to neutralize the German defenses known to exist on the NEPTUNE coast would require a naval force far beyond anything the NEPTUNE planners could expect to get; the drenching of the beaches and neutralization of known strong points would require about twenty battleships or cruisers and 100 destroyers.

Yet experience also indicated that despite its limitations, naval gunfire was more accurate and effective than aerial bombardment in silencing strongpoints, and 21 Army Group, wanting 7,800 tons of explosives hurled against the enemy shore in the last half hour before the landings, desired as much as possible of the tonnage to issue from naval guns. The air forces gave some of their attention to German coastal batteries through the spring, but the bombers had so many other tasks, and it was expected in any event that they could accomplish little enough, that from mid-April to D-Day only about 10 percent of their total bombing was directed toward such targets. Of this amount, concealment of the intended invasion area dictated that only about one-third fell on the NEPTUNE beaches. Counterbattery work had to come back to the ships.

Early in the year, Admiral Ramsay could assign only one battleship, one monitor, seven cruisers, and seven destroyers to the Western Naval Task Force to provide escort in addition to fire support to the convoys destined for UTAH and OMAHA Beaches. Few American warships were expected to be available to help the British, yet the Royal Navy not only had to support both the American and British invasion forces; the Admiralty also thought it must hold strength in reserve lest the German navy venture forth for a miniature Jutland. The consequent disparity between available fire support and the NEPTUNE planners' desires notwithstanding, Admiral Ernest J. King, Commander in Chief United States Fleet, was loath to release American vessels from his navy's battles in the Pacific. King's resistance even to small sacrifices by the Pacific Fleet for the sake of the campaign in Europe was a bitter draft for his countrymen in England, who both perceived Germany as a more dangerous adversary than Japan, and believed that for the climactic effort against Germany, American soldiers deserved the formidable fire support of their own country's ships: an American destroyer had nearly the firepower of a British light cruiser, and an American cruiser a weight of guns in similar proportion.

Over dinner at the Connaught following the Norfolk House Landing Craft Conference in February, Admiral Hall commented explosively about this situation to King's chief planner, Rear Admiral Charles M. Cooke. Though Cooke felt obliged to reprimand Hall for his choice of language, the episode served to wring from Washington an additional destroyer squadron and the ancient battleships *Arkansas*, *Texas*, and *Nevada*. The first of these was a product of Theodore Roosevelt's naval program, authorized by Congress in 1909; the other two came from the William Howard Taft programs of 1910 and 1911, respectively. Still, the 12-inch guns of *Arkansas* and the 14-inchers of *Texas* and *Nevada* would be more than welcome. *Nevada* joined Force "U," and General Collins of the VII Corps issued a specific request to assure that her main batteries would fire against the concrete seawall of UTAH Beach. Eventually, King added enough ships to Ramsay's fleet that Force "U" would have a bombardment fleet, beyond its escort ships, of *Nevada*, a British monitor, two American and one British heavy cruisers, two British light cruisers, eight American destroyers, and a Dutch gunboat. Force "o's" bombardment fleet would include *Arkansas* and *Texas*, two British and two French light cruisers, and nine American and three British destroyers.

Still, the NEPTUNE planners could count on the navies for only 2,500 of their desired 7,800 tons of explosives on the beaches before touchdown, which accounts for the tonnage figures allocated to the final preliminary bombing by the Eighth and Ninth Air Forces. During the final run-in of the assault craft to the shore, the lighter naval vessels would make a last effort to saturate the enemy defenses, especially machine-gun positions. After both the air forces and the big ships had to lift their bombardments for the safety of the invading troops, fire support was to continue from craft accompanying the landing waves: LCT(R)s and LCGs (landing craft, gun) armed with rockets, LCT(A)s and LCT(HE)s equipped to carry medium tanks in firing position, LCT(5)s carrying 105-mm. self-propelled howitzers in firing position. Once the troops were ashore, naval fire-support control parties would call on the ships' guns to assist the advance inland. Forty aircraft of the British Fleet Air Arm, assisted until noon on D-Day by RAF reconnaissance planes, would provide aerial observation for the naval gunners.

As May gave way to June, German intercepts of Allied radio were crackling as they had for weeks, with the traffic of the First United States Army Group, commanded by the dashing battle captain of America's North African and Sicilian campaigns, Lieutenant General George S. Patton, Jr. In German appraisals, the Allies knew, Patton was the most likely leader of the coming invasion. The intercepts showed the Germans that his army group was poised to assault the Pas de Calais. Information from German spies in England amply confirmed to Hitler the troop concentrations and growing readiness of Patton's army group all over the east of England; the Germans did not know, of course, that their entire intelligence network in Britain had been turned around by British counterintelligence and was relaying just what the British wanted them to hear.

While Operation FORTITUDE, the Allies' deception plan, thus misled the enemy, the real OVERLORD invasion force, as well as the absence of much real substance in Patton's army group, lay concealed under a ban against visitors throughout a ten-mile coastal strip between Land's End and the Wash from April onward, and by a suspension of diplomatic correspondence out of the United Kingdom except that of the British themselves, the United States, and the Soviet Union. By late May, the invasion troops were sealed in their marshaling areas, the crews of the invasion fleets sealed in their vessels, and all mail of NEPTUNE participants impounded until further notice. The Luftwaffe's limited reconnaissance in the face of Allied air supremacy could do no more than confirm that immense preparations for an amphibious operation were going forward. Dummy camp sites and deceptive troop movements in eastern England could assure the Luftwaffe that an army group stood poised to fall on the Pas de Calais. So completely had Allied air won the battle for control of the skies that German planes achieved only one bombing strike of any consequence against the tempting targets of Allied troop concentrations, a raid on the night of May 30 against a camp near Falmouth that inflicted several casualties on an American ordnance battalion.

General Patton, impatient in his passive role as a decoy, drove to Bristol on the 1st of June to say goodbye to the real commander of American troops in the invasion, General Bradley. Bradley had graduated from West Point six years after Patton and was his subordinate as recently as Sicily, but then the two slapping incidents involving hospitalized soldiers he thought cowards threw Patton's career into shadow. The chastening had not altered the style that made Patton so conspicuously excellent a decoy: "General George Patton arrived in Bristol on Thursday evening in a huge, black Packard automobile, eloquently outfitted with silver flag staffs and a plethora of stars. We met him with a great convoy of chattering motorcycles, knowing of his fondness for noisy escorts." (Referring to the slapping incidents, Bradley's aide Major Hansen recorded: "When I told the Captain of the MPs to provide a motorcycle escort for Patton's arrival, he grinned and asked, 'Shall we have them wear boxing gloves?'")

The next day, Bradley and Patton said goodbye. Once Bradley's First Army and the British Second had assured the lodgment, Bradley would move up to command an American army group and Patton would depart from the deception plan to lead the American Third Army into the battle. At Bristol, "Patton clenched Bradley's hands, hitched up his trousers under the custom tailored British tunic to say, 'Brad, the best of luck to you. We'll be meeting again—soon, I hope.'"[8]

In the same first days of June, Allied soldiers marched through the greenery of the English springtime down to their ships. At homes along the way, "Now and then a mother would hold up her child to see the passing troops, as if she wanted him to be able to say when he was old that he had seen the soldiers march off to attack the distant shore."[9]

On Saturday, June 3, Bradley and his staff boarded Admiral Kirk's flagship, the heavy cruiser *Augusta*, which would carry them to Normandy. The same day, as scheduled, the old battleships and other bombardment vessels of the Western Naval Task Force slipped out of Belfast Lough, and the minesweepers sailed into the Channel.

Also on that day, however, the weather forecasts for the prospective D-Day, June 5, began to appear increasingly unfavorable. By Sunday the 4th, the weather outlook for Monday was hopeless. Eisenhower believed the invasion must have the full support of the air forces; the margin for success would be too narrow to risk proceeding if weather prevented the airplanes from lending all the help of which they were capable. Early on Sunday morning, the Supreme Commander postponed the invasion.

Therefore the ships had to steam back to their ports, the small craft by now tossed by heavy seas, and Eisenhower had to ponder whether to begin again under the forecasters' offer of an uncertain possibility of a brief break in the weather on Monday night and on Tuesday, June 6. The alternative was to postpone the invasion all the way to the next favorable moon and tides. The tides would not be auspicious again until June 18–20, and the moon and tides both not for another month. There could be no cautious compromise choice of June 7, because with many vessels having already started from their ports, by that time some would need refueling. On Sunday evening, Eisenhower met with his ground, sea, and air commanders at Admiral Ramsay's headquarters, Southwick House, a country place a short distance north of the Portsmouth docks. Admiral Kirk had to be notified within little more than half an hour of the meeting time, if there was to be a June 6 D-Day, to turn his bombardment ships south into the Irish Sea again. Under this pressure, Eisenhower decided tentatively to risk using the hoped-for short interval of rainless skies and moderating winds, with a cloud base just high enough to permit spotting for naval gunfire. Montgomery and Ramsay supported him, and his decision would have been firm had not Leigh-Mallory demurred.

So the navies set forth. On Monday morning, though the wind still drove the rain in horizontal sheets, SHAEF's chief meteorologist, Group Captain J. M. Stagg, RAF, gave a firmer promise of two days of fair weather beginning early Tuesday morning. At 4:15 A.M., June 5, Eisenhower spoke his now famous: "O.K., let's go."

More difficult still than the weather decision, the Supreme Commander later said, was watching the 101st Airborne Division take off that night. By then the rain had long since ceased and the winds abated, but Eisenhower feared he was seeing the last of men who were going on his orders to their slaughter.

The plan for the 101st and the 82nd to drop into the Cotentin had had to be changed. Leigh-Mallory insisted that the 82nd's parachute regiments could not be fully reinforced by the division's glider regiment until dusk on D-Day, lest the gliders suffer prohibitive losses as they tried to land by daylight. Accordingly, the paratroopers would have to fight almost a whole day alone. Mainly they would have to fight with hand weapons, rifles, grenades, pistols, and bazookas against tanks and whatever else the Germans could throw against them—though an initial series of gliders would bring in some 57mm. antitank guns at daybreak. Worse, in late May the Germans had moved their strong 91st Division into reserve in the Cotentin. To try to seal off the peninsula by dropping the 82nd Airborne across its southern base as earlier planned would scatter the 82nd too widely in the teeth of this enemy concentration and probably assure the airborne division's destruction. Thus under new VII Corps orders of May 18, the 82nd and the 101st were both to drop behind UTAH Beach, the 101st shifting its drop zone slightly southward, the 82nd to go down astride the Merderet River to secure a bridgehead from which to reach westward toward the upper Douve. Still, experience in Sicily suggested that airborne troops should not be landed where they would immediately confront the kind of heavy opposition the Germans could now promise to give them.

Leigh-Mallory urged Eisenhower to cancel the Cotentin drop altogether. In a letter of May 29, he warned that the airborne landings could not yield the results originally hoped for, that their failure could jeopardize the landings from the sea, and that at most 30 percent of the glider units would get into action effectively. Deciding that the letter was not strong enough, the AEAF commander went to see Eisenhower on May 30, to enlarge his forecast with a warning of the "futile slaughter" of two fine airborne divisions, whose casualties he predicted might run as high as 70 percent.[10]

"It would be difficult to conceive of a more soul-racking problem," Eisenhower said later.[11] But General Bradley believed the airborne landings were indispensable to the success of UTAH Beach and consequently to the early capture of Cherbourg. Without the airborne landings, Bradley would scratch UTAH itself. So Eisenhower decided the drop of the 82nd and the 101st must proceed. But if they failed, then, by both Bradley's and Leigh-Mallory's reckonings, the UTAH landings would probably also fail.

Under the British system of double daylight saving time, it was not yet dark at 10 P.M., June 5, when 822 transport planes of the Ninth Air Force's IX Troop Carrier Command began taking off and assembling in great Vs of Vs, to fly more than 13,000 men of the two airborne divisions' six parachute regiments to the Cotentin. RAF night fighters rose up to fly escort, and Stirling bombers flew ahead to drop radar-deceiving WINDOW—sheets of metal-coated paper that produced echoes on enemy radar receivers comparable to those created by planes—to simulate an airborne attack well south of the real landing sites. By the time the leading C-47 transports were over France, a rising moon lighted every field, hedgerow, and farm building below. There was no interception by Luftwaffe fighters.

Major General Matthew B. Ridgway, commanding the 82nd, had not undergone a paratrooper's jump training and had never jumped in combat. But to be where the division commander was needed, he decided he must make this jump with his men. He landed almost exactly where he was supposed to. Promptly he met a cow, which he later remarked he could have kissed, because her presence in the landing field meant that the field was not staked with a "Rommel's asparagus" of sharp posts connected to mines to touch off explosions in series when troopers struck the obstacles. Quickly, Ridgway was able to collect his eleven-man command group and set up his division command post in an apple orchard just where it was supposed to be.

By that time, however, "The finest fireworks display I ever saw was going on all around me,"[12] for despite the Stirlings and WINDOW, German radio had given warning of large formations of planes northwest of Cherbourg, and all the transports except a few of the leading waves had to fly through heavy bursts of flak. Furthermore, cloud cover and fog soon closed in to obscure the initially clear view. C-47s lost their places in the formations, and even experienced pathfinders could no longer locate the drop zones that they were supposed to mark with flares. Enemy fire grew especially heavy west of the Merderet, the drop zones there were never effectively marked with lights, the few troops who fell in scattered bands west of the river found themselves entangled in marshes, and so the westward reach of the landings was even more limited than the revised plan envisaged.

But, as by ones and twos and squads the paratroopers began to find each other, clicking toy crickets for identification, there was also no evidence that casualties had been severe. Leigh-Mallory had erred again. If the paratroopers were scattered unduly, the scattering confused the Germans as well, and to enhance this effect the Americans and the French Resistance busied themselves cutting communication lines. The commander of the German 91st Division, Generalleutnant Wilhelm Falley, trying to regain effective contact with his troops, took his staff car out into the patternless shooting of the night, and Ridgway was soon to learn that his paratroopers had killed this opposing general.

Toward dawn, Lieutenant Malcomb D. Brennan, commanding Headquarters Company, 3rd Battalion, 508th Parachute Infantry, had found four of his men and was trying to learn his location from a sleepy French family at the edge of a town —Picauville—when a German staff car came speeding by. Instinctively, the Americans spun around and opened fire, sending the car swerving out of control into a stone wall and its occupants spilling into the street. One of the Germans shouted out in English, "Don't kill! Don't kill!" but all the while reached for his pistol, which had tumbled from its holster. Because of that motion, Brennan shot him. The name in his cap indicated he was General Falley.

The great invasion had begun.

PART TWO : NORMANDY

5: The Beach

A<small>N AMPHIBIOUS</small> assault is a frontal attack, with all the perils thereby implied. The assaulting troops have no room for maneuver. They cannot fall back. They have only a limited ability to outflank strong points. They can do nothing subtle. They must simply generate enough striking power to penetrate whatever crust of fortifications they find, yet not so overburden themselves with heavy weapons that they risk losing the mobility necessary to exploit a penetration and advance inland.

Against the hard crust of Hitler's Atlantic Wall as reinforced by Rommel, General Bradley's First Army planners calculated that their assault divisions at best would not move inland very far with any speed. Consequently the First Army stripped these divisions of many of the vehicles and support troops that ordinarily gave them their overland mobility, but the army enhanced commensurately their firepower. Each assault regiment was to have a tank battalion attached, some of the tanks to be DDs to be launched offshore and to swim in ahead of the infantry, some of the tanks to be loaded on LCTs to touch down with the initial wave of infantry. The first tanks would be used simply as close-support artillery. This role is not ideal for tanks, especially for Shermans which were designed for movement more than for hard punching; but only guns protected by armor were likely to survive on the beaches. The main job of the tanks was to neutralize the enemy pillboxes by firing into their embrasures, thus helping the infantry approach the pillboxes with flame throwers and explosives to destroy them.

The leading infantry would come ashore immediately after the first tanks. For the occasion, one platoon of every rifle company was to have an 81mm. mortar and a heavy machine gun, and the other two platoons would each have a 60mm. mortar. Every rifle platoon would also have a wire-cutting team, a bazooka team, a flamethrowing team, and a demolition team. Each platoon would be divided into two sections of twenty-nine men and one officer, a force that could be accommodated in an LCVP. Once ashore, the infantry were to clear the beaches and cover the landing of engineer demolition teams, naval demolition units, and tankdozers that would clear and mark lanes through the underwater obstacles before the rising tide covered them.

Subsequent assault waves would be mostly infantry, with some additional engineers to help complete the clearing of the beaches and to go to work on mine fields farther inland. Artillery was to begin going ashore about an hour and a half after the first landings. Vehicles of all kinds would begin to debark after about three hours. By then, the infantry were expected to have opened exits from the beaches and to have pressed inland.

The problems of grasping a foothold were the tactical problems of a soldiers' battle. Once the landings began, the high command must leave the fate of NEPTUNE to the bravery and skill of the soldiers and of their company- and field-grade officers—to skill as well as to bravery, because though all units had rehearsed carefully, and every soldier was to have seen a model of his unit's landing beach and objectives and to know his unit's part in the plan, Allied intelligence could not have pinpointed every enemy stronghold, nor predicted the effects of the preliminary bombardment. The final problems were not for the NEPTUNE plans but for the men under fire.

OMAHA

Off UTAH Beach, General Collins of the VII Corps sailed with Admiral Moon on the attack transport *Bayfield*. Off OMAHA, General Gerow of the V Corps shared space with Admiral Hall on the amphibious command ship *Ancon*. General Bradley and Admiral Kirk plugged their ears with cotton at 5:30 on D-Day morning and the 8-inch guns of the *Augusta* began rocking the ship as they blasted away at OMAHA Beach. The smoke of the naval and aerial bombardments soon thickened a morning mist over the shoreline; but while the generals offshore could see little, they soon had cause for worry.

In the lee of the Cotentin, UTAH was partially shielded from wind and weather. There, though restless Channel waters swelled ominously, all but four of thirty-two DD tanks with the first wave reached shore. The casualties came when an LCT carrying the rest struck a mine.

At OMAHA, in contrast, the sea was so choppy that Admiral Kirk was sure the DDs would be swamped if the LCTs did not carry them all the way to the beaches. On his instructions, one battalion of the amphibious tanks accordingly rode to the beaches in their LCTs, whence they emerged a minute before H-Hour with their guns blazing. But elsewhere in "O" Force, the plan and the lower-echelon officers had already taken over from the generals and admirals, and another battalion of DDs, attached to the 16th Infantry Regiment, was launched 5,500 meters offshore despite the rough surf. These tanks promptly fulfilled the Admiralty's original fears, foundering right and left, and only five of thirty-two made it to the beach. Three of the five survivors were from LCT-600, whose commander, Ensign H.P. Sullivan, had the presence of mind to pull up his ramp as soon as he saw the first DD go down, and beached the others he was carrying.

Worse followed. H-Hour on the American beaches was 6:30. By 8:30, the troops were supposed to be breaking through the beach exits toward higher ground along Route N13. But at that hour, the corps and army commanders had no confirmation that the V Corps had so much as effected a landing. Like the DDs, the OMAHA assault in fact was coming close to total foundering. The attacking infantry had been transferred from ships to LCVPs sixteen to twenty kilometers offshore, and at least ten of the LCVPs sank. So did the craft carrying almost all the 105mm. howitzers that were supposed to be the first artillery ashore after the tanks. The V Corps was assaulting with two regiments of the 1st

Division abreast, on the right the 16th Infantry, on the left the 116th, attached to the 1st from the 29th Division. They debarked from the LCVPs in heavy seas and under heavy fire from enemy fortifications upon which the preliminary bombardment seemed to have had little effect. The troops found themselves in water often up to their necks, their burdensome equipment dragged them back and down as they tried to wade free, bullets chopping away at them, with drowning the almost certain fate of the wounded.

Most of those men who crawled ashore to the first oddments of shelter—usually parts of enemy obstacles—then discovered that a strong lateral current had combined with smoke and mist to divert them from their assigned touchdown points. They saw none of the landmarks they had been trained to expect, and the smoke and enemy fire also combined to isolate small parties and to separate soldiers from the officers who might have begun reorganizing and redirecting them. In the 116th Infantry of the Virginia National Guard, furthermore—the old Stonewall Brigade of the Confederate States Army, which had earned its sobriquet in the first great battle of the Civil War—events developed less propitiously than in that earlier baptism of fire. Three-fourths of the 116th's radios failed to function. When company officers tried to scramble from group to group to regain contact and control, they made targets of themselves enough to fall killed and wounded in demoralizing numbers.

Not until almost ten o'clock did Bradley receive any report from that other Virginian, Gerow. Then it was mostly confirmation of trouble: "*Obstacles mined, progress slow. . . .*"[1] The generals could see for themselves little more than a perilous congestion of landing craft apparently unable to touch down because the beaches were jammed. Admiral Kirk's gunnery officer, Captain Timothy A. Wellings, and General Bradley's aide Major Hansen went in close riding a torpedo boat but still found "it is difficult to make sense from what is going on."[2]

Major General Clarence R. Huebner of the 1st Division had enlisted in the 18th Infantry Regiment in 1910 and fought with the Big Red One from Lunéville and Cantigny through the Meuse-Argonne in the First War. He had taken command of the division in 1943 in the midst of the Sicilian campaign. Now he was aboard the *Ancon* with Gerow and receiving nothing but gloomy tidings even from his veterans: "There are too many vehicles on the beach; send combat troops. 30 LCTs waiting offshore; cannot come in because of shelling. Troops dug in on beaches still under heavy fire."[3] Huebner responded by ordering his old regiment, the 18th, to land at once as a reinforcement; but only one battalion of the regiment had assault craft, and the others, needing to be transshipped from LCTs, would not be able to go ashore until afternoon despite the order.

Gerow, studiously calm under pressure—he held to the old style of gentlemanly self-control in leadership—could do no more for the moment than dispatch his assistant chief of staff, Colonel Benjamin A. Talley, in an amphibious dukw for yet another look close enough to try to make sense from what was going on. Talley's radio reports amplified the themes already developed: the beaches were jammed with infantry under heavy fire, while reinforcing troops were held up in LCTs milling offshore like "a stampeded herd of cattle."[4]

The enemy's guns, big and little, still blazed away. Because of cloud cover at first light, the Eighth Air Force heavy bombers had had to make their runs by instruments, and it was becoming apparent that in their caution to avoid hitting the assault craft they had bombed well inland, missing the beach defenses at OMAHA. Underwater obstructions were doing much to hold the landing craft under the muzzles of the enemy's unharmed artillery; the demolition teams like the infantry had been swept wide of the places where they were supposed to open paths. These specialists were suffering heavy losses of equipment as well as manpower. On the 116th Infantry's beach, it was to turn out that only three of sixteen bulldozers could be put to work. The rising tide halted demolitions before more than six paths could be opened into OMAHA Beach. So many marking buoys and poles were lost that only one of the paths was marked. At that, landing craft from all units were gravitating toward the "Easy Red" segment of OMAHA where the few paths had been opened, thereby snarling themselves in an accumulating traffic jam off that part of the shore.

By about noon, furthermore, Gerow's V Corps headquarters knew that the 1st Division was not grappling merely with the low-quality garrison fomations the NEPTUNE planners hoped to find. Even with ULTRA, order-of-battle information could be less than perfect. Allied intelligence had shown the static 716th Division, including many East European troops, to be holding the Calvados coast from the Orne River to the Vire. The 716th was still there, but so also was a mobile, full-attack division, the 352nd. Eight enemy battalions defended where the Americans had expected to strike four. British intelligence had feared the arrival of the 352nd Division in May, but the American command had doubted the slender evidence on which this concern rested. Just before the departure from England, Bradley's First Army G-2, Colonel Benjamin A. Dickson, concluded that the 352nd had indeed shifted from reserve around St. Lô in the interior to an exercise on the beaches; but there was no time to pass this word to the assault companies, and now confirmation of the unit's location was arriving in a way that posed for General Bradley his first decision of the campaign. In fact, the 352nd had been on the coast for almost three months.

Against the resistance of good German troops, the frontal assault on OMAHA Beach seemed to be approaching the predictable fate of frontal assaults against good troops well positioned. At noon, the V Corps told Bradley that the struggle for the four vehicle exits out of OHAMA Beach was "still critical."[5] Bradley felt obliged to consider diverting the OMAHA followup troops to UTAH or the British beaches, from which reports were much more encouraging. With only a fraction of the first OMAHA assault force of 34,000 troops and 3,300 vehicles as yet ashore, the followup force of 25,000 troops and 4,000 vehicles was about to arrive at the transport area, that is, the area where the troops would leave larger vessels for the assault craft. Proceeding on schedule might only render the congestion offshore hopeless. On the other hand, not reinforcing would almost assure the vulnerability of OMAHA to a counterattack, and not holding OMAHA would leave UTAH and the spearhead directed against Cherbourg isolated from the British beaches. The whole buildup plan would then be precariously out of balance.

General Bradley

Bradley at least was fortified for this crisis of OMAHA Beach by previous exposure to the harsh pressures of command on the battlefront to an extent unmatched by any other senior American officer in the NEPTUNE invasion. This was true despite the fact that, like his 1915 West Point classmate Dwight Eisenhower, he had missed overseas service in the

First World War and feared for a time that the lack of such service might permanently stunt his career.

But in 1929, the homely and homespun Missourian had become an instructor in battalion tactics at the Infantry School at Fort Benning, and a year later he was chief of the weapons section. Here Bradley caught the attention of Lieutenant Colonel George C. Marshall, then assistant commandant of the school. After Marshall became Chief of Staff, it eventually became known that with systematic forethought he had kept on file his evaluations of officers potentially qualified for high command in war. Bradley made Marshall's list. In 1940, he became Assistant Secretary of the General Staff, then in 1941 commandant of the Infantry School. Upon reactivation of the 82nd Infantry Division, the "All-American" National Army division of World War I that had shared the fame of its Sergeant York, Bradley received the division's command. Thus he was first to shape the unit that would become the crack 82nd Airborne. He took command of the 28th Division of the Pennsylvania National Guard after it was nearly wrecked by cannibalization of its cadres for other formations, with the wreckage torn also by National Guard internal politics; Bradley contributed mightily to making the Keystone Division an effective unit as well. Early in 1943, he was about to move up to a corps command when Marshall decided that General Eisenhower's multiple political and strategic responsibilities in North Africa required that he have a deputy to stay close to the front and act as his eyes and ears and be a troubleshooter. Eisenhower and Bradley had seen little of each other since West Point, but nevertheless Bradley was among Eisenhower's suggestions to fill the post that Marshall had conceived. His situation awaiting orders for corps command made him available, and Marshall gave Bradley the job.

He arrived at the American front in Tunisia, held by Major General Lloyd R. Fredendall's II Corps, just after the February defeat in the Kasserine Pass. The corps was only beginning the effort to restore its psychological and material balance from a setback so complete that it raised once more, among allies and enemies alike, the troublesome old question that had been the bane of General Pershing in World War I: whether the New World armies of America, with no ancient tradition and experience of European war, could ever match European military standards. Rommel had heard that British and French officers captured by his troops disparaged the Americans as "our Italians," and he accepted this evaluation seriously enough to choose to hit the Americans hard at Kasserine so he might impose a German moral ascendancy over them once and for all. He succeeded well enough, too, that Bradley decided the II Corps could be saved only by a thorough overhaul. From division chieftains downward, the corps had so completely lost confidence in General Fredendall, and Fredendall's dispositions before Kasserine had in fact been so faulty—with isolated infantry pockets scattered among the Tunisian djebels, armored reserves also strewn about in bits and pieces—that to begin with, Fredendall must surely go. This judgment seconded Eisenhower's. The new commander of the II Corps, drawn from garrison command of the I Armored Corps in Morocco, was the flamboyant General Patton. Of all American senior officers, Patton seemed most likely to rescue the American army from contempt as the Allies' Italians. But Patton for his part, not wanting a free-ranging emissary of the Supreme Commander peering over his shoulder, persuaded Eisenhower to make Bradley the deputy corps commander, though Bradley retained the right to represent Eisenhower.

As Patton's deputy, Bradley supplied quiet administrative and tactical competence to complement Patton's dramatic command style and operational boldness. Together Patton and Bradley revitalized the II Corps until it could even its score with the Germans at the Battle of El Guettar on the Gafsa-Gabès road. When Patton moved on to plan the invasion of Sicily, Bradley took over the II Corps and further restored hope for the American army's fitness to wage European war. Where Patton the cavalryman, with his deep spearhead aimed down the Gabès road toward the German line of communication, had offered early evidence of a special talent for swift, long-range movement, Bradley the infantryman showed promise in the more constricted manipulation of units on a tightly contested battlefield to probe and then penetrate the enemy's weak points, in the fight for Hill 609 and for the road to Bizerte.

In Sicily, Bradley's II Corps was the sole corps in Patton's Seventh Army. Sicily afforded Bradley experience in conducting an amphibious assault, a share in the first spectacular unleashing of Patton's flair for swift and deep penetration at which the North African campaign had hinted, and an opportunity to temper Patton's excesses of zeal as the army commander drove recklessly as well as relentlessly along the northern coast road from Palermo to Messina. Bradley also demonstrated a better sense of the logistical practicalities than Patton; and for this reason, though in General McNair's scheme of army organization the corps was expected to be an exclusively tactical organization, with supply responsibilities left to the army above it and the divisions below it, Bradley's II Corps assumed much of the logistical administration that ordinarily would have belonged to the Seventh Army. Altogether, Bradley's calm stability as contrasted with Patton's impetuousness, combined with Bradley's accumulation by the end of the Sicilian campaign of more combat experience than any other corps commander, led Marshall to choose Bradley when it became imperative to establish an American field army headquarters in England. Eisenhower concurred.

It had been fortunate for the American interest in OVERLORD planning to that point that COSSAC, General Morgan, "is so heavily on our [American] side now . . . that it may be embarrassing in his relation to the British Chiefs of Staff in London. . . ."[6] Otherwise, the early OVERLORD planning would have been almost exclusively dominated by British viewpoints. In 1943 the commanders of the European Theater of Operations, United States Army—Lieutenant General Frank M. Andrews and, after Andrews's death in a plane crash in May, Lieutenant General Jacob M. Devers—tried to keep their hands in the invasion planning; but they lacked an appropriate staff to do so. Theirs was an administrative command. Even the American part of Morgan's COSSAC staff was merely on detached service from the G-5 (Plans) section of ETOUSA. On the tactical level, 21 Army Group, the British Second Army, and the Canadian First Army all had functioning headquarters participating in the planning for weeks while the highest American tactical headquarters in the United Kingdom remained Gerow's V Corps.

General Devers repeatedly importuned the War Department to set up American headquarters parallel to the British, to assure suitable American representation in operational planning. At length, at the beginning of September 1943, Bradley received orders to proceed from Sicily to England, there to establish both an army and an army group headquarters. Over both he was to hold at least temporary command: First Army, whose command post he set up in the Gothic buildings of Clifton College, Bristol, in southwest England where the American invasion forces would muster, and First United States Army Group, in West End flats in Bryanston Square near Marble Arch.

Among the reasons for Marshall's lack of a sense of urgency in creating these commands was the continuing uncertainty, in the summer and through much of the autumn of 1943, about the yet higher levels of the OVERLORD chain of command. The War Department at that time still expected that Marshall himself would eventually be named Supreme Commander. The North African model of Allied command, as established in January 1943, would have provided for ground forces, navy, and air chiefs directly subordinate to the Supreme Commander. But especially if the Supreme Commander was after all to be an American, a ground forces commander would probably have to be British. Foreseeing the eventual heavy numerical preponderance of American over British troops in Europe, the War Department did not like that idea at all.

Nor did the War Department welcome the COSSAC proposal that a British field army should command the initial assault. Rather, Washington wanted the American First Army to command the whole of the amphibious attack, albeit at a time when an American, a British, and a Canadian corps were envisaged as participating. The compromise of American and British views eventually arrived at had the American First and British Second Armies commanding the assaults on their own respective beaches, with 21 Army Group supervising the armies' planning and exercising overall command while the lodgment was being secured.

Once an American army in addition to the First joined the battle, the First U.S. Army Group would take over American field forces in France, and 21 Army Group would revert to command over the British and Canadian armies only. A critical feature of this design was that, contrary to the North African model, but in a compromise of British claims to superior experience with eventual American troop predominance, there would be no overall ground commander following the initial phase of the invasion. Montgomery would be overall ground commander at first, but only at first. Though probably the only practical adjustment of conflicting national claims, the design was one to which the British, and particularly Montgomery, reconciled themselves only after months of controversy, if ever.

General Marshall wanted to secure the independence of American field headquarters from their own army's administrative headquarters as well as from the British. Upon the transfer of Bradley to England, Devers proposed a United States GHQ in the United Kingdom, commanding both operations and administration, on the model of General Pershing's American Expeditionary Forces headquarters of the First World War. GHQ would have been formed out of ETOUSA. Marshall, in contrast, wanted the combat headquarters free to focus on combat. He told Devers: "I desire that the organization of the Army Group headquarters be initially controlled directly by Bradley under your supervision and that it not be merely an offshoot, or appurtenance to ETO headquarters."[7] It was on Marshall's recommendation that the army group headquarters was separated physically from ETOUSA's Grosvenor Square establishment. Eventually, when Eisenhower became Supreme Commander, he also took Devers's place in command of ETOUSA. He then commanded the administrative and support apparatus of the American army in Europe in his ETOUSA rather than his SHAEF capacity, further assuring the separation of these functions from the operational headquarters' focus upon combat. Direct control of

ETOUSA and thus of supply and administration was actually exercised by Eisenhower's deputy commander of ETOUSA, formerly chief of ETOUSA Services of Supply, the arrogant, unlikable, but efficient Lieutenant General John C. H. "Court House" Lee, West Point 1909. (Or, as the troops came to interpret his initials, "Jesus Christ Himself." Other generals wore the stars of rank on the front of their helmets; Lee wore the stars both fore and aft.)

Headquarters, First United States Army, which had commanded a training army on the east coast of the United States, arrived in the United Kingdom on October 19, 1943. By that time, Bradley had already brought up from the Mediterranean a staff nucleus from the II Corps. These two groups combined to form the new headquarters, but Bradley naturally tended to award the key positions to the II Corps officers tested by battle and by the amphibious assault on Sicily. The transfers from the Mediterranean included the G-2, Colonel Dickson, "the Monk," and the G-4, the supply chief, Colonel Robert W. Wilson. Both of these men were Philadelphians, both had served in the First World War—Dickson as a West Point graduate of 1918, Wilson as a civilian become artilleryman—and both had spent the interwar years in private business. Though Dickson prided himself as a raconteur—less winning than he imagined—and Wilson was taciturn, both shared an uncomfortable prickliness. Astringency still more characterized another Mediterranean transplant, the chief of staff, Major General William B. Kean, Jr. General Bradley said that it was a result of less than happy relationships with Seventh Army headquarters, while the II was in the awkward role of that army's only corps, that this staff "in its later relationships with the other Armies and especially with higher commands . . . was critical, unforgiving, and resentful of all authority but its own."⁸ Surely there were deeper reasons of character and experience. In any event, while Bradley gave the First Army a competent staff, it was one that needed to have ruffled feathers smoothed continually by a cool, quiet, and dominant commander.

Bradley himself supplied these qualities. A less proven figure was the deputy commander of the army, who would probably succeed Bradley at the head of the army when Bradley's army group became active on the Continent. The deputy was Lieutenant General Courtney H. Hodges. Hodges was older than both Bradley and Eisenhower. He had entered West Point in 1904, had fallen afoul of mathematics, but enlisted as a private in the Regular Army and earned his second lieutenant's commission only a year after his class graduated from the Point. (Patton, too, had entered the Military Academy in 1904 and suffered academic deficiencies; but he managed to stay on, repeat his plebe year, and graduate to receive his commission in the same year as Hodges, 1909.) Hodges showed himself a good fighting infantryman with the Pershing Punitive Expedition and with the 6th Regiment, 5th Division in France in 1918, where he won the Distinguished Service Cross. Just before the Second World War he was Bradley's immediate predecessor as commandant of the Infantry School, and in 1941 he became Chief of Infantry.

Some considered Hodges another Bradley—a calm, careful infantry tactician. Bradley himself called Hodges "a military technician" of "faultless techniques and tactical knowledge."⁹ But those who knew him as commander of the Third Army in training in 1943 had doubts. At Third Army he had followed another tough non–West Pointer, Lieutenant General Walter Krueger; but where Krueger had contrived to make a difficult headquarters staff function as a team, under Hodges the staff had begun to pull in different directions, and some thought Hodges had retreated to let his chief of staff run the army. Now in Kean the First Army had the sort of chief of staff who might readily jump the traces if his commanding officer were anything less than completely in control. And critical associates thought Hodges the reverse of a strong military commander, but instead the model of a rumpled, unassertive, small-town banker.

For the NEPTUNE planning, nevertheless, and under Bradley's close direction, Hodges had proven an effective alter ego to Bradley, enabling the army group and army commander to shuttle back and forth between Bristol and London with no interruption of the steady advance of invasion preparations.

As his chief of staff at First Army Group headquarters, Bradley chose yet another non–West Pointer (commissioned 1916) and former commandant of the Infantry School, Major General Leven C. Allen. Allen had presided successfully over an immense wartime expansion of the Infantry School. He operated a less taut and nervous but better disciplined shop than Kean. At first, there was a relative lack of urgency in the army group's planning tasks, for these tasks did not include the immediate direction of a segment of the NEPTUNE assault. Indeed, an army group was so new to the American army that there was scarcely an American doctrine for its functioning, and the role of the army group and its relations with army headquarters remained to evolve under experience and Bradley's inclinations in France.

Bradley had activated the First Army Group officially on October 16. The First Army took over operational control of American ground forces in the United Kingdom on October 23. This start was late enough that the American commands never quite caught up with British shaping of OVERLORD and NEPTUNE. But the crisis confronting Bradley at OMAHA Beach on D-Day also suggested that the American commands might be suffering from other problems more fundamental than a late start.

The Question of American Military Skill and Experience

The midday crisis of June 6, 1944 facing General Bradley at OMAHA Beach could suggest that American generalship and planning, still new to European war, had failed to catch up with the British in qualitative terms. The first effort to climb ashore in France can be interpreted as evidence of the American army's persisting unreadiness for war against German professional soldiers. The British Second Army won its D-Day foothold just to the east of OMAHA with no comparable crisis but instead with surprising ease. To the writer of the first comprehensive history of the Anglo-American campaign of 1944, the Australian Chester Wilmot in his *The Struggle for Europe*, the difference between the events of OMAHA and those of JUNO, GOLD, and SWORD was the difference wrought by superior British military experience and skill.

General Montgomery had allowed Bradley a wide range of discretion in choosing the means by which the American First Army would fulfill assignments given it by 21 Army Group. In refraining from a constant watch over Bradley's shoulder, Montgomery deferred both to American national sensitivity and to American customs of command, which favor prescribing a subordinate's mission rather than the details of how he is to accomplish it. Over the British Second Army, Montgomery's army group exercised tight tactical control; with the American First Army, Montgomery confined himself, in what was for a general of his temperament and habits a considerable exercise in restraint, to American-style definitions of mission. It was Chester Wilmot's contention that the Americans failed to merit the breadth of discretion and responsibility accorded them.

Wilmot conceded that the American landings at OMAHA suffered from heavy seas and from the unexpected strength of the German garrison. But he pointed out that the British obviously had to overcome the same bad weather and rough surf, and he argued that the Americans imposed on themselves avoidable difficulties with the seas by launching their assault craft at excessive distances from the shore. He also contended that the Americans relied too much on infantry unshielded from the enemy's fire and not enough on armor, especially to clear mines and other beach obstacles. Most fundamentally, he argued that underlying the "grave defects" in the American plan was "the American predilection for direct assault. The plan for OMAHA was a tactical application of the head-on strategy which Marshall had so consistently advocated in pressing the case for cross-Channel invasion."[10]

Wilmot's criticism of the launching of the American assault craft bears consideration, though it applies particularly to the navy. The Americans launched their assault craft almost twenty kilometers from the beach, while the British lowered theirs only about twelve kilometers out. The leading American craft had to begin their runs while it was still dark. Thus was aggravated the tendency of wind and tide to drive the first assault waves off their targets; the British made considerably fewer mislandings than the Americans. Obviously, the longer passage also aggravated the changes of foundering, to say nothing of the sufferings of the soldiers from seasickness.

The question of armor in the NEPTUNE assault may reflect General McNair's whole design of the wartime American army, with the infantry rather than the armored divisions conceived as the core of its power to break resistance. It may also reflect differences between the American and British armies almost as fundamental as those between peripheral, attritional strategy and a strategy of applying overwhelming power to destroy the enemy. Though the British army between the world wars had not dealt kindly with its prophets of armored warfare, the very memories that nearly stifled British resolve to launch a cross-Channel invasion—the ghosts of 1916—also drove some Britons to a desperate search for an alternative to the infantry charges of the Somme and Passchendaele. So the British prophets of armored warfare continued to make their way and to attract and hold something of a following despite the antipathy of the army's highest levels.

Along with Fuller and Liddell Hart there were less famous figures, such as Major General Sir Percy Hobart. In 1934, Hobart commanded the British army's first post–World War I tank brigade, and it was he who developed in Britain much of the tactical application of the pioneers' theories. Because Hobart believed firmly in the utility of armor, the British high command, which did not, could scarcely have elevated him to head its first armored division, the Mobile Division; this division went initially to a gunner and then to a cavalryman. But Hobart received the consolation of organizing the armor in Egypt, creating what was to be the renowned 7th Armoured Division of the desert war. Retired early before he could test this creation in battle, he was pulled by Churchill from a corporalship in the Home Guard and set to work developing specialized armored vehicles and tactics for the invasion.

On D-Day, Hobart commanded the 79th Armoured Division, elements of which accompanied all of the assault battalions to the British beaches. The equipment of the 79th included not only DDs but "Crabs," Shermans with flailing arms to beat paths through minefields; "Crocodiles," flamethrowing tanks to deal with pillboxes; and "AVREs"—Armoured Fighting Vehicles, Royal Engineers—which served a remarkable variety of purposes. The basic AVRE was a Churchill IV tank mounting a mortar, called a petard, which threw a 25-lb. charge in a "flying dustbin" to destroy fortifications and beach obstacles. The AVRE could also carry a "Small Box Girder Bridge" in front of itself, fire a small charge to release the tackle that held it, and drop the bridge to span a ditch or crater. Other AVREs carried fascines to drop into and fill antitank ditches, or to roll over walls to soften landings on the other side. Sometimes on the British beaches, one AVRE would lay an SBG bridge over a sea wall, another would cross the bridge to lay a fascine in an antitank ditch, and a Crab would then cross the bridge and the fascine to clear a path through mines.

General Montgomery ordered Hobart to offer one-third of his gadgets—or rather, in British army talk, his bobbins—to the Americans. Except for the DDs, which were so plainly related to the perilous amphibious part of the invasion process, Bradley and his staff were not interested. The Americans went ashore with no armored protection of direct application to the beach obstacles save the light armor of bulldozers, and they had to clear barbed wire and concrete walls with explosives manually placed, and to lift mines by hand. Their lack of interest seems odd among a nation so often mesmerized by mechanical contrivances, but part of the explanation may be linked to the larger American attitude toward tanks as instruments of mobility rather than of breakthrough power. The Americans had not suffered the Somme and Passchendaele. Their memories of the First World War were mainly of the heady offensive victories at Soissons, St. Mihiel, and the Meuse-Argonne, won by their infantry.

Could the unarmored infantryman still penetrate the strongest of the enemy's defenses as he had the Kriemhilde Stellung in 1918? Was it true, as Chester Wilmot alleged, that the Americans embraced the tactical equivalent of their strategic tradition, holding that in tactics as well as in strategy it is best to confront the enemy's strength head on, under the assumption that if his main strength is knocked out all else will follow?

To a degree, the American NEPTUNE planners had to believe that, or they would not have been willing to send the First Army against OMAHA Beach. Along the whole stretch of coast assigned to the Americans, OMAHA was the only place between Arromanches and the mouth of the Vire where a landing could be made on a level beach. Everywhere else, there were cliffs rising sheer from the sea, or rocks offshore. The Germans on this part of the Calvados coast concentrated almost all their attention on OMAHA. Yet the American planners readily accepted the task of going ashore there. They did not suggest a shift to an altogether different stretch of coast, or Corlett's idea that with enough amphibious tractors and other suitable equipment an amphibious assault does not require a flat beach.

OMAHA is a crescent-shaped beach stretching 6,500 meters between cliffs more than thirty meters high at Pointe et Raz de la Percée to the west and just beyond the village of Colleville-sur-Mer to the east. A gently sloping sand beach some 100 meters deep was backed by a fairly sharply rising embankment of loose stones, or shingle, as much as fourteen meters across. In the Vierville sector, on the 116th Infantry front in the western area of the beach, the shingle piled up against a part-masonry, part-wooden sea wall. On the rest of the beach the shingle was backed by sand dunes. The dunes and, for the most

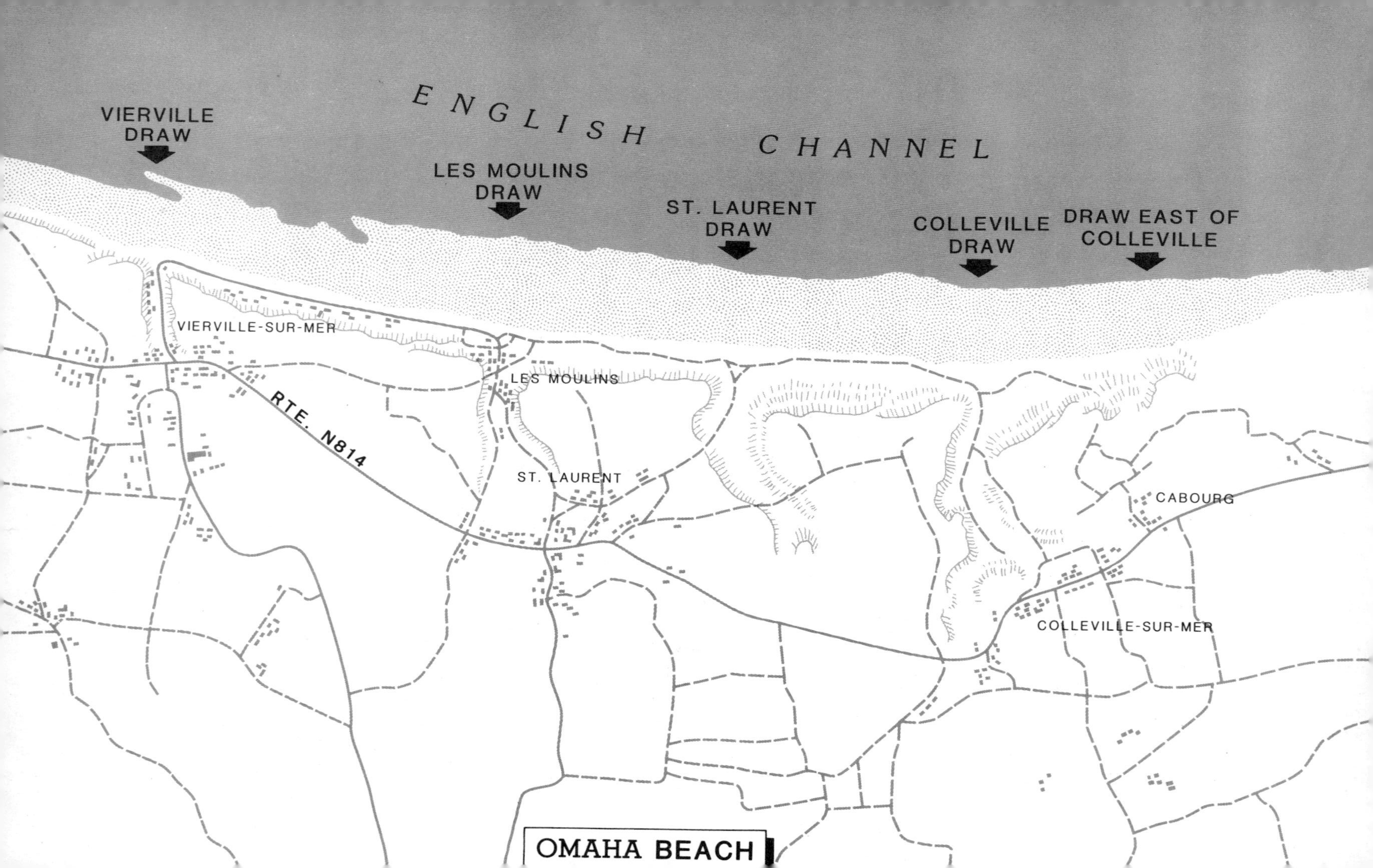

ENGLISH CHANNEL

VIERVILLE DRAW

LES MOULINS DRAW

ST. LAURENT DRAW

COLLEVILLE DRAW

DRAW EAST OF COLLEVILLE

VIERVILLE-SUR-MER

LES MOULINS

ST. LAURENT

CABOURG

COLLEVILLE-SUR-MER

RTE. N814

OMAHA BEACH

part, the shingle were impassable to vehicles. Beyond the dunes rose scrub-covered bluffs thirty to fifty meters high and merging to east and west with the cliffs. The bluffs were of varying steepness but rough and impassable even to tracked vehicles except at a few places. The exits inland were unimproved roads running through four or five draws that cut the bluffs. One of these roads connected with a road closely paralleling the coast, Route Nationale 814, at Vierville-sur-Mer; two others connected at St. Laurent-sur-Mer, and one at Colleville-sur-Mer. The latter places, thus commanding every exit, were stout stone villages admirable for defense. The fifth draw, northeast of Colleville, contained only a trail and was expected to be developed as a vehicle exit only after the beach was secure.

The plan, naturally, was to seize the exits as quickly as possible and reach not only Route N814 but the high ground along the main Paris-to-Cherbourg highway, Route N13. Optimistically, the plan scheduled the exits to be open as early as H-Hour plus 2, to accommodate a flow of vehicular traffic that would permit the V Corps to push on to its ambitious D-Day objectives. On the west flank, the 29th Division was to come ashore, resume command of its 116th Regiment, and turn right to clear the whole area between the coast and the Aure as far as Isigny. The 1st Division was to turn left to link up with the British at Port-en-Bessin, while also pressing south to gain a bridgehead over the Aure east of Trévières. By nightfall, the planners hoped the beachhead would be twenty-five kilometers wide and eight or nine kilometers deep.

Just as naturally as the American plan aimed for the beach exits, the Germans recognized the importance of the exits and fortified them heavily. In front of the fortifications, under German guns sited to sweep with crossfire practically the whole of OMAHA Beach, the American attack thus stalled throughout D-Day morning, to oblige General Bradley to ponder evacuation. It was painful pondering, in which he might not have had to engage had he himself and all the American planners not so blandly accepted the translation of head-on, power-drive strategy into tactics of head-on infantry assault.

The Fight up from OMAHA

The officers and NCOs and natural leaders among the privates on the beach spared Bradley a final decision. Perhaps without a combat-experienced division, the 1st, as the core of its landing force, OMAHA Beach could not have been taken. In late morning, by example and by exhortation, the bravest of the leaders began to gather growing clusters of followers around them, and to urge the men forward into the hills bordering the exits. Colonel George A. Taylor of the 16th Infantry enjoined the men around him: "Two kinds of people are staying on this beach, the dead and those who are going to die—now let's get the hell out of here."[11] The navy turned much of its effort to the vital exits. LCT-30 and LCI(L)-544 steamed full ahead through the obstacles off Colleville firing all weapons at the fortifications of the Colleville draw. The destroyer *Thompson* devoted her attentions to the Les Moulins draw, the more westerly of the two exits leading to St. Laurent. With soldiers and combat leaders displaying more ingenuity than the planners, who had called for concentrations directly in front of the beach exits, by afternoon knots of infantry were moving through the cover provided by irregularities in the bluffs on both sides of the exit draws, to take the defenses of the draws from flank and rear.

Company C of the 116th Infantry, urged on by the regimental commander, Colonel Charles D. W. Canham, and by the assistant commander of the 29th Division, Brigadier

General Norman D. Cota, moved up west of the Les Moulins draw and worked its way to the crest of the bluffs, to permit General Cota to open his command post there. The 5th Ranger Battalion followed closely. Canham persuaded men to advance by pointing out that they were being murdered as long as they remained on the beach—they might as well move up and take their chances of being murdered inland. Cota found a bulldozer abandoned just where it could have broken the antitank wall at the exit from the beach. "Who drives this thing?" he asked. No one answered. "Hasn't anyone got guts enough to drive the damn thing?" he demanded again. A soldier slowly rose and deliberately approached the bulldozer, saying, "I'll do it." Cota responded, "That's the stuff. Now let's get off the beach," and other men began to rise, too.[12] Both Canham and Cota thus won the Distinguished Service Cross.

There was nothing mysterious about their accomplishment in arousing men apparently paralyzed by fear. What they did took courage, but not extraordinary magnetism. In training, soldiers feel the presence of their comrades, their squads, platoons, companies, and battalions around them, and the awareness of the presence of others does much to hold the individual soldier to his duty. On the battlefield, in contrast, everyone goes to ground under the shock of enemy fire, and the soldier abruptly finds himself apparently alone. Even the enemy is usually unseen; nothing was more frightening about the Second World War battlefield than its emptiness. At OMAHA Beach, the enemy lay in careful concealment, and his heavy fire drove the attackers immediately to ground as soon as they reached any semblance of dry land and cover; wrecked equipment was all about, yet living humans were almost nowhere to be seen. The great armada just off the beach notwithstanding, OMAHA was a battlefield of somber loneliness exceptional even by the standards of World War II. Feeling alone, many men did not fight because the accustomed presence of officers and comrades was not there to prod them. Many others did not fight because it was the sense of aloneness that added the final paralyzing dimension to fear. Canham, Cota, Taylor, and others like them assured just enough men that they were not alone.

Just enough. A few men, a few companies carried a disproportionate share of the D-Day fighting. In the Stonewall Brigade, the 3rd Battalion clambered in small, scattered groups to the crest east of the Les Moulins draw. Nuclei of Companies G and E of the 16th Infantry found their way up the least defended draw, the one east of Colleville with only a trail. They were followed, on Colonel Taylor's exhortation, by parts of the 2nd and 1st Battalions of their regiment, while Company E turned west at the summit to hit from the rear the guardians of the St. Laurent draw. Meanwhile other men of the 3/16th had knocked out the main enemy fortifications in the easternmost draw, fortifications bypassed by the first advances along the trail.

Wherever there were minefields, the absence of mechanized antidotes to them made for hesitant, groping, often single-file American probing. The British with their mine-sweeping tanks could advance more readily. Still, by the approach of dusk the Americans were at last breaching the German positions on the coastal road, N814. There remained much cause for concern. The lodgment along the road between St. Laurent and Colleville was nowhere more than two kilometers deep, and thus extremely vulnerable should the Germans be able to mass reserves for a counterattack during the night. Fighting continued in the villages, to make title to them questionable. To the west, the 116th Infantry and the 5th Ranger Battalion grasped another foothold on the coast road at Vierville, but this pocket was separated from the main line. Three companies of the 2nd Ranger Battalion in a remarkable effort had scaled and seized the sheer cliffs of Pointe du Hoc about five and a half kilometers west of OMAHA. They intended to capture what Allied intelligence considered "the most dangerous battery in France"[13]—only to discover that the six 155mm. guns they sought to take were no longer there, and to find themselves at nightfall still another isolated pocket, and a very weak one at that.

Everything needed for further advances was lacking—ammunition, artillery, armor, vehicles. Elements of five artillery battalions had landed during the afternoon but had lost twenty-six guns while doing so. Two antiaircraft batteries scheduled to land on D-Day had been postponed.

Yet the initiative, the bravery, and the tactical skill in the indirect approach among the soldiers on the beach had between midday and darkness turned General Bradley's thoughts from withdrawal to reinforcement. The casualties on OMAHA had been high, and made higher by such mistakes as the premature launching of so many DDs—about 2,000 killed, wounded, and missing in all. But mainly, the casualties reflected the toughness of the German resistance. Significantly, the British to the east, who did not have to face cliffs and steep bluffs like those at OMAHA, had an easier time of it—everywhere but on their extreme right, around the village of Le Hamel, where their 50th Northumbrian Division collided with the right of the same enemy 352nd Division that defended OMAHA. There, the British fared scarcely better than the V Corps.

UTAH

The VII Corps had a more fortunate day than the V. On UTAH, the preliminary aerial bombardment was conducted by the medium bombers of the Ninth Air Force rather than the heavies of the Eighth. Brigadier General Samuel E. Anderson of the IX Bomber Command received permission to bomb visually under the overcast, and the German defenses were hit much more effectively than they were at OMAHA. More important, because of the flooding just inshore and then again at the base of the Cotentin, the enemy did not perceive UTAH as a promising place for the Allies to land, and the defenses were not as strong as farther east and the defenders more casual. At UTAH, too, although the lee of the Cotentin afforded the DDs and the assault craft relative shelter, the still-choppy seas early swamped two control vessels, and the invaders consequently came ashore about two kilometers south of where they were supposed to be—with fortunate results. The defenses were weaker here than at the prescribed landing place. The assault waves of the 4th Division quickly grasped enough of a foothold for demolition teams to clear paths for followup waves by midmorning.

The major problems arose when the 3rd Battalion of the 22nd Infantry in the assault waves, and then the rest of the 22nd and the 12th in the followup, turned north to clear the originally intended beaches. They soon met heavy resistance and could not take the guns on a ridge line from which the Germans were shelling the landings.

But before the morning was over, the infantry were already on the causeways leading across the inundations, with DDs protecting their flanks. One causeway proved undefended and unmined. Major General Maxwell D. Taylor's 101st Airborne Division was already in control of the western ends of four others.

This latter fact alone amply vindicated Bradley's insistence and Eisenhower's decision that the airborne attacks must proceed. In addition, the 101st achieved its

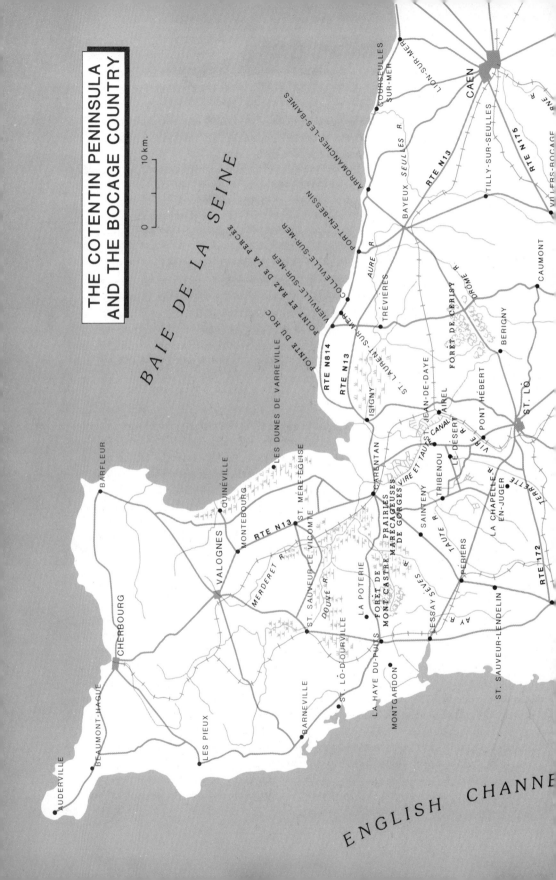

THE COTENTIN PENINSULA
AND THE BOCAGE COUNTRY

0 10 km.

BAIE DE LA SEINE

ENGLISH CHANNEL

AUDERVILLE

BEAUMONT-HAGUE

CHERBOURG

LES PIEUX

BARNEVILLE

MONTGARDON

LA HAYE-DU-PUITS

ST. LÔ-D'OURVILLE

ST. SAUVEUR-LE-VICOMTE

LA POTERIE

FORÊT DE MONT CASTRE

MERDERET R

DOUVE R

VALOGNES

MONTEBOURG

RTE N13

QUINÉVILLE

BARFLEUR

LES DUNES DE VARREVILLE

ST. MÈRE-EGLISE

POINT ET RAZ DE LA PERCÉE

POINTE DU HOC

VIERVILLE-SUR-MER

COLLEVILLE-SUR-MER

PORT-EN-BESSIN

ARROMANCHES-LES-BAINES

COURSEULLES-SUR-MER

LION-SUR-MER

CAEN

RTE N13

BAYEUX

SEULLES R

TILLY-SUR-SEULLES

RTE N175

VILLERS-BOCAGE

ORNE

AURE R

TRÉVIÈRES

ST. LAURENT-SUR-MER

ISIGNY

RTE N13

RTE N814

CARENTAN

CANAL

VIRE ET TAUTE

JEAN-DE-DAYE

AIREL

LE DÉSERT

PONT HÉBERT

VIRE R

ST. LÔ

FORÊT DE CERISY

DRÔME R

BERIGNY

CAUMONT

PRAIRIES MARÉCAGEUSES DE GORGES

SAINTENY

TRIBENOU

TAUTE R

SAINT ÈVES

ESSAY S ÈVES

PÉRIERS

LA CHAPELLE-EN-JUGER

TERRETTE R

RTE 172

ST. SAUVEUR-LENDELIN

AY R

second objective of occupying the line of the Douve River to shield the southern flank of the VII Corps and to serve later as a springboard from which to drive through Carentan to link up with the V Corps. Here the airborne position was much more tenuous, and it was a disappointment that no bridgehead was secured south of the Douve; but while the Germans seemed to be building up a superior force along the Douve to counterattack, the very shock of suffering airborne assault, the confusion and uncertainty about where the airborne center of gravity might lie and what the Americans intended, appeared to be staying the Germans' hand. As it happened, furthermore, the German buildup against the 101st, palsied by confusion though it was, diverted part of the 352nd Division from OMAHA Beach during the critical hours when the battle there was most uncertain.

The situation of the 82nd Airborne was less satisfactory. By nightfall, the seaborne 4th Division had not yet linked up with the 82nd to the north and west, and the 82nd had failed to win a firm foothold west of the Merderet River. General Ridgway's division nevertheless was drawing itself together around Ste. Mère-Eglise, and from the German perspective this meant for practical purposes the loss of the ground from the coast to the Merderet for eight kilometers north from the Carentan Canal. With American paratroopers beating about west of the Merderet, furthermore, the Germans perforce were also chasing through that area, once more in apparently greater strength than the Americans but not sure enough of it to use their strength effectively. All the achievements of the 101st and 82nd Divisions came at a D-Day cost recognizable on the spot as not prohibitive—especially in proportion to the value of the causeways out of UTAH Beach—and eventually proving to add up to 1,259 killed, wounded, and missing. On UTAH itself, thanks in part to the airborne, the 4th Division's D-Day casualties were fewer than 200.

The Defense

Thus the UTAH force suffered less on D-Day than it had when the E-boats got in among its rehearsals at Slapton Sands. This fact indicates also that the Allied success owed much to the failure of the German navy to interfere effectively on D-Day. Here, the storm that postponed the invasion by a day and caused the Allied command so much worry helped the Allies by aggravating the enemy's naval weakness. The commander of Germany's Naval Group West, Admiral Theodor Krancke, was lulled by the storm into believing that the invasion could not come for at least some days more; without meteorological observation in the Atlantic, the Germans could not forecast the temporary break in the weather that permitted Eisenhower to say "Let's go" for the 6th of June. The Allied invasion fleet met no German patrols as it crossed the Channel. The only naval contact during D-Day occurred when four enemy torpedo boats reached the Eastern Task Force late in the afternoon and sank the Norwegian destroyer *Svenner*, fortunately missing the battleships *Warspite* and *Ramillies* which lay just beyond the victim. After launching eighteen torpedos, the German vessels turned away into a smoke screen and fled eastward.

The Allies eventually learned that fifteen E-boats based at Cherbourg had headed for the Bay of the Seine, but the rough seas discouraged them and they returned without accomplishment. The U-boats in Brittany and the Bay of Biscay were too distant to reach the invasion fleet for several days.

German mines were thus the most dangerous naval threat to the invasion fleet on D-Day, but this menace also proved smaller than it might have been. Rommel had not been able to prevail on the navy and the Oberkommando der Wehrmacht to renew the mine belts already laid in the Channel as often as they should have, let alone to complete all the minefields he would have liked. The Germans had not gotten around to laying their new "oyster" pressure mines, which either could not be swept at all or could be swept only in the most favorable weather. Admiral Ramsay had feared the enemy would sow oyster mines in the invasion ports in England, where he thought they would have played havoc. Such mines did not turn up even on the French coast because, it later appeared, the Germans did not have enough to cover the whole invasion coast and were afraid that by using a few they would permit the Allies to capture one and learn the secret of its operation. Moreover, the Allies were able to make their way to the coast largely through the channels the Germans had kept open for themselves—which were mapped for the Allies by ULTRA. On D-Day underwater mines sank only the American destroyer *Corry* off UTAH; PC-2161, a 173-foot patrol craft; three LCTs; and two LCIs.

The Luftwaffe, so fearsome to the Allies in the earlier, 1940 battle of France, intervened on D-Day with even less effect than the Kriegsmarine. In the twenty-four hours of D-Day, the Allied air forces flew more than 14,000 sorties. The American Eighth and Ninth Air Forces alone flew 8,722. The Americans lost seventy-one planes, to flak and in aerial combat. They claimed only thirty-one enemy planes destroyed, which does much to indicate the scale of the German countereffort. The German records eventually captured show that Jagdkorps II, the tactical arm of Luftflotte 3 in the invasion area, had only from 50 to 121 fighters available. Jagdkorps II recorded only 250 sorties against the landings—or rather, almost wholly against Allied shipping, not the troops ashore—none with substantial effect. Other German aerial operations on June 6 in France were mainly far inland, against Allied air penetrations. Four Heinkel bombers appeared near JUNO Beach about dusk and dropped their loads, but a squadron of Spitfires destroyed all of them.

Without such complete Allied air superiority, the unsubtle frontal assault that was the amphibious invasion could have had scant hope of success. The completeness of Allied air superiority and the limited cost of D-Day in Allied lives—compare even the 2,000 casualties of OMAHA with the more than 12,000 of the Union army at the Battle of Antietam on September 17, 1862—were paid for at other times and places. The Fw 190s and Bf 109s were not in France but back in Germany, if they could fly at all, primarily because of General Spaatz's daylight bombing of the Reich. In this and the other campaigns in which the AAF and RAF had prepared the way for the invasion, the Allied air forces had lost 12,000 air crewmen and over 2,000 planes in the two months preceding D-Day.

By nightfall, none of the Allied landings had reached the lines drawn on the NEPTUNE planners' maps as D-Day objectives. But only at OMAHA was the beachhead shallow and incoherent enough to make this fact a cause for reasonable concern. British 30 Corps, assaulting GOLD Beach to the immediate left of OMAHA, met relatively light resistance except from the right flank of the 352nd Division. The corps's failure to capture Bayeux and otherwise to attain its full objectives was due less to any stoutness in the defense than to the caution of its commanders. Falling short of its objectives, 30 Corps still carved out a foothold about ten kilometers by ten and linked up with 1 Corps on JUNO to its left. From JUNO, the 3rd Canadian Division of 1 Corps pushed its advance some eleven kilometers inland. On the extreme Allied left, two parachute brigades of the

British 6th Airborne Division had dropped during the night simultaneously with the American airborne attack and carved out a bridgehead east of the Orne.

The only semblance of a German threat to develop on D-Day beyond the beaches took shape in the center of 1 Corps, where during the evening a tank battalion of those old desert adversaries, the 21st Panzer Division, drove a spearhead between the 3rd British and 3rd Canadian Divisions to the sea. But not only did Allied fighter-bombers harry the efforts of other panzers to follow along; the Germans seemed incapable of bringing up infantry to consolidate the panzers' gain. Able at best to advance only at the pace of horses and men on foot unless it rode the rails, the German infantry evidently found that the Allied aerial assault on Normandy's highways and rails left them altogether incapable of the kind of movement necessary to apply reinforcements in the critical first hours of the invasion.

By the end of D-Day, said Major Hansen, "Bradley shows no sign of worry. He told Collins, however, 'They are digging in on Omaha Beach with their fingernails. I hope they can push in and get some stuff ashore .' "[14] He also soon said to Montgomery: "Someday I'll tell Gen[eral] Eisenhower just how close it was those first few hours."[15]

6: Cherbourg and Caumont

THE GERMANS' inability to reinforce or to replenish losses with the speed requisite for turning back the invasion grew more reassuringly evident in the days immediately after June 6. Especially was this true opposite the V Corps. In a kind of providential compensation for its hard fight to dig in its fingernails on D-Day, the OMAHA force soon found itself favorably engaged against the weakest opposition of any of the assault corps.

Tough as the enemy's 352nd Division proved to be, Allied ground and air power chipped away at its strength in the first days of battle to visible effect. The only substantial reinforcement to come up alongside the 352nd was the 30th Mobile Brigade, whose mobility was that of bicycles. It began arriving from Coutances on June 7. Thus, American reinforcements from the sea built up an increasing local numerical advantage for the V Corps over its German opposition, and the American advantage in turn hastened in geometric proportion the erosion of the enemy's will to persist in the fight.

As early as D plus one, the V Corps had five regiments ashore. That day the 18th Infantry of the 1st Division, taking over the advance from the bruised 16th Infantry, carved out two bridgeheads across the River Aure. The Big Red One's 26th Infantry, attacking eastward toward a junction with the British, fared less well, and it was not until June 8 that it made firm contact with 30 Corps across the Drôme River. At that, skillful defensive fighting and a well executed withdrawal on the night of June 8–9 enabled part of the 726th Regiment of the 352nd Division, along with the 30th Mobile Brigade, to escape a potential Anglo-American trap. Similarly, the inexperienced American 29th Division had trouble pushing westward to relieve the three Ranger companies isolated at Pointe du Hoc. The Rangers were cut down to fewer than a hundred effectives and in real danger of extinction before the 116th Infantry, reinforced by other Rangers, at last relieved them during the morning of June 8. Still, the evidently deteriorating forces confronting the V Corps were no longer capable of anything like the resistance posed by accumulating panzer reserves opposite the British, or the hornet's nest the VII Corps had entered in the Cotentin.

The Battle of the Cotentin

As soon as the Allies touched down in Normandy, the Germans of course had no trouble in perceiving the importance of Cherbourg to the coming contest of the buildup, on which the ultimate fate of the campaign for France would hinge. Furthermore, during the month before the invasion the Germans formidably reinforced the Cotentin; Hitler, Rommel, and Admiral Krancke had all begun to feel unease and intuitions about Normandy. The Germans supplemented the static 709th Infantry Division on the east coast of the peninsula and the 243rd Division on the west coast with the strong and more mobile 91st Division in time to unhinge the NEPTUNE planners' idea of dropping the American 82nd Airborne across the Cotentin's southern base. The Germans further reinforced the 91st Division by attaching to it the 6th Parachute Regiment. About the same time, the 206th Panzer Battalion—a separate tank battalion—along with the Seventh Army Sturm Battalion and several other reinforcements of similar size entered the peninsula.

During the night of June 6–7, a patrol from the 82nd Airborne's core position at Ste. Mère-Eglise made contact with General Barton, commander of the 4th Infantry Division. Some concerting of plans between the airborne and the infantry from UTAH could then take place, which was fortunate, because early the next morning a strong German counterattack came pushing down Route N13 against Ste. Mère-Eglise. The Seventh Army Sturm Battalion, an elite unit as its name implies, led the way, with a miscellany of other formations in its wake, including a company of the 709th Antitank Battalion with ten self-propelled 75mm. guns. The lightly armed paratroopers who had assembled in the town, even more a miscellany than the enemy as far as company and battalion organizations were concerned, soon felt themselves hard pressed and in danger. But the previous night's contact permitted General Ridgway to call on General Collins through the 4th Division for reinforcement. Help came in the form of a task force of the 746th Tank Battalion, which splintered the attacking Germans into a number of separate groups and threatened to isolate some of them in turn.

Nevertheless, with its main force thus occupied, the 82nd could do nothing to revive its D-Day objective of a firm bridgehead across the Merderet. Similar enemy counteractions meanwhile isolated the parts of the 101st Airborne that had reached the north bank of the Douve. At the same time, the 4th Division was finding the high ground and gun positions north of UTAH Beach still less penetrable than on D-Day.

Because of this evidence of stiffening German resistance against the critical effort to take Cherbourg, Montgomery and Bradley agreed in a shipboard meeting on June 7 that joining the OMAHA and UTAH beachheads for the most rapid possible buildup and concentration against Cherbourg should have the Americans' first priority. Visiting the beaches with Admiral Ramsay that day, General Eisenhower reached the same conclusion.

Consistent with the developing post-D-Day pattern of German resistance, the V Corps had an easier time than the VII in completing its share of the mission. During the night of June 7–8, the 29th Division's 175th Infantry Regiment, Maryland National Guard, with the 747th Tank Battalion attached and Shermans leading the way, took off westward from the OMAHA beachhead toward the small port and Camembert cheese center of Isigny. The Marylanders and the tankers met only scattered pockets of the enemy. Aided by naval gunfire, they broke the pockets without much trouble. They entered and cleared Isigny the next night. In doing so they added to the woes of the enemy 352nd Division by snapping the divisional left flank loose from the sea and leaving it dangling in air.

The 101st Airborne, in contrast, acting for the VII Corps, though General Collins freed it from other missions to concentrate on taking Carentan with its glider regiment as well as its paratroopers, found itself stalled by parts of the German 6th Parachute Regiment and 77th Infantry Division, the latter of which Rommel had ordered east from

Brittany on D-Day; somehow, the 77th had gotten to the front with relatively little interference by Allied air.

The 101st had to execute much of its effort single file along causeways over the flooded Douve River and Carentan Canal, a tactical method that obviously did not speed the way. By June 10, the 327th Glider Infantry at length achieved tenuous contact with Company K of the 175th Infantry, which had crossed the Vire River west from Isigny. Not until June 12 did concentric attacks by the 101st occupy Carentan, and not until June 13 did the contact between the V and VII Corps become firm. By then, the linking of the corps flanks had a Civil War atmosphere beyond that suggested by the meeting of the Blue and Gray Division with the Screaming Eagles of the 101st, whose shoulder patch memorializes Old Abe, the eagle mascot of the Army of the Tennessee. Both the airborne troopers and the National Guardsmen had been in contact with German infantry transport long enough that many were mounted on horseback.

Bradley and his staff on their visits to the VII Corps found "a good deal of ginger." Youngish, handsome General Collins was "trim and austere without a tie," says one diary entry; "independent, vigorous, heady, capable and full of vinegar. Needs a check rein if anything," says another.[1] But all its own and its commander's ginger and vinegar did not save the corps from trouble on its north flank as well as the south. Collins hoped to plunge directly north to Cherbourg to capture the vital seaport as quickly as possible, without consuming time in a lateral thrust across the base of the Cotentin in the preliminary move envisaged by the planners. To that end he left to subordinates on the one hand and to Bradley and Hodges on the other the main work of supervising the junction between his corps and the V, whatever its formal priority, while he himself concentrated on driving his troops toward a breakout from UTAH northward. Yet capturing even the D-Day objectives immediately north of UTAH proved to require not a day but a week of hard fighting by the 4th Division, the 505th Parachute Infantry of the 82nd Airborne, and eventually the 39th Infantry of the 9th Division, the latter thrown in against the enemy's coastal fortifications on June 12. The reward for these units' efforts was a ridge line westward from Quinéville to the Merderet and the freeing of UTAH Beach from the worst of an artillery bombardment that had continually plagued unloading. By the time this success was achieved, Bradley had decided on June 9 that he must insist on Collins's completing the planned attack across the southern Cotentin to the west coast, despite loss of time, to ensure Cherbourg's eventual fall by preventing its reinforcement.

In that western direction, a similar interval and effort had already had to pass before the enemy's stubborn Cotentin garrison yielded the D-Day objective of a Merderet bridgehead large and firm enough to serve as a launching pad for the strike across the southern base of the peninsula. According to Bradley's latest plan, the fresh 90th Infantry Division was to relieve the 82nd beyond the Merderet and, while Ridgway's troopers guarded its southern flank, to carry most of the burden of the westward push.

Brigadier General Jay W. MacKelvie's 90th began landing on UTAH Beach before D-Day was over, and it attacked through the lines of the 82nd west of Ste. Mère-Eglise on June 10. The 90th had been a National Army division drawn from Texas and Oklahoma in the First World War; its shoulder patch, a T crossing an O, symbolized its origins. Without combat experience, it was abruptly contending against the enemy's high-quality 91st Division. Immediately it found itself in trouble. From the outset it had to plunge into the Bocage—"Damnedest country I've seen," Bradley was already calling it[2]—where the hedgerows cancelled any chance that superior American mobility might compensate for the absence of battlefield conditioning. The UTAH assault division, Barton's 4th, had to master similar problems, but at least the 4th benefited from a more gradually developing encounter with German veterans in massed strength, and first it had bolstered its self-confidence with its well-executed, and lightly opposed, assault landing. The NEPTUNE planners, in their neglect of the implications of the Bocage, had not prepared any other formation better than they did the 90th for confinement among the hedgerows; everybody was having to find his own solutions there. But the difficulties of the 90th seemed to be worse than those of other outfits in similar predicaments. In the Germans' opinion, a majority of American infantry units lacked aggressiveness and were overly bound to their artillery and inclined to substitute saturation fire from the guns for maneuver and assault. By its own historical account, the 90th suffered such handicaps with special severity.

On June 13, the 90th was still fighting in the vicinity of the D-Day objectives of the 82nd. General Collins, full of vinegar, thereupon relieved two regimental commanders and General MacKelvie. He gave the division to his deputy corps commander, Major General Eugene M. Landrum, who had fought in the Aleutians and recaptured Attu from the Japanese in May 1943. Bradley and Eisenhower supported Collins's dropping of the axe; Eisenhower concluded that the 90th "was not well brought up"—though as far as MacKelvie's responsibility for its training was concerned, he had commanded the division only since January, after a tour as its artillery chief.[3]

A new division commander could not remedy improper nurturing overnight, so Collins also reorganized the westward assault. Bradley kept himself in close touch with his corps and division leaders, including Collins, but with the aggressive chief of the VII Corps he was inclined to defer to forthright requests to let corps headquarters do things its own way. Collins's way now was to turn the main thrust over to the combat-experienced Regular Army 9th Division, which since the latter part of the Tunisian campaign had been commanded with conspicuous boldness and skill by the florid, hearty Major General Manton Eddy, a non–West Pointer but a veteran of Pershing's old AEF. The 90th would turn north to cover the right flank of the 9th as the latter took up the big westward push, with help from the 82nd. Risking no undue setbacks, Collins also asked Bradley to give him the 79th Division, in case the new leadership failed to improve the 90th rapidly enough. Bradley agreed.

"Lightning Joe" Collins's style of corps command was one of highly personal leadership, the corps chieftain close to the front, hastening by scout car from one division, regiment, or battalion to another to solve problems directly and to urge everybody forward. His handling of the 90th suggested that his peppery vigor harbored something of the ruthless intolerance of a Philip H. Sheridan toward leaders less impatient than himself for success. If in addition, early indications that Collins possessed the larger aggressive attributes of a Phil Sheridan should mature, then, unlike the Army of the Potomac, the American First Army in Europe could prove fortunate enough to have found its Sheridan at the very outset of its campaigns.

Like that earlier fighting Irish-American, Collins came to corps command in one army after leading a division in another far away. He had graduated from West Point in April 1917. After training commands in the United States until the Armistice, he served in the Army of Occupation in Germany, and then spent much of the interwar period as a student and instructor in the army's service schools, graduating from the Command and General Staff School, the Army Industrial College, and the Army War College, and teaching at the War College. In May 1942 he received his second star and the 25th Division. By the beginning of 1943, this unit had relieved the 1st Marine Division on Guadalcanal and was beginning its own initial offensive there. The 25th had dubious antecedents: it had been formed around a cadre drawn from the prewar Hawaiian Division, now the 24th Division, a Regular Army formation but as a garrison division one long regarded as distinctly less than first rate. Yet the 25th had to fill the shoes of the 1st Marines on Guadalcanal; trained by Collins and led by him in combat, it did so without embarrassment. The division codename, LIGHTNING, became aptly associated with Collins himself.

Guadalcanal provided useful preparation for the hedgerows. Collins decided that the hedgerows were as bad as much of the jungle growth of Guadalcanal, which was saying a great deal; but at least, after that fetid island hardly anything could seem worse, or any geographic problem insurmountable. The Bocage of the Cotentin was among the most troublesome in Normandy, its hedgerows peculiarly thick. Bradley, reflecting the planners' negligence about preparing the field commanders for the Bocage, asked a tank officer: "Can't we run tanks up there and chew those ditches apart with a few shells and a burst of machine gun fire?"[4] The hedgerows did not yield so easily. Standing firm, they permitted the artillery the barest fields of fire, and the tanks could scarcely deploy. Collins decided to push his advance on regimental fronts of only a thousand meters. Each of his spearhead divisions had only two regiments in line, since the 39th Infantry of the 9th Division was still away on the east coast of the peninsula, and the 508th Parachute Infantry of the 82nd Airborne was busy maintaining contact with the 101st on the division's left, while the 505th had been attached to the 4th Division. The 9th and 82nd Divisions thus moved west along the two main roads out of Ste. Mère-Eglise, each division bestriding its road with its regiments abreast in column of battalions.

The drive proceeded in brief, hard thrusts, maintaining its pace through relief of the leading battalions two or three times a day. On the maps, the flanks were insecure, but Collins knew from his South Pacific experience that an enemy with relatively poor communications and few tanks would not be able to exploit such an opening if the advance kept on moving. Whatever danger there was in this arrangement was aggravated because the 90th Division continued to make a poor showing on the right flank; Landrum's men were meeting more and more elements of the German 77th Division as the enemy's 91st Division was worn down. Still, the Germans somehow failed to interpose their fresher and stronger units in front of the main attack. By June 15, the 325th Glider Infantry was within 1,000 meters of St. Sauveur-le-Vicomte, the choke point near which the 82nd Airborne would have dropped according to the early NEPTUNE plan, on the only good road into the central part of the peninsula from the south. Because the 9th Division had been slowed by a counterattack, Collins decided to send the 82nd across the Douve into St. Sauveur no matter what progress the 9th made farther north. The orders for June 16 called for the 82nd and the 9th to advance echeloned to the right rear, each regiment refusing its right to tie in with its neighbor to the north.

Before noon the next day, the 325th was on the right bank of the Douve opposite St. Sauveur. General Ridgway asked Collins's permission to cross without delay. Receiving it, he sent the newly rejoined 505th and 508th Parachute Regiments over to carve out a bridgehead. Sensing then that the German 91st Division was crumbling in front of him, Collins countermanded his earlier orders to the 9th Division and directed General Eddy to hasten forward toward alignment with the 82nd Division along the Douve. Before the day was over, part of the 2nd Battalion of the 60th Infantry of Eddy's division also had a bridgehead west of the stream, opposite Ste. Colombe.

Until D-Day, the Allied aerial bridge-busting campaign had spared the crossings of the Loire lest the pattern of the campaign should too evidently outline the invasion area. With NEPTUNE ashore, the Loire bridges became fair targets, and by June 15 at least eight of them were destroyed and all were badly damaged. The German Seventh Army between the Seine and the Loire thus could receive only a trickle of reinforcements and supplies. By now, furthermore, bombing in combination with the activities of the French Resistance had also almost cut the routes between Normandy and Brittany. More than ever, the Germans' battle in Normandy and the Cotentin would have to be fought with the men and matériel already there. In addition, the enemy's use of his relatively fresh 77th Division mainly against the secondary activities of the American 90th Division suggested that he was hoarding his best troops in the northern Cotentin for the direct defense of Cherbourg. To do so while Collins was destroying all vestiges of connection between Cherbourg and the rest of Europe was hardly consistent with sound strategy, but it was consistent with Hitler's established penchant for demanding the last-ditch defense of fortified strongpoints, such as Cherbourg.

Thus Collins's aggressive instincts were altogether correct when he decided to leap the Douve between St. Sauveur and Ste. Colombe, believing that no effective resistance or danger to his flanks remained to thwart the progress of his spearheads to the sea. On June 18, the 9th Division cut the west coast road at Barneville.

It would be difficult to assert with confidence that any other Allied corps commander would have paused as briefly as Collins after completing this sweep across the south base of the Cotentin. General Bradley helped keep the VIII Corps in motion by promptly transferring the 82nd Airborne and 90th Divisions to Major General Troy H. Middleton's newly operational VIII Corps, and making Middleton responsible for guarding the line across the peninsula against counterattack from the south. But it was the Collins touch that had the VII Corps—now, from right to left, the 4th, 79th, and 9th Divisions— all in line ready to attack northward toward Cherbourg by the morning of June 19.

In the 9th Division, which had to make the sharpest turn just after completing its drive to the Cotentin's west coast, it was also Manton Eddy's touch. Eddy was a heavy-set man who always kept a comfortable headquarters, an excellent chef, and an elegant table; but he was also a hard driver for all that. As Bradley described his division's turn:

> . . . for Eddy's 9th it demanded an unbelievably swift change in direction. Manton had not reached his final objective on the Cotentin west shore until 5:00 A.M., June 18. Within 22 hours he was expected to turn a force of 20,000 troops a full 90 degrees toward Cherbourg, evacuate his sick and wounded, lay wire, reconnoiter the ground, establish his boundaries, issue orders, relocate his ammunition and supply dumps, and then jump off in a fresh attack on a front nine miles wide. Eddy never even raised his eyebrow and when H hour struck, he jumped off on time.[5]

It was with good reason that Eisenhower rated the 9th and the 1st as the two best American divisions in his theater.[6] The smooth functioning of the 9th reflected not only the division's seasoning and the abilities of its commander and headquarters staff, but also Eddy's command arrangements, modeled on German practice. The assistant division commander habitually remained at the division command post, with Eddy roaming among the troops. The assistant commander both made emergency decisions and supervised the "operational group" at headquarters, the G-2 (Intelligence) and G-3 (Operations) sections. The division chief of staff supervised the "administrative group," the G-1 (Personnel) and G-4 (Supply) sections. Eddy himself could be relied on to be almost always in the center of the action, where the most critical decisions had to be made most quickly.

Collins was all the more intent on turning northward toward Cherbourg rapidly because Allied intelligence—specifically, ULTRA—revealed that a tug-of-war was going on between Hitler's desire to hoard troops directly in front of Cherbourg and the hopes of Rommel and the Seventh Army to strike at the line across the base of the Cotentin while it was still thin. One effect, Collins learned, had been to disrupt the 77th Division, half committed to the battle for communication with the rest of France, half held back for the coming fight for Cherbourg. Thanks to ULTRA, the American high command knew, too, that the Führer's preferences had produced an order to Generalleutnant Karl-Wilhelm von Schlieben of the 709th Division, now commanding the defense of Cherbourg, granting permission for a general withdrawal into the Cherbourg fortifications, Landfront Cherbourg. The VII Corps commander wanted to catch as many of the enemy as possible in the vulnerability of retreat. The destruction of German land lines by air attack and the Resistance did much to account for the rising ULTRA productivity through which Bradley's G-2s could guide Collins.

Hoping to discomfit the Germans also by forcing a rapid shift of attention from their right to their left, Collins had Barton's 4th Division open the attack by advancing on both sides of Montebourg near the east coast at three in the morning. Against well-prepared defenses shielded by darkness, the Ivy Leaf Division gained no headway. In daylight on June 19, the story grew different; the defenders' exhaustion again became the primary element in the battle, and the 22nd Infantry Regiment was able to capture Montebourg by late afternoon. Farther west, moreover, Collins was rewarded as he expected to be by hitting little but disorganized fragments in retreat. In the first day's action after its rapid change of direction, Eddy's 9th Division smoked out almost no resistance. The 79th had a more difficult time of it; but this Organized Reserve division, commanded since May 1942 by Major General Ira T. Wyche, West Point 1911, was not only luckier than the 90th in the quality of its first opposition, but also seemed from the outset "well brought up." So thoroughly did Schlieben's left and center crumble on impact, indeed, that by the next morning the 4th Division found only open country ahead of it. The worst problems for the VII Corps on June 20 were those created by bad weather.

And bad weather made Collins's drive for Cherbourg still more urgent. Against the crucial race to build up men and supplies on which holding the OVERLORD lodgment depended, and against the danger that adequate ports would not be captured and opened in time, the British had built at Prime Minister Churchill's urging and at immense cost in scarce materials two artificial harbors, one for their own beaches, one for the American, codenamed MULBERRIES. Protected by breakwaters of sunken ships and floating steel, and consisting of concrete caissons and piers designed to rise and fall with the tide, the

MULBERRIES were supposed to permit enough unloading across the invasion beaches to keep the invasion alive. To the logisticians' view,

> It must be remembered that an amphibious landing is fundamentally a supply project rather than a tactical maneuver. For a few hours, while the assault troops are fighting on the beaches, tactics and logistics meet, but once the infantry begins to slash its way inland, the beach area ceases to be a battlefield and becomes a highly specialized port and depot whose main purpose is to insure a steady flow of supplies and reinforcements to the front.[7]

In terms of this interpretation, and given British doubts about the whole OVERLORD enterprise, it is no exaggeration to say that without the prospect of the MULBERRIES to permit the beaches to function as ports, Churchill and his government would probably have backed away from OVERLORD after all. Now a Channel storm wrecked the American MULBERRY beyond repair and put the other one out of service.

The literature of the invasion is replete with vivid descriptions of the fury of "the Great Storm." It was furious enough. Ninety ferrying craft and indeterminate numbers of larger vessels, in addition to MULBERRY A, were lost on OMAHA alone. Some 800 vessels were stranded on the American and British beaches. Still, Captain Robert C. Lee, USN, investigating for SHAEF G-4, concluded that the storm proved the dubiety of the artificial harbors, in effect that they had been an unsound project all along. The wind, Lee pointed out, had seldom exceeded Force 6—up to thirty miles an hour—which seamen describe as a "strong breeze," and never exceeded half-gale force—thirty-six miles an hour. "The Great Storm" was not a great storm measured against what could be expected from Channel weather.

Some materials were salvaged from MULBERRY A to put the British MULBERRY B eventually back into use. Still, after the British had come to believe and many Americans were persuaded that the MULBERRIES were indispensable to the invasion, to survey them smashed and useless as they were by June 21 was a hard fate. That day, General Collins issued orders for the climactic attack on Cherbourg, telling his VII Corps that a new urgency attended "the major effort of the American army."[8]

All three of Collins's divisions by now stood poised at the circumference of the Cherbourg fortifications, built by the French beginning generations ago and much strengthened by the Germans. During the night of June 21–22, Collins sent a surrender demand to General von Schlieben, but the deadline of nine in the morning of the 22nd passed without answer. In consequence, at 12:40 P.M., eighty minutes before H-Hour for Collins's infantry, the final assault on Cherbourg began with the most formidable Allied aerial operation since D-Day.

Major General Elwood R. "Pete" Quesada, commander of the Ninth Air Force's IX Tactical Air Command, was a rarity among senior AAF and RAF officers. In those air services, whose very existence as autonomous military commands sprang from the doctrine of strategic bombing as a force that could by itself win wars, Quesada was a proponent of close cooperation with the ground forces. Brereton had been brought from the Middle East largely because of his experience in support of the ground war there, in the theater where the RAF had also developed such doctrine as it cared to nourish on the subject. But Brereton nevertheless displayed scant enthusiasm for close aerial support of the ground campaign, and Leigh-Mallory cared still less. (Spaatz, though wholeheartedly a strategic bomber, was different, because he was never a man of dogma but always a pillar of common sense; the ground commanders found they could always talk with Spaatz, and the prevailing circumstances of air–ground communication were such as to make this a high tribute.) But Pete Quesada, who had won his spurs as a fighter commander in North Africa, was everything the ground soldiers looked for and could not find in most air commanders; and just as important, batting about from one airfield to another in a P-38, he communicated his attitudes to his subordinates. "Your airmen reflect your enthusiasm," Bradley told him, adding the more general observation: "I have yet to find a division commander with a division that is not just as good as he is."[9]

In the early days of the invasion, air support of ground operations was more cumbersome and less effective than usual because AEAF insisted on channelling requests from the beachhead back through air headquarters in England. Apart from the immediate delays caused by this system, it permitted little consultation and sharing of planning between ground and air. As soon as he found it feasible, however, on June 18, Quesada set up his advanced headquarters at Au Gay in Normandy, separated only by a hedgerow from Bradley's First Army headquarters.

Quesada worked mainly out of this advanced headquarters and in close contact with the ground command. He encouraged frequent visits to Bradley's G-2 and G-3 by his equivalent A-2 and A-3, and return visits from the First Army. Quesada helped whet Bradley's appetite for another concentrated application of air power to hurry along the land battle, and on June 21 Bradley, Collins, and Quesada met together, with the redoubled desire for Cherbourg suggesting the target.

Collins was already close enough to Cherbourg that everything had to be done in haste. With the main weight of Allied aerial command still in England, the final plans had to be fixed upon late in the day and flown across the Channel that night. At Ninth Air Force headquarters at Uxbridge, General Brereton and his staff coordinated preparations with AEAF and the Second Tactical Air Force, but with no representative of the ground command participating at this stage. General Spaatz offered the heavy bombers, but Brereton's planners rejected the offer with thanks because they perceived no suitable objectives. Collins wanted "air pulverization" of some twenty square miles, but the air commanders believed it would be more realistic to aim not at pulverizing resistance but simply at disruption of communications and demoralization of the garrison. Sometimes it was the ground commanders, not the airmen, who advanced exaggerated notions of what air power might be able to do. The airmen would employ 557 fighter-bombers and 396 mediums of the Ninth Air Force and 118 planes of the Second TAF, but they planned to drop only about 1,000 tons of bombs over the large target area, a relatively modest amount.

Collins's artillery laid on counterbattery fire against the German antiaircraft batteries and sought to mark the landward boundaries of aviation's target area with white smoke. In skies at last auspiciously clearing after the Great Storm, the Second TAF opened the air assault with six squadrons of strafing Mustangs and four of rocket-firing Hawker Typhoons covering the target area from west to east. Twelve groups of IX TAC fighter-bombers followed, bombing and strafing until five minutes before H-Hour. As the infantry began to advance at 2:00 P.M., all eleven groups of the IX Bomber Command took over with attacks on eleven strongpoints. Some twenty-nine planes fell to German flak, but there was no aerial opposition at all.

It was a spectacular fireworks display, but the VII Corps found the payoff disappointing, at least initially. Two regiments of the 9th Division and one of the 4th complained of strafing by friendly aircraft. According to General Bradley, "parts of the 9th Division were doggedly air shy" for the rest of the war.[10] When they began advancing after the air show, Collins's three divisions still made only scant progress through the rest of June 22 against three ridges anchoring the Cherbourg defenses. By nightfall, they scratched out a foothold on each, but they were having to make a fight for every pillbox—fighter-bombers and artillery driving the enemy into the shelter of the concrete bunkers and pillboxes, infantry advancing under artillery cover to within 300 or 400 meters of these emplacements, machine guns and antitank guns firing into the embrasures while demolition squads worked around to the rear doors, the demolition teams finally blowing up the doors and thrusting pole-charges and phosphorous grenades inside.

In retrospect, the aerial preparation came to seem more worthwhile, for the defenders though stubborn were evidently stunned, slower than usual in their reactions, and in a mood of despair. Bradley, in fact, began pondering a similar use of air power, but on a larger scale, when the time came to lunge out of the beachheads southward. During June 22, Hitler enjoined Cherbourg troops "to defend the last bunker and leave to the enemy not a harbor but a field of ruins. . . . The German people and the whole world are watching your fight," the Führer said; "on it depends the conduct and result of operations to smash the beachheads, and the honor of the German Army and of your own name."[11] But Collins's troops were taking not only German but also French, Russian, and Polish prisoners, whose compatriots probably had very little susceptibility to appeals to the honor of the German army. By June 23, resistance was noticeably weakening. The 12th Infantry of the 4th Division, hitherto barely moving against fortifications so thick that there were no routes wide enough to bring up tanks, found more open ground and attached two Shermans to each of the forward companies, whereupon the advance grew faster. On June 24, Collins's infantry closed in on the city itself, despite Schlieben's efforts to stimulate resistance by means of a promiscuous distribution of Iron Crosses specially flown in for the purpose.

On June 25, Rear Admiral Morton L. Deyo, to whom on June 15 Admiral Kirk had entrusted all naval gunfire support in the American sector, responded to Collins's surprisingly belated request for assistance by bringing in the battleships *Arkansas*, *Texas*, and *Nevada* along with four cruisers and their screening destroyers to duel with the guns of three of the German shore batteries and to fire at additional targets on call. Air spotting for the ships' guns was by RAF Spitfires, some of them flown by United States Navy pilots normally assigned to the big ships' Kingfisher observation planes and familiar with American naval procedures. In a contest of *Arkansas* and *Texas* against Battery Hamburg, four 280mm. (11-inch) guns well protected by steel shields and concrete casemates, *Texas* knocked out one of the 280mm. guns with a direct hit. But this was a lucky shot, and in general Cherbourg demonstrated once again the historic truism that because of the flat trajectories of naval guns and the relative instability of ships as gun platforms, duelling with shore batteries is not ideal employment for warships. Two hundred six

14-inch shells from *Texas*, fifty-eight 12-inch shells from *Arkansas*, and 552 5-inch shells from five destroyers left Battery Hamburg with its casemates pockmarked but, except for the one lucky hit, otherwise unharmed. Fortunately the ships emerged undamaged, but they had to maneuver violently at times to escape German salvos.

Still, the ships were more useful in on-call firing against lesser strongpoints such as batteries of 88s, and apparently the naval intervention was as demoralizing to the Germans as the earlier air attack. By the end of June 25, the Americans could reckon the German left and right as collapsed, while Wyche's 79th Division in the center, though meeting fanatical resistance at a strongpoint called Fort du Roule, had won part of the main defenses of the fort and was beginning to receive piecemeal surrenders. The next day, Eddy's 39th Infantry learned from a prisoner that General von Schlieben had his headquarters in a tunnel in the southern outskirts of the city. When the general refused a new surrender demand delivered directly to his shelter, tank destroyers began firing into two of the three tunnel entrances. A few rounds sufficed to flush out Schlieben, along with the naval commander for Normandy and about 800 other Germans. Schlieben still declined to order the capitulation of the rest of the Cherbourg fortress, but news of his capture helped precipitate the surrender of another 400 of the enemy later in the day around the city hall, and of Schlieben's deputy, Generalmajor Robert Sattler, with yet another 400 on June 27. With that, organized resistance in Cherbourg itself practically ended.

Eddy's 9th Division still had to fight hard for Cap de la Hague, the northwest tip of the Cotentin, where 6,000 prisoners were gathered in by the end of the month. Barton's 4th Division, taking over the whole of the city while the 79th Division went south to participate in new campaigns, had to mop up the last forts in the harbor, a task it completed by June 29. Considering the strength that the enemy concentrated in the Cotentin just before and immediately after D-Day—to the end of June, the VII Corps captured 39,042 prisoners—the capture of Cherbourg was achieved creditably close to the pre-D-Day First Army estimate of D plus fifteen days. The accomplishment reflected primarily the ability of the Americans to reinforce, while the Germans could not; after early June, the German command could give Schlieben little more than the shipment of Iron Crosses plus adjurations to resist fanatically. Gaining Cherbourg so early also reflected, however, the tireless drive of the commander of the VII Corps and the exceptional efficiency of the commander of the 9th Division under him. Eisenhower and Bradley could well conclude that neither Collins nor Eddy had yet reached the limit of his powers.

The achievement was to appear still greater in postwar retrospect, when the Allies learned that the Germans had counted on a much longer, if not indefinite, resistance despite their inability to reinforce. Their hopes of destroying the Anglo-American lodgment in France hung mainly upon their ability to deny the invaders a port, and they had believed that their concrete and steel coastal fortifications were equal to the challenge. Now they knew, as Rommel sorrowfully told Rundstedt, that "Even the strongest fortifications were demolished section by section," principally by "the massed operations of the enemy air force and naval activity."[12]

The Battle of the Buildup

Yet though Cherbourg had fallen, the Germans were not without comfort. Schlieben surrendered only after he assured the Seventh Army that the "Navy considers [Cherbourg] harbor has been destroyed for good."[13] Colonel Alvin G. Viney, author of the American plan to reopen the harbor, confirmed when he saw the place that "The demolition of the port of Cherbourg is a masterful job, beyond a doubt the most complete, intensive, and best-planned demolition in history."[14] Planning estimates based on the experience of reopening the port of Naples after German demolition—which was accomplished within three days—proved absurdly inapplicable.

The enemy had strewn Cherbourg harbor with a variety of mines, blocked all port basins with sunken ships, destroyed all cranes, demolished the Gare Maritime which housed the electrical control system and heating plant for the port, and blown 18,000 cubic meters of masonry into the deep basin that had housed the transatlantic liners. The work of rehabilitating the harbor began before the last forts surrendered, but it was to be months before Cherbourg could handle cargo in quantity.

The Allies had come to Normandy to get ports, but they did not have ports—at least not in the condition they expected. Furthermore, stiff German resistance on or near the coast had caused unloading across the beaches to fall behind schedule. At OMAHA, beach unloading had to compete for nearly a week after D-Day with persistent and unanticipated chaos, because the foothold remained exceeedingly narrow. During the first three days, unloading at OMAHA proceeded at little more than a quarter of the anticipated level. At UTAH, the ease of the first landings and of capturing the causeways permitted unloading as early as D plus 2 probably to exceed the planned estimate of 3,300 tons for the day; but the delay in capturing the ridge to the north kept the beach and thus unloading activities under at least sporadic artillery fire until June 14, and delayed the expansion of the organizing facilities necessary for proper handling of supplies. The same slow movement inland that hampered use of the beaches also reduced demand for certain kinds of supplies, notably petroleum, but heavy resistance meanwhile increased the need for other supplies. By June 12 the Americans were facing a shortage of some important calibers of ammunition, particularly 155mm. shells.

Prospects seemed to improve toward the end of the second week. On D plus 9, June 15, the target for supplies unloaded at OMAHA and UTAH was actually exceeded, 15,000 tons for the day against a planned 13,700. By D plus 12, June 18, combined daily discharges at the two beaches were averaging about 14,500 tons, just below expectations. By that date, accumulated discharges had reached 72.8 percent of the tonnage planned, 116,065 as against 159,350 tons, and there was much hope of catching up. The Americans had 314,504 troops and 41,000 vehicles ashore. The British had landed 102,000 tons of supplies, 314,547 troops, and 54,000 vehicles. MULBERRY A was in partial operation.

Then came the Great Storm and the dismaying completeness of the demolition of the port of Cherbourg. The storm destroyed hopes of remedying the ammunition shortage and left the specter of insufficient artillery ammunition if a crisis should arise to haunt the Americans for weeks, even months. Only a three-day supply was on hand in First Army dumps when the storm abated. Bradley had to call off a southward attack by the VIII Corps to assure enough ammunition for Collins's drive on Cherbourg. He also limited the

V and the newly operational XIX Corps each to twenty-five 155mm. rounds per day, and even cut Collins's allowance for the Cherbourg offensive by one-third.

One redemptive element in this crisis over ports and supplies had begun to develop, fortunately, before the storm. It had helped produce the optimism of the second week and at least slightly relieved subsequent pessimism. It was that the beaches themselves, once cleared of enemy fire and the chaos of frantic and thus nearly indiscriminate unloading of supplies, proved far more satisfactory ports than the Allies had expected. Under pressure of the initial disruptions of unloading schedules, LSTs began to be "dried out" on the beaches, as early as D plus 2 on OMAHA and D plus 3 on UTAH. That is, the ships were grounded on a falling tide and unloaded directly on the beach, then refloated by the rising tide. This method, urged by army officers in both the V and VII Corps, had been rejected by the naval planners for fear that ground inequalities on the beaches would break the ships' backs. But the ships survived. More than 200 LSTs were dried out on OMAHA in the first two weeks without damage, with immense saving of time by avoiding the use of ferrying craft. As the storm abated on June 22, five coasters bearing ammunition were beached on OMAHA to be unloaded directly into trucks. On June 23, amidst the work of clearing the wreckage left by the storm, 10,000 tons were unloaded on OMAHA and 6,400 on UTAH. In the last week of the month, OMAHA unloaded an average of 13,500 tons a day, UTAH 7,000 tons—113 percent and 124 percent, respectively, of planned capacity. Without benefit of a MULBERRY—though with the MULBERRY breakwater of sunken ships offshore (called GOOSEBERRY) subsequently strengthened—OMAHA and UTAH Beaches long remained the principal American ports. In July, there were to average together 15,680 tons a day, almost exactly fulfilling the schedule anticipated had MULBERRY A remained. For months, the beaches overshadowed Cherbourg.

With a few minor ports, mainly Isigny and Grandcamp, added to the beaches, American unloadings in July were to average 17,875 tons daily. Still, the planned total capacity of American-held ports for July was to have been 725,000 tons, and only 446,852 tons were actually discharged during the month. General von Schlieben had cause for satisfaction with the Cherbourg demolitions, and the lag in unloading was yet to hinder escape from the constricting land of the hedgerows into which the Americans had come in search of a port. Meanwhile, the search for a port had monopolized American attentions and activities perhaps excessively.

The Allies had assured more than amply that the greatest amphibious assault of history had received the lavishly detailed planning it merited, generated alike by American enthusiasm for the project and by British misgivings and fears of failure. Nevertheless, however essential it may be, the most careful of planning still bears its own dangers of fostering rigidity. Concentration upon attaining planned objectives may divert attention from other opportunities. It is even possible to anticipate too carefully the enemy's likely responses, and then to be blind to reality when the enemy fails to perform according to the plans drawn up in his behalf.

Because the OVERLORD planners rightly emphasized that outracing the Germans in the buildup of men and matériel in Normandy would become the critical contest to accomplish control of the province once ashore, the capture of Cherbourg had received its priority as the first major objective of the American army beyond OMAHA and UTAH Beaches. In assigning this objective to the urgent and aggressive Lightning Joe Collins of the VII Corps, Eisenhower and Bradley made almost an inspired choice of the right commander to win a victory that had to be swift, to give them Cherbourg with the requisite speed despite both determined enemy resistance and the hesitancy inevitably accompanying the first movements inland by largely inexperienced troops. And yet, the knowledge in hindsight that Cherbourg would be long in regaining utility anyway induces reflection upon what Collins's style of leadership might have accomplished elsewhere on the Normandy battlefront. The Anglo-Americans were not always so aggressive as he was. And there were times and places that cried out for unhesitating, driving leadership to snatch unplanned-for opportunities, and to exploit the enemy's neglect to do always what the Allied planners expected of him.

The Caumont Gap

Late on June 7, another old Regular Army division began landing on OMAHA, Major General Walter M. Robertson's 2nd. Like the Big Red One beside which it took up its positions, the 2nd boasted a proud First World War record—it was the division of Belleau Wood—and had appeared on the active roster without interruption since 1917. On June 8, Major Hansen noted, "everywhere along the road you can see the distinctive Indian head of the 2nd Inf. which they have placed on their fatigues." By midday of June 9, the division was operational in the V Corps center between the 1st and 29th Divisions. Its initial objective was the Forêt de Cerisy astride the Bayeux-St. Lô road, high ground that dominated the OMAHA beachhead and seemed a likely assembly area for a German counterattack. By late the next day, to the surprise of V Corps and First Army headquarters, the 2nd had already crossed through the forest. German opposition in front of it had almost evaporated, and only twice during June 10 did the division so much as hear enemy artillery.

On the left of the Indian Head Division, the Big Red One was experiencing a similar disintegration of the opposing front during June 10 and 11. Thus the 1st advanced with surprising ease and rapidity toward a still more dominating height than the Forêt de Cerisy, in fact the most important objective between the road junctions of St. Lô and Caen, the bold hill of Caumont. American possession of this hill would drive deep into the German Seventh Army's defensive front a salient exploitable toward either of the latter road junctions, the anchors of the German line. Yet the German defense had lost its stubbornness, where it had not completely disappeared. The V Corps had entered upon the full benefits of the earlier German collapse on both flanks of the 352nd Division, which left that initially stubborn enemy formation with its flanks in thin air even as the failure of reinforcement exhausted its own troops. As early as the night of June 9–10, the 352nd was in full retreat southwestward, refusing its right, toward the line of the little Elle River in front of St. Lô.

The First Army did not, however, envisage for General Gerow's V Corps an advance as urgent as Collins's against Cherbourg. Furthermore, the OVERLORD planners had anticipated that by this stage in the invasion, the enemy would surely be assembling his armored and motorized troops for a counterstroke. If such a stroke were to develop against the American front, almost certainly it would not voluntarily entangle itself in the inundations farther west but would hit the V Corps, where it could move in concert with the panzer formations already in action to the eastward against the British. First Army headquarters, with its eyes focused on Cherbourg, and fearful of any other commitment that might prove to be an expensive diversion, thus continually warned the V Corps of the likelihood of a strong enemy countermove on the Forêt de Cerisy-Caumont front. Responding to rumors gleaned from prisoners and civilians as well as to its own fears, First Army G-2 passed on to the V Corps reports of large enemy concentrations in the Forêt de Cerisy even as the 2nd Division was pushing readily through the forest. "No surprise should be occasioned should this cover produce an armored or motorized division," Colonel Dickson's office cautioned late on June 9,[15] and the notion of a waiting armored concentration persisted.

Then, after June 10, the 1st Division began to make contact with troops of the 17th SS "Götz von Berlichingen" Panzer Grenadier Division. It was easy for intelligence to believe its suspicions were confirmed. Nevertheless, the First Army prescribed a renewal of the V Corps advance toward Caumont on June 12. But because General Huebner of the 1st Division feared that the 17th SS might attack the right flank of his advance, because he knew that the Panzer Lehr Division was by now operating against the British on his immediate left, and because a gap eventually opening to twelve kilometers was developing between his left and the British in that very sector, he restricted his troops to a cautious advance by phase lines. The 1st Division was to pause to prepare for defense at each successive phase line and, except for aggressive reconnaissance, was to progress from one phase line to the next only on divisional orders. Huebner and Gerow impressed their worries upon Bradley, who responded by making the newly arrived 2nd Armored Division available as a reserve behind the Caumont salient; but this assurance had hardly been received before one of the 2nd Armored's combat commands had to be shunted westward to deal with a threat to the V Corps-VII Corps linkup at Carentan. This threat seemed to pose still more reason for caution about a coming enemy counterstroke.

As the 1st Division shifted into low gear for a slow and methodical advance, Gerow's headquarters instructed the 2nd and 29th Divisions to tailor their advances to conformity with the 1st, but with objectives echeloned to the right rear for yet more caution. Gerow felt this fastidiousness about his right especially necessary because he could get little reassurance from the British about the safety of his left. General Montgomery's latest planning made the potential importance of Caumont all the greater, but little in Gerow's neighbors' actions reflected such a turn in 21 Army Group thinking.

Having failed to achieve the planned capture of Caen on D-Day, General Dempsey's Second Army had spent the intervening days in futile direct assaults upon the city. By June 9, Montgomery decided to shift to an indirect approach against Caen, specifically to drive with his right from Bayeux through Tilly-sur-Seulles to Villers-Bocage on the Caen-Avranches highway, then to drop the 1st Airborne Division south of Caen to link up with the Villers-Bocage force around Evrécy, and thus to envelop Caen. American possession of the high ground at Caumont would shield the right flank of this maneuver.

For the drive through Tilly to Villers-Bocage, Montgomery chose the 7th Armoured Division, the most famous of all the constituent formations of his old Eighth Army. Once the solitary armored force to face the enemies of the British Empire in the Middle East, this creation of General Hobart's had contended with Marshal Graziani and then with Rommel and the Panzerarmee Afrika through the Western Desert campaigns from Sidi Barrani onward. Unfortunately, the Desert Rats of the 7th Armoured found the constrictions of the Bocage peculiarly oppressive after the vast expanses of open terrain to which North Africa had accustomed them. Also unfortunately, they were victims of the British tendency toward overspecialized, separate cavalry and infantry tank types. They were equipped with Cromwells, cavalry "cruiser" tanks designed for swiftness, sometimes satisfactory in the desert, but inappropriate to the Norman hedgerows and to combat with German battle tanks. The Cromwell shared with the Sherman the disadvantage of a short 75mm. (6-pounder) gun; its weakness in armor made it even less a match for German tanks than the Sherman. The 2nd Armoured Brigade, leading the 7th Armoured Division, made good progress southward, swinging west of Tilly and around the flank of Panzer Lehr on June 12, and sending its leading tank squadron through Villers-Bocage on the morning of the 13th; but east of the village, the Cromwells met Tigers.

The panzers isolated and destroyed the leading Cromwells something over a kilometer northeast of Villers-Bocage on the road toward Caen. During the afternoon, the British managed to repulse several tank attacks on Villers-Bocage itself. These attacks were mounted by elements of the 2nd Panzer Division, a disconcerting new presence that the American 1st Division had also encountered, beginning the previous afternoon when the 26th Infantry Regiment reached the edge of the town of Caumont. Meanwhile, around Tilly, on the left of the 7th Armoured, the 50th Northumbrian Division was achieving no progress against Panzer Lehr. In this situation the commander of 30 Corps, Lieutenant General G.C. Bucknall, perceived the 7th Armoured, strung out snakelike from just east of Caumont to Villers-Bocage, as perilously exposed. Despite the arrival of fragments of the 2nd Panzers, there was still not much weight in front of the Americans on his right; so he might just as well have perceived it as a saber embedded deep into the German front. But instead of reinforcing the relative success of the 7th Armoured, Bucknall tried to spur on the 50th Division in its frontal assaults upon Panzer Lehr to the east, thus to bring the 50th abreast of the Desert Rats. He was not in a sanguine mood, however, because when he returned to his headquarters from a visit to the 7th Armoured late on June 13, both of his escort tanks were, as he announced with agitation to his staff, "knocked out by a Tiger."[16] When the 50th Division failed again on the morning of June 14, Bucknall was psychologically prepared to withdraw the 7th Armoured from its salient and back to the neighborhood of Caumont. He did so.

That day Gerow conferred with Bradley. As Major Hansen described it:

> Gerow worried about his 1st Div salient, fears that counterattacks may squeeze from right and left. . . . 50th Div (assailed and tired) are back seven miles, opening Gerow's left flank to attack. Brit 7th armored moved down through 1st Div sector to front, hooked off to the left in a long enveloping move to take objectives and cut off e[nem]y but attack has not progressed. . . . Get more sense of a drive among Amerks than you will among Brits. Gerow: "I'm worried. I wanted to show it to you and see if it looks the same to you that it does to me. He may come in through here (St. Germain d Elle and Barigny and bet. St. Paul du Verna and Caumont) pinch off that stuff and sweep me up. I've got nothing in depth, nothing to stop him with." Wants CC "A" and tanks now with paratroops [of the 101st Airborne around Carentan] in their effort. But Taylor also needs them there. Brad: "Yes, I know. I'm worried about that too. But I just had to send [Brigadier General Maurice] Rose and CC "A" of the 2nd Armored to Carentan until that situation clears up. They've hit tanks there. He may try to hit us in the center, break through and destroy the flexibility we now have."[17]

It was the bulk of the 17th ss Panzer Grenadier Division that had shown up in the counterattack against the V Corps-VII Corps juncture between Isigny and Carentan, rather than in front of Caumont as expected; but this development simply renewed Bradley's concern that there should be no diversion from the main effort of the First Army, Collins's drive against Cherbourg. So the 1st and 2nd Divisions received new orders to conduct aggressive patrolling and give the enemy the impression that they intended continued offensive efforts, while actually finding suitable defensive positions and digging in.

History has called the affair that of "the Caumont Gap." Notwithstanding the frequent success of Allied intelligence in discovering the enemy order of battle, the Anglo-American armies evidently did not know that on June 10 a front of more than fifteen kilometers, from the right of the 352nd Division around Berigny on the St. Lô-Bayeux road, to the left of Panzer Lehr just west of Tilly, was held only by the Reconnaissance Battalion of the 17th SS Panzer Grenadiers—the force whose discovery fueled fears of a counterattack by that entire division. During June 10, a reinforced regiment of the 3rd Parachute Division narrowed the gap slightly by extending the right of the 352nd to St. Germain d'Elle. The 2nd Panzer Division, whose arrival the Germans had hoped for much earlier, did not begin to throw any appreciable strength into action in the gap until June 12. The 2nd Panzers had to travel from Amiens. Like so many earlier German reinforcements, they were harried from the air as they moved, and not until June 13 were they able to counterattack the 7th Armoured. Even then, they struck with two infantry regiments supported by two battalions of artillery but with no tanks. At least the hill of Caumont paid a dividend during this action, because V Corps artillery firing from the heights helped break up the assault upon the British. But after General Bucknall decided to reinforce the failures of his 50th Division instead of the successes of the 7th Armoured, and withdrew the Desert Rats from Villers-Bocage, it was to take another six weeks for the Allies to return to the latter place. The opportunity for envelopment lost, the battle for Caen meanwhile ran a costly and controversial course, encouraging the Americans' feeling of "more sense of a drive among Amerks than you will [find] among Brits." But the cautiousness was not all British.

There were a number of reasons why the Caumont Gap beckoned to the V and 30 Corps, and the Germans remained desperately short of reinforcements to hem in the Allied lodgment. Not only did German troops advancing toward the front have to run gauntlets of aerial and French Resistance harassment, and to cross the unbridged Seine and Loire. Through June, the Germans of their own volition continued to hold eighteen divisions of their Fifteenth Army in the Pas de Calais. The few divisions brought to Normandy from north of the Seine during the first few days were replaced in the Pas de Calais by additional divisions from Norway and Denmark. Only at the end of June did the Germans move an additional panzer division and two infantry divisions from the Fifteenth Army westward across the Seine.

The German military command, having believed before June 6 that the invasion must strike the Pas de Calais, refused to change their minds. They convinced themselves that the Normandy invasion had to be a mere feint, designed to draw their strength away from the more vital Kanalküste north of the Seine, and they determined that they would not be misled. Hitler strangely abandoned his pre-D-Day intuition about Normandy and applauded their resolve—an instance in striking confirmation of Albert Speer's judgment that the Führer's leadership deteriorated when he forsook intuition for reason.

Wishful thinking helped keep so much German attention fixed on the Pas de Calais. On the night of June 12–13, their Flak Regiment 155 at last commenced the V-weapon offensive against England. The difficulties of completing preparations in the face of the Allies' CROSSBOW attacks prevented launching the grand opening salvo of sixty-four V-1 flying bombs that the Germans desired. Instead, only ten V-1s were fired the first night, of which four crashed immediately, two simply vanished, and only four reached England, one falling in Sussex, the others near Gravesend, near Sevenoaks, and at Bethnal Green. But within three days, the Germans were able to send off 244 V-1s inside twenty-four hours. Their barrage, mainly hitting London, took 2,752 lives in its first three weeks.

The Allies wondered why the V-bombs had not been used against the concentrations of invasion troops and shipping, but the moral strain of the new "blitz" was heavy in a London so recently relaxed by the happy news of D-Day. The Germans felt sure that if the Allies had not already planned an invasion of the Pas de Calais, the V-1s would oblige them to do it. As the Germans yielded hope of forcing the Normandy landings back into the sea, they even yearned for new landings on the Kanalküste. Hitting where they were best prepared, such landings ought surely to fail, and in their failure carry the Normandy beachheads away with them.

After all, as the Germans saw it, the Anglo-Americans possessed ample strength to mount additional landings on the Continent. As Allied intelligence was pleasantly aware, the Germans were continuing to buy the Allied deception operations codenamed first JAEL and then BODYGUARD, which had helped considerably to divert the enemy's attention from the Norman coast before D-Day and were now performing the still more remarkable feat of diverting attention from Normandy after D-Day. These operations included the ZEPPELIN activities that threatened an invasion of the Balkans and contributed to the Germans' stationing twenty-six divisions there by the eve of D-Day. They included Operation FORTITUDE's gestures toward a Norway invasion, so that in early 1944 the Germans had sixteen divisions there and in Denmark. Most important of all, the BODYGUARD activities included the main FORTITUDE deception scheme to misguide the enemy about the time and place of the principal Allied thrust into France. The pièce de resistance of FORTITUDE remained the fictitious placement of the most successful and famous American combat commander, George S. Patton, at the head of an additional United States army group, poised to fulfill the enemy's expectations about the Pas de Calais.

7: The Bocage

UPON HOLDING as many Germans as possible in the Pas de Calais as long as possible hinged issues greater than maintaining the local numerical superiority that the V Corps enjoyed just after D-Day. The FORTITUDE deception was also wedded closely to the prospect of a breakout from the Normandy beachhead.

When he spoke at St. Paul's School, the euphoria of the auspicious occasion may have tempted General Montgomery into excessively optimistic remarks forecasting a tank knockabout toward Falaise. But Montgomery never gave voice to mere casual speculation. His idea of a tank knockabout had firm roots in the OVERLORD planners' conception of a breakout. If they could establish their beachhead, the Allies from the beginning intended to attempt as their next step a breakthrough to rupture whatever defenses the Germans could form against the beachhead, followed by exploitation in a breakout from Normandy deep into France. Planning beyond the amphibious assault was not as thorough as it should have been, but breakthrough and breakout appeared consistently on the Anglo-American planners' agenda.

Almost as much as they feared failure to win a foothold on the continent, the American and especially the British governments feared a stabilizing of the Norman battlefront around the beachhead. A stabilized battle implied a return to the old Western Front, the Somme and Passchendaele all over again. This stabilization was the grim prospect against which the ghosts of 1916 cried out so piercingly to Winston Churchill. It was the prospect, too, against which the planners labored to prepare a breakout from Normandy.

The Breakout Issue

Stabilization was the more frighteningly real a prospect—and the continued success of FORTITUDE the more vital—because the demands of the logistical buildup of the beachhead in matériel, the limitations of British manpower, and the design of the American army all combined to assure the Germans a superiority in military manpower in France during a considerable period after the cross-Channel invasion, even should the Allies otherwise forge ahead in the race for the buildup.

> If the Germans are not compelled to withdraw formations from the West to the Russian front [said a SHAEF G-3 estimate on May 31, 1944], and if they suffer no extremely heavy losses, it is unlikely that the Allies will have superiority in infantry until at least D plus 200. Even at this time superiority will not be gained if the Germans are able to bring further reinforcements to the west by evacuation of Norway, Italy, etc.[1]

In spite of this handicap, the same SHAEF estimate argued, the Anglo-American armies must achieve a breakthrough to permit breakout conditions in which they could exploit their advantages in realms other than infantry manpower, and particularly to exploit their mobility:

> . . . we shall be superior to the enemy in air power, sea power, airborne lift and armour; but NOT in infantry; and . . . we must exploit this superiority to the full by bringing the enemy to battle in good tank country, by using "end run" operations, by "canalising" enemy communications by attacks on bridges over the numerous river lines and by using airborne forces to the full.
> . . . .
> It follows, therefore, that we must do out utmost to prevent a German withdrawal "according to plan," as our advance North-Eastwards would then be conducted against an enemy who would exploit the numerous and traditional river lines to delay our advance and who would be little inferior in defensive warfare. Such a situation would be likely to result in prolonged delays in our advance due to the necessity for mounting a series of major river crossing operations.
> Our object must be to force the enemy to fight on ground favourable to armoured forces and in front of areas where communications offer suitable targets for our superior air power. After every such action we should use our air and armoured forces to harass the enemy's retreat and give him no time to reform, at the same time using our airborne forces to facilitate the crossing of river and other natural obstacles.[2]

On April 15, the Supreme Commander at last had ordered his naval and air commands and the SHAEF staff divisions to prepare a series of forecasts of developments following NEPTUNE. The resulting documents consistently emphasized the fear and peril of a stabilized front enclosing the Normandy lodgment. On June 10 there appeared a staff study addressed specifically to avoiding stabilization. It offered three possible remedies if stabilization should begin to set in: an amphibious or airborne operation to effect a deep envelopment of the enemy front, an amphibious or airborne operation in direct support of a breakout offensive, or a concentration of "all possible air and ground forces for a determined effort to force a breakout from the bridgehead itself."[3] In the absence of numerical superiority on the ground, except possibly in localized actions, the planners looked to air power as a decisive element in the breakout:

> The Allied air forces are so powerful that is is probable that they could create the situation necessary for a tactical break out from the stabilised area, provided all their efforts were concentrated on the task for the requisite time. The method of producing this situation would be by paralysing the enemy's lines of communication and disrupting his reinforcement programme, combined with heavy attacks on the troops containing the beach-head in order to shatter their will to resist. This air action will be combined with a maximum effort at a break through on the part of the ground forces.

Thus the planners chose the third option as the means to break through and break out from a stabilized front: "In the event of stabilisation the best course would be to concentrate the Allied air effort in conjunction with a determined offensive by the land forces to force a break out from within the bridgehead itself."[4]

On May 7, SHAEF had begun the practice of sending the War Department in

Washington a weekly planning cable to provide regular outlines of the progress of planning. Once NEPTUNE was ashore, these cables indicated the prompt turning of the planners' attention to breakthrough and breakout. Weekly Planning Cable 8 of June 22 reported that for the preceding week, in addition to possible airborne seizure of a Breton port, planning had been directed to:

> Examination, particularly from a logistical point of view, of a plan to exploit a deterioration in German ability to resist our advance from OVERLORD bridgehead. Exploitation to consist of an all out drive from the bridgehead towards the Seine in an effort to defeat the German forces before they cross the Seine: followed up by the forcing of the Seine and capture of Seine ports. . . .
>
> Study as to best method of crossing the Seine as a first step in post-NEPTUNE advance.[5]

Caen

Where was the breakthrough to occur? From what sector of the Allied bridgehead should the breakout leap forward?

Following the war, when he was a field marshal rich in honors, Viscount Montgomery of Alamein made it his custom to claim that his victorious battles had gone always and altogether according to plan. Thus he made yet more a virtue of his reputation as the forever-careful planning general, the sovereign of the set piece. In this manner, Montgomery stated in 1946 that the OVERLORD planning always contemplated only a holding action in the British sector around Caen. The British were to act out sufficiently convincing threats of a breakthrough to draw upon themselves the bulk of German reinforcements, and especially of armor. Thereupon the Americans would be able to mount the real Allied breakthrough and breakout farther west. The Allies would "threaten to break out of the initial bridgehead on the eastern flank—that is, in the Caen sector . . . draw the main enemy reserves into that sector . . . keep them there . . . [and] make the break-out on the western flank, using for this task the American armies under General Bradley."

He went on to say that

> strong and persistent offensive action in the Caen sector would achieve our objective drawing the enemy mobile reserves on to our eastern flank. This was my original conception of the manner in which the Battle of Normandy was to be developed. From the start it formed the basis of all our planning, and was the aim of our operations from the time of the assault to the final victory in Normandy. I never once had cause or reason to alter my plan.[6]

In 1958, in his *Memoirs*, Viscount Montgomery similarly wrote:

> My master plan for the land battle in Normandy I have described already. Briefly, it was so to stage and conduct operations that we drew the main enemy strength on the front of the Second British Army on our eastern flank, in order that we might the more easily gain territory in the west and make the ultimate break-out on that flank—using the First American Army for that purpose. . . .
>
> I never once had cause or reason to alter my master plan.[7]

By 1968, nearly a quarter-century after the great invasion and following considerable critical dissection or the Normandy battle, Montgomery was hedging these assertions slightly in his *History of Warfare*. Following another repetition that his plan was "so to conduct the land battle that the British would draw the main German strength . . . to fight it and keep it there," Montgomery softened absolute fulfillment in favor of saying merely: "So, more or less, the battle developed."[8]

More or less. His remarks over the relief map at St. Paul's School, predicting an early tank knockabout from Caen to Falaise, suggest that the really appropriate word is "less." So does the concentration of the first Allied armored formations to be landed in the Second Army, not the First Army. The British would promptly have three armored divisions plus seven independent tank brigades, in contrast to two armored divisions for the Americans—a British edge of two to one in armor. The Americans would not be strongly equipped for armored warfare until late July. By that time, even the planning that Montgomery committed to paper—he was always careful to guard what the written record would show he had promised in advance—had the Second Army thrusting well beyond Falaise to Argentan and Alençon: just as though the tank strength of the Second Army was intended not only to attract and then hold off the enemy's panzers, but to engage in the sort of armored offensive that Montgomery had suggested at St. Paul's School.

More or less, Montgomery went to Normandy with such a master plan as he said he had for what to do once ashore—bearing in mind that the overwhelming preoccupation of most of the Allied planners before June 6 was simply with getting ashore and staying there, and that while there was a determination to escape a stabilized front by means of breakthrough and breakout, these ideas received little attention compared with the NEPTUNE amphibious assault. The COSSAC plans that preceded Montgomery's arrival at 21 Army Group called for the British to stage a major offensive effort through Caen, to deny the Germans that road junction for their lateral movements against the Americans' Cherbourg drive, to utilize the port of Caen, and most important, to achieve the most direct possible release from the entanglement of the Bocage, launching Allied mobility into the open country beyond Caen and also onto the shortest road to Paris. In addition, there were the excellent airfield sites of the Caen-Falaise plain. General Morgan more than the larger planning staffs that took over from COSSAC had maintained a cautious awareness of the hedgerow problem waiting behind the Normandy beaches, and his proposal to advance into the rolling plain to the eastward reflected his concern about the hedgerows. When Montgomery arrived in England, however, he characteristically removed from the written plans any explicit commitment to mount the principal Allied offensive from the Second Army sector. Instead he began pointing to the likelihood of a panzer buildup against the Allied left. Yet while removing any commitment or promise that he would achieve the breakthrough around Caen, Montgomery obviously went on contemplating the possibility.

Thus, Caen itself remained a D-Day objective of the Second Army. The NEPTUNE Initial Joint Plan of February 1, 1944 still stated that the immediate postinvasion mission of the Second Army was to penetrate south of the line Caen-St. Lô to gain airfield sites, as well as to protect the First Army's Cherbourg drive. Phase lines drawn at 21 Army Group on February 26 still showed the Second Army beyond Argentan and in Alençon by D plus 25. Certainly it was General Eisenhower's impression that Montgomery intended a major offensive effort on the Allies' eastern flank, not merely an absorption of German reserves. Montgomery later claimed that this impression was a mistaken one flowing from

Eisenhower's lack of combat experience and strategic grasp—by implication, from his obtuseness; but the record of Montgomery's own statements and activities before and after D-Day should have led anyone to the same conclusion as Eisenhower's.

When the Second Army's first push ashore and immediately subsequent grapplings with the 21st and soon the 12th ss Panzer Divisions failed to win Caen, Montgomery on June 8 nevertheless instructed General Dempsey "to develop operations with all possible speed for the capture of Caen."[9] When head-on efforts did not suffice, Montgomery devised the right hook through Villers-Bocage to envelop Caen. When 30 Corps's failure to complete the right hook caused cancellation of the airborne drop that would have sealed the envelopment, Montgomery returned to a major frontal assault. During this period General Eisenhower expressed his disappointment at the delay before Caen and kept urging Montgomery to hasten on to the early capture and—more to the point—the exploitation that the Supreme Commander had been led to expect. "The Chief of Staff tells me the attack is to start tomorrow morning after a forty-eight hour delay," Eisenhower wrote Montgomery on June 18 regarding a projected new attack. "I can well understand that you have needed to accumulate reasonable amounts of artillery ammunition but I am in high hopes that once the attack starts it will have a momentum that will carry it a long ways."[10]

The Great Storm frustrated this particular set of high hopes, but Montgomery rescheduled the attack for June 25. This time the newly operational British 8 Corps was to open an enveloping drive midway between Tilly and Caen with two infantry divisions supported by a tank brigade and by the 11th Armoured Division. Once this advance was well underway, 1 Corps was to join in and squeeze Caen with attacks both immediately east and west of the city. Montgomery promised Eisenhower a "blitz attack."[11]

Under yet more rainfall, which curtailed air support, the British blitz turned out to consist of only slight gains of a few kilometers. The Second Army nevertheless kept plugging away at the attack until June 29, when the Germans opened a counterattack spearheaded by the 9th ss Panzer Division, one of the two divisions of the II ss Panzer Corps newly arrived from eastern Europe.

Drawing this additional powerful formation upon the Second Army indicated that Montgomery was amply fulfilling the defensive purposes that his caution had left as the only plainly stated part of the British mission. This was the more true in that Allied intelligence believed, correctly, that Rommel wanted to draw armor out of his front-line defenses in favor of infantry. Rommel hoped to concentrate his panzers as a mobile reserve, so he could eventually stage the kind of large-scale counterstroke that had so far been prevented by Allied aerial and French Resistance interference with the panzer divisions' movement to Normandy, and by the necessity to commit formations piecemeal to stem one emergency after another. But every gesture toward pulling German armor into reserve was promptly frustrated by renewed British pressure against Caen and the direct road to Paris. Allied intelligence estimates also approximated the facts that by the end of June seven and a half panzer divisions confronted the British while only half a panzer division faced the Americans. One hundred fifty serviceable heavy tanks, including Tigers and the new, yet more strongly armored King Tigers, and 250 medium tanks were opposite the Second Army, while only twenty-six Panthers counted as heavies and fifty mediums opposed the First Army.

Nevertheless, SHAEF remained disappointed. On June 30, the day following the 9th SS Panzers' counterattack at Caen, Montgomery issued a new directive that more clearly than any previous statement anticipated his postwar version of planning and events. He emphasized the holding mission of the Second Army so firmly, and so emphatically laid responsibility for major offensive progress upon Bradley's First Army, that he seemed as never before to concede that an early tank advance into the Caen-Falaise plain would not occur. As Eisenhower's chief of staff, General Walter Bedell Smith, described it: "By June 30th the British Army had *not* captured Caen, and now Montgomery issued his first directive that showed *an intention of holding on the left and breaking through on the right*. He directed the British forces to contain the greatest possible part of the enemy forces."[12] Montgomery and his defenders would say that Smith's reference to a "first" directive showing an intention merely to hold on the left demonstrated that Smith like Eisenhower misunderstood everything Montgomery had said until now. But while Eisenhower's manner could sometimes—deceptively—suggest slow mental processes, his chief of staff has so rarely been accused of sluggishness in any degree that the notion of his misconstruing Montgomery for months carries no conviction whatever.

In any event, contrary to his postwar assertions, Montgomery's headquarters was still planning at the end of June for the British eventually to accomplish the breakout. On June 27, the planning section of 21 Army Group had issued an outline of Operation LUCKY STRIKE, a "general operation to exploit enemy weakness by drawing east with our major forces."[13] The staff appreciation outlining LUCKY STRIKE anticipated Montgomery's directive of three days later by conceding that steady attacks by the Americans in the Bocage would have to precede a new major effort eastward. The Americans must join in the work of depleting the enemy's armor as well as his strength generally, and because the Bocage offered the Germans so many opportunities for delaying actions, it must "be our object to drive the enemy out of as much of the 'bocage' area as possible prior to the drive east so that the mobility of all forces may be exploited to the utmost and thereby our chances of preventing the enemy's escape increased."[14] Once the Americans had thus weakened the enemy and cleared the greater part of the Bocage, however, the British would take up the main offensive burden. If the Germans' strength deteriorated enough to invite a breakout effort, but the enemy retained relatively strong formations between the Loire and a line Laval-le Mans-Chartres, then "From the firm base as outlined [Montgomery would] drive east with First Canadian Army, Second British Army and a portion of First US Army, with the rest of the First US Army holding the Southern flank. . . ."[15] If the enemy's strength had altogether deteriorated north of the Loire and west of Laval, then an armored thrust along the north bank of the Loire would be added to the scheme; but the major participants would remain the First Canadian Army, the Second British Army, and only a portion of the First American Army.

The object remained breakthrough followed by breakout.

> The present appreciation of the enemy's intentions [said the 21 Army Group planners] shows that he is prepared to engage our forces in a decisive battle along the present beach-head lines in the effort to contain us. Such action by the enemy may give us the opportunity to deal him a decisive defeat in the near future. . . .
> There is a comparatively small number of enemy infantry formations engaged in the beach-head battle and these are not of a high standard of training or

equipment. This has the effect of requiring the use of Panzer formations to hold forward lines in the 'bocage' country or to react piecemeal to our successes. . . .[16]

Unless the enemy can improve his situation, the opportunity may arise for dealing him a major defeat on the beach-head line or in the 'bocage' and then, by the means of a rapid drive towards the east, with maximum forces, of destroying the balance of his mobile and high-grade formations before they cross the Seine or escape through the Paris-Orleans gap. If we move boldly to pursue our advantages, a considerable shortening in the war may result. . . .[17]

Having reached the Seine with our main thrust, and having destroyed what enemy forces we have trapped, [the intent is] to force a crossing with the least possible delay and secure the Seine ports and a sufficient area to guarantee their safe repair and operation.[18]

If our operations to this point [the crossing of the Seine] have been successful, the enemy should be so disorganised as to permit additional pursuit within maintenance limitations by the balance of Second British Army and by a portion of First US Army.[19]

The LUCKY STRIKE plan to use the American First Army in support of and protecting the right flank of a British drive implied the possible extension of 21 Army Group's command of the First Army beyond the time when the American Third Army would go into action on the American right, and thus postponement of American army group command on the Continent. Montgomery broached this unwelcome possibility to Bradley at a conference on June 29–30; the subject matter may have had something to do with Bradley's aide's finding Montgomery more aloof and even less amiable than usual:

Went to tea with Monty and found him oppressive. Monty is beginning to believe in the Monty legend, that he is a great man of history, fully convincing himself of his godlike role. . . .
The word my recurs in his conversation. And he moves his face briskly and searchingly about the table in an attempt as though discovering whether or not you were listening to him.[20]

For the present, Bradley was able to evade the issue of prolonged British command of American troops, and Montgomery had to defer his visions of a destiny to command the breakout to and beyond the Seine, because the two commanders also had before them the immediate issue of a major American battle to deplete the enemy in the Bocage. The victor of Alamein was still far from his postwar claim that he had planned all along for the Americans to lead the way out of Normandy; but simply to prepare for LUCKY STRIKE, the Americans must be next to move the ball.

Hostile Terrain and Armies

Gossip flowed freely from Montgomery's headquarters to Bradley's "that 21 Hqrs looked askance at the Amerk effort. . . . Have never lost their superior opinions of their own arms."[21] This was the opposite side of the coin, the reverse of the Americans' questioning of British drive, of American impatience at the stalled offensive before Caen, of American "wondering when the Brit. are going to move."[22] Montgomery hoped to reserve the breakout role for 21 Army Group in part because he doubted the Americans had the combat experience and capacity to perform the role. Because each ally knew the other's feelings, Bradley was all the more impatient for his immediate opportunity to move the ball. He hoped to attack southward only five days after the fall of Cherbourg: for Collins's corps, one day of rest, two days of movement, one day of reconnaissance, and then attack. He apologized to an equally impatient Eisenhower when he decided that the delay imposed by the Great Storm on VIII Corps arrivals in Europe, the ammunition shortage, and the cleanup work in the northern Cotentin required a postponement until July 3. He hoped, nevertheless, to generate from his attack more than simply a prelude to a British breakout. "I am very anxious," he told Eisenhower, "that when we hit the enemy this time we will hit him with such power that we can keep going and cause him a major disaster."[23]

At the very least, Bradley wanted "to keep going without any appreciable halt until we turn the corner at the base of the peninsula,"[24] and Montgomery's June 30 directive, written in consultation with Bradley, instructed him to wheel the First Army in a wide turn pivoting on Caumont to reach the line Caumont-Vire-Mortain-Fougères. Fougères would allow the American right to "turn the corner" into Brittany. Thereupon General Patton's Third Army was to become operational and move south and west into Brittany to afford OVERLORD logistics a mighty boost by capturing the Breton ports. Not the least of Bradley's concerns about Montgomery's LUCKY STRIKE project was the fear that the British would go gallivanting northeastward before Allied port capacity could sustain a long drive; Bradley thought the Breton ports indispensable for this purpose, and American logisticians reckoned that LUCKY STRIKE and the clearing of the Breton ports could not progress simultaneously, because the Allies did not have enough troops or support.

The new VIII Corps was to lead off Bradley's attack. Because of Bradley's principle that units are never better than their commanders, the First Army chief and the Supreme Commander looked with particular interest to General Middleton's debut at the head of the corps; British attitudes also made the Americans peculiarly sensitive to the lack of experience in their higher leadership. Eisenhower himself was insisting to the War Department that proven combat performance must be a major criterion for senior command, and that divisions and corps should go only to those commanders of regiments and combat commands who excelled under fire. Though new to a corps, Middleton had the next best credentials. He was a proven administrator of a large organization, because after retiring from the army in 1939, he had returned to Louisiana State University, where earlier he was professor of military science, to become a successful dean of administration and comptroller. More to the point, after graduating from Mississippi A & M College in 1909 and enlisting in the army as a private, by the Armistice of 1918 he had commanded both the 39th and the 47th Infantry Regiments in combat, won his eagles as the youngest colonel in the AEF, and earned George Marshall's judgment, later entered in Middleton's 201 file: "This man was the outstanding infantry regimental commander on the battlefield in France."[25] Returning to the army from retirement, Middleton had taken over the 45th Division in training and added to his combat laurels through his command of it in Sicily and Italy.

In Italy, Middleton had had to give up the 45th Division and go into a hospital at Naples and then to Walter Reed Hospital with a painful knee, diagnosed by various physicians as caused either by arthritis or an injury. There are two versions of his coming back from this disability. Omar Bradley's version has Marshall responding to objections to Middleton's fitness by saying: "I would rather have a man with arthritis in the knee than one with arthritis in the head." Eisenhower said he himself asked Marshall for Middleton but it was Marshall who replied: "Fine, I agree with you in his value. But he's in Walter Reed Hospital with his knees." To which Eisenhower replied: "I don't give a damn about his knees; I want his head and his heart. And I'll take him into battle on a litter if we have to."[26]

So into battle Middleton would go, despite the gimpy knee. If he and his VIII Corps were to achieve Bradley's aims, they must do it not only despite the American limitations in combat experience that gave the British pause—and were caustically described in captured German intelligence documents—but also despite the obstacles that had led General Morgan to urge from the first COSSAC plans onward that the Allied left carry the main offensive burden. The British faced the bulk of the German tanks, but armor was supposedly an Allied strong suit—at least quantitatively—in which the Allies could achieve predominance. The Americans might face fewer panzers, but they confronted the best defensive country in France, the hedgerows that cancelled out Allied advantages in mobility and relegated decision in battle mainly to the infantryman. No forebears of the First Army fighting Indians in the North American forest had ever grappled in a country so conducive to ambush.

Where there was not bocage in front of the Americans there was something worse. Across Bradley's front west of the V Corps lay the flooded marshlands of the Cotentin plain. Here the so-called prairies marécageuses, along the Merderet, Douve, Taute, and Vire Rivers, and the twenty square kilometers or so of the Prairies Marécageuses de Gorges are bogs dangerous to foot travelers and impassable to vehicles at best. The German flooding operations had assured that the only routes across them were the narrow, tarred causeways. Occasional islands or peninsulas cropping up out of the prairies marécageuses were crisscrossed by hedgerows more frequent and more luxuriously overgrown than those of the rest of the Bocage, and their fields were not much firmer than the surrounding marshes.

Surely Hitler would insist on the most determined exploitation of the defensive advantages of the Bocage and the Cotentin plain. He almost never yielded ground willingly, most especially not ground as good as Normandy's. The Führer had prohibited, in fact, the preparation of any intermediate defensive lines rearward in France. The German army would fight in the hedgerows with the knowledge that no comparably adequate line lay between them and the West Wall on the border of the Fatherland.

The Caumont Gap no longer yawned invitingly in front of the V Corps on Bradley's left. In the middle days of June, the enemy's 3rd Parachute Division marched into the gap, and though it arrived in driblets, all three regiments were in line and substantially intact by June 17. Traveling under strict discipline only at night, avoiding main roads, and keeping careful camouflage during the day, the 3rd Parachute came up almost without damage from Allied airplanes. Even with such opposition in place, Caumont might have remained an inviting area for Bradley to open his attack, for the ground at least was dry. Despite the 3rd Parachute Division and the projected pattern of the First Army's turning movement, Bradley might yet have begun here—except that the stalled condition of the Second Army not only placed the offensive burden upon his army in the first place, but dictated that a renewed advance around Caumont might well become a more dangerously exposed salient than existed already.

So Bradley decided to lead off with Middleton's VIII Corps attacking on his extreme right, followed by Collins's VII Corps moving southward on Middleton's left and General Corlett's newly committed XIX Corps on Collins's left, the whole pivoting on the V corps. This sequence had the advantage of moving first with the corps that, after the V, had been longest in position and had enjoyed the most time to prepare itself. If it had not been for the ammunition shortage, Bradley would have had Middleton attacking southward as early as June 22.

The respite thus afforded the enemy to strengthen his defenses opposite Middleton was to prove one of the least pleasant consequences of the storm. Under Bradley's final orders, the VIII Corps attack on July 3 would be followed by the VII on the 4th of July, Collins thus receiving another extra day to complete the turnaround from Cherbourg, and the VII Corps artillery becoming available to support the VIII Corps's opening moves. The XIX Corps, whose 30th Division was just completing its arrival at the front, would follow on July 7. This attack in sequence seemed the best arrangement possible if anything were to be started off promptly, if there were to be no further delaying of the drive. In practice, the plan was to suffer the usual penalty of attacks in sequence; it permitted the enemy to shuttle his reserves from one threatened point to another.

The initial objective was the line Coutances-St. Lô-Caumont. Attaining this line would put the flooded prairies of the Cotentin plain behind all four of Bradley's corps, placing the whole First Army on dry ground for the next wheeling attack to Caumont-Vire-Mortain-Fougères. Until the initial objective line was reached, the prairies marécageuses would compel the VIII, VII, and XIX Corps all to advance on narrow fronts delectable to the defense. Middleton's corps had the greatest distance to go, thirty-two kilometers simply to Coutances; but on the west coast of the Cotentin it had the widest table of firm ground over which to move, eleven kilometers at its narrowest, between the Prairies Marécageuses de Gorges and the tidal flats of the Ay River. This was the route the Germans had taken northward into the Cotentin in 1940. The VII Corps would have to move down the very narrow corridor of less than firm ground between the Prairies Marécageuses de Gorges and the Taute River—only three to four kilometers wide—from Carentan to Périers. the part of the XIX Corps west of the Vire River would follow the slightly wider corridor from Carentan toward St. Lô, between the Taute and the Vire.

When the Allies came ashore on D-Day, the German Seventh Army's LXXXIV Corps had held the entire front against them. By the beginning of July, despite restrictions on German reinforcement self-imposed and otherwise, and despite battlefield attrition, a formidable array awaited Bradley's attack and held fast the Second Army around Caen. There were in fact too many units for Seventh Army headquarters to handle properly, so on June 28 a headquarters called Panzer Group West took over from the Seventh Army a front of four corps from the Caumont area eastward. Before D-Day, Panzer Group West had commanded Rundstedt's armored reserve, withheld from the control of Rommel's Army Group B as part of the difference of opinion among the Germans over the proper role of reserves. When it became in effect an army headquarters, Panzer Group West was assigned to Army Group B rather than continuing to report directly to OB West. Facing the American First Army, the German Seventh Army had the LXXXIV Corps on its left, from the west coast to the Vire River, and the II Parachute Corps on its right, from the Vire to the Drôme River in the St. Lô-Caumont area. Comprising the Seventh Army were three relatively fresh infantry divisions, four divisions already hard used, an independent parachute regiment, and three Kampfgruppen—mobile regimental-sized combat teams.

The Seventh Army's edge over the First Army in the greater combat experience of its leaders would be partially offset by a series of command changes at the end of June and the beginning of July. These left Rommel the only high-ranking German officer in Normandy accustomed to his post as well as further seasoned in combat against the Anglo-Americans by the first month of the Normandy fighting. General der Artillerie—a general of a specific arm was equivalent to an American lieutenant general—Erich Marcks of the LXXXIV Corps had been killed by American fighter-bombers on June 12 while trying to shore up the Caumont Gap. Marcks would be badly missed; he was both a skillful General Staff planner—one of the principal authors of the Operation BARBAROSSA plan of 1941—and a hardened veteran of the Eastern Front. At the beginning of July, Generalleutnant—equivalent to an American major general—Dietrich von Choltitz had just arrived from Italy to take over the LXXXIV Corps as interim commander.

Generaloberst—full general—Friedrich Dollman had commanded the Seventh Army on D-Day as he had done since September 1939 and through the victorious battles in France in 1940; but after the stagnation of four years' garrison duty, the strains of June 1944—climaxed by word that Hitler blamed him for the premature fall of Cherbourg and had ordered a court-martial inquiry—were too much for him. Dollman died on June 27, according to German reports at the time "in action," according to later reports of a heart attack, and according to the recent testimony of Generalmajor Max Pemsel, his chief of staff, from poison self-administered. Generaloberst Paul Hausser, who had led the II SS Panzer Corps to the west, succeeded Dollman at Seventh Army.

General der Panzertruppe Leo Freiherr Geyr von Schweppenburg had led Panzer Group West since Rundstedt's desire for an armored reserve caused its inception; but Geyr, a supercilious officer out of the best—or worst—red-trouser-striped German General Staff mold, in late June incautiously criticized the conduct of the Normandy battle in a report that reached Hitler's eyes. This misstep provoked his imminent relief by an armor expert from the Eastern Front, General der Panzertruppen Heinrich Eberbach.

Similarly, Rundstedt himself grew so pessimistic over the eventual prospects of the German army in Normandy, and so fearful that the Anglo-Americans would in time not only execute a breakout but in doing so envelop the Seventh Army, that at Berchtesgaden on June 29 he joined a still more pessimistic Rommel in trying to persuade Hitler that there must be a strategic withdrawal behind the Seine. Needless to say, the effort was futile. Thereupon Rundstedt for once shed his usual dignified acquiescence in the Führer's generalship and vented anger. On July 1, he is supposed to have snapped at Generalfeldmarschall Wilhelm Keitel, head of OKW: "Make peace, you fools, what else can you do?"[27] The old Prussian promptly gave way as Oberbefehlshaber West to one of Hitler's favored army group commanders from the East, Generalfeldmarschall Hans Günther von Kluge, "der kluge Hans," the clever fellow who had shown himself an adroit manipulator of battlefield tactics again and again since the Polish campaign of 1939, and of professions of loyalty to the Führer even longer.

So the old German order of command changed; but for the present, given Hitler's stand-fast determination, command on so high a level mattered less than good company officers and good soldiers.

The Battle of the Cotentin Plain

Mont Castre is scarcely more than 100 meters high, but the *Guide Michelin* considers its view worth a star. To the left wing of General Choltitz's LXXXIV Corps, the view merited more than one star, for along with other abrupt hills around la Haye-du-Puits, Mont Castre permitted Choltitz's men to observe virtually every movement of General Middleton's VIII Corps. Middleton had General Wyche's 79th Division on his right to assault the Montgardon Ridge and Hill 121 west of la Haye-du-Puits; General Ridgway's 82nd Airborne in his center to attack the Poterie Ridge just north and northwest of the town; and General Landrum's 90th Division on his left to advance on Mont Castre, the Roman cantonment site that commands the Cotentin plain for miles.

The 82nd, in line since its early morning drop on June 6, was reduced to half the strength it had brought to Normandy. After taking the Poterie hills it was slated to be pinched out by a converging advance of Middleton's other divisions and to go back to England for refitting. A veteran division, as airborne troopers exceptionally well trained to be aggressive and resourceful, and now encouraged by the prospect of returning to England to finish the job at hand quickly, the 82nd overcame the Germans' advantages of observation and position, advanced more than six kilometers in three days, and inflicted some 500 casualties in addition to taking 772 prisoners. The troopers did so at heavy cost to themselves. After four days the rifle companies of the 325th Glider Infantry, for example, ranged in size from 57 to 12 men, and the regiment itself was down from its authorized 135 officers and 2,838 men to 41 officers and 956 men. But the 82nd gained its objectives.

The rest of the VIII Corps did not. Mont Castre shadowed every effort of the 90th Division. From its heights, the Germans shelled attempts to swing around its base and frustrated head-on assault. German defensive doctrine prescribed continual local counterattacks to give the enemy offensive forces no rest and no security in their gains, and to bite back everything possible. If German infantry could not counterattack immediately, German artillery would hit a newly lost position with guns already zeroed in—making it important for the Americans never to stop in a strongpoint just gained. To counter these tactics demanded all the skill and stamina of the veterans of the 82nd; against less experienced and less aggressively trained American infantry, the incessant counterstrokes were all too likely to spawn demoralization and defeat. Leadership in the unlucky 90th Division remained less confident and energetic than it might have been. Infantry and tanks still failed to communicate or cooperate adequately. The troops seemed unable to coordinate their actions well enough to give substance to the theory of fire-and-maneuver tactics: the firing elements failed to pin down the enemy, the maneuverers would not probe forward aggressively. Two companies of the 357th Infantry became isolated, and one of them surrendered while the other was overrun and practically destroyed. General Landrum, who was supposed to shake up the division but had received scant time in which to do it before the Mont Castre test, relieved one of his regimental commanders while another was being evacuated for wounds; but General Bradley was close to making up his mind that Landrum, too, would have to go and a third commander be found for the 90th Division.

Yet the 79th Division, which had earned a favorable reputation during its debut in the Cherbourg fight, succeeded scarcely better, with nothing quite so ominous as Mont Castre to overcome. General Wyche's Cross of Lorraine Division lost 2,000 casualties in five days of battle and, while reaching the crest of the Montgardon Ridge, failed to grasp a secure hold on it. The casualties of the 79th for five days were practically identical to those of the 90th, and its advance of about six kilometers was comparable.

To the American command, this combination of high casualties and small progress did not seem good enough. Bradley believed the whole campaign so far had confirmed that American small-unit training was less thorough than it should be. The First Army after-action report on the Normandy battles was to cite as the principal tactical lesson learned "the urgent need for the development of an aggressive spirit in the infantry soldier. . . . The outstanding impression gained from a review of battle experience is the importance of aggressive action and continuous energetic forward movement in order to gain ground and reduce casualties."[28]

Bradley favored putting four instead of two or three infantry divisions, along with one armored division, into the usual corps; then he might be able to deal with the developing problems of high infantry casualties and high rates of fatigue by rotating divisions out of the line for fifteen days after they had fought for thirty. So early in the campaign, he was already grappling with a lack of enough divisions: "You always need one more division than you've got," he remarked to Hodges.[29] Though to him the most feasible solution seemed to be to employ more of the same, he was also grappling with the deficiencies of the American infantry division in generating the combat power appropriate to a strategy of head-on power drives like his attack southward in the Cotentin.

Distrusting independent tank power, General McNair's design of the army had attached tank battalions in effect permanently to the infantry divisions; but the infantry generally, by no means only the 90th Division, had trouble making good use of the armor they had with them. The First Army report on Normandy also concluded:

> Initial operations in Normandy indicated that insufficient training had been conducted in infantry–tank cooperation prior to entry into combat. . . . Many of our infantry commanders do not possess sufficient knowledge of the proper employment of tanks as an infantry support weapon and insufficient opportunity is given the infantry division in training to become familiar with and work with the separate tank battalion.[30]

Part of the problem was the difficulty of mere communication between infantry and tanks. American troops began to improvise the attachment of a telephone or microphone to the outside of a tank, connected with the intercommunication system inside, so an infantryman could talk with a tank crew by stepping up to the tank and using the phone. Otherwise, the troops had to work out their own signal systems using hand gestures, smoke grenades, or pyrotechnics. Increasingly the rifle companies sought to improve liaison by designating one rifle squad to work consistently with the attached tank platoon. Especially in the close country of the Bocage, the designated rifle squad would move with the tank platoon, protect its flanks, and scout routes of advance.

The limited power of the Shermans themselves was also becoming an increasingly evident factor in the problem of generating adequate American combat strength. Against the well-beveled heavy armored surfaces of the rival Panthers and Tigers, the Sherman's 75 had almost no effect. Even the new long 76 proved a disappointment in its first trials; it was a better antitank gun than the short 75 but carried an insufficient charge in its high explosive ammunition to perform up to expectations against the unarmored targets it took on when it was not fighting tanks. Major General Edward H. Brooks of the 2nd Armored Division thought the solution was a general adoption of the British 17-pounder as Allied tank armament; but production difficulties stood in the way.

The immediate tactical problem of tank-versus-tank confrontations became finding a means to halt the Panther so the more numerous Shermans could maneuver around to fire on its vulnerable sides. Available tank destroyers and antitank guns did not offer enough high-velocity penetrating power in combination with mobility. Bradley's troops wanted an equivalent of the German 88; Bradley offered the 90mm. antiaircraft gun, more and more turned to a dual purpose like the 88. The 90mm. AA had reasonably adequate penetrating power; its mobility left something to be desired.

The Bocage aggravated all these inherent limitations of the American army and its weapons, all the more because the planners had neglected tactical preparation for this obstacle behind the Normandy beaches. It was now, belatedly, that Montgomery's headquarters conceded: "Experience gained to date in Normandy has shown that the 'bocage' country is most unsuitable for large scale armoured action and, further, that it would offer the enemy limitless opportunities for delaying actions during a withdrawal." Major Hansen, speaking for Bradley's headquarters, said: "Hedgerow fighting has been far more difficult than we anticipated."[31] It was too bad that these revelations had to wait upon experience. Tactics and weapons for coping with the Bocage were only now being improvised; hammering them out by trial and error in combat cost time and lives.

> The most effective method of attack proved to be by the combined action of infantry, artillery and tanks with some of the tanks equipped with dozer blades or large steel teeth in front to punch holes through the hedgerows. It was found necessary to assign frontages according to specific fields and hedgerows instead of by yardage and to reduce the distances and intervals between tactical formations. Normal rifle company formation was a box formation with two assault platoons in the lead followed by the support platoon and the weapons platoon.[32]

At the beginning of July, much of that remained to be worked out, particularly the adaptations of the tanks for breaking through the hedgerows. Under the circumstances, the American infantry relied more than ever on tactical air support. Because of persisting difficulties of calling in the fighter-bombers, despite Quesada's efforts, and the close-quarters nature of the fighting, they relied still more on the sovereign American remedy for battle problems, the artillery. Against the tough and stubborn German defenders of Normandy, shielded by the hedgerows and armed with a formidable array of automatic rifles, machine guns, cannon, antitank guns, Panzerfäuste, and panzers, American infantry tended to transpose the doctrine of fire and maneuver into one of maneuver and fire: instead of using fire to fix the enemy and maneuver to trap and destroy him, troops maneuvered to find the enemy and then called in aerial and artillery firepower to try to destroy him.

Artillery promptly impressed friend and foe alike as the outstanding combat branch of the American ground forces. The opposite side of this coin was Patton's agreement with an old French army friend, General Koechlin-Schwartz: "I reminded him that at Langres [the World War I AEF staff college] he had said, 'The poorer the infantry the more artillery it needs; the American infantry needs all it can get.' He was right then, and still is."[33]

To a point, of course, reliance on the guns saved lives and was tactically sound. When the Germans on one occasion laid down a heavy concentration of artillery fire with devastating effect on some American infantry, an American gunner remarked that the Germans must finally have found an American artillery manual to tell them how to mass their fire.[34] On the other hand, artillery and even combined aerial-artillery barrages proved again and again to produce limited results against an enemy skillfully dug in. To capture ground and to capture or destroy enemy formations, the lavish application of heavy firepower was no adequate substitute for aggressive maneuver. Exceptionally successful American infantry officers testified that while the enemy feared American guns, he feared aggressive infantry even more. Said one, "We have learned to keep moving forward. If there is anything the Germans hate it is close fighting." Another advised: "Move forward aggressively. The German is a poor marksman under the best conditions. In the face of heavy fire and an aggressive enemy his fire becomes highly ineffective."[35]

In the Cotentin, this sort of aggressive American infantry fighting was rare. Nevertheless, the Germans found American pressure so unremitting that Hausser of the Seventh Army had to open a stream of appeals for reinforcements. From the Panzer Group West sector he got part of the 2nd ss "Das Reich" Panzer Division, a bogeyman to Allied intelligence whose commitment had been long awaited; the Germans put it in against the 79th Division on the west coast of the Cotentin. Similarly, despite the disappointments it gave the American command, the 90th Division troubled the enemy enough to draw upon itself the only OKW reserve remaining in northwestern France, the 15th Parachute Regiment. Against this formation plus parts of the enemy 91st, 265th, 77th, and 33rd Infantry Divisions, the 90th was cast in a duel against numbers at least equal if not superior to its own—some 5,600 front-line combat troops.

For all the disappointment occasioned by Middleton's slow pace of advance, furthermore, there was no reason to think the VIII Corps commander had developed arthritis in the head or heart. The personal leadership of Lightning Joe Collins could accomplish no more when the VII Corps resumed action on the Cotentin front. The VII moved out on July 4 between the Prairies Marécageuses de Gorges and the Taute River on a front so narrow that Collins could deploy only one division, the 83rd, advancing down the Carentan-Périers road with two regiments abreast in column of battalions, the 330th Infantry to the left of the highway, the 331st to the right. The 83rd, the Thunderbolt Division, with its "OHIO" monogram on its shoulder patch, had relieved the 101st Airborne when the Screaming Eagles returned to England for refitting. In Major General Robert C. Macon, a 1912 graduate of Virginia Polytechnic, the 83rd had a commander experienced in regimental leadership in North Africa; but the division itself was another raw one. Collins characteristically did all he could to compensate for its inexperience with close control from corps headquarters. Starting about five kilometers south of Carentan, if the division could drive forward about three kilometers to Sainteny, as Collins hoped it could do in one day, then it would be about halfway from Carentan to Périers, and the corps commander planned to insert elements of the now relatively experienced 4th Division to help carry on with the rest of the drive.

But after the June rains, even the highest ground of the Carentan-Périers isthmus was sodden and almost a marsh, with mud holes waist-deep. Infantry could barely move cross-country, let alone tanks and tank destroyers. Infantry heavy-weapons companies could not slosh through the bogs well enough to provide adequate fire support. The Germans had the road and the occasional approximations of good footing carefully covered by machine guns and mortars sited behind hedgerows and in log pillboxes reinforced by sandbags. When one infantry battalion achieved a slight advance but then paused for others to catch up, Collins exploded, "Don't ever let me hear of that again," and insisted that any battalion in the lead must push on to cut behind the defenders.[36] All Collins's prodding, however, and Macon's similar prodding with Collins breathing down his neck, failed to spur the 83rd Division forward for more than a few hundred meters along the Carentan-Périers road on the 4th of July, at a cost of almost 1,400 casualties.

The 5th of July gave the VII Corps little more cause for celebration than this inglorious 4th. In return for another 750 casualties, the 83rd drove its total two-day advance to about a kilometer and a half. With this scratch into the defenses, the isthmus widened just enough that Collins decided he could shift the 83rd Division to the left of the road on July 6 and commit Barton's 4th Division on the right. Adding this blooded formation—all too literally blooded, since it had suffered 5,400 casualties since D-Day, for whom it had received about 4,400 replacements—did not elevate Collins's now more realistic expectations above reaching Sainteny, originally the first day's objective, by nightfall on July 7. Yet this new and modest hope also failed of fulfillment. More rains on the 7th wiped out an air strike. By evening, the 83rd and 4th Divisions were not quite two-thirds of the way from the July 4 line of departure to Sainteny.

Collins had kept up a steady stream of adjurations to his division commanders, and Macon had responded with equal demands upon his regimental and battalion commanders: "You tell him that he must take that objective and go right on down regardless of his flank; pay attention to nothing, not even communication." "Never mind about the gap; keep that leading battalion going." "To hell with the fire, to hell with what's on your flank, get down there and take the area."[37] To little avail. The German army's better formations in the Second World War had no superiors in the world in two military skills particularly: exploiting the offensive breakthrough, and holding ground tenaciously on the defense. In front of the VII Corps, the Germans not only had superb terrain for tenacious holding, but the 83rd and 4th Divisions were facing some of the best enemy troops in the West, the 17th ss Panzer Grenadier Division, reinforced by the 6th Parachute Regiment. When Hausser added the rest of the 2nd ss Panzer Division, the enemy alignment facing Collins was altogether calculated to nourish the weary GI's delusion, complained of by many a commander, that every panzer grumbling out of the hedgerows was a Tiger, and every gun an 88.

Yet there was advantage to the Americans in the arrival of Das Reich, for on the same drizzly 7th of July when these ss troopers rolled into position outside Sainteny, the American XIX Corps on Collins's left joined the attack, and the enemy no longer had reserves at hand.

General Corlett, the XIX Corps commander, West Point 1913 and an infantryman, would never be associated with such a codename as Lightning—the Marine Corps found his methods, and the army's generally, in the assault and capture of Pacific islands painfully slow and labored. But Corlett rightly had a reputation as a tough customer who was calmly competent under fire. After his corps moved into the line between the VII and the V on June 12, he was so eager to launch probing attacks despite Bradley's preference for clearing Cherbourg and the northern Cotentin before taking on anything else that Bradley commented half ruefully about all his corps commanders' brimming over with "piss and vinegar."[38]

Like Middleton, unfortunately, Corlett had health problems; and Corlett's, though less a cause for initial misgiving, were to prove more troublesome as time went on. The Pacific's extremes of climate had eroded Corlett's strength, and after a few nights of sleeping on Normandy's wet ground he came down with a severe cold complicated by a bladder infection. For about two weeks, Major General Walton H. Walker, slated to command the XX Corps in Patton's army, filled in for Corlett in the field, while Corlett kept an uncertain grip on corps planning from his headquarters.

His headquarters had to devise plans more complex than those of Collins and Middleton farther west. The XIX Corps first had to get its right-flank division, the 30th, across the Vire et Taute Canal and the Vire River, along the north and east banks of which the division front formed an arc. The canal, little more than five meters wide, could be waded at several places; but the Vire River where it flowed past the 30th Division was some eighteen meters wide and two and a half to four meters deep, with steep banks over two meters high. It would have to be crossed in boats until bridges could be laid down or repaired.

Against the kind of resistance the First Army was meeting elsewhere, such water crossings were expected to present formidable problems. Corlett and Major General Leland S. Hobbs, West Point 1915, the division commander, planned assault, bridge construction, and followup elaborately, the more so because intelligence reported part of the 17th ss Panzer Grenadier Division as well as remnants of the tough old 352nd Division and the 275th Division in the triangle between the waterways. There were meticulous rehearsals, featuring model performances by the 30th Division's 117th Infantry Regiment, which happened to have been a demonstration regiment for river crossings at the Infantry School at Fort Benning. There was a strong artillery preparation, including plastering of all buildings suspected of housing German strongpoints and a rolling barrage ahead of the assault. Corlett was a stickler on artillery support, as suggested by his concern over low ammunition allotments in Europe as compared with the Pacific. Though on July 7 the weather cancelled the air strikes for Corlett's attack as it had earlier for Collins's, much of this preparation proved happily superfluous.

The earlier attacks to the westward had drawn away most of the German strength from the wedge of the Vire et Taute Canal and the Vire, leaving only three battalions of the 275th Division and a handful of panzer grenadiers. General Hobbs's Old Hickory Division of the Carolina, Georgia, and Tennessee National Guard crossed the river and canal with relative ease. The crossings went so well that during the afternoon of July 7, General Bradley decided to give Corlett the 3rd Armored Division. This unit had been blooded in a limited action at the end of June on the V Corps front; its casualties in the action—about 400—mounted so high so quickly that the commander, Major General Leroy H. Watson, immediately became conspicuous in the chorus calling for more heavily gunned tanks.

General Bradley failed to make clear the use to which he intended Corlett should put the 3rd Armored, or even how much of the division ought to be inserted into the Old Hickories' still constricted bridgehead. Having received early rumors that he might get the 3rd Armored, General Corlett had begun planning to pass it rapidly through the 30th Division and to send it on toward a ridge west of St. Lô for later operations against that road-junction town, thus exploiting Hobbs's initial success before the enemy could regroup. Unfortunately, Corlett's illness had sent him to bed, and he was unable to develop this plan in detail. On the afternoon of July 7 he telephoned Watson and told him to cross the Vire as soon as possible and to drive south. "How far do you want me to go?" Watson asked. "The Germans have little or nothing over there," Corlett answered; "just keep going."[39]

The 3rd Armored thus entered its first major effort with its commander's lacking a precise conception of what was intended of it. This uncertainty did nothing to ease the minds of inexperienced subordinates soon troubled also by the perplexities of passing the armored division through a narrow bridgehead just captured by another division, a movement that got started late enough to have to be conducted mostly after dark. Because it was Combat Command A that had absorbed the casualties of the division's earlier action, Watson decided that Combat Command B, under Brigadier General John J. Bohn, should move first into the Vire bridgehead. With only one bridge as yet available for westbound crossing of the Vire, and that one under heavy enemy fire as well as being much used by the 30th Division, CCB took all night and much of July 8 for the crossing. Because of the absence of opportunity for detailed preparation and coordination of the move and the inexperience of almost everyone involved, a constant succession of traffic jams and arguments about priority of movement developed to irritate all hands, especially the 30th Division, which naturally regarded the bridgehead as its own, and its commander General Hobbs, who was known to be mercurial anyway.

Hobbs imagined that in compensation for his annoyance and the disruption of his division's progress, he might enjoy the benefits of an armored spearhead leading the way for him down the main road southward, capturing the crossroads town of St. Jean-de-Daye, which his infantry had barely failed to reach, and rolling on through Pont-Hébert toward St. Lô. Watson, however, instructed Bohn to turn left as soon as he crossed the Vire and to proceed southward on unimproved roads and trails hugging the bank of the river. There were two reasons for Watson's instructions. First, he feared the exposure of open flanks in a drive straight down the main road. Second and more important, Watson was mindful of the superiority that German antitank guns were habitually demonstrating over American tank armor. Perhaps he exaggerated the proportion of 88s scattered among 75s and lighter guns in the enemy's antitank arsenal; almost all Americans did. Watson's CCA in its brief earlier combat had responded to the antitank gun problem by avoiding direct confrontation with the German guns on the roads, taking to movement cross-country and along small trails. This procedure was consistent with the 3rd Armored's training, which had stressed the techniques and value of tank movement cross-country.

The west bank of the Vire, however, was an area of exceptionally numerous and narrow hedgerowed fields and lanes, where CCB's attempts to apply its training in cross-country advance achieved little progress. One effect was to destroy the last of General Hobbs's patience, for he could now perceive no compensation at all for the troubles to which the armor had put him. Hobbs told corps headquarters he preferred to take his chances without the help of the 3rd Armored. Corlett roused himself to reply that the armor was available now and Hobbs had to use it. "Every road is blocked by [our own] armor," Hobbs responded.[40] To try to resolve the issue, on the night of July 8 Corlett ordered Hobbs to take over operational control of CCB himself, and to use the command as he saw fit—but he must use it.

On July 9, Hobbs employed the extravagance of language that went with his impatient personality to flay General Bohn for attempting to move cross-country, insisting Bohn must get CCB on the roads and pick up speed. The perversities of this situation included the fact that moving cross-country had been Watson's idea, not Bohn's, and Bohn would have preferred all along to travel as much as possible by road. By now, however, CCB was so entangled in hedgerows that breaking free to the roads was much more easily said than done. Anyway, such roads as existed in the area along the Vire River where Watson had committed CCB were so narrow and so readily, and regularly, barricaded by felled trees that they were hardly better than the hedgerows. Hobbs sent his assistant division commander to prod Bohn onto the roads. Bohn was already prodding his lead task force commander to the same effect, while the latter responded with citations of the divisional training doctrine favoring cross-country movement. Hobbs finally warned the unlucky Bohn that unless he moved faster and advanced some five kilometers to capture a place called Hauts-Vents by five o'clock in the afternoon, Hobbs would relieve him of his command.

Hauts-Vents was an aptly named site where Hill 91, swept by winds from the sea, overlooks and dominates the St. Jean-de-Daye–Pont-Hébert–St. Lô road and particularly its crossing of the Vire. It had become Hobbs's latest immediate objective not only for this obvious geographic reason but also because American intelligence had learned that the Germans were trying to rectify quickly the weakness that their displacements westward had created in front of the XIX Corps. Elements of the 2nd SS Panzer Division were on their way from the west—so that Corlett's headquarters soon committed the 3rd Armored's CCA to meet them on Hobbs's right. The full remaining strength of Panzer Lehr, released from Panzer Group West, was approaching from the east.

General Bohn did not capture Hauts-Vents in time to save his job from the repercussions of Hobbs's irritated mood. Instead, in a comedy of errors, the Americans went up the hill and down again three times before they finally stayed, and in that interval Hobbs's deadline passed and, after a five-hour grace period, he removed Bohn. During July 9, meanwhile, Bohn in his desire to take the objective and retain his job had sent an advance party of eight tanks hastening toward Hill 91 in front of the rest of CCB. They had almost reached Hauts-Vents when they took a wrong turn, northward and westward back toward St. Jean-de-Daye. Near that town they collided with the 3-inch guns of the 823rd Tank Destroyer Battalion, which mistook them for the 2nd SS Panzers. Losing two of their tanks before they extricated themselves, the advance of CCB then turned back in the correct direction and climbed to Hauts-Vents just before darkness. There, fresh from their battle with American antitank guns, they were strafed by American airplanes, because General Hobbs had given up for the day and ordered a halt short of Hauts-Vents, but the word had failed to reach the leading tankers. After a night without a sign of friendly support, the six advance tanks retreated northward to rejoin their comrades of CCB on the morning of July 10.

During that day, Hobbs became discontented all over again, this time with the new commander of CCB, Colonel Dorrance S. Roysdon, because the command had trouble regaining the hill that its six advance tanks had held without support through the previous night. By now Panzer Lehr was arriving in the neighborhood, and a CCB thrust that reached the top of Hill 91 late on July 10 was soon forced off by enemy artillery and mortar fire. An attack the next morning carried the crest a third time, only to be blown back again, before Colonel Roysdon himself at last led a charge that stayed on top late in the afternoon of the 11th. Once the hill was captured, Hobbs calmed down enough to concede he had probably acted too hastily when he sacked General Bohn.

For these chaotic events yielded unexpected benefits. The confused actions of CCB around Hauts-Vents turned out to be extremely well timed to confuse the enemy more than the Americans, and thus to blunt what was intended as a major counterattack by Panzer Lehr. First, going up and down again with CCB at Hill 91 prevented Panzer Lehr from having all its armor and guns in position where they should have been for a counterattack scheduled to jump off early on July 11. Then the Germans' effort to stage a converging attack on St. Jean-de-Daye from both right and left was split into two mutually unsupportive prongs by the presence of CCB in strength along the axis reaching north from Hauts-Vents. Finally, CCB's capture of Hill 91 during the 11th, in the midst of the German attack, deprived the Germans of the high ground from which they might have brought their two columns back into coordination and dominated the battlefield.

Thus aided, troops of the 30th Division repulsed the weaker of Panzer Lehr's prongs, its right flank attacking along the west bank of the Vire River, before noon on July 11. The left and stronger prong might have caused a good deal more trouble, had it not happened to crash head-on into Manton Eddy's exceptionally capable 9th Division. This American formation was in the area because General Collins at VII Corps had decided, in consultation with General Hodges and at Hodges's suggestion, that it might help the stalled VII Corps advance along the Carentan-Périers isthmus to throw in the 9th east of the Taute River, to menace the flank of the Germans facing Collins. General Bradley accepted the suggestion, too, and while he perceived the 9th as also assisting the advance of Corlett's XIX Corps, he left Collins in control of Eddy's division, moving the boundary between the VII and XIX Corps eastward to split the peninsula between the Taute and the Vire. In any event, the 9th Division crossed the Taute et Vire Canal on July 9 and was preparing to attack southward on the morning of July 11 when it was struck unexpectedly by Panzer Lehr—unexpectedly, because all levels of American intelligence had misinterpreted the noise of tank motors in the 9th Division sector as mere cover for an enemy withdrawal.

No matter; the effect was still to reverse the usual pattern of the Normandy fighting. This time it was the Germans who by attacking were exposing themselves to a battle-wise enemy who enjoyed the advantages of a terrain that seemed deliberately fashioned for defense. Panzer Lehr's left Schwerpunkt—two battalions of panzer grenadiers, a company of tanks, and two companies of self-propelled guns—came barrelling along determinedly enough to score two penetrations, one along a regimental boundary within the 9th Division, one along the boundary between the 9th and the 30th. So it was no doubt a fortunate chance for the Americans that the strength of the 9th had been added to the sector. But almost everything else also went the Americans' way. General Collins estimated that on July 11 his corps destroyed more than thirty German tanks, mostly in front of the 9th Division; while the 30th Division along with CCB claimed about twenty

German tanks for the day. Panzer Lehr itself acknowledged losing a quarter of its effective combat strength. The next day the 9th Division resumed its own interrupted attack.

Nevertheless, another apparently inviting opportunity for the Americans had disappeared without effective exploitation. Where the advance across the Taute et Vire Canal toward Pont-Hébert and St. Lô had begun so promisingly against only light and scattered opposition, the intervention of the 3rd Armored Division had failed to capitalize on the possibilities, and Panzer Lehr now barred the gate, injured but in an American assessment still "great big husky boys, and arrogant . . . not beaten at all."[41]

On the far right of the stumbling American attacks, General Middleton was preparing to commit in the center of his VIII Corps the newly arrived 8th Division of Major General William C. McMahon. Built from an old Regular cadre, the 8th was supposed to be one of the best-trained fresh divisions in the European Theater. To give it elbow room, Middleton narrowed the zone of the 79th Division, once it had completed clearing la Haye-du-Puits, to a narrow coastal strip which General Wyche's men were to scour as far south as the Ay River estuary. The 82nd Airborne had a last hurrah in helping the 90th climb Mont Castre, a job mostly completed on July 10 before the 82nd began returning to England on the 11th. The 90th Division like the 79th henceforth was to confine itself to a narrow zone of advance, southeastward to the Sèves River near Périers where it would be pinched out against the right flank of the VII Corps.

This concentration of the VIII Corps effort on the central drive by the undepleted 8th Division produced little improvement. Whatever its reputation for having been exceptionally well brought up, the 8th displayed about as many symptoms of inexperience, with as much lack of cohesion under pressure and hesitation and inertia under fire, as had the unlucky 90th. Within four days, Middleton relieved General McMahon and replaced him with Brigadier General Donald A. Stroh, assistant commander of the 9th Division. Manton Eddy of the 9th provided perhaps the best schooling in divisional command to be had in the American army, and Stroh was able to get the 8th Division moving forward, with a series of sideslipping maneuvers to flank the main obstacles in its path. By July 14, the 8th had reached a ridge overlooking the Ay River.

That same day, the 79th arrived at the Ay estuary, and the 90th reached the Sèves and made contact with the VII Corps. The opposing LXXXIV Corps was everywhere falling back behind the Sèves and the Ay. The Battle of the Cotentin Plain nevertheless had to be considered a grave disappointment, both in its rate of advance and in the combat showing of most of the American divisions involved. The VIII Corps had consumed twelve days and 10,000 casualties to cross eleven kilometers of the Bocage, and the line of the Ay and the Sèves was only one-third of the way to the original corps objective, the dry ground of the Coutances-St. Lô ridge. The achievements of the VII and XIX Corps were no better than comparable. At First Army headquarters, General Bradley perforce was scanning his maps to look for possible new means of cracking the defenses in front of him, rather than persist in the slow slugging match endured so far.

Caen Again

General Eisenhower at least had an alternative to studying maps of the Bocage. He could look east toward Montgomery and the British Second Army, beyond the flooded prairies marécageuses and the worst of the Bocage. Seen from SHAEF, the battle was assuming all too grimly the feared stability, the lineaments of a new Western Front on the 1914–1918 model. While the Americans thrashed about awkwardly and painfully in the Bocage, "on the British side we are approaching the limit of our available resources," since the British had committed about all the soldiers their population could afford. "Very soon, also, we will be approaching the limit in the capacity of the ports now in our possession to receive and maintain American troops." The effect would be a German capacity to build up men and resources faster than the Allies. The Anglo-Americans might actually face "the necessity of fighting a major defensive battle [against superior German concentrations] with the slight depth we now have in the bridgehead." "I am familiar," Eisenhower assured General Montgomery, "with your plan for generally holding firmly with your left, attracting thereto all of the enemy armor, while your right [the American First Army] pushes down the [Cotentin] Peninsula and threatens the rear and flank of the forces facing the Second British Army." But what if geography and enemy strength combined to frustrate movement by the Americans? What if enemy armor departed from the British front anyway, to form reserves and to block Bradley?

"It appears to me," Eisenhower therefore told Montgomery on July 7, "that we must use all possible energy in a determined effort" toward a breakthrough. Bradley had thrown a hard punch in the Bocage but little had come of it. Meanwhile, "We have not yet attempted a major full-dress attack on the left flank [by the British] supported by everything we could bring to bear."

Montgomery, to be sure, scarcely needed Eisenhower to remind him that "on the British side we are approaching the limit of our available resources." That was the stumbling block to all Montgomery's aspirations for a breakthrough with his left: he dared not risk "a major full-dress attack" on any scale that might expend his country's last field army. The limits of British manpower also represented the basic flaw in the reasoning of Eisenhower's July 7 communication; they were the other horn of the Allied dilemma the first horn of which was the geographical intractability of the Bocage.

Nevertheless, Eisenhower persisted, and with at least a partial recognition of the fundamental restraint upon Montgomery's freedom to attack:

> I know that you are thinking every minute about these weighty questions [he went on in his letter to Montgomery]. What I want you to know is that I will back you up to the limit in any effort you may decide upon to prevent a deadlock and will do my best to phase forward any unit you might find necessary. For example, if you could use in an attack on your left flank an American armored division, I would be glad to make it available and get it in to you as soon as possible.[42]

Eisenhower's generosity with American armor would have held no charms for Bradley. The First Army commander was just now congratulating himself on fending off Montgomery's direct request for an armored division, which he accomplished by agreeing to take over an additional section of the Caumont front instead.

Eisenhower's purpose in writing to Montgomery, according to Tedder, was simply to "tell Montgomery tactfully to get moving." According to Bedell Smith, Eisenhower's allusion to the absence of a full-dress British effort so far "referred to the fact that attacks by the Second Army, during this phase, had been made on a scale of two or three divisions. It was the Supreme Commander's conviction that a fully coordinated attack by the entire army would put our left flank in motion."[43] If geography prevented the Allied right flank from moving, then in Eisenhower's judgment the left clearly had to move. The trouble was that a promise of an armored division, or even several, was small potatoes compared with risking the British army.

As Eisenhower was well aware, Montgomery was already preparing another attack on Caen for the next day—but only by a single corps. At 9:30 P.M. on July 7, 460 Wellingtons of RAF Bomber Command began a forty-minute drop of 2,300 tons of 500- and 1,000-lb. bombs on a carpet 4,000 yards wide and 1,500 yards deep. Six hours later, before dawn on July 8, three British and Canadian divisions of 1 Corps attacked directly across the carpet and into Caen, with three armored brigades in immediate support and a fourth in reserve. Unfortunately, the heavy bombs had so badly cratered the area that bulldozers often had to fill in the holes before the troops could cross them. Though many of the Germans in the area were stunned by the aerial bombarment and isolated from support, most resisted with their customary tenacity.

During the day, Bradley met with Montgomery and other British leaders at 21 Army Group headquarters. Bradley seconded Eisenhower's pleas for a major British effort by expressing his doubts that his Americans could quickly enough overcome the marshes and the hedgerows. To be able to use American material strength and mobility to advantage, the First Army had to reach the St. Lô-Périers line at the least, and preferably the St. Lô-Coutances line, the original objective of the July 3 attack. Even when by means of such a gain he held reasonably firm ground, Bradley would have to restock his ammunition dumps after the heavy expenditures of the Battle of the Cotentin Plain. Neither the grasping of good ground nor the restocking was in immediate prospect. Montgomery in reply assured Bradley that he might take all the time he needed and that the Second Army would be able to go on holding the Germans at bay. To both Eisenhower and Bradley, Montgomery maintained with consistent equanimity that the danger of a stabilized front was nonexistent. But the conference ended with Bradley still the one who was to move the ball. To be sure, Bradley again showed no willingness to lend Montgomery any large American formations.

After Bradley's departure, Montgomery's British army commander, the tall, angular General Dempsey, himself urged the army group commander to give the Second Army a larger offensive role. Dempsey, too, urged that it was only in the British sector that terrain favored the Allies, and he suggested yet another effort, and on a large scale, to drive a tank offensive into the Caen-Falaise plain. For the present at least, Montgomery refused. Meanwhile the current 1 Corps attack was advancing well enough to capture the section of Caen west of the Orne during the next day, July 9, but thereupon this thrust bogged down like all its predecessors. It carried no farther than the Orne.

The Birth of the COBRA

General Bradley returned to his own complex of headquarters trucks and tents at Au Gay to resume pondering upon escape from the Bocage. By July 10, he had worked out with Hodges, Kean, Dickson, and Colonel Truman C. Thorson, his G-3, the outline of a scheme that Thorson codenamed COBRA. Thorson, who had come with Bradley from Sicily but had joined Bradley's old II Corps there too late to suffer a full infection of the irritable suspiciousness that vexed most of the First Army staff, was perhaps the most able as well as the most amiable of the group. Discovered by Bradley at Fort Benning as the author of an impressive defense plan for the many military installations in the state of

Georgia, Thorson was tough enough to be "Hard Rock Harry" to the troops he commanded, but gaunt enough to be inevitably "Tubby" to the First Army staff.

More fearful than Montgomery that the front was stabilizing, Bradley also showed more concern about the race for the buildup. No other officer outside the services of supply was so consistently mindful as Bradley of the Breton ports. To Bradley, Brittany was the necessary foundation on which to build the American army group he would soon command and the logistical strength to carry the Allies out of stalemate and into victory. COBRA took for its purpose a breakthrough and breakout to the Breton ports.

COBRA abandoned, however, the prospect of simply persisting in the current Battle of the Cotentin Plain directly southward through la Haye-du-Puits and Périers to Coutances and thence to Avranches to turn the corner from Normandy into Brittany. Rather, it acquiesced in the St. Lô-Périers road as a compromise, second-choice objective of the current slugging through the Bocage. On the north side of the St. Lô-Périers road, the plan assumed, the ground was high and dry enough, and beyond the road the hedgerows thinned out just barely enough, that this highway might serve as a substitute line of departure for the next offensive, for the big effort to force a breakthrough.

To assist shoving the First Army's way to a section of the road, Bradley shifted his corps boundaries again. Collins's VII Corps yielded the Carentan-Périers isthmus to Middleton's VIII Corps, while Corlett's XIX Corps yielded the 30th Division to Collins. The forceful Collins was to drive the 9th and 30th Divisions to the St. Lô-Périers road, and thence he was to lead off the new offensive by attacking across the road in heavy force on a narrow front. After the 9th and 30th Divisions had opened the new attack, Collins was to have the rested and now motorized 1st Division to throw in as well, along with the two American armored divisions available in France, the 2nd and 3rd Armored. The 1st Infantry motorized and the 2nd and 3rd Armored were to employ their mobility to spearhead a thrust through the gains of the 9th and 30th Divisions rapidly southwestward to Coutances. The 9th and 30th Divisions thus would break through the German crust, whereupon the 1st Infantry and the 2nd and 3rd Armored would break out. COBRA's mobile divisions would take Coutances not head-on as the July 3 attack had sought to do but from the flank. In doing so they might accomplish yet much more: the opening of the doorway into Brittany as the logistical foundation of further success, and the trapping of the German LXXXIV Corps between the American VII and VIII Corps, to begin fulfilling the constant desideratum of American strategy, the destruction of the enemy army.

The desperation of the Bocage deadlock had driven Bradley and his staff to a plan uncharacteristic of the American army both in its emphasis on concentrated power on a narrow front for the breakthrough, and in its vision of the indirect approach and a possible envelopment of enemy strongpoints as eventual dividends of American mobility. Adversity indeed has its uses; it had pushed Bradley to contrive an excellent plan.

The key to the initial breakthrough, to bursting the infantry stalemate, was to be partly Collins's heavy attack on a narrow front, the concentration unusual in American planning. Still more, air power was to provide the key. As Collins came into the planning, he and Bradley together called on their memories of the air strike preceding the entrance into Cherbourg. If the object was to escape a deadlock reminiscent of the First World War, they could call on a weapon never available in 1914–1918, a truly massive aerial bombardment that could exceed by many orders of magnitude any artillery preparation possible on the old Western Front. The thinner protective casing of bombs in contrast to artillery shells gave the bombs a considerably greater destructive charge in proportion to their weight. Bradley planned a carpet bombing of a rectangular area just south of the St. Lô-Périers road, to employ both the fighter-bombers and mediums of the Ninth Air Force and the heavies of the Eighth. In the sector intended for the attack by the 9th and 30th Divisions, the road was a long straight line. One of the main reasons why Bradley selected the road as his next objective and as the line of departure for the big attack was its quality as a landmark readily recognizable from the air. "I've been wanting to do this now since we landed," said Bradley of the intended bombing. "When we pull it, I want it to be the biggest thing in the world. We want to smash right through."[44]

On July 19 at Leigh-Mallory's headquarters, the famous Battle of Britain Fighter Command nerve center at Bentley Priory, Stanmore, a somewhat awed Major Hansen accompanied Bradley into the Gothic chambers for a "great conference of marshals"— the air marshals—to hammer out the details of the COBRA bombing: Leigh-Mallory himself, disliked and distrusted by most Americans but a "top dog" who had to be reckoned with; Tedder, "lean, small, wiry and quivering with alertness"; Coningham, "with a chin he sticks out at you, a heavy jaw, large teeth and an aggressive attitude"; the American General Brereton, "trim, small and stony faced." Solly Zuckerman was there too, a "small mysterious man with old unpressed tweed suit."[45] By two means, Bradley and the airmen hoped to improve upon the RAF strike that had preceded Montgomery's July 8 attack on Caen and to give the new bombardment unprecedented effectiveness. First, an area 250 yards deep and 7,000 yards long just beyond the road would be attacked only by fighter-bombers, strafing and glide bombing with light fragmentation bombs. The fighter-bombers of course could hit with unexcelled accuracy, and their methods and their bomb loads would ensure against the deep cratering that had obstructed Montgomery's 1 Corps. Even the heavy bombers, saturating an area one mile deep and five miles long beyond the fighter-bomber zone, would be restricted to relatively light fragmentation bombs. The medium bombers would follow the heavies and concentrate on enemy strongpoints, especially those out of reach of American artillery. American armor would be able to mount its effort against an enemy who had been pulverized but across ground not necessarily made impassable by the pulverizing. The second critical point in the air planning was that by relying on the accurate fighter-bombers in the attack zone closest to the troops, Bradley hoped to keep his troops close to that zone and to advance immediately after the air strikes, without the long delay between air and ground attacks that the British had imposed on themselves at Caen.

The Battle of St. Lô

Before the COBRA could be loosed, the First Army must fight its way to the St. Lô-Périers road. To protect the left flank of Collins's COBRA strike from enemy observation and fire based on dominating ground, the First Army must also capture the ancient market town of the sainted Bishop Laudus of Coutances. Commanding the Vire from rocky promontories, St. Lô, the Briovera of the Romans, was no stranger to battles and sieges. In 1574, when it was a Calvinist stronghold, the Catholics stormed it and put many of its citizens to the sword.

General Collins took control of the new VII Corps front between the Taute and the Vire at midnight on July 15–16. Until he reached the St. Lô-Périers road, there was

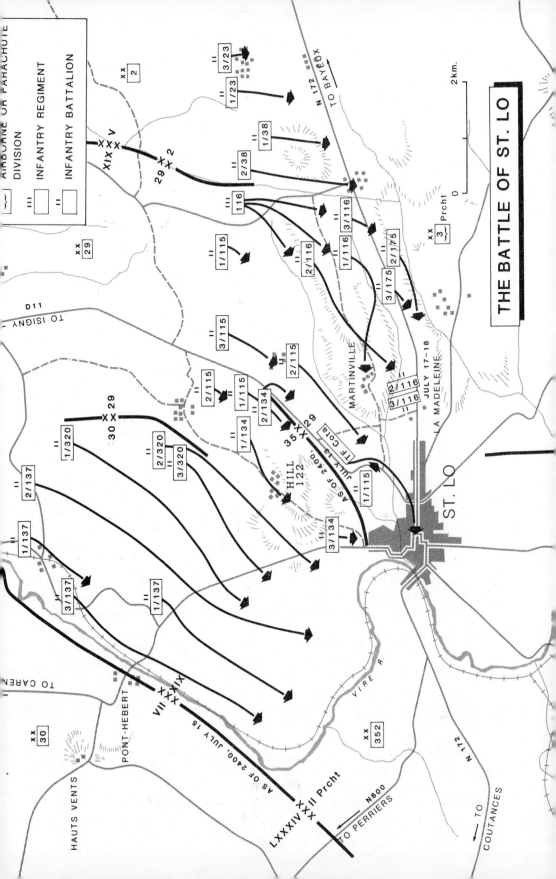

THE BATTLE OF ST. LO

KEY:
- Airborne or Parachute Division
- Infantry Regiment
- Infantry Battalion

Units and locations shown on map:

2/23, 1/23, 1/38, 2/38, 1/16, 1/115, 2/116, 1/116, 3/116, 2/175, 3/175, 3 Prcht, 2/116, 3/116, 3/115, 2/115, 1/115, 2/115, 2/134, 1/134, 3/134, 1/115, 2/320, 3/320, 1/320, 1/137, 2/137, 3/137, 1/137

XXX XIX, XX 2, XX 29, XX 30, XX 29, 29 XX 2, XXX VII, XXX XIX, LXXXIV Prcht, XXII Prcht, XX 352, XX 30

ST. LO

MARTINVILLE

LA MADELEINE

JULY 17–18

HILL 122

TE Cota

JULY 16

AS OF 2400, JULY 15

AS OF 2400, JULY 15

HAUTS VENTS

PONT-HEBERT

VIRE R.

TO BAYEUX — N 172

TO ISIGNY — D 11

TO CAREN...

TO PERRIERS — N800

TO COUTANCES

N 172

2 km.
0

3/23

nothing to do but to slog ahead as before—a depressing prospect rendered worse because Collins had to surrender most of the 3rd Armored Division from the battlefield so it could reunite and flex its muscles for COBRA. On the VII Corps's new right flank, Eddy's 9th Division was enduring a plague of gnat-bites: attacks by small German groups still nesting in the inundations along the Taute River. On the left, Hobbs's 30th Division was now moving south along the Hauts-Vents ridge line but similarly subject to infiltrating jabs into its left from out of the Vire bottomlands. Both divisions suffered similarly as well from recalcitrant Germans holding out in the small Terrette River valley. The bloody but unbowed Panzer Lehr Division still stood in front.

By July 17, the 330th Infantry of Macon's 83rd Division, attached to the right flank of the 9th Division to clear the east bank of the Taute, had fought its way through a sea of mud spotted with German tanks and assault guns dug in and seemingly floating, almost to the St. Lô-Périers road. Its right flank thus reasonably secured, the 9th Division thereupon initiated a thorough sweep of the Terrette valley. By July 20, both the 9th and the 30th Divisions were in positions overlooking the road. When preliminary efforts to clear the road failed, Bradley decided that for the time being, he had enough. His guns dominated the road. He had an adequate line of departure for the coming big push. He had also paid enough: more than 3,000 casualties in the 30th Division to advance thirteen kilometers since July 7, some 2,500 casualties in the 9th Division since July 10.

General Gerow's V Corps and General Corlett's XIX worked meanwhile against the heights of St. Lô. The V Corps had halted only a few kilometers short of the town when the Germans plugged the Caumont Gap in June. Thereafter, Bradley had delayed further direct attack in hopes that the 30th Division's drive toward Pont-Hébert might carry close enough to St. Lô to pry the place from the enemy's grasp. Now the tactical importance of the St. Lô hills demanded an assault on the town, direct if need be.

Both Gerow's and Corlett's corps had to participate because, while St. Lô lay within the XIX Corps zone, taking it demanded taking also Hill 192 in the V Corps zone, about six kilometers east of the town, the culuminating height of the Martinville Ridge which rises gradually from the eastern edge of St. Lô. General Robertson's 2nd Division had expended more than 1,200 casualties in three days during efforts against Hill 192 in June. While the V Corps was to take on this eminence once more, the XIX Corps hoped to avoid direct attack against another height just north of St. Lô, Hill 122, by threatening to encircle its defenders. This object was to be accomplished by means of menacing gestures to the north of the hill at the same time that Corlett's troops also availed themselves of Gerow's expected capture of Hill 192 to direct their main effort down the Martinville Ridge from east to west, south of Hill 122.

The German defenders were General der Fallschirmtruppen Eugen Meindl's II Parachute Corps. Meindl had the 3rd Parachute Division on his right and Kampfgruppen of the 353rd, 266th, and 352nd Divisions on his left, the Kampfgruppen reporting to the headquarters of the latter familiar, battered, and respected formation. Some of the Kampfgruppen with which the Germans began the July operations had been selected mixed-arms task forces; Meindl's Kampfgruppen ran to a second type, the scrapings of the remnants of ruined units. The 3rd Parachute Division, in contrast, was a tough outfit that had given the Americans unpleasant proof of its prowess during the June fighting to close the Caumont Gap.

The American 2nd Division surprised itself, therefore, when its new effort against Hill 192 and the 3rd Parachute Division captured the height in one day's fighting, July

11. The 2nd accomplished this feat, in addition, despite more of the chronic bad weather that had plagued the Allies since the beginning of June and now cancelled the scheduled supporting air strike. It did so also despite the misfiring of an elaborate scheme to deal with the hedgerows. Opposite the divisional line of departure, the hedgerows were quietly hollowed out except for a thin shell facing the enemy, so when the attack began the Shermans would be able to crash straight through. A slight withdrawal the night before the attack, for safety against the supporting air strike that never came, nullified this preparation; the Germans discovered the withdrawal and advanced into part of the abandoned ground, enough to put themselves in front of the Americans' main artillery preparation, and then they disabled or drove back all six tanks in the first wave of one of the assault battalions. Nevertheless, exceptionally good divisional training during the past month in tank-infantry-engineer teamwork, plus exceptionally heavy and accurate artillery support, permitted the Indian Head Division to push the German paratroopers off the hill.

Corlett's XIX Corps began attacking with General Gerhardt's 29th Division the same day. This division had now been continuously in the line longer than any other American division in France. It was a tribute to its short, dapper, peppery cavalryman commander—West Point 1917—in his polished boots and Sam Browne belt, that it could still put on an exceptional show of military ceremony whenever a distinguished visitor arrived—and that General Corlett could still call on it to lead the way into St. Lô. Counting on the 2nd Division to take care of his left flank and rear, Gerhardt intended to launch the 116th Infantry in column of battalions southward against the Martinville Ridge from a parallel ridge where it was entrenched; the historically minded executive officer of the Stonewall Brigade's leading 2nd Battalion noted apprehensively that in terms of relative elevation and separation of the ridges, this was like assailing Cemetery Ridge from Seminary Ridge at Gettysburg, a bad omen for a Virginia regiment. Despite the auspices, however, the 116th took the crest of the Martinville Ridge. The real trouble came afterward, when the troops had to make a sharp right turn to travel down along the crest of the ridge toward St. Lô. The turn exposed their left flank to German fire from two parallel ridges to the south, along one of which ran Route N172, the Bayeux-St. Lô road. If the Stonewall Brigade should shift to the north slope of the Martinville Ridge to shield themselves from the worst of this fire, the effect would be exposure to Hill 122, to escape whose guns they had swung around to the Martinville Ridge in the first place.

Gerhardt therefore decided to persist in running the gauntlet of fire from the south, as the lesser evil. But losses were heavy—almost 500 men on the first day—and on July 12 German artillery disrupted the effort to pass the 175th Infantry through the 116th to give new impetus to the division's attack, inflicting another 500 or so casualties. The next day the 175th managed to mount an attack on a new German line running across the crest of the Martinville Ridge in front of St. Lô, but it achieved scant progress. Corlett and Gerhardt then changed their minds and concluded that Hill 122 would have to be assaulted directly after all, to clear the way toward accomplishing anything else. With the 29th Division tied down on the Martinville Ridge, Corlett had to assign Hill 122 to his other, and inexperienced, division, Major General Paul W. Baade's 35th, built from the Missouri, Kansas, and Nebraska National Guard.

Like the attack of the 2nd Division on Hill 192, this sequel turned out better than anybody could reasonably have expected. The 35th Division had arrived with an advance reputation for good leadership and good training, but so had other fresh divisions that proved disappointing in combat. Baade's Sante Fe Cross Division, however, came late enough to benefit from a measure of preparation, including psychological preparation, for what they would find in the hedgerows, even if the reality was a good deal worse than the part of Cornwall used by Baade as a stand-in during training. Furthermore, the enemy's 352nd Division was at long last reaching the end of its tether. On July 14 Baade's right-flank regiment, the 137th infantry of the Kansas National Guard, attacked along the east bank of the Vire River. Aided by General Hobbs's 30th Division on the opposite bank, the 137th reached the Pont-Hébert–St. Lô road on high ground just west of St. Lô. The 352nd Division, heavily shelled by American artillery during the previous three days, appeared to be nervously preparing to flee the scene. General Meindl had to shovel in reserves to stiffen this long-suffering formation. The reserves slowed the 137th, but thereupon the old 1st Nebraska Infantry of Civil War days, now the 134th Infantry, reinforced with tanks, tank destroyers, and combat engineers, found the enemy in its front weakened enough that at twilight on July 15 it could scramble to the crest of Hill 122.

Late that same afternoon, the Stonewall Brigade came back from a brief, two-day rest behind the lines to attack behind an aerial and artillery bombardment west along the Martinville Ridge. The advance of Major Sidney V. Bingham's 2nd Battalion broke through to a crossroads village called La Madeleine, only about a kilometer from St. Lô. But the Germans were able to cut most of the 2nd Battalion off from the 1st Battalion, some 650 meters back. For two days Bingham's men found themselves under siege, sustained only by the ammunition and rations they had with them at the beginning, and with radio communication faltering uncertainly. Still, the ordeal proved for the Americans a blessing in disguise. The Germans' inability to deliver the knockout punch proved to both sides the accelerating exhaustion of their striking power, while the desire to rescue the lost battalion restimulated attacks all along the 29th Division's line. On July 17 Major Thomas D. Howie's 3rd Battalion of the 116th made contact with Bingham, only to lose its commander and join the 2nd Battalion in isolation. But another old Confederate outfit, the 175th Infantry—elements of the 5th and 53rd Maryland, C.S.A.—hastened to aid the remnant of the Stonewall Brigade in its efforts to rescue their comrades from this new Cemetery Ridge; and at the same time, General Gerhardt decided to punch hard with the 115th Infantry between the Martinville Ridge and Hill 122, and to push toward this northeastern gateway to St. Lô in addition a task force of the division's supporting arms under the assistant division commander and D-Day hero, General Cota.

The shift in direction worked. Without the support of Hill 122, the German defenses in the northeast corner of the city proved too weak to stop the 115th Regiment and Cota's Task Force C, and on July 18 Cota entered St. Lô. Task Force C carried with it Major Howie's body, because when asked whether he could both relieve Bingham and drive his own battalion into the town, Howie had replied without hesitation: "Will do." Placed high on a bier of rubble in front of the ruins of the sixteenth-century Church of Notre-Dame, the flag-draped body of the "Major of St. Lô" became the symbol of the battle and of its over 5,000 American casualties—more than 3,000 in the 29th Division, more than 2,000 in the 35th Division. Because the battle for the largest town in the region—population 11,000—and the capital of the Department of Manche came eventually to seem the climax of the whole campaign in the Bocage, the Major of St. Lô also symbolized all 40,000 American casualties lost in July from the Carentan plain to the verge of the St. Lô–Périers road.

High as it is, the figure 40,000 does not adequately express the cost of the campaign. It does not include the especially heavy toll of psychologically wounded imposed by the Bocage, the victims of combat fatigue severe enough to cause at least temporary disablement, who numbered an additional 25 to 33 percent of 40,000.

Some 90 percent of the casualties were concentrated among the infantrymen. In the hard-used 90th Division, for example, the first six weeks of fighting compelled replacement of the enlisted infantrymen at a rate of over 100 percent, and the infantry officer replacements reached almost 150 percent. By mid-July, infantry replacements were so scarce in the European Theater that 25,000 had to be requested from the United States by the fastest transportation possible.

In return for these casualties, the First Army had advanced about eleven kilometers west of the Vire River and about half that distance east of the Vire. Reflecting on his own regiment's fight on the Carentan-Périers causeway, the Battle of St. Lô, and all the rest of the July battles in the Bocage, the historian of the 83rd Division's 329th Regiment offered an apt summary: "We won the battle of Normandy, [but] considering the high price in American lives, we lost."[46]

8: COBRA

A FTER GENERAL BRADLEY departed from the conference of July 10, and after General Dempsey urged that the Second Army ought to strike the very kind of offensive blow that Bradley had urged, the victor of El Alamein sought as usual the solitude of his trailer quarters in which to reconsider a full-blooded attack by his British troops. Undeniably, the British faced far more favorable ground than the Americans; Bradley might be concocting plans for a breakthrough, but in the conference he displayed little conviction that he could achieve it. Just as surely in Montgomery's mind, the British were the better soldiers of the Grand Alliance. And equally surely, the British tank knock-about toward Falaise, once perhaps rashly forecast, still offered the brightest available prospect of a triumph to match El Alamein: there lay the bulk of the panzer divisions, the heart of the enemy strength, whose defeat would signify the defeat of the German army.

There lay Rommel's panzers: but perhaps by now as in October 1942 the attrition already imposed on the panzers and the penchant of the Desert Fox, however bold he could be in the offensive, to yield despairingly to setbacks represented opportunity as well. The War Office already was cautioning Montgomery that manpower replacements could continue flowing to the Second Army at the existing rate for only a few weeks more. So attrition was expending Britain's last army even when Montgomery used the army with great caution; while handled properly, an offensive might represent the lesser risk for the army after all. Perhaps, moreover, an immense aerial preparation such as Bradley was planning, but applied to the British front, correcting the defects of the July 7 attack on Caen, might work even better for the British, free from the impediments of the Bocage, than for the Americans.

Before the 10th of July was over, Montgomery had not only changed his mind but issued his first instructions to the planners and to Dempsey for what was to become Operation GOODWOOD. The codename, borrowed from a famous English racecourse, surely implied breakout.

GOODWOOD

General Dempsey's instructions charged him to prepare a "massive stroke" from Caen to Falaise. The principal instrument of the stroke was to be the 8 Corps of Lieutenant General Sir Richard O'Connor, who had commanded the British army's first great westward race across the North African desert from Sidi Barrani to El Agheila in 1940–1941. Attacking out of the bridgehead east of the Orne, 8 Corps was to have a concentration of three armored divisions. But this time the offensive would not be limited to a single corps, for 12 Corps was to open the game with a diversionary attack from the

British right, and the Canadian 2nd Corps was to attack simultaneously with 8 Corps to complete the conquest of Caen. For the armored 8 Corps, said Dempsey, "What I had in mind was to seize all the crossings of the Orne from Caen to Argentan," which would spring a bigger trap than the proposed dash of the American VII Corps from just west of St. Lô to Coutances. If Dempsey succeeded, he would bag the better part of Panzer Group West.[1]

Argentan, Dempsey's goal, is seventy-two kilometers from Caen, twice as far as Falaise. Montgomery, his caution about explicit commitments reasserting itself, ordered Dempsey to erase even the name of Falaise from the Second Army plan. Still, informing Eisenhower that he intended to attack on July 17 and "that the whole weight of the air power is to be available on that day to support my land battle," Montgomery promised that "the whole eastern flank" would "burst into flames" in a "decisive" victory. Eisenhower anticipated "a brilliant stroke which will knock loose our present shackles."[2]

When the persistence of abominable weather threatened the aerial preparation for GOODWOOD, Montgomery postponed the attack from July 17 to dawn of the 18th. The 18th was the date on which Bradley had hoped to unloose COBRA, when he first began planning that offensive; but the slow American advance to the necessary preliminary objectives was compelling a postponement of COBRA in any event, and now, so GOODWOOD and COBRA could both have maximum aerial support, Bradley's attack was rescheduled to follow GOODWOOD by three days.

The preliminary attack of 12 Corps from the British right commenced as early as July 15. Unfortunately, it failed to divert the Germans' attention from the impending main effort. During the next two days, Second Army intelligence reported a thickening of the German defenses in front of 8 Corps. The British thought the defenses reached back five to six kilometers; Rommel was actually completing multiple belts of defenses with a total thickness of about sixteen kilometers. On the Bourguébus Ridge overlooking the projected battlefield, behind three main defensive lines and a reserve line, the British knew the Germans had a gun line studded with 88s and other artillery pieces. But there were not enough airplanes available to extend the preparatory bombing carpet far enough to include this line. The gun line also happened to be at the extreme range of most of Dempsey's artillery. The airmen offered to return and hit the gun line at noon, but Dempsey refused in the belief that by then his tanks would have reached the Bourguébus Ridge if they were going to reach it at all.

More than 2,000 heavies, mediums, and fighter-bombers of the RAF and AAF dropped over 8,000 tons of bombs to open GOODWOOD, three times the weight that had preceded Dempsey's July 8 attack. British warships in the Bay of the Seine joined in. The bombardment produced most of the desired effect of stunning those Germans within the carpet who survived it; prisoners were so deafened that they could not be interrogated for another twenty-four hours. Montgomery's first dispatch of the offensive announced: "Early this morning British and Canadian troops of the Second Army attacked and broke through into the area east of the Orne and south-east of Caen": broke through![3]

Then the attack struck the gun line. By the time the spearheads advanced this far, most of the British force had fallen well behind, entangled in congested crossroads villages. Against the 88s on the Bourguébus Ridge, the spearheads faltered. General O'Connor, still aggressive despite the sojourn in Axis prison compounds that had cut short his brilliant career in the Western Desert, decided in the early afternoon that he must hurl everything available head-on at the Bourguébus Ridge, casualties be damned. But the routes open to his armor were so narrow—including the lanes opened by his engineers through British mine fields—that everything available no longer amounted to very much; his tanks were mostly strung out beyond supporting distance of his spearheads. By dusk his vanguard seemed to be making progress anyway; but then it crunched against infantry of Adolf Hitler's Lifeguard, the 1st SS Panzer Division, fresh from Eberbach's reserves.

July 18 cost the Second Army 270 tanks and 1,500 men, without cracking the Bourguébus Ridge. The next day, the British persisted in local attacks. By the third day, July 20, these efforts drove the enemy from most of the northern slope of the Bourguébus Ridge. But the Germans clung to the crest, and on the 20th a thunderstorm erupted, to make a quagmire of the area of the bombing carpet through which reinforcements and supplies must pass to assail the ridge. That was the end of GOODWOOD, sealed by a German counterattack on the 21st.

To the Supreme Commander, SHAEF headquarters, and the Americans, GOODWOOD was a sad disappointment. General Montgomery claimed to be satisfied with the latest attrition of German strength and the diversion of attention from Bradley's front. The Second Army had completed its occupation of the ruins of Caen and expanded its bridgehead east of the Orne for total territorial gains of some fifty-eight square kilometers. But these accomplishments were small when set against Montgomery's prebattle pledge of a decisive victory, or his report on the opening day of the battle. Why did Montgomery use the words "broke through" if, as he subsequently claimed, a breakthrough on the Allied left not only failed to occur but was never intended?

At SHAEF, staff members guessed who would be Montgomery's successor, because even Eisenhower with his carefully self-imposed patience toward his British Allies made no secret of his belief that the Second Army again did not press as hard as it might have. The Supreme Commander went so far as to urge Prime Minister Churchill "to persuade Monty to get on his bicycle and start moving."[4] On July 21, General Eisenhower also pleaded with Montgomery directly to renew the offensive, reminding him that eventually the strength of the American army on the Continent would overshadow the British, and urging that therefore, "while we have equality in size we must go forward shoulder to shoulder, with honors and sacrifices equally shared." But he also told Montgomery: "Now we are pinning our immediate hopes on Bradley's attack."[5]

The rumors about who might take Montgomery's place had at least a slight foundation, in the presence at SHAEF of senior officers never well disposed toward the arrogant, hawklike loner at 21 Army Group, and now out of patience with him. Notable among these opponents of Montgomery was the Deputy Supreme Commander, Air Marshal Tedder. When there was a SHAEF discussion on the 21st about dealing with the V-weapons, and Bedell Smith remarked that it would be a long time before the Allies got to the launching sites in the Pas de Calais, Tedder responded: "Then we must change our leaders for men who will get us there." Tedder said he was ready to write to the British Chiefs of Staff about Montgomery's deficiencies.[6] Eisenhower, in contrast, however disappointed, never moved in that direction. He soon muted his misgivings about GOODWOOD. To charge that the Second Army could have pushed harder was dubious anyway. As it was, GOODWOOD cost the British 36 percent of the tanks they had in France.

The casualties amounted to 4,000 in 8 Corps alone. The Second Army could not have risked losing much more.

Yet the possibilities within GOODWOOD had been so great that disappointment must linger—the terrain so much better than in front of the Americans, Dempsey's proposed trap along the Orne potentially so ruinous to Panzer Group West and the whole Seventh Army. If the Allies had to pin their hopes on Bradley and the Americans, it remained too bad that unquestioned assumptions about the logistics of the invasion had placed the Americans where they must fight the Bocage as well as the Germans.

The COBRA Strikes

The Allied command would not be changed, but the German would. It was Rommel's habit to visit the front daily. On July 17 he drove back toward Army Group B headquarters at la Roche Guyon from an inspection of Panzer Group West's dispositions against the anticipated Allied attack that proved to be GOODWOOD. His big Horch command car had just rolled out of Livarot toward Vimoutiers on Route N179 when two low-flying RAF Typhoons roared down the road, guns blazing. An explosive 20mm. shell struck the car, and Rommel was hit on the left temple and left cheek by flying glass and stones and instantly knocked unconscious. The driver was also hit and lost control, the Horch struck a tree, and Rommel was hurled onto the road. He suffered a fracture of the base of the skull, two fractures of the left temple, a broken-in left cheekbone, a damaged left eye, and severe concussion. Doctors at a Luftwaffe hospital at Bernay doubted his survival. The Germans tried to conceal the incident, but Allied intelligence promptly learned that Hitler's most famous general was out of action.

The new OB West, Field Marshal von Kluge, took over direct command of Army Group B. Three days later, on July 20, the conspiracy against Hitler from within Germany failed when a bomb set off in the Führer's East Prussian headquarters wounded but did not kill him. Kluge, it happened, had—like Rommel—been in limited contact with the conspirators and, not knowing they intended tyrannicide, had shown them mild and guarded sympathy. As the inevitable ruthless SS search for every hint of complicity in the assassination attempt produced in the subsequent weeks more and more tortured confessions and lists of conspiratorial names, and Kluge more and more nervously awaited what might be charged against him, the German command in the West found a new motive for holding its lines as tenaciously as possible. Allied intelligence, learning of the July 20 Attentat, briefly hoped for a general rising against Hitler and a defection of the Wehrmacht, but allowed no false hopes to grow among the staffs and troops now readying for COBRA.

If COBRA offered terrain and strategic possibilities inferior to GOODWOOD, at least the Americans had reached ground drier and more open than the Cotentin plain. At the St. Lô-Périers road, the prairies marécageuses and the artificial inundations for the most part lay behind the First Army. In the fertile, rolling countryside to the southward, the hedgerows enclosed larger pastures and apple orchards growing heavy with the source of the brandy of the Calvados. Roads became more numerous, many tarred and two-lane, but with a few wider highways. Rising hills and ridge lines could offer a new impediment to mobility; but as Collins pointed out to Bradley early in the COBRA planning, reaching

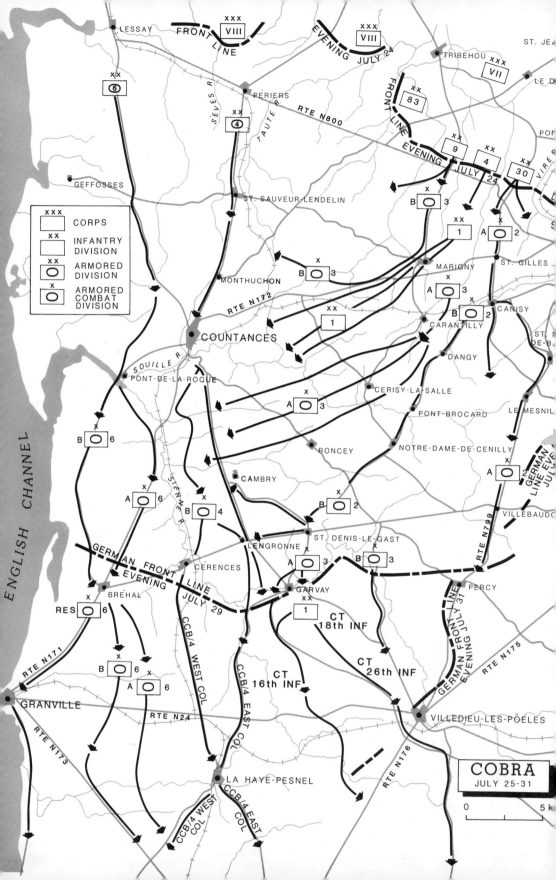

COBRA
JULY 25-31

0 ⎯⎯ 5 km

Marigny not far past the potential breakthrough zone would give the VII Corps a sheltered valley between the ridges through which to travel southwest to Coutances.

In the final days before COBRA, there was even hope of crashing armor through the hedgerows. From the beginning of the Bocage fighting, soldiers in the field experimented with the sort of devices for countering the hedgerows that the invasion planners might have thought about earlier had they comtemplated the Bocage. Improvisation supplemented the First Army's few tank dozers—tanks mounting bulldozer blades—by attaching blades to ordinary Shermans; but it often took a satchel charge in advance to permit even a tank dozer to penetrate a hedgerow. Individual units contrived their own kinds of hedgecutting equipment, such as the XIX Corps's "salad fork" of frontal prongs on a tank, intended to bore holes in the hedgerows so demolition charges could be planted there, but sometimes found capable of acting like a fork to lift enough of the hedgerow that the tank could push through the rest. On July 14, at General Gerow's invitation, Bradley visited the 2nd Division to see the device invented by Sergeant Curtis G. Culin of the 102nd Cavalry Reconnaissance Squadron: heavy steel tusklike prongs welded to the front of a Sherman in such a way that when the tank butted into a hedgerow, the prongs pinned the tank so it would not belly up over the obstacle; then the Sherman was able to drive through the hedgerow by main force. Culin had fashioned his prongs from a German roadblock. Bradley was so impressed that he ordered German underwater obstacles from the beaches used to mass-produce the tusks, and he instructed his ordnance chief to comb England for as much arc-welding equipment and as many welding crews as he could get, and to have tanks in England equipped with prongs as well. Sergeant Culin's "Rhinoceros" or "Rhino" was on three out of five First Army tanks by the beginning of COBRA. No Rhino tank was allowed to go into action before COBRA, to ensure the enemy's surprise when the Shermans began plunging straight through the barriers that until now had so thoroughly hamstrung and depressed the American army.

In a war and an army where command decisions tended to ooze slowly and gelatinously out of a morass of staff work, it was a rarity that COBRA was preeminently the design of just two generals, Bradley and Collins. Not only did Bradley entrust his hopes for breakthrough and breakout to the proven aggressiveness of the conqueror of Cherbourg and the northern Cotentin. The two men worked easily together, Bradley with his studied calmness offering softspoken suggestions, Collins a "powerhouse ready to drive through,"[7] Bradley shaping the total design but quick to accept Collins's proposals for modification. Within the VII Corps, as the corps history of COBRA put it, Collins "For all practical purposes . . . was his own General Staff. He not only made the final decisions but personally put together the jigsaw pieces which added up to the decisions."[8]

The breakthrough was to be sought against roughly the 7,000 yards pommeled by the air bombardment along the St. Lô-Périers road. When Manton Eddy nevertheless argued that more strength had to be added to his own 9th and Hobbs's 30th Division to assure the desired penetration, and Collins seconded him, Bradley immediately said, "Well how about another division?" and offered Barton's 4th, recently pulled from the line for a rest. (During the trip back to his own headquarters, Bradley smiled to "Tubby" Thorson, "Gosh, I never thought I'd ever be in the position where I could give away a division that easily.")[9] Three divisions, the UTAH veterans of the 4th in the center, would try to break the German crust.

With his eye on the protected way between the ridges and on Route N172 running straight along that way from Marigny to Coutances, Collins also suggested that the main thrust by his exploiting troops be directly down the road. The First Army plan had called for wider, more circular sweeps, by way of Carantilly and Canisy. But the army plan had thereby cautiously emphasized the establishment of blocking positions against possible counterattack from the southeast; bold Collins was more concerned with dealing with the German formations in front of the VIII Corps, and with ensuring that the main drive would cut across the rear of the current German lines. Bradley accepted the change in plan.

For the principal exploitation, Collins chose Huebner's motorized 1st Infantry Division and CCB of Watson's 3rd Armored. To retain what he thought an adequate measure of protection against the possibility of counterattack from the south and southeast, he would send CCA of the 3rd Armored on the longer sweep toward Coutances by way of Carantilly. He would also send Brooke's 2nd Armored through le Mesnil-Herman to take up blocking positions farther south.

While Collins's more direct thrust through Marigny along N172 to Coutances increased the chances of cutting behind more Germans to entrap more of them, Collins also modified the program to emphasize not so much the laying of a trap—which on the American flank of the Allied lodgment would be at best a limited trap anyway—but further exploitation beyond the immediate operation, into an accelerating and expanding breakout. The First Army plan had the exploiting armor going all the way to Bréhal virtually on the Cotentin west coast. Collins instructed his exploiting force to halt at Coutances and at Cérences south of Coutances, to position itself in a manner that would provide a protected corridor for the VIII Corps to break out of the Cotentin down the peninsula's west coast. Otherwise there would be "a hell of a scramble" as VII and VIII Corps units met along the coast.[10] With this modification, moreover, there were new potentialities for Bradley's injunction that while COBRA was striking at the Coutances-Caumont line, the army should be ready to go on moving rather than consolidate on that line, should be alert to exploit enemy disorganization to the fullest. Collins still more than Bradley was emphasizing breakout beyond breakthrough.

Giving Collins the 4th Division put virtually every combat soldier at Bradley's disposal into the line for the supreme effort to break the deadlock of the Bocage. G-3 Thorson commented that the First Army had no reserve except the 99th Norwegian Battalion. "Collins interrupts to say he has never had a reserve in any of his fights. Brad laughs, 'I went all through Tunisia and Sicily without a regiment of reserve.'"[11]

Bradley and Collins grew "warmed up in enthusiasm": "Bradley also tells Collins ... that he is going to have the fighters drop bellytanks of this flame thrower fuel on the area after they finish their escort mission. That's giving them the works all the way around."[12] The troops understandably retained greater apprehensions: "Meanwhile infantry elements of the 30th Division were marching down the road, widely spaced to avoid enemy shellfire. Many of them were replacements, with the division only three or four days and scared to death of the ordeal now facing them. Some of the replacements were only several days out of Camp Walters, 21 weeks in the army from the time of their induction."[13] Some of the soldiers' uneasy premonitions were well founded; the great offensive proved to open in tragedy.

In Bradley's discussions with the airmen, the margin of safety between the aerial bombardment and the American troops had become a vexing question. Bradley, wanting to avoid the defects of earlier aerial preparations and to afford the enemy no opportunity to recover from blast and shock, hoped the VII Corps could attack across the St. Lô-Périers road virtually as soon as the bombardment ended. He proposed to withdraw his troops only 800 yards behind the target area south of the road. To guard adequately against the bombers' hitting his men despite this narrow margin, he recommended that they fly their bomb runs parallel to the front, rather than perpendicular to the front with an approach over the heads of the American troops. The airmen countered that they could not assure the troops' safety with a buffer zone of less than 3,000 yards. They also objected to lateral bomb runs, arguing that thus approaching the target area on its narrow rather than its wide side would cause excessive congestion and would not permit completing the bombardment within the short time that was desirable. They pointed out, too, that a perpendicular approach would permit less enemy interference and would thereby help the planes to bomb accurately. To deal with this latter objection, Bradley urged that a morning attack could come in from east to west out of the sun, partially blinding the enemy's guns and interceptors.

After Bradley for a time insisted that there would be no withdrawal of more than 1,000 yards—some of his commanders expressed unwillingness to give up even an inch of the ground for which the First Army had fought so hard—the conferees compromised on a 1,200-yard safety margin for the fighter-bombers, with the less accurate heavy bombers to strike no closer to the troops than 1,450 yards. With this agreement, Bradley also developed the impression that the airmen had acquiesced in bomb runs parallel to the front.

The aerial bombardment was to begin at eighty minutes before H-Hour with 350 IX TAC fighter-bombers striking mainly against the 250-yard strip just south of the St. Lô-Périers road. After twenty minutes of fighter-bomber activity, 1,800 VIII Bomber Command heavies would take over, saturating the carpet south of the narrower strip in a one-hour strike, to a depth of 2,500 yards from the road. Immediately thereafter, 350 fighter-bombers would again hit the narrow strip for twenty minutes, during which time the troops were to move up to their line of departure, to jump off at the very time the bombardment ended. Ten minutes later, 396 IX Bomber Command mediums would attack the southern half of the target area for forty-five minutes. With the Ninth Air Force completely committed to the bombardment, eight groups of VIII Fighter Command would fly bomber cover.

Collins's artillery would supplement the aerial bombardment with the preparatory fire usual for a major attack, for which the VII Corps artillery was reinforced with much of the artillery under First Army control: nine of twenty-one heavy battalions, five of nineteen medium battalions, and all seven of the First Army's nondivisional light battalions. Nondivisional guns under VII Corps control would total 258; Collins would have more than 1,000 guns in all. Unfortunately, the shortage of artillery ammunition restricted what the guns could do. Enemy strongpoints considered vital were to be taken under fire in the preliminary bombardment, but many merely suspected German centers of resistance would have to wait for artillery attack on call when the assault moved forward. There was no overall corps fire plan; division artillery commanders planned their own fires. The nondivisional guns under corps control fired only a counterbattery and counterflak shoot. Relatively little fire fell beyond the enemy's immediate front lines.

The air plan was all the more crucial because it would have to do much of the work ordinarily expected of artillery.

The heavy bombers were to drop more than 3,300 tons of high explosive and fragmentation bombs, the mediums 137 tons of high explosives and 4,000 260-lb. fragmentation bombs, the fighter-bombers 212 tons of bombs and a great deal of the infernal substance whose advent Bradley hailed so delightedly, napalm. Though only half the aerial preparation for GOODWOOD, the total scheduled effort amounted to a considerably heavier barrage than Bradley thought he could get when he first began the COBRA planning, and he looked forward to the attack feeling well compensated for having yielded on the safety zone, and for having to accept somewhat larger bombs than the 100-lb. fragmentations which he had wanted as a limit to reduce cratering.

Because the ground offensive was to be built upon its aerial support, Leigh-Mallory received authority to fix the date and time for COBRA. The July 21 date set after Montgomery initiated GOODWOOD passed without action because of the same installment of the summer's chronically wet weather that helped mire GOODWOOD. By the night of July 23–24, though Eighth Air Force meteorologists felt uneasy, the forecasts were encouraging enough that Leigh-Mallory scheduled COBRA for the 24th. Setting H-Hour for 1:00 P.M., by which time an overcast sky was expected to have cleared, the AEAF commander traveled to France in the morning only to find the overcast persisting and visibility inadequate. So he postponed the operation again.

But only after six groups of IX TAC fighter-bombers and three bombardment divisions—about 1,600 planes—of Eighth Air Force heavies had taken off. Three of the six fighter-bomber groups received the recall order before they attacked, but the others bombed the narrow strip south of the highway and a few selected strongpoints north of the road. No radio channels had been designated for emergency communication with the heavies, and the only way to try to recall them was to broadcast on frequencies to which they might be listening. When the first formation of 500 heavies reached the target area, they found visibility so poor that they did not bomb. The second formation similarly found the overcast so bad that only thirty-five planes dropped their loads. But with some breaks in the clouds, over 300 bombers in the third formation dropped almost 700 tons before word of the postponement finally reached them.

"Suddenly," wrote Major Hansen, "there was a sharp deadly screaming whistle. I had heard it before in Tunisia when we were bombed at El Guettar. We dove to the ground. . . ."[14] The bombing killed twenty-five and wounded 131 soldiers of the 30th Division. The casualties occurred mainly when the lead bombardier of a sixteen-plane formation had trouble moving his bomb-release mechanism and, trying to correct it, dropped his load prematurely; the other planes of his formation followed his lead. Furthermore, to Bradley's surprise and dismay, the heavies came in perpendicular to the front, and the American troops could readily become their inadvertent targets.

Bradley returned to VII Corps headquarters where he found General Quesada of IX TAC and learned that Quesada had already telegraphed General Brereton about the short bombing. Brereton's reply was also already in hand, stating among other things that Bradley had been informed that the bombing would be perpendicular to the road. On the contrary, said Bradley, Quesada as the airman in closest touch with him had been unwilling to believe when he saw it that the bombers were coming in directly from the north, and for himself, "Had I known of air's intent to chance the perpendicular approach, I would never have consented to its plan."[15] Yet Bradley had no choice but to let the bombers fly in over the heads of the soldiers again on the next try; the airmen said they could not attack the next day if they had to devise a new bombing plan. The best they could offer was to arrange additional precautions against short bombing, including visual bombing by the heavies at minimum altitudes, more use of red smoke shells fired by the troops as markers, and cerise and yellow panels to mark the VII Corps's forward lines.

Bradley accepted these arrangements as preferable to further delays, because the bombing of July 24 had already given the Germans an obvious warning that something was about to happen on a narrow front along the St. Lô-Périers road. As some small consolation, the attack divisions were at least able to fight their way back across the safety zone to their original positions and projected line of departure without meeting much opposition; Collins had feared the enemy would respond to the bombing by moving north of the road in the hope of escaping a second bombing attack farther south. Unlucky elsewhere, the 30th Division was especially lucky in its return to its original front, meeting almost no Germans in the process.

So, under newly encouraging weather forecasts, the Allied commanders prepared to try again on July 25. The predicted good weather arrived, and IX TAC's fighter-bombers began striking again at 9:38 A.M. on the 25th.

Late in a morning of nervous waiting and listening to the roar of the air fleets at Collins's CP, Tubby Thorson handed Bradley a message and commented: "They've done it again." Under the strain of flying at the relatively low altitude of 12,000 feet, with consequent recomputation of the bombardiers' calculations, heavier enemy flak, and loosening of formations, and with the artillery's smoke markers obscured in the dust and smoke of the bombardment, a considerable portion of the Fortresses' and Liberators' bombs fell outside the target area, the bombs of thirty-five aircraft striking to the north of it. Forty-two mediums of IX Bomber Command also short-bombed.

The commander of Company B, 8th Infantry, in the 4th Division described it:

> The dive bombers came in beautifully, dropped their bombs right in front of us just where they belonged. Then the first group of heavies dropped theirs in the draw several hundred yards in front of us. . . . But then the next wave came in closer, the next one closer, still closer. The dust cloud was drifting back toward us. Then they came right on top of us. At least three plane loads fell in the next 10 or 15 minutes right on the first and second platoons. We put on all the orange smoke we had but I don't think it did any good; they could not have seen it through the dust. . . . The shock was awful. A lot of the men were sitting around after the bombing in a complete daze. . . . I called battalion and told them I was in no condition to move, that everything was completely disorganized and it would take me some time to get my men back together, and asked for a delay. But battalion said no, push off. Jump off immediately.[16]

The casualty toll of the bombing errors was 111 Americans dead and 490 wounded. In the 9th Division, the 3rd Battalion of the 47th Infantry lost its whole command group, except for the CO himself, and suffered so many other casualties that it had to be replaced in the attack by the 1st Battalion, 39th Infantry. The American advance in this battalion sector was delayed for an hour to an hour and a half. The 30th Division was hard hit for a second time.

Dejection "settled over us like a wet fog," said General Bradley,[17] and despite the orders to push on it was questionable whether the attacking troops could recover rapidly enough to take advantage of whatever effects the bombing might have had on the defense. In the 119th and 120th Infantry of the 30th Division, the commanders seemed as concerned about finding ambulances for the wounded as about getting the attack started. "I was pretty foggy," the company executive officer added to the account of Company B, 8th Infantry:

> I knew there was something I had to do but I was not quite sure what it was. It reminds me of an occasion when I was boxing and was knocked down. I jumped up immediately and fought through three more rounds winning the fight, but I don't remember it and remember very little that happened for the next six hours. I was in much the same condition 25 July. The next thing I remember is moving forward with my platoon but I don't know how much later that was. Lt Burris was with me and I remember that he was very impatient with me about something.[18]

So much had the generals depended on and expected from the carpet bombing, and so much had the generals' expectations filtered down to the troops who watched the thousands of friendly planes stream over them and felt the earth shake, that anything less than complete pulverization of the enemy in the target area was sure to aggravate the fog of dejection. And though the first advancing troops found disabled German vehicles, shattered corpses, and stunned and disoriented survivors everywhere in the bombing carpet, they also found the veterans of Generalleutnant Fritz Bayerlein's Panzer Lehr Division "doing business at the same old stand with the same old merchandise—dug-in tanks and infantry."[19] Indeed, the Germans had even infiltrated the safety zone north of the bombing, and the Americans had to fight for that ground all over again. German artillery fire was so heavy in front of the 30th Division that the division G-2 reported disgustedly, "enemy artillery was not touched by our bombing."[20]

The three assaulting infantry divisions were supposed to reach Marigny and St. Gilles before Collins committed the three mobile exploiting divisions. On July 25, the assault carried only about two kilometers at best, and got nowhere near those two crossroads. It would not have progressed as well as it did had it not been for the lack of a connected enemy line. There were enough gaps in the German positions to permit sideslipping and flanking operations. In the 9th Division, the 1st Battalion of the 47th Infantry spent three hours in frontal assaults against an irregularly shaped woods north of the St. Lô-Périers road, where the Germans could command excellent fields of fire across flat meadows to the north with well sited automatic weapons and Panzerfäuste placed in covered foxholes and concealed by underbrush. Bloodied and repulsed, the American battalion found an opening to cross the highway east of the woods and then take the defenders out from the southeast. When darkness came, some Germans were still in the woods annoying the battalion's rear.

The 120th Infantry of the 30th Division attacked in column of battalions astride the paved St. Jean-de-Daye–St. Gilles road. When a roadblock featuring three Panthers and automatic weapons defied the lead 2nd Battalion for several hours and knocked out three supporting tanks, the regimental commander sent the 1st and 3rd Battalions on flanking marches to the east and west. These movements eliminated the threat of the roadblock, and the 3rd Battalion picked up enough momentum that it was soon able to penetrate what seemed to be the enemy's main line of resistance.

The best gain of the day, surprisingly, was scored by the 1st Battalion, 39th Infantry, filling in for the bomb-ravaged 3/47th. Though stalled through most of the afternoon by another woods—in this instance, an orchard—full of concealed and well-placed German guns, once the battalion had cleaned out the area among the trees it was able to leap all the way to la Chapelle-en-Juger, almost two kilometers south of the St. Lô-Périers road.

General Collins took careful note that the resistance, while disappointingly stubborn, was scattered in pockets susceptible to flanking. This could mean that the July 24 bombing had forewarned the enemy and he had withdrawn his main line of resistance southward, where for the most part it remained to be met. The meaning could also be, however, that the main line of resistance had already been fragmented, despite the pessimism of reports from the front. In this event, exploitation ought to begin before the enemy could consolidate a new position and bring up reserves. Furthermore, Bradley had lined up for July 26 another program of air support on a scale too lavish to be maintained day after day. Combining these considerations, General Collins decided on the afternoon of July 25 that he should gamble by ordering two of his three mobile columns to begin their attacks the next morning.

Breakout

The gamble, said Collins, "is we shouldn't count too much on fast movement of armored divisions through this country; if we make a break-through it is OK but until then . . . [the armor] can't move any faster than the infantry."[21] The result might be congestion to snarl everybody's movement.

So Wednesday, July 26 was a day of suspense. The divisions scheduled for exploitation were being committed with their first mission now simply the deepening of the first day's disappointing penetration. The inevitable rearrangements produced their unfortunate effects immediately. The 1st Division had to shuffle its column to put assault troops in the lead, instead of the reconnaissance units that would have headed up a lightly opposed exploiting march. On Collins's right, General Eddy had to hasten to clear the Marigny road of his own 9th Division as well as the Germans so the 1st Division and CCB of the 3rd Armored could get under way.

Directed with Eddy's customary skill and flair, however, the 9th Division performed its chores and in doing so pressed four kilometers south of the St. Lô-Périers road and almost three kilometers west from the Marigny road. Still, the advance of the Big Red One and CCB hit German reinforcements—including two tank companies of the 2nd SS Panzer Division—north of Marigny and by nightfall penetrated only into the outskirts of the town. CCB advanced along the Marigny road. The 1st Division advanced in a column of regiments just to the east of the road and parallel to it, the 18th Infantry in column of battalions leading the division, the 1st Battalion in column of companies leading the 18th Regiment, a tank dozer in front of the column because moving cross country required cutting through every hedgerow. The cutting process averaged two and a half minutes per hedgerow. Hearing a false report that CCB was inside Marigny, the 1/18th in the late afternoon headed for a dominating landscape feature, Hill 100, south of the town. Somehow the battalion got lost at this juncture, and after dark the regimental commander, Colonel George Smith, Jr., discovered abruptly that despite previous contrary information, Germans full of fight were still in front of him both at Marigny and on Hill

100. Collins had ordered the 1st Division to push the attack during the night, but Smith decided that coordinated attacks on the town and the hill by daylight would cost less and have a better chance of success.

This situation prompted Collins to chance yet another gamble. For July 27, he told CCB to take off down N172 from Marigny toward Coutances even though the enemy still held Marigny.

Collins judged the new gamble acceptable because the signs were that the earlier, bigger one was beginning to pay off. On the VII Corps left, where the 2nd Armored Division was supposed to execute the lesser, covering strike to protect the movement through Marigny, the 30th Division initially had more trouble than the 9th in clearing its roads—the macadam St. Jean-de-Daye–St. Gilles road and an unpaved parallel route— for the mobile troops. During Wednesday afternoon, however, Hobbs's men began to find resistance crumbling. When Brooks of the 2nd Armored instructed Maurice Rose to take CCA down the path cleared by the Old Hickories and above all to keep moving, Rose complied by hurrying his lead tanks through St. Gilles by midafternoon. CCA's recent days of combined training with the attached 22nd Infantry Regiment paid off richly; at every cluster of resistance, the infantry would dismount from their vehicles, fix the enemy positions, and lead the tanks in to finish them off. At dusk the tanks and mounted infantry passed through Canisy, the west side of the town aflame from a fighter-bomber attack and the armored column silhouetted against the blaze. South of Canisy, Rose pushed the column onward through pitch darkness, saying when subordinates requested a rest stop that the whole American offensive depended on his forward motion, and that he would not stop short of his planned objectives however black the night or heavy his losses.

Like Collins, Rose sensed that the time for gambling was at hand, the hour when opportunity must be seized lest it not return again. In the darkness, a halftrack and trailer persisted in passing vehicles and working their way to the head of the column until the commander of the lead tank grumbled as they crawled past him, "Hell, I'm supposed to be leading this column."[22] Then he realized they were German vehicles whose crews must have thought they were in a German column, and he opened fire and knocked out the halftrack. This incident was not the only such indication of enemy flight and confusion during the night.

About three in the morning, Rose reached CCA's first COBRA objective, a road junction just north of le Mesnil-Herman, where at last he called a halt and prepared to take up blocking positions. When news of Rose's march climbed up the chain of headquarters, its meaning was unambiguous. The German crust in Normandy was broken at last; CCA, 2nd Armored, had rolled clean through the enemy's defenses.

The reports from the 4th Division's 8th Regiment in Collins's center spelled out the same meaning. Adhering to Collins's orders to maintain pressure through the night, elements of the 8th twice during the dark hours collided with a strong force of German tanks, armored vehicles, and infantry. On both occasions, the panzers merely fired to cover the escape of the rest of their column, and then drew away themselves. By dawn, the 4th Division's spearheads were eleven kilometers south of the St. Lô-Périers road.

Meanwhile the 30th Division made contact with the XIX Corps on its left at the Vire River bridge leading out of St. Lô and captured two other bridges on the main roads south from St. Lô. By noon of July 27, Eddy's 9th Division had so completely fulfilled its assignment of penetrating the German defenses on the right of the assault, and resistance in its sector had evaporated so completely, that Collins sent the division into reserve.

When Colonel Smith of the 18th Infantry opened his attack against Marigny at seven A.M. on Thursday morning, he discovered the enemy had withdrawn southward to Hill 100 during the night. Part of his 3rd Battalion supported by a platoon of tanks fought all day without taking the crest of Hill 100, the Germans enjoying excellent observation and protection behind hedgerows and trees, and Smith's infantrymen deciding they were under the heaviest volume of enemy fire they had yet found in France. But Marigny was secured, and CCB of the 3rd Armored was driving down N172 so readily that it could put the light armor of its reconnaissance battalion in the lead, with two task forces each composed of a company of Shermans and a company of armored infantry moving abreast close behind. The contrast between the tough opposition persisting directly south of Marigny and the almost open road to the southwest suggested that the enemy had not expected the unsubtle Americans to shift direction, but rather thought they would continue charging straight southward.

The chief danger to the CCB column came from Germans retreating from other actions and cutting across its rear. To move gasoline, ammunition, and rations to the front and prisoners to the rear, tanks had to escort the supply convoys. German staff cars, Volkswagens, motorcycles, and ambulances continually blundered into the American column not knowing it was there. With the Americans busily cutting enemy communications by breaking telephone wires and knocking down telephone poles as they progressed, panzers in good positions were often struck unaware and overwhelmed before they could put up much of a fight. This virtual road march was war such as the American army was designed for, especially the American armored divisions. Appealing also to the passion for moving on that is so much a part of the American character and heritage, it brought out the best in the troops, their energy and mechanical resourcefulness. General Watson of the 3rd Armored could feel a lot better satisfied with his CCB on the road toward Coutances than he had among the narrow hedgerows near the Vire et Taute Canal.

In the afternoon, CCB's right task force struck off three kilometers across country to take a commanding hill near Camprond. About this same area but south of N172, the 1st Division's 16th Infantry came up on CCB's left during the night. By this time, however, the going was becoming tougher again, with increasing enemy harassment of the flanks of the narrow CCB column—which extended only one hedgerow to the left and one hedgerow to the right of the highway—and with stubborn oddments of resistance coagulating in front, bits and pieces of the 2nd SS Panzer Division, the 17th SS Panzer Grenadier Division, and the 353rd Infantry Division. The arrival of these Germans to annoy the VII Corps's main spearhead reflected the impact of Collins's advance upon the neighboring VIII Corps sector.

Bradley's COBRA plan stipulated that as Collins's principal mobile column drove across the rear of the enemy facing the VIII Corps, General Middleton should advance to crush his opponents between the closing jaws of his own corps and Collins's. Middleton was to kick off a day after Collins. When Middleton accordingly renewed his southward attacks across the Cotentin plain on July 26, he assigned the main burden to Stroh's 8th Division, between the Ay and the Taute Rivers, and to Landrum's 90th, astride the Taute but with its center of gravity to the east of it. He did not choose these divisions because he considered them his best. On the contrary, since its insertion into the line between the 79th and 90th earlier in the month, Middleton had already relieved two regimental commanders as well as the original commanding general of the disappointing 8th, and he was on the verge of seeking yet another new CG for the still uninspired 90th. Rather, the maddening geography of the Cotentin plain gave only these two divisions suitable corridors of dry ground.

July 26 produced the same old bloody repulses and minuscule gains on the VIII Corps front. Patrols moving out on the morning of the 27th discovered, however, that the enemy was gone. By afternoon, if not before, Middleton had the decidedly mixed satisfaction of knowing the enemy had folded his tents and silently moved away in fog and rain during the night and early morning all across the VIII Corps front. The Germans had given him the slip—but the VIII Corps could join in the pursuit. Behind them the Germans had left the worst mine fields Middleton had ever seen, Schu mines, Teller mines, mustard pot mines, box mines, antitank and antipersonnel mines, ubiquitously obstructing the still-constricted roads and lanes where vehicular traffic was possible.

General Patton had arrived in France on July 6 to prepare to make his Third Army headquarters operational when the breakthrough came and he could lead his army into Brittany. On July 14, General Eisenhower authorized Bradley to establish an American army group on the Continent and activate the Third Army as soon as he found it convenient and practicable. The VIII Corps would become part of Patton's army for the turn from Normandy into Brittany, and when Bradley learned that Middleton's corps was able to leap forward and join the breakthrough, he telephoned Patton's headquarters in the afternoon of July 27 to authorize Patton to take immediate control of the VIII Corps, for the time being in the capacity of deputy army group commander to Bradley. The next day Bradley wired Eisenhower that he was publishing an order to make his army group and the Third Army operational at noon on August 1. Naturally, Patton had barely been able to contain his impatience to join the action; Eisenhower told Bradley that George made him a semi-jocular offer of $1,000 for each week by which the Supreme Commander would hasten his operational command. Now Patton himself hastened to see Middleton, "but conducted everything very casually so as to not get people excited at the change. . . . Felt much happier over the war. May get in it yet."[23]

Despite the mines, Patton and Middleton agreed they should put the VIII Corps's armor in the van of the pursuit. Middleton ordered Major General John S. Wood's 4th Armored Division to move out at five in the morning of July 28 to drive south on the Périers-Coutances highway as far as Monthuchon, where Wood was to coordinate the advance through Coutances with the oncoming VII Corps before barrelling farther southward. Major General Robert W. Grow's 6th Armored Division, which Bradley gave Middleton during the afternoon of the 27th, received orders to move south from Lessay, bypass Coutances to the west, and drive on to Granville. Grow had Troop A of the 86th Reconnaissance Squadron starting out to reconnoiter the zone of advance as early as 4:30 on Thursday afternoon.

That night General Bradley reacted further to the opening of the VIII Corps front and the renewed clotting of resistance in front of the VII Corps east of Coutances by reassigning from Collins to Middleton Monthuchon, high ground north of Coutances, and a zone south of Coutances. The precise boundary between their two corps was to be worked out by Collins and Middleton themselves. This order confirmed Bradley's determination to push the pursuit as rapidly and uninterruptedly as possible, without pause at Coutances. The order also confirmed that the offensive was becoming less an envelopment and more a simple breakthrough and pursuit. The enemy was getting away: the VIII Corps captured only about a hundred prisoners on July 27, and the 1st Division had taken only 565 in the three days since COBRA struck.

On Friday, the 28th, resistance in front of CCB, 3rd Armored continued to stiffen and to hold Collins's main spearhead east of Coutances. CCB of General Wood's 4th Armored entered Coutances that evening, which not only meant that Collins's corps, as its history put it, "lost the race to Coutances"[24] to Middleton's corps, but more importantly, that the 1st Division and CCB, 3rd Armored could not block the enemy's escape south of Coutances as the COBRA plan had intended. Nevertheless, Bradley and Collins still had another card to play.

Brigadier General Isaac D. White's CCB of the 2nd Armored Division had followed closely upon the rapid advance of General Rose's CCA as far as Canisy. At midday of July 27, White had received orders to turn quickly southwestward and take up blocking positions facing not south against German reinforcements from the interior of France but north—for another try at entrapping the LXXXIV Corps. Responding to the German withdrawal from in front of Middleton, White's superiors gave him to understand that he was in a race with an opponent who had a head start, and that he should proceed accordingly.

He did so. While he moved, higher headquarters wavered again over whether the primary object was envelopment or further exploitation of the pursuit, and White was told first to drive all the way to the Cotentin west coast, and then to stop about fifteen kilometers short, presumably again to allow a corridor for the VIII Corps's pursuit. In any event, White's CCB hastened on by outflanking a roadblock three kilometers southwest of Canisy, leaving it to be knocked out by artillery and IX TAC. Notwithstanding numerous other obstructions and reliance on only a single much-damaged road, the combat command made eleven kilometers from Canisy by nightfall, to the village of Notre-Dame-de-Cenilly halfway to the latest objective, Lengronne. Their progress through a small cluster of houses called Dangy was so rapid that they passed unknowingly right by General Bayerlein of Panzer Lehr, who was holding a conference there.

The remaining dash to Lengronne the next morning was spearheaded at eighty kilometers an hour, and it either put under strong guard or prepared for demolition all but one stubbornly held bridge across the Sienne River along the way. Late in the day, General Collins told White orally to prevent any German escape southward between Lengronne and Notre-Dame-de-Cenilly.

That night and the following day brought the climax of COBRA's entrapment phase. Down upon General White's loose cordon of blocking positions came one after another of the remnants of the LXXXIV Corps—once more into the breach the 2nd SS Panzers, the 17th SS Panzer Grenadiers, the 6th Parachute Regiment. Before dawn a self-propelled 88 led some thirty tanks and other vehicles into two American companies, one tank and one infantry, near Notre-Dame-de-Cenilly. A bitter little battle ensued, with the 88 overrunning the American defenses until Sergeant Robert Lotz of Company I, 41st Armored Infantry, destroyed the gun's periscope and then shot its commander. The Americans won the fight. During Friday morning, the 8th Infantry Regiment began arriving to shore up White's defenses. About 9:00 A.M., some of the newcomers were driven in and fifteen German tanks and several hundred paratroopers got in among the guns of the 78th

Armored Artillery Battalion. Many of the gunners and an attached antiaircraft section lowered their pieces for direct fire, and they prevented the Germans from gaining control of the melee until part of the 41st Armored Infantry arrived to turn the tide. The Germans pulled away leaving 126 dead and nine tanks destroyed.

The very concentration of their remaining mass that the Germans needed to muster if they hoped to penetrate the American cordon increased their vulnerability to Allied air power when the skies cleared on Friday afternoon. Against a hive of vehicles around Roncey often bumper-to-bumper, the P-47s of IX TAC's 405th Fighter-Bomber Group rotated squadrons systematically for more than six hours. American artillery, informed of the attraction, also pumped in shells. "I have been to two church socials and a county fair," said one Thunderbolt pilot, "but I never saw anything like this before!"[25] Two days later, American troops moving into the area counted 66 tanks, 204 vehicles, and 11 guns destroyed, and another 56 tanks and 55 vehicles damaged. The Americans thought such a clot of stalled traffic could be explained only by the enemy's running out of fuel; but in fact the hail of aerial and artillery fire had simply caused the drivers to flee on foot.

During the night of July 29–30, the Germans were still trying hard to break away. About 1:00 A.M., some 1,200 men from the 2nd SS Panzers and the 17th SS Panzer Grenadiers, supported by about ninety tanks, assault guns, and other armored vehicles surviving from the Roncey concentration, pierced the cordon of the 3rd Battalion, 67th Armored Regiment just north of St. Denis-le-Gast. A Panther's gun appeared poking over the hedgerow that lined the battalion command post and began methodically knocking out the command vehicles. Their way lighted by the burning American transport, Germans overran the CP and then attacked the command post of the Division Reserve, the 41st Armored Infantry Regiment Reinforced. Here clerks, cooks, radio operators, and everybody joined in the defense. Lieutenant Colonel Wilson D. Coleman of the 2nd Battalion, 41st Armored Infantry personally accounted for a tank with a bazooka. Soon afterward, he was killed. Fortunately for the Americans, the enemy's intent was only to escape, not to exploit their penetration by rolling up the American line to the right and left. While many Germans did escape, their limited intent helped the Americans reform their defenses. When the smoke cleared, the Americans had taken over 500 prisoners. Some of the Germans who had fled through St. Denis somehow turned west and collided with more Americans around Lengronne, where another 200 or so became prisoners.

About the same time as the St. Denis battle, another 2,500 Germans of the 2nd SS Panzers and miscellaneous formations struck Company E of the 67th Armored Regiment and Company I of the 41st Armored Infantry near Cambry north of Lengronne. For six hours the terrible earsplitting crash of high-velocity tank guns rocked the opposing troops while the Americans wrestled to fend off enemies outnumbering them four to one. Yet the Germans achieved less than the smaller force at St. Denis and lost about 1,000 prisoners and 100 vehicles, while the remainder mostly scattered in disorder hither and yon. When Captain James R. McCartney of the tank company surveyed the wreckage by daylight, he remarked that if he had known what he was facing he probably would have advised withdrawal. The executive officer of the 2nd Battalion, 67th Armored called the piles of bloody, dismembered, and cremated German dead "the most Godless sight I have ever witnessed on any battlefield."[26]

COBRA Dissected

"We shall continue attacking," General Bradley told his staff on July 28, "never give him a chance to rest, never give him a chance to give in." Bradley believed that COBRA had not only broken the front but might be breaking the German army itself. "If there is an armistice for the air war while Germany is negotiating for peace," he continued, "there will be no halt in our attack. We shall never stop until the army is beaten and until the army knows it is beaten."[27]

In the same mood, Bradley wrote to Eisenhower:

> To say that the personnel of the First Army Headquarters is riding high tonight is putting it mildly. Things on our front really look good.
>
> Late yesterday afternoon [July 27] seeing that we had practically accomplished our mission of reaching Coutances, I called in Gerow, Corlett and Collins and gave orders for the second phase of this attack which was, in substance, that Gerow would take over everything east of the Vire River and would keep up his attack to the south. . . . Corlett was to take over a sector west of the Vire . . . and I gave him . . . an objective, the forest and high ground west of the City of Vire and Vire itself. Collins was told that as soon as he gained contact with Middleton coming down from the north, he was to change his direction to the south with a mission of taking the road center at Villedieu-les-Poeles. I directed Middleton to take his 2 Armored Divisions south, the 4th along the road Periers-Coutances-Cerences . . . , and the 6th Armored Division to move by Lessay-Coutances-Brehal. . . .
>
> . . . Middleton has been directed to follow these two Armored Divisions as fast as possible with the 79th and 8th Divisions. He expects to reach the high ground north of Coutances before dark. He will renew the advance in the morning toward the south following the 4th and 6th Armored Divisions. I told Middleton to continue tomorrow morning toward Avranches and go as far as resistance will permit.
>
> When we reach the Granville-Vire line we will not stop but will keep pushing on to the south and try to force the crossings of the See and La Selune Rivers. This is really the third phase of this operation as I originally planned it.
>
> Although the instructions have been issued placing the . . . Army Group in operation at 1200 hours on Tuesday [August 1], I have directed Hodges to keep close track of the three left Corps and I have directed Patton to form the six divisions now on the right into two Corps while they are on the move, interjecting [Major General Wade H.] Haislip's [XV] Corps headquarters so that when we reach the corner [of Brittany] it will not be necessary to stop and reorganize. This splitting of the two Corps should be made while the troops are on the move. I have asked Patton to keep active track of the operations of these two Corps after the XV Corps comes into the picture so that he will be thoroughly familiar with the tactical situation when he takes over next Tuesday.[28]

Expressing regret that Eisenhower had not been present at the front to witness the breakout—the Supreme Commander had been with Bradley only on COBRA's first day, when depression still reigned—Bradley added to his promise to drive the front unceasingly forward his second thoughts about the role of air power: "This operation could not have been the success it has been without such close cooperation of the Air. In the first place, the bombardment which we gave them last Tuesday [July 25] was apparently highly successful even though we did suffer many casualties ourselves. The cooperation of Quesada's IX TAC Air Command has been outstanding. He has kept formations over the advancing columns continuously."[29]

Bradley thought Ike needed the reassurance. The COBRA carpet bombing had been principally Bradley's idea, and after the short bombing on both the 24th and 25th and the first day's disappointing ground operations, Eisenhower declared he would never again use heavy bombers in tactical operations. "I gave them a green light this time. But I promise you it's the last."[30] As the ground troops pushed across the bombing carpet, however, they were more and more impressed by the terrific impact on the enemy, even if their own progress was slowed by the cratering of the roads and the pulverizing of the ground despite the limitations on the size of bombs that had been used. If the fragmentation bombs that made up much of the aerial barrage required direct hits to produce casualties and made little impact on German tank armor, they nevertheless shredded unarmored vehicles and broke the treads of tanks. The ruin of German communications became apparent because enemy "Units resorted to the radio in the clear and they report with some anxiety that their position is critical indeed."[31]

It was grimly fortunate that the earlier battles had already driven almost all French civilians out of the whole St. Lô area. The COBRA carpet bombing merely completed the transformation of fertile Norman fields and ancient turreted towns into a desert—or a Mondlandschaft, a moon landscape, as General Bayerlein of Panzer Lehr described it.[32] For the present, any American misgivings about the French population of the district and their possessions were submerged in the exultation over victory and in admiration of the equally spectacular contribution of air power as breakthrough gave way to pursuit.

In any event, air power had partially compensated for the shortage of artillery ammunition. Collins was to testify that "I can recall no real supply difficulties that hampered the actual operation," but other commanders at the time and soldier-historians studying COBRA in close detail thereafter concluded: "If [artillery] ammunition had been unrestricted, all commanders would have fired considerably more and the initial advance would probably have been faster and our own casualties less."[33] The relatively indiscriminate power of aerial bombardment remained only a partial substitute for the more selective force of artillery.

If anything, General Bradley was in the process of shifting from depression over the short bombing and the enemy's initial tough resistance toward the opposite extreme of crediting the bombing excessively as the sine qua non of the breakthrough. The circumstances in Normandy were ripe for a concentrated attack such as Collins's to penetrate the German defensive crust even if the aerial preparation had been considerably less massive. The main source of COBRA's success was concentration; but even after a victorious application of the principle of concentration, the Americans were loath to acknowledge its value.

American intelligence had actually underestimated the numerical strength of the German forces opposite the VII Corps on the eve of COBRA, counting only 17,000 rather than the 30,000 troops who actually occupied that sector of the LXXXIV Corps front. Nevertheless, the stretch of the St. Lô-Périers road chosen for the assault was held only by Bayerlein's Panzer Lehr Division and some attached units of other depleted divisions. Panzer Lehr was already so badly wasted by its fights with the British and such actions against the Americans as its counterattack along the Vire River in early July, that even with its attachments it numbered less than half of its authorization of about 15,000 men and over 200 tanks and assault guns. In his main line of resistance at the beginning of COBRA, Bayerlein mustered only 2,200 combat troops and about forty-five serviceable armored vehicles. Behind him, the constant pressure imposed by the Allies to force the shoring up of one part of the German front after another had left almost no German reserves. The LXXXIV Corps had another tired and depleted division, the 353rd, in reserve around Périers. The Seventh Army reserve consisted of the 275th Division and two infantry and two tank companies of the 2nd SS Panzer Division. The 275th was practically destroyed on the first day, by a fighter-bomber attack as it was marching toward the front from Marigny, and then by American infantry. The companies of the 2nd SS Panzers were among the few formations to pose effective resistance after July 25. The LXXXIV Corps as a whole was in much the same shape as Panzer Lehr: weary survivors of the campaign in the Bocage that was described by General von Choltitz, the corps commander, as "one tremendous bloodbath, such as I have never seen in eleven years of war."[34]

The Americans had endured the bloodbath too, but their divisions received replacements, and the German divisions mostly did not. Against Choltitz's depleted corps, Collins's VII Corps with its six divisions had been reinforced for COBRA virtually to the dimensions of an army. General Bradley's First Army opened COBRA with fifteen divisions in its four corps, against all—meaning all that was left—or elements of some eleven divisions in the German Seventh Army.

With the attainment of the St. Lô-Périers road from which to launch COBRA and the invention of the Rhino tank to cut through the hedgerows, the First Army at last had dry ground for exploiting both the strength it had assembled and the mobility of American arms, along with a means of dealing with the principal remaining terrain obstacle in the arena of battle. Throughout COBRA, German armor remained restricted to the roads; American armor could surge forward off the roads, thanks to the Rhinos. As events developed, the COBRA penetration was so rapid and so complete that the American tanks could usually exploit along the roads after all and rarely left them. But it was an inestimable psychological boon—the breaking of the melancholy spell cast by the hedgerows during the Battle of the Bocage—to know that movement did not have to be road-bound, and that flanking maneuvers through the hedgerows were at last possible to the Shermans.

Confined for the most part to movement on roads, the German army was ripe for the penetration of its defenses also because the American capture of the road center of St. Lô and the bringing of the main roads both east and west of that town under the fire of American guns denied the Germans any convenient route of lateral movement westward and eastward across their front to reinforce against such a concentration as Collins's. The one likely chance the Germans could have had to stop the COBRA penetration was to strike quickly against it with an armored counterblow, as they had done against the various British offensives around Caen. In this regard, General Montgomery's attacks had served the Allies invaluably despite the disappointments they occasioned, because when COBRA began the Germans still faced the fourteen front-line British divisions with fourteen German divisions equipped with the bulk of the German armor, six panzer divisions in contrast to only two confronting the Americans. Montgomery's pressure and the geography of the Caen-Falaise plain had held German attention locked on what proved to be the wrong place. When COBRA struck, the German Seventh Army had most of its two panzer divisions in the line and unavailable for counterattack, while the larger body of German armor in Panzer Group West was too far away to hit back, and the Allied domination of the most direct roads assured that the situation could not be corrected before the COBRA penetration became uncontrollable.

Confined for the most part to movement on roads, German armor also remained thereby more vulnerable to constant harassment by American aircraft. In North Africa and at least through the early part of the campaign in Italy, the Americans had continued to lag abysmally behind German standards of tactical communication and cooperation between the air and the ground. The difference reflected the contrasting histories of the German and the American air services. Denied military aviation by the Treaty of Versailles, the Germans were obliged to conceal their evasions of the treaty within the cloak of their army through most of the years between the two world wars. Hitler made bold to unveil the Luftwaffe on March 16, 1935, but its air officers had so long operated thoroughly within the discipline and traditions of the army that they were little inclined to question the primacy of the army's needs. In Germany, moreover, the army was unquestionably the central military service, the premier bearer of the German military tradition. After 1935, furthermore, the drive toward rapid building of a large air force militated against big, expensive strategic bombers and in favor of smaller tactical aircraft, while the Luftwaffe's one conspicuous proponent of strategic bombing, Generalleutnant Walther Wewer, happened to die in a plane crash in 1936. Thus the Luftwaffe developed principally as a highly mobile artillery supporting the ground forces. The American Army Air Corps, though organizationally part of the army, was pushed by national history and international legalities into no such identification with the traditional army. Long since, it dedicated itself not only to a primary mission of strategic bombing independent of the army, but also to operational independence in the course of supporting the ground forces.

The AAF thus developed jealously the doctrinal proposition that when giving support to the ground, air power must not be tied to any specific division, corps, or even army but should range over the entire theater of operations; if more direct tactical support could not be avoided, the decision to fly a mission must remain with the air officer commanding the supporting aerial units. Despite the complaints of General McNair and other ground forces officers about the unsatisfactory quality of air support throughout the 1940 and 1941 maneuvers that did so much to shape the American army for war, the Army Air Forces managed to insist that FM 31–35 of April 1942, the latest relevant field manual, should prescribe that the ground commander request air support through his air liaison officer, who would then relay the request via his own communications to the nearest appropriate air headquarters. There the decision to employ the air weapon would be made, and there the pilots would receive their orders. The doctrine did not provide for communication between the pilots and the troops they were supposed to support. By the time the planes arrived at the battle, this final deficiency might not matter, because the reason for the original request might be gone.

In Italy, where a common interest in winning the war shared with the ground forces came to seem to airmen a more pressing urgency than doctrinal purity suitable to an autonomous air arm, practice eroded the FM 31–35 prescriptions. Army and AAF headquarters frequently were planted side by side. AAF officers allowed ground commanders to explain their viewpoints and problems to pilots. The air liaison officer, now called the controller or "Rover" control, habitually rode forward in a jeep or flew ahead of the ground forces in a small liaison plane, from either vantage point radioing air support directly against suitable tactical targets.

Under Pete Quesada of IX TAC, doctrine yielded still more to the question of how best to help the ground forces. Quesada had shocked the RAF by suspending bombs from Spitfires to convert Britain's finest fighter into a ground-support fighter-bomber. The RAF protested loudly enough both that such use of a classic fighter was unseemly and that anyway it was impossible, until Quesada remarked of the aircraft in question: "But they're not your planes any more—they're mine. And I'll do anything I want to with them."[35] If he could hang bombs on a little Spitfire, Quesada could and soon did burden his big Thunderbolts with pairs of 1,000-lb. bombs. Reaching for the nub of effective air-ground coordination, Quesada persuaded Bradley to give him a Sherman, so he could experiment with installing AAF very high frequency radios directly in tanks, to permit his air support parties—the latest term for the liaison officers—to ride at the head of the tank columns instead of in open jeeps. For a while Quesada's tank failed to be delivered, because Ordnance could not believe IX TAC was the right address for the recipient.

By July 25 and the opening of COBRA, twelve of Quesada's fighter-bomber groups had moved to bases in France. On July 20, Quesada had issued his orders for the fighter-bombers' armored column cover armed with bombs or rockets to help hasten along the anticipated mobile exploitation:

> Each of the rapidly advancing columns will be covered at all times by a four ship flight . . . [which] will maintain a close armed recce in advance of the . . . column. They may attack any target which is identified as enemy, directing their attention to the terrain immediately in front of the advancing column. The combat command commander may monitor [radio] channel "C" to receive any information transmitted by the flight of FBs which is covering him. [He] may also request this flight to attack targets immediately in front of him. Targets which require more strength than the four ship flight will be passed back through ASP [air support party] channels and the missions will be accomplished by FBs on ground alert.[36]

Thus, during COBRA a typical radio communication from tank to plane began: "Is the road safe for us to proceed?" "Stand by and we'll find out," came the reply, and the four covering Thunderbolts found four German tanks up ahead. The P-47s disposed of the panzers and then radioed: "All clear. Proceed at will." With such communication and with the First Army's columns displaying bright fluorescent panels to identify themselves, the airplanes sometimes attacked tanks and strongpoints little more than 100 meters in front of their own troops. The concentrated stream of fire of a Thunderbolt's eight .50-caliber machine guns was a superb killer of enemy vehicles, ripping through thin-skinned vehicles or ricocheting off roads into the soft underbellies of tanks. Even better for tanks or fixed emplacements were rockets launched from rails under the wings, introduced by the British in a 3-inch model for their Typhoons in 1943, eventually carried by Thunderbolts, Lightnings, and Mustangs in batteries of ten 5-inch rockets. From the beginning of COBRA to the end of July, fighter-bombers in the VII Corps zone alone claimed 362 enemy tanks and assault guns destroyed and 216 damaged, 1,337 other vehicles destroyed and 280 damaged. The number of burned-out vehicles along the roads confirmed that these claims suffered relatively slightly from the airmen's usual vice of exaggeration.

On the Eastern Front, Germans and Russians alike were accustomed to using their tanks in huge concentrations. Germans on the Western Front had to be skeptical about the relevance of the experience brought by reinforcements from the East, particularly on this point; officers from the East tended to take too long to learn that tank concentrations just would not suit in the West, even when enough tanks were available. Anglo-American air power made Eastern-style massing of German tanks suicidal.

"This man Quesada is a jewel," General Bradley assured the chief of the Army Air Forces, General Henry H. Arnold, about the spirited commander of IX TAC:

> I cannot say too much for the very close cooperation we have had between the Air and Ground. In spite of the fact that we had no time for training together in England, it did not take long to work out a system of cooperation. Quesada was a peach to work with, because he was not only willing to try everything that would help us, but he inspired his whole command with this desire to such an extent that these youngsters now do almost the impossible whenever they think we need help. In my opinion, our close cooperation is better than the Germans ever had in their best days.[37]

"Quesada acquired an armored force of his own," Bradley said of his gift of a Sherman,[38] but IX TAC repaid by giving Bradley's exploiting columns an accompanying reconnaissance and artillery force skillfully adapted to enhance the ground forces' mobility. And now that COBRA had achieved the breakout, and the most mobile army in the world for the first time since D-Day could capitalize on its mobility, the issues confronting the army became for the first time in Europe strategic rather than tactical. The soldiers' battle of Normandy was about to become the generals' battle of France, testing whether American generalship possessed a strategic flexibility and deftness to match the mobility of the army it commanded.

The Eastern Flank

Conditions had been ripe for the breakthrough with or without an aerial barrage on the scale of COBRA's because the fighting men of the Anglo-American 21 Army Group had already won the soldiers' battle of Normandy before the July 25 attack jumped off. The COBRA breakthrough was confirmation of a victory already achieved but hitherto not apparent. Confirmation came also with the inability of the Germans east of the COBRA penetration, and especially their concentrations of armor opposite the Second Army, to join the battle in any way that could counteract the breakthrough and breakout farther west.

Like Middleton's VIII Corps to the west of Collins, the American and British formations east of the VII Corps attacked in support of the main effort. On July 23, Lieutenant General H.D.G. Crerar's First Canadian Army had taken over from the Second Army the left of the British front, and on July 25, simultaneously with COBRA, Crerar's Canadian 2nd Corps opened an attack from Caen astride N158, the main highway to Falaise. The Canadians faltered against the heavy enemy concentration on the old Bourguébus Ridge battlefield of the GOODWOOD offensive, so General Montgomery, always wary of a possibly costly battle, closed out the attack on the second day. Nevertheless, the Canadian effort provoked a counterattack by the 9th SS Panzer Division, and through the critical first hours of COBRA the Canadians reinforced Field Marshal von Kluge's fatal conviction that the Anglo-Americans remained principally interested in rolling across the Falaise plain, and that it was the American attack farther west that was diversionary. Kluge himself went to the Caen front.

Pete Corlett of the XIX Corps, feeling and looking better than in early July, thought that by capturing St. Lô his and Gerow's troops had made COBRA possible and therefore merited a more conspicuous role in the offensive than simply staging diversionary shows. Pointing to the potential threat to COBRA from the German armor to the east, Corlett had suggested to Bradley that his own XIX Corps sector be shifted to the west bank of the Vire so it could better focus its efforts upon shielding Collins's eastern flank. Baade's 35th Division thus should be reassigned to Gerow. Once the effort began moving, Hobbs's 30th Division should be returned to the XIX Corps along with the part of the 2nd Armored that staged COBRA's southwestward exploitation. With Gerhardt's 29th Division and the new 28th as well as these forces, the XIX Corps should then drive the 30th Division-2nd Armored left-flank thrust of COBRA still farther southeastward, on toward the town of Vire. Thus Corlett could build an extended but firm shoulder against German intervention from the east. Bradley accepted Corlett's proposal; it was to bring all that Corlett could have wanted of the prominence that comes from fierce fighting.

For Gerow's V Corps, Bradley continued to prescribe only a diversion, with no specific plan or objectives assigned by army headquarters. The British had not revealed any immediate plans to advance south of Caumont on Gerow's left flank, so there remained the danger that a V Corps attack might give Gerow an exposed flank as had happened earlier when the 7th Armoured Division foundered at Villers-Bocage. Though he consistently worried about this peril, Gerow nevertheless devised a supporting attack that would be a COBRA in miniature. His 2nd and 5th Divisions were to try to break the crust of the German defenses in his immediate front along the St. Jean-des-Baisants ridge. If they achieved a breakthrough, exploiting columns were to wheel southwestward to envelop the enemy troops facing the 35th Division and holding the first ridge south of St. Lô, called Hill 101.

The parallel with COBRA proved to extend further than could have been anticipated. The 2nd and 5th Divisions gained some ground but did not achieve the penetration Gerow wanted, and therefore the southwestward envelopment was abortive. Difficulties stemmed partly from the inexperience of Major General S. LeRoy Irwin's 5th Division. Yet the 35th Division, still in the XIX Corps at the opening of the attack, found the German grip loosening on its front; and just as in COBRA it was the VIII Corps moving straight ahead that took Coutances, so in this secondary attack it was the 35th Division of the XIX Corps moving straight ahead that on July 27 took Hill 101. Thereupon Bradley conducted his shuffle of the 35th from Corlett's to Gerow's command.

American intelligence soon reported the enemy was flexing his muscles for the countereffort from the east that Corlett had predicted and against which he proposed that the XIX Corps should guard. Between the night of July 26–27 and the morning of the 28th, Kluge began shifting the 2nd Panzer Division, from Panzer Group West reserve, and then the 116th Panzer Division, released at last by the Fifteenth Army in the Pas de

Calais, from the Orne toward the Vire. To command the effort Kluge inserted into his order of battle the XLVII Panzer Corps headquarters of General der Panzertruppen Hans Freiherr von Funck. Coming into the Seventh Army line between the collapsing LXXXIV Corps and the II Parachute Corps, Funck also took over the remnants of Panzer Lehr, the 2nd SS Panzer Division, and the 352nd Division. As Corlett meanwhile took command of the 30th Division and Rose's CCA, 2nd Armored and pushed forward also the 29th and 28th Divisions up the west bank of the Vire, the effect was a sharp, jarring collision on July 28 between Corlett's spearhead and Funck's.

The impact shook the relatively fresh 2nd Panzer Division especially hard and in doing so broke the momentum of Kluge's counterstroke before much momentum had gathered. To hold its advantage, the XIX Corps had to fight the Battle of Tessy-sur-Vire, the American army's toughest battle since the beginning of COBRA. Kluge's reinforcements of armor from the eastward made the XLVII Panzer Corps a most formidable organization. The XIX Corps halted Funck's advance, but not even accelerated aerial strikes from IX TAC in combination with the forays of the XIX Corps could compel these Germans to recoil. North of Tessy-sur-Vire, far short of Corlett's objective, which was the neighborhood of the town of Vire, the opposing American and German corps fed into the battle everything they had. By the time the 116th Panzer Division joined the 2nd on the German side during the morning of July 30, the Germans were threatening Corlett's line of communication back to le Mesnil-Herman, and for a while supply vehicles headed for Rose's CCA at the tip of the American spearhead around Villebaudon had to spurt across road intersections at irregular intervals to dodge German artillery fire. It was the Americans who on this part of the front were now fighting defensively; and through much of Sunday, July 30, holding Villebaudon seemed more than they might be able to achieve.

On Monday, the 30th Division's attached 743rd Tank Battalion found itself ground down to an effective strength of only thirteen Shermans, but the battalion managed to poke its way into the town of Troisgots. Its small triumph signaled a new shifting of the initiative. By now, as General Corlett rightly suspected, not the fortunes of the local struggle but events elsewhere were most likely to govern German conduct—and to put an end to the XLVII Panzer Corps's furious resistance. Corlett alerted his troops to guard against and to harry any retreat during the night. Rose's CCA and Hobbs's 30th Division complied with sufficient diligence that they were able the next day to follow the enemy closely into Tessy and, after yet more hard fighting, to capture the place.

A large part of the reason for Funck's withdrawal was a threat to his own line of communication, as a combined Anglo-American drive threatened to descend upon the town of Vire behind him. Disappointed that the enemy still locked his troops in a slugging match as if nothing had changed since the beginning of July, Gerow nevertheless kept up the pressure of his diversionary attacks east of the Vire from July 25 onward. On July 29, he received the welcome news that the Second Army on his left was about to attack southward again the next day. General Dempsey's latest effort, Operation BLUECOAT, launched 8 Corps south from Caumont toward both Vire and the Mont Pinçon Ridge, a dominating system of high ground eight to thirteen kilometers south of the Caumont–Villers-Bocage line. Montgomery believed the capture of the ridge would deny the enemy the pivot he would need to consolidate a new westward-facing front against the Americans.

As usual, the British seemed to suffer more than their share of misfortunes. The skies clouded over again for Montgomery's now-customary aerial bombardment to lead off the attack, and some 200 of more than 1,200 planes had to return home with their bomb-bays still full. The hilly terrain proved both crisscrossed with exceptionally numerous hedgerows—except that it was dry, it was some of the worst of the Bocage— and liberally sprinkled with mines. When 8 Corps captured crossings of the Souloeuvre River, they proved to be within the V Corps zone, and Gerow's men thus helped themselves to them with a resultant tangle of British tanks and American infantry impeding everybody's progress. On the other hand, because the town of Vire was also within the American zone, the British stopped about eight kilometers short of it after their reconnaissance cars probed it and found it almost deserted on the night of August 1-2. (British news reports subsequently claimed credit for the capture of Vire anyway, to the Americans' disgust at what they perceived as an increasing tendency for London to take credit for everything.) Instead of entering Vire, Dempsey concentrated on the Mont Pinçon hills, which was probably a mistake though understandable and characteristically gentlemanly; Dempsey was one Briton whom the Americans could rarely accuse of trying to hog the headlines. But Dempsey's move both softened the pressure on the rear of the XLVII Panzer Corps and sent 8 Corps to crack a tougher nut.

The cracking was all the more readily stymied because on the left of 8 Corps, 30 Corps and its 7th Armoured Division once again failed to perform with the aggressiveness expected of them. Montgomery thereupon made almost a clean sweep of their principal commanders, but not in time to save the 8 Corps flank from yet another westward-moving German armored formation, the absolute last German reserve in Normandy, the 21st Panzer Division. Still, BLUECOAT was satisfactory enough to SHAEF and the Americans, because they no longer had to count on Montgomery for the breakthrough, and the operation ensured that every German soldier in Normandy would be too much occupied elsewhere to rebuild the shattered German left flank. BLUECOAT helped the XIX Corps put a favorable end to the Battle of Tessy-sur-Vire on July 31, and it permitted the V Corps at last to begin hastening forward against only sporadic opposition the same day.

Unfortunately, Gerow had hoped to snatch a bag of prisoners before the enemy departed, but like Middleton before him he had discovered that Germans withdrawing in the night were expert in completely giving their opponents the slip. Into the first days of August, Gerow was driving his troops forward restlessly, determined both to prevent the enemy from consolidating a new line and "that they would not let the enemy pull such a neat trick again."[39]

9: The Crossroads South of Avranches

THE FIRST ARMY had grown unwieldy. The First Army's four corps together had fifteen divisions in the front lines as COBRA began, with an infantry and an armored division in reserve and another armored division about to land. A single army headquarters could no longer maintain satisfactory control. The necessity for activating an American army group on the Continent loomed still greater when all the American divisions now arrived in England were included in the reckoning: a total of fourteen infantry, six armored, and two airborne divisions were in the European Theater of Operations by July 1944, and four more divisions were expected in August. By July 29, there were 903,061 American soldiers in France (along with 663,295 British), and 858,436 tons of supplies and 176,620 vehicles had been landed for the American army (along with 744,540 tons and 156,025 vehicles for the British).

On July 14, General Bradley changed the designation of his army group from the First to the 12th, so that a fictitious First U.S. Army Group could remain in England to prolong the deceptions of Operation FORTITUDE about a coming invasion of the Pas de Calais. Because General Patton would soon emerge on German intelligence charts as the commander of the Third Army in France, another senior general of suitable prestige had to ornament the headquarters of the First Army Group in Patton's place. With the organization and training of ground combat units virtually completed, General McNair was an obvious choice for this role. Tragically, McNair traveled to the front to observe the payoff of his previous labor in the unloosing of COBRA and fell a victim of the short bombing of July 25. A search of the cratered area where he was watching produced a portion of his ring finger with his West Point class ring. For the sake of FORTITUDE, the death was concealed as long as possible; only Bradley, Hodges, Patton, Quesada, Major General Ralph Royce, deputy commander of the Ninth Air Force, and McNair's aide attended the funeral. Lieutenant General John L. DeWitt was summoned from the command of the Army and Navy Staff College to emerge when necessary as the new chief of the First Army Group.

Bradley had insisted on postponing the activation of the army group and Third Army headquarters until after COBRA, ostensibly because he thought control by a single army could ease the anticipated traffic jam when the VII and VIII Corps met around Coutances, more probably because Bradley distrusted Patton's impetuosity too much to risk giving him leadership in the critical effort to escape the deadlock in the Bocage. Close friends in North Africa, Bradley and Patton since Sicily had come more and more to regard each other warily under an outward show of continued camaraderie. Bradley feared the activation of Patton's army as the inauguration of a generalship reckless to the point of utter irresponsibility. Patton in turn disdained Bradley's generalship as insufferably orthodox, predictable, and cautious. Despite his efforts to keep up appearances, Bradley's feelings were plain enough to his staff; those devoted followers of the unassuming, softspoken army group commander—Bradley's Lincolnesque, homespun kindliness readily inspired devotion—developed a strong dislike for the bombastic, egotistical "gorgeous George" with his tailored green jackets, bright buttons, fancy leather belt and boots, and initialed pistols (though the famous pearl-handled pistols had gone into storage after Patton's recent bouts with bad publicity). When George came visiting at Bradley's headquarters, the staff made no effort to be more than lukewarm, and when possible "after dinner we quickly turned him to a movie" to be rid of him.[1]

It was Eisenhower who throughout July pressed Bradley for the change in command lest the troop commitment exceed the First Army's span of control, until Bradley at last issued his orders to activate the Third Army and the 12th Army Group on August 1. The OVERLORD planners had anticipated that when Bradley took this step, and General Montgomery's 21 Army Group consequently reverted to command only of the Second British and First Canadian Armies, Eisenhower would add the functions of overall ground commander to those of Supreme Commander. The planners had also anticipated, however, that by the time so many Allied troops were in France, the lodgment area would have been pushed much farther inland than it was as COBRA first began to unfold, and that SHAEF headquarters consequently would have moved to the Continent. Because in fact Eisenhower and SHAEF were still quartered in England, it now seemed unwise for Ike to attempt to direct the ground battle from across the Channel. An emergency might catch him with communications out. Eisenhower thus decided that for the time being Montgomery should continue as ground commander, temporarily acting as the Supreme Commander's agent to direct the 12th Army Group as well as his own 21 Army Group.

This sound decision led to a contretemps whose very absurdity throws light on the tensions partially concealed by the rhetoric of both British and American leaders who extolled the Grand Alliance. These tensions in turn shaped the conduct of the campaign to a much greater extent than Eisenhower liked to admit. Further to attempt to conceal them, the Supreme Commander tried to employ British and American armies as though they were interchangeable, sending the British to good tank country and the Americans to the hedgerows and morasses of the Cotentin plain as though it made no difference, ignoring the British inability to risk sustained big battles and to absorb heavy losses as well as other differences between the two nations' armies.

On August 14 an Associated Press reporter circumvented censorship with a dispatch indicating that Bradley and the 12th Army Group were now coequal with Montgomery and his command. The report provoked an uproar from the British press, much of which regarded the notion of American equality with the masterful and experienced hero of El Alamein as an insult, a virtual demotion for Montgomery and yet another instance of the increasingly overbearing Americans' effrontery. Of course, the report surfaced at a bad time for British military prestige, when COBRA had turned the Americans loose in France while 21 Army Group was still not much beyond Caen. SHAEF's Public Relations Division chose characteristically to salve British pride by merely denying that Bradley's place in the hierarchy was equal to Montgomery's, without telling the whole story. Predictably, the next furor was in the American press, much of which thought it was high time that American equality in command matched the growing American predominance in contributions to the war. This sentiment could be placated readily enough when, as planned, Eisenhower did assume the ground command, on September 1, and Montgomery reverted to equality with Bradley after all. His Majesty's Government thereupon soothed both the British press and the national military hero by promoting Montgomery to the rank of field marshal. But neither press nor hero, as events were to prove, could be reconciled to the loss of the ground command.

To Eisenhower, more than anyone else charged with preserving the harmony of the alliance, such events were a plague and a sore disappointment. To Bradley, who bore lesser diplomatic responsibilities and therefore thought he could afford to nurse grievances, they fueled a growing suspicion that Monty and the British would never acknowledge true equality between the leaders of the 12th and 21 Army Groups; grievance and suspicion would more and more shadow all Bradley's relations with the Allies. To Patton, everything that discomfited Montgomery was nectar to be savored—for Patton and Montgomery, equally thirsty for applause, had seen each other as rivals at least since they commanded, only formally in tandem, the American and British armies in the Sicilian campaign.

In July and August 1944, Patton was receiving much to relish for the first time since November 1943 and the public revelation of the soldier-slapping incidents in Sicily. Not that public applause had yet returned; for as long as possible, SHAEF wanted the Germans to believe Patton was still in England poised to lead the second Channel crossing. But by the time of COBRA, two of his corps headquarters as well as Patton's army headquarters were in France waiting to take command of troops, and a third corps headquarters was about to arrive. When COBRA achieved the breakthrough, Bradley saw the hour as almost uniquely opportune for the very rashness that made him distrust Patton in other circumstances, and thus Bradley made his decision to give Patton early charge over Middleton's VIII Corps, a fourth corps scheduled for Patton's army.

When with Middleton's agreement Patton pushed the 4th and 6th Armored Divisions to the forefront of the VIII Corps advance, he was hurrying to the front armored divisions that had trained under his direct supervision in England and were nurtured in his passion for mobility as the essence of mechanized war. The 4th Armored in particular had served as a test division for the development of Patton's theories of tank-infantry cooperation. In both armored divisions he had instilled his belief that armor should strike swiftly and deeply, flowing around enemy strongpoints to plunge far into vulnerable rear areas. Mobility is not the same as maneuver. The American army's historic dedication to mobility had failed to develop in most American commanders a corresponding penchant for strategic maneuver. Patton was an exception. He was one American general who believed that mobility must be exploited into the strategic maneuver of the indirect approach.

Pursuit

Annoyed at the substantial German escape from the VIII Corps front, and eager both to catch up with the fleeing foe and to invoke the devastating impact of far-ranging armored columns, Patton and Middleton at midnight on July 28 ordered the 4th and 6th Armored Divisions to extend their objectives to Avranches and the crossings of the Sée River. These targets were more than fifty kilometers beyond Wood's and Grow's lead tanks. To back up the armor, Middleton attached forty quartermaster trucks to the 8th and 79th Infantry Divisions, so each could motorize a regimental combat team to follow close behind the 4th and 6th Armored, respectively.

Like St. Lô a medieval walled town and, more pertinently, a road nexus, Avranches occupies a sixty-meter bluff at the base of the estuary of the Sée and Sélune Rivers, looking out to the Bay of Mont St. Michel and its rock and monastery clearly visible thirteen kilometers away. Avranches is the junction of roads from the Norman towns of Granville, Coutances, Villedieu, and Vire. These roads crossed the Sée over two bridges and became a single road before diverging to east, south, and west again after crossing the Sélune at the village of Pontaubault, some six kilometers south of Avranches. Thus Avranches-Pontaubault is the gateway between western Normandy and either Brittany or the major land mass of France. Here, if the Americans followed the thinking of the OVERLORD planners, they could turn the corner into Brittany and head for the abundant Breton ports whose proximity to the Cotentin had contributed so much to bringing the Allies ashore in Normandy.

But with the German left shattered and the rest of Field Marshal von Kluge's forces too busy elsewhere to lend prompt assistance, did the ports still matter so much? Should the Americans turn from Normandy not right into Brittany but left, east and southeast into the ancient County of Maine and Duchy of Anjou and toward the Île de France? Did not the completeness of the collapse of the German left beckon strategy in this direction— toward encirclement of the remaining German forces in Normandy, toward a Cannae battle, toward the classic battle of envelopment which since Helmuth von Moltke's day had been the hallmark of German strategy, but might now be turned upon its foremost modern practitioners?

First, the Americans must take Avranches, the exit either to Brittany or to the heart of France. In England, Middleton's VIII Corps staff had developed with care at least five plans for the exploitation out of the Cotentin, but now events moved so rapidly that none of the plans was applied. "The plan the VIII Corps used in finally breaking out of the peninsula was played by ear—strictly off the cuff," said Middleton later. "Our action depended on what the enemy had done and was doing."[2] On July 28, Patton and Middleton expected General Wood's 4th Armored Division to move southeast from Coutances through Cérences to cross the Sée and Tirepied above Avranches, shielding the key crossings of the main highways but yielding the honor of first entering Avranches to General Grow's 6th Armored Division. But during the next day, the 4th advanced with so much flair and speed as well as skill that by evening of July 29, Middleton decided it was in a better position than the 6th to capture Avranches, and he awarded it the prize. Middleton like Patton could take personal satisfaction from the 4th's performance. Against the advice of armored experts, in early July Middleton had assigned it a defensive tour in his lines. Thereby the division had received just enough seasoning to give it a battlefield sharpness uncommon to new divisions by the time it became a corps spearhead.

Brigadier General Holmes E. Dager's CCB of the 4th Armored on July 30 discovered both bridges over the Sée at Avranches intact and entered the undefended city early in the evening. Dager outposted Avranches and immediately sent a small force east along the north bank of the Sée to secure the bridge at Tirepied. During the night and into Monday, July 31, CCB had to fight for Avranches after all, for a time giving up one of the Sée River bridges. At first, the enemy seemed to be mounting a serious counterattack, but he proved to be merely scrambling to get out of the Cotentin. So intent were the Germans in the western Cotentin on flight alone that on Monday afternoon a task force of Colonel Bruce C. Clarke's CCA, 4th Armored raced across the Sélune River bridge at Pontaubault, dispersed a feeble counterstroke, and thus completed assurance that the VIII Corps could burst out of the Cotentin.

The fighting around Avranches occurred because Middleton's armored columns had caught up with the Germans who decamped from the VIII Corps front on the night of July 26–27 despite the enemy's thirty-hour head start over the 4th and 6th Armored. From July 26 through 28, the VIII Corps had captured only 372 prisoners. On July 29, Middleton's men took another 200. But as the VIII Corps caught up, the bag rose dramatically: 1,321 prisoners on July 30, some 7,000 on July 31. The haul of about 8,300 prisoners on the last two days of July was the largest yet taken in a comparable time by any corps of the Allied armies. In the bag was represented every major German unit that had been in front of the VIII Corps when COBRA began.

The prisoners came streaming in even though Middleton told his commanders that taking prisoners must not delay the advance: "Send them to the rear disarmed without guards."[3] For the 4th and 6th Armored were setting new Allied records in rapidity of advance as well as in prisoner hauls. General Dager's CCB covered sixty-eight kilometers between Périers and Avranches in three days. When Colonel Clarke's CCA crossed the Sélune, it had traveled eighty-seven kilometers in four days. No other Anglo-American units had yet done so well.

To move so fast required accepting risks, for especially between the Sée and the Sélune the vanguard of the VIII Corps had broken out in front of the rest of the First Army and was ranging forward with its left flank completely exposed. Though the advance was a pursuit from July 27 onward, the spearheads remained alert against any kind of trouble the enemy might have in store. The fighter-bombers of IX TAC prowled overhead throughout the daylight hours and harassed the enemy wherever they found him. The armored combat commands advanced in balanced task forces of tanks, armored infantry, tank destroyers, armored artillery, and armored engineers. In general the task forces drove ahead with the armored version of marching fire, a specialty of the training Patton had given his armored troops. As a column approached any likely strongpoint, a road junction, a defensible terrain feature, a man-made structure that might be fortified, it automatically took the possible obstacle under fire. Some task forces automatically sprayed all hedgerows with fire as they passed. To keep the enemy off balance, telephone lines were systematically cut and telephone poles regularly overturned. The VIII Corps lost only 673 casualties from July 28 through 31, only 160 during the two days when it was taking more than 8,000 prisoners.

So they could continue rolling forward, the armored divisions had overstocked themselves with supplies before setting out. As the s-4 of the 37th Tank Battalion in the 4th Armored Division described it:

> The rapid movement south would have been impossible with the regular allowance of gasoline. The regular allowance to be carried in the train was over 5,000 gallons (1059 five-gallon drums). Actually, this amount was doubled. The kitchens were taken from the regular 2½-ton cargo carriers and stored in the trailers or other available places so that the cargo carriers could carry more gasoline, oil, etc.

The kitchens were not used during this period because of the rapid movement. K rations and 10-in-1 rations were the order of the day.[4]

Turning the Corner

Chary though he was, and had to be, of risking British lives, General Montgomery was a commander of greater audacity than the Americans sometimes liked to admit. He was the first senior Allied commander to recognize enough to define them the full opportunities opened by the collapse of the German left in front of Collins and Middleton—opportunities for a battle of envelopment to trap the German Seventh Army between the Allied forces and the bridgeless River Seine. Encouraged by their chief, and building upon his and their LUCKY STRIKE conceptions for a primarily British breakthrough and breakout, the 21 Army Group planners in late July weighed the OVERLORD plans' emphasis on the Breton ports against the new strategic situation created by COBRA. Montgomery and his planners decided that the latter made the former obsolete. At most, Montgomery quickly decided, not Patton's Third Army as prescribed in the OVERLORD plans but only a single corps should turn right from Avranches into Brittany. The great bulk of the American forces turned loose by the breakout should instead hasten eastward toward the successive lines Laval-Mayenne and le Mans-Alençon to trap the Germans against the Seine. If the German forces west of the Seine could be destroyed, then the whole Western Front might open, and the war might be won speedily enough that the Breton ports would not be needed. At the least, other ports could be opened farther to the Allied left, and "the main business lies to the East."[5] It required considerable badgering from the logistical experts to hold Montgomery to the commitment of even a single corps to Brittany.

By August 2, the Supreme Commander's thoughts were running in a similar direction. General Eisenhower's sense of the possibilities turned first to a lesser encirclement of the Germans west of the Vire, to be accomplished by the closing of a pincers through the town of Vire upon Bradley's pincers through Avranches. But such a success could lead to a larger envelopment. With the closing of the first trap, "I would consider it unnecessary to detach any large forces for the conquest of Brittany and would devote the great bulk of the forces to the task of completing the destruction of the German Army, at least that portion west of the Orne, and exploiting beyond that as far as we possibly could."[6]

On August 2, Bradley was still thinking less boldly and more in terms of the OVERLORD plan. He clung to the invasion of Brittany as the next main effort of his armies after the Normandy breakout, and he intended to commit the entire Third Army to capturing the Breton ports. By the next day, Thursday, August 3, Bradley had shifted his judgment to the hope that Patton could clear Brittany with "a minimum of forces,"[7] while the bulk of the American armies moved eastward to expand the lodgment area in that direction. But where Montgomery was planning an encirclement, Bradley's design envisaged advancing all along the American line. He also expected to have to stop well short of the Seine. "Gen hopes," Major Hansen wrote on August 6, "to build up on Domfront-Le Mans and there collect supplies necessary for movement. Supply may limit the rapidity with which we move towards Paris. Gen hopes to get going by September." Bradley was also concerned about defending what he had already gained. He still feared a

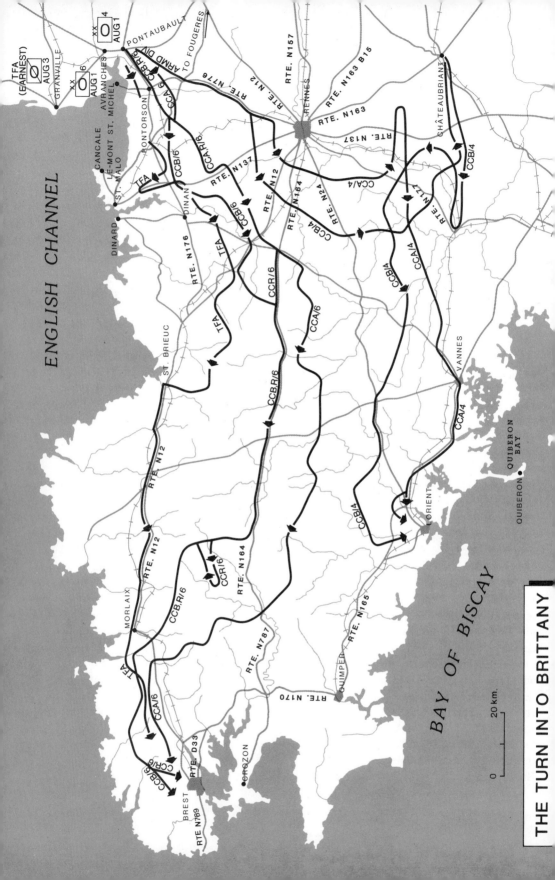

THE TURN INTO BRITTANY

German counterattack into the area where the American First and British Second Armies met: "Attack of First Canadian army for tomorrow if successful to Falaise should clean out much resistance and take flanks with it to straighten line, permit us to build supplies without threat of Ger attack on the hinge north of St. Hillaire."[8] Still more, Bradley feared for the gap that was opening as the Third Army began turning at least part of its force west into Brittany while other Americans moved eastward. Bradley ordered Patton to commit newly operational units of the Third Army to close the gap, by holding a ninety-five-kilometer stretch of the north-south Mayenne River between Mayenne and Château-Gontier, and by guarding the line of the Loire River west of Angers.

The distrust between Bradley and Patton arose partly from the differences in outlook between the infantryman and the cavalryman. "I am also nauseated," Patton grumbled, "by the fact that Hodges and Bradley state that all human virtue depends on knowing infantry tactics." To Patton, Bradley was never audacious enough: "Bradley and Hodges are such nothings. Their one virtue is that they get along by doing nothing. . . . They try to push all along the front and have no power anywhere."[9] Yet despite such criticism of Omar, "the tent maker," Patton like Bradley—and unlike Montgomery—hesitated to diverge too far from the long-standing plan that placed his Third Army's first mission in Brittany. The British military critic B.H. Liddell Hart later testified that on the eve of D-Day, he found Patton skeptical that the Allies would be able to repeat in France in 1944 anything like the swift and deep armored drives of the Germans in 1940. Rather, said Liddell Hart, Patton spoke of going "back to 1918 methods."[10]

One of the few officers in the Allied armies whom Liddell Hart found alert to the possibilities offered by his own strategic theories of deep armored envelopment and the indirect approach was the much more junior General John Wood of the 4th Armored Division. Like Patton bred as a horse soldier—albeit, with Wood, horse artillery—and something of a protégé of Patton's, "P" (for "professor," a moniker earned while tutoring at West Point) Wood was a student of cavalry exploitation in the best tradition of the old horse soldiers.

On the afternoon of August 1, Wood pushed the spearhead of his 4th Armored Division right on across the Sélune bridge at Pontaubault and forward for over thirty kilometers more, almost to the city of Rennes. Augustus Hare had called this capital of the Duchy of Brittany, mostly rebuilt after an eighteenth-century fire, "the dullest, as it is almost the ugliest" city in France, [11] but it was scarcely either to the Americans. A city of over 80,000, Rennes was the hub of ten main highways. Some ninety kilometers southwest of it is Quiberon Bay, where the OVERLORD planners, anticipating German destruction of the major existing ports, envisaged Allied building of a new seaport. But almost equidistant to the southeast is Angers on the Loire, the historic capital of Anjou, on the road to Orléans and, beyond that, to Paris.

Wood wanted to turn east, both to keep his division where he believed the biggest action would be, and in quest of strategic opportunity for the whole Allied cause. After he decided on August 2 that Rennes was too strongly held for his division to take it quickly—some 2,000 German troops had gravitated into the place from all points of the compass—he proposed to General Middleton the next day that the 8th Division, following him from Avranches, should take up the time-consuming task of capturing Rennes. The 4th Armored should bypass the city around a wide arc west of its defenses, but thence the division should not drive on to Quiberon Bay but rather turn southeast to Châteaubriant, almost fifty kilometers from Rennes on the road to Angers. By this means, the 4th Armored would isolate Rennes on three sides until the followup infantry captured it, and would still move far enough south to block enemy traffic to and from the Brittany peninsula. Wood let the merits of the eastward thrust speak for themselves. Anticipating approval, he ordered his division to begin the movement.

Presently there came to Wood a corps order prepared earlier and reiterating that Quiberon Bay was a primary objective of the VIII Corps advance into Brittany and that as the southern spearhead of the corps, it was the 4th Armored's task to reach the bay. The language was explicit enough that Wood had no choice but to rescind his own most recent order; but while transmitting to his division the instructions from corps, he added, almost as though it were incidental, a proviso that the troops should remain prepared to swing east to Châteaubriant. Beginning to circle around Rennes on the morning of August 3, by late afternoon Wood's CCA was at Bain-de-Bretagne and CCB was at Darval, fifty and sixty kilometers south of Rennes. They had cut seven of the ten main roads converging on Rennes and had met almost no opposition to their sweep.

By this time, Middleton had acknowledged Wood's movements and thus seemed implicitly to have approved them. Circumspection on Middleton's part was transmitted to Wood only in the form of an order that Wood must capture Rennes quickly, not remain content to isolate it. This order in itself was not unduly frustrating. Wood could make good use of the Rennes road nexus to ensure the communications of his eastward turn anyway, and he was already sending the regimental combat team that had been motorized with quartermaster trucks and attached to him, the 13th Infantry, toward a rapid, August 3 assault on the city. With its leading battalion plunging into the attack from route column march formation as soon as it reached the defenses, the 13th scored a quick penetration. The defenders, evidently disheartened before they entered Rennes, withdrew over secondary roads and cross country during the night. The bulk of the 8th Division promptly followed the 13th Infantry into Rennes and garrisoned it.

Also late on August 3, however, Middleton's concern for his corps's responsibility westward into Brittany led him to add another cautionary exception to his apparent acceptance of Wood's activities. Wood was to leave adequate blocking forces at the bridges of the Vannes River, which flows southwestward from Rennes to empty into the sea about halfway between St. Nazaire and Quiberon Bay. These blocking forces would help assure the sealing off of Brittany, for the American higher command to choose to do with the peninsula whatever it wished.

Wood had not received this order when he conferred with Middleton face-to-face. As Middleton later told the story, Wood radioed him and asked urgently to see him:

> I asked him [said Middleton], "Where are you?" He replied, "I'm just outside Rennes." I asked, "How are you getting along?" And he replied, "I've got to see you, I can't tell you." I said, "When?" He said, "Right now; get in your Jeep and come on down here."
>
> Well, it wasn't like driving out to pay a call on a neighbor. It was enemy country, and there were Germans everywhere. So I got a couple of halftracks, a couple of Jeeps and a few soldiers. We got to Wood's headquarters about daylight. Wood was stripped to his waist, near a little trailer with his maps all out on the ground. He came over and threw his arms around me. I said, "What's the matter,

John, you lost your division?" He said, "Heck no, we're winning this war the wrong way, we ought to be going toward Paris."[12]

But Middleton felt obliged to pass the word that higher headquarters were still essentially following the OVERLORD script for the westward turn into Brittany. Obliged to confront Wood's improvisations directly, Middeleton decided: "So I had to get him back on the track and get him started toward Lorient—much to his disgust."[13]

Wood and Middleton were soon to receive further confirmation that their seniors had not changed the OVERLORD design. On August 5, Patton's chief of staff, Major General Hugh J. Gaffey, read a routine VIII Corps list of the missions assigned the corps's component units. Therein he learned how Wood and—notwithstanding the meeting with Wood—Middleton seemed to be still engaged in modifying the plan for the Third Army to capture the Breton ports. Gaffey promptly told Middleton that General Patton "assumes that in addition to blocking the roads . . ., you are pushing the bulk of the [4th Armored] division to the west and southwest to the Quiberon area, including the towns of Vannes and Lorient, in accordance with the Army plan."[14] Gaffey also got off a direct message to Wood, with a copy to Middleton, explicitly sending the 4th Armored to Vannes and Lorient, westward into Brittany.

Wood was bold enough to bend instructions from Middleton, but word from Patton's headquarters was another matter. Already slowed by a shortage of gasoline catching up with the heads of Wood's columns, the 4th Armored drive to the east had to end on the morning of August 5. By evening, the leading units of Colonel Clarke's CCA had shifted far westward to the town of Vannes, which with the help of the French Forces of the Interior they captured so swiftly that the Germans could not prepare demolitions. Lorient proved more resistant, perhaps because artillery fire from the defenses prompted an exceedingly cautious, probing approach. In any event, Wood did not consider assault upon strong prepared defenses a proper use of an armored division. From August 6 to 10, while trying to talk Lorient into surrender, the 4th Armored otherwise did little more than contain the garrison and wait for some other formation to arrive to free the armor for a return to cavalry warfare.

Wood could not keep his eyes away from the east. Knowing he could not, Middleton turned to him when Patton called on the VIII Corps to relieve a battalion of the 5th Division that was containing the enemy garrison of Nantes, 130 kilometers east of Lorient. Middleton instructed Wood to dispatch a combat command, and Bruce Clarke's CCA began the move on August 10 and arrived the next day. During the following night the Germans inside Nantes blew up ammunition dumps, and French civilians reported that the garrison was preparing to flee. Thereupon Wood told Clarke to attack. CCA captured Nantes on August 12.

Patton had expected Middleton to send not Wood's men but 8th Division troops from Rennes; but with half Wood's force already so far east, the Third Army acquiesced. The 6th Armored Division relieved the 4th Armored at Lorient on August 15, and Wood's whole division again faced toward Paris. But ten days had gone by since the division had last done so. Wood was bitter about the strategic consequences when he later told Liddell Hart that the American command had proven incapable of appropriately prompt reaction when COBRA with unexpected swiftness opened the door out of Normandy at Avranches:

When it did react, its order consisted of sending its two flank armored divisions [Wood's 4th and Grow's 6th] back, 180 degrees away from the main enemy, to engage in siege operations against Lorient and Brest. August 4 was that black day. I protested long, loud, and violently—and pushed my tank columns into Château-briant (without orders) and my armored cavalry to the outskirts of Angers and along the Loire, ready to advance (east) on Chartres. I could have been there, in the enemy vitals, in two days. But no! We were forced to adhere to the original plan—with the only armor available, and ready to cut the enemy to pieces. It was one of the colossally stupid decisions of the war.[15]

Middleton, with a moderation and tolerance that were characteristic of the fatherly ROTC instructor and university dean, tried after the war to split the difference between Wood and the higher command: "Looking at it with hindsight, Wood was right, of course. But the high command at the time was absolutely right in . . . [wanting] the ports."[16] Though kind, this was misguided. Wood and the higher command held opposite views on the value of turning the armored divisions into Brittany and could not both be right.

Brittany

Nothwithstanding the affair of the 4th Armored Division, General Patton's reputation for bold and swift, even reckless advance was amply merited. Racing armored columns offered the nearest possible equivalent of an old-time cavalry pursuit, and like "P" Wood, George S. Patton, Jr., was preeminently a horse soldier.

Patton's love of horses stemmed from his well-to-do Virginia and southern California antecedents and upbringing. It was especially the speed of the mounted arm that he cherished—the speed of mounted advance and pursuit, and also the speed with which the traditional cavalryman had to thrust and parry with his historic weapon, the saber; for Patton's first professional writing he had taken the sword as his subject. Patton had competed in the modern pentathlon at the 1912 Olympics and performed best in horsemanship and fencing, giving the eventual French fencing winner his only defeat. In 1913 Patton became the first American officer to be awarded the title Master of the Sword by the French Cavalry School at Saumur. Though he commanded the largest American tank force to go into action in World War I, the 304th Tank Brigade, he remained true to his first love, the old-style cavalry, over any mechanical mounts and weapons, and returned again from the horse cavalry to tanks only with wistful reluctance on the eve of World War II.

Patton the horse soldier expressed the strongly traditionalist bent of Patton's character. In his own imagination, he was the knight in armor. Nevertheless, his nostalgia for saber and spurs, free from the chronic mechanical failures of the tank and from its dependence on a gasoline umbilical cord, signified also attitudes more appropriate to modern war: Patton's quest for the headlong mobility of the old free-ranging cavalry.

At its headquarters, Patton's Third Army was a cavalry army, with movement and pursuit the passions not only of the commanding general but of the whole army command. Patton surrounded himself with cavalrymen and armored specialists. His chief of staff, General Gaffey, like Wood had come from the field artillery; but Gaffey had transferred to armor early in the American preparation for war and led the 2nd Armored

Division in Sicily. The deputy chief of staff, Brigadier General Hobart R. Gay, had been Patton's chief of staff in North Africa and Sicily and would have been the army commander's first choice to remain as such had he possessed sufficient seniority; Hap Gay was a well-known horseman and riding instructor in the old army. The G-3, Colonel Halley G. Maddox, was also best known to the army as a horseman. Throughout, the Third Army staff had worn crossed sabers on their lapels or early wore the tank insignia.

"P" Wood's swift drives followed the methods he and Patton had worked out during the 4th Armored's training in England—in particular one of Patton's favorite injunctions: "Our basic plan of operation is to advance and to keep on advancing regardless of whether we have to go over, under, or through the enemy."[17] Whatever Patton might have said to Liddell Hart about returning to 1918 methods, he used nothing of the sort when he impatiently activated Third Army headquarters at noon on August 1. His style of army command included hurrying from one subordinate unit to another by jeep, escorted by an armored car, stopping wherever he saw mistakes to be corrected or courage and intelligence to be commended, and forever pushing "to advance and to keep on advancing." In early August, in the flush of renewed action after exile, he played this role to the hilt.

Still, as to Brittany, he accepted Bradley's and not Wood's view of what constituted boldness: it was reckless enough to diminish the planned Third Army invasion of Brittany from army strength to a single corps. So at first it was away from the main enemy and westward into Brittany that Patton hurried and pushed.

Moving in any direction whatever from Avranches-Pontaubault was a problem through much of the first part of August because all traffic had to converge through wreckage and rubble in Avranches upon a single road. Some of Patton's energy, and that of many other senior officers, went into assisting the military police as traffic cops. On Monday, July 31, Middleton instructed Grow of the 6th Armored that for the time being his division would have to remain at Pontaubault simply guarding the bridgehead there. Grow posted his reserve combat command directly at the bridgehead; CCR had fewer command tanks, headquarters personnel, and radios than the other combat commands of an armored division and was generally used in relatively static roles. By early Tuesday, however, Middleton was feeling Patton's hot and impatient breath intensely. In consequence, changing his instructions to Grow and ordering him to move into Brittany, he so emphasized speed that Grow led off with CCR rather than delay to pass another combat command through it.

Speed was surely what Patton wanted. Presently he found Grow directing traffic at a crossroads and told him he had a five-pound wager with Montgomery that American troops would be in Brest by Saturday night. That major port near the western extremity of the Brittany peninsula was about 300 kilometers away. The German XXV Corps was in Brittany, including many weary Normandy survivors but of uncertain overall strength, and doubtless operating under Hitler's standard directive that major seaports must be regarded as fortresses and held to the last. Nevertheless, Patton put his hand on Grow's shoulder and said: "Take Brest." Intermediate resistance should be bypassed.

The 6th Armored like the 4th had trained for such a mission under Patton's tutelage, and like Wood of the 4th, Grow of the 6th Armored had a cavalryman's experience and taste for just the sort of rampaging dash that Patton wanted. By nightfall of August 2, Grow's CCB had passed through CCR and was near Bécherel, sixty-five kilometers west of

Pontaubault, having bypassed strong resistance at Dinan. CCA was fifteen kilometers still farther along at Quédilliac. The 6th Armored was so far west, in fact, that General Middleton at corps headquarters just north of Avranches found communication with it "practically nil." "The expensive signal equipment at the disposal of the Corps," he later said, "was never designed apparently for a penetration and pursuit of the magnitude of the Brittany operation."[18] Telephone cables could not be laid fast enough; supposedly high-powered long-distance radios worked only sporadically.

Ignorance of what his spearheads were doing, and where, aggravated the concerns of Middleton, who was not a cavalryman, that his units were ranging too far too recklessly without enough regard for the safety of their flanks. Middleton was by no means a timid officer, as his considerable acquiescence in Wood's bending of orders had shown; but having his corps charge off in opposite directions at once without communication and thus without central control was too much for him to accept. Moreover, by August 2 he was out of touch with Patton, who was chasing his army's spearheads and also unreachable from corps headquarters. But while Patton was out of touch, Bradley showed up at Middleton's command post on that second day of his translation to the role of army group commander exclusively, and Bradley proved to perceive events as Middleton did.

Bradley's role as commander of an army group operational in the field was not only new to him but unfamiliar to any American officer. Previous American experience with an army group had been limited to about two weeks at the close of the First World War, when two American armies fought along the Western Front and Pershing commanded them as a group of armies from his AEF headquarters. But Pershing relied on that already existing headquarters, which was mainly concerned with AEF administration. During the interwar years, American theory of the nature of an army group headquarters had developed in Chapter 6 of the standard manual FM 100–15, *Field Service Regulations, Larger Units*, into the concept that an army group is purely a tactical unit. It is a headquarters for directing operations on a scale too large for the grasp of a single army headquarters. It is not, however, an administrative or territorial headquarters; observation of the British arrangement of Allied army group headquarters in North Africa and Italy, commanding American as well as British units, added practical insight to American theory and convinced Americans that they should adhere to their theory and not add administrative and territorial duties as the British did. The effect   of British practice in making the army group an administrative command, they concluded, was to expand the army group staff so greatly that the headquarters became immobilized and its tactical leadership suffered. Administration should be left to the theater command—in the European Theater, to J.C.H. Lee's organization. For all that, as an American officer soon to wrestle with creating a second American army group was to remark of army group command, "as late as 1944 . . . the number of officers in our Service having a reasonable knowledge of it totaled exactly zero."[19]

An additional part of the theory formulated in FM 100–15 was that as a tactical headquarters, the army group directs operations but does not conduct them. To permit his span of control to remain large enough to encompass several armies, the army group commander would have to rely on "mission orders": he must prescribe missions, but not attempt to control in detail how his subordinates from army command downward might carry out the missions. American theory of command tended toward a preference for such mission-type orders at virtually every level, extending a wide discretion to the responsible officer on the scene to accomplish the tasks assigned him according to his own judgment of his circumstances. (German theory and practice exhibited the same tendency, only more so.) But the army group commander even more than others must content himself with the assignment of missions, leaving the conduct of operations to others. Thus the army group headquarters was to be large in its span of control but small, mobile, and flexible in the size and functions of its staff.

On this second day of his operational army group command, Bradley began to show signs of departure from this theory that were to swell the size of his headquarters—more than 900 officers by the end of the war—and involve him enough in the conduct of operations that 12th Army Group Headquarters tended to become indistinguishable in tactical function from an army headquarters, operating at a more senior level. Hearing Middleton's troubles and surveying the map displays of the scattered condition of the VIII Corps, Bradley grumbled, according to Major Hansen: "Some people are more concerned with the headlines and the news they'll make than the soundness of their tactics. I don't care if we get Brest tomorrow or ten days later. If we cut the peninsula, we'll get it anyhow. But we can't risk a loose hinge." The hinge that worried Bradley and Middleton was Avranches. For a second day, the Luftwaffe had managed a resurgence of bombing and strafing activity upon the Avranches bottleneck, and the army group and the corps commanders both feared this aerial effort might presage a German ground counterattack to break through to the sea at Avranches and cut the lines of communication of the VIII Corps troops already south of the bottleneck. Middleton had little force with which to guard Avranches and was allowed little by Patton's orders to hasten everything into Brittany.

Noting that Wyche's 79th Division was just north of Avranches though loading up for an advance into Brittany, Bradley said to Middleton: "I want the 79th Division down near Fougères and I want to build up there. It would be very embarrassing to George [if the Germans broke through]. George is used to attacks from a single division. He's buttoned up well enough for that. But he's not used to having three or four German divisions hit him. He doesn't know what it means yet."[20] Fougères is thirty-five kilometers southwest of Avranches and a good shielding position.

Like Middleton unable to reach Patton from VIII Corps headquarters, Bradley hastened to the advance headquarters of the Third Army. There he found Patton. "For Christ's sake, George, what are you going to do with this open flank you have?" said Bradley. "I've sent the 79th down there and I hate to have to bypass a commander. It's your army." According to his diary, Patton's reply was something about Bradley's "getting the British complex of over-caution," but otherwise he took Bradley's intervention in stride. Above all, he was exhilarated to be back in the field and did not want to risk his position.[21]

Placing the 79th Division at Fougères was precisely what Middleton himself wanted to do. Thus encouraged by Bradley, the corps commander took another step the next day to bring his units under control. On August 3, the 6th Armored Division had traveled about half the 300 kilometers from Avranches to Brest when a communication from corps headquarters got through to Grow. Reaching him first by radio and then by courier, Middleton instructed him not to bypass the strongholds of Dinan and St. Malo, but instead to concentrate for an attack on the latter seaport.

If he obeyed, Grow could hardly expect to reach Brest by Saturday, so he protested the order. He also obeyed it. Unable to reach CCB by radio, he caught up with this unit far west of Dinan near Loudéac, and finding it there he decided to compromise matters by holding it in place, well out toward Brest, rather than calling it back. But other parts of his division would pause to capture St. Malo.

The next morning, Friday, August 4, Grow and his staff were in a wheatfield near Merdrignac working out a plan to fit the new corps orders when General Patton's jeep came driving up, unheralded. Patton jumped out with his fair complexion reddened by the effort to repress an eruption of anger: "What in hell are you doing here? I thought I told you to go to Brest."

"My advance was halted, sir," Grow replied.

"On what authority?"

"Corps orders, sir." Grow's chief of staff already had his hand in his pocket to produce the courier-delivered order from Middleton, which he had not yet had a chance to file. Patton read the note, put it into his own pocket, and muttered about its author, as though to himself, "And he was a *good* doughboy, too." Then he turned to Grow. "I'll see Middleton," he said. "You go ahead where I told you to go."[22]

To handle an army commanded as this one was, Bradley's expansion of the functions of the army group may have been necessary. A few minutes later, Grow received another message from Middleton—returning the 6th Armored to its original mission against Brest. The day before, after sending the order that angered Patton, Middleton had learned from aerial reconnaissance that Grow was much farther beyond Dinan than he thought. With this new information, Dinan and St. Malo seemed clearly to be problems for Brigadier General Herbert L. Earnest's Task Force A (mainly the 15th Cavalry Group and the 6th Tank Destroyer Group), which was moving along the north coast of Brittany to secure the railroad line there, and for Macon's 83rd Division, designated to replace the 79th as a followup for the armor in Brittany. Middleton had been trying without success to reach Grow and renew the charge toward Brest since late Thursday afternoon.

Grow turned his division westward again as quickly as he could; but by the time his orders had circulated and everyone was ready to move, it was late Friday afternoon, and the movement against Brest had been delayed almost a day. With a full moon and clear skies, Grow ordered a night march. Continuing to bypass enemy strongpoints, the vanguard of the 6th Armored reached the neighborhood of the city by nightfall on Sunday, August 6. But it was in no position to attack the city, and Monday had to be consumed in deploying the whole force in three columns against the Brest defenses.

As that work proceeded, harassing artillery fire from the defenses indicated both that there would be no surprising the garrison and that the fortified seaport was held in strength. On the morning of Tuesday, August 8, Grow submitted to the German command in the city his formal call for a surrender, which predictably was refused. He then requested air support for a major attack on August 9, but this assault did not occur. Before Tuesday was over, Grow learned that large parts of the German 266th Division were approaching his rear from the interior of the Brittany peninsula. By the time the 6th Armored had reversed in place to dispose of that threat—and dispose of the threat it did, for the 266th was a garrison division and not overly formidable—further reconnaissance of the Brest defenses afforded the unpleasant assurance that the garrison and fortifications were too strong to be overcome by a single armored division, even one reinforced by the infantry that Middleton had mounted in quartermaster trucks way back before

Avranches. When corps headquarters digested the information that reached it from Grow and from the AAF, Middleton sealed this conclusion by ordering Grow to contain Brest with one combat command while relieving the 4th Armored at Lorient and Vannes with the others.

The delay caused by Middleton's orders of August 3 became a subject of controversy, on the ground that Middleton allowed the Germans to withdraw their coastal garrisons from all over western Brittany into Brest, and thus to make formidable a fortress that Grow could have taken if he had arrived there a day earlier. The 6th Armored's encounter with the 266th Division is an example of the enemy's activity in consolidating his forces in the area. The charge that an opportunity was lost gains plausibility from the fact that the enemy's exceptionally well trained 2nd Parachute Division joined the 343rd Division in garrison only on August 9, slipping past the Americans from the south. These Fallschirmtruppen eventually proved the core of the defense. Nevertheless, the fortifications of Brest were so large and complex—extensive caves and bombproofs developed by the Germans from strong old French works—and the determination of the enemy to hold on to major ports was so intense, that it seems impossible that Grow's division alone could have captured the place even before the garrison attained its full eventual strength of 38,000.

Thus the division's disappointment at the end of its 300-kilometer odyssey should not obscure its accomplishments. Besides moving at a pace that rightly warmed the hearts of founders of American mechanized forces such as its army commander, it took 4,000 prisoners, while losing itself only about 130 killed, 400 wounded, and 70 missing. "We are having one of the loveliest battles you ever saw," Patton wrote to an old friend. "It is a typical cavalry action in which, to quote the words of the old story, 'The soldier went out and charged in all directions at the same time, with a pistol in each hand, and a saber in the other.'"[23]

The real question raised by the plunge into Brittany is not whether Brest might have fallen to the 6th Armored had it not been for the delay on August 3–4, but whether the soldier should have been charging in all directions at the same time. The charge into Brittany yielded the Allies little. Brest did not fall until September 19, by which time other ports far to the northeast had been captured. When Brest fell, the customary methodical German demolitions had yet to be cleared, and so by the time Brest was safe and operating the war had left it too far behind to make much of a contribution to Allied logistics. The Americans eventually abandoned its rehabilitation with the work incomplete. Lorient and St. Nazaire remained in German hands until the end of the war. The new port on Quiberon Bay was never built, because the rapid race of the war eastward promptly made the expense of construction patently out of all proportion to any conceivable utility. St. Malo fell to the 83rd Division on August 17 after a siege tenaciously and well conducted on both sides. The deep-water channel to St. Malo and also the lesser ports of Granville and Cancale could not be used until the Île de Cezembre surrendered on September 2 under air and artillery bombardment and the threat of amphibious assault.

On August 25, meanwhile, the Communications Zone had decided to clear the German demolitions from and to develop the Breton ports of St. Malo, Cancale, Morlaix, and St. Brieuc, as well as Granville near the southwest corner of the Cotentin. These harbors were so small, however, that the combined capacity for which the rebuilders would aim was only 20,000 tons a day. Eventually, the biggest of them, St. Malo, was returned to the French on November 21 with reconstruction incomplete because the Americans decided again that the dividends of rebuilding were not worth the effort. Nevertheless, the initial American reaction to tough German resistance at Brest and other Breton ports had been not to write off the Brittany campaign as a bad investment, but to consider diverting more strength from the campaign eastward to move in the wake of the VIII Corps westward. It required Montgomery's stubborn resistance to any such diversion to prevent the investment in Brittany from growing more disproportionate still.

The Americans entered Brittany without complete knowledge of German strength in the peninsula, but with enough knowledge to have predicted that the enemy could defend the ports for a considerable time, and with enough awareness of Hitler's attitude on the necessity of retaining "fortress" ports to recognize that as long as the enemy was able to defend, he almost certainly would defend. The Germans' devastation of port facilities likewise was altogether predictable, especially after the Cherbourg experience. Thus the unwisdom of the turn into Brittany by even an entire corps, and especially by armored divisions, becomes if not as obvious as General Wood's angry remarks to Liddell Hart would have it, at least an issue to be pondered. Up to a point, General Bradley had displayed admirable flexibility in leaving open his course of action after COBRA. When COBRA broke the German left in Normandy more completely than Bradley had dared to anticipate, he did not stop his troops when they reached the Coutances-Caumont line that was the formal objective, but capitalized on the mobility of the American army to keep them moving onward at a pace that strained supply lines. Nevertheless, perhaps in part under the weight of his new responsibilities as operational commander of an army group, Bradley was inflexible about Brittany. The OVERLORD plan called for the thrust into Brittany, and amid the bewildering rush of events at the end of July and the beginning of August, Bradley evidently found an anchor of security in the plan.

To be sure, there was the matter of containing the German XXV Corps in Brittany. Bradley later justified a prolonged and costly siege of Brest, even after any need for the port had manifestly passed, on the ground that vigorous offensive action was required to restrain the large enemy garrison from making mischief in the Allied rear. While the Americans entered Brittany without full knowledge of German strength in the peninsula, however, among the things that they did know was that the enemy's XXV Corps had lost most of its best and most mobile troops to the defense of Normandy. The Americans were aware that three of the remaining four divisions—the 2nd Parachute Division was the exception—were weak, static formations, ten understrength battalions in all. The XXV Corps remained capable of stubborn defense of fixed positions; large-scale offensive movement across the Brittany peninsula was something else.

Furthermore, the French Forces of the Interior had an exceptionally strong organization among the proud, individualistic Bretons, and in preparation for the Allied invasion the FFI in Brittany had been exceptionally—though certainly not lavishly—well armed by Allied air drops. One of the main reasons why Patton's armored columns could race so swiftly through the peninsula was that the FFI had already captured almost the whole countryside and driven the Germans into the port cities. With some 30,000 armed Bretons (thought by the Allies to be 50,000), backed up by perhaps another 50,000 carrying grenades, intermingled with small but highly trained bands of French and British parachutists, and centrally commanded by Colonel Albert M. Eon who had been parachuted in from Charles de Gaulle's Free French forces in England, the FFI had a considerable capacity to contain static German divisions.

At the beginning of August, when newspapers in Britain and America alike were dominated by exciting reports of the American breakout from Normandy, Prime Minister Churchill looked for a means of recapturing for British soldiers a due proportion of news space and credit for Allied achievements. He found a partial solution in the public announcement of General Morgan's role in the planning that necessarily preceded the great invasion. Morgan as conciliator between British and Americans as well as for so long the principal OVERLORD planner deserved all the public credit he might get. Nor should his unusual achievements among the planners be overlooked; more than most, he had feared the Bocage, and therefore he had urged that the breakthrough effort be mounted toward the Caen-Falaise plain on the Allied left. Nevertheless, the timing of the announcement was ironic, with Allied flexibility at this very moment impeded by the constraints of the planning. For the planners had planned too much; preoccupied with the amphibious assault and with keeping it ashore, they had become almost obsessed with port capacity, and now their designs for obtaining ports were distracting attention from more immediate and much larger opportunities.

PART THREE : FRANCE

★ ★ ★

10: The Short Envelopment

As THE soldier who charged in all directions at the same time, General Patton assisted in distracting the Allies from their main offensive purpose, which should have been to pursue the German armies eastward to their destruction. But Patton's charging aggressiveness also helped stimulate movement in the proper direction of opportunity and ultimate purpose. He himself merited the primary credit for hastening as many as seven divisions through the Avranches-Pontaubault bottleneck in only seventy-two hours despite stubborn German aerial attack. This force was larger than even Bradley wanted to consign westward to Brittany, so some of it was available for other uses than assailing the Breton ports.

When General Bradley ordered Wyche's 79th Division of Patton's army into a shielding position at Fougères, this defensive reaction also provided Patton with a foundation for yet another offensive. The Third Army commander liked to declaim about letting flanks take care of themselves, while forcing the enemy to attend to *his* flanks. In action as distinguished from rhetoric, he was not so heedless in such matters as Bradley feared. About the same time that Bradley dispatched the 79th Division to Fougères, Patton himself was ordering Major General Lunsford E. Oliver's 5th Armored Division to the same area. Once each level of command became aware of what the other was doing, Patton found himself with a force around Fougères strong enough to take initiatives as well as to shield.

With Middleton's headquarters clearly involved in too many efforts at once, Patton shifted the 79th Division to Major General Wade Hampton Haislip's XV Corps. To this newly activated corps headquarters, Patton assigned the task of seeing to Bradley's injunction that he close the gap between the First Army and his own by patrolling the Mayenne River south of the town of Mayenne. Already, Patton had also transferred the 90th Division from the VIII Corps to the XV and sent it through Avranches and thence eastward into a blocking position between the Sée and Sélune Rivers from Juvigny to St. Hilaire-du-Harcouët, with a bridgehead south of the Sélune toward Louvigné-du-Désert.

The 90th, whose brief history in France was already so troubled, got off to an unhappy start with the impatient Patton when he encountered it on the march between the Sée and the Sélune on August 2: "The division is bad," he decided, "the discipline poor, the men filthy, and the officers apathetic, many of them removing their insignia and covering the markings on helmets."[1] But Middleton and Bradley had given up on the unfortunate General Landrum, and everyone might hope for improvement under the division's third commander since going into action, Brigadier General Raymond S. McLain. McLain was a National Guardsman, a banker from Oklahoma City who had been artillery commander of the 45th Division. How much he had impressed his superiors in combat in the Mediterranean Theater was implied by the rarity of a National Guard officer's getting the command of a non–National Guard division such as the 90th. To execute this upward jump, McLain had to be an exceptional soldier, so there was hope for the 90th still.

Indeed, despite what Patton saw, the division vanguard conducted a swift and efficient descent and attack on St. Hilaire on the morning of Patton's visit to other parts of the formation, and with similar efficiency the 90th had taken up its whole assigned line south from Juvigny by shortly after midnight.

The next day, August 3, the 79th Division occupied Fougères in force and made contact with the right flank of the 90th. The 5th Armored was still preparing to move through Avranches to extend the right flank still farther. On August 5, Haislip sent the 90th Division forward from St. Hilaire toward Mayenne, and the advance contributed again toward the improvement of the divisional image by covering almost fifty kilometers to the west bank of the Mayenne River in less than half a day. The town of Mayenne, with its highway bridge intact, fell to a frontal assault during the afternoon before a flanking force could get into position. The 79th encountered more numerous roadblocks and moved a little less rapidly in its simultaneous advance from Fougères toward Laval, and it found the Mayenne bridges at Laval destroyed. But it crossed the river and captured Laval on the east bank during August 6, and had a treadway bridge spanning the stream soon after midnight. Catching up, the 5th Armored reached the Mayenne at Château-Gontier by evening of August 6.

Because General Bradley had also instructed Patton to patrol the Loire west of Angers, the Third Army was in process of committing yet another new corps, General Walker's XX, to take over the front south of Château-Gontier on the Mayenne. Walker's leading division would be Irwin's 5th Infantry, now seasoned by its fighting around Vire. Without waiting for Walker's troops to begin arriving, Patton asked and received Bradley's permission to send Haislip's corps on to le Mans, another seventy kilometers to the east—though the move would test Patton's dictum that it should be the enemy who worried about his flanks, for both flanks of the XV Corps would be open. Between Haislip and le Mans lay the Sarthe River, enough of a stream to constitute a respectable military obstacle, while le Mans itself was a city of 75,000 which had long been headquarters for the German Seventh Army.

Yet Patton pushed onward and Bradley approved because Haislip's march so far made plain that only disorganized German fragments barred his way at present. Casualties were extremely light; hauls of prisoners ran into the thousands. G-2s from army group to XV Corps had worried for days that they knew nothing about the enemy in the corps area, but now it was apparent that they had known nothing because there was no

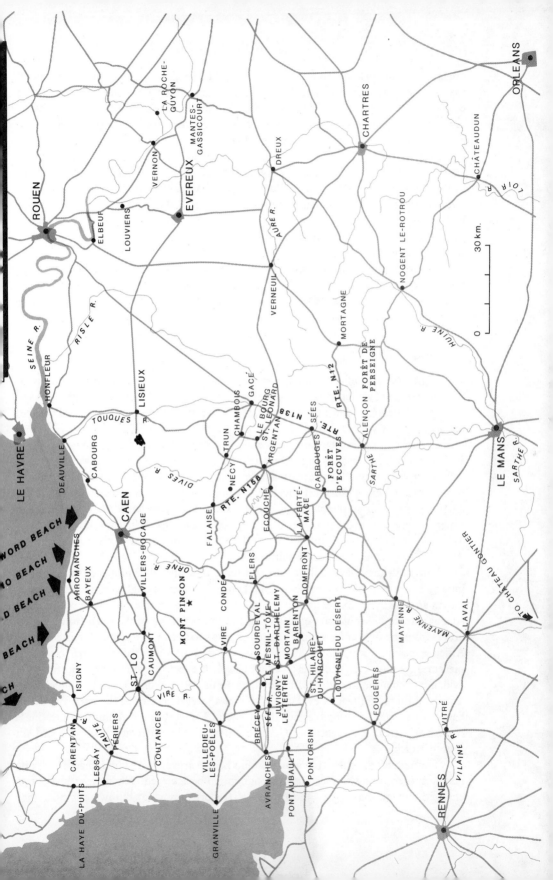

organized enemy to know about, at least short of the neighborhood of le Mans. All hands were now sensing in this eastward direction something of the opportunity that Wood had discerned while almost everyone else was still thinking about Brittany. "Don't stop" again became Patton's prescription for troops who met pockets of resistance; such resistance should be bypassed. Perhaps a division like the 90th seemed to be picking up pep and ginger not only because of the new commander but because swift movement was what the American army was best designed for, including the infantry divisions. Swift, dashing movement also tapped the deepest American military traditions: General Haislip, West Point 1912, Virginian namesake of one of R.E. Lee's great cavalrymen, urged his commanders "to push all personnel to the limit of human endurance." ". . . action during the next few days," he predicted, "might be decisive for the entire campaign in western Europe."[2]

The exhilaration of the chase after the long stalemate had much to do with such a promise; but there was more to it than that. Patton suggested to Haislip, as the XV Corps crossed the Mayenne, that he should not be surprised if he soon received orders turning him northward, into the rear of the Germans who were still fighting on the old Normandy front.

The Battle of Mortain

Some stout panzer and infantry formations still fought to the eastward on that front, and they were not yet incapable of dangerous responses to the American charge south and east from Avranches. But the response they apparently had in mind posed still further opportunities as well as danger.

Until the ULTRA secret was revealed in 1974, historians could only say—as Ladislas Farago did in his biography of Patton—that General Bradley's repeated warnings to his commanders, at this otherwise exuberant moment, to beware of a German counterattack were "based on exceptional intelligence, the origin of which was never disclosed."[3] On August 3, the ULTRA intercepts of enemy communications encoded by the German Enigma machines revealed to the Allied high command that Hitler was directing Field Marshal von Kluge to counterattack with at least four panzer divisions against the Avranches bottleneck, still only thirty kilometers wide.

During the next several days, ULTRA listened in while Kluge protested with surprising vigor that he could not extricate from battle elsewhere enough armored divisions to mount an effective counterattack, and that in trying to assemble even an approximately adequate force he would run excessive risk of the rupturing of the Caen front. Earlier orders from the Führer for similar counterattacks had been shortcircuited, moreover, by Allied pressure compelling the Germans to commit their troops defensively and piecemeal. Thus, even the interception of explicit enemy communiqués did not offer evidence conclusive enough for Bradley to make outright predictions of a counterattack. Yet in addition to ULTRA's evidence of Hitler's intentions and of the enemy order of battle, there was the tangible fact that General Hodges's First Army was meeting a pattern of resistance suggesting German determination to retain a springboard for counterattack.

Throughout the COBRA planning, Collins had been even more intent than Bradley on readiness to exploit whatever breakthrough might be achieved. When the COBRA design changed enough that it was Middleton's VIII Corps, moving southward, rather than

Collins's VII, moving westward, that captured Coutances, Collins was quick to turn as much of his own corps as he could southward for exploitation as well. For several days at the end of July, much of the VII Corps had to continue facing northward and westward to seal off the Germans in the Roncey pocket. Like Patton, Collins also had to become his own traffic cop to extricate his troops from the Avranches bottleneck. Collins later said:

> Sensing that there would be some inescapable difficulties in coordinating the movement to the south of the 3rd and 4th Armored Divisions, I personally went to Coutances [on July 30] . . . and then headed south on the Coutances-Gavray road. Progress south of Coutances was slow because of the fact that the approaches to the bridges over the Soulle River south of Coutances had not yet been fully cleared of rubble and because of the steep grades leading from the valley of the Soulle on the road to la Belletiere. . . .
>
> I drove by jeep via the la Belletiere-Roncey road. The traffic was halted because of sporadic German resistance, but primarily from the fact that the road was blocked with German equipment which had been destroyed either by our tanks, artillery, or by fighter-bombers. I finally came upon Brig. Gen. Doyle Hickey [of CCA, 3rd Armored] in the town of Roncey where the entire city square was blocked with well over a hundred German motor vehicles that had been caught by our fighter-bombers and burned to a crisp. It took some time to pull these vehicles out of the way. South of Roncey a similar group of vehicles amounting to a hundred or more had been caught on the road double-banked. These had likewise been destroyed but were a serious obstacle to traffic. I took steps to see that bulldozers were placed at the head of each column in order to assist in clearing these vehicles and others off the road.[4]

Before noon on July 30, Collins had Watson's 3rd Armored on his right, its combat commands reunited, and Barton's 4th Infantry Division on his left advancing southward from around Gavray toward Villedieu-les-Poëles. The objectives included the town of Villedieu, a road junction about halfway between Granville on the Cotentin west coast and the town of Vire, and high ground east and west of Villedieu.

Despite his personal efforts on the roads, the 3rd Armored Division failed to advance rapidly enough for Collins's taste. Disappointment with this division among the higher command had begun early with its part in the fizzle of the 30th Division's Vire River bridgehead and the action around Hauts-Vents. In COBRA, the 2nd Armored had moved faster and contributed more to exploiting the breakthrough than the 3rd, even though the plans had given the 3rd the primary role. Collins thus decided that the 3rd Armored was not as aggressive as it ought to be. So he separated the division's combat commands yet again, assigning CCB to the 4th Infantry Division and CCA to the 1st, leaving the headquarters of the 3rd Armored virtually as a mere administrative command.

With this change, and two first-rate division commanders—Huebner of the 1st and Barton of the 4th—heading the southward advance, Collins's new drive picked up speed, though against real opposition and thus at nothing like Patton's pace. On July 31, CCA of the 3rd Armored led a 1st Division advance cutting the Granville-Villedieu road, Route N24, some eleven kilometers south of the previous day's line of departure. Collins immediately instructed Huebner to press forward another nineteen kilometers to Hill 242 south of Brécey. Speeding through Brécey, finding the town's Sée River bridge destroyed but fording the stream, the head of the column was on the north slope of Hill 242 when it halted for the night.

While the 4th Division pushed through Villedieu toward the Sée near St. Pois, Collins next pivoted the 1st Division eastward toward Mortain. Mortain was a place of fewer than 3,000 inhabitants in peacetime, ornamented by its medieval parish church and a nearby twelfth-century convent, but it possessed conspicuous military importance because from it radiated seven main roads, and it occupies a commanding, rocky hill above the gorge of the Cance, a tributary of the Sélune, midway between the Sée and the Sélune. Duke William the Bastard, the future King William the Conqueror, in 1049 took the comté of Mortain from a cousin and awarded it to his half-brother Robert. Thereafter the medieval counts of Mortain tended to be just closely enough related to the kings of England to get along badly with them and become their rivals—Robert's son William rebelled against Henry I, and while Richard I occupied the English throne the count was his scheming brother John—so the name of Mortain already bore a certain dubious historical renown.

Despite difficult, broken terrain and narrow, twisting highways, CCA rapidly led the way for the 1st Division's entrance into Mortain on the afternoon of August 3, driving back not only German infantry formations but also, with more ominous implications, the Reconnaissance Battalion of the 2nd Panzer Division. Huebner promptly occupied the desired high ground, reaching eastward beyond the little town.

Meanwhile, on August 2 the 1st Division's right flank had linked up with the left of the 90th Division of the XV Corps at Juvigny. This meeting eased one of General Bradley's worries by closing the gap that had opened between the First and Third Armies.

While at least part of the First Army's VII Corps thus shared much of the Third Army's ability to advance eastward, all the Allied forces north of Mortain in contrast were again grappling with German resistance little less stubborn than before COBRA. This circumstance made it questionable whether Collins should maintain his momentum from Mortain toward Domfront on the Varenne River, a stream flowing almost directly southward into the Mayenne, toward which river in turn the Third Army was moving. In Bradley's mind, the impulse to give Collins free rein was tempered both by the ULTRA intercepts and by the continued presence of Germans in strength north and east of Mortain. Especially strong clusters of the enemy seemed to populate the difficult hill country of the Suisse-Normand just to the north. Unlike the 1st Division, Barton's 4th collided with almost unyielding enemies around St. Pois on August 2 and thereafter barely made headway. Similarly, the enemy had stiffened again in front of the XIX and V Corps and pressed back into Vire—Gerow need not have worried so soon about another clean getaway—and along with 8 Corps the XIX and V were locked in a bitter contest around Vire. By now all three corps of Dempsey's Second Army were also involved in a persistent struggle for Mont Pinçon.

During the night of August 6–7, the Stonewall Brigade of the XIX Corps finally cleared the streets of Vire, though the immediate German response was to bring the town under heavy shelling. During the same night, tanks of the 13th/18th Hussars led the British army up a narrow track with a sheer bank on one side and a sheer drop on the other to the 365-meter summit of Mont Pinçon. Vire and Mont Pinçon could thenceforth be regarded as the scenes of small triumphs of simple hard fighting in the manner of the landmarks of the first month of the invasion; but other gains currently scored north of Mortain were merely those of following up the shortening and straightening of the German lines, and all of the enemy's activity in the area gave additional indications of new fish frying on the other side of the hill. In short, just north of Mortain the enemy clung stubbornly to a salient well suited to be the launching area for a counterattack, and every type of evidence appeared to confirm his intention to mount just such a riposte.

So Bradley for the most part chose caution, not halting but nevertheless slowing the eastward progress of his southernmost forces. He allowed Hodges and Collins to shift the 1st Division south of the Sélune River to Ambrières-le-Grand and thence on to Mayenne, to relieve the 90th Division and to remain close enough to the further eastward progress of the XV Corps to permit coordinated action. But Hobbs's 30th Division, which had been pinched out of the XIX Corps front, replaced the 1st Division on the strategic hills of Mortain. Part of Bradley's thinking was that continued pressure from Collins's right wing and from Patton to the south of the main German strength, along with Hodges's pushing between St. Pois and Vire, might yet forestall the expected German counterattack as similar applications of constant Allied pressure had broken up other incipient German counterstrokes of which ULTRA had warned earlier. But Bradley's mood was mainly one of watchfulness. And by the night of August 6, Patton, who had been scoffing at Bradley's apprehensions about the counterattack forecast by ULTRA, also sensed that the enemy was genuinely up to something. "Personally," said Patton, "I think it is a German bluff to cover a withdrawal, but I stopped the 80th, French 2d Armored, and 35th [Divisions] in the vicinity of St. Hilaire just in case something might happen."[5]

The destruction of the German left flank obliged the enemy to choose between two courses of action. So rapidly did the Americans exploit their advantage and send their armored vanguards circling round the dangling remnants of the German left that to go on withdrawing surely meant to retreat to the line of the Seine. No intermediate line could be made defensible under Allied pressure. The Seine itself probably could not be held for long; the winding course of the river would create too extended a front with too many vulnerable crossing sites. At best the Seine would no doubt be a temporary position before a withdrawal to the Somme and the old First World War lines, or posssibly the line of the Albert Canal and the Meuse, either of these latter fronts anchored in the Vosges Mountains on the south. In truth, no defensive position short of the permanent fortifications of the West Wall on Germany's frontier offered so many defensive strengths as the Normandy line the Americans had just breached and turned.

Thus it hardly required Hitler's famous aversion to yielding ground for the Germans to think seriously about the other possibility, a counterattack to try to restore the Normandy front. Much as the Germans—not Hitler alone, but millions of his people— loathed the Slavic Russians and all they stood for, the Red Army was still far away in Poland, or at worst on the fringes of East Prussia; so that if the real alternative to restoring the line in Normandy was the West Wall, almost on the edge of the Ruhr, the Anglo-Saxons now posed the greater immediate peril, even in Hitler's reckoning. It was the shadow of such dire eventualities that made the cross-Channel invasion the climactic event of the war; if it was now too late to hurl the Western Allies back into the sea, the next best hope for Germany was to ensnare them again in the hedgerows. The Allies were well enough aware of such reasoning for it to add to the significance of the latest ULTRA readings and of the gathering of a panzer concentration north of Domfront.

Still, success is a heady wine, and it was hard for Allied commanders to take altogether seriously the notion of a counterattack by an enemy so many of whose soldiers were running away or surrendering. General Montgomery felt sure that the next decisive battle would be fought not against a German counterattack but for the crossings of the Seine. With that in mind he was planning for August 8 yet another assault upon the Bourguébus Ridge down the Caen-Falaise road, Operation TOTALIZE, to bring the British in for the kill when Patton's Americans came wheeling down the Seine shutting off the crossings. As rational a commander as he was, Montgomery simply noted that the German concentration north of Domfront was insufficient to generate a counterattack of enough tactical strength to reverse the battle, however desirable it might be for the enemy's strategy to restore the Normandy lines. True, the Germans had shifted two divisions—the 84th and 85th—from their Fifteenth Army in the Pas de Calais, possibly because the emergence of Patton on the battlefield had at last undermined the FORTITUDE hoax. But this was much too little and too late. From August 2, the 84th Division already had all it could handle in helping stem the Americans west of Vire. Meanwhile the German tanks forgathering near the Americans had come partly from Panzer Group West, which should render TOTALIZE so much easier.

Montgomery's optimistic reasoning prevailed in most Allied headquarters over Bradley's forebodings, or even Patton's sense of caution. ULTRA notwithstanding, therefore, on the night of August 6–7 General von Funck's XLVII Panzer Corps was able to roll out of the darkness against the 30th Division at Mortain and, without the warning of an artillery preparation, to achieve tactical surprise.

General Hobbs's Old Hickory Division was weary from its long exertions in the hedgerows, including the COBRA breakout, and tired, too, because it had just completed its journey down from the Vire River when the enemy hit it. The 2nd SS Panzer Division, reinforced by the remnants of the 17th SS Panzer Grenadiers, advanced against the 30th in two columns, overran Mortain from north and south, and plunged on southwestward almost to St. Hilaire by noon. The 30th Division's positions had been prepared by the 1st Division merely as forward posts from which to launch further attacks, not for stout defense. The Germans who brushed past them might have charged on through St. Hilaire and to Avranches without delay, for there was little in front to stop them. They seemed troubled, however, by a fragment of the 30th Division, much of the 2nd Battalion of the 120th Infantry along with Company K of the 3rd Battalion, which held out though isolated on Hill 317, a rocky bluff just east of Mortain. These Americans could survey the whole arena of the counterattack, the Sélune River valley from Domfront twenty-five kilometers eastward, to the Bay of Mont St. Michel beyond Avranches thirty-two kilometers to the west. They could call down artillery fire on all the columns of the 2nd SS Panzer Division.

The 2nd SS Panzers had jumped off shortly before midnight. A few hours later, the 2nd Panzer Division struck farther north along the Sée toward le Mesnil-Tôve, where Eddy's 9th Division had recently moved back into the line. Before striking up a battlefield acquaintance with the 2nd Panzer Division, American intelligence had rated it as of only moderate quality, on the ground that it had been recruited largely in Austria, with about half its rank and file Austrian. Upon closer intimacy, the 2nd was rising in American esteem to rank second to none among German panzer units, despite its lack of the special favors shown SS formations; and its commanding officer, General der Panzertruppen Heinrich Freiherr von Lüttwitz, a veteran cavalryman, clearly stood in the top rank of his profession. On this occasion the 2nd Panzers drove straight across the path of and through the 39th Infantry Regiment, which had been attacking northeastward, and separated the regimental command post and most of the cannon and antitank companies from the infantry battalions. Another part of the 2nd Panzers attacked about dawn into St. Barthélemy and thus between the two earlier German thrusts, overrunning two companies of the 30th Division's 117th Infantry and almost encircling the rest of the regiment before American artillery forced the Germans to halt and to settle down for a prolonged fire fight with the American infantry.

General Collins's VII Corps headquarters had received enough additional intelligence that it had distributed a warning about an imminent counterattack near Mortain just before the 2nd SS Panzers struck. By morning, Bradley, Hodges, and Collins were worried both about the immediate condition of the VII Corps and about the presence in the area of two more German armored divisions, the 1st SS Panzers and the 116th Panzers. There were twelve American divisions south of the Avranches bottleneck by now. Considering his unexpectedly rapid progress so far and his still uncommitted force, the enemy might after all be able to tear through these divisions' supply areas and across their lines of communication—destroying the Avranches and Pontaubault bridges—to inflict enough damage to cripple their further exploitation of COBRA. Bradley was later to say that he felt the decision to continue pushing the southern divisions forward in face of the risks was the most critical he had yet to make.[6] ULTRA's warnings had not forearmed the Americans but merely permitted them, in effect, to read tomorrow's newspaper today without doing anything about it.[7] The Battle of Mortain had immediately erupted into a more severe test of their soldiers' resolution and their generals' will than they had anticipated. Nevertheless, Bradley let the southern divisions go on moving eastward.

A main reason why he was willing to accept the risk was the availability of the excellent General Barton and his 4th Division in VII Corps reserve, resting just north of the Sée River near the right flank of the German spearheads. American tactical doctrine prescribed that in case of such a penetration, the first task should be to seal off the flanks and prevent the penetration from becoming an expanding torrent to right and left. Barton had acted immediately on this prescription as soon as he knew what was afoot, laying down a heavy artillery fire across the Sée and assembling his division to defend against a German crossing of the river. Fortunately, too, CCB of the 3rd Armored, just released from its attachment to Barton's division, was also still in the area, and Collins gave it to Hobbs, who used it to shore up the south bank of the Sée.

Initially, Collins's idea was that Hobbs could use CCB to start plugging the dangerous and conspicuous gap in front of the 2nd SS Panzers around St. Hilaire; but Hobbs chose to turn to this purpose a somewhat bigger force that was near at hand, the 2nd Armored Division less its CCA. Except for the latter combat command, General Brooks's "Hell on Wheels" veterans were fortuitously on their way from the Vire toward the American right. They were able quickly to lend their strength to the beleaguered 39th Infantry and permit that regiment to reassemble. Then Brooks's armor swung to the south to hem in the left flank of the German penetration as Barton was confining the right.

Near Barenton, southeast of Mortain, part of Hobbs's 30th Division meanwhile had joined part of the 1st Division's recent coadjutor, CCA of the 3rd Armored, in a local counterattack just before the enemy struck. When the 2nd Armored Division rumbled into the area, General Brooks took this whole Barenton contingent under his command. With considerable chunks of both of the big, old-style armored divisions, he had collected a strong holding force on the southern flank.

For the counterattack, the Germans had risked concentrating their panzers enough to violate their Western Front policy against offering big targets to Anglo-American air power. With daylight, the fighter-bombers consequently took the skies with special relish and anticipation. In one of the campaign's best examples of interallied cooperation, Second TAF's Typhoon squadrons joined the fray as quickly as the Thunderbolts, Lightnings, and Mustangs, the RAF's fighter-bombers flying 294 sorties around Mortain on August 7.

So far so good, especially since the 116th Panzer Division, though in position on the north flank of the advancing Germans, inexplicably failed to weigh in until late afternoon. (The 116th was another exceptionally good division, as its troops would often remind the Western Allies almost to the last day of the war; the Americans could not know, however, that its current commander, Generalleutnant Gerhard Graf von Schwerin, had been involved in the July 20 plot and no longer had his heart in the war. He would later become one of the fathers of the postwar Bundeswehr.) By the time the 116th Panzers were on the move, General Eddy's 9th Division had time to prepare a suitable reception.

Furthermore, when the 1st SS Panzer Division—nothing less than the Leibstandarte Adolf Hitler, having evolved out of the original SS Life Guards Regiment—at length joined in the attack about noon, August 7, luckily for the Americans it supported the 2nd Panzer Division. In this sector Collins had more strength to resist than if these troopers had followed their SS comrades of Das Reich division toward St. Hilaire. The Germans failed to heed the maxim that it is success that should be reinforced.

For on the road to St. Hilaire the counterattack had scored its greatest advances, reaching within fifteen kilometers of Avranches, and toward St. Hilaire Hobbs's gravest danger lay. In that direction, besides trying to rally his now battered and widely dispersed as well as weary Old Hickory Division, Hobbs could do little but await the arrival of Baade's 35th Division. The 35th, also veterans of the fighting farther north and west, had been among the troops that Patton's foreknowledge and instincts had led him to hold back. When the enemy struck, Baade's men were around Fougères and Vitre awaiting commitment to the Third Army advance as a newly assigned part of the XX Corps. Bradley promptly gave the division to Collins, but it was evening of August 7 before the men of the Santa Fe Cross were on their way to assist the Old Hickories. Meanwhile, Hobbs worked to restore communications among numerous scattered small components of his division, attempted to distract the enemy with company-size attacks, and hoped the 700 men with the 2nd Battalion of the 120th Infantry could hold Hill 317 despite their encirclement.

The 2/120th had lost its command post, and the officers of its command group had fallen prisoners while trying to reach the companies on the hill. Captain Reynold G. Erichson now had the command, and he also had almost constant assault from the 17th SS Panzer Grenadier Division, attached to the 2nd SS Panzer Division, with which to contend. But Erichson felt no inclination to surrender a position from which he could call down shells on much of the German advance, and which would obviously also give the enemy a grandstand view of the VII Corps if it fell into German hands.

Erichson's attitudes extended all the way up the chain of command. For a time on

August 7, many American G-2s were ready to reinforce Bradley's worst fears by predict-ing that Field Marshal von Kluge could make the position of the twelve American divisions south of Avranches logistically untenable; but by the second night of the battle these intelligence officers were mostly reverting to optimism, concluding that the four panzer divisions committed to the counterattack mustered a total of only 250 tanks. With this intelligence judgment, Bradley could regard the Battle of Mortain as an enhancement of the COBRA opportunities rather than a threat. He went so far as to arrange for radio transmissions and reports by Allied-controlled double agents to suggest to the enemy an increase in the forces entering Brittany, as bait to tempt the Germans to persist in their assaults around Mortain.

Having been alerted by ULTRA to the possibility of a German counterattack, General Eisenhower had planned before the blow fell that on Monday, August 8 he would visit Bradley's headquarters at St. Sauveur-Lendelin. There Bradley discussed with the Supreme Commander the opportunity to repay the enemy for the unwariness of moving his center of gravity so far westward, by entrapping him around Mortain. Bradley and the 12th Army Group G-2 and G-3, Brigadier Generals Edwin L. Sibert and A. Franklin Kibler, had developed a plan: "Let's talk big turkey," Bradley had said to the staff officers. "I'm ready to eat meat all the way."[8] With Eisenhower at his side, Bradley telephoned Montgomery for a three-way discussion of the plan.

General Haislip's XV Corps by now was well past Laval and should soon be in le Mans. Previously, the design growing out of COBRA was that Haislip should continue to lead Patton's Third Army to the Paris-Orléans gap and the Seine, to trap the Germans remaining in Normandy against the crossings of the river. Now Bradley proposed a shorter envelopment, but one that seemed to promise still surer results. At le Mans, the XV Corps should turn north to Alençon, forty kilometers distant, and on toward Argentan.

If Haislip did so, he would be moving toward a direct meeting with the Canadian First Army, which that day opened its TOTALIZE attack from Caen toward Falaise. TOTALIZE of course had been designed for the large encirclement along the Seine, but it fitted Bradley's new plan for the shorter envelopment still better. If the Canadians could take Falaise while the Americans occupied Alençon, the Allies would control two of the three main east-west roads between the German forces in Normandy and escape to the Seine and eastward. Only some fifty-five kilometers separate Falaise and Alençon, and if the Canadians and Americans should go on to meet about halfway, they would, as Montgomery expressed it, "put the enemy in the most awkward predicament."[9] Patton said it more directly: "The purpose of the operation is to surround and destroy the German army west of the Seine."[10]

In fact, two German armies aggregating over 100,000 men were to be encircled. Since August 5, Eberbach's Panzer Group West was the Fifth Panzer Army. So Bradley resisted the fears that would have had him call back troops from his right flank to assist at Mortain. Rather, he committed his remaining reserves to the encircling army swinging eastward. Since the boundary between the 12th and 21 Army Groups had already been drawn along a line just north of Domfront and Carrouges to Sées, the Allied commanders at first envisaged the Canadians and Americans as meeting at Sées, on the army group boundary, just south of Argentan. But while Bradley instructed Patton to "advance on the axis Alençon-Sées to the line Sées-Carrouges," he also told him to be "prepared for further action against the enemy flank and rear in the direction of Argentan"—implying an advance into the British zone, if necessary to close the pincers upon the enemy.[11]

Another visitor to Bradley's headquarters on August 8 was Secretary of the Treasury Henry Morgenthau. Bradley says he told the Cabinet officer he had "an opportunity that comes to a commander not more than once in a century. We're about to destroy an entire hostile army." Pointing to the map, Bradley explained: "If the other fellow will only press his attack here at Mortain for another 48 hours, he'll give us time to close at Argentan and there completely destroy him. And when he loses his Seventh Army in this bag, he'll have nothing left with which to oppose us."[12]

It was better not to discourage the Mortain counterattack too completely, at least for the moment, and the American troops aready committed around Mortain would have to go on carrying the burden. They did so in a seesaw battle that the 30th Division G-3 said "Looks like hell. We are just mingled in one big mess, our CP is getting all kinds of fire, tanks within 500 yards of us."[13] While the high command was reaching its decisions on August 8, General Baade of the 35th Division attacked with two regiments abreast against the 2nd SS Panzer Division spearhead to try to advance through St. Hilaire to the Mortain-Barenton road. The black-shirted SS retaliated with relentless counterstrokes. The following day Baade had to throw in all three of his regiments. Then his progress accelerated slightly, but it remained painfully slow and costly.

That day and the next, the 119th Infantry of the 30th Division and CCB of the 3rd Armored fought the 2nd Panzer Division and the 1st SS Panzers in le Mesnil-Tôve, eventually clearing the place on Friday, August 11. On Saturday, the 117th Infantry recaptured St. Barthélemy. By then, four days of fighting and more than 700 casualties had carried the 35th Division thirteen kilometers and across the Mortain-Barenton road, and Baade's National Guardsmen were assaulting the south slope of Hill 317 to relieve the North Carolinians of the 2nd Battalion of the 120th. Since their isolation early on August 7, the troops on the hill had been resupplied less than satisfactorily with food and ammunition by air drop—at least half the supplies falling outside their perimeter—and more satisfactorily with essential medical items fired to them in artillery smoke shells. They also received chickens, vegetables, and encouragement from French farmers. At noon on August 12, the 35th Division made contact with them. Some 300 of the original 700 had been killed or wounded, but the survivors walked off only after they were relieved a little later on August 12 by their comrades of the rest of the 120th Regiment. The old 1st and 11th North Carolina from which the 120th descended had never fought a better battle.

The relief of Hill 317 sealed and symbolized the outcome of the Battle of Mortain. Repulsed and then driven back by American infantry, battered all the while by artillery and aircraft, the Germans failed to break through to Avranches and lost heavily in the attempt. After the battle the Americans found nearly 100 German tanks abandoned in the immediate vicinity of Mortain. The 2nd Panzer Division lost virtually an entire regiment around le Mesnil-Tôve. To be sure, ULTRA, luck, and German mistakes greatly assisted the Americans. Bradley had held back some of his troops in response to the ULTRA warnings, but many of those who played critical roles in the repulse, such as the 2nd Armored Division and CCA of the 3rd Armored, just chanced to be in the right place at the right time. If Kluge had reinforced success and pushed hardest southwestward through

St. Hilaire, he probably could have entered Avranches at least for a brief time and scored at least something of a psychological victory.

All that was past, and the attention of both sides shifted hurriedly from the Battle of Mortain to the Battle of the Falaise-Argentan Pocket; for by the time Hill 317 was rescued, the Germans were perceptibly and according to ULTRA moving eastward again to deal with the American and Canadian columns that threatened to encircle them. In fact, Bradley thought more of them had already moved east than really had, a judgment that was to affect the course of the battle.

The Battle of the Argentan-Falaise Pocket

General Haislip's XV Corps took the former Seventh Army headquarters city of le Mans against inconsequential opposition on Tuesday, August 8 and prepared bridges, roads, and assembly areas for a jump-off northward early on August 10. To assist the corps in a rapid closing of the southern jaw of the proposed pincers, General Patton gave it an additional armored division.

Veterans of fighting in Africa and now reequipped by the Americans and organized on the pattern of an American armored division, the 2ème Division Blindée was the first French regular division to join with the Anglo-Saxons and the FFI irregulars in the struggle to liberate the homeland. It had landed on the Normandy beaches on July 30 without fanfare but created an immediate sensation in the villages and towns through which it rolled as the citizens caught sight of the tricolor painted on its tanks.

The commanding officer was Général de Division Jacques Philippe Leclerc—the nom de guerre adopted by Philippe François Marie de Hautecloque to protect his family when he joined the Free French. Leclerc had taken command of the Gaullist outpost of the Chad in West Africa in December 1940. After leading a series of successful raids into Libya, in December 1942 he marched the Régiment de Tirailleurs Sénégalais du Tchad across the Sahara from Fort Lamy to Tripoli to join the British Eighth Army. Reinforced by Free French from all over the French Empire, this regiment served as the nucleus around which grew the French 2nd Armored Division.

The division joined the XV Corps at le Mans on August 9. Haislip was an appropriate corps commander, for he was a graduate of the École Supérieure de Guerre.

For the attack next day, Haislip put General Oliver's 5th Armored Division on the corps right, followed by Wyche's 79th Division, to move through Mamers to Sées. Leclerc's 2ème Blindée, followed by McLain's 90th Division, was to move through the road junction city of Alençon—where the Paris-Rennes (N12) and Rouen-Bordeaux (N138) highways cross—and thence to Carrouges. The corps would attack with the same absence of intelligence about the enemy in front to which it had grown accustomed since practically its entrance into the campaign.

August 10 produced a series of short but sometimes fierce tank combats and the development of the presence in Haislip's front of the German LXXXI Corps. This corps had the 708th Division forming its right and the 9th Panzer Division, recently arrived from southern France and initially intended for the Mortain counterattack, on its left. Backing up these divisions were the remains of the much-traveled and much-battered 352nd Division and Panzer Lehr. Though the 9th Panzers and the 352nd claimed that together they knocked out thirty-six Allied tanks, these German forces were not enough even to slow down the XV Corps appreciably. As far as delays were concerned, traffic jams were about as bad a nuisance as the Germans. The 708th Division, a garrison unit, was already much weakened from earlier encounters with the 90th Division in the latter's eastward sweep. The 9th Panzers happened to have committed their Panther battalion to the battle against the Canadians farther north. Haislip's troops had to circle around the dense Forêt de Perseigne, which was suspected of harboring strong clusters of the enemy; but artillery interdicted the exits from the forest, a napalm attack was laid on by the air force, and the Germans turned out to have evacuated the area.

Another forest and yet another traffic jam produced somewhat more serious problems after the 5th Armored Division took Sées and the 2ème Blindée captured Alençon on Saturday, August 12. On the basis of the "further action . . . in the direction of Argentan" implicitly authorized in Bradley's instructions to Patton, Haislip now directed the 5th Armored to move without pause northwestward from Sées to secure Argentan, while the 2ème Blindée continued on its way to Carrouges. Blocking the southern approaches to Argentan was the Forêt d'Ecouves. Haislip ordered Leclerc to pass his division around the west of the forest, bypassing any Germans who might be lurking in it to use the woods to slow the closing of the Allied pincers. But by circling westward, Leclerc was also to keep the highway from Sées to Argentan east of the forest open for the unimpeded use of Oliver's 5th Armored. In his impetuous eagerness to place his French division in the forefront of the liberation of France, Leclerc nevertheless divided the 2ème Blindée into three columns, sending one of them west of the forest as ordered, but hastening a second through the forest and the third up the Sées-Argentan highway, N158, to the east. This latter French combat command blocked 5th Armored fuel trucks on N158 long enough to delay refueling and the attack of one of Oliver's combat commands on Argentan by six hours. In this time, by late afternoon of August 12, the Germans interposed a battalion of the 116th Panzer Division in Oliver's path. Argentan, which might have fallen easily a few hours before, would have to become a prize of battle.

ULTRA intercepts had kept the Allies aware of the outline of the German shift eastward that had moved this vanguard of the 116th Panzers from the north flank of the Mortain front to Argentan. After the Americans halted the Mortain counterattack of August 7, given the stakes involved Hitler predictably demanded that Kluge try again. Over Kluge's renewed objections to any weakening of the defenses south of Caen, the Führer insisted on transferring the 9th, 10th, and 12th ss Panzer Divisions from the Fifth Panzer Army to the western salient. The opening of TOTALIZE abruptly changed this design and obliged even Hitler to acquiesce in retaining all but the first of these units—the 9th ss Panzers had already begun moving—on Kluge's eastern flank. Still Hitler remained so insistent on a renewed Mortain attack, delivered with all the weight possible, that in the midst of the Fifth Panzer Army's battle to hold off the Canadian attack toward Falaise, he deprived that army of its commander, Eberbach, whom he shifted to lead the new charge toward Avranches. Eberbach was thought to be a dedicated Nazi, and the motivation apparently included a characteristically Hitlerian concern for party loyalty and zealotry above all else. In fact, Eberbach had been flirting with the dissidents. But Hitler's idea was that when Panzer Group Eberbach took over the command at Mortain from the XLVII Panzer Corps, a general with a reputation for unflinching Nazism would eclipse General von Funck, who to Hitler's horror had once been a protégé of Generaloberst Werner Freiherr von Fritsch, a supposed nemesis whom Hitler had removed from command of the army in the purge of 1938.

However full of zeal—or recently and secretly lacking in it—Eberbach could not fulfill the Führer's hopes. Kluge had already postponed the renewal of the attack from August 9 to August 11. When Eberbach surveyed the Mortain scene, he said he could not be ready until August 20. Hitler insisted on August 11, but the new attack never occurred. By evening of August 10, the left turn of the American XV Corps northward out of le Mans was making plain the threat of a double envelopment. In a series of Enigma communications between Kluge and Hitler during the night and into the next day, OB West informed the Führer—and inadvertently the Allies—that both General Hausser of the Seventh Army and Eberbach agreed with him that further efforts toward Avranches had no prospect of success and must be broken off to permit an attack to blunt the American XV Corps spearhead around Alençon. After wasting August 11 in argument, Hitler conceded much of Kluge's view but approved only a minor withdrawal around Mortain, to await a later renewal of the counterattack toward the Atlantic. He modified Kluge's proposal for an effort against Haislip's advance into a more southerly drive against the XV Corps west flank. Kluge had already issued tentative orders for the reversal of direction, pending Hitler's approval, and his troops were ready to move fast enough to put part of the 116th Panzers astride the path of the 5th Armored below Argentan the next afternoon.

While Kluge was engaged in his long-distance debate with Hitler, simultaneously on August 11 General Montgomery was reviewing the question of how best to complete the double envelopment that Kluge feared. The immediate issue before him was the boundary between the army groups. As the Germans prepared to react to the threat of the Allied pincers, either by shifting forces from Mortain or by committing additional troops from farther east, Montgomery decided they would probably throw the bulk of their strength against the American pincer, "to have the benefit of the difficult 'bocage' country," which reappeared in the Alençon-Argentan area.[14] The Americans therefore would probably make less rapid progress in the next few days than the Canadians. The Canadians would probably reach Argentan from the north before the Americans got there from the south. In 21 Army Group, Montgomery was by no means alone in such thinking. General Dempsey had a friendly bet with Bradley about which Ally would reach Argentan first. Thus, despite rethinking the issue, Montgomery decided to retain the existing boundary. He ordered the Americans to stop Haislip's XV Corps just south of Argentan.

Montgomery of course recognized the risks, and he reminded his commanders that they should be prepared to return to the longer envelopment at the Seine in case the jaws approaching Argentan and Falaise failed to close. His decision was already a dubious one, because the Canadian attack so far had improved disappointingly little upon previous efforts along the Caen front. By August 11, the Canadians had been bogged down for three days.

General Crerar of the Canadian First Army had confided immediate direction of TOTALIZE to the most experienced Canadian senior officer, Lieutenant General G.C. Simonds of 2nd Corps. Simonds had commanded an infantry division in Sicily and an armored division in Italy. He responded to Crerar's trust by devising an original and promising plan of attack. To open TOTALIZE on August 8, Simonds proposed to dispense with the now-habitual aerial carpet bombing in front of the attack, and thus to escape its cratering and rubble as impediments to his advance. Instead, the RAF's night bombers should strike simultaneously with the ground attack and try to seal off its flanks by saturation bombing on both sides of it: the night bombers, because Simonds planned to attack in the darkness of August 7–8, to minimize the terrible effect of the German artillery on Bourguébus Ridge that had halted GOODWOOD. The 2nd Canadian and 51st Highland Divisions were to attempt to penetrate between German strongpoints by moving in six long, narrow, compact columns of tanks, self-propelled antitank guns, and infantry riding in the chassis of self-propelled artillery from which the guns were removed—a device conceived by Simonds and later called "Kangaroos." Simonds hoped to keep the columns on the proper tracks through darkness and confusion by guiding them with radio directional beams, green target-indicator shells fired ahead upon their objectives, bursts of tracer fire on the flanks, and searchlights supplementing moonlight.

Though some wrong turns and traffic jams developed anyway, the attack gained its first objectives by dawn of August 8, penetrating the first two German lines and advancing about five kilometers. But a ground mist in the early daylight hours delayed further advance and gave the enemy time to organize a counterattack spearheaded by two Kampfgruppen of the 12th SS Panzer Division. The chances of turning the penetration into another COBRA-like breakthrough nevertheless seemed good enough that Simonds committed the two armored divisions that were supposed to do for him what the 2nd and 3rd Armored had done for Collins.

Unfortunately, Simonds's exploitation divisions, the Canadian 4th Armoured and the Polish 1st Armored, were inexperienced and fell into the usual consequent errors, particularly that of pausing to deal with strongpoints rather than bypassing them. They also closed down the attack overnight on August 8–9. Aggravating their shyness was another miscarried air attack during the preceding afternoon, whose short bombing killed twenty-four men and wounded 131, mostly among the Poles. The Germans thus enjoyed leisure to withdraw to a new line of prepared positions along the Laison River, where they halted the Allied advance on August 9. The sinister Bourguébus Ridge no longer barred the Canadians' path, and 2nd Corps had gained some thirteen kilometers. But an approximately equal distance remained between the Canadians and Falaise.

Montgomery's decision to retain the old army-group boundary demanded that the Canadians renew their drive promptly and vigorously. Crerar, one of those Allied officers apt to condescend toward the American command for its lack of experience, nevertheless spent the days from August 9 to 14 demonstrating what really battlewise generalship could do by regrouping and mounting diversionary attacks. Montgomery might have helped get him moving by reinforcing the relatively small Canadian army with a loan of some British divisions, of which a number might have been spared while the Second Army was launching only limited secondary attacks on Crerar's right. When Crerar was ready on August 14, Simonds staged an assault much like TOTALIZE, except that this time he relied on smoke rather than night to obscure his columns in the face of German artillery concentrated on a hill line, the Potigny Ridge. The tanks and infantry steered toward the sun, seen through the smoke as an angry red disc and offering better directional guidance than the elaborate devices of the night attack. At dusk, the Canadian 3rd Division was within five kilometers of Falaise. Through August 15 and into the 16th, the rump of the 12th ss Panzer Division, 500 troopers and fifteen tanks aided by twelve 88s, clung to the last ridge before Falaise. But on August 16 the Canadian 2nd Division entered the town by way of a flank attack from the west. In a hard day's fight through August 17 the prize that had once glittered in Montgomery's eyes as almost attainable on D-Day was at last secured.

So much, however, for Montgomery's expectation as late as August 11 that the Canadians would beat the Americans to Argentan. As early as August 12, Bradley's staff were grumbling that "the British effort . . . appears to have logged itself in timidity and succumbed to the legendary Montgomery vice of overcaution."[15] If the charge was less than fair and the vice less than real, nevertheless the Americans were in Argentan for more than a day before Crerar even began his attack along the River Laison. On August 16, a gap twenty-five kilometers wide still separated Simonds's 2nd Corps at Falaise and Haislip's XV Corps. Through the gap, by that time, Field Marshal von Kluge's armies were racing to escape the Allied envelopment. Their ability to do so, however, involved debatable decisions by the American as well as the British and Canadian commands.

Those decisions extended all the way back to "P" Wood's inability to persuade Patton and Bradley to allow his 4th Armored Division to continue pushing eastward from Rennes, and to Bradley's decision to turn an army corps with two armored divisions from Avranches into Brittany. For the presence of even one more armored division toward the point of the American pincer near Argentan would have been highly comforting, and perhaps productive of desirable aggressive action, when Panzer Group Eberbach turned from Mortain to assail the XV Corps left flank.

In fact, Wood's 4th Armored was among the divisions that Patton specifically alerted on August 11 for possible movement eastward into Haislip's pincer. Doubting Montgomery's ability to strike south through Falaise rapidly enough to close the Argentan-Falaise gap before the Germans escaped, Patton that day told Haislip to be ready to push his XV Corps straight on north through Argentan to Falaise. Haislip, however, expressed misgivings whether his corps was strong enough to close the gap and hold it closed when the bulk of Army Group B came pounding out of the west to escape. Both flanks of the XV Corps were suspended in thin air. The corps was also far out on a limb: once its left spearhead reached Carrouges, some forty kilometers separated it from the VII Corps right at Mayenne. So Patton made his call to Wood. He also directed General Walker to move up the XX Corps from the Mayenne-le Mans area toward Carrouges to cover Haislip's left, and asked Bradley to return the 35th Division to the Third Army for similar work.

But it was late to be seeking this extra strength. Patton's diary records that returning from seeing Haislip, he "Got home to find that Gaffey had not yet got VIII Corps going, so we can release the 4th Armored [from Brittany]. I was quite angry."[16] Wood's 4th Armored now had to await part of the 6th Armored, to relieve it from the siege of Lorient, which Patton now considered an infuriating diversion, and which Wood had thought a mistake from the beginning.

On Saturday, August 12 at 11:30 P.M., Haislip informed Patton that the 5th Armored was on the verge of securing Argentan and reminded the army commander that he had assigned no mission beyond Argentan. Despite Haislip's concern about his left flank, if Patton authorized it he would continue northward to meet the Canadians. Patton replied that he would telephone Bradley and get back to Haislip. Bradley soon heard Patton's high-pitched voice: "We now have elements in Argentan. Shall we continue and drive the British into the sea for another Dunkirk?"[17]

But Bradley told Patton, "Nothing doing. You're not to go beyond Argentan. Just stop where you are and build up on that shoulder. Sibert tells me the German is beginning to pull out. You'd better button up and get ready for him."[18]

Patton nevertheless had Gaffey instruct Haislip to "push on slowly direction of Falaise allowing your rear elements to close. Road: Argentan-Falaise your left boundary inclusive. Upon arrival Falaise continue to push on slowly until you contact our Allies."[19]

In the late morning of August 13, however, the 12th Army Group chief of staff, General Leven Allen, called Gaffey to reiterate and underline Bradley's decision to restrict Patton to the interallied boundary. Under no circumstances, said Allen, was that boundary to be crossed. The XV Corps must halt at once.

As soon as Gaffey told him of the call, Patton himself was on the phone to Bradley's headquarters again. Bradley turned out to have gone to SHAEF Advance Headquarters, but a call there did not reach him either, and Patton had to settle for a conversation with Allen. When Patton pleaded with him at least to urge Bradley to speak again with Montgomery, Allen telephoned SHAEF and managed to talk with Bradley, who was with the Supreme Commander. Thus the issue reached Eisenhower. But on Bradley's urging that the army-group boundary ought to be observed, Eisenhower agreed to let the halt order to Haislip stand. Allen was instructed to inform Patton accordingly.

In the meantime, Bradley's G-3, General Kibler, had in fact telephoned 21 Army Group to seek Montgomery's permission for an advance beyond Argentan. Here too, the chief of staff, General de Guingand, dealt the ambitions of the Third Army another rebuff.

Yet another call from Patton to Allen changed nothing. When Patton hung up, he told Gaffey: "The question why XV Corps halted on the east-west line through Argentan is certain to become of historical importance. I want a stenographic record of this conversation with General Allen included in the History of the Third Army."[20]

At 2:15 P.M. of Sunday, August 13, Haislip as a result of these developments received Patton's order through Gaffey to halt at Argentan, to recall any units that might have advanced further northward, and indeed to "assemble and prepare for further operations in another direction"[21]—implicitly, the long envelopment on the Seine.

> I believe [Patton glumly told his diary three days later] that the [halt] order . . . emanated from the 21st Army Group, and was either due to jealousy of the Americans or to utter ignorance of the situation or to a combination of the two. It is very regrettable that the XV Corps was ordered to halt, because it could have gone on to Falaise and made contact with the Canadians northwest of that point and definitely and positively closed the escape gap.[22]

Haislip's efforts to move on toward Falaise earlier in the day, before he received the halt order at 2:15, might nevertheless have lent conviction to the decision of higher headquarters. The stiffening resistance that the XV Corps had begun to meet the previous evening now grew worse, and progress toward Falaise had practically halted before 2:15 P.M. Leclerc finished circling and clearing the Forêt d'Ecouves, captured Carrouges, and got a patrol into Argentan by afternoon; but German tanks soon forced the patrol to retire. The 5th Armored struggled unsuccessfully to nail down a firm penetration into Argentan or to work around its eastern outskirts. The 116th Panzer Division had been joined by elements of the 1st SS and 2nd Panzer Divisions—a remarkably rapid movement by Panzer Group Eberbach over cratered roads and under harassment from the air. For the moment, the enemy appeared to have assembled a considerable array of strength.

He appeared to have done so: in fact, except for artillery well placed on a ridge north of Argentan, the German front was more sound and fury than substance. By Eberbach's estimates, the 116th Panzer Division was reduced to only fifteen tanks, the 1st SS to thirty, the 2nd to twenty-five. If the XV Corps had continued pushing forward and had pushed as hard as Haislip could make it, the German strength in front of the corps could not have held it for long. Despite the corps's experiences of the morning and early afternoon of August 13, the true reason why the German front held at Argentan was the halt order.

Contrary to Patton's diary, nevertheless, the German line held and the XV Corps had to halt as much because of Bradley's decisions as Montgomery's. Bradley himself recorded: "In halting Patton at Argentan, however, I did not consult with Montgomery. The decision to stop Patton was mine alone; it never went beyond my CP."[23]

If the Germans did not have enough strength in front of Haislip to hold him long, Bradley still feared the total German force in the pocket and the weight it might throw at Haislip's left and against the gap between Carrouges and Mayenne. This fear is the most convincing consideration that Bradley later offered for not seeking Montgomery's agreement to allow the XV Corps to advance farther north, and for recommending to Eisenhower that there should be no change of the interallied boundary. In his memoirs, Bradley argued that while Patton might have closed the Argentan-Falaise gap, it was doubtful he could have kept it closed. "Nineteen German divisions were now stampeding to escape the trap." Haislip's four divisions were already blocking the escape routes through Argentan, Sées, and Alençon. Had they stretched themselves to Falaise, they would have been extended across sixty-five kilometers. "I much preferred," said Bradley, "a solid shoulder at Argentan to the possibility of a broken neck at Falaise."[24]

On August 13, however, when by Bradley's orders Haislip withheld his punch, it was not true that nineteen German divisions were stampeding to get out of the Argentan-Falaise pocket. As Bradley knew from ULTRA, the enemy had deferred a renewed attack at Mortain so Panzer Group Eberbach could deal instead with Haislip; but the armored divisions of the panzer group were already badly battered, and the bulk of the Fifth Panzer and Seventh Armies in the pocket were still occupied trying to hold the front to the west and north. The Germans had not decided to flee the pocket.

Furthermore, during August 13 Haislip's vulnerability to counterattack was being reduced by the hour, and the Carrouges-Mayenne gap in particular was rapidly disappearing. Not without minor mishap; Patton's efforts to shore up the XV Corps with Walker's XX Corps partially misfired. The only division Walker had immediately available, Major General Horace L. McBride's inexperienced 80th, accomplished scarcely more on August 13 than to entangle itself with the 90th Division on the roads approaching the Forêt d'Ecouves west of Alençon. One source of the trouble was the scantiness of the Third Army's knowledge of the precise location of its units during the rapid movements since the army's commitment. Fortunately, the march of the 80th

Division was almost superfluous, because on August 13 General Collins's VII Corps was advancing rapidly northeastward from Mayenne. General Hodges had ordered the First Army to return to the offensive as early as August 9, but it was not until the German Seventh Army broke off the action at Mortain that Hodges's corps commanders could consolidate their forces enough to do so. On August 12, the V and XIX Corps had renewed their pressure southward and pivoting eastward against the northwestern circumference of the pocket now containing the German armies. Readjustment after its defense of Mortain caused Collins's corps to take a day longer to get underway. By that time, Collins had released the 35th Division back to the Third Army and received a reunited 3rd Armored Division under a new commanding officer, Maurice Rose. Now wearing a second star, Rose had well earned a divisional command through his aggressive handling of CCA of the 2nd Armored in COBRA. With Barton's 4th Division back in reserve, Collins advanced with Huebner's 1st Division on his left, Eddy's 9th in his center, and Rose's 3rd Armored on the right. By August 14, the VII Corps had substantially closed the Mayenne gap.

Bradley gave an additional reason for halting the XV Corps at Argentan. He was "reluctant to chance a head-on meeting between two converging [Allied] Armies as we might have done had Patton continued on to Falaise." He feared that without a halt at the prearranged boundary, the XV Corps and the Canadians might not have recognized each other before they began spilling each other's blood. Particularly, there was danger of friends' falling under each other's artillery. Yet as Bradley pointed out in his memoirs almost in the same breath, a distinctive terrain feature could have been agreed upon as a boundary marker to permit American movement farther north. Or, as Bradley also pointed out, Montgomery "might better have shifted his weight to the east and closed the trap at Chambois"[25]—or for that matter the Americans might also have shifted east or west of N158, the Argentan-Falaise road, the shift of either Americans or Canadians avoiding a crash of the heads of their columns along the road and forming a double barrier to German escape.

Other observers offered other possible explanations for not closing the gap. To bring the American and Canadian troops closer to each other could have interfered with aerial and artillery devastation of the Germans as they fled through the crowded, narrow gap. As it was, to avoid hitting friendly troops the tactical air forces constantly had to shift bomb lines—beyond which aerial attack was not permitted—and to strike with delicate care. Leigh-Mallory wanted to abolish bomb lines in the area and allow fighter-bombers to hit any identified targets, believing that the bomb lines restricted close air support and allowed many enemy troops and much equipment to get away. In any event, closing the trap and capturing troops and equipment seems the better solution. Still less weight attaches to a rumor current at the time that troops could not enter the Argentan-Falaise gap because the air forces had dropped time bombs along the highways. They had, between August 10 and 13, but the bombs were fused for a maximum of twelve hours' delay and could not have endangered an advance.

The fragility of Bradley's and other explanations for not pushing hard to close the Falaise gap, with the possible exception of the argument about the weakness of the XV Corps, is all the more remarkable in light of the inconsistency of Bradley's positions. In his later account, Bradley not only took full responsibility for the halt at Argentan and attempted to justify it; at the same time he also implied it was a mistake not to close the gap and that the mistake was Montgomery's. He noted, accurately enough, that when the Canadian advance toward Falaise bogged down, instead of using troops from the British Second Army to reinforce the critical drive, Montgomery proceeded to use the Second Army "to squeeze the enemy out toward the Seine. If Monty's tactics mystified me, they dismayed Eisenhower even more. And . . . a shocked Third Army looked on helplessly as its quarry fled, [while] Patton raged at Montgomery's blunder."[26]

If failing to close the gap was a blunder, however, the fault was also Bradley's, for discouraging whatever might have been done to rectify the blunder—even discouraging on August 13 a call from the Supreme Commander to Montgomery about the interallied boundary. Late in the war, with another opportunity for an envelopment before him, Bradley was thinking about Falaise. As Major Hansen recorded it:

> By his tone this morning the General indicated he will not delay in pressing [to capture] a bag as he did at Falaise when he was told by the British that they would push south to close it and he stopped his forces at Argentan. When he speaks of decisions, he often says that is the only decision he has ever questioned. The burden was not his. But he feels that had he forced the issue and insisted on the advance of our troops, our bag at Falaise might have been considerably more than it was.[27]

Toward the Seine

On August 14, with Collins's VII Corps rapidly closing the Mayenne gap that separated it from Haislip's XV, Haislip's corps could have resumed its advance through and north from Argentan under much less of the danger that Bradley said influenced his halt order of the day before. Nevertheless, Bradley still refrained from lifting a finger to change the interallied boundary so Haislip might proceed northward. Rather, because Montgomery did not change the boundary on his own initiative, and because Bradley now concluded—erroneously—that most of the Germans had already escaped from the Falaise pocket anyway, Bradley shifted the main effort of his armies toward the east. He did so with the impetuous Patton's approval and perhaps under his inspiration. "I then flew back," said Patton of this Monday, ". . . to see Bradley and sell him [Patton's] plan. He consented. . . ."[28] If Patton was not allowed to move full speed ahead in one direction, he would try for another. According to the plan, Bradley instructed Patton to send Haislip eastward with two of his divisions, to resume the effort toward the long envelopment at the Seine. The other two divisions of the XV Corps, reinforced by the 80th Division and supported by the VII Corps, were to remain at Argentan to continue forming the southern arm of a pincer operation upon which Montgomery's northern arm would presumably close sooner or later. Whereas the previous day Bradley by his own testimony had not pushed the closing of the Falaise-Argentan gap because the XV Corps did not have enough strength in the area, now he was actually depleting the XV Corps around Argentan. With the trap only partially closed, Bradley and Patton were impatiently beginning the movement of the 12th Army Group in pursuit of different objects.

Major Hansen's diary entry for Monday, August 14 illuminates the mood as well as the reasoning at Bradley's headquarters:

> It is now definitely established [said Hansen, repeating Bradley's error of fact] that our opportunity to close the pincer and trap the German army has been lost for reasons which now appear both apparent and difficult to understand. It is possible that Montgomery has subscribed to the vice of extreme over-caution and has made

the error of many commanders in denying sound tactics for the prestige value of the objective. . . . However, it would be folly to criticize Montgomery due to his great prestige position among the British and he occupies an almost professional papal immunity in his position.

All of us are anxious that the SHAEF Operational Hqs come in soon and take command of the situation, thereby relieving us from 21 Group control.

. . . Speed seems essential in forcing the Seine and as it is now evident that the German is preparing a position east of Paris on the Marne where the Allies made their stand in the last war.

Patton, exuberant, calls Brad "the Eagle" [EAGLE was the code name for 12th Army Group headquarters, in response to which Montgomery chose LION for 21 Group], admits with pride that he is the general of the war and wishes, like everyone else, that we can soon escape restrictive tactical control of 21 Group.[29]

The passage suggests some of the feelings that restrained Bradley even from picking up the telephone to talk to Montgomery about the interallied boundary. Patton's dramatic transformation in less than two months from bête noire to hero among Bradley's staff was a direct function of the correspondingly swift decline of the hero of El Alamein; that Patton, so recently loathed in these quarters, could now be welcomed so enthusiastically implies much about the amount of poison that had so quickly seeped into the relationship between the two army groups. The arrogance and coldness of the 21 Army Group commander with "his sharp beagle like nose, the small grey eyes that dart about quickly like rabbits in a Thurber cartoon,"[30] his impenetrable self-satisfaction, all formed the nettle around which animosity clung; but that suspicion and dislike had grown so rapidly out of so little apparent controversy indicates sources far deeper than Montgomery's unamiable personality, old distrusts between Americans and British far stronger than the rhetoric of the Grand Alliance.

As for the more specific issues of the diary entry, it is of course the G-2s rather than Bradley and Patton directly who must be faulted for the belief that it was "definitely established that our opportunity to close the pincer and trap the German army has been lost"—though the possibility of so rapid a movement by the bulk of both the Fifth Panzer and the Seventh Armies as well as Panzer Group Eberbach, along bombed, strafed, and constricted roads, might have seemed worth questioning. Yet if Bradley believed that the Germans could get away so readily, then it is also questionable whether he should have attempted the short envelopment at all. If a twenty-four-hour delay in closing the Falaise gap made the design not worth pursuing, then should time and energy have been expended on it in the first place? Should not the Third Army have continued moving toward the Seine and the long envelopment without interruption? Or on the other hand, if the short envelopment at Falaise and Argentan was worth essaying at all, should not Bradley have pursued it with a bit more persistence?

On Tuesday, August 15, the 5th Armored and the 79th Divisions moved eastward toward Dreux, followed by General Haislip's XV Corps headquarters and the corps artillery. A skeleton corps headquarters remained behind to oversee the 2ème Blindée and the 80th and 90th Infantry. That day, slackening contact with the enemy all along the Argentan shoulder appeared further to confirm the idea that most of the Germans had already fled the pocket. The next day, however, as the 90th Division was preparing to move out northeastward to look for the enemy, searching abruptly became superfluous.

Elements of the 2nd SS and 116th Panzer Divisions hit surprisingly hard at a 90th Division roadblock at the village of le Bourg-St. Léonard, nine and a half kilometers east of Argentan and five kilometers south of Chambois, on the forested ridge line between the watersheds of the Orne River to the west and the Dives to the east. The Germans drove the Americans from the village, American tanks and infantry recaptured it after dark, and the battle for its possession thundered into the next day.

If the Germans in fact had not yet escaped, they would be further imperiled by Allied observation from the le Bourg-St. Léonard ridge commanding the Orne and Dives valleys below. Their strong attack on le Bourg-St. Léonard was one portion of an accumulating flood of evidence on August 16 that the Germans had not yet escaped the pocket after all, but rather were just beginning a serious effort to do so.

The new evidence rekindled Allied interest in closing the Falaise gap. On August 16, the day the Canadians at length entered Falaise, Montgomery telephoned Bradley to get everybody available advancing toward another effort to complete the short envelopment. Montgomery suggested, however, a meeting not directly between Falaise and Argentan, but eleven kilometers northeast of Argentan, between Trun and Chambois on the Dives River, in hopes of increasing the bag of captures by looping a little farther east.

The Battle of Chambois

Bradley's abrupt reversion to the long envelopment on August 14 had weakened the American forces around Argentan from four divisions and fifteen artillery battalions to two divisions and seven artillery battalions, for on August 16 the 80th Division was still southwest of Alençon. Since there was also no real corps headquarters on the scene to direct an attack, Patton created a provisional corps under his chief of staff, General Gaffey. With the 80th Division now hastening forward, Gaffey ordered the 2ème Blindée on his left and the 90th Division on his right to be ready to attack by 10:00 A.M., August 17.

The troops did not move out on schedule, mainly because Bradley intervened to give them a regularly constituted corps headquarters, with confusion the immediate result. The V Corps having been pinched out of the line to the north by the Second Army's moving across its front, Bradley ordered Hodges to send General Gerow and his staff to take charge at Argentan. Gerow later told how on the night of August 16–17:

> I took a part of my staff along, I should say about ten officers, travelling in three jeeps. We proceeded to [First] Army as rapidly as we could go. At Army I talked to Hodges and the First Army staff. I was told that I was to take command of three divisions and that I was to proceed to close the pocket. I asked, "Where are these Divisions?" and I was told, "We do not know, you will have to locate them." I then asked about the enemy situation and was again told by the staff of the First Army that they knew nothing of the enemy situation. We left the conference in the middle of the night and drove on. It was raining like hell. We had in the beginning one car with a radio but we soon found that the radio was out of order and we were out of communication with all other headquarters; for all practical purposes V Corps that night was composed of ten rain-soaked officers in three jeeps out searching the countryside for three divisions, with only a general knowledge about the area of the search. We found the 90th Division and we proceeded to set up Corps Headquarters at the Hq of the 90th, using their facilities, including their communications.

However, General Gaffey had arrived a few hours earlier, having been sent by General Patton with four officers to do the job which we were supposed to do. Gaffey had already located the three Divisions and had issued instructions that the Divisions were to attack on his order. He had prepared an attack order which I read and did not or could not entirely approve, but for the time being I simply stood by and waited for a favorable chance to take over. Meanwhile Gaffey withheld any orders for an attack and that afternoon I took over from him. On the following morning I ordered the 90th Div to attack, which it did.[31]

In the interval, Gaffey, Patton, and Bradley had all been in contact with each other, and Bradley had confirmed that he wanted Gerow in command with the mission of securing the line Ecouché-Argentan, capturing Chambois, and advancing on to Trun unless it had already been taken by Allied troops moving down from the north—in short, closing off the Falaise pocket. Patton, repeating a favorite phrase, said Gerow should push right through to "Another Dunkirk."[32] On Gerow's urgent orders, General McLain's 90th Division struck just after dark on the night of August 17–18 to regain firm possession of the ridge at le Bourg-St. Léonard, whence it was to move on the next day against Hill 129 and other high ground just southwest of Chambois. The night attack succeeded; the 90th at last had firm possession of le Bourg-St. Léonard by about midnight.

Gerow wanted the 2ème Blindée on his left to form a strong protective shoulder holding the enemy north of the Orne River around Ecouché, and to assist by fire the attack of his two infantry divisions. The 80th Division in his center received the long-deferred task of capturing Argentan itself. As might have been expected, however, the 80th displayed the customary symptoms of rawness, as described by Colonel Harry D. McHugh, commanding officer of its 318th Infantry:

> I attacked . . . and had no real trouble till we got to the Argentan-Paris road. There were hedgerows up to the road and beyond the road there were two hedgerowed fields, then a considerable stretch of perfectly open ground. The Germans were well placed behind the hedgerows, in the open field and beyond it, and commanded a beautiful field of fire. This was our first real fight and I had difficulty in getting the men to move forward. I had to literally kick the men from the ground in order to get the atk started, and to encourage the men I walked across the rd without any cover and showed them a way across. I received no fire from the enemy and it was a big boost to the men. A tank, 400 yds to our front, started firing on us and I called up some bazookas to stalk him. However the men opened fire at the tank from too great a range and the tank merely moved to another position. I walked up and down the road about three times, finding crossings for my troops. We advanced about 100 yds across the rd and then the Germans opened up with what seemed like all the bullets and arty in the world. I called up my tanks. . . . When my tanks came up we lost the first four tanks with only eight shots from the Germans.[33]

No units of the 80th Division made much progress. The 90th, which had been all through such growing pains, was finally beginning to convince itself it could live up to the old World War I nickname suggested by its Texas-Oklahoma T-O monogram, "tough 'ombres," and it pressed on from its ridge line to cut the le Bourg-St. Léonard–Chambois road about halfway to Chambois. But the Germans were still giving ground in front of it too stubbornly for the division to attain its full objective, the high ground just outside

Chambois. On the night of August 18–19 there remained an opening through which Germans could still flee out of the Falaise pocket and across the Dives.

Some of the tough 'ombres fought their way into Chambois on the morning of August 19. Meanwhile the Canadians had gone on pressing southward after clearing Falaise on the 17th. The Fifth Panzer Army, commanded since Eberbach's departure by Generaloberst Josef "Sepp" Dietrich of the I ss Panzer Corps, resisted Crerar's army almost as stoutly as ever until Saturday the 19th, when at last the toll of exhaustion and attrition began to become visible to Dietrich's enemies. That day the Canadian 3rd Division advanced down the east bank of the Dives between Beauvais and Trun, threatening the German escape crossings farther south, and the Polish 1st Armored Division captured Hill 262, the northern part of Mont Ormel, which dominates the countryside south to Chambois. In the process the Poles collided with a long column of German tanks and other vehicles and destroyed it. Furthermore, troops from the Polish right flank worked their way around a dangling German flank and eventually pried themselves into Chambois from the south. There these Poles, part of the 10th Regiment of Dragoons, met Company G of the 359th U.S. Infantry.

Poles and Americans together cleared Chambois, and the Poles handed over to the 90th Division 1,300 prisoners and their own wounded, because they had no means of attending to them. The reason for this latter circumstance was that the closing of the Falaise gap was still tenuous in the extreme. The Poles inside Chambois had lost contact with the rest of their division. The largest portion of the Polish 1st Armored, some 1,500 infantry and eighty tanks, was cut off on Mont Ormel from the rest of the Canadian 2nd Corps and during the night of August 19–20 had to hunker down in a perimeter defense to try to hold the high ground. When morning came and a dawn mist lifted, the Poles on Mont Ormel saw the whole plain west and south of them crawling with German vehicles making their way northeastward. Polish artillery began taking the wealth of targets under fire, but soon the Poles had their hands full with the efforts of the 2nd ss Panzer Division to break their perimeter, overrun them, and free the Germans below from their observation and harassment. Presently the Poles found themselves under heavy mortar and artillery fire from almost every direction, and Germans from a multiplicity of units, including crack paratroop infantry as well as ss panzer grenadiers, were mounting wave after wave of coordinated attacks to smash them.

The perimeter on Mont Ormel compressed but did not break, yet the pressure on it freed the enemy below to continue the flight over secondary roads and cross country through the remaining holes in the Allied cordon across the gap. Meanwhile the rest of 2nd Corps farther north was kept too much occupied all through August 20 to give the Poles any help. By nightfall, the perimeter contained about 300 wounded lying in the open without adequate medical care, some 800 restless prisoners, and discouragingly little ammunition with which to maintain the fight.

By nightfall also, the Poles and Americans down below in Chambois similarly wondered whether they could hold the positions they had just taken. The salvation of all concerned lay in German behavior during the night of August 20–21, which bespoke the enemy's conviction that this might well be the last night for escape and that any other activity had to be subordinated to getting away. The 90th Division artillery on the le Bourg-St. Léonard ridge was enjoying an "artilleryman's dream" against every conceivable kind of motorized or horse-drawn vehicle passing through its sights. In addition,

American ammunition, gasoline, and rations got into Chambois late on August 20, to be shared by the Americans and Poles. Finally, though the Poles on Mont Ormel endured another bad morning and afternoon on August 21, including a climactic suicide attack of German infantry straight into Polish machine guns, in midafternoon the Canadian army at last reestablished contact and brought up supplies.

With that, the Falaise gap was closed not only on the maps but in reality. A week and a day had passed since the XV Corps halted at Argentan; the 80th Division had finally captured Argentan on August 20. The delay became the center of the historical controversy that Patton had predicted when Bradley told him to halt, over whether the entrapment of the German forces west of Argentan and Falaise could have been made practically complete, and whether the war in the West might thereby have been hastened to an end before the coming of winter.

As it was, the Germans had surely suffered a crushing defeat, and the Allies could enjoy the satisfaction of a spectacular victory. But the incompleteness of the closing of the trap left doubt even about the dimensions of the victory that in fact occurred, to say nothing of Allied disappointment not to win more. Of the Seventh Army, the Fifth Panzer Army, and Panzer Group Eberbach, all but two corps of the Fifth Panzer Army had been inside the Falaise pocket at the time of the Allied decisions of August 13. By the end of August 20, Army Group B was reporting that from 40 to 50 percent of the encircled troops had escaped. No doubt this German estimate erred on the side of optimism. Later estimates by the Germans themselves set the total who escaped between 20,000 and 40,000 men. Since support units had gone out first, sometimes dispatched on a division's own initiative, those who made it out of the pocket were disproportionately noncombat troops. The average combat strength of German divisions as they reassembled east of the pocket was only a few hundred men, though a few came close to 3,000. In the haste and chaos of the final days of the pocket, the Allies lost count of how many prisoners they captured. Probably the Americans took about 25,000, the Canadians and British an equal number. The Allies also found some 10,000 German dead within the pocket.

German equipment losses were heavier. Very few tanks, guns, and vehicles succeeded in running the gauntlet of aerial and artillery bombardment in addition to the eventual infantry and tank cordon. On August 17 the gap became so narrow that no bomb line remained in the Falaise pocket, and aerial harassment at least theoretically ceased; but in the meantime the dense throngs of fugitive Germans and their vehicles offered an airman's as well as an artilleryman's dream. On August 14, as the 405th Fighter-Bomber Group was strafing northeast of Carrouges, Germans in the road waved white flags, whereupon the Thunderbolts buzzed the road and herded the Germans into a column that they marched off to the American lines to surrender. Often German traffic jams themselves so paralyzed movement that drivers abandoned their vehicles, sometimes to Allied soldiers who found the motors still running. An incomplete count of the ruined and abandoned vehicles and ordnance in the pocket tallied 220 tanks, 160 assault guns, 700 towed artillery pieces, 130 antiaircraft guns, 130 half-tracks, 5,000 other motor vehicles, and 2,000 wagons. There were also 1,800 dead horses.

At least symbolically, the Falaise pocket fell short of being another Stalingrad because there was no general surrender. It was of more than symbolic importance that German higher headquarters for the most part escaped the envelopment, as the Allies were to learn when these headquarters demonstrated the remarkable rapidity with which they could reconstitute divisions and corps around themselves. Of fifteen divisional commanders in the pocket, only three did not get away. Only one of five corps commanders did not reach safety. Hausser, Dietrich, and Eberbach all escaped, though the latter was badly wounded. The survival of cadres and headquarters influenced the whole German conception of the battle, with much benefit to German morale apart from their practical utility in repairing shattered organizations; officially, the Germans proclaimed the struggle in the Falaise pocket a noble achievement of their arms, because they extricated as much as they did to fight another day. This interpretation is not without merit.

Nevertheless, the battle destroyed Field Marshal von Kluge. After failing for several days to persuade Hitler to authorize as rapid a withdrawal as he thought necessary for safety at least from the western part of the pocket, Kluge visited the front on August 15 to see for himself how bad things were. He left Dietrich's headquarters early in the day to meet with Hausser and Eberbach at Nécy, but did not keep the rendezvous and vanished from sight and radio contact for almost the whole day. He arrived at Eberbach's headquarters after dark to explain that he had been caught in an artillery bombardment, that fighter-bombers had knocked out his radio car, and that he had spent most of the day in a ditch. It would be two weeks before Kluge was shown to be implicated in the July 20 plot, yet Hitler's customarily suspicious mind was hypersensitive after his narrow escape from assassination, and by the time Kluge resurfaced, the Führer had decided that his OB West must have run off to contact the Western Allies and surrender the western German armies. The most tenuous of evidence since released on the Allied side suggests the possibility of some truth in Hitler's suspicion, though probably the Allies knew of no such intentions on Kluge's part.

When Kluge's first act upon reappearing proved to be the sending of a message to OKW advising that in his and his army commanders' opinion the pocket must be evacuated immediately, Hitler decided to summon Generalfeldmarschall Walter Model from the Eastern Front to replace him. Model, commander of a panzer division in the invasion of Russia in 1941, had grown to be a superb defensive specialist. Since the autumn of 1943 he had commanded in succession Army Groups North, South, and Center and had halted a Soviet onslaught against each. At least as much to the point, Model was unquestionably loyal to the Führer. On August 17 he arrived at Army Group B headquarters at the château of la Roche-Guyon with orders to relieve Kluge and, ominously, for Kluge to report to the Führerhauptquartier. Kluge thereupon wrote to Hitler a last letter about the hopelessness of the war and then, the next morning while traveling toward Germany, bit into a phial of potassium cyanide and died.

In his letter to the Führer, Kluge excused himself for his defeats by blaming the insufficiency of German numbers and equipment in contrast to the wealth of the Allies. He did not admit to inferior generalship, and in truth, although he had made mistakes, no such admission would have been appropriate. He had commanded about as successfully as anyone could have with the resources at hand and under the peculiar circumstances of his tenure in the West. These circumstances of course were such that, while at first glance Kluge seemed to have too much to do, as both OB West and commander of Army Group B, in fact once the COBRA breakout began Hitler himself assumed at least the functions of OB West, and for most purposes directed operations in enough detail to be counted as army group commander, too. In the limited sphere left to him, Kluge displayed tactical proficiency—his mistakes at Mortain were mainly those implicit in acting in haste, in a venture he did not approve—and in his dispatches he described to OKW with reasonable truthfulness the realities of the Western Front on which Hitler might base his actions. It was not his fault that Hitler devised strategy and operations in disregard of those realities. But Kluge, whose relationship with the July 20 plotters had been ambivalent, was also ambivalent toward Hitler to the last, and he only most indirectly included the Führer in his apportionment of the blame for defeat. In this silence, there was a measure of justice, for Kluge's rise to a marshal's baton and the highest military commands had been accomplished through his carrying into execution, in France in 1940 and in the early campaigns in the East, strategic designs that were Hitler's. But now Hitler's powers as a strategist had sorely failed, and it was the Führer who had offered the Allied generals an opportunity for a double envelopment so inviting that merely competent generalship was enough to grasp massive victories.

On the Allied side, it was somewhat more than mere competence and the material superiority cited by Kluge that achieved the victories. How much more, in the realm of generalship, is debatable. Taking advantage of the stubborn perseverance of the divisions around Mortain on the defense, the American command had earned credit by its adroit juggling of the forces nearby as well as by its refusal to be panicked into retracting its right hook that was ranging to the east. The degree of surprise suffered at Mortain may be excused, despite ULTRA, because it was the Allies' recognition of the strategic folly of the German counterattack that created their skepticism that it would occur. On the offensive, Patton's energetic driving of the right hook provides the one example of genuinely inspired leadership in the Mortain-Argentan-Falaise campaign. On the level of corps command, Collins lived up to his previous record of accomplishment in his closing of the Mayenne gap, and Haislip emerged as another corps commander to be watched for the further development of a possible unusual measure of aggressiveness. But in the critical decisions about how to capitalize on Hitler's strategic blunders, Montgomery not only erred but persisted in error for days on end in his judgment of the Canadians' pace toward Argentan. Bradley, having set the stage by urging Eisenhower and Montgomery to grasp the opportunity of a short envelopment at Falaise-Argentan, failed to persist in completing his own design. He abandoned the short envelopment before its potential was achieved, and meanwhile he had delayed the long envelopment at the Seine, to which he abruptly returned.

Eisenhower's abstention from intervening to hasten the closing of the Falaise gap was consistent with his perception of his role as Supreme Commander. As long as Montgomery remained the Allied ground commander, Eisenhower would not dictate the operational and tactical method of execution of strategic designs. At the same time, the fumbled closing of the Falaise gap indicated the urgency of Eisenhower's taking over as ground commander. At the very least, the distrustful unwillingness of Bradley and Montgomery to communicate frankly with each other was a defect in the Allied command system replete with possibilities for further misunderstanding. At the worst, the Allied armies in Europe simply lacked one of the prerequisites of military success, unity of command.

Against an enemy in as much disarray as the Germans, the Allied command system nevertheless was almost good enough. The German army remained highly dangerous. An American battalion commander found the pursuit not "a game of Allied hounds coursing the German hare" as suggested by some press accounts, but rather the hunt after "a wounded tiger into the bush; the tiger turning now and again to slash at its tormentors, each slash drawing blood."[34] Yet the German army at last was a badly beaten army, and if the short envelopment had not succeeded as fully as it might have, the long envelopment remained in process.

And to aggravate the Germans' disarray, August 15 brought Hitler the news not only of Kluge's disappearance and of the almost certain need to abandon the Falaise pocket and the Mortain counterattack, but also of Allied landings in the south of France and the threat that there, too, a German army group might be cut off.

11: The Riviera and the Rhône

HAPPILY, the prolonged interallied debates over ANVIL, the invasion of southern France, do not fall within the province of this narrative. They made a dreary and depressing subject. After General Eisenhower and the American Joint Chiefs of Staff acquiesced in the impossibility of staging ANVIL simultaneously with OVERLORD because not enough landing vessels were available, they hoped nevertheless to reschedule ANVIL as soon as possible. ANVIL had been discussed by Anglo-American strategists as early as April 1943, and the First Québec Conference had put it formally on the planning books in August 1943. When Stalin gave decisive interallied impetus to the American strategy of a direct cross-Channel assault against northwest Europe instead of British peripheral strategy at Tehran in November 1943, he also encouraged the Western Allies to proceed with ANVIL, to form with OVERLORD a double envelopment so gigantic that its arena would be the whole of France. But the British resisted ANVIL all along, and after the postponement they strove for permanent abandonment. Winston Churchill in particular returned again and again to the assault upon ANVIL, and he did not yield his struggle until five days before the eventual D-Day of August 15.

Most American strategists, in contrast, believed ANVIL was virtually imperative. With the postponement, the course of the campaign in northern France made the reasons if possible still more compelling than they were before. OVERLORD failed to produce usable ports as promptly as the Allies had hoped; Eisenhower therefore believed he must have Marseille. Marseille is one of the great ports of Europe, bigger than the most capacious Brittany ports or any of the Channel ports short of Antwerp. In Allied hands it could sustain a major share of the support of a drive from France into Germany. It could also receive many of the trained divisions still in the United States and too numerous to enter Europe through the Channel ports. Marseille is about 150 kilometers closer to the German frontier than is Cherbourg. The navigable Rhône River, a major railroad, and good highways could link Marseille to the advance of the Allied armies. If he did not get Marseille, Eisenhower believed, then he must have Bordeaux; but to seize Bordeaux without unduly diverting the forces in northern France would require a landing in southern France anyway.

In addition, divisions coming up and supplied from the Mediterranean coast could help Eisenhower form a front along the whole German border from the North Sea to Switzerland, to stretch the German army as perilously thin as possible for its defense of the Fatherland. ANVIL would bring into the main campaign aimed at the heart of Germany some of the American divisions otherwise being employed to doubtful purpose in the secondary Italian theater. ANVIL could also bring an eventual field army of French divisions, reequipped by the United States and naturally eager to join in liberating their own country. Since they were already in the Mediterranean Theater, the south coast of France was the obvious place at which to commit the French divisions to the cause that was their raison d'être. Landed in southern France, French troops could quickly make contact with some of the strongest bands of the French Forces of the Interior, who had carved their domain in the Massif Central.

If the lengthy campaigns already waged in the Mediterranean had a central purpose at all, it was to secure the sea for Allied commerce; but currently the Germans were greatly strengthening their submarine pens at Marseille and Toulon, building concrete roofs seven meters thick. Clearly an invasion of southern France would cancel this menace. Less urgently, because Germany's Army Group G in southern France was already much depleted, an invasion of the south would spare Eisenhower the necessity of guarding a long open flank at the Loire and eastward as he turned toward Germany. Small detachments, the destruction of the Loire bridges, and aerial patrols did this job in early August, but it would be better to destroy Army Group G between the hammer of OVERLORD and the ANVIL.

Nearly all these considerations hung upon the American conception of the overwhelming primacy of the campaign in France in Allied strategy against Germany. Even in the summer of 1944, however, Prime Minister Churchill and many other British leaders were unwilling to concede that sort of primacy to OVERLORD. The prestige of the British Empire, and thus Britain's weight in peacemaking and postwar politics, would better be served by maintaining continued prominence for the campaign in Italy. With a British theater commander in the Mediterranean, a British army group commander leading all the Allied ground forces in Italy, and a British contribution to the Allied Mediterranean forces proportionately far larger than Britain's coming share in the battles of vast armies on the Continental land mass, Italy was peculiarly Britain's campaign. Many British leaders preferred that the American divisions now in Italy should contribute to as glorious as possible an outcome for the effort there, rather than merely swell Eisenhower's American armies to the northward. If the Americans could be retained to contribute to an advance from Italy into the upper Danube valley, to Vienna and Budapest, then the outcome would be glorious indeed—and well worth the risk of acrimonious debate with the Americans.

ANVIL–DRAGOON

Rome fell to the Allies on June 4, two days before D-Day in Normandy. On June 7 General Sir Henry Maitland Wilson announced the readiness of Allied Force Headquarters in the Mediterranean to launch an amphibious operation somewhere about August 15. On June 11, three of the American Joint Chiefs, Marshall, King, and Arnold, met in London with the British Chiefs of Staff to discuss the site of such an operation. Because the British remained unwilling to pledge themselves to ANVIL, the Combined Chiefs of Staff decided to order the drawing of plans for optional three-division assaults. Eisenhower was to prepare for an invasion in the Bay of Biscay, Wilson for an invasion of the southern French coast around Sète or, in accord with British aspirations, for an invasion of Istria.

Eisenhower soon replied that aiming for the port facilities of Bordeaux by direct invasion from the Bay of Biscay was logistically impracticable. Marshall and Arnold,

THE CAMPAIGN
IN SOUTHERN FRANCE

TO LYON (28km.)

VIENNE

ST. RAMBERT

ST. VALLIER

TOURNON

BOURG-DE-PEAGE

RTE N86

RTE N7

VALENCE

CHABEUIL

ISÈRE R.

GRENOBLE

COL DU MT. CENIS (20

FRANCE

ITALY

COL DE GALIBIER (2556m.)

COL DE LAUTARET
(2058m.)

COL DE MONTGEN
(1854m.)

BRIANCON

RTE N85

COL DE MENÉE (1440m.)

LIVRON

ALLEX

CREST

DIE

COL DE LA
CROIX HAUTE (1179m.)

COL BAYARD (1246m.)

LA COUCOURDE

MARSANNE

ROUBION R.

BONLIEU

N540

N538

MONTELIMAR

DIEULEFIT

DONZÈRE

GRÂNE

SAILLANS

DRÔME R.

N93

COL DE CABRE
(1180m.)

ASPRES-SUR-BUECH

N94

GAP

COL DE VARST (2

DURANCE R.

RTE N85

COL DE MAURE (1347m.)

RTE N94

AYGUES R.

OUVÈZE R.

SISTERON

RHÔNE R.

RTE N7

ORANGE

N85

DIGNE

AVIGNON

CASTELLANE

RIEZ

RTE N85

GRÉDOUX

VERDON R.

DURANCE R.

RTE N7

ARLES

RIANS

BARJOLS

DRAGUIGNAN

CANNES

1   TF

RTE N7

FREJUS

CALANQ
D'ANTHE

AIX-EN-PROVENCE

BRIGNOLES

ST. RAPHAEL

GOLFE DE
LA FRÉJUS

CAME

PORT-DE-BOUC

STE. MAXIME

BAIE DE DELTA F

MARSEILLE

ST. TROPEZ

PAMPELONNE

CAVALAIRE

ALPHA FO

LA CIOTAT

TOULON

HYÈRES

BAIE
DE
CAVALAIRE

C. NEGRE

0   30km.

MEDITERRANEAN SEA

RADE
D'HYÈRES

ÎLE DU
LEVANT

SSF   1

PORQUEROLLES

ÎLES
D'HYÈRES

PORT-CROS

meanwhile, flew to the Mediterranean to meet with Wilson on June 17. Marshall brought Wilson at least partially around toward appreciating the merits of ANVIL by convincing him, in Wilson's words, "that there are between 40 and 50 divisions in the United States which cannot be introduced into France as rapidly as desired or maintained there through the ports of Northwest France or by staging through the United Kingdom. . . ."[1] Thereupon, though not yet fully persuaded, Wilson made an important contribution by suggesting that if ANVIL were to happen, the Allies ought to strike around Marseille and Toulon rather than farther west around Sète, to open the port of Marseille more quickly, to hit the submarine pens directly, and to make rapid contact with the strongest FFI concentrations.

SHAEF and Wilson's Allied Force Headquarters proceeded to arrange the necessary cooperation, such as transfer of landing vessels and warships to the Mediterranean. SHAEF insisted on retaining the landing vessels until July 15 because of OVERLORD's logistical troubles, and on keeping gunfire-support warships until Cherbourg fell.

Meanwhile, detailed planning for ANVIL was already under way. The American Seventh Army, headquartered at Palermo, had received orders from AFHQ to begin the planning as early as December 19, 1943, while Patton, who had led this army through Sicily, still commanded it. A planning group called Force 163, headed by Brigadier General Garrison H. Davidson, the Seventh Army Engineer, continued the planning without interruption through the change from Patton to Lieutenant General Mark W. Clark as army commander, through an interval when there was no Seventh Army commander because Clark's urgent duties leading the Fifth Army in Italy had divorced him from active oversight anyway, and on into the tenure of Major General Alexander M. Patch at the head of the army, beginning March 2, 1944. Like Collins and Corlett, Patch, West Point 1913, was a veteran of the war in the Pacific, having commanded the United States forces on Guadalcanal in the final phase of the battle for the island; and while Corlett was disgusted that the OVERLORD commanders appeared to think his knowledge of amphibious war in the Pacific of no relevance to NEPTUNE, Patch's experience seemed to carry more credit among the Allied Mediterranean leadership. Patch added members of his own staff to Force 163.

The prolonged uncertainty over whether ANVIL would occur, the fluctuations of Seventh Army command, and the complete uncertainty even into the spring of 1944 as to which troops would mount the operation assuming it took place, all gave the planning group an unusual autonomy. The ANVIL blueprint more than OVERLORD or almost any other major operation of the war was the planners' rather than the potential operators' design. Fortunately, Force 163 did its work well. Established at the École Normal at Bouzareah just outside Algiers, the planners were in the midst of the governmental offices of Free France, and surrounded by French speculation about a coming invasion of southern France so loquacious and insistent that it became a test of the will to sustain a pretense of indifferent aloofness toward any such enterprise.

Captain Robert A. J. English, USN, headed the naval planning contingent representing the prospective commander of the invasion force, Vice Admiral H. K. Hewitt, USN. Group Captain R. E. Lees, Royal Australian Air Force, represented the Mediterranean Allied Tactical Air Force. Apart from informal French efforts to pry out information concerning the proceedings, General de Gaulle's insistence that the French army reconstituted in North Africa and in part fighting in Italy must join in the liberation of France led to early agreement on a prominent French role—it suited the Americans to have French political support against the British, as well—and the injection of a French component into Force 163, under Colonel Jean L. Pettit. France's Army B, the planners decided, would promptly follow the American divisions ashore and would participate in the campaign initially as part of the American Seventh Army. De Gaulle expressed his willingness to subordinate French generals to Americans of lesser rank if it would help hasten the French army into the battle.

The commander of French forces in the Mediterranean Theater except Italy, Général d'Armée Jean de Lattre de Tassigny, thus was to serve in effect as a corps commander under an American lieutenant general (a rank attained by General Patch on August 7). Meanwhile de Lattre contributed to the planners an ambitious proposal that reflected French divorcement from the mainstream of Western military thought since 1940 by suggesting landings on two separate fronts east and west of Toulon. General Patch had to point out to de Lattre that such dispersion of force would proportionately reduce air cover, naval gunfire support, and logistical efficiency. In an amphibious assault, even the Americans worshipped concentration, and rightly so. Delay in capturing Toulon was not too high a price, said Patch, to pay for a concentrated assault on the most favorable terrain.

Toulon, nevertheless, was the first major objective already chosen by Force 163, to be confirmed with the help of General Wilson's preference for it over Sète. The same imperative that had shaped OVERLORD, the necessity for early access to a port, focused the planners' attention on the coast east of Toulon: the beautiful shore of eastern Provence, the French Riviera between St. Tropez and Cannes, where the snow-capped Alpes Maritimes tower up abruptly behind the beaches. The mountains obviously might cause problems, but worse difficulties loomed to the westward nearer Toulon and Marseille. Between the Îles d'Hyères and Marseille, the coast itself is forbiddingly rugged, and this stretch also lay mainly within range of the 340mm. guns guarding France's principal naval base at Toulon. From the Golfe de Fréjus between St. Tropez and Cannes, moreover, the valley of the Argens River forms a path through the mountains, between the Massif de Maures nearest the coast and the Provence Alps farther inland, with a choice of exits to Toulon, Marseille, and the Rhône, and level ground for a parachute drop to supplement the amphibious assault. The Route Napoléon—now N85—from Cannes through Grenoble and Lyon, the course of the Emperor's triumphant march on his return from Elba, is also accessible as an avenue northward to supplement the traditional major route from southern France, the Rhône valley.

For the assault, the planners chose eight kilometers of beaches within a seventy-two-kilometer stretch of coast between the Baie de Cavalaire, southwest of and behind St. Tropez, and la Calanque d'Anthéor, across the Golfe de la Napoule from Cannes.

In June, after the fall of Rome, the 3rd, 36th, and 45th Infantry Divisions were withdrawn from the Fifth Army and reassigned to Patch's Seventh Army as the initial assault force. Their origins were, respectively, Regular Army—the 3rd Division was the "Rock of the Marne" and shared with the 1st and 2nd Divisions the distinction of never having been deactivated since 1917; Texas National Guard—the 36th Division was the "Texas army"; and Arizona, New Mexico, Oklahoma, and Colorado National Guard—the Southwest symbolized by the 45th's Thunderbird shoulder patch. The divisions immediately began retraining for amphibious assault, though all boasted amphibious experience. The 3rd, whose own ebullient commander, Major General John W. O'Daniel, supervised its amphibious exercises at Pozzuoli, had gone ashore in Morocco, in Sicily, and at Anzio. Major General John E. Dahlquist's 36th and Major General William W. Eagles's 45th exercised along with prospective supporting units under the direction of an Invasion Training Center. But the 36th had been first ashore at Salerno, and the 45th had been part of the first assault on Sicily. Salerno was the appropriate locale of the 36th's and 45th's rehearsals: "The same beaches, the same hills, the same dust and sand" as the previous September, said a member of the 171st Field Artillery Battalion, "but conditions have altered the situation, and though we expected the whine of shells and the roar of German planes, we found a refreshing, reassuring stillness, serene and peaceful."[2]

Together, the assault divisions would form the VI Corps, under Lieutenant General Lucian K. Truscott, Jr. It would have been hard to find a better commander for the amphibious assault. A polo-playing friend of Patton's in the old army—though he was not a West Pointer but a 1911 graduate of the Oklahoma Normal School at Norman, commissioned second lieutenant of cavalry in 1917—Truscott combined a horse soldier's dash with a wealth of amphibious experience. On April 20, 1942, he had won from General Marshall the assignment as first head of the American section of Britain's Combined Operations Headquarters. He oversaw the creation and training of the 1st Ranger Battalion, and when fifty of his Rangers joined in the Dieppe raid, Truscott went along. From the nurturing of Ranger battalions he moved to the 30th Infantry of the 9th Division, leading the 30th in the amphibious assault against Mehedia in Morocco. This was an exceptionally difficult first attack for the regiment and its commander, because it required moving directly from the beaches into boats again, to cross a watercourse called the Wadi Sebou on the way to Port Lyautey. After commanding the 3rd Division by the final phase of the Tunisian campaign, Truscott also took that division ashore west of Punta San Nicola in Sicily in an operation characterized by divisional staff planning of meticulousness exceptional even by the standards of an amphibious assault. Truscott's division entered Italy through Salerno after the beaches were secured; but it was in the Anzio battle from the beginning, and on February 22, 1943 Truscott took charge of the battle and the VI Corps to inject into both a new vigor and to rescue the unhappy Anzio campaign from utter fiasco. All three prospective ANVIL divisions were with Truscott in the breakout from Anzio and the march on Rome. By that time, not a few Allied leaders, including Eisenhower and Bradley, saw Truscott as a potential commander of an army.

At the beginning of July, ANVIL received the new codename DRAGOON. The operation had been so much bruited about that the Allies feared the security of the term ANVIL might have been compromised. Anyway, Churchill wanted to indicate that he had been "dragooned" into accepting the project. Though Churchill was still resisting, on July 8 General Wilson ordered his forces to proceed with it. The planning staff now moved to Naples and henceforth worked in direct contact with the main headquarters of the Seventh Army and the VI Corps. A Commanders' Conference on July 12 resolved the final disputes and details among the planners and the ground, naval, and air commanders. The planners were able to allay several of the fears natural to Truscott's immediate past experience. They assured him they had taken adequate inventory of German beach obstacles and provided an adequate concentration of Allied force to avoid entrapment on the beaches like the "stranded whale"[3] of Anzio.

H-Hour and D-Day would be 8:00 A.M., August 15. For the first time a Mediterranean landing was to take place by daylight. The Normandy experience helped the navy persuade the army planners that the value of preliminary bombardment outweighed that of more complete tactical surprise. A last-quarter moon, rising at 3:15 A.M., would provide enough light for commando raids and a parachute drop preceding H-Hour.

Air support was to come principally from the Twelfth Air Force's tactical command, XII TAC, under Brigadier General Gordon P. Saville, with reinforcement by the RAF. The air commander for the Mediterranean, Air Marshal Sir John Slessor, offered assurance that his forces could simultaneously take on southern France and continue with the Italian campaign, because by now the Luftwaffe could "virtually be ignored."[4] On August 4, the air forces announced their plan for a pre-D-Day campaign in two phases. From D minus 10—the next day, August 5—to D minus 6, air would neutralize what remained of the Luftwaffe in southern France, interdict communications, and attack submarine bases. From August 10 to D-Day, air would neutralize the main coastal batteries and radar stations and use any surplus strength to finish off earlier targets. For deception, the attacks on coastal defenses would range all the way from Sète to Genoa. The principal platform for launching the air effort would be Corsica, within convenient fighter range of the invasion coast. Since January, Corsica had been so thoroughly developed as a base for the invasion that by summer the stocks there needed no enlargement, merely replenishment to keep them at existing levels. Especially in the days immediately before the invasion, the heavy and medium bombers in the Mediterranean were to join in the preparations, striking particularly at railroads and oil installations. Between 5:50 and 7:30 on D-Day morning, twelve groups of heavy bombers and two wings (six groups) of mediums were to hit the assault beaches along with all the strength of XII TAC, to try to paralyze the defenders.

ETO had to lend the Mediterranean 416 tow planes and 225 glider pilots to build up air transport to the three troop carrier wings needed to mount and support the proposed airborne landings that were to cut roads and create diversions inland from the beaches. The transports and gliders formed Brigadier General Paul L. Williams's Provisional Troop Carrier Air Division. Since there were no longer any airborne divisions in the Mediterranean, a provisional one was improvised for the work at hand, called the 1st Airborne Task Force and led by Major General Robert T. Frederick. Frederick was experienced in improvised commands and bold operations akin to airborne assaults. He had largely created and then commanded the 1st Special Service Force—the "Devil's Brigade" of postwar romance—picked American and Canadian soldiers trained in parachute jumping, amphibious landings, mountain fighting, and demolitions. This force had spearheaded the recapture of Kiska in the Aleutians, and its performance added a ray of much needed brightness to the Anzio campaign.

Frederick received the help of thirty-six imported staff officers, mostly from the 13th Airborne Division in the United States. The 517th Parachute Infantry, the 1st Battalion of the 551st Parachute Infantry, the 509th separate Parachute Infantry Battalion, the 463rd Parachute Field Artillery, the 550th Glider Infantry Battalion, the British 2nd Parachute Brigade Group, and various special units scraped together formed his division. They trained near Rome during July; without opportunity for a full-scale rehearsal, much of the practice consisted merely of jumps by two or three men at a time from the same airplanes they would use later.

In his Western Naval Task Force which would conduct the amphibious assault, Admiral Hewitt had no larger vessels at hand for fire support than the light cruisers *Brooklyn* and *Philadelphia*, so he asked Admiral King to arrange to have something more sent down from the English Channel. He received the heavy cruisers *Augusta*, *Quincy*, and *Tuscaloosa* and five veteran battleships, the trusty old *Nevada*, *Texas*, and *Arkansas* along with the Royal Navy's *Ramillies* and the French navy's *Lorraine*. Large numbers of destroyers also sailed south, in addition to landing vessels. One of the exceptions to the generally American cast of DRAGOON was the aircraft carrier force of seven British and two American escort carriers. Their decks were to launch spotting planes for naval gunfire as well as Seafires, Hellcats, and Wildcats to supplement XII TAC's Thunderbolts, Lightnings, and Spitfires in aerial support.

Hewitt divided the Western Naval Task Force into three subsidiary forces. ALPHA Force would carry the 3rd Division and Combat Command Sudre of France's 1ère Division Blindée to beaches on the Baie de Cavalaire and the Baie de Pampelonne, whence the Rock of the Marne and its supporting armor were to squeeze in a pincers the hill towns, pine forests, vineyards, and olive groves of the Presqu'île de St. Tropez. DELTA Force would set down the 45th Division on a 4,500-meter continuous beach in the center of the landings, just northeast of the Golfe de St. Tropez. The 36th Division was to be taken ashore by CAMEL Force on constricted beaches pressed closely by the cliffs facing the Golfe de Fréjus, where the Argens River empties to offer the vital route into the interior. Eight hundred eighty ships and landing vessels would participate in the invasion, carrying more than 1,370 landing craft on their decks and in davits.

This armada was the mightiest the Allies had yet gathered in either Europe or the Pacific save for NEPTUNE, and the defenses seemed to pose good reason for the flexing of such muscles if DRAGOON were not to become another Salerno or Anzio. On the French Riviera, the Germans had not built an equivalent of the Atlantic Wall. But the land mines on the beaches were more numerous than anywhere on the periphery of Europe except the Channel coast; the array of defending artillery included such items as a 220mm. gun in the DELTA area camouflaged to look like the garden of a villa—rosebushes painted into the concrete; and while the underwater obstacles were less numerous than in Normandy, the slightness of the Mediterranean tide—eight inches or twenty centimeters on D-Day—meant that these obstacles would remain submerged and hard to deal with. Devices concocted to try to eliminate submerged obstacles included the Apex drone boat, a remote-controlled landing craft loaded with high explosives to be detonated above the obstacles, and "Reddy Fox," a pipe filled with explosives to be sunk next to the obstacles and detonated. None of these contraptions proved reliable in rehearsals, and forty-one eleven-man teams of frogmen had to be assembled to try to do the dismantling job on the day of the assault.

Enemy troop strength presented a rather less discouraging picture but could not be taken lightly. Generaloberst Johannes Blaskowitz's Army Group G, defending the south of France under the direction of OB West, had never rivaled Army Group B in strength and by August was much diminished to reinforce the north. The German First Army, the garrison of southwestern France, withdrew most of its forces in early August to try to build a defense line along the Seine southeast of Paris, leaving only the LXIV Corps in the south. Along the Mediterranean coast, the Nineteenth Army of General der Infanterie Friedrich Wiese had four divisions between the Spanish border and the mouth of the

Rhône, two divisions at Marseille and Toulon, and a reserve division in the immediate DRAGOON area. On D-Day the formidable 11th Panzer Division proved to be en route from the Bordeaux area to the Rhône; the Allies could guess the reason, which was that German air reconnaissance had spotted Allied convoy activity on August 13. The captors of Belgrade in 1941, Generalleutnant Wend von Wietersheim's 11th Panzers had won in Russia the sobriquet "the Ghost Division," a testament to their dazzling mobility as well as to many a famous victory carved out by their firepower. Sent to quiet southern France to refit, the 11th Panzer Division had rested and regathered strength around its veteran leaders and cadre long enough to cause the DRAGOON planners some of their deepest worries. Altogether, the Germans had about 30,000 troops in the assault area and over 200,000 within a few days' march.

The final assemblage of the DRAGOON forces was hasty, and the training and rehearsals of many of them for this particular operation were slight. The creation and training of the airborne force presented an especially acute example of haste and improvisation; but there were enough similar examples that Prime Minister Churchill could repeatedly cite the peril of a disastrous miscarriage by unprepared forces as one of his reasons for opposing the enterprise—ignoring, to be sure, the fact that his prolonged foot-dragging was one of the reasons why the force had to be pieced together as it was. However sincere Churchill's resort to the unpreparedness argument may have been, a most disturbing indication that DRAGOON might fire half-cocked was the suicide of Rear Admiral Don P. Moon. The commander of "U" Force in the Normandy landings, Moon came down to the Mediterranean late in July to lead CAMEL Force. After a few days of hard work putting together rehearsals, and a few nights of no sleep because so much remained to be done, on August 4 he implored Admiral Hewitt to postpone the invasion, because the participants could not possibly be ready by August 15. Hewitt tried to reassure him but promised that if the final rehearsal was not satisfactory, he would discuss postponement with General Wilson. Not satisfied, Moon took his own life the next day. His death could be attributed to the strain of overwork, having plunged into a new invasion project so soon after leaving UTAH Beach. On the other hand, Moon was an experienced officer who knew what an amphibious assault force ought to be.

The Battle of Provence

Yet the invasion proceeded almost without a hitch. The main parachute lift of 396 airplanes took off about 3:30 in the morning from ten Italian airfields. Though there was a heavy mist over the countryside, and only one of three pathfinder teams preceding the main force jumped into its assigned drop zone, radar and radio-compass homing devices guided about 60 percent of the main body to their proper zones or the immediate vicinity. No casualties marred the journey, every plane returned safely to its base, and the drop was one of the most accurate of the war. With much help from the FFI, the paratroopers carried out their tasks of blocking roads, seizing towns, and fending off counterattacks.

To divert the enemy from the real airborne assault, six planes had earlier approached the Baie de la Ciotat between Marseille and Toulon, dropping the metal strips called WINDOW or CHAFF that appeared on enemy radar as a large flight of aircraft, and then unloading several hundred parachute-borne dummies, accompanied by noise makers to simulate gunfire. For a time the Germans were taken in by the ruse, which according to Radio Berlin "could only have been conceived in the sinister Anglo-Saxon mind."[5] More substantial diversions included the landing from the sea of General Frederick's old command, the 1st Special Service Force some 2,000 strong, on the Île de Port Cros and the Île de Levant on the left flank of the main invasion beaches. In addition to distracting the enemy, the Devil's Brigade was to capture a battery of three 164mm. guns on the Île de Levant. The battery proved, however, to consist of wooden "Quaker" guns, a deception no doubt to be attributed to the sinister Teutonic mind.

The 1,000-man French Groupe de Commandos landed at Cap Negre on the mainland west of the principal beaches for yet an additional divertissement and to block the coast and inland roads from Toulon. The mission was successfully accomplished. Some of the commandos landed on the wrong beach but served to add to the enemy's confusion. Another French force, a naval assault group specializing in demolitions, landed east of the main beaches but were less fortunate. They were supposed to cut the road from Cannes, but they stumbled into a big field of land mines, whose explosions aroused a large enough force of defenders to drive the French back into the sea. Then their boats were machine-gunned by friendly airplanes, obliging them to jump overboard and swim ashore, where they were captured. More luckily, casualties were few and the prisoners were rescued the next day.

Other Allied boats roamed ostentatiously along a considerable stretch of coast, listening to the screams of German sentries being knifed by the successful commandos, and trying to create still further misconceptions about where the main landings would put down. Though the Germans had enough experience fighting amphibious invasions that small-boat sideshows did little to deceive them, it made scant difference to the main assault. The morning mist required Admiral Hewitt's fleet to do a lot of "blind firing" guided by gridded shore maps—at dawn the peaks of the Alpes Maritimes were just beginning to rise above the haze—and aborted one-third of the scheduled aerial sorties, but the effects of the remaining bombardment on beach defenses and underwater obstacles were more satisfactory than anticipated. The floating gadgets for exploding the obstacles also worked better than in the rehearsals. O'Daniel's 3rd Division landed virtually without opposition, except from land mines, and entered St. Tropez in the afternoon to find the town already liberated, not only by the FFI but by some of the few paratroopers who had come down in the wrong place; the airborne men had captured two coastal batteries, an antiaircraft battery, and a garrison of 240 Germans. Eagles's 45th Division experienced scarcely more trouble, and before the day was over it made contact with the paratroopers inland.

Only Dahlquist's 36th Division had to go through a real fight before establishing itself ashore. In its sector, the underwater mines were exceptionally numerous, so were the land mines, and the narrowness of the beaches and the abruptness of the cliffs created still more difficulties. The Germans exploited these features to put up an exasperating though not especially persistent opposition. One of the beaches was secured only on the second morning, by the expedient of going around to its rear through the town of St. Raphaël and thence bulldozing a row of "bathhouses" behind the beach that turned out to be a camouflaged antitank wall.

"It is inadmissable," General de Gaulle had announced, "for French troops at this stage to be used elsewhere than in France."[6] General Patch had responded wholeheartedly to this sentiment by insisting that the French components of his army should have the responsibility and the honor of capturing Toulon and Marseille. The II Corps of General de Lattre's Army B began landing through the Americans on August 16 to undertake this mission. De Lattre naturally would have preferred to be in on the first assault, but Admiral Hewitt had been able to persuade him that the intricacies of an amphibious assault are sufficient unto themselves without adding a language barrier.

The 1ère Division Motorisée d'Infanterie and the 3ème Division d'Infanterie Algér-ienne debarked at the Baie de Cavalaire and on Plage La Foux at the head of the Golfe de St. Tropez. Though they were greeted by a surprising Luftwaffe attack that caused eighty casualties, in the next few days they advanced westward so rapidly, overrunning roadblocks and strongpoints, that they outpaced the navies' ability to keep up with them while the ships were also knocking out German batteries along the coast. The 9ème Division d'Infanterie Coloniale and two groups of Tabors of Goums along with various special forces and the remainder of the 1ère Division Blindée followed beginning on August 18 to complete the French II Corps.

The DRAGOON planners had felt obliged to assume that Toulon and Marseille might not be captured until D plus 40; but by August 20, de Lattre's troops were already fighting in the outskirts of Toulon, and within a few more days both port cities came under heavy attack by land as well as by sea and air. On Cap Cépet, commanding the Toulon roadstead and the sea approaches to both Toulon and Marseille, the French had planted before the war two casemated turrets of 340mm. guns from the battleship *La Provence*. By the time the DRAGOON expedition arrived, French workmen had already sabotaged two of the guns, but the 340mm. guns of the battleship *Lorraine* now had the interesting chore of a duel with the guns that had served a sister ship. *Lorraine* led off, but she received the help of *Nevada* and *Ramillies* as well as a bevy of cruisers. With the advantage of a land battery against ships, however, the Germans held off the Allied fleet from August 19 to 26, when the Allies simply ran past the battery with one of its big guns silenced but the other still firing.

Toulon and Marseille had both received the Führer's designation as fortresses and the concomitant no-surrender orders. They were garrisoned by a division each, the 242nd in Toulon and the 244th in Marseille. But they were out of reach of any prospect of effective help and, unlike the Brittany ports, by the time they came under siege they were genuinely needed by the Allies and the targets of overwhelming concentrations of force. At Toulon, where all approaches were blocked by forts, pillboxes, mine fields, and antitank obstacles, the French nevertheless assailed and captured early the three moun-tain forts of Caumes, Faron, and le Coudon. Commanding the city from these vantage points, they thereafter relied heavily on artillery, B-26s, and P-47s. Marseille was less strongly fortified and more vulnerable to infantry assault, and with the help of the FFI de Lattre's infantry pushed inexorably through the streets and toward the docks. The French were still underequipped by American standards, but the élan of their assaults on both major seaports amply justified Patch's decision to grant them so conspicuous a part in DRAGOON. Toulon and Marseille both surrendered on August 28.

The Battle of Montélimar

General Patch meanwhile had his American VI Corps striking as fast as it could move for the Rhône and the interior of France. The purpose was to trap as many as possible of the Germans in southwest and south-central France by closing off the Rhône as a route of retreat. The Seventh Army's ability to pursue this purpose with a headlong march was another triumph of ULTRA, a more substantial triumph than ULTRA's contribution to the Battle of Mortain, because on this occasion fewer other sources and military instincts confirmed the relevant messages from ULTRA. ULTRA consistently assured that Patch could hasten his troops inland and up the Rhône without dropping off major units to protect the right flank, because the Germans were not shifting substantial forces from Italy to threaten Patch from the east.

To lead a rapid advance inland, General Truscott was as good a choice to head the VI Corps as he had been for the amphibious assault. He possessed the cavalryman's passion for mobility to an exceptional degree, and he had trained his own 3rd Division in the "Truscott trot," whereby troops carrying weapons and full packs could cover thirty miles in less than eight hours; they marched at five and a half miles per hour for the first hour, four for the next two, and three and a half for the rest.

While the Americans trotted up the east bank of the Rhône, the French were to follow as soon as possible up the west bank. As quickly as the capture of Toulon and Marseille was assured, de Lattre extricated the 1ère D.M.I. and the 1ère Division Blindée from the coastal fighting to cross the Rhône. Handicapped by low gasoline supplies and the destruction of the Rhône bridges, the French nevertheless hastened temporary bridging across the Durance River and ferries across the Rhône, and they reached the west bank around Avignon, Tarascon, and Arles on August 29.

From his first introduction to the ANVIL planning, Truscott had applied his zeal for mobility to the plan by projecting the entrapment of the enemy's Nineteenth Army in retreat. The geography of southern France would naturally canalize the German retreat, like the principal Allied advance, into the Rhône valley, between the Massif Central to the west, with its sharp face to the Mediterranean, and the lofty Alps-Jura system to the east. Roads cross the Massif Central from Nimes through le Puy to Lyon, but the way is winding, difficult, and over 150 kilometers longer than the direct route to Lyon up the Rhône valley. In the valley, railroads and two highways follow the Rhône. Route N7 on the east bank is straighter and more level than N86 on the west bank, where the hills more often encroach closely upon the stream. ULTRA early showed the enemy assigning to his 11th Panzer Division the missions of protecting the east face of the Rhône delta and Highway 7 from Avignon south through Aix-en-Provence against Allied incursion, while less mobile divisions of the Nineteenth Army began withdrawing up the Rhône. The panzers would then act as a continuing escort up N7 through the valley. From the first, Truscott had envisaged a flanking movement to block such a retreat well to the north, at the Gate of Montélimar.

Between Lyon and its entrance into the delta at Avignon, the Rhône follows an almost straight north-south course for over 200 kilometers. Proceeding upstream, the traveler along the river finds a broad, dry loam plain from Avignon to Orange. He then enters a relatively narrow corridor extending for some eight kilometers, before the valley opens outward again. Thereafter, additional narrow defiles continually interrupt the riverside plains. Just north of Montélimar, some seventy kilometers above Avignon, between the Montélimar Plain to the south and the Valence Plain to the north, the valley closes in dramatically through the Cruas Gorge, or the Gate of Montélimar. Heavily forested hills rise to 300 or 400 meters on the east bank of the river, and there are cliffs considerably higher to the west. Here the Romans for obvious reasons had built a fortress. Passing to the family of Adhémar, the fortress became in time the Monteil d'Adhémar, then simply Montélimar. Militarily famous for Gaspard de Coligny's defense against the Huguenots in the Wars of Religion, the Gate of Montélimar now offered General Truscott a superb site for the blocking of Route N7 and the trapping of the Nineteenth Army.

The Americans could approach the gate from the east, by following the Route Napoléon from their beaches to Gap, and thence traveling via N94 and N93 and down the Drôme River. To spearhead the VI Corps's exploitation from the beaches, Truscott promptly assembled a mobile group under his deputy corps commander, Brigadier General Frederick B. Butler, another veteran Mediterranean campaigner who had fought from El Guettar to Cassino. Task Force Butler, or the Provisional Armored Group, was built around the 753rd Tank Battalion, with the 2nd Battalion on the 143rd Infantry, motorized, from the 36th Division; the 59th Armored Field Artillery Battalion; the 117th Reconnaissance Squadron; and companies of tank destroyers and combat engineers plus other appropriate attachments. Conceived before the departure from Naples, Task Force Butler moved out from the beachhead as early as August 18 to strike ahead through Draguignon and Riez toward Grenoble. Dahlquist's 36th Division was to follow toward Grenoble through Castellane and up N85. The 3rd and 45th Divisions advanced instead up the Argens corridor toward the Rhône, the 3rd traveling directly along N7 and fighting its way into Aix-en-Provence on August 21. The 45th grappled for Barjols to clear its route to crossings of the Durance River, whence, with the 3rd gathering satisfactory northward momentum, the Thunderbirds could sideslip rightward to join the march on Grenoble to provide insurance between Task Force Butler and the Texas Division. If Truscott's design succeeded, the 3rd Division would drive the enemy up N7 into roadblocks closed by Task Force Butler and the 36th Division at the Gate of Montélimar.

The German 157th Reserve Division was at Grenoble and dispatching elements southward to harass the Americans. On August 20, however, the main column of Task Force Butler captured the Col de la Croix Haute, a mountain pass 1,179 meters high on Route N75 north of Aspres; another column with the aid of the FFI drove a German force from Gap, capturing a thousand prisoners. The effect was to block further German movement from Grenoble toward the beachheads. That done, Truscott instructed Butler at 8:45 P.M.: "You will move at first light 21 August with all possible speed to Montelimar. Block all routes of withdrawal up the Rhone Valley in that vicinity. 36th Division follows you."[7]

Dropping roadblocks north of Gap and near the Col de la Croix Haute until the 36th Division could relieve them, Butler accordingly turned west. During the day a Seventh Army conference considered the recommendation of the FFI that the VI Corps might move on northward through Grenoble because the Resistance already controlled the Rhône valley. The decision was not to rely on the French but to persist with Truscott's plan. Events supported this verdict before the day was over. By nightfall Butler's vanguard had reached the Rhône valley, but there they met a German convoy of some thirty vehicles moving out from the Gate of Montélimar north of Livron. They attacked and destroyed the convoy, but reconnaissance patrols attempting to cut N7 around La Coucourde collided with superior German forces. Butler was able to do nothing more than occupy high ground overlooking the highway a few kilometers north of Montélimar.

One of Butler's roadblocks farther east, a reinforced company of the 117th Reconnaissance Squadron, had to fend off an estimated two-battalion attack at the Col Bayard north of Gap during August 21, but the next day the 36th Division relieved the roadblocks and went on to take Grenoble before sunset. The division's 141st Infantry Regiment, supported by two battalions of field artillery, turned west at Aspres under orders from Truscott to reinforce Task Force Butler with all possible speed. By midnight, the artillery was in position around Marsanne, ready to fire all the way across the Rhône valley.

Yet the American advance had been not quite fast enough. Butler knew by now that there were German tanks as well as troops holding three hill masses north of Montélimar. These hills dominated the highways running both northward and eastward from the town: Ridge 300, some four kilometers north and east of Montélimar; Hill 294, just southeast of the ridge; and Hill 430, just east of the northernmost portion of the ridge. When reinforcements from the 36th Division began to arrive, the 2nd Battalion, 141st Infantry attacked Montélimar from the north and northeast on August 23, supported by a platoon of tanks, a platoon of tank destroyers, and some FFI. German artillery from the town and from Ridge 300 readily broke up the attack.

Coming close but not entering Montélimar or seizing the dominant hills meant that American strength in hand, already apparently insufficient to control the situation, had to be dissipated further. As long as the Germans held Montélimar they could move out the road along the Roubion River eastward from the town as well as northward on N7. Along the Roubion there was good, firm tank country. Thus the Germans not only retained an alternate route of escape, but they could threaten the tenuous line of communication between the VI Corps advance around Montélimar and Grenoble, Gap, and the corridor to the beachheads. As more of the 36th Division arrived, consequently, the 142nd Regiment and the 111th Combat Engineer Battalion had to be used not offensively but to extend the line from the Marsanne vicinity through the village of Bonlieu to the Roubion. Artillery fire had to be divided between Highway 7 and protection of the line of communication.

In the afternoon of August 25, Germans of the 198th Infantry Division infiltrated into Bonlieu, through which a company of the 111th Engineers were strung out along a front well over a kilometer long. This German effort, by a company and a couple of tanks, proved to be a diversion preceding an attack toward Marsanne in battalion strength, supported by six Tigers. The main enemy effort ruptured the American line, and it was not until the next day that the final regiment of the Texas Division, the 143rd, repaired the breach. Meanwhile Germans filtered northward through the opening and across the Drôme, probably in considerable numbers.

When the 2nd Battalion of the 157th Infantry, 45th Division, arrived in the battle zone on August 26, Truscott ordered it to set up roadblocks at Crest and Allex on the Drôme, to narrow the Germans' escape routes to the western extremity of that river, near Loriel. In addition, American artillery and aviation pounded the Drôme bridges. But in late summer the river is readily fordable, and the Germans brought the 110th Panzer Grenadier Regiment of the 11th Panzer Division to the scene to hold back the Americans from the crossings near the mouth. The German exodus continued.

Closer to Montélimar, the VI Corps was trying again to block Route N7 directly by setting up roadblocks north of the town. Task Force Butler tried its hand in the morning of August 25, the 141st Regiment twice in the afternoon, and Task Force Butler again on the morning of August 27. Enemy infantry and armor consistently broke through. At least the Americans as well as the Germans had the Rhône valley under artillery fire, so the retreating Nineteenth Army was suffering heavy losses in men and equipment even if it was not being stopped. But with the artillery, there was a problem in bringing up enough ammunition via the difficult and circuitous route from the beaches. Within the battle area, every available man had to be set to carrying shells from battery to battery and from gun to gun, to try to assure that whoever had the most remunerative targets at any given moment would have something to shoot in their direction. Nevertheless, the guns did their usual good work. On August 26, the 133rd Field Artillery Battalion scored a series of direct hits on a railroad train of fifty-five cars, stopped it, and blocked two other trains for further working over. Increasingly the Germans felt obliged to shift their highway traffic to the narrower and more winding road on the west bank. Late on August 27 the 141st Regiment reported that artillery had accomplished what the infantry and Task Force Butler had been unable to do, creating a roadblock on N7—a barrier of enemy vehicles wrecked by the guns.

Realizing that much of the Nineteenth Army had already slipped farther northward, Truscott by that time had shifted his main effort to pushing all the way down the north bank of the Drôme to its mouth to cut N7 near Livron. The 157th and 142nd Regiments together fought this battle, and by late morning of August 28 they had Livron surrounded and N7 closed. That morning, moreover, the 3rd Division, driving up N7 from the south, pressed into the town of Montélimar. With the enemy losing the town, the 141st Regiment was able at last to climb the commanding hills just north of it. But no one found more than scattered enemy fragments. The Nineteenth Army had already slipped through Truscott's fingers.

The extended line of communication from the beaches up the Grenoble corridor through Gap and thence westward down the Drôme had deterred the Americans from putting quite enough power into the enveloping force to close the Gate of Montélimar while the enemy was still using it. The Seventh Army had repeated the experiences of the Allied armies to the north; somehow, American envelopments seemed always to fall just short of completion.

From Montélimar, major portions of the German 189th, 198th, 338th, and 716th Infantry Divisions, as well as the 11th Panzer Division, got away. General Blaskowitz of Army Group G had been out of Hitler's favor at least since the Polish campaign of 1939, for faults both in military élan on the attack and Nazi party zeal. But Blaskowitz was too skillful a tactician for the Führer to prevail on the Wehrmacht to dismiss him altogether. Holding open the Gate of Montélimar was his first exhibition of his tactical abilities to the Americans.

Still, the Germans left behind some 2,000 to 3,000 vehicles, more than eighty artillery pieces, and five big railway guns, captured when the three immobilized trains were eventually occupied. The battle of Montélimar was a notable American victory however incomplete, confirming the judgment of his superiors that Lucian Truscott was about as promising a corps commander as any in the American army in Europe.

Consolidating a Mediterranean Base

Before the big port cities fell and they could know how soon the docks there could be usable, Admiral Hewitt and General Patch decided to secure as a stopgap the Golfe de

Fos, thirty kilometers west of Marseille. From Port de Bouc on this gulf, a canal big enough for an LCM leads to the Rhône at Arles. The Germans evacuated Port de Bouc on August 21 before the Allies arrived, but sweeping the entrance free of mines proved a tough task, and a torpedo boat had its stern blown away and five men killed simply in the process of reconnoitering. Seabees and army engineers occupied Port de Bouc on August 27, and on September 1 the first LCMs set off for Arles. Though the prompt capture of the larger ports minimized the need for this supply route, the landing craft sent through the canal provided useful ferries to carry troops across the Rhône.

As early as August 16 and 17, the rapidity of the Seventh Army's first advances out of the beachheads required an airlift to supplement overland supply. On those two days, thirty-nine troop-carrier planes dropped 123,000 pounds of gasoline, ammunition, and rations to keep the advance going. Allied aviation's own earlier work now complicated Allied logistics. On August 25 and 27, General Saville of XII TAC urged the theater air command that bridge-busting be suspended. "Any bombing in France now within range of medium bombers hurts us more than the Germans," he said, because the object was to drive forward the American and French spearheads as rapidly as possible.[8] Fighters could best be employed not to escort the B-25s and B-26s but to harry the fleeing enemy. Major General James K. Cannon, commander of the Twelfth Air Force, responded by ordering on August 30 that henceforth the mediums be used only to create a more northerly line of interdiction, from Nantes eastward to northwest of Dijon, to interfere with the flight of the German First Army remnants from southwestern France.

To the east, while the bulk of the Nineteenth Army made its way through the Gate of Montélimar, the 148th Reserve Division withdrew instead along the easternmost French coast toward Italy. The 157th Reserve Division responded to the bloodying of its nose around Grenoble by also moving eastward. Reports of the transfer of two unidentified German divisions in northern Italy toward France suggested the possibility of a small counterattack against the lengthening right flank of the VI Corps, although ULTRA continued to offer assurance that nothing big would come through the Alpine passes. To be safe, nevertheless, the 1st Airborne Task Force staged a limited offensive eastward between St. Vallier and the coast, designed to capture Cannes and Nice and to force the enemy far enough back into the passes so that aggressive activities on his part would become still less likely. Because General Frederick's British contingent returned to Italy, the 1st Special Service Force joined his ad hoc division. The 509th Parachute Battalion captured Cannes on August 24 and Nice on August 30, and while avoiding the risk of casualties that might come with heavy attacks into the mountains, the airborne troops remained busy enough to occupy the enemy's attentions along the Franco-Italian frontier.

North of the Airborne Task Force, the 45th Division briefly took on similar responsibilities for protecting the right flank. In the final days of August, however, the Seventh Army freed the Thunderbirds from so static a task by putting together odds and ends to form the Provisional Flank Protection Force: a cavalry reconnaissance troop, three chemical companies, two infantry antitank platoons, and a field artillery battery. Aided by the FFI, this force experienced some sharp fighting against infiltrating Germans around Briançon, but no heavy attack materialized. Eventually the French brought into the Italian border area the 2ème Division d'Infanterie Morocaine, the 3ème Division d'Infanterie Algérienne, and the 9ème Division d'Infanterie Coloniale, to activate their I Corps and take over the permanent defense of the region.

Toward the Belfort Gap

When the trap at Montélimar failed to close, Patch and Truscott wasted no time before trying to set another one. The French II Corps came charging up the right bank of the Rhône, and the 36th Division resumed the American advance up the left bank. Although he felt obliged to hold the 3rd Division back for a short time to mop up around Montélimar, Truscott also ordered the 45th Division to hightail it to the roads running eastward out of Lyon, to try to cut off any German turn eastward there. By compelling the Nineteenth Army to continue moving farther north, Truscott hoped to push it into the maw of General Patton's oncoming Third Army, or to drive his own main force between the Germans and the border of the Reich.

Eagles's Thunderbird Division moved with speed enough to satisfy even the impatient Truscott. By the last day of August, its 179th Infantry Regiment had preceded the enemy to Pont d'Ain, midway between Lyon and the Swiss frontier, and the division quickly began setting up blocks on every road coming toward it from Lyon.

Dahlquist's 36th Division reached high ground overlooking Lyon from the south the following afternoon, and by early afternoon of September 2 FFI reports and Texas Division patrols alike established that the enemy was not about to fight for the third city of France, but rather had virtually completed his evacuation. Truscott's headquarters nevertheless instructed Dahlquist not to send his troops into the city, except for small patrols and liaison parties, but to leave the honor of liberating it to the French II Corps. The 1ère Division Motorisée d'Infanterie was already entering the western outskirts, and this unit paraded into the customary melee of welcoming tricolors, wine bottles, and grateful feminine arms the next day.

Mere escape, not the defense of even so large a city, preoccupied the Germans. On September 1, while the Texas Division was approaching Lyon, the 179th Infantry of the Thunderbird Division had its hands full of enemy armor at its roadblock southwest of Meximieux on N84, the main Lyon-Geneva highway. The 11th Panzer Division came barreling along in the morning with tanks, assault guns, and infantry. It broke through the roadblock and fought the Thunderbirds for the town all afternoon. The Germans surrounded the defenders, forced the 179th to throw kitchen personnel and everybody else into the firing line, repeatedly plunged deep down the streets, but were unable to take Meximieux. The Ghost Division then slipped away in the night.

While this battle was going on, the 180th Infantry continued moving up the east bank of the Ain River north of Meximieux at the same time that Germans were marching along the opposite shore. The next day there was further sparring between the 45th Division and the 11th Panzers along the line of retreat, with the VI Corps claiming the destruction of fifteen tanks that Saturday. Earlier plans drawn up by the Seventh Army and approved by General Wilson at Allied Force Headquarters had called for a pause to regroup after the capture of Lyon and then a further advance on the line Autun-Dijon-Langres. During the night of September 2–3, however, Truscott dispatched a messenger to Patch's headquarters, citing the events of the past few days to urge that the enemy was in full retreat and no longer capable of more than scattered delaying actions, and seeking permission to press on without pause along the axis Lons-le Saunier-Belfort: to close the Belfort Gap. Truscott's new entrapment plan was to deny the Nineteenth Army the historic route between the High Vosges and the Jura to the Plain of Alsace, the Rhine, and Germany.

Patch and Wilson both agreed. They also ordered the French to support Truscott's "hot pursuit" with their II Corps advancing up the Saône River on the VI Corps's left while their I Corps guarded Truscott's right. Truscott pushed the vanguard of the 117th Cavalry Reconnaissance Squadron into Bourg-en-Bresse during Sunday, September 3, ahead of the 11th Panzer units that had fought the Meximieux battle. Some of the panzers rolled into Bourg during the night, to touch off a free-for-all with the American cavalry. The Germans wi th their heavier armament predictably prevailed, and Troop B of the 117th was almost wiped out; but the cavalry clawed the Germans enough that the panzers nevertheless pulled away to avoid further contact.

The next day, September 4, Truscott's advance was delayed only by road obstacles and blown bridges. These were troublesome enough, because they often forced detours into muddy, winding secondary roads, and any slowing of the pace reverberated over a long distance; virtually the entire VI Corps was trying to advance along a single main highway, Route N83 through and north from Bourg.

The Germans turned to try to hold open the Belfort Gate into their Fatherland by standing at the ancient Roman fortress center of Besançon. Nestled in a bend of the River Doubs, Besançon had been more recently fortified by Vauban, and again by the French after 1870 with the intention that its defenses should cover a French field army operating on the left flank of a German invasion. As the VI Corps approached the place on September 5, American intelligence estimated that some 3,000 enemy soldiers garrisoned Vauban's Citadelle, on a high hill in the neck of the loop of the Doubs, and the numerous thick-walled outlying redoubts on both banks of the river.

Truscott refused to halt the 45th Division, driving it on around Besançon up the Doubs toward Baume-les-Dames. But he felt compelled to deploy the 3rd Division to assail the fortified city. With tanks and tank destroyers as well as artillery pounding away at a stream of German vehicles that struggled doggedly through Besançon up the Belfort road—"I never saw such confusion in my life," said a tank destroyer commander of the effects⁹—the American infantry closed in from the north, west, and south. During September 6 and on through the following night they gradually took over the outlying fortresses, to stage a final bombardment and assault against the Citadelle on September 7. When American soldiers had crossed the moat and were scaling the walls, the garrison surrendered.

The same day, the 45th Division crossed to the north bank of the Doubs upstream at Baume-les-Dames and thereby precipitated a general scurrying northeastward on the part of all the Germans still downstream. The next day, September 8, Truscott prodded his corps with a reminder of the motives that had guided their incessant movement since they hit the beaches:

> The purpose of this operation is to destroy by killing or capturing the maximum number of enemy formations.
> Therefore the following should be observed:
> a. Make every effort to entrap enemy formations regardless of size. Long range fires, especially artillery, will merely warn and cause a change in direction.
> b. All units, but especially battalions and lower units, must be kept well in hand. Commanders of all ranks must avoid wide dispersion and consequent lack of control.
> c. Tanks must accompany leading infantry elements and tank destroyers must

accompany leading tanks. All must be supported by artillery emplaced well forward.

    d. Reconnaissance must be continuous and thorough—foot elements to a distance of five miles, motor elements to contact the enemy.

    e. Contact once gained must be maintained. The enemy must not be allowed to escape.

    f. Every attack must be pressed with the utmost vigor. Be vicious. Seek to kill and destroy.[10]

No American commander drove harder than Truscott, and none clung more steadfastly to the principle that destroying the enemy army was the goal. Perhaps if he had led more than three infantry divisions that were constantly outrunning their supplies, he might have succeeded in the complete destruction of the enemy in his front which had consistently eluded the American generals. But the German Nineteenth Army also moved fast—with the speed of desperation—and the detours and the Battle of Besançon held up the Americans just enough that as the adversaries closed in on the Belfort Gate, Truscott became dependent on the French on his right to impose a similar delay on the Germans. Admirably as they had won Toulon and Marseille, the French remained underequipped, without either the mobility or the power to match even a depleted panzer division.

On September 6, the French I Corps took St. Hippolyte along the slopes of the Jura, on the north-south road nearest the Swiss border, N437. The next day the corps vanguard pushed on toward Montbéliard and halted within little more than ten kilometers of Belfort. On September 8, however, tanks and infantry of the 11th Panzers lashed out in a counterblow and drove the French from their forward positions. The French I Corps did not have the strength to resume its advance once the panzer division was well anchored in its front.

Simultaneously the French II Corps, on Truscott's left, was pushing north from Lyon through Chalon-sur-Saône—captured on September 5—not only to help VI Corps against the Nineteenth Army, but also to attempt to cut off the escape route of some 100,000 bedraggled remnants and followers of the German First Army fleeing from southwestern France. Kampfgruppen of the 716th Division and of a newly created 30th SS Infantry Division contested the way. This particular SS division was hardly an elite formation, but rather a collection of Eastern European "volunteers" with only about 10 percent of its members German. On September 14, one of its battalions, mostly Ukrainians, killed their officers and joined the FFI. The II Corps captured prisoners in batches of hundreds all along its front. The 1ère Division Blindée liberated Dijon on September 10. But like the VI Corps farther east, the II Corps was advancing not quite fast enough to close its traps.

On September 12 and 13, the 1ère Division Blindée had to fight a stubborn battle to occupy Langres and its citadel. By that time, the 45th Division similarly was no longer charging forward in pursuit, but grappling against renewed enemy tenacity along a line from l'Isle-sur-Doubs to Villersexel. The 3rd Division in the VI Corps center and the 36th on the left enjoyed pursuit warfare a few days longer than their neighbors, but by the middle of the month their progress toward Lure and Luxeuil also slowed to be measured in meters instead of kilometers. Drizzling rain, quagmire battlegrounds, and poor visibility did not help; but the salient fact was that having reached the Belfort Gate ahead of the Allies, the German Nineteenth Army felt secure enough to pivot on the 11th Panzer Division and form a northwest-to-southeast defensive line along the broken, advantageous ground between the Doubs and the Moselle. Already the Germans had turned to contest the Third Army's passage of the Moselle with even greater tenacity just to the north. The ANVIL-DRAGOON campaign was about to merge into the main Western European battle just as that battle itself turned a new and, for the Allies, ominous corner.

Notwithstanding the disappointments at Montélimar and Belfort, the fathers of DRAGOON could be pleased with their child. In the first two weeks of the campaign, the Allies had captured 57,000 German prisoners with only 4,000 French and 2,700 American casualties. Almost equally favorable casualty rates followed DRAGOON all the way to the River Doubs. By September 28, when the DRAGOON invasion beaches were closed as ports of entry, 380,000 troops had landed across them. By the end of the war, 905,512 troops were to land at Marseille, Toulon, and Port de Bouc. Yet more important was the logistical support, much of which could have reached General Eisenhower's armies by no other route. When the French liberated Marseille and Toulon, German demolitions proved almost, if not quite, as complete as at Cherbourg. Nevertheless, three Liberty ships laden with port construction workers and equipment standing by at Marseille were unloaded at anchorage by dukws—two-and-one-half-ton amphibious trucks—immediately.

Clearing and rebuilding progressed so rapidly that Marseille was ready to receive its first Liberty ship for direct ship-to-shore discharge on September 15. Within ten more days, sixteen alongside berths and twenty-three offshore berths were operating. Toulon went into service on September 20. Port du Bouc with its canal to the Rhône meanwhile served especially well for carrying bulk gasoline and oil. By October, the southern French ports were handling 524,894 tons of a total of 1,309,184 tons of American supplies reaching Europe. In November, December, and January, the southern ports received 1,434,930 tons of a total discharge of 4,459,168 tons. By the end of that period, Marseille had seventy-two berths.

As the American Seventh Army approached a junction with the Third Army in mid-September, the pace of the Allied advance since the COBRA breakthrough was about to create a crisis in supply. Without the southern French ports, this crisis would have been insurmountable. Without the southern French ports, a tactical crisis yet to come would also have been far more desperate than it proved to be—and for a time this tactical crisis of December was to be bad enough.

ANVIL-DRAGOON contributed directly and mightily to bringing the bulk of the American army to grips with the German army in the West, to defeat and destroy it. If the ANVIL-DRAGOON strategy was wrong, and using many of its troops in the secondary Italian theater would have been better, then the whole American wartime strategy of gathering massive armies to overwhelm the enemy's main strength—the OVERLORD enterprise itself—should be judged questionable as well.

12: The Seine

WHEN A thousand hurtling events crowd themselves into a brief moment of time, the haste and turmoil of the hour seem to speed the passage of the minutes ever faster; but in retrospect the brief interval may come to seem long, because only a considerable span of time would appear able to contain so much activity. Thus it was that when General Patton paused after his daily staff conference on August 14 to offer a little speech about the accomplishments of the Third Army so far, it scarcely seemed possible that the achievements he was recalling were those of a mere two weeks—the entire time span since his army had been committed. In those two weeks, however, Patton could boast, "the Third Army has advanced further and faster than any Army in the history of the war."[1]

It was still advancing. With the headquarters and two divisions of General Haislip's XV Corps diverted on the day of Patton's backward historical glance to take up the long envelopment on the Seine in place of the short envelopment at Argentan, Patton was about to order Haislip to hasten Oliver's 5th Armored and Wyche's 79th Infantry Divisions across the Eure River at Dreux. General Walker's XX Corps, thus far operating for the most part with only Irwin's 5th Infantry Division in hand, had captured Angers on the Loire—coveted by "P" Wood of the 4th Armored in that seeming long-ago of the Third Army's infancy—and closed up to the le Mans-Mayenne line. Major General Lindsay McD. Silvester's 7th Armored Division had joined the 5th Infantry on Walker's front, and Patton's next orders to the XX Corps, delivered August 15, would direct it toward the Eure at the cathedral city of Chartres. Major General Gilbert R. Cook's XII Corps had practically completed the administrative task of receiving Third Army units as they arrived in France from England, and was sweeping the north bank of the Loire with a small part of its force to guard the army's long, exposed right flank; but Cook was ready to move with his main force, Baade's 35th Division and the vanguard of Wood's 4th Armored, against Orléans and Châteaudun. The Third Army was heading for the Seine.

Patton was "very happy and elated"[2] to be racing forward in pursuit again, for that is what the shift away from Argentan and Falaise permitted him to do. The stronger portions of the German First Army of General der Infanterie Kurt von der Chevallerie, up from the Bay of Biscay, were trying to organize a defense in front of Patton, and fresh enemy divisions were also coming down from the Pas de Calais. But for the time being at least, Patton's three corps rarely met more than discouraged fragments of German units and weak roadblocks. Haislip's XV Corps capped a ninety-kilometer advance from Argentan with the 5th Armored's capture of Dreux on the afternoon of August 16, while the 79th Division was displaying its Cross of Lorraine shoulder patches on the east bank of the Eure at Nogent-le-Roi only fifty kilometers from Paris. The 35th Division and

Bruce Clarke's CCA of the 4th Armored captured Orléans for the XII Corps the same day, and the next morning the 35th also secured Châteaudun. Major Hansen of Bradley's staff described a First Army outfit traveling near Patton's left flank, but his word picture could have applied to any of the American divisions hurtling forward:

> Fourth div rolling up the road [near Chartres], 8th Infantry and many of them, battlestained with dirt, huddling tightly in the vehicles against the cold rain, wear their unit citations and combat infantrymen badges over their dirty uniforms. Intently proud of them. Soon the sun came out and everyone felt better. Blankets were hung in the speeding trucks to dry as they sped along, infantrymen sprawled everywhere, hanging from the railboard, their feet out along the side, asleep on the decks of the weasels, piled all over the cats that pull the ninety's of the AA bns. One truck with GI pouring wine he had picked up from Fr. civilian where carnival spirit prevails all along the route. Another held up and flew as a flag a fancy embroidered slip with trappings which caused French to laugh uproariously.
>
> Another wore fancy brass fireman's helmet. Still another wore Beret French fashion with long cigaret holder and his fancy pose with rifle.[3]

Only at Chartres was there a semblance of determined resistance to Patton's men. There the green 7th Armored's assault on August 16 met such resilient old adversaries as the remains of the 352nd Infantry Division and the 17th ss Panzer Grenadier Division, as well as a conglomeration of newcomers such as the students of an antiaircraft training center. The Americans were handicapped, too, because their habitual reliance on artillery to blast their way through tough defenders had to yield to unwillingness to ruin the great cathedral. So Chartres held out until August 18 before falling to the combined efforts of the 7th Armored and 5th Infantry Divisions. The nervous new soldiers of the 7th Armored went on firing occasionally at the cathedral towers and threatening to damage them after all, out of fear of snipers, until some American correspondents climbed up and unfurled a tricolor as reassurance.

Meanwhile, on Wednesday, August 16, General Bradley annoyed Patton once more by instructing him to hold and go no farther at his latest prizes, Dreux, Chartres, and Orléans. A combination of factors motivated this latest vacillation: logistical problems brought on by the rapid advances of the past three weeks, with a gasoline shortage taking shape as an especially threatening cloud on the horizon; Bradley's belated renewal of interest on this date in the short envelopment at Argentan-Falaise, and the consequent restoration of first logistical priority to that effort; fear for Patton's left flank if the Third Army continued hurrying eastward while much of the First Army remained held up around Argentan; the persistent influence of the pre-D-Day OVERLORD plans, which called for a pause to consolidate on reaching the limits of the lodgment area between the Seine and the Loire, not a rapid thrust through the Paris-Orléans gap such as Patton was now on the verge of making.

Yet the attractions of keeping the enemy on the run—and the injunction of all military experience that it was the correct thing to do—beckoned Bradley as well as Patton. After a conference with General Hodges and the restless Patton, Bradley lifted his hold order on August 17 to the extent of allowing Haislip's XV Corps to roll on to the Seine at Mantes-Gassicourt, some forty kilometers in a straight line northwest of Paris. Walker's XX Corps was to relieve the XV at Dreux, and Cook's XII was to remain in place to conserve fuel. Bradley's decision of August 14 to revert to the long envelopment

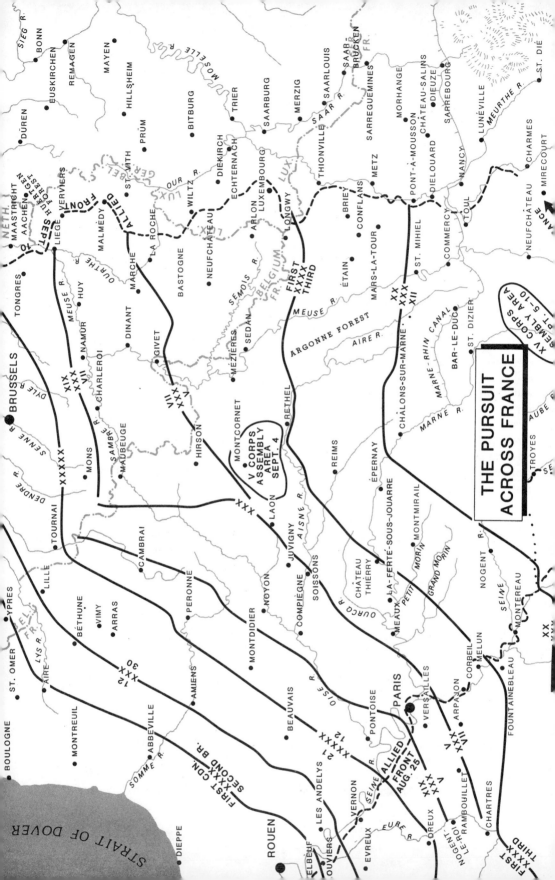

THE PURSUIT
ACROSS FRANCE

at the Seine, even if he had compromised that decision on the 16th, virtually impelled him to permit at least one corps to advance toward the rear of the remaining bulk of Army Group B, still west of the Seine and north of Mantes.

Haislip's 5th Armored and 79th Infantry Divisions rambled to Mantes-Gassicourt without trouble on August 18. The next day, General Eisenhower met with Bradley and Montgomery to review one of the issues that troubled Bradley, the OVERLORD plan and its specifications of a halt at the Seine to reorganize and build up supplies before advancing beyond the lodgment area. The gasoline shortage grew more troublesome by the day and presented a strong argument for maintaining the plan. The logistical problems were all the more troublesome because no consistent, orderly buildup of supplies and transportation facilities had yet been possible. Because of the prolonged deadlock in Normandy, on D plus 49 the Allies had still been where they were supposed to be on D plus 20, and to that point they had needed more ammunition and less transport and fuel than the planners foresaw. But now, on August 19, D plus 74, the race since the breakout had carried them to or near the extreme boundaries of the lodgment area, which the planners had expected to reach only by D plus 90. Still, the same considerations that had goaded Bradley to lift part of his August 16 hold order also drove the Supreme Commander and his other principal subordinates. Montgomery had anticipated for weeks the possibility of the long envelopment at the Seine. Haislip's capture of Mantes suggested a XV Corps left turn to drive down the river, pushing the Germans toward the wide and bridgeless lower reaches and the coast. Intelligence estimated that 75,000 enemy troops and 250 tanks remained west and south of the Seine to be caught in such a trap.

Once again, the envelopment design put the interallied boundary at issue. At Mantes, the XV Corps had already entered the 21 Army Group zone. To advance farther would carry Haislip squarely across the paths of the British Second and Canadian First Armies. Bradley offered Montgomery a loan of American trucks to carry British troops to Mantes to execute the envelopment. The British declined the offer with thanks lest administrative confusion be compounded. Anyway, the prospect of completing the long envelopment rendered Montgomery's mood expansive. He authorized the Americans to ignore the interallied boundary and to strike on down the west bank of the river. The senior Allied commanders also agreed that Haislip should exploit his capture of Mantes by establishing a beachhead on the right bank as well.

Both Patton and General Wyche of the 79th Division had already been wondering whether to seize an opportunity to cross the river. At 9:35 in the evening of August 19, Wyche received the order to go across that very night. Once his infantry was east of the Seine, he was to build a bridge for heavy vehicles and to advance the beachhead enough to protect the bridge from medium artillery fire—some six to nine kilometers. The Seine at Mantes is 150 to 250 meters wide. Fortunately, the Germans had only partially destroyed a dam, which could still serve as a footbridge. In darkness intensified by a downpour, the 313th Infantry Regiment crossed single-file on the dam, each man clutching the man in front of him. The next morning, the 314th Infantry followed in assault boats and rafts. By afternoon, the division engineers had a treadway bridge ready, and the 315th Infantry crossed in trucks. Tanks, tank destroyers, and artillery followed. The crossing of the Seine flushed out the Luftwaffe, but antiaircraft guns were ready around the bridge by the time the enemy planes appeared, and the guns claimed a dozen aircraft in the first day, fifty in the first four days.

The expansion of the beachhead quickly carried the 79th Division into Army Group B headquarters at the château of la Roche-Guyon, where in the shadow of the ancient Norman round tower Rommel had planned the defense of the Atlantic Wall. Model's staff had to scurry east to Soissons. Once more emboldened by continuing success, Bradley now authorized Patton to resume the advance of the XX and XII Corps, to pass through the Paris-Orléans gap to the Seine above Paris. From Dreux and Chartres, Walker's XX Corps was to move out on August 21 for Melun and Montereau. From Orléans, Cook's XII Corps was to push to Sens on the Yonne River, a tributary of the Seine, more than 100 kilometers east. Patton said he gave the corps commanders "one word, 'Proset,' which means 'halt in place,' to be used in case Bradley loses his nerve at the last moment."[4]

Meanwhile, on August 20 General Oliver's 5th Armored Division of Haislip's corps executed its left turn and headed down the Seine, aiming at Louviers, fifty kilometers from Mantes. A conference among Montgomery, Bradley, and Hodges produced a decision to order General Corlett's XIX Corps of the First Army, long since pinched out of the northern front, to hurry into line on Haislip's left to reinforce his blow. Both the XV and the XIX Corps were to push downstream toward Rouen. Between Mantes-Gassicourt and Rouen, the Seine averages about 150 meters in width, and the retreating Germans could improvise bridges to cross it with relative ease; but below Rouen, escape eastward would have to overcome the vagaries of a tidal stream 300 to almost 400 meters wide.

Manton Eddy had to move up from the 9th Division to take over the XII Corps from Cook, who was felled by a circulatory ailment. According to Patton's account, Eddy immediately asked him how much he needed to worry about his flanks as he moved east from Orléans. "I told him that depended on how nervous he was." And Patton added: "He has been thinking a mile a day good going. I told him to go fifty and he turned pale."[5]

To help him keep in touch with his farflung columns, Patton had transformed the 6th Cavalry Group into his Army Information Service—more familiarly, "Patton's Household Cavalry." The group encompassed a varying number of reconnaissance platoons formed into troops under two squadron commands, to bypass the usual channels of communication and range far and wide to keep the army commander in touch with scattered units and subordinates.

Since the activation of the Third Army, Patton also had his own tactical air command from the Ninth Air Force, Brigadier General Otto P. Weyland's XIX TAC, to help him with communications and intelligence as well as to provide air cover. In the manner of Pete Quesada, Weyland had his headquarters set up next to Patton's own, and Weyland's A-2s and A-3s kept themselves in constant touch with Patton's G-2s and G-3s, to pool information about where units were and where they were going.

For the best possible armed aerial reconnaissance and armored column cover in front of his rapidly moving troops, Patton recommended that bomb lines be abolished and the fighter-bombers be allowed to attack freely against any clearly recognizable targets of opportunity. The sort of accomplishment that could follow was demonstrated by the Thunderbolts of the 362nd Fighter Group on August 20, when ground reconnaissance troops of Walker's corps were already ranging to Rambouillet and the Seine in preparation for the corps's main advance next day. The 7th Armored Division reported a cluster of panzers ahead. The planes found six camouflaged tanks. Because Walker's troops were very near, the squadron leader came down low to fix the location of the target, then from a high altitude talked in his P-47s for attacks that wiped out the panzers.

"I have used one principle in these operations. . . ," Patton wrote to his son on August 21, "and this is to—

    'Fill the unforgiving minute

    'With sixty seconds worth of distance run.'

"That is the whole art of war, and when you get to be a general, remember it!"[6]

Patton and the Whole Art of War

It was the essential Patton who gave such advice, but the advice hardly encompassed the whole art of war. Nor did the Third Army's headlong advance since Avranches, aiming at fifty miles a day with strongpoints bypassed and no worrying about the flanks.

The 5th Armored Division had advanced only about thirteen kilometers downriver from Mantes on August 20 when it struck stubborn opposition. The delay was all the more infuriating because it was imposed by the kind of scratch force that it seemed should have been easy to brush aside: enemy tanks and infantry in a hodgepodge from almost every division in northern France. But the enemy's good selection of commanding sites, plus the rains that had made miserable the first crossing of the Seine on the broken dam the night before—and that now curbed air support—added just enough advantages to the exasperating stubbornness of the Kampfgruppe to enable it to stop Oliver's division cold.

On August 21, enough elements of the 1st ss Panzer Division arrived in the area to extend the intractable resistance from the Seine westward to the Eure. As the XIX Corps came up west of the Eure to assist the XV, it met no comparable opposition at first—only Germans intent on running to the Seine—and for several days Corlett's troops made good progress. But on August 24 around the southern outskirts of Elbeuf, some fifty kilometers north of where the 5th Armored was bogged down, the XIX Corps found the scrapings of some eight panzer divisions in front of it, and again a nondescript Kampfgruppe proved capable of baffling recalcitrance.

Corlett managed to capture Elbeuf next day with a coordinated attack by CCA of the 2nd Armored Division, now under Colonel John H. Collier, and part of the 28th Division. The latter, the Keystone Division of the Pennsylvania National Guard, had stumbled through almost all the muddles that could plague a new division when it fought earlier on the Vire front, but it had enjoyed an impressively swift rise to respectability since General Norman Cota, of conspicuous D-Day memory, took over on August 13. Still, the delay inflicted on the XIX Corps by scrapings from the bottom of the enemy's barrel was not encouraging, and the five-day struggle required before the 5th Armored finally ruptured the Kampfgruppe north of Mantes was worse.

For Patton's army to falter before the resistance of such limited and hastily assembled forces raised anew some of the questions about the aggressiveness of the American soldier that had been generated by the fighting in the Bocage. The affair also raised questions concerning Patton as a general. Of course, the ability of an impromptu Kampfgruppe—which proved to have been pieced together by an ss captain on the spot—to hold off the 5th Armored Division was in part merely a testimony to the inherent advantages of the defense, especially when benefiting from strong positions. Americans on the defense had similarly displayed and exploited those advantages on several occasions during the campaign, notably against Panzer Lehr's counterattack along the Vire on July 11, and in the 2/120th Infantry's defense of Hill 317 near Mortain. But there is also the troublesome fact that the Germans, on the receiving end of American attacks, consistently gave a low rating to American aggressiveness under fire.

Naturally, the Germans were prejudiced observers, and some of their prejudice is plain enough in the repetition of variations on one of Hitler's favorite themes: "America will never become the Rome of the future. Rome was a state of peasants." Because Americans were not peasants, they presumably lacked the solid, tough, uncomplaining staying power of the historic great armies of Europe. Generaloberst Alfred Jodl, head of the planning staff of OKW, the Wehrmachtführungsstab, was in a position to synthesize reports from the front; he conceded that American paratroops were "useful," but concluded that the rest of the Americans "surrender the moment the position is hopeless" and " never attack as long as a single gun is left firing from the German lines."[7]

In an effort to counter such German criticism, the Australian journalist Chester Wilmot argued that it was precisely because they were not peasants that American soldiers developed their most characteristic virtues. Hitler

> did not realize that America's strength lay in this very absence of the 'peasant mentality', with its narrow horizons, its acceptance of the established order, and its ignorance of machines. The basic German miscalculation was the failure to appreciate that America's military prowess was a logical consequence of her industrial power. The Germans learned by experience that this power had given the American forces boundless equipment, but they did not realise that it had also provided a vast reservoir of manpower skilled in the use of machines.[8]

Thus the Americans, masters of machines, and accustomed by their frontier heritage to vast distances, were able to roll across Europe at a speed that astonished the Germans and that no other mass army could match—as Patton had boasted when he reviewed the first two weeks of the Third Army's operations.

It is rare enough to find praise of Americans in Wilmot's history of the war in Europe; his compliments in this instance remain somewhat lefthanded. They deal with the Americans' pace of advance once COBRA broke the front open. They do not meet the issue of "never attack[ing] so long as a single gun is left firing in the German lines." Instead, they imply not only strengths, but also the very weaknesses that led American infantry to rely on their artillery and airplanes to smother the enemy's resistance.

They imply, too, the questions that can be raised about Patton's generalship. The speed of the Third Army's advances—650 kilometers by August 26, liberating about 77,000 square kilometers of French soil—was based on the Americans' machinery and their mechanical aptitudes and love of movement. It was also based on Patton's injunctions, "Don't stop"—on bypassing resistance, going around trouble and leaving it behind. The speed of the Third Army's advance was accomplished in large part through the avoidance of fighting. The army inflicted a respectable number of casualties on the enemy in its first month of operations, but not an especially high number in proportion to the distances advanced and the extent of territory overrun: 16,000 killed, 55,000 wounded, 65,000 captured. When the Third Army could not bypass opposition, its record was not nearly so impressive as its performance traveling on the open road.

Patton's biographer Ladislas Farago, in commenting on these aspects of the campaign, suggests that Patton's preference for bypassing centers of resistance stemmed from an admirable capacity to face hard facts: "To a considerable degree," says Farago, "it was caused by his realization that the American infantryman fighting under him at this stage was not yet quite as proficient in war as this do-or-die confrontation with the Germans required."[9] In short, the Germans' skeptical appraisals of the American soldier were not without substance.

Farago makes other points as well. When Patton had applied his preference for bypassing resistance during maneuvers in 1941, General McNair had been critical to the point of exclaiming: "This is no way to fight a war." The reason for McNair's displeasure was that he saw Patton's methods of generalship as occupying ground but not destroying enemy forces. And indeed when Patton passed from maneuvers to war, Farago concedes of his rapid marches that

> while he did penetrate to the enemy's rear in these lightning raids, he usually confined his piecemeal operations to skirmishes with stragglers, instead of interfering strategically with the enemy's communications zone. While he did succeed in places and in parts in preventing the enemy from forming a front, he did not destroy enough of his units to make more than a dent in his strength.[10]

Sir Basil Liddell Hart admired Patton's generalship—though he criticized all the generals responsible for the right turn from Avranches into Brittany—because Patton's readiness "to exploit in any direction" and keen sense "of the key importance of persistent pace in pursuit" carried him as close as any Allied commander in the Second World War to realizing Liddell Hart's strategy of the indirect approach to the enemy's strategic rear.[11] Unfortunately, as Farago indicates, Patton's realization and application of the potential of the indirect approach were not complete. He did not ruinously disrupt the enemy's communications zone. His traps failed too often to close on the enemy's main forces. Principally, he occupied ground rather than destroying armies.

Or the criticism of Patton's generalship might take another turn. Many American strategists doubted the merits of Liddell Hart's indirect approach. Captain Reuben Jenkins's *Military Review* comments on the 1939 FM 100-5 had come closer to the heart of American strategic thought with the observation: "the price of victory is hard fighting and . . . no matter what maneuver is employed, ultimately the fighting is frontal." McNair notwithstanding, the public and his peers widely regarded Patton as the epitome of the aggressiveness of the American army. Yet Patton's aggressiveness was not that of Jenkins's maxim either. Patton's was an aggressiveness of speed and mobility, not of the application of overwhelming power to crush the enemy. The most aggressive senior American commander remained a soldier of saber and spurs.

The Long Envelopment

Once the XV and XIX Corps broke through the Kampfgruppen below Mantes and around Elbeuf, they drove all the way across the British Second Army front and into the zone of the First Canadian Army. Their advance unhinged the enemy's brief hope of defending at least an interim line along the Touques River short of the Seine.

While the German First Army tried to contain Patton on the upper Seine, Field Marshal Model had consolidated the Fifth Panzer and Seventh Armies under Fifth Panzer Army headquarters—perhaps because General Hausser of the Seventh Army was wounded during the flight from the Falaise pocket—and given Sepp Dietrich the task of guarding the Touques or at least the Seine from the latitude of the northern outskirts of Paris to the sea. The relatively intact right-flank units of the Fifth Panzer Army still treated the Canadians to a hard fight when General Crerar's army began attacking eastward across the Dives River near the coast on August 16. The Canadian army did not reach and cross the Touques until August 22. Yet by now the Germans were fighting only to prevent their latest retreat from deteriorating into a rout, and to escape across the Seine before Haislip and Corlett broke through the ragged forces composing the Fifth Panzer Army's southern flank.

Still, the jaws of the long envelopment, like those of the short envelopment before it, failed to close until the bulk of the enemy's personnel, if not his equipment, got away. The Canadians made contact with the XIX Corps around Elbeuf on August 26, and General Dempsey's Second Army promptly met Corlett's troops as well along the Risle River. While the XV and XIX Corps withdrew southward into the American zone, the British and Canadians closed up to the Seine from Vernon to the coast during the last week of the month. The mere administration of the American withdrawal was a delicate but well organized task, for the Americans and their Allies frequently had to pass through the same crossroads alternately, the Americans going south, the British east. Aided by the persistent return of the rains that had plagued Allied air power in July, the Germans meanwhile fled over the Seine by every available means—sixty ferries between Elbeuf and the sea, several pontoon bridges, rafts improvised from cider barrels or from tree limbs lashed together by telephone wires, eventually by swimming. In the first days of the mass crossing, between August 20 and 24, they moved 25,000 vehicles to the east bank. Once again, as at Falaise, almost all German higher headquarters escaped. The final major crossings took place during August 26 and 27, with some of the ferries still functioning even by daylight, and as the Germans saw it, the British and Canadians not pressing very hard.

Americans might, of course, have been waiting on the east bank, if the 79th Division's crossing at Mantes had been exploited to send the main enveloping column down that side of the river instead of the west bank. The Germans believed they were so weak on the right bank that this maneuver might well have assured the entrapment of the remains of Army Group B, in a worse debacle than the Falaise pocket. A wide and probably irreparable gap would then have opened between those parts of the Fifteenth Army in the Pas de Calais that had not yet been committed to battle and the First Army trying to organize the defense of the upper Seine. But this idea of a right-bank envelopment seems never to have been much developed by the Allied commanders. It was easier to dispatch the XIX Corps to the support of the XV west of the Seine, and the river did not endanger the communications of a pincer moving west of it. Yet the Germans were in no condition to put American communications across the Seine into much jeopardy, especially if an entire American corps had operated on the east bank. Once again, American conduct of the campaign did not altogether accord with the emphasis of American strategic thought on the destruction of the enemy army as the first strategic object. The Germans, the former masters of the Kesselschlacht, the battle of envelopment, were finding this operational method a menace in their enemies' hands, but not quite the deadly weapon it had been under the guidance of their own Helmuth von Moltke.

Nevertheless, the German escape across the Seine was disappointing enough to put Allied commanders in a churlish mood. The usually amiable General Dempsey gave the London *Daily Telegraph and Morning Post* an interview, printed on September 5, in which he complained of the Americans' getting in his way and delaying his advance from Falaise to the Seine. Bradley angrily took up the matter with Eisenhower: "I consider General Dempsey's statement to be a direct criticism of American forces and very unfair."

> When the British Second Army started its advance east after cleaning up Argentan [said Bradley], it naturally advanced very rapidly, as all enemy forces had been forced north. Dempsey and Hodges worked out a very orderly arrangement of passing the British troops through to the Seine and the withdrawal of American forces to the south. The movement of the British forces was made through territory already taken by American forces and without opposition. If we had not carried out this operation, they would have had to fight all the way to the Seine, and it would, in my opinion, have taken much longer than any delay of which Dempsey speaks.[12]

So British-American relations had slipped still another step downhill; but Bradley's irritation would no doubt have been worse had he been more interested in completing the envelopment. Major Hansen's account places the focus of Bradley's interests elsewhere at the time. Hansen has Bradley looking not toward the long envelopment but straight east into Germany: "79th Div has crossed the Seine at Mantes-Gassicourt. Monty directive has ordered a turn north to further bottle off the German effort and Bradley accedes although he is more particularly desirous of driving eastward into Germany and taking a force into that country for the tremendous psychological effect it would have on the people."[13]

"This may be the turning point," Hansen again reported Bradley's thoughts a few days later, "and if we do not quickly follow up our advantage to slam through into Germany and end the war on his ground, we may be forced into a longer fight in the lowlands where the terrain is better suited for defense and where he will have time to make a stand and prepare a line."[14]

Every disagreement with the British seemed to draw Bradley and Patton closer together. Patton also saw the greatest opportunities beckoning not toward an envelopment on the Seine but eastward. On August 24, the XV Corps passed out of the Third and into the First Army anyway. Even earlier, on August 21, Patton recorded in his diary the racing of his plans far beyond the Seine: "We have, at this time, the greatest chance to win the war ever presented. If they let me move on with three corps, two up and one back, on the line of Metz-Nancy-Epinal, we can be in Germany in ten days."[15]

General McNair had been right to worry in 1941 about the consistency of Patton's dedication to destroying the enemy army as the first object of war.

To Troyes, Fontainebleau, and Montereau

On the day of the diary entry, Patton's XII and XX Corps set off through the Paris-Orléans gap to cross the upper Seine. The advance immediately added substance to Bradley's and Patton's hopes that they could score a quick entrance into Germany. Belying Patton's first fears that as a corps commander he might prove too timid about his flanks and not speed along at a Third Army pace, General Eddy leaped the XII Corps 110 kilometers from Orléans to Sens on the Yonne River in a single day. At Sens, Eddy's vanguard captured a party of German officers who were visiting the twelfth-century cathedral of St. Étienne as tourists; the officers had thought that even a weakly-held front was too far away for Sens to be in any danger.

That other officer who rivaled Patton in intense appetite for the swift advance, Wood of the 4th Armored, spearheaded the XII Corps drive. At Montargis on the Loing River, Wood had met fairly strong opposition; but in the customary Third Army fashion he sent his CCA on a bypassing route, leaving the town to be dealt with by CCB and General Baade's 35th Infantry Division. By August 22, Colonel Bruce Clark's CCA was through Sens and across the Yonne. After a short pause to assure communications through Montargis, which fell on August 24, CCA advanced another sixty-five kilometers from the Yonne to attack Troyes on the upper Seine on August 25.

Troyes was defended. Clark's tanks charged the defenses frontally, in spread formation with about 100 meters between Shermans, guns blazing continuously, across five kilometers of open ground in front of the city, as though the Champagne pouilleuse were the Western Desert and they were the Desert Rats invoking the old tactics of North Africa again. The armor rumbled into the city, but it required street fighting through the night and the next day, as well as a turning movement into the German rear, to complete the capture of the marriage place of King Henry V of England and Catherine of France. By that time, some of Wood's troops had crossed on the evening of August 25 to give the Third Army another bridgehead over the Seine.

Against somewhat more numerous clusters of opposition from the enemy's First Army, conditioned partly by proximity to Paris, Walker's XX Corps on Eddy's left advanced only slightly less rapidly, and by August 25 gained three Seine bridgeheads. On Walker's left flank, armored infantry of the 7th Armored Division's CCA crossed the river in boats and carved out a small bridgehead at Tilly near Melun, some forty kilometers above Paris, on the evening of August 23. Melun itself lies mainly on the east bank, where dominating high ground can aid a defender. CCR drew the job of attacking Melun but failed to satisfy the corps commander with the vigor of its charge, so Walker took a personal hand in the fighting. His intervention could be dramatic, for he was both fat enough and pugnacious enough to alarm the observer on both counts—Patton once remarked that Walker would go far if he didn't blow up first. On this occasion, however, his belligerent taking-over served chiefly the seriocomic purpose of inadvertently liberating the inmates of a prison on an island in the middle of the Seine. Despite the contretemps, Walker was able to count Melun as secure early on August 25.

Walker's other division, General Irwin's 5th Infantry, had advanced some sixty-five kilometers from Chartres across the Essonne River toward Fontainebleau and Montereau on August 21. Leaving the 2nd Infantry Regiment behind to deal with a bypassed garrison at Étampes, Irwin had his 11th Infantry in Fontainebleau, some ninety-five kilometers beyond Chartres, by noon of August 23, Lieutenant Colonel Kelley B. Lemmon, Jr., thereupon swam the Seine, found five small boats on the other side, tied them together, paddled them back, and with them ferried the beginnings of a bridgehead force to the east bank. The next day Irwin's remaining regiment, the 10th Infantry, captured Montereau, some 110 kilometers from Chartres, and planted yet another bridgehead there.

Paris

Eisenhower and Bradley alike would have preferred to wait a little for Paris. The OVERLORD planners had intended that it be bypassed and encircled, because they expected the Germans to fight hard for the French capital, and they did not relish either the military and civilian casualties or the damage to the city and its monuments implicit in a prolonged bout of street fighting. Such dangers aside, the American command was in no hurry to take on responsibility for feeding and otherwise supplying Paris. Allied bombing and the diligence of the French Resistance had almost isolated the city. Its people were on the verge of famine in electricity, gas, and coal as well as food. SHAEF calculated that it would take over 4,000 tons of supplies a day to sustain the city. Converted into gasoline for the armies, this tonnage would represent a three days' march toward Germany. If delaying Allied relief to the Parisians posed an ethical and humanitarian problem, the SHAEF planners were able to argue the problem away on the ground that hastening the end of the war would ensure more rapid complete relief from war's incidental horrors, and thus be more humane in the long run. In any event, the Anglo-Americans also wanted to steer clear as long as they could of the political entanglements of restoring French authority in Paris.

All these motives for procrastination collapsed when events in Paris took on a momentum of their own. As American armies approached their gates, the Parisians understandably grew impatient for liberation. Beginning about August 15, strikes began to paralyze the city's services. By August 18, the police had practically disappeared from the streets, armed members of the FFI ambled to and fro in open defiance of the German occupation, and posters called for a general strike. The next day, some 3,000 armed gendarmes took over the Préfecture of Police, and during the following night the uprising spread out to occupy the Hôtel de Ville, the Palais de Justice, and a number of other government buildings.

Many leaders of the Paris Resistance nevertheless feared the reprisals that the guns of the German army might yet visit upon the populace. Such leaders were happy to accept the good offices of the Swedish consul general, Raoul Nordling, when he volunteered to negotiate a truce with the Paris fortress commander, General von Choltitz, late of the LXXXIV Corps in Normandy. Choltitz, who was nominally under the First Army, had about 5,000 troops, fifty light and medium guns, and sixty airplanes. The bulk of the German troops around Paris were in the environs to face the oncoming Americans. Because Choltitz was as uncertain as the Resistance leaders that he could either prevent chaos from exploding or emerge victorious if it did—his garrison obviously enjoyed no excess of strength or guns, and its morale was hardly high—and because Choltitz saw his principal responsibility as the maintenance of order for a safe German withdrawal through the city, a truce proved possible. But the terms were vague. Each side distrusted both its own strength and its rival's enough to agree to an armistice, at first for a few hours, later extended indefinitely. Choltitz promised to treat members of the Resistance as soldiers and to regard certain—undefined—parts of the city as Resistance territory. The French said they would allow German troops unhindered passage through other parts of the city.

For nobody to trust anybody else was an attitude perhaps typically Parisian. It was also an attitude well founded. Neither side could prevent sporadic outbursts of shooting. Both sides still feared a sudden plunge into anarchy. The French leaders sent representatives, official and otherwise, to General Eisenhower, to try to persuade him to hasten his occupation of the city. On August 21, the Supreme Commander received similar representations of de Gaulle himself, delivered in person. The timing was unfortunate, because the Allied armies were still involved in closing off the Falaise pocket. But the determination of the French to rescue Paris from some unpredictable catastrophe was underlined when de Gaulle followed up his visit by dispatching Général d'Armée Alphonse Juin later the same day with a letter to Eisenhower, politely threatening to send French troops to Paris without reference to SHAEF. Moreover, the commander of the French troops in question, General Leclerc of the 2ème Blindée, not only talked but acted. Aptly described by Patton to Wood of the 4th Armored as "a bigger pain in the butt than you are,"[16] the independent-minded Leclerc that evening sent about 250 men in ten light tanks, ten armored cars, and ten personnel carriers as his advance party from Argentan toward the city.

Fortunately for the prevention of chaos in the Allied command structure as well as in Paris, Eisenhower was already in the course of changing his mind. The next day the change was completed by two impressions conveyed to him by representatives of the French Resistance: that the truce was about to end at noon, with much bloodshed as the likely sequel unless Allied soldiers entered Paris quickly; and that Choltitz was willing to yield without a fight if confronted with strong, regular Allied force. Neither impression was precisely accurate; but Eisenhower sent Bradley flying to Hodges's First Army headquarters to instruct Gerow to turn the V Corps toward Paris. At the airstrip serving Hodges, Bradley encountered Leclerc, whom he ordered to Paris forthwith. After all, it was with exactly this mission in mind that the 2ème Blindée had been detached from the French Mediterranean forces and joined with Eisenhower's armies.

Leading the V Corps advance, Leclerc's division made unexpectedly slow progress. Germans still hanging on around the city's perimeter put up occasional fights, the excited officers of the division provided less than first-rate leadership, and crowds of jubilant citizens jammed traffic in every town and hamlet. It was evening of August 23 before Leclerc's main force was as close to Paris as Rambouillet.

Gerow had sent General Barton's reliable 4th Infantry Division to function as a reserve for Leclerc and to seize crossings of the Seine just south of Paris. By August 24, Barton discovered that enemy resistance beyond Rambouillet had prompted Leclerc to swing part of the 2ème Blindée south of Paris and across Barton's lines of advance. Meanwhile tension in and around the city was growing apace, for Hitler had ordered Choltitz to prepare to demolish all the Paris bridges and not to abandon the city "except as a field of ruins,"[17] and some idea of the Führer's intentions was reaching French leaders and neutrals in the city, all of whom with any access to Choltitz were urging him to do otherwise. Exasperated, Gerow requested permission to send Barton straight into Paris, and Bradley decided: "To hell with prestige, tell the 4th to slam on in and take the liberation."[18]

The 4th had reached Arpajon. Barton chose the 12th Infantry Regiment, torn by more than a thousand casualties when it was attached to the 30th Division around Mortain, to bear the honor of breaking into Paris on the morning of August 25. Starting to move from Athis-Mons toward Villeneuve-le-Roi, the 12th was diverted from this approach to the Seine by German gunfire from the right bank. The Americans turned to enter the city through the Porte d'Italie and passed through the Place d'Italie and thence down the Avenue des Gobelins and the Rue Monge toward the Île de la Cité. The 102nd Cavalry Group screened the way. By noon, the white-starred vehicles of the United States lined up before the Cathedral of Notre-Dame.

But poetic justice also prevailed. During the night of August 24–25, Leclerc attempted one last stab to beat the Americans into the city, and he succeeded. He could not make contact with his most advanced combat command, Colonel Paul Girot de Langlade's, which had tanks across the Seine at the Pont de Sèvres. Colonel Pierre Billotte's combat command, with which Leclerc was in touch, was still eight kilometers from the nearest entrance into Paris at the Porte d'Orléans. Nevertheless, Leclerc ordered Billotte to infiltrate into the city with a small detachment of tanks and half-tracks under cover of darkness. The detachment took side roads and back streets, entered Paris through the Porte de Gentilly, crossed the Seine by the Pont d'Austerlitz, and was in front of the Hôtel de Ville before midnight of August 24.

Choltitz felt he no longer had the strength to fulfill Hitler's order to destroy the city, nor did he wish to do so; he afterwards cited both explanations for his conduct. The French dash into Paris during the late hours of August 24 was the last straw, and during the night Choltitz ordered a withdrawal behind the Seine. Thereupon the German defense of Paris caved in. While the Americans enjoyed their triumphal advance to Notre-Dame, impeded in the last stages only by celebrating Parisians, the French column hitherto stalled at Sèvres rolled to the Arc de Triomphe and thence to meet Combat Command Billotte at the Rond Point des Champs-Elysées.

Scattered parties of Germans were still shooting, and about 2,000 held out in the Bois de Boulogne. It could be hoped that Choltitz's formal surrender might put a stop to hostile activities, and a little after noon on August 25 French tanks surrounded his headquarters at the Hôtel Maurice on the Rue de Rivoli. French soldiers made him a prisoner and carried him off to Leclerc at the Préfecture of Police. There Choltitz signed an act of capitulation, which Leclerc and the commander of the Paris FFI accepted, not as representatives of the Allied command in Europe, but in the name of the Provisional Government of France.

By that time Leclerc's commanding officer, General Gerow, was also in Paris, establishing his headquarters in the Gare Montparnasse. Gerow's exasperation with the French was only beginning, for their indifferent neglect of the senior Allied officer present in the city when they took the surrender was merely the signal that they intended to pay no particular attention to the American commander when he attempted to restore and assure order more generally.

In such circumstances, the Americans might be pardoned for finding perverse pleasure in the discovery of the persistent incompleteness of Choltitz's authority even when he surrendered. The Germans in the Bois de Boulogne, for example, had to be rooted out after the surrender. Furthermore, American skepticism about whether de Gaulle's acceptance by the Parisians was as complete as he let on proved not altogether unfounded. De Gaulle and his minions professed that the Americans had nothing to do with the liberation of Paris, but that did not prevent de Gaulle from reminding Eisenhower continually of the gravity of the city's supply situation and its need for Anglo-American assistance—Paris became as much a drain on Allied logistics as anticipated—or from requesting that two American divisions make a show of force in his behalf in the city.

Besides allowing de Gaulle to retain the 2ème Blindée until order was assured, Eisenhower complied with the French leader's wishes to the extent of marching General Cota's 28th Division down the Champs-Elysées on August 29. The occasion served among other purposes to remind the Parisians that the American army, after all, had something to do with their liberation. De Gaulle, Leclerc, Bradley, and Gerow took the Keystone Division's salute from an improvised reviewing stand, an upside-down Bailey bridge. General Montgomery wisely and discreetly turned down the Supreme Commander's invitation to share in the spectacle, thus remaining aloof from the vexed question of Allied versus French authority in Paris. General Gerow could rejoice that he was about to escape this question as well, for yet another purpose of the march was to pass the 28th Division rapidly through the city to join the V Corps's renewal of the offensive beyond the Seine.

13: The Meuse

THE ALLIES had neglected the opportunity to translate the long envelopment into the more deadly design of sending its American pincer down the east rather than the west bank of the Seine. Nevertheless, Generals Eisenhower, Montgomery, and Bradley were hardly so cautious as to cling to the OVERLORD plan for a pause at the Seine when the Germans were fleeing across the river in disarray. At their conference of August 19, the three Allied generals decided to cross the river on the run. It was a decision that Montgomery had foreseen as early as June as implicit in the strategy of forcing a breakthrough and breakout from Normandy, and his LUCKY STRIKE plan had summarized the reasoning:

> The original concept of the forcing of the line of the Seine . . . was that a deliberate advance to the Seine, opposed by strong co-ordinated opposition, would be followed by about a three weeks interval prior to the crossing for the necessary dumping of bridging stores, ammunition, petrol etc. It was expected that the crossing would be strongly opposed from well-prepared defences. Under LUCKY STRIKE conditions [which COBRA proved to create] neither the opposition to the advance to the Seine nor the crossing of it are likely to be against a strong scale of opposition, although it is possible that some enemy forces will have moved south from the coast defences of the Pas de Calais to defend the river line. It will obviously be most undesirable to give the enemy a chance to catch his breath and prepare his defence by pausing for three weeks south of the Seine. Every endeavour will therefore have to be made to force the crossing without pause. . . .
>
> If our operation to this point has been successful, the enemy should be so disorganised as to permit additional pursuit [beyond the Seine] within maintenance limitations.

Thus the Anglo-American armies should "force a crossing with the least possible delay" and press on eastward as far as maintenance limitations—the iron bonds of logistics—might permit.[1]

Thus also, the Allied commanders must now decide without pause on the shape of their campaign beyond the River Seine. In their directive to the Supreme Commander, the Combined Chiefs of Staff had prescribed the object of his campaign beyond the Channel beaches as an offensive "aimed at the heart of Germany and the destruction of her armed forces."[2] They had not suggested to Eisenhower a specific route into the heart of Germany. Taking up this more specific issue, the OVERLORD planners had recognized Berlin as what might well be meant by "the heart of Germany," but they had concluded that the enemy capital was too far east to be a realistic goal. Instead, they designated as the proper first major target inside the Reich the Ruhr industrial region, an area of vital economic importance an attack on which would compel the enemy to commit his remaining armed forces so that the Allies might bring them to battle and destroy them. To reach the Ruhr, the OVERLORD planners had proposed two routes, a primary route and a secondary one.

The first route was the most direct path from the lower Seine, through Amiens, Maubeuge, and Liège to the Ruhr. The proposed secondary route was that from the upper Seine through Metz and the Saar Basin to Frankfurt-am-Main. Like the more direct, northerly route to the Ruhr, this was one of the historic avenues of invasion between France and Germany, for the road through Verdun and Metz is the shortest route between Paris and the Reich. But the secondary route had been chosen mainly during eras when marching through the Low Countries was politically unacceptable, and also before the Industrial Revolution enhanced the relative importance of North Germany as compared with the South. The reasons for its relegation to secondary status were apparent, and of course had shaped the famous Schlieffen Plan as well as Allied planning in 1944.

Along the planners' secondary route lay more difficult terrain than on the Schlieffen route. First, there were the military barriers raised by the escarpments of the Lorraine plateau. Furthermore, to reach the Ruhr by the southern route, it would be necessary to make a left turn at Frankfurt and proceed through a difficult passage down the Rhine, much constricted by the Mittelgebirge thrusting up east of that river. The OVERLORD planners had contemplated using the secondary as well as the primary route in spite of these considerations mainly to force the Germans to meet multiple pressures and thus the better to ensure that their front would have to break somewhere.

It was when the questions of routes beyond the Seine became an immediate one that it began to become entangled in the Anglo-American jealousy that surfaced almost simultaneously, among numerous other symptoms, in the dispute between Bradley and Dempsey over whether the American First Army slowed the British Second on its way to the Seine. The British as well as the American planners had agreed that both the primary and the secondary routes should be followed eastward. Only on August 15, apparently, did General Montgomery move toward a different view, which was to exacerbate international jealousies and also to offer a perennial topic for debate among soldiers and historians. In the following few days, Montgomery began to propose that virtually all the Allied divisions be concentrated for a single thrust into Germany along the northerly route through the Low Countries.

On August 23, Montgomery advanced this proposal in two conferences. Flying to 12th Army Group tactical headquarters at Laval, he discussed plans with Bradley. Then, later in the day, he conferred directly with Eisenhower, who drove to 21 Army Group tactical headquarters at Condé-sur-Noireau. Montgomery had been upset to learn from Bradley on August 20 that, while scrapping the OVERLORD plan for a pause at the Seine, Eisenhower still clung to the planners' design to use the two routes into Germany. It was Bradley's impression, in fact, that Eisenhower "favors the Brad[ley] plan of driving eastward to Germany rather than diverting too much strength up over the northern route to the Lowlands and into Germany from that direction."[3] Montgomery's new object was to change such thoughts and to shift all effort to the north and to his own 21 Army Group, suitably reinforced by the bulk of Anglo-American strength.

On August 23, however, advocacy of a single Allied thrust by the northerly route suffered the handicap that Montgomery's 21 Army Group had only begun its crossing of the Seine, through a small Second Army bridgehead at Vernon. None of Montgomery's armored divisions had reached the river, and it would be nearly the end of the month before the British and Canadian armies could close up to the Seine enough to stage their major crossings. By August 23, Patton's Third Army was already far to the east on the upper Seine. General Eddy's XII Corps spearhead in fact was more than 150 kilometers beyond the longitude of Vernon. Patton was belaboring Bradley for permission, a few more divisions, and the fuel and other supplies he needed to grasp his "greatest chance to win the war ever presented." As Patton saw it, the difficulties of the terrain in front of him mattered little compared to his position far closer to Germany than any other of the Allied armies, with no apparent organized opposition in front of him. If only he could keep on moving, he saw no reason why he should not crash straight through the West Wall fortifications on the German frontier before the enemy could get troops into the pillboxes.

But everything depended on speed, on keeping the Germans on the run and giving them no chance to regroup. "No one realizes the terrible value of the 'unforgiving minute' except me," Patton complained to his diary.[4] No one else had yet moved so rapidly, either. The realities of the armies' positions on August 23 and of Patton's performance since the beginning of the month made his and Bradley's arguments to turn the secondary offensive into the major thrust exceedingly cogent. At least the Germans thought, and feared, so.

The Miracle of the West

On the day following the liberation of Paris, a SHAEF G-2 summary stated: "Two and a half months of bitter fighting . . . have brought the end of the war in Europe within sight, almost within reach. The strength of the German Armies in the West has been shattered. Paris belongs to France again, and the Allied armies are streaming towards the frontiers of the Reich."[5] The description of the condition of the German armies was substantially accurate even though neither the short nor the long envelopment had achieved all that might have been hoped for, and the condition of the enemy's armies in turn gave warrant for the hope of a quick end to the war.

Since D-Day, the fighting in the West had cost the German army nearly 300,000 dead, wounded, and missing. An additional force of over 230,000, including 85,000 troops of the Feldheer, the Field Army, had to be written off, as far as the main battle for the Reich was concerned, because they had gone into the fortress cities along the French coast. The Germans had committed some 2,300 tanks and assault guns to the struggle against the Western Allies. General der Infanterie Günther Blumentritt, the OB West chief of staff, estimated that only 100 to 120 had returned to the east bank of the Seine. On August 29, Field Marshal Model told Hitler that the eleven panzer and panzer grenadier divisions that had retreated across the Seine averaged five to ten tanks each. These eleven divisions might be reconstituted into eleven regimental-strength Kampfgruppen—if they received prompt replacements of men and equipment. The sixteen infantry divisions brought back across the Seine might be reconstituted into four divisions—if they received heavy weapons, since almost nothing but small arms remained to them.

Hitler expected Model to form a new line along the Somme and the Marne, some 110 kilometers east of the Seine. Model was trying. He had General der Flieger Karl

Kitzinger, military governor of France, hard at work using Organization Todt construction forces and impressed civilians to build this "Kitzinger Line." But Model, who did not mince words however loyal to Nazism he might be, had already told OKW that to hold at the Somme and the Marne he would need thirty to thirty-five divisions, plus twelve panzer divisions as a mobile reserve, plus another fifteen divisions to defend a left flank extending from Troyes through Dijon to the Jura. With such reinforcements, he might restore approximate parity with the fifty Allied divisions he estimated he would be facing by the beginning of September. In the manner of generals everywhere, he credited the Allies with somewhat more strength than they actually mustered, but not by much.

Model's reinforcements were hard to come by. While suffering 300,000 casualties in the West, the Germans had also endured over 900,000 losses against the Russians in June, July, and August. Against the Soviets, they believed they had to maintain armies of more than two million men. Of the 3,421,000 troops on the rosters of the Feldheer at the beginning of September, 2,046,000 belonged to the East Army. At that, the Germans had lost the Ploesti oil fields, their major reserve of natural petroleum, to the Russians at the end of August.

Nevertheless, Hitler was trying with all the desperate energy he could generate under pressure to meet Model's needs. Thanks to the extent to which Germany could still count on impressed foreign labor to man its industries, he was enjoying enough success in stamping divisions out of the ground to confirm Patton's fears about the unforgiving minute. In late July, the Führer ordered the formation of eighteen new divisions, and by September 1 two of them had already been sent to the West. Also in July, Hitler ordered that some 100 fortress infantry battalions, being used in rear areas, be transformed into replacement battalions for the front. About four-fifths of these were destined for the West, and they were to begin going into action in mid-September. In the middle of August, Hitler directed the creation of twenty-five new reserve divisions, to be called Volksgrenadier divisions, the foundation of a People's Army eventually to replace the old army of the July 20 plotters that had failed and betrayed him. The eighteen divisions called for in July were also now to receive the honorific title of Volksgrenadier. To assure appropriate dedication and zeal, the Volksgrenadier divisions would receive their indoctrination and training from Reichsführer Heinrich Himmler and the SS.

Ten new panzer brigades numbered 101st through 110th were also in process of formation, concocted in large part out of fragments of armored forces battered but experienced on the Eastern Front, and some were ready to go into action by the beginning of September. As early as June 26, Hitler had ordered that because of tank losses to the numerous American Shermans in Normandy, German tank production must seek more than ever to match Allied quantity with quality, and for every Pzkw IV built by German industry, one Pzkw V Panther henceforth must also roll out of the factories. During July and August, accordingly, the Germans stepped up their building not only of Panthers but also of Tigers; 373 Panthers delivered in July, 358 in August; 140 Tigers in July, 97 in August (as well as 282 Pzkw IVs in July and 279 in August). In early August, Hitler ordered that the West receive priority in delivery of the new tanks, which were to go first to the new armored formations rather than to depleted panzer divisions. This latter part of the directive was of dubious wisdom, considering the leadership talents among the veteran panzer divisions; but it assured that the new panzer brigades could be built, for the most part, around a battalion of forty Panthers each.

As the front moved eastward, the Germans' logistical problems diminished, while the Allies' naturally grew. Allied fighter-bombers still harried everything German that moved on the roads, but the roads were not so long between the German armies and the three major supply depots recently established, in Luxembourg near Arlon, around Nancy and Toul, and around Belfort. Nor was it only newly created combat forces that Hitler could spare to resist the impending Allied rush to the Reich itself. As a necessary price of DRAGOON, the Allies had to ease their pressure in Italy, and from the Italian front the veteran 3rd and 15th Panzer Grenadier Divisions were on their way to France.

Their destination was the German First Army. During the first days of September, the First Army was built up along the Moselle River from three and a half divisions to a force of three panzer grenadier divisions (the 3rd, the 15th, and the reconstituted 17th ss), four and a half infantry divisions (among them the 553rd and 559th Volksgrenadier), and the 106th Panzer Brigade with its new Panther tanks. General der Panzertruppen Otto von Knobelsdorff, an armored specialist who had distinguished himself at the head of three different panzer corps in the East, had replaced the infantryman General von der Chevallerie in command of the army. In early September, Knobelsdorff's command was easily the strongest German army in the West. Its power and location indicated where the Germans thought the gravest threat now confronted them. Already the Germans had done much to correct the odds on Patton's front in their favor; Patton's two corps racing toward Germany, the XII and the XX, had just received two additional infantry divisions, but apart from the VIII Corps far away in Brittany, the Third Army had only two armored and four infantry divisions.

Appropriately, Patton's G-2, Colonel Oscar Koch, submitted on August 28 an intelligence estimate less optimistic than most of those emanating from SHAEF and other Allied staffs:

> Despite the crippling factors of shattered communications, disorganization and tremendous losses in personnel and equipment, the enemy nevertheless has been able to maintain a sufficiently cohesive front to exercise an overall control of his tactical situation. His withdrawal, though continuing, has not been a rout or mass collapse. Numerous new identifications in contact in recent days have demonstrated clearly that, despite the enormous difficulties under which he is operating, the enemy is still capable of bringing new elements into the battle area and transferring some from other fronts.
>
> . . . barring internal upheaval in the homeland and the remoter possibility of insurrection within the Wehrmacht, it can be expected that the German armies will continue to fight until destroyed or captured.[6]

The wounded tiger could still slash at its tormentors. The German army was not yet beaten, especially in front of Patton. To the Germans, the recovery of the late summer and early autumn of 1944 would soon become celebrated as the Miracle of the West. For the Allies, the German army's dramatic resilience made the choice of the best possible plan of campaign a matter indeed of the unforgiving minute.

The Vengeance Weapons Again

The German dispositions implied that the enemy perceived Patton's offensive, already so far east of the other Allied armies, as the most dangerous. Nevertheless, in the

August 23 conference between the Supreme Commander and the leader of 21 Army Group, General Eisenhower proved remarkably receptive to Montgomery's recently developed arguments, and willing to go far toward sacrificing Bradley's and Patton's direct eastward thrust toward Metz and the Saar in favor of the more northerly advance against the Ruhr from the lower Seine. Where the OVERLORD planners had intended that both the American First and Third Armies would take the Saar route into Germany, Eisenhower proved willing in fact to divert Hodges's army northeastward. Then the American First Army would form the right flank of a 21 Army Group drive through the Low Countries to the Ruhr.

Not the least of the reasons for Eisenhower's attitude lay in the assault of Hitler's V-weapons upon England. By late August it was plain that capturing the launching sites was the only fully satisfactory means of dealing with the V-weapons, and this fact pointed to as rapid as possible an Allied advance up the Channel coast—Montgomery's offensive, not Patton's.

In the two months since the launching of the first V-1s against England, the flying bombs had killed over 5,000 people, injured another 35,000, and destroyed some 30,000 buildings. At first, on June 16, Prime Minister Churchill declared that he would not allow the bombs to interfere with Allied concentration upon the battle in Normandy. He nevertheless assembled the entire War Cabinet that morning to prepare countermeasures, and within two days, believing the onslaught more than his war-weary people should have to bear, he asked Eisenhower to make the launching sites the first-priority target for the Eighth Air Force and Bomber Command. On June 18 Eisenhower directed Tedder in writing that CROSSBOW "targets are to take first priority over everything except the urgent requirements of the battle."[7]

The new aerial campaign proved a sore disappointment. The big ski sites on which the early CROSSBOW effort had concentrated seemed no longer to be in use; the smaller improvised launching sites that the Germans were employing did not make good targets, especially for the heavy bombers. The bad weather over the Continent in June and July was no help. Despite the weather, Bomber Command flew against the V-1 targets every day except one from June 16–17 to the end of the month, 4,057 sorties dropping 15,907.2 tons. Beginning June 19, the Eighth Air Force flew 2,149 sorties against CROSSBOW targets through the rest of the month, dropping 5,524 tons. The Ninth Air Force, preoccupied with the land battle, did not resume CROSSBOW missions until June 23, but in what remained of the month it flew 1,500 medium bomber sorties, dropped 2,000 tons, and—significantly—achieved the best results. Nevertheless, the V-1s continued to soar against England at an average rate of 100 per day.

The combination of a large aerial countereffort with disproportionately meager results touched off another squabble among the airmen. With NEPTUNE safely ashore, General Spaatz strained with impatience to return his United States Strategic Air Forces to the bombing campaign against German petroleum that he believed could win the war. Already on June 8 he had issued an order to both the Eighth and the Fifteenth Air Forces that henceforth their primary strategic purpose was to deny oil to the German armed forces. Spaatz recognized that British morale required an impressive show of effort against the flying bombs. But he believed that morale as well as every other purpose could be served best by ending the war as quickly as possible, and on June 29 he delivered personally to Eisenhower a strong letter asking the Supreme Commander to free the Eighth Air Force for its proper missions of denying the German ground forces the means to continue resisting—that is, oil—and of suppressing the Luftwaffe. On days when the weather permitted bombing Germany, Spaatz argued, missions there should have overriding priority, with only two exceptions: a major emergency in the land battle, or attacks against the large CROSSBOW sites. In effect, Spaatz hoped to downgrade attacks on the smaller CROSSBOW sites as unsuitable for heavy bombers.

Eisenhower demurred. The same day, he replied that V-1 sites—implicitly, all of them—should continue to receive "our first priority."[8]

Spaatz did not surrender. Characteristically, he proposed better methods for overcoming the V-1: hitting the Pas de Calais electrical system, on which the launchings surely depended; dispatching pilotless, worn-out bombers, carrying excess loads of explosives, by radar to crash against V-1 targets (a method not developed soon enough to be attempted on more than a limited scale); attacks on V-1 storage depots; attacks on the factories that made the V-1's gyro compass. Other Americans urged also a trial of the fighter-bomber attacks recommended long ago by the AAF's Eglin Field experiments; after all, the Thunderbolts, Lightnings, and Mustangs were scoring very well against such similar small targets as bridges. But this idea was encrusted with too much of the animosity stirred up when Leigh-Mallory first rejected it to be accepted now. To a considerable extent, the evident ineffectuality of bombing the launching sites did turn the air forces to the alternative of hitting the logistical systems behind the V-1, but this tactic was not a howling success either. Meanwhile, despite Eisenhower's rebuff, Spaatz contrived in practice to divert most of the heavies' CROSSBOW effort to Bomber Command, and when the weather was clear, the Eighth Air Force flew to Germany. Twice in August, Tedder asked General Doolittle of the Eighth why he was scheduling missions into Germany instead of the CROSSBOW missions required by SHAEF. Doolittle answered that he thought he was striking the more important targets and went his own, and Spaatz's, way.

The V-1s continued to come buzzing, abruptly cutting their engines, and crashing into England. When the Allies crossed the Seine, the enemy abandoned his launching sites south of the Somme, and the assault on England partially eased. But this event merely confirmed that depriving the Germans of launching sites was the only surely effective remedy, and thus emphasized the V-weapon menace as a strong argument for a concentrated thrust under Montgomery's command up the Channel coast. The V-weapon menace: by now the necessity to overrun the launching sites was all the stronger, because Allied intelligence knew the Germans were about to add a V-2 assault to the V-1. The V-1 pilotless bomber flew on a preset course at about 400 miles per hour and was, albeit to an unsatisfactory degree, vulnerable to antiaircraft fire and to interception by the RAF's fastest low-medium altitude fighter, the 435-miles-per-hour Hawker Tempest, introduced into combat on June 8, five days before the first V-1 attack. Tempests eventually exploded some 630 V-1s by hitting them over the Channel. The V-2, frighteningly, was a rocket-launched ballistic missile rising to an altitude of ninety to slightly over a hundred kilometers and hurtling down to earth at five times the speed of sound. It could not be seen, heard, or intercepted. Overrunning its launching sites would not be only the most effective remedy, but simply the only remedy.

The Single Thrust

Even more cogent an argument for first priority to an offensive up the Channel coast was the need for seaports. With the Brittany ports unavailable—General Middleton's VIII Corps was due to open a major attack against Brest on August 25—and the speed of the armies' advance already outrunning the ability of logistical support to keep pace, Eisenhower needed more ports as quickly as possible, especially ports close enough to the German frontier to support a climactic campaign into the Reich.

Most of the Channel ports—Calais, Dunkirk, Nieuport, Ostend—were only river mouths transformed into small harbors by means of artificial locks and basins; their limitations had helped direct NEPTUNE to Normandy. But ahead of Montgomery's armies there was also Antwerp. If Marseille provided an imperative argument for ANVIL-DRAGOON, Antwerp posed a yet more irresistible reason for hastening up the French coast and into Belgium. Ninety kilometers up the Scheldt estuary, Antwerp had a thoroughly sheltered harbor, but also one with a minimum depth of eight and a half meters, so that large seagoing vessels could be received at all stages of the tide. Some five and a half kilometers of quays lined the right bank of the Scheldt. Northeast of the city, eighteen wet basins that were reached from the river through four locks provided yet another forty-two kilometers of quays. The docks were equipped with more than 600 hydraulic and electric cranes, along with many floating cranes, loading bridges, and floating grain elevators. In 1938, Antwerp had registered 12,000 vessels and handled almost 60 million tons of freight. In short, Antwerp ranked with New York among the great seaports of the world. And its clearance facilities included more than 800 kilometers of rails, extensive marshaling yards, and excellent linkage with the Belgian network of over 5,000 kilometers of railroads and 2,200 kilometers of navigable waterways. Beyond Antwerp, furthermore, for later Allied use, lay one of the few seaports of the world boasting comparable capacity, Rotterdam, also beckoning as a prize for a rapid march northeast along the coast.

An offensive from the lower Seine also promised Allied naval power in the Channel as protection for its left flank, good airfield sites on level ground, and convenient access for medium bombers and fighter-bombers still based in England. It would bring to battle—or perhaps isolate and trap large segments of—the enemy's Fifteenth Army in the Pas de Calais, much reduced now by the shifting of troops to the Fifth Panzer and Seventh Armies but still a relatively well organized force.

Yet none of these considerations, not Antwerp, not even the elimination of the V-weapon sites, was the decisive reason for hurrying northeastward. The governing consideration was the race for the Ruhr. The northeastern route to the Ruhr was the direct route. If the Allies reached the Ruhr before the German armies could reorganize a stable defense, without the Ruhr's industry the Germans would never be able to reestablish such a defense. From their industrial plant in eastern Germany they might be able to sustain their Ostheer, but not their armies on two fronts. If the Allies could quickly capture the Ruhr, all other considerations would become irrelevant, because the war in the West would be over. And the Germans were not yet organizing their defense of the Ruhr on a scale comparable to their preparations to receive Patton farther south.

So compelling, then, Patton's progress notwithstanding, was the pressure for hurrying through Amiens and Liège toward the Ruhr that on August 22, the day before his meeting with Montgomery, Eisenhower had already seemed to be turning toward a still greater emphasis on the northern route than the OVERLORD planners had given it. That Tuesday, the Supreme Commander proposed to deploy Bradley's 12th Army Group east and northeast of Paris in such a way that "it can either strike northeastward, thus assisting in the rapid fall of the Calais area and the later advance through the Low Countries or, if the enemy strength in that region is not greater than I now believe, it can alternatively strike directly eastward, passing south of the Ardennes."[9] By the time Eisenhower had conferred with Montgomery, his shift in favor of the northern route had lost this latter, rather muddy equivocation and become clear. "For a very considerable time," he now told General Marshall, "I was of the belief that we could carry out the operation in the northeast simultaneously with a thrust eastward, but later concluded that due to the tremendous importance of the objectives in the northeast we must first concentrate on that movement." He would direct Bradley "to thrust forward with the bulk of his offensive units along the right boundary of the 21st Army Group so as to assist in the rapid accomplishment of the missions in that area." Bradley was also to continue assembling forces for the eastward thrust toward Metz and the Saar, but the northern advance would come first and it would receive the bulk of Bradley's strength, as well as all the weight of Montgomery's army group.[10]

Eisenhower apparently had come around to Montgomery's plan of action. So Bradley and especially Patton interpreted it when they heard the news. But the 21 Army Group chieftain and the Supreme Commander did not depart from their conference on August 23 in quite as complete agreement as Eisenhower seems to have thought or Bradley and Patton feared. Montgomery's plan for an offensive as he had described it in writing to Bradley was for a single massive thrust along the northeastward route to the Ruhr by almost all the Allied forces:

1. After crossing the Seine, 12 and 21 Army Groups should keep together as a solid mass of some forty divisions which would be so strong that it need fear nothing. This force would move north-eastwards.
2. 21 Army Group, on the western flank, to clear the channel coast, the Pas de Calais, West Flanders, and secure Antwerp and South Holland.
3. 12 Army Group to form the eastern flank of the movement and to move with its right flank on the Ardennes—being directed on Aachen and Cologne.
4. The whole movement would pivot on Paris. A strong American force to be positioned in the general area Orleans-Troyes-Châlons-Reims-Laon, with its right flank thrown back along the R. Loire to Nantes.
5. The Dragoon force coming up from southern France to be directed on Nancy and the Saar. We ourselves must not reach out with our right to join it and thus unbalance our strategy.
6. The basic object of the movement would be to establish a powerful air force in Belgium, to secure bridgeheads over the Rhine before the winter began, and to seize the Ruhr quickly.[11]

Montgomery commented in his *Memoirs*: "In its simplest terms this was the German 'Schlieffen Plan' of 1914 in reverse, except that it would be executed against a shattered and disorganised enemy. Its success depended on the concentration of Allied strength, and therefore of maintenance resources, on the left wing."[12] As outlined by Montgomery, the plan indeed demanded strengthening the left even more disproportionately than

Schlieffen had "kept the right wing strong." The 12th and 21 Army Groups currently comprised some thirty-eight divisions. The precise number cannot be stated because three or more had been withdrawn for reequipping, and Montgomery may have assumed that there were more than forty and that he was not asking for everything. Nevertheless, "a solid mass of some forty divisions" would have left almost nothing for the 12th Army. Group right wing—the Third Army—in what would be in any event a passive role, guarding the flank from Laon back to Nantes.

Thus Montgomery urged Eisenhower in the August 23 conference that Patton's advance be stopped and all supplies to him cut off. This was more than Eisenhower could concede, if for no other reason than that political considerations would not allow an American army to be completely halted as its advance neared flood tide. Eisenhower nevertheless gave Montgomery's northeastward offensive first call on supplies. In particular he allocated the bulk of the 12th Army Group's gasoline to the northeastward advance, to the extent that Patton would have to halt anyway, not immediately but within a week: about as far toward fulfilling Montgomery's every desire as any American officer would have dared to go.

Eisenhower also offered Montgomery his decision that Hodges's First Army should move on the right flank of 21 Army Group in the offensive toward the Ruhr. Thus the Supreme Commander solidified his promise to give the northeastward advance the bulk of Bradley's offensive strength. The First Army had four corps; the Third Army had only two assigned to its eastward advance. Including the VIII Corps in Brittany, Patton had some 669 medium tanks, a relatively small number for a field army; his army consistently averaged 150 to 200 fewer medium tanks than the First Army.

Though Patton thought otherwise and many Americans have agreed with him, Montgomery's design for a single concentrated thrust could not be considered simply a plan for the aggrandizement of the British role in the final drive into Germany while reducing the Americans to spear carriers. When Eisenhower's judgment of what was practical limited the American contribution to the northeastward advance to the First Army, the Americans retained a leading part in Montgomery's proposal. According to 21 Army Group instructions, General Crerar's First Canadian Army would clear the Channel coast, including the Pas de Calais. General Dempsey's Second British Army would move into southern Belgium by way of Beauvais, Amiens, Lille, and Ghent. The Canadians and British both would have to advance across the old battlefields of Flanders, traversing again the multiple rivers, canals, drainage ditches, marshes, and inundations of the humid plain that had plagued armies for many centuries and bedeviled their own fathers in 1914–1918. Once they escaped the mud of Flanders, both armies of Montgomery's group would find their advance foreshortened by the Scheldt estuary. To the First American Army, in contrast, Montgomery's plan left the best of the historic invasion routes, the relatively level, dry, straight roads from Paris through Charleroi, Namur, and Liège—the routes of the Schlieffen Plan. This indeed was the only northeastward route that had been favored by the OVERLORD planners; they had rejected the Flanders plain, over which the British and Canadian armies were now to move.

General Hodges's troops would advance first to the Peronne-Laon line and thus through the Seuil de Vermandois, the best northeastward avenue out of Paris, the natural gateway formed by the saddle between the Ardennes foothills to the right and the chalk uplands of Artois to the left. They would skirt waterlogged Flanders. No obstacles of consequence, natural or artificial, would stand in their way before the West Wall around Aachen. So favorable was the First Army zone of advance, in fact, that Bradley was willing to suggest to Montgomery a modification to give the British slightly more elbow room, curving the interallied boundary eastward around Tournai to allow the British to wheel through Antwerp and past the Scheldt to the Rhine and the Ruhr, thus continuing to cover Hodges's left flank. Montgomery agreed.

To Verdun and St. Mihiel

While the high command deliberated, General Patton went on driving still farther beyond the advance of the other armies—as long as he had gasoline in his tanks—to keep a question mark attached to Eisenhower's decision of August 23. Patton did so with Bradley's acquiescence and sometimes encouragement, because Bradley was not as ready as Eisenhower to transfer overwhelming priority to the northeastward advance, and still preferred to maintain pressure against the Germans on a broad front from Lorraine, the Saar, and the upper Rhine to the North Sea. For that reason, Bradley had fleshed out Patton's advance by sending McLain's 90th Division from Argentan to join Walker's XX Corps and McBride's 80th Division from Orléans to Eddy's XII Corps. He also prepared to restore Haislip's XV Corps to the Third Army. Furthermore, the First Army took over the Melun bridgehead from Walker, freeing the whole of the XX Corps to advance eastward rather than northeast; while Patton freed the XII Corps by assigning the watch over the Loire River flank, previously Eddy's responsibility, to the VIII Corps all the way from Orléans westward.

On August 23, the day of the conferences, Patton's restless mind turned briefly from the eastward gallop to the possibility of yet another envelopment. The Third Army commander proposed to 12th Army Group Chief of Staff Leven Allen to swing the Third Army northward from the upper Seine to Beauvais and thence on a course parallel with the river to the Channel, to cast another net for the Germans who were about to escape across the Seine. When Bradley was told of the plan, he was unresponsive, and Patton's real passion was not fighting Kesselschlachten anyway. The Beauvais envelopment proved stillborn, and by the time the XII Corps completed the capture of Troyes, Patton's discussions with Bradley concerned how far east the Third Army should go. On August 28, Patton proposed the Meuse as his next objective. Bradley suggested he settle for the Marne; the day before, the army group commander had to reduce authorized levels of POL—petrol, oil, lubricants—to five days' supply, instead of the customary seven days'. The Third Army had so outrun the major supply depots far back on and near the Normandy beaches that its actual stocks were well below the new authorization. Nevertheless, Patton did not find it hard to argue Bradley into approving an advance to the line Verdun-Commercy on the Meuse. Fortunately for the Third Army, moreover, the XII Corps found thirty-seven carloads of German gasoline and oil, over 100,000 gallons, at Sens; in the usual if dubious fashion, nobody in Patton's army was telling any higher authority about it.

So the Third Army set out to traverse the American battlefields of the First World War, and the greatest of the French battlefields as well. A story circulating among the staffs had a general telling a regimental commander: "Colonel, we had better bypass that next city: I made some pretty tall promises to a girl back there in 1918."[13] The shortage of supplies, particularly gasoline, was a threat no longer remote; the tanks might run dry any day now. But there was much cause for the good cheer that seemed to make Patton's jeep sprout gaudier ornamentation every day. The Third Army would be moving in the direction in which the plateaus of central France, rising gradually from west to east, favor the offensive; the sharp, abrupt scarps of the Marne and the Meuse face eastward. There was no cause to expect a revival of strong opposition short of the West Wall, if then—which was the justification for Patton's haste. The prospect of a race over the famous battlefields of the past was even more bracing than the army's usual zest for the chase, especially to Patton himself, who had been there in 1918. And both Patton and Bradley believed there was "Some question now as to whether the violation of German border would not be worth more than destruction of the German army." Their hope was to "head for the German border, break through the Siegfried Line while the enemy is disorganized and before he can plug it, make for the Rhine and drop paratroops to protect the Bridge crossings."[14]

On August 28, Bruce Clarke's CCA of Wood's 4th Armored led off for the XII Corps with a charge of eighty kilometers from Troyes across the storied Marne at Vitry-le-François. The next day the combat command moved down the east bank of the Marne toward Châlons-sur-Marne while General McBride's 80th Division approached the same target from the west. By noon of Tuesday the 29th, the XII Corps had captured this ancient garrison city of the French army—and another cache of over 100,000 gallons of German gasoline as well. All along the way, resistance was sporadic and dealt with in the usual Third Army fashion.

Walker's XX Corps had moved from Melun and Montereau to mount their attack of August 28 from the vicinity of Provins toward Reims. In 1918, the battered cathedral of Reims had suffered so much in the battles for the surrounding projection of the Marne escarpment into the Champagne lowland that it became a symbol for the whole agony of the Western Front. Now Reims witnessed no renewed agony of assault and counterassault, but another swift and almost bloodless conquest by the Third Army. General Silvester's 7th Armored struck for the Marne on August 28 with two combat commands abreast, in six columns of armor, hoping to capture somewhere an intact bridge. The method paid off when armored infantry seized and crossed a bridge at Dormans. Expanding the bridgehead, CCB pushed on from Epernay around the east of Reims toward the River Aisne. CCA and CCR moved through Château-Thierry, where the 3rd Infantry Division had won its fame as the Rock of the Marne in July 1918. On August 29, these two combat commands crossed the Vesle River at Fismes, for which the 32nd Division had struggled house by house at the beginning of the Allied counteroffensive in 1918. Encircled, Reims fell easily to the 5th Division on August 30.

That same Wednesday afternoon, the XX Corps headed off in column of divisions toward the fortifications of Verdun, just over 100 kilometers away. The tour toward Verdun included the jagged hills and deep ravines of the Argonne Forest, the "Thermopylae of France," but on this American visit nobody was guarding the pass. The FFI saved the Meuse bridges at Verdun from German demolition, and by noon on Thursday some of Silvester's tanks were across the river and inside the most famous French garrison city of all.

On Eddy's front, CCA of the 4th Armored reached and crossed the Meuse at Commercy the same day. A light tank company in the vanguard raced into town so fast that it shot up the defending German gun crews before they could remove their breechblock covers, and captured a bridge intact. The next day, September 1, the 80th Division established yet another Meuse bridgehead near where Patton had first led tanks in battle, at St. Mihiel.

By the beginning of September, then, both the XX and XII Corps were firmly across the Meuse, and their patrols were already ranging to the Moselle near Metz and Nancy. "General [Bradley] expects to be on the Rhine a week from Sunday if Ike will give him the go ahead sign," wrote Hansen in his diary.[15] From the Moselle, the Rhine was just over 150 kilometers farther, the West Wall in the Saar region barely half that distance. The Third Army sweep across the Meuse produced two immediate, but somewhat contradictory, results. It drained all the gasoline from the army's tanks, thus halting it, and also prompted Eisenhower to rethink his August 23 decision about strategy.

On Friday, September 1, as earlier planned, General Eisenhower assumed direct operational control of the ground forces in northern France, and Montgomery reverted to a position of equality with Bradley as an army group commander, with whatever consolation he might find in his new rank of field marshal. In the August 23 conference, Montgomery had resisted the change and insisted on the principle of an overall ground commander, professing to value the principle so much that he would serve under Bradley if need be. Eisenhower was not deterred, but nevertheless he took up his new job with a measure of reluctance. He had wanted to delay it until he could move SHAEF's main headquarters to the Continent, complete with ample communications. In late August, his headquarters commandant and the chief of his Signal Division chose a site at Jullouville, a small town just south of Granville on the Cotentin Peninsula, where they assured the Supreme Commander an adequate communications net could be established promptly enough for the September 1 changeover. But Granville was far from the front, and communications did not prove satisfactory.

Eisenhower found he had to keep in touch with Montgomery and Bradley largely by traveling by plane and jeep to see them; otherwise he was dependent on letters or the insecurity of wireless telegraphy. There were neither telephone lines nor a radiophone link between Granville and the armies. Yet Eisenhower had no real choice about the ground command. Since the public furor over the command question in August, pressure from the United States had grown intense and Marshall insistent. The conduct of the August operations, and particularly of the Argentan-Falaise envelopment, surely dramatized the need for a unified command.

On September 2, Eisenhower inaugurated his efforts to create appropriate contact with the front by flying to Bradley's tactical headquarters, now at Chartres, to meet with the 12th Army Group commander and the leaders of his armies and the Ninth Air Force. The occasion was notable not least because it was the first time Eisenhower and Patton had seen each other since the Third Army joined the battle. The two had become friends when they met in the old Tank Corps at Fort Meade just after the First World War, when their relationship had been somewhat that of Patton the older patron (in the war a temporary colonel commanding the largest American tank formations in action in France) and Eisenhower the younger protégé (in the war a temporary lieutenant colonel commanding a tank training center at Gettysburg). The friendship had cooled when the soldier-slapping incidents in Sicily caused Eisenhower to resent not only Patton's irresponsibility but also the burden placed on him as theater commander to shield his impetuous subordinate from public and official wrath. Since their last meeting, Patton's regard for Eisenhower in turn had not been improved by SHAEF's refusal to acknowledge publicly the presence and achievements of the Third Army and its commander until almost the end of August, in an eventually absurd effort to continue the FORTITUDE deception; finally, SHAEF had to confirm the Germans' broadcasts about Patton.

Believing nevertheless that he had to impress the Supreme Commander if the Third Army's offensive was to remain alive, Patton told Eisenhower that he had patrols on the Moselle and—stretching the truth—in Metz. "If you let me retain my regular allotment of tonnage, Ike, we could push on to the German frontier and rupture that Goddamn Siegfried Line. I'm willing to stake my reputation on that."

Animosity surfaced with Eisenhower's rejoinder: "Careful, George, that reputation of yours hasn't been worth very much," and Patton's riposte: "That reputation is pretty good now."[16]

The reputation had certainly become too good to ignore—especially since Bradley had overcome misgivings about Patton that were stronger than Eisenhower's as recently as the beginning of August. Importuned by Bradley as well as by Patton, Eisenhower agreed to hedge his August 23 decision with a slight shift toward the wishes of the 12th Army Group. The northeastward offensive would retain priority; but as soon as the Calais area was cleared and secured, the Third Army might advance toward Mannheim, Frankfurt, and Koblenz. According to Patton, Eisenhower also conceded that the Third Army might cross the Moselle as soon as it had enough fuel. On September 4, new orders from SHAEF confirmed the shift by stating among the missions of Bradley's army group: "To occupy the sector of the Siegfried Line covering the Saar and then to seize Frankfurt. It is important that this operation should start as soon as possible, in order to forestall the enemy in this sector, but troops of Central Group of Armies operating against the Ruhr north-west of the Ardennes [that is, Hodges's troops on Montgomery's right flank] must first be adequately supported." The next day, Eisenhower wrote in a memorandum for his own record: "I now deem it important, while supporting the advance on eastward through Belgium, to get Patton moving once again so that we may be fully prepared to carry out the original conception for the final stages of the campaign."[17]

SHAEF followed through by increasing the Third Army's fuel allowance. During the spectacular advance from the Seine to the Meuse between August 26 and September 2, Patton's army consumed from 350,000 to 400,000 gallons of gasoline per day, but received an average of only 202,382 gallons a day. Without the captured German stocks, the advance could not have reached the Meuse. By September 2, the Third Army's gasoline receipts were down to 25,390 gallons. Already on August 30, Eddy had visited army headquarters to report an "extreme shortage of gasoline within his Corps" and an imminent halt short of the Moselle. Patton "desires that you keep moving and get that crossing," Chief of Staff Gaffey told Eddy. "He says if necessary to drain the gas from some tanks and put it in others, and go on."

"Is it OK if I become immobilized?" Eddy responded.

"Yes," said Gaffey, whose deputy added in his diary: "Patton directs that the advance continue—until all tanks are dry. Also—that 3rd Army is aware of the plot to stop Patton," which is how Patton interpreted the cause of his woes.[18]

By September 2, Patton's headquarters was hearing from one formation after another that was stranded without fuel. Luckily, the next morning Eddy reported that his men had found another 100,000 gallons of German fuel. Still more fortunately for

Patton, Eisenhower's change of mind helped bring 240,265 gallons to the Third Army on September 5. During the following three days, 1,396,710 gallons more arrived. Patton could resume his march to the Moselle. But with this development, Montgomery was furious. To the field marshal, at least, Allied planning seemed to have slipped into total disarray.

14: The Twin Tyrants: Logistics . . .

EVERY INFORMED Allied officer had foreseen the fuel crisis. Its coming was implicit in the decision not to pause at the Seine. A staff study ordered by the SHAEF G-4 in July had affirmed the impossibility of the kind of accelerated pace of advance that the American armies subsequently achieved in August. Risking the logistical crisis was a price the field commanders decided was worth paying for the chance of hastening the end of the war.

Not only had the Allies moved eleven days ahead of the OVERLORD planners' schedule by reaching the Seine on August 24, D plus 79, instead of on D plus 90. As recently as D plus 49, the deadlock in the Bocage had still held the Allied armies on the D Plus 20 line. Thus, in the thirty days between D plus 49 and D plus 79, the armies had traversed a distance that, according to the plan, was to have taken seventy days. Naturally, they had consumed fuel much more voraciously than the OVERLORD plans anticipated.

After the crossing of the Seine, the logistical situation went from bad to worse. September 4 was D plus 90. According to the OVERLORD plans, on that day the American Zone of Communications was to be supporting twelve United States divisions on the Seine. The plans did not envisage supporting these divisions in an offensive beyond the Seine until D plus 120. In fact, on D plus 90, sixteen United States divisions were already over 200 kilometers beyond the Seine.

Because the demands of the logistical buildup of an amphibious invasion were so difficult, the OVERLORD planners had believed that even their cautious forecasting of phase lines represented virtually the maximum extension of support of the armies that could be achieved. To create their cautious forecasts, they had also relied on having several ports operating by D plus 90; in fact, on that day the Allies had only one port of consequence, Cherbourg, plus the beaches.

To some extent, the long delay before reaching the D plus 20 phase line was a logistical blessing, which helped make possible the great leap forward after D plus 49. Although the fighting around Caen and in the Bocage swallowed tons of ammunition, and an ammunition shortage developed early, the stationary front permitted other kinds of supplies to accumulate—particularly fuel. Despite the disappointment of not capturing additional port facilities, the prolonged stability of the front in June and July and the consequent limited consumption of supplies meant that there was no immediate shortage on the Continent at the beginning of September, except in ammunition. Port capacity might soon become a problem—American port discharges were averaging less than 35,000 tons a day—but for the moment, the needed supplies were present in France. As

September began, the quays of Cherbourg were piled high with more than 70,000 tons of cargo that could not even be moved to supply depots. The problem was transport.

The accelerated advance of the armies had outrun the ability of the Communications Zone to keep pace with them in carrying supplies from the depots on and near the Normandy beaches, 600 kilometers behind the American spearheads. The transport problem was all the worse because the accelerated advance demanded that almost all transportation be by truck. The slower pace contemplated by the planners would have permitted considerable rebuilding of the French railroads to help with supply. Now, the railroads remained devastated—by the Allied bombing and the FFI activities that had sealed off Normandy so well from German reinforcement and resupply. The first train from Normandy reached Paris on August 30, and then by a circuitous route. It did not herald a beginning of extensive and sustained rail transport.

The Paris rail yards were largely wrecked and provided only the narrowest of funnels through which to forward supplies beyond the Seine, into the area to the east where the railroads were in better condition. Such tonnage as found its way to Paris mostly had to remain there anyway, to feed and fuel the city. Not Paris but Dreux and Chartres became the railheads for the First and Third Armies, respectively. But the pace of railroad rebuilding is reflected in the movement of only seventy trains carrying slightly over 30,000 tons from le Mans to Chartres between August 24 and September 2. The principal historian of American logistics recorded that operations, especially signals, "resembled those of a third-class Toonerville Trolley," so "the ghost of Casey Jones shadowed many an engineer . . . , as it did on 5 September at Maintenon, northeast of Chartres, where a blacked-out trainload of high-octane gas roared around a downgrade curve and crashed into another train, sending flaming Jerricans into the night."[1]

Air also failed to carry as large a burden of supply as the OVERLORD planners had hoped. Here the source of the problem was different: it was simply the limited capacity of the transport aircraft of the time, however reliable and sturdy the workhorse Curtis C-47 might have been. Of course, there were also inadequate landing fields, bad weather, and, despite the sorry state of the Luftwaffe, occasional enemy interference. Frequently, C-47s were taken out of support service to be assembled for prospective airborne operations. Eighteen airborne drops were planned in late August and early September, three almost reached the point of launching, but all were cancelled because the pace of the ground advance would have made them meaningless.

Except for airborne operations, the field service regulations prescribed that air supply should be used only in emergencies—though this restriction had not prevented the OVERLORD planners from anticipating its use, nor SHAEF from promising as early as August 12 that it would try to make available 1,000 tons of air supply per day. Two days later, Montgomery's headquarters called instead for 2,000 tons per day to the American armies. When the first air shipments got under way on August 19, delivering rations to a newly opened field at le Mans, the best average that CATOR (Combined Air Transport Operations Room, a branch of AEAF) could achieve was 600 tons per day. On August 26 and 27, air shipments hit a peak of almost 2,900 tons as the two-day total (including, however, shipments to Paris). Thereafter, new withdrawals of airplanes for projected airborne operations caused shipments to fall to 500 tons daily through early September, despite attempts to relieve the deficit of C-47s by converting Fortresses and Liberators into transport craft. The total tonnage carried by American planes to the 12th Army

Group from August 19 to September 16 proved to be only 13,000. When every drop of gasoline was precious, anything helped; but the front needed a lot more.

Thus the trucks, which were not supposed to have to work more than about 250 kilometers beyond railheads, had to carry almost everything, from the beaches to Verdun. Because the planners had not foreseen this burden, there were not enough trucks. The Transportation Corps had calculated in 1943 that operations in Europe would require 240 truck companies. The European Theater of Operations, trying to save ship cargo space for combat troops and gear, wanted to cut the figure to 100 truck companies. Eventually, all concerned compromised at 160 companies. But the companies were slow to arrive in the theater. As they came in, they turned out to be equipped disproportionately with light trucks. Heavy-duty trucks for long hauls fell far below the two-to-one ratio over light trucks sought by the truckers. Without enough big trucks, the Transportation Corps in the ETO also found itself unable to train enough drivers for long runs. It also failed to receive enough drivers to keep its trucks rolling twenty-four hours a day.

When Eisenhower decided to jump the Seine and keep moving, the Communications Zone estimated it must place 100,000 tons of supplies, not including POL, in the Chartres-Dreux-la Loupe depot triangle by September 1. At first, its planners assumed that the railroads would be repaired enough to haul one-fifth of this tonnage. When they discovered that, instead, trucks would have to carry practically everything, they conceived the famous truck service that henceforth tried to keep pace with the rush across France: the Red Ball Express, a one-way loop highway using every available truck and working around the clock, with blackout rules ignored and headlights burning at night. The name derived from railroaders' lingo for a fast freight.

Without the Red Ball Express, the armies could have advanced nowhere near the Franco-German border by the beginning of September, and there would have been no hope of ending the war before the snows fell. Tribute paid to the Red Ball included a song in the Broadway musical *Call Me Mister* and a 1952 movie named for the express starring Jeff Chandler. Its fame was richly deserved. But any enterprise involving thousands of American truck drivers hurrying to their destinations was bound to be chaotic, so the Red Ball was far from the orderly operation its planners envisaged; trucks were supposed to drive back and forth on parallel highways between St. Lô (actually the beach depots, but St. Lô was the marshalling point) and Chartres, with the highways reserved for exclusive Red Ball use, all traffic moving in one direction, all trucks organized into convoys, all convoys divided into smaller serials, twenty-five miles per hour maximum speed (to avoid excessive wear), no halting except for specified ten-minute breaks at exactly ten minutes before each even hour, all vehicles maintaining a sixty-yard interval with no passing. There were not enough MPs to enforce such regulations, not even enough to prevent a small but appalling number of drivers from turning off to sell their cargos on the French black market. Of some 22 million Jerricans shipped to France to carry fuel, careless handling had lost about half by the beginning of September. Vehicles ignored convoys, went their own way, spent much of the time driving at twice the speed limit, and altogether—as British lorry drivers put it—the only way to escape oncoming American trucks was to "not only get off the road but climb a tree."[2]

Until September 10 the Red Ball was supposed to go only as far as Chartres, leaving transportation beyond that depot to the armies' internal trucking. One result was that many of the irregularities involved more or less legalized hijacking of the convoys to supply dumps farther and farther east. So complete was the confusion behind the armies' rapid advance, and so quickly did supply units and depots move on from one point to another, that convoys and truckers often had to "peddle" their loads until they found someone who would take them—desperate as were the needs of the spearheads.

The Red Ball began rolling on August 25 and delivered 4,482 tons to the Chartres-Dreux depots that day. By August 29, the express had 132 truck companies running 5,958 vehicles and delivered 12,342 tons of supplies (almost as much as the air deliveries of the whole emergency period). August 29 proved, however, to be a peak that could not be reached again, as road discipline deteriorated and, worse, so did the trucks under the strain of continuous operation. Deliveries fell off to an average of about 7,000 tons daily. By the beginning of September, about 115 truck companies worked the Red Ball on any given day (though more than 130 companies remained assigned, and the Communications Zone now had 185 truck companies). To keep this much truck transportation functioning, the Communications Zone had to do a lot of cannibalizing: two engineer general service regiments were reorganized into seven truck companies each, a chemical smoke generating battalion became a truck battalion, antiaircraft units formed another ten truck companies, and three recently arrived infantry divisions (the 26th, 95th, and 104th) were immobilized and their vehicles formed into truck companies. Out of apparent chaos, in ultimate confirmation of what marveling foreign historians such as Chester Wilmot say about the American genius for movement, came the delivery of an indispensable 89,939 tons to the armies in the eight days between August 25 and September 6. (Everything exacts a price; the Red Ball Express also consumed some 300,000 gallons of gasoline a day.)

The armies, too, had to scrounge for trucks for hauling from the Red Ball depots to the front—and occasionally for ranging all the way back to the beaches in search of hard-to-find items. As early as August 22, General Bradley ordered both his armies to leave their heavy artillery west of the Seine and to use the artillery transport vehicles to carry supplies. By the end of August, the First Army was also using engineer tactical transport for supplies. Soon the trucks of eighteen battalions of its artillery had joined its logistical services, and another 340 trucks were taken from antiaircraft artillery. Any units with trucks—signal depot and repair companies, ordnance maintenance companies, mobile refrigerator companies—were likely to have to give them up to haul supplies. The infantry either marched or moved forward in shuttles on the few trucks remaining with tactical units. The Third Army resorted to similar expedients.

Because the race toward Germany demanded that everything on wheels continue rolling, either in the forward units or to supply them, maintenance was neglected. By early September, if trucks and tanks did not run out of gas, they soon broke down. By mid-September the 3rd Armored Division, for example, had only seventy to seventy-five tanks in condition for front-line duty out of an authorized medium tank strength of 232. Frantic attempts at minimal maintenance created a shortage of spare parts everywhere near the front, with truck tires a dangerously scarce commodity.

Clearly, the race across France could not proceed indefinitely into Germany. Could it go on long enough to seize the unforgiving minute by capturing targets vital enough to the enemy to win the war?

How Much and How Far?

Even as General Eisenhower met with his American commanders and shifted back toward reopening General Patton's drive across the Moselle toward the upper Rhine, his SHAEF logistical planners and 12th Army Group headquarters were completing a study of the material restraints on the Third Army offensive. Their conclusions were not encouraging. They assumed that Patton's army might be given first call on all available supplies, to the extent of halting the other Allied forces. The British might remain near the Seine; American divisions outside the Third Army might become inactive. Transport would be beefed up by using all troop carrier planes to lift supplies and by using bombers generously as well. With these arrangements, the planners concluded, the Third Army would be able to push a force of ten to twelve divisions to the Rhine. But the army would not be able to advance much beyond the Rhine—perhaps to Frankfurt.

Ten to twelve divisions was a small force compared with the remaining and regathering strength of the German army. On the upper Rhine, Patton would strike no target essential to the enemy. His force would have stretched itself so deep into enemy territory—its exposed northern flank would run through about 500 kilometers of hostile country—that even Patton would have to worry a great deal about his flanks and his lines of communication. The remaining, immobilized Allied forces could do little to aid him. Fighter cover would be hard to maintain, because establishing advanced airfields would consume scarce supplies and transport.

The logistical planners' analysis of the northeastward offensive was not much more encouraging—but the posssibilities it offered were somewhat brighter. It was highly relevant, after all, that Montgomery's armies were much closer to ports than Patton's, and would enjoy an increasing advantage as the Channel ports opened. During the first days of September, the SHAEF G-4 staff estimated that three British and two American corps striking northeastward might be supplied in an offensive aimed at Berlin itself, though only three corps could actually be sustained all the way to the German capital. One of the British corps would have to be grounded around Bremen-Hamburg, one of the American corps around Magdeburg. To mount such a drive, 489 truck companies would be required, British and American. Only 347 happened to be available, but G-4 was willing to assume an airlift making up much of the deficit by carrying 2,000 tons a day, the equivalent of sixty truck companies.

Previous performance made this latter assumption doubtful, and even with a full air lift, there would be only a narrow margin of sustenance for the troops pushed deep into Germany. Furthermore, the offensive would be possible only if ten American divisions were altogether immobilized, and another twelve were left "quiescent." In short, once more there would be a force deep in Germany—deeper than Patton's in the alternative scenario—with long, exposed flanks and with the rest of the Allied armies so deprived of transport that they would not be able to move effectively to its aid.

At that, G-4's Berlin scenario involved still further conditions. Railheads must be available not only at Paris but at Châlons-sur-Marne and Brussels. Antwerp must be discharging cargo at a rate of 1,500 tons per day by September 15. By that same date, all the main forces of both Montgomery's and Bradley's army groups must have reached the Rhine, to provide an adequate launching platform for the climactic thrust.

The field commanders and Eisenhower might well have attached to these logistical estimates their own qualification, that the estimates derived from the same planners who had thought the pursuit to the Seine impossible at the pace at which it had occurred, and who had thought a dash without pause beyond the Seine still more out of the question. In this light, it might appear most significant that such extremely cautious logisticians dared even conceive of the northeastward offensive's charging all the way to Berlin. Toward the northeast, there was a hope of winning the war quickly that was tangible enough for the most inveterate pessimists to grasp. The Ruhr, moreover, was a lot closer than the logisticians' hypothetical objective of Berlin.

At least as much to the immediate point, despite their giving consideration to the southern as well as the northeastward offensive, the effect of the logisticians' studies was practically to write off the strategic significance of Patton's latest spectacular dash, from the Seine to the Meuse. They did so at the very moment when Montgomery reentered the lists on behalf of the northeastward offensive with the strongest argument of all. He spurred even the British armies—in American eyes laggards—to a pace of advance beyond the Seine rivaling Patton's own. By the first days of September, when the gasoline shortage hit Patton's army hardest, the northern armies drew almost abreast of him.

The Mons Pocket

The northern armies' most aggressive corps under their most aggressive commander led off the northeastward advance beyond the Seine. J. Lawton Collins's VII Corps headquarters, furthermore, now commanded three of the most proven divisions in the American army: General Huebner's North Africa, Sicily, and D-Day veterans, the Big Red One; the equally veteran 9th Division, so well brought up and well commanded so long by General Eddy, now under Major General Louis A. Craig (Hansen had written of the 9th: "Everyone has great affection for it; Has always been overshadowed by flashier and showier 1st Div"[3]); and the 3rd Armored Division, at first a disappointment but in the past few weeks transformed by Maurice Rose, as Collins put it, "into a marvelous thing."[4]

The First Army sent the VII Corps across the Seine through the Melun bridgehead already captured by the Third Army. Collins attacked toward Laon and the historic invasion gateway to Belgium on August 26. Rose's 3rd Armored tankers crossed the old Château-Thierry battlefield on August 28—the same day as Silvester's 7th Armored—and before nightfall they had also passed across the 1918 battlefield of Soissons, where the 1st Division along with the 2nd had broken the right flank of Ludendorff's Marne salient and thus led off the Allied offensive that did not end until the Armistice.

Those events of 1918 were much in everyone's mind, for, notwithstanding such cautious intelligence estimates as those of Patton's G-2, the German armies surely appeared to be in worse shape now than they had been when Berlin abruptly cried for peace in 1918. By August 30, the VII Corps had reached Laon, whereby Collins turned the flank of the enemy's Kitzinger Line along the Somme and mocked all Hitler's imprecations against a rupture of the Somme positions. Notwithstanding Model's earlier efforts to comply with the Führer's wishes, Collins's men met no stronger opposition along the way than had Patton's to the southward. In fact, though many of the remnants of the Fifth Panzer and Seventh Armies were somewhere in the Somme neighborhood, on August 28 Model had sent his surviving panzers off to help form the eventual resistance to Patton, in keeping with the Germans' perception of priorities.

Montgomery launched 21 Army Group's major offensive across the Seine on August 29. His instructions were as appropriate to the occasion as anything Patton could have ordered:

> The proper tactics now are for strong armoured and mobile columns to by-pass enemy centres of resistance and push boldly ahead, creating alarm and despondency in enemy rear areas. Enemy by-passed will be dealt with by infantry columns coming on later. I rely on commanders of every rank and grade to "drive" on ahead with the utmost energy; any tendency to be "sticky" or cautious must be stamped out ruthlessly.[5]

Even in Montgomery's army group, closer than Bradley's to the beaches and its depots, the supply pinch was so bad that Montgomery had to ground 8 Corps and most of his heavy and antiaircraft artillery to permit 30 Corps to move rapidly at the head of the Second Army advance, with 12 Corps cleaning up behind it. Montgomery felt new confidence that 30 Corps would strike forward in the spirit of his instructions, because he had just placed Lieutenant General B.G. Horrocks in command. This lean, lithe personification of one of the standard physical stereotypes of the English soldier had commanded 12 Corps in Montgomery's Eighth Army at Alamein and led 10 Corps in the flanking attack that turned the Mareth Line and carried the Eighth Army into Tunisia. Just before the invasion of Sicily, Horrocks had been hit by a falling antiaircraft shell, and in September 1943 he had flown with Bradley from North Africa to England, apparently facing an invalid's life and the end of his military career. In June 1944, the doctors were still telling him he would never again lead troops in the field. By late August, he was restoring in the hitherto disappointing 30 Corps something of the dash its divisions had shown long ago in the desert.

Bad weather, minefields, and pockets of the principal forces remaining to the Fifth Panzer and Seventh Armies held Horrocks to a thirty-kilometer advance out of the Vernon bridgehead on August 29. The next day the sun came out, resistance diminished, and 30 Corps began rolling. His appetite for speed whetted, Horrocks ordered the drive to continue through the night, with the result that the British carried their First World War logistical center of Amiens on August 31. With the help of the FFI, they took Amiens with several of its Somme bridges intact. They also gobbled up General Eberbach, the latest commander of the German Seventh Army, just after he signed an order for the defense of the Somme. The enemy now retained no plausible line short of the Albert Canal and the Meuse, and Patton had already compromised that.

General Haislip's XV Corps was currently slated to rejoin Patton's army, but the First Army's other corps followed Collins by jumping off the same day as the British, August 29. Collins would form the right of General Hodges's army. Gerow's V Corps would advance in the center, and Corlett's XIX on the left. The 28th Division's parade through Paris and on to the northern outskirts put it in contact with Barton's 4th Division, which had helped capture the city, and these two infantry formations led Gerow's advance until General Oliver's 5th Armored Division passed through them two days later. Initially, the V Corps march repeated the rapid progress now customary, but at the Forêt de Compiègne—famous as the site of both the 1918 and 1940 armistices—the 5th Armored met uncommonly stiff opposition from remnants of the LVIII Panzer Corps. The tankers therefore let the 4th Division pass through them to clear the forest and the city of Compiègne. Barton's men accomplished the task with enough dispatch to carry the corps advance across the Aisne between Compiègne and Soissons by September 1.

Meanwhile General Corlett took over the Mantes-Gassicourt bridgehead along with the 30th and 79th Divisions from the XV Corps on August 29. Adding General Brooks's 2nd Armored Division, Corlett started off forthwith for Montdidier and Péronne; but he was diverted two days and eighty kilometers farther on, when his XIX Corps was between Beauvais and Compiègne, because Bradley and Hodges had decided to seize yet another opportunity for an envelopment.

Their decision to do so produced the Battle of the Mons Pocket. ULTRA intercepts confirmed that the greater part of the bedraggled survivors of the Fifth Panzer and Seventh Armies, nominally some two panzer and eight to ten infantry divisions, might be cut off by a swift First Army turn northward to block the highways leading to Brussels through Tournai and Mons just across the Belgian frontier. Montgomery was planning an airborne assault to put Allied troops into Tournai before the Germans got there. Bradley had consistently opposed the whole series of planned air drops of the past few weeks, holding them to be mere wasteful diversions of badly needed air transport, and he considered the repeated preemption of the proposed airborne targets by ground advances to be an ample confirmation of his judgment. Rather than suffer a yet more prolonged diversion of air transport, by actually mounting an airborne attack instead of just planning it, Bradley now determined to hasten Hodges's troops into Tournai before Montgomery's design could take effect. Doing so would entail putting the First Army back into what had become the British zone of advance after Bradley's suggestion that 21 Army Group should not have its path cut short at the Scheldt estuary; but since it was Bradley's own generosity that had placed Tournai north of the interallied boundary, the 12th Army Group commander thought he was entitled to reabsorb Tournai in a good cause. No doubt the growing belief that fastidious adherence to boundaries had cost large opportunities at Argentan entered into Bradley's thinking.

In any event, Tubby Thorson, Hodges's G-3, carried his cadaverously thin person to Corlett's headquarters on August 31 to order the XIX Corps to capture Tournai—more than 150 kilometers beyond the corps spearheads—within forty-eight hours, or by midnight September 2 at the latest. That done, the corps was to press on to Ghent. Corlett promptly motorized two regiments of Wyche's 79th Division and one regiment of Hobbs's 30th. With Brooks's 2nd Armored leading the way, the motorized bulk of the XIX Corps then set out to march by night, bypass islands of resistance, and confirm Brooks's promise to Corlett that Tournai was "in the bag."[6] Colonel John Collier's CCA of 2nd Armored crossed the Somme early on September 1 after bypassing resistance at Montdidier, which Wyche's Cross of Lorraine Division mopped up, and by 10:00 P.M. of September 2 Collier had reached Tournai.

By that time, Montgomery had protested to Bradley about the violation of the interallied boundary, but the Americans told 21 Army Group it was too late for orders to stop Corlett short of Tournai. A subsequent show of politeness did halt the XIX Corps on a line running from about fifteen kilometers short of Tournai to just beyond the city—as emptied gasoline tanks would have done anyway.

There would be no air drop, but there would be bigger consequences of the First Army's northward turn. Like Corlett, Gerow responded to the order for the turn and for a quick march north by motorizing as much of his infantry as he could. Most of his V Corps ran out of gas on September 2 near the old tank battlefield of Cambrai, short of the Belgian border, where late orders from Hodges called for a halt in any event. But Colonel John T. Cole's CCB of the 5th Armored had already driven almost to Leuze, directly east of Tournai, and had put patrols into the town. The August 31 orders meanwhile had turned Collins's VII Corps north from Rethel and Montcornet through Avesnes and Maubeuge toward Mons. Here, around the capital of Hainault, amidst its dreary belt of industrial and coal-mining towns, where the Germans at the beginning of their twentieth-century march of conquest had beaten the British Expeditionary Force in August 1914, Collins was to complete the closing of a First Army trap.

The spearheads of Rose's 3rd Armored Division were almost in Mons by nightfall of September 2. Hodges had to send them yet another halt order, prompted by the gasoline shortage, but the order arrived too late to stop them short of the city. On the morning of September 3, General Rose's division controlled Mons and stretched back along the road to Avesnes, the 1st Division was around Avesnes just behind the armor, and the 9th Division had slipped east to Charleroi.

So far, the First Army's northward turn had bagged few prisoners. Not only had there been little opposition to the advance; there was little fresh evidence of Germans in the neighborhood, and another envelopment seemed about to end in disappointment. Nevertheless, the 3rd Armored went about the business of establishing roadblocks between Avesnes and Mons, and the 1st Division moved northwest from Avesnes to try to smoke out some enemies. The sense of disappointment proved premature; there were plenty of enemies close at hand. Hit by the Big Red One, a mass of Germans sprang to life and began thrashing about in search of a direction in which they might move without further immediate Anglo-American entanglements. But the XIX Corps was west of them, the V Corps was south of them, the British had advanced beyond Tournai and were closing in from the north, and the 3rd Armored Division blocked the paths to Germany.

Most of the German soldiers thus pocketed had endured too much and felt too exhausted and discouraged to go on trying to escape, if trying meant fighting. Few higher headquarters staffs were with them to incite them to do battle. (Those few that were, mainly parts of the LVIII Panzer Corps and II SS Corps headquarters, once again largely escaped.) The fighter-bombers of IX TAC were pouncing upon the German soldiers and their equipment, afterward claiming the destruction of 851 motor vehicles, 50 armored vehicles, and 652 horse-drawn vehicles. The enemy troops simply gave up. On the afternoon of September 3, between 7,500 and 9,000 fell into the hands of the 3rd Armored and the 1st Division alone. Altogether, the closing of the Mons pocket netted some 25,000 prisoners.

Despite the escape of the headquarters staffs, it was the most complete and most satisfying of the encirclement efforts, albeit a miniature operation compared with the Falaise pocket or what might have been at the Seine. It might be significant that closing an envelopment satisfactorily involved entrusting the trap to Joe Collins and the VII Corps. It is surely significant that, throughout the operation, Collins retained his ability to keep sight of all possible objectives and advantages. Just as in COBRA he more than any other American commander planned and acted to ensure that an effort to trap German troops would not hinder the exploitation of the breakthrough toward possibly still greater advantages, so now when he was ordered to turn north from Rethel and Montcornet,

Collins's first thought was that any undue slackening of the drive eastward toward Germany, or a widening of the gap between his corps on the First Army right and the Third Army to the south must be prevented. He asked Hodges about these problems, was told they were his problems, and reinforced the 4th Cavalry Group to maintain the eastward march while the rest of his corps was going north, and to fill the gap south to the Third Army's left flank. Collins gave the 4th Cavalry Group a battalion each of light tanks, motorized artillery, tank destroyers, and infantry, along with three engineer companies, and further instructed it, while it was about its job of keeping contact with Patton, to establish a bridgehead over the Meuse at Mézières.

Encroaching into the British zone of advance or not, the First Army had bestowed upon Montgomery a brilliant counter to Patton's claims that demonstrated achievement had won for the Third Army first call on supplies. Nor, with 30 Corps rejuvenated under Horrocks's leadership, were Montgomery's British soldiers far behindhand in awarding their commander new cards to play in his contest for the priority of the northeastward advance. While the Canadian army dropped off forces to capture the Channel ports, the British Second Army sped across the Flanders battlefields of 1914–1918 and into the heart of Belgium. At dawn of September 3, the Guards Armoured Division of 30 Corps was in the vicinity of the Belgian border a little over 100 kilometers from Brussels. While the Americans cleared the Mons pocket, the Guards drove into the Belgian capital that Sunday afternoon—despite more impediments from welcoming crowds than usual, for the Belgians could offer British soldiers a more unrestrained and wholehearted gratitude than the proud French could ever find in their hearts.

Meanwhile Horrocks's other spearhead, the 11th Armoured Division, bypassed Brussels and struck for Antwerp. German disarray remained so pervasive that, when the division rolled into the port city on Monday morning, almost nothing of the expected demolition had occurred. Some damage to the locks would preclude immediate use of the wet basins, three railroad bridges were destroyed, and two sunken coasters would have to be removed from the estuary. But when the 11th Armoured reached the docks in the early afternoon, they found the quays in good condition, warehouses and sheds mostly intact, and even the port's cranes and other electrical unloading machinery practically untouched and almost all in working order.

Strategy and Logistics

It was on that day, September 4, that Eisenhower issued his new directive confirming the restored emphasis on Patton's advance, to which he had been led by Patton's crossings of the Meuse and the conference of Saturday, September 2. The combination of circumstances drew a predictable response from Montgomery, in a new missive to Eisenhower stating:

> I would like to put before you certain aspects of future operations and give you my views.
> 1. I consider we have now reached a stage where one really powerful and full-blooded thrust toward Berlin is likely to get there and thus end the German war.
> 2. We have *not* enough maintenance resources for two full-blooded thrusts.
> 3. The selected thrust must have all the maintenance resources it needs without any qualification, and any other operation must do the best it can with what is left over.

4. There are only two possible thrusts: one via the Ruhr and the other via Metz and the Saar.

5. In my opinion the thrust likely to give the best and quickest results is the northern one via the Ruhr.

6. Time is vital and the decision regarding the selected thrust must be made at once and para. 3 above will then apply.

7. If we attempt a compromise solution and split our maintenance resources so that neither thrust is full-blooded we will prolong the war.

8. I consider the problem viewed as above is very simple and clear cut.

9. The matter is of such vital importance that I feel sure you will agree that a decision on the above lines is required at once. If you are coming this way perhaps you would look in and discuss it. If so delighted to see you lunch tomorrow. Do *not* feel I can leave this battle just at present.[7]

The condition of SHAEF's communications at Jollouville lent a certain warrant to Montgomery's otherwise arrogant recommendation about how to conduct a discussion, for Eisenhower's usefulness was limited while he was confined at SHAEF Forward. Nevertheless, the Supreme Commander did not choose to call on Montgomery for the moment. Illustrating the communications problem, however, Eisenhower's "Most immediate" reply, sent at 7:45 P.M. September 5, reached Montgomery in two parts, the first not arriving until 9:00 A.M. September 7, and the second coming to Montgomery near Brussels only at 10:15 A.M. September 9. Paragraphs three and four reached Montgomery first, with paragraphs one and two following.

Thus on the morning of September 7 Montgomery heard in reply—from Eisenhower's paragraphs three and four—that it was essential to open Le Havre and Antwerp to sustain a powerful thrust into Germany, and that while the offensive toward the Ruhr as always had priority, it was Eisenhower's "intention to initially occupy the Saar and the Ruhr, and by the time we have done this, Havre and Antwerp should be available to maintain one or both of the thrusts you mention."[8] In short, the Supreme Commander was holding to his revised plan of September 2 as affirmed in his directive of September 4.

Montgomery responded on September 7:

Have just received paras. 3 and 4 of your message of 5 September. First part of message has not arrived yet so do not know what it contains. My maintenance is stretched to the limit. First instalment of 18 locomotives only just released to me and balance still seems uncertain. I require an air lift of 1000 tons a day at Douai or Brussels and in last two days have had only 750 tons total. My transport is based on operating 150 miles from my ports and at present I am over 300 miles from Bayeux. In order to save transport I have cut down my intake into France to 6000 tons a day which is half what I consume and I cannot go on for long like this. It is clear therefore that based as I am at present on Bayeux I cannot capture the Ruhr. As soon as I have a Pas de Calais port working I would then require about 2500 additional 3-ton lorries plus an assured air lift averaging minimum 1000 tons a day to enable me to get to the Ruhr and finally Berlin. I submit with all respect to your para. 3 [about Le Havre and Antwerp as essential] that a reallocation of our present resources of every description would be adequate to get one thrust to Berlin. It is very difficult to explain things in a message like this. Would it be possible for you to come and see me?[9]

Two days later, Montgomery received the missing first part of Eisenhower's message of September 5. It stated, to Montgomery's surprise, that Eisenhower agreed "with your conception of a powerful and fullblooded thrust to Berlin." But it also stated, contradictorily, that the Allies "must immediately exploit our success by promptly breaching the Siegfried Line, crossing the Rhine on a wide front and seizing the Saar and the Ruhr"—the September 2 decision again reiterated.[10] More to the point, however, Montgomery's message of September 7 meanwhile had expressed enough urgency to bring Eisenhower flying to 21 Army Group after all, on September 10.

The incidental surroundings of the visit were not happy. It chanced that on returning to Jollouville from the September 2 conference with the American commanders, Eisenhower's liaison plane had to make a forced landing on the beach of the Cotentin. In trying to help the pilot move the light plane away from a rising tide, Eisenhower wrenched his knee, so badly that he had to spend the next few days in bed and wear a plaster cast. When he called on Montgomery, he could not leave his plane, and the conference had to take place inside it.

If these circumstances did not sufficiently abbreviate the short temper that lurked behind Ike's conciliatory demeanor, Montgomery acted to cut the fuze closer. He insisted that Eisenhower's chief administrative officer, Lieutenant General Sir Humphrey Gale, vacate the premises, while equally insisting that his own chief administrative officer should stay. He conceded that the Deputy Supreme Commander, Marshal Tedder, might remain. But lest this generosity mislead Eisenhower about Montgomery's conception of their respective credentials, the field marshal opened the proceedings with a lecture on strategy delivered in a fashion suitable for an audience of dull-minded schoolboys. As it continued, this performance also gathered invective directed at the conduct of the campaign since D-Day, until at last Eisenhower put his hand on Montgomery's knee and cautioned: "Steady, Monty! You can't speak to me like that. I'm your boss."[11]

It is thus remarkable that there emerged from the meeting another shift in strategic direction, in favor of Montgomery's northeastward thrust. In particular, closing an issue that had been much discussed in the preceding several days, Eisenhower confirmed that Montgomery should receive the one substantial reserve in SHAEF's possession, the airborne forces recently gathered in the First Allied Airborne Army. This army should be employed in an airborne operation of Montgomery's conception, designed to cross the Rhine in Holland, outflank the West Wall, and place the Allies immediately on the doorstep of the Ruhr: Operation MARKET-GARDEN.

The next day Montgomery attempted to press his advantage by means of a warning message to Eisenhower that current allocations of supplies still would not permit MARKET-GARDEN to be launched before September 23 at the earliest and possibly September 26. Eisenhower promptly reaffirmed the latest direction of strategy by dispatching Bedell Smith to Montgomery's headquarters with new assurances. As Montgomery understood it, Eisenhower's chief of staff promised that the Saar offensive would be halted after all, that the bulk of the 12th Army Group's logistic support would go to the First Army on Montgomery's right, that Montgomery would be entitled to deal directly with Hodges to ensure the First Army's close cooperation, and that the transport of the three grounded American divisions would be used to sustain 21 Army Group. Immediately, SHAEF began delivering Montgomery's requested 1,000 tons a day to Brussels by road and air. The next day, SHAEF refined the promise to continue such deliveries by extending the Red Ball Express to the Bayeux-Brussels route for delivery of 500 tons a day, arranging an air lift of another 500 tons daily, and preparing an additional air lift by bombers to deliver POL. A pleased Montgomery promptly scheduled MARKET-GARDEN for September 17.

Ready to intrude upon this unwonted harmony, however, were certain still unresolved misunderstandings between the field marshal and the Supreme Commander. Montgomery was still talking about "one really powerful and full-blooded thrust towards Berlin." In fact, nevertheless, he was no longer contemplating any effort resembling the forty-division offensive of his mid-August proposals. By early September, he had conceded enough to the constraints of logistics that he was planning rather a sixteen- or eighteen-division advance across the Rhine and into Germany—in effect, a march by the British Second and American First Armies.

It was unfortunate and incongruous that Montgomery accompanied this concession to straitened supply with an ambitious extension of his objective: no longer was he aiming, as in August, for the Ruhr; he was heading "towards Berlin." By September 18, "towards Berlin" was to harden into: "I consider that the best objective is the Ruhr, and thence on to Berlin by the northern route."[12] Berlin was still some 650 kilometers away. To plan a rapid thrust "on to Berlin" by sixteen or eighteen divisions was to substitute for "one really powerful and full-blooded thrust" the kind of offensive Eisenhower had feared Montgomery intended all along, and which Eisenhower doubted could accomplish much that was useful. After the war, Eisenhower was to describe Montgomery's designs as involving all along "a single knife-like and narrow thrust into the center of Germany," or a "pencillike thrust into the heart of Germany."[13] Montgomery was to deny that he intended anything merely "knife-like" or "pencillike," pointing to his forty-division proposal. But an offensive by only sixteen to eighteen divisions would surely approach the "knife-like" or "pencillike."

And the difference between a genuinely full-blooded offensive and a knife-like thrust was crucial. Liddell Hart has argued in favor of Montgomery's design for a quick punch into Germany by pleading that the circumstances of September had outrun any need for a broader offensive:

> [The] 'broad-front' plan of advance on the Rhine, designed before the invasion of Normandy, would have been a good way to strain and crack the resistance of a strong and still unbeaten enemy. But it was far less suited to the actual situation, where the enemy had already collapsed, and the issue depended on exploiting their collapse so deeply and rapidly that they would have no chance to rally. That called for a pursuit without pause.
>
> In these circumstances, Montgomery's argument for a single and concentrated thrust was far better in principle.[14]

The trouble with this interpretation, and with the latest version of Montgomery's northeastward offensive, lay in the question whether "the enemy had already collapsed." There still appeared to be little respectable opposition on Montgomery's immediate front, but as early as September 9, General Eisenhower felt obliged to moderate the optimism of some of the earlier SHAEF intelligence estimates and to shift closer to Patton's

Colonel Koch's assessment of the enemy: "Enemy resistance, which has shown signs of collapse during the past few weeks, is stiffening somewhat as we approach the German frontier."[15] Against the reorganized German forces that Hitler was gathering within the Reich, a force of only eighteen divisions trying to plunge all the way to Berlin would suffer from badly exposed flanks and from a line of communication stretched so perilously that adequate logistical support might at last become impossible. In short, Montgomery's concessions to logistical reality combined with the apparent expansion of his ambition, to reach all the way to Berlin, nourished Eisenhower's misgivings: "There was still a considerable reserve in the middle of the enemy country and . . . any pencillike thrust into the heart of Germany such as he proposed would meet nothing but certain destruction."[16]

Yet Montgomery had been unable to avoid lowering his logistical sights from arguing for a forty-division offensive to settling for an eighteen-division advance. For one thing, he had on his hands an embarrassing fiasco of British logistics which increased his dependence on American help. Some 1,400 British three-ton lorries, plus all the replacement engines for this model, had been discovered to have faulty pistons rendering them useless. They represented the loss of 800 tons a day.

At that, Montgomery might still have been able to push nine divisions of the British Second Army into the Ruhr. Assuming as the Allied logisticians did that each division required 650 tons per day, nine British divisions needed 5,850 tons of supplies daily. By early September, the French railways were repaired enough to carry 2,800 tons daily into the excellent and largely intact Belgian rail network. Eisenhower had promised another 500 tons daily from the Bayeux-to-Brussels Red Ball Express. The promised air lift, 500 tons daily carried by transports and an additional amount by bombers, might reach 1,000 tons per day. Receiving 4,300 tons from these sources, Montgomery would have to haul another 1,550 tons daily himself. To accomplish this, according to standard SHAEF calculations that a truck company could carry 200 tons 100 miles per day, would require forty-six or forty-seven truck companies taking six days for the 600-mile round trip between Bayeux and Belgium. To carry the nine divisions on into the Ruhr, a two-day round trip totalling about 250 miles (and thus stretching the companies somewhat beyond the 100-miles-per-day standard travel distance) would require another fifty-eight or fifty-nine truck companies. Montgomery's army group had 140 truck companies, so thirty-four to thirty-six companies would remain to support the six divisions of the Canadian First Army and for port clearances while the Second Army advanced. It might just have worked—as far as the Ruhr, not Berlin.

But the supply situation of Hodges's First Army, intended to advance in tandem with the Second Army in Montgomery's design, presented more difficulties. The SHAEF logisticians of course calculated that Hodges's nine divisions also consumed a total of 5,850 tons daily. (In early September the First Army was actually reduced to eight divisions, the 79th Infantry having been returned to the Third Army, leaving the XIX Corps with only two divisions.) Even after Eisenhower's August 23 decision vesting supply priority in the First Army over the Third, however, the greater distance between the American beaches and ports and the American front, plus the general disruptive effect of the headlong advance upon the American Communications Zone, limited COMZ's supply deliveries to Hodges to 2,225 tons daily at the end of August—this at the time when the Third Army was in a worse case and practically brought to a halt by dry gasoline tanks. Using its own transportation, Hodges's army was able to increase its daily receipts to 3,000 tons.

On September 5, an improvement in American supply deliveries after several days' suspension of Patton's advance encouraged Bradley to anticipate total receipts of 7,000 tons daily. In accordance with Eisenhower's strategic shift of September 2–4, Bradley revoked Hodges's priority and announced an equal split of this tonnage between the First and Third Armies, 3,500 tons daily to each. As events developed, COMZ proved unable to deliver 7,000 tons. During early September, the First Army received about 3,300 tons per day, the Third Army 2,500 tons. To bring up an additional 2,500 tons daily from the railheads west of the Seine, needed to provide Hodges with 5,800 tons, would have required about thirty-six additional truck companies. To sustain the First Army into the Ruhr would have required yet another fifty-eight or fifty-nine truck companies, just as with the Second Army. With the demands of the Red Ball Express, the ninety-four truck companies of this calculation could not have been found even if the Third Army and the operations against Brest had been stripped of nonorganic transport altogether.

Of course, Hodges's army could have made up some of the difference by using its organic trucks, as it had done when it increased its receipts from 2,225 tons to 3,000, and as it did customarily in any event. In addition, the 650-tons-per-division-per-day figure has to be regarded as another specimen of the logisticians' habitual caution. Consumption during the race across France had been closer to half that figure. The Germans when they were on the offensive in Russia had allotted only some 300 tons per day to their mobile divisions, and Rommel's divisions in North Africa had sometimes held the offensive with much less. On the other hand, if the Anglo-American allowance of 650 tons per division per day was lavish, it was this very generosity of support that gave the Western Allies their unique capacity for sustained rapid movement. The pursuit across France had been accomplished on a supply scale of about 300 tons a day, but the result was that by September many vehicles were simply wearing out, whether they had gasoline in their tanks or not. Considering how badly worn Hodges's vehicles already were, how many Shermans already could not move or fight until they were repaired, it would have been unrealistic to expect the First Army to penetrate the Ruhr on an allowance much lower than 650 tons per division per day. American divisions could get by with less for a time; but they had already been doing so for 400 to 600 kilometers.

Despite Bradley's promise of more, Patton's Third Army between the Meuse and the Moselle continued to receive only about 2,500 tons a day through the whole first half of September. This was only about 500 tons per day above its receipts in the first few days of the month, when dry gasoline tanks had stopped the army in its tracks. The margin of tonnage between allowing Patton a measure of movement again and reducing him once more to paralysis was insufficient to count on it for maintaining a "full-blooded thrust" even if all of it had been diverted to Hodges, and the Third Army had been immobilized all over again.

Even the emaciated version of Montgomery's "full-blooded thrust" was beyond the capacity of Allied logistics. Montgomery surely erred in speaking to Eisenhower about a thrust "towards" or "on to" Berlin; his doing so could only cause Eisenhower to doubt the field marshal's sense of responsibility and his motives. At most, for Eisenhower to give priority to Montgomery's northeastward offensive, even to the point of paralyzing Patton again, might have permitted parts of the British Second Army and the American

First Army to hasten to the Ruhr—but not on a scale of sixteen to eighteen divisions. Nevertheless, Eisenhower was willing to gamble that this venture might pay satisfactory dividends. He virtually halted Patton again so Montgomery might try to launch a spearhead across the Rhine. The first part of the gamble was to be Montgomery's Operation MARKET-GARDEN.

The Battle of Brest

To consider why armies with the wealth of the United States behind them should have arrived at this logistical predicament, it is useful to turn back 800 kilometers westward from the Meuse and the Scheldt to Brittany, to the battle for Brest.

General Middleton's VIII Corps of the Third Army began the sustained battle for Brest on August 25, the same day that Paris fell and the bulk of the Third Army began the pursuit east of the Seine. Middleton had shifted the 6th Armored Division east from Brest for the mobile part of his corps's work, covering the 12th Army Group's southern flank along the Loire, and meanwhile gradually moving far enough eastward to be able to rejoin Patton's main body on short notice. For the attack on Brest, Middleton had three infantry divisions plus General Earnest's Task Force A. Stroh's 8th Division, already with the corps when it entered Brittany, had been joined by Robertson's 2nd and Gerhardt's 29th. Middleton's intelligence estimated that some 16,000 German troops had to be overcome in the Brest area—a figure more than slightly in error, for eventually the Battle of Brest yielded 38,000 German prisoners. To subdue the numbers he thought were in Brest, Middleton asked the Third Army for an initial stock of 8,700 tons of ammunition, with a replenishment allowance of 11,600 tons for the first three days. Already strapped for adequate supply tonnage in its eastern spearheads, the army at first allowed Middleton only 5,000 tons of ammunition for the whole operation, increasing this amount to 8,000 tons only on Middleton's most urgent pleas. Eventually the battle grew so fierce, and supplies had to be diverted from the eastward advance at such a rate, that Middleton had 25,000 tons of ammunition in his corps supply depot when the port actually fell.

The fight became so fierce because Brest was well protected by hills and ridges separated by deep, narrow valleys crossed by numerous streams; by defensive works ranging from pillboxes to an elaborate interconnecting system begun by Vauban, greatly strengthened in the nineteenth century, and given modern artillery by the Germans; and by a garrison built around the elite 2nd Parachute Division, under a commander, Generalleutnant Hermann B. Ramcke—a hero of the 1941 battle for Crete—who took seriously the Führer's injunctions about defending fortresses to the last extremity.

Task Force B under Brigadier General James A. Van Fleet, assistant commander of the 29th Division, led off promisingly in a preliminary action beginning August 21. Van Fleet captured Hill 154, which dominates a rocky promontory overlooking the approaches to Brest from the south. But for many days thereafter, the VIII Corps enjoyed little comparable success. The battle for Brest had to become a patient, grinding, probing action lurching from strongpoint to strongpoint. Middleton called in heavy air strikes whenever the weather was good enough—much of the time it was dismal—but against defenders thoroughly dug into the ground or holding well-constructed permanent casemates, the effects were minimal. So were those of shelling by H.M.S. *Warspite*. Flame throwers and demolitions charges often had to do the final job of cleaning out a strongpoint. On August 28, two leading companies of the 8th Division's attack were cut off and captured. On September 1, corps artillery fired 750 missions in twenty-four hours, and known enemy gun positions were kept under continuous fire, but despite such support the infantry gained only a few hundred meters. Middleton wrote a pessimistic letter to Bradley, complaining about his supply situation and air support, and saying that the troops were "none too good"—the now-familiar problem of American infantry's lack of aggressiveness in a head-on fight.

After September 10, Patton far to the east no longer had to concern himself directly with this stubborn battle in his rear, because the VIII Corps passed to Lieutenant General William H. Simpson's Ninth Army. The Ninth had become operational five days earlier at Rennes and assumed responsibility for patrolling Bradley's southern flank as well as for Brittany. The tall, lean, egg-bald, restrained, and modest General Simpson took over direct control of the 6th Armored Division and the 83rd Infantry Division along the Loire, to allow Middleton to give all his attention to Brest.

By that time, progress was at last becoming visible enough to restore optimism. On September 7, the 2nd Division had captured Hill 92, commanding the northeast approaches to Brest. On September 8, Company G of the 29th Division's 115th Infantry captured the Kergonant Strongpoint, which had been defying the division for ten days. As S.L.A. Marshall described the Maryland company's action:

> The task was truly formidable. The Company had to charge 700 yards across an open field to close on the enemy works. It made this move at one bound, with the men firing from the hip and shouting the division battle cry as they ran. A few were cut down, but the others continued the run until they flopped down next to the hedgerow which covered the enemy's inner fire line. The charge lasted five or six minutes. It was executed with such dash and vigor that most of the members of the enemy garrison fled their works and escaped via a sunken road to the rearward.[17]

To complete the job, Lieutenant Robert W. Rideout, the company commander, had to reach the strongpoint itself at the head of his reserve squad and a platoon on loan from another company, a total of seventy-three men, because his own company was reduced to eighty men and for the time being fought out. "None too good" was not a description applying to all American infantry. And Kergonant opened a general advance by the whole Blue-Gray Division.

On September 10, the 8th Division reached the city wall of Brest. Two days later, Ramcke declined an offer of surrender, but the end was coming, and Middleton responded to Ramcke's rebuff by telling his troops: "Take the Germans apart."[18] That afternoon, the 29th Division's other Maryland regiment, the 175th, captured Fort Keranroux, one of the old French works. On September 16, the same division's Virginia regiment, the 116th, broke a still tougher ancient obstacle, Fort Montbarey, with the aid of tanks from the 141st Regiment, Royal Armoured Corps. Two days later, two of the main groups of defenders surrendered. Ramcke escaped across the harbor to a strongpoint on the Crozon Peninsula, but on September 19 the 8th Division overran the peninsula's main defensive lines and most of its troops, and in the afternoon Ramcke gave himself up. He claimed to have fired the last shell from his remaining 75mm. gun. Task Force A rounded up the last resistance the next day.

To capture the port and the 38,000 prisoners, the VIII Corps had suffered 9,831 casualties. To accumulate the eventual surplus of 25,000 tons of ammunition had required continual exasperated appeals from Middleton to Bradley and from Bradley to the Communications Zone—whose own communications, in the most literal sense of the word, were so defective that it took two days for a message from Bradley about Brest, dated August 28, to be delivered to COMZ headquarters. To deliver so great a tonnage of ammunition, not counting other supplies, demanded also a considerable diversion of scarce transport along the 130 kilometers from Cherbourg to Brest. The fact that through much of the battle there was not enough transport explains why throughout most of the operation Middleton was exasperated. Eventually, for two weeks beginning September 5, 3,000 tons of ammunition per day went to Middleton in landing craft. This transport also could have served other purposes, by going to beaches beyond the Seine.

Middleton's troops around Brest, along with the rest of the forces in Brittany, mainly around Lorient and St. Nazaire, numbered some 80,000. Bradley was so concerned about Brest that on September 10 he gave Middleton first priority in supply, ahead of the divisions pressing toward Germany. Air support for Brest did not so directly affect the advance farther east as supply priority, but what happened was significant. For nearly a month, a considerable part of the AAF's European strength was diverted from other operations to aid Middleton. The VIII Corps received continuous support except during bad weather. Fighter-bombers on alert status flew about 430 separate missions involving more than 3,200 sorties. Fighter-bombers of XIX and IX TAC also flew planned missions against fifty targets between September 4 and 7. Medium and heavy bombers frequently hit the Brest fortifications. Between August 26 and September 18, XIX TAC flew the majority of its missions against Brest on every day except three.

For what purpose? According to Patton, Bradley told him: "I would not say this to anyone but you, and have given different excuses to my staff and higher echelons, but we must take Brest in order to maintain the illusion of the fact that the U.S. Army cannot be beaten." Patton's own comment was: "More emotion than I thought he had. I fully concur in this view. Anytime we put our hand to do a job we must finish it."[19]

Bradley's explanation of the Brest action in his memoirs carries an aura of defensiveness, as if he were offering one of his "different excuses." Acknowledging almost 10,000 American casualties, he asks: "Why not rope off Brest as we did Lorient and St. Nazaire—or as Montgomery did the Channel ports?" In answer, he points to the aggressiveness and fanaticism of General Ramcke and the 2nd Parachute Division, arguing that it would have been too expensive to contain soldiers like these. "I went ahead with the costly siege of Brest, with Eisenhower's approval, not because we wanted that port, but because Ramcke left us with no other solution." Bradley fails to note that Ramcke had no tanks and little transport, so that his aggressiveness could have found only very limited outlets, or that when the sustained effort began, American intelligence thought he had only 16,000 troops.[20]

Whether to contain Ramcke or to guard the prestige of the American army when it put its hand to a job, the end of August and the beginning of September represented a singularly ill-chosen time to divert a large effort to Brest. If either of the cited reasons actually compelled the Americans to capture Brest, surely the supreme effort did not have to occur at the time when a crisis of supply was certain to develop farther east—as everyone foresaw when the armies crossed the Seine. If Brest had to be taken sometime, surely it did not have to be assailed at the very moment when Bradley himself believed that the armies moving eastward ought to "throw everything we've got into Germany" because Germany might then collapse—but that the danger lay in not having enough supplies to go far enough.[21]

The only persuasive explanation for the Americans' persistence in attacking Brest, particularly at the critical time when they did so, is that they still allowed themselves to be bound by the constrictions of the OVERLORD planning, and thus by the old fears of dangers so perilous in an amphibious assault and buildup that nothing beyond getting ashore and staying there had been adequately thought out. They were still impeded by the inheritance of Gallipoli. The excessively cautious concern of the planners for the postinvasion buildup and thus for ports had turned the Third Army into Brittany from Avranches at the beginning of August, when far greater opportunities beckoned to the east. Now the dead hand of the planning still held an excessively large corps in Brittany and diverted first priority in supply tonnage westward to Brest when it was most desperately needed on the German frontier.

The battle for Brest reflects the excessive caution of the planners, and of a generalship that persisted in relying on the OVERLORD plans, in a still deeper sense. Just as the planners' preoccupation with merely getting ashore and staying there had failed to lay an adequate foundation for a breakout from Normandy—from the placement of the Americans on the right flank of the invasion and therefore in the Bocage on through every other aspect of the planning—so when a breakout nevertheless took place, the plans offered no adequate means of seizing the opportunity. Even if the OVERLORD logistical planners had not thought anything resembling the Avranches breakout and the pursuit without pause across the Seine likely, they might have made some provision for the bare possibility. To be caught utterly unprepared for opportunities that are possible and foreseeable, even if unlikely, is among the worst forms of a generalship that takes counsel of its fears. Yet that was exactly the condition of OVERLORD logistical planning. When the opportunity to leap the Seine proved irresistible even to field commanders otherwise so cautious that they played out the whole Brest drama to its tedious conclusion, the still more cautious logisticians proved never to have considered that flexibility might be a military virtue.

15: . . . and Time

IT WAS thin gruel that remained to the Anglo-American armies in lieu of the capacity for "one really powerful and full-blooded thrust" to the Rhine and the Ruhr, but after all, General Eisenhower on September 10 had committed whatever he possessed to the strategy of Field Marshal Montgomery. On September 12, the Supreme Commander reiterated and reinforced the commitment in the message that Bedell Smith carried to Montgomery, and again Eisenhower underlined his assurances in a cable to 21 Army Group the next day. Restating in writing General Smith's pledge that American transport would provide Montgomery the 1,000 tons of supplies daily beyond his own logistical capacities that he needed for his forthcoming operations, Eisenhower also affirmed that General Hodges's First Army would receive adequate maintenance for the supporting operations Montgomery desired on his right. Most importantly, Eisenhower was prepared to adopt any necessary emergency expedients "to enable you to get across the Rhine. . . . every day gained will be to our advantage. . . ."[1]

On September 20, in a message stating, "I cannot believe there is any great difference in our concepts," Eisenhower's commitment to Montgomery became still firmer:

> Never at any time have I implied that I was considering an advance into Germany with all armies moving abreast.
> Specifically I agree with you on the following: My choice of routes for making the all-out offensive into Germany is from the Ruhr to Berlin.[2]

By that time, the best approximation of an "all-out offensive" that Montgomery could achieve was already under way.

The Field Marshal

How good would Montgomery's best be? As far as the generalship of the newly commissioned field marshal was concerned, his campaign from the beaches to Brussels offered promising auguries. Though his role in the OVERLORD planning had certainly been pivotal enough that he must bear considerable responsibility for the conspicuous caution of the plans, since D-Day Montgomery had been among the few consistently aggressive and energetic senior commanders in Eisenhower's armies. If he had brought upon himself a nagging American resentment through his failure to execute a breakthrough around Caen, the disappointment came mainly because he had seemed to promise too much beforehand. The frustrations of Caen should have been expected, by the Americans as well as by Montgomery himself, because they originated not in a lack of vigor on Montgomery's part but in the inherent limitations of the British army, in that army's inability to absorb the casualties of a major offensive effort against strong defenses. Under the circumstances of his command, Montgomery at Caen had displayed all the aggressiveness that could have been expected. His limited attacks to keep the enemy off balance and to draw German reserves into his sector were almost continuous. Short of accepting the intolerable casualties of a full-scale attempt toward a break-through, his probing had been so vigorous that he provoked War Office complaints about exceeding the nation's capacity to produce replacements. But he persevered.

Once the Americans had introduced mobile warfare by accomplishing the break-through and breakout that Montgomery's British forces could not afford to achieve, Montgomery was bolder even than Patton in his willingness to discard the plans for Brittany in order to hasten all possible strength eastward. The Brittany diversion in early August might well have been worse had it not been for Montgomery's influence. Montgomery erred in overestimating the Canadian army's ability to drive forward through Falaise, and thus he contributed more than his share to the incompleteness of Allied success at the Falaise pocket. Once launched eastward to the Seine and beyond, however, he pressed General Dempsey's Second Army onward to Brussels and Antwerp at a pace rivaling the Americans'—this although another, if far less fundamental, difference between the British and American armies lay in the superior American equipment for sustained rapid movement. The British lacked a lorry comparable to the workhorse American two-and-one-half ton truck, and they did not have bridging gear and boats on the American scale for crossing the rivers of northern France.

Given Montgomery's record so far in France and his determination to launch a decisive offensive toward the Ruhr while the German defenses in his front remained in disarray, there is nothing surprising about the boldness of his conception for Operation MARKET-GARDEN, his design for employing the priorities that Eisenhower assigned him in early September. The conception was hardly without flaws, especially in its tactical requirements; but the strategic design was both sound and, in the context of Anglo-American generalship in France, refreshingly daring.

Vertical Envelopment

From Washington, General Marshall and General H.H. Arnold, the commanding general of the AAF, had been urging Eisenhower since the breakout from Normandy to use his airborne reserve the better to exploit the fluidity of the pursuit. The causes of Arnold's interest in airborne assault are evident. As the ranking American airman, he had invested large resources in transport capacity for airborne operations. The AAF would have preferred, at heart, to devote these resources to the strategic bombing campaign, which Arnold and most of his commanders believed could win the war independently. Nevertheless, if higher authority dictated a ground assault upon Germany in addition to the Combined Bomber Offensive, Arnold wanted assurance that the resources the AAF turned to support of the ground arm would not be wasted, and that the AAF should make an appropriate contribution and receive appropriate honors in return. General Marshall, for his part, had long sponsored strong airborne forces in the belief that they offered a trump card to break the tactical deadlock that had so often stultified modern war. If Marshall had won his way, the airborne operations of D-Day would have become not a shallow but a deep and bold vertical envelopment, striking eighty or ninety kilometers behind the Atlantic Wall. Since he had not had his way on the 6th of June, the test of a deep vertical envelopment remained to be attempted, and Marshall would not rest nor allow Eisenhower to forget his desires until it occurred.

On August 8, as the pursuit across France and its possibilities for airborne exploitation were opening, General Brereton left the Ninth Air Force to take command of the First Allied Airborne Army. (Major General Hoyt S. Vandenberg shifted from deputy commander of AEAF to succeed Brereton with the Ninth Air Force.) It was for elements of Brereton's army, and to satisfy Marshall's and Arnold's prodding, that the eighteen abortive airborne missions of August and early September were planned, each of them cancelled by the rapidity of the advance of the ground forces. When Eisenhower confirmed on September 10 that Montgomery should have Brereton's army for the priority northeastward drive, Montgomery immediately began detailed planning at his own, Dempsey's, and Brereton's headquarters for an idea he had already conceived to use the airborne reserve.

Montgomery proposed that the airborne troops should be dropped as a carpet in front of Dempsey's army across the many water obstacles of Holland, all the way to and over the Rhine. Without a series of airborne coups de main against the bridges, the Second Army's advance through Holland might consist of one difficult battle after another for the water crossings. Probably, in fact, a ground advance alone would not reach the Rhine before the Germans repaired their defenses in Montgomery's front, for the combination of logistical strain with the necessity to mask or clear the Channel ports and deal with the Fifteenth Army, still hovering on Montgomery's northern flank, restricted 21 Army Group's spearhead to Horrocks's 30 Corps alone. With Operation MARKET, however, the proposed airborne assault, Brereton's troops were to come out of reserve to seize all the Dutch water crossings almost simultaneously; and in coordination with MARKET, Operation GARDEN was to carry 30 Corps swiftly across the bridges seized by the airborne army, to the farthest MARKET outpost and beyond the Rhine. Because the West Wall ended at Cleve some forty kilometers south of MARKET-GARDEN's prospective Rhine crossing at Arnhem, 30 Corps reinforced by the airborne army would thus outflank that barrier and enter the northern doorway of the Ruhr. This was not even the sixteen-division assault on the Ruhr; but it offered a way to arrive there before the Germans could regroup and despite all the vexations of Allied logistics.

German resistance in front of Dempsey's Second Army was already rallying enough, and the fragility of a single-corps spearhead was already creating enough problems in dealing with the resistance, to slow the British advance markedly since the rush into Brussels and Antwerp. On September 7, nevertheless, the Guards Armoured Division won a foothold across the Albert Canal at Beeringen, and on September 10, while Eisenhower and Montgomery were conferring at Brussels, the Household Cavalry found an opening for the Irish Guards to race across a bridge of the Meuse-Escaut Canal between Bourg Leopold and Hechtel. This bridgehead, touching the Belgian-Dutch border at De Groote Barrier, was to be the springboard from which 30 Corps would launch the ground advance, Operation GARDEN, over the carpet formed by Operation MARKET's airborne landings. Because Montgomery proposed an airborne seizure of the Arnhem highway and railway bridges across the Neder Rijn just over ninety-five kilometers away, the test of a deep vertical envelopment so long desired by General Marshall was about to occur.

**CROSSINGS
OF THE
MAAS–WAAL
CANAL**

1. HONINGHUTJE
2. HATERT
3. MALDEN
4. HEUMAN

NORTH SEA

THE HAGUE

ROTTERDAM

UTRECHT

NEDER RIJN

ARNHEM

OOSTERBEEK

DRIEL

ELST

NIJMEGEN

CLEVE

GOCH

GROESBEEK

MOOK

GENNEP

VENLO

GEILENKIRCHEN

SITTARD

MAASTRICHT

MAAS–WAAL CANAL

MAAS R.

WAAL R.

OSS

GRAVE

GEMERT

HELMOND

DE GROOTE PEEL

MEIJEL

WEERT

BREE

HASSELT

'S-HERTOGEN-BOSCH

VEGHEL

ST. OEDENRODE

BOXTEL

BEST

BOZON

EINDHOVEN

VALKENSWAARD

DOMMEL R.

BEERINGEN

LOUVAIN

ZUID WILLEMS CANAL

WILHELMINA

TILBURG CANAL

BREDA

MEUSE–ESCAUT CANAL

DE GROOTE BARRIER

TURNHOUT

HERENTHALS

BRUSSELS

OVERFLAKKEE

SCHOUWEN DUIVELAND

THOLEN

NORTH BEVELAND

SOUTH BEVELAND

WALCHEREN

BRESKENS

TERNEUZEN

BRAAKMAN INLET

ANTWERP

ALBERT CANAL

ANTWERP TURNHOUT CANAL

GHENT

ESCAUT (SCHELDT)

NETHERLANDS
BELGIUM

LEIE (LYS) R.

ESCAUT (SCHELDT) R.

CANAL DE LA DERIVATION DE LA LYS

LEOPOLD CANAL

GHENT CANAL

ZEEBRUGGE

BRUGES

**MARKET-GARDEN
AND THE
APPROACHES**

Eight water obstacles lay between the Irish Guards' bridgehead over the Meuse-Escaut Canal and the north bank of the Neder Rijn at Arnhem: three major rivers ranging from 200 to 400 meters in width, the Maas (the Dutch portion of the Meuse), the Waal (a major outlet of the Rhine), and the Neder Rijn (Lower Rhine) itself; two lesser rivers, the Dommel and the Aa; and three large canals, the Wilhelmina, the Willems, and the Maas-Waal. From the resources of the First Airborne Army, the MARKET-GARDEN planners chose General Maxwell Taylor's veteran American 101st Airborne Division to land between Eindhoven and Veghel and secure a twenty-five-kilometer path crossing the Dommel River at Eindhoven, the Wilhelmina Canal at Zon, the Dommel again at St. Oedenrode, and the Willems Canal and the Aa River at Veghel. The still more experienced 82nd Airborne Division, now under Brigadier General James M. Gavin, was to drop around Grave and Groesbeek. It was to seize the Maas crossing at Grave, the Waal bridge at Nijmegen, and crossings of the Maas-Waal Canal in between. From the Groesbeek drop zone it was also to hold the Groesbeek Ridge, an elevation rising southeast of Nijmegen and extending into the Reichswald across the German frontier, only about 100 meters high at most but among the loftiest hills in Holland and vital to the defense of the carpet against counterattacks from Germany. The most distant objectives, the Neder Rijn bridges at Arnhem, were to be captured and held by the British 1st Airborne Division, a formation built around a nucleus of veterans of Britain's first airborne assault, the commando raid against the German radar station at Bruneval on February 27–28, 1942, and experienced as a division in the Mediterranean theater. The 1st Polish Parachute Brigade and, as soon as landing strips could be prepared, the 52nd Lowland Division (Airportable) were to reinforce the "Red Devils" of the 1st Airborne Division.

Brereton's First Airborne Army had two corps headquarters, the American XVIII Airborne Corps, to which General Ridgway had been promoted, and the British 1 Airborne Corps, under Lieutenant General F.A.M. "Boy" Browning. Because Browning was also deputy commander of the Airborne Army, he was chosen to land with the 82nd in the central air drop and to exercise immediate command of MARKET through his corps headquarters. Perceptive observers in touch with the planning might have interpreted this choice as a first, unsettling warning that the execution of MARKET-GARDEN might not match the laudable boldness of the strategic concept. Although two of the three divisions initially under Browning's command would be American, "Boy" was the kind of supercilious English aristocrat for whom Americans are likely to feel an instinctive dislike: "Tall, moustache, well poised. Too deliberate a smile, cool and polished manner of a British gentleman." In fact, the American airborne leaders did strongly dislike him, especially Ridgway. Two reasons, and a yet more pointed cause for unease, lay in General Bradley's reaction to word that Browning had been selected over Ridgway to lead one of the earlier, eventually aborted airborne assaults: "Christ, why don't they use Ridgway? He's a fighter and knows more about airborne than all of them."[3]

The boldness of MARKET-GARDEN lay most particularly in throwing airborne troops ninety-five kilometers in front of the nearest ground support. Despite General Marshall's long advocacy of it, so deep a vertical envelopment was a perilous adventure, which would certainly demand a fighter in the airborne command. Responding to Marshall's disappointment at his refusal to include a similarly deep airborne envelopment in NEPTUNE, Eisenhower had specified what was perilous: the superior mobility of airborne troops disappeared the moment they hit the ground. On the ground, they were among the least mobile of Allied forces, with little vehicular transport. They were also among the least well armed, without tanks or artillery except for very light guns. On the ground, airborne troops lacked both mobility and power to contend against a well equipped adversary, and therefore they soon could become a liability rather than an offensive threat. If deep vertical envelopment had been less inherently dangerous to the envelopers, the enemy would have shown greater fear of the Allied capacity for it. Indeed, Eisenhower had told Marshall:

> The German has shown time and again that he does not particularly fear what we used to refer to as a "strategic threat of envelopment." Any military man that might have been required to analyse, before this war, the situation that existed in Italy on about January 24 [after the amphibious envelopment at Anzio more than ninety kilometers in the enemy's rear], would have said that the only hope of the German was to begin the instant and rapid withdrawal of his troops in front of the Fifth Army. The situation was almost a model for the classical picture for initiating a battle of destruction. But the German decided that the thrust could not be immediately translated into *mobile tactical action*, and himself began attacking. The Nettuno [Anzio] landing, due to the incidence of bad weather, was really not much heavier in scale than an airborne landing would have been during those critical days when time was all-important. The force was immobile and could not carry out the promise that was implicit in the situation then existing.

The Anzio adventure was saved from disaster, Eisenhower reminded Marshall, only because it was an amphibious and not an airborne envelopment, so that "our complete command of the sea allowed us to continue to supply and maintain and reinforce the beachhead." A deep vertical envelopment would lack this advantage. It would therefore violate what Eisenhower regarded as a cardinal rule governing the division of forces for an envelopment: "There must exist either the definite capacity of both forces to combine *tactically*, or the probability that each force can operate independently without danger of defeat."[4]

In MARKET-GARDEN, the airborne forces would not be able to operate independently without danger of defeat, because of their limited mobility and weaponry. But could there be "the definite capacity" of the GARDEN and MARKET forces to combine tactically, when a ninety-five-kilometer gap lay between De Groote Barrier and Arnhem? Eisenhower and his chief of staff, Bedell Smith, remained gravely doubtful. Yet Montgomery was pressing them hard, and the dwindling chances for rapid victory seemed to demand exceptional willingness to take risks. If MARKET-GARDEN was to succeed, however, it would most emphatically demand tactical execution as bold as the strategic conception.

Auguries

Other auguries besides the appointment of Browning were less auspicious than they might have been. Bold tactical execution would be demanded particularly of 30 Corps, to reach the airborne troops with tanks and artillery before the enemy could exploit the inherent weakness of 1 Airborne Corps to overpower it. Field Marshal Montgomery directed, in the spirit of his strategic conception, that the ground advance must be "rapid and violent, and without regard to what is happening on the flanks."[5] The planners' timetable called for 30 Corps to cover the ninety-five kilometers to Arnhem "before the end of D plus 3." In fact, the spearhead was to push on to the IJsselmeer—the Zuider Zee—160 kilometers from the departure line, within "six days or less."[6] Despite the pace at which he had driven 30 Corps northeastward from the Seine, General Horrocks had enjoyed only a very short time to rid the corps of the habitual hesitancy that made it a disappointment from Normandy to the Seine—and that the Americans and Germans both suspected was inherent in the British army.

The advance from the Seine notwithstanding, Horrocks's generalship did not always seem to be what it had been before his wounding. For example, his own timetable for his corps called for a D-Day advance—beginning one hour after the first air drops—of only eleven kilometers, from De Groote Barrier to Valkensward, eleven kilometers short of Eindhoven and the linkup with the 101st Airborne Division. Horrocks spoke informally of hoping to be in Eindhoven by the end of D-Day—but then why not schedule officially an advance to Eindhoven that would have been more in keeping with the four-day schedule to Arnhem?

Indications that things were not yet quite right with 30 Corps persisted, especially at the moment of triumph on September 4 when the 11th Armoured Division barreled into Antwerp and captured the place with docks almost intact. In the excitement, the British neglected to take the bridges over the Albert Canal on the northern edge of the city. By the time Major General G.P.B. Roberts of the 11th Armoured got around to trying for the seizure two days later, on September 6, the Germans had rallied enough to permit him only a small bridgehead, which was promptly destroyed. The excuse later offered by the division historian was: "Had any indication been given that a further advance north was envisaged, these bridges might have been seized within a few hours of our entry."[7] There could scarcely exist a more devastating commentary on the spirit and principles instilled by the responsible division and corps commanders.

Pausing to savor the triumph at Antwerp was to produce yet worse results. If Roberts had pressed on to take the canal bridges while they remained undefended, his division and the infantry in its wake could also have moved swiftly to cross the twenty-nine kilometers to the eastern base of the South Beveland peninsula, not far across the Dutch border. Doing so would have trapped altogether the remnants of the persistent menace from the Pas de Calais, the German Fifteenth Army. As it was, the British advance to the Scheldt had nearly isolated this force; but because Roberts failed to seal off South Beveland, a precarious route of escape still existed. The Fifteenth Army's current commander, General der Infanterie Gustav von Zangen, left a few units to resist on the south bank of the Scheldt west of Antwerp, while he commenced laboriously ferrying the bulk of his troops across the estuary to Walcheren Island and thence to South Beveland and union with the German forces remaining on the Dutch mainland. Besides casting doubt on the quality of leadership in 30 Corps, these events were also sending Zangen's troops directly toward the prospective left flank of MARKET-GARDEN. The Fifteenth Army might be a shadow of its once formidable self—but within two and a half weeks, by September 22, Zangen was to evacuate to the mainland more than 86,000 men, with over 600 artillery pieces, 6,000 vehicles, and 6,000 horses. Meanwhile, any threat to the long flank of the airborne corridor to Arnhem would be a most serious matter. Given the immobility on the ground and the light weaponry of the airborne troops, Montgomery's design depended on the continued disarray of the enemy, until GARDEN was across the Rhine.

Thus the suddenly stiffening resistance in front of 30 Corps between the Albert and the Meuse-Escaut Canals was also a bad sign. Horrocks's pause to "refit, refuel, and rest"[8] from September 4 to 7—though his petrol tanks, unlike Patton's, were not dry—looked all the worse when thereafter the Guards Armoured Division required until September 10 to cover the twenty-nine kilometers from the Albert Canal to the Meuse-Escaut, with some Germans left behind still resisting in scattered crossroads towns along the division's line of communication. The defenders' numbers were small, but the terrain favored them—swampy heath and watercourses that confined vehicles to the roads—and they fought with a tenacity that the Allies had rarely encountered since far back to the west of the Seine. For, in addition to tatters of the Seventh Army, 30 Corps was meeting reconstituted Luftwaffe ground units, particularly the 2nd and 6th Parachute Regiments, the latter of which was one of the most imposing collections of tough fighting men to have disheartened the Americans in the Bocage.

The loss of Antwerp had frightened the Führer into a number of actions that still further rebuked the British pause from September 4 to 7. The Anglo-Americans would not immediately feel the priority Hitler now gave the Western Front in new artillery and assault guns, though combined with the West's priority in new tanks this gesture could become troublesome if the Allies did not hasten to grasp every opening toward a rapid victory. It meant prompt trouble, furthermore, that Hitler acted to fill the gap between the Fifteenth Army and the Seventh by hurrying to the Netherlands Generaloberst Kurt Student and the headquarters of the First Parachute Army. This "army" had been merely a training command, but it brought to the West a capable and energetic commanding officer and those reconstituted parachute regiments, built around the cadres of their veteran officers and NCOs, that impeded Horrocks's progress even before he reached the Meuse-Escaut Canal.

Student's skeleton of an army took flesh squarely in the path of MARKET-GARDEN. Student borrowed the headquarters of General der Infanterie Hans Reinhard's LXXXVIII Corps from the Fifteenth Army, gave it the 719th Division from the Netherlands garrison, and set as its first task to hold open the escape route for Zangen's army from South Beveland to the mainland. Reinhard promptly took under his wing also a higher quality though conglomerate division-sized force, Kampfgruppe Chill, which Generalleutnant Kurt Chill of the Seventh Army's 85th Division had pulled together along the Albert Canal from oddments of his own and other retreating divisions plus Luftwaffe, navy, and military government troops. Chill helped contest the British advance out of the Beeringen bridgehead over the Albert Canal, confined the advance to a narrow corridor, and ensured that MARKET-GARDEN would have a vulnerable left flank and the Fifteenth Army a path from which to strike it. Under a Colonel Walther, Student assembled the 6th Parachute Regiment, a battalion of the 2nd Parachute Regiment, and a newly formed parachute regiment as Kampfgruppe Walther directly in front of the Guards Armoured Division. On Walther's left he formed Parachute Training Division Erdmann, commanded by Generalleutnant Wolfgang Erdmann, his chief of staff, and comprising three additional new parachute regiments.

Student's abrupt conjuring up of at least the semblance of an army was especially menacing because from De Groote Barrier to Arnhem the terrain would favor the defense just as it had helped the first arriving German parachutists to accomplish much with small numbers between September 7 and 10. In MARKET-GARDEN, the Allied airborne troops would have to seize and hold open, and 30 Corps would have to traverse, a narrow corridor through additional swampy heath all the way to Arnhem—in fact a single two-lane highway, bounded immediately by small, open, cultivated fields hedged in by poplar trees and surrounded by drainage ditches. Occasionally the road ran past thick pine forests. Up the road the Irish Guards would lead 30 Corps on a front two tanks wide. To meet his time schedule for reaching Arnhem, Horrocks planned to move 20,000 vehicles over this highway from Eindhoven to Arnhem in sixty hours, which would be a considerable logistical feat—even if the Germans close in on the flanks proved unable to interrupt the traffic flow, and even if the advance maintained its schedule under the circumstances that had slowed the Guards Armoured Division to a crawl from Beeringen to De Groote Barrier.

All of which raises the question whether Montgomery's bold strategic conception could not have been applied in an area posing fewer problems of tactical execution. Horrocks's encounters with Student's newly arrived parachute formations, and the disappointingly slow pace that the enemy immediately imposed on the 30 Corps advance, prompted General Dempsey to ask that very question. Dempsey also noted that choosing the Eindhoven-Arnhem route to cross the Rhine and outflank the West Wall deviated from the essence of Montgomery's own strategic goal by assuring still further that there would be no "really powerful and full-blooded thrust," even in the Allies' northeastward advance. To take the road to Arnhem was to carry Dempsey's army off on a tangent away from General Hodges's American First Army, which in accordance with Montgomery's August desires, as accepted by Eisenhower, was still following the path out of Charleroi, Namur, and Liège into Germany. Thus at the very time when MARKET-GARDEN was being planned, the First Army was crossing into the Reich near Aachen, over 100 kilometers south of Arnhem. Every kilometer that the MARKET-GARDEN troops advanced would carry them farther from the First Army on their right and create a wider gap in the Allied front. Dempsey therefore proposed that the airborne bridgehead across the Rhine be carved out not at Arnhem but at Wesel, just behind the northern limit of the West Wall at Cleve, cutting its distance from Hodges nearly in half.

But once more the Germans' V-weapons exerted their malevolent influence. Montgomery's choice of Arnhem as the airborne objective had been assured two days before his conference with Eisenhower at Brussels when, on September 8, the first of the long-dreaded V-2 rockets hit London. They were launched near The Hague in Holland; hence Montgomery believed he must overrun Holland as rapidly as he could.

Other malevolent objects appeared in Holland at almost the same time. By September 10, the Dutch resistance was reporting to the Allies that panzer formations were resting and refitting in the Arnhem area. Within a few days these formations were identified as the 9th and probably the 10th ss Panzer Divisions. The condition of their equipment was not clearly reported, but even a few tanks could sorely menace airborne troops. The probable presence of the panzers around Arnhem contributed to Dempsey's preference for shifting the airborne objective south to Wesel. The panzers so alarmed Bedell Smith that he received Eisenhower's permission to fly to Montgomery with a warning that either the equivalent of a second British division ought to be dropped around Arnhem, or one of the American airborne divisions should be moved north and added to the Arnhem drop. Montgomery was unimpressed by the danger, and the planning did not change.

Not even as his own preparations increasingly underlined the limitations constricting the airborne operation did Montgomery allow stiffening German resistance to impress him. MARKET would be the largest aerial assault ever attempted, but the limitations nevertheless would be severe. Major General Paul L. Williams of the American IX Troop Carrier Command would direct the aerial part of the operation, and he would have at his disposal 1,545 transport planes and 478 gliders. Nevertheless, even this armada could carry no more than half of the 101st, 82nd, and 1st Airborne Divisions to their targets in a single lift, to say nothing of supplementary forces. The troops and their equipment would have to fly in relays. The division commanders asked for two missions on D-Day, to have their strength consolidated by sundown. The aerial commanders demurred, arguing that two lifts in a single day would not allow enough time for minor repairs and maintenance and resting the crews. Brereton accepted the aviators' view and scheduled one lift per day, with three and a half divisions to be carried to the drop zones by D plus 2. This decision naturally made three, or at least two, days of good weather imperative; the meteorologists warned that this was a great deal to expect along the English Channel at the approach of autumn.

Brereton accordingly scheduled the six parachute regiments of the 101st and 82nd Airborne Divisions all to land on D-Day, September 17. The 101st was to get its glider infantry on D plus 1. The 82nd, with the likelihood of heavier work to do—such as fending off counterattacks from the Reichswald—was to receive its glider artillery on the second day. On D plus 2, the 101st would get its glider artillery and the 82nd its glider infantry. Meanwhile, the British 1st Airborne Division would drop on D-Day a parachute brigade—roughly equivalent to an American parachute regiment—along with part of a glider brigade and a regiment of air landing artillery. The rest of the 1st Airborne would arrive on D plus 1. The 1st Polish Parachute Brigade would reinforce the British on D plus 2. It was fortunate that British airborne regiments were better equipped with antitank artillery than American; the 1st Airborne was likely to need all the guns it could take to the drop zones. This prolonged schedule, so dependent on the weather, embodied little of the daring of Montgomery's strategic conception; nor did many other of the tactical or logistical details.

Yet everywhere along the Western Front, the week of planning on the eve of MARKET-GARDEN witnessed the same ominous rallying of the enemy and toughening of his resistance. From the upper Moselle to the Meuse-Escaut Canal, almost all the Anglo-American forces noted particularly an unpleasant result of the incompleteness of the Falaise and Seine envelopments. As the G-2 of the 82nd Airborne expressed it, the experienced officers and staffs of the enemy's higher headquarters who had escaped the encirclements retained a "degree of control exercised over the regrouping and collecting of the apparently scattered remnants of a beaten army [that was] little short of remarkable. Furthermore, the fighting capacity of the new Battle Groups formed from the remnants of battered divisions seems unimpaired."[9]

Presiding over the recovery since September 5 was a familiar adversary. Generalfeldmarschall Gerd von Rundstedt was again Oberbefehlshaber West. Much of his importance was merely symbolic. Rundstedt was old and tired, and his subservience to the

Führer had grown almost obsequious; having repented the uncharacteristic "Surrender, you fools" outburst that precipitated his earlier departure as OB West, he had spent the late summer presiding over a Court of Honor to expel from the Wehrmacht those officers who were implicated in the July 20 plot. But Rundstedt represented to friend and foe the triumphant Wehrmacht of 1940, whose panzers had concentrated in his Army Group A for the invasion of France. There remained a touch of magic in his name and in his erect Prussian presence. Furthermore, the significance of Rundstedt's return was not simply symbolic. Relieved of dual responsibilities, Model could now give his full attention and skill in defensive war to Army Group B in front of Montgomery's 21 Army Group and Hodges's First Army; while at the same time Army Group G in front of Patton and the DRAGOON forces could receive a fuller share of the efforts of OB West.

The Americans Reach the West Wall

General Hodges, "neat and trim in his battle jacket and [with] cigaret holder"—somehow his clothes seemed to rumple when events went badly, but events in his army were still progressing well enough in the late summer of 1944—impressed Bradley's headquarters as "more positive now, he has found himself with a command."[10] He hurried his First Army onward almost without impediment from the enemy as late as September 10, the day of Eisenhower's decision to support MARKET-GARDEN. The logistical problem had grown so severe that Hodges halted his weakest corps, Corlett's XIX, around Tournai for several days after the Mons battle to afford the remainder of the army enough fuel to drive forward. But the XIX Corps was due to resume its attack on Monday, September 11, crossing the Albert Canal initially over bridgeheads won by the VII Corps on its right and 30 Corps on its left at Liège and Beeringen. Meanwhile General Gerow's V Corps and General Collins's VII were on the verge of the first Allied intrusions across the German frontier.

Gerow's corps had assembled around Montcornet on September 4 to take over Hodges's right flank and, with the rest of the army remaining to the northward after its turn toward Mons, to resume what had earlier been Collins's drive toward the historic battlegrounds and crossings of the Meuse around Mézières and Sedan. This line of advance carried Gerow into the wooded and deeply scored plateau of the Ardennes, where the relatively few good roads tended to run diagonally across his path rather than to assist him. But this broken country so seemingly hostile to an army moving on wheels and tank tracks had of course been the scene of the German panzer breakthrough into France in 1940, and now its obstacles did not prevent the V Corps from sweeping across it rapidly enough to win the honor of the first entry into Germany.

Nor did the gasoline shortage. Initially, Gerow had the 102nd Cavalry Group on his left and Oliver's 5th Armored Division on his right leading the way across and beyond the Meuse, with Barton's 4th Division following the cavalry and Cota's 28th Division trailing the armor. Despite Hodges's grounding of the XIX Corps, the 5th Armored Division ran out of gas on September 7. Thereupon Gerow passed the 28th Division through the 5th Armored and diverted his supplies of fuel to the infantry, which used less of it. When the 5th Armored gassed up again on September 9, it fanned out southeastward over a front about fifty kilometers wide to make contact with the left flank of the Third Army. Marching in triumph through welcoming crowds in the city of Luxembourg on Sunday, September 10, the 5th Armored sent a patrol of the Second Platoon, Troop B, 85th

Cavalry Reconnaissance Squadron wading across the Our River from Luxembourg into Germany near the village of Stalzemberg at 6:05 P.M. on Monday.

Before Monday evening was over, a reinforced company of the 28th Division's 109th Infantry Regiment had also entered Germany, crossing the Our on a bridge at the northern tip of Luxembourg, into the German village of Sevenig. Almost simultaneously, a patrol of the 4th Division's 22nd Infantry also crossed the Our, southeast of St. Vith, Belgium, near the German village of Hemmeres. This patrol brought back a packet of German soil, as well as a German cap and currency.

On Bradley's instructions, issued reluctantly to comply with Eisenhower's latest award of priority to the northeastward offensive, Hodges kept his center of gravity toward the left of his army to support the right flank of 21 Army Group. The halting of Corlett's corps to help keep Gerow as well as Collins moving is a limited exception to this generalization, and the British-Australian champion of Montgomery's strategy, Chester Wilmot, gives some emphasis to Hodges's effort to maintain contact between the First Army and the Third, on the ground that it constitutes an example of the Americans' betrayal of "one really powerful and full-blooded thrust." "Thus the result of giving Third Army sufficient petrol to carry it to the Moselle," says Wilmot, "was that First Army had to drive forward on its right to cover Patton, instead of on its left to support Montgomery and the drive for the Ruhr."[11] Wilmot scores a point; but as the 5th Armored Division's two days of empty gas tanks indicate, the scale on which Hodges was supporting the effort to keep in touch with Patton was scarcely lavish, and not enough to have made a critical difference in behalf of Montgomery's advance—the same conclusion that applies to the whole American right-flank effort in the crucial days of September. Furthermore, the XIX Corps's pause did not materially injure its support of the Second Army's right flank, because the advance of 30 Corps after September 4 was itself so leisurely (which is not to detract from the service 30 Corps rendered the XIX Corps by sharing the bridgehead it had won at Beeringen). A much worse blow to Hodges's moving in tandem with Dempsey came when Montgomery overruled Dempsey's suggestion to aim the airborne assault at Wesel and decided instead to go off on a tangent to Arnhem.

In the V Corps itself, Hodges and Gerow concentrated the weight of the corps mainly on its left, where it could support Collins and the First Army's main drive on the right flank of Montgomery's armies. To cover the fifty-kilometer front between the concentrated strength of the 4th and 28th Infantry Divisions and the boundary with Patton's Third Army, Gerow practically relegated the 5th Armored Division to the screening functions of a cavalry group. The stretching of the 5th Armored so Gerow's main weight could serve Hodges's commitment to help Montgomery was to result, as we shall soon see, in the sacrifice of one of the Allies' brightest opportunities for an early rupture of the West Wall.

Hodges naturally wanted to penetrate the West Wall while German troop strength in front of him remained slight, before the enemy's rallying under Rundstedt and Model could give the border fortifications stout garrisons. The very existence of a belt of fortifications in front of Hodges's army immediately shifted logistical urgency from fuel to ammunition, because even lightly held fortifications would almost certainly demand more fighting than the First Army had done since it crossed the Seine. In the race across France, ammunition shipments had been neglected to bring in as much fuel as possible. On September 10, SHAEF's ever-cautious logisticians informed Hodges that they could not fill his magazines with enough ammunition for five days' hard fighting until Friday, the 15th. Hodges was unwilling to wait quite that long to assail the West Wall, and he ordered the VII and V Corps to plan coordinated attacks for the morning of September 14, with active reconnaissance in the meantime.

Collins of the VII Corps ran true to form by requesting permission to make a reconnaissance in force as early as Tuesday, September 12, to advance as far as he could into the defenses along the German border. If the going continued easy, he would push into the West Wall without waiting for more ammunition. As usual, Collins's inclinations were both bold and militarily sound; he was aware as Patton of the unforgiving minute. Also as usual, the commander of the First Army deferred to Collins; Hodges granted the request, and instructed Gerow to begin a similar reconnaissance in force. If the Germans responded with solid opposition, Hodges cautioned, Collins and Gerow should halt in place and await the ammunition supplies.

Collins hoped quick action would produce a quick rupture of the West Wall, because the fortifications were not of overwhelming intrinsic strength. They could not compare, for example, with the defenses of Brest. This much the Americans knew; they did not know altogether how weak the West Wall was. Begun in 1936 after the remilitarization of the Rhineland, the West Wall fortifications had been intended to frighten the French and British away by the mere appearance of strength—while Hitler attended to desired projects eastward—rather than actually to bolster a defensive campaign inside the Reich frontier. A defensive campaign was not the sort of war Hitler intended to wage against the Western democracies. Leisurely construction of a short band of fortifications along the Saar River opposite the Maginot Line accelerated in May 1938 into activity on a much larger scale, when Czech resistance to German demands raised the threat of a war with both Czechoslovakia and her supposed guardians in France and Britain. The Western powers insisted on calling the German West Wall the Siegfried Line, after a portion of the enemy's Western Front fortifications of the First World War, and the misnomer persisted among the British and Americans in 1944. Fritz Todt, the builder of Hitler's Autobahns, spent the summer of 1938 and on into September supervising the intensified work along the "Siegfried Line"-West Wall, using the labor of thirty-six infantry battalions, thirty battalions of sappers, ten batteries of artillery, twelve antitank companies, and 190 sections of the labor service—500,000 workers in all. His efforts consumed about a third of Germany's annual production of cement. Nevertheless, when Hitler surveyed the West Wall on the eve of the Munich crisis, his candid if inelegant assessment was: "Ein Hundsfott wer diese Stellung nicht hält!"[12]

The Czech crisis evaporated at Munich, and not much was done on the wall thereafter, not even between 1938 and 1940. Between 1940 and August 1944, the wall was neglected and much of its armament removed. The patrol of the 5th Armored Division that first entered Germany saw about twenty concrete pillboxes of the West Wall, around one of which somebody had built a shed for chickens.

The Maginot Line was a system of large, self-contained forts. The West Wall, in contrast, was a band of small pillboxes. To the extent that it had more than a propaganda function, it was intended not to repel a strong attack but to delay it until mobile reserves could counterattack. The pillboxes were six to seven and a half meters high, measuring six to nine by twelve to fifteen meters in width and depth, with reinforced concrete walls one to two and a half meters thick, the concrete strengthened by wire mesh and steel rods and beams. These structures were located for mutual support, but in certain portions of the line they were rather thinly scattered. Only in limited areas did the pillboxes form a tight pattern of clusters in a forward line supported by an additional line of clusters to the rear; unfortunately, from Geilenkirchen past Aachen in front of Collins's VII Corps was one such strong area, because geography otherwise favored the Liège-Aachen invasion route.

Where there were obstacles such as rivers, lakes, railroad cuts, and forests, the West Wall utilized them for antitank protection. Elsewhere, German engineers had constructed up to five rows of "dragon's teeth," heavy posts or steel beams or most often pyramid-shaped reinforced concrete projections, rising in height from a little under a meter in the first row to almost a meter and a half in the fifth row, with a single concrete foundation that rose three-quarters of a meter above the ground on the approach side to form an additional obstacle. Roads leading through the dragon's teeth were obstructed with steel gates and with steel beams embedded diagonally in concrete foundations.

The neglect of the West Wall since 1940 had been so complete that when the Allies approached, staff officers at OKW had to scurry around in near-panic to find the keys that opened the entrances. No mines or barbed wire supplemented the works when the German army fell back on them, and there were few communications wires and few weapons. Most of the pillboxes could not accommodate artillery larger than the 37mm. antitank gun of the 1930s. A few large pillboxes could house a 75mm. antitank gun, but even this weapon was of limited utility against the heavier armor of 1944. The embrasures of the smaller works could not accommodate the standard German M1942 model machine gun. Although the lack of recent intelligence about the West Wall—itself an evidence of the Germans' neglect—was somewhat disconcerting to the Allies, they knew just enough about the enemy's deficiencies that as the 12th Army Group approached the wall, its commanders sloughed off their discouragement over the supply crisis and Ike's apparent favoritism toward Monty, and their spirits and intelligence assessments alike approached a new peak of optimism. Supply problems notwithstanding, they were about to assail the West Wall with missiles a lot more formidable than the gaseous subject of Hitler's disparaging remark; they were confident they would plunge through.

Supply shipments were gradually improving, and the American commanders resolved to demand that COMZ do still better. "Many of our ground forces have done the impossible," said Bradley; "let S[ervices] O[f] S[upply] try the impossible for a while. I am not convinced they are doing all that can be done." Patton echoed the army group commander: "Hell, have 'em get off their asses and work the way our troops have."[13]

"The strategic opportunity offered at the moment to the First U.S. Army is enormous," Monk Dickson, Hodges's G-2, suggested on September 15. To Dickson, the very stiffening of the enemy's resistance north and south of the First Army augmented the opportunity:

> . . . It is now apparent that after the Allies had crossed the Seine the German concentrated his forces in the North and in the South, leaving a gap from Trier to Maastricht [directly in front of Hodges] which he is now attempting to fill with everything on which he can lay his hands. His fear that the main Allied drive on the Reich would follow tradition [the historic invasion routes through the Low Countries to the north or through Metz to the south] has proved his undoing.

b. Police, L of C, Signal and other service units, hastily gathered and thrown in to man the West Wall may yield an additional 20,000 to 30,000 men in the zone of action of the First U.S. Army. However, the training, physical fitness, morale and equipment of these people are probably miserable. Moreover, the character and quality of the leadership of these rear service units will be of a low order.

c. A great shortage of [German] artillery is to be expected.

Dickson believed the bagging of the Mons pocket offered the final assurance that a virtual vacuum lay before the First Army. The inferior German troops hurried forward to try to fill the vacuum might display a temporary stiffening of morale because they would be defending their homeland, but "It is doubtful whether this can be sustained for any length of time because of the effect on the soldier of a thoroughly warweary population. . . ." The enemy would surely order a stand "on the West Wall for reasons of prestige"; but, far from being able to garrison the wall in time, "Unless troops are evacuated successfully from Finland, Norway and the Balkans, he will not have the manpower necessary to man [even] the Rhine." Thus the great strategic opportunity for Hodges:

A breakthrough in the sector of the V and VII Corps of the West Wall offers the possibility of a swift advance to the Rhine. This would force the enemy to evacuate the Rhineland because he would then occupy a compromised line with an obstacle at his back. The cutting of strategic roads and bridges and the prevention of withdrawal across the Rhine could effect the destruction of the remaining enemy western field forces. Having pierced the first belt of the West Wall south of Aachen the VII Corps has the glittering possibility of rapidly piercing the second, and proceeding via Stolberg-Duren to Cologne. The V Corps has the possibility of continuing its advance north of the Moselle along the valley of the Ahr to Andernacht. . . . exploitation of the strategic possibilities would . . . reduce the enemy to a third capability [after minimal resistance and retreat], that of collapse and surrender.[14]

"Brad and Patton agree neither will be too surprised if we are on the Rhine in a week" Hansen recorded on September 15. "Prepared the general's map for next phase of operations which extends from Rhine to the city of Berlin. . . . General anxious to slam on through to Berlin. . . . Marked bullseye on Berlin."[15]

Into the West Wall

But the First Army's attack on the West Wall was not quite early enough. On Friday, September 15, while Hansen marked his bullseye, Dickson was recording established fact when he said the VII Corps had "pierced the first belt of the West Wall south of Aachen"; but already Hodges's drive was slowing.

On Tuesday, September 12, the thin German garrisons in front of Collins had displayed skill enough in exploiting good defensive ground to halt the VII Corps reconnaissance in force short of the pillboxes. Characteristically, Collins persisted in the offensive nevertheless, ordering what amounted to a full-scale assault for Wednesday, though he did not call it that. Whereas his corps had been charging forward with its three divisions abreast on a broad front, however, Collins realigned his troops for a breakthrough on a narrow front, to be followed by an encirclement maneuver which, in conjunction with action by the XIX Corps, ought to isolate Aachen. Maurice Rose's 3rd Armored Division was to seek the breakthrough by avoiding the urban sprawl of Aachen

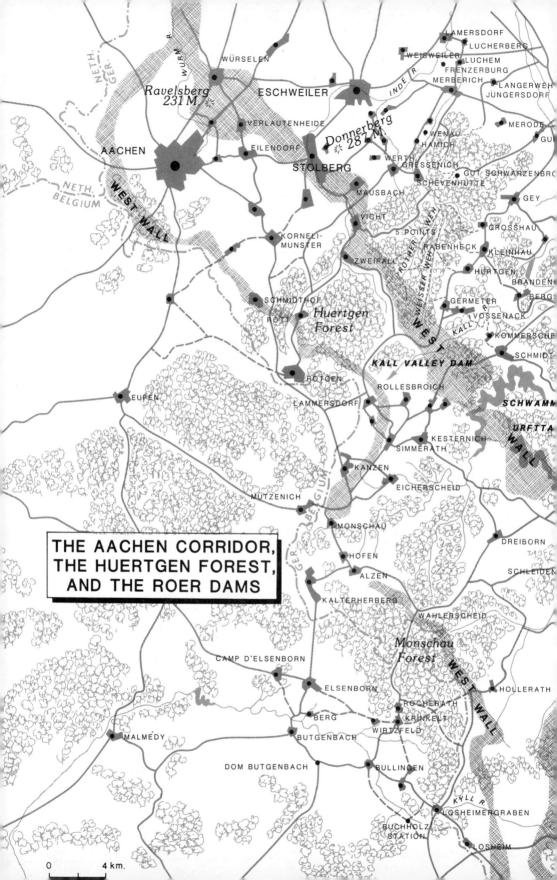

THE AACHEN CORRIDOR,
THE HUERTGEN FOREST,
AND THE ROER DAMS

as much as possible and punching up the suburban corridor through Stolberg to Eschweiler, through both bands of the West Wall. The 1st Division would screen the armor's left by reaching out from the corridor south of the city to capture high ground east of Aachen. The 9th Division would protect Rose's right by penetrating toward Düren through the forest barrier south of Aachen; here wooded hills signalize the near encroachment upon the Aachen invasion route of the rugged high ground of the Ardennes or, as its German extension is called, the Eifel.

In several days' stubborn fighting, Rose's tanks and armored infantry, aided by the 16th Infantry and a battalion of the 26th Infantry from the 1st Division, scored the desired rupture of both bands of the West Wall in two places. Part of General Hickey's CCA crossed the dragon's teeth of the first band as early as Wednesday afternoon, traversing a fill of stone and earth that local farmers had made. Brigadier General Truman E. Boudinot's CCB blasted a path straight through the teeth. By Wednesday evening, the spearheads of both combat commands had left the first belt of the wall behind them. Crossing the interval between the two belts on Thursday, CCB pushed its leading task force all the way through the second belt by Friday afternoon, September 15, and by that evening CCA also had most of the second belt behind it and only a few scattered pillboxes remaining in front.

Much as they spurred hopes everywhere from Bradley's headquarters to Rose's, nevertheless, these two penetrations through the Stolberg corridor toward Eschweiler accomplished little more than to signify what might have been possible had the Americans assailed the West Wall a few days earlier. Such German reinforcements as the 9th Panzer Division were already beginning to arrive. And Rose owed most of his success to encountering largely Landesschützen—home guard—troops under the headquarters of the 353rd Division; while at the same time, wherever the VII Corps struck enemy units that could be rated as high as mediocre, the inherent strength of the West Wall pillboxes worked wonders for the defense. The West Wall was not the mightiest of fortress complexes, but even in neglect its obstructions and the interlocking fire of the pillboxes became formidable obstacles if the strongpoints were garrisoned by anything resembling a proficient formation. The old First World War axiom that the attacker needed three times the combat manpower of the defender seemed to apply at the wall; some German defenders thought six to one was a still more accurate estimate of the predominance the Americans would require. American training in attacks against field fortifications could have been better; the technique of getting close enough to pillboxes to blow them open had to be learned for the most part by trial and error. The 90mm. antiaircraft guns that had become the American equivalent of the German 88s proved of little use against concrete fortifications. Bazookas with their rocket-fired shaped charges were more effective, but training in their use remained sketchy. American intelligence regarding the West Wall was still more sketchy, to the point that detailed information on pillbox locations was nonexistent; and pillboxes and bunkers were often exceedingly well camouflaged.

Thus on the right of the 3rd Armored, where the 9th Division met the German 89th Division, General Craig's men were unable to duplicate General Rose's penetration; the 89th Division had lost almost all of its organic troops in France and by now was decidedly rag, tag, and bobtail; but its cadre remained to stiffen newcomers, and in the West Wall that was enough. The 89th clung to the Monschau bend in the West Wall, which gave the Germans a salient pointed deep into the 3rd Armored's flank and rear.

By September 16, Collins found his corps through the wall in two almost needle-thin penetrations, but with the immediate flanks of his advance forces constricted and threatened by Germans still in the wall, and his more distant right flank and rear menaced by the recalcitrant Monschau bend. On the left flank was the urban complex of Aachen, a maze that Collins did not wish to enter, however battered the 116th Panzer Division remnants in garrison might be. The rival armies were in delicate balance; but at this juncture a fresh, well-trained, well-equipped enemy division of tough, young soldiers, the 12th Infantry, began appearing on Collins's front. When the 3rd Armored tried to renew its advance on Sunday, September 17—D-Day for MARKET-GARDEN to the north—Rose's troops collided head on with the German 12th Division, also attacking. The two sides fought each other to a standstill. The veteran Americans imposed alarming casualties on the German newcomers, a process methodically continued through the night by the fearsome American artillery. Yet the battle with the 12th Division was the last straw for the American command's hopes of a quick rupture of the West Wall on the VII Corps front. If only Collins's corps could have dealt merely with troops like the 353rd Division—but that would have required the Americans to hit the West Wall just a few days earlier, or that the enemy's capacity to rebuild his armies around the cadres escaped from France might have been just a few days slower.

As it was, the Germans could throw in a reserve division and Collins could not. Though ammunition was beginning to come up, Collins's unwillingness to await its arrival before he jumped off had badly depleted his supplies, particularly for the 105mm. howitzers. The VII Corps was also still suffering other penalities of its headlong August advance. The 3rd Armored remained at little more than half its authorized tank strength, and as many as half the tanks in service were unfit for front-line duty. All through the attack on the West Wall from September 13 onward, furthermore, the weather denied Collins his accustomed air support. His decision to attack early to test the West Wall was the right one, because German reinforcements began filling the works opposite him only at the eleventh hour, so his gamble nearly succeeded. But on September 18 Collins ordered his troops to hold and consolidate, except for the 9th Division which must try to improve the security of the right flank.

Farther south, it was almost night on September 11 before Gerow received Hodges's order of that date acceding to Collins's desire to hasten the First Army attack. Since it was than too late for the V Corps to prepare a strong effort for September 12, Gerow confined himself to preparatory activities through both of the next two days and attacked the West Wall as originally scheduled on Thursday, the 14th. When he did so, the V Corps met opportunities and frustrations very similar to those of the VII Corps. But describing Gerow's opportunities raises an additional question about Allied strategy that must be deferred until later. The suspension of Collins's offensive in the Stolberg corridor meanwhile restored Montgomery's effort to almost as full a priority as the field marshal had ever desired. MARKET-GARDEN became the sole remaining repository of SHAEF's hopes for an enormous strategic opportunity, and the recipient of all available resources. And by now, Montgomery's plan had turned into action; MARKET-GARDEN was launched.

PART FOUR : THE DISPUTED MIDDLE GROUND

★ ★ ★

16: Holland

ALL THE auguries had pointed to the same conclusion: MARKET-GARDEN was sure to demand tactical execution equal in boldness to Field Marshal Montgomery's strategic conception.

The initial tactical execution could hardly have been better. Lancasters and Mosquitoes of the RAF flying by night on September 16–17, RAF bombers escorted by Spitfires in the early hours of Sunday morning, Eighth Air Force Flying Fortresses escorted by Mustangs later in the morning, all pounded enemy interceptor bases and struck hard at flak installations to prepare the way for the airborne assault. Three hundred seventy-one Spitfires, Tempests, and Mosquitoes provided by Air Defence of Great Britain escorted the C-47s and gliders carrying the 1st and 82nd Airborne Divisions across the Scheldt Estuary and into Holland from the north. Five hundred forty-eight Mustangs, Thunderbolts, and Lightnings of the Eighth Air Force escorted the 101st Airborne's transports and gliders across Belgium and then through an abrupt left turn north to Eindhoven. Two hundred twelve Ninth Air Force attack planes meanwhile hit the flak positions again, while 2nd Tactical Air Force raided German barracks at Arnhem, Nijmegen, and points nearby.

Using the two aerial routes was a compromise between the greater distance over enemy-held territory on the northern route and the greater concentrations of flak near the front lines on the southern route. Losses proved lighter on the northern route; but altogether, of 1,546 transports and 478 gliders dispatched, 1,481 and 425 respectively made their drops practically on target. The British lost not one 1st Airborne troop carrier or glider to enemy action.

Brereton had decided on a daylight drop because there were no amphibious landings with which to coordinate the airborne assault as in Normandy, and because daylight ought to allow better aiming at the drop zones. Furthermore, there was good reason to expect even less interference from the Luftwaffe than on the 6th of June. In the event, the German air force managed to fly some 100 to 150 sorties, and they shot down only one fighter escorting the aerial convoys.

[305]

Coming in at one o'clock on a clear Sunday afternoon, all three airborne divisions enjoyed the most accurate drops they had ever experienced, in training or in combat. Nearly all of 16,500 paratroopers and 3,500 glidermen assembled quickly on the ground.

From that point onward, however, tactical execution deteriorated. Trouble unbounded already lurked in the choice of the drop zones where the Red Devils of the 1st Airborne Division so neatly came down. When the British 6th Airborne Division was charged with capturing the much smaller bridges over the River Orne on D-Day in Normandy, it had landed detachments virtually on the bridge approaches. Such action was consistent with the doctrinal principle that airborne assaults should be landed as close to the target as possible because the attackers became relatively immobile as soon as they hit the ground. At Arnhem, nevertheless, the First Airborne Army and 1 Airborne Corps planners decided to set down the 1st Airborne Division in landing zones on the north bank of the Neder Rijn some nine and a half to thirteen kilometers distant from the main target, the Arnhem highway bridge. They argued that, near the bridge, flak would be too heavy and the available landing sites excessively soft fenland. General Williams of IX Troop Carrier Command pleaded "that the flak in the [entire MARKET] area appeared to be the most difficult element to combat," and he "was quite concerned about it."[1] The division commander, Major General Robert Urquhart, felt misgivings about the distance to Arnhem; but while he was a combat veteran of the Mediterranean theater, he had no previous airborne experience, and his lack of expertise led him to acquiesce.

The 1 Airborne Corps After Action Report was later to state: "The difficulties in selecting DZ's and LZ's in Holland was [sic] greatly overestimated. Landings could have been made almost anywhere as far as the terrain was concerned."[2] Ironically, when the 101st Airborne had been briefly selected for the Arnhem part of the operation, the 1st Airborne objected by claiming it had better knowledge of the ground; it had been involved in planning an Arnhem drop for one of the earlier, smaller, abortive projects, Operation COMET.

The Battle for Arnhem

The British chose to send their gliders in first. Although none of their 358 Horsas and Hamilcars were shot down, thirty-eight failed to arrive at the landing zones, mainly because their tow-ropes broke. By extreme bad luck, the missing gliders happened to contain almost all the armored jeeps of the 1st Airborne Division Reconnaissance Squadron. With the jeeps, the squadron was supposed to compensate for the distance between landing zones and Arnhem by rushing to the railway and highway bridges and seizing them by coup de main. The bulk of the 1st Air Landing Brigade and a regiment of airborne artillery fanned out to protect the landing zones, and it was not until the 1st Parachute Brigade dropped following the glider troops and marched a detachment to Arnhem on foot—a matter of four hours—that an effort could be mounted against the bridges.

North of Arnhem was high ground. Like that near the 82nd Airborne's landing zones farther south, it was only about 100 meters high, but in Holland it was enough of an eminence to command the Arnhem bridges. Therefore the 1st Parachute Brigade sent one of its battalions toward the high ground, leaving only two battalions for the bridges. The battalion marching toward the ridge north of Arnhem had the misfortune to encounter armored reconnaissance patrols of the 9th SS Panzer "Hohenstaufen" Division; the Germans halted the paratroopers about three kilometers northwest of Arnhem's western suburb of Oosterbeek. One of the battalions marching toward the bridges met other elements of the 9th SS Panzers and were similarly stopped short at the western outskirts of Oosterbeek.

These mishaps left only Lieutenant Colonel J. D. Frost's 2nd Parachute Battalion on the move toward the division's principal objective, the bridges. Frost, a veteran who had led the Bruneval raid, bypassed most resistance by detouring over a secondary road near the river bank. He detached C Company to take the railroad bridge, but the structure blew up in the paratroopers' faces. He had to detach B Company to deal with Germans nestled in outlying houses of Arnhem about three kilometers from the highway bridge. With A Company and the battalion headquarters, he pressed on to the highway bridge, found it intact, and seized the north end at 8:30 P.M. of D-Day. C Company worked its way through to join Frost during the night, but only tatters of B Company reached him. At its greatest, Frost's strength at the divisional target and the ultimate objective of the whole of MARKET-GARDEN was 500 men.

During the night, Frost tried to capture the whole bridge, first by attacking across it, then by sending a platoon across the Neder Rijn in rowboats. Both efforts failed.

MARKET-GARDEN was already in deep trouble. If Urquhart could have pressed toward Arnhem and the highway bridge with everything he had with him even in the late hours of September 17, his force probably would have been sufficient to break through to join Frost, despite the fact that the Germans had reacted promptly and their SS panzer strength fortuitously in the area was concentrating fast. But Urquhart could not do anything of the sort, because he had to hold the landing zones for the remainder of his division and equipment and supplies, due to arrive during the next two days. Pointing to the supreme importance of the Arnhem highway bridge, he had pleaded to have enough air lift transferred from the American divisions to land almost the entire 1st Airborne Division on D-Day. If his request had been granted, he would not have been in his present predicament; but it had been denied. It is still more pertinent to wonder why, even if the D-Day landings had to take place so far from the Arnhem bridges, subsequent landings could not have been planned to come down much closer to Arnhem. If Urquhart had not been tied to the distant landing zones, he probably could have captured the whole Arnhem highway bridge by D plus 1, and the second air drop would not have had to worry much about flak at the bridge. If even with his full D-Day strength Urquhart might have chanced not to take the bridge, this failure would have signified a desperate enough situation to justify grave risks, such as those of staging the D plus 1 landings at the bridge—because it is better to endure heavy losses in payment for accomplishment than to endure them to no purpose.

September 18 revealed that the 1st Airborne's efforts were most likely to no purpose. The better part of the 9th SS Panzer Division came into the battle, along with possibly some of the 10th SS Panzer "Frundsberg" Division and Division von Tettau, an amalgam of the defense and training battalions of Armed Forces Command Netherlands under the deputy head of that German command, Generalleutnant Hans von Tettau. Responding to radio appeals from Frost, the remaining two battalions of the 1st Parachute Brigade tried to slip around the south flank of the Germans who had held them up on D-Day, but they collided with a counterattack by heavy enemy forces that not only stopped them cold but inflicted severe casualties, isolated several companies, and altogether left the battalions shattered. The 140 surviving effectives of one of the battalions made a final lunge toward the bridge late Monday afternoon and failed again.

Fog in England delayed the D plus 1 reinforcement, but about three in the afternoon the 1st Airborne Division at length received its 4th Parachute Brigade and the rest of the 1st Air Landing Brigade. Holding one of the new parachute battalions as a badly needed reserve—because the Germans were already beginning to press hard against the landing zones themselves—division headquarters sent another battalion to try again to capture the high ground, and the third new parachute battalion went out on the trail of an understrength landing battalion already following the 1st Parachute Brigade toward the bridge. At the end of Monday, this latest reinforcement for the fight in Arnhem had not been able to force its way through SS troopers far enough to catch up with the earlier, stymied reinforcements. General Urquhart himself had been cut off from his troops and was hiding in the loft of a Dutch house. Because the division's radios had proven incapable of effective operation among either the houses of Arnhem or the trees surrounding the landing zones, division headquarters not only had no idea where Urquhart was, but had lost contact with Frost and all the other elements of the 1st Parachute Brigade. The division was unable to inform 1 Airborne Corps or any other headquarters about its bad and deteriorating condition. Brigadier General Floyd L. Parks, the First Airborne Army chief of staff, attempted on Tuesday to arrange for contact with Urquhart through the Dutch underground; by late that afternoon he learned that, as of Monday morning, "a parachute battalion had captured the northern end of the bridge at Arnhem but had been unable to capture the other end. The glider elements were occupying the defensive positions around the DZ's and LZ's as planned."[3] Meanwhile members of the underground reached American paratroopers by telephone with a simple message, transmitted up the chain of command as: "Dutch Report Germans Winning over British at Arnhem."[4]

Much depended on the 1st Polish Parachute Brigade, due to reinforce the 1st Airborne Division on D plus 2—and to land near the Arnhem bridge. Whatever the Poles might be able to do, 30 Corps had better move swiftly.

The 1 Airborne Corps planners had assumed that "the flight and landings would be hazardous, that the capture intact of the bridge objectives are more a matter of surprise and confusion than hard fighting, that the advance of the ground forces would be very swift if the airborne operations were successful, and that, in these circumstances, the considerable dispersion of the airborne forces was acceptable."[5] But after the landings themselves, all did not go well for the 1st Airborne Division, and the advance of the ground forces to the rescue was proving a good deal less than very swift.

At the southern end of the MARKET airborne corridor, the 101st Airborne Division's 506th Parachute Infantry, dropped between St. Oedenrode amd Zon, had as its primary task the capture of the highway bridge over the Wilhelmina Canal at Zon, to be followed by a march south to clear Eindhoven. Major James L. LaPrade's 1st Battalion of the 506th, accompanied by the division commander, General Taylor, bypassed the town of Zon and approached its highway bridge from the west, while the other two battalions moved straight down the highway through the town. Apparently expecting the flanking battalion to take the bridge, the rest of the regiment knocked out an 88 in the streets but then settled for a leisurely progress through Zon, taking time to sweep up the enemy from houses along the way. The 1st Battalion unfortunately encountered another 88, firing from good cover in the Zonsche Forest and hard to eliminate. By the time the eliminating was accomplished, both American forces approached the bridge simultaneously—only to have it blow up and shower them with debris when they were only 100 meters from it.

Major LaPrade, a lieutenant, and a sergeant swam to the south bank of the Wilhelmina Canal, while a larger party ferried itself across in rowboats. The bridge's center trestle was still standing, and when Dutch civilians pointed the way to a cache of black-market lumber, a platoon of engineers used the wood and the center trestle to improvise a footbridge. By that means, the whole 506th Regiment crossed before midnight. Nevertheless, the commander, Colonel Robert F. Sink, was reluctant to push on into Eindhoven because there were Dutch reports of a large enemy garrison in this industrial city of 100,000. General Taylor acquiesced in Sink's view, which involved risks of its own in light of General Horrocks's informal remarks that he would drive 30 Corps all the way to Eindhoven on D-Day.

As events turned out, this particular retreat from tactical boldness on the part of the 506th Regiment caused no harm, because it was dusk by the time the Irish Guards spearhead of 30 Corps reached the day's formal objective of Valkenswaard, nine and a half kilometers short of Eindhoven, and the British stopped there for the night. The Guards Armoured Division had jumped off from De Groote Barrier at 2:35 P.M. to begin the difficult job of plunging straight up the highway through Kampfgruppe Walther's strong roadblock, which was buttressed by antitank guns and Panzerfäuste stationed among cypress plantations on the flanks. Aided by an artillery barrage and constant relays of Typhoons striking at targets within 200 meters of the Guards' tanks, the job was done, but it took time and sapped energy.

By noon of D plus 1, Colonel Sink's regiment had pressed into Eindhoven, where it found only about a company of Germans and captured four bridges over the Dommel River and a local canal. Eindhoven burst into celebration, with the Dutch tricolor waving everywhere, but Maxwell Taylor and his officers worried through Monday afternoon about where the British might be. Sporadic radio contact indicated the Guards were having another tough fight south of the city, and the main British column did not link up with the 506th Regiment on the southern outskirts of Eindhoven until about seven in the evening of the second day of the operation.

The radio contacts had also warned Horrocks of the destruction of the Zon bridge, so British engineers hurried through Eindhoven to erect a Bailey bridge over the Wilhelmina Canal. They labored through the night, and the first tank crossed at 6:45 A.M. on D plus 2, September 19. Horrocks was at least thirty-three hours behind schedule.

The Guards hastened through Zon, St. Oedenrode, and Veghel under the protection of the 101st Airborne, which was receiving a hard enough time from German troops converging on its drop zones to make "Hell's Highway" the GIs' fond designation for the road. Especially troublesome was the enemy's 59th Division, the vanguard of the Fifteenth Army's escape from isolation by way of the door left open from South Beveland. Attached quickly to Student's army, the 59th prevented the 101st Airborne from capturing an alternate Wilhelmina Canal bridge at Best and dealt the 502nd Parachute Infantry heavy casualties in the process. Fortunately, while they were no longer gaining much new ground, Taylor's men were able to fend off the enemy successfully enough to afford the British a swift passage beyond Zon. The Guards linked up with the 82nd Airborne south of Grave, having traveled some fifty-five kilometers beyond Zon, as early as 8:20 on Tuesday morning. This was less than two hours after the first armor crossed the Wilhelmina Canal. But Horrocks had not bitten substantially into the lost thirty-three hours; and to the north—unknown, of course, to 30 Corps—the reinforcing battalion of the 4th Parachute Brigade had just reached the remnants of the other battalions west of Arnhem, yet the composite force still could make no headway toward Colonel Frost at the Arnhem bridge.

General Gavin's 82nd Division had faced more complex tactical problems than Taylor's 101st. To contribute its share to the advance of GARDEN toward Arnhem, the 82nd had to capture and hold the nine-span, 550-meter highway bridge over the Maas River at Grave and the great 600-meter highway span over the Waal at Nijmegen, plus at least one of the four possible crossings of the Maas-Waal Canal between the rivers. If the bridges were to be held and kept usable, moreover, Gavin's division also had to capture and retain the 100-meter eminence of the Groesbeek Ridge between Beek, east of Nijmegen, and Mook, on the Waal east of Grave, to fend off counterattacks from the nearby Reichswald in Germany itself. Some reports placed concentrations of German armor in the Reichswald. To accomplish all these tasks and to hold so much terrain would dangerously, perhaps excessively, scatter the three parachute regiments scheduled to land on D-Day. Because Gavin believed that everything else depended on holding the ridge—with the Germans in control of it, the bridges would be worthless—he set its capture as the 82nd's first task. Because the highway and rail bridges at Nijmegen would also be useless if 30 Corps could not cross the Maas and the Maas-Waal Canal to reach them, the bridge at Grave and a canal bridge received secondary priority. Taking the longest bridges, the highway and railway spans across the wide Waal, would be the 82nd's final task.

General Browning, whose British Airborne Corps headquarters would be located in the 82nd's sector, agreed wholeheartedly with these priorities. In fact, he felt more confident that they were in proper order than Gavin did. The division commander worried whether he should not strike more promptly for the Nijmegen bridges; as late as the afternoon of D plus 1, Browning rejected a plan for a strong effort against the Nijmegen rail and highway bridges and instructed the 82nd to concentrate on holding the Groesbeek Ridge instead.

Well before that time, Gavin's concern about the Nijmegen bridges had grown acute. About seventy-two hours before his planes took off for Holland, he had decided that "if I could possibly spare a battalion, I knew I had to commit it to the Nijmegen [highway] bridge as quickly as I could send it in that direction."[6] He later testified that he instructed the regimental commander of the 508th Parachute Infantry, Colonel Roy E. Lindquist, to that effect:

> I told him that if, in his opinion, the situation along the Groesbeek high ground was quiet in the late afternoon of the day of our landing, he was to send a battalion against the Nijmegen bridge that night. I further cautioned him to send it off over the flat ground under the cover of darkness and not through the city. A few well-placed automatic weapons could hold up a battalion indefinitely in narrow city streets.[7]

Lindquist, however, somehow had a different impression of his instructions.

On D-Day, the 82nd's model jump was followed by rapid capture of the Grave bridge, intact, and seizure of the Heumen bridge over the Maas-Waal Canal after a sharp fight. The Germans destroyed two other canal bridges, at Malden and Hatert, but on D plus 1 a platoon of Colonel Lindquist's regiment took the fourth canal bridge, at Honinghutje, although the structure had been weakened by a German demolition attempt. Gavin's troops also took up their defensive positions on the Groesbeek Ridge, finding no German tanks and hearing from local civilians that the reports of armor in the Reichswald were false. But because Lindquist understood that he was to send no troops to the Nijmegen bridges until all his regiment's other objectives were secured, Lieutenant Colonel Shields Warren's 1st Battalion did not go quickly toward the bridges as Gavin anticipated it would in the prevailing quiet circumstances. The battalion merely assumed a defensive posture on the outskirts of Nijmegen, tying in with the defenses of Heumen canal bridge and the Groesbeek Ridge, under instructions from Lindquist to be prepared to enter Nijmegen later.

Colonel Warren himself sent a rifle platoon of c Company and the battalion intelligence section on a reconnaissance into the city about 6:30 P.M. He had heard from the Dutch that only eighteen Germans were guarding the highway bridge, and he ordered the patrol to take the south end if they could. The Dutch report about the weakness of the bridge's defenses remained fairly accurate for a number of hours after the 82nd had landed and was within striking distance. By the time Warren's patrol approached, however, the Germans had grown strong enough to deal with so small a force, and because the patrol's radio failed it could not report to Colonel Warren.

About dusk, Gavin learned enough about these occurrences to order Lindquist "to delay not a second longer and get the bridge as quickly as possible with Warren's battalion."[8] Warren instructed Companies A and B to rendezvous south of Nijmegen about seven with a Dutch civilian he had found, who said he could both guide the troops to the bridge and on the way check with Resistance headquarters in the city to learn the Germans' current condition. Company B got lost and failed to show up at the rendezvous, so about eight o'clock Warren began moving toward the bridge with Company A. The Dutchman led the way into the very sort of entanglement in the city's streets against which Gavin had warned, then disappeared into the darkness of the night. Moving cautiously and searching buildings as they went, Company A groped on until at about ten o'clock a burst of automatic weapons fire—the characteristic "Brrrrrrrp" that gave German guns, with their high cyclic rate of fire, the familiar name of burp guns—tore at them from a traffic circle. This circle surrounded the Keiser Karel Plein, a park near the center of the city. As Company A formed up to attack the source of the shooting, a motor convoy rumbled into the circle from the opposite side and German soldiers poured out of the trucks. When Company A advanced again, ss troopers counterattacked, and Company A might have been overrun had not Company B put in a timely appearance.

Warren ordered the remainder of Company c to come up as reinforcement and reported these events to Lindquist. Meanwhile, Captain Jonathan E. Adams, Jr., of Company A heard from civilians that the Germans' control mechanism for demolishing the highway bridge was housed in the post office, a few blocks north of the Keiser Karel Plein. Adams personally led a platoon who bypassed the traffic circle, fought past some guards into the post office, and destroyed what seemed to be the mechanism. Then they found that Germans had closed in behind them, and with some helpful civilians they had to withstand a three-hour siege until relief arrived.

Toward morning, Warren mounted another attack, but again it was engulfed in a counterattack. Gavin arrived during the melee and decided there were too many Germans and too much congestion in narrow streets for this approach to the bridge to succeed. Calling off further effort by Warren's battalion, Gavin ordered Lindquist to make a try with Lieutenant Colonel Louis G. Mendez's 3rd Battalion. This unit was at the north end of the high ground east of Nijmegen and might still be able to reach the bridge through the city's less constricted eastern district.

Captain Frank J. Novak's Company G had already occupied Hill 64 about a kilometer and a half from the south end of the bridge, and at 7:45 A.M. on Monday this company pushed on into the city. Along its route, however, was another defended traffic circle, just south of Hunner Park on the southern approaches to the bridge. A lofty seventeenth-century tower, the Belvedere, surrounded by stout walls, gave the enemy excellent observation. When Company G approached, the Germans sprayed them with weapons ranging from small arms to an 88. Captain Novak deployed his men and attacked. Company G drove within a block of the traffic circle but could advance no farther.

Colonel Mendez could not reinforce Novak, because he needed his other companies on the high ground. Another of Gavin's regiments, Colonel Reuben H. Tucker's 504th Parachute Infantry, had long since captured the Grave bridge and helped to capture the Heumen bridge over the canal, and thereafter had been engaged mainly in patrolling. "When we looked back on the situation years later," Gavin was to write, "we realized that it should have been obvious that Tucker's 504th was much better prepared to spare a battalion to go to the Nijmegen bridge" than Lindquist's 508th.[9] On Monday, all the strength that the 508th could spring loose from the bridge area, along with the 505th Parachute Infantry, had to join urgently in clearing landing zones on which the D-plus-1 glider reinforcement was about to arrive, but which had been recaptured by Germans spilling out of the Reichswald. The 505th cleared one of these zones with half an hour to spare. Colonel Warren's battalion hit the other after a thirteen-kilometer forced march from Nijmegen, charging headlong downhill to chase the Germans from their 20mm. guns just as the gliders were coming into view.

Clearly the 82nd was feeling the pinch of too few men and too many diverse responsibilities. The arrival of the gliders, with the division's glider artillery and one parachute and two glider infantry battalions, would help; but at the same time the enemy continued to increase his pressure from the Reichswald, even if with Landesschützen and not panzers.

Browning now requested from Gavin a plan for seizing the Nijmegen highway bridge that night. Gavin responded with a design for enveloping the approaches from both east and west with the full 508th Parachute Infantry reinforced by a battalion of the 504th. It was this plan for taking the bridge that Browning thereupon disapproved after all, because he believed the other responsibilities of the 82nd ought still to take priority over the Nijmegen bridge. As reported in the division files, Browning based this view and his lack of a sense of urgency on "the situation in the 30th Corps."[10]

It was true enough that 30 Corps was nowhere near being able to use the Nijmegen bridge even if it had been in friendly hands. Horrocks's troops were still two and a half hours from contact with the 101st Airborne below Eindhoven. Whether it was the situation of 30 Corps that should have governed action, or the possible predicament of the

1st Airborne Division, from which nothing had yet been heard, was another matter. Of course, Browning and Gavin had to consider the pressure on the 82nd from the Reichswald, including fresh reports that enemy tanks were massing there. This danger appeared great enough to persuade Gavin to endorse Browning's decision. In its practical effect, however, the decision implied there would be no further effort to capture the bridge until 30 Corps arrived to assist the 82nd Airborne.

After the linkup with the Guards Armoured Division had at length occurred during the morning of D plus 2, Gavin met with Horrocks that afternoon to outline a new plan for the bridges. Lieutenant Colonel B.H. Vandervoort's relatively fresh 2nd Battalion, 505th Parachute Infantry, hitherto in division reserve but relieved in that role by a battalion of the Coldstream Guards, was to renew the attack on the south ends of both the highway and the railroad bridges. "I had ordered the seizure of the railroad bridge," said Gavin, "because we had learned in our fighting in Sicily that such a bridge could quickly be converted into a jeep bridge and to a tank bridge if captured intact. In any event, it would be able to take infantry that could cross during darkness."[11] The crucial effort, however, was to be made by another force, crossing the Waal in boats to attack the north ends. "In the American army," Gavin recorded in his memoirs, "a corps acting in an independent role, such as 30 Corps in the Holland situation, would have an engineer battalion or regiment attached to it, and that would include a company of boats. As we stood talking, I asked General Horrocks about it, and he said he thought they had some boats well down the road in the train somewhere."[12] Horrocks's staff revealed that the boats would be canvas, not plywood like American assault boats. Thirty-three of them ought to be available, but they would not be able to work their way up the congested highway until the next morning, Wednesday, D plus 3. Meanwhile, Horrocks offered a company of infantry and a battalion of tanks for immediate assistance to the 2/505th.

When Wednesday morning came, the probable arrival time for the boats was, in the customary manner of such promises, pushed back to noon. Gavin felt unable to schedule the crossing for earlier than 2:00 P.M. In the meantime the German defenders at both bridges were turning back repeated assaults by paratroopers and Guards, whether the attackers advanced by the direct route through Nijmegen or the circuit through the eastern fringe earlier attempted by Captain Novak's company. Gavin's G-2 now estimated that 500 first-rate SS troopers with considerable artillery would have to be overcome at the highway bridge alone. Furthermore, the D-plus-2 reinforcement scheduled for Tuesday had failed to come in because bad weather intervened; without the scheduled arrival of the 325th Glider Infantry, Gavin tried to compensate for his shortage of troops by putting 450 glider pilots into the line, an expedient that aroused no one's enthusiasm. The same bad weather kept the Polish Airborne Brigade from reinforcing the Red Devils at Arnhem. That morning, as Brereton prepared to brief SHAEF, Chief of Staff Parks signaled him: "Dear Boss: . . . Don't worry. We are all doing everything possible to relieve situation for 1st British A/B. Will get them something today if humanly possible."[13] But by now, nobody could repress worry.

Gavin's shortage of infantry became all the more ominous while he awaited the canvas boats, because by Wednesday morning it was not merely Landesschützen but troops of General Meindl's II Parachute Corps who were coming out of the Reichswald, aided by scattered armor and including two battalions of the feared and famous 6th Parachute Division. The 82nd as yet had only five battalions of its own to hold the

Groesbeek Ridge against such an eruption. At mid-afternoon, Meindl was threatening the Heumen bridge across the Maas-Waal Canal, over which 30 Corps's armor was moving north, and tanks of the Coldstream Guards had to join in and bolster the American infantry to make the highway secure again. All along the high ground on the 82nd's east flank, intense fighting raged throughout Wednesday afternoon. Colonel Mendez of the 3/508th had to shift his platoons back and forth like fire brigades. (During Wednesday there arrived with 30 Corps the first American trucks supposedly carrying additional ammunition for Gavin's artillery; but some proved to have the wrong kind of shells, and others had never been loaded.)

All in all, General Browning would clearly have to forgo his wish to have everything else tidied up before a climactic assault on the Nijmegan bridges. At three o'clock on Wednesday afternoon, September 20, Major Julian A. Cook's 3rd Battalion, 504th Parachute Infantry at last launched the river crossing in 30 Corps's boats. Typhoons bombed and strafed the north bank for a half hour before H-hour, and British artillery along with tanks track to track pounded the far shore, while other guns laid down a white phosphorus smoke screen. But nothing could offer much encouragement to the troopers who had to cross in twenty-six—not thirty-three—boats which they first saw only twenty minutes before the latest H-Hour, and which proved to be the frailest of tiny craft, six meters long, of canvas with a reinforced plywood bottom.

The Waal is almost 400 meters wide at the crossing site, with a swift current of about fifteen kilometers an hour. The current prevented launching at a concealed place that Gavin had chosen, within the mouth of the Maas-Waal Canal, lest the boats be carried too far downstream; so they had to be launched within full view of the enemy in the bridge towers and dug in beyond a 200-meter stretch of open shore on the north bank. German shellfire began as soon as Cook's battalion approached the launching site, a steep enbankment. The water close to the south bank is shallow, and the paratroops had to wade far into the Waal before climbing into their boats. As soon as they struck deep water, the current seized them wildly, at least one boat whirling in circles for a time, while, without enough paddles, some men tried to propel their craft with rifle butts. "Had it not been for the gruesomeness of the situation," said Captain Henry B. Keep, "the sight might have been ludicrous." But "It was a horrible picture, this river crossing," Keep also said, writing to his mother, "set to the deafening roar of omnipresent firing. It was fiendish and dreadful . . . defenseless, frail canvas boats jammed to overflowing with humanity, all striving desperately to cross the Waal as quickly as possible, and get to a place where at least they could fight."[14]

Half the boats reached the north bank and deposited their sickened, vomiting, exhausted troops. Cook's men pulled themselves up to stumble pell-mell across the open beach and eventually to fight their way to a diked road about 800 meters from the river. Engineers ran the gauntlet again with the remaining boats, and eleven made it to the north bank carrying a second wave. In time, six crossings reinforced Cook's 3/504th with Major Willard E. Harrison's 1st Battalion. The individual companies were supposed to set out on various assigned missions, but the crossings mixed up units too much for anything to be done except by individuals and impromptu groups.

It was mainly parts of Companies H and I that first converged on the north ends of both the railroad and highway bridges. Meanwhile, aided by Cook's spectacular distraction, Colonel Vandervoort's 2/505th along with infantry and tanks of the Guards had at last begun to make headway against the traffic circle at Hunner Park. Just as British tanks approached the south end of the highway bridge, their crews saw the Stars and Stripes go up across the river. The flag was actually flying from the railroad bridge, but the tankers assumed it meant they could cross the highway span. Out they went onto the bridge, firing into the towers and girders all the way. Three tanks reached the north end almost simultaneously with three privates of Cook's battalion.

When General Dempsey of the Second Army next saw Gavin, he expressed his feelings about the assault on the Nijmegen bridges by saying: "I am proud to meet the commander of the greatest division in the world today."[15] Soldiers of the 82nd were less happy with the British and the way they used the hard-won victory at the bridges. From the time of the first contact between the Guards Armoured Division and the 82nd, almost thirty-five hours had already passed before British tanks met American infantry at the north end of the Nijmegen highway bridge, at 7:10 P.M. on D plus 3, September 20. It would take 30 Corps almost another twenty-four hours before the advance began rolling again.

To be sure, the night and part of Thursday were required to root out all the German defenders still squirreled away in the metalwork of the Nijmegen bridges. More importantly, the pressure of the II Parachute Corps from the Reichswald was judged to compel Horrocks to hold back the Coldstream Guards Group as a reserve for the 82nd Airborne, leaving him only two armored groups, and little infantry, with which to forge ahead. But 30 Corps was now only fifteen kilometers in a straight line from Oosterbeek, so there was intermittent radio contact with the 1st Airborne, where Urquhart was back in command; and however garbled they were, it should have been clear from the messages that the Red Devils were in desperate trouble. The latest report indicated Frost was still hanging on at the north end of the Arnhem bridge, but needing help very, very soon.

Sensing the true situation, Major General E. Hakewill Smith of the 52nd Lowland Division offered to take a brigade to Urquhart by glider. Browning responded: "Thanks for your message but offer not repeat not required as situation is better than you think."[16]

When a small force of Horrocks's armor advanced out of the bridgehead across the Waal late on D plus 4, September 21, they moved only five kilometers before they struck a roadblock at Ressen, held by two enemy battalions, including one of ss troopers, with tanks and 88s. Because the highway remained flanked by soggy bottomland, tanks could not maneuver, and Horrocks was stymied again. Typhoons were prowling overhead but could not be guided in on the roadblock because the radio sets in the available RAF ground liaison car would not work. About nightfall, the British 43rd Wessex Infantry Division began rolling into Nijmegen in trucks, the road congestion having required it to consume three days to drive ninety-five kilometers; it might as well have marched. This infantry would not be able to join the vanguard at Ressen until Friday morning.

The weather in England had cleared enough on Thursday, September 21, that the Polish Parachute Brigade was flown to Holland to try to reinforce the 1st Airborne Division; but the weather over Arnhem was still so bad that only fifty-three of 110 planes dropped their loads. Because Urquhart's airhead north of the Neder Rijn by now was severely constricted by enemy pressure, the transports had to deposit the Poles south of the river near Driel. From there the Heveadorp ferry had continued shuttling to the north bank amidst chaos. As the kind of luck becoming characteristic of MARKET-GARDEN would have it, the Germans captured the north end of the ferry line and sank the ferry boat just before the Poles arrived—the unforgiving minute yet again. The Poles would have to wait for assault boats. Across the river, the 1st Airborne was compressed into a perimeter west of Oosterbeek less than a kilometer wide and a kilometer deep, pounded by artillery and continually assailed by local attacks.

There was no other 1st Airborne perimeter, for radio contact on Thursday brought 30 Corps the news that the previous evening's report about Frost's holding out at the Arnhem bridge was wrong. During Wednesday afternoon, Frost's survivors had been driven away from their last foothold on the bridge approaches. Tanks and guns of the II ss Panzer Corps had been rolling across the Arnhem bridge to reinforce the defenses around Nijmegen at the very time when the much-postponed Allied attack on the Nijmegen bridges finally succeeded—the unforgiving minute with a terrible vengeance.

The Germans thus could readily reinforce their roadblock north of Nijmegen. The Allies, in contrast, were about to lose part of their narrow lifeline from the Belgian-Dutch border. The British 8 and 12 Corps, advancing on the right and left, respectively, of 30 Corps, had achieved progress aptly described by Field Marshal Montgomery as "depressingly slow."[17] Contending with the wet polderland, Student's First Parachute Army on the left, and LXXXVI Corps (Parachute Training Division Erdmann and the 176th Division) on the right, they had pushed no farther than abreast of Eindhoven. The 101st Airborne Division consequently found itself, as General Taylor described it, fighting like a wagon train in the American West, forming circles to fend off the hostiles at one place after another. Taylor tried mounting small attacks of his own to keep the enemy off balance, but on Friday he was unable to hold back simultaneous attacks from east and west that broke Hell's Highway between Veghel and Uden by afternoon. About a day passed before the road was opened again, only to be broken once more between St. Oedenrode and Veghel on Sunday, September 24. The 101st with British aid could not repair this rupture until Tuesday, September 26.

Such distractions did not prevent the Allies from resuming their efforts to reach the 1st Airborne Division, but the Germans reinforced their roadblock north of Nijmegen during Thursday night, September 21–22, and when the British 43rd Division attacked, it drove forward a short distance, to Elst, but no farther. This was less than half way from Nijmegen to Arnhem.

Horrocks decided meanwhile to send a left hook over secondary roads toward the Poles and the ferry site. Poking their way through early morning mists on Friday, armored cars of the Household Cavalry soon appeared among the Poles. Infantry of the 43rd Division and dukws for crossing the Neder Rijn made a much more leisurely progress behind them, halting to stage elaborate attacks on small roadblocks. Horrocks and Browning had abandoned any thought of early capture of the Arnhem bridge, but they hoped that through Driel they might relieve and reinforce the 1st Airborne to retain a bridgehead across the Neder Rijn for later development. Unhappily, it was discovered that night that the river banks were too soft and steep to launch the dukws. The best the relief column could accomplish during darkness of September 22–23 was to use improvised rafts to ferry about fifty Poles and a little food and ammunition to the 1st Airborne.

When 30 Corps, 1 Airborne Corps, and Second Army headquarters digested this latest bad news, their hopes of retaining a foothold beyond the Neder Rijn almost died. Dempsey authorized withdrawing the 1st Airborne Division to the south bank if necessary. Horrocks grasped at the straw of getting up assault boats to ferry the Poles and some

British infantry on the night of September 24–25. But the cutting of Hell's Highway prevented the arrival of enough assault boats. With eight boats, about 250 soldiers of the 4th Battalion, the Dorsetshire Regiment, crossed that night, only to be scattered by the current and readily hemmed in by the Germans before they could reach the airborne perimeter.

That did it. On D plus 8, Monday, September 25, Urquhart learned he was to pull back his perimeter to the river for withdrawal during the night. Only fifteen boats were available, and these ferried back and forth through a night fortunately darkened, though made still more miserable, by heavy rain. At daybreak, some men began swimming as machine-gun fire terminated the ferry service. Some 2,163 men of the 1st Airborne Division and the Glider Pilot Regiment, along with 160 Poles and 75 Dorsets, reached the south bank safely. Some 300 wounded inside the perimeter and another 200 Dorsets were taken prisoner. The Germans captured more than 6,000 prisoners in all north of the Neder Rijn, nearly half of them wounded. A few hundred British and Polish soldiers remained at large, helped by the Dutch and gradually finding their way south of the river.

MARKET-GARDEN Assessed

Field Marshal Montgomery has incurred considerable criticism over the years because of MARKET-GARDEN; it was his design, and it failed with tragically high losses. The Arnhem bridge was *A Bridge Too Far*, the argument most often goes. It was unreasonable to believe the 1st Airborne Division could hold out through the time 30 Corps would need to travel more than ninety kilometers from De Groote Barrier, or that 30 Corps could thrust up the highway to Arnhem on a two-tank front in the three days of the planners' schedule.

The problems inherent in an airborne assault once the troops reach the ground—the relative immobility and the light weaponry of airborne forces—make this criticism not unreasonable. Especially does the criticism acquire added force when MARKET-GARDEN, involving the largest and most ambitious employment of airborne troops in the Second World War, is considered in the context of the entire history of the war's airborne operations. Despite the diversion of large amounts of energy and resources to the training, equipment, and transport of airborne formations, and the assignment of leaders and soldiers qualified to make airborne divisions genuinely elite units—Dempsey's praise for the 82nd at Nijmegen was merited—never in the war did airborne troops make a decisive contribution to any Allied victory. They may have come closest in Normandy; but the cross-Channel invasion would have succeeded without them.

Nevertheless, while MARKET-GARDEN thus demanded accepting high risks, it is the essence of effective command in war to take high risks when the risks are appropriate. A great commander—and Montgomery ranked himself among the great commanders—does not take counsel of his fears. In September 1944, MARKET-GARDEN offered the best remaining opportunity for the Allies to win the war that autumn. It was by no means a "full-blooded thrust" to the Rhine and the Ruhr, but it was the nearest approximation that the Allies' logistical predicament allowed. If it had succeeded, MARKET-GARDEN would have put the Allies across the Rhine, turned the flank of the West Wall, and opened a door to the Ruhr. Furthermore, its chances of succeeding were good enough that, with such stakes involved, the risks were worth running.

For it could have succeeded. It suffered from an extraordinary streak of bad luck, beginnning with the presence of the 9th and 10th SS Panzer Divisions near Arnhem for refitting (though Montgomery should have paid more heed to reports of their presence). The bad luck included also, as the Allies were to learn later, an American officer's improper decision to carry with him a copy of the Allied operational order, and the capture of this order on D-Day when his glider was shot down near General Student's headquarters. Student soon had the order on his desk, and so did Field Marshal Model, who happened to be headquartered at the Hartenstein Hotel at Oosterbeek, almost within the 1st Airborne Division's drop zones, so that he was in an excellent position to coordinate German ripostes based on the captured order. There was also the bad weather, which prevented the Poles and the 82nd Airborne's glider infantry from landing on D plus 2 when they were so sorely needed. Montgomery blamed the weather for the failure; on the other hand, bad weather had to be expected in Holland by mid- to late September. Nevertheless, bad luck, like bad weather in northern Europe, has to be included in the military commander's calculus of risks, and MARKET-GARDEN could have succeeded in spite of bad luck.

The critical flaw was not in the strategic design but in the tactical execution. General Brereton said: "It was the breakdown of the 2nd Army's timetable in the first day—their failure to reach Eindhoven in 6 to 8 hours as planned—that caused the delay in the taking of the Nijmegen bridge and the failure at Arnhem."[18] This evaluation is self-serving, in its removal of the blame from Brereton's own First Airborne Army, and it is unfair; but it is a partial explanation, because much of the tactical failure lay in the slow advance of the Second Army, including 12 and 8 Corps on the flanks but most especially 30 Corps. The first day's delay was probably most critical; but there was no determination to advance proportionate to the plight of the 1st Airborne Division when 30 Corps confronted the bridges at Nijmegen either, or along the final miles between Nijmegen and Arnhem.

Even if 30 Corps had advanced faster on D-Day, however, it would have met trouble at the blown bridge over the Wilhelmina Canal at Zon. If the 101st Airborne had heeded a suggestion by Montgomery that it drop troops on both sides of the Zon bridge, as the 82nd in fact did at Grave, 30 Corps might not have had to delay still longer while its engineers threw down a Bailey bridge.

If the 82nd Airborne had attacked the Nijmegen bridges soon after landing, as Gavin just before D-Day was inclined to believe it ought to do, the next big delay at the crossing of the Waal might not have occurred. During the subsidiary contest for bridges over the Maas-Waal Canal, Gavin chanced to meet General Ridgway, who was roaming about unhappily without an operational command. Perhaps unfairly, anyone familiar with Ridgway's career must wonder what would have been the outcome if the operational corps commander at Nijmegen had been not "Boy" Browning of 1 Airborne Corps but Matthew Ridgway of the XVIII Airborne Corps.

Finally, if the 1st Airborne Division had dropped near the highway bridge at Arnhem, instead of nine and a half to thirteen kilometers away, or even if it had moved its whole strength to the bridge at the end of D-Day, then the Arnhem bridge might have been held long enough for 30 Corps to reach it in spite of the other delays, especially because the II SS Panzer Corps could not have used the Arnhem bridge to hasten reinforcements to the roadblocks between the Waal and the Neder Rijn.

Altogether, if the boldness of tactical execution had approximated the boldness of Montgomery's strategy, MARKET-GARDEN should have succeeded. But it failed, and with it failed the hope of a prompt penetration of the Ruhr; for by now the Third Army far to the south as well as the First Army at Aachen had stalled against German troops rallying behind strong defenses.

17: Attack in the Ardennes (I)

THE OVERLORD planners actually had considered four possible routes toward Germany from the OVERLORD lodgment area, though they had rejected two of them forthwith. In addition to the classic route Amiens-Maubeuge-Liège and the Metz-Saarbrücken-Frankfurt route, the SHAEF planning staff had pointed briefly to the Flanders plain and to the Ardennes. Though the low, wet ground caused them to rule out Flanders, the necessity to clear or contain the Channel ports and eliminate the V-weapon launching sites eventually made this route a subsidiary path for 21 Army Group nevertheless. It was only the Ardennes that was altogether rejected.

The reasons for its rejection are obvious. Deeply scored, abrupt ravines break the surface of the Ardennes plateau, and there are many streams, a heavy forest cover, and a shortage of good roads, with even the secondary roads running for the most part diagonally across the invasion path. Thus, in SHAEF planning both of General Bradley's armies were slated to bypass the Ardennes, initially by moving south of the area. When General Eisenhower decided to strengthen the Amiens-Liège thrust, General Hodges's First Army was directed to shift its route to go around the northern border of the Ardennes, while General Patton's Third Army would continue to skirt the Ardennes on the south.

But the Ardennes merited more serious consideration than it received. The impediments of the terrain notwithstanding, the Germans in 1940 had sped mechanized columns through the Ardennes with spectacular effect—and were to do so again. For the Allies now as for the Germans on other occasions, the very difficulties of the terrain could have rendered the defenses to be penetrated otherwise less formidable. Despite the Germans' own 1940 campaign, the West Wall was only a single thin band of fortifications behind the Ardennes, not the double band of the Aachen corridor or of the Saar.

By advancing north of the Ardennes along the historic route of the Schlieffen Plan but in reverse, Hodges's First Army benefited from the best invasion route of all—but only as far as the German frontier. Once Hodges entered Germany, he had to contend with the combined problems of one of the heaviest fortification complexes of the West Wall and a narrow approach corridor without space for maneuver as he struck the fortifications. His route was obstructed, moreover, by the urban sprawl of Aachen itself, a city of 165,000 before the war, which narrowed his practicable route to the Stolberg corridor through Aachen's southern and eastern suburbs. The outlying hills and forests of the Eifel, notably the Huertgen Forest, encroached on this route from the south. Just ahead lay the Schwammenauel and a series of other dams on the Roer River and its tributaries, which if opportunely ruptured by the Germans could flood Hodges's invasion path and effectively close it for several weeks. The Huertgen Forest and the Roer dams were soon to cast their shadows over almost every movement of the First Army. By the time of MARKET-GARDEN, Hodges's army already had its first taste of the West Wall defenses in the Stolberg corridor, and the taste was bitter.

Eisenhower's decision in August to add Hodges's whole army to Montgomery's northeastward offensive committed the First Army to this constricted approach to the West Wall. If the Supreme Commander had retained the earlier SHAEF design for avoiding the Ardennes, holding both the First and Third Armies south of that plateau, the approach to Germany would also have been dangerously constricted; for the Lorraine Gap between the Ardennes and, to the south, the Vosges is barely wide enough to accommodate the advance of a single field army of the 1940s type. As events developed, however, Eisenhower's decision to send Hodges and Patton on divergent paths to the north and south of the Ardennes had the highly unfortunate result of dissipating the most powerful, concentrated blow he could have struck. To have hurled the American First and Third Armies against the West Wall in such a way that these two most powerful offensive ground weapons in the Allied arsenal could have assailed the wall within mutual supporting distance would have afforded the Allies their best opportunity to break through the wall early. To put Hodges instead on the right flank of 21 Army Group not only condemned the First Army to entanglement in the heavy defenses around Aachen, but yoked the First Army to the British Second Army. The limitations of the British forces, especially in manpower, made this combination a considerably less imposing one than closely linked assaults by the First and Third Armies would have represented. The only means, however, by which the First and Third Armies could have assailed the frontiers of the Reich in deadly combination and with adequate space for maneuver would have been to risk an advance through the Ardennes by the First Army, in conjunction with the Third Army's assault through the Lorraine Gap.

The First Battle of the Schnee Eifel

Operations were to produce further evidence that the Ardennes and the Eifel might have received fuller consideration as a route of advance toward and into Germany. When General Collins's VII Corps kicked off the First Army's attack up the Stolberg corridor, Hodges wanted General Gerow's V Corps on Collins's right to support it with an attack from the Ardennes across the German frontier into the Eifel. When upon Collins's urging, Hodges on September 11 moved up the date of the army's attack from September 14 to September 12, Gerow was included in the instructions to begin at least a reconnaissance in force on Tuesday, the 12th. Though Gerow's corps, strung out loosely across the Ardennes, and for the most part more distant even than the VII Corps from supply depots, could not be ready for a respectable assault even by September 14, Gerow attempted to comply with orders as best he could, insisting on probing efforts on September 12 and 13 and the fullest possible facsimile of a big attack on September 14. When this latter effort reached out, the West Wall opposite the Ardennes proved so weakly held that the V Corps promptly broke through in two places. The most promising penetration was scored, in fact, by the 5th Armored Division, the part of the corps that was most loosely dispersed.

Gerow's two infantry divisions, Barton's 4th and Cota's 28th, were bunched fairly closely together on the corps left flank, the better to support Collins. The 4th Division

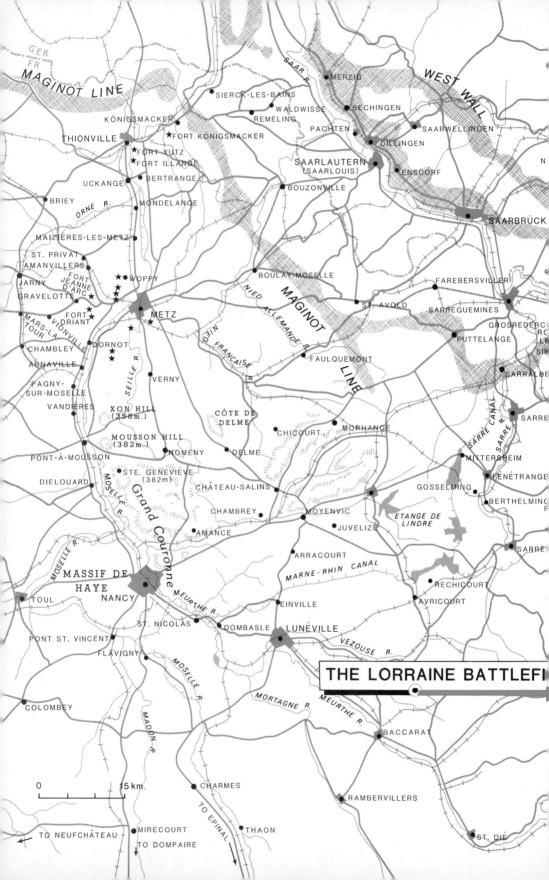

faced the escarpment of the Schnee Eifel, a 700-meters-high wooded ridge barring the entrance into the Eifel opposite St. Vith, Belgium, and extending some twenty-five kilometers from Stadtkyll to Brandscheid. The Losheim Gap reaches around the northern edge of the Schnee Eifel on the 4th Division's left flank, but the gap is so narrow that Gerow assigned the 4th mainly the work of striking the escarpment to divert the Germans from the 28th Division's attack. Cota's Keystone Division would advance over relatively more hospitable ground, south of Brandscheid where the Schnee Eifel blends into a more open plateau.

Over Cota's objections but on Hodges's insistence, the 28th Division had lent its 112th Infantry Regiment to help flesh out the much extended 5th Armored Division. Cota's remaining two regiments pressed toward the West Wall on the border of the Eifel without such equipment as explosive charges and flame throwers, usually necessary in attacking pillboxes. The division's attached tanks and self-propelled tank destroyers were behind the lines repairing the wear and tear of the long pursuit. For direct fire support the infantry had only 57mm. antitank guns and a few towed tank destroyers. There was not enough ammunition on hand for more than light combat.

Opposite the northern flank of the V Corps was the I SS Panzer Corps, with the 2nd Panzer Division opposing Cota's troops. General von Lüttwitz's division could muster only three tanks, but its cadre maintained the professional skills of an organization the Americans had come to regard as the best panzer division on the Western Front. Yet the panzers were so few, and the Germans were so strained to find anyone to reinforce Lüttwitz in the pillboxes—the Americans captured a forty-year-old cook who had been at the front only two hours—that by September 14 both of Cota's regiments had achieved encroachments into the West Wall. On Friday, September 15, ten unarmed engineers, each carrying fifty pounds of TNT, blew a roadblock and thereby permitted the 110th Infantry to storm and capture Hill 553 within the wall. That night the standard German counterattack overran and almost destroyed Company F, but the next day the 1st Battalion nevertheless pushed forward to capture two higher adjacent hills. Now the Keystone Division possessed not only the highest ground for miles around but also, except for a few scattered pillboxes, a clean break through the West Wall.

At first, Barton's 4th Division to the north enjoyed even better success, because the other division of the I SS Panzer Corps, the 2nd SS Panzers, was less ready than Lüttwitz's efficient 2nd Panzers to receive the first assault. Once the 2nd SS Panzers, got themselves uncoiled for battle, however, the harsh terrain of the Schnee Eifel assisted them in creating the expected virtual deadlock, with strong roadblocks to frustrate both further adventures on the escarpment and a probing attack through the Losheim Gap. For four days, Barton's division persisted in throwing punches, but the breaks it scrounged out of the West Wall led to no roads or objectives of consequence.

The Battle of Wallendorf

But to the south, General Oliver's 5th Armored Division met no resistance comparable even to that contrived by two battered panzer divisions. The 5th Armored faced a pair of narrow but negotiable corridors into Germany converging on the Eifel region's road center at Bitburg. There was a southerly corridor through Echternach and a northern one through Wallendorf. When Oliver ordered his CCR to probe the West Wall in conjunction with the reconnaissances begun by the rest of the V Corps on September 12 and 13, the combat command approached Wallendorf on Wednesday, the 13th, and found itself at the very edge of the West Wall without having drawn a single hostile shot. Gerow thereupon ordered Oliver, while continuing patrol activity and keeping up contact with the Third Army, to use one combat command plus the 1st Battalion of the 112th Infantry to attack through Wallendorf to Bitburg.

Just after noon on Thursday, CCR crossed the Sauer River into Germany, at a ford below the confluence of the Sauer and the Our. The tankers smoked out nothing more than a home-guard Alarmbattaillon in Wallendorf and pushed right through the town and past the first pillboxes of the West Wall. Despite fog, roadblocks, a gorge at the crossing of Gay Creek, and several Pzkw IVs—apparently from the remnants of Panzer Lehr—by afternoon of Friday, September 15, CCR and the attached infantry battalion were all the way through the West Wall and across the westernmost section of the Eifel plateau, as far as the banks of the Prüm River. This was the same day that the 28th Division scored its first major penetration of the West Wall with the capture of Hill 553, and Gerow decided to combine the two successes by instructing General Oliver not only to continue his move on Bitburg but at that place to turn north to Pronsfeld and the town of Prüm, taking the I SS Panzer Corps in rear.

The 5th Armored had been fortunate enough to strike the West Wall south of the left flank of the I SS Panzer Corps, and below the left flank of the German Seventh Army and Army Group B as well. Nominally, Wallendorf was in the sector of the LXXX Corps of the German First Army, which since September 8 had again been part of General Blaskowitz's Army Group G. In fact, a gap lay open between the two enemy army groups, and Oliver had marched straight into it. Poor enemy troops might manage to make good use of the West Wall pillboxes; but the pillboxes were useless if they were garrisoned by no enemy troops of any description.

The new commander of the enemy's First Army, General von Knobelsdorff, had been brought from Russia precisely because he was thought to have enough courage and energy to deal with this kind of emergency. While appealing to Rundstedt for reserves, and getting two grenadier battalions and a flak regiment, Knobelsdorff hastily shuffled his own units to free a regiment of the 19th Volksgrenadier Division, which he began moving by truck toward the Wallendorf penetration on the night of September 15. Within two days, Knobelsdorff had the remaining two regiments of the 19th VG Division on the way. Meanwhile the handful of Germans already on the scene, such as the Panzer Lehr remnant, prepared to hang on until help arrived. They would use the customary method prescribed by their doctrine, incessant local counterattacks, especially against the American flanks.

On the evening of September 16, such a counterattack struck American engineers who were investigating how best to improve the difficult crossing of Gay Creek. At this defile the Germans were also able to halt the progress of artillery on its way to join the American spearhead. CCR sent a platoon of mixed infantry and tanks back to clear the crossing, but the lieutenant in command met some supply trains east of the creek, assumed therefore that the crossing was open, and failed to carry out his mission. Traffic consequently jammed up under German fire at "Deadman's Ford" until late on Saturday, the 16th, and then an American attack brought only a brief interval of safe crossing before German tanks showed up.

Colonel Glen H. Anderson, commanding CCR, postponed any further advance until he could be sure that artillery would be able to reach his front. Thus a whole day was lost. By Sunday, elements of the 2nd Panzer and 5th Parachute Divisions were making disconcerting nuisances of themselves around the penetration, and two days later the 19th VG Division launched a large-scale counterattack, supported by still other reinforcements that Knobelsdorff's energy had conjured up, such as the 108th Panzer Brigade and part of the 36th Infantry Division. CCR and the 1/112th repulsed the Germans everywhere, with the aid of the first good weather and the first considerable air support since the operation had begun. On the new 108th Panzer Brigade, the Americans inflicted a loss of ten tanks. Nevertheless, there was no longer an opportunity, with the limited strength available to Oliver, to exploit quickly the penetration of the West Wall. On September 21 Oliver pulled back behind the Sauer River.

American knowledge of the West Wall was so limited that it is not clear whether any Americans were aware the 5th Armored Division had penetrated it, or thus that a large opportunity beckoned. In any event, Gerow had called off the offensive all along the V Corps line as early as September 16. By that date, he sensed that the amount of opposition his advances were provoking was beyond the capacity of his far-flung corps to handle, especially when it remained starved for ammunition and for maintenance of its vehicles.

Gerow was understandably vexed about the entire disposition of his corps and had exchanged harsh words about it with Hodges. At this juncture, the army commander seemed unresponsive to any of his corps commanders except Collins; the self-confidence that had blossomed in Hodges during the pursuit seemed to be slipping away, and he was withdrawing deep into his headquarters behind his protective and assertive chief of staff, in a manner that might have aroused uncomfortable memories among those who had known him when he commanded the Third Army back in the States.

The nub of Gerow's discontent was that using an armored division as though it were a cavalry group, extended over a front of some fifty kilometers, and yet expecting the division to mount an offensive at the same time was nothing that would have been contemplated in the orderly precincts of the War Plans Division which Gerow had headed before he took a field command. If Gerow had been less the kind of careful master of detail who becomes a senior General Staff planner, he might have been less troubled by his troops' awkward dispositions and more eager to try to drive forward in spite of them. Had he been as eager as Collins to attack, he might have hit the West Wall harder while the Germans were even weaker than his troops found them as they penetrated the wall on September 15 and 16. Still, Gerow received no encouragement from Hodges either to attack early and hard or to persist when trouble began to develop. Despite Hodges's attack order that reached Gerow late on September 11, Gerow had the "definite impression" that Hodges did not want him to become "involved" in the West Wall before September 14.[1]

Gerow's concerns about his dispositions and supply shortages were well enough founded to make it highly doubtful that his corps could have sustained any momentum in pressing beyond the West Wall against the sort of reinforcements Knobelsdorff so rapidly mustered. Not that the German reinforcements were in any way overwhelming— which is the point on which the history of the brief Ardennes-Eifel campaign of September 1944 must turn. Here more than anywhere else, the Allies reached the West Wall before the rallying Germans did, and here the limited and dispersed strength of the V Corps was sufficient to plunge through the wall. But more than the V Corps was needed to exploit the unparalleled opportunity. If the SHAEF planners had not ruled out the Ardennes as an invasion route, if the Schwerpunkt of Hodges's First Army had been aimed here instead of at the heavy fortifications in the narrow Stolberg corridor, if the First Army had not been yoked to the British Second Army and the latter's weaknesses but had moved in tandem with the Third—these are probably more critical might-have-beens than the much debated ones of Field Marshal Montgomery's early-autumn frustrations.

18: Lorraine (I)

FAR FROM attacking in tandem with the First Army, but rather 130 kilometers south of the infantry concentrations of the V Corps, General Walker's XX Corps on Patton's left was sharing in more than ample measure the frustrations of its impatient army commander. Patton's dry fuel tanks of the first days of September had not merely permitted the Allied armies farther north almost to draw abreast of the Third Army. Because of the eastward curvature of the German frontier as it trends south, the fuel shortage had halted Patton well short of the West Wall. Despite their lead in the August race across France, his troops would not have the honor of first assaulting the West Wall. They faced different problems and, in the XX Corps sector on the Third Army's left, the ancient and famous—and as events proved, in many ways more formidable—defenses of Metz.

When the XX Corps prepared to resume its movement once there was gas in its fuel tanks again, General Walker proposed that parts of the 7th Armored Division should demonstrate in force northeastward toward Sedan. The purpose was to deceive the enemy into believing the Third Army might execute a left turn to rejoin hands with Hodges after all. In fact, at the end of August, Walker was already drawing up orders both for a thrust straight east through Metz and—assuming as his G-2 believed that his armor would roll again before the Germans could do much to defend Metz—for a plunge to the Rhine at Mainz and on across the great river to Frankfurt, 280 kilometers away, before the corps might have to pause again. The hope was that the speed of the advance would preclude a strong German defense either at the West Wall or on the Rhine. "The American successes during August apparently justified such an ambitious and optimistic program," wrote some of the earliest official historians of the campaign. "The assignment of remote objectives seemingly impossible of attainment had paid handsome tactical dividends during the August pursuit across France. XX Corps units had chased the retreating Germans approximately 500 miles in 26 days."[1]

The assumption of a rapid sweep past Metz was based on ignorance of the fortifications as well as on confidence that the Germans remained too disorganized and demoralized to garrison them. The Deuxième Bureau had supplied the Americans with information about the condition of the forts as they were in 1940, but no one knew how much the Germans had changed them. The American advance had outrun the ability of the G-2s to disseminate their information widely, and intelligence concerning historic fortresses was further limited by lack of interest. Brest had not yet provided its warning of the remarkable resiliency of defensive works built in years long past, and so old forts were not regarded altogether seriously.

Remains of the earth-and-log fortifications of the Romans can still be seen around

Metz. The Romans called the place Divodurum or, as the chief town of the Mediomatrici, Mediomatrica. After the legions departed, the province of Lorraine or Lothringen became for centuries the cockpit of the endless struggle between French and German cultures and states for ascendancy in the disputed middle ground between their respective heartlands. Lorraine was the nucleus of that middle section of Charlemagne's empire inherited by Lothair, whose capital was Metz. For the Germans, this Lothringen section of the middle kingdom was the best road to Paris; for the French, it was the best road to Bavaria, the upper Danube, and eventually Vienna. After the dissolution of Lothair's kingdom, and as long as Franco-German rivalry remained poised indecisively enough to allow the middle ground political independence, medieval Lorraine focused upon the three bishoprics and autonomous imperial cities of Metz, Toul, and Verdun. Always, in this historic killing-ground, the cities had to be fortified. The medieval city walls of Metz gave way to more modern ramparts by 1550, and a citadel was added a few years later. By the time Louis XIV declared the three bishoprics annexed to his realm in 1680, Vauban had already redesigned the Metz works to face them definitely eastward. Napoleon III added a circle of detached works, and by 1870, having fallen to no enemy since the Huns in the remote fifth century, fortified Metz had long been called "La pucelle," the virgin city.

The faulty generalship of the Second Empire might have been thought to have ended all that when, on October 14, 1870, Marshal Bazaine surrendered the Army of the Rhine of 180,000 men along with the city and the forts; but it could still be said that no one since Attila had taken Metz by storm. Germany annexed Lorraine and from 1870 to 1918 turned the forts westward, incorporating them into the formidable Metz-Thionville Stellung. After the French regained Lorraine, they made some limited efforts to tie the Metz defenses into the Maginot Line. Nevertheless, the strongest and most modern parts of the Metz defenses faced west.

An inner circle of fifteen forts, begun under Vauban and completed in 1866, could not accommodate large modern ordnance and in the twentieth century had to serve mainly as infantry strongpoints. Most of Metz's casemated guns lurked in an outer ring of twenty-six fortresses about ten kilometers outside the city, constructed by the Germans between 1871 and 1912. Each fortress of this system was actually a complex of strongpoints designed for self-sufficiency. The main fort of each complex, two stories deep, contained headquarters, control centers, and living quarters under arched concrete ceilings often more than three meters thick. The guns were fired from rounded revolving steel turrets that barely protruded above the surface of the ground. Only a direct hit by a bomb of 500 lbs. or more was likely to do much damage to the turrets. Each main fort was supported by two or three subsidiary forts with interlocking fields of fire, covering the surrounding deep dry moats and minefields. Underground passageways linked the forts of each complex. A telephone system of deeply buried double lines connected the various strongpoints both directly and through a central exchange in Metz. To offset the anomaly of infantry strongpoints inside the ring of artillery emplacements, the Germans had dug entrenchments along the edges of thick woods that grew around the forts. They placed antitank guns in these works well forward with the infantry.

Marshal Bazaine notwithstanding, Metz still wore the aura of La pucelle. General Patton enthusiastically encouraged Walker to drive for Metz. Like his subordinates, Patton had no adequate intelligence maps that might have shown details of the fortifications; having outpaced the supply of such materials, he was drawing his plans from a Michelin roadmap. The Michelin showed plainly enough that Metz commanded the most direct route from Verdun to the Rhine. More than that, to assault a famous and legendarily impregnable fortified city was a challenge scarcely to be resisted by a soldier with Patton's sense of his military destiny.

Arnaville and Gravelotte

To expect, like Walker's G-2, that the Germans would attempt no more than a delaying action in Metz was to ignore Adolf Hitler's fascination with famous battlegrounds, fully equal to Patton's. In consonance with the style of Patton's generalship, neither Patton nor Walker intended to strike the heaviest fortifications head on; the XX Corps would swing across the Moselle north or south of Metz and thus envelop the city. But some head-on grappling with the forts was inevitable if the Germans made a contest of it, because the Metz fortress system was too big to leave as a thorn in the line of communication.

Between the Meuse at Verdun and the Moselle at Metz, the ground drops off abruptly from the Côtes de Meuse, the Meuse heights just east of that river, into the desolate, wet plain of the Woëvre, then rises gradually into the more pleasant and fertile countryside of the Moselle plateau. This plateau is one of the series of heights gradually ascending eastward all the way from the Paris region to the Rhine. Like the other elevations in the series, it has an abrupt escarpment facing eastward. The Moselle escarpment rises just east of the Moselle River, for, like the Meuse, the Moselle in this area no longer flows along the eastern base of the heights bearing its name, but has trenched the backslope of the heights slightly west of the escarpment. Advancing eastward, the Americans continued to be spared a perennial problem of the Germans in their westward invasions, the assault of the steep eastward-facing escarpments. On the other hand, as the Third Army approached Metz, the gentle rise of the western face of the Moselle plateau formed a prolonged natural glacis to be swept by the guns of the Metz defenders. With the western edge of the plateau marked roughly by the Conflans–Mars-la-Tour–Chambley road, the glacis extends for about fifteen kilometers. Its eastern half, averaging 370 meters in height, is rugged, wooded, and broken by ravines and draws—excellent ground for screening the dispositions of the defenders, for compartmentalizing the defenses into numerous small tactical pockets, and for staging the standard German counterattacks.

In contrast to the Americans' paucity of detailed knowledge of the Metz forts, the Germans had used Metz as a military school center before the First World War and again since 1940, and from their school exercises they knew every fold of ground intimately. Feeling their way, the Americans opened their drive toward Metz on the morning of Wednesday, September 6, with Walker sending General Silvester's 7th Armored Division to assess the ground and the resistance. Cavalry squadrons were to scout for suitable crossings of the Moselle, CCA to reach out to the north of Metz, CCB with CCR following to probe toward the south. CCB's course would follow a historic military landmark famous in the annals of the Franco-Prussian War, the Rupt de Mad gorge, and two other generally parallel ravines extending southeastward toward the river. The effect was to confirm a nagging worry: the few days' halt to await gasoline might indeed have been a few days too many, the enemy's special efforts to concentrate his reorganized and rejuvenated First

Army in front of Patton seemed to be paying off for him, and Metz might prove a hard nut to crack after all.

The Germans were not yet strong enough to prevent Silvester's combat commands from circling the fortifications to arrive at the Moselle north and south of the city on September 7. But Colonel Dwight A. Rosebaum's CCA, followed by General McLain's 90th Division, could not risk a crossing against the fortifications it could see beyond the stream until the corps situation clarified itself elsewhere; and the form such clarification took on September 13 was an order to shift weight southward to relieve other elements of the 7th Armored and the 2nd Infantry Regiment of the 5th Division, which had become ensnared upon the western face of the Metz fortresses.

Still farther south than the scene of this contretemps, Brigadier General John B. Thompson's CCB and General Irwin's 5th Division actually secured a bridgehead across the Moselle at Dornot south of Metz on September 8, and the 5th Division achieved another crossing at Arnaville on September 10. The Dornot bridgehead was harried, however, by the guns of Fort Driant atop a 360-meter bald hill on the west bank of the river immediately north of the crossing, as well as by vigorous counterattacks. The Germans' fire was too heavy to permit building a bridge, and the bridgehead could not be expanded enough to afford adequate ground for offensive maneuver. The Dornot foothold had to be abandoned on the night of September 10–11. Though also plagued by Fort Driant as well as by batteries of 88s in nearby woods, the Arnaville bridgehead received a bridge built under cover of darkness on the 10th–11th, as well as gradual reinforcement. Nevertheless, development of the bridgehead was slowed by continual determined counterattacks, mounted by troops who displayed as sharp a fighting edge as any remaining in the German army. The unit identifications included practically every organization assembled to stop Patton, including the 3rd and 15th Panzer Grenadier Divisions just up from Italy—some of their members still fighting in tropical uniforms— and the familiar 17th SS Panzer Grenadier Division.

In front of Metz, the 2nd Infantry Regiment had stepped off past the French and German military cemeteries of earlier wars to assault an exterior German line along the Gravelotte-Amanvillers-Roncourt ridge, flanked on the south by the defile of the Manse rivulet, and on the north connected with the general Moselle plateau by a saddle from Amanvillers west toward Doncourt. In 1870, German attacks had melted and fabled German discipline dissolved all along this same ridge line when the men in spiked helmets threw themselves against well-positioned ranks of chassepots. Now the roles were reversed, and the Germans enjoyed the advantages of the defensive—with a similar outcome. East of Malmaison at the Moscou Farm, whose buildings formed a fortress in miniature, the French in 1870 had broken a converging attack by the German VII, VIII, and IX Corps; now the 3rd Battalion of the 2nd Infantry was halted on September 9 by Germans in the same buildings—reinforced by pillboxes—and further torn by crossfire from the same defile east of Gravelotte, on the Verdun-Metz road, that had helped throw the three German corps into confusion during the 1870 battle. On September 11, the 2nd Battalion lost about half its men in attack and counterattack along the same ridge, east of Verneville. Battalions now fought where whole army corps had gathered in serried ranks, but so firm is the grasp of terrain and its obstacles, natural and manmade, upon the shape of war, that the same battles seemed to repeat themselves on the same battlefields after more than three generations. Frustrated as he was in his hopes of resuming the headlong chase, Patton must yet have been enthralled by the demonstration of the constancy of the face of battle.

The colonel of the 2nd Regiment, A.W. Roffe, protested to General Silvester about the uselessness of hurling infantry against "20 odd forts."[2] The forts in front of him, moreover, were garrisoned by German troops at least as good as those hemming in the Arnaville bridgehead to the south, albeit their units were not so famous as the veteran panzer grenadiers. The 2nd Infantry Regiment had struck Division No. 462. This was an improvised formation one of whose regiments was a mediocre security formation—the 1010th Security Regiment—of overaged soldiers, but whose other two regiments were exceptionally sturdy and skillful, assembled as they were from the Metz military schools—the Unterführerschule Regiment of NCO trainees and the Fahnenjunkerschule Regiment of officer candidates. The latter, young, tough, and zealous, along with some of the 17th ss Panzer Grenadiers, held the 1870 battleline so unbendingly against the 2nd Infantry that General Walker had to shift the 90th Division rightward to take over part of Colonel Roffe's front before resuming the attack on September 15.

Not that the Germans in the Metz area were all supermen. On September 7, when Walker's new offensive was first getting started, General von Knobelsdorff decided to try to spoil the effort by thrusting the 106th Panzer Brigade into the left flank of the 90th Division. The flank was exposed and echeloned northeastward because the V Corps had not quite come up even with it. The panzer brigade managed to find a way down side roads between the 358th and 359th Infantry Regiments and, in the dark morning hours of September 8, came roaring into the 90th Division command post. Whether or not the American high command had exaggerated the early deficiencies of the 90th, General McLain's "tough 'ombres" were the wrong outfit against which to attempt this sort of maneuver. Once alerted, the Americans fought with every kind of weapon at hand. The strung-out column of Germans was soon surrounded, and few of the enemy vehicles that approached McLain's CP found their way back to the German lines. By the end of the day, the 90th Division captured or destroyed thirty tanks, sixty half-tracks, and about a hundred other vehicles.

Still, the XX Corps was finding the Metz defenses not merely the thinly held, obsolete works that its G-2 had hopefully guessed lay ahead, but rather the sort of defenders' dream combination of strong works and difficult terrain that would put backbone into almost any garrison—and the panzer grenadiers and officer and NCO candidates were not just any garrison. By September 16, the 90th Division's 359th Infantry had joined the historic list of attackers to be stopped and cut up in the defile of the Verdun-Metz highway just east of Gravelotte. For the XX Corps, the pursuit was over, and hard fighting was the only immediate prospect.

The Battle of Nancy

General Patton may have been working from a simple Michelin map, but he had traveled all over the Lorraine area during the First World War, and he was more than enough of a military historian to know the significance the Lorraine gateway had held between France and Germany ever since the French and the Germans had evolved as different peoples. The plain of Lorraine—which in fact consists of rolling hills marked by lakes and often forest-covered, scored by many streams, but fertile with fields of grain and prosperous with factory towns—offers a passageway from France to Germany between the forbidding Ardennes to the north and the much more forbidding Vosges to the south. The plain is the crossoads, too, for travelers among the headwaters of the Seine, the Rhône, and the Rhine, all readily accessible.

On Patton's Michelin map, Nancy would have appeared to be as likely a point of departure as Metz for a march through the Lorraine gateway to the Rhine. Unlike Metz, however, Nancy has not been strongly fortified in modern times. When after 1870 General Sere de Rivières planned the new French border fortresses to guard the new frontier against Germany, he decided it was wise to leave it so. Instead, he planned two systems of gros ouvrages, leaving between them in southern Lorraine an open gateway. To the north, there was the Verdun fortress system extending to Toul on the Moselle. To the south, another chain of fortresses reached up the canyon of the Moselle from Épinal and across the Vosges to Belfort, where the Belfort Gap opens as another gateway between France and Germany, though much narrower than that of Lorraine. The unfortified area, centering on the town of Charmes, was to form a trap in which the invading German armies would be destroyed when the French armies engaged them in the "Bataille de la Trouée de Charmes." Delayed and finally held at the Meurthe, Mortagne, and Moselle River barriers that cross the "trough" of Charmes, the Germans would then be taken in flank from the plateaus to the north and the higher ground of the Vosges—and 1870 would be avenged.

So, at least in part, events transpired in 1914, when General Noël de Castelnau skillfully extricated his Second Army and General Auguste Dubail's First from the Battle of the Frontiers, and with Dubail's army strung across and holding the Trouée de Charmes, Castelnau's took the Germans in flank and rear and drove them into headlong retreat.

Patton's offensive through the Lorraine gateway would draw his troops into the Trouée de Charmes in the reverse, west-to-east, direction. But as the Germans perceived when they set out in 1914 to offset the lost Bataille de la Trouée de Charmes, the capture of Nancy and the heights surrounding it would unhinge the entrapment mechanism of the Charmes trough by depriving it of its northern anchor; and, more directly to the Americans' purpose, Nancy would open to them one of the main roads to the Rhine.

Just on the eve of the First World War, Castelnau's concern lest the Germans outflank the Charmes trough at Nancy had brought about some belated, hasty fortification. Earlier defenders of Nancy had rallied on the city's natural bastions, which are considerable. Approaching from the west, the Third Army would have to traverse the untamed Forêt de Haye, on the rugged upland triangle, cut by deep chasms, surrounded by the natural moats of the Moselle bend to the west and the gorge of the Meurthe on much of the eastern side, between Nancy and Toul. The historic associations of the Massif de Haye were partly American, because this inhospitable area was one of the first places where the old A.E.F. had entered the Western Front. East of Nancy, the strip of the Moselle plateau east of the river erupts into a high bastion of scarps and buttes commanding the countryside for miles around, the Grand Couronné de Nancy. The heights on the east bank dominate the Moselle itself, and the river in this area is often more than fifty meters wide and more than two meters deep.

On September 4, General Eddy of the XII Corps received Patton's green light to resume the advance on the right of Walker's XX Corps. Eddy was to cross the Moselle around Nancy, to secure the city and its barrier uplands. He planned that the 319th

Infantry of General McBride's 80th Division should cross the Moselle at the river's westernmost extremity near Toul, whence, centuries before, the Moselle had flowed on into the Meuse, and march against Nancy directly through the Forêt de Haye. This head-on attack was to be a diversion, however, to distract attention from the main effort, an envelopment of Nancy from the north. About thirty kilometers north of Nancy, the Grand Couronné is broken by a fairly broad opening, through which a highway crossing the Moselle at Pont-à-Mousson proceeds southeast toward Château-Salins. The Pont-à-Mousson gateway is flanked by bluffs both 382 meters high, the Ste. Geneviève plateau on the south and Mousson Hill on the north; but despite these guardian pillars, it has been for centuries one of the favored military routes across the Moselle. General Eddy's plan called for McBride's 317th Infantry Regiment to win a bridgehead at Pont-à-Mousson, through which Bruce Clarke's CCA of General Wood's 4th Armored Division and a battalion of the 318th Infantry would move swiftly to circle south and east into Nancy.

The XII Corps's collision with the preparations that the Germans had made while the army paused to await gasoline came yet more abruptly than Walker's. On September 5, the 317th Infantry was unable to force a crossing of the Moselle at Pagny-sur-Moselle on its north flank, and at Pont-à-Mousson a tiny bridgehead was wiped out by a German counterattack, with 160 officers and men missing. The 319th had succeeded in crossing into the loop of the river near Toul late on September 4, but it made additional headway only slowly against good troops, the 3rd Parachute Replacement Regiment, who exploited some of the old French fortresses of the Verdun-Toul system.

General Eddy, whose 9th Division had changed front with such remarkable promptness months ago on the Cotentin Peninsula, with similar promptness formed a new design: a double envelopment. His third division, General Baade's 35th, had been held back at first to protect the Third Army's south flank; but General Bradley's solicitude for the Third Army—carrying his hopes for an all-American thrust to the Rhine—now brought the XV Corps back into Patton's fold and to the right flank, freeing Baade from patroling duties. Eddy thereupon decided to use the 35th Division to win a bridgehead over the Moselle south of Nancy, through which General Dager's CCB, 4th Armored would hasten to envelop Nancy from the southeast. When the enemy shifted his attention to contain this stroke, the 80th Division would again essay a crossing north of Nancy. CCA, 4th Armored would join whichever thrust showed the greater promise, reinforcing success.

General Baade's 134th Infantry Regiment, the old 1st Nebraska Volunteers, found a bridge across the Moselle near Flavigny on Sunday, September 10, and its 2nd Battalion crossed. But, as additional evidence of the new order of things across the lines, troops and tanks of the newly arrived 15th Panzer Grenadier Division forced the National Guardsmen to return to the west bank during the night. Still, the Germans did not have enough reinforcements to hold the Moselle in strength everywhere along Patton's front, and on Monday morning the 137th Infantry, Kansas National Guard, along with CCB won crossings farther south, around Crévéchamps and Bayon. These footholds soon attracted more of the 15th Panzer Grenadiers, and the Americans faced slow going.

The ensuing commotion south of Nancy seemed to make the moment ripe for a new effort by the 80th Division north of the city, at some place other than Pont-à-Mousson and the strongly held hills flanking and commanding the Pont-à-Mousson gateway. The place selected was Dieulouard, about six kilometers south of Pont-à-Mousson; the occasion would be the first major World War II offensive of McBride's Blue Mountaineers, whose divisional antecedents lay in western Virginia and West Virginia and among Stonewall Jackson's men. McBride assigned the 317th Infantry the assault crossing again, with the further duty of pushing as far as the summit of the Moselle plateau east of the river. The 318th Infantry was to follow and turn north, mopping up the high ground all the way to Mousson Hill. McBride took special care to conceal from hostile eyes the shift of his attention away from the Pont-à-Mousson crossing site, and his care paid off. The Moselle plateau opposite Dieulouard proved another of the places that the Germans had not gotten around to reinforcing. The Americans crossed at two fords or in assault boats during the early morning hours of Tuesday, September 12, against only occasional fire from light enemy outposts. Obscured by low clouds and a drizzling rain, the engineers soon threw bridges across. The 317th Infantry captured the Ste. Geneviève heights, and the 318th pushed north as far as the town of Atton on the way to Mousson Hill.

The crossing happened to have struck a loosely held part of the 3rd Panzer Grenadier Division's sector, but by Wednesday this formation was reacting with counterattacks vigorous enough to threaten yet another American withdrawal. By that time General Wood and Colonel Clarke had decided, and Eddy had agreed, that Clarke's CCA should be committed at Dieulouard, so the counterattacks soon had to tangle with American armor as well as McBride's infantry. The commander of Clarke's spearhead, Lieutenant Colonel Creighton W. Abrams of the 37th Tank Battalion, took charge of the fighting at Ste. Geneviève, cleared the counterattackers from the town of that name, and then despite continued chaos to his rear set out on the kind of armored ride deep into enemy territory in which the Third Army specialized. Abrams's destination was the road junction of Château-Salins, by way of a swing north from the bridgehead to the main eastward road out of Pont-à-Mousson. His tank gallop reminded General Eddy of Jeb Stuart's ride around the Army of the Potomac outside Richmond in June 1862. Smashing through enemy roadblocks, Task Force Abe laagered for the night around Fresnes-en-Saulnois, almost thirty kilometers beyond the bridgehead and only five kilometers short of Château-Salins. On the way, Abrams lost only twelve dead, sixteen wounded, and no tanks. He took 354 prisoners and captured or destroyed twelve tanks, eighty-five other vehicles, and five large-caliber guns.

Enough Germans were in the neighborhood to test whether "P" Wood's superbly aggressive division could fight as well as it could raid and pursue. The next day, September 14, Wood ordered Colonel Clarke to bypass Château-Salins and proceed instead to Arracourt, farther south and east, to make contact with General Dager's CCB coming up from the south, and to help CCB bridge the Marne-Rhin Canal just south of Arracourt, CCB having used up most of its bridging equipment in crossing the Meurthe River as well as many lesser streams in addition to the Moselle. Task Force Abe again led the way, and promptly it met part of the 15th Panzer Grenadier Division traveling to join a German concentration to the southeast. The day's score for CCA was 409 prisoners taken and twenty-six armored vehicles, 136 other vehicles, and ten 88s captured or destroyed, in exchange for losses of ten men killed, twenty-three wounded, and two Shermans destroyed. Around Arracourt during the night, the combat command began bagging Germans who were retreating eastward unaware of any American presence in the area.

Meanwhile the advance out of the bridgehead south of Nancy had also gathered momentum in the past two days, and late at night patrols of CCA and CCB met to complete the double envelopment of Nancy.

The Nancy pocket within the envelopment remained crawling with stubborn Germans, the 553rd Volksgrenadier Division as well as elements of the 15th Panzer Grenadiers and a miscellany of other units. By September 15, the morning after the CCA-CCB linkup, the 80th Division was having so much trouble fending off counterattacks at Mont Toulon and Mont St. Jean, a second outcropping of hills east of the Moselle commanding CCA's route to Arracourt, that CCA had to release the attached 1st Battalion, 318th Infantry and send it back to help stem the tide. The 3rd Panzer Grenadier Division was spearheading the enemy's counterefforts from the north designed to break the envelopment from outside, and these Germans found the broken hills of the eastern extremity of the Moselle plateau ideal for their stock in trade of constant local harassment. Daily morning fog helped them mount continual surprise attacks bursting from behind cover against American parties more or less isolated on the rough ground. A typical German foray would pin Americans in positions with fire, encircle them, and often overrun them. On September 14 the 3rd Battalion, 318th had taken the crest of Mousson Hill, only to be cut off from assistance for much of the next day.

To the south, the 35th Division moved northward on the left flank of CCB, and by September 15 this whole force had either crossed to the north bank of the Marne-Rhin Canal or closed to the south bank. That Friday, furthermore, a task force of parts of both the 35th and the 80th Divisions aided by the FFI entered the city of Nancy from the Toul road. East of Nancy and north of the canal, nevertheless, the fighting grew as bitter as McBride's troops were finding it around Ste. Geneviève and Mousson Hill.

On Sunday, September 17, while MARKET-GARDEN was being launched far to the north, General Baade's Santa Fe Division opened a battle for Mont d'Amance and the Pain de Sucre, a mesa and a butte isolated east of the main bulk of the Grand Couronné, but the focal points of the contest in which Castelnau had driven back the Germans in the 1914 Battle of the Grand Couronné. It was now the Americans' turn to assail the heights that had foiled the Germans in 1914. With the aid of P-47s slashing at the dug-in defenses, Baade's men captured the Pain de Sucre on Monday, September 18. But Patton had concluded that Baade's infantry needed reinforcement by the armor of CCB of General Grow's 6th Armored Division, which Grow had contrived to shift eastward from Brittany in his effort to rejoin the main battle. On September 22, Colonel G. W. Read's CCB joined the 137th Infantry in an assault on Mont d'Amance as part of a coordinated attack all along the 35th Division-80th Division front to break the enemy in the pocket east of the Moselle. CCB cut into the rear of the Amance hill while the Kansas infantry charged in front and Thunderbolts again banged away at the summit. The mesa fell. On Saturday, September 23, there was a tangible slackening of resistance and evidence of a German intent to try to flee the pocket.

The Battle of Dompaire

Whoever held the heights flanking the Trouée de Charmes on the north need not fear the trap the French General Staff had long ago seen in the trough. By the time General Haislip's XV Corps could resume a role in the Third Army's advance, this time on the army's right flank, the XII Corps battles around the Grand Couronné had gone far

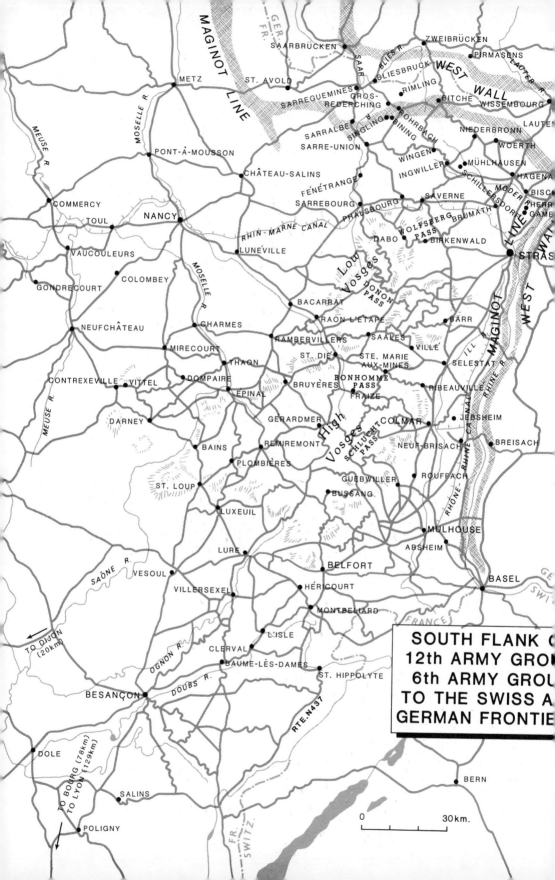

MAGINOT LINE

MEUSE R.

MOSELLE R.

SAAR

BLIES R.

LAUTER R.

WEST WALL

SAARBRÜCKEN
ST. AVOLD
SARREGUEMINES
GROS-REDERCHING
SARRALBE
SARRE-UNION

ZWEIBRÜCKEN
PIRMASENS
BLIESBRUCK
RIMLING
BITCHE
WISSEMBOURG
ROHRBACH
SINGLING
BINING
NIEDERBRONN
WOERTH
WINGEN
INGWILLER
MÜHLHAUSEN
HAGENA
SCHILLERSDORF
BISC
RHERR
GAME

METZ
PONT-À-MOUSSON
CHÂTEAU-SALINS
FÉNÉTRANGE
SARREBOURG
PHALSBOURG
SAVERNE
BRUMÄTH

WEST WALL
MAGINOT LINE

COMMERCY
TOUL
NANCY
RHIN-MARNE CANAL
LUNÉVILLE
DABO
WOLFSBERG PASS
BIRKENWALD

VAUCOULEURS
COLOMBEY
Low Vosges
DONON PASS
STRAS

GONDRECOURT
NEUFCHÂTEAU
CHARMES
BACARRAT
RAON L'ETAPE
SAALES
BARR
VILLE

MIRECOURT
RAMBERVILLERS
ST. DIE
STE. MARIE AUX-MINES
SELESTAT

CONTREXEVILLE
VITTEL
THAON
DOMPAIRE
BRUYÈRES
BONHOMME PASS
FRAIZE
RIBEAUVILLE

DARNEY
EPINAL
GERARDMER
High Vosges
COLMAR
SCHLUCHT PASS
JEBSHEIM
BREISACH

BAINS
REMIREMONT
NEUF-BRISACH

PLOMBIÈRES
GUEBWILLER
ROUFFACH

ST. LOUP
BUSSANG

LUXEUIL
MULHOUSE
ABSHEIM

LURE
BELFORT

VESOUL
SAÔNE R.
VILLERSEXEL
HÉRICOURT
BASEL

MONTBELIARD
GER.
SWIT.

L'ISLE
FRANCE

CLERVAL
BAUME-LÈS-DAMES
ST. HIPPOLYTE

OGNON R.
DOUBS R.
BESANÇON
RTE.N437

TO DIJON (20km)

DOLE

TO BOURG (78km)
TO LYON (129km)
SALINS

BERN

POLIGNY

FR. SWITZ.

SOUTH FLANK C
12th ARMY GROU
6th ARMY GROU
TO THE SWISS A
GERMAN FRONTIE

0   30km.

enough toward assuring the safety of the northward heights that Haislip could regard the trough not as a trap but rather as an inviting west-to-east runway. The XV Corps reassembled southeast of Troyes and began its advance on September 11. For the present, the corps contained only two divisions: the 2ème Blindée, which with extreme reluctance had wrenched itself out of liberated Paris, and the 79th Infantry, the Cross of Lorraine Division having completed the long journey from its regiments' native Pennsylvania to the province whose symbol it wore as an emblem of martial prowess on its shoulder patch. That Haislip could bring even an additional two divisions to the Third Army in September was evidence of General Bradley's bending SHAEF directives as far as he could to assist Patton; the 79th had moved nearly 500 kilometers south from Belgium at the height of the fuel and transport shortage.

For the time being, Haislip would have to march toward Charmes with part of his small corps echeloned southwestward, guarding the Third Army's right flank. But his front was an area that the Germans had not yet been able to reinforce, and only scattered enemy detachments, largely Landesschützen, guarded the Charmes runway. The detachments were under the command umbrella of the German LXVI Corps, part of General Blaskowitz's Army Group G. The LXVI Corps was supposed to be holding a door open north of Dijon for the escape of the Germans fleeing the DRAGOON forces. By now, the Nineteenth Army coming up from southwestern France was locking its fairly firm front upon the Swiss frontier on its left; but still straggling along from the Bay of Biscay was a motley collection of some 80,000 men and 2,000 women, called the LXIV Corps, unable to flee by the most direct route across the Massif Central because the French Resistance was in control there, and harried by the French wherever their circuitous route carried them. In early September the German 16th Division was hastened along in advance of this exodus, and it soon formed the best force with which the LXVI Corps could confront Haislip to protect the escape hatch. But the 16th Division was not as impressive as its low number might imply; it was a recent amalgam of the 16th Luftwaffe Field Division and the 158th Reserve Division.

Anyway, the hatch was about to close. On the night of September 10–11, patrols of the 2ème Blindée met the advance of an Armored Reconnaissance Group of General de Lattre's Army B at the village of Sombernon just west of Dijon. On September 12 there was another meeting of patrols of the 2ème Blindée and the 1ère Division Motorisée d'Infanterie at Châtillon-sur-Seine. On September 15, the linkup between the XV Corps and the DRAGOON forces became firm, although as usual, most of the German fugitives somehow squeaked through before that happened.

With the 2ème Blindée tending to the army and corps right flank, Haislip began his movement of September 11 by motorizing the 314th Infantry of General Wyche's 79th Division—stripping two corps artillery battalions of transport to do it—and ordering the 314th down the trough from just north of Neufchâteau to Charmes. Sweeping across the front of the enemy's 16th Division, whose escape-hatch duties had it facing northward, the regiment reached Charmes by evening and captured the town in a day-long fight on September 12. Though the enemy blew the Charmes bridges across the Moselle, the Americans found a ford.

By that time the other regiments and combat commands of Haislip's two divisions were also moving forward, and Combat Command Langlade of the 2ème Blindée was almost as far east as Dompaire. Outside Dompaire on the late afternoon of September 12,

Colonel Langlade heard from civilians that a large German tank force was approaching from the direction of Épinal. Reconnaissance confirmed many German tanks in Dompaire that night. Langlade prepared to give battle next day by sending one column to the right to cut the Dompaire-Épinal road, while another column—under Lieutenant Colonel Jacques Massu, of later fame as a leader of rebellious French regulars unwilling to yield independence to Algeria—hit the Dompaire concentration head on.

The Germans proved to be the new 112th Panzer Brigade, sent to counterattack complete with its Panther and Pzkw IV battalions. After some preliminary skirmishing by Langlade's right column, the French colonel sent armored infantry advancing in front of Massu's tanks as a feint, with the purpose of drawing the enemy army in on well positioned tanks and field guns. The maneuver worked, and the enemy was hit hard not only by the ground weapons but also by the Thunderbolts of the 406th Fighter-Bomber Group, summoned all the way from Brittany. During the day, the P-47s flew four air strikes, following each of which the French moved forward under cover of orchards and woods, compressing the Germans into an ever narrower mass in the valley bottom in which Dompaire lies. When another column of German tanks turned up approaching from the southeast to strike the French rear, it was already too late to save the German main body, and Langlade was ready enough to receive the newcomers for his guns to knock out seven Pzkw IVs in the first exchange.

Optimistic Allied estimates of enemy losses—the 406th Group alone claimed thirteen tanks destroyed and fifteen damaged—were eventually confirmed when the Allies learned that the 112th Panzer Brigade had extricated only four of its Panthers from its first battle, and lost twenty-six Pzkw IVs as well. It detracts little from the brilliance of the French action to say that the Battle of Dompaire together with the recent battle of the 106th Panzer Brigade against the 90th Division suggested a certain unwisdom in Hitler's committing his brand-new tanks largely to brand-new formations, rather than replenishing the veteran panzer divisions. Even if the officers of the new panzer brigades had experience in Russia, that was not enough preparation to meet the air-ground teamwork of the Western Allies.

Despite the outcome of the Battle of Dompaire, the presence of so much enemy armor suggested caution until the XV Corps right should be no longer open but in firm alignment with the Seventh Army coming up from the Mediterranean. During the next few days, Patton and Haislip contented themselves with closing the corps up to the Moselle. Their wisdom was confirmed when Combat Command Billotte, feeling its way over onto the enemy side of the Moselle on September 16, ran into about fifteen Panthers and two infantry battalions of the 111th Panzer Brigade. Again, the French scored a decisive small victory—an officer prisoner said the Germans lost five Panthers and 200 men—but the accumulation of German armor surely suggested that something was in the wind.

The Battle of Arracourt

The threat materialized on Monday morning, September 18, when German armor in two main columns emerged from forests to the east and south in a concentric attack against the vanguard of the 4th Armored Division around Lunéville. Because the 553rd VG Division and other Germans were still fighting inside the Nancy pocket, in General Wood's rear, the 4th Armored's position might readily become precarious. The panzer attack proved to be the culmination of Hitler's persistent efforts to accumulate a mass of maneuver in front of Patton, and was conducted by a reconstituted Fifth Panzer Army into which a major share of German tank production had been poured; resolution of the threat would have to take the form of the biggest tank battles the Americans had yet fought in Europe.

One German Schwerpunkt, General der Panzertruppen Walter Krüger's LVIII Panzer Corps, attacked due west toward Lunéville between the Seille River and the Marne-Rhin Canal, a stretch of excellent, open, rolling tank country. The other spearhead, the familiar XLVII Panzer Corps reconstituted under General von Lüttwitz of 2nd Panzer Division fame, came up from the southeast to converge with Krüger at Lunéville. Commanding these corps from headquarters, Fifth Panzer Army since September 11 was General der Panzertruppen Hasso-Eccard von Manteuffel, a diminutive but highly energetic hero of the armored battles in the East. Manteuffel's army had been inserted into Blaskowitz's Army Group G front between the First and Nineteenth Armies.

None of the German dispositions and intentions were clear to the Americans on the morning of September 18. Instead, Lunéville became a scene of confusion as German tanks beat back the light armor of American calvary east and south of the town and sent the cavalry retreating into streets where the course of events was already so chaotic that both sides claimed to possess Lunéville. American intelligence had thought the panzers were assembling for an effort farther south, and the troops around Lunéville had not expected to be hit. Nevertheless, Wood's 4th Armored Division demonstrated that it was not to be pushed around easily by such stuff as the 111th Panzer Brigade which led Krüger's charge. Colonel Wendell Blanchard's CCR, Wood's main force inside Lunéville, stood up so stoutly that the Germans shifted their main effort northward the next day, to strike around Arracourt where some of the pocketed 553rd VG Division lay not far to the west.

Still unaware that Monday's flight for Lunéville had been anything more than an unusually determined specimen of the enemy's continual local counterattacks, Wood had massed General Dager's CCB around Fresnes-en-Saulnois, about twenty kilometers northwest of Arracourt, in compliance with orders from corps and army to resume the advance toward Sarreguemines on Tuesday. CCA was strung out in a light defensive screen from Chambrey just south of Château-Salins almost to the Marne-Rhin Canal, with Colonel Clarke's headquarters, the field artillery, and a platoon of tank destroyers in and around Arracourt. Colonel Abrams with part of his 37th Tank Battalion was out in front at Lezey, and during Monday night and early Tuesday morning his and other advanced detachments heard a good deal of ominous clanking and whirring of tracked vehicles in front of them. American artillery fire quieted the noise, but several brushes between hostile patrols struck sparks in the early morning fog.

Out of that morning fog there soon rumbled big, hulking Panthers. A section of Shermans south of Lezey abruptly saw a Panther take form out of the mist scarcely seventy meters away. Within seconds the Sherman knocked out this and two following Panthers, and the crew heard other German tanks apparently drawing back. Clarke got the word at Arracourt and dispatched a platoon of the 704th Tank Destroyer Battalion toward Lezey. They arrived just west of Bezange-la-Petite in time to deploy in front of another force of German tanks and to open fire at about 150 meters. The Germans knocked out three of four tank destroyers, but the Americans disabled seven Panthers in return. Meanwhile four of Abrams's tanks followed up the retreat of the first Germans by racing the withdrawing armor some 3,000 meters to a ridge west of Bezange. The Americans arrived on the crest about three minutes before eight Panthers appeared. The Shermans blasted four of the Panthers out of action before the Germans could return the fire, then withdrew behind the crest, shifted position under concealment, and returned to finish off the other four Panthers.

Thereafter the battle developed around a series of attacks by the 113th Panzer Brigade toward both Lezey and Bezange, the enemy looking for an opening in CCA's defenses, the Americans bringing reinforcements from both Lunéville and Chambrey onto CCA's flanks. The initial American successes owed much to the fog, which nullified the range advantage of the Panther's long 75 over the Sherman's short 75. At close range, the Shermans and the Americans' self-propelled tank destroyers could also count on a slight edge in maneuverability. Beyond these assets, and the defects of inexperience in another of the new enemy panzer brigades, the quality of "P" Wood's 4th Armored Division also played a part. The division had engaged in just enough serious fighting during its career of headlong pursuits that the tankers could hone their skills under an especially demanding leadership, but a leadership that at Wood's insistence stressed cooperation and mutual responsibilities rather than competition among tanks, platoons, companies, or battalions. The Sherman crews of the 4th Armored had developed to a fine pitch the knack of offsetting their tank's shortcomings with maximum exploitation of its maneuverability and its motorized—against the Germans' hand-traversed—turret. By late Tuesday, CCA reported forty-three German tanks destroyed, mostly new Panthers (a tally close to the enemy's report of fifty tanks destroyed or damaged), against five Shermans and three tank destroyers lost.

Patton himself came to Arracourt, and at day's end he judged that CCA reinforced by CCR could take up the advance toward Sarreguemines on Wednesday morning; CCB had attacked on schedule and was now fighting its way through Château-Salins. But eight German tanks again appeared at Arracourt on September 20 after most of CCA had moved on, and while the rear guard readily repulsed them, Clarke led the whole combat command back to sweep the area "once and for all." The sweep set off a mid-afternoon battle west of Ommeray against Pzkw IVs and 88s in defensive alignment among low hills, with each side losing eleven or twelve tanks.

The Americans were soon to learn that the reversion to large-scale counterattacks had also produced the relief of General Blaskowitz from command of Army Group G. Blaskowitz had never been a favorite of the Führer's; his four years of occupation duty in France at the head of the First Army and then Army Group G had represented as much as Hitler felt he could do toward putting a senior general and a protégé of Rundstedt's on the shelf. The skillfulness of Blaskowitz's retreat from the Mediterranean availed him nothing with the Führer, who simply awaited a pretext to sack him now that his front was active, and for whom the fizzle of the intended major counterstroke against Patton was not merely a pretext but a cause for fury.

Blaskowitz's successor was General der Panzertruppen Hermann Balck. The name was thoroughly familiar to American soldiers of Patton's era, because Balck's father, Generalleutnant Wilhelm Balck, had written a treatise on *Tactics* that had been a standard reference work in English translation for a generation.[3] The younger Balck had added to the family's renown in 1940 when his 1st Rifle Regiment of the 1st Panzer Division spearheaded the assault of Guderian's XIX Panzer Corps beyond the Meuse. Since then Balck had led the 11th Panzer Division, the XLVIII Panzer Corps, and the Fourth Panzer Army on the Eastern Front, all with both offensive and party zeal. Personally brave—he was six times wounded—he inspired others to bravery by projecting a sense of sure confidence in the ultimate triumph of the Third Reich in spite of all adversity.

Bruce Clarke's CCA spent Thursday, September 21, completing its sweep around Arracourt. The enemy proved to have grown so docile, and in fact was so little in evidence, that General Wood gave the combat command Friday as a day of rest and rehabilitation before rejoining CCB in the offensive against what was proving a stubborn target at Château-Salins. Balck's arrival at the opposing army group headquarters made itself felt immediately, however, in yet another procession of tanks out of the fog on the morning of CCA's intended day of rest.

This day the sun broke through relatively soon after the fighting began, and Colonel Abrams had P-47s of the XIX TAC overhead when he led his 37th Tank Battalion and the 10th Armored Infantry Battalion in a counterstroke toward the town of Juvelize north-west of Lezey. Some of Abrams's tanks and artillery made a flank march that put them on a hill commanding the road down which German reinforcements were moving into the battle, and they quickly destroyed fourteen German tanks and mortally wounded the chief of the 111th Panzer Brigade, Oberst Heinrich Bronsart von Schellendorff, whose family name is even more famous than Balck's in German military writing. It did the Germans no good to throw in the remnants of the 113th Panzer Brigade in support of the 111th; the effect was merely to complete the wrecking of another two of the new armored formations.

Bruce Clarke's CCA had borne almost the whole brunt of the German counterattack because Lüttwitz's XLVII Panzer Corps to the south had never been able to get its intended complementary efforts off the ground. Instead, the American XV Corps by resuming its advance occupied Lüttwitz with the defense of his own left flank, obliging him to face southwest rather than to strike to the northwest and north. On Tuesday, September 19, both of General Haislip's divisions attacked Lüttwitz's left-flank screen along the Mortagne River, and they crossed the river and penetrated the screen in half a dozen places. Lüttwitz was trying to hold here with the 21st Panzer Division; but this veteran unit, the first armored division to grapple with the Anglo-American invaders on the 6th of June, was now reduced to a weak infantry formation with a handful of tanks. Lüttwitz tried to bolster it with the survivors of the 112th Panzer Brigade, but that was hardly enough. By September 21, Haislip's troops were knocking at the doors of Lüttwitz's next defensive line along the Meurthe River—and, more than that, taking the line in flank by crossing the river over the XII Corps's bridges at Lunéville.

That day the Germans' resistance stiffened, because Lüttwitz could take advantage of forest cover, both to counterattack into Lunéville from the adjacent Forêt de Parroy, and to resist a 79th Division bridgehead across the Meurthe in the Forêt de Mondon. He now had much of the 15th Panzer Grenadier Division committed to his fight against the XV Corps. Haislip required three days' struggle and heavy casualties to break the line of the Meurthe and the Germans' hold on the forests before Lüttwitz fell back to the next river line, that of the Vezouse.

Despite this frustration of the redoubtable Lüttwitz and his XLVII Panzer Corps, and the rebuffs administered the LVIII Panzer Corps at both Lunéville and Arracourt, the Third Army learned from prisoners that the enemy intended to counterattack yet again. The blow fell on Sunday, September 24, this time against the 4th Armored's CCB between Château-Salins and Fresnes-en-Saulnois, for the enemy's failures farther south had persuaded him to shift the efforts of Manteuffel's Fifth Panzer Army northward once more so that Knobelsdorff's First Army could join in on Manteuffel's right. Unfortunately for the Germans, Manteuffel's two panzer corps had absorbed so thorough a battering that the combined aggressive drive of Manteuffel and Balck could not suffice to prepare the Fifth Panzer Army soon enough to attack in coordination with the 559th Volksgrenadier Division of the First Army. The battle on September 24 thus became a contest between the 559th VG and General Dager's CCB—plus the Thunderbolts of XIX TAC, because the usual fog broke just in time for General Weyland's fighter-bombers to turn a chaotic melee into an American victory, which the Germans fled leaving eleven ruined tanks and some 300 dead behind them.

Manteuffel at length returned to the charge the next day, reinforced by parts of the 11th Panzer Division transferred to him from the Nineteenth Army. Wisely, he chose the reliable Ghost Division as the spearhead of his attack, to drive through Moyenvic southeast of Château-Salins and north of Arracourt. In a rainstorm that kept the hated P-47s away, the 11th Panzers drove through light cavalry opposition past Moyenvic to fan out south and west, making contact with the 559th VG Division on their west flank. Manteuffel thereupon ordered the attack broadened across the whole front of the LVIII Panzer Corps, with Lüttwitz and his XLVII Panzer Corps to join in at least to the extent of providing counterbattery fire from below the Marne-Rhin Canal against gun concentrations behind the American front.

As soon as the Germans took on the main concentrations of CCA, Manteuffel's optimism had to yield to another replay of a now-familiar script. Northeast of Juvelize, ten German tanks struck Shermans of Abe Abrams's 37th Tank Battalion, deployed in superior numbers across commanding ground. The Germans had to withdraw. Farther southeast, German infantry and tanks attacked armored infantry and cavalry throughout the afternoon and into the evening, but without breaking them.

During the night of September 25–26, General Wood moved CCB from his left to his right flank, to hold from the right of CCA around Réchicourt to the Marne-Rhin Canal. The 35th Division moved into CCB's old positions. Wood's shift proved prescient, because on September 27 Manteuffel made still another change in the axis of his thrusting. Hoping he had drawn the Americans northward, he drove up the road along the canal against CCB's new front, seeking to break it and then swing north to envelop a camelback rise of two hills south of Arracourt whence the Americans had enjoyed excellent observation of much of the past days' battlefield. More specifically, Manteuffel attacked CCB in the fashion he and Balck had come to favor through their long experience on the Eastern Front, a concentration of the bulk of the tanks available into a single array—some twenty-five tanks from the 11th Panzer Division, the 15th Panzer Grenadier Division, and the 111th and 113th Panzer Brigades. General von Wietersheim of the 11th Panzers objected that such a concentration of armor was unsuitable to the Western Front; but Manteuffel replied that the Luftwaffe had promised him fifty planes to fly cover, and he persisted in the plan.

Krüger's LVIII Panzer Corps opened diversionary attacks all along its front at eight in the morning of September 27. Some of its stabs made slight penetrations into weak sections of the 4th Armored Division's line. About ten o'clock, the German armored concentration began the main effort, but American artillery halted its advance with dismaying abruptness. Nevertheless, the canny Wietersheim used the uproar to screen the infiltration of some of his panzer grenadiers into positions from which they could readily assault the higher hump of the camelback. Fighting thereupon surged back and forth around this crest all day and into September 28, when the Americans recaptured the peak in the morning, lost it again, retook it about noon, and lost it again after darkness, to fight back to the top yet again during the early morning of September 29.

The Germans meanwhile had carved out strongpoints on the slopes and in the forests surrounding the camelback, but when the morning fog cleared on the 29th, the Americans on the summit used their vantage place to direct the fighter-bombers of XIX TAC onto knots of German armor, including what remained of Manteuffel's main assemblage. Simultaneously, the American ground troops opened a general series of counterattacks. Despite such mishaps as some planes' dropping propaganda leaflets instead of bombs, the Americans pushed back the enemy everywhere around Arracourt. By afternoon, the exhausted Germans seemed on the verge of rout. A few panzers standing stubbornly in defensive deployment averted this possibility, but the enemy infantry's entrenching gave evidence that the German effort was spent.

So, for the time being, was Wood's 4th Armored Division. It had proven itself as admirable a formation in hard defensive fighting as on the racing pursuit, but for the present it must dig in and husband its strength. Its soldiers and officers still expected that Patton's major offensive might resume soon, and that they might yet recapture something of their pace across France and be into Germany and across the Rhine within a matter of weeks. The senior officers knew, after all, that Patton had been about to jockey his three corps into position for a heavy, concentrated blow by all the corps each advancing in column of divisions when the Fifth Panzer Army's counterattack forestalled him. Yet by the end of September, the expectation of a rapid final offensive into the Reich had faded into a far less substantial hope than it had seemed when the Allies drove headlong across the First World War battlefields a month before. If the Germans could mount at Arracourt the most formidable tank attacks since the battles against the British around Caen, their recovery had exceeded the expectations even of Patton's sober G-2—and the West Wall still lay ahead everywhere, and unbroken.

Patton in September

On the other hand, while it had been months since the enemy could muster the kind of strength he pressed into the tank battles around Arracourt, Manteuffel's panzer concentrations never approached the scale of those that had confronted Montgomery around Caen. Disconcerting as the German counterattacks might be after the Allies' great expectations of the beginning of September, they could also have been worse. Allied intelligence had gathered some awareness that the enemy intended a much more powerful countereffort than the September 18–29 attacks of the LVIII and XLVII Panzer Corps proved to be. Since August, the Germans had been hoarding on Patton's front and right flank all the main weight of the reserves and the new formations their rally and recovery so extraordinarily accumulated. They transformed Knobelsdorff's First Army into the most powerful on Germany's Western Front, and then added the armor of Manteuffel's Fifth Panzer Army. The intent had been to store up enough strength first to hold Patton on the Moselle, and then to hurl a mass of maneuver—Manteuffel's army—against Patton's vulnerable southern flank and northward into his rear. Hitler envisioned a grand offensive striking from the Meuse to the Marne and beyond. His dreams no doubt exceeded the potentialities of any recovery of which Germany remained capable. Nevertheless, the counterstroke against Patton, a month in preparation, might have become considerably more dangerous to the Allies had not Patton, with General Bradley's support, repeatedly compelled a piecemeal commitment of German reserves by persisting in his own offensive despite logistical crisis and the vacillating but genuine tendency of SHAEF to restrain the Third Army in favor of Montgomery.

That tendency became most pronounced with the September 10 decision for MARKET-GARDEN just before Patton's crossings of the Moselle opened the major fighting in Lorraine. On September 12, Bradley felt the pressure of the MARKET-GARDEN decision enough to warn Patton that if the Third Army could not cross the Moselle with the mass of its forces by the evening of September 14, Patton's offensive toward the Saar and the upper Rhine would have to be discontinued, and the Third Army must revert to some sort of support for the First Army's right flank. Bradley, of course, wanted Patton to be able to continue onward in his own way, and by the September 14 deadline Patton had sufficient troops beyond the Moselle for the none-too-difficult purpose of convincing Bradley he should proceed further.

By proceeding, the XV Corps overran the Trouée de Charmes, though it had been the German intention to move Manteuffel west through the trough to Neufchâteau and thence northward, in this way turning the Meuse escarpment and nullifying its defensive advantages to the Americans. By proceeding, Patton also tied down or chewed up important segments of the enemy's intended mass of maneuver. Already the advance of the XX Corps against Metz had led to the premature commitment and the evisceration of the 106th Panzer Brigade. The 2ème Blindée's advance through the Trouée de Charmes not only deprived the enemy of his geographical springboard but worked ruination upon the 112th Panzer Brigade. The 15th Panzer Grenadier Division was partly in motion to join Manteuffel's army when the XII Corps offensive cut the roads east of the Moselle over which it was moving. Much of the same division, moreover, Knobelsdorff could not spare from his defensive battle against the XX and XII Corps, even to begin the shift toward Manteuffel. Neither the 15th nor the 3rd Panzer Grenadiers ever received enough relief from Patton's relentless pressure to play the counteroffensive role Hitler had intended when he brought them up from Italy.

If Patton had not maintained his offensive in early and mid-September, the German counterstroke would not have been wasted and blunted before it could begin. If Patton's logistical support had been cut back as completely as Montgomery desired—to immobilize Patton's divisions—it is difficult to conceive how the Third Army could have countered the greater German offensive that Hitler would then have been able to marshal against it—and the effect would have been severe embarrassment to the entire Allied front. Surely no logistical allotment that would have permitted Patton the ammunition and fuel he needed to withstand German counterattacks could have afforded Montgomery enough additional tonnage over what he actually received to have made a decisive difference in the course of his battles.

The Allied Right Flank

Having raced to within a few kilometers and a few hours of closing the Belfort Gate against the southern wing of Army Group G, General Wiese's Nineteenth Army, the DRAGOON forces like Patton's divisions had to settle for a slugging match against consolidated and reinforced German defenses.

General Devers as Deputy Supreme Allied Commander in the Mediterranean had been exercising general supervision of the DRAGOON forces on behalf of the Mediterranean chief, General Wilson, from an Advance Detachment of Wilson's Allied Force Headquarters. The Combined Chiefs of Staff had long since planned that when DRAGOON linked hands with General Eisenhower's armies, the DRAGOON forces should shift from Wilson's to SHAEF's control, and Devers should head a new army group, the 6th, on Eisenhower's southern flank. Devers had activated 6th Army Group headquarters on Corsica as early as August 1. With the meeting of the DRAGOON forces and Patton's army consummated, the 6th Army Group officially became operational on the southern section of the front at one minute past midnight on September 15. Devers, who wanted to keep his headquarters small, lean, and mobile in the spirit of FM 100–15's prescriptions for an army group—and who was destined to succeed in that effort considerably better than Bradley, with much less duplication of the functions of the army headquarters subordinate to him—made the change at the front largely by the simple expedient of transforming the Advance Detachment, AFHQ, into 6th Army Group.

Not until September 19 did the 6th Army Group or Southern Group of Armies have more than one army to command. On that date General de Lattre's Army B was redesignated the First French Army and transferred from Seventh Army to 6th Army Group control. This change in turn left General Patch's Seventh Army with only one corps, General Truscott's VI.

SHAEF was not yet ready to take up logistical support of the 6th Army Group. Indeed, SOLOC—the Southern Line of Communications—was never to become completely disentangled from the Mediterranean Theater. The Twelfth Air Force, the American tactical air force in the Mediterranean, relinquished control of the Seventh Army's partner in arms, the XII Tactical Air Command, to the Ninth Air Force. The aerial partner of the French First Army was to be the French First Air Force. In October, this French aerial command and XII TAC were brought into the First Tactical Air Force (Provisional) under Major General Ralph Royce, thus according the 6th Army Group its own coordinate air headquarters. General Vandenberg's Ninth Air Force, once again minus XII TAC, reverted to working with the 12th Army Group.

While these organizational changes sorted themselves out at higher levels, the VI Corps was no longer going anywhere rapidly: its nerves and energy were frayed by thirty-five days of pursuit, its supply line stretched as thin as anybody's. In mid-September, Truscott's men were fighting their way through Luxeuil, Lure, and Villersexel with no more ambitious immediate goal than simply reaching the Moselle. By September 20, the corps had pushed far enough that Truscott could issue his orders for crossing that river. His next purpose, apart from maintaining constant pressure against the enemy, was to grind his way through the considerable obstacle of the Vosges to reach the Plain of Alsace and the Rhine. Unless events elsewhere precipitated a change of enemy dispositions on his front, this process was bound to consume a good deal of time.

General Eagles's 45th division, relieved in the Villersexel area by the First French Army, shifted from the right to the left of the VI Corps to cross the Moselle at the communications center of Épinal, thence to move northward through Rambervillers and Baccarat to force a passage of the Saverne Gap, which opens between the Low Vosges to the north and the High Vosges confronting the bulk of Truscott's troops. General Dahlquist's 36th Division in Truscott's center was to cross the Moselle around Éloyes and head northward for St. Dié and the Saales Pass, the least arduous route through the High Vosges to Strasbourg and the Rhine. General O'Daniel's 3rd Division was to cross the Moselle around Rupt to advance toward the Schlucht Pass, the route to Colmar.

Of Truscott's divisions, the Texas Army leaped the Moselle first. A sixty-year-old French naval officer who was now mayor of Raon-aux-Bois near Éloyes, M.R.M. Gribelen, led the 141st Infantry through a forested shortcut which he was in the habit of following to visit his daughter in Éloyes, but which was unknown to the Germans and led to a convenient ford where the 1st Battalion crossed the river without opposition. The enemy promptly woke up and repulsed an attempted crossing by the 3rd Battalion at another site, but by late afternoon of September 20 the 143rd Regiment was across along with the larger part of the 141st, and Texas had a firm bridgehead. The next night, September 21–22, the 45th Division availed itself of the convenience of a XV Corps bridgehead at Châtel, just north of Truscott's sector; but the enemy was paying so little attention that the 3rd Battalion of the 157th Infantry easily waded the Moselle in its own sector while the 1st Battalion was using the XV Corps bridge. The Thunderbird Division had to pay its toll elsewhere, in the 180th Infantry's fight for Épinal, a contest that the Germans protracted from September 21 through 24. The 3rd Division around Rupt proved to face a difficult passage through well-defended woods still between it and the Moselle at the time when Truscott issued his crossing order; its compensation was the 7th Infantry Regiment's discovery and capture of a bridge intact during the night of September 23–24.

In the steep, forested hills of the Vosges beyond the river, only the 45th Division, with the least unfavorable terrain, achieved any semblance of encouraging progress during the next several weeks. Elsewhere, the fighting in the woods and hills was a bitter business in which the Germans were forever sending down a hail of lethal missiles by bursting shells high among the tree branches, and continually infiltrating back into forest patches the Americans thought they had gained. The VI Corps's final thrust to the Rhine was turning into a depressingly prolonged journey.

19: The Reich Frontiers

A s LATE as September 15, two days before the launching of MARKET-GARDEN, General Eisenhower had remained euphoric about the prospects for an imminent ending of the war. On that date he issued a circular letter to his army group and air and naval commanders, based on the assumptions that the Allied armies were about to close up to the Rhine, that "the Germans will have stood in defense of the Ruhr and Frankfurt and will have had a sharp defeat inflicted on them," and that it was time to plan the final offensive: "Clearly Berlin is the main prize, and the prize in defense of which the enemy is likely to concentrate the bulk of his forces. There is no doubt whatever, in my mind, that we should concentrate all our energies on a rapid thrust to Berlin." On September 24 a detailed SHAEF G-3 planning document seconded the Supreme Commander, offering a disquisition on the theme:

> Our main object must be the early capture of Berlin, the most important objective in Germany.
> Speed in our advance to Berlin is essential if the enemy is not to be given a breathing space to build up his forces by withdrawal from other countries, to carry out demolitions and to prepare defenses.[1]

Even by September 15, however, speed in advance and attack was rapidly fading from possibility. Against Patton in the south, the enemy had already gathered the forces that were to check the XX Corps around Metz, and the bulk of the forces that were to curb the XII Corps by lashing out in counterattack east of Nancy. Elsewhere the enemy's recovery had not yet rallied armies quite so formidable, but by deliberate decision the Allies lacked sufficient power in the Ardennes to seize opportunity there, while the West Wall in combination with the restricted maneuver ground of the Aachen corridor was about to halt the VII Corps—so the possibility of realizing Eisenhower's hopes narrowed down to MARKET-GARDEN. As bold in strategic conception as was appropriate to these circumstances, MARKET-GARDEN's failures of tactical execution dashed the Supreme Commander's hopes.

With failure and frustration came recriminations. For all disappointments, Montgomery blamed inadequate commitment to his strategy of the concentrated full-blooded thrust into the Reich. In his view, MARKET-GARDEN, and with it the prospect of rapid victory, failed not because he himself had taken insufficient pains to assure that tactical execution would match the spirit of his strategic design, but because Eisenhower had not accorded him enough resources for the northeastward advance. Montgomery and Eisenhower were soon quarrelling again.

   Montgomery's response to the circular of September 15 was a pestering one, but it was consistent with Eisenhower's own apparent meaning. The field marshal seized upon the suggestion "that we should concentrate all our energies and resources on a rapid thrust to Berlin," to comment that Eisenhower evidently had accepted Montgomery's strategy of concentration, and to try to brace the Supreme Commander toward still firmer commitment in that direction. Once more Montgomery reiterated his theme that the Allies could not support all their armies advancing everywhere, and that consequently "I consider that the best objective is the Ruhr, and thence on to Berlin by the northern route."[2]

   Thus Montgomery wrote on September 18, when confidence in MARKET-GARDEN was still high. By the time Eisenhower got around to replying, it was September 20, and the prospects no longer seemed so pleasing, either for MARKET-GARDEN or for anything else. So while Eisenhower's reply included a conciliatory observation that "I cannot believe there is any great difference in our concepts," a note of impatience also intruded. In effect, Eisenhower told Montgomery that the two of them were no longer talking about the same thing. Montgomery was still dwelling on how to arrive at the Ruhr and the Rhine. Eisenhower had moved on to consider how to proceed after the Allied armies had closed to the Rhine. Once at the Ruhr and the Rhine, "Never at any time have I implied that I was considering an advance into Germany with all armies moving abreast." Presumably, that is, Eisenhower's call for concentrating on a rapid thrust to Berlin would eventually mean just what Montgomery thought it should mean. Nevertheless, Eisenhower proposed to advance all the armies up to the Rhine before the final offensive commenced: "What I do believe is that we must marshal our strength up along the Western borders of Germany, to the Rhine if possible, insure adequate maintenance by getting Antwerp to working at full blast at the earliest possible moment and [then] carry out the drive you suggest."[3]

   Montgomery can be pardoned for thinking that, at the least, Eisenhower had altered the terms of the discussion confusingly. Adding to that all the implications of Eisenhower's statement, it is little wonder that the field marshal was provoked in turn to yet more impatience. Closing up everywhere to the Rhine before doing anything else had hardly been the apparent intent of Eisenhower's recent concessions to Montgomery at the time of the MARKET-GARDEN decision. With his temper not improved by MARKET-GARDEN's crashing down around him, Montgomery answered Eisenhower forthwith, on September 21, insisting that "I cannot agree that our concepts are the same and I am sure you would wish me to be quite frank and open in the matter. I have always said stop with the right and go with the left, but the right has been allowed to go on so far that it has outstripped its maintenance and we have lost flexibility." Furthermore, whatever subject Eisenhower intended to be talking about, getting to the Ruhr was still the issue at hand. The Allies were not there yet, and "The net result of the matter in my opinion is that if you want to get the Ruhr you will have to put every single thing into the left hook and stop everything else. It is my opinion that if this is not done then you will not get the Ruhr."[4]

   Eisenhower meanwhile had decided that his inability to understand and be understood in his dealings with Montgomery indicated a need for a conference of all the army group commanders along with the principal officers of SHAEF, to thrash out strategy face to face. He convened the meeting on September 22 at Versailles, where SHAEF had moved in quest of better communications, among other amenities. If we need hardly wonder at

Montgomery's irritation over Eisenhower's vacillating policy pronouncements, still there is no acceptable excuse for the field marshal's not deigning to attend the conference. The excuse he offered was that MARKET-GARDEN demanded his attention. But if he was exerting so much detailed control over the operation that he could not leave his headquarters, then the question naturally arises, why was he not correcting MARKET-GARDEN's tactical errors?

Because Montgomery's excuse for nonattendance was a transparent pretext—so consistent with his recent behavior that SHAEF staffers had been taking bets on whether he would show up—Chester Wilmot tried to offer a deeper explanation. Montgomery's refusal to journey to Versailles was "a tacit acknowledgment of his own limitations" as a military diplomat. His strategy had brought early victory within the Allies' grasp,

> But the cup of triumph had been dashed from his lips by men who, according to his standards, had barely begun to understand the profession of arms. Now when all his warnings had been fulfilled, when the great opportunity that he had foreseen so clearly had been cast away, he did not trust himself to meet them at so 'public' a gathering as this conference in Versailles. He feared that, if he did go, he might do more harm than good.[5]

So he sent in his place his chief of staff, "Freddy" de Guingand, who arrived looking harried, as well he might, but who possessed diplomatic skill and whom the Americans liked.

Thus bickering and pettiness again were conjured up by Montgomery's ego in collision with Eisenhower's inability thus far to steer the kind of consistent strategic course that might have assured Montgomery of the firmness of Allied direction. At the least, the Supreme Commander's efforts to explain why Patton had not been immobilized completely and altogether might have carried more conviction had they not been clouded by periodic reversions to reciting broad-front strategic doctrine, which Eisenhower had not employed anyway—yet. In fact, Eisenhower so far had yielded to Montgomery all the resources he dared to; to have yielded more would have run intolerable military and political risks. To have granted Montgomery all that the field marshal desired might well have brought military disaster to the southern flank of the 12th Army Group, as well as political disaster to the Grand Alliance. Given these circumstances, it was the field marshal himself, Eisenhower's strategic vacillations notwithstanding, who finally had dropped the cup of triumph from his own lips. Montgomery himself failed to carry to success the fullest commitment to the northeastward strategy that the Allies could afford. Montgomery himself botched the tactical execution of MARKET-GARDEN.

On the other hand, Eisenhower was about to embrace strategic consistency at last, but for Montgomery it would be consistency of the wrong kind. Since early September, the strategic and logistical equations had changed on both sides of the Western Front. In late September, Eisenhower no longer saw the German disarray that in August and early September had drawn him to the single-thrust strategy. Montgomery's unwillingness to journey to Versailles had at least the warrant that Montgomery was correct in sensing he had lost the strategic debate even while he was also losing MARKET-GARDEN. Hitherto, Eisenhower had tried to go Montgomery's single-thrust way; but Eisenhower's September 20 message to Montgomery—the complications about what to do beyond the Rhine aside—spelled the end of the single-thrust experiment and Eisenhower's return to the

American predilection for the strategy of the broad front. With the failure of MARKET-GARDEN, a strategic corner had been turned.

The Estuary of the Scheldt

Whatever the merits and deficiencies of Montgomery's generalship and the twists and turns of strategic debate, the end of the pursuit and the Germans' restoration of a stable front point once again to the misfortune of the British position on the Allied left. Despite the waterlogged terrain of much of the Low Countries, the best remaining routes into Germany lay there. The troops coming up from the Mediterranean faced not only the barrier of the Vosges, but worse geographic barriers in Germany across the upper Rhine, and few critical objectives. Patton's Third Army found the ancient fortress complex of Metz an obstacle scarcely less formidable than in the wars of the past, surrounded by much other terrain conducive to the defense of the Reich frontiers, along a path leading to targets in Germany that were secondary compared with the Ruhr. Between Patton's Third and Hodges's First Armies, the Ardennes posed difficulties of terrain supposedly so severe that the Allies had written off the area—perhaps mistakenly, but understandably. The main effort of the First Army had to strike the West Wall straight through the narrow corridor at Aachen. The unexpected strength of the West Wall fortifications and the failure to pass through them before they were garrisoned had stripped the First Army's invasion route of the attractions it held when Montgomery had seemed generous in suggesting this route during the high summer. But some thirty kilometers north of Aachen the West Wall ended, and only on their northern flank did the Allied armies enjoy adequate space for maneuver unmenaced by strong and numerous permanent fortifications. Yet there the British carried the ball, and they did not have enough men.

General de Guingand signaled Montgomery from the Versailles conference of September 22: "Excellent conference. Ike supported your plan one hundred per cent. Your thrust is main effort and gets full support."[6] No doubt the field marshal himself would have felt less enthusiastic, because Eisenhower also adhered to his September 20 prescription that all the Allied armies must form up along the Rhine before the concentrated drive toward Berlin could begin. Nevertheless, the Supreme Commander testified again to the overwhelming geographical and tactical advantages of the Allied left flank by describing the envelopment of the Ruhr by 21 Army Group, supported by the First Army, as "the main effort in the present phase of operations."[7]

At the same time, Eisenhower assigned Montgomery's army group the task of opening Antwerp to Allied shipping as a matter of urgent priority. Montgomery's initial neglect of this detail had provoked increasingly frequent reminders from SHAEF of the logistical importance of Antwerp all through September; but as long as MARKET-GARDEN might succeed, Eisenhower acquiesced in deferring the Antwerp task out of the hope that the war might yet end promptly enough to make the port capacity of Antwerp unnecessary—or at least that the Allies could cross the Rhine and enter the Ruhr before having to pause to develop the port. With German resistance now restored everywhere, ammunition requirements consequently growing, and the logistical pinch still excruciatingly tight, opening Antwerp could no longer be postponed. For their offensive into Germany, the Allies would need a major port close behind their lines. The Canadian First Army had taken Dieppe on September 1, Ostend on the 9th, and Le Havre and Bruges on the 12th. Dunkirk was to be masked, and Boulogne and Calais were scheduled for prompt attack.

But these Channel ports would not be enough to support the heavy fighting now in prospect.

The Germans remained ensconced on both sides of the Scheldt along much of its ninety-kilometer course from Antwerp to the open sea. Geography assisted them in creating formidable problems for any troops who might try to break their grip on access to the port. On the south bank of the West Scheldt, the German Fifteenth Army had left behind the 64th Infantry Division, strengthened by the usual hodgepodge of additional fragments, to hold what became known as the Breskens Pocket, from the Braakman Inlet west to the mouth of the Leopold Canal opposite Zeebrugge. In front of the pocket, the Braakman Inlet, the Canal de la Dérivation de la Lys, and the Leopold Canal formed an almost continuous defensive moat. On the north bank of the West Scheldt, the German 70th Division had two regiments on heavily fortified Walcheren Island, one on South Beveland. Orders called for Walcheren to be defended as Cherbourg and Brest had been. If the 70th Division was perhaps oddly chosen to mount so stubborn a resistance—it was called the White Bread Division, because to simplify ration problems the Germans had created a whole division of men with stomach disorders (Teutonic logic fashioned similar "stomach battlions," "ear battalions," and what not)—in compensation the 70th had an exceptional complement of artillery, some 177 pieces including sixty-seven fixed naval guns. Even to grapple with Walcheren from the mainland, moreover, the Allies would have to fight their way to the narrow, readily defensible South Beveland isthmus through the static 711th and the more powerful 346th Divisions, with additional units of the Fifteenth Army close at hand—another penalty of the failure to charge on to the isthmus as soon as Antwerp fell.

Consistent with his generalship throughout the campaign, Montgomery aggressively refused to tie down more than a bare minimum of his troops to deal with these defenders of the Scheldt Estuary. Instead, he proceeded from his optimistic pronouncement that MARKET-GARDEN "was ninety per cent successful"[8] to try to mount a new offensive from Nijmegen against the northwest corner of the Ruhr. Such an effort seemed appropriate to the Versailles decision that Montgomery's drive to the Ruhr should be the main Allied thrust, and Eisenhower at first endorsed it. The practical effect, however, was that opening Antwerp fell to the Canadian First Army alone, while the British Second Army busied itself toward the Ruhr. The Canadian army attacked from Antwerp toward the South Beveland isthmus on October 2, and on the 6th opened operations against the Breskens Pocket. It soon became evident that the German defenses of the Scheldt were so strong that the Canadians' small army of two corps—2nd Canadian and 1 British—would be occupied an intolerably long time if it did not receive help. This would have been true even if Montgomery had not also assigned the Canadian army the task of clearing the left flank of the corridor created by MARKET-GARDEN.

Nor did the British Second Army have enough troops to take full advantage of its prime location to advance into Germany. Montgomery liked to regard the MARKET-GARDEN salient reaching out across the Waal at Nijmegen as a dagger pointed at the Ruhr. But the salient also added about 200 kilometers to the 21 Army Group front, almost doubling its length. To secure the salient while maintaining any hope of a new offensive, Montgomery had to hold the American 82nd and 101st Airborne Divisions in Second Army. General Brereton protested that such use of airborne troops as ordinary infantry was a violation of their very reason for being, and he warned Eisenhower that "Further combat will deplete them of trained men beyond replacement capacity."⁹ Eisenhower nevertheless decided he must acquiesce, at least until Antwerp was open.

On the south flank of the corridor to Nijmegen, the divergence of MARKET-GARDEN northward from the easterly path of the American First Army had created a German-held salient of more than 800 square kilometers between the corridor and the left flank of General Corlett's XIX Corps eighteen kilometers north of Maastricht. Montgomery's weakness in manpower prompted the Versailles conference to shift northward the left boundary of General Hodges's army and give Hodges the task of clearing out this potentially troublesome enclave as far as the west bank of the Maas. Hodges did not like the change, and for good reason, because east of the Maas the interallied boundary was to remain as before; thus the First Army would have to divert its left flank into a pocket and then funnel it out again. Still, Hodges was to be given General Silvester's 7th Armored Division from the Third Army and General Gerhardt's 29th Infantry Division from Brest, and he agreed to use the armored division against the salient, along with the 113th Cavalry Group and, on loan from Montgomery, the 1st Belgian Brigade.

The most conspicuous and disturbing terrain feature of Hodges's new sector was De Peel, or the Peel Marshes, a lowland of some ninety square kilometers between the Maas and Eindhoven in the upper western part of the area. To conquer the marshes and cut off the rest of the German salient, Hodges proposed to pass the 7th Armored through the British zone to move southward through De Peel, while the 113th Cavalry Group and the Belgians mounted a converging, secondary attack northward from the main XIX Corps area. Unfortunately, this scheme was based on a consensus supporting the XIX Corps G-2 estimate that only two or three thousand Germans remained in the salient. When the Americans and Belgians opened their attack on September 29, they quickly discovered that the enemy must be much more numerous.

In fact, there were at least eight times as many Germans as Allied intelligence had thought, in the LXXXVI Corps of General Student's efficiently commanded First Parachute Army. The enemy included Kampfgruppe Walther, with the 107th Panzer Brigade, and Parachute Training Division Erdmann, as well as two numbered divisions. The marshes confined the attackers' tanks to the few roads, and the roads were well mined. The infantry had to take on the main burden of slogging through the fens. By October 5, six days of effort had earned the 7th Armored an advance of less than three kilometers toward the town of Overloon, with losses of twenty-nine Shermans, six light tanks, forty-three other vehicles, and some 452 men. The lightly armed cavalry and the still less well equipped Belgians were accomplishing less.

By this time, moreover, Hodges had committed the rest of the XIX Corps to another attack eastward against the West Wall, and the only source of help in immediate prospect was the British Second Army, despite the manpower strain that had sent the Americans into the Peel Marshes in the first place. Because Montgomery remained intent on jumping off from Nijmegen into the Ruhr as soon as possible, he believed the threat to his right flank from the Peel Marshes had to be eliminated, and he and the Americans struck a deal. The field marshal confessed candidly to SHAEF that he did not have enough men for all his responsibilities. He also suggested, yet once more, that the root problem was one of command, hinting that the American First Army ought to be attached directly to 21 Army Group. Eisenhower responded that command had nothing to do with the current difficulties, but he offered Montgomery a choice between a further and fuller shift of

Hodges's boundary northward, or two American divisions for 21 Army Group. Montgomery picked the latter, and received from Bradley the 7th Armored plus the 104th Infantry Division, grounded until now by the cannibalization of its transport.

Eisenhower had never stopped insisting that before the Allies could consider going far into Germany, they must open Antwerp. In this light, the Supreme Commander evidently anticipated that Montgomery would employ his additional strength to put more weight into the battle to clear the Scheldt. Instead, Montgomery promptly issued a new directive, on October 9, paying lip service to the priority of Antwerp but giving the Canadian army no help. He directed the Second Army to prepare the way to the Ruhr by assuring the safety of the Nijmegen corridor and sweeping the Peel Marshes.

The same day, the Royal Navy gloomily prognosticated that at the rate things were going it would be some time in November before the Canadians opened the Scheldt estuary. Meanwhile the autumn gales in the Channel had commenced their expected work of reducing imports across the beaches. Eisenhower lost patience and got off to Montgomery about as concise and pointed a message as he could write, on the theme that "of all our operations on our entire front from Switzerland to the Channel, I consider Antwerp of first importance, and I believe the operations designed to clear up the entrance require your personal attention."[10]

Relations between the Supreme Commander and the field marshal had reached such a pass that any such missive was bound to touch off a new bout of argument. Montgomery replied the same day that the navy had evidently been making "wild statements," and that anyway on October 7 he had suspended operations toward the Rhine so he could "get Antwerp"; but he also reminded Eisenhower of the September 22 decision to make the Ruhr the main effort, and pointed out that the previous day he had received a copy of a telegram from SHAEF to Bradley saying that gaining the Rhine was still the first mission of both army groups. In his *Memoirs*, moreover, Montgomery took the position that the October 9 message was the first he had received in which Eisenhower gave Antwerp absolute priority. The debate went on; Eisenhower in turn told Montgomery yet again on the 10th "that no matter how we adjust missions and objectives for both groups in their offensive actions toward the east, the possession of the approaches to Antwerp remains with us an objective of vital importance."[11]

Montgomery's actual focus at the moment was upon the Peel Marshes. Receiving the 7th Armored Division, he assigned it to General O'Connor's 8 Corps, and ordered O'Connor to mount an early offensive against the marshes, citing again the necessity to clear the Second Army's right flank before advancing into the Ruhr. In British planning, the 7th Armored reverted to a defensive role, to hold along with the Belgian Brigade a line of some fifty kilometers within, west, and south of the marshes, while the British 3rd Infantry Division resumed the attack from the north. O'Connor advanced on October 12. Building on the gains of the American armor, the British captured Overloon the first day. But they met the same kind of obstacles and resistance that had plagued the Americans, and it took them until October 17 to cover the five kilometers between Overloon and the most important road center in the area, Venray, while the Germans gave no sign of weakening.

Clearly, a rapid breakthrough was not to be expected against the tough core of paratroopers and panzers who so well exploited the defensive assets of De Peel, nor was there any prospect of a rapid resumption of the attack from Nijmegen. Confronted by these unpleasant realities and badgered by Eisenhower about the Scheldt—a new, strong communiqué arrived from SHAEF on the 13th—Montgomery at length capitulated on October 16 to the necessity of turning his attention to Antwerp. On that day he gave Antwerp "complete priority . . . without any qualification whatsoever," and dispatched "the whole of the available offensive power" of the Second Army to help the Canadian army.[12]

The whole available offensive power of the Second Army consisted of four divisions of 12 Corps that Montgomery could spare to face northward on the Canadian right flank, to clear the south bank of the Maas in support of the Canadian effort to seal off egress from South Beveland. They attacked on October 22 and completed their task by November 5. Meanwhile Montgomery also reinforced the British 1 Corps of the Canadian army with the 49th Division, and the American 104th Division went to the same corps. Consisting now of the British 49th, the American 104th, the Polish 1st Armored, and the Canadian 4th Armoured Divisions, this corps renewed its attack toward the south bank of the Maas east of a line Turnout-Raamsdonk, and on October 24 it turned its left flank into the South Beveland isthmus. The 104th Division had been organized and trained by one of the first American heroes of the war in North Africa, Major General Terry de la Mesa Allen, who had commanded the 1st Division in its first campaign of the war; Eisenhower and Bradley had eventually felt obliged to remove him because they thought he misidentified the interests of the 1st Division with those of the whole army, a common affliction in the proud Big Red One. But there had never been any question about his competence as a trainer, organizer, and inspirational battle captain, and the 104th immediately showed it had been well brought up.

The Canadian 2nd Corps had destroyed the Breskens Pocket by October 21, just as this new assistance on its right was about to come forth. On October 31, the Canadians' first effort to gain a foothold on Walcheren Island by amphibious assault was repulsed; but they managed to get ashore and stay the next day. So did British Commandos landing at the eastern end of the island, and so did troops of the British 1 Corps coming from South Beveland on November 4. On the 8th, the last resistance on Walcheren ended, and the Scheldt was open to Antwerp. Minesweepers had already begun their work. The first Allied convoy reached the Antwerp docks on November 28.

This was eighty-five days after the 11th Armoured Division had captured the docks and port equipment almost intact. The long delay testified to Montgomery's persistent underestimation both of the importance of Antwerp—granted he was right to concentrate on reaching the Rhine as long as there was a chance of quickly ending the war—and of the German strength that had to be overcome to free the port. The long delay also testified to British manpower weakness; if Montgomery had had more men to spare, he probably would have moved vigorously against the Scheldt sooner.

While he was turning his main effort toward Antwerp at last, the shortage of men continued to haunt him elsewhere, too. Lack of satisfactory progress in the Peel Marshes along with the Antwerp issue caused Montgomery to suspend the 8 Corps attack in De Peel on October 15. The Germans used the lull for a counterattack of their own. Early on the morning of October 27, a forty-minute German artillery barrage exploded upon the long and thinly held defensive positions of the 7th Armored Division. Behind the barrage spearheads of the 9th Panzer Division lunged forward. The Germans captured the town of Meijel and forced their way across the Deurne Canal. The next day General Silvester's

Americans rallied and counterattacked in turn. But they made little progress toward recapturing lost ground, even though O'Connor brought British troops southward to shorten Silvester's front. The 7th Armored found itself contending with the 15th Panzer Grenadier Division as well as the 9th Panzers; commanding both enemy divisions was General von Lüttwitz's XLVII Panzer Corps, like the 15th Panzer Grenadiers brought up from Patton's front to mount a counterthrust that caught Allied intelligence completely by surprise—a bad omen.

So Montgomery had to shuffle his scarce divisions again, bringing the British 15th and then the 53rd down from 12 Corps. Fortunately, the battle to clear the south bank of the Maas on the Second Army front had been won by this time. Perhaps equally fortunately, the Germans evidently had not intended more than a limited local attack in De Peel, for they did not renew their assaults. Though the 7th Armored fought stoutly enough after the first day, and its headquarters had been far from alone in being surprised, Bradley had long felt there was a dearth of energy and dash in this unit, and he now made up his mind that Silvester was not up to snuff and relieved him.

Ominously, despite the suspension of the German attack, General von Manteuffel's Fifth Panzer Army headquarters followed Lüttwitz's corps to the Peel Marshes area, being inserted into the Army Group B front between the First Parachute and Seventh Armies. The Germans' apparent strong interest in the sector led Montgomery to bring the whole 12 Corps down from the lower Maas to assist 8 Corps in sweeping De Peel. With so much of the Second Army concentrated here, Montgomery could spare the 7th Armored Division, and on November 7 he returned it to Bradley. But two British corps spent the month of November doing the job that the unlucky Silvester was initially to have accomplished with his single division and a few auxiliaries. It was not until December 3, more than two months after the 7th Armored had opened the Battle of the Peel Marshes, that 8 and 12 Corps at last won the battle.

Only then could Montgomery return to preparations for a big push toward the Rhine. He had found it a bitter autumn, and he would never stop blaming the "men who, according to his standards, had barely begun to understand the profession of arms." But the failure of MARKET-GARDEN had simply left 21 Army Group with too many tasks to be done and too few men to do them.

The Balance of Strength

If only the Americans had fought on the left, where the opportunities were greatest, the means to grasp fortune at its September flood would have been far more ample. But on their long front reaching southward, even the Americans had none too plentiful resources of manpower for the autumnal campaigns.

It might not have appeared so on September 15, when the juncture of the Third Army with the DRAGOON forces added the 6th Army Group to Eisenhower's command. Shortly thereafter, in another encouraging development, General Simpson's Ninth Army advanced from Brittany to the German frontier. As yet, this army consisted only of General Middleton's VIII Corps, with the 2nd and 8th Infantry Divisions. On September 19, the VIII Corps turned Brest over to the Brittany Base Section of the Communications Zone, and on the 26th the corps headquarters and the two divisions began to move by rail and road to the Ardennes-Eifel area. Small as the Ninth Army still was, by taking over from the V Corps the sector from St. Vith south to the Third Army boundary near

Echternach it allowed Hodges to concentrate north of the Ardennes. To complete the arrangement whereby each American field army worked in tandem with a tactical air command, the Ninth Air Force on September 14 had activated the XXIX Tactical Air Command (Provisional) under Brigadier General Richard E. Nugent, attached temporarily to IX TAC, and then becoming operationally autonomous as the Ninth Army entered the line on October 1.

Thus on September 15, Eisenhower commanded three army groups, eight field armies (including the First Allied Airborne Army), and fifty-five divisions on the European continent. Four of the armies and twenty-eight divisions were American. These included twenty infantry divisions (in order of arrival in the European Theater, the 29th, 5th, 28th, 2nd, 1st, 9th, 8th, 4th, 30th, 90th, 79th, 83rd, 35th, 80th, 94th, 3rd, 36th, 45th, 104th, and 44th), six armored divisions (the 3rd, 2nd, 4th, 5th, 6th, and 7th), and two airborne divisions (the 101st and 82nd; the 6th Army Group included the First Airborne Task Force, of divisional size but not usually listed in the accounting of divisions). Two additional American infantry divisions (95th and 26th), one airborne division (17th), and one armored division (9th) had arrived in the United Kingdom and awaited shipment to the Continent. Of the fifty-five Allied divisions under Eisenhower's command, the remaining twenty-seven included eighteen British and Canadian, one Polish, and eight French. By the afternoon of September 11, 2,168,307 men and 460,745 vehicles had entered Normandy. By mid-September, another 380,000 troops and 69,312 vehicles had entered France across the DRAGOON beaches. Casualties in the 21 and 12th Army Groups from June 6 to September 11 had been 39,961 killed, 164,400 wounded, and 20,142 missing, a total of 224,569, or about ten percent of the force committed.

Against the Allies' forty infantry and airborne and fifteen armored divisions, Rundstedt's OB West in theory mustered some forty-eight infantry and fifteen panzer and panzer grenadier divisions. Scarcely a German division was anywhere near full strength. The Germans had lost about 300,000 casualties since June 6, another 200,000 of their men were penned up in coastal fortresses or on the Channel islands, and all Hitler's efforts had not sufficed to replace the losses at all fully.

In military hardware, the Allies had a much greater superiority than in men: at least 2½ to 1 in guns (although this advantage was curtailed by the ammunition shortage) and 20 to 1 in tanks. In the air, the disparity was still greater, badly constraining the ability of the Germans to utilize such tanks as they had for fear of the dread Allied "Jabos," the Jagdbomber or fighter-bombers. In the United Kingdom and France on September 1, the Allies had 5,059 American bombers, 3,728 American fighters, and 5,104 RAF combat aircraft. On September 15, the Germans redesignated the air command facing the Allies in France from Luftflotte 3 to simply Luftflotte Kommando West. The command had only some 573 serviceable planes; the whole Luftwaffe had only 4,507.

An impressive Allied array—yet in manpower, the Allied advantage was not all that great, especially against enemy soldiers shielded by the pillboxes and dragons' teeth of the West Wall, or by such a fortress complex as encircled Metz. So the only offensive the Allies could mount toward the Rhine in October proved scarcely overwhelming, and it practically ended the last lingering hopes of victory in 1944.

The Battle of Aachen

For Montgomery's soldiers, opening the Scheldt and guarding the exposed flanks of the Nijmegen corridor provided more than enough occupation throughout October.

Thus it remained to Hodges's First Army alone to sustain any active semblance of fulfillment of the theoretical Allied commitment to a major effort toward the Ruhr.

Hodges's job remained the unsubtle one of a head-on assault against the West Wall in the narrow Aachen corridor between the fens of Holland and the uplands of the Ardennes-Eifel. The strategy that had linked his march from France to Germany to the right flank of 21 Army Group had committed the First Army to this corridor. The commitment was more firm than ever now that the Ninth Army had taken over the Ardennes, where the 5th Armored's breakthrough had tempted Hodges momentarily in September.

At least, Hodges now had his strength well concentrated to punch through the corridor. Corlett's XIX Corps, held back behind the VII Corps by the supply crisis of early September, and then compelled to use one of its two divisions as flank guards when 21 Army Group diverged northward, became the recipient of Gerhardt's 29th Division from Brest; Gerhardt took over the role of shielding the left flank, freeing Hobbs's 30th Infantry Division and the 2nd Armored Division, now under Major General Ernest N. Harmon, for more active tasks. Gerow's V Corps moved up from the Ardennes-Eifel to take over some twenty-five kilometers of the VII Corps front around Monschau. This shift reduced Collins's VII Corps line to about thirty kilometers. With his three corps in hand, and with the principal offensive hopes of the Allies resting on him, Hodges aimed to push through the West Wall to the Rhine from Düsseldorf to Bonn.

To do so, he would at last have to face up to the urban congestion of Aachen, or the XIX Corps north of the city would become separated from the rest of the First Army, and the line of communications would become unconscionably insecure. Hodges's plan was to begin by encircling the city. The XIX Corps should penetrate the West Wall north of Aachen and then turn south to the area of Würselen, east of the city. As Corlett's troops approached Würselen, the VII Corps was to attack north from Eilendorf, also east of Aachen, penetrating the second band of the West Wall at Verlautenheide, and meeting the XIX Corps around Würselen—to envelop the city. Thereupon part of the VII Corps could reduce Aachen at leisure, while the rest of Collins's corps and Corlett's pushed on east and northeast.

Though enclosed between two bands of the West Wall, Aachen was not fortified on the scale of Metz. Its position opposite Belgium rather than France, and the relative recency of the restored importance of the northern invasion route between France and Germany, gave Aachen no history comparable to Metz's as a pivot of military strategy. Nevertheless, the Americans had been in no hurry to assault it, not only because the buildings of a city whose prewar population had been 165,000 were bound to make for slow and costly street fighting. In addition, the Germans surely would contest Aachen with special stubbornness, as their first major city to face capture, and as the seat of the First Reich and consequently a place of significance to the Führer of the Third Reich. For Aachen, with its medicinal springs, the Aquisgranum of the Romans—named for Apollo Granus, a deity associated with hot springs—and the Aix-la-Chapelle of more recent history, was the city of Charlemagne and of the coronations of the Holy Roman Emperors. Here Charlemagne probably was born in the palace of his father, King Pepin; under the dome of the cathedral, according to tradition, Charlemagne's tomb was opened in the year 1000 by the Emperor Otto III to disclose the body of the great Charles wearing white coronation robes and seated upon a marble chair; in the Hungarian Chapel, Charlemagne's bones have rested in later centuries. From Louis the Pious, son of Charlemagne, in 813, to Ferdinand I in 1531, the emperors customarily were crowned in the cathedral and banqueted in the coronation hall.

In the usual pattern of American attack, Hobbs's 30th Division was to lead off for the XIX Corps north of Aachen, with Harmon's 2nd Armored to follow. In an unusual departure that Hodges thought dictated by the congestion of factory towns in its vicinity, however, army headquarters prescribed that Harmon not exploit but instead follow Hobbs's penetration and then turn north to shield the flank and rear of Hobbs's southward turn toward Würselen. Harmon, an old cavalryman and an armored pioneer who had earlier commanded the 2nd Armored in North Africa, thought such a defensive mission inappropriate to a force built for mobility, and the acerbic "Old Gravel Voice" expressed his discontent with Hodges's plan in outspoken terms that did nothing to improve relations between army headquarters and the XIX Corps. These relations already were not good. Corlett, sensitive that generals whose whole combat experience was in Europe thought him an interloper from the Pacific, and morbidly conscious that his illness in Normandy had not gotten his European service off to an auspicious start, could readily feel aggrieved. In this mood he thought himself and his corps neglected in favor of Hodges's close relationship with Collins. Hodges never gave Corlett any warmth or encouragement and rarely visited him. The corps and the army commanders simply did not get along.

Corlett and Hobbs chose to cross the Wurm River and strike the West Wall on a narrow front, just over a kilometer wide, near the villages of Marienberg and Rimburg. Some fourteen kilometers north of Aachen, Hobbs would avoid urban congestion in his initial attack, and some five kilometers south of Geilenkirchen, he would also avoid the strong West Wall defenses around that town. While awaiting resupply, especially of ammunition, before his October 1 D-Day, Hobbs had time to rotate his battalions in and out of the line and refresh their training in the tactics of assaulting pillboxes and of infantry-tank coordination. Duckboard footbridges were readied for the infantry to use in crossing the narrow Wurm. Tankmen and engineers prepared contrivances of logs bound together in metal, which the men called "culverts," for the river crossing; tanks were to pull them to the stream, and tank dozers to shove them into it.

Preparations and rehearsals were elaborate enough to call forth memories of the set-piece attacks of the First World War—so much had the German rally restored the campaign to stasis and near-deadlock. In the fashion of the old war, the artillery was to open its preliminary bombardment on September 26, four days before the infantry assault, in an effort to knock out all the pillboxes directly in front of the attack. General Corlett decided to risk cutting deep into his scarce ammunition supply for maximum effect at the outset, hoping to compensate somehow later; as the bombardment progressed, warnings from his staff of an increasingly acute shortage forced curtailed firing after all.

In this war, naturally, the systematic working-over by the artillery was to be supplemented by aerial bombardment. As so often happened, however, the air's advantage over an old-fashioned artillery barrage, greater explosive power in proportion to weight of projectiles, proved a doubtful asset. The Old Hickory Division was dubious about preparatory air attack in any event, remembering its losses of seventy-five killed and 505 wounded in the carpet-bombing along the St. Lô-Périers road before COBRA. General Hobbs and his staff tried again to insist on bombing parallel to the front; the airmen again found arguments why they would have to attack perpendicular to the front. At least, the heavy bombers were unavailable, and the ground troops felt somewhat less fear of the B-26s and A-20s of the 9th Bombardment Division (as IX Bomber Command was redesignated on September 25) and of the P-47s and P-38s of IX TAC. At that, as early as September 22, P-38s dropped four napalm bombs within Hobbs's lines and killed two men and wounded four while destroying an American ammunition dump.

October 1 brought a heavy overcast at dawn and a downpour later, and the attack had to be postponed a day. When the airplanes opened the proceedings under scattered overcast the next day, they did not hit the 30th Division, but they did not hit many of their assigned targets either. Corlett listened in while two P-38 pilots accustomed to working with his corps tried frantically but unsuccessfully to make radio contact with the medium bombers to guide them to the proper targets; finally one of the Lightning pilots exclaimed in despair, "Let's shoot the son of a bitch down."[13] An hour after the air strike began, the commander of one of Hobbs's two assault regiments reported that no bombs had fallen in front of him.

The only reasonably effective strike was by mediums that came in so late they forced fighter-bombers to scurry out of their way, whereupon the mediums bombed targets that had been marked with smoke for the Jabos. Forty-five kilometers west of the target area, other mediums bombed a Belgian town, killing thirty-four civilians and wounding forty-five. In the target area, not one pillbox was hit. Because ground and woods were wet from the previous day's rain, napalm had little effect. When military operations are of such a nature that they are likely to kill or injure any civilians at all, they ought to receive hard moral scrutiny; when an operation produces so little of military value as this West Wall air strike, while exacting a grievous civilian toll in a not uncommon kind of miscalculation, the effort should cause a moral revulsion whose apparent absence in October 1944 is a testament to the deterioration of ethical values produced by the war so far.

Corlett decided he must compensate for the ineffectual bombing by blasting away again with his guns. He was down to 2,000 rounds beyond allotments not yet released by army headquarters, but his artillery chief smiled at the order. "The 30th Division was definitely and irrevocably committed," Corlett wrote later. "To save lives and to give them a chance of success they must have support and right away."[14]

Despite all the overtones of the old Western Front, including mud that made a chaos of the crossing of the Wurm on duckboards and nullified the culverts by trapping tanks on the shores of the stream, the ground assault gained headway. Hobbs's refresher courses in pillbox warfare paid off. Well-handled flame throwers, pole charges, hand grenades, and bazookas commenced so systematic a destruction of the pillboxes that many defenders—who included Landesschützen and other kinds of home guards who were scarcely the best of the German army—became intimidated and proved willing to surrender on demand. At the end of October 2, Hobbs's right-flank regiment, the 119th Infantry, was pinned down at a railroad embankment close enough to the east bank of the Wurm that the Germans could keep the crossings under small-arms fire; but on the left the 117th Infantry had breached the first line of pillboxes and held high ground around Palenberg. Engineers had built treadway bridges. Corlett decided he could commit the 2nd Armored the next day, if not to exploit at least to widen the breach.

Both Corlett and Hobbs remembered well how a similar early commitment of armor through the 30th Division bridgehead over the Vire et Taute Canal and the Vire River had created a fiasco, so in the circumstances the decision required more than a little boldness. The decision proved correct. For a while on October 3, congestion on the approaches to the small foothold across the Wurm produced a bumper-to-bumper jam of tanks under enemy shellfire; but the early crossing put the 2nd Armored's CCB in position to help repulse the standard German counterattack on October 4. In this counterattack the enemy expended all his immediately available offensive strength and spirit, and the Americans thereupon returned to the systematic elimination of the pillboxes, with tanks now assisting the infantry. Forward observers would bring down artillery on a pillbox to clear the enemy from subsidiary positions; tanks would then blast entrances and apertures with armor-piercing ammunition; infantry would close in, at which point the Germans frequently surrendered.

By October 6, the German Seventh Army had brought up reserves to mount another counterattack; but by this time the 30th Division was itself well ensconced in the West Wall, and CCB had built up a firm line on the northeastern flank. About the same time, Generals Bradley and Hodges visited the headquarters of their corps commander who was the latest to breach the West Wall. Bradley said little; Hodges indulged himself in dressing down Corlett for his heavy expenditure of artillery ammunition on the first day of the attack. Corlett indiscreetly lashed back with an angry reply to his commanding officer.

Consuming ammunition was a serious enough business, because the most troublesome enemy activity now came from his artillery, and the ammunition shortage compelled the XIX Corps to limit its response to about twenty-four rounds per enemy battery—not enough for permanent silencing. Nevertheless, on October 7 Hobbs was able to report to Corlett that his battle for the West Wall was over. After helping the 30th Division in its final push through the fortifications, the 2nd Armored's CCA had joined CCB in the defensive shield on the left flank. The 30th Division was at Alsdorf, only about five kilometers from Würselen, its planned meeting place with the VII Corps; Hobbs was ready to turn south to complete the encirclement of Aachen. Losses in the two divisions Corlett had committed to the battle were 1,800, including about 200 killed; CCB had lost fifty-two medium tanks.

Corlett believed the enemy in front was so badly injured that the XIX Corps ought to press onward to the Roer River; this objective, which he thought now within reach, was destined to cost the American army dearly in later months. Army headquarters preferred to complete its plan for Aachen and the securing of the line of communication for a subsequent advance to the Roer. Hobbs thereupon recommended that the VII Corps now open its attack northward to meet him, and late on October 7 Hodges endorsed this suggestion. The Big Red One on Collins's left flank was to form the southern pincer of the Aachen envelopment, and General Huebner ordered the 18th Infantry Regiment to begin the push against Verlautenheide in the second band of the West Wall before dawn of October 8.

Heubner's choice of regiment reflected the toll that the fighting in the Aachen corridor had already wrung from the 1st Division's manpower and offensive capacity. The 16th Infantry was pinned down in defensive positions from near Eilendorf to Stolberg. The 26th Infantry was holding a defensive line south of Aachen facing the city; it might attack Aachen once the circle was closed at Würselen. To free the 18th Infantry for the attack, the 1106th Engineer Combat Group had to go into the line, also south of Aachen. The 1st Division's only reserve as the attack began was one battalion of the 26th.

Fortunately, both the XIX and the VII Corps G-2s performed excellently during the encirclement effort. Accurate assessment of German strength and locations had contributed much to Corlett's rapid penetration of the West Wall north of the city. Collins and Huebner were also accurately informed of German strength in Aachen—an estimate of about 12,000 troops, with the 246th Volksgrenadier Division as their core—and knew how much, or how little, strength they could afford to apply. The 18th Infantry like Corlett's assault regiments was well rehearsed and well organized for overcoming pillboxes. A battery of 155mm. guns and a company of tank destroyers, both self-propelled, were assigned to accompany the infantry to pour direct fire into the defenses. The attack gobbled up Verlautenheide before daylight and before the defenders had emerged from sheltering themselves against the preliminary artillery barrage. In the afternoon the Americans captured Crucifix Hill (Hill 239), another strongpoint about a thousand meters northeast of Verlautenheide. By evening of October 9 they were atop their final objective, the Ravelsberg (Hill 231), where they were to await the XIX Corps. The next morning the men on the Ravelsberg were favored with a hot breakfast, compliments of German cooks who did not know the hill had been taken.

The Ravelsberg and the 18th Infantry's adjacent conquests were also soon favored by the predictable rash of local counterattacks. These came mainly from the enemy's recently committed 12th Division and were therefore about as formidable as German skill could make them. Supplementing the counterattacks were heavy concentrations of artillery fire, accurately aimed because the Germans knew perfectly well the map coordinates of the defenses they had just vacated. For several days, heavy morning mists never completely dissipated, and neither American artillery nor airplanes could do effective counterbattery work. The 18th Infantry had to huddle in shelters, surfacing only when a counterattack seemed about to hit. Day after night after day constantly under fire began to spawn evident nervousness and fatigue; troops laying antitank mines on the Ravelsberg exploded one of their own devices and set off a chain reaction of twenty-two blasts, inflicting thirty-three American casualties. General Huebner had no reserve adequate to offer relief.

The 30th Division meanwhile was approaching from the north with excruciating slowness. When he turned southward from Alsdorf on October 7, Hobbs expected to cross the intervening five kilometers and be at Würselen awaiting the 1st Division by the next night; but with the 2nd Armored left behind to protect his rear, he had to drop off so much of his strength for flank protection against the enemy's pesky counterattacks that his spearhead was too weak for any such progress. Particularly, the XIX Corps G-2 warned that the 108th Panzer Brigade had arrived with the seeming intent to assail Hobbs's eastern and southern flanks, and that further enemy reserves might well follow against the same targets. Such forward progress as Hobbs carved out was with "close in pill box and village street fighting where panther tanks in pairs guarded every crossroad."[15] The snail's pace of the advance provoked Hodges to badger Corlett with a stream of prodding telephone calls. When the corps commander heard from one of his staff officers that a member of the army staff had remarked that the XIX Corps couldn't be fighting very hard because it wasn't suffering enough casualties, Corlett mounted his jeep to visit Hodges's headquarters for another venting of his spleen. Hodges proved to be not at home, but the chief of staff, General Kean, and the army G-3 received an undiplomatic invitation from Corlett to visit his front and see for themselves what was going on.

Intelligence, at least, was still functioning very well. Just as Corlett's G-2 predicted, the tanks of the 108th Panzer Brigade, incorporated into a strong task force including three infantry and three assault gun battalions and called Mobile Regiment von Fritzschen, came out of the morning mist against the 117th Infantry on Hobbs's east flank on October 8. They isolated a platoon, killing or capturing twenty-six of its members and knocking out three of four supporting tanks; then cut off another platoon, of which only six men returned to the American lines; and left one company with only thirty-three effectives. Other parts of Mobile Regiment von Fritzschen fought their way briefly into Alsdorf. These scored less heavily but helped increase Hobbs's wariness about his flanks.

Worse, after several more days of tedious progress and frequent entanglement with armor as well as enemy infantry, on October 12 the 119th Infantry at North Würselen collided with the 60th Panzer Grenadier Regiment, a unit of the 116th Panzer Division. The same afternoon, Hobbs's troops also identified SS-Battalion Rink, part of the 1st SS Panzer Division. Corlett's irritability and sensitivity did not prevent his passing a strong note of worriment up the chain of command: "If the 116th Panzer and [Leibstandarte] Adolf Hitler are in there, this is one of the decisive battles of the war."[16] Hobbs seconded Corlett by pleading for assistance; his division's losses since crossing the Wurm totaled 2,020, mostly riflemen. But Hodges had little help to offer; the best he could do was to place the separate 99th Infantry Battalion in XIX Corps reserve. He also stepped up the flow of strong hints to both Corlett and Hobbs that they might soon be awaiting new assignments if the 30th Division did not hook up with the 1st Division fast.

Hodges was not altogether wrong to interpret the latest German arrivals less ominously than did his corps and division commanders. SS-Battalion Rink proved to be merely an element of Kampfgruppe Diefenthal, which was a thin shadow of the old 1st SS Panzers. The 116th Panzer Division was in better shape; but as usual, the Americans' offensive pressure drove the Germans to commit their reinforcements piecemeal instead of in the concentrated dosage that General der Panzertruppen Erich Brandenberger, now commanding the Seventh Army, and Field Marshals Model and von Rundstedt clearly would have preferred. In addition, on the same day when the frightening new arrivals were identified, the sun came out, and IX TAC could return to its work of revising battlefield odds in the First Army's favor.

The enemy had again slowed and even shaken Hobbs and Corlett, but he did not halt their glacial progress, and on October 15 he shifted his main attention to the southern pincer of the Aachen encirclement. This time the fire brigade that Model conjured up for Brandenberger turned out to be the much-traveled 3rd Panzer Grenadier Division, which tried to separate the 18th Infantry's Verlautenheide-Ravelsberg salient from the rest of the 1st Division. Fortunately for the Americans, the brunt of the attack struck the 16th Infantry rather than the weary 18th. Fortunately, too, intelligence again did its job, and both division and corps artillery were primed to welcome the panzer grenadiers warmly. At that, Tigers and—according to the GIs—some captured Shermans (one still bearing 5th Armored Division markings) kept right on rolling and almost accomplished a rupture of the 16th Infantry's left and its connection with the 18th. Again the heavens favored the Americans at a critical turning point, and P-47s came to the rescue, bombing and strafing low.

The 3rd Panzer Grenadiers persisted in their attacks through October 16, but by the second day they had evidently lost their sharp edge. On that day, furthermore, Hodges's caustic prodding impelled Hobbs to try a new scheme for closing the gap to the Ravelsberg. He would shift the 119th Infantry westward to attack toward Aachen along both banks of the Wurm, mud and the separation of his troops by the river notwithstanding, in hopes of turning the strong defenses that his earlier attacks had provoked the Germans to create. The 117th and 120th Infantry would stage diversions along the old route of advance.

The gambit worked. The 119th Infantry achieved more rapid progress than Hobbs's division had enjoyed since its turn southward. Despite the diversions, the 119th attracted punishing gales of artillery fire, but at 4:15 P.M. its 2nd Battalion met soldiers of the 18th Infantry on the Ravelsberg. Aachen was encircled.

But the new pattern of the war had also been underlined. The 30th Division had required nine days to close the last five kilometers from Würselen. Since the start of the drive, the division had lost some 3,100 men.

The closing of the circle also came too late to save Corlett. On October 18, General Bradley relieved him. The army group commander and General Eisenhower tried to assure both Corlett himself and General Marshall that the reason for the relief was Corlett's uncertain health and need for rest; Eisenhower indicated he would be willing to have Corlett as a corps commander again, after a rest. But Hodges was clearly happier with the XIX Corps under someone else. Corlett's chief of staff brought the news to Hobbs's headquarters, where Corlett was visiting. The mercurial Hobbs wept, feeling it was he and his division who had let Corlett down. Corlett would have liked to weep: ". . . leaving the XIX Corps, every man and officer of which I loved, was just plain heartbreak."[17]

It remained to close the ring inward upon Aachen. The 18th Infantry's capture of the Ravelsberg on October 9 had prompted General Huebner to demand the surrender of the city on the 10th, threatening ruthless air and artillery bombardment if the garrison did not yield. The demand involved a degree of bluffing, because, as Huebner knew, the garrison outnumbered the two battalions of the 26th Infantry he had available for an assault. Still, Huebner could fulfill his warnings about air and artillery, and he did. After the Germans refused his terms, four groups of IX TAC Thunderbolts and Lightnings plastered Aachen on October 11. Division and corps artillery hurled almost 5,000 rounds into the city.

The 2nd Battalion of the 26th opened the assault into the main industrial and residential wards, the kind of house-to-house fighting the Americans had hoped to avoid. A tank or tank destroyer accompanied each infantry platoon and kept each building under fire until the infantry were ready to push into it. Then the armor would shift to the next building. Machine guns firing up the streets helped keep the Germans pinned down. When the riflemen moved into a building, the enemy usually had been driven into the cellar, where he could be rooted out with hand grenades and, if necessary, flame throwers and heavier explosives. Meanwhile artillery and mortar fire would be sweeping ahead systematically block by block, to prepare the way for the armor and infantry.

The 3rd Battalion of the 26th meanwhile assailed the high ground on the west of Aachen, hills called the Lousberg and the Salvatorberg and Farwick Park, where the Palast-Hotel Quellenhof and the Kurhaus presided over the hot springs. On October 21, the 3rd Battalion was about to call 155mm. rifle fire on a bunker at the north end of Lousberg Strasse, whence the commandant of the garrison, Oberst Gerhard Wilck, had been radioing exhortations to fight to the last. Nevertheless, before his refuge was blasted, Wilck sent out two captured Americans and two German officers under a white flag to make the contacts necessary for surrender. By the end of the day, virtually all resistance in Aachen had ceased.

In the Battle of Aachen, the 30th Division had taken 6,000 prisoners and the 1st Division almost as many, including 3,473 within the city. But the 1st Division also suffered casualties comparable, in proportion to the number of its troops engaged, to the 30th's 3,100. With both these divisions depleted and exhausted, Hodges and Bradley alike believed the First Army must be reinforced before it could take the offensive again. In the battle for Aachen, the final spasmodic effort of the once-overwhelming Allied onslaught of July and August clutched at a local victory, and then died.

Allied intelligence estimated German effectives on the Western Front at close to three times their numbers of the beginning of September. Against the German Miracle of the West, neither the British nor the Americans had as yet enough men to break the line.

The First Battle of the Huertgen Forest

Life magazine told its readers that the Battle of the Huertgen Forest was taking its place in American military history beside such classic struggles as the Wilderness and the Argonne Forest.[18] The comparison was apt, and for deeper reasons than those of a setting of dense, blackened woods where the attacker could never exploit any advantage in firepower, and the defender could nestle his guns and traps in a thousand places of concealment to demand an almost intolerable toll of attrition for every foot of ground. In the Huertgen Forest, war returned fully to the pattern that had become normal for it since such Civil War battles as the Wilderness first revealed the deadly firepower of modern rifled weapons, a pattern solidified by the addition of the machine gun to the rifle on such grisly World War battlefields as the Argonne. Wherever two armies confronted each other with approximate equality in numbers, weapons, and tactical skill, deadlock ensued. Not even Napoleonic genius in a commander could produce any longer the decisive margins of battlefield victory that Napoleon had scored; for the most brilliantly executed Napoleonic maneuver against the enemy's rear or flank now usually collapsed in the dissolution of the maneuverer's offensive strength under thunderstrokes of firepower as the defender changed front to meet the menace to his flank or rear—as Union army rifles, for example, mowed down Longstreet's flanking attack in the Wilderness. Battle had lost its capacity to produce decision at reasonable cost.

Eisenhower's armies had endured the characteristic deadlock of modern war in the Bocage, then had escaped it when the partial destruction of the German Fifth Panzer and Seventh Armies in the Falaise pocket deprived the enemy of that approximate equality of strength on which the deadlock rests. Now that the Germans had restored themselves to rough equality in numbers at the front—they actually had an overall numerical superiority in the West—their well-honed tactical skill, bolstered by strong fortifications, compensated for their shortcomings in equipment, and the battlefield deadlock returned.

But the Huertgen Forest lent the deadlock added dimensions of horror. While awaiting reinforcement and replenishment of supplies to resume the main offensive, the First Army tried to clear its right flank of the indeterminate numbers but menacing presence of the Germans among the dark evergreens of the Wenau, Huertgen, and Rötgen woods, known collectively and simply to the Americans as the Huertgen Forest— and altogether an eerie, haunting region fit for a witches' lair. The woods extended across some eighty square kilometers of a triangle formed by Aachen, Düren, and Monschau. From southwest to northeast through the forest two ridges point toward the Roer River. The northern ridge, harboring the towns of Huertgen, Menhau, and Grosshau, is about five kilometers long. The southern ridge extends from Lammersdorf to Schmidt. Between the ridge lines is the deep gorge of the Kall River. The ridges were largely cleared of timber and thus all the more dominated the forest below, where densely packed firs rose high up from rough, rocky, deeply scored hills and a damp carpet of evergreen needles that provided superb concealment for mines. Mines, barbed wire, and camouflaged pillboxes with interlocking fields of fire clotted the forest. On the brightest day, little sunlight filtered through the tall trees to the gloomy darkness of the forest floor.

To General Collins, a soldier of World War I, the shadow of the Huertgen on his right flank duplicated almost precisely the menace of the Argonne Forest on the left flank of Pershing's great 1918 offensive. Whether such a perception of the Huertgen Forest was warranted was a question meriting fuller consideration than it seems to have received in the autumn of 1944. As American intelligence knew, the German troops within the forest were yet another motley assemblage of conglomerate units, by no means first-rate in their personnel, largely commanded by the 353rd Infantry Division during September, then from the beginning of October under the direction of the 275th Division. Information reaching the Americans indicated that neither the enemy's morale nor the combat coherence of his units was impressive. Could such a German force seriously threaten offensive activity against the right flank and line of communication of the First Army? And was there any reason to expect the Germans would put anything more formidable into the forest, when the density of the woods and the absence of roads precluded their using the Huertgen to screen any large concentration of armor?

The most likely way to make the Huertgen a menace to the American army was to send American troops attacking into its depths. An army that depends for superiority on its mobility, firepower, and technology should never voluntarily give battle where these assets are at a discount; the Huertgen Forest was surely such a place. The German 275th Division and its successors in the Huertgen could not be much of a threat if they ventured outside the forest; but within the dark woods, battle would become a fragmented series of infantry contests, the unit cohesion lacking in the Germans' Huertgen forces would count for little anyway, American fighter-bombers, tanks, and artillery could barely make themselves felt, and the shelter of the trees would lend strength even to unskilled and irresolute defenders.

The 60th Infantry Regiment of the 9th Division had already endured a hard attrition attempting to penetrate the Huertgen in September. The arrival of the Ninth Army on the old V Corps front in the Ardennes-Eifel and the consequent shortening of the First Army sector permitted the commander of the 9th Division, General Craig, to employ two of his regiments in a new attack on the forest in October. While the 47th Infantry Regiment had to continue facing northward defensively at Schevenhütte, near the apex of the Aachen-Stolberg corridor, Craig could send both the 60th and, on its right, the 39th Infantry into the forest in pursuit of General Collins's determination to clear it.

The most specific target for the 9th Division was the crossroads village of Schmidt, taking which would add certain positive advantages to the mere securing of the VII Corps line of communication. At Schmidt, the 9th Division would overlook the Roer River from one of the highest ridges on the flank of the Aachen corridor, a suitable point from which to strike back southwestward to take Monschau from the rear and a possible launching pad also for eventual further attack east and north into the valley of the Roer.

But these possible positive assets were not overwhelmingly important; the motives for fighting in the Huertgen remained largely negative. And it was this fact that might have caused reconsideration at least when Craig's two regiments proved not enough. The Germans sheltered in the pillboxes and bunkers studded through the woods could direct mortar and artillery shells to burst in the treetops and shower the Americans below with ricochet fragments. Each American regimental sector had only one narrow trail, and because the trails and firebreaks were blocked with mines and felled trees, tanks could not support the infantry. Incompletely trained in woods fighting, the Americans found merely maintaining their sense of direction an almost insuperable problem. For company officers—let alone higher grades—to maintain control of their units was a worse problem. Attacking on October 6, the 60th Infantry required four days and the 39th five to advance about a kilometer and a half to the first clearing inside the forest. Then the infantry had to pause while engineers hacked wider trails through the woods so tanks could come up before the riflemen exposed themselves in the open ground. To advance this far cost the two American regiments almost a thousand men.

To advance this far also provoked the enemy to counterattack, striking hard against the 60th Infantry's exposed left flank with a regiment of good troops brought up from a quiet sector near Luxembourg. With the whole strength of the 9th Division committed either in the forest or at Schevenhütte, the regimental commanders had to rob Peter to pay Paul in a series of attempts to deploy reserves at any threatened spot. By October 16, the division held the first clearing and a few trail junctions, but it had paid 4,500 casualties to push its advance to three kilometers. The only experienced riflemen who had survived were drained of strength and initiative, inexperienced replacements often fell dead or wounded before they learned the names of their comrades, and the 60th and 39th had to be relieved and rested.

Therefore General Hodges shifted his corps boundaries to give General Gerow's V Corps responsibility for Schmidt, and on November 2 General Cota's 28th Division began trying its hand at the Huertgen Forest. Cota was to attack with all three of his regiments, and Gerow reinforced him with three engineer combat battalions, a battalion of towed tank destroyers to supplement the usual attached tank and self-propelled tank destroyer battalions, and a chemical mortar battalion. He placed eight battalions and a separate battery of V and VII Corps artillery in direct support and received six additional batteries of VII Corps artillery for preparatory fire. For the time being, the Huertgen Forest was to feel the primary attention of IX TAC; but the significance of this promise, uncertain enough in the forest, was still more doubtful because wet weather had set in and seemingly come to stay. The autumn was to prove the wettest thus far in the century.

The Keystone Division had to move up through the dank woods rendered yet more dismal by the wreckage of the 9th Division's battle, and to relieve tired, frightened men.

To everyone's surprise, undaunted by the prospect, Lieutenant Colonel Albert Flood's 3rd Battalion of the 112th Infantry nevertheless advanced nonstop across the Kall gorge and up into Schmidt by evening of the second day, November 3.

The success proved almost too early and too critical. On the high ground of Schmidt, at the northeastern apex of the more southerly ridge across the Huertgen, the Americans threatened both Monschau's rear and, eastward in the Roer valley, a series of objectives whose military value they had so far ignored: the dams of the Roer River and its tributaries, which if opened could cause floods of several weeks' duration downstream, to the immense embarrassment of any effort by the VII or XIX Corps to cross the lower Roer toward the Ruhr. In so sensitive a place, the Americans at Schmidt naturally became a magnet drawing German reinforcements and counterattacks from far and wide.

Furthermore, the battalion at Schmidt could readily be cut off from effective help because through the deep gorge of the Kall River only a narrow dirt trail, with a steep wall on one side and a precipitous drop on the other, connected it with the main body of the 28th Division. Late in the afternoon of November 3, a company of tanks began trying to negotiate the trail to link up with the 3/112th. Merely to begin, they had to move an abandoned weasel carrier that was blocking the trail. In gathering darkness, the lead tank slipped and almost dropped off the trail into the gorge. Engineers nearby had only hand tools and one bulldozer, which broke down in the early hours of the next morning. On November 4, three tanks led by 1st Lieutenant Raymond E. Fleig managed to make their way through to the imperiled infantry, leaving another tank with a disabled track partially blocking the trail, yet another with a thrown track stuck in the mud, and the cliff edge of the trail badly chewed up even by the successful passage.

The Americans had foreseen that infantry at Schmidt might thus have to fight with little or no armor in support, but they had counted on the same difficulties of negotiating the Kall gorge, plus artillery and air power, to keep panzers away from Schmidt as well. They did not realize that the Germans had better roads into Schmidt, and they did not appreciate how completely the woods and the bad weather would shield enemy armor from their observation and from artillery and air strikes. By early morning of November 4, tanks of the 116th Panzer Division were already counterattacking Flood's battalion, helped by infantry of the German 89th Division which chanced to be passing through the area just when the Americans broke into Schmidt. By this time, furthermore, Cota had felt obliged to commit elsewhere the only infantry battalion he had held in reserve because the Germans had already begun counterattacking hard against his right flank near Monschau.

During the morning, the Germans overran Schmidt. With escape routes through the Huertgen all infinitely precarious, the retreat of Flood's battalion quickly degenerated into near-panic. About 200 men fled in a wrong direction, southwestward, still deeper into German territory.

Others, more fortunately, rallied upon Major Robert T. Hazlett's 1st Battalion, which had also climbed up the southeast side of the Kall gorge and had reached Kommerscheidt just northwest of Schmidt. Here Lieutenant Fleig's three tanks showed up just in time to confront at least five advancing Pzkw IVs and Vs. Fleig in the lead Sherman first took on a Panther, but his high-explosive ammunition bounced off its armor, and his armor-piercing shells were outside his turret in the sponson rack. Turning the turret while under the Panther's fire to get at these rounds, Fleig and his crew retrieved an armor-piercing shell, got it into their gun, and with it cut the Panther's gun barrel in two. Three more good shots opened the Panther's side and set it afire. Altogether, Fleig's three tanks took out three German tanks, while a P-47 killed another and a bazooka rocket yet another. With such doughty assistance, the 112th Infantry clung to Kommerscheidt.

But an unhappy precedent had been set: the 28th Division by its very initial success had overextended itself so much that the counterattacking Germans, not the Americans, appeared to hold the initiative. Until November 8 the Keystoners battled grimly back and forth for possession of the Kall gorge and for Kommerscheidt as a foothold toward Schmidt beyond, but they could never gain firm enough possession of the gorge—and the trail through it was not good enough anyway—to match the concentrations of strength, including armor, that the Germans could throw against the Schmidt ridge. Meanwhile the strain of trying to hold Kommerscheidt, added to the normal attrition of fighting in the Huertgen, helped thin the 28th Division elsewhere, and on November 6 the 2/112th was overrun and routed on the northerly ridge. On November 7, Cota recommended withdrawing the bridgehead from around Kommerscheidt back across the Kall.

The next day, the Huertgen Forest reached the agenda of a conference including Eisenhower and Bradley as well as Hodges, Gerow, and Cota. Hodges grumbled over his disappointment with the performance of the 28th Division and again was in a mood to chop heads, particularly Cota's. By now there should have been enough experience with the Huertgen to raise doubts whether any other division or commander could have done better, but Hodges was a hard man to placate. He eventually agreed to let Cota pull back across the Kall provided that the 28th Division continue to cling firmly to the northerly ridge near the town of Vossenack, which is at the base of the ridge just across the Kall gorge from Schmidt; that the division also assist the newly committed 12th Infantry of the 4th Division to capture an alternate launching site toward the Roer still farther north around the town of Huertgen; that Cota continue to press south toward the rear of Monschau; and that he send a regiment to join with General Oliver's 5th Armored Division in a frontal attack on Monschau.

Hodges was asking a great deal of an already battered division. If this point needed any clarification, the newly arrived 12th Infantry Regiment provided it, by starting into the Huertgen Forest fresh and near full strength on November 8, but losing more than 500 casualties for little accomplishment in the next five days. Nevertheless, Cota tried to help, to the point of committing in aid of the 12th three companies of the 1/109th that numbered only sixty-two, fifty-five, and seventy-three men. One of the companies reached its assigned objective, was cut off for three days, and returned with thirty-three men.

On November 13, Hodges relented and ordered the 28th Division to be relieved by exchanging places with the 8th Division of the VIII Corps. In its part of the battle of the Huertgen Forest, the Keystone Division had lost 6,184 casualties. The 112th Infantry alone had lost 2,093. These 2,093 included 544 nonbattle casualties; snow had become mixed with the incessant rain, and there were many frostbite and trench foot cases at the medical aid stations.

Even now, the American high command did not reexamine the wisdom of doing battle in the Huertgen. Hodges did, however, reconsider tactics. The 9th and 28th Divisions had spread their forces across much of the width of the forest and by their dispersal invited counterattacks and the isolation of small units, thus aggravating the tendency of the forest to minimize the attacker's assets and magnify the defender's. Hodges now contemplated a concentrated drive into the forest by a powerful, cohesive column. The next problem, however, was where to find the manpower for the concentrated column. It was not to be had; there was no First Army reserve. Believing now that only a power drive was likely to overcome the horrors of the Huertgen, Hodges nevertheless settled in the meantime for still further dispersed efforts for the sake of keeping any activity at all in motion, notwithstanding the almost certain result of draining still more his army's already thin files of riflemen.

20: Autumn Interlude

T HE HUERTGEN FOREST had for the time being consumed the combat power of two divisions, the 9th and the 28th, and Aachen had come close to paralyzing the 30th and the 1st. The American command proposed to deal with the disturbing depletion of its combat manpower by means of the obvious expedients of hastening the flow both of individual replacements and additional divisions into Europe. Yet neither of these solutions seemed altogether satisfactory. Both, rather, pointed to still more problems, fundamental to the shape of the American army and the American participation in the Second World War.

Manpower

The casualties that dangerously thinned the combat ranks, as well as the fatigue that drained the efficiency of the survivors, fell always disproportionately upon the infantry, and yet more disproportionately upon the riflemen. The reader will recall how the battles in the Bocage caused casualties of more than 100 percent among the riflemen of the 90th Division, and of some 150 percent among that division's officers, within the first two months of fighting. Before D-Day, American planning had modestly anticipated that infantry would incur about three out of four casualties suffered in Europe. More precisely, in April 1944 the War Department yielded to the pleas of the European Theater of Operations that the proportion of infantry in the replacement pool must be raised from 64.3 to 70.3 percent. The first month of combat in Normandy promptly demonstrated that the modesty of this expectation was excessive, for infantry losses proved to comprise 85 percent of the casualties. By mid-July, when the Bocage fighting was at its height, the commander of the ETO Ground Forces Replacement System, Brigadier General Walter G. Layman, lifted the estimate of infantry casualties to 90 percent of the total. These figures, furthermore, referred to infantry in general; the War Department had calculated that 76 percent of infantry replacements must be trained as riflemen and heavy weapons personnel, but experience soon showed that this figure should have been about 95 percent. The rifle platoons of a full-strength division totaled 3,240 men. Reflecting on these figures, it requires little imagination to recognize that, considering the 28th Division's 6,104 casualties in the Huertgen forest, Hodges was asking a great deal in the tasks he imposed on the division late in the action as conditions for its withdrawal from beyond the Kall.

Of the first three months' casualties after D-Day, about 30 percent were killed, captured, or missing, 70 percent wounded. Of the 70 percent who were wounded, 45 percent could be expected to recover and return to general assignment duty, while 11 percent could be placed in limited assignment duty. Forty-six percent of the wounded could return to some kind of duty within 120 days, and thus could figure importantly in replenishing losses. It was significant that most of them expressed a strong desire to return to their old units, so strong that many took the risk of going AWOL, leaving the replacement pipeline when they felt trapped in it, to find their way back to their former companies. Even in the American army, with its relative lack of unit traditions and limited encouragement of primary-group loyalties, men felt "driven by the instinct to return to one's own people which only the 'regimental soldier' can understand"—the words of a British soldier who "clawed my way back" from a hospital at Cairo to fight with his field battery at El Alamein.[1]

In the name of administrative efficiency, too much of this potential for replenishing losses was wasted, and the army frustrated the desires of the very men who wanted to return to where they were needed. To guard against the possibility of overstrengths in some units while others remained understrength, army policy declared that men discharged from hospitals who were still qualified to perform the duties of their old Military Occupation Specialty should be returned to their former units whenever practicable—but this meant only if requisitions were on hand from those units to fill vacancies. This policy was closely tied to a theater requisition policy that forbade a division to requisition replacements for an understrength regiment if the division as a whole was overstrength. At the same time, however, recognizing the advantages of returning a soldier to his old unit, the theater G-1 also decreed that casuals—hospital returnees—should not be used as replacements for other units than those they had come from, unless no other replacements were available. The effect was to compel thousands to sit around in replacement depots doing nothing—for the depots were barely equipped to accomplish anything constructive in the way of training new soldiers, let alone utilizing the time of experienced ones. The casuals grew bitter, some to the point of striking out on the AWOL route back to their buddies, in hopes that their officers could set things right. Meanwhile field force commanders pleaded for the automatic return of casuals to their old units. Still, as late as November 1944, bureaucratic reasoning not only prevailed but scored a new triumph by proclaiming that casuals were to be held in forward replacement depots only ten days; if no requisition from a soldier's former unit justified by actual vacancies was forthcoming within that time, the casual was to be used to fill any requisitions. In practice, some replacement depots violated this order and held casuals until there were requisitions from their old outfits, but this tactic in turn aggravated the problem of lost time spent waiting.

Field-grade officers were eventually exempted from the rules and returned to where they belonged. When the 6th Army Group found itself in especially dire need of replacements at the beginning of 1945, General Devers, habitually a voice of common sense, used his influence to persuade SHAEF to return all enlisted casuals from his army group to their former units. Devers proved to have broken the log jam, for later in January 1945 SHAEF suspended the old rules for 12th Army Group enlisted men as well. In March, common sense was applied at last to company-grade officer casuals, too; and at the end of the month the theater finally rescinded all the regulations keeping returning casuals away from the places where they could best be used. It had taken most of the war for the combined forces of reason and compassion thus to prevail.

Where reason and compassion ought to converge to maintain more generally the fighting strength, integrity, and morale of units long exposed to the hard attrition of combat was a yet more vexing question. In fact, the United States Army has never in its long history discovered a satisfactory method of doing so. In its first war requiring massive forces, the Civil War, the United States Army simply held a regiment's nose to the grindstone of combat until that regiment was no more. With minor and usually ineffective exceptions, there was no replacement system. Union army regiments with a table of organization strength of 845 to 1,025 were down to an average of about 375 by the time of Gettysburg, only halfway through the war. New regiments were raised to take the places of the depleted ones, an unconscionable waste of the experience of veteran officers and enlisted men. To avoid such waste, in the world wars the army gave depleted units infusions of individual replacements. This method kept regiments and divisions somewhere within hailing distance of their authorized strength—though not really at authorized strength, because among other impediments units were not allowed through most of 1944 to requisition on the eve of combat in anticipation of losses, and they had to requisition on the basis of assigned rather than effective strength (a man who was AWOL, for example, was carried as part of assigned strength for a year). While units did not simply fade away as they had in the Civil War, there remained the Civil War problem, aggravated by the more continuous combat of the twentieth century, that once a unit entered the lines it stayed there until the end of the war. Divisions occasionally went to quiet sectors to rest and refit, but not often enough or according to any system. The German army almost until its final extremity rotated units out of the line more frequently and regularly than the American army. The effect was to undermine an effective American division's asset of experience by sheer weariness.

Once an individual soldier was committed to combat, he had to count on remaining under fire until the war ended or he was so badly wounded he could not return—or until he was dead. For all its faults, nevertheless, this system was preferable to the British practice, followed in North Africa and fortunately less evident in Europe, of rotating units out of the line so frequently that relatively raw or rusty British formations were forever being chewed to pieces by veteran German divisions. The American replacement system of World War II was also far superior to the Korean and Vietnam War systems, which rotated individuals, officers as well as men, out of both their units and combat as soon as they had served under fire for a stipulated time. In the Korean and Vietnam Wars, the United States Army virtually returned to the short enlistment periods that had been the bane of American armies in the Revolution, the War of 1812, and the Mexican War—under pressure, of course, of political circumstances very different from those of World War II. But the urge of the World War II casual to return to his unit suggests that the absence of a rotation system that would have assured at least periodic relief from combat did not damage morale as badly as might be supposed. And the World War II replacement system had the great virtue of sustaining unit integrity as well as numbers; the later Korean and Vietnam replacement system practically destroyed unit cohesion.

Or more specifically, the World War II replacement system at least nourished the individual soldier's sense of identification with his unit once he was there long enough to know to which regiment and division he belonged, and who were his officers and comrades. Too often the system of individual replacements flung a lone man into a group of strangers, with no chance to get to know them before he entered combat with them. Too often, the replacement arrived at night and did not even see his comrades' faces before the battle resumed. Not the least of the defects of a program that did not regularly rotate divisions out of the line was the lack of opportunity to absorb replacements under conditions that allowed some introduction to the unit's members and history, to say nothing of a measure of training with the unit.

The War Department's initial shipments of replacements to Europe did not meet even its own limited expectations about the casualty rate among infantrymen and particularly riflemen. On D-Day, only 52 percent of the 76,000 replacements in the European Theater were infantry-trained. The May, June, and July shipments of infantry replacements contained, respectively, only 35, 58, and 50 percent riflemen.

The theater in turn was slow to perceive the implications of these figures. As late as July 11, ETO headquarters actually reduced its September replacement requisition by 15,000 men, albeit in favor of hastening shipment of full divisions. Early efforts to improve the prospects of replenishing infantry losses were limited to a theater survey to find whether there was an excess of personnel in the Communications Zone, along with a directive to COMZ section commanders to release any such excess. Since the theater offered neither incentives for releasing men nor penalties for not doing so, compliance was minimal. Some 4,800 men eventually moved into the replacement system by this means, but General Layman complained about how few of them were fit for training as riflemen—which raises questions about the real motives when a COMZ section chief chose to put somebody into the pool.

Before July was over and COBRA was under way, ETO had to take a more urgent view of replacements. Its requests to Washington for infantry replacements sought abruptly to cancel earlier deletions and to hasten shipments as rapidly as possible. The theater soon began fishing from the replacement pool men trained for combat arms other than infantry—field artillery, tank destroyer, and antiaircraft men—and ordering that they be converted as quickly as possible to infantrymen. By August, the Replacement System had retrained about 5,500 soldiers as riflemen. All the facilities of the American School Center at Shrivenham, England were turned to that purpose. Nevertheless, by September 1 ETO had 42,000 infantry replacements on hand against a calculation that for safety it needed 55,000. Of those it had, only some 15,000 offered the vital MOS 745 classification of rifleman. This was when the August pursuit across France had dramatically reduced casualties, and renewed hard fighting had yet to make matters worse.

At this juncture, the issue of replacing combat infantry casualties almost disappeared into a bureaucratic morass. Though ETO was admittedly short of riflemen, according to the War Department it had been hoarding a consistent surplus of almost every other category of soldier. In July, Washington had accused the theater of harboring 130,000 men above its allowance. By September, the Inspector General of the army was visiting the theater, finding in its replacement pool an excess of 49,000 above the 70,000 authorized, and threatening immediate retribution. The theater responded that much of its apparent overstrength in noninfantry categories resulted from necessities unforeseen, or at least unprepared for. Without enlarging truck companies, for example, to make it possible to run trucks both day and night, there could have been no Red Ball Express. General Eisenhower himself became ensnared in a prolonged haggle over accounting methods, which differed considerably between the War Department and ETO with complicated consequences for their respective reckonings of how many men the theater had on hand.

Behind this often petty wrangling over details and definitions lay some basic issues.

The War Department insisted on chiding ETO and even Eisenhower not only because the bureaucrats relished springing a trap on deviant accounting practices, but also because if ETO were to receive the infantry replacements it needed so much, it must clean house elsewhere in its own replacement system. The total number of available replacements was decidedly finite. By D-Day, the army had contrived to exceed slightly its authorized strength of 7,700,000 men under the modified 1943 Troop Basis; but hereafter the limits of the Troop Basis decreed that new demands for strength in one part of the army would have to be met by reducations in other parts. Furhermore, by late 1944 the pool of men in the prime eighteen-to-twenty-six age group who had not been deferred for industrial or farm purposes was almost exhausted. Obviously, only a limited number of men entered this age group each month. The War Department eventually agreed with Selective Service to reexamine about 30,000 men previously rejected for service but regarded as borderline cases, and it was considering reduced physical standards. But Selective Service was a dwindling asset, which also decreed that unless exemptions for maintaining the American economy were drastically changed, the army would have to replace its combat losses almost exclusively from within its ranks.

As early as February 10, 1944, General Marshall had anticipated these developments by cutting back the Army Specialized Training Program, a program for college education of some of the more intelligent inductees, to 30,000 men. At this stroke of his pen, he released some 120,000 soldiers for redistribution, 73,000 of whom went to the Army Ground Forces, the rest almost entirely to the Service Forces. The army also reassigned 24,000 surplus aviation cadets to the Gound Forces. The Ground Forces in turn used almost all these men as infantry replacements for depleted divisions. Even before D-Day, furthermore, the War Department began an accelerated deactivation of tank destroyer and antiaircraft units to transfer their personnel mainly into the infantry. By August 1944, nevertheless, the War Department had to warn ETO that the manpower well was so nearly dry that from the beginning of the new year it would not be able to meet the theater's replacement needs.

Meanwhile, the War Department could reasonably contend that it was doing more than ETO to comb out needed replacements from less essential units. Lulled by the relatively light casualties of August and early September, and by the expectation lingering into October that the war was nearly won, the theater still bestirred itself less than might have been expected. In September, in response to earlier War Department reductions throughout the army of the number of privates in unit tables of organization, ETO ordered that all soldiers so released should be retrained as infantry rifle replacements. By the end of October, however, the theater seemed satisfied to have brought up its pool of replacement riflemen to 30,000, though this figure remained well below its own announced margin of safety. By that time, Aachen, the Huertgen Forest, and deadlock along the whole line already forecast a coming demand upon the pool at least as great as that imposed by the battles in the Bocage.

ETO showed a larger sense of urgency about bringing in new divisions, despite the heavy strain that moving whole divisions and their equipment placed on overworked ports and transport. In September, every American division in the line was holding about twenty kilometers of front, and the commanders thought this frontage excessive. The larger urgency was occasioned in part, too, by the increasingly apparent ravages of fatigue upon the effectiveness of the veteran divisions, including the best of them—evident in the almost somnambulist plodding of the 1st Division during the late days of the Battle of Aachen. As early as August, Eisenhower responded with enthusiasm to a War Department offer to speed up the flow of divisions. The first, small result was to advance the arrival of the 26th and 104th Divisions from early September to late August. Immediately afterward, Eisenhower embraced the prospect of receiving in September not only the three divisions scheduled for that month, but also all five divisions scheduled for October. With the logistical crisis burgeoning, the Communications Zone grumbled about moving so many new troops so quickly; but Eisenhower wanted the divisions.

When the War Department offered still further acceleration of division shipments, at some expense to the combined maneuver training and the completeness of heavy ordnance equipment of the divisions involved, Eisenhower continued to choose the fastest possible schedule. This schedule worked out to include one more division in November, five in December, three in January, three in February, and one in March. ETO deferred to the Communications Zone and the logistical crisis to the extent of requesting that three of the October divisions enter the Continent by way of Marseille. Lack of transportation also kept seven American divisions waiting in the United Kingdom at the beginning of November, though SHAEF had hoped to cut the number to four at most. Lack of port capacity also obliged Eisenhower to curtail in October a plan of Marshall's for further acceleration of infantry regiments to Europe ahead of their parent divisions, so tired veteran regiments could be relieved by assigning new regiments temporarily to front-line divisions. Meanwhile, accelerating the arrival of divisions aggravated ETO's quarrel with the War Department about excess noncombat troops in the theater because Eisenhower's headquarters claimed that the multiplication of divisions justified a proportionate multiplication of service troops, especially truck drivers, while the War Department persistently tried to cut service troop allotments to find men to meet combat demands.

For SHAEF and its fighting line, badly strained by the German recovery, the new divisions could not arrive too soon. Without them, it was a luxury to consign to rest and refitting so badly battered a division as the 28th. Given the edge in numbers as well as equipment that the October battles showed the American army still needed to attack successfully against Germans, the whole resumption of the offensive in November by Bradley's First and Ninth Armies waited on their getting even one more division: the return of Terry Allen's 104th from British to American control.

But given the ninety-division gamble, the end of the parade of divisions was as clearly in sight as the bottom of the manpower barrel.

Guns and Shells

With American combat manpower and divisions so limited, the army had to play two other cards to offset the approximate equality in numbers that the Germans had reestablished in combination with their deadly combat proficiency. One was quantitatively superior artillery, employed with the concentrations of fire characteristic of American artillery doctrine. The other was tactical application of air power. But both these American assets labored under disadvantages in the autumn of 1944.

For the artillery, there remained the shortage of ammunition that had developed soon after D-Day. In ammunition, the Americans lacked even the quantitative advantage that their war production, for which they sacrificed numbers of soldiers and divisions, was supposed to ensure. In the principal types of artillery ammunition—for the main divisional artillery support weapon, the 105mm. howitzer; for the 155mm. howitzer; for the 240mm. howitzer; for the 8-inch gun—stocks in Europe had never reached the levels authorized to assure ample reserves. Restrictions on firing introduced in Normandy to conserve ammunition had stayed in effect consistently, except for a short period during the pursuit when the absence of sustained combat reduced expenditures. Even then, a brief relaxation of the restrictions promptly depleted ammunition reserves to within two weeks of exhaustion, just as hard fighting resumed in Lorraine and along the West Wall.

The 12th Army Group, driven by uncertainty to allocate ammunition for periods of only eight days, curbed the September 27–October 5 expenditures to 3.8 rounds per gun per day for the 240mm. howitzers and 3.1 rounds for the 8-inch guns. The 6th Army Group had fallen upon similar hard times. On October 1, a meeting of 12th Army Group and Communications Zone officials slightly increased the allocations for Bradley's troops only to discover two days later that the supplies they had theoretically doled out existed neither in field-army depots nor in Communications Zone stocks. On October 11, the 12th Army Group devised yet another new allocation, in which all available ammunition was assigned to one or another of the field armies, but with the warning that no additional amounts would be issued until November 7. The assignments for the one-month period were often smaller than the earlier eight-day allocations. Because the new allocations were also retroactive to October 5, some of the ammunition had already been spent.

The immediate cause of this October pinch was inadequate unloadings at the beaches and ports. At the beginning of the month, the arrival of autumn storms in the Channel brought the long awaited disruption of beach unloadings. Only about 1,000 tons of ammunition came ashore daily in the first week of October. General Lee responded with an urgent program for getting more ammunition ships into the port of Cherbourg, while also accelerating ammunition unloading at other ports and trying to restore beach unloadings. He aimed at 6,000 tons daily. The 6th Army Group aimed for similar acceleration at Marseille. For the future, the 12th Army Group devised a new distribution system which gave the armies a previously absent incentive to conserve ammunition by allowing them to accumulate credits from one allocation period to the next.

Urgent effort paid off to the extent of passing Lee's 6,000-tons-daily goal on October 23 with 7,617 tons. From October 16 to November 12, daily discharges averaged 6,614 tons. But improvement at the ports and beaches helped unveil a deeper problem: despite warnings from ETO since March 1944 that ammunition expenditure would surely exceed the War Department's allocations to the theater, Washington had failed to contract for enough ammunition production. Another exchange of rival salvos of accounting statistics between ETO and the War Department obfuscated the facts, but the essentials were that on October 30 Washington acknowledged to General Eisenhower that it had almost completely drained its own stocks to meet the latest ammunition crisis in the theater, adding a week later that there was no assurance of filling ETO's demands for the next three to six months.

Ammunition production had been cut back a year earlier, in the autumn of 1943, under congressional criticism of the accumulation of large stocks in North Africa. In April 1944 the War Department had begun to try to restore production. But tooling up for ammunition manufacture was so complicated—making a 155mm. shell required some forty separate operations—that many months would pass before the American troops in Europe could expect to be free from the predicament they had reached by November 1944: ammunition stocks already in the theater and en route now represented total resources.

The armies would have to make do under persistent severe restrictions on firing. One expedient was to use captured guns and their ammunition. Another was to use German ammunition in American guns, which could be done with the 155mm. howitzer and the 81mm. mortar. In a renewal of the fighting around Metz, General Walker's XX Corps fired a time-on-target mission on October 10 using German 88s and 105mm. howitzers, Russian 76.2mm. guns, and French 155mm. howitzers besides American pieces. In this engagement and others up and down the front, the Americans also made much use of tanks, tank destroyers, and antiaircraft guns as artillery, because 75mm., 76mm., 3-inch, 40mm., and 90mm. ammunition was relatively plentiful.

In the XX Corps, the artillery commander also forbade the use of artillery for anything except repelling counterattacks that endangered the American positions, counterbattery fire against active enemy guns, and observed fire against the most lucrative targets. From October 11 to November 7, the Third Army limited its total expenditure in all calibers to 76,325 rounds, which was less than the army would fire in a single day in the great battle coming in December. In the DRAGOON forces, the artillery commander of the VI corps could spend only enough ammunition to support one division in the attack at a time. Hoping to take the offensive in November, Bradley's armies were to be rationed under a plan that would give the First Army 50.1 percent of the available supply, the small Ninth Army supporting the First 22.8 percent, and the Third Army 27.1 percent.

The Air Arm

On October 22, General Marshall told Eisenhower that the Combined Chiefs of Staff wanted to study ways they might possibly generate an all-out offensive in Europe that might yet reverse disappointment and restore early Sepember's prospects of winning the war before the end of the year. Marshall and his colleagues and advisers had in mind particularly the release of new weapons whose use had been restricted lest their methods of manufacture fall into the hands of the enemy. The variable time (VT) or proximity fuze was the most notable example of such a weapon. The fuze triggered a shell electronically when it neared a target, and the British credited it with the success of their antiaircraft batteries against the V-weapon threat. But the "funny fuze," as Patton was to call it, had been kept out of ground combat to prevent the enemy's capturing a specimen. In addition, Marshall and the CCS were considering immediate commitment of reserves and stockpiles of men and equipment without regard to what might remain at the end of the year. They also contemplated eliminating all strategic air force operations that did not immediately reduce German combat capacity.

The latter suggestion can be interpreted as a partial implied acknowledgment that too large a share of Allied resources might have been devoted to strategic bombing. Though he was first a ground soldier, Marshall had been a consistent advocate of the Combined Bomber Offensive, and he probably would have made no explicit admission of doubt about strategic bombing. Still, not the least disconcerting aspect of the German revival was the continuing rise of German war production in the face of the Bomber

Offensive. The only critical shortages hampering German war industry in the autumn of 1944, after a summer in which the Allied heavy bombers had returned their main effort overwhelmingly to their independent campaign, were in oil and communications.

Not until September 14 had the Combined Chiefs directed Eisenhower to restore General Spaatz's United States Strategic Air Foces and Air Chief Marshal Harris's RAF Bomber Command to direct CCS control. Until then the command arrangements for OVERLORD had persisted, and Spaatz as well as Eisenhower would have preferred to continue them indefinitely. The British had urged a change, however, at the second Québec conference in August 1944, because the Chief of Air Staff, Marshal Portal, and the Air Ministry wanted to regain firmer control over Harris, a willful gentleman.

In the spring, the British had resisted SHAEF control of Bomber Command in part so they could keep at least one major segment of the war effort as long as possible distinctively British. Now, strange to tell, Portal's motive was largely the reverse of that. The Chief of Air Staff had become a convert to Spaatz's Oil Plan as the true medium for fulfilling the old promises of victory through air power. Portal wanted to remove Bomber Command from Eisenhower's tolerant and minimal control, to have a go at forcing Harris's Lancasters and their huge bombloads into the campaign against petroleum.

General Arnold, chief of the AAF, went along with Portal's desires largely because removing Spaatz from subordination to Eisenhower would come close to making Spaatz coequal with Portal, as Arnold's delegate in exercising CCS authority and as commander of all American air power in Europe. Eisenhower objected, but the two air members of the CCS together prevailed and the change occurred, though Eisenhower retained the right to call for direct support of the ground forces by the heavy bombers. Yet the new arrangements made little difference to the heavy bombers' availability for the ground campaign, Harris's participation in the Oil Plan, or anything else. Eisenhower possessed at least the prestige and the strength of character to control Harris on those occasions when he wanted to. Portal did not. Harris became more independent than before.

However that might be, Spaatz had amply earned Portal's conversion to the Oil Plan. As early as June 8, two days after D-Day, Spaatz had taken advantage of Eisenhower's generously loose rein upon the strategic bombers to order both the Eighth and the Fifteenth Air Forces that the denial of oil to the enemy's armed forces should be their primary aim. German aircraft and armaments production were specified as secondary targets, with ball bearings to receive particular attention. Even with Ike's generosity, diverse calls upon the heavy bombers, including CROSSBOW raids as well as support of the ground forces, restricted oil targets to 11.6 percent of the American strategic bombers' efforts in June, 17 percent in July, and 16.4 percent in August. Yet this restricted effort cut the amount of aviation fuel produced for the Luftwaffe from 156,000 tons in May to 54,000 tons in June, 34,700 in July, 17,000 in August, and 10,000 in September—while the Luftwaffe had consumed 165,000 tons in April alone. Production of other petroleum products dropped by similar disastrous proportions. Even to the extent that they could scrounge up oil for combat, the Germans could no longer afford to expend it for adequate training of either Luftwaffe pilots or tank crews; the contrast between the usual quality of the German army and the frequent ineptitude of the newly formed panzer brigades was an index to the merits of Spaatz's Oil Plan. In September 1944, there impended for Germany a paralysis of all its internal combustion engines that threatened the immediate undermining of the whole Miracle of the West, and the immediate defeat of the Reich, despite MARKET-GARDEN and the stoutness of the West Wall.

But Portal could not prevail on Harris to bring the great weight of Bomber Command to Spaatz's aid; and after a massive late-summer climax of the Oil Plan—USSTAF attacks sending 1,136, 888, and 718 aircraft against synthetic oil plants on September 11, 12, and 13 respectively—a rainy autumn closed in and the oil campaign fell off. Not knowing how much Spaatz was accomplishing, other Allied commanders, ground and air, still failed like Harris to offer full support, diversions still carried the Fortresses and Liberators elsewhere, and when diversions combined with autumn weather, the Reich oil supply received the respite it needed. Production of aviation fuel recovered to 21,000 tons in October, 39,500 tons in November, and 24,500 tons in December, other types of petroleum production again responding proportionately. The Allies had held victory through air power in their grasp but had not persevered to the kill.

In part, the failure to persevere sprang from disillusionment flowing from other phases of the Bomber Offensive. During the summer months of 1944, both USSTAF and Bomber Command reached the peak of their activity and power. At the same time and into the autumn, German war production also achieved ever higher peaks. The reasons for this dismaying juxtaposition were complex, and they by no means altogether discredited the Combined Bomber Offensive. One of the most basic factors was the failure of Germany to mobilize fully heretofore, so there had remained a considerable excess capacity in the German economy, waiting to be turned to war production. Nevertheless, a full summer of intense strategic bombing, with growing ability to find industrial targets on overcast days, appeared to have failed either to cripple the German economy in anything like the measure for which the prewar prophets of air power had hoped, or to influence the land battle decisively.

In these circumstances, Marshall's suggestion to reexamine bombing strategy in search of a means to end the war quickly helped prompt Marshal Tedder and the Air Ministry to revive the Transportation Plan, to be directed this time against the Reich itself. Tedder issued on October 25 a paper describing the existing strategic bombing campaign as a "rather patchwork" effort.[2] He argued that the German rail and water transport system was essential to the functioning of everything else in the enemy economy, and he suggested that if the Allies concentrated their whole aerial effort against this transport system in the western part of Germany, they might produce a German collapse within a matter of weeks.

The American Joint Planning Staff in Washington was skeptical, and senior American air officers for the most part supported Spaatz's predictable defense of the oil campaign. Tedder's proposal was debated at a conference of senior SHAEF officials on October 28. Spaatz restated his arguments for first priority for oil, but he conceded that Tedder's Transportation Plan might get a trial as the strategic bombers' second-priority effort, displacing armaments depots. Spaatz and the British were then able to reach quick accord on a detailed plan for the transportation attacks. They divided Germany into nine zones, of which the approaches to the Ruhr, Frankfurt-Mannheim, and Cologne-Koblenz were to be the three accorded greatest attention. In these zones the heavy bombers would attack marshaling yards, mediums and fighter-bombers would strike railway repair installations and power centers and finish off smaller targets that might escape the heavies within the main rail centers, and fighter-bombers would cut lines and shoot up rail traffic whenever opportunity offered. RAF Bomber Command was to take on the waterways as well as the marshaling yards.

One reason for such ready agreement was the absence of the irritating personality of Leigh-Mallory. The Americans had just succeeded, on October 15, in removing him and his AEAF headquarters from the scene. Disliking AEAF as much as its chief, and thus leaving it largely to British direction, American air officers took the opportunity of Eisenhower's assuming direct command of the ground forces to suggest an arrangement for air command parallel to the ground arrangments. Just as each of the army group commanders reported directly to SHAEF, so the tactical air forces supporting the army groups might logically be coordinated by SHAEF. Tedder joined the RAF staff members of AEAF in arguing, rather, that there ought to be an overall Allied air command—not necessarily AEAF—reporting to a small air staff at SHAEF. Without unified air command, they argued, an already overburdened Eisenhower would have to decide too many questions concerning air power and outside his expertise.

Given the shortcomings of such central command as SHAEF provided even for the ground forces, this latter objection to divided air command was scarcely unreasonable. American officers at AEAF grasped at Tedder's suggestions to accept the idea of a new Allied air headquarters but to draw up details that would assure American domination of it. Since transferring another Allied agency to practical American control was not what the British had in mind, agreement did not yet emerge. Instead, everyone at length fell back on an air staff at SHAEF, but one large enough to shield Eisenhower from most air decisions. Air Marshal J.M. Robb headed the new staff. Most Americans found him more agreeable than Leigh-Mallory but, not having got what they wanted, they allowed his organization to remain mostly British. Effective coordination of tactical air with the ground forces still had to occur at other levels, often informally. As for Leigh-Mallory, he was reassigned to the China-Burma-India Theater and lost his life in an air crash on the way.

Whatever complaints there were about SHAEF's being too remote from the battle front, Eisenhower was too close and possessed too much common sense to expect that any of this juggling of commands, priorities, and strategic expedients would accomplish General Marshall's objective of a rapid end to the war. Marshall urged Eisenhower to "Be frank with me"[3] about the prospects. With Antwerp still closed at this juncture, Eisenhower replied that his principal efforts had to be directed toward Antwerp and better logistical support, without which little else could be achieved. He still needed "infantry under an accelerated flow," but logistics was already getting in the way of that object. As for bombers, Eisenhower still favored the oil program. The heavies had not been used recently in direct tactical support of the battleline for two reasons. "First, practically all of our heavy bomber work has had to be done through overcast with special technique and this technique is not repeat not suitable for tactical work. Second, we know that in these conditions our best bet is to keep hammering constantly at the enemy's oil."[4]

This candid analysis notwithstanding, and despite a climate of disillusionment with the strategic bombers that had penetrated the air forces themselves, it remained hard to abandon all hope that the war might end before the new year, and that somehow air power might rescue the deadlocked ground armies to do the job. Despite the disappointments of the Combined Bomber Offensive, Tedder was describing the American as well as the British army when he wrote to Portal on October 25: "As you are aware, the British Army have for months now been allowed to feel that they can, at any time, call on heavy bomber effort, and it will be laid on practically without question. . . . I am doing my best to get things straight, but I am sure you will realise that, the Army having been drugged with bombs, it is going to be a difficult process to cure the drug addicts."[5]

The American drug addicts had made it almost an article of faith that the COBRA bombing accounted for the COBRA breakout. When General Bradley and his army commanders planned for a resumption of the offensive in November, they requested an aerial preparation to dwarf COBRA.

On November 7, American air and ground commanders conferring at Ninth Air Force headquarters approved a plan for Operation QUEEN, a new lunge toward the Roer and the Rhine by Hodges's First and Simpson's Ninth Armies. The QUEEN air plan contained three variations to allow for vagaries of weather. If weather permitted, QUEEN was to open with the aid of 4,500 airplanes, about half of them heavy bombers. Its aerial preparation would exceed both the COBRA effort of 1,495 heavies and 338 fighter-bombers, and the GOODWOOD assault by 1,676 heavies and 343 mediums and lights.

In front of the First Army, three divisions of Eighth Air Force heavies, more than 1,200 Fortresses and Liberators, were to attack personnel and field installations in the Eschweiler-Weisweiler industrial area and the Langerwehe-Jüngersdorf urban complex. To protect Hodges's troops from bombing errors, the heavies were to drop their loads at least three times as far in front of the line of departure as the 1,200-yard COBRA safety zone. While the B-17s and B-24s attacked obstacles in the immediate path of the First Army's projected advance, an equal number of Bomber Command aircraft were to assail the towns of Düren, Jülich, and Heinsberg, somewhat farther to the rear, to block roads and intersections over which German reinforcements might move. Of eleven groups, some 600 planes, of the 9th Bombardment Division, part would similarly bomb the towns of Linnich and Aldenhoven in front of the Ninth Army. The remaining mediums would attack personnel and field installations around the villages of Luchem, Echtz, and Mariaweiler, in front of the First Army. The fighter-bombers were to operate mainly on call in support of their usual ground partners, though three groups from IX TAC were to hit three specific areas in the direct path of the main ground attack. Some 750 fighter-bombers would be available. Many more American and British fighters would escort the heavy and medium bombers.

Beyond increasing the safety zone between the ground troops' line of departure and the bombing area, the Americans planned other elaborate safeguards against repetition of COBRA's short bombing. Two giant white panel markers behind the First Army were to guide pilots toward the target areas. About three kilometers behind the front, eleven captive balloons borrowed from the British were to fly at about 600 meters in a line parallel to the front. The troops would display brightly colored panels, four to a mile, 500 yards behind the front. Bomb bays were to be opened and locked over the English Channel to assure against accidental droppings during the opening process.

The depressingly familiar bad weather of the autumn postponed QUEEN from the target date of November 11 to November 16, when the commanders decided the ground attack must begin with or without aerial preparation. During the morning of the 16th, the skies cleared over the Continent. Though fog persisted in England and interfered with takeoffs, 1,191 Eighth Air Force heavies, 1,188 Bomber Command heavies, and eighty mediums made their runs, along with numerous fighter-bombers. The air attacks killed only one American soldier, when apparently a faulty release mechanism dropped four bombs early. But neither did the air attacks produce any military damage to the enemy proportionate to the costs and the risks. Pushing back the bomb line to protect American troops also protected the Germans' front-line troops; casualties among them were few. German artillery absorbed somewhat harder blows, and its fire was relatively light during the rest of the first day of the offensive. Jülich, Düren, and Eschweiler were devastated, with harmful results to German communications, and with the near-annihilation of an artillery battalion and other units of the 47th Volksgrenadier Division that happened to be detraining at Jülich. Bradley implied his extravagant anticipations but accurately summed up the effects: " . . . though the air bombing had shattered an enemy division and churned up the neighboring terrain, it failed to tear a hole in the line through which our infantry and tanks could be pushed to the Rhine."[6] It did not even permit a first day's advance of more than three kilometers on the Ninth Army front, and much less on the First Army front. In succeeding days, QUEEN stumbled; the bombing did not open the way to another breakthrough.

21: Lorraine (II)

IN A MORE realistic mood than when he dreamed that QUEEN's air attack might blast open another breakthrough in the COBRA style, Bradley wrote later that "Allied superiority on the ground was not calculated to inspire long odds on any winter offensive."[1] Hodges's First and Simpson's Ninth Armies together had only fourteen divisions on the ninety kilometers of their front north of the Ardennes. Patton's Third Army, which had given up the XV Corps to Patch's Seventh Army so the corps could be supplied through Marseille, had nine divisions spread over a 135-kilometer front. None of Bradley's armies could take the offensive with more than a nominal reserve.

Nevertheless, when Eisenhower had met with his senior officers at Brussels on October 18, the idea of digging in for the winter received only perfunctory, pro forma attention. The Allies were not so weak that they must award the enemy a whole season's respite for further recovery. Though the drive to open Antwerp was still incomplete, and access to the Scheldt would be necessary to support any drive far into Germany, a month of relative stability had improved the logistical outlook enough to encourage the notion of a November push aimed at the Rhine. The Brussels site for the conference assured that Montgomery would have no excuse not to attend. His presence guaranteed another reprise of the single-thrust versus broad-front debate. In the American perception of him, Monty came into the conference "as a little monarch with a fantastic parachute scarf wrapped around his battle jacket and hanging halfway to his knees."[2] But by now the field marshal was too much ensnared in the toils of the Scheldt to urge that his 21 Army Group carry the major eastward burden very soon. Once the Scheldt was open, Montgomery would still have the Peel Marshes to deal with before he could go forward. With Montgomery thus constrained to temporary acquiescence, there was nothing to prevent the conference's endorsement of a November effort to close up to the Rhine along a broad front.

To carry out the conference's decisions, Eisenhower issued the orders that Bradley fashioned into the plan for QUEEN. The First Army was to attack as soon as possible, preferably between November 1 and 5, to reach the Rhine and grasp a foothold on its east bank at Cologne. The Ninth Army was to attack on the left flank of the First, because Bradley had decided on October 9 to shift control of the VIII Corps in the Ardennes to the First Army, and to move Simpson's headquarters northward for insertion between Hodges and the British. Simpson initially took over the XIX Corps. Bradley foresaw that, sooner or later, Montgomery's shortage of manpower would persuade Eisenhower to yield to the field marshal's requests for a full American army in 21 Army Group. When that happened, Bradley did not want to give up his most experienced army, his own first command on the Continent, to Monty. Moreover, the prickly General Hodges presided over a staff headed by the prickly General Kean, and over an army so accustomed to being first in priority as well as in name among American forces that First Army headquarters treated primacy as a natural right; this combination of temperaments and attitudes would not have boded well for harmonious subordination to such a personality as Montgomery. Besides, while returning to the broad-front strategy, Eisenhower continued to insist that the main effort should be north of the Ardennes; sending the Ninth Army north fitted this strategic conception, while also promising to allay the persistent shortage of troops along the interallied boundary.

Simpson was instructed, in fact, that once he reached the Rhine, his troops were to turn northward to help the British clear the region between the Rhine and the Maas. The enemy salient in that area, its intractability under pressure, and within a few days the spoiling attack that the XLVII Panzer Corps launched from it, so troubled Montgomery that, following his unwonted docility at Brussels, he also begged off the assignment in Eisenhower's postconference directive to attack southeast from Nijmegen. He could do so, Montgomery said, only after he had cleared the Peel Marshes, a task that could begin only after the Scheldt was well in hand, and that in fact began only on November 14. In November as in October, Hodges would have to sustain the principal Allied offensive, though aided now by Simpson.

Eisenhower's directive for the new offensive looked also toward an eventual attack by the First and Ninth Armies beyond the Rhine to encircle the Ruhr, the First Army enveloping the industrial region from the south, the Ninth Army from the north. But this scheme probably awaited a fairly distant future; mentioning it may have been intended as much as anything to appease the continuing delusion in Washington that there might yet be a rapid end to the war.

As for Patton's Third Army, it still waited at the far end of the logistical queue. On September 21, Bradley approved a daily allowance of supplies giving 700 tons to the still-small Ninth Army, 3,500 tons to the Third Army, and all that was left, with a guaranteed minimum of 5,000 tons, to the First Army. The Brussels conference set no date for Patton to renew the offensive, agreeing only that the Third Army would advance again "when logistics permit," driving northeastward to cover Hodges's right flank.[3]

The immediate future of Devers's 6th Army Group depended on Patton's actions. Patch's grinding October advance through the western foothills of the Vosges was slowly carrying Devers's troops toward one of the historic gateways into Germany, the Belfort Gap, the low pass little more than 300 meters high and some twenty to thirty kilometers wide between the Vosges on the one hand and the Jura Mountains and the Swiss border on the other. Though Marius had halted the Teutons in the Belfort pass at Aquae Sextiae, and Caesar had defeated Ariovistus near present Mulhouse, for centuries thereafter the Germans had more successfully used Belfort as their gateway to the Rhône valley and the south: "The Pass of Belfort is the strategic key to Central Europe."[4] But the Seventh Army's deadlock near the Moselle had set Devers to rebuilding roads, railways, and bridges along the 800 kilometers back to Marseille as a necessary preliminary to exploiting the gateway, and even with his logistical house in order Devers would need additional help. The French First Army was practically immobilized by the process of "whitening" its colonial divisions, whose African troops were already troubled by the cold of the Vosges in the autumn months; integrating into the ranks detachments of the FFI, furthermore, was a delicate political process with large implications for the hitherto rightist army of the French Republic. For the time being, an attack by Devers's army group would have to be an attack by Patch's army; but Patch himself lacked the means to regain headway through the Vosges alone, and so would have to depend on help from Patton.

With Devers's plans thus hanging on Patton's course, and Patton left in suspense by the Brussels conference, Bradley again came to the rescue of his most dependably aggressive subordinate. Bradley was beginning to contemplate a deeper encirclement of the Ruhr than that envisaged by Eisenhower's latest directive. The commander of the 12th Army Group could conceive of the Third Army's closing the ring on the Ruhr from a wide sweep across the upper Rhine and thence far eastward and northward into the Reich. With such thoughts for the future, Bradley issued his instructions for immediate activities to his army commanders on October 21, the day of the fall of Aachen. He confirmed that the First and Ninth Armies should attack on November 5. While he did not believe the Brussels decisions permitted him to award Patton a more generous allocation of supplies than the 3,500 tons he stipulated this same day, he decided nevertheless that he could allow Patton to attack under the Third Army commander's promises that his staff had designed a strictly limited, controlled, secondary operation to cross the Sarre River and thus bring the Third Army up to the West Wall. Bradley gave Patton a starting date—November 10.

With friends and enemies alike, Patton could be depended upon to exploit any opening he perceived. Bradley and Leven Allen visited Patton on October 22. Though Patton could joke by greeting such callers with "Well, what are you going to take away from me today?" it was he who invariably assumed the offensive in conference as eagerly as in the field. If Bradley intended to let him attack on November 10, why not now? Bradley agreed to November 5 as a compromise date for Patton to move—the same day assigned to Hodges and Simpson. Of course, Patton as usual was working upon Bradley's own inclinations: "General [Bradley] reluctant to push first one army and then the other but would rather hop them off together to prevent German from playing reserves before us."[5]

In the event, the shortage of men and divisions gave Patton the satisfaction of starting first. Bradley decided to wait for the return of the 104th Infantry and 7th Armored Divisions from the British before launching his northern armies. Awaiting these formations would yield the additional advantage of British activity on Simpson's left—Montgomery's drive into the Peel Marshes—soon after the First and Ninth Armies kicked off. Simpson might also be able to begin with the new 102nd Division in hand, now just arriving, and perhaps with the new 84th as well. But, impatient for action to resume somewhere, Bradley asked Patton on November 2 whether the Third Army could begin the attack alone. The answer was not surprising. Bradley and Patton agreed that the Third Army would advance as soon as weather was favorable, and whatever the weather, no later than November 8.

Metz and the Lorraine Gateway

The rains that had fallen with extraordinary persistence through June and July had abated for little more than a month, in August and early September. Now again they fell incessantly, to minimize the American advantages in air power, mobility, and quantities of equipment in general. The Third Army proved unable to march until November 8, and then it went forward without aerial preparation, slogging through sheets of cold rain, with the muddy clay of Lorraine clinging to its boots and tank treads, and a flooded Moselle in the path of its left wing. "I hope that in the final settlement of the war, you insist that the Germans retain Lorraine," Patton wrote Secretary of War Henry L. Stimson, "because I can imagine no greater burden than to be the owner of this nasty country where it rains every day and where the whole wealth of the people consists in assorted manure piles."[6]

While officially at rest and replenishing supplies during October, Patton had occupied the month with local attacks to keep his army's combat edge sharp and to improve his launching ground for the next offensive. The 90th Division refreshed its aptitude in the assault upon fortifications by means of a miniature but prolonged battle for the factories and slag piles of the industrial town of Maizières-lès-Metz, to close up to the Moselle just north of the city of Metz. In the 5th Division south of Metz, Colonel Charles W. Yuill of the 11th Infantry Regiment proposed to utilize leisure for a meticulous set-piece attack by his 2nd Battalion, suggested by the battalion commander, against Fort Driant. From its hilltop south of the city and just west of the Meuse, this fort had helped ruin the Dornot bridgehead and would continue to harry any crossing south of Metz or any effort to strike down the Moselle from above the city. It could also turn its guns northward to enfilade the right flank of troops advancing on Metz directly from the west.

Unfortunately for the idea of a meticulously planned assault, Yuill was unable to lay his hands on detailed diagrams of Fort Driant until after his attack had begun. Then the plans were discovered in Lyon, where a French officer had hidden them in 1940. It did not require the plans, however, to inform the American command that Driant was one of the strongest and most modern of the Metz fortifications, built in 1902 by the Germans and later strengthened by both French and Germans, its main enceinte guarded by four outlying casemate batteries, each with three 100 or 150mm. guns, and with a fifth battery further detached and covering the southern face. Colonel Yuill's division commander, General Irwin, was skeptical of the idea of an assault, but he allowed Yuill to sell his plan to General Walker, who in turn sold it to Patton. The redeeming feature of the plan was intelligence's assurance of the weakness of the Driant garrison.

The attack began September 27. Having the plans before the first effort might have saved some casualties, but it would doubtless have made no difference in the outcome. As Irwin anticipated, Driant proved much too strong, whatever the deficiencies of the garrison, to be captured by a battalion or by Yuill's whole regiment, except perhaps with prohibitive losses. Yuill's men worked their way to the top of the fort readily enough, but worming into the tunnels simply led to bloody head-on assaults against German barricades along the way. Neither high-explosive bombs nor napalm dropped from P-47s did much damage, nor did such artillery concentrations as the ammunition shortage permitted the XX Corps to work up. An 8-inch howitzer scored eight direct hits on one of the turrets, only to have the turret return its fire fifteen minutes later. "Snakes," long tubes filled with explosives and intended to be pushed through barbed wire, broke almost immediately against the German wire. Day after day of battle confused the Germans enough that an American messenger was able to wander by mistake into the guard room of the enceinte and walk out again, but this little contretemps told nothing about the enemy's determination to go on resisting. By early on October 4, Captain Jack S. Gerrie of Company G reported:

> The situation is critical. A couple more barrages and another counterattack and we are sunk. We have no men, our equipment is shot and we just can't go on. The troops in G are done, they are just here, what is left of them. We cannot advance, nor can K Co. Co. B is in the same shape as I am. We cannot delay any longer on replacement. We may be able to hold till dark but if anything happens this afternoon I can make no predictions. The enemy artillery is butchering these troops until we have nothing left to hold with. We cannot get out our wounded. . . . They have all of these places zeroed in by arty. The forts have 5 to 6 feet thick walls inside and 15 foot roofs of reinforced concrete. All our charges have been useless against this stuff. The few leaders are trying to keep what is left intact and that is all they can do. The troops just are not sufficiently trained and what is more they have no training even in basic infantry. Everything is committed and we cannot follow the attack plan. This is just a suggestion but if we want this damned fort let's get the stuff required and take it and then go. Right now you haven't got it.[7]

Having allowed himself to accept Yuill's plan, and having explained it in glowing terms to Eisenhower when the Supreme Commander visited the Third Army on September 29, Patton responded to frustration by telling Walker on the day of Gerrie's message that he must seize Driant "if it took every man in the XX Corps, but he could not allow an attack by this Army to fail."[8] As at Brest, the American army had put its shoulder to the wheel.

Yet beneath Patton's damn-the-torpedos façade was a considerable measure of good sense, and in spite of his histrionics—or perhaps because of the self-protection they afforded him—he was enough surer of himself than Bradley had been at Brest to concede at least tacit admission of a mistake. Notwithstanding the October 4 message to Walker, five days later Patton sent the trusted Hap Gay to the front to talk frankly with Walker, Irwin, and their principal subordinates about breaking off the engagement. Gay ordered the effort abandoned and Fort Driant evacuated of Americans. All were withdrawn by the night of October 12–13. Patton, Gay, Walker, and their staffs returned to planning the capture of Metz by envelopment.

On November 3, the day after Bradley asked the Third Army to open the offensive alone, Walker's headquarters issued its directive for the taking of Metz and the destruction and capture of its defenders. The actions at Driant and Maizières-lès-Metz had not distracted XX Corps headquarters enough to keep Walker's staff from compiling a plan so detailed that its maps showed every building in the city that was known to be occupied by the enemy—a remarkable change from the free-wheeling style of the Third Army in August, and another indication of the reversion of warfare to much of the manner of World War I.

For the new assault on Metz, Patton had arranged for the XX Corps to be reinforced to three infantry divisions and one armored—the familiar 5th and 90th Infantry, Major General Harry L. Twaddle's new 95th Infantry, and Major General W.H.H. Morris's new 10th Armored.

The 95th Division took over the 90th's sector west of Metz, permitting the 90th to shift north. Opposite Königsmacker, where there were outlying works of the fortress system some nine kilometers northeast of Thionville, the 90th was to cross the Moselle and swing southeastward. Simultaneously the 5th Division would attack from its hard-won bridgehead beyond the Moselle south of the city and press northeastward to converge upon the 90th. Meanwhile the 95th Division was to contain the German salient west of Metz. Once the circle had closed east of the city, the 95th would advance across the Moselle to capture Metz.

Patton believed Metz must be taken despite its demonstrated recalcitrance because otherwise it would be too dangerous a thorn in the side of the Third Army's main immediate operation, to drive to and across the Sarre River to the West Wall. To hasten this main purpose, while part of the 10th Armored Division moved on the 90th Division's right to help close the encirclement, another part was to push east toward the Sarre to prepare for the whole division's eventual crossing around Merzig. Furthermore, the XX Corps effort against Metz was not to be the first move of the Third Army's offensive. Rather, Walker's attack was to follow by one day the opening of General Eddy's XII Corps drive toward the Sarre from Eddy's bridgehead east of Nancy.

Eddy did not confront fortifications such as those of Metz. The Nancy sector presented natural barriers instead. Here the Third Army advance had carried roughly to the 1871 Franco-German border. The XII Corps lay on the Lorraine Plain among the slight hills and dales of the lowland through which flows the meandering Seille River. Just ahead lay another of the succession of heights that rise gradually across France from Paris to the Vosges, these less elevated above the surrounding countryside than many, but nevertheless offering advantages of observation and defense sufficient that at least one of them, the Côte de Delme, is reputed to have shaped the pre-1914 boundary—the victorious Germans of 1871 having been careful to include it within the Reich. At the beginning of November 1944, the exceptionally steep western slope of the Delme Ridge faced General McBride's 80th Division across the Seille on the XII Corps left.

Farther south, the center and right of Eddy's corps confronted two hill bastions projecting westward from a higher hill system. These are known usually by the names of the nearest towns, the northern bastion as the Morhange plateau for Morhange (Mörchingen) at its southeastern base, the southern one as the Dieuze plateau for Dieuze near its south-central base. Both are sometimes named, too, for the forests that cover large parts of them, the Forêt de Château-Salins climbing over the southwestern part of the Morhange plateau, the Forêt de Bride et de Köcking overlying nearly all of the Dieuze plateau. From the XII Corps positions, one road toward the Sarre River rises from Château-Salins up and across the Morhange plateau through the road center of Morhange itself and on to Sarreguemines. The attacker traversing it would be fighting along a narrow forest trace easily blocked. But the alternative road from Moyenvic through Dieuze to Mittersheim, and thence northeast to Sarre-Union or southeast to Sarrebourg, runs through a fringe of marshes and is dominated by the Dieuze plateau just to the north. Between the Morhange and Dieuze plateaus a railway follows the constricted valley of the Little Seille, shadowed by both bastions. Once past these various obstacles, the attacker would find himself having to cross the Sarre River on a narrow front between the Saar Heights on the north and, on the south, a tangle of forests, swamps, and lakes within the triangle Dieuze-Mittersheim-Gondrexange. The Lorraine gateway is a classic invasion route between France and Germany, but its advantages clearly are relative.

From much the same positions that the Third Army occupied, Castelnau's French

Second Army and the left wing of Dubail's First Army had commenced General Joffre's invasion of Germany via the Lorraine gateway on August 14, 1914. The opposing German line then as in 1944 stretched along the crest of the Côte de Delme and thence across the Morhange and Dieuze plateaus, its observers and guns looking down on the entire Seille lowland. Already in 1914, the Germans had created much the kind of trench system that was to become grimly familiar throughout the Western Front for the next four years, and remains of the system were still usable to the defender's advantage in 1944. The French in the 1914 Battles of the Frontier elected to screen the Côte de Delme while making their main efforts against the slightly less forbidding Morhange and Dieuze plateaus. Their XV Corps slipped along the southern base of the southern bastion to Dieuze, only to find itself on August 19–20 unable to climb out of the marshes against the fire of the Germans on the plateau north of them. General Ferdinand Foch's XX Corps of Castelnau's army penetrated up the valley of the Little Seille and across the western tip of the Morhange plateau, but by August 20 Foch too was hurling his troops vainly against the steep southern face of the plateau he must conquer, just short of Morhange. Once the French had exhausted themselves, the German Sixth Army of Prince Rupprecht of Bavaria counterattacked, its infantry pouring down from both plateaus and in a torrent into the valleys, immensely aided by the ability of heavier German guns to silence the French 75s. Foch's corps fought a rearguard action at Château-Salins while Castelnau prepared for the defense of Nancy in what was to become the Battle of the Grand Couronné.

In 1944, the shoe was on the other foot as far as weight of munitions was concerned; otherwise, Patton and Eddy could have expected nothing more than to recapitulate the unhappy experiences of Castelnau and Foch. But as the new, 1944 Battles of the Frontier had already amply shown, the American advantage was slight unless the rains relented enough to let the Jabos attack. The mud was sure to undercut American superiority in quantities of tanks, especially because the wider treads of German tanks made them better performers in bad weather. The terrain that had served the Germans so well thirty years ago had not changed.

From the Côte de Delme to Faulquemont

Rain persisted through the first days of November with no promise of remission. Late on November 7, General Eddy urged that the downpours, the mud, and the swollen rivers demanded postponement of the offensive. Patton invited him to name his successor. The corps commander thereupon bit his tongue, and on November 8 Patton ordered the Third Army to "Play ball!"

Echoing again the First World War, Patton and Eddy had decided to forego surprise in the hope of devastating the enemy's forward positions with an intense artillery barrage, all the more important because the rains kept the airplanes grounded. In accordance with the Third Army's current style of planning, the artillery had received an elaborate scheme of instructions by November 5 and carefully registered its guns. Seventeen battalions of corps artillery were to fire a preliminary bombardment for three and a half hours, from H-Hour minus sixty minutes to H plus 150. Twenty battalions of division artillery were to join in for the first thirty minutes. Close behind the infantry advance, the 90mm. antiaircraft guns, the 3-inch guns of the tank destroyers, and the 105mm. howitzers of the regimental cannon companies would also contribute to the plastering.

Like Walker's XX Corps, Eddy's XII had been reinforced for the new offensive. It was an impressive aggregation of three infantry and two armored divisions. Alongside the veteran 35th and 80th Infantry, Eddy had Major General Willard S. Paul's new 26th Division, built upon the New England National Guard, one of the most famous American World War I divisions and in that war one of the first to enter battle. In armor, Eddy was privileged to command both Wood's 4th Armored and Grow's 6th Armored, as formidable a combination of tanks and tank leaders as the American army had to offer.

Colonel Koch, the Third Army's consistently effective G-2, had fortified Eddy with what proved an accurate estimate of the enemy's front-line strength. About 15,000 men and twenty tanks or assault guns of the 48th Division and the 559th Volksgrenadier Division, XIII SS Corps, held the German right to just west of Moyenvic. The 361st Volksgrenadier Division of the LXXXIX Corps held the enemy left from near Moyenvic to the Marne-Rhin Canal. Behind the front, General von Knobelsdorff's First Army had the 11th Panzer Division in reserve. Though weakened in the Arracourt tank battles, the Ghost Division still needed no descriptive comment to emphasize its quality. The 48th had been hard hit while retreating through Luxembourg in September, and overaged men had replaced its losses. The 559th VG was known to Eddy's men from their first battles in Lorraine; it was good. The 361st VG had been formed from sailors, Luftwaffe ranks, and other miscellanies but had veteran officers and NCOs; its artillery and train were entirely horse-drawn, so it had brought to the battlefield and was able to maneuver its full complement of guns, the petroleum shortage notwithstanding.

This array of German strength no longer matched the kind of power the enemy First Army had mustered when it was initially reconstituted to stop Patton. German formations were being spirited away from the front for purposes unknown, about which the still-confident Americans failed to develop as much curiosity as would have been healthy. Nevertheless, German strength favored nothing like Patton's boast that he would reach the West Wall, sixty-five kilometers from the XII Corps, "in not to exceed D plus 2 days."[9] He may have been playing his confidence-man routine to make sure that Bradley and Eisenhower did not turn off the green light for his attack.

The American disinclination to concentrate power was rarely more apparent. While the First and Ninth Armies planned to attack with ten divisions on a thirty-eight-kilometer front, the XII Corps alone had a front of nearly fifty kilometers, the XX Corps an even longer front with a number of salients and reentrants—yet the Third Army was to leap forward virtually along the whole line.

For all the handicaps, the strong artillery preparation got Eddy's XII Corps advance off like a well-executed First World War attack. With the additional difficulty that McBride's 80th Division was to capture rather than merely screen the Côte de Delme, Eddy had little choice but to duplicate Castelnau's tactics of 1914 and charge headlong against the Morhange and Dieuze bastions. If the plan was unsubtle, at least the Americans enjoyed tactical surprise in the timing of their jump-off. The surprise was remarkable not only in light of the artillery preparation, but also because American troops were notoriously garrulous about their army's intentions and notoriously inclined to discuss them over the radio, and because like the French army in 1914 they found German informants exasperatingly numerous in Lorraine. Yet the first German prisoners were both dazed by the artillery and astonished to be hit at all. Evidently the enemy had considered his locks on the Lorraine gateway too secure to be tested, at least in a rainy

November. With this uncanny good luck, the XII Corps almost everywhere attained its first day's objectives.

In 1914–1918, the pace would almost certainly have slowed drastically after the first day through lack of mobility. But Eddy had his two armored divisions, and progress was good enough for him to commit Grow's 6th Armored and CCB of Wood's 4th through the 80th and 35th Divisions on November 9. CCA of the 4th Armored moved up through the 26th Division on November 10. Before nightfall on Thursday the 9th, a task force of the 4th's CCB uncovered the southern flank of the Côte de Delme, permitting infantry of General Baade's 35th Division to take the town of Delme, and forcing the enemy's 48th Division to abandon the commanding Delme ridge to the 80th Division's simultaneous pressure from the front. By that time, Americans were also astride both the Morhange and Dieuze plateaus. The Germans were alarmed enough to begin committing the 11th Panzer Division.

But American and German tanks did not altogether change the pattern of the 1914 fighting. The weather had improved slightly on November 9, to permit XIX TAC to intervene with particularly good effect at the Delme Ridge; but Friday's weather reverted to the usual bad form. Mud, woods, and rugged terrain confined the tanks almost completely to the few good roads. On the ridges, it was Patton's infantry that had to carry the battle against networks of German trenches, foxholes, breastworks, dugouts roofed with concrete and steel, barbed wire, and machine guns. The woods and the enemy's inveterate counterattacks and infiltration back into any vacuum forced the Americans to drop more and more of their strength to guard their lines of communication.

Patton insisted on marching fire as the surest tactical means of keeping the advance going under such circumstnces. Though slowed down, by November 12 the 35th Division and Wood's CCB had crossed the Nied Française River and cleared the Forest of Château-Salins, to approach Morhange itself. Prisoners said the 559th Volksgrenadiers had orders to hold Morhange to the last man, and General Baade's soldiers found German resistance yet more bitter than usual. Nevertheless, Baade took the town on November 15 and reached the Metz-Sarrebourg railway beyond it that afternoon. To the south, the 26th Division and Wood's CCA found the going at least as tough against the 361st VG Division, and Panthers of the 11th Panzer Division drove two task forces of CCA out of the town of Guébling.

Altogether, the American gains were substantial but far short of any hopes for a rapid leap to the West Wall, let alone a new breakthrough, and the costs were high. The persistent rains and increasing November cold exacted a heavy toll in trench foot and exposure beyond the heavy attrition of close infantry combat. The 26th Division managed to clear the forest atop the Dieuze plateau, but its 328th Infantry Regiment had to evacuate 500 noncombat casualties in the first four days of the offensive. The rifle companies of the Yankee Division's 104th Regiment—the 10th Massachusetts—sank to an average of about fifty men; some companies of the 1/104th were cut down to eight to fifteen effectives. In the 35th Division, a company of the 2/134th Infantry lost all its officers in the course of capturing a suburb of Morhange. While the 80th Division and the 6th Armored had easier going for a time after overrunning the Côte de Delme, by mid-November they ran up against the outlying works of the Falkenberg Stellung, a well prepared defensive complex on the slopes of the Falkenberg of Falquemont. The 48th Division in front of them was being stiffened by the 36th Volksgrenadier Division, whose

Generalmajor August Wellm bore an exceptional reputation as a tactician. Besides, the 80th had an exposed left flank, because the XX Corps to the north had been detained in trying to apply itself as a nutcracker against Metz.

The Taking of La Pucelle

Because Walker's corps kicked off a day later than Eddy's, the interlude of better weather on November 8 afforded Walker a measure of preliminary air support, though not nearly as much as scheduled. The heavies and mediums mostly had to bomb by instrument, so their effectiveness was minimal; but it was good to have XIX TAC at work. Because the 90th Division in launching the main attack north of Metz had to begin by crossing the flooded Moselle, the supporting artillery was careful to do no unusual firing until the infantry were under way in assault boats; surprise was essential to a successful crossing. To help assure that the main effort should indeed prove a surprise, the 95th Division's 1st Battalion, 377th Infantry made a diversionary crossing during the preceding night from Uckange south of Thionville.

The desired surprise was achieved. German intelligence in Lorraine was not quite as good as the Americans' sense of the inhabitants' coldness might have implied. With partial inadvertence, the XX Corps had sowed confusion when it shifted the 95th Division into the former positions of the 90th west of Metz. The 95th had gone through an earlier tour in the 5th Division bridgehead south of the city, and German intelligence combined these facts, according to a prisoner, to arrive at the conclusion that the 5th and 90th Divisions had lost so heavily the Americans had consolidated them as the 95th. The Germans did no better in divining where the XX Corps would cross the Moselle. When the vanguard of the 90th Division crossed on the morning of November 9, it found almost no opposition beyond the swirling torrent of the river. Even the flooding of the Moselle was not altogether a problem, because it inundated extensive German mine fields on the east shore, so the assault craft could simply float over them.

Inland, east of the highway and railroad leading south to Thionville and Metz, other minefields eventually halted the progress of the 90th in the early November dusk. Though the Germans had not anticipated an American crossing in this area, they had at least taken the precaution of compensating for a lack of infantry and antitank weapons in the sector with a promiscuous strewing of mines. Many of the tens of thousands of these infernal devices were new plastic and wooden box mines immune to standard mine detectors.

The Germans needed all the help of this sort that they could find. The LXXXII Corps of their First Army held a long front from Metz north to the confluence of the Sarre and the Moselle with only three divisions of doubtful quality. In Metz and its fortifications, OKW had given Division No. 462 a bad bargain: honorific redesignation as the 462nd Volksgrenadier Division, at the very time when the officer- and NCO-candidate regiments that had made the division so potent were replaced by assemblages of overaged and sick troops. North of Metz, the 19th Volksgrenadier Division held the line to a point between Métrich and Königsmacker, and the 416th Division extended for all of fifty-five kilometers thence to the Sarre. Both these divisions, especially the 416th, had more overaged and undertrained than first-rate soldiers. The German First Army called the 416th the "Whipped Cream Division."

Still, the Germans had Lorraine's usual strong positions on which to rally, including

Fort Königsmacker and smaller but similar works at Métrich a little over a kilometer southeast. These the French had incorporated into the Maginot Line, which extended along a ridge southeastward from Königsmacker. Off and on since 1940, the Germans had talked about turning the Maginot Line around to face an invasion from the west. They had never gotten around to doing it, but the guns in the Maginot forts around Königsmacker nevertheless could be pivoted enough to face an attack coming lengthwise along the ridge, and the Americans having selected this sector for their advance had little choice but to mount such an attack.

Fortunately, the 90th began the November offensive as a thoroughly good division. General McLain's handling of it had earned him a corps—the XIX, in succession to Corlett—and since October 15 the 90th was equally well commanded by Brigadier General James A. Van Fleet. A West Point classmate of Eisenhower and Bradley and a wounded veteran of the Argonne, Van Fleet saw his rise in the World War II army strangely stunted; eventually it turned out that General Marshall had confused him with somebody else of similar name, whose competence Marshall distrusted. By D-Day, Van Fleet nevertheless commanded the 8th Infantry Regiment, which he had trained, and led it onto UTAH Beach. Since then he had been making up for lost time with a combat record that removed all doubts about his capacities or identity. At St. Lô and Brest, he was assistant commander of the 2nd Division. In October after coming to the 90th, Van Fleet had planned a coup de main against Fort Königsmacker, which was a miniature version of Fort Driant. Driant had helped teach the Americans not to go down into the tunnels of such works, but to persist in chipping away with satchel charges, thermite grenades, TNT blocks, and dousings of gasoline from above. Infantry and engineers stormed to the top of Fort Königsmacker early on the first day, got themselves well established on its west side by nightfall, and with systematic blasting away at its ferro-concrete forced its surrender as a gift to General Patton on his birthday, which was also Armistice Day (of which convergence of anniversaries Chester Hansen remarked, "The two are incompatible"[10]).

The Moselle was still rising, its inundated area as much as two kilometers wide, and not until the night of November 10–11 were engineers able to complete a bridge, at Malling. Until then, no tanks, tank destroyers, or trucks could cross. Van Fleet had cause to be thankful that the XII Corps, by attacking a day before him, had already begun attracting the 11th Panzer Division to its front. Not until the early morning of November 12 was Army Group G able to work up a counterattack against the 90th Division, executed by a Kampfgruppe of the 25th Panzer Grenadier Division. With some ten tanks and assault guns, this effort broke through the 359th Infantry just east of Kerling and came sweeping down the road toward the American bridge at Malling. At a crossroads south of Petite-Hettange, Lieutenant Colonel Robert Booth of the 2/359th slowed the Germans with a band of cooks and clerks and an intelligence and reconnaissance platoon, wielding bazookas as well as small arms. Two American tank destroyers then crossed the bridge just before the Germans' guns knocked the bridge away. Joining the scuffle at the crossroads, the tank destroyers wrecked two assault guns and immobilized a third, which was enough to cause the Germans to pull back to lick their wounds. Taking a page from the Germans' doctrine, however, Booth gave them no rest, but led a charge of Companies E and G into the flank of the retreating column. Thus he turned retreat into rout.

Working along the Maginot Line ridge and adjacent parallel heights was never easy, and periodically the 90th stumbled into new fields of plastic and wooden mines. But on

November 13 the division completed another Moselle bridge at Cattenom, whereupon all of Van Fleet's heavy supporting equipment could begin coming over. It was a good thing, too, for the advance had gone far enough that the 90th was about to outrun the range of its artillery.

South of Thionville, the 95th Division sent a second battalion over the Moselle into its Uckange bridgehead on Armistice Day, and by November 14 these neighbors of Van Fleet's had captured Forts Yutz and Illange, more of the pre-1914 but troublesome works that seemed to sprout from every other hill. On the same day, the 90th and 95th Division bridgeheads linked up.

The next day, General Twaddle of the 95th gave Colonel Robert L. Bacon all of the division's troops east of the Moselle, the two infantry battalions plus two companies of tank destroyers, one of tanks, and some artillery. Bacon's orders were to clear the east bank of the river south into Metz.

General Morris's 10th Armored Division had been fretting while Walker at corps headquarters hesitated to send it across the 90th Division's bridges as long as the floods as well as German artillery made those spans doubly precarious. The expansion of the 95th Division bridgehead permitted engineers to build a Bailey bridge at Thionville, where there were high retaining walls to confine the Moselle. Here CCB of the 10th crossed on November 15. With the Thionville bridge as an insurance crossing if the floods downstream worsened, Walker also committed CCA over the repaired Malling bridge beginning the same day. The armor proceeded to swing wide eastward and southward to hasten the encirclement of Metz. Roadblocks and enemy antitank guns appeared often enough along the way that Morris had to change his plans to the extent of substituting Shermans for reconnaissance vehicles as his vanguard. But resistance was so spotty that narrow and muddy roads posed at least as much of a problem, and the 10th Armored had to splinter itself into numerous small columns scudding through the mire of the byways. Not until the armor was far enough east to seem to threaten the Sarre River did the Germans bestir themselves to stiffen their resistance.

South of Metz, General Irwin's 5th Division was on its way to meet the three American divisions approaching from the north. Irwin moved out on November 9 almost simultaneously with Van Fleet. Already across the Moselle, the 5th aimed for an area astride the Nied Française River some sixteen kilometers north and east of the line of departure, where the junction completing Metz's envelopment was to occur. The route led through one of the more inviting sections of the Lorraine plain, with no important natural obstacles except the Seille and Nied Rivers, which ordinarily would have presented few difficulties. At the moment, however, both streams were in flood, the Seille nearly 200 meters wide. The crossings were guarded, furthermore, by no less an opponent than the 17th SS Panzer Grenadier Division, filled up with replacements until it was actually overstrength in personnel, though it had few tanks and assault guns.

One compensation for these potential problems proved to be the early establishment of close cooperation between Irwin's infantry and the tanks of CCB of the 6th Armored Division, operating on the neighboring XII Corps left flank and frequently weaving across the corps boundary to the gratification of the 5th Division. Despite the veteran cadres of the 17th SS Panzer Grenadiers, moreover, the replacements were so unpromising that the division had by no means been restored to the standards that had plagued its previous American opponents since Normandy. By November 12, the 2nd Battalion of the 2nd Infantry Regiment had crossed to the east of the Nied Française and was affording welcome assistance to the left flank of the XII Corps's 80th Division. The commander of the 80th, General McBride, had earlier been disturbed about this flank because he had been misinformed that the XX Corps would attack at the same time as the XII on November 8. Just as he was gratified, the Germans evidently were disturbed by this apparent widening of the XII Corps drive toward the Sarre, and they reinforced the 17th ss Panzer Grenadiers with elements of the 21st Panzer Division, to counterattack against the 2nd Infantry on November 13. The counterattack failed, but the XX Corps nevertheless promptly disappointed General McBride again by suspending offensive activity in the Nied bridgehead. Thus the insecurity of McBride's flank as he approached the Falkenberg Stellung. The reason for the change was that Irwin had heard from Walker of a new corps plan; the 5th Division had performed so well against some of the better German formations in the area that Walker was transferring to it from the 95th the task and the honor of capturing the ancient fortress city of Metz.

The 95th Division's seizure of Fort Illange and adjacent works on November 15 had broken contact between the garrison of Metz and the 19th VG Division to the north. About 10:30 A.M. on November 19, Van Fleet's 90th Reconnaissance Troop met the 735th Tank Battalion, attached to the 5th Division, at Pont Marais on the Metz-Saarlouis road, and the encirclement was complete. Knowing Patton's impatience to reach the Sarre River—as in the promise to Bradley to get to the West Wall in two days—Walker immediately turned the 10th Armored from its now redundant wider encirclement onto the roads leading to that river.

American intelligence could deduce an ambivalence in the enemy command about how long to fight for Metz. About the time Patton's November offensive commenced, Hitler had disgorged his usual decree that Metz must be held as a fortress with no withdrawal and no surrender. Marshal von Rundstedt at OB West and General Balck at Army Group G could be assumed not to relish the sacrifice of yet another 14,000 or so troops. While Balck was more likely than Rundstedt to comply with the Führer's wishes in good faith, rather than try to evade them, Balck had notably failed to send any valuable new equipment into Metz. Just before the garrison lost contact with the rest of the LXXXII Corps, OKW gave Hitler's desires as much tangible reinforcement as that loyal headquarters could find by assigning Generalleutnant Heinrich Kittel to the Metz command. Kittel was a specialist in forlorn causes from the Eastern Front, where he had twice defended cities encircled by the Russians and eventually extricated his troops. Unfortunately for the Germans, his pronouncements as well as his actions in Metz promptly betrayed the customary underestimation of Anglo-American air power and mobility characteristic among officers from the East. Kittel evidently entertained real hopes both of holding the city for a long time and then of capping the defense with another escape coup.

Chimerical though such ambitions might be, his fortifications and garrison were still capable of troubling the Americans. On November 14, General Walker decided that the encirclement effort east of the city had proceeded far enough that he could open a frontal assault with the 95th Division from the west. That day Companies A and B of the 379th Infantry attacked along the road from Gravelotte to assail a series of lesser forts, which the Americans called the Seven Dwarfs, between Fort Jeanne d'Arc to the north and Fort Driant to the south. They captured three of the Seven Dwarfs, but the October failure to take Fort Driant returned to plague them in the form of a deadly flanking fire. Worse, there was the vexing presence of the famous draw along the road just east of Gravelotte. The best remaining element of the 462nd VG Division, the 462nd Füsilier Battalion, used the draw to infiltrate across the Gravelotte road and cut off the two companies of the 1/379th.

The next day, the Gravelotte draw once more became the scene of a vicious battle, as Companies C and L of the 378th Infantry tried to fight their way through to the isolated companies. In the afternoon, the relief companies at length broke the defense of the draw and pushed on to the Seven Dwarfs; but by this time part of the 2/379th was perilously close to succumbing to another German encirclement effort at Fort Jeanne d'Arc. The next day the 3/379th had to fight yet another Battle of the Moscou Farm. This affray ended with the Americans in possession of the farm, yet it was as though a film made in 1870 on these old battlegrounds so propitious for defense, having been given a repeat showing in September, was now being reeled off once more.

But not quite. The main effort of the 95th Division was not its battering at the front door from the Gravelotte road but an attack by the 377th Infantry southward along the west bank of the Moselle. The 90th Division's October capture of Maizières-lès-Metz had established the necessary line of departure. Beginning at Maizières on the morning of November 15, by darkness the 377th was fighting at Woppy, less than five kilometers from the center of Metz. Thus the Americans turned the right flank of the city's westerly defenses. Kittel could scrounge up no adequate reserves to counter this threat, and the further effect was to demoralize the Germans fighting around Gravelotte, with Americans about to thrust between them and the Moselle bridges. Their resistance collapsing, the Germans blew the charges on the bridges on November 18, destroying all but one. Walker ordered that the forts still resisting be contained and not assaulted.

For the Germans who were not already surrounded and contained, the main goal now was flight from the Metz area. East of the Moselle, the 5th Division reached the city limits on November 17. Irwin then shifted much of his strength northward around the rim of forts under Patton's and Walker's urgings to complete the ring around the city. Before this task was accomplished on the 19th, Germans had escaped "in droves," according to 5th Division patrols, but just how numerous they were is unknown.

Much of Irwin's division was already well inside Metz as early as the day before the closing of the ring, and the 377th and 378th Regiments and Task Force Bacon of the 95th Division all penetrated Metz on November 19. Thus it might be said that Metz was after all taken by assault before the Third Army's more sophisticated plan of envelopment achieved completion. Yet it was the gradual closing of the pincers east of both the Moselle and the city that had undermined German resistance; more demoralizing than the knowledge in the forts west of the city that the 377th Regiment was approaching the Moselle bridges was the awareness of all the Germans everywhere in the defenses that every escape route would soon be barred. And while once again too many Germans slipped between the jaws of the American pincers before they closed, and the sequence and timing of events did not quite match the American plan, Patton still prided himself on being the first conqueror to capture the historic fortress city by assault since Attila the Hun in A.D. 415.

The Führer's orders notwithstanding, the Germans failed to fight for the inner city house by house. The destruction of communications ended Kittel's overall command on the evening of November 17. Thereafter his soldiers surrendered in small groups. A 95th Division patrol captured Kittel himself, badly wounded, on November 21. Patton staged his triumphal entry on November 25, to review some of his conquering legions and to tell them: "Your deeds in the battle for Metz will fill pages of history for a thousand years."[11] The remaining German forts capitulated gradually during the next few weeks, Driant finally yielding on December 6, Jeanne d'Arc, the last to go, on December 13.

To the Sarre River

The Third Army and its leader could use a little Pattonesque rhetoric and a moment of regarding themselves as historic conquerors. The taking of Metz softened awareness that in most ways the great November offensive was hardly proving glorious.

Whether or not Patton had seriously expected to reach the West Wall in two days, he had not anticipated slogging along well short of it as the end of the month approached. German officers captured at Metz scarcely masked behind their politeness an infuriatingly smug conviction that the Third Army had been far too slow about capturing the city in light of the quality of the formations defending it; good German troops, they clearly believed, would have made a much quicker job of it—as they had with similar permanent fortresses in Belgium in 1940. It had to be conceded that such episodes as the October fiasco against Fort Driant had left the Third Army's subsequent approaches to formidable works distinctly cautious—and in the background were Patton's own long-standing doubts about the aggressiveness of American infantry. Whatever the merits of implied German criticism about Metz, moreover, November made the earlier logistical frustrations of September and October seem still worse: if only Patton's tanks could have charged across Lorraine before the continual downpours of autumn turned the clay subsoil into an endless muddy trap.

Over this betrayal of his destiny by the fates—or rather, by Eisenhower, who was "unwilling or unable to command Montgomery,"[12] and whose Anglophilia and absence of strategic sense had sacrificed Patton to the field marshal—Patton could only brood and lament; for his own flair for generalship seemed somehow drowned in the mud along with his tanks' and his troops' capacity for rapid action. Beyond castigating his obtuse superiors to his diary and to presumably discreet staff officers and visiting friends, and exercising his passions for discipline and martial neatness in a campaign against trench foot, Patton could stalk the front and urge on his subordinates to more mighty exertions, as he did General Irwin to hasten the 5th Division's closing of the Metz encirclement. But he could not execute grand operational designs. The immobilizing mud and the enemy's recalcitrant resistance had fragmented the battle into affairs of squads, platoons, companies, battalions—of divisions and corps at most—and Patton's juniors more than he controlled the course of action, to the extent that control was possible.

The Third Army's limited advances might have seemed to be taking a slightly more hopeful turn in the final days of November, at least had not the abysmal weather grown still more abysmal. The obvious cause of the ambivalence with which the enemy military command had responded to Hitler's desire to make Metz an unyielding fortress was the danger that when the place did fall, the sacrifice of its garrison would leave a gaping hole in the front of the German First Army. This fear was as well taken as it was obvious, and despite precautions it was in considerable measure fulfilled. After the collapse of Metz, the Germans could stabilize no line of resistance in front of the XX Corps's further eastward advance short of the Saar-Höhen Stellung, the Saar Heights Position, a series of heights just west of the Sarre River and just east of the German frontier. The Saar Heights presented the usual natural glacis up which the attacker from the west must climb, but beyond their natural advantages they were strengthened only by field works, not permanent fortifications.

Toward the heights the XX Corps began moving on November 25, as soon as most of the corps had broken free from the congestion of Metz. The 5th Division remained behind temporarily to occupy the city and deal with the holdout fortresses. The rest of the corps advanced with the 10th Armored on the left, the 90th Division in the center, and the 95th Division on the right. General Walker's orders called for the 95th Division to make the first crossings of the Sarre, between Saarlautern and Pachten, where a bridgehead of relatively level ground reaches from the east to the west bank of the river. Once across the Sarre, the 95th was to push its bridgehead northward to create crossings for the 90th.

With rolling country extending before them, broken only by minor streams short of the Sarre, and the enemy in disarray after his losses at Metz, Walker's divisions briefly enjoyed a northeastward progress almost reminiscent of the glorious days before the German rally. The muddy roads and still-swollen streams caused almost as much trouble as the sporadic resistance of knots of the 19th VG and 347th Divisions. The Maginot Line shouldered its diagonal northeast-southwest course across the line of advance, but the Germans' procrastination about turning the works westward reduced it to a locale for only a few delaying actions. By November 29, the 95th Division reached the Saar Heights where they thrust toward the west in front of Saarlautern.

Here the advance halted, however, before the enemy's evident determination to make the strongest possible defense. The determination was embodied in elements of that old nemesis the Panzer Lehr Division. Still, just as evidently, the Germans' intent to hold in front of the level river crossings at Saarlautern found expression at the expense of other parts of the front, because north of the Nied River the 90th Division pressed its patrols all the way to the Sarre.

But in this cold and overcast November, something was always bound to go wrong. The latest fiasco developed on Walker's left wing. Because Patton was aiming for Frankfurt and eventually either a turn down the Rhine or a wide envelopment of the Ruhr, he wanted his crossing of the Sarre to extend as far north as possible, preferably to the junction with the Moselle, so he could move on toward the Rhine with his left flank brushing and shielded by the Moselle. He had hoped to use for this purpose the 83rd Division, on loan from Bradley until the 12th Army Group should decide it was needed for the supposedly higher priority attacks to the north; but Bradley recalled the loan with exasperating abruptness. Thereupon Patton instructed Walker to send a combat command of the 10th Armored northward to clear the triangle between the confluence of the Moselle and the Sarre. These instructions carried General Morris's CCA straight into the dragon's teeth of the Orscholz Schnenstellung or Switch Line, the "Siegfried Switch" as some Americans soon called it. It was an east-west extension of the West Wall stretching along a ridge line to bar access to the Moselle-Sarre triangle and thus to shield the communications center of Trier and also prevent any turning of the north flank of the Saarlautern-Merzig section of the main wall. Unaccountably, though at least some members of the G-2 section of the XX Corps staff were aware of the existence of the switch, both the XX Corps and the Third Army had issued orders as if altogether ignorant of it.

Patton had optimistically professed to hope that armor handled with proper aggressiveness could plunge straight through the West Wall. The Orscholz Switch Line soon demonstrated otherwise. On November 21, its antitank ditch backed by dragon's teeth and pillboxes brought CCA to an abrupt halt. The 10th Armored had to turn to methodical reduction of the pillboxes by dismounted infantry and engineers. The casualty rate skyrocketed. After two days, Morris committed the 358th Infantry, on loan from the 90th Division. The infantry regiment was able merely to duplicate the experience of the armored force, that is, to grasp tenuous footholds through the dragon's teeth and among the pillboxes at extortionate expense.

The Metz fighting had reduced the 358th to 63 percent of its normal strength. After three days' fighting at the Orscholz Line the regiment was drained of offensive power. The Third Army abandoned the assault, assigned the 3rd Cavalry Group to screen its north flank, and added CCA to the advance northeastward. The setback was a minor one, but its implications were grim—confirming, of course, experience gained long since by Hodges's troops farther north—for Patton's desire to smash through the West Wall.

The Saar Heights setback proved more temporary. On December 1, with strong artillery preparation and a sufficient break in the weather for at least a small contribution by the 9th Bombardment Division and XIX TAC, General Twaddle's troops renewed the attack against the stiffened German resistance. There was hard fighting, but the 378th Infantry, coming out of reserve and advancing through the files of the 377th to add fresh impetus to the latter's attack, pushed two battalions to the edge of Saarlautern. Evidently despairing of further resistance west of the Sarre without excessive loss, along much of the division front the enemy withdrew across the river during the night. House-to-house fighting nevertheless was raging in Saarlautern the next day when an artillery observation plane discovered a bridge intact between Saarlautern and a suburb across the river. Colonel Bacon, commanding the 379th Infantry, early next morning sent his 1st Battalion across the Sarre downstream in assault boats to circle in on the far end of the bridge and rush it, cutting the demolition wires. The maneuver succeeded. L Company, reinforced, meanwhile fought its way to the southern end of the bridge and was ready for a quick assault in response. The Americans captured the bridge, sent tank destroyers across by nightfall, and repelled German efforts to roll tanks filled with explosives onto the span to blow it. The XX Corps had a bridgehead over the Sarre, which Walker could hope to develop as initially planned.

On the XII Corps front, troops of the 4th Armored Division had crossed the river as early as November 23 on the corps's south flank; but Eddy's men had not yet closed to the Sarre generally along their front. Hitler had not imposed on the forces facing the XII Corps any abrupt loss comparable to the substantial isolation and destruction of the Metz garrison. Eddy had to settle for the very gradual attrition of a defense stiffened by the 11th Panzer Division.

The Falkenberg Stellung, moreover, had proven sufficiently impermeable that after mid-November Eddy ordered the 80th Division to content itself with screening that position. The 26th and 35th Divisions continued their grinding advances along the Dieuze and Morhange plateaus, the 6th and 4th Armored Divisions still moving with the assaulting infantry, but the troops never achieving a breakthrough to permit Eddy to unleash the armor. On November 19, the 26th Division captured the town of Dieuze and thereby turned the main German line on the southern plateau, which opened the way to an advance relatively rapid by post-September standards—some nine kilometers by November 21. But the enemy had additional well-prepared defenses in the rear, utilizing woods, nearly every house in every village, and—to greater effect in this sector than most—the Maginot Line. Always there was mud, and as the rains turned cold and merged into sleet and snow, exposure and trench foot became almost the obsessions of army, corps, and divisional orders.

By the beginning of December, the latest tactical focus of the XII Corps was upon the bleak industrial town of Sarre-Union, just beyond the Sarre River. To come within grasping distance of Sarre-Union, the corps had advanced about thirty kilometers since November 8. Its new 26th Division had lost 661 killed, 2,154 wounded, and 613 missing. The toll in the 35th Division was 349 killed, 1,549 wounded, and 115 missing; the 35th's edge in experience no doubt explains most of the difference between its losses and those of the Yankee Division. All combat formations in the corps had suffered heavily as well from exposure, trench foot, and fatigue. All formations had grown weak in infantry; 88.8 percent of the XII Corps's November casualties fell on that arm, with the riflemen of course being hit still more disproportionately. Almost every infantry regimental and battalion commander expressed doubts about his unit's coming performance, because so many in his ranks were replacements.

Even the 80th Division reached the end of November with 513 killed, 2,215 wounded, and 373 missing, though it was to have spent the second half of the month more or less passively watching Faulquemont. Still, one of November's brighter moments partially explained the 80th's statistics. As he restlessly made his rounds of the front, seeking to allay frustration with mere motion, Patton found the 80th Division on the defensive and asked why. General McBride decided he should respond to the army commander's mood by asking General Eddy's permission to attack Faulquemont anew despite earlier corps orders. Eddy consented. The reward was an unexpected discovery of an undestroyed bridge over the Nied Allemande River. McBride hastily moved the bulk of his troops northward beyond the river to assault the Falkenberg Stellung from a direction the Germans had not anticipated.

On November 25, after a five-minute artillery preparation, all three infantry regiments of McBride's division charged forward, supported by a tank battalion and two tank destroyer battalions. To almost everyone's astonishment, they quickly overran the main works, took 600 prisoners, and left recalcitrant pillboxes to the tank destroyers. General Wellm, the German tactical expert in command, attributed the remarkable event, predictably, to the deadly American artillery and, astonishingly, to the prowess of the American infantry. The 80th Division's infantry, said Wellm, advanced through the heaviest fire "with their weapons at the ready and cigarettes dangling from their lips."[13]

Momentarily cheered, Patton himself was not sure how he ought to assess the balance of advantages in the November campaign. "I believe the enemy has nearly reached his breaking point," the general wrote on December 5. "As a matter of fact, we are stretched pretty thin ourselves." The Third Army was thin to the extent of an 11,000-man shortage in authorized strength, and with very little apparent prospect of getting some replacements.

People do not realize that 92% of all casualties occur in the infantry rifle companies, and that when the infantry division has lost 4,000 men, it has practically no riflemen left. Therefore, with 11,000 odd short in an Army consisting of three armored and six infantry divisions, we are closely approaching a 40% shortage in each rifle company.[14]

In the XX Corps's 95th Division, the 377th and 378th Regiments fought their way to the Sarre with four of their six rifle battalions reduced to 55 percent of normal strength or less. On December 2, the division's G-3 Periodic Report described the remaining soldiers as "tired" and for the first time did not rate overall combat efficiency as "Excellent" or "Superior." Yet it was the next day that the division's 379th Regiment captured the Saarlautern bridge, and along with it two bunkers commanding its northern exit. These bunkers were part of the West Wall. The Third Army had at last fought through the old French fortresses to the border fortifications of the Reich.

22: Alsace

THOUGH PATTON habitually decried generalship that worried about the security of flanks—the enemy should be forced to worry about *his* flanks—he just as habitually attended with care to the safety of his own. It was the usual Patton disjuncture between reckless words and sound tactical practice. When it became evident at the end of October, then, that the Third Army might be allowed to open the November offensive before the First and Ninth Armies, Patton qualified his assurance to Bradley that he could attack on twenty-four hours' notice by inquiring into Devers's plans for his south flank.

When Devers's 6th Army Group took over General Haislip's XV Corps on September 29, Eisenhower assigned to Devers along with it the responsibility to safeguard the important Lunéville position on Patton's right, whence the Fifth Panzer Army had already attempted to drive a spearhead down the good tank avenue along the Marne-Rhin Canal into what the Germans hoped might be Patton's soft underbelly. Now the hearty, generous Devers—the 1909 classmate who had consistently stayed a step ahead of Patton in the army hierarchy despite an absence of anything like Patton's flamboyant visibility— promptly vouched for the Seventh and French First Armies to afford all the cooperation desired. The 6th Army Group would launch a new offensive toward the Belfort and Saverne Gaps of the Vosges two days after Patton opened his attack.

The promise proved overoptimistic, because Devers was still sorting out both his manpower and logistical problems. But the very fact that he, and particularly his French formations, suffered from severe problems, and that everybody, most especially including the Germans, knew it, constituted a circumstance preparing the way for a remarkable success. Furthermore, Patton found Devers so eager to be helpful that, briefly at least, he wished his Third Army might be in the 6th rather than the 12th Army Group. When Devers attacked, Patton also soon found himself envious: "The Seventh Army and the First French Army seem to have made a monkey of me this morning," he wrote his wife on November 20.[1] At the Brussels conference on October 18, Eisenhower and his 21 and 12th Army Group chieftains had practically written off offensive contributions by the 6th Army Group, but Devers in November was ready for his demonstration of how to turn widely advertised adversities into advantage.

Belfort and Strasbourg

To be sure, it was General der Infanterie Friedrich Wiese's Nineteenth Army that confronted the 6th Army Group, and the Nineteenth Army was not the equivalent of the First Army that the Germans had assembled to stay the hand of Patton. The backbone that had held the Nineteenth Army together and saved it from General Truscott's potential entrapments on the long retreat from the Mediterranean was the 11th Panzer Division, but the Ghost Division had now gone off to join the array against Patton. The Fifth Panzer Army and its two excellent corps headquarters, the XLVII and LVIII Panzer Corps, likewise had departed the Lunéville area, for Marshal Model's Army Group B farther north. Of the 136,161 officers and men carried on the troop lists of General Balck's Army Group G on November 1, only 49,539 belonged to the Nineteenth Army. Wiese's true combat strength was considerably less. Balck received a few hundred replacements before the Americans and French opened their November offensive, but most of these, like the best divisions already on hand, went to Knobelsdorff's First Army.

The Nineteenth Army straddled the barrier of the Vosges, which had been enough to stop Devers in September when the Americans and French outran the logistical support and the energy that had carried them nonstop from the coast of Provence. Yet the enemy could not be counting on the Vosges to permit such a force as Wiese's to stand indefinitely. Troublesome though the forested slopes had proven for overstretched armies and understrength battalions, and although the Vosges reach elevations of 1,500 meters—or about 1,300 meters above the Rhine valley at their eastern base—their western slopes up which the Americans and French must advance are relatively gentle, without abrupt cliffs and declivities. The passes are relatively wide and low, the Belfort gateway only 305 meters above sea level, the Saverne Gap 404 meters but with a gradual enough gradient that the Marne-Rhin Canal passes through it. It was true that, defended by the historic and elaborte fortress of Belfort, the Belfort Gap had not fallen to the Germans in either 1870 or 1914 (the 1870 resistance commemorated by Bartholdi's famous Lion of Belfort), while in 1940 it was finally traversed by Panzer Group Guderian from the rear. But for symbolic as well as strategic reasons, the French traditionally had guarded the gateway with proportionately and qualitatively more of their strength than the Germans could spare for the south flank in the autumn of 1944.

So while the Vosges were no trivial obstacle, it was not their inherent defensibility on which the Germans had to be counting opposite the 6th Army Group. Rather, the Germans looked to the weakness of Devers's French army and to what lay behind the Vosges. The Allies might penetrate the Vosges to the upper Rhine; but directly across the Rhine rises the abrupt scarp of the Schwarzwald, the mountains of the Black Forest, a most forbidding fortress wall raised by nature against invasion of south Germany from the west. Rather than try to climb this escarpment, Napoleon and other eastward-moving invaders had instead continued up the Rhine and thence from its headwaters to the Danube. But such a march in 1944 would carry the 6th Army Group on a tangent away from the latter-day major prizes in northern, industrial Germany. The lack of accessible strategic objectives beyond the Vosges did much to account for the thinness of the German defense. By the same token, the question of where to go next after crossing the Vosges was to vex the 6th Army Group before it was fairly across. Still, Devers must attack, if only to safeguard Patton's flank.

If the rains of November 8 when Patton said "Play ball!" warned that the Third Army might be attacking in Lorraine a month too late, it was worse when Devers started out on November 13. The 6th Army Group attacked into a snowstorm. Nevertheless, General de Lattre's French First Army achieved an astonishing immediate rupture of the autumnal deadlock and drove through the Belfort Gap on November 16. The 1ère

Division Blindée, spearheading the French I Corps, plunged into Alsace along the French-Swiss border and on November 20 reached the Rhine. Circling northwest, part of the division entered the suburbs of Mulhouse the same evening. The attack had proceeded with such speed and had taken a direction so unexpected by the Germans that when French tanks clattered into Mulhouse the next morning, the headquarters of the Nineteenth Army had to decamp in disarray.

By this time, de Lattre's troops were also fighting within the city of Belfort: the key fortress of Salbert, barring the northwestern approaches, had fallen to a surprise attack by 1,500 Commandos d'Afrique who silently stole past the outpost guards and scaled the ramparts during the night of November 19–20. To liberate le beau pays d'Alsace, the reorganized French First Army was displaying a boldness of both operational design and tactical execution that Patton could well envy.

The Germans counterattacked southward from Burnhaupt, about midway between Belfort and Mulhouse, to try to cut the line of communication of the French column that had reached the Rhine. De Lattre countered by directing his columns to converge on Burnhaupt from both Belfort and Mulhouse. On November 28 he closed the trap on several thousand of the would-be entrappers of the Mulhouse column.

These rapier thrusts of the French I Corps, furthermore, now greatly eased the tasks of the remainder of the 6th Army Group. The American VI Corps, which had advanced 650 kilometers from mid-August through September but only twenty-five in October and the first half of November, did not proceed at a much more rapid pace than its recent one during the initial days of the new offensive. Nor did the French II Corps, between the VI and the French I. The VI and II Corps were still slugging uphill toward the Saales and Schlucht passes when the I Corps threat to German lines of communication and retreat commenced loosening their opponents' grip.

Nevertheless, there had been some reason for Devers to be hearty and confident in his assurances to Patton that the German grip in front of Patch's Seventh Army was about to loosen in any event. Both of Patch's corps had been reinforced for the new offensive. The VI Corps had two new infantry divisions, Major General Withers A. Burress's 100th and Major General Charles C. Haffner, Jr.'s 103rd, and was about to receive Brigadier General Albert C. Smith's new 14th Armored. The bold General Truscott was gone, departed for a command appropriate to his accomplishments—a new army in Bradley's army group. Truscott was bound to be missed, but Major General Edward H. Brooks, commander of the 2nd Armored Division in Normandy and across France, was a solidly competent successor. And even with the 45th Division out of the line for refitting, Brooks now had a powerful, oversize corps of four infantry and one armored divisions. Opposite his corps were four divisions notably understrength even by German standards of the autumn of 1944 (from north to south, the 708th, 716th, 16th, and 360th Cossack).

The VI Corps also went into the new offensive with a certain tactical finesse. The 36th Division and elements of the departing 45th demonstrated as though Brooks intended to shift his main effort southeastward through Fraize toward the Schlucht Gap. While this deception was occurring, General O'Daniel's workhorse 3rd Division quietly moved from the corps right flank to a sector north of St. Dié to mount the true main effort by turning the defenses of that important road junction and driving for the Saales Gap and, beyond it, the city of Strasbourg and the Rhine. The slow pace of the first few days of the attack carried Brooks's left and center divisions to the Meurthe River northward from

St. Dié, where the enemy had been digging in to form what he hoped would be his "Winter Line." Against opposition beginning to show signs of faltering under the combined threats of the weight of Brooks's numbers and the French maneuvers to the south, the 100th Division on Brooks's left flank penetrated the Winter Line on November 19 by capturing Raon-l'Étape on the east bank of the Meurthe. The next day the 3rd Division staged a major assault crossing of the river between Clairefontaine and St. Michel, the artillery laying on its biggest barrage in support of the Rock of the Marne since Anzio, XII TAC exploiting a break in the weather for a busy morning of close support.

The Winter Line quickly crumbled. Prisoners said they were not surprised by an assault in this sector but were simply outmanned and overwhelmed. While the 3rd Division hastened toward the Saales Gap, O'Daniel forming the 1/15th Infantry, reinforced, into a motorized "Task Force Whirlwind," the 103rd Division crossed the Meurthe through the 3rd's bridgehead on the night of November 20–21 and entered St. Dié on November 22. The town had a special significance for Americans; here was published in 1507 the *Cosmographiæ Introductio*, in which the New World was first called "America." Now, sadly, General Haffner's soldiers found the place a smoldering shambles. Several days before, the Germans had imposed a forced evacuation, and then they pillaged and burned St. Dié. Neighboring villages were similarly devastated. The enemy seemed to be inaugurating a scorched-earth policy. But the Allies were moving too rapidly to afford time for thoroughgoing destruction to be inflicted on much of Alsace.

The success of the French I Corps to the south had also helped spring loose General Haislip's XV Corps on the north flank of Devers's army group; and Haislip was lunging forward so fast that, despite the 3rd Division's breakthrough, on November 21 Seventh Army headquarters directed that the XV Corps instead of the VI might capture Strasbourg if it could get there first. Haislip had attacked with General Wyche's 79th Division on his right and Major General Robert L. Spragins's 44th Division, whose regiments had been gradually introduced to combat during October, on his left. The first objective was Sarrebourg, the major shield in front of the Saverne Gap. General Leclerc's 2ème Blindée waited in the wings to exploit any incipient breakthrough. As early as November 16, Haislip began advancing the armor through the 79th Division. On November 19, he ordered the 2ème Blindée to execute the divisional plan for opening the Saverne Gap.

For the purpose, Leclerc had organized his division into four combat commands, one to probe through secondary roads north of the Saverne Gap, one to probe similarly through the narrow Wolfsberg Pass south of the gap, the other two to follow up any advantage. Moving out from Cirey in the early afternoon of November 19, Combat Command L met growing opposition as it pressed into the Wolfsberg, but the next day Leclerc decided its progress was promising enough to commit Combat Command V behind it. The reinforcement allowed Jacques Massu's task force to break free from the battle and drive out of the mountains onto the Plain of Alsace at Birkenwald south of Saverne in the afternoon of November 21.

To the north, Task Force Rouvillois of Combat Command D followed a more widely sweeping arc through minor roads around the Saverne Gap to reach the Plain of Alsace at Bouxwiller on the evening of the same day. Task Forces Massu and Rouvillois converged on the town of Saverne the following afternoon and readily overran it. Leclerc's success having persuaded General Patch to authorize a XV Corps descent on Strasbourg, only one task force of the 2ème Blindée turned west to sweep Route N4 through the Saverne Gap and link up with Haislip's main force. Task Force Minjonnet of Combat Command L entered Phalsbourg the next day and there met the 79th Division coming from the west, the French and Americans together scooping up about 800 Germans who had been trapped in the pass. Meanwhile, most of Leclerc's division raced eastward by diverse routes toward Strasbourg.

The metropolis of Alsace, junction point of the main roads of the province and of the Marne-Rhin and Rhin-Rhône Canals with the crossings of the Rhine, depended principally on the barrier of the Vosges for its defense against attack from the west. Sixteen forts with impressive names such as Ney, Ducrot, Marshal Foch, and Marshal Pétain guarded the main highways entering the city, but they were not major works and lacked emplacements for big guns. Nevertheless, Leclerc believed that speed of advance and attacks from multiple directions were necessary to prevent the enemy from rallying to make a fight for Strasbourg. The Germans proved him right by holding up the first elements of the 2ème Blindée to reach the outskirts of the city from the northwest and west on November 23. Task Force Rouvillois, however, departing the Saverne Gap slightly later than the two vanguard combat commands, raced straight along the north bank of the Marne-Rhin Canal to Brumath, there turned due south to approach Strasbourg directly from the north, and found the defenses unready. At 10:30 A.M. on the 23rd, three hours and fifteen minutes after its departure from Saverne, Task Force Rouvillois radioed Leclerc's headquarters: "Tissue est dans iode." It was the coded signal that Rouvillois was in Strasbourg.

The city's outer defenses now collapsed everywhere. To the tanks of the 12ème Régiment de Cuirassiers went the mission of hastening to the principal military objective, the Pont de Kehl across the Rhine. While other forces grappled with pockets of resistance on their flanks, the cuirassiers rolled straight on past the Place Kléber, down the present Rue de la Division Leclerc and Rue de la 1ère Armée, out of the city and on to the Rhine at the bridge. Protected by permanent blockhouses and by artillery beyond the river, the bridge was not crossed. For the moment, the 2ème Blindée had done enough. The tricolor snapped again from the tower of the cathedral. On November 26, after the last German diehards in the city had been subdued, General Leclerc took the salute of soldiers and citizens at the Place Kléber. Elsewhere the Boche might still cling to scattered handfuls of French soil, but the liberation of the capital of Alsace symbolized the fulfillment of the liberation of France.

More mundanely, with Strasbourg there came into Allied hands documents to inspire sighs of relief among a few knowledgeable leaders. The papers showed that the Germans had not progressed far toward making an atomic bomb.

The Battles of Rauwiller and Bärendorf

The Germans could shrug their shoulders and endure French jubilation over yet another change in the fluctuating ownership of Strasbourg; they could not so well endure the military implications of a loss of the Vosges that was unexpectedly rapid even allowing for the depleted state of the Nineteenth Army. Just as the French I Corps had turned the whole Nineteenth Army line in the Vosges, so the abrupt collapse of the Nineteenth Army threatened to turn the German First Army's line facing Patton. And while Germany could afford an Allied penetration to the Rhine opposite the inhospitable

Schwarzwald escarpment, in front of Patton lay the thickest section of the West Wall, shielding the mines and industries of the Saar Basin; these defenses must not be turned.

German retaliation therefore was swift. By evening of November 23, the Panthers and Pzkw IVs of Fritz Bayerlein's Panzer Lehr Division, hastened out of a training ground, were driving in the north flank of the XV Corps. Haislip's cavalry screen, the 106th Cavalry Group, fell back before two enemy columns, one striking through Weyer, the other through Hirshland, both toward Route N4 where it led eastward into the Saverne Gap. Early the next morning, the eastern German column was grappling around Ischermuhl with the 114th Infantry of the 44th Division; the western column had struck the same division's 71st Infantry at Rauwiller, a place that the Germans quickly enveloped. The 71st had to withdraw to a new line farther south, and Haislip had to order the 114th into retreat as well, to protect its own and its sister regiment's flanks. Haislip also cancelled the movement of the remainder of the 44th Division into the Saverne Gap.

That Friday, November 24, Eisenhower and Bradley entered the 6th Army Group zone on their way to consult with Devers about the further development of the offensive. Their cars rolled up to Haislip's headquarters as Haislip came running out to shout to Eisenhower: "For God's sake, sir, I was just on my way down to tell you not to come. Please go on. We don't want you. There is a report of an armored breakthrough on the front held by our cavalry." Staffs and drivers noted that Haislip's headquarters group was preparing to make its own defense, and drivers commented that when the headquarters troops had to fight, it was time indeed for generals to get out.

But Eisenhower laughed and said to Wade Hampton Haislip, "Dammit, Ham, you invited me for lunch and I'm not going to leave until I get it."[2]

Ike and Bradley stayed for lunch, yet the experience may have reinforced the cautious mood the Supreme Commander displayed later in the day with Devers and Patch. Despite the unpromising terrain across from Strasbourg, the Seventh Army by now not only had its plans well along to embrace opportunity by forcing the Rhine, but dukws were assembled for the crossing and ready to move to the river. General Patton was about to confide to his diary that, in Eisenhower's place, he would send at least the VI Corps across the Rhine; ever the opportunist, Patton believed that opportunity in war is too rare to be missed.[3] Eisenhower, in contrast, now insisted to Devers that the front of the 6th Army Group was surely not the place to cross the Rhine. Rather, said the Supreme Commander, Devers and Patch should turn the XV Corps northward to join in Patton's assault upon the Saar Basin.

In part, Eisenhower's recommendation was the course of action the enemy evidently feared. Nevertheless, Eisenhower's proposal would also ease for the present the threat of the Allies' turning the south flank of Knobelsdorff's German First Army, by calling at least part of Haislip's vanguard back westward. Still again, the proposal would also ease the danger posed by Panzer Lehr to Haislip's own flank, by permitting the XV Corps to shift its center of gravity to concentrate against Bayerlein.

Into this complex interplay of pressures there came also help for the 44th Division from the neighboring Third Army. On the critical morning of Eisenhower's arrival at Haislip's headquarters, when Panzer Lehr was tearing into General Spragins's left flank, CCB of General Wood's 4th Armored Division was crossing the Sarre River at Romelfing and Gosselming. These crossings were within the XV Corps zone of advance. Wood had received permission to use them to turn the enemy's positions facing the XII Corps along the Sarre farther north. Officers in both the XII and XV Corps recognized that Wood's maneuver might incidentally assist Haislip as well, though no one foresaw how much.

CCB brushed aside weak detachments of the 361st Volksgrenadier Division in the immediate crossing area and then drove northeast straight for Panzer Lehr's right flank. Quickly CCB's lead tanks and armored infantry drove German armored infantry—mostly new soldiers fighting their first battle—from the village of Bärendorf. Bayerlein had to turn around his western column to deal with the 4th Armored.

His method was yet another outflanking of a flank attack, coming out of the morning mists of November 25 against the north flank of the Americans in Bärendorf. But there the Americans had disposed themselves in a perimeter defense for just such an occasion, and Shermans were able to knock out assaulting Panthers as they crossed a bridge over a small creek.

Bayerlein's eastern column, obliged to carry on alone, was meeting a different but familiar American menace, a heavy concentration of artillery. The guns of the 17th and 961st Field Artillery Battalions first blasted and broke a Panzer Lehr attack just as it was about to strike the 114th Infantry, then found a long column of tanks and trucks strung out on a road in the German rear and poured shell on it for an hour and a half. The combined effect of these actions was to throw Panzer Lehr onto the defensive.

In the next four days, the 4th Armored Division completed the favor it had already done the Seventh Army and XV Corps, by destroying the salient the German counterattack had carved into Haislip's flank. Though the battle pitted armored division against armored division, there were no tank duels resembling the Arracourt battles of September. The mud confined both sides' tanks to the roads, and wear and weather quickly reduced the roads themselves almost to impassibility. German and American tanks alike were limited practically to serving as artillery for the armored infantry and engineers. Panzer Lehr, furthermore, reconstituted and retrained just before the battle, grew so weakened that the enemy had to replace it with the 25th Panzer Grenadier Division. On November 29, the 4th Armored captured high ground around the village of Durstel, within about nine kilometers of Sarre-Union, and the flank was secure enough for the division to resume its previous course toward the West Wall. The riposte to Devers's spectacular advance had failed.

Seventh Army to the Maginot Line and the West Wall

General Eisenhower's cautious decision against crossing the Rhine had also ensured that the advance of the 6th Army Group would no longer be spectacular. If the Supreme Commander had entertained any second thoughts about turning Devers's forces away from adventurous designs, the experiences of the French First Army soon appeared to vindicate caution. On his visit to Devers, Eisenhower warned even against any major effort to advance northward from Strasbourg along the left bank of the Rhine until all resistance farther south in Alsace might be eliminated. The Allies had already dropped off too many troops to contain rearward islands of Germans. Eisenhower's warnings referred specifically to the pocket of enemy soldiers holding out around Colmar, separating the French up the Rhine near Mulhouse from the French and Americans downstream around Strasbourg. Eisenhower thought Devers should send the VI Corps to the aid of de Lattre's army in destroying the pocket. Devers argued that the remnants of the Nineteenth Army in the Colmar pocket no longer formed a coherent tactical force, and that the French army thus was easily strong enough to allow the VI Corps to move northward.

Devers was wrong. The impressive campaign to Belfort and Mulhouse notwithstanding, the French First Army had shot its bolt. Its losses of African troops to the coming of autumn had never been fully repaired, the drains on its strength to police other faraway German pockets still persisted, its government remained unable to resolve fully the political complexities of integrating the FFI into the army. Consolidated into a compact defensive mass, the supposedly defunct German Nineteenth Army repulsed de Lattre's attacks toward Colmar in a manner suggesting it was ready to hold the French to a tactical deadlock indefinitely.

For that matter, even as Eisenhower restrained Devers, the American advance through Alsace was already reverting to dogged battle in any event. While most of the 2ème Division Blindée raced for Strasbourg, General Leclerc had detached one of his four combat commands, CCR, to turn south from Saverne along the eastern fringe of the Vosges toward Mutzig, to help pry loose the opposition in front of the VI Corps. This service proved useful; but a similar effort toward a further enveloping sweep by CCA of the 14th Armored Division south from Mutzig soon floundered amidst blown bridges, big minefields, and fresh German infantry reinforcements wielding Panzerfäuste to make every village a fortress complex. South of Barr, ruined bridges halted the 14th Armored altogether. When army headquarters transferred the 2ème Blindée to the VI Corps for yet another but deeper enveloping maneuver, up the left bank of the Rhine from Strasbourg, the French armor collided with the same kinds of obstacles that had plagued the 14th, compounded by Panthers, 88s, and artillery fire from across the Rhine. When the infantry of Haffner's 103rd Division coming from the north and Dahlquist's 36th Division from the west converged at the beginning of December on the road junction town of Selestat, where Route N83 between Strasbourg and Colmar picks up several subsidiary roads, four of their battalions, two from each division, had to engage in a four-day house-to-house donnybrook to clear the place. By that time the main movement of the VI Corps was northward into a new direction of advance.

Though responding only in part to Eisenhower's caution, Devers had turned the Seventh Army away from the Rhine and north toward the West Wall, where the wall runs west to east between Zweibrücken and the Rhine. General Patch formed a new line astride the Low Vosges from the Rhine just north of Strasbourg west to the boundary with Patton's army near Fénétrange. A series of gradual shifts of the army's intercorps boundary eventually fixed the crest of the Vosges as the dividing line between the XV Corps zone on the west flank and the VI Corps on the east. The object was a general assault toward the West Wall in tandem with the Third Army's imminent attack upon the wall farther west and north, eventually to join Patton's troops in invading the Saar Basin and the Palatinate. Haislip's corps began shifting its attentions northward in the immediate wake of the Panzer Lehr counterattacks, while some of the corps was still also driving eastward. By December 5 Haislip's shift of direction was complete. The XV Corps now had Dean's 44th Division on its left, or west, flank and Burress's 100th Division, transferred from Brooks's corps, on its right, with Major General Roderick C. Allen's newly arrived 12th Armored Division in reserve. The VI Corps was to lead off the new northward effort with the 45th Division on its left—now under General Frederick, formerly Patch's airborne commander, because Eagles had been wounded—and

Wyche's 79th, transferred from Haislip, on its right along the Rhine; eventually Brooks was to insert the 103rd and the 14th Armored into his center. The 3rd and 36th Divisions remained farther south to help the French against the Colmar pocket.

Opposing Patch's northward drive would be General von Knobelsdorff's First Army. This army remained a more impressive force than the Nineteenth Army, even if in front of Patch it had to depend largely on a conglomeration of Kampfgruppen; but natural and manmade geographic obstacles again appeared more formidable than the troops and equipment the enemy could spare for Patch's part of the line. The VI Corps route of advance lay through the Hagenau Forest, some thirty kilometers from east to west and ten kilometers deep. A corridor of rolling farmland only five kilometers wide opened between the forest and the Rhine on Brooks's eastern flank. An opening of only nine kilometers lay between the western extremity of the forest and the Vosges, and this gap was broken by four rivers and numerous villages. North of the Hagenau was another rugged woodland, the Hochwald, and beyond that the Lauter River—the German border—and the West Wall. In front of the XV Corps, a cluster of the strongest of the gros ouvrages of the Maginot Line crowned a shelf of the Vosges around Bitche. Here, where the roads from Zweibrücken and Pirmassens in Germany cross the French lateral road from Lauterburg to Sarreguemines, the French had erected permanent fortifications since Vauban's day. The complex of Maginot fortresses called the Ensemble de Bitche had yielded to the Germans in 1940 only after the surrender of France. They were readily adapted to face southward. Intelligence suggested the Germans intended to make much more serious use of the Ensemble de Bitche than they had of most sections of the Maginot Line.

Against these defensive resources, the new drive of the Seventh Army in early December became a plodding affair similar to the Third Army's recent and concurrent attacks, or to the September to mid-November experiences of Patch's own troops. The 314th Infantry of General Wyche's 79th Division found the town of Hagenau another urban fortress that had to be chopped away house by house and street by street. Only the relative numerical weakness of the enemy kept him from turning the Hagenau Forest into another Huertgen, and at that the troops who fought there would remember bitterly another ordeal under the treetop shell bursts and their murderous hail of ricocheting debris.

Thanks to the enemy's manpower shortage on the one hand and the four-division power of the VI Corps on the other, Wyche's 313th and 315th Regiments nevertheless bulled their way across the Lauter and into Germany by December 15 and began grappling with the West Wall defenses on Saturday, December 16. The 45th and 103rd Divisions both crossed into Germany that same Saturday, also to collide with the West Wall. The 14th Armored, running slightly behind the rest of the corps, tried without success that day to carve out a lasting foothold on the German bank of the Lauter.

The XV Corps had achieved more rapid progress than the VI, until both its front-line divisions arrived around the Ensemble de Bitche on December 12. Both divisions mounted probing attacks against the Maginot forts during the next two days, and the spearheads of both fell back under a storm of shell from the gros ouvrages. The 44th and 100th Divisions both clearly would need to prepare strongly supported formal assaults. Engineers began planting explosive charges against turrets, and artillery and XII TAC tried to soften the objective, with discouraging results; 240mm. shells simply richocheted off the casemates. Even point-blank, direct artillery fire produced almost no visible effects. The infantry had to go in for the attack anyway, the Century Division beginning on December 17, the 44th on December 19. Before the attacks could penetrate far into the Ensemble de Bitche, disquieting news from elsewhere on the Western Front stopped the Seventh Army short.

23: Huertgen Forest and Roer Plain

G ENERAL BRADLEY was tired, visibly so, for the first time in the European campaign, and war weariness seeped through his headquarters. The autumn deadlock had persisted too long. Even Patton was less ebullient than usual. Hopes pinned on the new Hodges-Simpson offensive to be opened by air power in Operation QUEEN fluctuated with the extremes of mood felt by tired men: "The success of this effort can easily determine the length of the war. If we are able to drive through on the Rhine, perhaps seize an initial bridgehead, we will have destroyed the enemy's industrial potential, deprived him of the opportunity to replace the losses he is going to suffer." And: "This can end the war—with air we can push through to the Rhine in a matter of days." Yet, "Without success in this drive there is a grim possibility facing us that the war will drag into a spring campaign necessitating fighting up until next summer. War weariness is evident even among the headquarters personnel particularly those that have been over here for several years and in Africa and Sicily."[1]

At 12th Army Group and First Army headquarters, many officers believed that the outcome of the new offensive, and the difference between a prompt ending of the war and a long campaign into the summer of 1945, might depend on the air effort: "Bradley banks heavily on this effort as he did in the St. Lo breakthrough." When the weather repeatedly postponed the air's Operation QUEEN, the ground commanders grew testy. By November 14, Pete Quesada, also impatient but still the ground soldiers' loyal champion among the airmen, promised for the next target date: "Our airplanes will be there with them if we have to crash land every one of them in a field." Quesada did not need to go so far; on November 16 the sun broke through:

> Hodges joined us [the 12th Army Group and First Army staffs] at breakfast after the others were seated at the table, came down with Kean who was looking bright and happy this morning with a wide grin to replace the heavy sober mien that generally concealed his feelings. There was an air of celebration at the table. Shortly the clouds rolled still farther back. . . .
> Hodges turned around when the sun first showed itself under the clouds. "Look at that ball of fire," he said, "that's the sun." We looked and laughed.
> Hodges was cautious. "Don't look at it too hard," he cautioned, "you'll wear it out and chase it away." But we couldn't keep our eyes from it. . . . This was the sun and the sun spelt a chance. God how pleased we were to see the sun.[2]

The First Army's offensive was to be the Allies' main November drive. Patton's attacks in Lorraine and Devers's in Alsace were only adjuncts. QUEEN in turn was to assure that the main drive should yield a full triumph, to bring deadlock and war-weariness at last to an end.

The Battle of the Hamich Corridor

For General Bradley's large and even desperate purposes, nevertheless, neither QUEEN nor a massive, hour-long artillery preparation achieved what was hoped.

There were major differences betwen QUEEN and the aerial phase of COBRA, which accounted in part for the dashing of hopes. QUEEN spared American troops the casualties of the COBRA bombing; but because the heavies bombed two miles in front of the line of departure to avoid a repetition of the COBRA tragedy, the bombing did not much injure the enemy's main line of resistance either. At the time of COBRA, the Bocage fighting had the German defenders groggy and reeling before the blow struck; this fact may well have been the real foundation of COBRA's success. When QUEEN opened Bradley's main November offensive, the Germans opposite did not seem in much better condition. But the enemy had assets denied him when COBRA uncoiled.

Bruised and battered the Germans certainly were. The 246th Volksgrenadier Division that confronted the Ninth Army was a ghost from the Battle of Aachen. The 3rd Panzer Grenadier Division, straddling the American interarmy boundary to face both Simpson and Hodges, retained some measure of the prowess that had won it fame in the Mediterranean Theater, but since departing Italy it had wasted flesh, spirit, and equipment in one long journey and one weary retreating battle after another. The 12th Division (now honorifically the 12th Volksgrenadier Division), was so exhausted after stemming the Americans' September attacks in the Stolberg corridor that it was due for relief by the 47th Volksgrenadier Division. The 275th Division in the Huertgen had not been rated highly by Germans or Americans from the time the forest battle began, and surely the Huertgen was taking its toll of defenders in the process of draining two attacking divisions. On the other hand, the West Wall and the Huertgen Forest afforded these German defenders barriers against the attacker and reinforcement to their own strength such as General Hausser's men along the St. Lô-Périers road in July had in no way possessed. Not the least of the defensive advantages in November was the inability of the attackers to maneuver. Bradley, Hodges, and Collins could plan no envelopment comparable to Collins's turn westward after he had crossed the St. Lô-Périers road. Between the continuation of Aachen's urban sprawl and outlying hills on the left, and the Huertgen Forest on the right, the main drive still had to thrust through the narrow prolongation of the Stolberg corridor. Only after they had penetrated six and a half kilometers of heavy defenses in the corridor could the Americans conceivably be able to widen their attack, and to maneuver, as they reached the plain of the Roer.

If the First Army was to mount the Allies' principal November thrust, it went almost without saying that within Hodges's army, General Collins and the VII Corps would strike the primary blow—for many more reasons than the corps's geographic position in the corridor. Attacking through the corridor, however, would once again necessarily cramp Collins's strongest asset, his flair for swift, aggressive maneuver. Bradley might hope for opportunities comparable to COBRA's, but realistically Collins had to plan for yet another straightforward slugging match such as had engaged his corps and drained its vitality since the crossing of the Reich frontier.

The Big Red One, with replacements and a few weeks' rest since its endurance trial in Aachen, would attack from Schevenhütte down the center of the narrow corridor toward the Roer plain. The earlier fighting in the Stolberg corridor had put the West Wall behind this part of Collins's front, but General Huebner had to deal with well prepared defenses on an elevation called the Hamich Ridge in front of him and in the fringes of the Huertgen Forest on his right flank. To open the offensive, Huebner received a loan of Maurice Rose's 3rd Armored Division to operate in the left portion of the 1st Division zone, permitting him to concentrate his own attacking force on a narrow three-kilometer front, with the 18th Infantry Regiment in reserve. After the Hamich Ridge was taken, Huebner would spread out his front, and the 3rd Armored would leave the line in preparation for passing through the infantry for exploitation into the Roer plain.

Also on loan to Heubner was the 47th Regiment, the only regiment of the 9th Division not mauled in the Huertgen Forest. The 47th was to attack just to the right of the 3rd Armored, to take the town of Gressenich and thus open the main road toward the town of Hamich. The 16th Infantry would attack on the right of the 47th, from Schevenhütte through Hamich to Hill 232, the main elevation of the Hamich Ridge. The 26th Infantry on the divisional right would attack through the Huertgen Forest east of the Schevenhütte-Gressenich-Hamich-Langerwehe highway. The 1st Division's three infantry attacks were interdependent to an exceptional degree. The 16th might take Hamich even if the 47th failed to capture Gressenich, but then there would be no adequate supply route into Hamich. But unless the 16th gained Hill 232 and a related series of hills west of the highway, and the 26th captured four hills within the Huertgen east of the highway—a difficult feat requiring it to fight its way through more than three kilometers of forest—the road could not be used.

The constrictions and difficulties of the attack corridor did not end there. For the Americans to fix themselves securely in the zone of advance assigned to the 3rd Armored Division, and thus for the left of the 1st Division to be secure, the Germans would have to be pried off a 287-meter hill called the Donnerberg, just east of the town of Stolberg. The 3rd Armored had already fought an unsuccessful battle for the Donnerberg in September. A principal reason why the American command chose to await Terry Allen's 104th Division before opening the November offensive was to assign to it the Donnerberg, permitting the 3rd Armored and the 1st Division to narrow their fronts as much as possible while still coping with this obstacle. The 104th was also to complete the capture of Stolberg's industrial maze, only about half of that town having yet succumbed to the Americans despite the battering it had received since September. Allen in addition was to move on through the Eschweiler Woods to Eschweiler. When he arrived to survey the scene in person, he decided that these latter tasks were dependent on first taking the commanding Donnerberg.

Both Hodges and Collins retained their abhorrence of the Huertgen Forest as a menace to the right flank and rear of the whole offensive in the corridor. Therefore the VII Corps right, now General Barton's 4th Division, was to clear the northern part of the forest, between Schevenhütte and the village of Huertgen. Optimistically, the high command contemplated the 4th's pushing on beyond the forest to the Roer River south of Düren.

The infantry attack of the great November offensive commenced in the early afternoon of November 16. The enemy's artillery seemed a trifle less industrious than usual. Otherwise there was little evidence that QUEEN and the American artillery preparation had produced any impact. The 16th Infantry, moving toward Hamich through the omnipresent mud, could make no headway against log-covered fieldworks in the fringes of the Huertgen until it called in tanks. With their help, the regiment reached the edge of the woods within sight of Hamich by dusk, but found the final unforested approach to the town covered by deadly interlocking gunfire, not only from the town but from Hill 232 behind it. The 47th Infantry meanwhile struck a house-to-house defense of Gressenich, which offered no prospect of an imminent opening of the highway to Hamich. The 26th Infantry in the Huertgen immediately began suffering all the customary trials of that hideous battleground: the infantry almost wholly dependent on its own resources because neither tanks nor artillery could function to much effect; enemy mines, mortars, and machine guns everywhere; the shellbursts in the trees the worst menace of all, so that where there was no overhead cover it was better for advancing troops sprayed from above to remain erect and hug the trees rather than hit the dirt. The lead battalion gained only a few hundred meters, and at that had to call for reinforcements to hold its flanks against the counterattacks that, here and along the whole front, came as surely as darkness. On the corps left, the 104th Division scratched out practically no gains whatever under the guns of the Donnerberg. The expectations of higher headquarters were already receding: "we shall be lucky to reach the Rhine by the first of December, very lucky indeed."[3]

The first day's ground attacks of COBRA had not achieved spectacular progress either; but this time Collins could sniff out no hints that the Germans nevertheless were on the ropes and ready for a knockout, the kind of hints that in July had prompted him to the swift and decisive commitment of his armored reserve. On November 16, the only semblance of a satisfactory advance was in a sector of the 3rd Armored Division front, where the ground was most open. Yet there was no chance of exploiting the advantage, because CCB, attacking on the open ground, was almost intolerably vulnerable to fire both from the Donnerberg on the left and from the Hamich Ridge on the right.

On the second day, the 26th Infantry paid an exorbitant price to advance another couple of hundred meters in the Huertgen. The 16th Infantry and the supporting tanks tried unsuccessfully to cross the clearing in front of Hamich. The 47th Infantry persisted in the slow task of street fighting in Gressenich. The 3rd Armored Division's CCB suffered so heavily from the guns on the high ground on its flanks that General Rose had to consider throwing in his reserve merely to hold firm. The 104th Division spent another day in futility against the Donnerberg.

Because the battle took a toll from the Germans, too, even if the lesser toll of the defender; because the American attacks were persistent; and because the Americans could at least partially press their material advantages—after clouding over again during D-Day, the skies cleared for IX TAC on the third day—the VII Corps eventually carved out gains. The first two days cut the lead battalion of the 16th Infantry, the 1/16th, to about 100 riflemen in one company and sixty or seventy in each of the other two. On the third day, the battalion confined itself accordingly to laying down suppressing fire while the 3rd Battalion took over the assault against Hamich. Under the 1st Division plan, the 3/16th was to have been saved for Hill 232, so this shift seemed to involve robbing tomorrow for today. Still, with the help of the 1st Battalion's base of fire and a strong artillery barrage, the 3rd Battalion contrived to dash across the open ground and enter some houses on Hamich's outskirts. The intervention of P-47s permitted them to stay when the Germans counterattacked with tanks. The regimental commander, Colonel

Frederick W. Gibb, hereupon decided that the enemy might be sufficiently off balance to make this the time to throw his remaining battalion at Hill 232. His judgment was as good as it was quick. Fifteen battalions of artillery laid on an intense preparation, and the 2/16th then charged to send the defending Füsilier Battalion of the 12th Volksgrenadiers scurrying in flight. The 16th Infantry had Hill 232.

On the same day, November 18, the 3rd Armored Division completed taking its assigned objectives. During the morning, the 104th Division attacked the Donnerberg with no more success than on the two preceding days—but, about noon, the defense abruptly began collapsing, either because the enemy had orders to withdraw or, more likely, because attrition had also taken the starch out of this section of the 12th Volksgrenadier front. By nightfall, the Americans had the Donnerberg.

The Second Battle of the Huertgen Forest

Because the Gressenich-Hamich-Langerwehe road hugged the edge of the Huertgen Forest, and because there was more high ground in the woods, none of these modest gains could be capitalized upon until the VII Corps right flank achieved genuine progress in clearing the fringe of the forest up to and including the elevations. It should come as no surprise that progress in the forest had so far continued unsatisfactory. What is remarkable, instead, is the perseverance of the First Army in throwing one division after another into the dark maw of the Huertgen on extended fronts and never in accordance with the fundamental military maxim: "*Concentrate Overwhelming Combat Power.* The attacker must develop superior combat power where and when he wants it; if he does this correctly, the time and place of his choosing becomes the decisive point and critical time."[4]

By November, constant shelling had stripped the trees of foliage and transformed the Huertgen into a witches' caricature of a forest. But the tree trunks and surviving limbs remained so densely crowded together that to see the sky was a rare privilege, and there was no change in conditions of combat that were so favorable to the dug-in defenders and so unfavorable to exploitation of American mobility and military technology: no change, except for the gathering depression of spirit and will as soldiers more and more struggled amidst the bodies and parts of bodies and other accumulated wreckage of earlier battles. In the Huertgen, it was enough to be digging constantly for self-protection, so there was no time to dig graves.

Barton's 4th Division, condemned to fight in the Huertgen on the VII Corps right flank, had already committed its 12th Regiment in relief of the 28th Division's 109th before the November offensive began. So close to disintegration was the 109th Infantry when the 12th moved into its lines that there was no opportunity to correct and consolidate positions. The 12th had to move quickly into the existing foxholes as the exhausted survivors of the 109th dragged themselves out. The German 275th Division saw what was happening and counterattacked immediately, leaving the 12th Infantry no chance to shield exposed outposts and salients. The 12th began losing ground before it had fairly found its way into the forest, and it never recovered enough to do more than cling by its knuckles in defense.

It fought on a plateau of the northerly ridge, between a creek running through the forest, the Weisser Weh, and the Germeter-Huertgen road. Here the 109th had been shielding the left of the 28th Division's costly attack toward Schmidt; here the 12th was to shield the right of the zone into which the rest of the 4th Division moved. But the crisis conditions of the 12th Infantry's entrance into its lines and the obscurity of communication and vision in the forest, along with the First Army's customary Huertgen Forest practice of assigning excessively wide regimental fronts, prevented the 12th from ever establishing a satisfactory connection when its sister regiment of the 4th Division, the 22nd Infantry, moved in on its left.

The 22nd was luckier than the 12th, but in the Huertgen Forest the Americans never found good fortune unalloyed. Attacking on November 16 simultaneously with the main drive from the Stolberg corridor, the 22nd had immediately before it in the Huertgen an elevation called the Rabenheck, the Raven's Hedge. The enemy proved to have little more than an outpost line in this area, but it still required three days of hard fighting for the 22nd to capture the Raven's Hedge. The triumph threatened to turn sour when the regiment's advanced line found itself precariously isolated, not only with its flanks exposed—in part because of the problems of the 12th Regiment—but virtually cut off from supplies and help from the rear. At a crossroads behind the 22nd, where trails that the Americans called Roads X and W crossed the Weisser Weh, the Germans poured shells so accurately on every attempt to rebuild a bridge that it seemed an enemy artillery spotter must be lurking in concealment. During the night of November 20, the engineers at last completed a bridge by constructing it elsewhere. The next day, the German artillery spotter was found. But the 22nd still had no reliable contact with the rear, because achieving it depended on opening Road W, a task defying the 4th Division's remaining regiment, the 8th Infantry, on the left of the 22nd. The 8th was stymied in a fight for a forest manor called Gut Schwarzenbroich, on the grounds of a ruined monastery.

On November 19, General Hodges responded to the 4th Division's several predicaments by reducing the divisional front by about a kilometer and a half, revising the VII Corps's right boundary and committing to the forest, in this area and southward, Stroh's 8th Division under General Gerow's V Corps. In terms of mustering the concentrated power appropriate for the attacker, this was a step in the right direction, especially because Hodges also relieved CCR of the 5th Armored Division from temporary attachment to the VII Corps and returned it to Gerow to help the 8th Division. But events proved that this step was not big enough.

The change in the intercorps boundary permitted the relief of the 12th Infantry, already exhausted in trying to defend the old lines of the 109th. Unfortunately, Colonel John R. Jeter's 121st Infantry of the 8th Division, which was to constitute the relief, was 172 kilometers away when it learned on November 19 that it was not only to be in line but to attack in the Huertgen at 9:00 A.M. on November 21. General Stroh got the 121st moving through the night of November 19, despite rain, fog, and mud; but it was almost dark on November 20 before the regiment dismounted from its trucks, and then it had to march about eleven kilometers to assembly areas behind the 12th Infantry.

The V Corps began its new attack in the Huertgen with heavy preparation by the artillery, in contrast to the VII Corps's having used almost no artillery to help the 4th Division on November 16; otherwise the 8th Division got off to no better start that its immediate predecessor. For three days the 121st Infantry tried to plod forward, its daily gains varying from nothing to about 500 meters. As the 8th Georgia, this regiment had fought at the Devil's Den at Gettysburg, but it would be hard to say that the old battle had been more devilish than the fight in the Huertgen. By November 24, the regiment was already so demoralized by the forest that one company collapsed under artillery fire. Colonel Jeter impatiently relieved both the company commander and his battalion commander. The new company commander was struck down by artillery the next day. In four days, Jeter relieved another two company commanders and a second battalion commander. In one company, every officer who did not break outright under the strain was judged by his superiors to have to be relieved anyway. The regiment's casualties numbered about 600 by the close of November 24, including fifty known dead.

General Stroh had hoped the 121st would advance enough to open Road W along the Weisser Weh for an attack by the armor of the attached CCR. Like everyone who worked for General Hodges under similar circumstances, Stroh himself was beginning to receive hints of impending removal from his command. Late on November 24 Stroh tried to break the deadlock by ordering CCR to attack straight for the town of Huertgen next morning at daybreak along the Germeter-Huertgen road, a better route of advance but one bordered by forest still under German control at least on one side. The result was a fiasco. Engineers were supposed to work on the road and clear it of mines during the night, but the first tank got stuck in a crater at the very beginning of the advance. Once the crater was bridged at midmorning, a mine disabled the next tank to try to go forward, and a gun wrecked the tank retriever that attempted to remove it from the road. All activity was torn by small arms and artillery fire, and CCR had to give up. Stroh relieved Colonel Jeter (who retained his rank and received another regiment in another division).

By this time, nevertheless, the progress of the 121st was accelerating slightly, aided by an advance by the 4th Division on its left. Furthermore, Stroh reinforced the 121st with the 1st Battalion of another of his regiments, the 13th Infantry. By midday of November 26, the 121st was within sight of Huertgen. A platoon of Shermans worked its way up to the infantry vanguard, and with this additional help the infantry took possession of the town during November 27 and 28.

The small victory did not change Hodges's and Gerow's latest decision, that General Stroh should join the list of commanders assigned a change of scene. They took into account his loss of his son, shot down over Brest, and gave him a leave of absence along with assurance that he would eventually lead another division. Brigadier General William G. Weaver, formerly assistant commander of the 90th Division, replaced Stroh at a juncture fortunate for himself by the standards of events in the forest. The capture of Huertgen permitted him to throw CCR into the battle after all, because a kilometer or so of road from Huertgen to the next village to the east, Kleinhau, ran through a clearing. Furthermore, on November 28 the sun came out, and IX TAC sent P-38s to soften the Kleinhau defenses. A CCR task force took Kleinhau on the 29th.

From Kleinhau, the drive turned southeast to take a continuation of high ground on which stand the villages of Brandenberg and Bergstein. Capturing these would at last bring the 8th Division almost to the Roer. Weaver's relatively easy debut as division commander now ended abruptly, however, because the Kleinhau-Brandenberg road proved another that was too well covered by German gunners in the woods on both sides. The infantry had to resume its hacking away before CCR could advance again, the weary 121st now aided by the 28th Regiment. When on December 2 the hour was deemed propitious for a cautious new commitment of the tanks, they soon found themselves among mines so thickly strewn that the engineers removed 250 from a single dip in the road.

With the aid of a few more breaks in the weather and therefore of P-47s, CCR tanks overcame the mines to fight their way into Brandenberg on December 3 and Bergstein on December 5. This approach to the Roer touched a more sensitive German nerve than the Americans knew, because it seemed to threaten those mysterious troop movements in the enemy's rear about which the Americans were less curious than they might have been. The Germans responded with reinforcements. They also stepped up their artillery fire. When the 28th Division had been around Schmidt, German gunners on the northerly ridge around Brandenberg and Bergstein fired across the Kall gorge to help ruin the Keystoners; now the enemy could reverse the process, raining down fire from Schmidt upon the 8th Division. Even the Luftwaffe brewed up as impressive an intervention in the ground war as it had mustered since D-Day, about sixty Messerschmitt Bf 109s strafing the V Corps on December 3. Parts of the 47th Volksgrenadier Division arrived from the Hamich corridor. New arrivals from the 272nd Volksgrenadier Division mounted a counterattack at Bergstein before daylight on December 6, accompanied by tanks or assault guns that wreaked havoc before it was light enough for the Americans to find them. Even when daylight came, the Americans might have had too much to handle in the form of well-placed panzers if it had not happened that a few of CCR's Shermans carried the new long 76mm. gun; those armed with 75s were ineffective in this battle.

At the eastern edge of Bergstein, the Germans held the Burgberg, which the Americans called Hill 400.5 or Castle Hill, an abrupt peak affording superb observation over much of the northerly ridge. From here the enemy could guide further counterattacks and, worse, vicious artillery fire. General Weaver had no force not otherwise pinned down or still strong enough to venture an attack against Castle Hill. Fortunately, V Corps headquarters commanded the 2nd Ranger Battalion, of Pointe du Hoc renown on D-Day. Hodges and Gerow agreed that the Rangers should be lent to Weaver. On December 7, two companies of Rangers charged up Castle Hill while the remaining company gave covering fire. As happened so often, the worst job was not taking the position but holding it against counterattacks. During the day, the enemy's efforts to come back wore down the Ranger assault companies to a total strength of twenty-five men. For the time being, Weaver could scrape up only a single platoon to reinforce these lonely survivors; but the CCR artillery observer with them called down so heavy a supporting barrage that the platoon was enough, until Weaver worked part of the 13th Infantry free to go to the Burgberg on the night of December 8.

The progress of the 4th Division on Weaver's left had opened the door to this succession of advances from Huertgen to Bergstein by exposing the flank of the Germans on the Germeter-Huertgen road back on November 21–24. Barton's division, in turn, had achieved its unusual pace, which had led to the further unusual progress, by means of a maneuver capitalizing on the mediocrity of the defenders of the Huertgen—particularly their lack of mobility—in a simple but hitherto untried way. Each of Barton's assault regiments, the 8th and the 22nd Infantry, had renewed its attacks on November 21 by moving a single battalion forward as ostentatiously as possible, with all sorts of weapons firing noisily in support. At the same time, each regiment sent another battalion stealthily around the flank and rear of the defenses it was trying to overrun. Both maneuvers worked, even though the enemy had just sent in a relatively fresh division, the 344th, to take over the Huertgen fight and absorb the remnants of the 275th.

Barton was able to follow up this coup with as close an approximation of an attack in concentrated strength as the Americans in the Huertgen had yet achieved. The change in the boundary between the VII and V Corps had freed the remnant of his 12th Infantry Regiment to become his center and to link the 8th and the 22nd Infantry firmly together for the first time in the battle. General Collins extended the 1st Division zone into the western part of the forest to reduce Barton's 8th Infantry front by about 800 meters. All Barton's regiments were now well in hand, on a front extending about two kilometers southeast from near Gut Schwarzenbroich.

The concentration came almost too late. Barton no longer commanded the same 4th Division he had led into the forest. During November, he received 170 officers and 4,754 enlisted men as replacements; he suffered from the old torment of not having enough experienced riflemen, or enough experienced company officers and sergeants either. On November 28, General Collins had to conclude that the 4th Division had spent its offensive power, and he moved to begin replacing it with the 83rd Division, which Bradley had returned to the First Army after its tentative assignment to Patton.

But even the seemingly endless Huertgen Forest had boundaries, and the Americans at last had nearly touched the northeastern limits. After a three-day pause in the attack, which was no pause in the action because the enemy kept up a constant harassment, Barton pushed his division onward again on November 29. Drained though it was, with five companies of fewer than fifty men each—and against yet another replenished German division, the 353rd—the 22nd Infantry with tanks and tank destroyers in the lead was just able to claw its way into the village of Grosshau during the night of the 29th–30th. Thereby the regiment entered a clearing east of which remained one patch of trees—and then the open valley of the Roer. CCA of the 5th Armored Division was waiting to go into the valley. From the combat command, Barton attached the 46th Armored Infantry Battalion to the 22nd Regiment and asked of the 22nd one more effort—to take the village of Gey beyond the forest. By nightfall on December 1, the regiment was dug in on a hill overlooking Gey. The same day the 8th Infantry Regiment dragged itself to within about a kilometer of the edge of the Huertgen.

With these efforts and the 8th Division's fight into Brandenberg and Bergstein, the Huertgen Forest completed its shattering of two more American divisions, to follow the 9th and the 28th. Since November 16, the 4th Division had suffered 4,053 battle casualties and lost another 2,000 men to trench foot, respiratory disease, and exhaustion. Since November 18, the 8th Division, CCR of the 5th Armored, and the 2nd Ranger Battalion together had lost some 4,000 combat casualties, and another 1,200 to the noncombat perils of the Huertgen. But the VII and V Corps had narrow spearheads inching out of the forest toward the Roer.

Into the Roer Plain

Because of the assumed menace of the Huertgen Forest to the VII Corps right flank and rear, General Huebner was concerned lest his 1st Division advance too far toward the mouth of the Stolberg-Hamich corridor while the fighting in the forest remained dead-locked and be cut off by a German thrust out of the forest. His concern made little difference, because progress through the corridor was only slightly less slow than through the forest anyway. On November 19, after four days of little gain, General Collins still professed to believe that with a couple of days' good weather the enemy crust could be shattered, and a breakthrough might yet occur. Two full, consecutive days of good weather were not forthcoming, but in any event nothing that took place tended to confirm such a hope.

Though the first few days of the offensive and the Americans' capture of the Hamich Ridge left the enemy's 12th Division gasping, the 47th Volksgrenadier Division took its place, and in doing so was to prove that the Americans ought not to take the new units labeled "Volksgrenadier" so lightly as was sometimes their custom. In fact, the 1st Division came to rate the 47th Volksgrenadiers as "the most suicidally stubborn unit this Division has encountered . . . on the Continent."[5]

The enemy earned this accolade through a series of battles in which he utilized almost every kind of military obstacle except mountains—pillboxes, antitank ditches, towns, farm buildings, forests, creeks, ravines, hills, and a fifteenth-century moated castle, the Frenzerburg. The arena of combat remained so congested that the obstacles were mutually supporting. Hills 187 and 167, targets of the 47th Infantry Regiment, dominated much of the zone of advance of all three American divisions in the corridor, from the 104th on the left through the 3rd Armored, still slogging along with the infantry, in the center, and well across the 1st Division zone on the right. To take Hill 187, twenty artillery battalions, including a 240mm. howitzer battalion and two 8-inch gun battalions, eventually fired a three-minute TOT concentration on an area of about 300 by 500 meters; this knocked out the opposition in the immediate area. The fight for the Frenzerburg produced such curiosities as a battle for a drawbridge and a tank's falling into the castle moat. After several days' struggle for the castle, three tank destroyers at length broke open the main gate for infantry to enter, but the German garrison escaped through an underground passage.

The Frenzerburg fell to the 47th Infantry on November 28. Capturing it helped open the main road to the industrial town of Langerwehe, which the 18th Infantry and part of the 26th mopped up the same day. That day, too, the 26th Infantry broke into the neighboring town of Jüngersdorf. Langerwehe and Jüngersdorf put the 1st Division at the exit from the Stolberg-Hamich corridor into the widening Roer plain. The division was about six kilometers from Schevenhütte, where it had jumped off on November 16. The intervening distance had cost the Big Red One 3,993 casualties, 1,479 of them in the 26th Infantry alone, which had fought mostly inside the edge of the Huertgen Forest. The 26th Infantry demonstrated the impact of its casualties on November 29 when it tried to capture Merode, a town just beyond the northeast fringe of the forest. The attack failed with the loss of two companies, cut off and virtually destroyed.

Terry Allen's 104th Division had disappointed General Collins at first, because he considered its attack on the Donnerberg lethargic. But in succeeding days the Timberwolves of the 104th reconfirmed the earlier good impression they had made while fighting with the British. General Allen had emphasized training in night fighting, in a manner appropriate to the Timberwolf patch, to correct a common American weakness and counteract a frequent German trump card; the enemy especially favored the night hours for his counterattacks. After capturing the Donnerberg, the 104th Division's 414th Infantry Regiment surprised the enemy by continuing to attack through the night of November 18–19 into the woods around the town of Eschweiler. This action not only mitigated Collins's fear that the 104th lacked energy, but it also opened a series of dividends from Allen's investment in night training. When the town of Eschweiler proved yet another tough nut to crack despite the progress of the 414th in the surrounding woods, Collins suggested that Allen bypass it. Instead of simply masking the largest remaining German city west of the Roer, Allen assigned it to the 415th Infantry, which was being pinched out by a narrowing sector of advance. The 415th surprised the last German defenders again by entering Eschweiler at night. When the town of Pützlohn and Hill 154 stymied the 413th Infantry by daylight on November 22, the regiment grasped the hill and a foothold in the town that night.

By then the 104th Division's attack, which had begun west of and echeloned behind the 1st Division, had carried four times as far as the 1st Division's. Much of the explanation lay in the circumstance that once Allen's men had cleared all of Stolberg plus Eschweiler and the surrounding woods, they were already in the Roer plain: open, rolling country with few natural obstacles. Still, although Collins had planned to have the 104th pinched out at the little Inde River, so that the old reliable 1st could spread out over a wider zone of advance, he was now impressed enough with the 104th to change his plan and instruct Allen to keep on moving across the Inde toward the Roer.

While the Roer plain was infinitely to be preferred as a battleground over the Huertgen Forest, the 104th by no means found easy going. The level plain bordering the Roer River, widening westward north of Aachen and merging eventually into the Low Countries, is part of the larger Cologne plain, the wide valley of the middle Rhine. Its hills and ridges are low; it averages under 100 meters above sea level. It was heavily populated and unforested, with many farming and mining villages of one to two thousand inhabitants, interspersed among fields of beets and cabbages broken by shallow ditches and low hedges. By the autumn of 1944 the German army possessed abundant experience in conjuring strong defensive positions out of plains more featureless than the valley of the Roer. In Russia they were doing it over hundreds of miles. Particularly, they had learned to transform every village into a menacing fortress, weaving around the compact stone buildings of the Roer villages a web of antitank ditches, fire trenches, foxholes, and communications trenches, covering the approaches with mines, concealing artillery behind walls and houses, cramming the trenches with mortars and automatic weapons, and clustering infantry in the cellars. Across the Roer plain, the villages and towns were so numerous that they readily formed in turn a great network of mutually supporting fortifications.

Even a slight elevation of ground, or a stream crossing, added to the defenses of the villages could reduce American progress to the pace of the Stolberg corridor, if not of the Huertgen Forest. The 104th Division discovered these unpleasant circumstances as it approached the Inde River, where the villages on the west bank were dominated by a low ridge across the stream, pockmarked with German artillery positions. On the division right, it required the week from November 23 to 29 to advance less than three kilometers through Weisweiler to the Inde. At the river, the division's penchant for night combat nearly boomeranged. On the night of December 2–3, I Company of the 415th crossed the stream to Lamersdorf using a wrecked railroad bridge, walking on one twisted rail while clinging to the other. But darkness failed to afford the desired completeness of concealment, and before another company could cross, the Germans isolated Company I. Most of the company were rescued the next day, but holding out until then required both hard fighting and a dash of luck in the form of a German medical officer's proposal of a truce to care for the wounded. Meanwhile the 2nd battalion had begun crossing the same night, over a ford between Lamersdorf and Lucherberg, and with orders to use only bayonets and hand grenades as long as darkness lasted; anyone who fired a shot would be considered a German and a legitimate target. This venture won the division its foothold beyond the Inde.

The westward reach of the northern part of the Roer plain put General Simpson's Ninth Army almost entirely in the plain from the beginning of the November offensive. The process of assembling divisions to activate the Ninth Army and of carving out a suitable sector for the army also happened to produce a heavy concentration of troops on a narrow front, an enviable asset otherwise unknown to the undermanned Allies in the autumn of 1944. Thus, there would have been good reasons to assign the army of likeable "Big Bill" Simpson the main role in the offensive. The only reasons not to were the newness of the army headquarters and some of the subordinate formations; Bradley's fear that too important a role for the Ninth might somehow redound to the glory of its neighbors, Montgomery and the British; and, as an express consideration, the dictum that one's outer wing should not make the primary effort—this latter academic thinking almost certainly a pretext rather than a genuine motive with such a commander as Omar Bradley. With its concentrated weight, the Ninth Army opened its first offensive on the Western Front under exceptionally favorable circumstances, notwithstanding November's rain, mud, sleet, and frostbite.

Then came the discovery by Simpson's G-2 that the army faced the most powerful German reserve immediately behind the front anywhere north of the Ardennes, General von Lüttwitz's XLVII Panzer Corps. Returned to reserve after its attack in the Peel Marshes, this corps lurked behind a boundary between two front-line German corps. South of the boundary was the LXXXI Corps, to which belonged the 12th and 47th Volksgrenadier Divisions facing Hodges's First Army, as well as the 246th Volksgrenadier and 3rd Panzer Grenadier Divisions which in whole or in part confronted the Ninth Army. North of the boundary was the XII SS Corps, holding the line opposite Simpson's left and on into the British sector. Lüttwitz's corps behind the seam now included, the G-2 noted, the 9th Panzer Division and the 15th Panzer Grenadier Division. An impressive number of its tanks and guns, by 1944 German standards, were known to have been restored to it; in fact, its two divisions between them had sixty-six tanks, forty-one assault guns, and sixty-five 105mm. and 155mm. howitzers.

The Ninth Army would begin from the bridgehead across the Wurm River won by the XIX Corps in October. With this corps now attached to Simpson's army and commanded by General McLain—the only National Guardsman and non-Regular among the corps commanders—the battle-wise, thoroughly reliable 30th Division was to carry the attack along half the corps frontage, a zone about eight kilometers wide, adjoining the First Army. Into the other half of the XIX Corps front, Simpson and McLain squeezed for the November offensive the 29th Division, in the center, and the 2nd Armored Division, on the left. By a new agreement with Field Marshal Montgomery, the XIX Corps, Ninth Army, and 12th Army Group left flank stopped short of the West Wall's northern anchor at Geilenkirchen. This target was allotted instead to 30 Corps, with the American 84th Division of the new XIII Corps on loan to the British to assist in taking it.

Once the 2nd Armored Division had pushed forward as far as Gereonsweiler, a communications center a little more than a kilometer short of the Roer, it was to pass into reserve to prepare to exploit a Roer crossing by the 29th and 30th Divisions. Its section of the front would be filled by inserting the XIII Corps. By then, the British presumably would have returned the 84th Division, and with that unit plus the 102nd and the 7th Armored, the XIII Corps under Major General Alvan C. Gillem, Jr., would give the Ninth Army a still greater concentration for its drive across the Roer toward the Rhine.

The 30th Division had yet to complete the clearing of the industrial town of Würselen, and its experiences there in October convinced General Hobbs that doing so would be the most difficult task in trying to get his division moving again. His wide front in comparison with the other elements of the XIX Corps was an advantage as well as a special responsibility against Würselen, however, because it permitted Hobbs to plan a wide envelopment. Two of his regiments would swing well north of the town, availing themselves of the better maneuver ground of the Roer plain, and then turn southeastward to cut Würselen's communications. Hobbs's attack was well rehearsed, the enveloping movement proved to strike another of the weaker areas of the German front—where mines were a greater problem than enemy soldiers—and it worked just as planned. Evidently fearing entrapment in Würselen, the 3rd Panzer Grenadier Division garrison, except for a stubborn rearguard, withdrew during the night of November 16–17. During the next several days the enemy failed to create more than delaying positions in the face of Hobbs's advance. The 30th Division paused on November 30 with its initial objectives achieved, awaiting the establishment of secure positions on its flanks by the 104th Division to the south and the 29th Division to the north.

The 29th's General Gerhardt planned an opening maneuver that was a mirror image of Hobbs's, enveloping with his right rather than his left. The strongly held obstacle comparable to Würselen that faced the 29th Division was the village of Setterich. It was located on the extreme north flank of Gerhardt's zone. In fact, had Setterich seemed an appropriate objective for armor rather than infantry, it would have been put into the 2nd Armored Division zone of advance. Once the village was taken, the interdivisional boundary was to shift a mile southward, and the 2nd Armored would take up the advance directly east of Setterich. Rather than grapple directly with the defenses of the town, Gerhardt proposed to swing around its southern flank before dispatching part of his division reserve against it.

Having long been occupied with the struggle for Brest, Gerhardt's Blue-Gray Division had not engaged in mobile warfare since the campaign in Normandy. Gerhardt's plan for Setterich not only paralleled Hobbs's for Würselen; it was also part of a larger conception of offensive warfare that Gerhardt brought from Normandy to the Roer plain. Not without reason did his colleague in division command, Cota of the 28th, think that Gerhardt was "the best combat commander in the European Theater."[6] Gerhardt intended to be meticulous in bypassing enemy strongpoints and in saving lives by infiltrating beyond the strongpoints to cut their communications. In the Roer plain, the towns and villages were the strongpoints; the 29th Division would try to concentrate its main efforts on the countryside, until the towns fell of their own weight.

Unfortunately for this reasoned design, the Germans facing Gerhardt proved less tractable than those opposite Hobbs, and the villages of the Roer plain were too numerous and thus too close together to permit safe infiltration between them. On

D-Day, November 16, the advance of the 175th Infantry on Gerhardt's right carried no more than 400 meters before it was pinned down in a drainage ditch by a hail of fire from a village on one side and a railroad embankment on the other. In the center, the 115th Infantry moved less than 600 meters before it, too, was pinned down, by fire from three different villages, including Setterich on its left flank. The 115th did not even have the shelter of a drainage ditch. Its men hugged the ground between rows of beets, many of them removing their combat packs because the packs protruded above the vegetables.

The 29th's lack of progress caused General Harmon of the 2nd Armored during D-Day afternoon to remind both Gerhardt and McLain that his division was counting on Gerhardt's to take Setterich quickly. The armor had to complete its initial business with dispatch if it was to prepare for the exploiting role. Advancing his CCB in three task forces, with support from the 406th Infantry of the 102nd Division, Harmon was moving more rapidly than Gerhardt. Despite squishing through mud, the armor was on its way toward gaining at least the first day's objectives and probably more in every part of its zone save one, where the town of Apweiler presented a recalcitrant defense in the center. But to maintain progress, Harmon needed Setterich, because the Aachen-Linnich highway passing through it was the only road that could afford his advance an adequate line of communication.

How much Harmon needed a good line of communication for reinforcement and relief, and part of the reason why the Germans insisted on denying him a possible defensive anchor in the town of Apweiler, began to emerge during the night as outposts repeatedly said they heard tracked vehicles moving behind the enemy front. In a mist-shrouded dawn on November 17, CCB's tanks were clattering into position to resume their attack when they were struck by heavy shell fire, followed promptly by Panthers and Tigers materializing out of the fog.

Caught in the open and in an offensive formation without depth, on soggy ground where wider tracks gave the German tanks superior mobility, the Shermans found their usual handicaps against Panthers and Tigers aggravated, and they were overborne. One enemy column hit Task Force X at Immendorf on the division left, where Harmon transferred the command to the colonel of the 406th Infantry and authorized him to commit his whole regiment if necessary. Another, stonger column—twenty to thirty Panthers and Tigers and a battalion of panzer grenadiers—struck Task Force 1 on an open hill northeast of Puffendorf on the division right. American artillery pinned down the panzer grenadiers, but German guns similarly immobilized the American armored infantry. The contest became simply a duel of tanks, and the German armor shoved the American off the hill and back into the shelter of the buildings of Puffendorf. The Americans wrecked at least eleven Panthers and Tigers, but their own tank losses were considerably worse. Lüttwitz's panzer corps was showing its hand. The Pzkw Vs and VIs belonged to the 9th Panzer Division.

CCB's remaining task force, called Task Force 2, tried to resume its attack on Apweiler despite the uproar on both its flanks; but the town's defenders proved at least as resistant as on the day before, and the long-range 76s and 88s of part of the 9th Panzers' counterattack force, firing from high ground near Gereonsweiler, made persistent American effort suicidal. Impatient about Setterich, Harmon had also scheduled for November 17 an attempt by part of CCA to open secondary roads around Setterich into Puffendorf. The effort stalled against the combined obstacles of a five-meter-wide, three-meter deep antitank ditch and the gunfire from around Gereonsweiler, which paralyzed gestures toward filling in the ditch.

The 9th Panzer Division had been refurbished impressively by the German standards of 1944, and Panthers and Tigers were always fearsome beasts. Nevertheless, the German standards of late 1944 were not the numerical standards of 1940, nor of an American armored division, and the 9th Panzers' counterpunch therefore possessed limited endurance. At Immendorf, the entire 406th Infantry proved unneeded; just one of its battalions rendered the enemy wary and was enough to hold the village. At Puffendorf, the panzers did not risk following the Shermans in among the houses, where the rapid traverse of the Americans' turrets would count for more than the panzers' superior quality as mudders, and close quarters would equalize the terms for the Shermans' 75mm. guns.

Nevertheless, fearing what the next day might bring, Harmon redoubled his pressure on Gerhardt and his persuasion of McLain to hasten the capture of Setterich, both to open the Aachen-Linnich highway and to secure a crossing of the antitank ditch, which angled out from Setterich. McLain, whose recognition of the sturdiness of the Setterich defenses had earlier persuaded him to show patience with Gerhardt's slow progress, now joined in insisting that Setterich must fall quickly.

On the second day, Gerhardt had adjusted his modus operandi in deference to the interlocking fields of fire of the numerous towns and the virtual impossibility of bypassing all strongpoints: but direct assaults on the towns, including Setterich, had not yielded results much more satisfactory than those of the first day. On the third day, November 18, Gerhardt modified his tactics yet again, drawing on the probable cause of the superior pace of advance achieved by the 2nd Armored at least until it struck the 9th Panzers. Gerhardt had believed the November mud made a battleground whose trials the infantry might surmount, but in which tanks would surely founder; accordingly, the 29th had attacked so far with little use of tanks. Now Gerhardt asked Harmon both to allow part of the 116th Infantry to pass through the 2nd Armored for an attack on Setterich's untested northern perimeter, and to help the Blue-Gray Division with tanks. Gerhardt proposed additionally to assail Setterich from the west and southwest with the remainder of the 116th, accompanied by the armor of the tank battalion already attached to his division.

As the first day's advance by the 2nd Armored suggested, such cooperation by tank-infantry teams was indeed the best available mode of tackling the defended villages. Forward observers could maintain artillery concentrations on the objective until the attacking troops were within a few hundred meters of it. Machine guns and mortars would help pin down the defenders until the advance masked their fire. Tanks attacking simultaneously with the infantry would both draw enemy fire and keep up a constant suppressive fire in the infantry's behalf, including machine guns rattling constantly and 75mm. gunfire when the supporting artillery lifted its barrage.

Pressured himself by McLain from above and by his colleague General Harmon, Gerhardt added to modified tactics his own pressure upon his subordinates: there could be no alternative to improved progress on November 18. He also watched carefully over every detail of the day's attack. The 29th Division began to reassert itself. By evening, the Stonewall Brigade had assured the capture of Setterich, though scattered enemy pockets and the antitank ditch remained to be mastered. Farther east, Gerhardt's 175th and 115th

Regiments took the villages of Siersdorf and Bettendorf and left the German 246th Division sagging enough to promise continued progress.

With Setterich almost in hand and the ditch running northeast from it soon to be crossed, Harmon could also think about resuming his attack. The 9th Panzers had evidently shot their bolt in the big tank battle of November 17. They made only a perfunctory show of resuming the counterattack on the 18th. That day Harmon bestirred his division to conceal its heavy tank losses by pressing the attack on stubborn Apweiler, with the 406th Infantry cast in the leading role, but with enough tank support to reflect a proper adherence to the lessons of the past few days. Apweiler finally fell.

The counterattack provoked by this gain took the form of the enemy's committing parts of the remaining division of Lüttwitz's corps, the 15th Panzer Grenadiers. Accompanied by tanks, the German armored infantry hit Apweiler before daylight on November 19. But Harmon had anticipated some such reaction, his own troops were therefore in defensive array, and the consequent struggle was nothing so desperate as the panzer battle two days before.

On November 20, McLain's corps could resume the advance all along the line. With the corps's techniques for assaulting fortified villages rapidly becoming routinized, the XLVII Panzer Corps licking its wounds, and the German 246th Division already a brittle shell because of its losses at Aachen, the advance accelerated and the Ninth Army exceeded the pace of the First. The 2nd Armored Division took Gereonsweiler, and the next day, November 21, it repulsed another counterattack on hills east of the town. From the hills, the Roer River was in sight.

To the south, the 29th and 30th Divisions had pressed to within two to five kilometers of the river. Since November 16, the XIX Corps had advanced about nine or ten kilometers, and its casualties were moderate.

Having captured its objectives, the 2nd Armored under the Ninth Army plan was to have yielded its sector to the XIII Corps, to prepare itself to exploit the forthcoming river crossings by the XIX Corps infantry. General Gillem's XIII Corps, however, was not quite ready to take up the advance on McLain's left flank. General Bolling's 84th Division had made an auspicious debut at Geilenkirchen, but the northern anchor of the West Wall had proven too resistant for the division to be able both to assist in overrunning it and also to move on almost to the Roer in less than a week.

American Ninth Army and British Second Army headquarters together had designed a scheme to bite off Geilenkirchen by closing just east of the place a set of jaws consisting of the 84th Division on the south and the 43rd Wessex Division on the north. Previous experience with the stronger sections of the West Wall, a description fitting the Geilenkirchen salient, led all concerned to agree that this attack should follow by two days the D-Day for the rest of the November offensive, in the hope that some enemy troops might thereby be drawn away. None were. But at least postponement may have helped lead the enemy to commit Lüttwitz's corps elsewhere, though a few elements of it proved to be on hand at Geilenkirchen. The defenders of Geilenkirchen mainly comprised the XII ss Corps of General der Waffen ss Günther Blumentritt, hitherto a staff officer of much experience on the Eastern Front. Blumentritt had two divisions of average capacity for the German army at the time, the 176th in the northern part of the Geilenkirchen salient and the 183rd Volksgrenadier in the southern.

The pursuit across France and Operation MARKET-GARDEN had displayed various British shortcomings in equipment, including the lack of a sturdy general-purpose transport vehicle equal to the American two-and-a-half-ton truck in long-distance capacity and endurance, quantitative deficiencies in bridging equipment, and the lamentably inadequate assault boats lent to the 101st Airborne for the crossing of the Waal. But in tanks the British still had the advantages of their menagerie of specialized vehicles, and it could be gratifying to Americans to have these "funnies" join in their battles. Flamethrowing Crocodiles, for example, assisted the 2nd Armored Division across the Roer plain. The 84th Division, similarly, was to stage its first attack aided by two troops of flailing Crabs. Under the beams of a British searchlight battery, these contrivances cleared a couple of paths through the Geilenkirchen mine fields before dawn on November 18. Because the British had kept their artillery much more generously supplied with ammunition than the Americans, and the 84th Division shared the blessings of 30 Corps artillery, General Bolling's first attack was also preceded by an exceptionally heavy supporting fire. Thus favored, the 84th Division's spearhead 334th Infantry Regiment took its D-Day objectives in good time. These were Hill 101 and the town of Prummern. The town had harbored infantry of the 9th Panzer Division to stiffen the 183rd Volksgrenadiers. The 334th also repulsed the panzer grenadiers' counterattack during the night, so altogether it was an excellent beginning for the Railsplitters, descendants of the old Lincoln Division, the Illinois, Indiana, and Kentucky National Army division of World War I.

But the first day was not to be matched for some time to come. On the second day, enemy resistance stiffened markedly. Intelligence soon rightly assessed as the ominous cause of this development the arrival of much of the 15th Panzer Grenadier Division. On the fourth day, November 21, the incessant rains reached one of their periodic climaxes in an overpowering downpour that turned all the ground and all but a few main roads into a quagmire. The British provided more Crocodiles, but they, too, faltered against the stubbornness of the panzer grenadiers and the trials of hauling fuel wagons through the mud. The garrisons at Müllendorf, Würm, and Beeck and the surrounding West Wall pillboxes refused to give way. General Bolling had only two of his regiments in hand because the 335th Infantry was serving as a reserve for the 30th Division farther south. He had to call on higher headquarters for help in order to retain any momentum at all. General Gillem sent the 405th Infantry from the 102nd Division.

For all that, the pincers formed by the 334th and by the British pressing around Geilenkirchen from the north were close enough to meeting that the Germans loosened their grip on Geilenkirchen itself. Bolling's 333rd Regiment was able to clear the town on November 19. Army group and army headquarters decided soon thereafter that the Geilenkirchen salient was sufficiently removed as a menace to the Ninth Army's flank that the XIII Corps could join the main offensive. On November 23, the 84th Division and attached units reverted from 30 Corps to General Gillem. On that date, according to the plans for the offensive, the XIII Corps was to launch its attack on the left of the XIX Corps. Between the hard fighting endured by the Railsplitters and part of the 102nd around Geilenkirchen and the necessity to reassemble the scattered 102nd, the date now had to be pushed back to November 29.

Therefore the 2nd Armored Division would have to fight on for a while longer beyond Gereonsweiler. More generally, the XIX Corps felt reason to regret the delay in turning the Ninth Army's full strength toward the Roer. For, on November 22, resistance on McLain's front also abruptly stiffened. The German 246th Division had been worn down to fewer than a thousand effectives, but the enemy responded by relieving it with the fresh 340th Volksgrenadier Division, plus a fresh infantry replacement battalion and fresh increments of artillery and assault guns. During the early morning of November 22, the German reinforcements rudely ejected the 29th and 30th Division vanguards from the villages of Bourheim and Lohn. Both XIX Corps infantry divisions spent the rest of the day trying to regain the lost ground and to resume their advance, but without success. To make matters worse, the Roer was now close enough that the enemy could throw smothering artillery barrages onto the Americans from the relative safety of the east bank.

The next day, General Bradley toured the Ninth Army, and for various reasons he indicated that the proper response to the enhanced resistance was a more cautious and even leisurely approach to the Roer. The relevant considerations included the inability of the VII Corps right wing and of the V Corps, still enmeshed in the Huertgen Forest, to match the pace of the Ninth Army. A still more fundamental factor was one hitherto strangely neglected: the existence of a series of dams on the upper Roer and its tributaries near Schmidt. Even if the Ninth Army reached the river, it could not be permitted to cross until the dams were in American control, lest the Germans flood the Roer plain and isolate a beachhead.

The XIX Corps now proceeded generally to alternate days of attack with days of consolidation. This new pattern proved a wise adjustment to all the current circumstances, since the Germans did not relent in their new determination to hold back the Ninth Army. Rather, the evident inability of the British to join in the November offensive, except for 30 Corps's limited effort at Geilenkirchen, permitted Rundstedt to begin shifting formations from Holland to add to the resistance to the Americans. After the 175th Infantry Regiment regained Bourheim on November 23, and the 116th Infantry took Koslar the next day, the Germans counterattacked on November 26 against both these regiments of the 29th Division. Fresh infantry of the 340th Volksgrenadiers, stiffened by Tigers as well as assault guns, punched holes in the American front and isolated two companies of the 116th for almost a day. By the time the XIII Corps joined the attack toward the Roer, its G-2s correctly reported that the 10th ss Panzer Division of MARKET-GARDEN repute was on its way to the corps sector, where the 9th Panzer Division and the 15th Panzer Grenadier Division had already been reassigned from Lüttwitz's corps to Blumentritt's XII ss Corps.

So the Ninth Army traveled slowly across the last few kilometers to the Roer. Nevertheless, it moved. By sending the 115th Infantry on a flanking march southward through the 30th Division zone while the Germans were preoccupied with their November 26 counterattack, General Gerhardt turned the flank of the counterattack. The resulting reversal of fortune carried the 29th Division to the river within the next several days, except where two small strongpoints held out in its rear. By capturing the town of Altdorf in a night attack on November 27–28, the 30th Division reached the Roer and then gradually closed up to the river along its whole front. The 2nd Armored also reached the Roer on November 28.

The XIII Corps was not entirely free of worry about the stump of the Geilenkirchen salient reaching along its left flank. General Gillem proposed to direct the 84th Division's principal effort against these pillboxes. In part, he would renew the assault upon Müllendorf, Würm, and Beeck; but mainly he would push east against Toad Hill (Hill 87.9) and another hill occupied by the town of Lindern, after which the old obstacles could be hit from the rear. Meanwhile the 102nd Division, on the right of the 84th, would stage a secondary attack directly toward the large town of Linnich on the Roer.

The trouble with this plan was that intelligence assessments gave no reason to think that Toad Hill and Lindern would be at all less resistant than Müllendorf, Würm, and Beeck, which had already frustrated the Railsplitters. On November 28, the eve of his attack, Gillem therefore rethought his plan and shifted to the 102nd Division in its Linnich attack the burden of his corps's main effort. In doing so, Gillem endorsed the earlier inclination of Major General Frank A. Keating, the 102nd's commander, to commit all three of his regiments. In addition, corps and division artillery would have to lay on a heavy program of counterbattery fire to protect the 102nd from the German guns across the Roer, and XXIX TAC would have to be as industrious as the weather might permit.

The shift in plans did not prohibit General Bolling's 84th Division from taking a stab at Toad Hill and Lindern on November 29. Bolling gave the task to the 335th Infantry, up from its attachment to the 30th Division. Artillery preparation was sacrificed in the hope of achieving surprise, and the Germans were caught napping enough that their defensive fire was slow to gain intensity. Two platoons of the 335th's Company K and one of Company I took advantage of this laxity to work their way across an antitank ditch and into Lindern. There, unhappily, the awakening of the Germans cut them off, about 100 men in all. A bullet broke the aerial of one radio and another malfunctioned, to deprive the three platoons of communications. Still other mishaps separated their parent companies from communication with regimental headquarters. Ignorant of the predicament of the isolated 100, and finding German resistance mounting as the enemy roused himself, the 335th made no hasty move to try to thrust any more strength into Lindern.

Ignorant as well of the isolated Americans' dispositions and weakness, the Germans brought up Tigers to assail them but merely probed cautiously in the face of bazooka fire. During the early afternoon, persistent tinkering with one of the silent radios, particularly the rigging of an aerial from a fence and some telephone wire, got a message out from the platoons in Lindern to an American tank. The commander of the 40th Tank Battalion immediately ordered a company of Shermans to the rescue. Six of them made it by about 2:30 P.M. Other reinforcements filtered into Lindern at dusk. Only after darkness did the Germans risk a counterattack in strength, and by then it was too late. A hundred American infantrymen had taken Lindern and thereby opened the way to reduce the remains of the Geilenkirchen salient from the rear.

In the 102nd Division, the 406th Infantry made surprising progress despite the shelling from across the Roer and captured Linnich on December 1. As intelligence had predicted, the 10th SS Panzer Division showed up to rally Blumentritt's resistance—but with few tanks. The SS troopers were not able to prevent the XIII Corps from gradually closing to the Roer along its whole front in early December.

By December 9, the Ninth Army had cleared the west bank of the Roer throughout its sector, from around Brachelen through Linnich and the ground opposite Jülich and on to Altdorf. Like Hodges's First Army, Simpson's Ninth had achieved nothing resembling a breakthrough. In twenty-three days of campaigning, the army had advanced only nine to twenty kilometers. It had lost 1,133 killed, 6,864 wounded, and 2,059 missing. How many German casualties the Ninth Army had inflicted was and is unknown, though the bag of prisoners was 8,321, and the army buried 1,264 enemy dead.

The comparative casualty figures suggest a mixed but generally favorable verdict on the offensive, beyond the disappointment over failure to break through. In its first major campaign, the Ninth Army had advanced more rapidly than the neighboring First Army. If more favorable terrain largely accounted for the more rapid pace, the advance was still to the army's credit. All principal headquarters had performed with quiet efficiency. Newness produced no major mistakes, on any level from army through corps headquarters to the cutting edge of the new divisions. The Ninth Army began to claim Bradley's affections as the army he could count on simply to go about its business uncomplainingly and effectively, in contrast to the bumptious, noisy Third and the jealous, prima-donna First.

Judging both from their appraisals of their principal subordinates and their conviction that openings in high command should go to battle-seasoned and proven veterans of the next lower levels of command, Eisenhower and Bradley would have preferred Collins as the next army commander in the 12th Army Group after Hodges and Patton. They appear to have gotten Simpson instead because General Marshall wanted to assure generals who trained large formations in the States, as Simpson had trained the Ninth, that they did not face dead ends, that they were not altogether excluded from leading their armies into combat. Simpson's continuing at the head of the Ninth Army into the European campaign seems similar to the elevation of General McLain with his National Guard background to a corps: it was an encouragement to a whole class of officers. In his army's first tests in combat, Simpson began repaying Marshall's trust.

Yet for all that was encouraging in the Ninth Army's first offensive, its slow pace despite a multiplicity of advantages also testifies to the enduringly formidable combat power of the Wehrmacht. Through every adversity and despite prolonged and apparently hopeless retreat, the German army still was able, company by company and regiment by regiment, at the very least to match the fighting qualties of the Americans— and in fact, still to raise questions about the ability of the American army to generate and focus the combat power appropriate to modern war.

Beyond the failure to break through, the Ninth Army's offensive would also have been more satisfactory if other commands' neglect of the Roer dams had not posed for the immediate future a halt of indefinite duration along the west shore of the Roer.

24: On the Eve of a Breakthrough

I F THE autumnal deadlock of 1944 placed in question the combat power of the American army, it also raised doubts about the overall level of American generalship, and particularly about the quality of aggressiveness. Patton in army command, Collins in corps command, and an occasional Wood in division command had long been exceptions, albeit none of them an altogether consistent exception, to a pervasive commitment to caution. Persistence in the cautious and the predictable in strategy, operations, and tactics had cost the Anglo-American Allies the timely closing of either the Falaise or the Seine pocket, with the resulting escape of the German headquarters staffs around which rallied the new enemy armies in their startlingly successful defense of the Reich frontiers in September, October, and November. The caution of the logistical planners who failed to foresee and attempt to provide for the fuel needs of a rapid drive into Germany, if not the caution of the operational commanders, cost the alliance whatever chance there might have been to win the war before the snows fell.

Caution—and in this instance Collins's caution, as well as Hodges's and Bradley's—mainly accounted for the long nightmare in the Huertgen Forest. The overriding motivation sustaining the battles in the Huertgen was caution for the safety of the First Army's right flank and rear. A less cautious and more genuinely offensive-minded planning could scarcely have neglected so long the only objective across the Huertgen that could at all have warranted the expenditure of lives and divisions in the forest: the Roer dams. If the object of the battles of the Huertgen Forest had been the offensive one of winning the dams, however, the full-scale clearing of the forest, the bitter combat for every obscure crossroads, need not have happened. A better route to the dams lay south of the bulk of the forest through the Monschau corridor. By this route, the Americans could have turned the defenses of the forest as well as more readily approached the dams. To seek to turn the forest rather than fight through it head on was all the more appropriate because of the immobility of all but a few of the enemy formations that defended the forest. These formations did not have the capacity to strike the offensive blows into the First Army flank and rear that the Americans feared from them. Rather, the situation of these immobile German units cried out for the Americans to take the defenders of the Heurtgen in flank and rear.

The Huertgen Forest resembled Grant's battle of the Wilderness, with bloodshed reminiscent of the appalling casualties of the spring of 1864 but without Grant's justification that geography offered no better place to grasp the enemy army in the effort to destroy it. The Huertgen Forest resembled Pershing's battle of the Argonne, without the partially redemptive circumstance that it was the plans of the Allies rather than American strategy itself that had driven the doughboys into the Argonne. The Huertgen Forest was a worse American military tragedy than the Wilderness or the Argonne.

The cautious American generals expected equal caution from the enemy. The Germans' Mortain counteroffensive, if nothing else, should have warned them that when the Führer was the opposing supreme commander, ordinary prudence did not bind the enemy's strategy. Even without Hitler's unpredictability, a cautious generalship's anticipation of equivalent enemy restraint becomes a paradoxical sort of recklessness if it rates the enemy's capacity for riposte so far below its true measure as the principal Allied headquarters did in early December 1944. Despite the German military recovery so indomitably embodied in the defense of the Netherlands, Lorraine, and the Reich frontiers since September, the Allied euphoria of late summer had not altogether dissipated by December. The American November offensive had become a slugging match rather than a breakthrough; but hopes for a sudden return to the slashing advances of August would not die—and surely, an enemy so recently gasping on the ropes would not abruptly come charging into full-center of the boxing ring again.

Euphoria dimmed intelligence and muted inquisitiveness about certain remarkable phenomena of the enemy order of battle. When the November offensive began, the G-2s of the 12th Army Group and its constituent armies believed that Hodges's and Simpson's soldiers would be doing battle against that old antagonist, the German Seventh Army. This belief was only partially correct. The November and December Battles of the Huertgen Forest were indeed waged mainly against the LXXIV Corps of the Seventh Army, to which the 272nd Division and its various successors and reinforcements in the wilderness were assigned. Following the November 16 D-Day, however, American intelligence found that the LXXXI Corps, resisting Collins's VII Corps and part of the Ninth Army, and the XII ss Corps, resisting the rest of the Ninth Army, had evidently been transferred to General von Manteuffel's Fifth Panzer Army. This headquarters had in fact been inserted into the enemy front between the Seventh Army and the First Parachute Army on October 30. After the belated discovery of its arrival, the G-2s continued to perceive its apparent presence throughout the American November offensive, since the Germans evidently designated their command immediately north of their Seventh Army as Gruppe von Manteuffel, i.e.—presumably—Manteuffel's Fifth Panzer Army.

The truth of the matter was that the Fifth Panzer Army had been withdrawn from the line on November 15 before the Americans decided it was in the line on this part of the Western Front. The day before the American D-Day, Manteuffel relinquished his sector to the command of General von Zangen's Fifteenth Army. So it was Zangen who controlled the LXXXI Corps, the XII ss Corps, and, initially in reserve, the XLVII Panzer Corps during the November offensive. But the Germans spared the Americans the mental strain of coming to terms with this latest change in command by masquerading Zangen's Fifteenth Army as Gruppe von Manteuffel.

Thus, of course, the Germans also spared the Americans the necessity of puzzling over what might have become of Manteuffel's Fifth Panzer Army headquarters, and what its shift out of the line might portend. Still further to relieve the Americans of troublesome puzzlement, the Germans concealed the departure of the Fifteenth Army from Holland by seeing to it that Armed Forces Command Netherlands, General der Flieger Friedrich Christiansen commanding, which took over there, pretended to be Zangen's

Fifteenth Army. The Allies were slow to discover these changes and deceptions, and thus slow as well to ponder their meanings.

The Roer Dams

The matter of the Roer dams falls into this same pattern of uninquisitive headquarters planning among the Allies during the late autumn. Unlike the whereabouts of the Fifth Panzer Army, the existence of the dams was certainly no secret. A Belgian agent's report on them to First Army headquarters on October 6 was drawn from the Baedeker guide to the Rhineland. (Despite its source, this report was forthwith classified Secret.) Nor was the potential of the dams to obstruct an offensive across the Roer hard to discern. On October 2, just before the 9th Division launched its unhappy October 6 attack into the Huertgen, the division G-2, Major Jack A. Houston, warned: "Bank overflows and destructive flood waves can be produced by regulating the discharge from the various dams. By demolition of them great destructive waves can be produced which would destroy everything in the populated industrial valley [of the Roer] as far as the Meuse and into Holland."[1] Nevertheless, the dams might as well have been a secret for several weeks thereafter, for all that they influenced the design of American efforts to reach and cross the Roer.

If the November offensive had broken through the enemy defenses and carried beyond the Roer, the Germans could have opened the dams to produce a flood isolating troops east of the river. The dams were seven in number, three of them actually located on tributaries rather than on the Roer itself. The principal dams were the Urfttalsperre, on the Urft River between Gemünd and Ruhrberg, and the Schwammenauel Dam, on the Roer about three kilometers southeast of Schmidt. Built, respectively, just after the turn of the century and in the mid-1930s, these two dams were intended to control the Roer and to provide hydroelectric power. The lesser dams were designed mainly to regulate the flow of the river. The Urfttalsperre was concrete, capable of impounding 45,500,000 cubic meters of water. The Schwammenauel was earthen with a concrete core, and able to impound 100,700,000 cubic meters. The principal military value of the Urfttalsperre was to allow the Germans to increase at will the amount of water behind the Schwammenauel downstream. The most likely way for the Allies to destroy the Schwammenauel was to break the Urfttalsperre, then to create a gap in the Schwammenauel downstream, and to let the erosive force of the water flowing from the Urft do the rest.

Despite the proximity of the Schwammenauel to Schmidt, the dams were not the targets of the early American battles in the Huertgen, not even of the sacrifice of the 28th Division around Schmidt. It was only about the time when the 28th's battle ended that higher headquarters began to pay any particular attention to the Roer dams. On October 3, the day after Major Houston's warning, the First Army intelligence section dismissed the problem by concluding that if the Germans were to blow all of the dams, the worst result would be local flooding for about five days. Two days later the First Army's chief engineer stated more circumspectly that the flooding might be widespread. Yet SHAEF evinced no concern until mid-November, and it was scarcely earlier that army group and army began taking a serious view of the dams. Some slight extenuation can be found in the circumstance that, during October, the reservoirs were filled only to 30 to 50 percent of capacity. The Germans began consistently raising the water level only in November.

On November 11, both the First and the Ninth Armies directed that no troops were to advance beyond the Roer except on order from army headquarters. The apparent reason was dawning recognition of the troublesome potential of the dams. On November 18, General Hodges began studying the possibility of destroying the dams by bombing them, and four days later he urged Bradley to support an aerial attack. In October, the Third Army had called on XIX TAC to help with a similar problem: a seventeenth-century earthen dam on the Étang de Lindre, a tributary of the Seille, had been built by French engineers as part of the Vauban defensive system with the express purpose of permitting flooding of the Seille, and the Germans might blow it to obstruct the coming XII Corps attack. Two squadrons of P-47s therefore breached it with 1,000-lb. bombs well before General Eddy's advance across the Seille, giving the waters time to recede. The Étang de Lindre dam was much smaller than the Urfttalsperre or the Schwammenauel, but the First Army planners thought that if aviation could break the lesser of these, the Urfttalsperre, then just a little more work at the Schwammenauel could open the way to ruinous erosion.

Bradley's G-3 for air passed the First Army's request to SHAEF, whence it was referred to the RAF. The reason for such referral was the reputation made by a precision-bombing faction within Bomber Command with a low-level attack on a series of Ruhr valley dams on May 16–17, 1943. The British had manufactured a famous victory out of severely damaging the Möhne and Eder dams—a disproportionately famous victory, in light of the failure of eleven of nineteen bombers to return, and of the survival of the most important dam, the Sorpe, unscathed, while two others intended as targets were not attacked at all. The popular, romanticized version of the tale of the "dam busters" notwithstanding, SHAEF air officers returned from consultation with the RAF bearing the verdict that bombing the Roer dams was impracticable.

By now the ground commanders were exercised enough that the 12th Army Group insisted on further efforts toward persuasion. At the end of the month, the RAF capitulated and agreed to have a go at the Roer dams. Thereupon three days of the customarily bad autumn weather prevented any action. One hundred ninety bombers were able to fly to the Roer on the fourth day, December 3, but they could not find the targets. The next day Bomber Command sent 200 planes, of which twenty-five Lancasters and three Mosquitoes actually attacked the dams, but without doing much harm. On December 5, the weather once more washed out any effort. Air Marshal Harris now tried to cancel further attempts as a waste, but Eisenhower insisted the bombing must go on. Two hundred five planes dropped 797 tons on December 8, scoring two hits on the Urfttalsperre and eighteen on the Schwammenauel but breaking neither. On December 11, 178 of 230 attacking Lancasters concentrated on the Urft dam with 1,065 tons. They created a small spill of no importance. Scheduled efforts on December 13 and 14 again yielded to the weather, and at last Harris was able to stop the whole business. This employment primarily of heavy bombers had proved to be another misapplication, for which the RAF had its own public-relations inflation of the Ruhr dams episode largely to blame.

Hodges still thought the airplanes should persevere—a 1,000-plane raid ought to do the job—but Harris's attitude had obliged him to commence drawing plans for a ground attack.

The Monschau Corridor

The Battles of the Huertgen Forest had surely sapped the ability of the Germans to defend the Roer dams, and had cleared much of the left flank of the best attack route. This route was the Monschau corridor, the thin band of open country between the

Huertgen and Monschau Forests. Appropriate regard for the importance of the dams would have directed a major effort into the corridor long since. Reasonable flank protection for such an effort could have been produced without the scale of bludgeoning in the Huertgen that had by now occurred.

The Monschau corridor would not be easy. Multiple streams and abrupt, steep gorges made it a natural setting little more attractive than the forest. The Germans had festooned it with two bands of West Wall pillboxes, against which part of the 9th Division had launched an abortive attack in September. Furthermore, the neighboring forests closed in on the eastern end of the corridor, and the final plunge would have to be across the Kall River gorge to Schmidt, places of notorious memory.

General Gerow's V Corps faced the Monschau corridor and thus received the task of attacking toward the dams. For the purpose, Hodges gave the corps General Robertson's veteran 2nd Division, recently recuperating in the Ardennes from its labors in Normandy and Brittany, and Major General Edwin P. Parker, Jr.'s new 78th Division, hoping for results appropriate to the bolt of lightning emblazoned on its shoulder patch. Gerow still had also the tired 8th Division, the 2nd Ranger Battalion, and CCR of the 5th Armored Division, all fighting near the eastern edge of the Huertgen on the left of the Monschau corridor. Major General Walter E. Lauer's new 99th Division was to guard the right flank of the attacking force, and part of the new 9th Armored Division was in corps reserve.

Gerow planned for the 78th Division to strike directly through the Monschau corridor to Schmidt, coming upon the dams from the north, while the 2nd Division turned the attack into an envelopment by moving through the Monschau Forest from the Belgian border villages of Krinkelt and Rocherath to approach the dams from the south. At a road junction where there was a forester's lodge called Wahlerscheid, Robertson's division was to fan out, part to press northwest to clear a ridge through Alzen and Höfen to Monschau, part to advance along the higher Dreiborn ridge to the dams.

It was consistent with a developing pattern, of which the 84th, 95th, and 104th Divisions had provided earlier examples, that the new divisions of the V Corps performed creditably from the start. More realistic training than the divisions mobilized earlier had received, based on American combat experience, probably helped reduce growing pains. It was probably of consequence also that the new divisions being committed in the autumn of 1944 often contained large quotients of men transferred from the Army Specialized Training Program, which had provided college courses for soldiers of high intelligence until the shortage of infantrymen prompted their reassignment. To the extent that divisions liberally laced with ASTP men performed exceptionally well, this outcome amounted to a tacit rebuke of the usual American practice of consigning only the least promising and least intelligent soldiers to the infantry. For an army that depended on its infantry for its sustained combat power to have used that infantry as a dumping ground for its least desirable personnel should, of course, have raised questions long before this demonstration of the contrary possibilities.

Thus, the 78th Division attacked without artillery preparation out of a heavy fog on December 13 and advanced two kilometers, winning all its initial objectives by taking the villages of Rollesbroich, Bickerath, and Summerath on a high plateau that was the first major terrain feature of the Monschau corridor. Two battalions of the 395th Infantry and one of the 393rd of the 99th Division also made good progress in clearing wooded high ground on the right flank of Robertson's zone of advance.

The veteran 2nd Division, in fact, had more initial trouble than either of its less experienced neighbors. The problem was the similarity of its attack zone in the Monschau Forest to the nearby Huertgen Forest. Once again explosives shattering the treetops rained showers of deadly debris on the troops below. Once again the advance had to funnel along a single road, the division pushing forward in column of regiments. Once again the forest denied any accurate perception of the enemy's strength or of the locations of his pillboxes and other strongpoints. For three days the 9th Infantry Regiment, leading the division, stalled short of the Wahlerscheid crossroads, suffering 737 casualties, about 400 of them from trench foot and exposure.

At length, on December 15, Lieutenant Colonel Walter M. Higgins, Jr., of the 2nd Battalion of the 9th learned that the night before a couple of squads had cut and slithered their way completely through the enemy's barbed wire. When the darkness returned Higgins sent a patrol through the wire by the same route, followed by Companies F and E. The 2/9th soon consolidated a foothold behind the Wahlerscheid defenses. Another battalion promptly followed. By morning of December 16, the 38th Infantry was passing through the 9th to advance northeastward along the Dreiborn ridge toward the dams.

By that time, however, the 78th Division had been halted at the fourth village of the Monschau corridor, Kesternich, and during the night of December 15–16 a battalion was isolated there. That veteran menace of the Huertgen Forest, the German 272nd Division, proved to be back in line to force the halt, aided by the thousand casualties—358 of them exposure cases—that the 78th had suffered in its first three days of action. By that time, too, there was abruptly increasing evidence that heavy concentrations of enemy troops lurked just beyond the 2nd and 99th Divisions, with aggressive rather than defensive intent. The commanders of both the 2nd and the 99th suspended their attacks to try to sniff out what was transpiring beyond the shadows of the Monschau woods, for fear they might catch a tiger by the tail.

The Saar

As yet, practically no American believed that the aggressive intent growing tangible beyond the Monschau Forest could assume more than local importance. Perhaps the enemy was ready for the expected commitment of his panzer reserves in a final effort to hold the Roer dams. His intending much more than that was unthinkable—in the most literal sense that nobody at all thought about it—because the first weeks of December were seeming to reveal at last the long-awaited softening of the resistance that had revived in September. The Americans' November offensive gained no COBRA breakthrough, but there was cause to believe that in the attrition it had imposed on the enemy it was at least analogous to the hedgerow battles: disappointing for the moment, the struggle might nevertheless prove to have exhausted the Germans to the verge of collapse, and the new COBRA might yet wait just ahead. The Huertgen Forest, the Aachen corridor, and Lorraine might yet emerge as the Wilderness, Spotsylvania, and Atlanta of U.S. Grant's and W.T. Sherman's military descendants—the bitter bloodbaths, heartbreaking in their tactical reverses as well as their toll of casualties, that nevertheless achieved the strategic ruination of the enemy, through their intolerable attrition of his armies.

The price to be paid for destroying the enemy armies by overwhelming them in head-on attack was high in casualties among one's own soldiers, but so it had been for Grant and Sherman too, and such was the consistent pattern of modern war. From the beginning of September until December 16, the American First Army had lost in battle 7,024 killed, 35,155 wounded, and 4,860 missing and captured. In its relatively short period of combat, the Ninth Army had lost 1,133 killed, 6,864 wounded, and 2,059 missing and captured. Through December 18, the Third Army's battle casualties since September amounted to 6,657 killed, 34,406 wounded, and 12,119 missing and captured. The First Army had suffered 50,867 nonbattle casualties, the Ninth Army 20,787, the Third Army 42,088. Equipment losses were heavy, too—550 medium tanks in the First Army, for example, about 100 in the Ninth, 298 in the Third. Yet though the comparable German figures were mostly unknown, the Americans could take comfort that the First and Ninth Armies had captured some 95,000 prisoners, the Third Army some 75,000.

Just as Grant's destruction of the Confederate army in the Wilderness-Spotsylvania-Cold Harbor campaign expended many proud old Union army formations as well—Winfield Scott Hancock's II Corps, until 1864 probably the best of the Army of the Potomac, was never more than a shadow of its old self after the 1864 summer—so the autumn attrition of 1944 removed veteran divisions at least temporarily from Eisenhower's line. In the V Corps, General Gerow could commit only two regiments of the 78th Division to the battle for the Monschau corridor because the third regiment had to bolster the shattered 8th Division farther north. Nevertheless, the 8th was incapable of renewing its attacks to add another prong to the December advance against the Roer dams. Collins's VII Corps resumed its push out of the Stolberg corridor and into the Roer plain on December 10 without the 4th Division, yet another victim of the Huertgen, or the 1st Division. The Big Red One's 26th Infantry Regiment had lost 165 missing on the single day of November 29 when two of its companies were isolated at Merode, and General Collins had to conclude that a fiasco so unprecedented in this division portended the necessity to rest the whole formation. Collins's latest attacks began with General Macon's 83rd Division, up from its brief assignment to Patton, in the place of the 1st in the opening onto the Roer plain, while General Craig's rehabilitated 9th Division replaced the 4th on the northeastern fringes of the Huertgen Forest.

About the same time, Patton in the Third Army concluded he must part at least for the time being with what had probably been the best of the armored divisions—Wood's 4th Armored—and more permanently with its commander. Wood's zeal to grasp the unforgiving minute, exceeding Patton's own when higher headquarters were ordering the turn from Avranches into Brittany, did not serve him so well when mud and a stubborn enemy mired the treads of his tanks. "Unquestionably," said Patton, "in a rapid moving advance, he is the greatest division commander I have ever seen, but when things get sticky he is inclined to worry too much, which keeps him from sleeping and wears him down, and makes it difficult to control his operations."[2] For weeks, Patton had hoped to find a kindly way to ease Wood out. Discovering none, he relieved him on December 3. General Gaffey moved over from the post of army chief of staff to succeed Wood. General Hobart Gay, the deputy chief of staff, always close to Patton personally, moved up to Gaffey's former place.

However tired he had grown, "P" Wood was so evidently one of the best of the division commanders—perhaps the very best—that suspicion of his superiors' motives has inevitably gathered around the question of his relief. Perhaps he had expressed his differences of opinion with the high command too forthrightly—and about Brittany, perhaps he had been too embarrassingly correct. Veterans of the division almost universally agree that they never found another leader to match him. Yet Manton Eddy had no ax to grind over such an issue as Brittany, and the XII Corps commander had nevertheless grown insistent that Wood's taut nerves would no longer permit him to command the 4th Armored.

How optimism and hope for a new breakthrough by the American army could be sustained despite such sacrifices to the autumn's hardships is partially explained by the subsequent performance of Wood's division. Even without Wood, even after the long weeks of fighting in the vanguard that had left its men and machines as much in need of rest as its old leader, the 4th Armored persisted. When December came, most of General Eddy's XII Corps paused to take breath—but the 4th Armored did not relent in its exploitation of the defeat of the Panzer Lehr counterattack, seeking to drive into and beyond Sarre-Union, across the ground over which Bayerlein's panzers had advanced. Together with the 101st Regiment of the 26th Division on its left, CCB fought its way into Sarre-Union on December 1. It drove back the 25th Panzer Grenadier Division despite a stiffening of tanks from both Panzer Lehr and the 11th Panzer Division. Though the battle for the industrial town seesawed for a while—the Germans rolled in again on December 2, and the 104th Infantry had to be committed to the battle—as soon as the place was secure, on December 4, General Gaffey sent CCA thrusting northward again. His next objective was Rohrbach-lès-Bitche, a road junction behind the German positions farther west facing the bulk of the XII Corps, and also astride the line of retreat of the Germans facing southward against the XV Corps of the Seventh Army.

At the village of Bining, on the main road from Sarre-Union to Rohrbach, the Germans proved to have massed more than enough artillery to discourage assault. The ground, as usual, was too soft for tanks to move cross country, so Abe Abrams, again commanding the advance, shifted to a secondary road a little to the west, approaching Rohrbach through the village of Singling and thereby outflanking Bining. Gaffey directed CCB toward Singling as well. When Abrams opened the attack against the latter village, on the morning of December 6, he soon found himself stymied yet again, by a combination of the Bitche complex of the Maginot Line and German artillery on hills to the north, plus tanks and assault guns—fixed and mobile defenses formidably coordinated. At nightfall American tanks and armored infantry fought into the village, but enemy guns made their position intolerable. Most leaders and formations would have subsided before this parade of frustrations; Abrams and the 4th Armored were different. Amidst a noisy furor of battle at Singling, a company of light tanks with an attached segment of the Yankee Division's 328th Infantry sidled off to Bining and captured it by indirection after all. The 4th Armored thereupon departed for rest and refitting, but it had opened a path for its replacement, Roderick Allen's new 12th Armored, to drive into Rohrbach on December 10.

The effect was to hasten a general enemy withdrawal before a renewed XII Corps offensive begun on December 4, and thus to strengthen the American impression that the strain and casualties of the past two months might be about to pay dividends. Baade's 35th Division in the corps center had led off without artillery preparation, followed by Grow's 6th Armored and McBride's 80th farther west with a preparatory blasting by the guns. The immediate aim was to cross the Sarre River and, in the process, to capture the industrial city of Sarreguemines, which straddles the river. Surprise in the center and artillery preparation on the left were equally effective, no doubt because the opposition, the 17th ss Panzer Grenadier Division, had been drained since Normandy beyond even the capacity of German leadership to rehabilitate it without prolonged rest and retraining. While McBride's 80th Division captured high ground around Farebersviller on the corps flank, both Grow's 6th Armored and Baade's 35th closed up to the Sarre by the end of December 6. Predictably, house-to-house fighting in Sarreguemines presented the most difficult problems of the attack; but it was less to clear the western portion of the city than to allow Paul's 26th Division to disentangle itself from Sarre-Union and close up on Baade's right that the advance paused at the river.

The 35th and 26th attacked in tandem before sunrise on December 8, the 35th readily crossing the Sarre, General Paul's division pressing into a sector of the Maginot Line. The standard, almost immediate counterattack against the 35th, conducted by tanks and armored infantry of the 11th Panzer Division, took so harsh a battering with the help of artillery from the Sarre's west bank that in Army Group G, the enemy henceforth felt obliged to modify a nearly sacrosanct article of his doctrine. General Balck ordered that hereafter, counterattacks should be launched only at twilight, during the night, in fog or bad weather, or from the concealment of woods. American artillery should be afforded no opportunity to break up the counterattacks before they were fairly formed.

In spite of snow and sleet, for four days the 35th Division struggled onward from the Sarre River to the Blies. During the same days the Yankee Division penetrated and passed the Maginot Line, assisted by the scouring of Rohrbach by the 12th Armored. Though the 26th Division had not been in the line as long as the 35th, the autumn campaign in Lorraine had imposed on it a hard initiation into war, and army and corps headquarters believed that Paul's troops ought to join the 4th Armored in refitting. After most of the division had gone back to Metz, the 328th Infantry remained in the battle long enough to inscribe the crossing of the German frontier into the division journal on the night of December 12–13.

The Blies River proved a tougher barrier against Baade's 35th Division than the Sarre, partly because its relatively high east bank offered the Germans a good artillery platform, partly because the 11th Panzer Division lay entrenched in a portion of the crossing area. The vanguard of the Sante Fe Cross Division nevertheless won a bridgehead on the east shore on December 12, but then it had to fight a battle for the town of Habkirchen so severe that the contest cost the 134th Infantry more than half its combat strength. Soldiers of the 35th soon came to believe, furthermore, that not only the presence of Wietersheim's Ghost Division but also the reaching of the international frontier and the challenge of defending Germany's home soil accounted for the harder going beyond the Blies. Still, by December 16 the 35th Division and Major General Frank L. Culin, Jr.'s new 87th had carried the XII Corps to the outworks of the West Wall, and the opposing German lines betrayed evidence of a promising thinness.

Patton's other corps, Walker's XX, was by then well established in the outer works of the West Wall. From the corps's first small encroachment into the wall, when General Twaddle's 95th Division captured the two bunkers facing the Saarlautern bridge, the 95th had gone on to serious grappling with the numerous bunkers and pillboxes that crowded the northern suburbs of Saarlautern. On December 6, meanwhile, Van Fleet's 90th Division on Twaddle's left crossed the Sarre around Dillingen and thus also reached the wall, which here abutted almost directly upon the east bank of the river. The pattern of fighting for both divisions became a slow crawl from pillbox to pillbox in the manner of the First Army's earlier penetration of the wall far to the north.

Indeed, the Saarlautern section was the strongest area of the West Wall, a double barrier even thicker than the similar double belt of fortifications around Aachen. Before the war, in January 1939, the German General Staff estimated that if the French attacked they would do so in this very zone where the XX Corps was now fighting, between Merzig and Saarlautern. Therefore the Saarlautern section had received special attention in 1939 and early 1940. It was also one of the few sectors of the West Wall to have received any serious strengthening later than 1940, in 1943 and early 1944. To wrestle with the XX Corps, in addition to the usual agglomeration of scratch formations, the German First Army had the remnants of the 21st Panzer Division, with few tanks but still with something of the fighting spirit that had made it fearsome long ago in the Western Desert, and the relatively fresh 719th Division, brought down from Holland.

Like Hodges's First Army before them, Patton's soldiers found when they hit the West Wall that their training in attacks against well-positioned, interlocking fortifications was not all that it might have been. Once again the bazooka proved more valuable against pillboxes than most soldiers' training in its use would have indicated, and bazooka instruction programs had to be improvised behind the lines. Furthermore, the 95th Division, as we have seen, was already drooping with exhaustion when it first struck the West Wall; and after a few days among the pillboxes on the east bank of the Sarre—while their own artillery and tanks were still west of the river—the infantry of the 90th Division were in no better shape. By December 12, the combat efficiency of Van Fleet's division was rated at 43 percent.

Yet the XX Corps wearily but steadily groped onward through the West Wall. By December 18, Twaddle's division had taken 146 pillboxes, 1,242 defended buildings, and over 3,000 prisoners since the beginning of the month. The 90th Division had crunched through the main belt of fortifications around Dillingen, leaving German resistance no longer a continuous line but a scattering of island strongpoints. The Germans were worried enough to need a scapegoat; General von Knobelsdorff, who had come to their First Army in late summer as the officer supposed to be able to turn back Patton, gave way on December 4 to General der Infanterie Hans von Obstfelder. Obstfelder was a defensive-minded protégé of Field Marshal Model.

American intelligence could enjoy the further comfort that the new First Army commander came in lieu of more substantial aid in reinforcements and matériel, which thanks to the autumn battles of attrition the enemy seemed unable to afford. On December 12, a 12th Army Group intelligence summary concluded from such developments: "All of the enemy's major capabilities, therefore, depend on the balance between the rate of attrition imposed by the Allied offensives and the rate of infantry reinforcement. The balance at present is in favor of the Allies. With continuing Allied pressure in the south and in the north, the breaking point may develop suddenly and without warning."[3]

Great Expectations

On the evidence and conclusions thus afforded him, it was not unreasonable for Eisenhower to respond to Montgomery's latest strategic complaints by saying:

I do not agree that things have gone badly since Normandy, merely because we have not gained all we had hoped to gain. In fact, the situation is somewhat analogous to that which existed in Normandy for so long. Our line as late as D plus 60 was not greatly different than what we hoped to hold in the first week, but I never looked upon the situation then existing as a strategic reverse. . . .[4]

By implication, that is, the autumn battles might yet prove the necessary preliminaries to a new breakthrough, as the battles in the hedgerows had prepared the way for COBRA.

Still, with the Roer dams presumably soon to fall and Allied freedom of maneuver north of the Ardennes thus to be restored, the method of seeking the breakthrough had to be planned. Montgomery, relatively quiescent as a grand strategist while 21 Army Group was preoccupied with opening Antwerp and clearing the Peel Marshes, had returned to counseling the Supreme Commander, and he raised the issue of method in a conference with Eisenhower on November 28 and a followup letter on the 30th. Naturally, Montgomery returned to urging a concentration of Allied resources upon an offensive by 21 Army Group in the north. Almost as naturally, the field marshal blended counsel with less than tactful criticism, which accounted for the first of Eisenhower's sentences quoted above, denying that affairs had gone badly since Normandy. Montgomery's offending observation had involved a new effort to propose an overall ground commander, or at least a single ground commander north of the Ardennes. In that connection, Montgomery had remarked: "Bradley and I together are a good team. We worked together in Normandy, under you, and we won a great victory. Things have not been so good since you separated us."

As anyone would have, Eisenhower inferred that Montgomery thought little or nothing had gone well since the activation of the 12th Army Group. When Eisenhower's written response of December 1 took issue with such a view, Montgomery retreated by pointing to the fact that he had also spoken of a specific and recent "strategic reverse," the failure to carry out SHAEF's operational directive of October 28, and saying he had meant no broader failure than this one. The October 28 directive had called for defeating the enemy armies decisively west of the Rhine and winning a bridgehead over the Rhine. "We have achieved none of this, and we have no hope of doing so. We have therefore failed; and we have suffered a strategic reverse."[5] Montgomery said his criticism involved nothing more than these circumstances which everyone acknowledged. Eisenhower responded, too generously, with "prompt and abject apologies for misreading your letter of 30th November."[6]

All of which hardly mattered. By now, Eisenhower's efforts to placate Montgomery while proceeding with operations different from the field marshal's desires were becoming a mere ritual. It is a pity that Montgomery remained incapable of reasoned argument for concentration in the offensive without Olympian arrogance to close the ears even of the patient Eisenhower—let alone Bradley and the other Americans—and without continual harping on the question of ground command, which more and more appeared churlishly self-serving. Montgomery's aspirations toward a larger command no longer possessed as much of a strategic foundation as they had two or three months earlier. In the flux of September, a single-thrust strategy might conceivably have dealt a knockout blow; in November and December, after the German recovery, a single-thrust strategy merely offered the enemy the opportunity to shift his meager resources from inactive sectors to threatened ones, as shown by the recent American encounters with German divisions brought south from Holland.

Hoping for more constructive planning toward the anticipated new breakthrough, Eisenhower assembled Tedder, Montgomery, and Bradley to meet with him on December 7 at Maastricht. The site was near enough to Brussels that Montgomery deigned to attend. But his presence hampered rather than assisted constructive discourse. All the old debates about the single thrust versus the broad front had to receive yet another tedious rehearsal, with as much futility as in the Eisenhower-Montgomery exchange of letters the previous week. Montgomery said, "The only real worth-while objective on the western front is the Ruhr," and that both his and Bradley's army groups ought to be concentrated completely north of the Ardennes to encircle the Ruhr. Montgomery's army group, reinforced with an American army of at least ten divisions, should cross the Rhine between Nijmegen and Wesel and attack the Ruhr from the north; the 12th Army Group ought to mount a secondary operation south of the Ruhr. Both these army groups north of the Ardennes should have a single commander. The Saar should be left to the 6th Army Group, to operate on whatever supplies might be left over. Eisenhower, in response, argued that Montgomery "put too much stress on the Ruhr; it was merely a geographical objective; our real objective was to kill Germans and it did not matter where we did it." Furthermore, the Frankfurt area was also a suitable target, and he was not about to halt Patton's offensive toward it. At the same time, Eisenhower also professed as usual to believe he did not substantially differ from Montgomery, and that they disagreed only about the point of origin of the secondary offensive. But such professions had become even more simply ritualistic than the larger pattern of these arguments. Eisenhower's judgments of December 7 were no longer his judgments of September 10, when he had authorized MARKET-GARDEN. Eisenhower's flirtation with the single-thrust strategy was over.[7]

"And so we really achieved nothing at the Maastricht conference," said Montgomery,[8] though from Bradley's viewpoint Montgomery still achieved too much. As Bradley had feared, Eisenhower decided that the Ninth Army, with ten divisions, ought to reinforce 21 Army Group. Beginning as early in January as possible, the British armies and Simpson's were to launch converging attacks from Nijmegen and the Roer to carry them across the Rhine north of the Ruhr.

Nevertheless, with Antwerp open, logistics in reasonably good order, and the enemy no longer in the disarray of September, there was no real doubt of the ascendancy of the broad-front strategy. The turn in strategy signaled by Eisenhower's September 20 letter resolving to close to the Rhine with all his armies had proven far more enduring than any of the Supreme Commander's earlier pronouncements about how to enter Germany. Simultaneously with the coming 21 Army Group offensive, Hodges's First Army would attack across the Roer to drive against the Ruhr from the south. Patton's Third Army was to go on attacking also, eventually to join Hodges in the southern assault upon the Ruhr. Patch's Seventh Army would continue thrusting forward through the West Wall in support of Patton.

And Patton might yet steal the show. While Bradley suggested that the problem of the Roer dams might delay the "main," northern attack at least until January 15, Patton and his staff along with the Ninth Air Force began preparing a Third Army offensive for

December 19. Bradley warned that Eisenhower's concessions to Montgomery on the secondary nature of the southern front were sufficient that Patton might have to attain considerable momentum within a week or suspend his effort; but the visibly staggering enemy in front of him and Patch caused Patton few doubts.

25: The Breakthrough

THE RIGHT FLANK of General Lauer's 99th Division, shielding the V Corps advance toward the Roer dams, trailed off into the Losheim Gap. Into this narrow corridor formed by the upper Kyll River, General Barton of the 4th Division had once hoped to throw a flanking force to turn the enemy positions farther southward on the Schnee Eifel. That was back in September, when the V Corps still thought of exploiting the enemy's weakness in the Ardennes and the Eifel to penetrate across these wooded plateaus into the Reich. Barton of course abandoned the project when his division, as well as Gerow's whole corps, became too patently overextended on the wide Ardennes front, and higher headquarters vetoed further offensive efforts there. In mid-December, no Americans any longer regarded the Losheim Gap as a corridor for offensive action. Their plans pointed in other directions, and the 3rd Battalion of the 99th Division's 394th Infantry maintained no real line in the gap, but only a succession of unimposing strongpoints. South of the gap, Major General Alan W. Jones's new 106th Division of the VIII Corps extended the front still more loosely into the Ardennes.

The 394th's Intelligence and Reconnaissance Platoon of some eighteen men guarded a crossroads near the village of Lanzerath, about three kilometers west of Losheim on the main road from Manderfeld to Losheimergraben, at a place where a lesser road forked northwest to a railroad station at Buchholz and to Honsfeld. If enemy troops should be able to move up the fork, they would turn the right flank of the 394th's 1st Battalion, which at Losheimergraben guarded a major crossroads, the junction of the lateral Manderfeld-Losheimergraben-Monschau road with the main highway through the Losheim Gap, running from Germany through Losheim and Malmédy back toward the Meuse at Liège. The I and R Platoon occupied foxholes, in front of a woods, that were dug deep and provided with good overhead cover by previous guardians of the Losheim Gap, General Robertson's 2nd Division. Also around Lanzerath were a few tank destroyers of the 14th Cavalry Group, attached to the 106th Division and representing the extreme left of the VIII Corps.

Before dawn on Saturday, December 16, an enemy artillery barrage far exceeding in volume anything the new troops of the 394th had ever witnessed rumbled back and forth across the eastward hills. Fortunately, the I and R Platoon was entrenched well enough to escape unhurt. But by the glow of the bombardment, the Americans could distinguish all too plainly the silhouettes of many tanks and assault guns on the hills around Losheim— so plainly that the tank destroyers decided they were excessively overmatched and pulled back toward Büllingen.

First Lieutenant Lyle J. Bouck of the I and R Platoon radioed the ominous news to regimental headquarters, which instructed him to send a patrol into Lanzerath just in front of him and report further. He led the four-man patrol in person. By first light he saw heavy columns of German infantry moving through the Losheim Gap in his direction. He called for artillery to hit the road; but, presumably because a large concentration of troops with offensive intent was not to be anticipated from an enemy as exhausted as the Germans, and because such a concentration would most particularly not emerge from the rugged Eifel, the requested fire support failed to appear.

Bouck's platoon prepared to defend its crossroads from the concealed foxholes with its own rifles, BARs, a submachine gun, and two .30- and one .50-caliber machine guns. Strangely, when the German infantry marched within range—wearing the uniforms and insignia of parachutists and thus presumably elite troops—they paid as little heed to the possibility of American resistance as most American headquarters were paying to the possibility of a large, aggressive German presence. So blandly did they parade along in column, without vanguard or flank guard, that Lieutenant Bouck decided to let some 300 pass before he sprang an ambush. Just as a cluster of officers appeared and he was about to give the signal to fire, a little girl ran out of a house and evidently warned the Germans that there were Americans nearby. Before the girl was under shelter again, the enemy had just enough time to begin leaping into ditches—and to escape the worst moment of surprise.

Still, well-placed and well-sheltered foxholes permitted the handful of Americans to put up a hard fight. Regimental headquarters now accepted the word that something big was going on—the same kind of news was coming from everywhere—but could offer little more help than an order to stand fast. Except occasionally, American artillery fire remained absent. As the day wore on, the Germans brought in mortar fire. More and more German infantry continued to arrive. By evening, those Americans who were not shot had expended their ammunition and had to surrender. Bouck felt the satisfaction of estimating they left some 400 enemy dead piled in front of their foxholes.

The Second Battle of the Schnee Eifel

The 394th Infantry began December 16 strung out along a thirty-kilometer front, between the well-concentrated American force battling for the Roer dams just to the north and the yet thinner lines of the VIII Corps to the south. Somewhere around midday, the regiment lost radio contact with its I and R Platoon—Bouck's radio was knocked out. The 3rd Battalion, on the regimental right rear, was being struck hard by Germans infiltrating toward the Buchholz railroad station. By the time the fate of the I and R Platoon disappeared into the swirl of combat, this battalion was protecting the regimental right by facing southwest along the railroad, which here paralleled the Losheim-Malmédy highway about two kilometers south of it. German troops were pushing through the chasm now yawning between the 394th and the VIII Corps. At Losheimergraben, the 1st Battalion was under severe pressure to abandon its crossroads, and the 3rd Battalion had to yield four platoons to reinforce the 1st. The shift left the 3rd Battalion with only about 100 men in line—but at least one company of the 1st was down to twenty men.

On the regiment's left flank, in contrast, the 2nd Battalion repulsed a head-on charge during the morning with little loss to itself and much loss to the enemy, and thereafter was little disturbed. All in all, just as the 394th Regiment stood midway between heavy

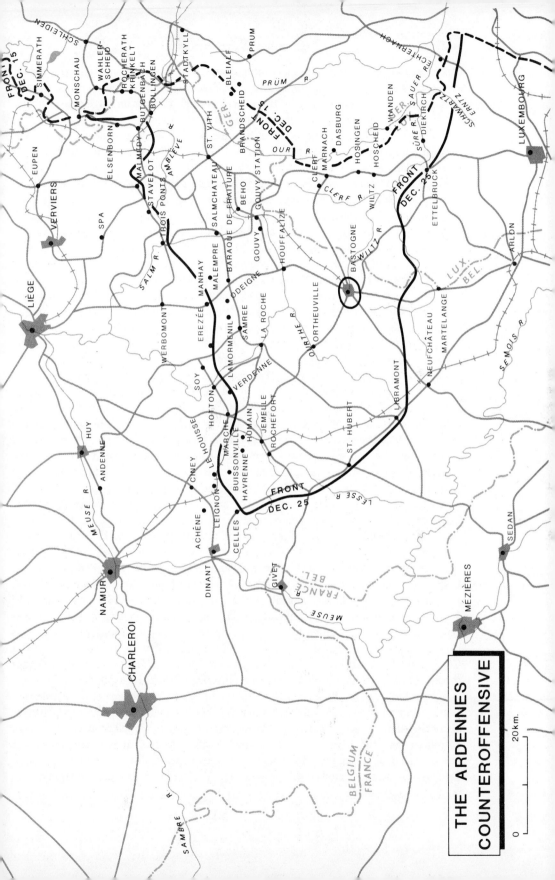

THE ARDENNES
COUNTEROFFENSIVE

concentrations to its left and the overextended VIII Corps on its right, so too its experiences of the day fell at about midpoint along the spectrum; its right and center precarious, its left reasonably solid, the 394th was worse off than its northern neighbors, but in a lot better shape than its comrades just to the south.

The entire V Corps front received the same kind of predawn artillery treatment as the 394th, with the Germans dedicating themselves particularly to counterbattery fire. At several places the enemy advanced under the glare of searchlights. On the 99th Division's left the 395th Infantry, two of whose battalions had advanced into the Monschau Forest in tandem with the 2nd Division, absorbed an early-morning attack in heavy but unknown strength. The attackers belonged to a newly arrived formation, the 326th Volksgrenadier Division. This same division was identified in attacks all the way north to the Monschau corridor, where General Parker's 78th Division had to send a fresh battalion to restore contact with the troops cut off in Kesternich and under heavy attack. General Gerow sent the 2nd Ranger Battalion to the assistance of the 78th. About noon, corps headquarters instructed the 2nd Division to release a battalion each of tanks and infantry to the 99th. But except out on the 394th Infantry's right flank, the V Corps found enough strength to retain its positions and the integrity of its units.

Apparently at the request of the First Army, General Gerow also ordered General Robertson of the 2nd Division to release CCB of the 9th Armored Division from attachment, and to send it south to the VIII Corps zone. On General Middleton's VIII Corps front, the Germans continued spilling out of the Eifel woods in greater and greater numbers as the day went on, and the consequences were perilous. Because the various Allied headquarters had rejected the Ardennes-Eifel as a route into Germany, and because intelligence rated the Germans as having no capacity for a counteroffensive and thought that if the enemy managed even a local counterattack, it would come along the Roer, Bradley and Hodges had turned the Ardennes into a rest area for old divisions and a training ground for new ones. There Middleton's troops held a front of about 145 kilometers with a mere four divisions. The new 106th Division on the corps left was intended to gain a gradual seasoning in war in the quiet Ardennes, while to the south the exhausted 28th and 4th Divisions recovered from their ordeals in the Huertgen. The 4th and the 106th had only recently entered the line, the 4th from December 7 to 13 to replace the 83rd Division, the 106th on December 11 and 12 to replace the 2nd. The 14th Cavalry Group, also present only since December 11, and portions of Major General John W. Leonard's 9th Armored Division filled in a few stretches of the VIII Corps line, and Leonard's armored infantry from time to time relieved battalions of the infantry divisions. Middleton had wanted to retain the 9th Armored as a reserve, but for various reasons only CCR was available in that capacity on December 16. Altogether, the VIII Corps had 68,822 officers and men that Saturday morning. The corps front was about three times the length American doctrine prescribed for a force of this size.

Patrolling as vigorous as the VIII Corps could manage would have seemed necessary to the security of so weak a front, no matter what higher headquarters might believe about the enemy's lack of reserves. Nevertheless, Middleton failed to insist on diligent patrolling, and the recency of the 4th and 106th Divisions' arrival hampered their perceptions of anything that might constitute unusual activity opposite them. The 83rd Division had demonstrated across the Sauer and Moselle Rivers in late October. The 2nd

Division had laid down a heavy barrage on the anniversary of the 1918 armistice. Nothing much had been done since then, and nothing had dispelled the impression—correct enough in October—that only low-rated divisions held the enemy front. The 14th Cavalry Group and the 106th Division had inherited the 2nd Division's defensive plans, but they were not granted much time to acquaint themselves with the details on the ground.

The 14th Cavalry Group had elements spotted along an eight- or nine-kilometer front across part of the entrance to the Losheim Gap, between the 99th and 106th Divisions. South of the cavalry, the 422nd Infantry Regiment occupied a part of the 106th Division front where the September offensive had carried into the West Wall and to the crest of the Schnee Eifel. Here the Americans could look down into the German positions eastward, but before December 16 they saw nothing unusual. Farther south, the 106th Division trended slightly to the west. The 423rd Infantry, though its left was on the crest, bent away from the Schnee Eifel into a valley. The 424th Infantry continued the front southwesterly through the valley, to a minimal connection with the 28th Division around Lützkampen.

The 14th Cavalry Group sector was traversed by a hard-surfaced east-to-west road around the northern edge of the Schnee Eifel from Hallschlag behind the German front through Manderfeld, the cavalry's command post, across the Our River at Schönberg, and on to the Belgian road-junction town of St. Vith, headquarters of the 106th Division. Another hard-surfaced road ran from Prüm inside Germany around the southern edge of the Schnee Eifel to Bleialf, in rear of the 423rd Infantry, and also on to Schönberg. A secondary road, which like all such in the area had many stretches barely negotiable by wheeled vehicles after the autumn rains, hugged the north edge of the Schnee Eifel to Roth and on to Auw and thence to Bleialf or Schönberg. Through the 424th Infantry a third good road reached northwest from Pronsfeld in Germany through Habscheid and Winterspelt and on to St. Vith. To describe hard-surfaced roads in the Eifel and the Ardennes as good is to use the adjective relatively. On the deeply scored plateaus, all roads descended abruptly on occasion into deep ravines and wound over hills and through woods via successions of blind curves.

The night of December 14–15, cold and clear, resounded with the clamor of many engines and tracked vehicles in motion east of the 106th Division, while German aircraft droned back and forth overhead, perhaps to distract American attention. But no one made any special effort the next day to discover the cause of the hubbub. On the 15th, General Jones's division took two prisoners, both of whom said that fresh troops were arriving constantly in the German lines and that a big attack was due in a day or so, certainly before Christmas. Even inexperienced intelligence officers knew, however, that prisoner statements about a forthcoming attack were to be expected routinely; the Nazis apparently tried to stimulate morale through promises of aggressive action. Noises again disturbed the night on December 15–16, accompanied again by ostentatiously busy German airplanes. Enemy patrols were also unusually active during the night, still without prompting much American concern.

Beginning at 5:30 in the morning of December 16, the left flank of the VIII Corps, like the I and R Platoon of the 394th Infantry just north of it, was awakened and awed, but not much injured, by the roar and glow of a German bombardment. Many telephone wires were cut, and radio communication grew difficult because the Germans began playing phonograph records on the American wave lengths. The 106th Division alerted the 14th Cavalry Group's reserve squadron and moved it closer to the potential action.

Only a single artillery salvo actually struck around the cavalry group positions in the villages of Roth and Kobscheid. By that time, German infantry were probably already in and around the villages. Daylight came slowly, with fog and drizzle. Once the cavalrymen were able to see, they discovered that Germans were all about them. Roth and Kobscheid were cut off. When light tanks hastened up from Manderfeld, they were stopped by Germans already in control of Auw. At Krewinkel farther north, a cavalry outpost repulsed an assault by parachute infantry only to have one of the departing enemy soldiers shout, in English: "Take a ten-minute break. We'll be back." They were. Without the manpower or armament for a defense in depth, their towed 3-inch tank destroyers incapable of movement rapid enough to deal with an enemy who had infiltrated in every direction, by noon the cavalry were simply trying to extricate themselves. They hoped to stand on a ridge around Manderfeld some 3,000 meters behind their initial positions. By late afternoon, the Germans were behind both flanks of the Manderfeld ridge and the surviving cavalrymen were pulling back again, to ridges around Andler in front of the Schönberg bridge.

The inevitable collapse of the cavalry against a German force big enough that elements of two divisions could be identified—the 3rd Parachute and the 18th Volksgrenadiers—turned the left flank of the 422nd Infantry on the Schnee Eifel. This regiment experienced little of the shock of the attack, but Germans were at Auw in its rear before anything could be done about it. During the early afternoon, under the inherited 2nd Division plan, the 422nd dispatched a task force to recapture Auw. The march was impeded by an abrupt snowstorm, and before the counterattack could be driven home, it was recalled by word that Germans infiltrating the Schnee Eifel by way of a sheltered ravine were threatening the regimental command post.

Because the 2nd Battalion of the 423rd Infantry was in division reserve, that regiment had compensated by devising an impromptu right wing from the regimental antitank company, a platoon of the cannon company, a rifle platoon, and Troop B, 18th Cavalry Squadron, the latter borrowed from the 14th Cavalry Group. Enemy infantry moving along the southern road around the Schnee Eifel drove this scratch battalion out of Bleialf early in the day. But the 423rd recaptured the town by throwing in the headquarters company and Company B, 81st Combat Engineer Battalion. Farther south, th 424th Infantry, also with only two regular battalions in line, almost exceeded this performance. It thrashed an attack on its center and right so soundly that the enemy gave up trying to infiltrate between the 106th and 28th Divisions. But the 1/424th, unfortunately, allowed itself to be driven off high ground that gave the enemy a wedge toward Winterspelt and the road thence to St. Vith.

All in all, December 16 showed not a bad day's work for the 106th Division. Victims of tactical surprise after only a short sojourn in an unfriendly environment—frostbite and trench foot had already begun their ravages—the troops nevertheless had overcome their inexperience and such incidentals of inexperience as their lack of the surplus of BARs and light machine guns that every veteran division hoarded. They gained at least a draw in every combat they fought save one.

But there was no cause for complacency. In the enemy force behind the left flank of the 422nd Infantry the division G-2 rightly discerned the shaping of that favorite German offensive gambit, an envelopment—to isolate the Schnee Eifel and the better part of the two regiments atop it. All through the night, furthermore, the Germans kept pressing their advantages and marching more troops into the threatened areas. General Middleton told General Jones by telephone that it was important to hold the Schnee Eifel but that the high ground was untenable unless its northern flank could be protected. Jones later telephoned Middleton, suggested that the Schnee Eifel would have to be abandoned, and predictably found the corps commander passing the buck back to him as the man on the spot. Nevertheless, Jones left Middleton with the impression that he would withdraw. Middleton then issued a "hold at all costs order" to the entire VIII Corps, but excluded from it positions east of the Our. In fact, Jones decided to try to hold on, perhaps because Middleton had assured him that armored help was on the way—not only CCB of the 9th Armored Division, returning from the V Corps, but also CCB of the 7th Armored, dispatched by order of SHAEF from the Ninth Army. Corps headquarters optimistically told Jones that the 7th Armored combat command would reach St. Vith the next morning. Anyone believing this was not looking carefully at his maps, but Jones accordingly diverted CCB, 9th Armored from his north flank to Winterspelt. Perhaps Jones's division had held up a little too well; December 16 had not dissipated the sanguine mood at division and corps as much as it should have.

The Skyline Drive

General Cota's 28th Division front extended along the Our River, a deep scouring of the landscape like most of the streams of the Ardennes, and in Cota's zone the boundary between Germany and Luxembourg. Replacements—or, as the supposed requirements of morale had newly decreed they be termed, reinforcements—had restored all three of Cota's regiments substantially to table-of-organization strength. Many new officers and men thus patrolled the Our border.

The 112th Infantry on the division left posted its main line of resistance on the German side of the Our. Its frontage of about nine and a half kilometers was, as usual in the Ardennes, too long for its strength. Its right flank bent west to the Luxembourg side of the Our and dwindled away in a series of outposts. No good roads traversed the regimental area of pine-forested hills, draws, and ravines; but there were several bridges across the Our that might become enemy objectives in the unlikely event of a German attack.

On December 14, a German woman fleeing the Nazis happened to reach the 28th Division. She told of woods near Bitburg jammed with troops, vehicles, and bridging equipment. This report interested the division G-2 enough, and seemed to be supported with enough circumstantial detail, that it was passed up to the VIII Corps and on to the First Army. The refugee was being questioned at First Army headquarters on December 16. The 28th Division, like the 106th, also heard the ominous sounds of tracked vehicles moving in Germany on the nights of December 14–15 and 15–16; but the 28th had been in the Ardennes long enough to know that such rumblings merely signified replacement units coming in and old formations going out.

The 112th Infantry received some of the German artillery bombardment on the morning of December 16. Shells screamed above the rearward command posts, evidently intended for American battery positions, and then dropped their range eastward toward

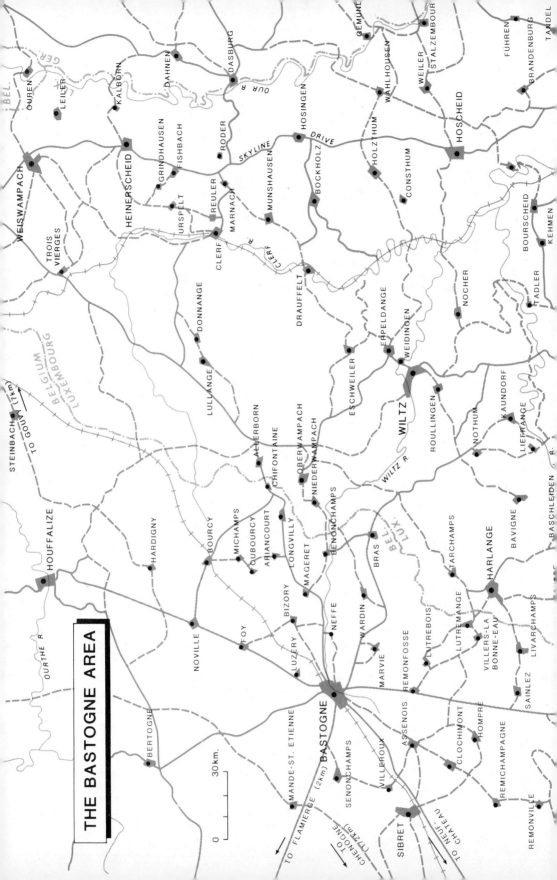

the Our. Presently, German searchlights flashed on. By dawn many German soldiers were already among or past the forward platoons. In the 3rd Battalion, a platoon of Company L was attacked by a German company while the men were eating breakfast. The company kitchen was captured, the platoon was overrun, and the enemy raced on to take a stone arch bridge over the Our south of Ouren. But much of the 3rd Battalion enjoyed the anchorage of West Wall pillboxes, and most of the troops rallied on the pillboxes to hold their main position. Two companies of the 2nd Battalion mounted a counterattack from west of the Our and recaptured the Ouren bridge. The 1st Battalion also yielded a kitchen truck at the first contact with infiltrating enemy infantry; but even without pillboxes, the battalion had sited its foxholes so well that their interlocking fields of fire began mowing Germans down and persuaded many to surrender. The veterans among Cota's troops soon concluded that much of the opposition this morning was exceedingly green. The judgment was correct; the 112th sector was allotted largely to the German 560th Division, composed of inexperienced garrison troops from Norway and Denmark. On the regimental left, the familiar 116th Panzer Division arrived on the scene, but flanking fire from the 424th Infantry hit this division so hard at the outset that even the tanks crunched forward with extreme caution when they began to be committed during the afternoon.

So the 112th Infantry held firmly to its positions throughout Saturday and administered more punishment than it received. Unfortunately, its situation nevertheless came more and more to resemble that of the 106th Division to the north of it; for the perils of the 106th were exposing the left flank of the 112th Regiment, while to the south the neighboring regiment of the Keystone Division was experiencing troubles that simultaneously unhinged the 112th's right flank.

The neighboring regiment was the 110th Infantry, which suffered the double misfortune of guarding a front some fourteen kilometers long and of standing in the direct path from Germany to the principal road center of the southern Ardennes, the Luxembourgian town of Bastogne. Furthermore, the 2nd Battalion of the 110th was in divisional reserve. The front was so long that the 110th made no pretense of maintaining a continuous line. Instead, there were merely company-sized strongpoints, distributed among the villages along the crest of the first ridge line on the Luxembourg side of the Our. From village to village along this crest ran the hard-surfaced, north-to-south, St. Vith-to-Diekirch road, part of the main road between Spa and the city of Luxembourg. The Americans called the road the Skyline Drive. It paralleled the Our two to three kilometers west of the stream. During daylight, the 110th customarily sent patrols down to the Our; but their efforts failed to keep the west bank clear of Germans even while the sun was up, and at night the wooded draws between the river and the Skyline Drive were German territory. This circumstance permitted the enemy to build up a heavy force there on the night of December 15–16 without the Americans' realizing that anything unusual was going on.

The German barrage beginning at 5:30 A.M. knocked out the 110th's telephone wires but did little other damage, and artillery radios continued to function. At dawn, however, German infantry charged out of the fog in numbers great enough to open a desperate close-range battle around nearly every American village strongpoint. The enemy's numbers, seemingly impressive everywhere along the VIII Corps front, felt yet more overpowering here. In fact, they were. The 106th was not fighting as many

Germans as it thought; the opponents of the 106th were scarcely more numerous than the division itself, but had simply concentrated against the weak points and especially the seams between units. Though General Jones's G-2 believed by Saturday evening that two different German divisions formed the prongs threatening to envelop the Schnee Eifel, actually both prongs belonged to the 18th Volksgrenadier Division. But it was different along the Skyline Drive; the 110th Regiment had to grapple with two divisions and the vanguard of a third before the day was over.

One of these was the 26th Volksgrenadier Division, a rested and refitted edition of an old-line infantry division which had fought on the Eastern Front from July 1941 to September 1944, and whose veterans considered the designation "Volksgrenadier" a doubtful honor for the Old 26th. Another of the 110th's assailants was the 2nd Panzer Division, which required no introduction; at its core it was still the unit the Americans had long rated the best panzer division on the Western Front, and it soon unveiled its generous resupply of Panthers and Pzkw IVs. Panzer Lehr, though less well equipped than the 2nd Panzer Division, also joined the attack, and it too had had its tanks replenished since its last battles, against the XII and XV Corps. (To be precise, the 2nd Panzer Division had fifty-eight Panthers and twenty-seven Pzkw IVs; Panzer Lehr, thirty Panthers and twenty-seven Mark IVs.) In short, the 110th Infantry proved to be confronting the whole of General von Lüttwitz's famous XLVII Panzer Corps—and the American regiment had a longer front than the German corps.

The villages the Germans evidently coveted most, and around which two of the 110th Infantry's fiercest battles developed, were Hosingen and Marnach. At Hosingen, Company D along with Company B, 103rd Engineer Battalion, held off Germans of the Old 26th who were trying to open the secondary road from an Our River bridge abuilding at Gemünd westward through Eschweiler to Bastogne. At Marnach, Company B of the 110th and a platoon of tank destroyers blocked the primary hard-surfaced east-west road through the sector. This road crossed the Our at Dasburg, where the 2nd Panzer Division sent panzer grenadiers and engineers across in rubber boats to assail Marnach while other engineers began erecting a bridge for the armor. As long as the enemy lacked his tanks and heavy weapons, Marnach might be able to resist him, but he wasted little time before infiltrating past the village and downward from the Skyline Drive toward the larger town of Clerf, where Colonel Hurley E. Fuller had set up regimental headquarters. When Company A from the north and Company C from the south tried to send help to Marnach along the Skyline Drive, they found some of the infiltrators strongly blocking the way.

To reopen the Drive and rescue his companies from isolation and defeat in detail, Fuller appealed to General Cota to return his 2nd Battalion. Cota thought the situation all along his front too fluid and unclear to risk yielding his principal reserve, but he tried to compensate by sending Companies A and B of the 707th Tank Battalion, two-thirds of his only other reserve. The opposing German army corps was already over the Our in such strength, making numbers and Panzerfäuste do the work of heavy weapons, that the tank companies promptly discovered they had all the fighting they could handle in merely approaching the Skyline Drive from the west, let alone reopening it. One of their platoons, directed toward Fuller's Company I on the Drive at Weiler, could not push through before the early winter darkness closed in, and the Weiler garrison then decided it had to try to make its way toward safety westward in small groups. Another tank platoon managed to punch into Marnach, but at dusk the garrison there radioed that it could hear German half-tracks approaching—the enemy's heavier strength was about to intervene—and battalion and regimental headquarters thereafter learned nothing more of Company B. By that time the engineers and infantry in Hosingen were grappling with Germans hand-to-hand in the streets and houses. To hold on, they said, they needed not only reinforcements but also rifle ammunition. Four Shermans fought their way into the village about ten that night, but they carried no rifle ammunition. Fuller's regiment was scarcely in fit shape to meet the panzers that were already doubtless crossing the Our at Gemünd and Dasburg, while the infiltrating enemy infantry columns were now pouring around the remaining Skyline Drive strongpoints and down into the valley of the Clerf River.

Cota's remaining regiment, the 109th, occupied perhaps the only place in the Ardennes where the American command had given serious thought to the possibility of even a local counterattack. The 109th extended the 28th Division front south to the confluence of the Our with the Sauer River at Wallendorf. Here a hard-surfaced road crossed the Our from Germany and continued up the valley of the Sauer—one of the few river valleys in the Ardennes wide enough to accommodate a highway—through Diekirch to Ettelbruck, where it branched southward and westward and also met the Skyline Drive. Cota had surmised that the Germans might try to move along this road to cut the roads and railroads running north from the city of Luxembourg. To guard against such an attempt, the 3rd Battalion of the 109th, though assigned over five kilometers of front, concentrated its strength in an almost continuous three-kilometer line on hills within the "V" of the river junction, commanding the road. The 1st Battalion lay in reserve at Diekirch. The 2nd Battalion, reaching northward to meet the 110th Regiment, had about seven kilometers of front, which it would try to defend from two company-sized strongpoints and a series of lesser outposts.

On the morning of Thursday, December 14, the 109th had sent a large combat patrol across the Our from a ruined château at Vianden, one of the 2nd Battalion outposts, only to contact no enemy whatever. But at 5:30 A.M. on Saturday, the Germans gave assurance of their return by including the 109th in the artillery barrage that resounded over the Our front. As elsewhere, by the time the big guns fell silent German infantry had already penetrated the fog all around the American strongpoints and outposts and at some places were well on their way into the American rear. The château at Vianden was overrun before any warning had sounded. When regimental headquarters first learned that outposts were under assault, the numbers of attackers seemed so small that for a while the regiment thought the Germans were merely patrols. But, once again, enemy numbers built up rapidly. Once more, American battalions were confronting whole divisions: the 5th Parachute Division mainly on the 2nd Battalion front, the 352nd Volksgrenadier Division—reincarnation of the old D-Day adversary—mainly on the 3rd Battalion front.

The fighting was most bitter at the remaining 2nd Battalion strongpoint, Führen, which commanded the road climbing up the hills from Roth, where the Germans began bridging the Our. Both German divisions contributed troops to the assault on Führen. Company E, the garrison, was quickly isolated. But the company held on, and so did the rest of the 109th throughout the day. The gravest trouble was that by dusk the Germans who initially infiltrated past the regiment's principal positions had been joined by many of their comrades. In the early morning hours on Sunday, regimental headquarters learned there was a heavy German force on the Skyline Drive in the 109th's left rear—for the eastward swing of the Our had put the 109th generally in advance of the 110th. Another ominous fact was the ability of the enemy to press the 109th almost to the breaking point on Saturday without his tanks and heavy weapons; though their bridge-building in front of the 109th seemed to be stumbling along with amazing slowness, the Germans would surely find a way to get these weapons into the sector soon.

Still farther south, the hills near the German border become rugged enough that this corner of Luxembourg is called "la petite Suiss." Here the 60th Armored Infantry Battalion of the 9th Armored Division occupied a line of about four kilometers on the right of the 28th Division. When a German infantry attack took shape out of the Saturday morning fog, this battalion also found itself the apparent target of an entire enemy division, the 276th Volksgrenadiers. Each American sector suffered its own peculiar problems of defense; with the armored infantry these took the form of deep, wooded valleys to shelter attackers working their way along either of the battalion flanks, the valley wherein the Our met the Sauer on the left, and a gorge called the Schwarz Erntz on the right. Mortar and machine-gun fire from the 3/109th's concentration above the two rivers stopped an enemy probe along the armored infantry's left, but the Schwarz Erntz and a series of lesser ravines and draws from the battalion right toward the center proved more troublesome. On Saturday afternoon, General Leonard of the 9th Armored stabilized the 60th Battalion's front by committing all the reserves he had at hand, amounting to his CCA. CCA headquarters took command of the fight on Sunday morning. Meanwhile, on this front at least there was no immediate threat to the American rear. Either the 276th Volksgrenadiers were the least enterprising German division to go into action on December 16, or it might be that here, far south on the beleaguered VIII Corps front, it was becoming possible at last to discern the southern edge of the German effort.

A G-2 drawing either or both conclusions would have arrived at part of the truth, but nevertheless the left of General Barton's 4th Division, beyond the 60th Armored Infantry, was not too far south to share in the enemy's attentions. Having just completed its shift from the Huertgen Forest on December 13, the 4th was still in bad shape. Replacements were coming in, but the infantry regiments remained 500 to 600 men short of authorized strength, and many rifle companies mustered only half strength. Many of the veterans were away on a well-earned leave in Arlon or Paris. Equipment had not been generally replaced since the division began fighting in Normandy; much of it was in the repair shops, and much of the rest in dubious condition. The attached 70th Tank Battalion had only eleven of fifty-four Shermans in running order. Yet the division held a fifty-five kilometer front, facing the Sauer and the Moselle to the Third Army boundary just south of the Luxembourg border.

Necessarily, Barton like his neighbors distributed his men in outposts and made no effort to defend a continuous line. In the 12th Infantry on the division left, for example, only five companies occupied the main line of resistance, if it can be called that, posted in the villages of Berdorf, Echternach, Lauterborn, Osweiler, and Dickweiler on the roads leading up from the deep trench of the Sauer. The company command post and a few additional men would occupy a village; the outposts fanned out over the nearby hills overlooking the river. The rest of the regiment, including the whole 2nd Battalion, lay in reserve. With thoughts roughly paralleling General Cota's, Barton feared an enemy effort to threaten the city of Luxembourg, little more than thirty kilometers from Echternach.

He counted on his large allotment of the available strength to his reserves to rope off such a drive. With the predawn bombardment on December 16, he thought the attack on the capital of the Grand Duchy was beginning.

Paris, Luxembourg, and Spa

"That the Ardennes Offensive . . . could have been foreseen," wrote Lieutenant Colonel Adolph G. Rosengarten, Jr., the ULTRA SLU officer at First Army headquarters,

> is submitted for the following reasons: (a) the enemy was defending on an artificial line with a major obstacle, the Rhine, astride his supply lines. (b) The German doctrine is an active defense. (c) The German situation, in the big picture, was so desperate that he could afford to take the longest chances and, (d) finally, the effect of our overwhelming air superiority was minimized by choosing a time when daylight was shortest, and the weather most likely to be bad. While the enemy had no cover plan to mislead us, his counter-intelligence was superb and merits very careful study. Some clues came from open sources but were not heeded as no clue came from ultra.[1]

No clue had come from ULTRA—itself a circumstance that might have aroused suspicions—and the German counteroffensive had gone unforeseen. When the unexpected blow fell, the disruption of American communications was bad enough, and events along the VIII and V Corps fronts confusing enough, that higher headquarters were slow to learn that anything of uncommon importance was happening. EAGLE-TAC, 12th Army Group tactical headquarters, was as close to the front as the city of Luxembourg; but as late as 9:15 on Saturday morning, Bradley's operations group reported to a daily briefing that there was no change on the VIII Corps front.

General Bradley himself was making the long drive from Luxembourg to SHAEF headquarters at Paris in his Cadillac staff car. Major Hansen had gotten only gloomy reports on flight conditions and suggested the car, but driving was little better than flying; the roads to Paris were sheets of ice, and the Cadillac barely missed colliding with a French car that shot from a byway with only a toot of the horn as a warning. "French are wild drivers—more menacing than the enemy sometimes."[2]

Bradley was sending his personnel officer back to Washington to plead against the diversion of replacements to the Pacific when so few were available for the European battle, and at SHAEF he wanted to underline his conviction of the importance of the mission with his own presence. He arrived late in the day. It was dusk when his meeting with Eisenhower was interrupted by Major General K.W.D. Strong, the SHAEF G-2, with an important message: the Germans had counterattacked in the Ardennes and scored penetrations at five places on the VIII Corps front. The enemy effort had begun early in the morning but its extent was still unknown. The most dangerous penetration seemed to be between the V and VIII Corps in the Losheim Gap.

The news did not prevent Bradley and Eisenhower from enjoying a round of champagne in honor of Ike's promotion to the new rank of general of the army, and the generals stayed up late to play five rubbers of bridge. In his memoirs, Bradley admitted forthrightly that he believed the Germans had launched a mere spoiling attack, to try to force a shift of Patton's troops from the Saar offensive back to the Ardennes.

But Eisenhower immediately sensed something bigger: "That's no spoiling attack."[3] The Ardennes itself offered no worthwhile objectives. If the Germans attacked there, they must be after bigger game. Eisenhower had felt misgivings about the weak VIII Corps front for a month; "the badly stretched condition of our troops caused constant concern," he said.[4] He had discussed the problem with Bradley, but his method of command forbade intervention. Yet his misgivings had grown with the recent identification of eight enemy divisions added to the German force opposite the Ardennes. He had been restrained from intervening also by his lack of reserves; he had hoped to build up a reserve corps but had accomplished little more than asking the army group commanders which divisions they could spare. SHAEF's only approximation of a reserve was the XVIII Airborne Corps, the 82nd and 101st Airborne Divisions, but these troops needed refitting after their withdrawal from Montgomery's lines in Holland. Studying his operations maps, Eisenhower noted, however, that the 7th Armored Division was still out of the line, in the Ninth Army sector, and the 10th Armored was uncommitted in the Third Army sector. "I think you had better send Middleton some help," he told Bradley. "These two armored divisions." Bradley objected that Patton would not appreciate losing the 10th Armored. Eisenhower overruled him, with a touch of impatience.[5]

By now, First Army and 12th Army Group headquarters had learned of captured orders that would vindicate the Supreme Commander's rapid and in part intuitive judgment. The captured documents began to solve recent mysteries of the German order of battle, and they pointed not to a spoiling attack but to a major strategic effort—a counteroffensive—in a desperate bid to reverse the course of the war. During the coming hours, the shape of two panzer armies emerged out of the Eifel-Ardennes, SS Oberstgruppenführer "Sepp" Dietrich's Sixth Panzer Army striking the V Corps, General von Manteuffel's Fifth Panzer Army striking the north wing of the VIII Corps. General Brandenberger's Seventh Army proved to have shifted well to the south of its old Huertgen Forest battleground, and it commanded the infantry divisions assailing the 109th Regiment, the 60th Armored Infantry Battalion, and the 12th Regiment. Field Marshal Model's Army Group B coordinated the three assaulting armies.

Eisenhower had to reach his quick appreciation of the force of the German drive without much prior help from the G-2s. About the beginning of October, Allied intelligence had become aware of the assembling of a number of panzer divisions behind the Germans' Aachen lines. The refitting and training activities of these divisions remained fairly conspicuous throughout the autumn—as the Germans evidently intended, for the location of the divisions reinforced a persistent Allied belief that the purpose was to defend the northern Rhine and the Ruhr, possibly by a counterattack after the Americans crossed the Roer. By the first week of November, the G-2s had identified the force as the Sixth Panzer Army, about the same time that this army was crossing from the east to the west bank of the Rhine. By the middle of November, SHAEF believed the enemy had contrived by "truly colossal effort" to form or recreate at least five panzer and five parachute divisions and to hold them in reserve for "a final showdown before the winter."[6]

Yet the intelligence staffs were not always as careful in choosing their words as their sensitive work might have dictated. Their inclination since August to believe that the enemy was on the verge of collapse led their more specific forecasts toward a surpassingly modest definition of "a final showdown." The Third Army's Colonel Koch, as usual, was something of an exception. Koch had never yet adopted the popular view that the German army was practically done for, and at least twice in the first half of December his summaries used the noun "offensive," with its connotations of a major strategic effort, to define the operation the Germans might attempt with the impressive reserve they were amassing. Still, even Koch spoke once merely of a "spoiling offensive," the adjective cutting the force of the noun, and on the other occasion he placed the likely "counter offensive" around Aachen and Düren.[7]

Colonel Dickson, the G-2 at Hodges's headquarters at Spa who was more immediately concerned with the Ardennes, issued a lengthy—and afterward much-debated—intelligence summary on December 10, designated Estimate 37. In it, the "Monk" went so far as to say that "The continual building up of forces to the west of the Rhine points consistently to his [the enemy's] staking all on the counteroffensive as stated in capability 2a (2)." Dickson was later to suggest that he thus foresaw and warned against the enemy's eruption into the Ardennes on December 16. Unfortunately, reference to the cited estimate of capability proves to diminish the force of Dickson's warning; in this estimate, he merely judged the enemy capable of "concentrated counterattack [rather than counteroffensive] with air, armor, infantry and secret weapons at a selected focal point at a time of his own choosing." The intelligence summary's other intimations of the enemy's possible aggressive intent and capability similarly warned not of a counteroffensive but of counterattack, with consequent limited, local, tactical rather than strategic connotations. The difference between an offensive as a large-scale operation of major strategic significance and an attack as a more limited effort of tactical scale was well enough established in military terminology that if the First Army intelligence staff really expected a counteroffensive, it should have avoided references simply to counterattacks.

If insisting on this distinction may nevertheless appear pedantic, in two further particulars Estimate 37 led away from rather than toward the German assault that occurred on the 16th. First, noting skillful handling and husbanding of forces by Rundstedt since his return as OB West in September, Dickson permitted himself a sarcasm addressed to the sort of German leadership that had directed the Battle of Mortain. Rundstedt, he said, "obviously is conducting military operations without the benefit of intuition." Nothing could have been more wrong. The error was fundamental, because the strategy of Rundstedt the conservative soldier was sure to be drastically different from that of the desperate Führer. It is hard to understand why as late as December 1944 any G-2 should have imagined Rundstedt rather than Hitler to be in effective command.

In any event, counteroffensive or counterattack, Dickson located the possible blow in the wrong place at the wrong time. Noting that the Germans' "armored reserve appears to be quartered in houses and barns along the railroads generally in a semi-circle from Duesseldorf to Koblenz, with Koeln as the center point," Dickson concluded that the "strategy in defense of the Reich is based on the exhaustion of our offensive to be followed by an all-out counterattack with armor, between the Roer and the Erft. . . . Indications to this date point to the location of this focal point [of the possible counterattack] as being between Roermond and Schleiden. . . . " Regarding the Ardennes, in contrast, Dickson spoke of "a definite pattern for the seasoning of newly-formed divisions in the comparatively quiet sector opposite VIII Corps prior to their dispatch to more active fronts."[8]

Colonel Rosengarten, the ULTRA specialist of the First Army G-2 section, amply summarized the geographic and temporal focus of Estimate 37:

The real intent of it was to warn that, despite the fighting that had taken place during the previous three weeks, Sixth Pz Army west of the Rhine was uncommitted and, therefore, available for a counter-offensive. This counter-offensive, it predicted, would most probably occur after our major forces had crossed the Roer River. It is beyond the scope of this report to examine the validity of the "ex post facto" constructions placed on it, that it intended to warn against the large scale offensive that actually occurred.[9]

Nothing in supplementary reports filed by First Army intelligence between December 10 and 16 changed anything. On the 14th, the First Army passed on to higher headquarters from Middleton's corps the refugee's report of equipment and troops massing around Bitburg. The next day, the First Army estimate cited reinforcements arriving between Düren and Trier plus prisoner interviews to suggest "it is possible that a limited scale offensive will be launched for the purpose of achieving a Christmas morale 'victory' for civilian consumption." Specifically, prisoners of war spoke of the "recapture of Aachen as a Christmas present to the Fuehrer."[10]

From the emergence of the German grenadiers out of the fog of the Eifel until his death in 1976, Dickson tirelessly reminded everyone who would listen that he had, after all, produced warnings. The Germans' seizure of the initiative was not, he insisted, the intelligence failure comparable to Pearl Harbor that some critics made of it. He had offered consistent and adequate admonitions that something was in the wind. A man possessed of considerable capacity for feeling wronged, Dickson believed himself victimized both by the Monday-morning quarterbacks after December 16 and by higher intelligence staffs beforehand—to say nothing of Generals Thorson and Kean at First Army, who he believed failed to take his warnings seriously. On this and other occasions, it is clear, Hodges's G-3 and chief of staff—the latter the key figure in the somewhat unhappy First Army headquarters—regarded Dickson as less than an oracle. Rosengarten spoke of Dickson's "relatively unimportant voice in the Army's cabinet."[11] Dickson's colleagues regarded him not only as bursting with the pretentiousness of a man deeply self-doubtful—when questioned too closely for comfort in staff discussions, his method of evasion was to show off his mastery of the German language—but as the stereotypical G-2 pessimist. A reputation for pessimism comes naturally to most G-2s; in Dickson's case, of course, such a reputation was scarcely warranted after the First Army G-2 summaries of the past August and September

Brigadier General Edwin L. Sibert, G-2 at 12th Army Group, was another target of Dickson's animus, the particular butt of Dickson's complaint that the flow of intelligence data was always upward, never downward—that the army G-2 never received pertinent information from army group and SHAEF to permit his completing the puzzles he was trying to assemble. Though he had cautioned against trouble impending, Dickson conceded he might have cast still darker auguries if he had been told about such things, known to higher headquarters, as the Germans' insistent attempts to get information on North Atlantic weather conditions that might affect central European weather in mid-December.

With ULTRA silent, the Americans still had aerial reconnaissance in the late autumn, curtailed by the storms and overcast skies of November and early December but surely not crippled as fully as the Germans might have hoped. The 67th Tactical Reconnaissance Group of IX TAC flew 242 missions labeled successful in the month before December

16. Along with the 10th Photo Reconnaissance Group of XIX TAC, it compiled a picture of impressive and growing buildups of German troops and equipment just west of the Rhine—and eventually moving toward the Eifel. The sightings included trainloads of Tiger tanks, fifty searchlights in one location, and concentrations of hospital trains. Night reconnaissance was limited—there were only two available squadrons of P-61 Black Widow night fighters, each averaging no more than ten planes operational—but reported plentiful lights indicating large-scale night movements. Much of the Eifel itself, of course, was heavily wooded, an admirable place in which to conceal a buildup from prying airplanes.

The evidence of German movement toward the Ardennes alarmed the SHAEF intelligence chief, General Strong. According to Strong's testimony, corroborated by Bedell Smith, Strong was so impressed and disturbed by the enemy's capacity to strike with his armored reserve in the Ardennes that about the first week of December, the SHAEF chief of staff suggested he visit the 12th Army Group and convey a warning directly to Bradley. Strong said he saw Bradley for about three-quarters of an hour, but that Bradley replied he was aware of the danger and "that he had earmarked certain divisions to move into the Ardennes should the enemy attack there. . . ."[12]

Bradley certainly had a kind of awareness of the danger. Eisenhower had reminded him of it several times. Visiting the VIII Corps front, Bradley discussed the matter with Middleton, who was sufficiently uneasy that he would have liked to withdraw from the Schnee Eifel, and reminded Bradley that the Germans had been able to attack through the Ardennes in 1914 as well as in 1940. But Bradley responded that no vital strategic objectives lay on the enemy's path through the Ardennes and assured Middleton that the Germans would not come this way again.

But if Bradley told Strong he had certain divisions earmarked for the region, it was not true. On December 16, Bradley hesitated over Eisenhower's removing the 7th and 10th Armored Divisions from the Ninth and Third Armies, particularly the latter; but he could propose no alternative.

From soon after December 16, through the writing of his memoirs and thereafter, Bradley argued with considerable elaboration that he had known he was taking a risk in the Ardennes, but that the risk was a calculated one. How much the risk was truly calculated—how much reasoned, foresighted weighing of dangers and advantages was involved—remains distinctly dubious. If the risk was calculated, it is strange that Bradley was so slow to acknowledge that the danger had materialized, and that there were no calculations for dealing with the danger. Bradley says that while he misread the enemy's intentions, his "estimate of his *capabilities* at the time was nearer right than wrong." But on the same page of his memoirs, Bradley confesses contradictorily, "I had greatly underestimated the enemy's offensive capabilities." His apologia is hardly a model of coherence.[13]

Nor is it fully convincing to argue, as Bradley does, that the allegedly calculated risk was run because there was no alternative except to abandon the Allies' autumn offensive. It was questionable in any event to rely on the Allied offensive to restrict the Germans to the defensive, when the Germans knew there would be no crossing of the Roer below the dams until the Allies had somehow solved the problem of the dams. As long as the Germans held the Roer dams, they also had the ability to weaken their front across the lower Roer to gain troops for use elsewhere.

Though Bradley claimed to have recognized the peril of a German counteroffensive through the Ardennes and to have foreseen the steps necessary to deal with it—to shift the direction of the First and Third Armies and "fling this mechanized strength against his [the enemy's] flanks"—it is curious also that if he foresaw and weighed the risks, Bradley should have adopted so injured a tone when he recalled the estimates of his intelligence staffs:

> During the middle of November, G-2 reported that the Sixth SS Panzer Army had been moved from its assembly point in Westphalia to an area nearer Cologne. Another Panzer Army, the Fifth, was reported to have massed its tanks a little farther north. So conspicuous were these telltale signs of von Rundstedt's apparent intent to nab us astride the Roer, that we should probably have sifted them for evidence of deception. But if anyone on that Western Front sniffed in those preparations an intent to mislead us on a German offensive elsewhere, he certainly did not share his suspicions with me.[14]

Note that Bradley shared the delusion that Rundstedt, not Hitler, was in command. The truth about Bradley's expectations and preparations surely lies less in the claim that his risks were calculated than in his confession that even when he heard the news from the Ardennes on his visit to Eisenhower, he "grossly . . . underrated the enemy's intentions in thinking the offensive a spoiling attack."[15] The truth about the extent of Bradley's calculations of risk is implicit also in his selection of the city of Luxembourg as the site of EAGLE TAC, his advanced headquarters. Luxembourg was no place from which "to fling this mechanized strength" of all of Bradley's armies against the flanks of a counteroffensive into the Ardennes, for a German incursion into the Ardennes was bound to weaken badly, if not to break, Bradley's grip on his northern two armies from Luxembourg, leaving him in firm contact only with Patton's army.

It was Bradley's headquarters, furthermore, that not only brushed off General Strong's concern about the Ardennes but seems to have gone out of its way to squash Dickson's warnings about some kind of counterstroke. Two days after the appearance of Dickson's Estimate 37, General Sibert published a 12th Army Group estimate directly at odds with it:

> It is now certain that attrition is steadily sapping the strength of German forces on the western front and that the crust of defenses is thinner, more brittle and more vulnerable than it appears on our G-2 maps or to the troops in the line. . . .
>
> These two basic facts—the deathly weakness of the individual [German] infantry division in the line plus the inevitability of the enemy falling still further in replacement arrears—make it certain that before long he will utterly fail in his current attempt to withdraw and arrest his tactical reserve so that he will be forced to commit at least part of his panzer army to the line. . . .[16]

On December 15, Sibert followed up Dickson's further warning of the 14th with an elaboration of what he had meant on the 12th:

> At no time since September has such a critical dilemma confronted the enemy. It would seem doubtful that the enemy can hold in the Aachen area without committing the Sixth Panzer Army. It also seems doubtful that he can hold the West Wall in the south without additional reinforcements including armor. The enemy may have to divide the Sixth Panzer Army, thus risking defeat both in the north and

in the south, or if he holds Sixth Panzer Army in the north, run a good chance of the Third and Seventh U.S. Armies reaching the Rhine this year in the area of Mainz. Finally, to solve this problem with reinforcements from the Russian front is to invite disaster in the east.[17]

If such estimates had not squared with Bradley's judgments, his headquarters would not have been likely to go on releasing them over a period of days. They do square with all we can learn about his expectations of the enemy's conduct. The risk to which Bradley subjected the VIII Corps on its long Ardennes front was not the carefully calculated one he later made it out to be. In war, caution can prove paradoxically reckless. Chary of offensive gambling himself, Bradley did not imagine a stroke so unorthodox as a beaten enemy's rising up for an armored counteroffensive through some of the worst tank country on the Western Front.

Bradley's British critics, from Chester Wilmot's early belaboring of the American command to Major-General John Strawson in his relatively recent *Battle for the Ardennes*, find the roots of Bradley's misperception of the Ardennes risk in the larger, more general American reluctance to concentrate.[18] The British critics are fond of arguing that the Americans relied too literally on the Lincoln-Grant strategy of the Civil War, in which Union armies had pressed the Confederacy all along its borders—the broad-front strategy—in the conviction that the inferior strength of the Confederacy could not match the superior strength of the Union everywhere, and if pressed everywhere must somewhere cave in.

Aside from ascribing to American generals a greater historical-mindedness than seems at all warranted, the weakness of this argument as criticism is that the Lincoln-Grant strategy is not necessarily a bad example to follow. It was a strategy that achieved its purpose. Like all military strategies, it ran risks to do so. Unless the strength of the superior contestant is unquestionably overwhelming, permitting him to press his inferior foe relentlessly, the broad-front strategy runs the risk that the inferior contestant will make sacrifices elsewhere—where he is in retreat anyway—to gather up a local superiority somewhere, and with it to loose a counterblow in an attempt to gain the initiative. When, with Lincoln at the helm, the Union was mounting offensives all along the Confederacy's circumference early in 1862, Stonewall Jackson with the help of R.E. Lee achieved just that kind of local superiority to capture a larger initiative in the famous Valley Campaign. More than two years later, when U.S. Grant as Union general-in-chief was affording the broad-front strategy more perfect coordination than President Lincoln alone had given it, the Confederacy nevertheless accomplished a similar kind of riposte in Jubal Early's march down the Shenandoah Valley and to the defenses of Washington. But the risk of the riposte does not invalidate the whole strategy.

In 1944, Bradley judged the risks in the Ardennes badly, exposed the VIII Corps to excessive peril, and should at least have attempted to hold the Ardennes front in greater strength. Yet these failings in themselves do not demonstrate error in the whole broad-front strategy. From December 16 onward, Eisenhower forthrightly shouldered the responsibility for what happened in the Ardennes. He did so not only because the responsibility was formally his, but also because while he had perceived the risks more clearly than Bradley, he had accepted them. Other factors beyond the discretion he habitually permitted his subordinates restrained him from doing anything to ease the risks. Eisenhower had not been sure how he could find troops to strengthen the Ardennes without halting either the First Army-Ninth Army or the Third Army-Seventh Army November offensive. Reducing the enemy's burdens either on the Roer or the Sarre might have multiplied rather than limited risks, by improving the Germans' ability to husband reserves. Already, the November offensives themselves suffered from the fact that the broad-front strategy was no longer all that broad. The relative inactivity of 21 Army Group was permitting the enemy to confront the American drives with troops brought down from Holland.

Hindsight after December 16 was to reveal the withholding of even limited reinforcement from the Ardennes as the graver danger after all. But Eisenhower's dilemma, when in November and early December he fretted over the Ardennes but perceived no satisfactory solution, points to a flaw in American strategy more fundamental than any excessive emulation of the Lincoln-Grant strategy of the Civil War. It was not that the broad-front strategy was wrong; the more basic trouble was that the Anglo-American alliance had not given Eisenhower enough troops to carry it out safely. The Lincoln-Grant broad-front strategy had depended on the Union's overwhelming manpower and material superiority against the Confederacy. When Union power was not applied overwhelmingly, a nasty reverse such as Stonewall Jackson's Valley Campaign or Jubal Early's Washington raid could result. Eisenhower had yet to enjoy the measure of manpower superiority over his adversaries on which Lincoln and Grant had counted. There were not enough Anglo-American divisions, or enough replacements for casualties in the existing divisions. Eisenhower could not create a reserve unless he abandoned the broad-front strategy. Far from creating a reserve, he could not even rest and refit exhausted divisions like the 28th and the 4th without risking them in the tissue-thin Ardennes line. More than the misjudgments of the commanders in Europe, the events unfolding in the Ardennes on December 16 indicated that the ninety-division gamble had gone sour. The American army in Europe fought on too narrow a margin of physical superiority for the favored American broad-front strategy to be anything but a risky gamble.

As for a single-thrust strategy, the Germans proved to be opening an exuberantly dramatic demonstration both of its merits and of its shortcomings.

26: The Doctrinal Response

THROUGH most of December 16, General Hodges insisted to General Gerow that the V Corps attack toward the Roer dams must persist. Hodges regarded the enemy lunge out of the Eifel as merely a spoiling attack to disrupt the drive for the dams, and he did not intend to dance to the Germans' tune. Hodges's supposedly pessimistic G-2, Colonel Dickson, was not on hand at First Army headquarters at Spa to sustain the more cautious mood of Estimate 37; he had chosen December 15—a strange time, if he foresaw danger as acutely as he later professed—to depart for Paris for a four-day leave.

Thus Bradley was not alone in believing the German effort a limited one, nor was General Jones of the 106th Division alone in his optimistic hope that the potential isolation of his 422nd and 423rd Regiments on the Schnee Eifel could be averted. Late on the 16th, V Corps headquarters telephoned VIII Corps to ask that contact be restored between their flanks. Colonel Mark Devine, commander of the 14th Cavalry Group, spoke to 99th Division headquarters and promised to comply with the request. After all, though Devine's own cavalrymen and certain other American units had been handled hard on December 16, at most places the Americans' Ardennes front still held.

From the Our to the Wiltz

More than Saturday, December 16, it was Sunday, the 17th, that was a day of decision. All through Saturday night the fighting persisted and the Germans continued pressing more troops forward. After five years of war, German doctrine remained puzzlingly unclear on whether infantry or tanks ought to spearhead a combined-arms assault; but it became apparent during the night that, at least on this occasion, infantry had been committed first to clear the ground for the armor—and that the panzers, in alarming numbers, were crowding in behind.

Whatever optimism General Jones felt about his 106th Division was based on his expectation of throwing his own armor into the battle—CCB of the 9th Armored Division on his south flank, the vanguard of the 7th Armored on his north flank.

After his long and successful leadership of the 4th Armored's CCA, Bruce Clarke, just promoted to brigadier, had received command of CCB of the 7th Armored as part of the effort to improve the division after its less than spectacular showing in the Peel Marshes. On Saturday evening Clarke was alerted that the 7th Armored was to move to Bastogne. The new division commander, Brigadier General Robert W. Hasbrouck, ordered him to hurry ahead to VIII Corps headquarters in that town, to learn what he could about the division's mission. Hasbrouck and Clarke were still unaware of Saturday's events in the Ardennes.

Starting out from near Heerlen, Holland, at about nine at night, Clarke reached Bastogne through rain, heavy traffic, and a near brush with a V-1 about four on Sunday morning. He promptly learned from General Middleton that more than enough work awaited his division. But after assuring Middleton that the 7th Armored was on its way with his own CCB in the lead, Clarke also soon learned that in fact the jammed roads and confusion in rear of the First Army had prevented his combat command from getting traffic clearance to leave Heerlen until almost five in the morning. Jones was unlikely to receive much armored help on his left flank during Sunday.

Despite his promise to the 99th Division, Colonel Devine had been pulling back his 14th Cavalry Group from one position to another all through Saturday evening and during the night, and there was no hope of the cavalry's restoring contact between the VIII and V Corps. With the buildup of German armor, Devine's light cavalry vehicles were confronting Tigers by Sunday morning. Early on December 17, the northern wing of the 18th Volksgrenadier Division captured Schönberg with its bridge across the Our. At 7:25 A.M., the southern wing of the same division once again and firmly captured Bleialf before the 9th Armored Division could intervene there. At 9:05 Jones got the news that these same Germans had pushed northwest from Bleialf to arrive at Schönberg, completing the envelopment of his northern two regiments.

The 422nd and 423rd probably were already aware of their entrapment; the 2nd Battalion of the 423rd had just tried unsuccessfully to blast its way into Schönberg from the east, with antitank guns in the lead. Division headquarters radioed the two regiments to withdraw if they had to and promised an effort to help during the afternoon. What force Jones expected to use to give help was unstated. This and subsequent reassurances of intended aid did nothing to hasten any further efforts by the entrapped units to break out westward on their own. Eventually the two regimental commanders decided to try for themselves, beginning at ten o'clock on Monday morning with their two regiments abreast in column of battalions. But by then the Germans had enjoyed far too much time to solidify their encirclement and to infiltrate the Americans' remaining positions. The two regiments lost effective contact with each other before their attack began. Promptly, enemy infiltration and the rough, wooded ground fragmented them further. The break-out effort failed.

During Tuesday, the 423rd Regiment was consistently pounded by German artillery and gradually overrun by infantry. With ammunition almost exhausted, its colonel surrendered the remnant about 4:30 P.M. The 422nd was enduring a similar process of attrition when the rumble of tanks approaching from the north raised hopes that American armor had arrived and broken through—but the tanks belonged to the elite, division-sized Führer Begleit Brigade, and the American colonel surrendered all his remaining troops about 4:00 P.M. Small bands separated from the main forces were still roving among the hills and ravines, but few ever found their way to the American lines. At least 7,000 soldiers surrendered or fell on the Schnee Eifel, probably more nearly 8,000 or 9,000, and a wide gap opened in the VIII Corps front. The old masters of the Kesselschlacht, the battle of envelopment, had executed yet another admirable, albeit miniature, example of the art.

St. Vith last heard from the isolated regiments on Tuesday morning, receiving a radio message sent out the previous afternoon that promised an effort to attack to the northwest. By the time this word reached Jones, the Germans had left only minimal forces to hold the encirclement and were continuing to pour westward. Their grasp had almost closed on St. Vith itself, with its numerous converging roads, and to the south, on the similar road junction of Bastogne.

For, east of Bastogne, the 28th Division, though it escaped a disaster comparable to the 106th's, had also seen a gaping hole punched through its front. Through the opening poured both General Walter Krüger's LVIII Panzer Corps and Lüttwitz's XLVII, the old antagonists of Patton's October battles with the Fifth Panzer Army. General Middleton had issued his hold-fast order to the VIII Corps during Saturday night, but the scattered village outposts of Colonel Fuller's 110th Infantry Regiment needed more help than that, and the help was unavailable. Tanks and assault guns of the 2nd Panzer Division of Lüttwitz's corps broke into the crossroads of Marnach during the night. About the same time, General Cota released all but one company—serving as division headquarters guard—of the 2/110th from reserve and agreed with Fuller that the battalion should attack eastward to Marnach. Cota also ordered the light tank company of the 707th Tank Battalion to attack toward Marnach southward down the Skyline Drive, while Fuller ordered a medium tank company and a rifle platoon from Company C to mount a converging effort from the southwest. But the pincers had much less chance of closing than had the smaller ones the day before. The 2/110th found the road into Marnach from the west swarming with enemy armor. These panzers, in fact, were already well along westward toward Fuller's headquarters on the Clerf River at the town of Clerf, or Clervaux.

The town might help out by posing problems for the panzers, because the main Marnach-Bastogne road and all the other streets wind precipitously downhill to the valley of the Clerf. Tanks and panzer grenadiers began showing up as early as Sunday morning, but parts of both the 1st and 2nd Battalions of the 110th plus a task force of the 9th Armored's CCR used the terrain in and around Clerf to keep their attack hesitant through most of the day. At the same time, the defenders cursed the increasingly familiar problem of an apparently endless buildup of enemy tanks, assault guns, artillery, and infantry, while the gradual overrunning of the last of the 1st Battalion's outposts farther north on the Skyline Drive exposed their left flank. At 6:25 P.M. Fuller telephoned division headquarters that his command post was under fire and about to go. He was captured soon afterward while trying to find a way out of town. About a hundred officers and men of the regimental headquarters company were still holed up in what the Michelin guides call "a picturesque feudal château," and there they continued fighting throughout Sunday night, holding off the Pzkw IV battalion of the 3rd Panzer Regiment, who were evidently fearful of taking risks against bazookas in the darkness. When the Panther battalion arrived in the morning, the tanks rolled on up the good paved road toward Bastogne, leaving infantry, engineers, and 88s to dither with the strongpoint for several more hours before finally setting it afire and forcing a surrender.

The little battle of Clervaux typified the multiple separate actions into which the Keystone Division's fragmenting defense resolved itself. As the division's center shattered, groups ranging from squads to battalions made nuisances of themselves wherever buildings or terrain favored a defensive stand. The American soldiers fought with exceptional bitterness and desperation because, beginning late on Sunday, rumors spinning through the front-line divisions told of SS massacres of unarmed GI prisoners, and of Germans in GI uniforms riding American vehicles behind the lines on errands of sabotage and assassination.

When the enemy entered Clerf, some of the 110th's original strongpoints were still holding out. At Hosingen on the Skyline Drive, Company K fought on with hand grenades after its ammunition was exhausted, and the Germans did not stifle the company until well into Monday morning. Other parts of the 3rd Battalion kept up the battle in Consthum, until during Monday afternoon tanks seemed about to overrun them; but a fog rolled in instead to permit their withdrawal.

Already at noon on Monday, the German spearheads had opened fire on Wiltz, the division headquarters, where Cota had constructed a partial perimeter out of the headquarters troops, including the band, paymasters, and the like, reinforced by the 44th Combat Engineer Battalion. As survivors of the 3/110th fell back from the battle of Consthum and other such actions as allowed escape, they joined the defense. Later on Monday, the Reconnaissance Battalion of Panzer Lehr, sure to contain some of the best troops and equipment of its division, came clanking toward the northern part of the Wiltz lines, having turned left at Eschweiler to seek in the Wiltz River valley one of the better secondary roads from the Our to Bastogne. The panzers pushed back the engineers and a little armor of the 707th Tank Battalion, but then apparently decided the welcome was too warm and turned away northward.

Cota's headquarters staff withdrew during Monday night to Sibret west of Bastogne, leaving the combat troops, improvised and otherwise, to fight on at Wiltz next day against the 26th Volksgrenadier Division and a large part of the 5th Parachute Division. The latter, fortunately, had been filled with recent Luftwaffe and navy replacements and was no longer quite the menace it had been in Normandy. But it was hardly a pushover either, and furthermore a scratch regiment could not hold back two divisions indefinitely. During Tuesday night the defenders of Wiltz tried to infiltrate westward through the cordon they found drawn around them. The provisional battalion of headquarters troops fought past two roadblocks—the second charged and overrun by a platoon of black soldiers relying on grenades and bayonets—but was trapped when an ambuscade erupted adjacent to a third roadblock. A breakdown in communications and consequent confusion turned the withdrawal of the 3/110th into disarray, and the remnant of the battalion lost most of its lingering cohesion.

When the Germans invaded this same area in 1940, they had not met anything resembling the 28th United States Infantry Division, and they reached the Meuse by the end of the third day. Now three days had gone by and they had not yet reached Bastogne, thirty or so kilometers from the Our and less than halfway to the Meuse. But for the moment, their path was again free from anything resembling the 28th Division as that division had been at dawn on December 16. The 3/110th was scarcely identifiable after the retreat from Wiltz. Only Company C of the 1/110th had emerged with organization reasonably intact out of the battalion chain of posts along the Skyline Drive. The fighting along the main highway to Bastogne from Marnach back to Clerf similarly shattered the 2nd Battalion. The fragments of both the 1st and 2nd Battalions found their way southwestward, eventually to fall in with parts of the 9th Armored Division. The gaping hole that had been the center of the 28th Division grew larger as enemy pressure forced Cota's flank regiments to pivot like opening doors.

The 112th Infantry on the north flank was another victim of the weakness along the seams between formations. By Sunday morning, the Panther battalion of the 116th Panzer Division was around its left flank between it and the 106th Division right. The northernmost battalion of the 112th, the 1st, had its left crushed and its center pierced before the morning was over, and the Germans were then in position to pulverize with artillery and roll over the remaining battalions. The 112th retreated northward during Sunday night, preserving its integrity and even extricating most of the 1st Battalion. One party, finding the bridge at Ouren in German hands, lined up in German march formation while officers shouted commands in German, and they strode across the bridge and on to safety. Eventually the regiment was amalgamated into the remains of the 106th Division and dug in, facing southward, between Malscheid and Leithum, with the 424th Regiment of the 106th on its left.

The Keystone Division's south-flank regiment, the 109th, similarly fought on through Sunday mainly in its original positions but with one of its battalions in deep trouble: no effective relief could force its way to Führen, the remaining strongpoint of the 2nd Battalion on the regimental left. The well-anchored southern portion of the regiment, on the heights above the confluence of the Our and the Sauer, nevertheless held their positions through Sunday night and on into Monday. Then the buildup of heavy weapons around them, including Tiger tanks, mounted rapidly; after two days' labor, the Germans had finally completed a bridge across the Our at Roth. The 109th Regiment had been holding off segments of three German divisions—5th Parachute and 352nd and 276th Volksgrenadiers—and on Monday it felt the full weight of the 352nd along with heavy weapons. No more word came out of Führen, and late in the day regimental headquarters had to ask, and received, permission to retreat to Diekirch. The 352nd Volksgrenadiers had spent so much of their energy in driving the regiment from the Our that they could not pull themselves together for an attack on Diekirch until Wednesday afternoon. Then the Germans' superior numbers threatened the Americans with encirclement, and the 109th retreated again, southwestward beyond Ettelbruck, to form a line facing north, in loose contact with elements of the 9th Armored that had also had to pivot away from the German-Luxembourg border.

The Northeastern Shoulder

They had not pressed past the Americans at anything like their 1940 speed, but the Germans nevertheless had given a textbook demonstration of the employment of concentration along a relatively narrow and vulnerable front to effect a breakthrough. Their display of the efficacy of the principle of concentration well applied was complete with lesser exercises in the skillful application of the military art, particularly on the front of Hasso von Manteuffel's Fifth Panzer Army. This force, long thought to have been resisting the Americans' Aachen attacks farther northward, was now identified as the hammer smashing through the 106th and 28th Divisions. Manteuffel's opening artillery preparation, for example, was savage but judiciously brief, shocking the defenders but not affording them time to recover from the shock before the guns lifted and they found infiltrating German infantry among them. The use of infiltration to penetrate the defenses before the battle began was a tactic applied with exceptional mastery and effect.

If the Germans had military textbooks and doctrine, however, so did the Americans; and all American commanders could at least feel confident that, the enemy breakthrough having unfortunately succeeded, their doctrine would assure common efforts to shore up the shoulders of the penetration and confine it to a narrow tunnel with vulnerable flanks—just as had happened, on a lesser scale, in the Mortain battle during the summer.

Fortunately, too, the resistant shoulders began to develop even before the First Army, 12th Army Group, and SHAEF, handicapped as they were by the shortage of reserves, could begin any shoring up coordinated by the highest headquarters. In the south, on the 4th Division front along the Sauer around Echternach, the shoulder held largely because the left flank of the enemy assault lacked the power—and particularly the armor—of the thrust farther north. To the north, above the Losheim-Losheimergraben-Malmédy road, the Americans already wielded the concentration they had mustered to assault the Roer dams.

For General Lauer's 99th Division, it was the resulting proximity of General Robertson's 2nd Division that made the division's situation, and fate, different from that of the 106th or the 28th. On the night of December 16, the right wing and center of the 99th were not so much better off than the two neighboring divisions just to the south. The left flank elements, the 38th Cavalry Reconnaissance Squadron and the 3rd Battalion of the 395th Infantry, both located astride relatively open hills north of the 2nd Division corridor into the Monschau Forest, proved to enjoy exceptional fields of fire across the ground over which the 326th Volksgrenadier Division tried to attack them. Their guns quickly piled German dead and wounded high in front of them. But the 393rd Regiment, Lauer's center, had to fight much harder to hold off the 277th Volksgrenadier Division and would face Sunday with its rifle companies already precariously thin; and the opening assaults of the 12th Volksgrenadier and 3rd Parachute Divisions, along with part of the 277th Volksgrenadiers, had battered the 394th Infantry on Lauer's south flank in the manner already detailed.

The road network, furthermore, made Lauer's division, like much of the 106th, a candidate for envelopment. The hard-surfaced road from Rohren in the German lines through Monschau and on toward Eupen in Belgium was one of the best in the Ardennes, an avenue obviously coveted if the intent of the German offensive was to reach the Meuse, and also a way past Lauer's left. While the cavalry and the 3/395th had stopped the enemy along this road at least for the first day, on the division right the Germans had not only pressed from Lanzerath toward Buchholz Station to make the 394th face south at the station; during Saturday night, furthermore, the decimated 394th could do nothing but watch and listen while a long procession of enemy tanks rumbled toward Honsfeld and Büllingen, past the division right and into its rear. From Büllingen, the Germans would be able to move on north over the paved road through Krinkelt and Rocherath toward Wahlerscheid, touring the rear of both Lauer's division and the 2nd Division salient in the Monschau Forest with its apex near Wahlerscheid.

Except among the open hills in the north around Höfen, Lauer's positions were inside the Monschau and neighboring forests. Though the Germans had shown in the Huertgen how well a properly trained defender could exploit the region's dark Teutonic woods, the forest was a mixed blessing for troops assailed by so many enemy divisions as was the 99th. The woods invited infiltration, to menace a formation already outflanked by creating multiple additional flanks and producing defeat in detail. To such use of infiltration against the 394th Infantry, the Germans added on the second day an advance by the armor of the 12th SS Panzer Division. Already fending off two infantry divisions and part of a third—of which the 12th Volksgrenadiers were among the best fighters of the enemy offensive—the 394th could not stave off the panzers as well. On top of everything else, the Germans called in Bf 109s to finish off Losheimergraben at the angle of the 394th's salient. The town fell late on Sunday, by which time the 394th was a collection of scattered detachments trying to dodge their separate ways to the rear.

But at this juncture there emerged the difference between Lauer's sector and those just to the south. In the early dusk of mid-December, the Germans built up troops to assail the survivors of the 394th as they straggled into Mürringen. Before the enemy could deliver this coup de grace, however, he had to deal with an irksome obstacle that had appeared on Mürringen's south flank: the 1st Battalion of the 23rd Infantry, the reserve regiment of the 2nd Division, had been thrown into neighboring Hünningen to backstop the 394th. Almost isolated though it was, the 1/23rd repelled everything the Germans were able to press against it throughout Sunday evening. Because this reserve strength was nearby, the 394th got enough of a respite to gather itself into a semblance of a regiment again at Mürringen and to retreat in good order toward Krinkelt. And upon that village and its twin, Rocherath, at the base of the 2nd Division corridor toward the Roer dams, considerable American strength was converging.

General Gerow of the V Corps had commanded Eisenhower at the beginning of the war, when he was head of the War Plans Division of the General Staff and Ike was his deputy; but giving Gerow so much as a corps had seemed something of a risk at the time the Allies invaded Normandy, because almost his entire career had been spent in staff work—and everybody remembered this limitation of his background, because in person Gerow was the epitome of the meticulous, painstaking staff officer, lacking Eisenhower's warm and ingratiating personality. By mid-December of 1944, however, Gerow was a veteran of corps command in combat, and he had developed—or as his record suggests, had always possessed—an admirable feeling for the ebb, the flow, the portents of battle. When the enemy charged so unexpectedly out of the concealing woods of the Eifel on December 16, Gerow was among the first American commanders to decide that a counteroffensive was at hand, not a mere local counterattack. By noon on Saturday he had ordered a halt to the 2nd Division attack toward Wahlerscheid. During Saturday afternoon, he asked Hodges's permission both to halt Robertson's attack and to withdraw the 2nd Division some eight kilometers to the defensive security of a forested ridge running north and south from Elsenborn.

Hodges's appreciation of what was occurring on December 16 resembled Bradley's of that evening, so permission was denied—although Robertson's attack did not resume. Late on Saturday, General Huebner, now Gerow's deputy corps commander, nevertheless warned Robertson to be ready for a quick change of plan. Early on Sunday, Gerow renewed his request to Hodges. The First Army commander now conceded that Gerow might do as he himself saw fit. Immediately—it was about 7:30 A.M.—Gerow telephoned Robertson and instructed him to fall back from Wahlerscheid, to secure Krinkelt-Rocherath as an intermediate strongpoint, and to hold the route thence through Wirtzfeld to Elsenborn.

Gerow already had felt obliged to attach two-thirds of Robertson's reserve, the 23rd Infantry, to the 99th Division, and the hard drive toward Wahlerscheid had already cut the 9th and 38th Infantry Regiments to no more than half their normal strength. These two regiments had all but one of their battalions thoroughly committed to the attack, and disengaging to retreat under fire is among the most difficult of military operations—even when the retreat does not have to follow a single forest road running parallel to another raging battle. Robertson planned to leapfrog his battalions rearward, beginning by pulling the most advanced ones back through the others. He soon learned the additional bad news that he could not depend on the 99th Division to hold Krinkelt and Rocherath on his route of escape because Lauer's division was already too far gone. Perhaps Hodges had waited too long to catch up with Gerow's perceptions of the strength of the German assault.

Lauer's 393rd Infantry was joining the 394th in disarray, under the combined pressure of the 277th Volksgrenadier Division and tanks from the 12th SS Panzers. Late on Sunday morning, under attack almost continuously since the previous morning and reduced to 475 effectives with only two machine guns, the 3/393rd fell back from in front of Rocherath through the battalion of the 23rd Infantry sent to assist Lauer's center. But that battalion, the 3/23rd, had arrived carrying few mines and little ammunition, while trucks trying to bring up a resupply ran afoul of the enemy in the rear around Büllingen. The 3/393rd had barely begun digging in along its new rearward position when the 3/23rd gave way in front of it. This latest retreat left another battalion of the 393rd, the 1st, isolated and trying to find a route back to safety. Fortunately, the 3/393rd, still attempting to shield Rocherath, received reinforcement from the 1st Battalion of the 9th Infantry before it had to resist another assault.

General Robertson was stalking up and down the Rocherath-Wahlerscheid road trying to hasten the withdrawal from the Wahlerscheid corridor, but meanwhile he and Lauer had shored up the Rocherath-Krinkelt position with every semblance of a reserve they could find. On Lauer's left, the 38th Cavalry Squadron was enduring another attack by the 326th Volksgrenadier Division—luckily, the enemy again chose a route that made his troops superb targets—but the 395th Infantry was not attacked on this second day; so in the afternoon the 395th and the attached 2/393rd fell back to form a defense on the north and northeast sides of Rocherath. A collection of antitank and service companies joined the Rocherath perimeter. The 3/38th, which had not been engaged at Wahlerscheid, contributed a company to Rocherath but went mainly to Krinkelt, where Robertson instructed it to face rearward toward Büllingen as well as southward and eastward.

The 1/9th was the last battalion of its regiment to be peeled away from the Wahlerscheid salient, beginning its march about 2:15 P.M. It moved rapidly and reached Rocherath for its opportune junction with the 3/393rd. By that time the 2/9th, which had been first to draw back from Wahlerscheid, had marched twelve kilometers and was deploying around Wirtzfeld with the remaining battalion of the 23rd, to hold open another part of the escape hatch to the Elsenborn Ridge, Here the 3/9th joined after dark.

The later withdrawals from the Wahlerscheid salient had to run an increasingly punishing gauntlet of German fire, but the last major unit, the 1/38th Infantry, deployed on a low rise along the Wahlerscheid road just northeast of Rocherath at dusk. Robertson, meeting the battalion on the road, commanded it to hold here until ordered to withdraw. Since stragglers were still out in the woods, Company B let some tanks and infantry pass through toward Rocherath about 7:30 P.M. before realizing it was the Germans who had arrived. A confused and bitter struggle flared up for possession of

Rocherath and Krinkelt, and it persisted with only the briefest of pauses through the next two nights and days.

A jumble of American battalions, fortunately including the better part of four tank destroyer battalions along with armor of the 741st Tank Battalion, attached to the 2nd Division, battled the 277th Volksgrenadiers, the 12th ss Panzers, and eventually the 3rd Panzer Grenadier Division. Amidst the chaos of battle, stragglers from the 99th Division, even truck convoys, continued lumbering in along with the Germans. Panthers and Tigers soon seemed to be everywhere, and General Robertson uttered his variant of the standard American comment on every tank battle of the war: "We could use the tanks mounting a 90mm." Still, the battle was fought mainly in fog and darkness, and Shermans could stalk the panzers' flanks or lie in wait behind walls and hedgerows for a shot at flank or rear. The 741st knocked out an estimated twenty-seven panzers in return for eleven Shermans. Two disabled Shermans parked in a hidden lane accounted for five Tigers. While armor dueled with armor, and infantrymen joined in taking on panzers with a veteran division's usual hoard of bazookas beyond regulation allowances plus Panzerfäuste, another component of American military power made its usual yet more decisive contribution. The artillery banged away from the Elsenborn Ridge against every German avenue of approach, concentration area, and string of foxholes. Seven gun battalions were firing by Monday, at least one of them shooting off more than 5,000 rounds on that single day.

It became clear that the Germans were hurling against the twin villages an effort extraordinary even by the standards of an offensive that must now be judged a major enemy operation all across the Ardennes. The ram battering at Rocherath and Krinkelt was nothing less than the Schwerpunkt of Sepp Dietrich's Sixth Panzer Army, that accumulation of armor so long eyed warily as it fitted out beyond Aachen. The proven but weakened Indian Head Division and the 99th Division in its first full-scale battle were holding off the bulk of Generalleutnant der Waffen-ss Hermann Priess's I ss Panzer Corps. A drive led by favored ss officers and units must surely be one of special consequence for the German offensive; significantly, it was on Gerow's V Corps front that the enemy starting gate was closest to the Meuse and to Liège, where the American army had created a major supply depot.

Sepp Dietrich's army had not opened the battle with the skillful infiltration tactics of Manteuffel's Fifth Panzer Army. So far Dietrich the butcher's son and butcher's apprentice—old-time ss bully boy and companion of Hitler at the Munich Feldherrnhalle in 1923, a German officer as far removed as possible from the educated, aristocratic product of Kriegsakademie and General Staff—had fought a butcher's battle of brutal head-on assault. But the Germans obviously believed they must gain the Elsenborn Ridge, and when mere weight of numbers and Tigers and Panthers could not budge Robertson's and Lauer's men from Rocherath and Krinkelt, even Dietrich's army could shift to more subtle methods. Robertson and Lauer had worried all along about the enemy in their rear at Büllingen. On Sunday, the German spearhead entering that town had slipped away again southwestward, but there remained too many Germans in the area for comfort. By Tuesday, the 12th ss Panzers were disengaging from the Rocherath-Krinkelt battle, and the 12th Volksgrenadiers were commencing a new effort to exploit the gap where the 99th Division had once linked up with the 106th. The Volksgrenadiers were driving from Büllingen toward Butgenbach and the back door of the Elsenborn Ridge; the panzers might be expected to join this movement.

Fortunately and characteristically, as early as 11:00 A.M. on December 16, General Collins of the VII Corps had sufficiently divined the possible danger to the V Corps on his south flank that he had put the 1st Division, refitting out of the line, on six-hour alert. By Saturday night the Big Red One was already on its way to Gerow. The next morning the vanguard of the 26th Infantry Regiment reported to the 99th Division. General Lauer began forming the regiment in a horseshoe curving southward from Butgenbach to hills near the hamlet of Dom Butgenbach. The 26th was not securely tied in with any other Americans, it had a front about six kilometers long, and its 2nd Battalion out on the forward curve of the horseshoe was especially exposed; but the regiment offered something of a shield for the right and rear of the 2nd and 99th Divisions. The oldtimers in the 26th had often fought alone and unsupported in the past—as long ago as Kasserine; but few oldtimers remained since the autumn battles, and the 2nd Battalion had only about a hundred men per rifle company, nine-tenths of them replacements.

The 26th nevertheless withstood infantry attacks supported by a few tanks on Tuesday morning, December 19. Frustrated again, the Germans again maneuvered leftward. They concentrated the 3rd Parachute Division south of Waimes for an evident movement around the flank of the 26th. Again Collins's prompt dispatch of the 1st Division permitted a riposte, for the 16th Infantry Regiment arrived on Tuesday in time for its vanguard to take position around Waimes and receive the paratroopers' first blows that afternoon. By evening, furthermore, General Hobbs's 30th Division, recently relieved from the Ninth Army's front lines, arrived to extend the defenses of the 16th Regiment westward and to cover the flank and rear of the Elsenborn Ridge as far west as the Malmédy area.

During the next several days, the Germans tested this rapidly forming north shoulder strenuously. Before dawn on Wednesday about twenty panzers and a battalion of infantry opened a series of assaults against the 2/26th salient at Dom Butgenbach. By Thursday, December 21, the 2nd Battalion was worn thin enough that panzers and panzer grenadiers of the 12th SS broke through the right portion of the salient. But once more it was American artillery to the rescue. The 26th Infantry's cannon company, the 1st Division artillery, batteries from the 2nd and 99th Divisions, and the 406th Field Artillery Group joined in fire support for the Dom Butgenbach salient—delivering over 10,000 rounds in eight hours. The fire sufficed to allow the infantry to restore their line.

Friday's action was almost a carbon copy, except of course that everyone still fighting had grown wearier, and both sides' forces were thinner from attrition. Once more the right of the Dom Butgenbach salient gave way, and once more artillery raked every German concentration and communication route and permitted the closing of the breach. During Friday night, the remaining regiment of the 1st Division, the 18th Infantry, came into the line to effect a more permanent seal. When the enemy's probes on Saturday, December 23 detected this additional presence, the Sixth Panzer Army conceded another defeat and turned its offensive attentions to other sectors.

But by this time the direct routes to Liège were barred to Sepp Dietrich everywhere. In late afternoon of December 19, with pressure against them reduced by the shift of the armor of the 12th SS, the defenders of Rocherath and Krinkelt successfully disengaged and withdrew through Wirtzfeld to the Elsenborn Ridge. As early as Sunday, December

17, moreover, the 47th Infantry of the 9th Division had begun arriving from First Army reserve at Eupen to help the 38th Cavalry Squadron clear away the remnants of that day's German attack around Höfen and Monschau. On Wednesday, December 20, General Craig's 9th Division relieved the 99th altogether of responsibility for the Höfen-Monschau sector. This sector as always, and now the Elsenborn Ridge to the south as well, offered the defenders the kinds of fields of fire that on December 20 and 21 permitted them to mow down German efforts to renew the attack. From Monschau to Malmédy, Gerow's V Corps now had the 9th, 99th, 2nd, and 1st Divisions in a well organized line that seemed proof against anything Sepp Dietrich might hurl against it.

The Valley of the Amblève

The hills around Dom Butgenbach not only guarded the rear of the Elsenborn Ridge. They also permitted American artillery to harry German armor, grenadiers, and trucks trying to use the roads from Büllingen and Honsfeld west through Schoppen. In this way, the artillery both hindered any effort to achieve a concentration against the 1st and 30th Divisions' westward extension of the northeast shoulder and helped determine the fate of the most dangerous enterprise so far mounted by the ss panzers in the Ardennes.

This enterprise involved Robertson's and Lauer's old fears of the German forces that had shown up at Büllingen, behind Krinkelt, Rocherath, and the Wahlerscheid corridor, as early as December 17 and before the evacuation of those exposed positions had begun. Robertson and Lauer had had ample cause for concern. When these early intruders into Büllingen passed the Buchholz railroad station, an American radio operator holed up in the basement there had sent General Lauer a specific report of their strength: by 5:00 A.M. on Sunday, December 17, he had already counted thirty German tanks and twenty-eight half-tracks among long columns of infantry, on their way around what was then Lauer's right flank and into his rear.

To Robertson and Lauer, it seemed almost a divine intervention that this imposing array turned at Büllingen and proceeded southwestward toward Schoppen instead of continuing up the road toward Krinkelt. Before leaving Büllingen, however, the German column appropriated some 50,000 gallons of gasoline and set American prisoners to work filling German gas tanks. The Germans' evident purpose had been to detour northward to seize this fuel before pursuing other objectives farther south and west.

The Germans' turnaround might have been the best possible development for the 2nd and 99th Divisions, which already had their hands full, and for the eventual solidifying of the northeast shoulder of the breakthrough. It still posed many dangers. The enemy armor, after all, was moving straight through the opening created by the splitting of the seam between the V and VIII Corps. Very little stood between it and a series of additional American fuel and supply dumps all the way back to the Meuse.

Before December 17 was over, the German column assumed a still more fearsome aspect, because it was found to be murdering American prisoners in cold blood. The column's ss panzer troops shot nineteen unarmed Americans at Honsfeld and another fifty at Büllingen. About noon, at Baugnez, the main crossroads between Schoppen and Ligneuville, the Germans intersected the path of the 7th Armored Division, hastening to the battle in accordance with Eisenhower's decision at Paris the night before. They just missed tangling with CCR. Instead they met Battery B, 285th Field Artillery Observation

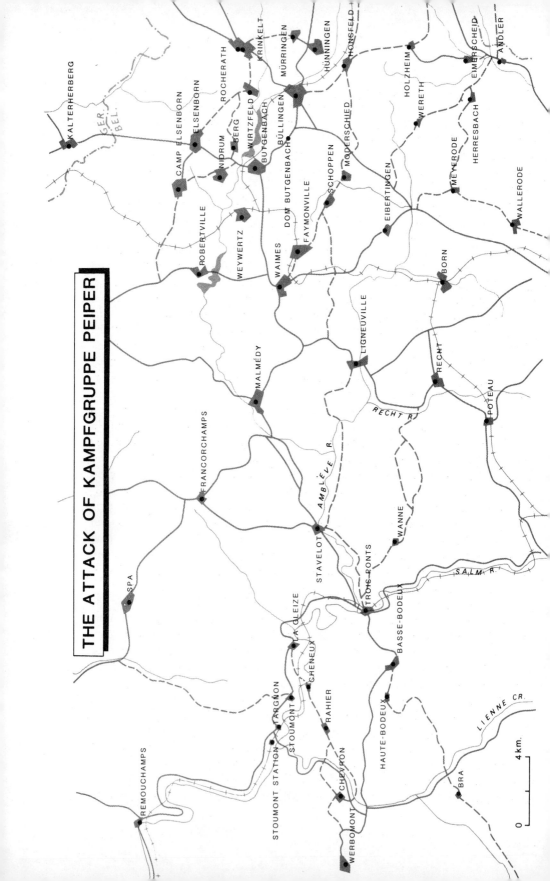

THE ATTACK OF KAMPFGRUPPE PEIPER

Battalion. These lightly armed Americans scattered for cover in ditches and woods, but some 150 of them were rounded up by troopers of the 1st SS Panzer Division—the Adolf Hitler Lifeguard—and marched into an open field. There they were mowed down by machine-gun and pistol fire. Some survived by feigning death. The wounded who cried out or moved were shot in the head. At least eighty-six were killed. The Germans quickly drove on, and about 2:30 P.M. a patrol from the 291st Engineer Combat Battalion reached the scene. Within three or four hours the inspector general of the First Army had the story, and by that evening news of the "Malmédy Massacre" was already circulating through the American front lines.

Complicating the tale by the next day were rumors of wandering Germans in American uniforms and jeeps, changing road direction signs and otherwise dispensing misinformation to confuse the reinforcement of the Ardennes front, and perhaps bent on additional murders. Here was the explanation of intelligence gathered earlier in December, which revealed that Hitler himself had ordered "the formation of a special unit for employment on reconnaissance and special tasks on the Western Front," whose personnel, "fully trained in single combat," were also to know "the English language and also the American dialect." All German formations were directed to turn in captured American clothing, equipment, and vehicles for these troops.[1]

On Monday, December 18, American headquarters and soldiers passed on reports that a few such masqueraders had been captured and that there seemed evidence of the activities of many more. One of the captured masqueraders had in turn heard rumors of an intent to assassinate Eisenhower; he told the story to his interrogators, with the effect that the Supreme Commander became almost a prisoner of his own security forces. For the next several days, General Bradley himself could not move through his command without being subjected to security checks questioning him about esoteric Americana designed to trip up Germans otherwise fluent in the "the American dialect." Lesser GIs naturally subjected each other to still more rigorous scrutiny.

For a while there seemed no end to the Germans' devilish ingenuity. Early on Sunday morning, December 17, the German paratroop force, in eclipse since Crete as actual parachutists, began dropping out of their old Junkers 52s again across a wide area of the northern Ardennes. Word of paratroops—and dummies of paratroops—spread through the American formations for the next several days, combining with and taking more frightening effect from the other varieties of menacing news. By Monday or Tuesday, the very breadth of the parachute landings, along with the failure of any concentrated paratroop force to take shape, suggested to every trained intelligence analyst a bungled drop that would not have been particularly formidable even if fully assembled. But it took time for this impression to filter through an army already jittery from too many unpleasant surprises.

Having contributed to this burgeoning of sinister shadows the only solid evidence of treacherous brutality, the Kampfgruppe of the 1st SS Panzer Division responsible for the Malmédy Massacre had hurried on westward. The commander and the leading units were already gone by the time the prisoners were rounded up and shot at Baugnez. The panzers appeared next at Ligneuville, a little before one o'clock on Sunday afternoon, their coming heralded early enough that most of the Americans in the town departed before they arrived, leaving half-eaten lunches for the Germans to finish. Of those GIs unlucky enough not to escape, another eight were shot. As the panzers were finding their way out of the narrow streets of Ligneuville in mid-afternoon, they collided with part of the trains of CCB of the 9th Armored Division, which were on their way to help shore up the 106th Division. A few Shermans and a tank destroyer put up a short fight, in which they killed the Germans' lead Panther and a few other armored vehicles and delayed the panzers' progress for about an hour.

While the detachment of the 9th Armored cleared out southward for St. Vith, the panzers went westward along the road that crosses to the south shore of the Amblève River about two kilometers outside Ligneuville. This road then parallels the river until it crosses northward again some five kilometers farther on at Stavelot. Like most of the streams of the Ardennes, the Amblève cuts a deep trench through the hills. It is not wide or deep but, partly because its banks are steep, tanks can cross it only by bridges. Stavelot, a town of about 5,000, has a few buildings on the south side of the river but mostly climbs up sparsely wooded bluffs on the north bank. The panzer spearhead approached at about dusk, when the north bank was alive with American trucks emptying a number of big gasoline dumps in the area. The Germans' road descended from heights on the south bank, passed through a narrow defile, and turned around a big rock to funnel into Stavelot's only vehicular bridge.

Here were the only American combat troops in the vicinity, a squad of the 291st Engineer Combat Battalion, dispatched from Malmédy to construct a roadblock. As the Germans' lead vehicle rounded the rock and headed for the stone bridge, it struck a mine laid by the engineers. The Germans then dismounted about sixty panzer grenadiers to assault the bridge, but antitank and small arms fire drove them off. During the night, the Americans could hear amidst sporadic enemy shelling plenty of tank noises coming up to reinforce the Germans. Until now, the 1st SS Panzer Kampfgruppe had displayed not only cruelty but also ample energy and resourcefulness; its spearhead was well to the west of any other German column on this second night of the battle. But the panzers surprisingly chose to push no more on the night of December 17–18.

The Americans also reinforced Stavelot during the night, but the First Army did not have much strength to spare. Major Paul J. Solis came in with a company of the 526th Armored Infantry Battalion and a platoon of towed 3-inch tank destroyers. Just before daybreak, Solis positioned two platoons of infantry and a section of tank destroyers on the south bank of the Amblève and the other infantry platoon and tank destroyer section in reserve around the town square north of the river. The Germans were sure to try for the bridge again with daylight, and this time they did so in force, brushing the Americans aside before they could get themselves fairly organized for defense and before they could blow the bridge.

After a brisk little fight in the Stavelot square, most of Solis's command retreated in a direction contrary to his orders, northeastward toward Malmédy. By doing so they exposed a big gasoline dump at Francorchamps just north of Stavelot, but Solis responded resourcefully by having his remaining troops pour out some of the gasoline— 124,000 gallons of it—in a deep road cut and set it afire. Thus he barred the Germans' path to enough fuel to have carried a large armored force the remaining sixty-eight kilometers to the Meuse.

The panzers turned back from the fire to Stavelot and moved on west along the Amblève toward Trois Ponts. Their lethargy of the previous night was about to cost them a good deal more than it had already, because the First Army's effort to stem their progress had sent Company C, 51st Engineer Combat Battalion to Trois Ponts during the night, and the place was well suited for even a company to hold up a big armored Kampfgruppe. At Trois Ponts the Salm River flowing from the south meets the Amblève. The road from Stavelot as it approaches Trois Ponts passes under a railroad and then turns sharply left to cross the Amblève into the town. From the town, two more right-angle turns lead to the other two highway bridges, westward across the Salm toward the Meuse and thus toward the panzers' presumed immediate destination. Major Robert B. Yates had deployed C Company to guard the underpass at the railroad and the Amblève bridge, and to be ready to blow all the bridges. When a lost 57mm. antitank gun and crew of the 526th Armored Infantry Battalion from the 7th Armored Division turned up, Yates commandeered them to stand near the underpass, covering a minefield. The vanguard of the 1st SS Panzer Division came clattering toward the gun a little before noon. The lead tank fired first, but the American gun managed to blow off a tread and cripple the tank before other German vehicles came up to knock out the gun and kill four of its crew. This encounter gave the engineers time to destroy the Amblève bridge and the first bridge over the Salm, while retiring into the houses of Trois Ponts.

It was apparent to the Americans by now that the enemy force at Trois Ponts and straggling back along the Stavelot road was the 1st SS Panzer Division's principal concentration of armored strength, including a strong detachment of Tigers in addition to a well-equipped division's allotment of Panthers and Pzkw IVs. But without yet having met major American opposition, this Kampfgruppe, doubtless critical to the enemy's plans, had gotten itself cooped up in the narrow valley of the Amblève, with no satisfactory route west to the Meuse. From the blown Amblève bridge at Trois Ponts, the panzers grudgingly turned away northward, to persist through the defile of the Amblève toward La Gleize, whence a narrow secondary road led to a bridge at Cheneux and a twisting route westward out of the valley. The Cheneux bridge proved intact, but the Germans had no sooner crossed it than they were beset by P-47s taking advantage of a brief break in the weather. And a short distance farther west was a still more insignificant stream, the Lienne Creek, but another watercourse requiring tanks to cross by bridge. Company A, 291st Engineer Combat Battalion, blew the bridge in the Germans' faces.

There were other bridges north and south along the Lienne, but none strong enough to support the weight of Tigers. A detachment of assault guns and half-tracks did cross during Monday evening, but the 2nd Battalion of the 119th Infantry was waiting to ambush and nearly destroy the detachment at Chevron. The panzers drew back from the Cheneux crossing to La Gleize, to continue on down the east bank of the Amblève toward Stoumont in search of another route of escape. The 119th Infantry was a part of General Hobbs's 30th Division, sent down from the Ninth Army. It had just arrived at Chevron. The Thunderbolts that hit the panzers near Cheneux, as well as liaison planes flying under the clouds, had reported thoroughly on the German column's whereabouts, and the rest of the 119th Infantry was arriving at Stoumont.

If the Germans had crossed the Lienne, only four more kilometers would have brought them to Werbomont, to a good road again, and to relatively open country through the remaining fifteen or twenty kilometers to the Meuse. The engineer detachments with their roadblocks and demolitions had delayed the Adolf Hitler Lifeguard just long enough to permit a major American combat formation to arrive before the Germans escaped the constricting canyons of the Amblève. With the placing of the Old Hickory

Division in front of the panzer Kampfgruppe, the American command was at length regaining a measure of control over the shape of the battle—the control it had lacked for three days since the enemy eruption out of the Eifel.

The Road Junctions

To regain control of the shape of the battle had of course been the special concern of General Middleton at VIII Corps headquarters at Bastogne. By evening of the first day, despite spreading communications failures, Middleton knew enough to begin resolving the apparently piecemeal German attacks of that morning into a picture of a major offensive seemingly aimed at reaching the Meuse at Liège. That evening Middleton still felt some hope that his brittle front line might hold—but not much hope. He ordered all his units to cling to their positions until they became "completely untenable."[2] Anticipating the rupture of the front nevertheless, Middleton resolved that he must block the few major road junctions of the Ardennes: St. Vith, Houffalize, and Bastogne, as well as the city of Luxembourg farther south. Whether or not the Germans in their probable thrust for Liège intended to bypass strongpoints, they would not well be able to tolerate an American presence in these communications centers in their rear, nor to maintain the momentum of their drive if the Americans held on to the principal road junctions along their lines of communication.

Unfortunately, it was inherent in the VIII Corps dispositions that had made Middleton's front line brittle that he possessed virtually no reserves with which to fulfill his resolve to defend the communications centers. In reserve he had CCR of the 9th Armored Division and four engineer combat battalions. He might call on another three engineer combat battalions belonging to the First Army but working in his sector. That was all. With these units he must do what he could.

More fortunately, General Eisenhower's rapid perception of the danger on the first evening gave Middleton assurance during the night of December 16–17 that the 7th Armored Division was on its way to him. He promptly directed Bruce Clarke and his CCB in the van of that division upon the most immediately threatened of the nodal points, St. Vith, behind the imperiled 106th Division. Middleton also directed some tank destroyers of the 9th Armored's CCR to Clerf, where they joined in the defense of that town and its crossing of the Clerf River, and ordered one of his engineer combat battalions, the 44th, to the battle farther south along the Clerf River, where it became part of the contest for Wiltz. He attached still another engineer battalion to the 4th Division to help shield the city of Luxembourg. On December 17, however, Middleton had to be chary in thus rationing out his scarce resources to bolster the front, because he was more likely to need reserves when the front collapsed. With this eventuality in mind, he accepted a proposal from the corps engineer to form a defensive line along the eastern approaches to Bastogne from Foy to Neffe, to be garrisoned by the 35th and 158th Engineer Combat Battalions, the latter one of the three in the corps sector that were directly under First Army headquarters.

On Monday morning, December 18, Middleton received word of a bad turn of events around St. Vith, the loss of the lesser road junction of Poteau west and north of it. Against the threat of Germans in that area, Middleton sent an assortment of engineer, ordnance, antiaircraft, and tank destroyer units to patrol bridges and intersections north from Bastogne to La Roche. He directed the trains of the 7th Armored Division to block the crossings of the Ourthe River to the northeast of Bastogne.

Additional bad news on Monday included word of the Germans' overrunning an engineer company command post at Steinbach, just east of Houffalize. Middleton had been hoping the 28th Division would hold long enough in front of Houffalize for the high command to have time to send him more help to throw into this communications center. Now it was evidently too late. Middleton's effort to recapture some control over the battle by retaining the road junctions was narrowing into an effort to defend Bastogne.

The means with which he had hoped to save Houffalize was General Gavin's 82nd Airborne Division. By December 17, General Hodges was coming to appreciate the true dimensions of the enemy's adventure, and feelings at First Army headquarters "swung precipitously from general optimism based on the long-term hopelessness of Germany's strategic position to calamity and woe, involving the imminent arrival of new divisions believed to be in the East (as well as invented ones), and new secret weapons."[3] Hodges signalized his new perception not only by giving Gerow a free hand to cancel the offensive toward the Roer dams and organize a defense of the Elsenborn Ridge, but also by calling on Bradley to ask Eisenhower to release the SHAEF reserve, such as it was, into battle: General Ridgway's XVIII Airborne Corps. This time it was Eisenhower who was reluctant to commit his remaining reserve so early in the confused action, but Bradley persuaded him to send the 82nd and 101st Airborne Divisions to the VIII Corps.

Recuperating from nearly sixty days of the kind of sustained battle for which airborne units were not designed, the two divisions were at Reims, some 150 kilometers from the battle. They possessed little organic transportation, but COMZ quickly found enough trucks and trailers to carry their infantry. The orders to move reached the divisions on Sunday evening. General Ridgway was in the Midlands of England observing the training of the newly arrived 17th Airborne Division, and the news did not catch up with him until later in the night. He flew to France as quickly as he could, just before fog closed down all flights out of England for forty-eight hours; but it would take time before he could rejoin his troops through the physical and operational fogs on the Continent. General Taylor of the 101st was on leave in the United States. Thus General Gavin became acting commander of the airborne corps. Because the 82nd had been out of the line a little longer than the 101st, it led the way.

When he learned gratefully that he was about to get the airborne divisions, Middleton felt no hesitation about where to put them: behind his broken center, to hold the Bastogne and Houffalize road junctions. Major General J.F.M. Whiteley, the SHAEF deputy G-3, had independently called the attention of Bedell Smith and Eisenhower to Bastogne, and SHAEF agreed that if the reserve were to be committed immediately, here was the place for it. Bradley had arrived at the same conclusion.

Evident though the importance of the Houffalize-Bastogne road network might be, some confusion still attended the airborne divisions' journey to the battle zone. Hodges early intended to use the 101st at Bastogne and the 82nd at Houffalize, and thus with the 7th Armored Division at St. Vith to cover all three principal road junctions. By Monday morning, however, when Gavin reported to First Army headquarters at Spa, Hodges's staff was worried most of all about the 1st SS Panzers' dash toward Werbomont and the Meuse. Colonel Dickson had returned from his Paris leave the night before after traversing a countryside trembling with alarums over the onrushing panzer

Kampfgruppe. The ultimate purpose in holding Bastogne was to deny the enemy the crossings of the Meuse, but the SS troopers already menaced the crossings elsewhere. So the First Army ordered Gavin to divert the 82nd to Werbomont, and for a time it appeared the 101st would follow. Thus Middleton lost the 82nd.

But Middleton got on the telephone to Bradley and persuaded the army group to reassign the 101st to Bastogne. When Colonel Thomas L. Sherburne at the head of the 101st column reached a road intersection at Werbomont, he found some MPs busily directing all airborne troops to Werbomont and others directing the same troops to Bastogne. He managed to sort out the confusion and to push troopers of the 101st toward Bastogne. Meanwhile Hodges confirmed Bradley's decision, assigned the 101st to the VIII Corps and Bastogne, and at the same time ordered Middleton to take his corps headquarters out of Bastogne. For the source of Middleton's latest urgency was the combination of the imminent loss of Houffalize with the crumbling of his last outposts east of the immediate Bastogne perimeter.

When he learned on Sunday that Clerf could not last long, Middleton sent CCR of the 9th Armored to set up two roadblocks on the Clerf-Bastogne highway: the first about seven kilometers west of Clerf, where the road from that town joins the highway from St. Vith, and the second about six kilometers farther west at Allerborn, where a secondary road from Wiltz, and thus from the German penetration into that area, meets the main road. About midday of December 18, strong enemy armored forces—the vanguard of the 2nd Panzer Division—surrounded the first of these roadblocks. They were well on their way toward the second before CCR and VIII Corps headquarters knew what was happening. There was no more strength to spare to rescue the roadblocks anyway. Late Monday afternoon, the Germans overran the second roadblock. Characteristically, their spearheads had already bypassed it and were almost at CCR headquarters at Longvilly, three kilometers farther on, before the battle at Allerborn was fairly joined. By evening, the headquarters and remnants of CCR were fighting for their very existence. Colonel Joseph H. Gilbreth, leading the combat command, had to call off an effort to escape toward Bastogne under cover of darkness because his fleeing troops met Germans already swarming west of Longvilly, and there was danger of panic and complete chaos.

The vanguard of the 10th Armored Division, Lieutenant Colonel Henry T. Cherry's Team Cherry, had reached Middleton in time to get involved in this fight at Longvilly—or, more precisely, part of Team Cherry was cut off there during the night along with the remains of CCR. The next morning the Germans gave a measure of their own sense of the importance of the Bastogne road junction when large parts of Lüttwitz's XLVII Panzer Corps converged to destroy the Longvilly obstacle on the Bastogne highway. Troops and vehicles of the 26th Volksgrenadier Division and Panzer Lehr joined the 2nd Panzer Division in the battle. Naturally, Longvilly was overrun. Colonel Gilbreth and other survivors of CCR escaped northward in scattered, small parties. The Team Cherry troops contributed at least their share to the battle at Longvilly and then in part made their way westward to join the bulk of their team and fight again at Mageret. This whole force was also about to be overrun when word arrived that it, too, should try to escape northward. Meanwhile Colonel Cherry himself and his headquarters troops were fighting the beginning of the battle of the Bastogne perimeter itself, two kilometers down the road from Mageret at Neffe.

The Germans clearly wanted to break their armor free to hasten to the Meuse even more than they wanted to overrun Bastogne, because during the day the 2nd Panzer Division tried to cut away toward Noville and whatever roads bypassed Bastogne to the north. Farther north, the 116th Panzer Division was bearing down along the south bank of the Ourthe River past Houffalize. In these areas, however, the panzers collided with more of the 10th Armored's CCB, at Noville, and with parts of Middleton's screen of combat engineers and the roadblocks erected by the trains of the 7th Armored. There was also the 705th Tank Destroyer Battalion, sent down by the Ninth Army and assigned by Middleton to the area of the Ourthe.

The defenses Middleton thus improvised from his scanty reserves after his center broke could not expect to endure for long, but they contrived to inflict disproportionate injury upon the German offensive. From Longvilly to Noville, pockets of Middleton's reserves somehow kept the 2nd Panzer Division tied up all through December 19. The 116th Panzer Division was evidently looking for good crossings of the Ourthe that would not deflect the division northward, like the Houffalize crossing, but would keep the armor bearing west toward the nearest crossings of the Meuse. When the 116th Panzers reached Bertogne on Tuesday afternoon, the Ourthe bridge just northwest of the town had already been destroyed, by whom it is not known. Farther west at Ortheuville, the Americans had failed to blow a Bailey bridge; but assorted engineers and eight of the 705th's tank destroyers had the bridge so well covered that late in the afternoon the Germans evidently decided an attempt to cross there would not be worth the price that the guns might extract. The head of the 116th Panzer Division turned back toward Houffalize, and with it the whole of General Krüger's LVIII Panzer Corps apparently prepared to detour northward after all.

It was a significant retreat. It represented, albeit in extreme form, a palsy that was beginning to afflict the whole German advance. On December 16 and 17, the Germans had achieved a textbook demonstration of applying the principle of concentration against weakness to rupture the American front in the Ardennes. But if they were to exploit their breakthrough despite the overall Allied superiority of strength on the Western Front, if they were to reach the Meuse and the supply dumps at Liège as they apparently intended, they must persist in racing swiftly forward before Allied units drawn from all along the front could converge against them. Instead, however, by Monday and Tuesday the German spearheads were moving cautiously and hesitantly. They had met so many pockets of American resistance that they moved as if they expected new resistance around every corner, and they allowed small roadblocks to hold up large forces.

It was especially significant that between the Ourthe and Bastogne the affliction gripped the Schwerpunkt of the Fifth Panzer Army. Until now, old German soldiers must have taken satisfaction from the success of Manteuffel's Fifth Panzer Army in contrast to the frustration of Dietrich's Sixth Panzer Army. Despite a heavier concentration on a narrower front, Dietrich's army built around SS formations could boast no success save the thin penetration by the 1st SS Panzer Division Kampfgruppe now blocked along the Amblève. It was Manteuffel's old army formations, with their more skillful tactics in the first assault, that had scored the massive breakthrough against the American center. Yet by December 18 and 19, it was Manteuffel's spearheads, the famous XLVII and LVIII Panzer Corps, with the reliable old 2nd and 116th Panzer Divisions and Panzer Lehr, that dithered while the Americans rushed to reinforce Bastogne.

Singleminded boldness more than material superiority had carried the Germans swiftly to the Meuse and beyond it to victory in 1940. As boldness was paid its reward in 1940, so hesitancy exacted its price in 1944. When the remnants of CCR, 9th Armored Division, struggled north from Longvilly and then west to Bastogne, as they approached the town they found themselves welcomed by troopers of the 101st Airborne. So did Team Cherry.

On Monday, December 18, VIII Corps headquarters had for the most part moved out of Bastogne as ordered by General Hodges, but Middleton and a few of his staff stayed to assure arrangements for the defense. General Ridgway arrived out of the fog that evening. He conferred with Middleton and Brigadier General Anthony C. McAuliffe, artillery commander and acting division commander of the 101st. In the morning Ridgway moved on to look after Gavin and the 82nd at Werbomont. Middleton helped McAuliffe make his first dispositions.

The 501st Parachute Infantry led the 101st Airborne column into Bastogne at midnight of the 18th. Considering they had traveled from Reims through rain, snow flurries, fog, and in large part darkness, the 101st made good time. Lieutenant Colonel Julian J. Ewell's 501st had been on the road for only eight hours, and McAuliffe had all four of his regiments in hand by nine o'clock on Tuesday morning. To supplement the light howitzers of the airborne, the 12th Army Group dispatched the 755th Armored Field Artillery Battalion of 155mm. howitzers, whose guns also arrived on Tuesday morning. That evening the 705th Tank Destroyer Battalion came in, after dropping two platoons at the Ortheuville bridge. The 969th Field Artillery Battalion, 155mm. howitzers, had been assigned earlier to support the 28th Division and wandered into Bastogne as it tried to find its way out of the 28th's debacle. With these units, the 101st had a suitable artillery complement for the defensive battle ahead.

The Battle of St. Vith

It was not only along the American front that the seams between units represented weakness. Every army faces this problem, and it was a flaw in the German plan that the other critical road junction, St. Vith, lay within the Fifth Panzer Army's zone of advance but so close to the northern boundary of that zone that an attack against a perimeter defense might well lack coordinated power.

General Bruce Clarke arrived at St. Vith on Sunday morning, December 17, to find General Jones's 106th Division command post sunk in gloom. Well it might be; Jones had received the news that substantial reinforcement from Clarke's 7th Armored CCB would be long delayed, and thus the full measure of the peril confronting the two regiments thrust out to the Schnee Eifel was being recognized for the first time. Jones's own son was out there. Jones and Clarke agreed on a plan to commit CCB when it arrived to an attack down the road to the Schönberg bridge, where the Germans were closing their noose only ten kilometers from St. Vith. Clarke's CCB would then turn south to reinforce CCB of the 9th Armored where it was trying to break the southern prong of the German pincers. But even in the making, the plan had the look of a theoretical exercise and no more. At the time, the 7th Armored Division was swimming against the current of a mass of vehicles, guns, and troops in retreat, and the reinforcing columns could make little headway. At Petit-Thier, Major Donald P. Boyer, Jr., S-3 of the 38th Armored Infantry Battalion of the 7th Armored's CCR, found that all traffic had stopped. In fact, it was the most perfect traffic jam I have ever seen. We had run into this hopeless mass of vehicles fleeing to the rear on a narrow road which would barely support two-way traffic at slow speeds. Vehicles streaming to the rear had attempted to pass each other in the intervals between the tanks of the 31st Tank Battalion, which was leading CCB, and now no one could move . . . .

It was already 1515 and from the looks of the road jam, neither the tanks nor anything else was going to reach St. Vith for a long time. Lieutenant Colonel [William H. G.] Fuller, Corporal Cox, and I took over the job of clearing a path for the tanks, and we started getting vehicles to move over to the sides. Slowly a path was beginning to open and the tanks began to roll along at a snail's pace with halts every 50 to 100 feet. Several times we had to wave the lead tank forward at full speed when some vehicles refused to pull over. Usually the sight of 30-odd tons of steel roaring down on him was all we needed to get the driver to move over.[4]

The 7th Armored could not make its way through the chaos rapidly enough to rescue the encircled regiments on the Schnee Eifel; the real issue was whether St. Vith itself could be defended. By mid-afternoon, German vehicles were seen west of Schönberg within seven kilometers of St. Vith. The only troops between the enemy and the town were the headquarters and service companies of the 81st and 168th Engineer Combat Battalions and the 106th Division headquarters personnel. Wielding bazookas and aided by a lucky brief appearance of fighter-bombers, the engineers put up the kind of stubborn show of resistance, disproportionate to their numbers, that was to become the speciality of their corps in the Ardennes. Probably the Germans west of Schönberg were still very few. If not, they were mysteriously hesitant for this early stage of the battle, and their hesitance afforded the Americans on the scene a misleading encouragement. Still, the fate of St. Vith so obviously depended on the coming of the 7th Armored that Jones turned over command of the town to Clarke.

By about 2:30 on Sunday afternoon some 7th Armored cavalry had struggled through the traffic jam to begin arriving at St. Vith. The first Shermans and armored infantry followed at dusk. The division was traveling southward in two columns, one through Stavelot, Trois Ponts, and Vielsalm, the other through Malmédy and Ligneuville. Some of the artillery in the eastern column had to detour to avoid tangling with German tanks around Malmédy—the Kampfgruppe of the 1st SS Panzer Division on its way to the valley of the Amblève. As units arrived piecemeal during Sunday night and into Monday morning, what would become a defensive perimeter was taking shape on a series of ridge lines screening St. Vith; but the arrivals were so piecemeal that battalions were broken up and the troops would have to fight in smaller units without the cohesion of the basic American tactical formation. On the other hand, so much had the German attack from Schönberg seemed to peter out, and so sketchy was the 7th Armored's knowledge of the scope of the German offensive, and thus of the likely enemy strength confronting them, that both Clarke and the division commander, General Hasbrouck, when the latter arrived on the scene, still contemplated an attack of their own as soon as CCB was well in hand.

The coming day partially clarified their peril but also suggested something about the lack of coordination that was to dilute German power around St. Vith and give them a fighting chance to fend off a juggernaut more massive than they yet imagined. Monday began with an overwhelming German strike against the town of Recht, on the north flank of the emerging St. Vith perimeter, where the enemy broke in remnants of the 14th Cavalry Group. Throughout the morning, the Germans pushed on irresistibly in this sector, continuing to drive a conglomeration of cavalry, parts of the 7th Armored's CCR, and other troops down the road to Poteau and past that town, and thus toward Vielsalm squarely in the rear of St. Vith. But abruptly, just beyond Poteau, the Germans again relented. They happened to be troops of the 1st SS Panzer Division. They were a different force from the Kampfgruppe that had perpetrated the Malmédy Massacre, but they belonged to the Sixth Panzer Army, not the Fifth Panzer Army in whose zone St. Vith lay. They had other fish to fry, farther north and west.

But the SS troopers had already broken the 7th Armored's best line of communication. And by the time their threat of a rearward envelopment abated, at least momentarily, St. Vith had so much to handle in front that the defenders were calling on Brigadier General William M. Hoge's CCB of the 9th Armored to hurry help up from the south. Hoge's force was too much occupied in battles of its own to send immediate assistance. The 18th Volksgrenadier Division thus was able to bend dangerously the line of the 38th Armored Infantry Battalion, though the ubiquitous engineers—the 168th Battalion, this time—plus additional armored infantry managed to stabilize the St. Vith front at nightfall.

Two circumstances that were mainly beyond the Americans' knowledge kept the barely contained German pressure from growing rapidly worse. One was the necessity for the 18th Volksgrenadiers to divide their attentions between St. Vith and extinguishing the resistance on the Schnee Eifel in their rear. The other was a traffic jam behind the German lines rivaling the Americans' tieup of the previous day, as columns of Dietrich's army overflowed into Manteuffel's zone. Once more, it was a saving virtue for St. Vith to lie so close to the enemy's interarmy boundary.

The German effort was restrained enough by these factors that, dangerous as it was, General Hasbrouck decided during Monday afternoon that he could spare his CCA to thrust back northwestward from St. Vith to try to recapture Poteau and thus restore the most direct line of communication to Vielsalm. A sharp fight crackled through Poteau for the second time in the day. Thanks to the withdrawal of many of the 1st SS Panzers, CCA recaptured the town. The road west remained under so heavy an enemy fire, however, that CCA was unable for the time being to reestablish contact with CCR, which was defending Vielsalm.

So Hasbrouck had spread his strength over an uncomfortably wide area, and he had not yet met the last of such demands. To attempt to maintain an alternate line of communication, he scattered detachments down the road and railroad from St. Vith through Beho and Gouvy. At the Gouvy railroad station, his men would eventually be hit by Krüger's LVIII Panzer Corps moving from the south bank of the Ourthe. Hasbrouck's trains and whatever combat elements were attached to them were forming, of course, the dubious defenses of the Ourthe still farther southwest. By Tuesday and Wednesday Hasbrouck found his communications decidedly precarious, as St. Vith became a lonely promontory around which the German tide rolled westward everywhere.

Early on Tuesday, December 19, messages dispatched the previous day reached 106th Division headquarters, now at Vielsalm, saying that the 422nd and 423rd Infantry were trying to fight their way off the Schnee Eifel. But nothing more was heard, the weather frustrated an VIII Corps effort to airdrop supplies, and not much hope lingered into Tuesday evening. Nevertheless, something was still preoccupying the enemy too much to permit him to mount more than probing attacks against the St. Vith perimeter that day. Further on the credit side of Hasbrouck's ledger, Hoge's CCB, 9th Armored had tied in during the night with CCB, 7th Armored. Also, the retreat of the 424th Infantry from the Our linked this regiment with Hoge's armor, to extend the St. Vith perimeter still farther to the right. Presently the commander of the 112th Infantry turned up at Vielsalm, having been cut off from his own 28th Division, and General Jones appropriated the regiment and ordered it to form on the right of the 424th during Tuesday night.

Amidst the turmoil that swept across the Ardennes all the way from the Elsenborn Ridge to Echternach, St. Vith had virtually lost contact with the VIII Corps, even by radio. Though the town was high on Middleton's list of road junctions that ought to be withheld from the enemy, for several days neither he nor any other senior officer knew much about what was happening there. On Wednesday, December 20, Hasbrouck slipped a liaison officer out to First Army headquarters, with a letter to General Kean describing the horseshoe line his own division and assorted increments were holding from Poteau in the north to Holdingen on the right flank of the 112th Infantry, but with the right dangling and exposed. Hasbrouck had heard that the 82nd Airborne was coming into the battle and reaching out toward his northern flank, which was correct. But he feared for his right, where the "TDs and stragglers we have collected and organized into defense teams at road centers" southwestward from Holdingen were his only protection, and those at Gouvy were already feeling the pressure of the 116th Panzer Division and the 560th Volksgrenadier Division, that is, the LVIII Panzer Corps. "VIII Corps has ordered me to hold and I will do so but need help," said Hasbrouck.[5]

The First Army replied that Ridgway's XVIII Airborne Corps was on the way with armor and infantry, instructing Hasbrouck that he would come under Ridgway's command once contact was established, and meanwhile confirming Hasbrouck's command of all the units in the St. Vith defenses. This latter had been hitherto none too clear, despite Jones's abdication of command to Bruce Clarke on December 17, because Jones was still active in the area and wore two stars to Hasbrouck's one; Middleton had said to Hasbrouck on Monday: "You two"—meaning Hasbrouck and Jones—"carry the ball up there for me."[6]

First Army headquarters could not give Hasbrouck what he needed most, help for his exposed right. Still, all through December 20, though the enemy had surged around St. Vith as far as forty kilometers to the southwest, Hasbrouck's front and flank remained strangely quiet. Why were the Germans so long in closing in? Surely Middleton was correct in his initial assessment that without the St. Vith road center, German lines of communication westward would be clogged. Making matters worse for the enemy, the German army with its limited motorization—horse-drawn vehicles often slowed tanks that were trying to break free to the Meuse—needed rail transportation to support any extended offensive, and St. Vith blocked the only rail line west through the Ardennes. The Americans in St. Vith confined the Sixth Panzer Army's penetration to a chokingly narrow corridor. Of course, St. Vith was not in the Sixth Panzer Army's zone, and we know now that Hitler himself had strictly prohibited deviations from the zonal boundaries. The German army hurt most by St. Vith could not attack it. Yet the Americans in St. Vith also choked off one of the Fifth Panzer Army's best routes to Bastogne, almost nullifying the significance of the captured road junction at Houffalize. Why, despite all these circumstances, the Fifth Panzer Army was so slow to hit St. Vith hard remains mysterious even today.

The Germans' interarmy boundary obviously continued to be part of their problem. Elements of Dietrich's army on their way westward went on colliding with the Poteau side of Hasbrouck's perimeter and then bouncing away. The boundary also limited the possibilities of maneuver for the corps directly responsible for St. Vith, General der Artillerie Walther Lucht's LXVI Corps of Manteuffel's army, the 18th and 62nd Volksgrenadier Divisions. Despite Hasbrouck's dangling right flank, the delineation of German corps sectors afforded Lucht little choice but to mount a frontal assault against St. Vith from the east. We know now also that the Germans had found Hasbrouck's perimeter so stubborn that they attributed to it much greater strength than it actually contained. This factor was crucial. It is not least among the laurels won by the St. Vith defenders that they so awed the enemy.

The Germans were also hampered by the very geography that had made their breakthrough possible. The roads of the Ardennes were too few, and in December the secondary roads were too soon churned into a mire, for reinforcement to reach Lucht's corps readily when St. Vith proved a tough nut to crack.

Late on December 20, American 90mm. tank destroyers near Hünningen just northwest of St. Vith caught four Panthers in their sights. Waiting on a reverse slope for such an opportunity, the tank destroyers fired seven rounds and knocked out all four tanks. The next morning, a force of panzer grenadiers infiltrated into woods somewhat to the west and attacked the 275th Armored Field Artillery Battalion. The artillerymen, veterans who had experienced this kind of combat before, turned away the attack; and to escape, the raiders had to evade a cordon of Shermans. These two jabs were the first attacks around St. Vith by the elite, overstrength Führer Begleit Brigade, which Manteuffel had persuaded Model to release from reserve to stiffen the drive on St. Vith. But Manteuffel had received the brigade on December 18, and it had taken until now to begin reaching St. Vith, with most of the tanks still somewhere on the congested roads to the rear. (The brigade's tank battalion came from the Grossdeutschland Panzer Division and caused American intelligence considerable confusion, and the defenders of St. Vith considerable apprehension, because the Grossdeutschland Division was supposed to be on the Eastern Front.)

The brushes with the Führer Begleit Brigade proved a prelude to the long-awaited major attack by Lucht's corps. On the afternoon of Thursday, December 21, an uncommonly ferocious and sustained artillery barrage heralded the advance of the 18th and 62nd Volksgrenadier Divisions. Though the St. Vith perimeter had not been seriously assailed since Monday, repeated probing attacks and constant exchanges of fire since then had eroded the defenders' numbers. The Germans' artillery preparation took an additional heavy toll, as well as inflicting the usual shock. By Thursday evening, a series of enemy attacks badly softened the defenses on the Schönberg road. Thereupon the Germans regrouped and concentrated on and near the road the main strength of the 18th Volksgrenadier Division. The Volksgrenadiers broke through, and they followed up by pressing hard along a draw between Clarke's CCB and Hoge's, where they scored another breakthrough. During Thursday night Clarke's CCB conducted a fighting withdrawal through a snowstorm to ground west of St. Vith.

The Americans were not yet ready to yield the Germans free use of the St. Vith road junction. Clarke's CCB formed on a ridge a kilometer west of town, and Hasbrouck's other units withdrew to fall into line with it. The previous morning's foray of part of the Führer Begleit Brigade proved at this juncture, however, to reward the Germans. During Thursday night the brigade used its first-hand knowledge of the terrain to infiltrate a force into Clarke's rear. At daybreak, these Germans were almost at Rodt, four kilometers west of St. Vith on the road to Poteau and Vielsalm, on an elevation commanding much of Clarke's position. The guns of Clarke's nearest Shermans could not reach the German panzers on the high ground, and Clarke's armored infantry was driven from Rodt. When CCA began coming down the road from Poteau to help, its Shermans became involved in an unproductive long-range duel with Panthers. Presently CCA had its hands full with yet another menace, as a hitherto uncommitted panzer division of Dietrich's army, the 9th SS Panzers, commenced knocking heavily upon the gates of Poteau. Meanwhile the 62nd Volksgrenadier Division stabbed a new thrust between the two CCB's. Clarke had no choice but to retreat again.

Hasbrouck now concluded that the whole St. Vith command must retreat or face destruction. Not only was his front crumbling, but intelligence indicated that the long-awaited threat to his open right might soon materialize with a vengeance, in the shape of nothing less than the 2nd SS Panzer Division, also newly committed to the battle. Soon there might be no line of communication, and perhaps no line of retreat.

Ridgway's corps headquarters sent a directive to hold on in a perimeter defense of the current positions, but corps was ignoring the circumstance that the St. Vith command now stood in a wooded area with only one poor road for lateral communication. Lightly equipped airborne troops, such as Ridgway was accustomed to leading, might have survived and operated in this environment; armor could not. Bruce Clarke, a blunt man, called the corps plan "Custer's Last Stand." Hasbrouck replied forthrightly to Ridgway's headquarters, cataloguing all his command's weaknesses, warning of the arrival of the 2nd SS Panzer Division, and stating: "The road net within our position is totally inadequate to the troops and vehicles concentrated therein." He had to add a postscript about the latest attack on his CCB: "A strong attack has just developed against Clarke again. He is being outflanked and is retiring west another 2,000 yards refusing both flanks. I am throwing in my last chips to halt him. Hoge has just reported an attack. In my opinion if we don't get out of here and up north of the 82nd before night, we will not have a 7th Armored Division left."[7]

General Jones sent a similar account and interpretation of events up the chain of command. General Ridgway, with his airborne training in perimeter defenses by isolated units, still believed that the St. Vith troops might hold on until his corps could counterattack. But he was the only one of Hasbrouck's and Jones's superiors to demur. Because the commanders on the scene and those at army and army group disagreed with Ridgway, the XVIII Corps granted Hasbrouck permission to withdraw.

With enemies prowling to the north, east, and south—the vanguard of the 2nd SS Panzers in fact was arriving on Hasbrouck's right—withdrawal itself would be a precarious journey to the Vielsalm and Salmchâteau bridges over the Salm River. Hasbrouck hoped to begin just after nightfall on Friday and to move through the darkness of December 22–23, but a new attack by the 62nd Volksgrenadiers pinned both Hoge and

Clarke in place. Luckily, the weather abruptly turned cold enough to solidify all but the most marshy surfaces, so Hasbrouck's vehicles could move along unpaved secondary roads and sometimes, when necessary, across country. Luckily, too, the Führer Begleit Brigade failed to exploit the possibility of moving from the rear of Clarke's morning position down across more of the American rear. The two CCB's eventually wrenched themselves from the grasp of battle, and, with timely aid from clearing skies and fighter-bomber strikes, Hasbrouck's command executed the most difficult of military maneuvers, a fighting retreat, with a skill worthy of comparison with their previous stubbornness in standing at St. Vith. The last of the northern elements of the command crossed the Salm at Vielsalm about seven in the evening on Saturday, the 23rd. The south flank, given a harder time by the 2nd SS Panzers, probably left a higher proportion of men and equipment behind, and its troops were still straggling across the Salmchâteau bridge all through that night.

American losses in the battle for St. Vith were severe, but have not been completely tabulated. The 7th Armored Division and the 14th Cavalry Group together counted 3,397 officers and men killed, wounded, and missing. The 7th lost fifty-nine medium tanks, twenty-nine light tanks, and twenty-five armored cars. In more than ample return, the St. Vith defense choked the advance of the Sixth Panzer Army, clotted the roads and rear areas of the Fifth Panzer Army, and gave the XVIII Airborne Corps time to form solid lines west of the Salm. It epitomized the Americans' application everywhere in the Ardennes of their army's tactical doctrine for countering just such a breakthrough as the Germans had achieved: constrict the avenue of the enemy's advance. But more perhaps than any other of the many defensive stands in the Ardennes—which is saying a great deal—it was the battle of St. Vith that bought the time required by Allied generalship to recapture control of the battle.

27: The Precarious Balance

GENERAL BRADLEY did not sleep well for a time, and at his morning briefings during the first week of the counteroffensive his customary folksy smile was lacking. His staff in contrast affected poses of cool assurance—Leven Allen "debonair as is his custom, again unmoved and unraveled by the quick succession of events," Raymond Moses, the G-4, "imperturbable as a rock." Only the G-2, Edwin Sibert, permitted himself to look tired, as his section of the staff "found itself confronted by a situation it did not believe possible." For by Sunday afternoon, December 17, Bradley had conceded misjudgment in his previous evening's modest estimate of the enemy effort. "This is Rundstedt's all-out attack," Bradley now announced. "Pardon my French—" he said over the situation map, "—I think the situation justifies it—but where in hell has this son of a bitch gotten all his strength?"[1]

By Monday, Bradley had concluded that the German objectives were the supply center at Liège and possibly even Antwerp. The following few days seemed to confirm this estimate: "Present counter offensive," it appeared by Tuesday, "attempt on major scale at lightning thrust to capture Allied supply base Liège and take Antwerp. Suggest Rundstedt now committed to all out gamble despite full knowledge serious threat to flanks especially Saar-Palatinate sectors. All reserves will be thrown in. Already 20 Divisions committed including 5 Panzers."[2] By the close of the week, as the defenders of St. Vith retreated behind the Salm, the shape of the counteroffensive had grown distinct enough that corps, army, army group, and SHAEF could form a reasonably clear conception of the significance of Hasbrouck's stand and of the affordability of his withdrawal.

The British Joint Intelligence Committee in London said on the Friday of the crossing of the Salm: "We believe present German offensive is fulfillment of basic strategy laid down by Hitler 3 months ago."[3] The assessment was remarkably accurate. On September 16, Hitler had announced to Keitel and Jodl of OKW and to Generaloberst Heinz Guderian, then Acting Chief of the General Staff, that he intended to reverse the course of the war in the West by hoarding reserves of men and new production of weapons for a massive counterblow in the Ardennes. Since then, all the resources Germany could spare by thinning out battle lines both east and west and risking their rupture had gone into the accumulation of strength for the Ardennes. OKW planned to muster a counteroffensive force of thirty-two divisions, including twelve panzer and panzer grenadier divisions; it did not fall far short of this goal. From October, all production of Tigers and Panthers was directed to the West. The Eastern Front had to make do with Pzkw IVs. In November alone, 1,349 new or refitted tanks and assault guns went from factories and repair shops to the West, and nearly 1,000 more were dispatched by Christmas.

The JIC's assessment of the respective views and influence of Hitler and his military commanders was also squarely on target by December 22—unlike the recent estimates that had Rundstedt calling the tune in the West—with only the slightest continuing exaggeration of the professional soldiers' influence and their enthusiasm for the Ardennes offensive:

3. Concept of large scale counter offensive probably in accordance with Rundstedt's views, provided execution of it not pressed dangerously far. Rundstedt may hope if offensive can get at least as far as Liège-Huy, German command of Meuse crossings would compel Allies withdraw from Aix-la-Chapelle salient and thus eliminate threat to Ruhr. Even if offensive does not get as far, Rundstedt may hope be able do great damage to Allied administrative areas and postpone Allied regrouping for next attacks. [The British had learned of Luftwaffe insructions to bomb the Meuse bridges north of Liège, but not those to the south; this information seemed to confirm an intent to cross the Meuse in the area Liège-Huy.]

4. Fact that all available German aircraft in West and almost all armoured reserves are being brought into the battle, suggests Hitler striving for some really big success. This supported by propaganda in German press to opening of offensive, by fact Hitler personally addressed Commanders in West immediately before the battle and by intensive activities of [Otto] Skorzeny sabotage units behind American lines [the Germans in American uniforms, now identified as a special unit trained and led by a daring commander famous for rescuing Mussolini from Italian antifascists].

5. Rundstedt would wish to watch situation to avoid placing his forces in dangerous position. Indeed is likely to urge halt in advance when assess Allied counter attacks are ready. Then probably prepared if necessary gradually withdraw, assured of having dislocated Allies' plans and of having denied them many of resources carefully collected over past few months.

6. If however Germans gain major successes, Hitler may demand exploitation beyond what OKW would consider sound strategy. This might lead to divergence of views between Hitler and his military advisers. In this event we think, if past form can be taken as a guide, Hitler likely prevail.[4]

The solidifying of the north shoulder of the German penetration and the constriction of its road and rail routes westward were encouraging, but on December 22 the Allied command could not yet feel at all sure that its gradual reassertion of control over the shape of the battle extended to the capacity to halt the enemy short of the Meuse. Once burned and twice shy, the G-2s now tended to put too high rather than too low an estimate on the Germans' still uncommitted reserves. An American assessment of December 21 stated:

Enemy drive is directed on Huy, Namur and possibly Dinant. 6 Panzer Divisions continue to spearhead the offensive [12th SS, 1st SS, 9th SS, 116th, 2nd, Panzer Lehr] with an additional Panzer division possibly committed [2nd SS]. 5 Panzer Divisions remain in reserve. Enemy Infantry Divisions are making poor showing especially those in Trier area with 276 [Volksgrenadier] Infantry Division well mauled. . . .
Enemy is capable of: driving to objectives at Huy, Namur and possibly Dinant on Meuse River; mounting an additional attack South of Schmidt in direction Liege with 2 SS Panzer Corps containing 3 SS Panzer Division[s]; mounting an attack in Trier area with Infantry supported by possibly 2 Panzer Grenadier Divisions.[5]

The Allies also feared the Germans remained capable of a bigger airborne strike than the scattered and so far impotent one of the beginning of their drive. Behind all other fears, furthermore, lurked the question of the security of the great port of Antwerp:

> Signal received 21 December states reliable news . . . of big concentration of airborne troops area Veluwer Bearn [in Holland] . . . . Airfields Deelen and Soesterberg will be used very shortly for take off with targets Brussels Antwerp and L[ine] of C[ommunication]. . . .
>
> Germans can probably put 125 Transport aircraft, mostly Ju 52, into the air carrying up to 1500 armed and equipped troops. Deelen and Soesterberg airfields both understood to be unserviceable although there are probably alternative strips near to each. Assume operation will not take place until weather conditions improve.[6]

Stoumont and Stavelot

Just as some places, like the draw in the road between Gravelotte and Metz, seem foreordained to be battlefields, others appear predestined for the more comfortable role of military headquarters. Such a place is Spa, where the mineral springs are reputedly the oldest known in Europe, where the fashionable of the whole Continent came in the time of Joseph II of Austria, and where the atmosphere affords the military commander that reassurance of stability and order so helpful when he must deal with equanimity in the life and death of multitudes and the destinies of armies and nations. Despite the noticeable fraying of the hotels and casino of Spa even before the First World War, it was here, from the "joli site, où sont soignés cardiaques et rhumatisants," that the Kaiser, Hindenburg, and Ludendorff presided over their German armies. Here the "station thermal célèbre"[7] also housed the more drab comings and goings of United States First Army headquarters late in 1944. Here, in the days following December 16, Lieutenant General Courtney H. Hodges strove first to comprehend what was happening to his army and then to rally the First Army and return it to its proper course. Unfortunately, the dignified antiquity of his surroundings did little for Hodges's self-confidence.

During the first days of the offensive, the most immediately dangerous enemy thrust took shape as the one also lapping almost at the gates of Spa. This was the bold foray of the 1st SS Panzer Division toward the Meuse along the road through Malmédy and Stavelot, barely more than ten kilometers down the highway from Spa. Hodges felt no inclination to witness the enemy's overrunning of his headquarters, and of course a precautionary removal of records commenced as soon as he discerned something bigger than local attacks. It was Kean, however, Hodges's chief of staff, who in the crisis was "a rock of Gibraltar there in the First Army,"[8] and who with special alertness saw to the more important moves. As soon as Eisenhower released the XVIII Airborne Corps to the First Army, army headquarters resolved to use the 82nd Airborne Division particularly to halt the 1st SS Panzers' Kampfgruppe short of both Spa and, above all, the Meuse.

On the morning of December 18, however, when General Gavin visited Spa as acting commander of the XVIII Corps, it was apparent that the 82nd could not be deployed around Werbomont before the next day, Tuesday, at the earliest. From liaison planes, First Army headquarters soon learned also that the troublesome panzer Kampfgruppe was already beyond Trois Ponts, moving north toward La Gleize and Stoumont.

On December 16, Hodges's First World War friend and fellow infantryman "Big

Bill" Simpson had already taken the initiative of offering the First Army the 30th Infantry and 5th Armored Divisions, both refitting in rear of Simpson's Ninth Army. Accepting the offer on December 17, Hodges had first sent General Hobbs's 30th Division toward the embattled 2nd and 99th Divisions on the right flank of Gerow's V Corps. On Sunday night, however, early reports of the adventures of the 1st ss Panzers prompted Gerow to divert Hobbs's men west toward Malmédy and Stavelot. Then, on Monday, Hobbs was summoned to Spa. While the 82nd Airborne was moving into position, his Old Hickory Division seemed to be the First Army's most likely instrument for curbing the panzers. Hodges and his staff judged that the armored Kampfgruppe might either go on north from La Gleize down the Amblève valley, thus threatening the First Army's rear areas, or break away from the Amblève through Werbomont, thus taking the shortest route to the Meuse. Consequently, Hobbs was ordered to block both the Amblève valley and the road through Werbomont.

The Old Hickories had Colonel Edward M. Sutherland's North Carolina regiment, the 119th Infantry, leading the way. Hobbs, always impatient, chose the most direct method to begin fulfilling both his tasks, by gambling on a split of the 119th. His haste paid off, producing the timely arrival of the 2/119th to ambush the German detachment that crossed Lienne Creek. The rest of the 119th similarly arrived just in time to form up in front of the panzer spearhead at Stoumont.

Hobbs's other troops, furthermore, were already engaged in additional plaguing of the Kampfgruppe. The 1st Battalion of the 117th Infantry was marching to Stavelot in response to Gerow's instructions of Sunday night when on Monday its commander, Lieutenant Colonel Ernest Frankland, met officers of the 526th Armored Infantry Battalion on the road and learned from them that the Germans had already taken Stavelot. Without hesitation, Frankland appropriated some of the armored infantry and a platoon of towed 3-inch tank destroyers of the 823rd Tank Destroyer Battalion and moved on, through the gasoline still flaming from the morning, for an afternoon attack on Stavelot.

With fortuitous help from the P-47s that had earlier hit the panzers around La Gleize, Frankland's men captured about half of Stavelot by darkness from whatever Germans remained there. Frankland also tied in with the 2nd Battalion of his own regiment and was joined by a tank platoon from the 743rd Tank Battalion, all of which was helpful because the Germans struck right back to try to regain Stavelot. Fighting seesawed through the town all night and next day. Elements of the 1st ss Panzers arriving from the east drove home two strong attacks, but American artillery arrived opportunely to help repulse them. By darkness of December 19, Frankland's battalion held Stavelot. Frankland had taken the precaution of blowing up the Amblève bridge against further enemy reinforcement from the east.

At Stoumont, the 3rd Battalion of the 119th Infantry spent Monday night preparing a foxhole line east, north, and south of the town and listening tensely to the rumblings that heralded German preparation for a heavy panzer attack. The battalion had the support of eight towed 3-inch tank destroyers and two 90mm. antiaircraft guns as well as three 57mm. antitank guns of its own. A company of Shermans from the 743rd Tank Battalion was on its way as reinforcement. But there was no artillery on hand. The infantry would need all the help against tanks it could get, because where the road along the Amblève passed through Stoumont, it leveled off atop a hill mass to ease tank operations, and the enemy Kampfgruppe now had a mass of Tigers, Panthers, and Pzkw IVs all well concentrated up front.

Attacking at dawn, the Germans drove the Americans through the town within two hours and badly chewed up the 3/119th while doing so. The Shermans of the 743rd joined the fight promptly, but the absence of the American ground forces' trump card, artillery, could not be remedied before the town was lost. Even with Yank artillery beginning to come into action, the Germans drove the Americans on down the road toward Targnon. If they could push the 119th far enough beyond this town to free from American fire the road leading south from it, they would have a route along the west bank of the Lienne Creek to Werbomont and the Meuse after all.

The Americans' ten Shermans managed to emerge from Stoumont still in action, and Colonel Sutherland began feeding his 1st Battalion into the battle to reinforce them. Hobbs, who was at Sutherland's command post, urgently appealed to First Army headquarters for more tanks because, aside from the 743rd Battalion's ten Shermans, the only armor between the 1st ss Panzers and the Meuse was another ten Shermans just out of repair shops and manned by ordnance mechanics. All that the army could spare for Hobbs was the raw 740th Tank Battalion, hastily equipped with duplex drive.

Driven through Targnon and Stoumont Station, the Americans formed on the 1st Battalion in the early afternoon to attempt a stand where the road curved between a hill and the river bank. Here, for the moment, came anticlimax. German armor poked gingerly at the American roadblock and then drew off. As Hobbs and Sutherland could soon surmise, the enemy had learned that his line of communication was cut at Stavelot. As they could also guess—for it was one optimistic consideration underlying the whole Ardennes battle—the enemy furthermore was running short of fuel. He had detoured to Büllingen to fill up with American fuel at the outset of his march, but he had been able to seize no large supply since then.

Without immediately knowing the reasons for the Germans' sudden shyness, the 119th and its attachments nevertheless seized the opportunity to begin feeling their way back up the Amblève road toward Stoumont, with the help of assorted tanks from the vanguard of the 740th Battalion.

About the time the enemy drew away from the roadblock, the 119th Infantry passed to the operational control of General Ridgway's XVIII Airborne Corps. Ridgway had the 82nd Airborne Division coming into line east of Werbomont, relieving the 2/119th along the Lienne Creek and preparing to move against the bridgehead the 1st ss Panzers had established south of the Amblève at Cheneux. Ridgway's corps had also received parts of the 3rd Armored Division. With these forces, Ridgway planned to clear both banks of the Amblève as far as Stavelot, link up with the 117th Infantry there, and do so in such a way as to envelop and then eliminate the advance Kampfgruppe of the 1st ss Panzers.

This Kampfgruppe, now contained at least for the moment between Stoumont and Stavelot, had assumed fairly clear lineaments on American intelligence charts. It comprised at least half the armor of its division, along with a strong detachment of panzer grenadiers. The remainder of ss Oberführer Wilhelm Mohnke's 1st ss Panzer Division were in three other groups still east of Stavelot, trying to push their way to a juncture with the advance Kampfgruppe and to reinforce its final plunge to the Meuse. The commander of the troublesome advance Kampfgruppe was ss Obersturmbannführer—that is, the ss equivalent of Lieutenant Colonel—Jochen Peiper. Though Peiper seemed junior in rank for so critical a command, the SS did not feel bound by military custom, and Peiper was a bold, ruthless officer who was at the same time intelligent and well-educated. He had made a name for himself on the Eastern Front such that, had the Americans known more of his career there, they would have been prepared both for the aggressive daring of his westward dash and for the evidence of atrocities that Kampfgruppe Peiper left in its wake. Captured troopers of the Kampfgruppe tended to be not tired Wehrmacht veterans but young, confident, cocky Nazis. It was part of the pattern that as the 117th Infantry cleared Stavelot and its suburbs, they found the bodies of 117 Belgian men, women, and children evidently murdered by the SS.

The sequel deserves mention. In 1945 a United States military court sitting at Dachau found seventy-three former members of Kampfgruppe Peiper guilty of war criminal charges arising out of the Malmédy Massacre. Forty-three, including Peiper, were sentenced to death, twenty-two to life imprisonment, eight to lesser prison terms. On the basis of technical errors, Peiper's sentence was later commuted to life imprisonment. Just before Christmas, 1956, he was paroled. In 1972, he took up residence near the village of Traves, France, along the Saône River about fifteen kilometers from Vesoul. On June 22, 1976, the Communist journal *L'Humanité* informed France of his past and his location. He received threats that he would be executed and his house would be burned if he did not leave Traves by Bastille Day. On Bastille Day, his home burned down and a corpse was found with an empty pistol beside it. The corpse was so badly burned that positive identification was impossible.

By December 19, 1944, Peiper and his Kampfgruppe had already given the American army more than ordinary cause to press the design Ridgway was about to unfold for the Germans' envelopment and destruction. "Sir, do you want to bother with them?" some soldiers of the 117th Infantry asked Captain John Kent as they brought in as prisoners nine of Peiper's men. With a certain hesitation, Kent ordered the prisoners escorted safely to the division cage.

Patton into the Battle

Before he knew the full scope of the German counteroffensive, Eisenhower was already determined that the Allies should turn the enemy's commitment of his forces to their own advantage. "Yesterday morning," he wrote to General Brehon N. Somervell of the Army Service Forces on December 17, "the enemy launched a rather ambitious counterattack out of the Luxembourg area where we have been holding very thinly. . . . However, we have some armour that is now out of the line and resting. It is closing in on the threat from each flank. If things go well we should not only stop the thrust but should be able to profit from it."[9]

The next day, Monday, December 18, the magnitude of the German effort was clearer, and so was Eisenhower's thinking about profiting from it. To his American army group commanders, Bradley and Devers, Eisenhower announced: "My intention is to take immediate action to check the enemy advance; to launch a counter-offensive without delay with all forces north of the Moselle." Devers's 6th Army Group was to abandon its own offensive and relieve the 12th Army Group westward to the Moselle. Its front thus shortened, Bradley's 12th Army Group was "To launch a counter offensive north of the Moselle. Attacks comprising this counter-offensive will converge on the general area

Bonn-Cologne."[10] The enemy's emergence from his defenses might prove the key to unlocking the autumn stalemate.

Threats must be contained before opportunity could be seized, and before Monday was over the still further unveiling of German offensive threats ruled out any immediate converging offensive from both the northern and the southern wings of the 12th Army Group. "In the north, where the weight of the German attack was falling," it became apparent, as Eisenhower later wrote in his memoirs, that "we would be on the defensive for some days. But on the south we could help the situation by beginning a northward advance at the earliest possible moment."[11] Eisenhower's underlying motive remained his belief "that by coming out of the Siegfried [Line] the enemy had given us a great opportunity which we should seize as soon as possible."

"By the night of the eighteenth," said Eisenhower, "I felt we had sufficient information of the enemy's strength, intentions, and situation, and of our own capabilities, to lay down a specific plan for our counteraction."[12] So he called Bradley, Devers, and Patton to meet with him and Tedder at EAGLE MAIN, Bradley's headquarters in a forbidding old French army caserne at Verdun.

Bradley and Patton were already thinking along similar lines. As Bradley recalled; "Although I would have preferred to clamp the Bulge in simultaneous attacks from both shoulders, it was clear that Hodges could not mount an offensive until first he checked the enemy's advance. And on December 19, the harried First Army was too preoccupied in stemming the German offensive to think about a retaliatory blow." On the other hand, "there was nothing to deter Patton from counterattacking against the Bulge from the south."[13] Bradley anticipated Eisenhower by calling Patton to EAGLE TAC at Luxembourg City on Monday to begin discussing such a blow.

Patton like Montgomery had brooded upon lost opportunities through the autumn. Each blamed Eisenhower's supposed preference for the other for the crippling of the offensives with which they might, by now, have won the war. Battle itself, and occasional happy incidents such as the triumphal entry into Metz, only momentarily relieved Patton's sense of grievance.

In November, Patton's discontent had fattened on new nourishment. He believed yet another grand opportunity had been snatched away from him. As the November offensive subsided into a dreary slugging match, Patton convinced himself that if the 83rd Division had remained on loan to him on the left flank of General Walker's XX Corps, as it was when the offensive began, the outcome would have been dramatically improved. With the 83rd Division at hand, Patton believed, he could have cleared out the triangle between the Moselle and the Saar, and this elimination of danger from his left flank would have given the Third Army, and particularly the XX Corps, the freedom from distraction and the power necessary to break across the Saar and through the West Wall quickly—to hurry on to Trier, and to add to the laurels of Metz the conquest of that other historic bishopric. Though the 83rd Division had always been merely on loan to the Third Army, Bradley restricting Patton to a limited "operational control" and forbidding any commitment of the division that would hinder a rapid transfer elsewhere, Patton's staff characteristically planned the November offensive in a manner that would have committed the 83rd deeply and made it an indispensable part of the campaign. But Bradley terminated the loan and recalled the division just as Patton's November offensive was beginning, in order to use the 83rd in the north with the First Army. The incident rekindled old suspicions of Bradley's likely jealousy, which Patton had repressed during the September and October days when Bradley supported the Third Army against Eisenhower's priorities for a northern offensive.

Patton allayed the hurt, as well as the frustrations of his slow November advance, by planning a new major offensive blow to break the West Wall, the hammer to fall on December 19. On December 6, Spaatz, Doolittle, and Vandenberg of the AAF visited Patton, to plan with him another overwhelming aerial bombardment with which to open his December 19 drive to the Rhine.

When Bradley called him from Versailles late on December 16 to take away the 10th Armored Division, it seemed to Patton a repetition of the Indian-giving of the 83rd. Once more Bradley was denying him a critical portion of his force just as he was about to launch a decisive offensive. Of his pleas to Bradley to forbear, Patton wrote in his diary: "Bradley admitted my logic but took counsel of his fears and ordered the . . . move. I wish he were less timid." In the privacy of his diary, Patton relented enough to add: "He probably knows more of the situation than he can say over the telephone."[14]

The Ardennes counteroffensive did not strike his front, was not thus his direct concern, and at first presented itself to Patton as merely another damnable obstacle in the way of his cherished design for a new Third Army offensive. In these circumstances, he was slow to concede the importance of the events that began on December 16. Though he had no choice but to yield up the 10th Armored, on the morning after Bradley's telephone call he indulged in another typical effort to preempt what he wanted. He instructed General Eddy of the XII Corps to get the 4th Armored Division so involved in action that it would not be possible to extricate the division from his lines.

Still, Patton's military intuition was as acute as any in the American army. He was so intent on attacking that it made him nervous not only to stand idle himself, but to observe idleness in any friendly troops on his flank. Whenever he had to halt his drives, he ordered vigorous local attacks to instill in the enemy the expectation of something bigger, as well as to maintain active reconnaissance against possible counterblows. Thus, during the weeks when Middleton's VIII Corps on his left flank had not done these things, Patton sniffed danger. "Furthermore, the First Army is making a terrible mistake," he confided to his diary on November 25, "in leaving the VIII Corps static, as it is highly probable the Germans are building up east of them."[15] By December 12, Patton's hunch about an enemy assault against the VIII Corps was strong enough that he instructed General Gay, his chief of staff, and Colonel Halley G. Maddox, his G-3, to study "what the Third Army would do if called upon to counterattack through . . . a breakthrough" in the VIII Corps front.[16]

Colonel Koch, Patton's dourly realistic G-2, stated forthrightly that the enemy's reserves were building for a "coordinated counteroffensive," though Koch's assessments did not go so far as Patton's intuitions toward predicting the locale.[17] When the Germans went into radio silence on the night of December 15–16, Patton reiterated to his staffs his conviction that the inactivity of the VIII Corps had invited trouble. He asked Gay and Maddox about the progress of their study of a Third Army counterattack into the Ardennes, and he instructed them specifically to develop the study into a plan for suspending the Third Army's eastward drive and turning the army ninety degrees to attack into Luxembourg.

At the morning briefing at Third Army headquarters on December 17, Patton invited Colonel Maddox to speak his mind freely about the proper course of action. Maddox proposed not a Third Army turn northward but an accelerated push eastward, into the rear of the Germans in the Ardennes. Then, he believed, Patton could break into the enemy's lines of communication and trap Rundstedt's main forces west of the Rhine. Patton agreed, but he said the plan would be too daring for the higher command. "My guess is that our offensive will be called off and we will have to go up there and save their hides."[18]

It was at 10:30 the next morning that Bradley telephoned Patton and asked him to come to EAGLE TAC with his G-2, G-3, and G-4 as soon as possible. Within ten minutes, Patton, Koch, Maddox, and Walter J. Muller were driving out of Nancy. At EAGLE TAC in the Luxembourg state railway building, Bradley's G-2 staff displayed its situation map estimating as many as seven panzer divisions might already be charging into the Ardennes. Deferentially, with evident expectation of an explosion from his headstrong subordinate, Bradley suggested that much of the Third Army would have to follow the 10th Armored Division northward to deal with such an enemy force. To Bradley's relief, Patton by now had prepared himself for this design and reconciled himself to it. He would have preferred to go on with his own offensive, he said, "But what the hell, we'll still be killing Krauts."[19]

Patton announced he would halt the 4th Armored immediately and concentrate it near Longwy starting at midnight. The 80th Division could set out for Luxembourg in the morning. The 26th Division could be alerted to move in twenty-four hours. In fact, as soon as he left the conference, Patton telephoned Gay to stop the 4th Armored and the 80th in their tracks and ready them for the northward turn. Gay should also brief Major General John Millikin of the newly arrived III Corps to prepare him to command the movement.

On Tuesday morning at seven Patton and his staff met with Millikin, Eddy of the XII Corps, and the VIII Corps artillery chief to outline his plans for using the 4th Armored, 80th, and 26th Divisions under III Corps headquarters, along with the VIII Corps which he assumed would be assigned to him, in an attack to rupture the southern flank of the German counteroffensive. He intended to drive, he said, along two of three possible axes—from the vicinity of Diekirch due north, from the vicinity of Arlon north to Bastogne, from the vicinity of Neufchâteau north against the western nose of the German salient. He wanted the plans completed for each axis of advance. Having received the call to meet with Eisenhower at EAGLE MAIN, Patton left a code name for each axis with Gay. The commanders were to be ready to move according to whichever code or codes he telephoned back from Verdun.

Thus, when Eisenhower, Tedder, Bradley, Devers, and Patton met about eleven that morning in the chill of the old Verdun caserne, Patton had already done his homework for accomplishing what the Supreme Commander would request. The 4th Armored Division was already in motion. Bradley remained uncommonly impatient and irritable that morning, but Patton could well arrive theatrically, in a jeep with plexiglass doors and a .30-caliber machine gun mounted on a post, his brass buttons gleaming, his jaws clamped on a cigar. He was confident enough of the immediate future to display characteristically possessive concern for the longer-range future. When Eisenhower repeated his proposal to shift the 6th Army Group boundary as far west as the Moselle,

Patton demurred. As Bradley tells it, Patton had accumulated a good deal of bridging equipment for the crossing of the Rhine, and he feared that Devers would appropriate it. A compromise accordingly left to the Third Army the existing XX Corps bridgehead across the Saar and into the West Wall; the new boundary separating the 12th and 6th Army Groups would run about midway between Saarlautern and Saarbrücken.

Devers like Patton was reluctant to abandon his own offensive plans but acquiesced in the necessity. Eisenhower for his part feared that the enlargement of Devers's zone would aggravate the problem of the Colmar pocket, an old sore subject between him and Devers. If the Germans in the pocket should become active, the Supreme Commander envisaged the 6th Army Group's withdrawing as far as the Vosges if necessary to prevent undue southern distractions and to preserve the integrity of Devers's front—thus giving up Strasbourg, a notion that inevitably precipitated an eruption from General de Gaulle when it soon reached his ears. Eisenhower's Colmar pocket worriment helped dictate also that, in exchange for the VIII Corps, Patton must yield some troops to reinforce Devers.

But the main theme of the conference was of course to counterattack. Eisenhower began by announcing—perhaps with an eye particularly on Bradley—that he wanted to see none but cheerful faces. "The present situation is to be regarded as one of opportunity for us and not of disaster," he said.[20] Patton was fully primed to enter into this spirit. He suggested they should all have the guts to let the Germans go to Paris: "Then we'll really cut 'em off and chew 'em up." Everyone smiled, but Eisenhower made haste to emphasize that the enemy would not be permitted to cross the Meuse: "Our weakest spot is in the direction of Namur," that historic strategic pivot at the junction of the Sambre and Meuse. "The general plan is to plug the holes in the north and launch coordinated attack from the south."[21] To lay his detailed plans, Eisenhower wanted to know how soon Patton could counterattack with at least six divisions.

Patton's answer created "a stir, a shuffling of feet, as those present straightened up in their chairs," and the stir has never quite abated. He could attack, Patton said, "On December 22, with three divisions, the 4th Armored, the 26th, and the 80th."[22]

No one but his own staff knew how much Patton had already prepared, and thus no one else thought he could disengage from one battle and turn ninety degrees into another battle so quickly. However much Patton had prepared, furthermore, as his biographer Martin Blumenson puts it: "Altogether, it was an operation that only a master could think of executing."[23]

A master's design, it was also to be an operation masterfully executed. But the operation should also be kept in appropriate perspective; it was not a unique stroke of genius. Other competent military commanders have accomplished similarly rapid disengagements, turns of direction, and recommitments. On the German side, for example, Heinz Guderian had accomplished at least an equal feat in 1941 with Panzer Group 4—the equivalent of an army—despite the handicaps of tired troops, who had been marching across the vastness of Russia and fighting incessantly for three months, and nearly worn-out equipment. Guderian shifted his panzer army "through 90 degrees in direction, from a posture of containment of the Kiev pocket on 26th September, to one of outright aggression on the 30th" northeastward to Orel. Indeed, Hitler's fluctuating whims had required Guderian to execute several such turns earlier, in France in 1940; but, partly because Guderian had then enjoyed ample resources and perhaps, as his biographer Kenneth Macksey observes, "because Guderian . . . made complexities of that sort seem simple," these maneuvers have received little notice, while "when Patton or Montgomery executed similar changes of direction in the years to come, their prowess was acclaimed to the roof-tops."[24]

The discrepancy between Patton's and Eisenhower's intentions should also be noted. Eisenhower had asked how soon Patton could attack with six divisions. Patton responded that he could attack within a mere three days with three divisions. Eisenhower doubted that three divisions could strike a hard enough blow and expressed a preference for less speed but greater force: "I did not want him [Patton] to start until he was in sufficient force so that, once committed, he could continue gradually to crush in the southern flank of the developing salient."[25]

At least on this occasion, no critic could complain about Eisenhower's lack of regard for the principle of concentration. Patton replied that he could beat the enemy with three divisions, and that if he paused to assemble more, he would forfeit surprise. Eisenhower, who had been first among the principal Allied commanders to recognize the German effort as a major counteroffensive, and who had been meeting resistance to this interpretation for three days, feared that Patton still underrated the Germans. Patton, thought the Supreme Commander, "did not seem to comprehend the strength of the German assault and spoke so lightly of the task assigned him that I felt it necessary to impress upon him the need of strength and cohesion in his own advance."[26] But when Patton agreed to reinforce his three-division attack with a larger attack in six days, Eisenhower yielded to the argument in favor of speed and surprise. As so often happened, the Supreme Commander may have left the conference thinking he had achieved greater agreement than actually existed. He informed Montgomery: "Patton moves north with six divisions and taking over VIII Corps temporarily will organize major counter blow with target date of 23d or 24th."[27]

Patton went from the conference to a telephone to call Gay. He gave his chief of staff the code words to move the 4th Armored and 26th Divisions at once by way of Longwy to Arlon—the capital of the Belgian province of Luxembourg, of which Bastogne is a market town—and the 80th Division on the city of Luxembourg by way of Thionville. He then drove to XX Corps headquarters to outline the situation to General Walker. He did not return to Nancy, but drove next day to the city of Luxembourg to begin establishing Third Army headquarters there.

Montgomery into an American Headquarters

While planning to cut into the southern flank of the German salient—the Bulge—to trap and destroy German divisions as well as to halt their offensive, Eisenhower did not want it forgotten that the enemy spearheads meanwhile must be stopped short of the Meuse. "This is just to remind you," he wired 12th Army Group and COMZ headquarters late on the Tuesday of the Verdun conference, "of the vital importance of insuring that no repeat no Meuse bridges fall into enemy hands intact. If necessary service units should be organized at once to protect them."[28]

Thereby Eisenhower jostled the cool posture of Bradley's headquarters, where the chief of staff, Leven Allen, grumbled: "What the devil do they think we're doing, starting back for the beaches?"[29] But Eisenhower remembered that the battle for the Meuse was still being fought.

It remained to be seen, for example, whether the trap could be closed firmly on Kampfgruppe Peiper, and whether the thin American positions on the Amblève east of La Gleize could prevent the rest of the 1st SS Panzer Division from reinforcing Peiper and restoring his momentum. At Stoumont, Peiper's men still showed plenty of fight on December 20, the day following the Verdun meeting. According to Ridgway's envelopment plan, the 1/119th with a tank company of the 740th Tank Battalion resumed its attack eastward toward Stoumont along the road from Targnon, while a detachment of the newly arrived CCB, 3rd Armored Division, attempted to press into Stoumont from the north along the road from Spa. This latter task force got stuck just outside the town when its lead tanks entered a stretch of sunken road and came under flanking fire from German tanks in hull defilade, that is, with all but their turrets behind cover. The American armor could not get off the road into position to hit the Germans, nor did forest cover and steep hills permit the accompanying American infantry to deploy properly. The 1/119th fared somewhat better in fighting its way down the Targnon road and into St. Edouard's Sanatorium at the western edge of Stoumont; but the sanatorium occupied elevated filled-in ground that American tanks could not climb, while German tanks could come up close along the more gradual eastern approaches. Just before midnight, the Germans mounted an infantry attack with strong tank support and threw the Americans out of the sanatorium. While the battle raged above them, some 200 civilians—patients and citizens of Stoumont—huddled in the basement of the building.

Another task force of the 3rd Armored's CCB had spent Wednesday trying to close in on La Gleize along the road from the northeast, but with results much like those befalling its companion detachment north of Stoumont. The Germans had set up a roadblock with a tank and two assault guns at a point where a ridge precluded the American tanks from maneuvering. This stopped the Shermans, while the enemy positions behind the roadblock were too strong to be carried by infantry working forward without tank support.

The 82nd Airborne meanwhile sought to eliminate the German bridgehead across the Amblève at Cheneux. Companies B and C of the 504th Parachute Infantry arrived at Cheneux late on Wednesday, the 20th, and attempted to attack under cover of darkness. To do so, they had to climb an open slope rising gradually toward German positions crisscrossed with barbed wire and replete with assault guns, flak pieces, mortars, and machine guns. The paratroopers had minimal heavy-weapons support. The Germans readily cut down two assaults. On a third try, assisted by a couple of tank destroyers, the Americans grasped a small foothold in the village.

The day's only noteworthy success against Peiper was achieved by a third, and the largest, task force of CCB, 3rd Armored. This detachment traveled south from Spa to cut the Stavelot-Stoumont road again in Peiper's rear, in the vicinity of Trois Ponts. It actually did so. Near Trois Ponts it collided with a column of enemy infantry, artillery, and trucks that proved to have crossed the Amblève on a reinforced footbridge east of the town. The Germans had been using this structure as a tenuous connection between Kampfgruppe Peiper and the rest of the 1st SS Panzers. The Americans mauled the German column and then set up three roadblocks between Trois Ponts and La Gleize.

The XVIII Airborne Corps hoped to augment this pressure on Peiper the next morning, Thursday, December 21. The day opened instead with a demonstration of the enemy's exasperating tenacity in clinging to his newfound initiative. Along the road from Ligneuville to Malmédy, where the 30th Division's third regiment, the 120th, stood guard with the separate 99th Infantry Battalion and assorted other units, including a company of tanks and two platoons of tank destroyers, there swirled out of neighboring woods a German attack that was as bizarre as it was unexpected. Some of the Germans wore American uniforms, others wore partial American uniforms, some drove American vehicles, others drove German vehicles fitted to simulate American tanks, armored cars, and jeeps and painted with the American white star.

The sequel was a day's hard fighting that gave the defenders of Malmédy a fuller acquaintance than they desired with the 150th Panzer Brigade. This unit constituted the main portion of ss Obersturmbannführer Otto Skorzeny's special force. Dietrich's failure to score a clear breakthrough had reduced Skorzeny's task from an intended dash to seize the Meuse bridges to ordinary line service; but his picked troopers nevertheless proved determined and resilient. Their weapons were oddly assorted but plentiful. For a while they seemed to have inserted a dangerous spearhead between the 120th Regiment and the 117th. Though the Americans rallied, Skorzeny's miniature surprise was an unpleasant reminder that American balance had not yet altogether recovered from Hasso von Manteuffel's and Sepp Dietrich's much larger surprise offensive.

The Tuesday evening when the XVIII Airborne Corps was preparing for its first, less than successful round of assaults on Stoumont, Eisenhower, back at SHAEF MAIN from the day's conference at Verdun, received from his chief of staff a suggestion that had originated with Generals Strong and Whiteley, SHAEF's G-2 and deputy G-3. When Whiteley had first proposed the idea to Bedell Smith about nine o'clock, Smith's hair-trigger temper snapped; his short fuze was a well-known characteristic of Ike's "small, pouchy" chief of staff "with a red face and stern eyes in a dynamo."[30] Smith sent Whiteley, aggrieved, from the office. But, on cooling off, the chief of staff decided the suggestion had enough merit that Eisenhower must hear it.

Whiteley and Strong proposed to transfer tactical command of all forces north of the German salient to Field Marshal Montgomery. They would leave under Bradley's 12th Army Group only the forces south of the salient. In effect, Montgomery would get the American First and Ninth Armies; Bradley would be left with only the Third. The compelling reason, as the two SHAEF staff officers saw it, was communication. So far only minor troubles had developed in telephone and radio contact between Bradley's headquarters south of the Bulge at Luxembourg and Hodges's north of the Bulge, moved during Tuesday from Spa to the less exposed location of Chaudfontaine. But critical to the army group's whole network of buried cables and open wires was a repeater station at Jemelle, which was squarely in the path of Manteuffel's Fifth Panzer Army between Bastogne and Dinant. Even if German possession of Jemelle should miraculously fail to occur, moreover, it is essential that a commander should be able to visit his principal subordinates, to feel the atmosphere at their headquarters and hold free and lengthy discussions. Bradley could no longer travel readily from Luxembourg to see Hodges. By evening of December 19, the only convenient method of doing so was by air, and flying obviously presented its own dangers and restrictions.

There was the additional, though lesser, consideration that with Montgomery in command everywhere north of the Bulge, British reserves might be more swiftly available for the battle. Already Montgomery had taken steps in that direction. Should the Germans cross the Meuse and penetrate into the heart of Belgium, 21 Army Group's communications and supply areas would be in bad shape. The assumption that Hitler controlled the enemy's movements and that the purposes were consequently ambitious suggested an effort to separate the British and Americans north of Aachen from the southern Allied armies—and as Montgomery remarked to the War Office: "We cannot come out through Dunkirk this time as the Germans still hold that place."[31] (This sentence was deleted from the version of the dispatch shown to Churchill.) Late on December 18, Eisenhower had alerted the 11th Armored and 17th Airborne Divisions, training in England, for immediate movement to the Continent, intending to use them to back up the line of the Meuse; but it would be several days before they could be in position. At the same time SHAEF had ordered the British 6th Airborne Division to come by sea as quickly as possible to join 21 Army Group for the same purpose; but it, too, would take time to arrive. By late on Tuesday the 19th, Montgomery believed there was little to prevent the Germans from "bounding the Meuse and advancing on Brussels."[32] Thus Montgomery sent reconnaissance troops of the British Special Air Services and tank replacement center troops into the First Army zone to help guard the Meuse bridges, and he began to move 30 Corps, which had been in reserve to prepare for his coming offensive, to concentration areas just north of the Meuse, around Hasselt-Louvain-St. Trond.

The objections to the proposed transfer of command were obvious. Eisenhower would seem to be yielding to Montgomery's long-standing and tediously repeated demand for unified control of the ground forces under himself. In a recent variation of that demand, Montgomery had called at least for a single commander north of the Ardennes. The field marshal and those British champions of his ambitions who never bothered much to conceal their disdain for American military inexperience and incapacity, such as Brooke, were sure to crow over the transfer as an American admission of the need for British tutelage. Montgomery and his champions had no more foreseen the German counteroffensive than anybody else; Montgomery had departed his headquarters to play golf on December 16, having stated on the 15th that the enemy's "situation is such that he cannot stage major offensive operations."[33] But the British have consistently contrived to present even their defeats as monuments to their military prowess, so they would surely not allow a few mere misjudgments of intelligence to get in the way of their claims to superior military knowledge and skill.

The originators of the proposed shift in command, Whiteley and Strong, were themselves British, which made matters worse; but they were by no means among Montgomery's circle of admirers—quite the contrary—and they believed the recalcitrant facts about 12th Army Group communications overrode the objections of which they were painfully aware. It was the recalcitrant facts that cooled Bedell Smith's temper, and they governed Eisenhower's decision. That same Tuesday evening, Eisenhower had Smith telephone Bradley to raise the issue with him. Naturally, Bradley objected. The shock, the hurt to his sensibilities, the inevitable inferences about his capacity to command no matter what might be said about communications lingered on to permeate his every remark about the event ever afterward. Even Bradley had to concede, nevertheless, that the logic of the shift was so apparent that he would not object if 21 Army Group were an American command, and "that if we play it the way you suggest, we'll get more help from the British in the way of reserves." His diarist-aide Hansen wrote: "This arrangement is probably reasonable inasmuch as contact and control of the First Army is now difficult since the interior lines of communication are subject to interference.

Moreover, it was felt that our headquarters is in danger of being overrun and should such a situation develop, control might suddenly become more difficult."[34]

When the usual SHAEF staff meeting began on Wednesday morning, Whiteley knew of nothing beyond Bedell Smith's eruption. He was surprised when Eisenhower called on him to present his idea about turning over the northern part of the battlefield to Montgomery. But a glance from Smith implied what had transpired and indicated Whiteley should proceed, so he offered the proposal. Eisenhower did no more than imply his own acceptance, but after the briefing Smith instructed Whiteley to write an appropriate operations order. Eisenhower telephoned Montgomery, and the change was effected.

The Supreme Commander himself had just been nominated to the newly legislated rank of general of the army. To emphasize that he had lost no confidence in Bradley, he recommended Bradley's promotion to full general. The Senate, however, had adjourned by the time Eisenhower cabled General Marshall, and no immediate action was possible.

Eisenhower defined the new boundary between Montgomery's and Bradley's army groups as a line extending from Givet on the Meuse through St. Vith to Prüm in the West Wall; a clarification put both the latter towns within Montgomery's sphere. Along with the transfer of the American First and Ninth Armies to 21 Army Group, IX and XXIX TAC passed to the operational control of the 2nd Tactical Air Force. Because the RAF had plenty of fighter-bombers of its own, enough planes were transferred from IX and XXIX to XIX TAC to give Patton's scheduled counterattack ample support from the air.

There were ways in which the change of command fulfilled Bradley's worst fears. Montgomery set out promptly for Chaudfontaine and instructed Simpson to meet him there. In the afternoon of December 20, he strode into Hodges's headquarters, as one of his own staff members described it, like "Christ come to cleanse the temple." He soon judged that under the strain of the battle Hodges was on his way to becoming one of the "cardiaques" who used to frequent the spas now inhabited by the First Army, and hinted to Eisenhower that Hodges might have to be removed. With Montgomery, the capacity to irritate was a source of perverse pride. His memoirs state with evident satisfaction: "I think the less one says about this battle [of the Ardennes] the better, for I fancy that whatever I do say will almost certainly be resented"—and despite the disclaimer, he goes on to describe the terrible mess the American command had left for him to clean up. "I found the northern flank of the bulge very disorganised. Ninth Army had two corps and three divisions; First Army had three corps and fifteen divisions. Neither Army Commander had seen Bradley or any senior member of his staff since the battle began, and they had no directive on which to work."[35] Such comment should be read in the perspective of the First Army's growing reassertion of control of events well before Montgomery arrived. Furthermore, while Bradley had not visited Hodges since the beginning of the battle, he had spoken with Hodges and Kean by telephone no less than half a dozen times on December 18 alone.

Worse displays of arrogance were to follow. But Montgomery took hold on the north flank with the energy and verve that were as characteristic as his peacockery. Already he had informed Hodges of the movement of 30 Corps to back up the Meuse line, and that the British would assume responsibility for the Meuse bridges at Namur, Liège, Huy, and Givet. This news brought a gratifying reduction of Hodges's worries. Montgomery employed a system of traveling liaison officers to keep himself in close contact with all principal headquarters under his command. This organization, called Phantom, already in touch with Hodges, now permeated the First and Ninth Armies and brought consistent assurance of support as well as a sustained effort to coordinate all activity. Montgomery concurred in the First Army's efforts thus far to shore up the north flank of the salient, particularly in the disposition of the XVIII Corps to try to fill the gap between the V Corps and the VIII.

The field marshal began immediately to plan for the husbanding of reserves for counterattack, although he evidently contemplated striking at the tip of the salient rather than cutting into its flank and enveloping Germans as Eisenhower, Bradley, and Patton were planning to do in the south. To command the reserves who gathered for the counterattack, Montgomery wanted the most aggressive corps commander available, and he would accept only one man: Collins.

Meanwhile, Montgomery was willing to yield ground the better to build up his reserves, or where the benefits of holding on would no longer match the cost. When Hasbrouck reported on December 22 that the time had come to abandon St. Vith, Montgomery decisively overruled Ridgway's disinclination, with characteristic words of encouragement for the defenders: "They can come back with all honour. They come back to the more secure positions. They put up a wonderful show."[36]

28: The Battles of Christmastide

O**N THE** fifth day before Christmas, December turned bitter cold. An ungloved hand unwarily touching the metal of a gun barrel was likely to freeze fast to the barrel. Digging a foxhole became a labor of Hercules. Until now, since the opening of the German offensive, fog had hung so low that drivers had to use headlights by day. Now the cloud cover rose higher, and within another two days snow was falling. The unwelcome white Christmas drove some Americans to wind themselves in sheets for camouflage, while others wore their white long johns outside their uniforms.

Because St. Vith had been denied the Germans so long, and because they had had to build up a powerful concentration of troops to capture it, they would require several days after December 22 to organize a reasonably smooth traffic flow through the town. Meanwhile, their traffic snarls at the St. Vith road junction were a godsend to the Americans, because the gap west of St. Vith remained only sketchily filled.

As Hasbrouck's intelligence had suggested, the 2nd SS Panzer Division, Das Reich, had come up and could spearhead the drive west from St. Vith once the Germans were able to move men and supplies with relative freedom through the town. The turning of General Krüger's LVIII Panzer Corps to the northward crossing of the Ourthe above Houffalize on December 19 also brought the 116th Panzer and 560th Volksgrenadier Divisions into the area west of St. Vith. On the American side, the 82nd Airborne was beginning to develop a fairly strong shoulder just south of the Amblève, but the XVIII Corps could spare nothing adequate to prolong the line beyond General Gavin's right flank. The opening first created in the American front by the breaking of the 106th and 28th Divisions remained an opening still, without even the semblance of a continuous defensive line, beckoning all the way to the Meuse.

The Salm and the Ourthe

Ostensibly, General Rose's 3rd Armored Division began moving into the threatened area beyond Gavin's right on December 20 to secure the line of the Bastogne-Liège highway between Manhay and Houffalize. Rose, however, had only a small fragment of his division, mostly CCR and a reconnaissance battalion. CCB was engaged against Kampfgruppe Peiper, and CCA was still in the north for the defense of Eupen. In fact, Rose felt able to send only three small task forces probing toward the highway.

Geography offered a small note of hope. Across the wide sweep of country between the Salm and the Ourthe, east and northeast of La Roche, there sprawled a high marshland, the Plateau des Tailles. Here cross-country movement was difficult even by the hard standards of the Ardennes, and control of roads and road junctions was even more than customarily important. Relatively few troops might achieve disproportionate results.

On Rose's right, Task Force Hogan (Lieutenant Colonel Samuel M. Hogan) moved out through the screen formed by the 7th Armored's trains at La Roche. It was soon stopped by a German roadblock a short distance south of that town. In the center, Task Force Tucker (Major John Tucker) joined another part of the 7th Armored screen at Samrée on the road from Salmchâteau to La Roche, but it did so just in time for both to be ejected from the town by prowling panzers. Unfortunately, 25,000 gallons of gasoline fell into enemy hands along with Samrée. On Rose's left, Task Force Kane (Lieutenant Colonel Matthew W. Kane) probed past the Manhay crossroads ten kilometers directly south of Werbomont and set up a roadblock at Malempré just beyond.

The task force so abruptly rebuffed at Samrée had been heading toward an important objective, the Baraque de Fraiture crossroads. This was a lonely intersection near the center of the Plateau des Tailles, the meeting place of the Liège-Bastogne-Arlon-Luxembourg highway with the road west from St. Vith through Marche to Namur or Dinant. Ridgway and Rose hoped at least to contest the Baraque de Fraiture. Rose therefore planned to begin Thursday, December 21 by striking again with his center, now reinforced as Task Force Orr (Lieutenant Colonel William R. Orr), to recapture Samrée. Before the attack could get started, however, patrols discovered that the Germans had pushed on with their spearhead so far beyond Samrée that they were already threatening Hotton. This place was 3rd Armored Division and CCR headquarters and, more importantly, the location of a bridge across the Ourthe.

Thursday's main battle in Rose's area thus became a struggle for Hotton. It was waged on the American side by the now-customary pickup team: headquarters and service detachments of the 3rd Armored, a detachment of the ubiquitous 51st Engineer Combat Battalion, and Colonel Robert L. Howse, Jr., counterattacking down the road from Soy to Hotton with the thin semblance of a reserve that CCR had been able to hold back from its earlier probes. The defenders had little artillery, and the foot soldiers had to rely mainly on their own weapons, aided by a handful of tanks and tank destroyers. Nevertheless, the American force proved sufficient to discourage the Germans from attempting an earnest grasp at the Hotton bridge; once again a few Americans achieved a great deal. Once again, furthermore, it was the tip of the LVIII Panzer Corps, of the 116th Panzers and the 560th Volksgrenadiers, that fell back from a crossing of the Ourthe. The retreat from the Ortheuville crossing had already cost Krüger a day; he had wasted two days entangled with the American detachments around Samrée and Hotton; now he was off on a new tack again, moving southward evidently to try to link up with the 2nd Panzer Division of Lüttwitz's XLVII Panzer Corps and cash in on its crossing of the Ourthe—for, by displaying a little more persistence and aggressiveness than Krüger's men, the 2nd Panzers had captured and on Wednesday night began crossing the Ortheuville bridge from which the LVIII Corps had earlier withdrawn.

Luckily for the Americans, once across the Ourthe the 2nd Panzer Division itself failed to sustain its old-time aggressiveness that had won it the bridge. Otherwise the Americans' troubles would have been considerably worse, because while elements of the 3rd Armored and their assorted coadjutors held the area north and east of the Ourthe only lightly, on December 21 the area west of that river was yet more sketchily defended. And the 2nd Panzers were now drawing perilously close to the goal of the Meuse: Marche, the principal road junction of the area they were entering, only twenty-four kilometers beyond Ortheuville, was practically undefended and only some forty-five kilometers from Namur or two-thirds that distance from Dinant by good roads.

The sluggishness of the hitherto excellent 2nd Panzer Division despite its refitting and reconditioning, and to a degree the sluggishness of the whole XLVII Panzer Corps under the division's former chieftain Lüttwitz, makes another of the mysteries of the Ardennes campaign. By the time the 2nd Panzers reached the Ourthe, their vehicles were developing the maintenance problems for which German machines of this period of the war were notorious. The men were tired (though the bicycle battalions had mechanized themselves with captured American trucks). But mechanical and human fatigue does not offer sufficient explanation; the 2nd Panzer Division and its parent corps had already moved with uncommendable hesitancy from Clervaux to Bastogne, where much of the corps was now being held up, and which greater aggressiveness might have brought promptly into German hands.

The 334th Infantry Regiment, the advance element of General Bolling's 84th Division, was just beginning to establish itself in Marche on Thursday morning, December 21. Most of the division was far enough behind that an energetic 2nd Panzer Division should readily have been able to outrace the Railsplitters to the Marche crossroads. The 84th, coming from Geilenkirchen, represented another thinning out of the Ninth Army to bolster the embattled First—partially explaining the disproportions between the two armies on which Montgomery commented adversely. Bolling's force was slated to become part of Collins's VII Corps for the counterattack against the northwestern penetration of the Bulge. For the moment, however, the 84th was to serve as another westward prolongation of Ridgway's XVIII Corps to try to close off the Germans' paths to the Meuse. Thanks to the 2nd Panzers' inertia, the only semblance of crisis faced by the Railsplitters on December 21 was a call for assistance by the outmanned agglomeration defending Hotton that day; the 84th was strangely slow to treat the appeal seriously, and by the time two companies of the 334th reached Hotton in the late afternoon, the enemy had drawn back.

Still, there were enough signs of Germans swarming just to the south that General Bolling called army headquarters late Thursday morning both to report the request from Hotton and to ask for clear instructions whether his thin strength was intended to hold the line from Hotton to Marche. Army headquarters and General Collins had been pondering that very question. The immediate danger in it was that of piecemeal destruction of the units intended to form the VII Corps counterattack before they could organize as a corps. Yet an unimpeded German dash from the Ourthe toward the Meuse would pose a greater peril. The answer to Bolling's question became yes.

While the enemy generously prolonged his pause, the bulk of Bolling's division came up during Thursday night to give respectable weight to the Hotton-Marche line by the morning of December 22. The countryside farther west remained open, so General Ridgway promptly thinned out the Railsplitters again by instructing Bolling to occupy the crossroads villages of Rochefort, Wanlin, and Beauraing. Among other purposes, Ridgway hoped to guard the repeater station at Jemelle, four kilometers east of Rochefort. These tasks stretched Bolling's right something over thirty kilometers beyond Marche. In addition, Bolling was to throw out a counter-reconnaissance screen along the line Harsin-Grupont-Wellin, some fifteen kilometers south of Marche. As detachments proceeded toward these places—Bolling sent a battalion each to Rochefort, Wanlin, and Beauraing—some of them had to fight or evade Germans along the way as the 2nd Panzer Division began moving again.

Naturally, Montgomery and Hodges were shifting yet more strength into the area, if only it could arrive in time. A happy dividend of the southward extension of 21 Army Group was the arrival of the British 29th Armoured Brigade, with fifty tanks. It appeared along the Meuse during Friday, to take over defense of the Namur, Dinant, and Givet bridges. The brigade had been refitting in western Belgium with new tanks, but Montgomery ordered it to climb aboard its old tanks and make haste to the Meuse. CCA of Rose's 3rd Armored Division arrived in Ridgway's corps area and was assigned to screen the west bank of the Ourthe between La Roche and St. Hubert; its vanguard got as far as Marche when it became caught up in the German probings against the 84th Division. General Harmon's 2nd Armored Division, also intended for Collins's VII Corps counterattack, arrived from the Ninth Army and would begin moving south in a sector west of Marche toward Ciney on December 23.

If only the added strength could concentrate in time: the Germans, despite their hesitations, still seemed to be leading the race toward a concentration between the Ourthe and the Meuse. On Saturday, December 23, the 3rd Battalion of the 335th Infantry with tank destroyer and engineer attachments, the 84th Division's garrison at Rochefort, came under attack from Panzer Lehr, which had broken free from Bastogne. Thus both panzer divisions of Lüttwitz's corps had joined the battle beyond the Ourthe. Meanwhile the 2nd Panzer Division cut the road between Rochefort and Marche and threatened another 84th Division garrison, at Buissonville in rear of both Rochefort and Marche. When CCA of the 2nd Armored Division began moving during Saturday night from Ciney to the relief of Rochefort and Buissonville, it had to fight through German guns as far north and west as the village of Leignon.

The opposite flank of the XVIII Corps also erupted with renewed dangers on Saturday, the 23rd. In that area, too, German hesitancy had spared the thin American screen any severe crisis since the fight for Hotton, though the task forces of CCR, 3rd Armored, were barely strong enough to hold their own against even an irresolute enemy advance. On Thursday, December 21, while the Hotton affair was transpiring, Task Force Hogan had found itself unable to fight its way out of the La Roche area to regain contact with other parts of CCR. Task Force Kane tried to reinforce the effort to retake Samrée, but instead the reinforcements were caught up in a battle that was beginning to take shape at the Baraque de Fraiture. Task Force Orr, far from being able to accumulate strength to recapture Samrée, fell back several times under German pressure and ended Thursday around Amonines, not far southeast of Hotton and Soy.

It was mostly the LVIII Panzer Corps, sprawled all over the area, whose elements caused the latter troubles. On Friday, December 22, Krüger tried to extricate the corps from its various entanglements so it could move westward again, in tandem with Lüttwitz beyond the Ourthe. In the process, Krüger's moving detachments collided yet more bruisingly with the bits and pieces of Rose's CCR. Task Force Hogan had to consider itself encircled and trapped. Task Force Orr was hurled back rudely when it tried to move south again from Amonines, and it might have had to fight more Germans than it could handle except that Task Force Kane stirred up a commotion in the enemy rear. Task Force Kane itself was soon pinned down at Lamorménil, with detachments also fighting at the Baraque de Fraiture.

Driblets of Americans had gradually been gathering at this latter crossroads since December 19. On that Tuesday afternoon, three 105mm. howitzers of the 589th Field Artillery Battalion, a splinter thrown off from the shattering of the 106th Division, had become the first defenses planted at the Baraque. Because their commander was Major Arthur C. Parker III, the Americans called the subsequent action Parker's Crossroads. Other elements turned up during the next several days: four antiaircraft half-tracks mounting four .50-caliber machine guns each, D Troop of the 7th Armored Division's 87th Cavalry Squadron, eleven tanks and a reconnaissance platoon from Task Force Kane. By Wednesday night, the Germans were beginning to probe at the garrison, and soon there arrived also adjurations from the 82nd Airborne and 3rd Armored Divisions to hold as long as possible. Considering the 3rd Armored's weakness behind the Baraque de Fraiture, General Gavin feared that a German thrust through the crossroads might lead to the turning of his division's right flank. On Thursday, in fact, Gavin sent as additional reinforcement the 2nd Battalion of the 325th Glider Infantry, which put one company into the crossroads but otherwise backstopped Parker on a ridge about a kilometer behind him. At the same time, however, the Task Force Kane tanks felt obliged to leave to participate in their parent body's business elsewhere.

Meanwhile the crossroads troops fended off probes, worried about periodic interruption of their communications by German columns passing across their rear, and worried still more because by Friday it seemed to be the relatively fresh 2nd SS Panzer Division that was building up in front. Important as the crossroads might be, no American commander for many miles around as yet had strength to counter anything like a major portion of this old and formidable antagonist. Sure enough, the 4th Panzer Grenadier Regiment of the 2nd SS Panzers charged the airborne troopers behind the crossroads before dawn on December 23. The 2/325th fought them off, but the weight of the attack made it apparent that here was a prelude to the main effort. Through Saturday morning and into the afternoon the defenders' apprehensive waiting continued, while the new-fallen snow starkly silhouetted their perimeter on the open plateau for the inspection of enemies concealed in encroaching woods. Then, late in the afternoon, came everything—artillery barrage, flares, tanks, grenadiers—in strength that boiled over the Baraque de Fraiture and poured on toward the Manhay crossroads only six kilometers distant, from which SS Das Reich would have its choice of good roads into the rear of either the 82nd Airborne or the 3rd Armored—or over some hills and thence straight to Liège.

So four panzer divisions—Panzer Lehr, 2nd Panzer, 116th Panzer, 2nd SS Panzer— were moving into the interstices of the thin screen that was all the Americans had hung so far across the gap in the old VIII Corps front. The one redeeming feature of the crisis remained the time the Germans had consumed in advancing this far. For that, thanks had to go again to the rookies of the 106th Division and still more to the tired but tough 28th, to the assorted defenders of St. Vith, and to the multiple scratch forces that had fought for so many crossroads from Marnach to the Baraque de Fraiture. Overreliant on his artillery he might be in the attack, but the American soldier was showing almost everywhere on the defense a stubborn resistance to being pushed around that was almost as unexpectedly heartening to his commanders as it was unexpectedly dismaying to the Germans.

Knowing what they did about German fuel shortages and the eagerness of the advancing columns to capture American fuel dumps, the Americans could guess that the amount of fuel consumed to maneuver and fight even against small roadblocks must be hurting the Germans by now, and must help to explain the enemy's fortunate hesitations. Still, the Americans also had to count it as sheer good luck that it was not into the open, inviting tank country between the Salm and the Ourthe that an enemy so aggressive and persistent as Jochen Peiper had charged, but into the constricting defiles of the Amblève. There Kampfgruppe Peiper, at least, might be stricken from the German arsenal.

The Death Struggle of Kampfgruppe Peiper

On the morning of Thursday, December 21, Peiper characteristically had antici-pated the American effort to regain St. Edouard's Sanatorium on the western edge of Stoumont. Peiper mounted an attack of his own. He drove back the 1st Battalion of the 119th Infantry and disorganized it enough that the short winter day was more than half gone before the Americans could revert to their planned assault.

Then there was merely renewed inconclusive jousting in the sanatorium. Nothing in the effort to eliminate Kampfgruppe Peiper went well that day. The weight of the 2nd Battalion of the 119th was insufficient to pry loose the German roadblock north of Stoumont, where the dilemma remained the inability of American tanks to progress along the sunken road or of infantry to make headway without tanks. The center of the three task forces of CCB, 3rd Armored remained hung up in practically the same predicament between Stoumont and La Gleize. The easternmost of the three CCB task forces, the one that had set up the roadblocks between Trois Ponts and La Gleize the previous day, moved some of its strength to the south bank of the Amblève to help cut off Peiper from the rest of his division; but this detachment absorbed about as much punishment as it dispensed. The 82nd Airborne at least completed the capture of Cheneux, but its ability to hold back any full-fledged effort by the remainder of the 1st SS Panzer Division to rejoin Peiper was no less questionable for that, especially because occurrences along the Ourthe rendered its right flank anything but secure.

So recalcitrant had the events of December 20 and 21 shown Kampfgruppe Peiper to be, encirclement notwithstanding, that both Ridgway at XVIII Corps headquarters and Hobbs of the 30th Division concluded that only fighter-bombers could break the various strongpoints where Shermans and available artillery seemed not to suffice. Second TAF was willing, but December 22 dawned with snow falling along the Amblève under a heavy overcast. The ground troops once again would have to go it alone.

During the night, however, an officer of the 740th Tank Battalion had contrived to build a ramp out of shell casings to enable Shermans to climb to the level of the sanatorium. Direct tank fire into the place delivered it firmly into American hands at last. (Astonishingly, the 200 civilians in the basement were not harmed.) This small victory put new life into the American effort to compress the encirclement, but the snow was falling heavily enough to delay any further thrust eastward into Stoumont. Patrols cautiously feeling their way into the town found it nevertheless remarkably quiet. When the snow tapered off and the 119th Infantry and its attachments resumed moving in earnest during the afternoon, the Germans were gone. Just as the Americans had almost given up to await a clear day and the air forces, Peiper's resolution had evidently begun to crack too, at least to the extent of his calling in all his remaining tentacles to hunker down in La Gleize.

He thus sealed his fate. Passive defense was not enough to save him, because his division commander, Mohnke, was behaving more like the diffident panzer leaders to the south than like the Peiper of December 17–21. Despite the deficiencies of airborne troops against armor, the 82nd found no serious trouble in fending off Mohnke's halfhearted jabs on the 22nd.

One source of German discouragement was the thorough working over being administered to the panzers' roads and assembly areas by American artillery. Artillery fire on December 23 also drove the remnants of Kampfgruppe Peiper into the cellars of La Gleize. The impact of the guns was enhanced by the high command's release of the proximity fuze for use in the land battle to deal with the emergency in the Ardennes. For all that, attacking infantry and tanks found pressing against Peiper little less difficult than before. The Germans still laid down a brutal defensive fire from their concealment and from dug-in tanks and antitank guns. The troops who had fought at Stoumont carried the brunt of the battle for the Americans, and their progress was slow whether they attempted to move into La Gleize directly from the Stoumont road or through woods north of the town. The overcast broke, but a tactical air strike scheduled for La Gleize hit Malmédy instead.

Yet it was only a matter of time, and during Saturday night Peiper made his move to slip away south of the Amblève. Several hundred Germans escaped—more precisely, some 800, the Americans eventually learned—to hide out in woods north of Trois Ponts on Sunday and cross the Salm Sunday night. Peiper had to leave his wounded and his vehicles behind. The Americans entered La Gleize on Sunday, the day before Christmas, to liberate 170 of their comrades, capture about 300 Germans, and find twenty-eight German tanks, seventy half-tracks, and twenty-five artillery pieces.

Peiper had lost many other tanks and guns, of course, in the fighting along the way. Thanks to the geography of the Amblève valley and the bravery and resourcefulness of a few engineers during the early going, as well as to the fighting qualities of the Old Hickory Division, the 3rd Armored, the 740th Tank Battalion, and their attachments at the end, the only reward for the most daring and ruthless German effort of the entire offensive was to cut the heart out of the 1st ss Panzer Division. It was Eisenhower's vision that the Ardennes counteroffensive should yet bring the equivalent result upon the whole Wehrmacht in the West.

Mostly, the idea was still visionary. On the day of Christmas Eve, while the troops of the 30th Division were counting Peiper's abandoned armor in La Gleize, the two panzer corps of Lüttwitz and Krüger at length embarked on their more powerfully armed bid for the Meuse. Before CCA of the 2nd Armored could bring help to the outmanned 3rd Battalion of the 335th Infantry, Rochefort fell to Panzer Lehr. On the right of Panzer Lehr, CCA arrived at Buissonville to find the 2nd Panzer Division already in possession. The 2nd Armored recaptured the town, but the reason for relatively easy recapture was that much of the 2nd Panzers' fighting power had already moved on westward. Second Armored headquarters began to receive numerous reports of German tanks around Celles; information was accurate as well as plentiful, because Lieutenant Colonel Merriam Wheeler of the division's reconnaissance battalion had discovered that in Belgium he could conduct reconnaissance partly by telephone, simply by alerting the local police and telephone operators in the villages all around to call in reports of German movements that they observed. Airplanes, however, sent to the Celles neighborhood to confirm the reports, were driven away by heavy flak. A strong Schwerpunkt of the 2nd Panzer Division was only six kilometers from the Meuse.

After a day of bitter fighting, furthermore, the 116th Panzer Division drove the 84th Division's left wing out of Verdenne and brought the Hotton-Marche road under short-range artillery fire. Its two time-consuming changes of direction notwithstanding, the 116th was now aligned with the right flank of the 2nd Panzer Division and giving Krüger's support to Lüttwitz's thrust to the Meuse. On the right of the 116th, in turn, the 2nd SS Panzers were pushing on from the Baraque de Fraiture toward the XVIII Corps rear.

The Battle of Bastogne

On the same Christmas Eve, the defenders of Bastogne were regrouping to squeeze the maximum defensive strength out of their fragile, encircled lines. They needed every ounce of strength they could get.

Even the Michelin guide, its editors as chary as any Frenchmen of memorializing the American contribution to victory over the Germans, has taken special note of American courage at Bastogne and essayed to capture for its readers something of the peculiarly American spirit of the defense: "Bastogne, réputée pour son fameux jambon d'Ardenne, a été rendue célèbre par l'héroïque résistance des troupes américaines encerclées par von Rundstedt, en décembre 1944. Invité à se rendre, le général Mac Auliffe [sic] fit cette réponse laconique et péremptoire: «Nuts» (litteralement: «des noix») . . . . "[1]

The whole battle of the Ardennes has tended to blur into the battle of Bastogne, an injustice to the resistance of other American troops who were not at Bastogne. General Fritz Bayerlein of Panzer Lehr, who was present at both Bastogne and Rochefort, testified, for example, that the resistance of the little battalion of the 84th Division at Rochefort compared in courage and significance to Bastogne. He had in mind the possible impact if the Germans had grasped the last few kilometers to the Meuse. Still, Bastogne was the final and most critical of Middleton's decisive crossroads. In American hands, it blocked the XLVII Panzer Corps's best routes to the Meuse and did much to explain why Lüttwitz initiated his climactic lunge for the river only on December 24, more than a week after the German counteroffensive had begun. The dénouement, furthermore, lent Bastogne something of the symbolic significance of the copse of trees at Gettysburg: from this point forever, the tide flowed in only one direction.

Though they came as a fire brigade, no one in the 101st Airborne Division including General McAuliffe foresaw that they were to be called on to be heroes. They did not know to what extent they would be dependent on their own resources—how complete, for example, was the shattering of the 28th Division. As late as December 20, McAuliffe sent a liaison officer to General Cota, now at Sibret southwest of Bastogne, to inquire whether the 28th could join the 101st in an attack toward Wiltz the next day. The men of the 101st did not know how much the 10th Armored would already have been chewed up and fragmented in its actions north and northeast of Bastogne by the time they made solid contact with it. In any event, McAuliffe was soon to expect that his troopers would promptly be joined by a second armored division, the 4th. Taking Patton too literally at his word, Middleton told McAuliffe on the evening of December 19 that one combat command of the 4th Armored was already well on its way. As late as December 21, rumor circulated in Bastogne that both the 4th and the 7th Armored were hastening to the rescue.

So the mood was no more apprehensive than in any other commitment to battle, and no doubt less than in an air drop, when McAuliffe marched the 101st eastward out of Bastogne in column of battalions on Tuesday, December 19, to locate both friends and enemy.

The mood began to change during the day, when beaten fragments of CCR, 9th Armored and CCB, 10th Armored fell back on the advancing 101st from the battles up the Longvilly and Noville roads. The airborne soldiers learned that many of the men of these commands were fugitives in the woods to the east and northeast. It was disconcerting, too, that when Colonel Ewell, learning of Team Cherry's loss of its roadblock at the Neffe railroad station, deployed the division's lead regiment, his 501st, astride the Bastogne-Neffe-Longvilly road, the paratroopers already could not occupy Hill 510. This eminence commanded Neffe and other towns just east of Bastogne.

Nevertheless, the 101st still regarded its immediate mission as setting up a linear defense facing eastward, while other units would extend its flanks. McAuliffe was considering a counterattack until well into the next day, December 20, as his communication with Cota shows. Until that Wednesday, the defensive line in front of Bastogne, reaching north and south in advance of the suburbs of Mont and Bizory, retained a northeastward projection all the way to Noville, which was defended by Team Desobry (Major William R. Desobry) of CCB, 10th Armored, built around fifteen Shermans.

Noville was an obstruction in the path of the 2nd Panzer Division as it tried to disentangle itself from the fighting around Bastogne to slide northwestward toward the Meuse. During December 19 and 20, the panzers applied extremely heavy pressure upon the place, committing as many as thirty-two tanks in a single attack. On December 19 Middleton had sent Desobry a platoon of the 705th Tank Destroyer Battalion, and McAuliffe dispatched the 1st Battalion of the 506th Parachute Infantry. But these reinforcements were not enough to bear the main weight of a panzer division, and on December 20 it required a local counterattack by several assorted battalions of the 101st merely to extricate the Noville garrison from impending entrapment. Without a heavy fog, evacuation might not have been possible. Thus abandoned, Noville had already done its work of helping delay Lüttwitz's Schwerpunkt for at least another day. Drawing back the Noville salient consolidated rather than hindered the defense of Bastogne.

Only gradually on Thursday, December 21, did the Bastogne defenders come to realize that a simple linear defense facing east was no longer their main problem. They were surrounded. Reports of Germans roving well to the west had reached them long since; it was evident enough that Bastogne, important though it was, was not the objective of the XLVII Panzer Corps, and that the enemy's armor was trying to break away to the Meuse. But not until December 21 did patrols moving on the road spokes fanning outward discover that every one of them was blocked by the enemy. The journal of the 101st recorded the blockage of every road at 10:30 A.M.; CCB, 10th Armored did not confirm that the southward road was definitely closed until late afternoon. Headquarters told the troopers about their surrounded situation quickly thereafter; it was a hallmark of their methods of command that McAuliffe and Colonel William Roberts of CCB, a veteran of combat in World War I, consistently let all their men know the score.

So, in an old American army tradition, the 101st would have to form a circle to fend off the Indians until the cavalry reinforcements arrived, in this instance in the form of

George Patton's Third Army tanks. For a perimeter defense, the 101st Airborne with its four regiments had a better organization, at least theoretically, than a standard triangular division. As the battle evolved, however, the perimeter took shape as a series of responses to local pressures rather than according to any organizational logic. The terrain was by no means ideal; Bastogne is a market town built on relatively level ground surrounded by wooded hills. The 501st Parachute Infantry continued to face east, its left flank on the railroad that ran to St. Vith and its right south of Neffe. To its left, the 506th extended from near the railroad to the town of Foy. Still farther leftward, the 502nd faced north from around Sonne-Fontaine to Longchamps. To the right of the 501st, the 2nd Battalion, 327th Glider Infantry faced southeast around Marvie. The division engineer battalion, the 326th, looked southward to extend the perimeter loosely across the Neufchâteau road. During the afternoon of December 21, McAuliffe removed the 1st Battalion of the 327th from attachment to the 501st and placed it to extend the engineers' right. The perimeter west of Bastogne had to be formed largely by portions of the division trains and service companies, along with the self-defense resources of the artillery that had been positioned here initially to fire eastward across the town. The 3rd Battalion of the 327th held a westward-reaching salient out the Marche-Namur highway to Flamierge.

Enough other troops had gravitated to Bastogne before its encirclement to fill out the light table-of-organization strength of an airborne division, particularly in artillery, to approximately the dimensions of a standard infantry division with the attachments customary in late 1944. The 705th Tank Destroyer Battalion from the Ninth Army arrived late on December 19; its equipment was not the old standard M10 tank destroyer with a 3-inch gun but the M18 with a long 76mm. gun that could duel on equal terms with any German tank armament except the Tiger's 88. The 420th Armored Field Artillery Battalion was present along with the 755th and 969th.

CCB, 10th Armored and CCR, 9th Armored retained about forty serviceable Shermans between them. These and an assortment of light tanks, cavalry assault guns, and quad-.50s—the quadruple-mounted .50-caliber machine guns on half-tracks—worked as mobile fire brigades, moving from one threatened section of the perimeter to another. The drop in temperature and the freezing of the ground beginning on December 21, just before the snowfalls, assisted mobility. It was also useful that Colonel Roberts was an expert on armor-infantry cooperation, having taught the subject at the Command and General Staff School; paratroopers were not trained much in such teamwork, but Roberts's knowledge and personality combined to remedy a good part of the deficiency.

Bastogne was also full of individuals and small units washed in from the wreckage of battle farther east. Roberts organized these men into a combat team, which its members called Team SNAFU. Numbering 500 or so, the team served as a badly needed reserve from which to draw emergency task forces or replacements.

Though encircled, the Americans were not in much danger of starving. Bastogne was normally a place of about 4,000 population and thus large enough to have some reserve food stocks. An American Red Cross dump proved to contain large quantities of doughnut flour, which could and did make numerous palatable pancakes. Medical equipment and assistance posed a graver problem, partly because on the night of December 19 a German raid had overrun the 101st Airborne medical company, killing or capturing all but eight doctors and forty-four men and destroying or taking all sorts of medical supplies. For the wounded, circumstances would not be propitious. For the defense, it was even worse that the 101st had been hurried into Bastogne with its ammunition and grenade pouches less than full, while 105 and 155mm. howitzer shells were in dangerously short supply well before the roads closed.

The main German pressure on December 21 was still against the eastern defense line. It came from the 26th Volksgrenadier Division. The division commander, General-major Heinz Kokott, had been left behind with a Kampfgruppe consisting mainly of his own troops, plus a grenadier regiment from Panzer Lehr, to take Bastogne while the mechanized forces of Lüttwitz's corps pressed on. The 26th Volksgrenadiers had shown their mettle by practically keeping pace with the panzers on the march from the Our; but McAuliffe could hope that they might now pay a price in fatigue.

For a time on December 21 the Germans drove a wedge along the seam between the 501st and 506th Regiments, but they posed a greater peril where, fortunately, they still had fewer troops, on the western side of the perimeter. There they almost broke through among the artillery groupment busily firing eastward. An encounter with some of the remaining tanks of CCR, 9th Armored east of Villeroux sounded the alarm just in time for the 755th and 969th Field Artillery Battalions to skedaddle to Senonchamps. There they had enough time to prepare something of a defense. Their own machine guns, a couple of stray tanks, and the quad-.50s of an antiaircraft battery halted the enemy at nightfall.

The next day the Germans adjusted their tactics by aiming their main efforts against this relatively weak western portion of the American circumference. They pushed hard from the Neufchâteau highway to Mande-St. Etienne just north of the Marche highway. The brunt of their effort fell on the 420th Field Artillery Battalion, organized as a mixed arms task force under the battalion commander, Lieutenant Colonel Harry D. Browne. Task Force Browne threw off assaults all day long, while also firing their 105mm. howitzers eastward into the more distant battle. Meanwhile their guns also offered a lucrative static target to German artillery, which cost them additional heavy casualties. The surviving tanks of CCR once more provided aid that was very likely indispensable.

It is not surprising that the enemy detected in the westerly battles a scarcity of American infantry grievous enough to warrant a surrender demand. About noon on December 22, four Germans under a flag of truce entered the lines of Company F of the 327th. A major, a captain, and two enlisted men, they described themselves as "parlementaires." The commander of the 327th could not immediately be found, so it was the regimental operations officer who received from the Germans a written note from "The German Commander," which he delivered to division headquarters. The note referred to the progress of German spearheads farther west toward the Meuse as evidence of the futility of holding out at Bastogne, which adds perspective to the importance of the battles concurrently being fought by the 2nd and 3rd Armored and 84th Infantry Divisions in front of the Meuse crossings. Thus suggesting that the German tide was irresistible anyway, the note demanded the surrender of the encircled town within two hours, on pain of annihilation of "the U.S.A. troops in and near Bastogne."

McAuliffe received this demand just as he was about to leave headquarters to congratulate the defenders of a roadblock who had given an especially good account of themselves. He dropped the message on the floor, said "Nuts," and left.

When he returned his staff reminded him of the message, and for the first time he gave it serious enough thought to ask what he should say in reply. His G-3 suggested, "That first remark of yours would be hard to beat."

"What did I say?" asked McAuliffe, and he was told. So the formal reply, typed on bond paper and delivered to the officer parlementaires at the F Company command post by Colonel Joseph H. Harper of the 327th, read:

To the German Commander:

Nuts!

The American Commander

Harper naturally found the parlementaires uncertain about the translation. He also found them apparently assuming their surrender demand would be met. Settling at first for advising them that the reply was decidedly not affirmative, by the time he had escorted the German officers back to the Company F outpost line, where they picked up the two enlisted men, Harper had pondered long enough on what he took to be their arrogance to send them off with: "If you don't understand what 'Nuts' means, in plain English it is the same as 'Go to hell.' I will tell you something else—if you continue to attack, we will kill every goddamn German that tries to break into this city."[2]

McAuliffe's G-2 saw that the story was circulated among the troops. Colonel Harper spent the rest of the day near his front awaiting the enemy's explosive reaction, which fortunately did not come: fortunately, because the exhaustion of artillery ammunition was now in sight. The respite carried the garrison into Saturday, December 23, the first clear day since the German crossing of the Our. Two hundred forty-one cargo planes each carrying 1,200 pounds attempted to drop ammunition and other supplies into the Bastogne perimeter, and the results were good. The sparkling winter's day of course brought out the fighter-bombers as well, a considerable American advantage when the Germans chose to resume their attacks against the western circumference. At that, McAuliffe's line nearly broke several times on Saturday, and he had to commit half of his mobile reserve, Team Cherry of the 10th Armored, to assure it would hold.

After dark the enemy went to work on the southeastern defenses as well, diametrically opposite some of the hardest fighting on the west. Not only did American artillery have to lay down a heavy fire toward Marvie while simultaneously fighting off their immediate assailants, but McAuliffe was obliged to throw the rest of Team Cherry into the battle. His G-3 telephoned the VIII Corps that the 4th Armored Division had better come quickly, because "it is getting pretty sticky around here . . . . The enemy has attacked all along the south and some tanks are through and running around in our area."[3] Which they were, though burning buildings silhouetted the marauding panzers to permit American tanks and tank destroyers to gun them down.

December 24 was a second clear day, and 160 planes of Troop Carrier Command dropped supplies. The near-ruptures of the perimeter the day and night before dramatized how much the garrison needed all the ammunition that could be flown in. Even with the supply drops of December 23, on Christmas Eve the 420th Armored Field Artillery Battalion restricted firing to five rounds per mission, and the 969th limited itself to thirty-nine rounds for the day, about one-fifth its earlier rate of firing. The fighter-bombers and the Germans' losses of the previous days fortunately restrained the enemy from much activity during December 24; the extent of their dependence on artillery and rockets in their assaults had indicated the Germans besieging Bastogne enjoyed no excess of manpower to expend. The garrison took advantage of the Christmas Eve respite to consolidate and reorganize its thin perimeter. The salient reaching west to Flamierge was retracted to establish a tight circle about twenty-six kilometers in circumference. Defense of the circle was apportioned among the four regiments of the 101st, each reinforced from the pool of other units to form a combined arms team. Colonel Roberts's CCB and Team SNAFU, now including the remnants of CCR, formed such reserve as there was, with about nine Shermans and five light tanks operational at any one time.

During the afternoon, VIII Corps headquarters relayed a message from General Patton: "Xmas Eve present coming up. Hold on."[4] But the garrison also saw apparent German reinforcements coming up, concentrating west of the perimeter. After the unusual spectacle of two Luftwaffe raids during the hours when Santa Claus should have been flying, German attackers in white snow suits strode out of the west before Christmas dawn.

They penetrated the 502nd Infantry's line around Champs, and a Schwerpunkt of tanks broke through the 327th east of Flamierge and rolled straight through the battery positions of the 755th Field Artillery. More and more Germans continued driving through the hole. They proved to be the enemy's reinforcements, the 115th Panzer Grenadier Regiment and other elements of the 15th Panzer Grenadier Division, newly committed to the Ardennes battle. Against the tank and grenadier penetration, the airborne troopers' training in fighting in all directions at once was an American trump card. American bazookas as well as tanks and tank destroyers turned up unpredictably and everywhere. It was soon the German hunters who became the hunted, their tanks ripped by crossfire, the panzer grenadiers who had ridden the tanks into battle dropping into surrounded knots to be gradually snuffed out.

But the weather turned worse on Christmas Day. Tactical air support fell off, cargo flights had to be cancelled, and the fiercest battle yet for Bastogne raged through Christmas and into December 26. On the 26th, the Germans launched yet another assault from Senonchamps toward Isle la Hesse and scored another penetration of the 327th— before the old reliable artillery, ammunition shortage notwithstanding, caught the penetrators on open ground and blasted them away.

By afternoon, fatigue on both sides reduced the fighting again to sporadic flurries of punch and counterpunch. At 4:50 P.M., the 326th Engineers on the southern edge of the perimeter reported seeing "three light tanks believed friendly."[5] Bastogne's isolation had ended: the tanks were the steel tip of the 4th Armored Division and the Third Army.

Patton's March from Luxembourg

General Bradley commented in his memoirs: "Until the Battle of the Bulge I did not share George's enthusiasm for his Third Army staff which, unlike those of both the First and Ninth Armies, lacked outstanding individual performers. Indeed, I had once agreed with the observation of another senior commander who said, 'Patton can get more good work out of a mediocre bunch of staff officers than anyone I ever saw.'"[6] This assessment was surely unfair to several of Patton's staff, particularly his prudent G-2, Colonel Koch. Bradley also had the emphasis a bit wrong. Any weakness in Patton's staff lay less in individuals than in organization. It was occasional bursts of individual exertion and ability that had to compensate for the lack of a consistently effective organization, which failed to manage the day-to-day activities of the Third Army with the consistency of staff supervision in the First or the Ninth Army. This absence of constant, detailed, untiring staff work at Third Army headquarters was at the same time a corollary of the personalized command that Patton exerted over his army in contrast to Hodges or Simpson. It was not Patton's design that his army should be directed by anonymous staff officers. He wanted no gray eminence at Third Army comparable to Bill Kean at First. The Third Army was commanded by George S. Patton, Jr., in person or through his Household Cavalry. It was not altogether exaggeration when Patton wrote his wife that on December 20, "the staff of the Third Army, which consisted of myself and Sergeant Mims [his driver], visited two corps and five division commanders, and telephoned for the engineers, tank destroyers, extra tank battalions, etc."[7]

It was because, administrative shortcomings notwithstanding, the Third Army staff had individual members capable of rising to a demanding occasion that Patton's ninety-degree turn from the Saar took place rapidly and efficiently enough to win the plaudits it has received. The movement produced its share of contretemps, but they were of the kind endemic to all improvisations under pressure, not specifically to be laid at the door of Third Army headquarters. The Third Army anticipated from December 18 onward, for example, that it would take over the VIII Corps; but it did not formally do so until noon of December 20, and meanwhile the advance detachments of the 4th Armored Division were not sure under whose orders they were functioning. In response to instructions from the VIII Corps staff, the 4th Armored's Task Force Ezell (Captain Bert Ezell) actually entered Bastogne on December 20 with a tank company, an armored infantry company, and a battery of self-propelled artillery—only to be ordered out again by General Gaffey's 4th Armored headquarters, which considered itself part of the III Corps. To make matters worse, Ezell had been in contact with McAuliffe but departed down the Neufchâteau road without informing the commander of Bastogne, because he had the impression someone higher up the chain of command was doing so. Still worse, of course, the incident raises the question why, if a small task force of CCB, 4th Armored could travel in and out of Bastogne on December 20, CCB itself was not used to keep the Neufchâteau road open.

Yet General Gaffey had what appeared to him a good reason for withdrawing Task Force Ezell, and the reason involved the principal command problem overshadowing the Third Army's entrance into the Ardennes battle. Gaffey feared that committing Task Force Ezell might prove to be the first step toward a piecemeal commitment of his whole division. Instead, he wanted to enter the battle in full power. Perhaps because he was still new to division command he may have been excessively sensitive to any possibility of losing control over part of his division, excessively intent on assuring himself full command of it. But Eisenhower also continued to fear that Patton's impetuosity might consign the Third Army to a piecemeal commitment. The danger was implicit not only in Patton's temperament but in the conflicting demands upon his army's intervention. While SHAEF wanted the Third Army to husband its forces for a major counterattack, all headquarters concerned also gave high priority to a rapid, narrow thrust along the Arlon-Bastogne road to relieve Bastogne. The Third Army turn to Bastogne was effectively enough administered by the Third Army staff; it is at the level of command decision beset by the conflicting pressures on the shape of the maneuver that substantial faults can be found. This was Patton's own level. Perhaps the faults arose in part because, assisted only by Sergeant Mims, Patton tried to do too much and thereby crowded his strategic and tactical vision with too many details.

"Drive like hell," Patton said to his commanders as he adjourned his final conference before the thrust northward. "Speed, speed. Obsessiveness with speed permeated our lives," says a 4th Armored tanker of the march toward Bastogne. "Within hours we were pushing so hard we were virtually maniacal."[8] Yet Task Force Ezell went into the Bastogne perimeter and out again, though the defenders of Bastogne had sore need of its tanks, guns, and men.

And while Patton's initial fast-moving narrow thrust thus misfired, under SHAEF's prodding for a big six-division attack Patton next forsook the advantages of a concentration that might quickly have redeemed the Ezell affair in favor of yet another broad-front effort to go forward everywhere. In the end, Patton accepted Eisenhower's adjurations to attack on a large scale with a literalness that undermined all ideas of going like hell. Patton's first instructions to his infantry divisions were to follow up the 4th Armored by striking northward in great depth, in column of regiments. Then he changed his mind and substituted breadth for depth, with two corps attacking northward along a wide front reaching all the way from the Neufchâteau road to the north-south section of the Sauer River. So wide was the front that, far from advancing in column of regiments, the divisions were hard put to keep their regiments in contact with each other's flanks.

The outcome was another slugging match in which the breadth of the front dissipated American strength enough to compensate considerably for German weakness. On December 21, Patton ordered the attacking divisions to wheel to the northeast as they moved, to seize crossings of the Rhine; but no race for the Rhine would occur. Progress instead lagged infuriatingly, the Germans received time to reinforce the south flank of the Bulge, and it was not until December 26 that the 4th Armored Division again made a connection with the defenders of Bastogne, and tenuously at that.

General Millikin, an old-time cavalryman who might have ridden out of a Remington painting, was untested in battle as a corps commander, but Patton had chosen Millikin's III Corps headquarters to lead the main drive to Bastogne because the corps was not engaged to the eastward. As Patton's plan jelled, Millikin was to have Gaffey's 4th Armored on his left from around Neufchâteau across the Arlon-Bastogne highway, while Paul's 26th and McBride's 80th Divisions extended the corps front to the Alzette River. On Millikin's right, General Eddy's XII Corps brought in Irwin's 5th Infantry Division and took over the 109th Infantry Regiment and miscellaneous units of the 28th Division, CCA of the 9th Armored Division, Morris's 10th Armored Division less its CCB, and Barton's 4th Infantry Division. Both the III and XII Corps were to attack on December 22.

Despite the Germans' initial disappointment at the Americans' ability to constrict the south shoulder of the Bulge, General Brandenberger's Seventh Army had projected its 5th Parachute Division about as far west as Neufchâteau. Brandenberger now faced south with two corps of two divisions each to fend off any American counterattack along the whole line east to the Sauer at Echternach. As Patton's army prepared to strike against this German line, American ignorance of the enemy's strength and dispositions was considerable. On the day scheduled for the attack, SHAEF was still appealing for intelligence of the enemy's order of battle. Saying that henceforth the issue would be decided by the commitment of reserves, SHAEF appealed to the three army groups "to know what formations the enemy is placing or can place in reserve . . . . Thus both positive and negative identification are of the greatest value to the Supreme Commander as elements in his decisions . . . . All identifications, whether repetitive or not, will be reported rapidly to G-2 . . . . " The south shoulder was one of the areas where identifications were inadequate.[9]

Especially east of the Arlon-Bastogne road, the south shoulder was also an area where terrain greatly aided the defense, as the weary Americans who had been holding on there knew. It was largely because of the terrain that the outmanned Americans had initially been able to firm up this shoulder from Echternach west just south of the Sauer and its extension the Sûre. All the disadvantages of the Ardennes as a military arena were amply in evidence: the wooded areas were numerous, large, and thick with trees; the ravines were many, steep-sided, and deep. Roads were fairly plentiful but tended either to run blindly through forests or to curve precipitously around steep slopes or down into the ravines. The Sûre-Sauer and Wiltz Rivers were deep defensive moats across the prospective III Corps front of advance. The Third Army launched its counterattack just as the snows and frigid cold came, so trench foot and exposure once more ravaged even veteran divisions.

The XII Corps attack was understandably late in getting started. For three days before the appointed Friday, many of Eddy's men were still busy with defense, trying to make sure that their line remained firm along the Sauer between Diekirch and Echternach. On December 22, Irwin's rested and refitted 5th Division began bolstering Barton's tired 4th, which had been compelled to give up ground again the previous day. By December 24, Irwin's division was ready to attack through Barton's, but the left of the division's 2nd Infantry Regiment and the right of its 11th promptly stalled in the gorge of the Schwarz Erntz. The 212th Volksgrenadier Division used the vantage points on the neighboring hills skillfully to seal off the gorge. The left wing of the 11th Infantry and elements of the 10th Armored Division attacking farther left made better initial progress against the less effective 276th Volksgrenadier Division which had disappointed the German command when on the offensive. Reaching high ground around Haller, the 11th was able thence to turn the hills immediately above the Schwarz Erntz on Christmas Day. Henceforth the 212th and 276th Volksgrenadier Divisions were pretty clearly engaged in nothing more ambitious than a fighting withdrawal across the Sauer, but they did this job far too well for the American commanders' peace of mind. Not until nightfall of December 26 was the south bank of the Sauer reasonably cleared of Germans, whereupon Patton, Eddy, and Irwin took up what was to prove a lengthy rumination on the merits of persisting in the notion of a hasty attack through the West Wall to the Rhine.

The 80th and 26th Divisions on the right and center of the III Corps enjoyed only two days of good progress at the opening of Patton's counterattack. The first day was so satisfying, in fact, that Patton told Millikin to keep the attack moving through the night, because he had a chance to win the war. By the third morning, December 24, the III Corps was astride the Germans' best road for maintaining their Seventh Army front facing southward, breaking at Ettelbruck and Heiderscheid the road from the Sauer to Wiltz. But such progress could be expected to provoke a strong enemy reaction, and before darkness fell on Christmas Eve, the 80th and 26th Divisions joined their comrades to the right in slugging matches painfully reminiscent of those they had recently endured on the way to the Saar.

Trouble began on December 24 with a strong German counterblow against the left flank of McBride's 80th Division around Heiderscheid and Eschdorf. It did not help that the front of the III Corps advance had opened so wide that there was a gap between the 80th Division and the 26th. Worse, the counterattacking Germans proved to be rested, vigorous troops exceptionally well trained in the use of small arms. The Germans did not have much artillery; but when they pinned down American detachments, they swept them with a devastating musketry and burp-gun fire, reinforced by just enough tanks and assault guns to complete the paralysis of a hitherto promising American operation. A large part of the newly arrived enemy was the 79th Volksgrenadier Division, hurried from OKW reserve when the Seventh Army front threatened to crack and thereby expose the whole southern flank of the Ardennes. While these Volksgrenadiers stymied McBride's division, Paul's 26th Division faltered before a formation that puzzled the G-2s and cast ominous shadows. This was the Führer Grenadier Brigade. It was an elite formation similar to the Führer Begleit Brigade, recruited from handpicked young Nazis and an offshoot of the Grossdeutschland Panzer Division—which created new suspicions that the latter famous and formidable unit had come to the Ardennes from the Russian Front.

The Führer Grenadier Brigade added Panthers and assault guns to well-trained infantry, and if it also aroused fears beyond its real merits, with its arrival the troubles of the 26th and 80th Divisions had grown more than ample. The new shape of the southern battle was typified by a series of costly frontal attacks, conducted against Eschdorf throughout Christmas Day by Task Force Hamilton (Lieutenant Colonel Paul Hamilton), which was built around the 2nd Battalion of the 26th Division's 328th Infantry. Eschdorf was indispensable if the Yankee Division were to cross the Sûre with adequate roads behind it. General Paul insisted the place must be captured. But the terrain and the Germans' positions allowed nothing but frontal assaults, up snow-covered slopes against grenadiers concealed in white capes and sheets on the reverse slopes.

When Eschdorf at last fell on December 26, who had captured it became an issue of bitter controversy between the 328th Infantry and the 104th, which had joined in the battle. The very bitterness of the dispute reflected the disappointment of high hopes, the mockery of Patton's promise to Millikin that the III Corps advance could win the war, the disintegration of the 26th and 80th Division counterattack into the same old facsimile of a stalemate, whose prize could no longer be the Rhine but only the little Sûre.

It is good for Patton's reputation that the relief of Bastogne is what is usually remembered about the Third Army counterattack. Despite the Ezell affair and a connection that remained uncomfortably fragile for a long time after December 26, the relief was the most successful part of Patton's operations in the Bulge.

Patton supervised the relief expedition in person, not only because of its urgency but because the 4th Armored and its commander were among his favorites. He personally prescribed the tactics the 4th Armored was to employ. He urged Gaffey that tanks, artillery, tank destroyers, and armored engineers ought to go in the lead. German doctrine might remain unclear on whether armor or infantry should take the van, but it was Patton's fixed conviction that "Whenever the ground permits tanks to advance rapidly, even with the certainty of a loss from mine fields, they should lead."[10] The frozen ground permitted rapid movement. Because Patton had grown acutely aware of the advantages of the Panther over the Sherman in gun and armor, the lead of the lead tanks should whenever possible be the newest Shermans with long guns and strengthened armor. The response to stiff resistance ought to be not head-on attack but envelopment. An envelopment should be relatively deep, started a mile to a mile and a half behind the enemy front and executing a right-angle turn.

Excellent as its record was, the 4th Armored Division was no longer ideally suited for the swift, slashing charge to Bastogne that Patton envisaged. Its casualties had been too many and the replacements it had received were too few. Few armored specialist replacements were still being trained in the United States. Worse, the division had received too few new tanks of any kind, let alone the improved Shermans. It was still driving too many of the same Shermans it had first brought to France in June. In the march to the Ardennes, one battalion alone left thirty-three tanks along the way because of mechanical failure. Some tanks could run only at medium speed. In others, the turrets had to be traversed by hand cranking. Most important, Hugh Gaffey was not "P" Wood, neither in consciousness of the unforgiving minute nor at least yet in self-assurance in division command. Over his months as Patton's chief of staff, both he and the army commander had come to take it for granted that Patton would dominate their relationship in every way. So both took it as natural that Patton should watch so closely over the 4th Armored's march to Bastogne, and Patton's tie to Gaffey helped cause the relative neglect of the other Third Army divisions and indirectly the misdesign of their attack.

As for the 4th Armored, General Middleton suggested to Patton that its best route to Bastogne might be on the III Corps far flank from Neufchâteau. On this road, elements of the 28th Division still held ground only about ten kilometers from Bastogne when Patton first turned north. Because making the main effort on the Neufchâteau road would have strained still more the extended III Corps line, however, both Patton and Millikin preferred to send Gaffey as directly as possible north from Arlon. On the 4th Armored's right, Brigadier General Herbert L. Earnest's CCA was to follow the main Arlon-Bastogne road. On the left, Brigadier General Holmes E. Dager's CCB was to take roughly parallel secondary roads just to the west of the main highway. The two combat commands were to draw within mutual supporting distance as they came close to Bastogne.

Obstructions on the roads—mostly demolitions performed by the VIII Corps in retreat—caused more problems than German resistance on December 22, but the secondary roads proved to be in better shape than the main ones. CCA was held up for a time by a large crater in the road near Martelange. After the crater was bridged, in the early afternoon the vanguard was stopped by a company of 5th Parachute Division infantry guarding the ruins of the Sûre River bridges at Martelange. Artillery could not reach the paratroopers effectively, and CCA was still grappling with them when CCB was as far along as Burnon, only eleven kilometers from Bastogne.

Patton ordered Dager to continue moving through the night, but now CCB also had to build a bridge, to replace a ruined span. Much of the night was required as well to clear stubborn Germans out of Burnon. There ensued a cautious, darkness-shrouded advance of a kilometer or so to the vicinity of Chaumont. Here at last the enemy seemed to be defending in force, with guns formidably mounted on surrounding hills to sweep the village, which occupies a saucerlike depression.

Dager formed his combat command early on December 23 for a formal assault on

Chaumont. Earnest, having captured Martelange with armored infantry during the night, labored that Saturday morning on the repair of the Sûre bridges for his vehicles. Patton grew impatient. "There is too much piddling around," he told III Corps headquarters. "Bypass these towns and clear them up later. Tanks can operate on this ground now."[11] But Patton was mistaken about the ground. Dager was preparing an envelopment, in accordance with Patton's instructions, but the sunlight of December 23 proved just warm enough to soften the ground so the enveloping tanks could not move across country. The tanks needed the roads, and therefore the 4th Armored had to take the towns. When the CCB attack, deprived of most of its subtlety, churned into Chaumont, the German guns on the encircling hills devastated the leading Shermans. Without effective tank support, Dager's armored infantry quickly took some sixty-five casualties and had to retreat. Having lost eleven Shermans, Dager was reduced to two platoons of medium tanks, and he spent December 24 doing little more than awaiting replacement tanks and sufficient progress by the rest of the division to reduce the pressure on him. At dusk on Christmas Eve, CCB was not much closer to Bastogne than it had been on the afternoon of December 22.

CCA had moved forward again late on December 23, but during Saturday night it ran into its own equivalent of CCB's Chaumont battle. At Warnach, just east of the Arlon-Bastogne road, Germans concealed in the buildings of the town let some tanks pass but then ambushed the first thin-skinned half-tracks to come past carrying armored infantry. CCA assaulted the buildings with a company of Shermans soon after midnight, but concealed antitank guns stopped the Shermans. Earnest had to await daylight and then fight an old-fashioned house-to-house battle, during which recalcitrant troopers of the 5th Parachute Division persisted in filtering back into the houses the Americans thought they had secured. "In their own way," wrote a tanker of the 4th Armored about the 5th Parachute Division in the fight for Bastogne, "these panzer-trained paratroopers were saying 'nuts!' to us." He added,

> I want to describe these bastards because some observers have underrated them. They were, to be sure, inexperienced [being recently reorganized], but I can only know that from a later look at relevant documents. The fact is, they didn't act inexperienced. They were slick, savage, continuously shooting, continuously moving forward, almost sullen in their bloody determination.[12]

By daylight, Earnest's Shermans could better make themselves felt, while the paratroopers did not have tanks. For that reason, the outcome was preordained even if prolonged. Warnach cost CCA sixty-eight officers and men. The Americans killed 135 Germans and captured an equal number.

The 4th Armored did not normally make tactical use of its CCR, but the reserve combat command under Colonel Wendell Blanchard also had to fight a battle at the same time that CCA was embroiled in Warnach. As early as December 22, Germans were reported moving into an open seam between the 4th Armored and the 28th Infantry Division. To respond, CCR skidded across icy secondary roads toward Bigonville on December 23, meeting Germans in woods south of that town during the afternoon. Mines halted an attempt to clear the way with a tank assault, and Blanchard decided to wait until December 24 to bring up his whole force before trying again. By that time, the Germans had withdrawn into the town, and another nasty house-to-house fight ensued. Eventually the Americans cut the northern exit road and trapped those Germans who were still resisting, capturing some 328 prisoners from the 5th Parachute Division.

Thus, by Christmas Eve, Gaffey's division seemed as much bogged down in infantry slugging as the rest of the III Corps. On December 24, the corps and division commanders therefore took two steps that might allay Patton's impatience and speed up the advance. Millikin transferred from the 80th Division to the 4th Armored the 1st and 2nd Battalions of the 318th Infantry, assigning them to CCA and CCB, respectively. If Gaffey must fight infantry battles, he had better be able to throw a bigger infantry punch. The infantry arrived late on Christmas Eve after a six-hour truck ride. Gaffey immediately sent them to the front, where they helped the combat commands crunch forward just a little farther on Christmas Day. Thus assisted, CCB at last captured Chaumont. Gaffey, meanwhile, had also decided to test a different route with armor: the Neufchâteau road suggested originally by Middleton. To that end he hastened CCR from its Bigonville battle to Neufchâteau, also on Christmas Eve.

In 4th Armored Division practice, CCR customarily absorbed battalions suffering from especially hard usage in the recent battles of the other combat commands. Accordingly, there assembled near Neufchâteau early on Christmas Day Colonel Abrams's 37th Tank Battalion and Lieutenant Colonel George Jaques's 53rd Armored Infantry Battalion, along with a self-propelled 105mm. howitzer battalion and a battery of 155mm. howitzers. They followed the main road from Neufchâteau through Vaux-les-Rosières and then turned off onto secondary routes hoping to meet fewer Germans. As they approached Remonville, however, either new information or soldierly intuition warned of a concentration of the enemy in the town, so the place was given a thorough blasting by artillery and tanks before tanks and infantry raced in. A whole battalion of the 14th Parachute Regiment proved to be holed up there, but they were pounded so hard by the guns and then hit so swiftly by machine guns and grenades that CCR practically destroyed the battalion, in remarkably short order for an element of the dangerous 5th Parachute Division. Blanchard's men counted 327 prisoners—making a good two days' work, for 328 prisoners had come in the day before.

Gaffey's principal expectation was that with this kind of help on its left flank, CCB should now be able to crash into Bastogne. Indeed, General Maxwell Taylor hitched a ride with CCB so he could rejoin his 101st Airborne as quickly as possible. Blanchard for his part instructed his battalion commanders on Christmas night that he intended to attack through Remichampagne and Clochimont the next day and then swing back to the main highway at Sibret for CCR's final plunge toward Bastogne.

On the morning of December 26, another clear day, P-47s bombed close in front of CCR to hasten the way through Remichampagne and Clochimont. The day was also frigid, and despite the sun the ground was hard enough again to allow tanks to roll across country. When the time came to turn toward Sibret, Abrams and Jaques conferred and decided on their own initiative to change the program. The Germans supposedly held Sibret in strength. Abrams's battalion was down to twenty tanks; Jaques was short 230 men. Instead of risking more losses against a strong garrison at Sibret, why not keep going straight ahead? Ahead lay the village of Assenois, but it ought to be a lesser obstacle.

There were problems of communication between CCR and division headquarters, but CCR nevertheless rounded up three CCB artillery battalions to join its own guns in a concentration on Assenois. The artillery opened fire at 3:35 P.M. Abrams's S-3, Captain William Dwight, led Company C of the 37th Tank Battalion and Company C of the 53rd Armored Infantry Battalion into Assenois so close behind the shells that friendly fire knocked out a half-track and sent others scurrying for shelter. Before the garrison could recover, five Shermans and a half-track were through the town. Jaques's infantry had to stay behind to grapple for Assenois with troops of both the 5th Parachute and 26th Volksgrenadier Divisions; the night was well advanced before the town was secure and some 500 prisoners were in Jaques's hands. Meanwhile, two of the lead tanks and the half-track were delayed by mines, but the other three Shermans pressed on and made the contact with the 326th Engineers in the Bastogne perimeter at 4:50.

Twenty minutes later, Colonel Abrams shook hands with General McAuliffe. After Assenois fell, Abrams's light tank company escorted forty trucks and seventy ambulances into Bastogne during the night.

Reserves Weak and Strong

Patton had gone over to the attack, and with the linkup to Bastogne he could forget his frustrations for the moment and simply relish the new triumph, the "Lovely weather for killing Germans,"[13] and the spectacle of his tanks rolling forward again—relish the moment all the more, because Bradley's hurt at the transfer of two of his armies to Montgomery left the army group commander so quiescent that Patton was practically acting on his own.

West of Bastogne, it took more time to go over to the attack. Too many gaps in the American front were slow to be filled, and for a week Montgomery's every effort to hoard a reserve for a northern counterattack succumbed to new demands to shore up the defensive.

Immediately west of Gaffey's triumphant 4th Armored Division, Middleton's VIII Corps was still trying to form a left flank for the Third Army out of a collection of fragments. Thus the Meuse above Givet had not yet been rendered at all as secure as the lower Meuse, where the British backstopped the First Army. Even Patton—or, given his knowledge of military history, especially Patton—still had to worry lest the panzer spearheads roving beyond the Ourthe past Marche and Rochefort might be aiming not for the junction of the Sambre and Meuse in the manner of 1914 and 1940, but for a southward turn to the 1870 killing ground of Sedan.

To protect the line by which supplies were reaching him, Middleton posted corps engineers at crossings of the Meuse and its tributaries the Semois and Chiers as far west as Bouillon on the Franco-Belgian border. To protect his corps against a wide turning movement, Middleton ordered his engineers to blow the Semois bridges west of Bouillon.

On December 20, General Lee's Communications Zone had received, in addition to all its other responsibilities—already enhanced by the apparent need to guard against Nazi saboteurs in American uniforms—the task of securing the line of the Meuse, particularly from Givet south. Lee began assembling four engineer service regiments along the Meuse. Slim reinforcements arrived in the form of a field artillery battalion, an antitank company, and six recently organized and poorly equipped French light infantry battalions. On December 23, these units passed to Middleton's VIII Corps, along with the responsibility for the Meuse from Givet to Verdun. Considering the meagerness of the troops involved, the effect was to aggravate rather than ease Middleton's burdens. Fortunately, Brigadier General Charles S. Kilburn's new 11th Armored Division began arriving the next day.

Still more fortunately for Middleton, and for Patton's counterattack, the Germans did not wheel south. Instead, the days just before Christmas brought a new turn to the threat to the lower Meuse from Givet to Liège.

As late as December 21 and 22, Sepp Dietrich's Sixth Panzer Army was still butting its head against the northeast shoulder of the Bulge on the Elsenborn Ridge. During the early morning hours of the 21st, the artillery of the American 1st, 2nd, and 99th Divisions expended 10,000 rounds against a 12th ss Panzer Division attack that overran Companies E and F of the 26th Infantry Regiment. Though these two companies of the Big Red One included few veterans, but rather were 90 percent replacements and nevertheless down to about 100 men each, they stayed in their foxholes to deal with the Hitler Jugend Division's grenadiers after its panzers had passed them by, until a counterattack relieved them. Again on December 22, all three regiments of the 1st Division had to go into action to seal off another penetration.

Yet already there were evidences of a shift of the Sixth Panzer Army westward along the northern flank of the penetration scored by the Fifth Panzer Army, and these evidences soon increased markedly. Except for the now isolated Kampfgruppe Peiper, Dietrich's ss divisions had so far failed to match the progress of Hasso von Manteuffel's Wehrmacht army; but Dietrich's troops could still be fed into the Bulge for a new start, to try to break open the north flank west of the recalcitrant American V Corps on the Elsenborn Ridge. Such appeared to be the meaning of the 2nd ss Panzer Division's emergence at St. Vith and its continued drive to the Baraque de Fraiture. Ridgway's XVIII Airborne Corps still grasped the area between the Salm and the Ourthe all too lightly for comfort, with no continuous line but instead a series of scattered strongpoints. The 2nd ss Panzer Division, now part of General der Waffen-ss Willi Bittrich's II ss Panzer Corps, might herald the approach of a formidable array catalogued by 21 Army Group intelligence on Christmas Eve: "2 ss . . . will still try with 9 ss [also of Bittrich's corps] to hook around Vielsalm NW using 3 P[anzer] G[renadier] Div and eventually possibly 10 and 12 ss."[14]

The Battle of Manhay

On the night of December 23–24, after the 2nd ss Panzers flooded out Major Parker's pickup team at the Baraque de Fraiture crossroads, Major Olin F. Brewster of the 3rd Armored Division assembled a similar team a couple of kilometers north on the road to Manhay. Brewster's force was built around a tank platoon and an armored infantry platoon from his own division and Company C of the 509th Parachute Infantry Battalion, with the usual assortment of stray accretions. Brewster put up a sufficiently convincing show of strength, from a sufficiently defensible position, and with enough aid from the fighter-bombers, that all through December 24 the 2nd ss Panzers merely probed at him. On the other hand, during the previous night the 3rd Armored Division's Task Force Kane had abandoned an outpost at Odeigne just west of Brewster's road-block. The abandonment had seemed necessary so Kane could withstand pressure from the 560th Volksgrenadier Division elsewhere, at Freyneux and Lamorménil; but it opened to the Germans a flanking route around Brewster.

Grateful nevertheless for the respite apparently being granted by the 2nd ss Panzers, the Allied commanders in the area spent the day of Christmas Eve trying to shore up their defenses between the Salm and the Ourthe. During the morning, Field Marshal Montgomery visited XVIII Corps headquarters and instructed Ridgway that the corps front must be consolidated on a tighter, more nearly continuous line. British critics argue with some merit that the American army, so unaccustomed to defeat, was excessively reluctant to yield even a meter of ground for the sake of larger strategic or tactical benefits—that the Americans often fought with a defensive inflexibility akin to Hitler's. It might be rejoined that this very stubbornness accounted for the impromptu defensive stands by overmatched scratch forces that had so invaluably delayed the German onslaught. As it happens, however, General Gavin of the 82nd Airborne had already reached independently the same conclusion as Montgomery.

The youthful paratrooper Gavin, commanding a division at thirty-seven, might have been considered the personal embodiment of the American army's youthful brashness if anybody was, and Gavin acknowledged that it was especially hard for him to give up ground because the 82nd had never done it before. But earlier in the day Gavin had already met with some of his principal officers to consider the implications of confronting elements of the 1st, 2nd, and 9th ss Panzer Divisions and the Führer Begleit Brigade from the long horseshoe-shaped line given the 82nd by the circumstances of its emergency arrival, rambling from Trois Ponts south and east to Vielsalm and Salmchâteau, and thence west to Fraiture, just short of the Baraque de Fraiture. Along much of this front, there were 200 meters between foxholes. The remnants of Kampfgruppe Peiper were still roaming in the rear. The American front to the right was even less solid. "If a major German attack developed from the south," thought Gavin, "threatening the right of the [82nd] division, its continued occupation of the salient . . . would be costly in life and to no advantage after the extrication of the St. Vith force."[15] Gavin believed he must pull his division back to an organized, dug-in position, protected by mines and wire, where he might be ready to face the attack of several panzer divisions by Christmas morning.

The division commander agreeing thoroughly with the army group commander, the 82nd Airborne accordingly withdrew under cover of the night of Christmas Eve to a straight line from Trois Ponts to Vaux Chavanne, just east of Manhay. During the move there were brushes both with Kampfgruppe Peiper, making its escape eastward, and with the 9th ss Panzer Division, closely following Gavin's retreat; but the Germans provided nothing the airborne troopers could not handle.

Meanwhile, under Montgomery's instructions the Americans were also attempting to build up a more solid front west of the 82nd. The abandonment of the St. Vith salient gave Ridgway General Hasbrouck's 7th Armored Division, covered with honor as Montgomery had said, but also with its ranks decimated, its equipment battered, and its surviving troops almost sleepwalking. Colonel Dwight A. Rosebaum's CCA was in the best condition of any of the division's combat elements, which was not saying much. Without rest after its escape across the Salm, CCA outposted Manhay and the roads radiating from it on December 24. Unfortunately, a blown bridge kept its left from direct contact with the right flank of the 82nd. Unfortunately too, the 3rd Armored to Rosebaum's right was part of the VII Corps, so Ridgway could not assure direct coordination between the two armored divisions; nor was the 3rd Armored well tied in to XVIII Corps communications.

The continuing effort during December 24 to consolidate the American front produced orders from corps for Rosebaum to move after dark to hills just behind Manhay, leaving an outpost at the Manhay crossroads. Rosebaum objected that he held better and higher ground south of the crossroads, but the order stood. The commander of one of Rosebaum's strongpoints, just north of Odeigne, was leaving his post to attend a conference to plan the withdrawal when a German armored attack struck. The attack came as a complete surprise, partly because the lack of communication with the 3rd Armored had deprived the 7th Armored of warning that the 3rd had pulled away its neighboring outpost screen. Led by a captured Sherman, the Germans were inside the 7th Armored strongpoint before the Americans realized they were hostile. The strongpoint collapsed, its survivors fleeing toward Manhay.

Another CCA strongpoint just to the north followed quickly. Rosebaum's headquarters group was beginning its planned withdrawal from Manhay when first the fugitives and then the Germans came streaming along. The Manhay crossroads dropped easily into German hands. Task Force Brewster, still far off to the south, soon realized that Germans were all over the roads in its rear. Brewster tried to slip away eastward toward Malempré, but enemy guns promptly knocked out his two lead tanks, and his task force had to abandon its vehicles and strike out northward on foot.

As became apparent eventually, the respite during the daylight hours of December 24 had lasted only as long as it took the 2nd SS Panzer Division to build a road capable of carrying its armor across the marshy Plateau des Tailles from the vicinity of the Baraque de Fraiture to Odeigne, whence to chop through Rosebaum's right to Manhay. The panzers' seizure of Manhay looked like a new bolt of lightning suddenly hurled toward Liège itself, for the consolidated XVIII Corps line had split before it was fairly formed, and the distance from Manhay to Liège was only fifteen kilometers by a good highway. Forthwith, General Hodges bestirred himself to insist of XVIII Corps that Manhay must be retaken, with no excuses for failure. He also appealed to Montgomery for more divisions to commit between Manhay and Liège. Montgomery himself believed the Germans had revealed their intention as a breakthrough across the Meuse between Liège and Huy.

On Christmas morning, however, Hodges and Ridgway breathed a surprised and guarded sigh of relief. Instead of barreling on toward Liège, the 2nd SS Panzers turned west at the Manhay crossroads toward Grandménil and Erezée. The Americans had no particularly ample powers of resistance in that direction, but the Germans' turn posed fewer immediate dangers.

At Grandménil was one of the outposts of Task Force Kane. Panthers pushed it aside during the early morning hours. Just to the west, the 289th Infantry of the new 75th Division was assembling to backstop the 3rd Armored. Again employing the ruse of following their captured Sherman, the enemy sailed through the 289th's first roadblock without a fight. The raw regiment's main foxhole line seemed scarcely likely to hold the panzers much longer.

Probably it would not have, except that one of the new infantrymen shot a bazooka round into the lead Panther just where the road skirted a high cliff. The rest of the SS armor could not pass the disabled tank. Apparently the Germans had no infantry on hand to assist the armor. Upon General Rose's appeal, the First Army released his division's CCB from La Gleize to hurry it south to bolster the rest of the 3rd Armored, hoping it would arrive before the 2nd SS Panzers could get moving again. The experience was similar enough to several others that 21 Army Group intelligence could eventually generalize: "One reason [for the] breakdown [of the] whole [German] scheme was reliance on using ingenious narrow routes stream valleys etc. for passing tanks through dense Ardennes. Equally ingenious American sappers found that if leading tank is stopped others cannot get by and fatal traffic blocks occur."[16]

But American luck turned bad in an unanticipated way. By Christmas afternoon, a company of CCB, 3rd Armored Shermans and a company of armored infantry were heading east to try to recapture Grandménil, when the 7th Armored vectored eleven P-38s onto them. This display of the importance of communication between neighboring units killed three American officers and thirty-six men. The weakened CCB task force nevertheless entered Grandménil, but it could not retain the place against a German counterattack.

Still, the Germans were unable to recapture their momentum of the previous night and the early morning. The 2nd SS Panzers could not turn their full force against the 3rd Armored because the XVIII Corps still had enough strength to visit plagues upon them from north of Manhay. Under Hodges's prodding, Ridgway in turn prodded Hasbrouck into counterattacking Manhay with whatever force the 7th Armored Division could muster. Hasbrouck's tanks sallied forth without making headway, but the attached 2nd Battalion of the 424th Infantry—raw and unblooded less than two weeks earlier, now the veteran survivors of the 106th Division—overcame 35 percent casualties to penetrate almost to the Manhay crossroads before they were called back. With that, plus American artillery concentrations on Manhay, plus a sky full of fighter-bombers, the 2nd SS Panzer Division had its hands too full to grasp the opportunities the Americans had feared were within its power.

Using the friendly darkness of Christmas night to regroup, the panzers tried to regain momentum by attacking eastward and westward simultaneously before dawn on December 26, to expand the breach in the XVIII Corps front. Their eastward column experienced the misfortune of striking the 325th Glider Infantry on the right flank of General Gavin's consolidated line; no American yielding was to be found there. Their main effort, toward the west, crashed head on into a renewed attempt by CCB, 3rd Armored to capture Grandménil. Here the Germans fared better, because such a battle favored the advantages of the Panther over the Sherman, and the CCB tank company that had arrived the previous afternoon retreated with only two of its tanks still functioning. But the bazookas of the 289th Infantry once again blocked the Panthers' passage, this time on a flanking road, and thereby CCB was afforded opportunity to put sixteen reinforcing Shermans into the battle before the Panthers could exploit their initial advantage. A three-battalion artillery concentration blasted the way for the additional Shermans to press into Grandménil in the early afternoon.

The 7th Armored Division remained too exhausted—only 40 percent of its tanks were running—to fight its way into Manhay, though Hodges's and Ridgway's importunities to Hasbrouck kept the division testing the 2nd SS Panzers from the north while the Germans were attempting their own attacks to east and west. To that extent the 7th served again to prevent Das Reich from concentrating its strength. Because Manhay still implied peril for Liège, no number of rebuffs could quench the high command's determination to retake it. Despairing of what Hasbrouck could do unaided, Ridgway brought in the 3rd Battalion of the 517th Parachute Infantry, a fresh formation. The paratroops attacked Manhay soon after midnight, December 26–27, and before daylight they cleared the village. On December 27, the 2nd SS Panzers made no effort to return either to Manhay or to Grandménil. The Sixth Panzer Army's fresh start between the Salm and the Ourthe had served the reputation of the Waffen-SS no better than the battle for the Elsenborn Ridge.

The Last Lunge toward Dinant

The evident explanation for the initial failure of the 2nd SS Panzers to drive north as soon as they took Manhay was that their aim was not Liège after all, but to plunge westward to support the other threat to the Meuse which had already climbed the final ridge before Dinant. SHAEF intelligence noted on December 26 that the "Germans [are] continuing buildup Marche Area and to west where Second Panzer Division halted along line Dinant-Ciney Road."[17]

When the 2nd SS Panzers made their left turn from Manhay to Grandménil and along the Erezée road, the 560th Volksgrenadier Division assailed the same road farther west between Soy and Hotton. This same road also continued on across the Ourthe to Marche and to the westernmost penetration of the 2nd Panzer Division near Dinant. On Christmas Eve, Task Force Orr of the 3rd Armored Division was again assailed at Amonines. The 560th Volksgrenadiers came so close to breaking the task force that Orr said they could have done it by throwing in three more riflemen. Before Christmas dawn and the probable arrival of three more Germans, the 289th and 290th Regiments of the 75th Division reached the scene, and Rose of the 3rd Armored used them, along with part of the 517th Parachute Infantry, to create some approximation—though hardly the full reality—of a continuous line. The men of the 75th had a harsh introduction to combat, with deep snow, bitter cold, and frostbite and trench foot to accompany the ferocity of an enemy whose last great gamble was turning against him; but the 560th Volksgrenadiers were at least as weary as they were desperate. The American front at last held from Grandménil to the Ourthe.

Moreover, while the Volksgrenadiers were expending their dying energies against this front, on Christmas Eve Task Force Hogan at last destroyed its serviceable vehicles and marched stealthily away from the ground where it had been encircled since December 21.

Christmas Eve and Christmas Day might well be judged the times of severest crisis in the Ardennes battle. At Bastogne, the encircled garrison inventoried its scarce ammunition on the evening of December 24 and wondered whether there was enough to hold off the next morning's attack, for which they had watched the Germans preparing all day. Would help or the end of the ammunition supply arrive first? At Manhay, the panzers rolled out of the Holy Night and drove the 7th Armored from the crossroads on the way to Liège. Just to the west, the 3rd Armored stretched so thin to fend off the 560th Volksgrenadiers that Colonel Orr thought the Germans could take the game with less than a squad of additional riflemen. On Christmas Eve west of the Ourthe, where General Bolling's 84th Division prolonged the front of the 3rd Armored's parent VII Corps, the Railsplitters lost Rochefort and much of the 3rd Battalion, 335th Infantry to Panzer Lehr on their right, while on their left the peripatetic 116th Panzer Division returned to the fray by infiltrating along the seam between the 334th and 335th Regiments to take high ground around Verdenne. By the time the Germans were discovered inside the American front, they had established themselves too strongly to be repelled without a major effort, and at Verdenne they had a springboard for a panther's leap on Christmas Day onto the Manhay-Grandménil-Hotton-Marche highway just northeast of Marche.

In fact, moving along forest trails during the night of Christmas Eve to position itself for joining a counterattack on Verdenne, Company K of the 334th Infantry stumbled upon enemy tanks still deeper inside the lines than they had been thought to be, in woods between Verdenne and Bourdon and thus practically on the highway. And the 2nd Armored farther west had been unable to forge a firm link with General Bolling's beleaguered men, while in its own front the 2nd sent out cautious fingers toward indeterminate numbers of tanks of the 2nd Panzer Division and Panzer Lehr between Rochefort and that last ridge overlooking the Meuse at Dinant.

The indecision that had become almost predictable in the 116th Panzer Division proved one of the first factors to shape a resolution of the crisis in the wide and dangerous area west of the Ourthe. Though in front of this division the Railsplitters stretched out thinly across a twenty-kilometer front even after their right flank was lopped off at Rochefort, the 116th failed to exploit the captured ridge of wooded high ground from Verdenne to the main highway at Bourdon. Instead, the Germans on Christmas morning seemed to be waiting for someone else to make something happen. While they waited, what happened was General Bolling's counterattack on Verdenne. In the now customary pattern, the Americans first softened the town with a powerful artillery concentration, which allowed the followup attack to move straight into the objective in short order. When two platoons of Company L, 333rd Infantry, found themselves menaced in the streets of Verdenne by superior numbers on three sides, Staff Sergeant Edward T. Reineke took careful aim at the commander of an enemy tank leading the charge against them, killed him, and then jumped onto the tank to lob a grenade into the turret. This exploit halted not only the tank but the worst of the German pressure. But many Germans remained holed up in buildings, and Christmas morning passed in another house-to-house battle to ferret them out. To add variety, two more German tanks lumbered toward the town about noon. Company B of the 771st Tank Battalion took them on, knocked out one, and was working on the other when seven more Panthers appeared. In an hour's fire fight, the American tank company eliminated them all.

The Railsplitters' recapture of Verdenne left the panzers farther on toward the vital highway still to be dealt with. These pocketed Germans took refuge in a declivity where it would be hard to get at them. The rim was high enough to prevent direct fire on targets inside, but if tanks climbed over the rim and down into the pocket they would be targets before they could bring their own guns to bear. The Americans waited until December 26 to mount a predawn infantry assault, which failed. The 84th then gave over the rest of Boxing Day to presentations of 8-inch and 155mm. howitzer shells, mixed with the offerings of a chemical mortar company animated by incendiary intent.

Unaware that the Rochefort garrison had been overrun, General Collier's CCA of the 2nd Armored Division planned to drive there from Buissonville on Christmas morning to relieve the place, and in the process to strangle the line of communication nourishing the 2nd Panzer Division spearhead that threatened Dinant. It was not until early Christmas afternoon that the 2nd Armored learned the fate of Rochefort, but by that time CCA's mission was scratched anyway. Collier had collided with Germans of Panzer Lehr who were in the act of bolstering the 2nd Panzers' thin lifeline, and the outcome was a day of battle around the towns of Humain and Havrenne.

Panthers had led Panzer Lehr columns into both towns about dawn. Humain, to the east of the Buissonville-Rochefort road, was simply outposted by American cavalry when the Germans arrived, and the cavalry had to run. At Havrenne, on the main road, a German officer wearing an American uniform and speaking American-accented English cleared an entrance into the town by ordering the first Shermans he met in the half-light of daybreak to return to their bivouacs. CCA soon recovered from this ruse, and superior numbers of Shermans chased a company of Panthers out of Havrenne, knocking out five of them.

Humain, however, represented a menace on CCA's left flank, or possibly to Marche should the Germans turn east, and a tougher problem to overcome. The Panthers there took shelter behind stone walls and throughout Christmas Day defied assaults by light tanks, tank destroyers, and finally reinforcements of Shermans. The Americans were roughly enough handled to decide that the town was decidedly misnamed. The resumption of action on December 26 revealed the reinforcement of Panzer Lehr by one of the fresh panzer divisions the G-2s had been warning about, the 9th Panzers. With evidently formidable added strength, the Germans sallied forth from Humain toward Havrenne and Buissonville again. General Harmon of the 2nd Armored responded by bringing all the artillery for miles around into a time-on-target concentration against Humain. The shelling seemed to dampen the enemy's enthusiasm for aggressive movement, but some Panthers and accompanying grenadiers had already reached Havrenne to open another combat there. Shermans, tank destroyers, and armored infantry had to repulse three separate attacks on Havrenne before night brought respite.

General Collins at VII Corps headquarters wanted to create a more ample buffer between the enemy and the Meuse by erecting an east-west defensive line along the L'Homme and Lesse Rivers. To that end the commanders involved decided during the night that CCA should resume its movement toward Rochefort on December 27 while Colonel Sidney R. Hinds's CCR came in to deal with Humain. Hinds proposed to encircle the place, sending his tanks around to the east, south, and west, while his armored infantry moved in from the north. When he closed this trap, the Panthers proved to have departed. Enough grenadiers remained to give CCR a full day's fight for Humain, but meanwhile the fighter-bombers were chopping up columns of German vehicles just to the south, and it was apparent that on the Rochefort front, too, the crisis had passed and the tide of battle had turned.

The final element of the Christmastide crisis, the shadow of the 2nd Panzer Division darkening the Meuse, had always possessed more drama than substance. To stick the pin representing the Schwerpunkt of Lüttwitz's XLVII Panzer Corps into the map practically at Dinant could frighten the fainthearted among the Allies and thrill the Führer, but what could happen next depended on the battles farther east fought by the 82nd Airborne, the 7th Armored, the 3rd Armored, the 84th Infantry, and the 2nd Armored's CCA and CCR, versus the 2nd SS Panzers, the 560th Volksgrenadiers, the 116th Panzers, Panzer Lehr, and the 9th Panzers. Still more, the outcome on the Meuse depended on Bastogne, as was to become more evident after Christmas than before. The 2nd Panzers near the Meuse could not roll on without additional strength and additional fuel, and stopping the Germans farther east deprived them of both.

As early as the evening of December 23, Allied intelligence had picked up a message from 2nd Panzer Division headquarters asking whether any fuel had been captured during the day. Montgomery saw this message as "the writing on the wall."[18] That night a jeepload of Germans in American uniforms turned up at Dinant, to be captured by the British, but the intercepted message explained why the panzers around Foy-Notre Dame, Celles, and Conjoux could accomplish nothing more threatening than such a raid. On December 24, these panzers became virtually inert.

Montgomery's expressed intent in moving Collins's VII Corps to the northwest flank of the Bulge had been to make it his striking force to counterattack. So far defensive battles had continued to absorb the elements of the corps as rapidly as they reached the front. While Collins never ceased searching for the opportunity to seize his corps's intended purpose, Montgomery was now applying a restraining leash, because he did not think the whole First Army front was stable enough as yet to permit lashing out at the enemy. Montgomery also believed that more of the enemy's reserves were still to be heard from; he did not want to entangle any troops prematurely in offensive action when he might need all the reserves he could find to deal with additional enemy strength.

The idleness of the 2nd Panzer Division's spearhead on December 24 struck General Harmon as an invitation to his uncommitted CCB, 2nd Armored to attack. In midafternoon Harmon telephoned VII Corps headquarters to ask permission to do so. Collins happened to be away visiting subordinate command posts, and the corps artillery chief, Brigadier General Williston B. Palmer, took the call. Knowing Montgomery's views, Palmer told Harmon to wait until Collins's rounds brought him to 2nd Armored headquarters; it was too late in the day to attack before Christmas anyway. Palmer felt sorry to have to discourage Harmon, however, and he was looking for a possibility of reversing himself when, a few minutes later, he received another call, from the First Army chief of staff, General Kean. Kean told Palmer that Collins was now authorized to commit his entire corps and to change his defensive line. He further told Palmer, guardedly, to look on the map for a town "H" and a town "A." Finding on the map what he wanted to find, Palmer saw the towns Le Houisse and Achêne south of the 2nd Armored. He decided to get back to Harmon. But the line to 2nd Armored headquarters had gone dead, so Palmer sent his aide looking for Collins with a message about Bill Kean's call:

> Bill was extremely guarded but indicated strongly that new dispositions would call for you to secure your west flank by preventing hostile movement to north or east of Meuse, mentioning a "pivoting move" and inviting attention to an "H" and an "A" (Le Houisse and Achene?)
> Commitment of 2d Armd Div for purpose of anchoring flank appeared to be what he was driving at.[19]

Meanwhile Kean experienced misgivings over the possible interpretation Palmer might have derived from his efforts to veil his meaning from prying enemy ears, so he telephoned the VII Corps again. "Now get this," Kean told Palmer. "I'm only going to say it once. Roll with the punch." A First Army staff officer would follow in person with more specific instructions. The notion of rolling with the punch sent Palmer's eyes backward on the map, to where he was appalled to find the towns Huy and Andenne on the Meuse. Hastily, he sent another messenger to find Collins: "He meant pivot *back*.

You can use Ernie [Harmon] any way you need but roll with the punch. Bolling says positive dope he gets socked tomorrow on his weak left. You better come home!"[20]

The second messenger caught up with the corps commander at Harmon's headquarters, where Collins and Harmon had responded to Palmer's first message by drawing up a plan for a 2nd Armored attack. Collins went home, but he also told Harmon to execute the plan unless he was instructed otherwise.

Presently the messenger from the First Army reached Collins's headquarters, confirming that the VII Corps was to remain on the defensive and indicating that Collins was authorized, at his discretion, to fall back on Hotton and Andenne. Montgomery and Hodges had agreed that the First Army front must be shortened and consolidated; this was the night, of course, when the 82nd Airborne was withdrawing to the straight line Trois Ponts-Manhay.

Collins consulted his staff, who agreed with him that the defensive and a retreat were not necessary for safety. Bolling's 84th Division indeed expected to be socked next day, by the 116th Panzer forces that had penetrated around Verdenne; but Collins was confident the Railsplitters could hold. To retreat would protect Liège, but at the cost of greater danger to Namur and the Meuse crossings farther south, particularly Dinant. Collins decided that the 2nd Armored Division should advance as planned. He was accustomed by now to proceeding as though the real command post of the First Army was the headquarters of the VII Corps.

Thus Harmon's CCA opened its abortive but nevertheless rewarding ride toward Rochefort, while Brigadier General Isaac D. White's CCB prepared to hit the 2nd Panzer concentration near the Meuse. Collins and Harmon had planned to divide White's combat command into two task forces to envelop and annihilate the German force around Celles. Task Force A would proceed from Ciney down the Achêne road, capture the Bois de Geauvelant west of the road between Achêne and Celles, and assemble on high ground southwest of Celles for a final assault. Task Force B would go from Ciney down the Conjoux road and circle through Trisogne to envelop Celles from the southeast. The 82nd Armored Reconnaissance Battalion would screen the right flank of the CCB sweep.

At Foy-Notre Dame, this reconnaissance battalion of the 2nd Armored Division encountered its equivalent in the German army, the Reconnaissance Battalion of the 2nd Panzer Division. The relatively fresh American unit had all the best of a fire fight with the overstrained Germans, capturing or destroying nineteen vehicles and one self-propelled gun and taking almost 150 prisoners, including the German battalion commander.

Meanwhile Task Force A rolled along past the Bois de Geauvelant, meeting virtually no opposition until it drew some fire from a farm off toward Foy-Notre Dame. Accompanying Lightnings flushed out four Panthers and silenced the trouble, at least for the time being. More Panthers turned up near Boisselles, but armored infantry were able to deal with them. By the middle of Christmas afternoon, the task force was firmly established on the desired high ground, blocking the roads west and southwest from Celles.

Task Force B even more readily swept its way to a ridge just southeast of Celles. The two task forces then converged on Celles and easily cleared the town. The enemy armor had pulled its horns back into woods to the northeast toward Conjoux, but the trap was closed. Harmon ordered White to scour the forest the next morning.

Artillery and mortars sprayed the woods with fire during the night. The 67th Armored Infantry Regiment turned back a breakout effort by panzer grenadiers with the capture of almost 300 prisoners, many of them not Germans but Poles. While White's armored infantry began beating the bushes in the morning to eliminate the surrounded Germans, several enemy attacks tried to punch into his circle from the south to reestablish contact with the pocket. Finding his hands full holding off some big German tanks in these attacks, White called on the nearby British 29th Armoured Brigade to arrange for help from rocket-firing Typhoons. Because American radios did not work on the same frequency as the British fighter-bombers, an American Cub liaison plane led the Typhoons to their target, where they destroyed seven of the panzers and chased off the rest. Thereafter White's sweep of the forest pocket proceeded without serious interruption. The woods and underbrush made for tough enough going that the effort had to extend into December 26, but the rewards were ample. Some 600 Germans escaped on foot, as the Americans learned later, but along with similar numbers of captives the 2nd Panzer Division lost all the equipment of its reconnaissance battalion, the 2nd Battalion of the 3rd Panzer Regiment, the 304th Panzer Grenadier Regiment, and three artillery battalions, as well as two-thirds of the equipment of the division flak battalion.

Altogether, in CCB's envelopment of Celles and the concurrent actions of CCA and CCR, mostly against the 2nd Panzer Division, the 2nd Armored lost 17 killed, 201 wounded, and 26 missing, seven light tanks, and twenty-eight mediums, twenty-six of the latter being returned to action by New Year's Day. The opposing 2nd Panzer Division lost 82 of the 100 or so tanks it brought into the battle, 83 assault guns and artillery pieces, 441 other vehicles, and 116 other heavy weapons, along with about 550 killed and 1,213 captured. The spearhead of Hitler's Ardennes offensive was gutted; there would be no German crossing of the Meuse; and no higher headquarters would question Collins's bold decision for an early turn to the counterattack.

General Eisenhower had hoped from the beginning that his forces might crush the whole of the Fifth and Sixth Panzer Armies as Collins had now wrecked 2nd Panzer Division. To accomplish the goal, however, would almost certainly require from other commanders a boldness comparable to Collins's; but so far in the counterattacks that quality had remained in short supply, as usual.

29: Attack in the Ardennes (II)

WHO ELSE besides Collins would respond to the occasion with boldness? There were two others who might claim to be the most imaginatively aggressive senior commanders in the Allied armies. But, in the counterattacks in the Ardennes, Patton's undeniable aggressiveness was stumbling again over unimaginative execution—the head-on, broad-front attack which through the autumn had too often tarnished Patton's laurels of the summer; while, in command of American troops, Montgomery's very aggressiveness itself was in strange abeyance.

Until now, throughout the European campaign the only risks that Montgomery had been unwilling to accept were those that might jeopardize the irreplaceable manpower of the British army, and thus Britain's claim to world power. Whenever the Allies could act boldly without bleeding away the Second Army, Montgomery had consistently championed boldness, from his support of the COBRA design to break out of Normandy, to his lonely opposition against diverting large forces west into Brittany, to his single-thrust design for the invasion of Germany and its MARKET-GARDEN variation in particular. Why he should have lapsed into cautiousness now is difficult to fathom, for the offensive instrument he held in his hand was not the fragile British Second Army but the American First and Ninth Armies. Did he simply so much distrust the military capacities of the Americans?

Did he, furthermore, genuinely believe what he said about a horrifying chaos in American command when he took over the First Army? Perhaps the German breakthrough had shaken whatever confidence he had developed, if not in the American soldier, then at least in American command and its ability to respond to his direction in the attack with the precise skill he expected of British officers. Perhaps long-standing British distrust of the professional qualifications and experience of American officers, muted in Montgomery by his close association with Americans since Sicily but always nourished by his patron Brooke, returned to vigor after the shock of the American defeats in the Ardennes.

When he took command of the First Army, Montgomery reported to Eisenhower that physical exhaustion might require some changes in command, though he was unwilling to relieve American commanders personally. Eisenhower replied that he should be apprised of any necessary changes, and he told Montgomery that "Hodges is the quiet reticent type and does not appear as aggressive as he really is. Unless he becomes exhausted he will always wage a good fight."[1] Apparently Hodges in particular raised Montgomery's doubts—though the field marshal responded to Eisenhower's reassurance by saying that while Hodges had been a bit shaken at the beginning and was very tired and in need of moral support, he was improving.

On December 20, Eisenhower asked Montgomery for his "personal appreciation of the situation on the north flank of the penetration particularly with reference to the possibility of giving up, if necessary, some ground on the front of the First Army and to the north thereof in order to shorten our line and collect a strong reserve for the purpose of destroying the enemy in Belgium." After his meeting with Hodges and Simpson that day, Montgomery replied: "I have every hope that we shall be able to restore the situation and I see no need at present to give up any of the ground that has been gained in the last few weeks by such hard fighting."[2]

This exchange is noteworthy in light of Chester Wilmot's allegation that it was habitually the American commanders who failed to emulate the laudable flexibility of their British coadjutors in willingness to yield ground, and particularly that the emotional source of American inflexibility lay in the desire to hold ground just because it had "been gained in the last few weeks by such hard fighting." At this early juncture it was also Eisenhower who, more willing than Montgomery to yield ground, was also more cautious than Montgomery about counterattacking too soon, especially fearing that Patton might go off half-cocked before a general, coordinated counteroffensive could get under way. Patton's "attack must be [by] phase lines with all forces held carefully together as to avoid dispersion and waste in strength before Montgomery can join the attack from the north."[3] Montgomery in contrast was insisting that Lightning Joe Collins must be hurried to the northwest flank of the Bulge to prepare a prompt counterattack.

During the next few days, however, the Supreme Commander and the field marshal reversed positions on these matters. After watching the First Army in continual retreat, Montgomery grew not only cautious, but even pessimistic. On December 22, he lamented: "From information available here I am not optimistic that the attack of Third Army will be strong enough to do what is needed and I suggest Seventh German Army will possibly hold off Patton from interfering with the progress westward of Fifth Panzer Army. In this case I will have to deal unaided with both Fifth and Sixth Panzer Armies. . . ." The next day Montgomery expressed his concern "at the weak local arrangements, particularly in infantry, of most of the divisions in the First and Ninth Armies."[4]

The next day, December 24, Montgomery insisted on the straightening and shortening of the XVIII Corps front, a sound tactical decision but also a reflection of the discouragement that led him to an insistence on the strict defensive and produced the confused interchange among Harmon, Palmer, Kean, and Collins.

On Christmas Day, when Collins allowed Harmon to counterattack despite 21 Army Group's instructions with such successful results, Montgomery was conferring with Bradley and pronouncing a counterattack by the First Army for the time being out of the question. In the kind of labored journey necessitated by the Bulge and the rumors of roving German assassins, Bradley had flown on Montgomery's invitation from Étain, some distance from his Luxembourg headquarters but the nearest airport deemed secure, to St. Trond, another small airport that was the best available for reaching Montgomery's command post. The travel arrangements were so uncertain that Bradley twice threatened to call the whole trip off and go home, the second time when there was no one to meet him at St. Trond. Bill Sylvan of Hodges's headquarters then showed up to drive Bradley to Montgomery. In further evidence of everyone's uneasiness, the signs pointing to 21 Army Group headquarters led only to a military police post, where "a tall slim sergeant washing out his messgear offered to show us the way."[5] These inconveniences as well as more profound causes probably did much to explain why Montgomery thought Bradley looked thin, worn, and ill at ease. Ever the master of tactful reassurance, Montgomery chose to cheer Bradley by remarking that if the single-thrust plan had been followed, none of the current troubles would have occurred; but "now we are in a proper muddle." "Poor chap," Montgomery described Bradley to Brooke; "he is such a decent fellow and the whole thing is a bitter pill for him."[6]

Nevertheless, neither his own travel fatigue and deeper disappointment nor Montgomery's crocodile tears and condescension prevented Bradley from urging more aggressive operations than Montgomery by now was willing to adopt. Bradley said the German offensive had spent itself and the moment had come to strike back. As Patton reported the conversation after Bradley summarized it for him, the field marshal rejoined that the First Army would be too weak to attack for at least three months. In the interval, the only offensive effort would be the Third Army's, yet Patton's army was also too weak for the tasks expected of it. To accumulate a sufficient reserve for Patton's plunge into the south flank of the Bulge, the southern armies would have to fall back to the line of the Saar-Vosges or to the Moselle.

Allowing for the chance that Patton, Bradley, or both might have exaggerated Montgomery's timorousness in the telling, Montgomery's latest report to Eisenhower was little bolder. He told the Supreme Commander that regaining the initiative would require more troops, who could be found only by withdrawing to shorter fronts. The southern front should be examined with this problem in mind.

Bradley's own recollection in his memoirs was that he returned to Luxembourg much troubled by Montgomery's attitude, because the field marshal expected one more big blow from the enemy and was unwilling to counterattack until the Germans had thereby exhausted themselves. Reluctant to postpone a First Army attack to converge upon the Third, Bradley asked that the American armies be returned to his command, and suggested that to coordinate them he could move 12th Army Group headquarters to Namur.

The next day Bradley also wrote a personal letter to Hodges, carefully noting that he was not giving instructions and that Hodges remained subordinate to Montgomery, but emphasizing as an old friend that the commander of the 12th Army Group did not view events in so grave a light as the commander of 21 Army Group. Bradley expressed his misgivings over any plan to yield ground that might be useful for future operations. He realized that the First Army had been hit hard, but he believed the Germans had also suffered heavily and were now weaker than Hodges's forces. If the Allies could recapture the initiative, he thought the enemy "would have to get out in a hurry." He advised Hodges to study the battle for opportunities to drive back the Germans "as soon as the situation seems to warrant."[7]

Hodges had already opposed even a limited abandonment of territory. So of course had that other weighty figure in the First Army, General Collins, who turned up at Hodges's headquarters the next day, December 27, with three plans for the VII Corps to spearhead an attack. Two of them aimed at meeting Patton around Bastogne, while the third proposed to cut off the Bulge closer to its base, at St. Vith. As events developed, the First Army in fact yielded no more ground. The reader will have guessed Patton's reaction in the meantime to the notion of a Third Army retreat south of the Bulge.

Eisenhower had expected to travel on the 27th to visit Montgomery. He had hoped, indeed, to see the field marshal three days earlier, but the uncertainty of weather and security discouraged air travel, and driving would take too long. Now he intended to go by rail, but his train chanced to be bombed by the Luftwaffe on the night of December 26, and the journey was postponed yet another day. During the 27th, however, Eisenhower heard an oral report that Montgomery was now again willing to consider a counterattack, and the Supreme Commander surprised his staff by exclaiming, "Praise God from whom all blessings flow!"[8]

On December 28, Eisenhower and Montgomery conferred at last at Hasselt. This location represented still another hitch; fog and ice had prevented Montgomery from driving to Brussels, where Eisenhower intended to see him. A more serious hitch was the revelation that Montgomery's new willingness to counterattack had evidently been exaggerated. He was engaged in removing Collins's VII Corps from the line to reassemble it for its original counterattacking purpose; but he remained unwilling to strike before the enemy made one more, last-gasp effort to break through on the northern flank of the Bulge. Montgomery was certain that such an effort would ensue, and he was certain also that the condition of the First Army dictated that the Allies must wait until the Germans thus shot their last bolt. Eisenhower conceded that intelligence suggested the likelihood of one more German assault; but the trouble with allowing Allied plans to depend on it was, of course, that it might never come, and meanwhile Allied delay would allow the Germans to shore up the gains they had already made.

The questionability of German intentions nagged at the Allied command. Since December 16, Allied intelligence was understandably reluctant to climb out on limbs. The surprising capacity of the Germans to hoard reserves for that first blow left the intelligence specialists uncertain how many more divisions they might have stashed away. The day before Eisenhower and Montgomery met, the British Joint Intelligence Committee attempted another distillation of available data comparable to its December 22 summary. The only guidance was toward caution. "So far as land forces are concerned, it is difficult for us to give any worthwhile estimate as to how long the Germans can maintain their existing forces in the present battle or what line they can reach. . . . We have, at present, inadequate information as to enemy dumps and reserve stocks in the battle area; and we have no information as to enemy capture of Allied material." The German offensive had not yet reached either its immediate or its long-range objective, and so the enemy might well release additional reserves for a final lunge:

> It seems clear that the immediate German objective is the Meuse. We believe, however, that the long term planning for this enterprise and the strict conservation of resources over a period of time point to more ambitious ultimate objectives. The insistence that the G.A.F. should on no account destroy the bridges over the Meuse indicates an exploitation beyond this river. . . .[9]

Montgomery's intelligence staff saw in an aerial reconnaissance report of a concentration of 500 enemy vehicles evidence that the 12th or perhaps the 10th ss Panzer Division was still moving up to add striking power to the north flank. "Northern line now takes firm shape with Panzer Divs stretched all along with possibility scraping together 1 more Corps behind to deliver next breakout." Though further German attacks might not be militarily sound, "Politics demanded another enemy bang though militarily he has failed in larger purpose. Model's known impulsiveness not to be disregarded. Another attempt by 2 ss Corps and 58 Corps to cross Ourthe likely and enemy possession of Hotton useful. [The enemy did not possess Hotton; that he did was for some reason a common misconception at higher headquarters.] May be essential clue. Note steady sid[e]step of Schwerpunkt left since offensive began."[10]

But the evidence pointing to another German lunge was by no means conclusive, and Eisenhower, though as his son writes he "had some sympathy with Montgomery's attitude," believed the Allies must resolve not simply to await the enemy. The Allies themselves must attack soon. As was customary with Eisenhower-Montgomery conferences, the Hasselt meeting reached no clear agreement. The most Eisenhower could achieve was to depart with an understanding that if the enemy did not launch his expected new attack by about January 3, then Montgomery would strike against the north flank of the Bulge.

Another customary result emerged from the Hasselt conference: the resurrection of that old Montgomery hobbyhorse, unified ground command. The field marshal might be uncertain about when to counterattack, but he was sure that he ought to command the counterattack—at least Bradley's army group as well as his own. His appetite whetted for the renewal of this familiar fray, Montgomery followed up the conversation with Eisenhower with a letter next day:

My dear Ike,

It was very pleasant to see you again yesterday and to have a talk on the battle situation.

2. I would like to refer to the matter of operational control of all forces engaged in the northern thrust towards the Ruhr, i.e. 12 and 21 Army Groups.

I think we want to be careful, because we have had one very definite failure when we tried to produce a formula that would meet this case. . . .

3. When you and Bradley and myself met at Maastricht on 7 December, it was clear to me that Bradley opposed any idea that I should have operational control over his Army Group; so I did not then pursue the subject.

I therefore consider that it will be necessary for you to be very firm on the subject, and any loosely worded statement will be quite useless.

4. I consider that if you merely use the word 'co-ordination,' it will not work. The person designated by you must have powers of operational direction and control of the operations that will follow on your directive.

5. I would say that your directive will assign tasks and objectives to the two Army Groups, allot boundaries, and so on.

Thereafter preparations are made and the battle is joined.

It is then that one commander must have powers to direct and control the operations; you cannot possibly do it yourself, and so you would have to nominate someone else.

6. I suggest that your directive should finish with this sentence: '12 and 21 Army Groups will develop operations in accordance with the above instructions. From now onwards full operational direction, control, and co-ordination of these operations is vested in the C.-in-C. 21 Army Group, subject to such instructions as may be issued by the Supreme Commander from time to time.'

7. I put this matter up to you again only because I am so anxious not to have another failure.

I am absolutely convinced that the key to success lies in:

(a) *all* available offensive power being assigned to the northern line of advance to the Ruhr;

(b) a sound set-up for command, and this implies one man directing and controlling the whole tactical battle on the northern thrust.

I am certain that if we do not comply with these two basic conditions, then we will fail again. . . .

> Yours always, and your very
> devoted friend
> Monty[11]

Eisenhower had intended that Montgomery's command of the American armies north of the Bulge should be temporary—command of the Ninth perhaps to continue until after the crossing of the Rhine, but the First to revert to Bradley as soon as the Bulge was erased. For security reasons the details of the change in command had not been made clear to the public, but enough was known to encourage the British press to suggest both that Monty had saved the Americans from the consequences of their follies and that he would rightly go on to lead all the Allies to victory. This newspaper theme had grown insistent enough by December 30, the day following Montgomery's engaging letter, that General Marshall felt obliged to cable Eisenhower that there were to be no concessions on the issue of command, and that "there would be a terrific resentment in this country" over long-run British command of the American armies.[12]

It had not required Marshall's encouragement for Montgomery's missive to stretch Eisenhower's temper at last to the breaking point. On December 31, the Supreme Commander sent Montgomery a copy of the SHAEF plan for resuming the offensive, with a covering letter that stated:

> You know how greatly I've appreciated and depended upon your frank and friendly counsel, but in your latest letter you disturb me by predictions of "failure" unless your exact opinions in the matter of giving you command over Bradley are met in detail. I assure you that in this matter I can go no further.
>
> . . . For my part I would deplore the development of such an unbridgeable gulf of convictions between us that we would have to present our differences to the CC/S. The confusion and debate that would follow would certainly damage the good will and devotion to a common cause that have made this Allied Force unique in history.[13]

Given the current American weight in the Allied war effort, referring unbridgeable differences between Eisenhower and Montgomery to the Combined Chiefs of Staff could produce only one result, the replacement of Montgomery. Several members of Eisenhower's staff, including Tedder and Bedell Smith, believed the time had come for such a showdown with the field marshal. Explicitly, their reason was Montgomery's supposed excess of caution; but Montgomery's hesitancy in attacking the north flank of the Bulge notwithstanding, the general charge of overcaution seems a polite rationalization for the decision that Montgomery's arrogance had become intolerable.

A talk with one of the British liaison officers at Bradley's headquarters had alarmed Montgomery's chief of staff about the rising feeling against the field marshal, and General de Guingand accordingly had telephoned Bedell Smith the previous day, December 30.

Because SHAEF headquarters had received Montgomery's letter of the 29th, the conversation with Smith alarmed de Guingand still more. He decided to fly forthwith from Brussels to Versailles to try to smooth the troubled waters. The weather had turned stormy again and the flight would not be easy, but de Guingand thought the emergency required persistence and risks. He reached Orly airfield late on December 30 after a journey through fog and snow and a final leg at treetop level along the Seine. At SHAEF, anger with Montgomery had simmered to the point of eruption. De Guingand found Eisenhower with the draft of a message to the Combined Chiefs, through Marshall, saying the chiefs would have to choose between Montgomery and himself.

De Guingand assured Eisenhower that Montgomery had no idea events had reached such a pass which, given the field marshal's insensitivity, was certainly true. The army group chief of staff urged postponing the drastic communication to the CCS until he could speak with Montgomery. Eisenhower and Tedder were disinclined to yield, but Smith displayed the patience and diplomacy habitually masked by his irascibility and persuaded them to give the generous, likeable de Guingand a chance; if ever a chief of staff complemented his master by embodying qualities the latter lacked, it was this one.

Montgomery soon received an urgent signal from his chief of staff saying de Guingand would fly to 21 Army Group tactical headquarters next day and that the two of them must talk. Returning to Belgium proved no easier than traveling to Versailles, but de Guingand reached Montgomery in late afternoon of the 31st for a candid conversation. Diplomacy was so little a part of Montgomery's qualifications for Allied generalship that he proved altogether astounded to discover that anybody at SHAEF was upset. Confronting the loss of his command, however, he could climb down quickly enough. He sent a message that Freddie de Guingand had already drafted for him:

> Dear Ike, I have seen Freddie and understand you are greatly worried by many considerations in these very difficult days. I have given you my frank views because I have felt you like this. I am sure there are many factors which have a bearing quite beyond anything I realise. Whatever your decision may be you can rely on me one hundred per cent to make it work and I know Brad will do the same. Very distressed that my letter may have upset you and I would ask you to tear it up. Your very devoted subordinate Monty.[14]

Eisenhower relented. He did no more than send Montgomery the stiff letter of December 31 already quoted, which crossed Montgomery's apology. Montgomery was chastened enough to have saved his job, but of course not enough to prevent his raising the command issue at least twice again later on, with the help of his almost equally tactless friend Brooke and the rest of the British Chiefs of Staff. For the time being, nevertheless, all concerned could go back to planning the Ardennes counterstroke.

Counterattack or Counteroffensive

One of the conditions without which Montgomery had predicted failure was "*all* available offensive power being assigned to the northern line of advance to the Ruhr." Here was a clue that Montgomery was not thinking about the Ardennes in terms of an offensive. His whole interest was in eliminating the Ardennes involvement to permit a prompt return to the offensive in the north against the Ruhr, the same design that had preoccupied him since the late summer, to be executed by his British 21 Army Group with as much American help as he could get.

In the Ardennes, Montgomery sought a counterattack, not a counteroffensive; he would pursue merely a tactical victory and proposed nothing larger. When the furor about command had blown over enough that he could comment on Eisenhower's outline plan, which had accompanied the Supreme Commander's letter of December 31, Montgomery regretted how long it was likely to take before the true offensive could follow a tactical victory in the Ardennes: "I suggest that tactical victory within the salient is going to take some little time to achieve and that there will be heavy fighting. . . . I also feel that after we have achieved tactical victory in the salient there may be a considerable interval before other offensive movements begin to develop. . . . "[15]

Eisenhower had something more in mind for the Ardennes than a tactical victory. It is true that he used the phrase in the outline plan he sent to Montgomery, saying he intended to leave existing command arrangements—Montgomery's command of the First as well as the Ninth Army—"undisturbed until tactical victory in the salient has been assured." But as early as December 20 he had told all three army group commanders that his intent in the Ardennes was "to take immediate action to check the enemy's advance and to launch counter offensives without delay on either side of the enemy salient with all available forces. In areas unessential to this main purpose I am prepared to yield ground in order to insure the security of essential areas and to add strength to our counter offensive." Eisenhower was thinking not merely of attack and tactical victory but of an offensive. In particular, he thought persistently about the offensive opportunity he had pointed out to the troops of the Allied Expeditionary Forces in a message to all of them on December 22. His object in the costly autumn battles had been to destroy the enemy armed forces, but the German defenses did much to frustrate this object. Now, "By rushing out from his fixed defenses," as Eisenhower told the troops, "the enemy has given us the chance to turn his great gamble into his worst defeat. . . . Let everyone hold before him a single thought—to destroy the enemy on the ground, in the air, everywhere—destroy him!"[16]

Eisenhower indicated he did not speak simply rhetorically of destruction when, in conference with Montgomery on December 28, and in his subsequent correspondence, he stressed that it was the opportunity for destruction that demanded a prompt counterblow on the north flank. The enemy, he wrote to Montgomery on December 29, must not be permitted "To introduce infantry divisions to hold as much of his present gains as he can, to withdraw his mobile forces into reserve. . . ." "Enemy action within the salient," he said to Montgomery on the 31st, "indicates his determination to make this battle an all-out effort with his mobile forces. *Therefore we must be prepared to use everything consistent with minimum security requirements to accomplish their destruction.*"[17]

Eisenhower wanted to exploit the opportunity created by the enemy in the Ardennes to destroy the German army west of the Rhine, especially its mobile forces. Montgomery's different design was merely, to quote the field marshal's words of a few days later, January 7, "to 'head off' the enemy from the tender spots and vital places. Having done this successfully, the next thing was to 'see him off,' i.e. rope him in and make quite certain that he could not get to the places he wanted, *and also* that he was slowly but surely removed away from those places."[18]

Eisenhower spoke of destruction. Montgomery spoke of slowly but surely moving the enemy away: slowly, because Montgomery retained so little confidence in the First Army command; surely, because Montgomery nevertheless was impatient to return to the only offensive business that truly interested him, the 21 Army Group offensive across the Rhine north of the Ruhr.

Within the First Army, Hodges, Collins, and Ridgway had difficulty dissuading Montgomery from the idea that when the counterattack came, it should be made at Celles, against the western tip of the Fifth Panzer Army. Montgomery's idea made no sense in terms of any large offensive purpose, particularly Eisenhower's purpose of destroying the enemy army. Montgomery sought no large offensive purpose. At that, to attack at Celles was so modest a method that Montgomery's preference for it can scarcely be explained, except as an expression of no confidence in the First Army's ability to accomplish anything more ambitious.

The obvious way to destroy the enemy armed forces within a salient is to lop off the salient at its base. By attacking at Celles, Montgomery would have chosen the opposite approach; but the American commanders did not choose to strike against the base of the Ardennes Bulge either.

Of course, the idea of doing so received consideration. Patton in particular argued that after the emergency project of relieving Bastogne, "I want to attack north from Diekirch," near the southeastern corner of the Bulge, to meet the First Army cutting southward from the northeast corner.[19] Collins wanted to shift his VII Corps east to attack the base of the Bulge from Malmédy. Bedell Smith, Hodges, and Gerow all favored the same principle. The problem, as usual, was the practical one: to make practice approximate obvious principle. Here was Clausewitz's problem of friction in war, that "Everything in war is very simple, but the simplest thing is difficult."[20] The Bastogne emergency had already pulled the greatest concentration of American troops on the southern front toward Bastogne. Not that Patton's concentration was a model application of the principle of mass against a strategic point; nevertheless, to attack from Diekirch would have required an awkward and time-consuming eastward shift of Patton's armored spearhead. This difficulty became aggravated in the last days of December, when firming up the 4th Armored Division's original tenuous connection with Bastogne necessitated committing the 6th Armored Division at Bastogne as well.

In addition, lopping off the salient at its base would have required the First and Third Armies to converge across a distance of sixty-five kilometers, the width of the base. The road net in this area was poor, especially leading southeast from the First Army shoulder on the Elsenborn Ridge. When they studied the problem, Hodges's commanders, Collins among them, had to conclude that the roads that far east would not support a swift, heavy armored stroke. The uncertainty of the winter weather aggravated the road problem and apparently decided Bradley against trying to cut the base. With the weather uncertain, air support as well as armored movement would of course also be uncertain, and Bradley feared a prolonged slugging match only slowly closing the shoulders of the salient. There might be a better chance of trapping more Germans by moving more swiftly if the Bulge were struck at its waist. On December 27, Bradley proposed to Eisenhower a Third Army drive from Bastogne and a First Army drive toward St. Vith, to meet around Houffalize. He was careful to note that this design was not Patton's, for the Third Army commander still preferred to go for the base of the salient.

In the Eisenhower-Montgomery conference of December 28, Montgomery seemed uncertain about the proper place as well as the timing of the northern drive, but he was receptive enough to an attack toward Houffalize that Eisenhower telephoned Bedell

Smith saying there appeared to be great possibilities in a Bastogne-Houffalize convergence. Montgomery would proceed with the relief of Collins's formations west of the Ourthe to permit a buildup of the VII Corps to attack toward Houffalize. Eventually, on the last day of December, the field marshal gave his definite agreement for the VII Corps, followed by the XVIII, to attack toward Houffalize and St. Vith respectively, beginning January 3.

Not only did Eisenhower propose to cut the waist of the salient using *"everything consistent with minimum security requirements to accomplish their* [the Germans within the salient] *destruction,"* but, unlike Montgomery, who wanted to drop Ardennes activity in favor of the offensive across the lower Rhine as soon as possible, he also proposed to convert counteroffensive victory in the Ardennes into the foundation of an offensive thrust into Germany. Since he hoped the Ardennes battle would end with an American concentration and a German vacuum in the area, Eisenhower proposed now to invade Germany through the Ardennes and across the Eifel after all—the route that had been deliberately neglected in the autumn.

Eisenhower's outline plan of December 31 called for Bradley to resume command of the First Army as soon as the First and Third Armies met within the Bulge: "Thereafter First and Third Armies to drive northeast on general line Prum-Bonn, eventually to Rhine." Montgomery would be allowed to retain the Ninth Army for 21 Army Group's offensive across the Rhine north of the Ruhr. The First and Third Armies would reach the Rhine south of the Ruhr in tandem and by way of the Ardennes and the Eifel.[21]

As Eisenhower's thinking was developing, furthermore, Hodges's and Patton's armies would then cross the Rhine and drive into Germany not in the Cologne-Bonn area just south of the Ruhr in support of Montgomery, but through the more favorable terrain of the corridor running from Frankfurt to Kassel. If the German army, and especially its mobile forces, could be destroyed in the Ardennes, then the rapid conquest of the Ruhr would become less urgent, because in any event there would be nothing to stop Hodges's and Patton's armies from driving swiftly across all Germany to a meeting with the Russians. For this purpose, the Frankfurt-Kassel corridor would provide the best opening. Though Eisenhower assured Montgomery and all concerned of the continued priority of Montgomery's northern offensive—and he could point to Montgomery's retention of the Ninth Army as an earnest of his sincerity—the battle of the Ardennes was drawing American strategy not only into the hitherto neglected Ardennes and Eifel, but southward toward the route into Germany that Patton had advocated all along.

But while it was the German counteroffensive that now provided the starting point for Allied strategy, it was the Allies who were shaping the strategy of the war again. They had regained command of the battle, and in such a way that they could discern the favorite desideratum of American strategy—the destruction of the enemy armed forces— just beyond the horizon.

The Battle of the Bastogne Corridor

Eisenhower was impatient to get rolling with the offensive to pinch off the salient. When he telephoned Bedell Smith on December 28, following his conference with Montgomery, and spoke of the favorable prospects for converging attacks on Bastogne and Houffalize, he tried to give impetus to the southern thrust by releasing to Bradley two divisions from SHAEF reserve. They were General Kilburn's new 11th Armored and

General Culin's 87th Infantry; Culin's division had gained brief battle experience with the XX Corps in Lorraine during the autumn. Bradley persuaded Patton to assign the two divisions to Middleton's VIII Corps, to afford Middleton the necessary muscle to attack in conjunction with a renewal of Millikin's III Corps drive on December 31. The effect again was to pull Patton's center of gravity farther west than he would have liked, though the Third Army commander tried to compensate by ordering Eddy's XII Corps to prepare itself for an eventual attack across the Sauer and northeast through Prüm. Meanwhile, from December 27 onward, General Baade's veteran 35th Division joined the III Corps battle at Bastogne, inserted between Gaffey's 4th Armored and Paul's 26th Infantry Division. Beginning on the morning of December 31, Millikin would kick off a strengthened effort to fortify the link with Bastogne and to drive on through Bastogne toward St. Vith. Middleton on Millikin's left would begin pushing around the northeast of Bastogne toward Houffalize.

The Third Army would need its new, extra muscle, for a reason directly related to the rather anticlimactic nature of the VII Corps's recent battle with the Fifth Panzer Army Schwerpunkt near the Meuse. Evidence was mounting that the Germans were withdrawing strength from the western tip of the salient to deal once and for all with Bastogne. Their failure to capture Bastogne early had thinned their drive toward the Meuse while congesting the available roads even for the weakened forces that did move west beyond the road-junction citadel. Their inability to open the good roads through Bastogne contributed to the fuel shortage that almost paralyzed Manteuffel's spearhead. As Montgomery's intelligence chief put it sharply on December 27: "Value Bastogne as thorn very evident. Result enemy stuck."[22] If the enemy were to have a chance of getting unstuck, he must capture Bastogne.

CCB of the 4th Armored had established an additional contact with the Bastogne garrison by nightfall of December 27, enabling General Taylor to enter the town and resume command of his division. But the Germans persisted in attacking the corridor between the Third Army and Bastogne with a ferocity that signaled they were not resigned to the lifting of the siege. During its first few days in the area, Baade's 35th Division was unable to draw abreast of the 4th Armored to build up a solid shoulder against enemy counterattack from the east. Yet more ominous was the Germans' accumulation of reinforcements.

After receiving his two new divisions, it was Middleton himself who had convinced Bradley and Patton that his corps ought to swing west of Bastogne and thus as much as possible avoid the congestion of the town, while as quickly as possible building up a shield west of it. To these ends, Middleton began pressing forward as early as December 27 with CCA of the 9th Armored Division, his right-flank element, to open the Neufchâteau road as the first step toward cutting the Bastogne-St. Hubert road. At first the VIII Corps enjoyed reasonably satisfactory progress, CCA capturing Villeroux on the night of December 27–28 and the next day emerging victorious from a hard fight at Sibret. But by December 29, CCA was stirring up German counterattacks, and the next day the source of stiffening resistance became apparent. The opening of the VIII Corps drive had begun pushing into the assembly area of German reinforcements. On December 30, furthermore, Middleton's men collided head on with the Germans' own counterattack against the Bastogne corridor from the west. When Middleton threw in the 11th Armored and 87th Infantry Divisions on CCA's left at dawn that Saturday, the VIII Corps promptly found itself entangled with Lüttwitz's XLVII Panzer Corps, the Führer Begleit Brigade and the 3rd Panzer Grenadier Division on Lüttwitz's left against CCA of the 9th Armored and CCB of the 11th Armored, Panzer Lehr coming up on the German right against the 11th Armored's CCA and the 87th.

Partly because Middleton had gotten his attack under way while Panzer Lehr was still in transit from the west, the VIII Corps at the very least held its own in this battle. Culin's 87th Division captured the crossroads village of Moircy as a first small step up the road that enters Houffalize from the west. The whole affray so distracted Lüttwitz that he made no impact against the Bastogne corridor.

But the Germans proved to have chosen December 30 for assaulting the corridor from the east as well, and there they were more ready to make their move and could accomplish more. The previous evening, Baade's 35th Division had entered the town of Lutrebois east of the Arlon-Bastogne road. In doing so, members of the 3rd Battalion, 134th Infantry happened to find a map showing the German attack plan for December 30. For some reason the map failed to reach higher American headquarters, and in the morning a Kampfgruppe of the 1st SS Panzer Division, soon followed by the 167th Volksgrenadier Division—yet more enemy reinforcement—came rumbling tanks foremost against the 35th Division in two columns, one heading for Villers-la-Bonne-Eau, the other for Lutrebois. At Villers-la-Bonne-Eau, the panzers not only captured the town but isolated Companies K and L of the 137th Infantry. Just north of Lutrebois they overran Company L of the 134th Infantry.

With the aid of XIX TAC and the 4th Armored—the guns of Gaffey's division were making their weight felt in the battles both east and west of the corridor—the Santa Fe Cross Division rallied, and the 1st SS Panzers ended up with another day of heavy tank losses; the Americans thought fifty-five. But the Germans had also eliminated three American infantry companies, driven a salient from Marvie to west of Villers-la-Bonne-Eau to Bavigne awkwardly close to the Bastogne-Arlon road, and forestalled any immediate contribution by the 35th Division to Patton's planned renewal of his attack.

For this big push scheduled for December 31, the plan had been that General Grow's 6th Armored Division would move through Gaffey's tired 4th Armored—which was down to forty-two tanks—and drive northeast out of the Bastogne perimeter. Meanwhile the 35th and 26th Divisions were to join in the attack on Grow's right. Naturally, Patton and Millikin were unwilling to let the panzer foray of December 30 spoil the whole scheme, so the 6th Armored rolled into battle as planned. CCA had to attack alone on December 31 because CCB had been held up when a misunderstanding forced it to share the Neufchâteau road with part of the 11th Armored. Nevertheless, the injection of relatively fresh but battlewise armor produced results as heartening to Patton as anything since December 26. CCA quickly captured Neffe and the adjacent woods, a bone of contention since the Germans first closed in on Bastogne half a month before. On New Year's Day, CCB joined in and captured Hill 510, which had frustrated the 101st Airborne on the first day of the division's entry into the battle for Bastogne. By midafternoon, Grow's tanks were through Mageret, to continue the reassuring litany of place names made well known when the Americans were going in the opposite direction.

But nowhere else on the III Corps front did Patton find much to cheer him. Trying to clear the Marvie–Villers-la-Bonne-Eau–Bavigne salient bound the 35th Division to a slugging match that persisted into the first days of January. This preoccupation of the

35th obliged the 26th Division to attack practically on its own, for it had no offensive support either on its left flank or on its right, where the loose connection with the XII Corps became looser still as terrain and the location of the resistance pulled the Yankee Division's direction of attack northwestward, back toward Bastogne. With the division flanks exposed, General Paul had to hold a regiment in reserve, and the attacking regiments had to move with their battalions echeloned rearward to guard the wings. Paul's men had crossed the Sûre on December 27, and their role in the army's December 31 attack was to be the breaking of the Wiltz-Bastogne road and thus one of the principal German lines of communication. But they had to face some of the roughest of the Ardennes terrain as they moved into the valley of the Wiltz River, together with a fresh German division—the 9th Volksgrenadiers—and roadblock after roadblock along the narrow, twisting routes of advance. One battalion after another wore itself out paying for a slow forward progress.

Despite thus having to carry the main III Corps thrust virtually alone, the 6th Armored Division was still gaining ground fairly rapidly on January 2; but its front had spread a good deal wider than armored-division doctrine would have allowed, the weather was turning stormy again to ice the roads and cut off tactical air support, and stiffening German resistance came close to isolating a tank detachment at Arloncourt and cost the 9th Armored Infantry Battalion 25 percent casualties in unsuccessful assaults across a little stream near Wardin. From the thickening of the enemy forces in front of Grow and elsewhere around the Bastogne perimeter, it required no special astuteness to conclude that the Germans were gearing up for one more counterattack, at least one more effort to throw the Americans back on the defensive and renew the siege of Bastogne.

A Southern Diversion

Furthermore, the Germans' December 30 attack on the Bastogne corridor barely missed coinciding with a major counterattack elsewhere on the Western Front, one purpose of which was obviously to divert Third Army troops from the southern flank of the Bulge and thus open additional German opportunities.

The shift of the bulk of Patton's army from the Saar to the Ardennes had left General Devers's 6th Army Group with a front of more than 300 kilometers. Eisenhower constantly worried about Devers's ability to hold it. Just as constantly, he urged Devers that if the Germans struck, he must be willing to sacrifice territory to maintain the integrity of his forces. Because as usual the Allies were receiving evidence that their own indifferent radio security was apprising the enemy of American movements, Eisenhower warned Devers and Bradley to "take every possible step to insure . . . the utmost possible secrecy" regarding the northward shift in the boundary between their army groups, "and that the fewest possible individuals in the command and staff setup are acquainted with the plans. Sixth Army Group should do everything possible to create the impression of an impending attack on the right flank of the sector."[23]

Eisenhower's concern was aggravated, and his exchanges with Devers touched with irritation, because the Colmar pocket added to Devers's vulnerability. This large German bridgehead and potential springboard for assault west of the Rhine, about eighty kilometers wide and deep, still existed, as the Supreme Commander saw it, because Devers had ignored his warnings in the autumn that the French First Army was not strong enough to eliminate it. Thus Devers had allowed the American Seventh Army to go off to other adventures without first securing its southern flank. Eisenhower's relations with Devers had none of the warmth or patience of the Supreme Commander's dealings with his friends in the 12th Army Group. Instead, there was a too-ready willingness to adopt an accusatory tone at the least hint of anything's going wrong.

The same weakness of the French First Army that had prevented its eliminating the pocket was now yet another cause to fear a German counterattack against the 6th Army Group. "The First French," Devers himself told Eisenhower on December 31, "is short approximately 8,000 Infantry replacements, is composed largely of Colonial Troops who are presenting a serious morale problem due to shortage of Officers with experience in handling Colonial Troops, and is badly in need of complete re-training and re-fitting. To bolster this army I am leaving the Third US Inf Div with it for the time being. . . ."[24]

In General Patch's Seventh Army, the situation at the end of December was not so much better. Patch's army had a front of nearly 200 kilometers, sixty-four kilometers along the Rhine and the rest facing the Saar. Allied headquarters calculated that the divisions of the Seventh Army held 15.1 miles each (the average French First Army division held 18.0 miles), in contrast to 12.4 miles per division for the Third Army, 8.0 miles per division for the Ninth Army, and 5.2 miles per division for the American First Army. "In Seventh Army," as Devers described it, "the 5 experienced Inf Divs are deployed facing the north, each occupying a frontage of from 10 to 15 miles. These Divisions are short approximately 9,000 Infantry and are in need of re-training and re-fitting. Although the need for replacements is immediate and compelling, none have been allotted for the month of Jan."[25] From left to right, the experienced divisions to which Devers referred were the 103rd, 44th, and 100th Divisions of Haislip's XV Corps and the 45th and 79th Divisions of Brooks's VI Corps. The 103rd and 100th were not all that experienced, so Devers could have depicted his weaknesses more dramatically had he wished.

He went on to depict further weaknesses that were severe enough. Three of his divisions, the 42nd, 63rd, and 70th Infantry, had arrived at Marseille early in December with only their infantry regiments and none of the normal divisional support; the War Department had accelerated their shipment in this stripped-down fashion in reponse to the autumn shortage of riflemen. On December 20, furthermore, to squeeze out infantry replacements for the Third Army for the crisis in the Ardennes, SHAEF had ordered these same three divisions stripped of their basic privates, that is, men normally included in tables of organization over and above specified job assignments as an advance provision for replacements; the basics usually constituted 10 percent of the table of organization strength of rifle companies or cavalry troops, since May 1944 half that proportion of the T/O strength of other units. Removing the basics from three of Devers's divisions yielded nearly 2,000 men for the Third Army but left Devers to continue his lament:

> Infantry Regiments of 42, 63 and 70 Divisions are being given intensive training, while at the same time being employed on organization of the ground and protection of the Rhine. These Regiments are short all basics and are not sufficiently trained for full scale combat operations.
> The 36 Div and 12 Armd Div are assembled west of the Vosges in SHAEF Reserve and 1 Combat Command of 14 Armd Div is in the reserve behind the XV Corps. The remainder of the 14 Armd Div is in reserve behind the VI Corps.
> . . . The rapid regrouping and movements required of Seventh Army by the

great extension of its front, coupled with the loss of 87 Inf, 12 Armd and 36 Inf Divs, have quite naturally brought about about a lack of cohesion that can only be corrected after all movements have been completed and troops and installations are again settled in their proper places. This will of necessity take time.[26]

There had been growing evidence of German intentions to attack the 6th Army Group. Prisoner interrogations, reports of rail movements, aerial reconnaissance, and above all ULTRA indicated a flow of replacements into the Colmar pocket throughout December and of reinforcements to the Saarbrücken area as well as Colmar late in the month. The special importance to Hitler of Devers's front along the sacred Rhine was probably signified by the reorganization of the defenders immediately along the Rhine on November 26, as Army Group Oberrhein; none other than SS Reichsführer Heinrich Himmler took command. Himmler not only had his separate army group, but he was independent of OB West.

While Himmler brought fanatical Nazism to the watch on the Rhine, significance of another sort, perhaps still more ominous for the Americans, attached to the return of Johannes Blaskowitz to his old command of Army Group G in place of General Balck on December 22. Army Group G still operated facing Patch's Seventh Army westward from the Rhine. Blaskowitz was a general who continually reappeared in critical commands, despite his notorious coolness toward the Nazis, on the simple ground of his military competence.

By Christmas Eve, Devers's intelligence had concluded: "Excellent agent sources report enemy units building up in the Black Forest area for offensive. Other indications for imminent enemy aggressive action exist. Imperative that all defensive precautions be immediately effective."[27] The most persuasive source was ULTRA. The likely dates were January 1 to 3. Devers flew to Paris to discuss the threat with Eisenhower. The Supreme Commander reiterated his theme that Devers should be prepared to yield ground. Eisenhower pointed particularly to the deep Lauterbourg salient where the Franco-German border, the West Wall, and the Seventh Army front all turned sharply west from the Rhine, as an area whose vulnerability exceeded its utility. Apparently he expressed an inclination to withdraw all the way to the Vosges, so Devers could release additional troops for the main battle in the Ardennes.

Devers believed no such drastic withdrawal was necessary. Nevertheless, he returned to his front to order rapid implementation of planning that was already under way, to prepare three fallback positions to which the forces in northern Alsace might retreat: the Maginot Line, several kilometers behind the Seventh Army penetrations of the West Wall; the Moder River from Wingen to Hagenau; and finally Eisenhower's preferred line, the Vosges. With a deference to French sensibilities about Alsace lacking in Eisenhower's current preoccupation with the Ardennes, Devers added to his instructions the proviso that Strasbourg and Mulhouse were to be retained if at all possible.

By the last day of 1944, when Devers wrote the assessments of his forces quoted above, the 6th Army Group expected the blow to fall that night or at least on New Year's Day. Devers's intelligence counted seven German infantry divisions in line on Army Group G's front with three panzer divisions, lately refitted, in reserve. This enemy force of fair to good divisions could be augmented quickly by three to five lower-quality divisions. The most dangerous threat would be a drive by Blaskowitz down the Low

Vosges toward Saarburg and Saverne, to expose the rear of the whole Rhine front north of the Colmar pocket. The Low Vosges would form a barrier fifteen kilometers wide against rapid reinforcement east and west along the Seventh Army front in the face of such a drive. Very likely, Blaskowitz's main attack might be combined with assaults out of the pocket, to keep the French busy and to enhance the danger of isolating the Lauterbourg salient. It seemed not unlikely that the enemy might also mount a direct strike across the Rhine against Strasbourg.

Devers's G-2 served him well. On New Year's Eve, Patch conferred with Haislip of the XV Corps and Brooks of the VI Corps at Haislip's command post at Fénétrange, reiterating that they could expect to be hit that night. One hour before midnight, without artillery preparation, the enemy began advancing from the north: NORDWIND was the codename he had given this attack.

The heaviest blows, delivered by the XIII SS Panzer Corps and spearheaded by the 17th SS Panzer Grenadier Division, struck General Dean's 44th Division in the center of Haislip's line between Sarreguemines and Rimling, aiming toward the much-contested Rohrbach road junction. Another German assault, south and southeast from Bitche, carried somewhat less power—it was mounted by the less formidable 256th and 361st Volksgrenadier Divisions—but it scored deeper inroads because the Low Vosges were held lightly by a cavalry task force on the left flank of the VI Corps—the 117th Cavalry Reconnaissance Squadron plus part of CCR, 14th Armored Division, a tank destroyer company, and a chemical mortar company. By dawn of New Year's Day the task force was in rapid retreat, the 117th Cavalry Squadron having to extricate itself from virtual encirclement. The XC Corps of the German First Army kept up the pressure along the mountain chain, and by January 4 it had punched the "Bitche salient" some ten kilometers deep into the Seventh Army front, reaching as far as the town of Wingen on the Moder River.

Combined with the assault of the XIII SS Panzer Corps farther west, the XC Corps thrust clearly was intended not only to reach the Saverne Gap and thus cut the line of communication of Patch's troops on the Rhine and in the Lauterbourg salient, but more immediately to envelop General Burress's relatively new 100th Division, which lay between the 44th Division and the VI Corps. The Century Division had to bend its front into a right angle to accommodate itself to the salient on its east flank.

The 44th Division fought a seesaw battle through the first day of NORDWIND, suffering a penetration of its 71st Regiment, mustering a rally, and then falling into another retreat, which was accelerated when the Germans set fire to farm buildings where the 2/71st had hoped to anchor a stand during the second night of the battle. By January 3, however, Patch and Devers had scrounged up reinforcements for the threatened area from Bitche to Rohrbach, notably General Leclerc's 2ème Division Blindée, which Devers had taken the precaution of shifting from the perimeter of the Colmar pocket in response to the intelligence warnings of impending attack. On January 4, as Leclerc's CCL backstopped the XV Corps, the enemy used captured Shermans in a ruse against the French as they had done earlier against the Americans in the Ardennes, successfully enough to capture Gros Rederching on the seam between the 44th and 100th Divisions. But this miniature triumph proved almost a last hurrah west of the Vosges; Haislip's corps still had the toughness to absorb plenty of punishment and was not the most suitable target for a major attack against Patch's army. Meanwhile, Patch and Devers had decided they would pull the overstretched VI Corps back to the first line of their fallback positions, the Maginot Line.

By this time, however, the enemy was turning his main attentions on Devers's front to the weaker formations east of the Vosges. Eisenhower feared, furthermore, that even successful defensive stands by the 6th Army Group ultimately served the enemy's purposes, absorbing troops that ought to be available should SHAEF want them for the bigger battle in the Bulge. When he learned of the enemy's NORDWIND attack, the Supreme Commander chose to believe that he had expressed himself to Devers about the dangers of Patch's extended line emphatically enough that the Seventh Army should have withdrawn to the Vosges before it was hit. Eisenhower promptly ordered Bedell Smith to "call up Devers and tell him he is not doing what he was told, that is, to get the VI Corps back and to hold the Alsace Plain with rec and observational elements."[28] Eisenhower thought the German attack would taper off soon enough that such light troops might prevent any thoroughgoing German reoccupation of Alsace; if not, the risk had to be run for the sake of the Ardennes. On this point Smith expressed his disagreement before he put in the call, arguing that Devers should be told either to try to defend his existing front or to withdraw to the Vosges completely. Nevertheless, Eisenhower was insistent; so Devers had to instruct Patch to pull the main body of the VI Corps all the way back to the Vosges, leaving only reconnaissance forces in the Alsace Plain.

The predictable first result was a cry of anger and alarm from the French generals and the chief of the French government, because Eisenhower's decision exposed Strasbourg to recapture. Strasbourg since 1871 had become far too much the symbol of victory or defeat for all France, the very touchstone of the rivalry across the Rhine, to permit any such loss to occur. On more practical grounds, there was the consideration that immediately crossed Patton's mind despite his supposed political naiveté: "It will . . . probably condemn to death or slavery all the inhabitants of Alsace and Lorraine if we abandon them to the Germans."[29] At least it might so condemn 300,000 or 400,000 of them in the Strasbourg area who de Gaulle thought would face reprisals. Quick as had been his perceptions in the Ardennes, the Allied Supreme Commander suffered from odd blind spots concerning policy as well as personalities on his southern flank.

Forthwith, de Gaulle threatened to remove his forces from Eisenhower's command if that proved necessary to save Strasbourg. The two chieftains met face to face over the issue on January 3, and de Gaulle's intransigence provoked an outburst of the temper that lurked not far beneath Ike's famous smile. The discharge of anger nevertheless helped ease Eisenhower's mind so he could rethink the problem, including the dangers that French discontent could pose for orderly Allied communications. The Supreme Commander agreed that the withdrawal of the VI Corps should be limited so its right wing would go on holding some distance north of Strasbourg.

Patch as well as General de Lattre and the French had been urging Devers that the abandonment of Strasbourg was required by no military necessity, Patch arguing that the simple withdrawal to the Maginot Line would leave Strasbourg covered while at the same time affording prepared defenses better than anything to the rear. Devers was at Patch's headquarters fending off this reasonable plea when Eisenhower's change of orders arrived. Patch could now do as he wished. The XV Corps was to continue defending in place; the VI Corps was to defend along the Maginot Line east to the Rhine and thence to bend southward, while continuing to prepare further defensive positions in the rear. The French First Army meanwhile would extend its responsibilities northward to encompass Strasbourg.

For a short time amidst the changing orders, Strasbourg lay practically undefended. Such evidence of Allied indecision may have encouraged Blaskowitz to attack from Wissembourg into the Alsace Plain, as he did beginning January 4, replicating one of the 1870 invasion thrusts. In addition, a portion of Himmler's army group crossed the Rhine near Gambsheim north of Strasbourg on January 5. Two days later, Army Group Oberrhein also began attacking against the French northward toward Strasbourg out of the Colmar pocket.

When General Brooks of the VI Corps learned of the Gambsheim thrust, he telephoned Wyche of the 79th Division, commanding in the area: "Get in there and get it—get it cleaned up—it's got to be cleaned up pronto—we can't let it get built up there." Something of the political sensitivity of anything at all near Strasbourg had communicated itself to the whole army group. But Wyche's long front along the arc of what remained of the Lauterbourg salient was fleshed out with Task Force Linden, the infantry elements of the 42nd Division, of which Brigadier General Henning Linden was commander; and notwithstanding its World War I fame as the Rainbow Division, the 42nd had suffered training difficulties this time around and would not have been given a share of the front without additional training except for the emergency. Wyche soon had to telephone Brooks that with the 42nd's "state of training, organization and operation," the fight around Gambsheim was developing badly: "I'm very sorry to have to present this situation, but that's the way it is."[30] Wyche's own Cross of Lorraine Division could not bolster Task Force Linden adequately to assure containing the Gambsheim bridgehead, because an obviously encouraged enemy was accelerating his pressure on Wyche's 315th and 313th Regiments, his left and center, from Wissembourg in the north as well as out of the Gambsheim bridgehead. Spearheading the pressure came no less redoubtable a foe than the 10th SS Panzer Division, with the 21st Panzer Division, the 7th Parachute Division, and the 25th Panzer Grenadier Division as coadjutors.

The 10th SS Panzers were newly released from OKW reserve near Bonn, where they had sat idly with eight consumption units of POL throughout the Ardennes battle. But now, when they struck elements of Roderick Allen's new 12th Armored Division sent to backstop the 79th, their experience paid off against American inexperience. Despite skies clear enough for XII TAC Thunderbolts to fly 190 sorties and claim twenty-seven tanks, the panzers knocked out seventy of the 12th Armored's vehicles and united the Gambsheim bridgehead with the Army Group G advance. Under the Germans' one-two punch from east and north, Brooks and Patch reluctantly decided to withdraw the VI Corps still farther, from the Maginot Line to the Moder River line, following the Rothbach River from near the XV Corps right southeast to Pfaffenhoffen, thence along the Moder to Bischweiler and south to Hoerdt, the boundary with General de Lattre's army.

Retreating in gloom deepened by steel-gray skies and icy roads, the VI Corps formed along its new line on the night of January 20–21. The soldiers' bleak mood notwithstanding, the retreat had its advantages, as a miniature repetition of the German withdrawal to the Hindenburg Line in 1917. That is, an enemy who had been fully poised to attack was instead embarrassed by the vacuum before him, and in need of his own tiresome marches and regrouping before he could hit the new positions. Nevertheless, the Germans maintained close enough contact with Patch's harried troops that Devers hastened Dahlquist's 36th Division, recently released by Eisenhower from the SHAEF reserve he was trying to accumulate, to aid the 12th Armored against the continuing insistent probes of the 10th ss Panzers. Meanwhile, to make sure that the hardships of marching and regrouping imposed on the Germans were properly exploited, Devers and Patch also augmented Wyche's 79th Division and Frederick's 45th in the new line with the 103rd Division, shifted from near the XV Corps left. To stiffen the 103rd, moreover, they had a new division commander skillful and resolute in defensive stands—Anthony McAuliffe of Bastogne, moved up from assistant command of the 101st Airborne.

The enemy charged the Moder River line on the night of January 24–25 with six divisions pushing out three spearheads. Prisoners taken from them boasted that the swastika flag would fly over Strasbourg again by the anniversary of Hitler's accession to the Chancellorship, January 30. While the 10th ss Panzers slammed into the 242nd Regiment of Task Force Linden in the 36th Division zone, and the 7th Parachute and 25th Panzer Grenadier Divisions led the latest assault upon the 79th Division—also hitting hard at another fragment of the Rainbow Division, the 222nd Infantry—an additional particularly formidable adversary tested McAuliffe's 103rd, the 6th ss Mountain Division. If the enemy was tired out by his pursuit across the ice, everyone in the beleaguered VI Corps was also on the knife edge of exhaustion, and for two days the Battle of the Moder River was perilously touch and go.

But a counterattack by the 410th Infantry of McAuliffe's division on the morning of January 25 cut the road between a German Schwerpunkt at Schillersdorf and its supporting forces three kilometers north at Mühlhausen, an event not only important in itself but typifying the last-gasp resolution of Brooks's men. Late on January 25, the enemy relented. During the next few days, evidence mounted that he was withdrawing to other fronts many of his best formations—the 25th Panzer Grenadier Division, the 7th Parachute Division, the 21st Panzer Division. The VI Corps could begin to catch its breath, while Devers laid plans to reinforce de Lattre with a strong American corps, the new XXI under Major General Frank W. Milburn, to pull the Colmar thorn at last from his and Eisenhower's side.

The Destruction of the Bulge

Signs similar to those that heartened Brooks, Patch, and Devers had long since shown the Ardennes counteroffensive expended, despite indications to the contrary at the beginning of the new year along the Bastogne corridor. Those ominous indications had found such fulfillment as they were capable of during the predawn hours of January 4, when both the XLVII Panzer Corps and the I ss Panzer Corps attacked the Bastogne perimeter from out of the north. The direction of this attack, however, constituted in itself a certain confession of German weakness, since the most dangerous German move would have been to try to break the still-narrow corridor reaching from Bastogne southward, as Manteuffel had attempted on December 30 and as the Americans thought he would do again.

The Americans were eventually to learn that, indeed, the Germans chose to strike the northern part of the perimeter simply because, having tested the flanks of the corridor without success, they hoped the defenses might be weaker in the north. The 15th Panzer

Grenadier Division of Lüttwitz's corps, soon backed up by tanks and assault guns of the 9th ss Panzer Division of the I ss Panzer Corps, struck the 101st Airborne around Longchamps and east to the Houffalize road. They gave the tired airborne troopers a hard fight all through the morning of January 4, but they could force no appreciable gains. Across the Houffalize road to the east, the 12th ss Panzer Division and the relatively fresh 340th Volksgrenadier Division progressed somewhat better, driving the 6th Armored back far enough that Mageret and Wardin changed hands yet again. But behind the towns, Grow's tanks pulled up on high ground where with artillery support they repulsed the panzers. The number of panzer divisions represented by a not altogether impressive accumulation of tanks implied that in the Ardennes, too, the Germans were now scraping the bottom of their barrel of armor. They were; the Americans would later learn that together, the 9th and 12th ss Panzer Divisions had fifty-five tanks, only one more than there were in a tank battalion attached to an American infantry division. By late on January 4, it was the Americans who were again on the attack.

To be sure, expending their offensive power did not mean that the Germans had lost their proverbial stubbornness and resourcefulness in defense. The next day General Baade asked permission to suspend his 35th Division's counterattacks against the enemy salient around Villers-la-Bonne-Eau because he was accomplishing only the attrition of his own division. The 35th reverted to aggressive patrolling; the Third Army was already at work on new plans to deal with the Villers-la-Bonne-Eau salient anyway.

Patton's attacks into the southern flank of the Bulge had to grapple with the strongest German concentration remaining in the Ardennes; the presence of the 1st, 9th, and 12th ss Panzer Divisions meant that in his determination to extinguish Bastogne, the enemy had stripped the Sixth Panzer Army on behalf of the Fifth. This shift at least provided Montgomery with the consolation that when eventually he sent the American First Army forward, the opposing lines would be thin.

At the end of December, the halting of the 2nd Panzer Division, Panzer Lehr, and the 116th Panzer Division west of the Ourthe, and of the 2nd ss Panzer Division between the Salm and the Ourthe, freed Montgomery to reassemble Collins's VII Corps for the counterattack. On December 28, Macon's 83rd Division and the 53rd Welsh Division began relieving the 2nd Armored opposite the Germans' western spearhead. On New Year's Day, the 53rd Welsh relieved Bolling's 84th Division as well. Harmon's 2nd Armored and the 84th shifted eastward, as did the 83rd also when more of 30 Corps came up, so the VII Corps could attack between the Ourthe and Lienne Rivers to converge with Patton's forces upon Houffalize. Montgomery had accepted this scheme for breaking the salient at its waist; he had also accepted January 3 as the starting date. On that morning, Collins would attack on a front of some twenty kilometers, the 2nd Armored Division leading off and the 84th Division following on his right, the 3rd Armored leading off and the 83rd following on his left. His corps would have Major General Fay B. Prickett's 75th Division in reserve. Ridgway's XVIII Airborne Corps was to attack to keep pace on the left of Collins's VII.

Collins's initial objective was to cut the La Roche-Salmchâteau road, the east-west highway through the Baraque de Fraiture crossroads and one of only two primary east-west highways the Germans had been able to seize for their line of communication. To reach the highway, Collins's troops would have to cross the troublesome ground of the

Plateau des Tailles marshland, where the bogs, added to the woods and sharp declivities common to the Ardennes, would aid the German resistance as they had earlier aided the American. Deep snow now concealed dangerous marshes while impeding movement everywhere. The persistent bitter cold still froze the oil in the combatants' guns.

The shortage of roads had shaped the earlier battles for the Baraque de Fraiture. Now General Rose's 3rd Armored Division would begin with only one road to follow, while Harmon's 2nd Armored would have only the Liège-Manhay-Baraque de Fraiture-Houffalize highway plus one secondary road. Collins's intelligence found the II ss Panzer Corps waiting in opposition. The corps was reduced to the 12th and 560th Volksgrenadier Divisions and the 2nd ss Panzer Division, all much depleted.

As the G-2s anticipated, this enemy force could barely match weather and terrain in obstructiveness. January 3 dawned overcast as well as bitterly cold. The fighter-bombers of IX TAC could not fly in support. The other supporting arm even more vital to American armor and infantry tactics, the artillery, would also be muffled by lack of observation, as well as by woods and rugged ground. Where the tanks could find level, open, solid footing, they were able to move cross-country over the frozen fields; but so much of the area was marshland, forested, and hilly that the armor usually had to stay on the roads, which were icy. The Ordnance Department had tried all manner of expedients but had never developed either rubber or steel tank treads that would grip on ice. Again and again the narrow, steep, high-crowned roads presented sharp turns at the crest of hills, and whenever a tank attempted to make such a turn or to pass a stalled vehicle, it was likely to skid into the ditch bordering the road.

Except for minefields, German resistance was light. The VII Corps advanced about three kilometers on January 3, approximately to the crest of the Plateau des Tailles and halfway to the La Roche-Salmchâteau road. During the next several days, the weather was as bad or worse and the enemy stiffened. In temperatures dropping below zero, the few clusters of houses and farm buildings became prizes richly to be desired and therefore fiercely contested. Roadblocks had to be flanked by infantry laboring through drifted snow. Where bridges were broken, infantry had to cross icy streams to create footholds on the south bank, while the tanks waited and German artillery often made bridge-building impossible until nightfall. The infantry divisions, initially cast in a supporting role, had to attach regiments to the armor to lead the slow, slugging advance.

On January 6, Rose's vanguard nevertheless reached and cut the La Roche-Salmchâteau highway. Because the mainstay of the defense, the 2nd ss Panzers, opposed Harmon farther west and slowed his advance, at the highway Rose turned west toward the Baraque de Fraiture to push into the 2nd ss Panzers' rear. Ice as well as enemy resistance still made movement difficult even on the highway, and late on January 7 a new snowstorm came swirling in just as Rose's men reached the intersection that the Americans called Parker's Crossroads.

Fortunately for the Americans, other factors now began to offset the weight of both weather and Das Reich in this westerly direction. After a week on the defensive, the Germans appeared to be deliberately retracting their far western flank out beyond Collins's right, and their withdrawals were developing an unintended cumulative effect adverse to them, destabilizing their defenses in front of the right flank of the VII Corps. Finding the Germans shaken loose in their front, American patrols entered La Roche on January 10. By that time, the British on the opposite bank of the Ourthe reported they had lost contact with the enemy. Under the circumstances, losing contact was not difficult; the British had been advancing cautiously, pressing just hard enough to relieve the Americans from damaging artillery fire from west of the Ourthe, because Montgomery wanted to spare 30 Corps for other enterprises.

There was no similar slackening farther east. The 83rd Division required two days to clear the village of Bihain a short distance south of the La Roche-Salmchâteau highway and another day to repel counterattacks. The 517th Parachute Infantry on the right flank of the XVIII Corps did not begin making substantial progress until January 7, when it flanked an enemy force and thus opened a path southeastward to the Salm. Here it established an east-shore bridgehead on January 9. In front of the 3rd Armored and the 83rd, however, the Germans were not only fighting stoutly in the wide forested area southwest of Salmchâteau but reinforcing the 12th Volksgrenadier Division with the 9th ss Panzer Division, brought north again from Bastogne. All the while Collins tried to hasten the advance with his customary personal pushing of his subordinate headquarters from division command posts to the front; but the ice, the snow, the cold, and the wooded, broken, road-poor countryside, if not the enemy, precluded the armored breakthrough on the COBRA model that he had hoped to repeat.

Patton still suffered the additional frustrations imposed by a stronger enemy. On January 2, General Culin's 87th Division on the VIII Corps left had cut the Bastogne-St. Hubert road at Bonnerue, but more than a week was to pass before the toehold became at all secure against the persistent counterattacks of Panzer Lehr. On January 3, General Kilburn's 11th Armored Division on the right of the 87th fought its way into the crossroads town of Mande-St. Etienne on the same highway, closer in toward Bastogne. Mande-St. Etienne had been the division's objective since it entered the battle on December 29. Kilburn's men had gone into their first fight on the morning of the 29th with virtually no rest after a 135-kilometer forced march through ice and snow; by the time they had advanced a little over nine kilometers in four days and captured Mande-St. Etienne, they lost 220 killed and missing and 441 wounded, along with forty-two medium and twelve light tanks. As early as January 2 General Middleton had decided he had to take them out of the line for rest and refitting, but the commander of CCB appealed successfully to be allowed to finish the job at Mande-St. Etienne. Major General William M. Miley's new 17th Airborne took over for the 11th Armored late on January 3, attacked on January 4, and hit the German meat grinder so hard in its first venture that the next two days had to be given over to reorganization before the division could attack again: this although one of its regiments, the 513th Parachute Infantry, had served as a school troop unit at Fort Benning and was a select outfit chosen largely from the best graduates of airborne training. In the winter of 1945, the German army retained the skills to deal harshly with even the best American units entering combat for the first time.

There were GIs in General Van Fleet's 90th Division—though not many of the riflemen—who could remember bitterly a similar baptism of fire. But the 90th was a veteran division now, and Van Fleet was near the top among division commanders in ability and potential. Patton chose the 90th to break the German salient still driven deep into the center of the III Corps. The battle the 90th fought came to represent at least a small turning point. On January 9, Van Fleet attacked through the 26th Division along the southeastern edge of the German salient. The 6th Armored opened a converging attack from the northwest, later assisted by the 35th Division. Both the arrival of the 90th

Division and the attack itself surprised the 5th Parachute Division; the Third Army staff had devoted unusual care to keeping the movement of the 90th secret and to covering it with false radio traffic. Despite another snowstorm and the now-familiar inability of the artillery to fire to full effect or the fighter-bombers to fly, the 90th gained a couple of kilometers and on the next day reached high ground dominating the enemy's only escape route out of the salient. The Germans held off the northwestern attack, but nevertheless they had to begin withdrawing during the night of January 10–11. When the 90th and 35th Divisions met on January 12, they bagged over a thousand prisoners.

During the same night when the enemy began pulling out from the Villers-la-Bonne-Eau salient, the 87th Division on the VIII Corps front to the left at last entered the town of Tillet, for which it had been battling more than a week. Thereupon the Germans evacuated St. Hubert and commenced a general withdrawal from the Bastogne-St. Hubert road, though they covered their retreat with numerous roadblocks and minefields. Meanwhile General Middleton returned Gaffey's 4th Armored to offensive action after its few days' rest, and its advance moved out along the boundary between the VIII and III Corps to seize Bourcy, overlooking the Bastogne-Houffalize road where it ran through the old Noville battleground.

Patton had to suspend much of this promising effort abruptly on January 10. That day Bradley telephoned to say that Eisenhower wanted at least an armored division taken out of the lines and sent to the XX Corps around Saarbrücken, lest the Germans' southern effort, still straining Patch's Seventh Army, extend itself northward. Bradley agreed with Eisenhower; 12th Army Group as well as SHAEF intelligence had not yet recovered from the once bitten, twice shy mood that set in on December 16. Patton's intuition as well as his own information assured him there was nothing to fear, but a meeting with Bradley at Arlon failed to dissuade the army group commander. Since the 4th Armored at the moment had only one combat command engaged, the generals decided this division should turn around yet again. The only positive aspect of the incident was Patton's satisfaction at the speed with which his favorite division shifted toward Luxembourg. "This is the second time I have been stopped in a successful attack due to the Germans having more nerve than we have," Patton lamented; "—that is, not me, but some of the others."[31] The first time was when the 83rd Division was taken from him in November.

Far from plotting new mischief, the Germans more and more evidently were retracting their spearheads from the Ardennes to avoid entrapment there. No other explanation could account for the simultaneous slackening of resistance against both the First Army's right and the Third Army's left on January 10. SHAEF's and 12th Army Group's bogeyman cost the Third Army about two days spent mainly marking time, but on January 12 Bradley gave Patton the green light again, and the VIII Corps resumed its attack with the 11th Armored Division reinserted into the line, between the 17th and 101st Airborne.

Like the First Army, the Third found the going much easier on its western than its eastern flank. The 87th Infantry and 17th Airborne Divisions reached the Ourthe on January 13 and 14, respectively, against light opposition, while the 11th Armored and 101st Airborne still had to contest almost every kilometer near and on the Houffalize road. Nevertheless, Patton's and Hodges's armies were drawing near enough to Houffalize to be able to see each other's artillery flashes at night. The 83rd Reconnaissance

Battalion of Rose's 3rd Armored Division had found a route over back roads and trails into the rear of the tough woodland resistance of the 12th Volksgrenadiers and the 9th ss Panzers. On January 13 Rose's armor began navigating this route and cut the Houffalize-St. Vith highway. Now it was the Germans who had to move along back roads, to avoid immediate entrapment.

In the afternoon of January 15, Bolling's 84th Division took without opposition a hill commanding Houffalize. Already a patrol representing all the battalions of Bolling's 334th Infantry had crossed to the south bank of the Ourthe in rubber boats, hoping to meet the vanguard of the Third Army. They met no one but Belgian villagers and farmers through the afternoon and night, but a little before nine in the morning of January 16 Pfc. Rodney Heinz, second in command of the patrol, saw an American soldier outside a farmhouse when the members of the patrol were all supposed to be inside. The man belonged to the 41st Cavalry Squadron, of the 11th Armored Division. Somewhat later, about 11:40 A.M., a patrol of the same 41st Cavalry Squadron met a patrol of the 41st Armored Infantry Battalion of CCA, 2nd Armored, southwest of Houffalize.

The Americans had cut the Bulge at its waist. In accordance with Eisenhower's earlier decisions, command of the First Army reverted from 21 Army Group to the 12th Army Group at the close of the next day, midnight, January 17. Exactly one month after the German counteroffensive had begun, the Americans had repaired the rupture of the front. Unfortunately, however much the convergence of the First and Third Armies upon Houffalize might have seemed at the end of December to offer the most feasible means of trapping Germans, one more opportunity for a mass envelopment had slipped away. The slow progress of Patton's wide-front attack along the southern flank, the lateness of Montgomery's attack in the north—perhaps unavoidable, but with the field marshal offering no stimulus toward an earlier start—and the admirably stubborn resistance of the German army everywhere, all combined to permit the bulk of German forces and equipment to escape eastward before the trap closed.

The rupture had been repaired, but the enemy was not yet back at his starting line behind the Our, and lesser opportunities for trapping Germans still remained. The gorge of the Our itself, with few bridges, would compress the retreat into a few vulnerable channels. This was one reason why Patton secured permission to open on January 18 the attack from the southeastern shoulder of the Bulge that he had wanted to attempt some three weeks earlier. Officially, the purpose of this thrust by General Eddy's XII Corps was to distract the Germans from the eastward drive of the III and VIII Corps and of the First Army on Patton's left; but Patton saw to it that Eddy kept an armored division in reserve to unleash if there should be a breakthrough.

The eastward push from the Houffalize area by Patton's two left corps and Hodges's army was Bradley's design. Though the general direction of the attack suggested that Bradley had reconciled himself to doing what Montgomery had wanted to do all along, merely seeing off the Germans to where they had come from, nevertheless the plan had its more imaginative aspects. Ridgway's XVIII Corps was to take over the main First Army effort from Collins; in fact, the VII Corps would be pinched out as the VIII and III Corps advanced northeastward. Ridgway's first objective was St. Vith. As the XVIII Corps moved toward that road junction, the V Corps was to join the battle by attacking out of the northeast shoulder to seize the Ondenval Defile leading southward along the upper Amblève River. Through this defile the V Corps was then to launch an armored division to meet Ridgway at St. Vith and bag as many Germans as possible between the pincers thus formed. Ridgway, meanwhile, conceived of his assault on the corner formed by the Salm and the Amblève as yet another envelopment. The rested 75th Division was to take the place of the 82nd Airborne on Ridgway's right and attack directly across the Salm toward St. Vith. While it did so, General Hobbs's 30th Division on Ridgway's left would attack south across the Amblève from around Malmédy, and with skill and luck a modest encirclement might trap the Germans who were still in the corner between the two rivers.

Ridgway's maneuver began developing as early as January 13, three days before the convergence at Houffalize. General Prickett's 75th Division struck out for St. Vith through the bridgehead east of the Salm already captured by the 82nd Airborne. Headquarters of the 106th Division, now under Brigadier General Herbert T. Perrin, tried to keep the Germans just to the north, the targets of the envelopment, suitably occupied. Perrin used for the purpose his division's own remaining regiment, the 424th, along with the 517th Parachute Infantry. The 30th Division's attack crossed the Amblève readily—once more the weather was more troublesome than the Germans—and by the end of the second day had gained six kilometers, to commanding high ground on the west side of the Ondenval Defile.

Unfortunately, the 75th Division, with the limited defensive combat experience it had acquired between the Salm and the Ourthe, could not yet match the pace of the 30th Division in the attack. It advanced slowly enough to permit the bulk of the German XIII Corps of two divisions to slip away to the south and east. By the time patrols of the 75th and the 30th met on January 19, General Hodges was again recommending the relief of one of his division commanders. Evidently the leader of the First Army had recovered his usual temper.

The V Corps kicked off its part of the attack on January 15, just as General Huebner took command of the corps from Gerow, who was moving on to head a new army, the Fifteenth. Huebner's old 1st Division, now under Brigadier General Clift Andrus, formerly its artillery commander, opened the attack against the heights bounding the east side of the Ondenval Defile. The 23rd Infantry of Robertson's 2nd Division attacked into the defile itself. In front of Huebner's advance, the enemy rallied to become as dangerous as the abominable weather. Having been fond of the envelopment maneuver in their own heyday, the Germans were adept at discerning a hostile envelopment in the making. They evidently perceived the intended trap for their defenders of St. Vith, and they responded by endowing their 3rd Parachute Division with more than the usual measure of artillery support. The 23rd Infantry cleared the defile on January 17, but the next day brought the predictable counterattack in more than predictable strength, at least a battalion supported by three tanks.

To exploit through the defile, the First Army appropriately had at hand General Hasbrouck's 7th Armored Division. January 19 slowed activity with another heavy snowstorm, but on January 20 Hasbrouck's tanks and armored infantry began rolling south through the Ondenval Defile and over a road captured by the 30th Division along the high ground to the west. On January 23, one day more than a month since the division had evacuated St. Vith, General Bruce Clarke's CCB led the way back into the ruined town. It was a moment worthy of celebration notwithstanding the enemy's blunting of the V as well as the XVIII Corps pincers, so that the First Army's maneuver east of the Salm had changed from an envelopment to a straightforward push southeastward.

There was consolation, too, because while January 23 was overcast as usual, the previous day had brought that rarity, clear weather. The fighter-bombers enjoyed a bonanza of flaying Germans now crowded into a compact pocket and wrestling with each other to move along the few roads to the few bridges crossing the Our. The enemy being driven by the First Army had little space for flight before colliding with the fugitives and debris pushed northward by Patton's battles. General Eddy's XII Corps had crossed the Sauer River in assault boats during the night of January 17–18.

A sick General Barton had reluctantly turned over his 4th Division to Brigadier General Harold W. Blakeley, who sent his troops into the angle formed by the Sauer and the Our. On Blakeley's left, General Irwin's 5th Division advanced on both sides of Diekirch, intent on a journey northward along the Skyline Drive. Patton's earlier counterstrokes against the Bulge had focused the attention of the German Seventh Army farther west. This circumstance helped Eddy's men duplicate the accomplishment of the first German attackers on December 16: they were over the river and infiltrating deep inside the enemy's positions before their opponents knew what was happening. H-Hour was three hours past before German artillery commenced firing. So sound asleep were the Germans and so dark was the night that at one point, American engineers quickly constructed a bridge of their assault boats, and at two other places Eddy's infantry walked across the Sauer because the engineers had been able to slip footbridges into place unobserved.

Before the day was over, tanks were crossing several treadway bridges and a vehicular ford, and the Americans had a bridgehead three kilometers deep from which they could bring two of the enemy's Our bridges under artillery fire. It was in such situations that the proximity fuze first came into quantity use in the ground campaign and could be applied to best effect, for it ensured the gunners as nothing else had ever done that their shells would burst squarely in the midst of the traffic jammed on the bridges.

Meanwhile General McBride's 80th Division on the XII Corps left had joined in the assault and promptly found the enemy crumbling before it. The whole right wing of the German Seventh Army was scurrying to the east to try to shore up and use its escape route. Thus the remnants of the Fifth Panzer Army fighting farther west and north were also imperiled, and it was not surprising that elements of Panzer Lehr from Manteuffel's army soon showed up to join the resistance against the XII Corps.

The resistance stiffened enough that the defenders of the Our bridge at Vianden were able to hold the tired and much understrength 4th Division at arm's length. On January 21 the 5th Division had to pause west of Vianden because there were rumors of counterattack and its right flank was partially exposed. Resting on the Skyline Drive, Irwin's men could pass the time as spectators of a headlong flight of Germans through the lower ground to the northwest—or rather of thousands of Germans caught in traffic jams backed up from the Our bridges, being heavily pounded by the XII Corps artillery. The melee among the enemy became yet more frantic and congested the next day as fighter-bombers joined the artillery in working the fugitives over. The battered knots of men and vehicles were all that remained of the enemy's former westerly spearheads. Meanwhile, vehicles of the 2nd Panzer Division as well as Panzer Lehr were trying to move at right angles across the path of flight, as what was left of the XLVII Panzer Corps attempted to bolster the dam holding back Eddy and thus save the bridges.

The highways' coating of snow and ice further complicated the enemy's frenzied movements, but it also hampered the American pursuit. Patton's III and VIII Corps almost lost contact with the retreating enemy on January 19. Except for a panzer ambush of a company of the 90th Division on January 22, these corps never again fought more than a patrol or skirmish action west of the Our. The roads grew so treacherous that much of the pursuit had to be dismounted; the passable roads were so few that pursuing units encroached on each other's territory. On January 23, both the 6th Armored and the 90th Divisions crossed the Clerf, and the 26th Division did so the next day. By January 23, however, the XLVII Panzer Corps had taken charge of the defense against the XII Corps, and Lüttwitz's battle-scarred panzer divisions retained enough spunk to keep Eddy's advance under control and the Our bridges open as long as any semblance of organized German forces pressed bumper-to-bumper across them. Also on January 23, Bradley began discussing with Patton a plan simply to flatten the last of the Bulge with the First and Third Armies in line, and thence, in the words of the Supreme Commander's December 31 outline plan, for "First and Third Armies to drive northeast on general line Prum-Bonn, eventually to Rhine."

The Morning After

Bradley and Patton planned for the First and Third Armies because the Ninth was definitely to remain with 21 Army Group for Montgomery's offensive to the Rhine. Bradley had hoped that Simpson's army might revert to his control at least briefly when the First Army did, "that we might complete the cycle and reclaim our command now that the Bulge had been flattened. But Ike replied that he was already exhausted in his struggle to block the British on a super ground command for Monty."[32]

Bradley fervently desired some kind of public testimonial that the temporary shift in command reflected geographic circumstances and not loss of Eisenhower's confidence in him. But Montgomery only rubbed salt into his wounds at the field marshal's notorious January 7 press conference.

On January 5, SHAEF had made its first public announcement of Montgomery's command of the First and Ninth Armies: "When the German penetration through the Ardennes created two fronts, one substantially facing south and the other north, by instant agreement of all concerned that portion of the front facing south was placed under command of Montgomery and that facing north under command of Bradley."[33]

So brief a statement left so much unexplained—in particular that Montgomery's new command was temporary—that it was ostensibly to clarify the whole affair, and to give everyone concerned his due recognition, that Montgomery met the press two days later. Whatever his motives, the field marshal surpassed himself in displaying what de Guingand called his " 'what a good boy am I' attitude."[34] He made certain that his relations with the Americans would be poisoned through the rest of the war—and this, less than a week after de Guingand's rescue of his job had left him professedly chastened. More inadvertently, however, Montgomery placed on display certain limitations of his own generalship.

Among the pertinent passages of Montgomery's text were these:

3. As soon as I saw what was happening [in the Ardennes] I took certain steps myself to ensure that *if* the Germans got to the Meuse they would certainly not get over that river. And I carried out certain movements so as to provide

balanced dispositions to meet the threatened danger; these were, at the time, merely precautions, i.e., I was thinking ahead.

4. Then the situation began to deteriorate. But the whole allied team rallied to meet the danger; national considerations were thrown overboard; General Eisenhower placed me in command of the whole Northern front.
   I employed the whole available power of the British Group of Armies; this power was brought into play very gradually and in such a way that it would not interfere with the American lines of communication. Finally it was put in with a bang, and today British divisions are fighting hard on the right flank of First US Army. You have thus a picture of British troops fighting on both sides of American forces who have suffered a hard blow. This is a fine allied picture.

5. The battle has been most interesting; I think possibly one of the most interesting and tricky battles I have ever handled, with great issues at stake. The first thing to be done was to 'head off' the enemy from the tender spots and vital places. Having done that successfully, the next thing was to 'see him off,' i.e., rope him in and make quite certain that he could not get to the places he wanted, *and also* that he was slowly but surely removed away from those places.
   He was therefore 'headed off,' and then 'seen off.' He is now being 'written off,' and heavy toll is being taken of his divisions by ground and air action.[35]

Thus the best general took charge in spite of "national considerations," and throwing "the whole available power of the British Group of Armies . . . [into battle] with a bang" he rescued the Americans from their predicament. Montgomery went on to say conventionally generous things about the gallantry of American soldiers, and very conventional, and inexplicit, words about how good it was to have Eisenhower as "the captain of our team." But these kindnesses were too perfunctory to be meaningful. As the British critic General John Strawson says of the main parts of the statement, "Montgomery as usual had the best of it—he did little and gave the world to understand he had done a great deal"; and in regard to the British armies' going in with a bang, "this distortion was really unforgivable." Prime Minister Churchill felt obliged presently to remind the House of Commons that "The Americans have engaged thirty or forty men for every one we have engaged and have lost sixty to eighty men to every one of ours."[36]

But the defects of character that crippled Montgomery as a coalition commander had already grown apparent. Less frequently commented upon is Montgomery's remarkable capacity to derive complete satisfaction from a victory so manifestly incomplete as the Ardennes. To be sure, he warned his listeners that as he spoke on January 7, the battle was not yet over and there remained much to do. Nevertheless, it was already evident that large numbers of the German troops and much of the equipment still fighting in the Bulge, almost certainly the bulk of them, would escape. The enemy in fact was not being "written off." Montgomery betrayed no regrets about this less than satisfactory outcome. He was well aware by now that his famous victory at El Alamein in the Western Desert could be criticized because he had simply seen off the enemy. Yet in the course of his statement he indulged his habit of holding up his North African triumphs as models of what victorious battles ought to be, with no recognition of their incompleteness. If he wanted to claim all the credit for the battles in the Ardennes, he should have reckoned that inseparable from the credit was the problem of generalship in the Ardennes counterattack—whether the counterstroke was prompt enough and properly placed.

Never, not even later when discussion could be more complete and candid than in January 1945, did Montgomery face up to the problem. To state the issue more broadly, Field Marshal Montgomery almost never paid so much as lip service to the dictum that the destruction of the enemy forces is the object of military strategy. He was to say later that he had tried to read Clausewitz but could not understand him, so he turned instead to military authors of his own language and nation. No doubt. His generalship had nothing in it of the Clausewitzian conviction that war is "an act of force to compel our opponent to fulfill our will," and that if he is to be made to fulfill our will, the opponent must be disarmed completely, or at the least threatened with complete loss of his capacity to make war.[37] Montgomery's aggressiveness was that of the energetic fencer, not that of the general who annihilates enemy armies, of Napoleon, of Grant, or of Moltke.

As an equally fundamental flaw, Montgomery's January 7 press conference epitomized his inability to be self-critical on any point. No victory is as complete as it might be; a major purpose of the soldier's reflection upon any campaign ought to be to discover how the military organization, the tactics, and the strategy might have been improved upon. The great general is not likely to be the smug general but the commander who scrutinizes his own operations so that his future operations may be better. Here Patton presents an instructive contrast to Montgomery—of all the contrasts between these two very different soldiers, one of those most in Patton's favor. Patton always regretted that he had not hurled his counterattack against the south flank of the Bulge north from Diekirch, instead of farther west:

> I have stated earlier . . . that Bradley did not in any way interfere with the combat of the Third Army [during the Ardennes battle]. In one case, while he did not order, he did strongly suggest, that, instead of attacking north of Diekirch . . . we should put in a new division southeast of Bastogne so as to insure the integrity of the corridor. I let myself be overpersuaded by him in this connection and assume full responsibility for the error of subsequently engaging the 90th Division too far west. Had I put the 90th Division in north of Diekirch, I am sure we would have bagged more Germans and just as cheaply.[38]

Even in public pronouncements at the time, as in a press conference just a few days before Montgomery's—New Year's Day 1945—Patton dwelt not so much on what had been accomplished as on what ought to be accomplished: "We want to catch as many Germans as possible, but he is pulling out." The "but" clause, the note of regret, the awareness of the imperfection of his victories typified Patton. Even Patton's self-confidence carried a healthy infusion of self-doubt: "Leadership . . . is the thing that wins battles. I have it—but I'll be damned if I can define it," he wrote to his son.[39]

And Patton certainly recognized the incompleteness of the victory in the Ardennes. He told the same January 1 press conference: "If you get a monkey in a jungle hanging by his tail, it is easier to get him by cutting his tail than kicking him in the face."[40] Kicking him in the face was what Montgomery proposed to do. The First Army-Third Army convergence on Houffalize was a compromise solution, and cutting the Germans' salient at its tail was never done. The enemy escaped.

30: "Inadequate Means"

G ENERAL PATTON's critical faculty was broad enough to recognize that the enemy escaped and victory was imperfect in the Ardennes not only because Allied generalship was flawed and the Germans fought stubbornly, but also because of deeper faults in the Allied war machine that it was too late to correct. When he was driving his generals and soldiers to attack and attack again at a time when he still hoped to destroy a considerable portion of the German army, he wrote in his diary: "We have to push people beyond endurance in order to bring this war to an end, because we are forced to fight it with inadequate means." In a letter to Secretary of War Henry L. Stimson, he was more specific about the inadequacy of means: "The two things which bother us . . . are replacements and ammunition." Furthermore, "things would be facilitated if we had more divisions, but as far as I know, there are no more, so we will have to get by with what we have."[1]

In November, Major General Harold R. Bull, Eisenhower's G-3, had traveled to Washington at the head of a special mission to present the European Theater's emergency appeal for action to ease the persistent ammunition shortage. By that time, the 12th Army Group G-4, Brigadier General Raymond G. Moses, had reached after a thorough study of the ammunition situation the simple but appalling conclusion that the War Department had allowed Operation OVERLORD to proceed without any certainty that there would be enough ammunition to overcome prolonged heavy resistance. Though Washington had remained consistently skeptical of Eisenhower's and his subordinates' laments, Moses's statistics were so compelling and unassailable, and Bull was a sufficiently prestigious and persuasive negotiator, that General Somervell and the War Department substantially conceded at last that a predicament existed. Having already admitted past mistakes to the extent of moving to create new production capacity, the War Department now agreed to all the expedients it could think of to replenish Eisenhower's arsenal until the increased production began to issue forth. The Army Service Forces had already ransacked military posts to find stray ammunition supplies to recondition and ship to Europe as soon as possible. Every feasible shortcut would be used to hasten the assembly of all components of ammunition on hand, to step up the December and January output. Similar shortcuts and special handling would hurry the delivery both of old stocks and new production to Europe.

General Moses's autumn assessment had concluded that existing rates of fire would exhaust ammunition reserves by December 15 and force severe rationing thereafter. In November, the First Army took an additional small step to meet the crisis by forming from the 32nd Field Artillery Brigade two provisional battalions to use forty-eight captured German 105mm. howitzers and the appropriate captured ammunition. Instead of severe rationing, however, the Ardennes counterattack compelled the 12th Army Group to allow the troops to fire freely. In almost every category, the December expenditures of ammunition were the heaviest of the war. The expedients won by the Bull mission partially offset this impact of the Ardennes. Nevertheless, the firing of 2,579,400 M2 105mm. howitzer rounds in December reduced the European Theater stock to 2,524,000 rounds, at War Department rates a twenty-one-day supply. The authorized level of reserves was 8,000,000 rounds. This shortage of ammunition for the workhorse gun of the American army was the worst aspect of the ammunition problem, but most other stockpiles were not encouragingly higher.

Reinforcements

Nor was the manpower situation consistent with the usual image of World War II America as a military giant bulging with surplus power. The Bull mission to Washington discussed replacements as well as ammunition, and Bradley was at Versailles when the German counteroffensive opened because he had wanted to ensure SHAEF's full support when he sent his personnel officer on a similar errand to pry replacements out of the War Department. On this issue, nevertheless, the War Department remained disinclined to assume any important share of the blame. The department still insisted that it had squeezed manpower as much as overriding national policies for economic and military allocations permitted, and that in contrast the European Theater was not as diligent as it ought to be in cutting fat from its Zone of Communications. In return for theater promises to try again to convert surplus soldiers from other branches into infantrymen, and to find more infantry officers from its enlisted ranks and from other branches, the War Department offered only narrow concessions. January shipments of replacements to Europe would be raised by 18,000 to 54,000; but this step involved borrowing from the future, because it could be accomplished only by reducing training from seventeen to fifteen weeks and cutting short the furloughs customary before shipment overseas. The department would also consider sending limited-assignment men to compensate for withdrawals of general assignment troops from service to combat units. It would provide training cadres for the European Theater's own program of converting miscellaneous troops into infantry and for a theater officer candidate school.

Then came the Ardennes. In the first week, the 12th Army Group believed it suffered 50,000 casualties, 40,000 of them infantrymen. Battle casualties for the month of December reached 77,700, nonbattle casualties 56,700.

The response of the European Theater partially vindicated the War Department opinion that in the past Eisenhower's forces had not worked as hard as they could have to find infantrymen for themselves. The theater command immediately speeded up its dispatch to the front of replacements already in the theater and in the pipeline. More to the point, it began a systematic combing out of units not essential to the battle. Similarly, after skimming the basics from the 42nd, 63rd, and 70th Divisions on December 20, the 69th Division, still in England, was yet more ruthlessly stripped a few days later, to hasten men into combat. By Christmas, such measures produced 30,000 replacements for the 12th Army Group, and the searching of the rear areas was still in its preliminary stages.

The theater command considered a sweeping withdrawal of combat-trained men from engineer combat battalions and general service regiments. For the time being, Eisenhower settled for the less drastic expedient of sending his own representatives throughout the Communications Zone to select men qualified to fight and to hasten them to the front. He also promised a pardon and a clean slate to soldiers under court-martial sentences who would go to the front and fight; everyone who faced fifteen years or more of hard labor volunteered. On December 26, meanwhile, General Lee of the Communications Zone offered "to a limited number of colored troops who have had infantry training, the privilege of joining our veteran units at the front to deliver the knockout blow."[2]

Lee had consulted with Eisenhower about this idea, as well as with Brigadier General Benjamin O. Davis, the army's first black general officer and currently Special Advisor and Coordinator to the Theater Commander on Negro Troops. General Davis, Brigadier General Henry J. Matchett of the Ground Forces Reinforcement Command, in charge of replacements, and the latter's G-1 had prepared a plan to train black volunteers as individual infantry replacements, thus breaking down the army's historic segregation of black soldiers into black units, as a means of easing the replacement crisis. Lee circularized all base and section commanders with orders for them to present his offer confidentially to his black troops.

Lee's expedient was more drastic than Eisenhower apparently recognized, especially because Lee promised that black volunteers would be assigned "without regard to color or race to the units where assistance is most needed." When Bedell Smith saw Lee's circular, he objected strenuously to Lee on the ground that such a promise contradicted War Department policy. When he failed to convince Lee that the circular must be recalled, he turned to Eisenhower, telling the Supreme Commander that Lee "believes that it is right that colored and white soldiers should be mixed in the same company. With this belief I do not argue, but the War Department policy is different." The effect, said Smith, was bound to be a furor at home, for "every negro organization, pressure group and newspaper will take the attitude that, while the War Department segregates colored troops into organizations of their own against the desires and pleas of all the negro race, the Army is perfectly willing to put them in the front lines mixed in units with white soldiers, and have them do battle when an emergency arises." Lee ought to be enjoined against issuing "any general circulars relating to negro policy until I have a chance to see them."[3]

Eisenhower, as a biographer comments, was "no more ready to promote a social revolution than Smith,"[4] and so he yielded to his chief of staff's urgings and personally rewrote Lee's circular. The revised version appeared over Lee's signature with the same date, file number, and subject as the earlier circular, but with a cover ordering all copies of the original returned and destroyed. The substitute circular was a generalized call for volunteers for combat service from among the Communications Zone troops, with an italicized sentence midway along specifying that the opportunity to volunteer was being *"extended to all soldiers without regard to color or race, but preference will normally be given to individuals who have had some basic training in Infantry."* The new circular also stipulated that "In the event that the number of suitable negro volunteers exceeds the replacement needs of negro combat units, these men will be suitably incorporated in other organizations so that their service and their fighting spirit may be efficiently utilized."[5]

There were no black infantry units and thus few blacks with infantry training in the European Theater. Several black artillery, tank, and tank destroyer units were on hand; a

SHAEF clarifying directive soon confirmed the implication that black volunteers who were retrained for combat would enter these units first. If a surplus remained, according to the directive, they would be formed into separate infantry units, with an initial goal of a single battalion.

Despite the discouraging restrictions, some 2,500 blacks promptly volunteered. By February, the number of black volunteers was up to 4,562, high enough that further rethinking of policy had to take place. SHAEF had also stipulated that only black privates and PFCs were eligible to volunteer; many black soldiers accepted a reduction in grade to get into combat in the face of this provision. A minor ripple in the troubled waters of the Ardennes battle, this affair of the black volunteers represented, in addition to its far deeper implications, one reason why the United States Army faced a manpower crisis. Some 10 percent of America's potential military manpower had been almost excluded from eligibility for combat.

As long as there was no implication of social policies that might, in Eisenhower's words, "run counter to regs in a time like this,"[6] the theater command had already gone far in the two months before the December crisis toward remedying the neglect of sources of combat manpower of which the War Department accused it. Field Marshal Montgomery's plaints about weakness in rifle strength (as well as in leadership) among the American formations that fell to his command prompted a pledge from Bedell Smith of 17,474 infantry-trained replacements to reach the First and Ninth Armies from December 24 to 31 inclusive; 2,200 of them were infantrymen from the 69th Division, but fully 40 percent were men already retrained in the theater during the weeks preceding the German counteroffensive. While Montgomery was receiving his infantry replacements, 12,309 more such replacements were to go to Patton's army, the same proportion of them retrained in the European Theater. Hitherto starved for replacements through much of the autumn by the priority given the northern offensives, Patton early in December had already transferred some 6,500 soldiers for infantry retraining in the Third Army's own replacement battalion at Metz.

Knowing these numbers that were in or about to go into the theater's replacement pipeline, the December mission from Eisenhower and Bradley to the War Department still had to report that the divisions in the European Theater would average only about 78 percent of their proper rifle strength by the end of the month. Nevertheless, the War Department replied that little more assistance could be offered beyond the small expedients already agreed to. Instead, the department would dispatch a manpower expert to Europe to survey the scene.

Reserves

With many divisions dangerously short of riflemen, the condition of the SHAEF reserve showed how small was the number of divisions themselves in proportion to the demands of the battle: the only way to find a reserve for the Ardennes had been to commit airborne divisions to prolonged slugging matches as ordinary infantry.

The German counteroffensive had, of course, also compelled Eisenhower to hurry to the front those divisions that were still in England on December 16: the 11th Armored, the 17th Airborne, the 66th Infantry (which arrived in France December 26), the 8th Armored (which arrived in France January 6), the 76th Infantry (reaching England December 21, and hurried to the Continent by January 17), and the 69th Infantry (at length assembled in France as a division on January 26). By mid-January, there were no more American divisions in the United Kingdom.

As previously scheduled, three divisions reached France direct from the United States in late January, the 65th and 89th Infantry and the 13th Armored. Only four divisions scheduled for the European Theater remained in the United States; only six divisions altogether remained in the United States.

General Marshall offered early in January to speed up the shipment of the four divisions allotted to Eisenhower. The latter agreed, and the 71st Infantry, the 13th Airborne, and the 16th and 20th Armored all reached France in February, each slightly ahead of its original schedule. By that time, Eisenhower had also appealed for the other two divisions, both slated to go to the Pacific. He got them, the 86th and 97th Infantry, early in March. With that, the American cupboard was bare.

Yet with nothing more to draw on from America, Eisenhower would scarcely enjoy a surplus of strength. The final two divisions arriving in March gave him sixty-one American divisions altogether. When the First Army joined the counterattack in the Ardennes on January 3, Eisenhower commanded forty-nine American divisions, twelve British, three Canadian, one Polish, and eight French. Of the total of seventy-three Allied divisions, forty-nine were infantry, twenty armored, and four airborne. Allied intelligence estimated that the seventy-three Allied divisions confronted some seventy German divisions.

The Enemy at Bay

This virtual equality in numbers of divisions could not be dismissed as altogether misleading. It was true that a German division, infantry or panzer, was no longer at all what it had been in 1940 or 1941. A German division of 1940 or 1941 had been so formidable compared with the equivalent organization in any other army that there had been a margin for plenty of deterioration, and the residue could yet remain a fearsomely tough and skillful combat force.

The advantages that the defensive would afford the Germans—and after the failure of the Ardennes counteroffensive, the Germans would almost certainly have to fight mainly on the defensive—meant that a margin of seventy-three attacking Allied divisions to seventy defending German divisions could be dangerously insecure. The margin remained insecure despite overwhelming Allied air superiority; leaving aside much of the Ardennes experience when the airplanes could not fly, the Germans had amply demonstrated during the near-deadlock of the autumn that the Allies' air power was a limited even if highly desirable asset on the battlefront.

Looking toward the late spring or early summer, Eisenhower expected to lead by then about eighty-five divisions. But if the Soviets did not soon launch a major offensive, or if they launched an offensive and the Germans contained it, he had to calculate that the eighty-five Allied divisions might face as many as 100 German divisions. The events of December had proven that the Allies dared not underestimate the capacity and willingness of the enemy to reinforce the Western Front at the expense of other battlegrounds.

Due to comparatively low scale of effort that the enemy is compelled to make on other fronts [Eisenhower wrote Marshall on January 7], an extremely high proportion of his personnel and material replacements is pouring into the Western Front.

Enemy units that have been badly cut up in the salient and at other places are persistently and quickly built up. Replacements in tanks and men reach the front in a matter of days from the interior of Germany. There is a noticeable and fanatical zeal on the part of nearly all his fighting men as well as the whole nation of 85,000,000 people, successfully unified by terror from within and fear of consequences from without. The Germans are convinced they are fighting for their very existence and their battle action reflects this spirit.[7]

The full story of the Germans' concentration of strength on the Western Front would have given Eisenhower even more reason for concern. As the new year opened, seventy-six German divisions in fact faced the Allies in the Ardennes and along the West Wall and the Rhine. The Western Allies confronted another twenty-four German divisions in Italy. Seventeen German divisions were pinned down in Scandinavia, another ten in Yugoslavia. On the Eastern Front, the Germans had cut back to 133 divisions notwithstanding the vastness both of the arena and of the opposing Red Army. About half the divisional strength of the Wehrmacht now faced the West. Seventeen German divisions that had helped hold the East on June 6, 1944 had been transferred to the West. Of twenty-three new Volksgrenadier divisions raised in the last three months of 1944, eighteen had gone to fight in the West. The West's continuing priority in German tank production had given the German armies in the West 2,299 new or refitted tanks and assault guns in the final two months of 1944, the Eastern Front only 921, mainly Pzkw IVs while the Panthers and Tigers still went west. As of January 5, all the German armies in the East had only two-thirds as many armored vehicles as had been used in the Ardennes. As the year turned, the Luftwaffe deployed 1,756 day fighters and 1,242 night fighters to support the Western Front or to defend the Reich against strategic bombing, only 520 day fighters and 47 night fighters on the Eastern Front.

After more than five years of war, the Germans had drawn so deeply into their manpower that some of their formations facing the Western Allies were indeed, as one of Patton's subordinates dismissed them, "nothing but Poles with ulcers."[8] But the main impression, driven hard upon the Allies by the Ardennes, was the Germans' almost uncanny ability to convert raw recruits into dangerous adversaries within a few weeks, and thus to maintain their divisions' quality. A SHAEF G-2 summary of January 3 put it thus:

> 3. Special units such as 150 Panzer Brigade and von der Heydt's Parachutists composed of extremely good type young soldier with high morale and considerable faith in victory. Some adopted view that it was either case of victory or death since nothing left if Germany lost war. ss Troops generally very high moral[e], who are fighting with good deal fanaticism.
>
> 4. Volksgrenadier Division rather mixed but generally good. As has been said previously good type men from Navy and Air Force [transferred to the Volksgrenadiers] and also young men newly called up resulted in good fighting spirit.
>
> 5. Not slightest doubt German Army in west went into battle offensively minded with the will to win. Now that battle has not gone so well signs that the first high spirit falling slightly and disillusionment in some cases setting in as result of reverses, but this by no means general. . . .
>
> 6. Generally German soldier is fighting with great determination and bravery. Desertions few, but have come from all types of units including ss. Only case so far

of unit desertion was surrender of 30 men from remnants of company from 3 Panzer Grenadier Division on 2 January.[9]

Even the Luftwaffe, Allied intelligence believed, could no longer be written off. When the Allied strategic air forces had returned almost their whole effort to the bombing of German oil, transportation, and industrial targets in the summer, and on well into autumn, they had frequently met no German fighters at all. In the autumn, resistance began to increase. For the Ardennes counteroffensive, the Luftwaffe was ready to intervene, if not dangerously at least troublesomely, in the ground battle. On December 24, the Germans mounted what IX TAC rated as their heaviest aerial effort of the European ground campaign. For a number of nights, they pounded Bastogne with multi-plane raids such as most American soldiers had never experienced; seventy-three German aircraft struck the town on the night of December 30. On New Year's Day an estimated 600 German planes took to the sky, hitting British airdromes at Eindhoven and Brussels with special force and wrecking 180 or more parked planes, including both Montgomery's and de Guingand's personal transports. ". . . they caught the British with their pants down so badly," the First Army heard, "that last night General Montgomery's G-2 sent a pair of suspenders as present to the G-2 of their Tac Air Force."[10]

Again the Allies were to learn the full magnitude of the German revival only after the war, but they knew the enemy was achieving near-miracles in fighter production. During most of 1944, the number of single-engine fighters reaching the Luftwaffe had risen steadily, from 1,016 in February to 3,013 in September. In the latter month, German industry turned out 4,103 fighters of all types, the highest production of the war.

It was mainly General Spaatz's oil campaign that blunted the teeth of the German aerial recovery, for in late 1944 the Germans had planes without fuel—and therefore planes without well-trained pilots too, because when enough fuel could be hoarded to muster such an effort as the 600 to 700 sorties flown by Luftwaffe fighters in support of the ground offensive on December 17, the pilots proved to have been too restricted by the shortage to develop skills and experience to match the Anglo-American aviators.

Yet the very quantity of German fighter production was disturbing—all the more because of what it implied about German determination and resourcefulness against the Allied bomber offensive. The Germans had dispersed aircraft production from twenty-seven main plants to 729 small ones, and they were achieving their peak output of the war from what resembled a handicraft industry. More than the thousands of Bf 109s and Fw 190s, furthermore, the Allies worried about the Messerschmitt 163 and 262 and the Arado 234: the German jets. The 600-miles-per-hour Me 163 single-engine and Me 262 twin-engine fighters had already been built by the hundreds. The Ar 234 bomber was just coming into production. Some Allied airmen feared that if the war lasted until June, the jets might yet restore control of German skies to the Luftwaffe. The Americans could not expect to use jets of their own until October 1945. As early as September 1944, Spaatz had given jet production priority second only to oil among his targets. On January 9, 1945, Spaatz and Bedell Smith agreed to accord the jets first priority, coequal with oil. The production plants, like those for Bf 109s and Fw 190s, were dispersed and hard to cripple; at least the bombers could pounce quickly on airfields that sprouted tell-tale long runways to accommodate jets.

Meanwhile the Ardennes battle sent the bombers back to targets they had neglected since the beginning of November, the factories that manufactured tanks, assault guns, ordnance, and trucks. Past experience indicated there was not much hope of crippling this production; but the Ardennes had just enough confirmed Hitler's belief that the quality of his Panthers and Tigers could offset the quantity of the Shermans, that the Allies wanted to reduce their encounters with the enemy's mechanical monsters to the lowest minimum possible.

Such was the resilient Wehrmacht against which the Western Allies must resume the offensive. Such was the resurgent Wehrmacht that the Americans had turned back, at least, in the Ardennes. When the battle had opened on December 16, some 200,000 Germans took the counteroffensive against 83,000 Americans. The German concentration in the zone of attack had given them a three-to-one advantage in infantrymen along the Ardennes front and a six-to-one advantage where their spearheads struck. The German concentration had afforded the Wehrmacht quantity as well as quality in armor at least at the beginning of the battle, a two-to-one margin in medium tanks, a four-to-one margin if their assault guns were counted as tanks. The toll in American casualties from December 16 to January 2, for the Americans the defensive phase of the battle, was 4,138 killed in action, 20,231 wounded in action, and 16,946 missing. From January 3 through 28, the attacks to eliminate the Bulge and if possible the Germans in it cost another 6,138 killed or died of wounds, 27,262 wounded, and 6,272 missing or known captured. Thus the total of American casualties in the Ardennes battle was 80,987. The total of German casualties is unknown. Railroad reports indicate that some 67,000 German troops were evacuated by rail from Army Group B during December. Estimates of German losses run from 81,834, the lowest German conjecture, to 103,900, the highest Allied estimate.

The victory in the Ardennes belonged preeminently to the American soldier. The generals failed to foresee the German counteroffensive, did not prepare for it as a contingency even to the extent they might have if they had been truly calculating the risks in the Ardennes, and then had to wait long and work hard before they could recapture a semblance of control over the shape of the campaign. They were able eventually to regain control because their soldiers' stubbornness and bravery did most of the job for them, gradually wresting the momentum of battle away from the enemy and in time restoring it to the Allied command. The history of American wars in the twentieth century has mainly witnessed the American armed forces in possession of enough material superiority that doubts can reasonably be raised whether a duel with an equally well equipped enemy might not find the American military a paper tiger, too dependent on material superiority to get along without it. The Ardennes battle, like Guadalcanal but on an immensely larger scale, is one of history's few means of reducing such doubts. With material superiority nonexistent in the Ardennes or nullified by the weather against a Wehrmacht that, if not in its high summer of 1940 or 1941 was still, in Drew Middleton's apt phrase, in the strength of its Indian summer—against these adversities and temporarily abandoned by many of his generals to his own resources, the American soldier won the battle. If the victory was less than complete, the fault lay mainly in generalship's failure to seize fully the opportunities created by the valor of the men at Lanzerath, Clerf, Stavelot, St. Vith, the Baraque de Fraiture, and scores of other places besides the fabled Bastogne.

PART FIVE : GERMANY

★ ★ ★

31: The Eifel

Perhaps second in importance only to his stubbornness in defensive combat, the mobility of the American soldier defeated the Germans in the Ardennes. The enemy failed to calculate how swiftly the Americans could reinforce the battleground. Even a grave American deficiency, frequently enjoined against in orders but never eliminated, had its positive aspect in enhancing mobility: the failure of American troops to maintain radio security regarding their movements. They continually informed the Germans where they were going; but their readiness to use the radio, even to excess, also helped keep roads and intersections clear—after the first few days' confusion—to speed American columns to their destinations. The Germans, with better radio discipline, constantly collided with each other and clotted their roads with traffic jams.

But long-distance movements nevertheless consumed time and tested the endurance of men and equipment, and for this reason General Bradley proposed that the coming offensive should carry the existing concentration of the First and Third Armies directly east from the Ardennes into the Eifel. Bradley believed that the advantages of avoiding another redistribution of the troops, and of continuing almost without pause from the elimination of the Bulge into a renewed invasion of Germany, overrode those disadvantages of poor terrain and limited roads in the Ardennes-Eifel that had previously sent his armies circling north and south around the region. His army commanders, Hodges and Patton, agreed.

General Eisenhower, as usual, agreed in part with his principal American subordinates; but he also felt obliged to respond to different pressures coming from Montgomery and, behind him, the British Chiefs of Staff, and his own inclinations for that matter differed from Bradley's. Though he obviously lacked Montgomery's all-consuming dedication to an offensive across the Rhine north of the Ruhr, and though in late September he had swung substantially to the broad-front strategy and had not wavered since as he had done earlier, Eisenhower remained more willing to grant first priority to his northern flank than Montgomery ever admitted. If the field marshal had not been too deficient in understanding and tolerance toward Ike to recognize this fact, he might have been able to exploit it to his advantage.

[575]

In his outline plan of December 31, the Supreme Commander had deferred to the developing Bradley-Patton design by proposing that after the destruction of the enemy in the Ardennes salient, "First and Third Armies to drive to northeast on general line Prum-Bonn, eventually to Rhine." He also said, however, that as soon as the salient was eliminated, 21 Army Group, including the American Ninth Army, was to resume its own preparations for attacking to the Rhine, and that after the Ardennes battle 12th Army Group headquarters was to shift north, in close proximity to 21 Army Group headquarters. He confirmed the implications of these latter provisos when he wrote to General Marshall on January 10:

> There has never been any question about our intentions of making the attack north of the Ruhr as strong as it possibly could be built up. . . . In every conversation with the CIGS and others that I have had on this subject, I have emphasized, therefore, the intent (1) to concentrate north of the Ruhr and (2) to launch a supporting attack with troops that were available after the complete satisfaction of the requirements of the main attack from such locality as study and continuous examination would indicate to be the best.[1]

Eisenhower was discussing strategy with Marshall in detail at this time, and the Chief of the Imperial General Staff entered into the discussion, because through Marshall and the Combined Chiefs of Staff the British Chiefs were again prodding Eisenhower to give still greater priority to Montgomery's northern offensive: to return to the single-thrust strategy. At least implicitly, the British Chiefs were also belaboring again the enlargement of Montgomery's sphere of command. Brooke and his colleagues in fact proposed to review SHAEF's strategy when President Roosevelt, Prime Minister Churchill, and their staffs conferred on Malta and at Yalta later in the month. Marshall believed he must acquiesce at least to the extent of airing the issues. Fearing that Eisenhower was again (in their interpretation) about to launch two major offensives when he had strength for only one, the British Chiefs had told their American counterparts that there must be only one major thrust and that overwhelming strength must be concentrated into it. Furthermore, one man must be responsible directly to Eisenhower for all the ground forces employed in the single thrust. Expressing also the anxiety of weary Britain that the end of the war dare not be unduly delayed, the British urged the Americans that to hasten a successful offensive in the spring, any aggressive activity during the winter preceding the major drive must contribute directly to the spring offensive. The British Chiefs did not see an attack in the Eifel as doing so.

Eisenhower sent Bedell Smith to represent him at the Malta meeting of the Combined Chiefs. Smith soon wired that the British Chiefs insisted on reassurance both that the northern drive across the Rhine would be the main effort and that Eisenhower did not intend to root out literally every nest of resistance west of the Rhine before he would allow Montgomery to cross the river. General Marshall, said Smith, suggested a statement that the SHAEF plan was: "(A) To carry out immediately a series of operations north of the Moselle with a view to destroying the enemy and closing the Rhine north of Duesseldorf. (B) to direct our efforts to eliminating other enemy forces west of the Rhine which still constitute an obstacle or a potential threat to our subsequent Rhine crossings operations."

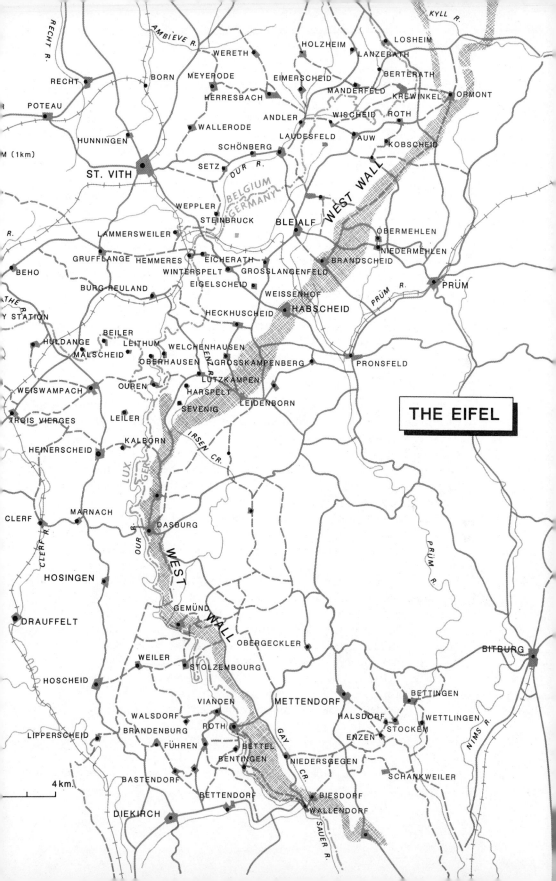

THE EIFEL

Eisenhower agreed that such a reassurance to the British would reflect his own concerns sufficiently that he should issue it. He added: "You may assure the Combined Chiefs of Staff in my name that I will seize the Rhine crossing in the north just as soon as this is a feasible operation and without waiting to clear the Rhine throughout its length. Further, I will advance across the Rhine in the north with maximum strength and complete determination immediately the situation allows me to collect necessary forces without incurring unreasonable risks. . . . "[2]

Marshall's belief that the British must be placated suggests the force of British pressure and concern. At the same time, the provisos about not leaving west of the Rhine German forces "which still constitute . . . a potential threat" and not "incurring unreasonable risks" left Eisenhower's broad-front strategy essentially unchanged.

The background light from the Ardennes gave new shadings to the old broad front versus single thrust debate. Eisenhower agreed with the British that "Terrain, length of our lines of communication and location of important geographical objectives in Germany, all confirm the necessity of making the principal invasion along the northern line."[3] In this judgment he obviously disagreed with Bradley and Patton. There is no reason to suspect, however, as Bradley and Patton did, that Eisenhower was merely kowtowing to Montgomery and Brooke; the conviction was undoubtedly Eisenhower's own. On the other hand, Eisenhower was most assuredly the strategic heir of Abraham Lincoln and U.S. Grant, and while conceding priority to the northern offensive he continued to insist upon attacking on more than one front, to prevent the enemy from concentrating against a single drive. The British interpreted the Ardennes battle as confirming the wisdom of their contrary view that attacking in several places spread Allied power thin so the enemy could concentrate dangerously against part of the thinness. Eisenhower, instead, interpreted the Ardennes as confirming the necessity for his broad-front strategy, particularly for closing up to the Rhine all the way to Switzerland. Otherwise, enemy pockets of resistance west of the Rhine would compel him to leave too many divisions merely containing the pockets.

Eisenhower's estimate was that, of his anticipated eighty-five divisions, "we will need in the defense and in reserve, (a) 25 if we have the Rhine, (b) 35 with the line as at present south of Bonn but Colmar pocket eliminated and (c) 45 if line is substantially as at present." ". . . *we must make certain,*" he told Montgomery, "*that he* [the enemy] *is not free, behind a strong defensive line, to organize sudden powerful thrusts into our lines of communication.* As I see it, we simply cannot afford the large defensive forces that would be necessary if we allow the German to hold great bastions sticking into our lines at the same time that we try to invade his country." Returning to one of his favorite themes, less favored by the field marshal, he suggested: "As an added thought, the more Germans we kill west of the Rhine, the fewer there will be to meet us east of the river."[4]

Thus, taking a different view from Montgomery's and Brooke's of what would constitute dispersion of effort, Eisenhower agreed to give Bradley a crack at an offensive through the Eifel. But the Supreme Commander's own preference for the northern offensive, along with the pressure he felt from the British Chiefs of Staff, decreed that Bradley must work on a short leash: "This attack will be pressed with all possible vigor as long as there is a reasonable chance of securing a decisive success. However, as an alternative we must be prepared to pass quickly to the defensive in the Ardennes sector, and to attack in the sector of the Northern Group of Armies."⁵ A decisive success evidently meant a rapid penetration of the West Wall.

Uncertainty in the High Command

Simpson's Ninth Army had shifted south to absorb the old First Army front opposite the Roer and its dams. On the southern part of Bradley's front, Walker's XX Corps of Patton's army held a sector of fifty kilometers from the Moselle to the junction with the 6th Army Group near Saarlautern. The bulk of the First and Third Armies thus lay concentrated against the Eifel. Twenty-one of forty-seven American divisions active on the Western Front crammed the area between the Huertgen Forest and the Moselle. Bradley planned to drive his main effort between the Huertgen and the Schnee Eifel, through a corridor some sixteen to nineteen kilometers wide. Doing so, his troops would pass south of the Roer dams as well as south of the dreaded Huertgen. Thus they would be able to reach the Rhine without danger of flooding from the dams. Moving diagonally northeast across the Eifel toward its transformation into the Cologne plain in the area of Euskirchen, a little less than fifty kilometers away, the offensive would have to travel some fifty-five to seventy kilometers from the Belgian border to the Rhine. It would arrive at the Rhine just south of Bonn, whence usable though hardly excellent routes would permit deeper penetration into Germany.

The Eifel is much more continuously wooded than the Ardennes and yet more deeply scored by watercourses. Among these watercourses, the Our and Prüm Rivers lay squarely athwart the path of the advance. Though German roads were better constructed and maintained than those of Belgium and Luxembourg, the roads of the Eifel even more than those of the Ardennes twist and turn up over hills, down into ravines, and through defiles. Except for Prüm and Bitburg, there are few towns and communications centers in the Eifel. The West Wall remained to be penetrated in the Eifel sector—the Ardennes counteroffensive had ejected the Americans from their few footholds—and across most of the path of Bradley's main effort the line of obstacles and fortifications was double. These were the patent disadvantages of the Eifel, which Bradley nevertheless believed would be offset by his existing concentration and by the prospect of turning the Roer dams.

General Ridgway's XVIII Airborne Corps was to jump off on January 28, with Hobbs's 30th and Bolling's 84th Divisions in reserve, Andrus's 1st Infantry and Gavin's 82nd Airborne in front. The 82nd on the corps right was to press through the historic invasion defile of the Losheim Gap, which at Stadtkyll would put it on the good, primary highway running from Prüm to Euskirchen.

General Middleton's VIII Corps of the Third Army was to join the attack the next day, January 29. On its left, the 87th Division would also move through the Losheim area and shield the XVIII Corps right. Blakeley's 4th Division and the 90th under Major General Lowell W. Rooks, Van Fleet having moved upward, were to take on the West Wall directly through the Schnee Eifel and just south of it. If they were successful they could—along with General Kilburn's 11th Armored Division from corps reserve—either join the advance northeast or roll up the West Wall southward.

On the third day, January 30, General Huebner's V Corps was to be ready to join in on Ridgway's left. Huebner planned to send Robertson's 2nd Division northeastward again over the familiar route of its critical rearguard action of the beginning of the

German counteroffensive, from the Elsenborn Ridge through the twin villages of Krinkelt and Rocherath to the Wahlerscheid road junction and customs house in the Monschau Forest. There Craig's 9th Division was to converge upon the 2nd, driving southeast from Monschau to do so. Lauer's 99th Division meanwhile would clear the triangle of the Monschau Forest west of the converging drives. Parker's 78th Division, though the shifting interarmy boundaries had assigned it to the XIX Corps of the Ninth Army, still lay just northeast of Monschau at the base of the Monschau corridor leading toward the Roer dams, toward which it had been attacking when the Ardennes battle interrupted it; the 78th had already pushed about three kilometers into the West Wall, and it was at last to resume its attack, to protect the V Corps left.

General Collins's VII Corps was now in reserve and ready to exploit success by either the XVIII or the V Corps. There was nothing subtle about Bradley's plan, but it had the rare virtue of concentration. Such a concentration for attack upon a relatively narrow front had been so infrequently achieved in the American campaign in Europe, and in its compacted force the concentration carried so much power and promise, that the mere existence of the concentration was indeed warrant enough for Bradley's desire to attack in the Eifel. The concentration might well have persuaded Eisenhower to grant Bradley a truly generous opportunity to see what could be accomplished, however troublesome the contrary pressures with which the Supreme Commander had to contend.

But the virtues of concentration did not rank high in Eisenhower's methods of generalship. They ranked so low, in fact, that the concentration was almost broken up before the offensive could get under way. Clearing the Colmar pocket was an obvious and proper ingredient of Eisenhower's desire to close up to the Rhine, but it had also become a virtual obsession. Eisenhower blamed Devers for the pocket's existence, and everything having to do with it was bound up with his increasingly evident penchant for nagging at Devers and finding fault with almost every move he made. Ike's unwonted coolness toward the 6th Army Group commander went beyond the usual and immediate explanation that Devers, unlike Bradley and Patton, was not an old friend and was Marshall's choice for his post rather than Eisenhower's; its touch of irrationality appeared especially in SHAEF's willingness to damage the Eifel offensive for the Colmar pocket.

On January 24, practically on the eve of the Eifel attack, General Whiteley called Bradley from SHAEF and told him he must yield several divisions to Devers for a drive against the Colmar pocket. Patton and Hodges happened to be meeting with Bradley, and Patton saw Bradley lose his temper as he had never done before in Patton's experience. Bradley flared up at Whiteley "that if he wanted to destroy the whole operation, he could do so and be damned, or words to that effect, and to take *all* the corps and divisions." Whiteley's superior, General Bull, came on the telephone and received the same kind of blast.[6]

In the back of every mind at Bradley's headquarters was Montgomery's condescension toward the American setback in the Ardennes and the fear that if the Eifel offensive went down the drain, so would the last chance for the American army, rather than the British, to redeem the Ardennes by launching the decisive offensive into the Reich. Patton's chief of staff, General Gay, was also present and recorded Bradley's outburst in detail:

"I want you to understand that there is more at stake than the mere moving of divisions and corps and of a certain tactical plan. The reputation and the good will of the American soldiers and the American army and its commanders is at stake. If you feel that way about it, then as far as I am concerned, you can take any goddam division and/or corps in the 12th Army Group do with them as you see fit and those of us that you leave back will sit on our ass until hell freezes. I trust you do not think I am angry, but I want to impress upon you that I am goddam well incensed."[7]

Patton in the background said in a voice loud enough to be heard over the telephone, "Tell them to go to hell and all three of us will resign. I will lead the procession."[8]

Under this barrage, SHAEF relented. According to Patton, he, Bradley, and Hodges were all confident that the Germans would soon evacuate the Colmar pocket anyway. Doubtful though that may have been, to risk the Eifel offensive for the Colmar pocket would have been virtually to announce that the principle of concentration retained no place whatever in SHAEF's military textbooks.

Against Snow and the West Wall

The abominable weather that had plagued the closing of the Bulge still harried the new attack into the Eifel. In subfreezing temperatures, men and vehicles had to plow through a snow cover of a foot or two everywhere and drifts as high as a tall man. The official historian says: "The story of all these first attacks could be told almost in a word: weather."[9] Plodding through the drifts left men exhausted even when they did not have to fight. The 1st and 82nd Divisions consumed four days in advancing the ten to sixteen kilometers between their jump-off positions and the last high ground before the West Wall.

Yet this offensive bore more potential than the hard hand of winter could overcome. Ridgway's two attacking divisions were, in their corps commander's words, "both veteran outfits at their highest state of combat effectiveness, attacking side by side. It was a joy to see. It was like watching two great racehorses, driving head and head to the finish line." From a general whose words as well as deeds always bespoke the toughness symbolized by the two omnipresent grenades strapped to his shoulders, such praise had to be well earned. Ridgway "had anticipated extremely heavy going and in my own estimate of the situation I had figured these two assault divisions would run out of steam just about the time they hit the first bunkers of the Siegfried Line." He planned that he would then pass the 30th and 84th Divisions through the 1st and 82nd. But the two old thoroughbreds were not so readily exhausted. "General Andrus's 1st and Gavin's 82nd were going with such momentum they smashed through the first zone and moved well inside" the West Wall.[10] By February 4 the two assault divisions had penetrated the dense first band of the wall to gain control of the first tier of villages inside Germany astride the Losheim Gap.

They were able to do so as much because of the weakness of the opposition as through their own fighting qualities. It became apparent that the Germans had not expected the Americans to reverse their habits of many months and strike into the rugged Eifel. Field Marshal Model's Army Group B had obviously sent much of its Ardennes concentration elsewhere—the Sixth Panzer Army had withdrawn from the front altogether—and the Eifel defenses were thin, with many pillboxes unoccupied. Otherwise, even Ridgway's old racehorses might have been stymied, because the roads behind them grew so snow-clogged that ammunition and food often could not get through, armor could scarcely move, and when Andrus's men first hit the West Wall, only one artillery battalion had pushed forward enough to support them.

Nevertheless, Ridgway's troops broke the wall, and Huebner's V Corps fared still better. Craig's 9th Division, able to jump off from positions within the West Wall captured earlier and still held, advanced southeastward almost to the Wahlerscheid road junction by evening of the second day of its attack, January 31. Then its patrols discovered that the Americans' December attack had led the Germans to face all their Wahlerscheid defenses southward, pointing away from the new advance of the 9th. Thus the division moved in among the fortifications the next day with relative ease. Robertson's 2nd Division meanwhile fought its way back through Krinkelt and Rocherath, and by February 1 it was able to join in clearing Wahlerscheid. The next day the 9th Division pushed some six kilometers beyond Wahlerscheid toward Gemünd, while the 2nd Division, diverging again from the 9th, drove about the same distance toward Scheiden. The V Corps attack thus had received some belated dividends from the earlier hard fighting in the Monschau Forest, and in addition had fortunately struck that proverbial weakness, an interarmy boundary, in this instance the seam between Manteuffel's Fifth Panzer Army and the Fifteenth Army just to the north of it. The V Corps was well along toward accomplishing one of Bradley's principal objectives, moving behind and around the Roer dams.

Yet this rate of progress was not enough. There had been penetration of the West Wall by the XVIII Corps but no breakthrough. The V Corps may have been on the verge of a breakthrough, but Eisenhower would not allow time to test the possibility. As Bradley understood the circumstances, the Supreme Commander had pledged to Montgomery before the German counteroffensive that if the First and Ninth Armies could not break free of the West Wall by the first of the year, the Allied main effort would go to 21 Army Group. While having allowed an extra month because of the Ardennes battle, Montgomery was now insisting that the pledge be fulfilled. Eisenhower felt he must honor it. Implicitly, at least, Eisenhower apparently had in fact promised Montgomery to decide the fate of the Eifel offensive by the beginning of February. Montgomery was free at last of vexatious diversions on the Channel coast as well as the need to backstop the Americans in the Ardennes, and he said his army group was ready to attack across the Rhine beginning February 8. Beyond any promises that might have been made, if Montgomery was ready, then Eisenhower's own priorities and the pressure of the Combined Chiefs of Staff dictated that Montgomery must receive his opportunity.

On February 1 at First Army headquarters, "The biggest and most unsatisfactory news of the day is that there will probably be a general regrouping and shifting of forces in order that the British together with the Ninth Army . . . may put on its [their] long planned and long wanted 'big show'. . . . General Thorson arrived back from Group tonight with this news and tomorrow Gen Bradley and Gen Simpson will arrive for a conference on details."[11] Eisenhower ordered Bradley to cancel the Eifel offensive and to be prepared to shift troops north from both the First and Third Armies to the Ninth Army. There were not enough divisions or replacements to permit these three armies to take the offensive simultaneously. The 12th Army Group was to revert to the defensive, except that the First Army must safeguard the Ninth Army's attack by capturing the Roer dams, and quickly. It would not suffice for the major, northern offensive to the Rhine to wait for the V Corps to go around the dams.

Eisenhower had suggested that Bradley move his tactical headquarters to Namur to be close to Montgomery and better able to confer and cooperate with him. His own unpleasant encounters with the field marshal notwithstanding, the Supreme Commander somehow retained misconceptions about Monty's willingness to confer with anybody, especially an American of approximately equal stature. The move put Bradley awkwardly far behind Hodges's headquarters, which had returned to Spa; it was also the first retrograde movement of 12th Army Group headquarters. The only real advantage was that, with his command post in the provincial palace, Bradley installed his living quarters in the Château de Namur and enjoyed a superb view of the convergence of the Sambre and Meuse.

The Battles of Prüm and Bitburg

Bradley's concentrated power-punch into the Eifel was cut short in mid-swing, even though Eisenhower as usual relented from his formal orders enough to give Bradley a measure of freedom for limited attacks. The Supreme Commander decided that while shifting troops to the Ninth Army and taking the Roer dams, Bradley might continue advancing until February 10 with the strength he retained in the Eifel, with the hope of gaining a line from Gemünd to Prüm that would secure the Losheim Gap for possible future utility. As for the Third Army, Patton might "continue the probing attacks now in progress," to prevent the enemy from concentrating against Montgomery in the north.[12] Eisenhower well knew that Patton would give the phrase "probing attacks" a generous interpretation.

Though starting a day later than Ridgway's XVIII Corps, Culin's 87th Division had approximated Ridgway's rate of progress and performed its assignment of shielding Ridgway's right; senior commanders were learning that where they saw the acorn badge of Culin's former Mississippi, Louisiana, and Arkansas National Army division, they could expect efficient performance under unassuming but thoroughly competent leadership. Farther south, however, terrain and the quality of the opposition had combined to restrict the Third Army's initial advances to a generally slower pace than those of the First Army. The partners of the 87th Division in Middleton's VIII Corps, Blakeley's 4th and Rooks's 90th Divisions, had to begin by crossing the Our River and its gorge directly into the teeth of the West Wall on the high opposite bank. While they both achieved crossings on the first day, in doing so they alerted the enemy and prepared him to contest their advance with considerable tenacity as they plodded through the snow into the Eifel. The backbone of the defense was the 9th Panzer Division, still a respectable opponent despite the cost of the Ardennes.

Nowhere had the VIII Corps reached the main defenses of the West Wall when Bradley gave to Patton the order to go over to the defensive, except for "probing attacks now in progress." Patton's response on February 3 was to instruct Middleton to keep moving, to drive through the West Wall to Prüm. To compensate as much as he could for the loss of the First Army's strength in tandem with Middleton, Patton also ordered Eddy's XII Corps into the battle, directing Eddy to attack northeastward from around

Echternach to take Bitburg. General Millikin's III Corps, between the VIII and the XII, might later join in to link its neighbors' zones of advance. To his staff and his corps and division leaders, Patton made no secret of his intention to force opportunities that would compel Eisenhower to let him resume a full-scale offensive after all.

It was the "rock soup" method of advance, of which Patton had made a dubious art since the gasoline shortage of the previous September:

> A tramp once went to a house and asked for some boiling water to make rock soup. The lady was interested and gave him the water, in which he placed two polished white stones. He then asked if he might have some potatoes and carrots to put in the soup to flavor it a little, and finally ended up with some meat. In other words, in order to attack, we had first to pretend to reconnoiter, then reinforce the reconnaissance, and finally put on an attack—all depending on what gasoline and ammunition we could secure.[13]

Patton enjoined his confidants to keep his aggressive intentions toward the Eifel secret from the rest of the world, particularly from Eisenhower, but he might as well have tried to silence the rumble of his tanks as to hide purposes by now so transparent and predictable. When he received a summons to a conference with Eisenhower at Bastogne, he feared he might be being called on the carpet for insubordination; but Eisenhower was no more ready than before to shackle Patton completely, and at the conference nothing was said about his supposedly surreptitious plans. On the other hand, seeing Patton for the first time since the crisis in the Ardennes, Eisenhower said nothing in praise of the Third Army's achievements around Bastogne either, thus wounding sensitive feelings. For all that, making "rock soup" in the Eifel proved to offer further indications of the success that might have crowned a continued concentrated drive by two armies.

When campaigns traverse battlefields of the past, the terrain tends to shape the new battles into recapitulations of the old. It is not often that it is the same troops who perform again under the familiar stage directions, but the 4th Divison was about to undergo this very experience as it attacked the West Wall on the crest of the Schnee Eifel north of the village of Brandscheid. This division had fought among the same pillboxes as part of the abortive V Corps advance into the Ardennes-Eifel in the late summer of 1944. Then as now in February, its penetration of the band of fortifications was remarkably easy, even considering that the band was as thin here as anywhere on the German frontier. Then as now, the test of the division's prowess and the offensive's potential came with the German counterattacks.

American intelligence estimated German strength in front of the VIII Corps as oddments of seven Volksgrenadier divisions with a total of only about 7,000 men, backed by three panzer-type divisions aggregating some 4,500, with about seventy tanks and assault guns. The latter included the 9th Panzers, who began giving Middleton's men tough going on the way from the Our to the Schnee Eifel. When the 4th Division resumed its efforts against the Schnee Eifel on February 4, events confirmed the G-2 estimate of enemy numbers as substantially and gratifyingly accurate. The panzers had evidently pulled back into reserve. The principal battle was against the tired infantry of the 326th Volksgrenadier Division, and the 1st Battalions of both the 8th and the 22nd Infantry Regiments won firm lodgments in the pillboxes along the crest around Brandscheid, with the intent that the remaining battalions would roll up the fortifications in the rest of the division sector and capture Brandscheid the next day.

This scenario continued to unfold, and Brandscheid fell, but the fighting on February 5 was distinctly tougher than on the first day and grew worse as the hours went by. The weather, as usual, contributed its share of troubles, this time with an unseasonable thaw that turned small streams into torrents and roads into treacherous slush and clinging mud. On the third day Rooks's 90th Division, previously just demonstrating, joined the attack in earnest, and that day enough Germans rose in counterattack at various points on the line that the rifles Rooks brought into the fray were exceedingly welcome to Middleton's whole corps. The 358th Regiment of the 90th was supposed to relieve the 22nd Regiment in Brandscheid so the 22nd could push on toward Prüm, while the 358th would move southeast in the direction of high ground along the Prüm River between Prüm and Pronsfeld. While the relief was in progress, before daylight on February 6, the enemy came charging out of sleet and rain to break the 22nd Infantry's line. Only the timely arrival of the 358th permitted the two regiments together to roll the Germans back.

Farther south, Rooks's 359th Regiment attacked Habscheid as the opening move in the 90th Division's advance toward Pronsfeld. Most of the 359th infiltrated into Habscheid before dawn, only to discover with daylight that the enemy still held pillboxes in the rear commanding a heavy gate of logs anchored in concrete on the road from the Our. When engineers tried to blow the gate so tanks and supplies could get through, the pillboxes sprayed them with intolerable machine-gun fire and called down heavier weapons on them. Without tank support, the vanguard fighting among other pillboxes in Habscheid came near being stymied. Eventually a self-propelled 155mm. gun approached to knock out the defenses at the gate and permit the engineers to open the way for tanks by nightfall.

The fortified gate had given the Germans an opportunity to cut off the 359th Infantry, but the enemy evidently could not muster the strength to do more than rattle his machine guns while the opportunity drained away. The Americans were hitting the Brandscheid area with two divisions now—plus the 87th clearing pillboxes on the left flank of the 4th—while in September they had had only one, and that one tired and without the support of an army headquarters convinced that the enemy's thinning of his Eifel defenses offered prizes not to be missed. These new ingredients broke the latest Battle of the Schnee Eifel free from the September pattern. While the 359th Infantry was fighting for Habscheid and thereby busying many of the defenders, the 22nd Infantry moved east out of Brandscheid into the first tier of villages beyond the West Wall. It was precisely here that the earlier drive of the 4th Division had halted, because General Barton did not have enough men to cross Mon Creek in the valley beyond the Schnee Eifel and to occupy another range of high ground farther east and commanding the creek, while no one believed in his attack enough to give him the necessary troops. But Blakeley had men enough for both the stream crossing and the high ground—he had not yet committed his third regiment—and he had the confidence of knowing there was still more power coming out of reserve; for Patton and Middleton were pleased enough with the battle that they promptly committed Kilburn's 11th Armored Division south of Habscheid.

Within four and a half hours the armor drove two kilometers into the West Wall and seized a fortified eminence, Losenseifen Hill, which had defied the V Corps in September and dominated a wide arena. By nightfall on February 6, the VIII Corps had broken the

West Wall on a front of eighteen kilometers. Corps and army headquarters were urging the divisions on to further achievement. Patton prepared to use the 11th Armored's advance to uncover an Our crossing for the III Corps.

The Germans might be too few for a stout defense even of dragon's teeth and pillboxes, but they remained customarily persistent in nagging counterstrokes. On February 7 the 22nd Infantry had to fight all day and sometimes to counterattack against counterattacks to hold or recapture the high ground commanding Mon Creek. The next day the 2nd Panzer Division—also a veteran of the earlier Eifel battles—came into the fight from the armored reserve. It contributed much to halting Middleton's advances everywhere except in the 87th Division sector on the northern flank, and it mauled Company G of the 22nd Infantry when tanks and grenadiers caught the company with no weapons but its small arms on the east bank of yet another troublesome creek, the Mehlen. Meanwhile another old adversary, the 352nd Volksgrenadier Division, was engaging the 357th Infantry of the 90th Division in an uncertain seesaw battle for a dominating elevation, Hill 511, along the Habscheid-Pronsfeld road.

Matters continued in similar suspense for two more days. An advantage overlooked by American intelligence when Middleton first attacked was his hitting another vulnerable interarmy boundary, between Manteuffel's Fifth Panzer Army and Brandenberger's Seventh Army; but the Germans had adjusted by giving the Seventh Army the whole threatened area, and Brandenberger in turn responded by reinforcing the battle against the VIII Corps with what remained of the 276th, 340th, and 352nd Volksgrenadier Divisions and the 5th Parachute Division as well as the 2nd Panzers.

These forces could slow Middleton's drive with a plague of counterattacks, but they did not have enough soldiers or weapons to stop it; the only men with the capacity to do that were at SHAEF headquarters on Patton's own side of no man's land. Late on February 10, German prisoners reported the beginning of the evacuation of Prüm, and the 4th Division entered the outskirts of the town the next day and cleared it on February 12. By that time, the 87th and 90th Divisions as well as the 4th had closed to the Prüm River. But the Third Army had just suffered the loss of an entire division, because on February 10 Bradley had informed Patton that he must transfer both an infantry division and one of his corps headquarters to the First Army.

This announcement was almost enough to cost Bradley all the credit he had earned with Patton when he stood up to SHAEF over the business of the Colmar pocket. As long as his troops were advancing, however, Patton's mood was likely to be ebullient, and thus he took his latest grievance in stride. For the corps headquarters with which to part, he chose Millikin and the III, informing his diary that Millikin was amateurish anyway—he had never commanded a division in action before he got a corps, a violation of Patton's precepts—and that it was better to have two big corps than three little ones. Patton gave Middleton General Grow's 6th Armored Division from Millikin's corps as well as control of the III Corps sector—the latter an index of Patton's steadily rising esteem for Middleton as the most consistently reliable of his corps chieftains, never spectacular but almost always cool and tactically skillful. Middleton's corps was about to pause at the Prüm River to let its supplies catch up; hard use and the thaw after the long freeze had played havoc with the roads. Before crossing the Prüm, Middleton could also take on the task earlier proposed for the III Corps, that of linking up the VIII Corps offensive with the XII.

General Eddy had opened his XII Corps drive from Echternach toward Bitburg on the night of February 6–7, and his experiences had largely paralleled Middleton's. Like the VIII Corps, the XII was restaging part of the September V Corps attack into the Eifel, indeed the part of it that had been most promising. In September the 5th Armored Division had scored a clean breakthrough past the West Wall and gone well beyond the village of Wallendorf up a narrow terrain corridor from the Sauer and Our Rivers toward Bitburg, only to be called back because there were no troops to keep the corridor open behind it, and no inclination at any headquarters to support an offensive into the Eifel by providing them. Like the VIII Corps, the XII was prepared this time to correct the deficiencies of the earlier attack, particularly by moving into the Wallendorf corridor only after it had secured the high ground commanding it, on the corps right flank in the area between the confluence of the Sauer River and the Prüm. Like the VIII Corps, the XII had to begin its attack with a difficult river crossing between high banks and into the teeth of the West Wall.

The Sauer River, swollen by the thaw to twice its usual twenty-five-meter width and with its current dangerously accelerated, gave Eddy's men a more troublesome crossing than Middleton's had had at the Our. General Irwin's 5th Infantry Division, protected on its right by the 417th Regiment of Major General William R. Schmidt's new 76th Division, was to cross between Bollendorf and Echternach to take on the main task of capturing the hills between the Sauer and the Prüm. General McBride's 80th Division was to cross farther north, between Wallendorf and Bollendorf, to shield the left of the 5th, and eventually to strike up the Wallendorf corridor toward Bitburg in cooperation with General Gaffey's 4th Armored Division. The crossings of both assault divisions turned into nightmares of capsizing and out-of-control boats, under mortar and artillery fire from the high eastern bank. Through the whole first day the 5th Division was able to land only two boatloads—eight men per boat—on the hostile shore, contriving to keep them there by concentrating all available artillery to lay down a screen around them, and bringing tanks and tank destroyers right up to the west bank of the river to take nearby enemy pillboxes under direct observed fire. The 417th Infantry was somewhat luckier and got a little over 100 men of Companies A and B across. The 80th Division began its crossing two hours later than the 5th. With surprise already gone, it used smoke to mark likely crossing sites and draw the enemy's fire, and then sent its boats over elsewhere. Eddy ordered Irwin to begin crossing 5th Division troops into the 417th Infantry and 80th Division bridgeheads.

Making the foothold secure nevertheless consumed three more days, because it was not until February 11 that engineers were able to overcome swollen current and machine-gun, mortar, Nebelwerfer, and artillery fire to bridge the river. Meanwhile at least a dozen bridges were lost in unsuccessful building attempts. Before a bridge was complete thirteen infantry battalions had crossed by boat, the 5th Division and the 417th Infantry had a foothold six kilometers wide and not quite two kilometers deep, and the 80th Division held two small separate footholds. The West Wall fortifications so badly impeded linking these positions that even Patton, when he visited on February 12, offered to let Eddy halt attacks for a day to regroup. Eddy declined, and indeed, with the 80th Division joining its two bridgeheads that morning, both divisions managed to link up during the evening.

Thereafter the parallels to Middleton's progress were striking. The Germans were strong enough to contest every hill and stream crossing, and to persist in their habitual counterattacks, but not strong enough to halt a steadily flowing American tide. The 80th Division found itself fighting the German LIII Corps, which had already yielded troops to reinforce the battle against Middleton. The 5th Division had to face reinforcements from the Trier area just to the south; but they amounted only to about two regiments, and the weakening of Trier brought a new gleam to Patton's eye. By February 24, the 5th Division cleared the triangle between the Sauer and the Prüm to within nine kilometers of Bitburg. Irwin then turned much of the area over to the 76th Division to concentrate his own strength for crossing the Prüm in a final drive on Bitburg.

By that date, too, the VIII and XII Corps together had cleared the space between their bridgeheads in the Eifel, called the Vianden bulge because it lay just east of that town on the Our. This task was a secondary one, but it was also difficult, because it involved scouring some of the most rugged country in the whole rugged Eifel, with especially deep and precipitous ravines breaking through irregular, forested hills. Against the bulge, the 80th Division attacked northeast from Wallendorf on February 18, while Middleton attacked south and southeast with no less than three of his divisions, from right to left the 6th Armored, the 90th, and the 11th Armored, screened by the 6th Cavalry Group along the Our.

The direction of the attacks saved the Americans for the most part from frontal assaults against the bulge's West Wall pillboxes from across the Our. Furthermore, when the 6th Armored went into action against the pillboxes on February 20, it demonstrated an effective technique that General Grow and his officers had contrived for the occasion. An intensive, twenty-minute artillery preparation preceded the assault on the West Wall by the division's CCB. The fire then lifted for ten minutes, to tempt the Germans out of their pillboxes and into more vulnerable field fortifications, whereupon all the artillery available plastered a one-minute TOT upon the first specific objective, a fortified hill. Then CCB went forward with much of its armored infantry organized into pillbox assault teams of half a platoon each. An assault team would approach a pillbox while an associated support fire team sprayed the embrasures with small-arms fire. On a prearranged signal, the support team would lift its fire while the assault team closed in with wire cutters, demolition charges, and rocket launchers. During a day of eliminating pillboxes, CCB lost only one man to small-arms fire.

On the evening of February 23, Middleton and Grow sent Task Force Duvall (Lieutenant Colonel Harold G. Duvall) of the 6th Armored driving across the front of the 6th Cavalry Group to hasten the meeting with the XII Corps. The mission succeeded; the task force met troops of the 80th Division the next morning just north of Obergeckler. Later in the day, the 90th Division of Middleton's corps also reached the intercorps boundary, and the Vianden bulge was effectively closed off. It was a most satisfactory little operation, for the enemy remained in his fortifications along the western edge of the bulge persistently enough that Patton's two corps swept up some 3,000 prisoners, while suffering only about 600 casualties themselves, including 125 killed.

The news from across the lines was that such misguided persistence still did not satisfy the Führer that his Seventh Army had clung to the West Wall with suitable stubbornness, and consequently General Brandenberger lost command of the army on February 20 to General der Infanterie Hans Felber. Felber had been leading the XIII

Corps against the northern flank of Middleton's drive to the Prüm. No previous change in the German senior command in the West, or pretext therefor, had been more utterly wrongheaded. And at last the disarray at the top of the German military hierarchy was beginning to be matched by the first signs of loss of cohesion in the units at the front. When the 5th Division crossed the Prüm during the night of February 24–25, resistance mostly melted away before it. Considerable numbers of German soldiers raised the white flag. The first visible cracks in the admirable cohesion and discipline of the German army were at length opening under the unrelenting pressure that Patton maintained despite every discouragement from his superiors. On February 26, pilots of XIX TAC reported the Germans were evacuating Bitburg.

The Battle of Trier

By the night of February 26, the 11th Infantry Regiment of the 5th Division was in the southern outskirts of Bitburg, and a task force of the 4th Armored Division was on the west bank of the Kyll River only three kilometers to the northeast. The Americans entered Bitburg in force the next day; Patton had left the West Wall behind him on a front of some thirty-five to forty kilometers and captured the two road centers, Prüm and Bitburg, that were the necessary bases for crossing the remainder of the Eifel to the Rhine. But his passion for retracing the paths of ancient conquerors, whenever doing so could at all plausibly be combined with present strategic or tactical advantage, had already diverted Patton's attentions for the moment to a different target. On the day the fighter-bombers reported the evacuation of Bitburg, Patton hastened to the headquarters of the right-flank division of the XII Corps, Schmidt's 76th, and struck the operations map where it marked the historic city of the Treveri, the possessors, according to Caesar, of the best cavalry in Gaul.

General Walker's overextended XX Corps was already nibbling in the direction of Trier with such resources as it could muster for the purpose from its fifty-kilometer front. By turning the 76th Division southward, Patton intended to convert the attack on Trier and on the triangle between the Saar and the Moselle in front of it into an envelopment. To lend the envelopment appropriate power, he hoped to inveigle SHAEF into granting him additional strength for the XX Corps.

While Twaddle's 95th Division and Paul's 26th together held about fifteen kilometers on Walker's right flank, and the 3rd Cavalry Group defended a similar distance in his center, Major General Harry J. Maloney's inexperienced 94th Division had occupied since January 7 some twenty kilometers on Walker's left. This division appeared to be of questionable quality on several grounds. Apart from its newness, it had the highest ratio of noncombat to combat casualties in the Third Army, and Patton had recently threatened Maloney with becoming a noncombat casualty himself if his men did not shape up.

The 94th faced generally north toward the Orscholz Switch, in the area where, back in November, Patton had hoped to use the 83rd Division before it was snatched away from him in one of the earliest of such infuriating incidents. The Orscholz Switch had thereafter defied the combined efforts of CCA of the 10th Armored Division and the 358th Infantry of the 90th Division. On January 12, Walker had ordered Maloney to begin a series of battalion-size probings against the Orscholz Switch, partly to prevent the enemy

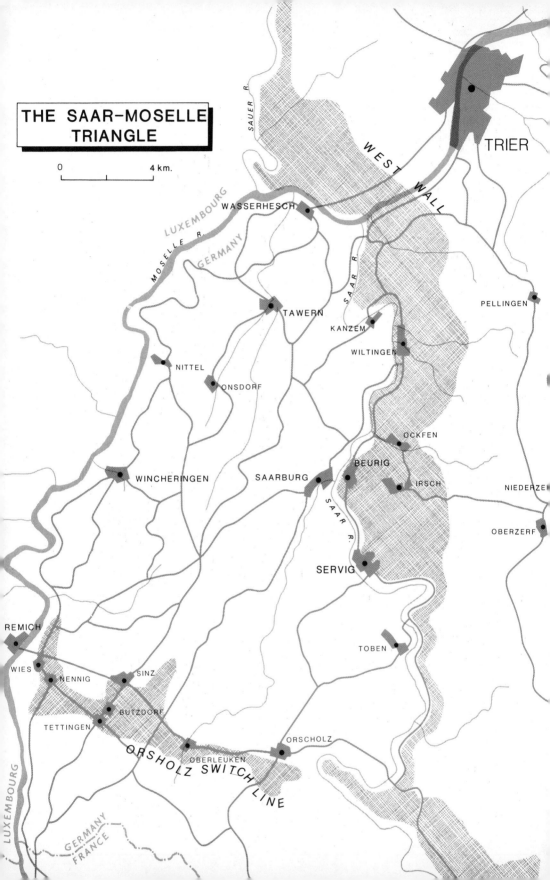

THE SAAR-MOSELLE
TRIANGLE

0   4 km.

TRIER

SAUER R.

WEST WALL

LUXEMBOURG

MOSELLE R.

GERMANY

WASSERHESCH

SAAR R.

TAWERN

KANZEM

PELLINGEN

WILTINGEN

NITTEL

ONSDORF

OCKFEN

BEURIG

IRSCH

NIEDERZE

WINCHERINGEN

SAARBURG

OBERZERF

SAAR R.

SERVIG

REMICH

TOBEN

WIES

SINZ

NENNIG

BUTZDORF

TETTINGEN

ORSCHOLZ

OBERLEUKEN

ORSHOLZ SWITCH LINE

LUXEMBOURG

GERMANY
FRANCE

from reducing his garrisons there to send reinforcements elsewhere, partly to add to the 94th Division's seasoning—it had helped earlier to contain Lorient and St. Nazaire—and especially to further Patton's developing designs upon Trier.

The Orscholz Switch lay in the domain of General Blaskowitz's Army Group G, which had strained its resources for the New Year's offensive in Alsace; thus the first American probe was able to achieve gratifying progress against weakly held pillboxes. The 1st Battalion of the 94th Division's 376th Infantry set out at dawn on January 14 toward Tettingen near the west flank of the switch, a village on a high ridgeline just behind the dragon's teeth. Despite having to plow through heavy snow, the attack pushed into Tettingen so readily that the regimental commander ordered it to keep going into the next village, Butzdorf, which it did. The next day the 3/376th continued the attack toward Nennig and two smaller adjacent villages, and while the resistance became a little stiffer, the day's objectives fell. In two days the 376th Infantry had broken the right flank of the Orscholz Switch.

The first of the enemy's ritualistic counterattacks were also overcome with relative ease. The prisoners were all from the German 416th Infantry Division, which evidently was holding the whole switch line with only two regiments. On January 16, however, aerial reconnaissance warned General Maloney to prepare for something tougher, because enemy armor was crossing the Saar in his direction. At dawn on January 18, no less an opponent than the 11th Panzer Division came pounding against Tettingen and Butzdorf, Pzkw IVs, assault guns, grenadiers, and all. If it was seasoning Maloney's men needed, General von Wietersheim's armored veterans were the best instructors in the art of war any raw American troops could be privileged to meet. But other Americans had already learned a great deal from German teachers since the 6th of June, 1944, and enough of the knowledge had found its way into training programs that new American divisions were no longer suffering the trials of initiation quite so painfully as had several in Normandy. In a five-day defensive battle worthy of comparison with Clervaux or Varenne or a score of others in the Ardennes, and despite the 94th Division's grave handicap of having no attached tank battalion, the 376th Infantry yielded Butzdorf and part of Nennig but otherwise held firm. The 11th Panzers could not restore the western anchor of the Orscholz Switch, and misgivings about the 94th Division could be laid aside.

General Maloney, in fact, thought the occasion ripe for a probe into the opposite flank of the switch line, where the town of Orscholz itself crowned another ridgeline. Unfortunately, the enemy was now more alert than he had been when Maloney's troops first struck, and the 1st Battalion of the 301st Infantry not only failed to break the fortifications but lost Company B, isolated and forced to surrender. But Maloney was by no means discouraged, and he returned to the charge on the western flank as soon as Wietersheim's assaults petered out. On January 23, the 376th recaptured all of Nennig and knocked out five Pzkw IVs while doing so.

The 376th enjoyed the assistance of some armored infantry of CCA, 8th Armored Division. Reinforcing success, Patton had decided that the Orscholz Switch was the place to blood this additional new formation, while affording the 94th Division some much-needed tanks. When the 11th Panzer Division, though thwarted in its own attack, proved predictably stubborn about yielding ground, General Walker further reinforced success by removing the restriction that had held each of Maloney's attacks to the size of a reinforced battalion. Maloney thereupon formed a neat plan to attack northeast from Tettingen and Butzdorf along their ridgeline to Sinz and Munzingen, beyond the fortifications. On January 26, the 302nd Infantry, now on his left, was to open a hole for CCA, 8th Armored, which would then roll up the defenders in front of the 376th Infantry.

The plan did not work out because the 302nd and CCA could not open the hole for exploitation; but the 376th drove forward anyway, and by January 27 its infantry and CCA tanks had at least reached high ground overlooking Sinz. At this juncture CCA had to be withdrawn for employment elsewhere, and the February thaw slowed the action by enmeshing everything in mud. Nevertheless, Maloney pushed forward as persistently as he could, and his persistence won its reward. The Germans had too few strong panzer divisions to expend the 11th in defensive battle; early in February, Wietersheim's men and armor began departing the scene. Immediately, Maloney found the going easier against the 256th Volksgrenadier Division, a unit recently beaten up in Alsace.

By mid-month, Maloney believed he was on the verge of a complete breakthrough past the Orscholz Switch, and he proposed to throw in his whole division, along with a tank battalion at last, the 778th, to drive up the ridge to Munzingen and apply the coup de grace. Walker and Patton agreed with Maloney's assessment of the prospects; the problem would be exploitation. This was where Patton's persuasive powers with SHAEF would have to come into play. The 8th Armored Division was gone. General Morris's 10th Armored had been attached to Walker's corps on February 11, but it could be employed only with General Eisenhower's specific approval, and neither the Saar-Moselle triangle in general nor Trier, just beyond the triangle, in particular appeared on SHAEF's agenda of Third Army "probing attacks now in progress."

On February 14, however, Patton had visited Paris on his first leave since October 1942; and besides shooting ducks at the Royal Preserve of the kings of France, taking in the Folies Bergère, and shopping, he used the occasion to call on SHAEF and talk up with Smith and Bull the wonders he might work with the 10th Armored. SHAEF eventually agreed that Patton might let Walker use Morris's division in one situation: if there was a clear breakthrough. Walker decided this was authority enough to order Morris to begin preparing for commitment and choosing zones of advance. Maloney's division opened its big attack before dawn on February 19. The results were as the generals expected. With the right flank of the Orscholz Switch already broken, the remaining Germans could not resist a division-strength attack. Maloney's 301st Infantry pressed its 1st and 3rd Battalions almost to Munzingen by daylight. Where occasional clusters of pillboxes resisted stoutly, the 778th Tank Battalion intervened to keep the advance moving. Mines were more troublesome than German troops. Before the morning was gone, Maloney urged Walker to commit the 10th Armored. Unable to reach Bradley by telephone, Patton called directly to Bull at SHAEF, who agreed he might use Morris's division, but only until the Saar-Moselle triangle was cleared—which still left out Trier. Nevertheless, the 10th Armored began rolling the next morning, and its progress proved that the 94th Division had achieved the stipulated clear breakthrough.

CCR headed up the western side of the triangle close to the Moselle, CCA up the center of the triangle. CCR with the 376th Infantry attached was aiming for the north tip of the triangle and toward throwing the Germans into sufficient disarray that CCA would be able to capture the Saar bridges at Kanzem and Wiltingen to assure a road to Trier. The 94th Division would sweep the countryside and the remains of the Orscholz Switch in the rear.

CCR met little obstruction except Germans wanting to surrender, and it reached the tip on February 21. CCA encountered somewhat more trouble, especially from mines, and it reached Kanzem and Wiltingen only after the bridges were blown. Walker nevertheless ordered an immediate crossing of the Saar, to keep the Germans on the run and prevent their regrouping in the West Wall on the east bank of the river, which dominates the western shore. He hoped the 10th Armored would cross during the night of February 21–22 northeast of Saarburg, the 94th Division the same night southeast of the town. Trucks were unable to carry the assault boats across the Saar-Moselle triangle until the morning of February 22; but fortunately it was not quite dawn, and a heavy fog had settled over the Saar, when the advance of the 301st and 302nd Infantry began crossing at Serrig and Taben, respectively. Though the Germans came back to life to resist strongly at Serrig, both bridgeheads were firm and the two were joined by nightfall.

Patton himself was on hand at Ockfen to hurry the 10th Armored across the Saar when its boats at last arrived about midday on February 22, but the Germans had been given enough time to reinforce the West Wall opposite, and they showered the western shore with so heavy a fire that the crossing could not begin. The attached 376th Infantry managed to grasp a bridgehead during the next night, but with heavy losses. By that time, Walker had formed a new plan. He sent the 5th Ranger Battalion through the 94th Division bridgehead during the same night to form a roadblock on the main east-west highway in the area, around Zerf, to slow the arrival of enemy reinforcements. The Rangers were in place by dawn. Meanwhile the 94th Division moved northward toward Beurig, across the river from Saarburg and where the road blocked by the Rangers crossed the river. The 10th Armored shifted to cross the Saar at the 94th Division crossing at Taben, where there was now a bridge, and then go north on the east shore, also toward Beurig. Thence the armor could turn east, relieve the Rangers, and be well placed for another move toward Trier.

This plan did not quite succeed, but Walker possessed flexibility and adaptability to match his aggressiveness, and a few mishaps made little difference. The principal trouble was that the 94th was unable to fight its way quickly into Beurig. But thereupon CCB, leading the 10th Armored, moved along a trail that took it to the Beurig-Zerf highway east of Beurig. On the afternoon of February 25, the armor was about to relieve the Rangers on the highway at Irsch when its column was ambushed by a Tiger, an 88, and two Panzerfäuste. These weapons knocked out three Shermans before the Rangers, reaching out to touch hands with their relief, in effect relieved the armor by helping to send the Tiger and its consorts packing. As the incident suggested, the Rangers had held their roadblock in good shape, despite strong counterattacks. CCB now pushed on through the Rangers eastward to the next main north-south road, which could take it to Trier, only eighteen kilometers away. Meanwhile the loss of the Beurig-Zerf highway evidently prompted the Germans to abandon Beurig, and the 301st Infantry cleared the town.

Walker and Patton were poised for their final plunge into Trier—assuming they could retain the 10th Armored, their use of which had already stretched SHAEF's instructions. With SHAEF badgering him and even Bradley warning that sending the division all the way to Trier would get him into trouble, Patton managed on February 23 to persuade SHAEF to give him a forty-eight-hour extension on the use of the division. "It always made me mad to have to beg for opportunities to win battles," said Patton.[14] When the forty-eight hours had passed, Patton appealed to his reliable—if sometimes complaining—champion, Bradley, who agreed to take upon himself the responsibility of letting Patton keep the 10th Armored until nightfall of February 27 for the specific purpose of capturing Trier. "The tent maker [Omar]," said Patton, "felt that we should stop attacking, and it took me and all three corps commanders half a day to get permission to continue the attack for another 48 hours, at which time if we have not taken a certain town then we will have to stop."[15]

At dawn of February 27, CCA had taken CCB's place in the lead up the main north-south highway from the Zerf area toward Trier, and Schmidt's 76th Division of the XII Corps had turned toward the city from the north. Alas, CCA struck a minefield south of Pellingen in mid-afternoon, lost two tanks, and had to halt for the rest of the day while engineers cleared the mines. The latest deadline passed with the 10th Armored still nine kilometers from Trier. Patton telephoned Bradley again. Bradley had heard nothing recently from SHAEF, and he said he would do nothing until he did hear—and he would stay away from the telephone for the time being.

CCA took Pellingen on the last day of February. On March 1, General Morris turned most of the combat command west to the junction of the Saar and the Moselle to prevent enemy troops from retreating north through the West Wall into Trier. Another CCA task force continued up the main road. CCB chose an alternate road to swing into the city from the east. At mid-afternoon, the main columns of CCA and CCB were both stuck against pillboxes and 88s at the city's outer defenses. Colonel Roberts of CCB—of Bastogne fame—detached a task force under Lieutenant Colonel Jack J. Richardson and ordered it to try to find a path into Trier by secondary roads between the main forces—and to head straight for the bridges over the Moselle.

Task Force Richardson got under way after dark but in clear moonlight. It met nothing except four antitank guns whose crews preferred surrender to a fight. Inside the city, Richardson split his task force to send a team to each of the bridges. One bridge proved to have been blown, but the Kaiserbrücke, some of whose piers and buttresses may date from 28 B.C., was intact. Covered by machine-gun fire from Richardson's own tank, a platoon of armored infantry and a platoon of tanks rushed it and got across in time to forestall the work of a demolition team on the west bank. Parts of both CCA and CCB fought their way into the city during the rest of the night, and the inhabitants awoke to learn that George S. Patton, Jr., had added his name to Julius Caesar's on the list of their conquerors.

Patton himself received that morning a new inquiry from Bradley about giving up the 10th Armored. He was ready to do so now; but the disparity between the accomplishments of the division and his haggling with the "the tent maker" and SHAEF over using it symbolized to Patton the differences between what he had already done and the greater accomplishments that might have been his and the Third and First Armies' if their concentrated invasion of Germany had not been cut short and scattered.

Fortunately, though his insatiable thirst for glory drove Patton to worry over his grievances to excess, it also pushed him constantly forward. Much opportunity still lay ahead. By crashing through the West Wall all the way from Prüm to Orscholz and crossing the lower Moselle, he was ready either to complete a sweep south along the Moselle that would place his army behind the West Wall defenses of the Saarland and threaten to trap the German First Army, or to turn north to meet Hodges's First Army on the Rhine in an operation, already well advanced in Bradley's planning, that might envelop both the right of the German Seventh Army facing Patton and the left of the enemy army opposite Hodges.

Patton savored his conquest of Trier on March 14, driving into the city along Caesar's road, where he "could smell the sweat of the legions," imagining them marching before him into the still-surviving amphitheater where the Emperor Constantine the Great had thrown his captives to the beasts. In the evenings, Patton was reading Caesar's *Gallic Wars*. But his ambitious soul could not rest. For all the triumphs of the offensive through the Eifel and the Saar-Moselle triangle to Trier, the Third Army had begun the campaign farther from the Rhine than any other army on the Western Front, and Patton still had so far to go that he feared his would be the last army to cross the Rhine, or at least not the first, as it ought to be. "We are in a horse race with Courtney," Patton wrote his wife as early as March 6. "If he beats me [across the Rhine], I shall be ashamed."[16]

32: Two Tumors Excised: Colmar and the Roer Dams

Eight of the Allies' divisions were French. This was one reason why General Eisenhower did not brim over with confidence when he counted Allied and German divisions. "The French divisions have at present," he said, "except for one [the 2ème Blindée], a low combat value. . . . French divisions are always a questionable asset."[1]

The basic reason continued to be the undermanning of the French First Army, no solution having yet been found for the effects of winter upon the colonial troops, or for the diversion of French forces to contain various German enclaves persistently holding out inside France. The many political disruptions of the French army in the past years; the creation of the existing army out of an amalgam of Gaullist, Vichyite, and FFI troops; the political conflicts accompanying the amalgamation; the consequent lack of uniform training standards, and particularly the lack of rigorous training among the FFI; the dependence of the French on American logistical and administrative support, for which they stood near the end of the line—all these circumstances contributed to the at least partial truth of Eisenhower's harsh judgment about his French formations.

The French naturally took a different view of the quality of their military contribution, and also with some warrant. In late January, Eisenhower betrayed part of his feelings about the French to de Gaulle and to the Chief of Staff of the French Ministry of Defense, General Alphonse Juin, telling them they would more readily get equipment for new divisions if they kept those they already had up to strength, and chiding Juin over that obsessive annoyance, the Colmar pocket. Both of the French leaders responded heatedly, Juin taking the opportunity to remind Eisenhower that the length of the French army's front had about doubled under the impact of the Ardennes battle and the German attack in Alsace, with no proportionate increase in French resources; yet the army had yielded no substantial ground and was preparing even now for a new offensive against the irritating pocket. Meeting one invidious judgment with another, Juin contrasted "the valiant efforts" of the French army with "the goings-on in the neighboring Army further to the North."[2]

The Colmar Pocket

It was true enough that holding the larger share of the 200-kilometer front of the 6th Army Group had kept General Patch's American Seventh Army precariously on the defensive through January, and that Patch's Seventh had yielded much more ground than the tiny corner north of Rhinau that General de Lattre's First Army gave up to the January 7 German attack out of the Colmar pocket. Happily, to force Patch's Moder River line against prepared defenses in a frontal assault through the snow proved

[596]

narrowly beyond the limited offensive strength of Germany's southernmost army groups. This the enemy conceded, not only by pulling many of his best units from the area soon after the failure of his January 24–25 attacks, but also by removing Heinrich Himmler from the scene. Himmler's anomalous Army Group Oberrhein returned to Army Group G and the jurisdiction of OB West.

It would not do, after all, for so eminent a Nazi to become involved in evident, unambiguous defeat. If the frustration of Germany's Alsace offensive was not quite that, the loss of the Colmar pocket would be. And on January 20, the French First Army had begun the promised effort that Eisenhower was determined should excise the vexatious pocket at last.

De Lattre led off with his I Corps against the southern flank of the pocket. On the night of January 22–23, his II Corps joined in against the northern flank. The object was to converge on Neuf–Brisach and the Rhine bridge at Breisach and thus to envelop the pocket. General O'Daniel's 3rd Infantry Division had been assigned to de Lattre's army since December but had recently withdrawn from the line to rehearse for the attack, its positions filled by Cota's 28th Division, slowly recuperating from the Ardennes. The 28th was to play an auxiliary role in de Lattre's attack, with the 3rd forming the II Corps spearhead.

At first, the weather conspired with the enemy to make it appear that once again the defenders of the pocket, now estimated at some 50,000, might hold off the entire French First Army. The snow was deep enough that progress would have been painfully gradual even without other obstacles, and other obstacles were plentiful, in the form of hundreds of mines as well as the machine guns, artillery, tanks, and troops constituting the bulk of the German Nineteenth Army. The 3rd Division attacked across the Fecht River near its junction with the River Ill, the 7th Infantry Regiment taking the town of Ostheim and feeling its way through the dense and densely mined Colmar Forest toward the Ill. The 30th Regiment captured a bridge over the Ill, crossed with much of its force, received a panzer counterattack, called up Shermans, and then saw the bridge collapse under the first friendly tank. The Germans as always proved quick to take advantage of an enemy's isolation, and through the rest of January 23 the 30th Infantry had to beat off almost constant counterattacks. When engineers completed a Bailey bridge at 7:30 the next morning, more Shermans made their way through a hail of 88 shells just in time to collide with a bevy of Pzkw IVs. The rival tanks rattled and rumbled against each other through most of January 24 before the American bridgehead could be deemed relatively secure.

Security was considerably less than anyone in the Allied camp would have wished because the 1ère Division d'Infanterie Morocaine, on O'Daniel's left and now filled with FFI troops, pushed forward only half-heartedly and thus exposed the 3rd Division's flank to still further enemy counterblows. Certainly O'Daniel could not risk driving southeastward across the Colmar Canal until the heavily fortified area around Jebsheim was cleared. General Devers, unable to hasten the French advance satisfactorily from his army group headquarters, betook himself to the front and on the evening of January 25 conferred with de Lattre and the principal generals of the II Corps. De Lattre also was impatient, but his own prodding failed to work much improvement upon the 1ère D.I.M.'s efforts toward Jebsheim.

O'Daniel, the proverbial pugnacious Irishman, had already moved to take matters into his own hands by concentrating the 254th Regiment of the 63rd Division, attached to the 3rd Division for the Colmar battle, and sending its 1st and 2nd Battalions in a power drive on Jebsheim following a four-battalion artillery preparation early on January 26. This frontal attack failed, but O'Daniel promptly responded by sending the 3/254th on an enveloping maneuver while the other two battalions kept the defenders occupied. The climactic effort against Jebsheim was preceded by an eight-battalion artillery serenade of fifteen minutes' duration during the night of January 26–27, following which the Americans entered the town. In friendly hands Jebsheim shielded the 3rd Division left flank, as O'Daniel resumed the advance with his own regiments. The left of the Jebsheim position was secured in turn by the French 1st Parachute Regiment, a crack outfit, and elements of the 5ème Division Blindée, both attached to O'Daniel's command.

Meanwhile, de Lattre consistently urged that more progress from his army depended on his getting more men, and as early as the second day of the attack, January 21, he had virtually demanded of Devers that the army group extract at least one more infantry division from the clutches of SHAEF. On January 24 Devers underlined his own latest appeal to Eisenhower by reporting that his shortages of riflemen replacements would reach 13,320 by the beginning of February. With the defensive battle on the VI Corps front still unresolved at this juncture, and Eisenhower still intent on eliminating the Colmar pocket, SHAEF relented by promising Devers five additional American divisions—to the subsequent dismay of Bradley and Patton—plus, later, 12,000 service troops for their support. This news heartened Devers to attach General Milburn's new XXI Corps to the French First Army, giving Milburn the 3rd Division, the 28th, the 75th—ordered to begin shifting from the Ardennes on January 25—and the 5ème Blindée. Milburn would take over the right of the French II Corps zone and the main effort to envelop the Colmar pocket from the north, while the II Corps contented itself with guarding his left and clearing that area to the Rhine.

The XXI Corps assumed command in its sector on January 28, and the 3rd Division attack carried across the Colmar Canal east of Colmar the next day. Cota's 28th Division attacked toward Colmar itself, and by the morning of February 2 the 109th Infantry Regiment was on the verge of entering; it stood aside to let the 5ème Blindée do the honors and receive the "delirious enthusiasm" of the populace. By that day, the 75th Division, now under Major General Ray E. Porter, had moved into the line between the 28th and 3rd and late in the afternoon reached the outskirts of Neuf-Brisach.

At last, de Lattre knew the complete liberation of Alsace could not be long denied; the Germans and the snow could accomplish no more than brief delays. Exhilarated, the French commander decided to punish the enemy's stubbornness with not one but two double envelopments. While the convergence on Neuf-Brisach continued, the fall of Colmar convinced him he should hasten a XXI Corps spearhead down the Colmar-Rouffach road to meet his I Corps around the latter place and instantly seal off all the Boche remaining in the Vosges. General Allen's 12th Armored had been added to Milburn's corps, and on February 3 it attacked southward through the Keystone Division. Parts of the armored division were held up by German hornets' nests still stinging on the very edge of Colmar, but the enemy neglected to put up equal resistance on the main road to Rouffach. Breaking through some roadblocks and bypassing others, one task force of Allen's CCA captured Rouffach early in the morning of February 5 while other task forces, encircling the place to cut off the garrison's escape, met the 4ème

Division Morocaine de Montagne of the I Corps. The Colmar pocket was split and the first of de Lattre's envelopments was complete.

Rouffach is famous for its formidable females who in 1105 supposedly divested the Emperor Henry V of his crown and scepter rather than complaisantly yield one of their number to his pleasure. The hapless Germans remaining in the Colmar pocket had lost the capacity for so much anger or formidability. De Lattre had initially intended that after taking Rouffach, the 12th Armored should exploit to the east, but the enemy now seemed so disorganized that mopping up appeared sufficient, and Allen's troops were simply to block off the Vosges between Rouffach and Colmar. Late in the same day that Rouffach fell, off to the northeast, patrols of O'Daniel's 30th Infantry Regiment arrived at the circumference of the walled town of Neuf-Brisach. As the Americans started forward the next morning to assail the walls, they met a Frenchman who led them to what he said was a secret way into the fortress, an eighteen-meter tunnel leading through the wall from the dry moat. A platoon cautiously followed the guide through the tunnel, entered the town, and found only seventy-six German soldiers. The prisoners said their officers had ordered them to resist to the last man, but the officers had decamped.

De Lattre's second envelopment barely missed completion. Some eight to ten kilometers south of Neuf-Brisach, the I Corps was pushing the last knot of German resistance into a narrowing bridgehead against the Rhine, whence the Germans were conducting an evacuation that, as the Allies were to learn, Hitler had prohibited until February 3. The French extinguished the bridgehead on February 9. As great a nuisance to the Allies as the Colmar pocket had been, especially in Eisenhower's mind, by clinging to it so long the Germans had finally turned it into an investment that cost them more than it was worth. The Allies lost 18,000 casualties in reducing the pocket but inflicted at least 22,000 and perhaps as many as twice their own. Of the eight German divisional formations in the final battle for the pocket, only the 708th Volksgrenadier Division escaped reasonably intact—because it led off the evacuation on February 3. More typically, the 2nd Mountain Division lost 1,000 combat casualties and 4,700 prisoners and virtually ceased to exist. The 198th Infantry Division extricated only about 500 troops. The 338th Infantry Division took out only about 400. The evacuation left behind some fifty-five armored vehicles and sixty-six artillery pieces.

The Battle of the Roer Dams

If there was another phrase that even more than "Colmar pocket" resonated with the Allied frustrations of the autumn of 1944, it was "Roer dams." The name conjured up all the battles of the Huertgen Forest as well as the inability of the American First and Ninth Armies to cross the last plain separating them from the Rhine. If Eisenhower's conception of the invasion of Germany demanded that the Colmar pocket be extinguished before the crossing of the Rhine, still more was it necessary that the menace of the flooding of the Roer by German destruction of the dams be overcome before the full weight of 21 Army Group launched the primary Allied offensive into the north German plain. With Eisenhower so committed to Montgomery's offensive as the primary one that he had sacrificed the American concentration in the Eifel in its behalf, the task to which the American First Army had to turn at the very time when the French First Army finally broke the Colmar pocket was the elimination at last of the problem of the Roer dams.

Montgomery's plan called for the Canadian First Army to begin the work of closing the 21 Army Group front to the Rhine by attacking southeast up the west bank from the Nijmegen salient. This phase of his plan was called Operation VERITABLE; D-Day was eventually set as February 8. Shortly thereafter, the Ninth Army was to attack from the Aachen area across the Roer to link up with the Canadians on the Rhine. This phase was Operation GRENADE; the opening date was to be February 10. The British Second Army, between the Canadians and the Americans, would attack from the Maas to help clear the intervening ground if necessary.

The target D-Day for Operation GRENADE left precious little time when at the beginning of February the American First Army called off its offensive in the Eifel and turned again to the capture of the dams, so the Ninth Army would be able to cross the Roer without danger of isolation on the east bank. Some preliminary movement toward the dams had already been accomplished as part of the Eifel offensive, but not much, considering the deadline. Protecting the First Army's left flank, General Parker's 78th Division of the Ninth Army, assisted by CCA, 5th Armored, had attacked on January 31 and on that day and the next pushed forward its penetration of the Monschau corridor from the fringe of the village of Kesternich, held since December, through the rest of the village and several adjacent settlements. The 272nd Volksgrenadier Division of the Fifteenth Army, an adversary too well remembered by American veterans of much of the Huertgen Forest fighting, manned the opposing lines and still resisted with its familiar tenacity and ingenuity. The gains of two days' battles did not look like much on the operations maps, but holding all of Kesternich gave the Americans high ground from which they could lay direct observed fire on the entire remaining defenses west of the Roerstausee, the reservoir behind the Schwammenauel Dam.

On February 2, the 78th Division returned to the First Army and the V Corps, as the First Army's principal mission became the capture of the dams. General Huebner's corps did not simply enjoy an accession of strength; in a general shuffling of responsibilities as the Eifel offensive ended and the better to support GRENADE, the V Corps front was extended southward to relieve the XVIII Airborne Corps, while both the XVIII and the VII Corps moved north of the V Corps to bolster the Ninth Army's south flank.

The same day his division rejoined the First Army, General Parker of the 78th received from General Huebner orders to capture Schmidt and the Roer dams, and to do it quickly. The very names of the objectives might have palsied a relatively inexperienced division and its commander; the scene could palsy the most experienced. General Gavin, whose 82nd Airborne had occupied this sector before the 78th, had walked the 28th Division's trail through the Kall River gorge toward Schmidt:

> It was obviously impassable for a jeep; it was a shambles of wrecked vehicles and abandoned tanks. The first tanks that attempted to go down the trail had evidently slid off and thrown their tracks. In some cases the tanks had been pushed off the trail and toppled down the gorge among the trees. Between where the trail begins outside of Vossenach and the bottom of the canyon, there were four abandoned tank destroyers and five disabled and abandoned tanks. In addition, all along the sides of the trail there were many, many dead bodies, cadavers that had just emerged from the winter snow. Their gangrenous, broken, and torn bodies were rigid and grotesque, some of them with arms skyward, seemingly in supplication. They were wearing the red keystone of the 28th Infantry Division.[3]

Appalled that the route through the Kall gorge had ever been attempted, Gavin had fought his division toward Schmidt along the paved, ridge road from Lammersdorf. While the gorge might be avoided, the imminent kickoff of GRENADE allowed no time for evading a battle for Schmidt itself, however many fearsome specters lay in wait there, because its ridge position so completely commanded the dams. From Parker's position in the Monschau corridor, the Wahlerscheid road led out of the open ground of the corridor into a dense evergreen forest considered by the Americans as part of the Huertgen. Shadowed by the trees for about two kilometers, the road emerged into open country again to climb over Hill 493 and then descend into Schmidt. A narrow feeder road paralleled the main road on the north before joining it in the woods about two kilometers west of Schmidt; at the junction there were barracks believed to be fortified.

Reinforced now by CCR, 7th Armored and an engineer combat battalion, and supported by V Corps and 7th Armored artillery in addition to its own, the 78th Division was to attack before dawn on February 5. Good news came just before the kickoff. General Craig's 9th Division, swinging north from the ground it had taken in the Monschau Forest around Wahlerscheid, had captured the second largest dam, the Urfttalsperre, almost without opposition, and found it apparently intact except for some damage to the outlet tunnels. Good news also came back to Parker's headquarters from the first efforts of his own men; similarly almost without opposition, his 309th Infantry Regiment slipped past pillboxes and bunkers and overran the barracks in the woods, catching some of the German occupants sleeping and others at breakfast.

Parker's plan, based on the expectation of stouter resistance, had called for the 310th Infantry to pass through the 309th beyond the barracks and to seize Schmidt. Unanticipated ease of success now produced unfortunate difficulty, as Parker and Huebner debated whether to allow the 309th to keep going. In the upshot, confusing and contradictory orders reached both regiments and led to alternate marching and waiting that cost time and left everybody tired and irritated as well as rain-soaked—the February thaw had come, but not an end to precipitation. Eventually there was agreement that the 310th should take over the advance the next morning. Meanwhile word reached Parker that General Hodges himself would visit division headquarters in the morning; under the circumstances the army commander was doubly certain to bring with him his customary threats of dismissal as the alternative to prompt results.

Perversely, just as Hodges arrived the battle turned bad. The 310th struck firm resistance as soon as it passed the 309th and remained pinned down in the forest a little beyond the barracks all day long. The monotony of its reports of frustration varied only when, about dusk, Company A was ambushed and severely mauled. Parker decided he must commit all three of his regiments on February 7, the 310th to continue pressing on the main road, the 309th on its left, the 311th, which had already been struggling cross-country through the woods south of the road, to try to swing into Schmidt from the southwest.

This heavier attack made better progress, but not enough to satisfy Hodges. The 310th Infantry climbed Hill 493, the eminence just outside Schmidt, and the 309th on its left captured the high ground at Kommerscheidt just north of Schmidt, another place of bad memories from the autumn. The 311th took advantage of the capture of Hill 493 to slip some men onto the main road between the hill and Schmidt and into the first houses of the town. But in the late hours of the day nobody could advance any farther, and

Hodges was acutely aware of the imminence of the February 10 D-Day for GRENADE. Hodges had returned to his headquarters, but he kept the line hot to General Huebner, and Parker was made thoroughly aware that his tenure in command was scarcely secure.

Hodges's whiplash method of command in combination with his large delegations of responsibility to his less-than-lovable chief of staff, Genral Kean, had made First Army headquarters less and less a happy place in the months since Bradley's departure. The deterioration had reached its nadir under the shock of the Ardennes—lending uncomfortable warrant to Montgomery's skepticism about the powers of American command—and neither Hodges nor Kean was a physician to heal wounds quickly. Bradley's aide Major Hansen, whose own past association with the First Army made him not unsympathetic, was appalled by a visit to the army at just this time:

> First Army has lost some of the cohesive quality General Bradley managed to give it as commander. Hodges has found it difficult to do this, lacking the warmth and personality of General Bradley. Hodges is essentially a brittle impersonal general to the bulk of his staff. Even tho appearing as a temperate quiet minded leader similar to Bradley, subordinates suggest that his grasp is not as great as that of Bradley, that during the Battle of the Bulge, when the situation was in a frightful state of turmoil during the rapid movements of men and material to meet the German threats, General Hodges was near exhaustion. It is evident that he relies more heavily upon Kean in technical matters whereas Kean, while functioning as chief of staff for General Bradley, devoted himself almost exclusively to administrative operations of our field orders and executions.[4]

General Gavin's recent service with the First Army had left him reflective not only about corpses in the Kall River gorge—and the generalship that had sent them there and persisted in assaulting the Huertgen Forest—but also about the impatient style of leadership whose hot breath Parker now felt. The specific source of Gavin's ruminations on the latter topic was the eventual removal of General Jones of the 106th Division after his travail in the Ardennes, but the reflections had a broader implication, especially in light of Patton's similar comments about Hodges's—and even Bradley's—style:

> In this case [said Gavin], one is particularly impressed by the manner in which Montgomery congratulated all those who fought at St.-Vith for the fine job they did. We relieved the two senior commanders, although one was restored [for when St. Vith was yielded, Hasbrouck of the 7th Armored was also briefly relieved]. In the situation at Arnhem, in our earlier battle in Holland, the British general lost three-quarters of his command and a battle. He returned home a hero and was personally decorated by the King.
>
> There is no doubt that in our system he would have been summarily relieved and sent home in disgrace. In the case of General Jones and his 106th Division, higher command knew no more about the German plans than he did. Higher command also knew of his dispositions and approved them. His leading green regiments were overwhelmed before they could offer much resistance, and there is little that he—or anyone else, for that matter—could have done about it. Summarily relieving senior officers, it seems to me, makes others pusillanimous and indeed discourages other potential combat leaders from seeking high command. . . . Summarily relieving those who do not appear to measure up in the first shock of battle is not only a luxury that we cannot afford—it is very damaging to the Army as a whole. We have much to learn from the British about senior command relationships.[5]

Such considerations no more restrained Hodges's pressure on Parker than they had saved Jones. When on the morning of February 8, General Craig of the 9th Division happened to visit V Corps headquarters, Huebner decided he had better substitute the veteran Craig for Parker in charge of the attack on the Schwammenauel. He would also beef up Parker's 78th Division with some of Craig's troops, whom the 2nd Division relieved.

Craig ordered his own 60th Infantry Regiment to take over from the 310th the drive along the main road. The 311th was to pass around Schmidt to clear the wooded hills north and northeast of the Roerstausee. Since some of Gavin's troops of the XVIII Corps, shifted to the north flank of Huebner's corps, had turned up at Kommerscheidt, the 309th Infantry was free for employment elsewhere; as soon as the drive along the main road had cleared Schmidt and the highway through it to the southeast to a point near the foot of the Schwammenauel, the 309th was to take off cross-country from that point and capture the dam.

Except for the addition of the 60th Infantry, this plan was essentially the same as Parker's. Despite the addition of the 60th Infantry, there was not much improvement in the pace of the advance during most of February 9. Late in the afternoon, however, Craig judged the 60th to be far enough along into Schmidt and up the road southeastward past the dam that the 309th could be released to go for the dam.

It was already dark when the leading battalion, the 1st, got started. As the men approached the Schwammenauel, they split into two groups, one heading for the lower level and the power house, the other, accompanied by a team of the 303rd Engineer Battalion, seeking the top of the dam and the disposal of any demolitions there. The lower group had to fear that the Germans might at any time blow the dam and bury them under concrete, earth, and water. The upper group were held back for a time by enemy fire, but after midnight they worked their way, still under fire, across the top of the dam to find a tunnel that according to intelligence ran down into the structure. Part of the spillway proved to have been blown already and the tunnel blocked. The engineers therefore had to slide down the sixty-five-meter face of the dam and look for the tunnel exit. They did so, found the tunnel, and—anticlimactically, after the long struggle for the dams—were not blown up but did not find any explosives either.

The Germans had simply destroyed the power machinery and the discharge valves. Similarly, they had diverted water from above the reservoir behind the Urfttalsperre to below the Schwammenauel. The effect was not a cascade of water but a great relentless flow that would flood the Roer valley for about two weeks.

Still, the Roer dams were in American possession and the end of their long menace was in sight. Furthermore, though Craig had led the final push, Parker kept his division after all—which was fortunate, because he would prove himself a good man.

GRENADE at the Ready

Above Düren, the banks of the Roer are high, and the destruction of the discharge valves was felt most evidently in an acceleration of the current, to as much as fifteen kilometers an hour. Below Düren, the Ninth Army stood poised for Operation GRENADE, with the codeword "Johnstown" ready for instant communication of the news should the dams be blown and the Roer come down in a torrent. Here, while there would be no Johnstown wall of water, the Roer nevertheless overflowed its banks. From a stream

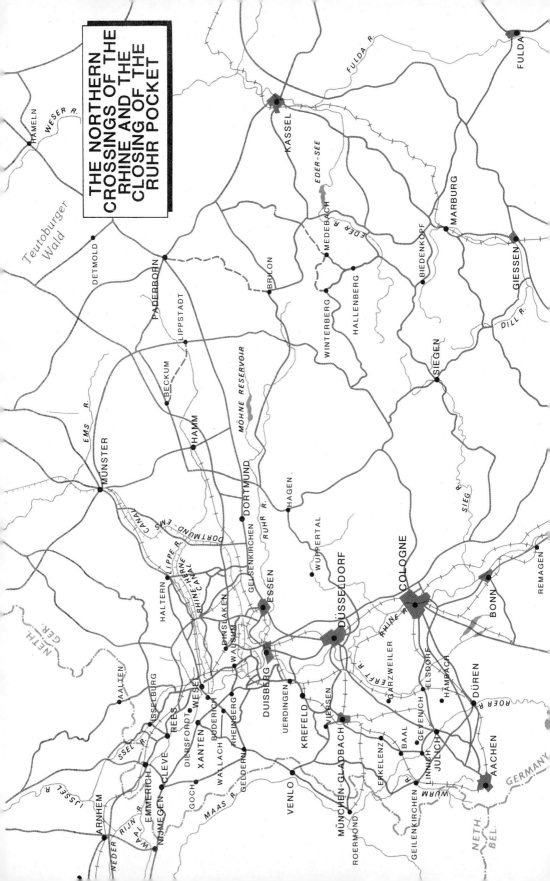

THE NORTHERN CROSSINGS OF THE RHINE AND THE CLOSING OF THE RUHR POCKET

normally some thirty meters wide, it swelled to 300 or 400 meters, and just north of Linnich to more than a kilometer.

D-Day for GRENADE had to be postponed day after day. This necessity, after the effort to capture the dams had rendered Allied intentions obvious, was among the reasons why Eisenhower tolerated Patton's February offensive despite SHAEF's formal directives; he wanted to discourage the enemy from shifting troops to the Ninth Army front notwithstanding the evident danger there. At last General Simpson fixed upon February 23 as the new D-Day for GRENADE. This was one day before by the engineers' calculations the reservoirs would be drained; but the river was already receding, its current was rarely swifter than ten kilometers an hour, and Simpson believed that by crossing before subsidence was complete he might yet gain a measure of surprise.

Fortunately, the Germans were incapable of using their respite to halt Operation VERITABLE, the Canadian army's attack from Nijmegen, which began on schedule on February 8. Hitler had been able to shift the Wehrmacht's center of gravity to the West in the autumn of 1944 in part because the Eastern Front fell quiescent during October. The Red Army, whose transport remained limited despite the acquisition of thousands of Studebaker and Dodge trucks via lend-lease, had to pause for resupply and regrouping after the mighty westward lunges of the summer. But on January 12, 1945, the Soviets opened their mightiest offensive of the war, a vast endeavor engulfing the entire Eastern Front from the Narew to the Danube. Every semblance of a reserve that Germany could still relinquish from areas not regarded by the Führer as absolutely vital hastened to the East. The Sixth Panzer Army, already vanished from the front lines in the West, soon disappeared from OKW reserve as well, to plunge into the eastern cauldron. Before a gun spoke from the Nijmegen salient to herald Eisenhower's primary offensive toward the Rhine and the Ruhr, the Soviets had drowned the Supreme Commander's fear of a German divisional parity that might renew the autumn stalemate, sweeping away such qualms in a Red Army tidal wave that overwhelmed the German defense of crucial sectors with a preponderance in men and tanks reaching six to one.

For on the 1,000-kilometer section of the Eastern Front from the Baltic to the Carpathians, where the Russians rolled toward or across Germany's own frontier, the Germans had only some seventy-five divisions, a smaller number than on the similar length of the Western Front, and with no fixed defenses equivalent to the West Wall. If the Germans had concentrated their remaining forces on their own country's eastern and western frontiers, they might have contrived a stout defense even after Stalin's armies began their climactic offensive. But Hitler's conception of absolutely vital areas not to be relinquished had quixotically dissipated the Wehrmacht to expose the Reich itself. The Western Front bent awkwardly and lengthily westward at its northern end so much of Holland could be retained to launch V-2s that Hitler hoped would close the port of Antwerp, though several months of such attacks had long since demonstrated their futility for any purpose beyond killing and maiming Belgian civilians. Seventeen German divisions remained in Norway and Denmark, principally to hold bases for the new electro-U-boats proclaimed by Hitler's fantasies a weapon that might yet win the war. Ten divisions were tied down in Yugoslavia, largely for the bauxite of Croatia, which was supposed to make the aluminum for the jets that might also turn the war around. Another twenty-eight divisions, with half the armor on the Eastern Front, guarded Hungary for its bauxite and oil. More than thirty divisions tried to hold Courland, Memel, East

Prussia, and the Gulf of Danzig, so the electro-U-boats would have training grounds in the eastern Baltic out of range of the Anglo-American bombers.

After Warsaw fell to the Soviets on January 17, the Germans at last began to rush divisions and armor to Poland and Silesia. In February, 1,675 new and repaired tanks and assault guns were shipped to the Eastern Front, only sixty-seven to the West. But it was too late to correct the earlier dissipation of force. The Soviets had already broken the front. Weakening the West only assured that Eisenhower's fears of a deadlock would evaporate and that the Anglo-Americans would break through as well.

Fittingly, it was General Horrocks's British 30 Corps, once fettered in the Nijmegen salient, that opened the attack out of the salient and into the Reichswald for the Canadian First Army. In opposition was Army Group H, which had grown out of General Student's original bolstering of Rundstedt's northern flank, to include the Twenty-fifth Army and, in the path of the Canadian attack, Student's old First Parachute Army. Initially Student had led the army group, but the Germans had just anticipated a major Allied thrust in the north by giving it to an old fireman brought up from the south, the politically undesirable but apparently indispensable General Blaskowitz.

Montgomery prepared for VERITABLE with a five-and-a-half-hour artillery barrage by 1,034 guns, the greatest artillery bombardment of the war in the West. Horrocks, with an un-American devotion to concentrating, threw five infantry divisions, three armored brigades, and eleven regiments of special armor, gadget-laden to deal with fortifications, against a narrow, twelve-kilometer front between the Rhine and the Maas. The West Wall did not reach this far north, but since September the Germans had industriously fortified Cleve and Goch and inundated much of the countryside. Obstructions and inundations, worsened by the February thaw, forced the heavy attack to clot along the only two paved roads that were available, and contributed at least as much as the enemy's active defenses to preventing the Allied concentration of power from generating a breakthrough.

Nevertheless, merely to hold Horrocks's attack to steady, remorseless progress instead of an outright breakthrough, western intelligence officers believed that during the first week the enemy threw into the battle from his slim reserves and from other parts of his line reinforcements including an infantry division, two parachute divisions, the 15th Panzer Grenadier Division, and the 116th Panzer Division. This effort apparently left the Panzer Lehr Division as the only armored reserve for either Army Group H or Army Group B, and at the end of the week Panzer Lehr also showed up in front of the Canadian army. Such movement of enemy forces was, of course, very good news for the Ninth Army. It should leave only about 30,000 men and seventy tanks to oppose Operation GRENADE.

And SHAEF's priorities had seen to it that the Ninth Army, in contrast, was heavily reinforced. Simpson's forces were to cross the Roer on a front of about twenty-five kilometers, from some eight kilometers above Jülich to just below Linnich. General McLain's XIX Corps on the right and General Gillem's XIII Corps on the left of the attack divided the front equally between them. McLain would cross the river with Hobbs's 30th Division on his right and Gerhardt's 29th on his left, with the 2nd Armored, now under Brigadier General Isaac D. White, and Macon's 83rd in reserve. Gillem would cross with Keating's relatively new 102nd Division on the right and Bolling's 84th on the left, with Oliver's 5th Armored Division in reserve.

To the right of Simpson's army, General Collins's VII Corps was to cross the Roer around Düren to protect the flank, with Weaver's 8th Division on the right and Terry Allen's 104th Division on the left, while an old favorite of the VII Corps, Maurice Rose's proud Spearhead Division, the 3rd Armored, waited in reserve. Major General John B. Anderson's new XVI Corps occupied the Ninth Army's northern flank, a longer sector than that of either of the attacking corps, some thirty kilometers from just below Jülich to the confluence of the Roer and the Maas at Roermond. Simpson had taken over this sector from the British Second Army to help Montgomery add punch to VERITABLE. To hold it, General Anderson had Baade's 35th Division and Brigadier General John M. Devine's new 8th Armored in the line, Wyche's 79th Division in reserve. On D-Day, Anderson's corps was to clear out a few German positions remaining west of the Roer in its sector and to simulate a crossing as a safeguard for the left flank of the assault. With ten divisions, the Ninth Army had some 303,243 men, with the additional 75,000 of the VII Corps to assist in the offensive.

Simpson also had the largest concentration of guns an American army had yet gathered for an offensive on the Western Front, over 2,000, giving the XIX and XIII Corps one artillery piece for every ten meters of front, in addition to their tanks, tank destroyers, antiaircraft guns, and infantry cannon. Because GRENADE would begin with a river crossing, a COBRA- or QUEEN-type aerial bombardment did not seem appropriate. Such a preparation would have required a daylight crossing, while the ground forces preferred to cross under cover of darkness. Heavy bombing of the east bank would also have required a withdrawal from the west bank for safety, inviting the Germans to retaliate with a heavy fire as the assault troops returned across relatively open ground by daylight to the launching sites. So, while XXIX TAC softened up and sought to isolate the target area, the immediate bombardment preparation would belong to the artillery. As the XIII Corps plan stated it, the Roer "crossing will be Sptd by fires of all AA, AT, TD and Tk weapons that it is possible to employ."[6] SHAEF's priority for the operation, plus careful rationing in the Ninth Army beforehand, fortunately secured an ample stock of artillery ammunition, though the overall American shortage still demanded the most careful control of allocations. Simpson would begin GRENADE with 46,000 tons of ammunition on hand, enough for at least twenty days' firing at normal rates of expenditure.

Simpson and his corps commanders initially laid plans to maintain their forces beyond the Roer with LVTs, dukws, treadway rafts, and an airlift, should they be ordered to cross with the Roer dams uncaptured and likely to be blown in their rear. When such orders did not come, the plan to cross before the floodwaters altogether receded still called for each assault division to carry five days' supply of rations and gasoline, for amphibious craft to ferry essential supplies, and for 500 C-47s to stand by loaded with enough supplies to maintain a division in combat for a day. The new plan was for corps engineers to build three vehicular bridges in each division sector beginning at H-Hour, but the army would be prepared to carry on if bridges went out.

Altogether, the Ninth Army's GRENADE planning was of the kind that rapidly won for this newest army committed to the Western Front Bradley's accolade as the easiest of his army headquarters to deal with—a painstaking, thorough, quietly competent command and staff.

If the decision to suspend the Eifel offensive and break up the American concentration there can be questioned, at least the American share in the substitute offensive to the north represented an only slightly less impressive concentration of power. Much of the credit must go to Montgomery, who insisted that once the Ninth Army was committed to the 21 Army Group offensive, it must be able to deliver the kind of massive, concentrated power punch that was his own offensive hallmark.

Montgomery's conception was admirable also, of course, in that on this occasion there could be no question of his design to erase large German forces from the board. Montgomery and other senior Allied officers believed that once the weapon of the Roer dams was gone, it would be foolhardy for the enemy to defend between the Roer and the Rhine; rather, he ought to retreat behind the Rhine. Because the Führer's conceptions of strategy made a defense of the Roer likely nevertheless, the Canadian First and American Ninth Armies if they converged as planned might well trap a major share of Army Group H's First Parachute Army and a smaller part of Army Group B's Fifteenth Army, facing Simpson, in their vise.

33: To the Rhine

GRENADE

Fᴿᴼᴹ ᴛʜᴇ Roer to the Rhine opposite the Ninth Army, the gound was level except for a plateau of nowhere more than about 120 meters reaching eastward across from Linnich. The land was mainly planted in grain and beets. On the north flank an extensive forest along the east bank of the Roer reached northward to the Dutch border, leading the Ninth Army to forgo an assault crossing by Anderson's XVI Corps. A somewhat smaller forest, the Hambach, lay astride the boundary between the XIX and VII Corps attacks; McLain's corps was to clear its northwestern third, Collins's corps the rest. Beyond the Roer another river, the Erft, flows diagonally northeastward across the Cologne plain, to enter the Rhine opposite Düsseldorf. The Erft is not a major stream, but it runs through boggy low ground about 1,000 meters wide; its course determined that the direction of the offensive should also be northeast toward Düsseldorf and Wesel, with the Erft to form the right boundary of the VII Corps and thus of the attack.

Across such terrain, the principal geographic obstacles were likely to be not natural features but towns. The Ninth Army's experience in the autumn campaign indicated the towns were sure to be fortified. The principal city, München-Gladbach, which with its suburbs had had a prewar population of over 300,000, Simpson intended to envelop. Gillem's XIII Corps would strike directly across the Roer for the plateau. After taking the relatively high ground, the corps would swing north to open an unopposed crossing for the XVI Corps. If the enemy's resistance began to yield quickly and the ground beyond the Roer was firm, the XIX Corps, traveling farther, would immediately envelop München-Gladbach and head for the Rhine. If resistance proved tougher, or soft ground kept the armor to the roads, the XIII and XVI Corps would instead carry the main burden, ensuring a secure line of communication by rolling up the German defenses from south to north up to Venlo and only then turning east to the Rhine.

The Roer itself would be the major obstacle before the Rhine whatever its breadth or current at the time of assault. General von Zangen's Fifteenth Army on the opposite shore had been so badly drained of manpower and equipment that Simpson could expect to follow the more optimistic of his two plans, or a yet more ambitious design. Field Marshal Montgomery called for "continuous and sustained operations . . . to keep up the momentum of the attack and thus force the battle to swing relentlessly our way." In the same spirit, Simpson instructed his commanders to be vigilant for an enemy collapse, and then "to conduct relentless pursuit in zone, . . . [when] phases will be abandoned in favor of taking full advantage of our opportunity."[1]

The crossings on February 23 were not easy but augured well. The artillery preparation began at 2:45 in the morning. Three-quarters of an hour later, infantrymen of four divisions in the Ninth Army and two in the First lowered assault boats into the Roer. Most of the first assault waves managed to plant a foothold on the opposite bank despite the buffeting of small craft by a swift and treacherous current; but almost everywhere the still-flooded river, abetted by German artillery fire, played havoc with bridgebuilding. The 119th Infantry of the 30th Division borrowed from the methods the enemy had used on December 16 to infiltrate infantry and engineers across the river before the artillery preparation began. By the time the artillery lifted its barrage, a footbridge was already in place. In the area of Hobbs's other assault regiment, the 120th, the current was so swift that the time just before the bombardment had to be spent less productively in anchoring a cable on the hostile shore for a cable ferry. Nowhere in Hobbs's sector, however, could the engineers finish a vehicular bridge before nightfall, and the assault infantry had to spend the whole day fighting without tanks or tank destroyers.

Bolling's 84th Division had practically the same experience, for a treadway bridge it laid down by eight-thirty that evening was immediately closed by a Luftwaffe strafer. Keating's 102nd Division had two footbridges and a bridge for light vehicles—some 57mm. antitank guns got across—knocked out before another light vehicular bridge and a treadway were completed about nine in the evening; thereupon the Luftwaffe wrecked the treadway just as the first tank destroyers were starting to cross. Only Gerhardt's 29th Division was able to get armor—and bulldozers to clear paths through the rubble of Jülich—across the Roer as early as the end of D-Day afternoon. Without generous application of smoke, laying bridges would have been close to impossible.

In Collins's sector the Roer swirled between higher banks, the current was swifter, and the crossings proved more difficult. Here the first assault waves sometimes failed to get across. In Allen's 104th Division, the first waves of the 415th Infantry generally made it; but the 413th got some of its boats stuck on a check dam, others came under intolerable artillery and machine-gun fire, and the 413th had to resort to crossing in the 415th's sector. In Weaver's 8th Division, only about three-fifths of the two leading companies of the 3rd Battalion, 28th Infantry completed their assault crossing, many losing their weapons on the way; and that was the biggest success the division scored. The 1/28th could not cross; the 2nd Battalion put across some 130 men of Company F, with thirty rifles among them. The 3rd Battalion of the 13th Infantry put thirty-six men on the hostile shore, contriving to reinforce them with two additional platoons later in the day. The 2/13th could do no better than to land twelve men of Company F. Not until the morning of the second day was there a bridge in the VII Corps sector, a Bailey bridge constructed on the piers of the former main highway bridge into Düren. No additional bridges served Collins's corps until the third day.

The bits and pieces of the VII Corps reaching the east bank were able to hang on mainly because the opposition, though it could pommel boats in the river, showed little stomach for a real fight. In Birkesdorf just north of Düren, for example, the 413th Infantry encountered the 12th Volksgrenadier Division of General Krüger's LVIII Panzer Corps. Since its commitment to the Aachen battles in the autumn, the 12th had given the Americans many a hard time. But the 413th readily captured a whole battalion of its 27th Volksgrenadier Regiment. The cracking of the morale of the German army, which Allied intelligence could scarcely perceive or dare to predict even at the close of the Ardennes battle, was at last becoming conspicuous reality.

For that reason, the assault crossings of the Roer proved indeed the most difficult phase of Operation GRENADE. Despite all the troubles with the bridges, the presence of parts of six American divisions on the east bank assured the outcome of the campaign, so weak was the enemy. In the whole course of the first day, it was only against the 102nd Division bridgehead around Gevenich and Boslar that the Germans staged their customary counterattacks in respectable strength. Against Boslar, they came on at least seven times, with tanks and assault guns, so the Americans sorely missed the antitank support that was still waiting west of the Roer. Nevertheless, with bazookas and the help of artillery from across the river, the 102nd stopped everything thrown at them, including Panthers.

Generals Simpson and McLain wasted no time in deciding the XIX Corps should make the wide pivot around München-Gladbach. The troubles of the VII Corps implied that by doing so McLain would be exposing his right flank, but the feebleness of the enemy seemed to justify the risk. The weather was good, and XXIX TAC had five groups of fighter-bombers ready to offer ample support. On the second day, the Old Hickory Division on McLain's right hurried through the northwestern reaches of the Hambach Forest to Steinstrass at the northern edge of the wood, meeting only scattered, local opposition. The Blue-Gray Division just to the left had a somewhat more difficult journey, with the result that the 102nd Division of the XIII Corps also had an exposed right flank as it pushed forward rapidly on February 24; but again the enemy failed to take advantage of this kind of opportunity.

To try to catch up with the Ninth Army, Collins ordered both the 104th and 8th Divisions to continue attacking through the night of February 24–25. With a bridge built, the VII Corps now had enough strength across the Roer to start to make headway by applying such continuous pressure. To the evident consternation of the enemy, who had grown accustomed to a respite from the Americans during the hours of darkness, the combination of battle experience and the tempting scent of breakthrough kept not only Collins's troops but too many of the Americans pushing persistently all through the night.

Not that all the Germans followed the example of the 12th Volksgrenadiers. The German army no longer boasted its former consistent toughness and professionalism, but many of its formations could still fight hard, like the troops of the 183rd Infantry Division of the XII SS Corps who held up the 84th Division's effort to turn northward down the Roer from the town of Baal and thus thwarted the plan to open an unopposed crossing for Anderson's XVI Corps. On February 25, consequently, to free the XIII Corps for other activities, General Simpson ordered Anderson to try to make his own crossing. Arranging to send one regiment, the 137th Infantry of Baade's 35th Division, into the 84th Division bridgehead to assist the main XVI Corps effort from the east bank, Anderson and Baade attacked the town of Hilfarth with the 134th Infantry before dawn on February 26. They chose the place because a highway bridge still spanned the Roer there. While the infantry fought into Hilfarth, artillery laid a steady fire around the bridge to try to keep German demolitions men away. The bridge was taken intact, and tanks rolled across by noon.

Freed of responsibility for getting the XVI Corps over the Roer, Gillem's XIII Corps had turned its whole attention northeastward. It drove almost without opposition into

Erkelenz some ten kilometers beyond the river. By now elements of the 9th and 11th Panzer Divisions had come into action against McLain's XIX Corps, but nevertheless on February 27 Generals Simpson and McLain thought the front was so near to breaking wide open that the principal question before them was whether McLain should commit the 2nd Armored Division. Should they exploit with armor immediately, or should they allow the infantry to go on leading the XIX Corps until the 30th Division overran a third and final line of prepared defenses, running through Garzweiler? Simpson decided to insert the armor as quickly as possible between McLain's assaulting infantry divisions and to instruct it to strike for the Rhine at Neuss opposite Düsseldorf; but the discussion about Garzweiler proved academic, because Hobbs's Division was in the village on February 28 before the armor could start rolling. Furthermore, as Hobbs's men wheeled around München-Gladbach, Gerhardt's 29th Division captured the city on March 1 almost without a fight.

During these same few days, Simpson and McLain were relieved of any concern about the security of the army and corps right flank. As early as February 26, General Collins had decided the time was ripe to commit armor to lead his corps to the Erft. The going had continued hardest on the VII Corps front, not only because its crossing of the Roer had been the most difficult, but also because Collins's troops collided with a stubborn Kampfgruppe of the 3rd Panzer Grenadier Division in addition to parts of the 9th Panzer Division. Once General Rose's 3rd Armored Division entered the battle, however, the American tanks found no great difficulty in breaking loose to reach the Erft late on February 27. In the course of that day's action, a new T26 Pershing tank armed with a 90mm. gun, one of the first twenty sent to Europe for testing, joined in against the 9th Panzers at the town of Elsdorf; it made an auspicious debut by penetrating the thick side armor of two Pzkw IVs and knocking them out at a thousand meters, and stopping a Tiger by hitting its turret joints. During the night of February 27–28, Collins's infantry waded the Erft to create two small bridgeheads.

GRENADE Exploited—to a Point

The firm anchoring of GRENADE's right flank on the Erft removed all question of Simpson's pulling out the stops, committing armor in every corps, and heading for the Rhine as fast as his men could move. With General Eisenhower breathing encouragement, the Ninth Army's immediate objective became nothing less than the seizure of a Rhine bridge, an unlikely but—with speed—possible prize. The mode of seeking the objective became pursuit, in the manner of the summer of 1944. By the first of March Simpson's columns were hastening forward at a rate of eleven to seventeen kilometers a day, with only occasional, unpredictably scattered opposition.

On March 1, General McLain committed his final division, Macon's 83rd. The very pace of the advance, following so closely upon the strain of the river crossings, was tiring his other troops, and he hoped a fresh unit might grasp for him at least one from among a railroad and two highway bridges at Neuss and another highway bridge just downstream at Oberkassel. Neuss fell that night. The highway bridges had been destroyed, but the division artillery laid fire around the east end of the possibly intact railroad bridge to try to keep demolitions men away, while with marching fire Company L of the 329th Infantry and a platoon of Company A, 736th Tank Battalion crossed open ground to assail an entrenched position at the west end. The advance presented a sufficiently remorseless appearance that the German defenders threw up their hands in surrender. A patrol hastened across the Rhine—only to discover that the eastern span had been blown.

The 330th Infantry grasped for the Oberkassel bridge by sending some of its riflemen and parts of the 736th Tank Battalion and the 643rd Tank Destroyer Battalion toward it through the night, with the tanks disguised to look like panzers, German-speaking soldiers riding on top, and infantry tagging along behind and at the sides as inconspicuously as possible. In the darkness, the task force passed a German column going the other way without trouble. But at first light a bicycle-mounted soldier in another German column apparently perceived the truth, was challenged by the Americans but raced away instead of halting, and had to be shot. The Americans got him, but in doing so they gave themselves away. The resulting fracas set the Oberkassel town siren shrieking, and the bridge blew up just as the first American tanks rumbled on to it.

So irresistible a prize was a bridge downstream at Krefeld-Uerdingen named for Adolf Hitler that the XIII and XIX Corps vied for the taking of it. A bridge so named beckoned with a special lure; in addition, a first-class highway lay along the east bank beyond the bridge, and at Krefeld the west bank was higher than the east to permit American guns to dominate the crossing site and ease the building of a new bridge even if the Germans blew the Adolf Hitler.

When White's 2nd Armored Division plunged within twenty-one kilometers of the bridge, Simpson alerted Gillem to be prepared to shift his XIII Corps boundary northward to make way for the armor of McLain's corps. On March 1 headquarters of the XIX Corps attempted to order the boundary change into effect. Gillem protested that the approaches to the bridge were a maze of canals and road and railroad embankments unsuitable for armor and that his own 84th and 102nd Divisions were already well on their way toward it. McLain conducted a personal reconnaissance, found Gillem's divisions entangled in knots of resistance, decided the 2nd Armored in fact had the best chance for the bridge, and persuaded army headquarters to let the boundary change stand. Nevertheless Gillem's corps, including its own armored division, Oliver's 5th, went on attacking toward the bridge, with orders from Gillem to halt at the new boundary only if the 2nd Armored was already on the scene. Meanwhile General Bolling of Gillem's 84th Division ordered his 334th Infantry, reinforced by most of the 771st Tank Battalion, to bypass Krefeld on the city's north side, rush the bridge, and try to cross the Rhine. In person, Bolling saw the column off. The sergeant in the lead tank passed him a cigar, saying, "Here, General, smoke this. Give me one across the Rhine." The tanks revved up to twenty-five miles an hour.[2]

When the 5th Armored Division reached the new corps boundary in the afternoon of March 2, there was the 2nd Armored, and reluctantly Gillem ordered his troops to observe the boundary. But the 2nd Armored was held up by the very obstacles that Gillem had cited, and meanwhile word of the controversy was unavoidably slow in reaching through the confusion of pursuit to the 334th Infantry. Thirteen kilometers from Krefeld when they began their dash, despite occasional obstacles and resistance the lead tanks of the 334th task force were in the suburbs within two hours. Then they took a wrong turn, into the city they were supposed to bypass. This mishap permitted enemy antitank guns to halt the procession and orders to arrive diverting the whole 84th Division downstream.

The 2nd Armored planned a set-piece attack on the bridge for early on March 3, while artillery using proximity fuzes kept the structure under fire in the manner that had worked at Hilfarth on the Roer. Attached to the armor was the 379th Infantry from the 95th Division, recently given to the XIX Corps from army reserve. Together, the 2nd Armored's CCB and the infantry fought their way to the west end of the bridge, but there they found a gaping hole in the road that tanks could not pass. Without help from the tanks, the infantry could not pass either, at least in daylight, for their attack had carried them into Blaskowitz's Army Group H sector, and from that formation's First Parachute Army there had arrived at the bridge not long before the Americans some tough paratroopers of the 2nd Parachute Division—"fine, young Dutch SS men," as CCB's Colonel Sidney Hines described them.[3] The First Parachute Army happened to be under orders from the Führer to retain a bridgehead west of the Rhine at all costs, not only because of Hitler's usual considerations of prestige, but also because, with its highways and railroads a mess, the Reich needed this section of the river and the waterways connecting with it for barge traffic into and out of the Ruhr to maintain a semblance of economic life. The commander of the First Parachute Army, General der Fallschirm-truppen Alfred Schlemm, was as tough a customer as his best troops and determined to fulfill the orders. So the resistance did not crack, and the Adolf Hitler Bridge remained near yet far.

Under cover of darkness, however, a six-man engineer patrol was able to creep past the defenders, make its way onto the bridge, and go all the way across and back again searching out demolition wires. But something went wrong. At seven the next morning, the bridge blew up anyway.

McLain next turned his attention to highway and rail bridges downstream at Rheinhausen, sending General Twaddle's 95th Division in their direction; but on the morning of March 5 aerial reconnaissance found these bridges also blown. The fates seemed determined to deny a bridge, but, nothing daunted, General Simpson was already looking forward to crossing the Rhine without one. He selected from plans projected by his staff a design to leap the river from the high western bank between Düsseldorf and Uerdingen, thence to turn down the right bank, clear the way for further crossings, and reach relatively open country not far away at the northern edge of the Ruhr. His objective would be the capture of Hamm, a rail center at the northeast corner of the Ruhr and the crucial outlet for shipment of the Ruhr's products to the Wehrmacht. Because the bulk of Germany's troops in the area were still battling to retain a foothold west of the Rhine, Simpson felt confident the crossing would meet little opposition, assure the desired entrapment of German forces on the west bank, and by catching the enemy surprised and unprepared reduce almost to insignificance the last major geo-graphic obstacle before the Ruhr and the heart of Germany.

While moving toward the Adolf Hitler Bridge, Colonel Hinds had passed a company of dukws and tried to get them assigned to him, because he believed an "instantaneous sneak amphibious crossing before the slow-reacting guards were aware of what was happening" was bound to succeed.[4] Hinds also suggested a swift parachute attack on the opposite bank. The latter idea collided with the customary problem that airborne assaults seemingly required considerable planning; the Allies' airborne weapon possessed high mobility only with a relatively long lead time. More pertinently, however, 21 Army Group was not responsive to either of Hinds's ideas. This indifference was a straw in the wind.

In the beginning, the untemperamental Simpson and his untemperamental, "uncommonly normal" Ninth Army staff had adjusted well to service under Field Marshal Montgomery. During the Ardennes battle, Simpson sent a personal message to Eisenhower assuring him

> that I and my Army are operating smoothly and cheerfully under command of the Field Marshal. The most cordial relations and a very high spirit of cooperation have been established between him and myself personally and between our respective Staffs. You can depend on me to respond cheerfully, promptly and as efficiently as I possibly can to every instruction he gives. . . .
>
> Yesterday the Field Marshal paid me a visit and at his request I took him to the Headquarters of my XIX Corps where I had all of my Corps and Division Commanders assembled to meet him. After all had been introduced to him, he made us a splendid talk on the present situation. Then we all had lunch together at McClain's [sic] mess.[5]

But Montgomery seemed bent on antagonizing every American. Trouble arose even before GRENADE was launched, when on January 21 the field marshal released his first directive for the crossing of the Rhine. He assigned command of the whole operation to the British Second Army. Altogether cut out of the command, under this directive the Ninth Army was to have only one corps participating. Montgomery's rationalization for such an arrangement was the necessity to unite a major operation under a single command. But the Ninth Army could not help beginning to share the suspicion nourished all along by Montgomery's and Brooke's insistence that the climactic blow against Germany must be delivered by 21 Army Group, the suspicion that had grown to be firm conviction at Bradley's and Patton's headquarters, that the British intended to hog the credit for defeating Germany—even as Montgomery in his celebrated press conference had attempted to monopolize credit for the victory in the Ardennes.

Simpson protested, and with General Dempsey seconding Simpson, Montgomery was persuaded to relent. He issued a new directive awarding the Ninth Army a share in the Rhine crossing. But the field marshal had planted a distrust that could not completely abate. Thus Simpson and his staff were dismayed, infuriated, but not really surprised when Montgomery vetoed Simpson's proposal to jump the Rhine on the run. Montgomery's excuse this time was that a crossing in Simpson's zone would lead directly to the industrial jungle of the Ruhr, an area that Eisenhower had always insisted must not become a battleground. This view ignored Simpson's point that a swift crossing would find too few Germans to make much of a battleground, as well as Simpson's intent to turn north immediately to rush into open country. Naturally, the Ninth Army staff decided that Montgomery's real motive was to deny any Americans the chance to steal the show from his forthcoming big set-piece crossing of the Rhine, which would still be a predominantly British operation. Of course Montgomery prevailed, and the opportunity for a swift Rhine crossing and a swift sealing off of the Ruhr went lost.

The Battle of the Wesel Pocket

It remained to dispose of the German forces still in Montgomery's sector on the west side of the Rhine. Closing the GRENADE pincer upon the VERITABLE pincer coming down from the north was the work of General Anderson's XVI Corps. A motorized task force of Baade's 35th Division and part of Devine's 8th Armored led the way for Anderson's men beyond the Roer. Joining in the race set off by the Ninth Army's breakthrough, the Santa Fe Cross Division pressed its vanguard into Venlo, more than forty kilometers from the Hilfarth crossing, as early as March 1; thus Baade took from the rear a historic fortress on the Maas once dreaded as an important obstacle on the path to the Ruhr. Anderson's columns then swung northeast to strike the Rhine between Duisberg and Wesel. On March 3, Baade's 134th Infantry met troops of the 53rd Welsh Division at Geldern, and the jaws had snapped shut.

The enemy, however, with his tactical skill triumphing as it so often did over Hitler's orders to stand fast, had by now moved most of his troops to the east side of the new Canadian First Army-American Ninth Army perimeter; and further progress toward the Rhine north of Duisberg became a fight again instead of a procession on the same day Simpson's army met General Crerar's. The Canadian 2nd Corps struggled with General Schlemm's paratroopers in the Xanten Forest. The British 1 Corps grappled with the First Parachute Army from the Xanten Forest to Geldern. Thence southwest to the Rhine, the Germans tried to hold off the onrushing Ninth Army, whose 5th Armored Division of the XIII Corps drove as far as Orsoy on March 5 and thereby interdicted traffic on one of the valuable barge canals, whose junction with the Rhine lay just opposite and now under American guns. North of Orsoy, however, even Simpson's charge was slowed. Schlemm stood on relatively high ground all around the Wesel pocket, as his west-shore bridgehead came to be called, and he held it with 50,000 troops, including Panzer Lehr, the 116th Panzer Division, and the 15th Panzer Grenadier Division as well as four parachute divisions.

Halfway between the northern and southern flanks of the German bridgehead a highway and a railroad bridge still spanned the Rhine to Wesel. The XVI Corps, which still seemed to face slightly less determined resistance than its neighbors, received the orders to lead off the attack against Schlemm's perimeter; Anderson was to drive relentlessly for the bridges, even though they lay within the Canadian zone. With CCB of the 8th Armored attached, Baade's division attacked astride the Lintfort-Rheinberg highway on March 4. Immediately the 35th found itself fighting as hard as anyone in 21 Army Group had done for the past week. When the next day Baade tried to shake loose a task force of the 320th Infantry on a diagonal march across country to the junction of the Geldern-Wesel and Rheinberg-Xanten roads, the Germans promptly isolated the lead platoon and forced the column to consume the entire day merely trying to rescue their comrades. Attempting to hurry his armor forward into Rheinberg, the commander of CCB got trapped in a house and had to spend the day there. Reaching the southern fringe of Rheinberg cost CCB thirty-nine of fifty-four tanks.

By now, however, the enemy had little to salvage west of the Rhine except a measure of prestige; he had been evacuating across the Wesel bridges as rapidly as he could. His remaining paratroopers and panzers fought stubbornly for four more days, but on the night of March 9–10 he blew up the bridges. The next morning the Allies found only rear guards facing them.

GRENADE ended in disappointment because no Rhine bridge was captured and, much more, because Montgomery did not allow the Ninth Army to speed on across the Rhine. On the credit side, the Ninth Army captured some 30,000 enemy soldiers and killed an estimated 6,000. Its own casualties were 7,300. Similarly, the Canadian First Army, whose earlier kickoff drew to it a larger share of German strength, took 22,000 prisoners while its own total casualties were 15,600. If the opposing German armies once again were not so totally destroyed as might have been hoped, Montgomery was correct enough in saying the enemy had lost the flower of his armies as well as the Rhineland. And 21 Army Group stood poised along the Rhine to execute the crossing that Montgomery insisted must be not impromptu but formally planned.

The Battle of the Cologne Plain

Collins's VII Corps of the First Army completed its role in GRENADE by driving on from its crossing of the Erft to follow the right bank of that river downstream to the Rhine, thus maintaining a shield along the Ninth Army's right flank. The arrival of the 9th and 11th Panzer Divisions in the area posed potentially a troublesome threat to Simpson's right, but Rose's 3rd Armored continued advancing swiftly enough and driving the panzers hard enough to prevent the enemy armor from assembling to deliver more than piecemeal counterattacks. As early as February 26, the consensus at First Army headquarters was: "Perhaps it is too early to be optimistic but everyone from the General down feels tonight that resistance is on the point of crumbling and that this time we are going to the Rhine quickly without being slowed down." By the next day, "the Boche, although not in any sense getting up and surrendering in mass, are fighting a disorganized defensive battle. Stiff resistance where it has been encountered has been centered in the small towns and usually after an hour or so of fighting, the soldiers have come out with their hands up. According to Col Dickson, all divisions that were in reserve on the western front have now been committed. . . ."[6]

Hodges was right about the swiftness of the march to the Rhine; Rose's vanguard reached the great German river near Worringen during the night of March 3–4, Lauer's 99th Infantry Division following not far behind in the area between the American armor and the Erft. By that time the 104th and 8th Divisions were fighting southwest across a low ridge broken by surface lignite mines, the Vorgebirge, in the direction of Cologne. Parts of the 3rd Armored were also turning southward toward that famous cathedral city, Germany's fourth largest.

Bradley and Hodges as much as Patton were still pressing to make sure that the 12th as well as 21 Army Group would soon cross the Rhine, and that their proposed drive to the Frankfurt-Kassel route eastward into Germany should be no more secondary to Montgomery's invasion than SHAEF directives made absolutely unavoidable. Unless the foundation for First Army and Third Army crossings of the Rhine were laid immediately, Hodges feared his army would join Simpson's in Montgomery's group, and Bradley feared that he might be left with a rump army group as in the Ardennes and with a nearly passive role. Thus the 12th Army Group leaders had planned that Collins must swing without pause from Operation GRENADE into the sequel designed by Bradley, Operation LUMBERJACK. LUMBERJACK proposed to grasp the Germans west of the Rhine in Bradley's sector within yet another envelopment much like VERITABLE-GRENADE—at length the Allied strategists were growing enamored of envelopment. With Collins's corps leading the way and the other corps of the First Army pivoting southeastward in succession to follow it, Bradley planned a meeting on the Ahr River between Hodges's men and Patton's coming northeast through the Eifel.

The detachments from Bradley to strengthen Simpson meant that the First Army-Third Army concentration was not all it had been in January, but Hodges still commanded nine infantry and three armored divisions, plus the reduced 106th Division, and Patton led seven infantry and three armored divisions. The January and February experiences in campaigning in the Eifel had shown that such a concentration was more than enough, in fact, to create logistic problems by breaking down the limited road net behind the front when the weight of transport combined with the ravages of alternate freezing and thawing; Bradley directed the packing of vital supplies at airfields in case an airlift proved necessary to keep LUMBERJACK in motion.

The weakness of the Germans in front of Hodges and Patton had offered a principal attraction of the earlier abortive Eifel offensive; and for the same reasons that the earlier First Army-Third Army concentration had been dissipated—Allied offensives elsewhere—the Germans had been unable to strengthen themselves in the Eifel or on the Cologne Plain since then. American intelligence estimated that only some 40,000 enemy troops faced the First Army and some 45,000 the Third Army. As Collins's corps turned toward Cologne to open LUMBERJACK, the enemy was engaged in yet another shift of his command arrangements, as though juggling headquarters might compensate for the absence of troops. Zangen's Fifteenth Army was taking over the former Fifth Panzer Army zone, generally opposite Hodges, while Manteuffel's headquarters moved down the Rhine to the better tank country to the north.

The Germans had not intended that any enemy should ever penetrate so deep into the Fatherland as the Anglo-Americans had already come. Therefore Cologne possessed only a weak outer ring of defenses, manned by bits and pieces of the 9th Panzer, 3rd Panzer Grenadier, and 363rd Volksgrenadier Divisions, and a weaker inner ring, manned by police and firemen and Volkssturm troopers. The Volkssturm was a militialike levy of old and young men under Nazi party command. Such defenses could not long delay Lightning Joe Collins. The 3rd Armored Division was inside Cologne on March 5, and Allen's 104th Division followed before the day was over. General Rose's tanks reached the Hohenzollern Bridge the next day but, predictably, much of the structure was resting in the water, and so were the rest of the Cologne bridges over the Rhine. Somehow the cathedral stood structurally almost intact, surveying a vast urban rubble, for Cologne had been an early and favored target of the area bombing of the RAF.

On the right of Collins's VII Corps was Millikin's III, wrested from Patton when Eisenhower and Bradley professed to be suspending his February offensive. To launch LUMBERJACK as promptly as possible, Bradley and Hodges had sent Millikin's divisions across the Roer beginning as early as February 25, as soon as Collins had enough strength on the east bank to make his contribution to GRENADE. Hodges prescribed that to avoid costly river-crossing assaults, Andrus's 1st Division on Millikin's left should use the VII Corps bridges and then move south to form its own bridgehead beyond the Roer. Once it had done so and put in its own bridge, Millikin's next division to the southward, Craig's 9th, should cross via the 1st Division bridge, and so on. Huebner's V Corps would follow Millikin's III according to the same method, each division crossing first into the bridgehead of its northern neighbor.

Employing this method, the V Corps began crossing the Roer on March 2, and by that time the III Corps had already broken any facsimile of a solid German line in its northwest-to-southeast swing toward the Ahr. Like Simpson's farther north, Millikin's advances became a procession reminiscent of last summer's pursuit—except that nighttime snow, turning into midday mud, aggravated the fatigue of continual movement.

Millikin's principal objective was to win crossings of the Ahr, so there would be a firm northern jaw upon which Patton's columns might close as they came up from the southern Eifel, to trap the German units still stubbornly clinging to the West Wall in front of Hodges's southern and Patton's northern flanks. Bradley and Hodges were insistent on the Ahr crossings as the III Corps goal, and Hodges underscored the insistence on March 5 by adjusting the boundary between Millikin's and Huebner's corps to provide Millikin a wider frontage on the Ahr. Nevertheless, the geography of Milli-kin's sector reinforced the siren song of the Rhine to draw his troops eastward toward the great river. With the heights of the Vorgebirge crowding the Ahr on the north and the tangled Eifel pressing hard upon it to the south, the Ahr itself pulled Millikin's men almost irresistibly toward its meeting with the Rhine near the town of Remagen.

The Battle of the Hohe Eifel

Bradley's insistence that Millikin anchor himself to await Patton on the Ahr, placing upon the First Army the primary responsibility for assuring a junction with the Third, deliberately freed Patton to think mainly of swift movement, of pushing for the Rhine, and of isolating as many Germans as possible in the process. Patton consequently instructed Middleton of the VIII Corps to advance from his line generally facing the Prüm River to reach the Rhine around Brohl, Eddy of the XII Corps to cross the Kyll River and head for the Rhine at Andernach. Both of these corps confronted some of the most rugged terrain of the whole rugged Eifel, the tumbled volcanic residue called the Hohe Eifel. Thus the swift movement that was Patton's passion and Bradley's obvious desire for the Third Army's share in LUMBERJACK would be possible only on the few roads—and difficult there. Patton accordingly instructed each corps commander that as soon as he had jumped the river barrier immediately in front of him, he should turn loose an armored division to charge along the roads. The infantry could lag behind to clean up the surrounding hills. Because Patton also wanted to keep open the possibility of a later southward campaign to envelop the Saarland, he instructed Walker of the XX Corps meanwhile to push one division from Trier along a narrow valley north of the Moselle eventually turning right to Bernkastel and toward the Saar.

The Third Army hurried into LUMBERJACK almost without pause from its Prüm-Bitburg and Trier campaigns. To the army's regret but scarcely its surprise, in that brief interval it had to part with Grow's 6th Armored Division, which Eisenhower purloined for his SHAEF reserve. Therefore Middleton had to assign the exploitation role in the VIII Corps to Kilburn's 11th Armored Division, which was far less tested, and for whose commander Middleton had felt steadily decreasing respect since the division's first battles in the Ardennes.

After Blakeley's 4th Division had suitably widened its bridgehead across the Prüm River around the town of Prüm at the beginning of March, the 11th Armored passed through on March 3 to strike on across the Kyll and thence northeast toward the Rhine. Unhappily, the difference between the 11th Armored and the 6th showed up quickly: the 11th hesitated at the wide bend of the Kyll southwest of Gerolstein, diffident lest in crossing there it expose itself to artillery and antitank fire from all around the bend. Kilburn asked that the 4th Division come up and that he be allowed to look for a better crossing site downstream. Middleton consented, and these arrangements naturally con-sumed time. It was not until March 6 that Kilburn was over the Kyll in a bridgehead he

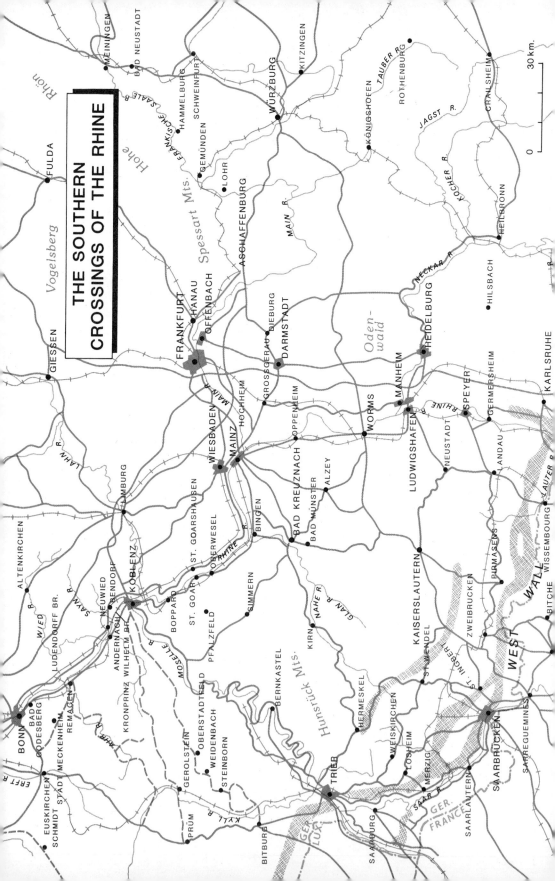

THE SOUTHERN
CROSSINGS OF THE RHINE

considered firm enough for further exploitation. By that time Culin's 87th Division on his left and Rooks's 90th on his right had caught up and also crossed the Kyll—the 90th at the bend that had stymied the armor. This site indeed proved so favorable that Kilburn's division backtracked and crossed over a Bailey bridge completed by the 90th on the night of March 6–7.

The contrast between this performance and that of the XII Corps spearhead, Gaffey's 4th Armored, made Middleton regret all the more the departure of Grow's 6th Armored. Eddy's XII Corps was already up to the Kyll when LUMBERJACK began, and Irwin's 5th Division forced a crossing on March 3 and put in a vehicular bridge by daylight of March 4. The Germans evidently regarded any neighborhood containing the 4th Armored as a danger zone, and they had their 2nd Panzer Division available to trouble the bridgehead with counterattacks. Nevertheless, Patton, Eddy, and Gaffey decided Gaffey's division should commence its exploitation on the morning of March 5. The plan was to drive two combat commands northward on parallel roads to Oberstadtfeld, which movement would cut the lines of communication of two of the German Seventh Army's corps, the XIII and LIII. From Oberstadtfeld, the armor was to turn northeast for Andernach and the Rhine.

Despite bad roads, bad weather—mixed rain and snow—and the 2nd Panzers, the plan worked almost to perfection. CCB, taking the better road from the Kyll toward Oberstadtfeld, advanced as far as Weidenbach the first day, with the hauling in of a thousand prisoners the major cause of delay, until a Nebelwerfer brigade slowed it up around darkness. The 4th Armored's only serious problem was the sorry condition of the secondary route traveled by CCA, so the next day Gaffey brought this combat command around to follow CCB. By that time the Germans had thrown some Tigers in CCB's path, but they showed up in driblets to be overwhelmed individually. As CCB repeated its triumphant progress of the day before, a German general came riding past in his command car. "Where do you think you're going?" asked 1st Lieutenant Joe Liese. Abruptly realizing he was no longer among his own retreating columns, the commander of the LIII Corps, General der Kavallerie Ernst Georg Graf von Rothkirch und Tritt, had to reply: "It looks like I'm going to the American rear."[7]

CCB traveled about thirty kilometers through rain and fog that day before darkness and broken road surfaces caused it to pause until it could better find its way again. Gaffey's spearhead was now far ahead of the XII Corps infantry, in possession only of the roadway; but the Germans approaching its flanks came mostly to surrender, and there seemed little danger in its exposure, even though the infantrymen in the rear were still meeting occasional pockets of stiff resistance. Gaffey's men pushed on as usual again on March 7, again found only scattered clusters of Germans who were willing to fight and many more who abruptly surrendered, and by nightfall reached the reverse slope of the last ridge before the Rhine. Granting the demoralized state of the opposition, still Bradley did not altogether exaggerate when he wrote that "in this attack Gaffey had staged the boldest and the most insolent armored blitz of the Western war."[8] From the crossing of the Kyll, the 4th Armored had driven some forty airline kilometers into the German rear, taking 5,000 prisoners, killing or wounding some 700 Germans, capturing tons of equipment—including thirty-four tanks and assault guns—and losing only twenty-nine killed, eighty wounded, and two missing.

The XIII and LIII Corps of the German Seventh Army and the LXVII and LXVI

Corps on the left of the Fifteenth Army were now all on the verge of entrapment, and those units that had not already crumbled were beginning a race to the Rhine that deteriorated swiftly into a case of sauve qui peut. For once, senior officers and headquarters fell into the American bag, to undermine the little capacity the Germans might still retain for rebuilding their formations. On the same day that the 4th Armored arrived at the hills above the Rhine, the southward progression of the First Army's attacks sent the 28th Division and the fragment of the 106th into action, and Cota's men overran the command post of the LXVI Corps, which had persisted in trying to defend the West Wall. The corps commander chanced to be away, but the chief of staff and most of the headquarters personnel trudged off toward American prison compounds. The 11th Armored Division, at last across the Kyll in force, barely missed capturing the headquarters and the new commander of the LIII Corps, Generalmajor Walther Botsch. Botsch had been hastened into the post of the captured General von Rothkirch so swiftly that he had been unable to brief his successor in his former command, the defense of the Rhine from Bonn to Remagen. The Rhine at Remagen, of course, was the destination toward which the valley of the Ahr was drawing part of the American III Corps, in spite of contrary intentions.

34: The Crossing of the Rhine

"IT WILL BE realized," General Eisenhower had reminded the Combined Chiefs of Staff on January 20, "that a crossing of the Rhine, particularly on the narrow frontages in which such crossings are possible, will be a tactical and engineering operation of the greatest magnitude." The Supreme Commander therefore envisioned an operation requiring the application of Allied power on the grandest scale, including strategic air support, airborne landings, and large numbers of every kind of amphibious craft. At that, "The possibility of failure to secure bridgeheads in the north or in the south can not, however, be overlooked. I am, therefore, making logistic preparations which will enable me to switch my main effort from the north to the south should this be forced upon me."[1]

The desire to have more than one card to play, then, was a major reason for Eisenhower's not staking all his plans for the crossing of the Rhine on the northern offensive by Montgomery's 21 Army Group, however much he might agree that Montgomery's crossing merited the highest priority. Moreover, Eisenhower had always maintained that there were good reasons for a southern crossing in addition to one in the north: too small a proportion of his strength could be driven deep into Germany if the Allies crossed the Rhine in Montgomery's sector alone—21 Army Group's own planners estimated that only thirty-five divisions at most could be supported across the Rhine below the Ruhr until railways were extended beyond the river; Eisenhower also felt the attraction of Bradley's idea for an envelopment of the Ruhr and the forces within it, by linking part of Montgomery's northern invasion force east of the Ruhr with Americans coming up from the south. For all of Eisenhower's conviction that Montgomery's invasion of Germany would carry most quickly over the best terrain to the most vital target—the Ruhr—it was also true, as General Bull was to remark to Bradley, that "Ike's heart is in your sector."[2] Bradley and Patton might rail at Ike for favoring the British, and Eisenhower might discipline himself to avoid favoring his own countrymen, but he wanted the American army to be deep in Germany for the final triumph.

Terrain still pointed so strongly toward Montgomery's invasion route that these reflections and inclinations left a puzzling problem: where to invade farther south? Even in attempting to defend his plan for a southern crossing of the Rhine to the skeptical British Chiefs of Staff, Eisenhower had to concede the geographic disadvantages upstream from the Ruhr, especially between Cologne and Koblenz:

> there is one [crossing] site on each side of Cologne suitable for a divisional assault crossing, but a crossing in this area would be tactically difficult, and after the seizure of a bridgehead, the hinterland is unsuitable for the development of operations against opposition. There are two isolated sites between Koblenz and Bonn, but

owing to the nature of the terrain operations would not be practicable except against very light opposition.[3]

In February, the Allied planners were still wrestling with the problem of southern crossing sites and invasion routes. All along, the most auspicious area for a southern crossing seemed to be from Mainz to Karlsruhe, where the planners discerned five suitable sites for division-size assault crossings, and where the transport facilities from the west would permit supporting as many as fifty divisions beyond the Rhine. But even here, the objectives beyond the Rhine were relatively much less important than those to the north, and the terrain relatively uninviting. To proceed straight east toward Schweinfurt and Nürnberg "may be ruled out as a method of reaching the heart of Germany, as it does not uncover or cut off any vital industrial area." The direction of advance would have to be northeast, but here the possibilities remained less than spectacular:

Important Objectives

24. Within approximately 30 miles of the Rhine in this sector there are a number of important industrial towns, lying roughly in two groups, i.e. Frankfurt-Mannheim and Karlsruhe-Stuttgart. Thereafter there are no really important economic objectives until an advance of some 150–200 miles from the Rhine has brought our forces to the Hanover-Brunswick or the Erfurt-Leipzig area.

Terrain.

25. An advance from the Mainz-Karlsruhe area North-Eastwards towards Kassel-Erfurt is bounded on the North-West by the Taunus, the Westerwald and the Rothaar hill masses. To the South-East there is no continuous boundary, but the Black Forest initially and the Thuringian Forest further North confine the flank at two points. The corridor, which is some 70 miles wide at the points of constriction, is divided roughly down the centre by the heavily wooded hill features of the Odenwald, Spessart, Rhon and the Harz mountains, but these do not form a continuous barrier. In addition, the river Main would have to be forced and the river Neckar divides our front initially.

26. The terrain over which the advance would have to take place between the difficult country mentioned above is fair only. Between Frankfurt and Giessen there is good going, but thereafter woods and hills increase. In the same way the going is generally fair to good on the general axis Karlsruhe-Heilbronn-Wurzburg but deteriorates thereafter.

Unimpressive as were any advantages in this area, the region from Mainz north to Cologne offered nothing better than the possibility of a turn southward to get back to the Frankfurt-Kassel-Erfurt corridor. From Bingen not far below Mainz to Koblenz, the Rhine itself "flows through a steep gorge with difficult forest country on both banks." Between Koblenz and Cologne:

Important Objectives.

15. With the exception of the Rhine towns of Cologne, Bonn and Koblenz, which could largely be neutralized without crossing the river, there are no important objectives other than the Ruhr about 30 miles to the Northwards, and the Frankfurt-Giessen area about 50 miles to the Southeastwards.

Terrain.

16. Apart from the Rhine plain itself which offers a narrow belt of good going to the East of the river, the whole region to the East is extremely difficult for cross

country movement. It is heavily wooded, undulating and broken in many places by narrow valleys with steep, thickly wooded sides. The only natural lines of Eastward advance are up the valleys of the Agger and Sieg which enter the Rhine near Bonn and offer progressively narrowing defiles towards Olpe and Singen. Thereafter, any further advance would have to be in a North-Easterly direction over further difficult country to avoid the still more unfavourable Rothaar Mountains region.

17. There is a possible alternative route into Germany from Cologne-Koblenz running South-Eastwards along the East of the Rhine, thence striking across through Limburg to Giessen and Kassel. This, however, is a round about approach to the Frankfurt-Kassel route.

Montgomery undeniably would enjoy not only the best path to the Ruhr but the best avenue into the heart of Germany thereafter. His prospective route into Germany lay between the Ruhr and, in the north, the excessively numerous waterways beyond a line Zwolle-Lingen-Bremen:

> The region between these boundaries, some sixty miles wide, is generally low lying and has few distinct features apart from the Teutoberger Forest, the river Ems and the Ems-Dortmund canal which cross the axis of advance, and the river Lippe and the Lippe canal running parallel to the Ruhr in the South. For the most part woods, bogs and heath increase towards the Dutch frontier, while towards the North, the ground is lower lying and more intersected by water courses and with a number of sandy tracts. To the South and East agricultural land and hedged-in fields predominate, with meadowlands along the rivers. The belt of country North of the Lippe is generally best suited to the employment of armour and is likely to dry earlier than the rest of this region.

Beyond the Rhine, the watercourses athwart Montgomery's path were not large enough to pose serious impediments to armies with bridging and amphibious equipment on the British, let alone the American, scale. Under the geographic circumstances, Eisenhower's mind was necessarily "up north," however much his heart might be in Bradley's sector.[4]

On the plans and preparations for the critical crossing up north, Montgomery lavished even more care than he had given to his great set-piece battle at El Alamein; the preparations rivaled those for NEPTUNE itself. In conjunction with SHAEF, 21 Army Group began its planning in October 1944, almost as soon as it was clear that MARKET-GARDEN's effort to seize a swift crossing of the Rhine had failed. Each of Montgomery's prospective assaulting armies had its engineer group planning with special care. Some 37,000 British engineers were to participate in the 21 Army Group crossing, along with 22,000 American engineers. To the engineer group of the Ninth Army came the largest of three naval detachments supporting the American armies in Europe, bringing twenty-four LCMs and twenty-four LCVPs to supplement army assault boats. The Royal Navy similarly supplied the same types of ocean-going assault craft to the British forces. The planners directed the accumulation of 118,000 tons of supplies for the British Second Army crossing, while the Ninth Army collected another 138,000 tons. Prime Minister Churchill of course followed avidly the preliminaries to the war's final great display of Britain's military might, and he prepared to travel to Germany to be a witness himself to the triumphant hour when the British army would carry out the first assault crossing of the Rhine in modern history.

While the Americans farther south were closing on the Rhine [Churchill was to write] Montgomery had made ready to cross it. Planning and assembling of material had begun several months before. Great quantities of stores, amphibious vehicles, assault craft, and bridging material were now brought up to the fighting zone, and troops concentrated on the near bank, behind constant smokescreens. . . .

All our resources were to be used. Eighty thousand men, the advance-guard of armies a million strong, were to be hurled forward. Masses of boats and pontoons lay ready. On the far side stood the Germans, entrenched and organised in the strength of modern fire-power.[5]

Such preparations consumed time. Having closed to the Rhine by eliminating the Wesel pocket on March 9–10, Montgomery looked toward March 24 as D-Day for the crossing.

Remagen

On March 5 General Hodges toured the front lines of the V Corps, learned from Collins of the VII Corps that Cologne was practically within his grasp, and "In celebration of the arrival of his troops on the Rhine, or as the General put it another way, to take the curse off the roast pork, he ordered champagne to be served during . . . dinner and Bill [Sylvan] proposed a toast 'to an early crossing' of the Rhine."[6]

Two days later, March 7, Hodges himself entered Cologne and its cathedral. Conferring with Collins, he was told that General Lauer of the 99th Division was imploring Collins "for permission to send across [the Rhine] two battalions of infantry but he naturally had to refuse. However, he [Collins] told General Hodges he hoped the Army would not make the mistake of waiting long enough to permit the Boche to pull back their strength. General Collins said he would put across his Corps any time General Hodges gave him necessary engineer equipment. As is always the case, he is raring to go, and does not want to stop."[7]

About six that evening, Hodges returned to his headquarters, a château overlooking Stolberg, where he had moved from Spa three days earlier. Pertinent news awaited him.

That morning, while the 4th Armored Division was hurtling from the southwest toward the Rhine at Andernach, and the 28th Division was about to overrun the headquarters of the German LXVI Corps, CCA of General Leonard's 9th Armored Division had jumped to the south bank of the Ahr. The immediate motive was to assure the destruction of both the LXVI Corps and its northern neighbor, the LXVII, by cutting their main escape route, the highway through the Ahr valley. Just the day before, III Corps headquarters had transmitted to the 9th Armored G-3 the high command's insistence that the Ahr was the division's primary objective. Therefore, although by reaching Stadt Meckenheim on the night of March 6 Leonard's CCB had approached within fourteen kilometers of the Rhine, the major portion of CCB was also heading for the Ahr on the morning of March 7.

The army, corps, and division commanders were mindful that Remagen near the mouth of the Ahr was the site of a railroad bridge across the Rhine, a structure completed in 1916 and named for a German hero of that year, General Erich Ludendorff. But the Americans had almost abandoned hope of capturing a Rhine bridge. Some time earlier, the III Corps G-3 had cooked up a scheme to seize the Ludendorff Bridge with paratroopers or Rangers, but there was not enough interest to advance the plan out of the corps operations section. Still, on March 6, III Corps headquarters restricted artillery fire against the bridge to time and proximity fuzes, and the corps also asked the air officer at First Army headquarters to leave off bombing the bridges at Remagen and Bonn. Furthermore, on the morning of March 7 the 9th Armored's CCB detached a task force comprised mainly of the 27th Armored Infantry Battalion and the bulk of the 14th Tank Battalion, placing it under Lieutenant Colonel Leonard Engeman and sending it toward the Ludendorff Bridge.

The morning was well along before bulldozers cleared a path through the rubble of Stadt Meckenheim for Engeman's lead tank platoon, equipped with the new T26 Pershings, to break free. Brushing aside sporadic light opposition, Task Force Engeman reached woods just west of Remagen a little before noon. Just before 1:00 P.M., 2nd Lieutenant Emmet J. Burrows, commanding the lead infantry platoon, emerged from woods onto a cliff overlooking the Rhine. Before him he saw, plainly enough despite a low haze, the town of Remagen and, still standing, the Ludendorff Bridge.

German soldiers were retreating across the bridge, and others, no doubt including the demolition team, were wandering about on the far side. Three arches resting on four stone piers crossed the Rhine between two grimy, forbidding, castlelike stone towers. The bridge was wide enough for two railroad tracks plus footpaths, and the tracks had been covered with wooden planking to permit troops and vehicles to cross. Just beyond the east end, the railroad tracks entered a tunnel through a black cliff.

Lieutenant Burrows quickly brought up his company commander, 1st Lieutenant Karl H. Timmerman, who in turn hurried the word to Colonel Engeman. While Engeman was instructing Timmerman to get his infantry into Remagen followed by the platoon of Pershings, the CCB operations officer, Major Ben Cothran, arrived and promptly radioed the CCB commander, General Hoge of St. Vith fame. Hoge came riding cross country, weighing as he did the prospects of losing a battalion when the bridge blew up versus the possibility of capturing it. Arriving about three o'clock, he ordered Engeman to seize the bridge as quickly as possible. Presently there arrived a report from CCB's main column, who had found a German civilian who insisted the Ludendorff Bridge was to be blown at precisely four o'clock.

By this time Lieutenant Timmerman's infantry and tanks had fought through most of Remagen against scattered resistance. It was almost four when they approached the bridge, dodging small-arms and 20mm. fire from the towers. An explosion lifted rocks and ground just in front of them, evidently intended to obstruct the approach against tanks. They could see Germans rushing around at the far end, surely about to set off the main explosion to destroy the bridge itself.

Nevertheless, Timmerman ordered his company to begin crossing. Thereupon the explosion erupted. There was a roar and concussion of sound; smoke, dirt, and timbers billowed into the air; and the bridge rose from its supports.

Then the smoke and dust cleared, and the Americans could see the bridge, big holes torn in the planking, but otherwise settled back on its supports.

The footpaths were intact, and Timmerman again ordered his men forward. They dashed from cover to cover under machine-gun fire, while the Pershings silenced some enemy riflemen who were on a barge in the river and kept the machine guns subdued enough to be tolerable. Three engineers followed Timmerman's infantrymen, cutting everything that might be a demolition wire. Timmerman and his company were soon across the 325-meter span. One platoon began climbing the cliff above the tunnel. The other men fanned out.

Among the first captives were Hauptmann (Captain) Willi Bratge, until the arrival of a major just before noon the area combat commander, and Hauptmann Karl Friesenhahn, the bridge engineer officer. There soon took form a story of confusion in German command and responsibility, partly occasioned by the departure of General Botsch to take over the LIII Corps; of reluctance to blow the bridge while it still represented escape to retreating German soldiers; and of a detonation system that when first activated did not blow at all, and then exploded ineffectually after a sergeant bravely dashed onto the bridge to ignite the primer cord. The Germans surmised that artillery fire had probably broken part of the circuitry.

General Hoge meanwhile had received orders to divert as much strength as possible from Remagen to a bridge across the Ahr that the main body of CCB had found at Sinzig. Hoge nevertheless ordered Engeman to send the rest of his armored infantry battalion across the Ludendorff Bridge immediately. His division commander, General Leonard, promptly confirmed "Let's push it" at Remagen. By 4:30, III Corps headquarters knew it had a bridge across the Rhine. General Millikin was away, but his chief of staff, Colonel James H. Phillips, ordered the 9th Armored to exploit the crossing.

Only a short time before, General Kean had reminded III Corps of standing First Army instructions that if anybody found a bridge across the Rhine, it should be exploited to the fullest. When Hodges returned to his headquarters about six and learned about the Remagen bridge, he spent most of the next two and a half hours with his staff trying to assure a firm and rapid grasping of the advantage. He changed the boundary between the III and V Corps to give Huebner additional territory so Millikin could concentrate on an attack into the bridgehead.

Hodges also telephoned Bradley. "Hot dog, Courtney," Bradley remembered himself saying, "this will bust him wide open. Are you getting your stuff across?" Hodges affirmed that he was, as fast as he could. Bradley told him to continue, and "button the bridgehead up tightly."[8]

But it was also true, as Major Hansen said, that "Tonight the war went to pieces. That is the war we had planned."[9] And not everyone was happy. General Bull from SHAEF chanced to be visiting Bradley when Hodges called. Bull's mission was "a larcenous proposal," as Bradley described it, to divert four divisions from the 12th to the 6th Army Group to assist Devers in the unfinished business of closing up to the Rhine in the Seventh Army zone. "There goes your ball game," Bradley told Bull. "Courtney's gotten across the Rhine on a bridge." Bull was less than elated. He remembered the staff studies showing that a crossing between Cologne and Koblenz would lead nowhere. He remembered the SHAEF plan that called not only for 21 Army Group to stage the primary crossing, but for a 12th Army Group crossing to take place between Mainz and Karlsruhe. Exasperated with such staff inflexibility, Bradley finally demanded: "What in hell do you want us to do, pull back and blow it up?"

Bradley sought a more sympathetic ear by telephoning Eisenhower, and initially he found the response he wanted: "Hold on to it, Brad. Get across with whatever you need—but make certain you hold that bridgehead." Four or five divisions ought to cross immediately, said Eisenhower.[10]

Debate between Bradley and Bull nevertheless persisted through the evening.

Bradley reminded Bull of the possibility of turning southward along the east bank of the Rhine to the corridor to Giessen—the Lahn River valley—and thus to the Frankfurt-Kassel corridor. When the planners had pointed out that this was a roundabout route to the same destination that Mainz-Karlsruhe crossings would reach more directly, they had not had in mind a free passage at Remagen. In the course of the evening, Leven Allen repeated to Bull again and again, "A bird in the hand is worth two in the bush." Bull conceded that perhaps the wrong troops were at the wrong place—perhaps Bradley and Patton ought to be in the north, ready to push for Berlin. Bradley repeated his fear that the northern crossings alone would be unable to support enough divisions beyond the Rhine: "Let's develop our strategy so that we can employ them all."

> Pinky [Bull] slumped wearily in his seat [says Hansen], the large leather chair before the brilliantly lighted map in General Bradley's ornate Namur office. Bradley sat quietly in another, flanked by his G's and General Allen while experts on terrain, movement and supply hovered in the background. Despite the drama of the moment, we were sleepy. It was midnight and we had eaten a heavy dinner. Sibert found it difficult to stay awake. Pinky, however, was still jostling.[11]

He continued "jostling" until nearly one in the morning, when Bradley finally agreed to yield up some divisions after all, and for his pains was assured that "The 12th Group is now harder to get along with than 21 and certainly no easier."[12] During the next few days, furthermore, Bull's unbending skepticism infected Eisenhower himself. It was not simply that SHAEF regarded an approved plan as equivalent to inscriptions on tablets of stone, though again there was influence from the staff conservatism that had earlier constrained the logistical planning for OVERLORD and thus helped stall the past summer's breakout. More important, Eisenhower's reasons for favoring Montgomery's crossings remained good ones, and the Supreme Commander still lacked enough divisions to have much strength to spare to funnel into Remagen. Perhaps yet more important, because of this paucity of reserve division, Eisenhower continued intent on closing to the Rhine along the whole front before he committed major forces anywhere beyond the river, lest the enemy use a bridgehead west of the Rhine to catch him off balance again in the manner of the Ardennes.

If the current Soviet offensive and the German collapse from Nijmegen to the Eifel made this policy appear cautious in the extreme, Eisenhower nevertheless felt assured enough of eventual victory to prefer caution over the risk of another setback. He had resisted the pressure of the British Chiefs of Staff to let Montgomery cross the Rhine before the Allied armies had closed to it, yielding only the most minute concessions during the Malta conference when even General Marshall was in a mildly appeasing mood toward the former senior partners of the alliance. If Eisenhower would not bend his determination to reach the Rhine along the length of his front for the British Chiefs of Staff, he would not do it for his American subordinates either.

Therefore, late on March 9 Bull enjoyed the satisfaction of telling Bradley that Eisenhower did not want the Remagen bridgehead expanded beyond the ability of five divisions to defend it. Bradley acquiesced by instructing Hodges to limit advances to about a thousand yards a day, just enough to prevent the enemy from mining and entrenching around the perimeter. At the Frankfurt-Ruhr Autobahn, less than ten kilometers away, progress was to halt until Eisenhower ordered otherwise. That day

Hodges had savored the congratulations of his peers at a meeting of Bradley's army commanders along with Juin, Simpson, Vandenberg, and Quesada at Namur; to this deflating news he returned.

The Battle of the Remagen Bridgehead

For the Germans, beyond its practical importance as the last barrier on which the invasion of the Western Allies might conceivably be halted, the Rhine's inviolability was crucial for symbolic reasons. The American crossing at Remagen cost Rundstedt his job as OB West; on March 8, Hitler called Generalfeldmarschall Albert Kesselring from Italy to replace the old Prussian aristocrat. Kesselring, an artilleryman turned aviator, had moved into the Mediterranean during the early phases of the war in the Western Desert at the head of Luftflotte II; he had gone on to become not only Axis commander in the theater but, in his masterful obstruction of the Allied climb up the boot of Italy, perhaps the supreme German defensive general of World War II. But Kesselring brought his skills to the Western Front too late to erase the Remagen bridgehead, and much too late to accomplish anything larger. Eisenhower had already advanced too far toward achieving one of his major purposes in wanting to close to the Rhine all along the front: the destruction of the Wehrmacht before it could make a stand behind the Rhine.

The destruction of those German forces caught between the First and Third Army pincers simultaneous with the Remagen crossing freed adequate American strength to hold a bridgehead that Eisenhower insisted must remain small anyway. The 11th Armored Division of Middleton's VIII Corps reached the Rhine at Brohl the day after the capture of the Ludendorff Bridge, forcing into desperate flight practically all that was left of German resistance to Bradley's armies south of the Ahr. The next day, the 2nd Division of Huebner's V Corps met the 11th Armored to close Hodges's and Patton's pincers. The pincers were slim enough that at first many Germans found means to slip through them—as usual—and then somehow ferried themselves across the Rhine. But since the beginning of the First Army's crossing of the Roer, Hodges's and Patton's men had captured about 50,000 prisoners, and to their gratifying haul of higher officers they added the commanders of the 3rd and 5th Parachute Divisions.

Millikin had hurried the vanguard of Craig's 9th Infantry Division to join Leonard's 9th Armored in crossing at Remagen, and Hodges had hurried up Parker's 78th Division from the left of the neighboring V Corps. Thus some 8,000 troops crossed the Ludendorff Bridge in the first twenty-four hours of American possession, including a tank battalion, a tank destroyer company, a battery and a half of antiaircraft artillery, and a platoon of armored engineers. On March 9, Millikin gave command of all activity in the vicinity of the bridge to Leonard of the 9th Armored, and of the east-shore bridgehead to Craig of the 9th Infantry Division.

For anyone other than that dominating personality Lightning Joe Collins, it was uncomfortable to work directly under the eye of Courtney Hodges, particularly in any operation that was critical enough to strain Hodges's nerves and to focus on the First Army attention that might become embarrassing to Hodges himself. On March 2, General Walker had remarked to Patton that the corps commanders of the Third Army did better than those elsewhere because they could feel that if they made a mistake, they would still be backed up.[13] Millikin at Remagen, so recently in the Third Army, had reason to regret he had passed from Patton's fatherly protection to Hodges's insecure impatience. In fairness it must be recalled that Millikin had by no means been Patton's favorite corps commander; but Patton's sporadic grumbling that the III was not administered as well as his other corps was nothing compared to Hodges's reluctance to concede that Millikin could do anything right at Remagen.

The expansion of the Remagen bridgehead was even slower than SHAEF's and Bradley's restrictions envisaged. To feed strength into the bridgehead, Millikin had to contend with the horrendous traffic tieups that inevitably accumulated on the west bank, and with the bottleneck of the bridge itself, which came under constant artillery fire and had to be the object of constant efforts at repair. The upstream truss having been ruined by the attempted German demolition, the downstream truss alone was precariously bearing all the weight of the structure, of thousands of marching men and vehicles, and of hundreds of nearby explosions. So the bridge had to be used with extreme caution. The early arrival of a naval unit bringing twenty-four LCVPs and of the 86th Engineer Heavy Ponton Battalion, which on March 9 began to operate three rafts each made of five pontons covered with wooden flooring, eased but did not eliminate the crossing congestion. Nor did the opening of a treadway bridge on March 11—delayed by the need to give combat units road priority to Remagen; for on March 13 the engineers decided they must close the Ludendorff Bridge completely for repairs.

In the bridgehead, initial hasty commitment of units left organizations intermingled and control difficult. The accumulation of problems led Millikin to order advances from the bridge to proceed gingerly to three successive phase lines: the first, four kilometers north and south along the river and three kilometers east, to free the bridge from small-arms fire; the second, far enough to prevent observed artillery fire; the third, north to Bonn, east beyond the Autobahn, and south to Andernach, to end all shelling of the bridge. By March 10, the bridgehead had expanded beyond the first phase line north and south along the river, but it still reached only about a kilometer into the hills east of the bridge. Much of the German artillery that had just fled across the Rhine concentrated in those hills to blast the bridgehead and impede its extension.

The next day Hodges paid his first visit to the bridgehead, disenchanted over both the lack of progress and Millikin's unaggressive management in general. The army commander's arrival was inauspicious. His jeep sped across the treadway bridge at a time when German shelling was luckily light, but as soon as he set foot in Craig's command post across the river, three shells dropped almost on top of the CP, one wiping out the adjacent latrine.

Millikin was preparing to concentrate his efforts eastward to get at the guns in the neighboring hills and southeastward to reach the Lahn River valley. Hodges preferred a big push northward to open a crossing for Collins and the VII Corps, but he had neglected to say so to Millikin until now, and even on the visit he issued no specific order to this effect. Millikin nevertheless responded by assigning the 78th Division a narrow sector in the north to facilitate a power drive, and by moving most of the 9th Division northward as well. Unfortunately for Millikin, the 11th Panzer Division began showing up in the enemy lines the same day, and around it the Germans built in the next few days a strong defense concentrated on the northern rim of the perimeter.

The Germans were sparing no effort to destroy the Ludendorff Bridge and contain the bridgehead. The Luftwaffe struck continually beginning March 8, affording a heavy grouping of antiaircraft batteries unaccustomed practice in the work for which they had primarily trained. Starting March 12, V-2s fired from Holland hurtled toward the bridge, one hitting a house only 300 meters east of it. German frogmen turned up on the nights of March 16 and 17, to be driven off on the first night and on their second try captured in the glare of welcoming searchlights. The principal menace nevertheless remained the semi-circle of German guns around the bridgehead, whose constant pounding of the bridge, men, vehicles, and supplies soon exceeded the narrow limits of General Hodges's patience.

If Hodges could not eliminate the guns, he would eliminate Millikin for not silencing them. On March 15 Hodges warned Bradley that this step was coming, and Bradley agreed to look for a new head of the III Corps. Two days later, General Van Fleet arrived at Hodges's headquarters to replace Millikin. "I have some bad news for you," Hodges telephoned Millikin. After hearing Hodges out, Millikin replied, "Sir, I have some bad news for you too. The railroad bridge has just collapsed."[14]

The Ludendorff Bridge had sagged abruptly and then fell apart with a roar, killing twenty-eight and injuring ninety-three of the men working on it. But it had already been closed, and under heavy smoke cover other bridges to supplement the first treadway were well under construction or promptly ordered. A second bridge opened later on March 17, another on the 19th, another on the 20th, and yet another on the 21st. There was no pause in the efforts to enlarge the bridgehead. As sure to turn in a pinch to his strongest corps commander as he was to hector and often remove less favored subordinates, Hodges had begun feeding the VII Corps into the bridgehead on March 15 and given Collins command of the northern part of the perimeter on the 16th. That same day, the steady if slow American advances that had been progressing all along despite Hodges's dissatisfaction cut the Frankfurt-Ruhr Autobahn at the northeast corner of the bridgehead.

The Germans continued to pile on reinforcements around the perimeter, until the operations maps showed the Americans ringed by at least nine enemy divisions in three corps. The greatest concentration of strength, including most of the panzers, still shouldered against the north rim, commanded by the veteran armor expert and old comrade of Rommel, General Fritz Bayerlein, long the leader of Panzer Lehr and now heading the LIII Corps. As in almost every critical battle since Normandy, however, the Germans' best formations arrived piecemeal and spent themselves in the same way, mustering only scattered, limited counterattacks instead of any major blow. The Americans were strong enough to brush aside such efforts and to persist in their own dogged attacks.

Eisenhower still proposed to limit Hodges's advances to points not much beyond Millikin's third phase line, despite Millikin's departure and against Hodges's wishes. Van Fleet's III Corps, profiting from the German concentration against Collins, made a second break in the Autobahn on March 18 and reached its stop line by March 20. The next day the 78th Division, now in Collins's corps, arrived at the Sieg River. This stream flows into the Rhine below Bonn and had become the prescribed northern limit of advance. Collins then sent a combat command of the 3rd Armored Division eastward along the south bank of the Sieg to complete the closing of the designated perimeter, an object achieved on March 22.

Hodges meanwhile had flown to Bradley's headquarters, on March 19, to discuss the rankling restrictions on advance. D-Day was imminent for Montgomery's massive set-piece crossing of the Rhine, and the Americans chafed more and more at the prospect of remaining spectators to this ostentatious display of British power, sure to be accompanied by the usual self-satisfied Montgomery press releases. Bradley at last had some balm to dispense. He had just seen Eisenhower, and the Supreme Commander had authorized him to increase the buildup in the Remagen bridgehead to nine divisions. Furthermore, from March 23 onward, Hodges was to be prepared to break out southeast toward the Lahn River valley and thence the Frankfurt-Kassel corridor. By that time, Patton's Third Army should be set to launch a converging attack on the east side of the Rhine; for the Third and Seventh Armies had enjoyed a spectacular success in clearing the Saarland and the Palatinate, the last German bridgeheads west of the Rhine.

The Battles of the Saar and the Palatinate

American field orders were stereotyped adaptations of Command and General Staff School models and therefore usually admirable in their clarity—the supreme desideratum of any military order—but altogether lacking in inspirational content. They pale beside Montgomery's field orders, which contain such adjurations as: "On no account can we relax, or have a 'stand still' . . .; it is vital that we keep going. There will be difficulties caused by mud, cold, lack of air support during periods of bad weather, and so on. But we must continue to fight the enemy hard. . . ."[15]

The field orders of General O'Daniel of the 3rd Infantry Division form an exception to the usual American model. When Patch's Seventh Army prepared as its part in closing to the Rhine to assail at last the West Wall from Saarbrücken to Lauterbourg—through most of that length the strongest frontier defenses the Germans had ever built—O'Daniel's Rock of the Marne Division was to attack in the center of Haislip's XV Corps toward Zweibrücken and on into the geographical corridor through Kaiserslautern to the Rhine. O'Daniel's orders began by bestowing upon the prospective phase lines names that recalled the 3rd Division's long roll of battles since North Africa: Fedela, Tunisia, Sicily, Italy, France, Germany, and Here We Come. Then he enjoined each assault regiment:

> Attack in zone with utmost speed and aggressiveness on D Day at H Hour. . . .
> Destroy all enemy encountered. . . .
> The attack will be pressed with the ruthless vigor that has routed every enemy formation opposing the 3d Div. All men will be brought to the highest possible state of offensive spirit prior to the jump-off. *Bayonets will be sharpened.* Maximum effort will be exercised at all times to seize and secure bridges.
> Commanders will exercise every measure to insure secrecy and tactical surprise. . . .
> All available means of motor transportation including tanks, but excepting vehicles marked with Geneva crosses, will be used for the transportation of the infantry. . . .
> O'Daniel
Comdg.[16]

Patch's army had spent February in filling up the divisions for which it had earlier received or retained only infantry, overcoming the ammunition shortage—for a time the 36th Division artillery was restricted to eleven rounds per gun per day, even while on a limited attack—and straightening the line of departure for the coming push against the West Wall. Dean's 44th, Major General Louis E. Hibbs's 63rd, Major General Allison J. Barnett's 70th, and Burress's 100th Divisions flattened the German salients around Gros Recherding, Rimling, and other scenes of the NORDWIND battles to carry the western part of the army front from Lorraine back across the German border and up to the outer defenses of the West Wall—on occasion slightly into those defenses. Farther east, however, Patch's front still sagged southward away from the Saar River near Sarreguemines along the Moder River line to the Rhine, leaving the northeast corner of Alsace in German hands.

Early in March, General Devers transmitted to SHAEF with his approval a Seventh Army plan for Operation UNDERTONE, to close up to the Rhine by means of a set-piece attack all the way from Saarbrücken to beyond Hagenau with Milburn's XXI, Haislip's XV, and Brooks's VI Corps abreast, from left to right. The going was sure to be hard in such a broad frontal assault, not only because the dragon's teeth and pillboxes of the West Wall still mostly lay ahead, largely in a double band with yet another line of fortifications some distance to the rear, but also because the advance would carry through the heavily urbanized Saar Basin and thence into mountains. The thickly wooded extension of the Low Vosges into the Hardt Mountains lay in front of Patch's right. The Pfälzer Bergland—the Palatinate Highland—was in front of his left. Separating the highlands was the narrow valley penetrating through Kaiserslautern toward the Rhine. Behind the Pfälzer Bergland lay the more formidable Hunsrück Mountains. Off on the east flank the Wissembourg Gap, a major invasion route for Blaskowitz in January and for the Prussians in 1870, bypassed the Hardt Mountains; but this path lay too far from the Seventh Army's center of gravity to be logistically attractive. Difficulties notwithstanding, SHAEF believed Devers and Patch must mount some such assault: to reach the Rhine all along Eisenhower's front, to gain possible additional springboards toward the Frankfurt-Kassel corridor, and to deny the enemy the output of the Saar, second only to the Ruhr as an industrial reservoir in the German West. The Saar produced ten percent of Germany's iron and steel and even in early 1945 sent twelve trainloads of coal east of the Rhine daily. About half Germany's chemical production came from the I.G. Farben plant at Ludwigshafen on the west bank of the Rhine. It was to find an armored division and three infantry divisions with which to beef up the Seventh Army for the Saarland offensive that Bull was visiting Bradley when the news about the Ludendorff Bridge arrived.

By the time Bull paid his "larcenous" call upon Bradley, however, the 12th Army Group had more to point to than the Ludendorff bridge to argue in resistance against so large a contribution to Devers. It had a Third Army plan passed on by Patton to Bradley for easing the Seventh Army's task by assailing the West Wall from the rear. Patton would take advantage of the Third Army's clearing of the southern Eifel to turn his troops east and southeast between Trier and Koblenz. Walker's XX Corps would attack east from its bridgehead across the Saar near Trier, while Eddy's XII Corps crossed the Moselle and struck across the Hunsrück Mountains toward Bingen, at the junction of the Nahe River with the Rhine, and Bad Kreuznach, up the Nahe. The two corps would converge on the Nahe.

Patton like most other American commanders had grown considerably more attuned to the potentialities of envelopment since the past summer. His design was that the pincers formed by the XX and XII Corps ought to trap much of the remnant of the German Seventh Army that had crossed to the south bank of the Moselle. Then the American Third and Seventh Armies should also trap between them the German First Army, now under General der Infanterie Hermann Förtsch. Though Patton did not say so in writing, he also reminded Walker and Eddy of a still further purpose: that they might rush on toward the Rhine between Mainz and Worms, the best stretch of the river for a southern crossing and one on which he had set his eyes at least since his race eastward the previous summer.

Devers briefly voiced doubts about Patton's plan, because there might be a collision between the Third Army and Patch's Seventh. But the advantages of driving toward the West Wall's rear so the defenders would be distracted while Patch attacked head-on were so obvious that Bradley had little trouble persuading Eisenhower. The Saar-Palatinate campaign would become a converging effort of two armies. Devers's fears were moderated by giving Patton and Patch authority to communicate directly with each other, bypassing their different army group headquarters, and according Patton's right-flank and Patch's left-flank corps commanders permission to do the same. With these agreements, Bradley's concession of divisions to bolster Devers and Patch was whittled down to two from the original four. The formations yielded were to be Blakeley's 4th Infantry and Grow's 6th Armored, the latter already in SHAEF reserve anyway.

Patch was preparing for a March 15 D-Day, but Patton intended to jump the Moselle without pause, giving the disarrayed formations he ejected from the Eifel no time to regroup. So intent was he on crossing the Moselle and hastening to the Rhine between Mainz and Worms, in fact, that Gaffey's 4th Armored Division may have missed an opportunity to capture the Kronprinz Wilhelm Railroad Bridge across the Rhine at Urmitz, midway between Andernach and Koblenz. The 4th Armored remained on the reverse slope of the last ridge before the Rhine through the night of March 7 and into March 8 to protect itself from German guns across the river while it awaited further orders. During March 8 its observers could watch Germans retreating toward Urmitz, but haze prevented seeing the bridge itself, and some prisoners and German civilians—though not all—confirmed aerial reconnaissance reports that the bridge had been destroyed. Curiosity piqued, CCA nevertheless planned an attack toward Urmitz for March 9; but before it launched the effort, orders arrived to turn the 4th Armored toward the Moselle. Later the Americans learned the Germans had destroyed two spans of the Urmitz bridge some time before but had hung a vehicular crossing between railway rails over the gap—which may have accounted for the contradictory reports. In any event, the Germans eliminated the crossing early on March 9.

Preceded by a brief—fifteen-minute—but extremely heavy artillery preparation, the XX Corps attack into the Saar-Palatinate triangle went forward in the early morning darkness of March 13. General Paul's 26th Division on the corps right opened a diversionary attack southward into the West Wall fortifications around Merzig. McBride's 80th Division in the center and Malony's 94th on the left, both already beyond the West Wall, carried the main effort into the wooded Hunsrück Mountains. Walker planned that once these two divisions had cleared the worst of the mountain barrier, by reaching a line Hermeskeil-Weiskirchen-Losheim (not to be confused with the Losheim of the Eifel) some eleven to sixteen kilometers distant, he would commit Morris's 10th Armored Division for exploitation. The German line opposing McBride and Malony proved so thin that the attack was virtually an infiltration, bypassing strongpoints that could be mopped up later. Despite forbidding terrain and limited, muddy roads, the attack carried some three kilometers and across the Ruwer River on the first day. The next day a regiment of the still-formidable 6th SS Mountain Division counterattacked the 80th Division, and McBride's progress slowed enough to arouse Patton's impatience. But the army commander could take comfort from the reports of his other attacking corps, which had completed its turn from the Eifel and jumped the lower Moselle that morning.

Eddy's XII Corps had to cross the river against high, forested bluffs up which there climbed only a few steep roads. A thirty-minute artillery preparation opened the predawn effort by Irwin's 5th Division and the 90th, now commanded by Major General Herbert L. Earnest, the hard-driving officer who had led Task Force Earnest in Brittany the past summer. Despite the bluffs, the crossing proved easy. Resistance on the south bank was almost nonexistent except in towns and villages. Once past the bluffs, the countryside opened into rolling ridge lines, and Eddy decided to turn loose the 4th Armored Division on the second morning.

Eddy's corps was opposing a battered skeleton, the German Seventh Army. Except for a few reinforcements such as elements of the 6th SS Mountain Division, the army that had contended against the Western Allies since D-Day in Normandy had at last been harried and pounded beyond its capacity to put up a good fight. Walker's corps was facing the German First Army, which remained in somewhat better shape than the Seventh and thus offered more obstinate resistance. But even in Walker's front, the enemy's formations began to crumble on the third day of the battle, March 15. Though at day's end the 94th and 80th Divisions were still generally short of the Hermeskeil-Losheim objective line, Walker saw fit to order the 10th Armored to ready itself for action by the next morning. Passing through the infantry during the night, Morris's armor found that a semblance of an organized German front remained to resist it on March 16; but by March 17 the armor had achieved a clear breakthrough, advancing thirteen kilometers to seize a bridge over the Prims River and then pushing on through the night over the remaining eighteen kilometers to St. Wendel on the Nahe.

Gaffey's 4th Armored had nourished Patton's affection for it by already reaching the Nahe. Its CCA passed through the 90th Division on March 15 and collided with some well-served antitank guns; but CCB plunged forward twenty-five kilometers in five hours, brushing aside occasional roadblocks, to rest for the night at Simmern before taking on the last terrain obstacle before the Nahe, the Soonwald. On March 17, this obstacle proved minor, and CCB raced another twenty-three kilometers to arrive at the Nahe three kilometers from Bad Kreuznach at noon. While CCB promptly established a bridgehead, CCA also broke free, to reach the Nahe across from Gensingen before dark.

Patton's brief impatience on March 14 had been provoked partly by fear that Patch's Seventh Army, kicking off on the 15th, might yet reach the middle Rhine before him. (As it was, Patch, having seen the Rhine in Alsace long since, would soon chide Patton: "George, I forgot to congratulate you for being the last man to reach the Rhine." To which Patton, remembering Patch's retreat in front of NORDWIND, replied: "Let me congratulate you on being the first man to leave it."[17]) To allay Patton's discomfort, there were now the far-reaching tentacles of the 4th and 10th Armored Divisions. Assuring him that he would beat Patch at least to the currently contested section of the Rhine, they also satisfied Patton by placing Patch in his debt. The American Seventh Army's formal frontal assault on the West Wall found no immediate easy going; but the defenders of the wall had to worry about Patton in their rear if they resisted Patch too long in front. So, while still having to fight hard to master tank traps and pillboxes, Patch's Seventh Army made better progress than had any earlier head-on confrontation with Germany's border fortifications.

Patch's army met its worst going, in fact, far from the West Wall, on its extreme right flank next to the upper Rhine. There the attached 3ème Division d'Infanterie Algérienne had to cross both the Moder River and a flat floodplain offering excellent defensive fields of fire, and after that to fight its way into an urbanized area. Yet by and large, Patch's progress satisfied all concerned. His Seventh Army did not even meet more than a handful of the usually ritualistic counterattacks; one of the few exceptions occurred in O'Daniel's sector, where the 17th SS Panzer Grenadier Division had the highest quota of armor in Army Group G and some of its old combative spirit. Yet to counterattack O'Daniel's veteran 3rd Infantry Division was assuredly to catch a tiger by the tail, and the panzer grenadiers won scarcely a pause in return for a strenuous and costly effort. With the enemy's main strength thus occupied, Burress's 100th Division captured again the much fought over road-junction town of Bitche.

Unlike the disintegration in front of Patton, for all that, the fight put up by the stronger troops in stronger positions on Patch's front had the quality of a well-controlled delaying action. Such an assessment much influenced a conference among Eisenhower, Devers, Patton, and Patch at Seventh Army headquarters at Lunéville on March 17. Eisenhower asked Patch if he had any objection to Patton's pressing forward across the Seventh Army zone of advance to trap as many Germans as possible. The easygoing, uncontentious Patch had none: "We are all in the same army."[18] The Supreme Commander proposed a new army group and army boundary running just north of Kaiserslautern to the Rhine at Worms. The irrepressible Patton thereupon suggested he penetrate still farther into Patch's zone, to encircle the whole section of the West Wall opposite the Seventh Army and meet that army's VI Corps on the Rhine. Patch again agreed.

Patton was not always so candid in announcing an intention to exceed his instructions, but he had been meeting with the Supreme Commander since the previous day and sensed that his recent triumphs had put him in better standing with Ike than at any time since his soldier-slapping outbursts long ago in Sicily. At last Ike had grown generous in his compliments, and on March 16 Patton had no trouble parlaying the breakout of the 4th Armored Division and the presumably imminent breakout of the 10th Armored into a promise to give the Third Army another armored division, Roderick Allen's 12th. Patton was also about to commit the 11th Armored on the XII Corps front; with Allen, he could add a second armored division to Walker's corps as well, the better to complete his race to the Rhine—and beyond.

Gaffey's 4th Armored was unable to resume its headlong progress on March 18, partly because Gaffey paused to repair tanks, partly because the division had to divert troops to clear Bad Kreuznach, perhaps partly because Gaffey's march had already posed so grave a peril to the rear of the West Wall, for there was also a certain stiffening of the opposition. On March 18 and 19 the 4th Armored advanced a mere sixteen kilometers, by its recent standards a letdown. But the 11th Armored, which crossed the Moselle early on March 18, had a new commander cut from the 4th Armored pattern, General Dager who had led Gaffey's CCB, and the division seemed determined to compensate for its earlier disappointments. The 11th promptly dashed thirty-four kilometers to the Nahe at Kirn. On March 19 it virtually duplicated this feat, and by nightfall it had reached the longitude of Kaiserslautern on the Kaiserslautern-Bingen highway. By that time the 10th Armored of Walker's corps was only some nine kilometers outside Kaiserslautern, having charged over thirty kilometers from St. Wendel, and the 12th Armored had covered about forty kilometers in two days to cross the upper Nahe.

Back on March 2, the Germans had transferred their Seventh Army from Model's

Army Group B to Army Group G, now under the wounded Normandy veteran Paul Hausser. The Eifel campaign had nearly split the Seventh away from Model's other armies in any event, and the primary mission remaining to the survivors of the Seventh was to try to prevent the Americans from exploiting their wedge northeast of the German First Army to isolate that stronger force. The realignment could not remedy the Seventh Army's weakness. By March 19, both of Hausser's two northern armies, the Seventh and the First, seemed on the verge of destruction. The tatters of the Seventh had been unable to hold the Moselle line or to form even a temporary defense on the Nahe, and Eddy's and Walker's infantry following the armored divisions were receiving large-scale surrenders. Along with three Volksgrenadier divisions, so impressive a catch as the remnants of the 2nd Panzer Division fell into the Third Army maw. Once more the higher headquarters tended to escape—Felber's army headquarters and those of two corps—but little else did. And meanwhile the German First Army was tangibly beginning to lose the control over the pace of its retreat before Patch's troops that it had so far maintained.

General Hibbs's 63rd Division of Milburn's XXI Corps on the American Seventh Army left had struck the West Wall immediately at the kickoff of Patch's March 15 drive and for several days thereafter endured as hard a fight as any unit in Patch's army. Late on March 19, however, the 63rd ruptured the main belt of the West Wall. Patch thereupon instructed Haislip to move a XV Corps task force through the gap opened by Hibbs, to come around to the rear of the fortifications that were still containing Haislip's attacks. On March 20, before this movement was well under way, General Frederick's 45th Division scored its own break through the West Wall. By that night, the whole XIII SS Corps in front of Haislip was abandoning the fortifications, and the XC Corps opposing Brooks's VI Corps farther east promptly fell back in conformance with the movement.

During the day, the Luftwaffe had staged another of its occasional heavy efforts, trying to hold the Americans at bay by assailing their columns with several hundred planes including Messerschmitt 262 jets; the jets had become an ominous factor intervening in the ground battle since VERITABLE and GRENADE. But despite the jets, it was XIX and XII TAC that were better able to make use of the clearing early-spring weather to harry the fleeing Germans who clotted the roads through the Pfälzerwald. The congestion of the retreat was all the worse because during the same eventful day one of the 10th Armored Division's columns drove nearly to Permasens on the western edge of that forest, while another column farther north was already approaching the eastern edge and a third was almost in Neustadt. The 12th Armored had leaped almost to Ludwigshafen on the Rhine. The Third Army was well along toward completing its semicircle around the German First Army rear to cut off retreat eastward across the Rhine as well as northward.

When Major General Harry J. Collins's 42nd Division resumed the VI Corps attack through the Hardt Mountains the next day, March 21, it found the enemy departed from its front. On March 22 the 17th SS Panzer Grenadier Division formed the core of successive defensive stands at Neustadt and Landau to try to slow the onrushing American tides from south and west, but the 12th Armored circling around the panzer grenadiers farther east had already passed through Ludwigshafen and was less than ten kilometers from Speyer. So the Germans blew the Speyer bridge over the Rhine on March 23, leaving themselves only the Germersheim bridge several kilometers upstream. It was no coincidence that on March 23 all the divisions of the VI Corps found the last enemy crust disintegrating before them. The Germans everywhere were making for the Rhine.

Patch loosed Major General Albert C. Smith's 14th Armored Division through the VI Corps infantry in pursuit, but a German rearguard action at Speyer, similar to the ones at Neustadt and Landau on March 22, held up the meeting of this Seventh Army armor with the Third Army's 12th Armored until March 24. That day both the 14th and the 12th Armored sent task forces racing toward the Germersheim bridge, but the Germans were not about to accept another Remagen. They blew the bridge in late morning before either American column entered the town. The Americans turned to mopping up stragglers.

While the Saar-Palatinate campaign had most conspicuously borne witness to the rapidity of the Wehrmacht's disintegration once disintegration set in, the campaign was notable also for its display of the American army's sharpening instinct for the jugular. The campaign's two envelopments, of the German Seventh Army by two columns of Patton's Third Army, and then of the German First Army by both Patton's Third and Patch's Seventh Armies, were models of how not only to gain ground but to destroy enemy forces. The Third Army netted more than 68,000 prisoners, Patch's Seventh Army 22,000. Patton's staff estimated the total German losses opposing them at 113,000, including the prisoners, in exchange for 5,220 Third Army casualties. The American Seventh Army, assailing the West Wall, lost more heavily, about 12,000. But in the brutal jargon of a later American war, the strategists could consider the campaign more than amply cost-effective. The Americans were probably not far wrong in estimating that the enemy had lost 75 to 80 percent of the infantry he had engaged in the battle.

And the extent of the American victory cannot be attributed merely to German decay. Some of the enemy's formations—the 6th SS Mountain Division, the 17th SS Panzer Grenadiers, a rested and refitted 159th Infantry Division that fought Patton in the Hunsrück—retained much of the old German savvy and toughness; still again the enemy extricated more of his senior officer and headquarters than the Americans would have liked. The American victory was in large part the product of mastery at last of a thoroughly mobile form of warfare genuinely aimed at the destruction of the enemy forces. Even in the glorious late summer of 1944, the American command had too often paid only lip service to the latter classical objective. Now, finally, the whole spirit of the battles of the Saarland and the Palatinate was that of O'Daniel's watchword: *"Bayonets will be sharpened."*

Montgomery's Mighty Crossing (I)

Of Montgomery's preparations to assault the Mareth Line in Tunisia early in 1943, the official United States Army history says that "the Eighth Army proceeded to the crucial battle with the majestic deliberation of a pachyderm."[19] The elephantine aspect of Montgomery's generalship was again much in evidence as, during the two March weeks of the American Blitzkriegs just described, 21 Army Group proceeded majestically, deliberately, even ostentatiously with its elaborate planning and preparation for the crossing of the lower Rhine, Operation PLUNDER.

A brief cause of concern, for example, was the impediment posed by the American ammunition shortage to the Ninth Army's meeting Montgomery's stupendous scale of ammunition supply, 600 rounds per gun. Strict conservation rules in the middle of

March helped Simpson accumulate enough to calm Montgomery's fears. To facilitate the collection of supplies on the left bank of the Rhine, Montgomery ordered that eight more bridges be erected to supplement the existing spans across the Maas. More than a quarter of a million men massed to execute and follow up Montgomery's assault: eleven divisions, three of them armored and two airborne, plus six independent brigades, in the Second Army; eleven divisions, three of them armored, in the Ninth Army; eight divisions in the Canadian First Army. For ten days before the assault, a massive chemical smoke screen concealed—or in a sense advertised—the preparations along a thirty-kilometer front. From the middle of February onward, RAF Bomber Command and the Eighth Air Force concentrated all the planes they could spare for an "Interdiction of Northwest Germany" program to seal off the Ruhr and break communications west of a line from Bremen to the Ruhr to the Rhine. Beginning March 11, 2nd TAF and XXIX TAC joined the campaign, directing most of their 7,311 sorties between that date and March 21 at the rail and road networks of the area. In the two weeks before the scheduled assault, the British and American air forces dropped 50,000 tons of bombs on targets whose elimination might ease Montgomery's way.

Not least, Marshal Montgomery delivered his customary exhortation to his troops:

> 6. 21 ARMY GROUP WILL NOW CROSS THE RHINE
> The enemy possibly thinks he is safe behind this great river obstacle. We all agree that it is a great obstacle; but we will show the enemy that he is far from safe behind it. This great Allied fighting machine, composed of integrated land and air forces, will deal with the problem in no uncertain manner.
> 7. And having crossed the Rhine, we will crack about in the plains of Northern Germany, chasing the enemy from pillar to post.[20]

Pachydermal preparation could on occasion be a military virtue. Another quality of Montgomery's generalship, similarly on display in the Tunisian campaign, was also surfacing again, and had far less to commend it. In Tunisia, Montgomery had tried to assure that the credit for the final entrance into Tunis would belong exclusively to him and his Eighth Army, though on that occasion the rival claimants were another British commander and army, General Sir Kenneth Anderson and the British First Army. In "a highly acquisitive mood," as General Sir William Jackson describes it, Montgomery then had badgered the Allied ground forces commander, General Alexander, and sought "to usurp his authority," to ensure that the First Army would be held back enough for the Eighth Army to claim the most conspicuous prize.[21] Montgomery had behaved similarly toward Patton and the American Seventh Army in Sicily. Now he was at it again.

As we have seen, while he insisted he must have the American Ninth Army to afford his British army group adequate power for the great crossing, his first plans for PLUNDER put the whole crossing under the command of the British Second Army. The Ninth Army would contribute a corps, but Simpson's army would not participate as such, and the spectacle presented to the world would be that of the first assault crossing of the Rhine in modern history conducted exclusively by the British Second Army. When General Dempsey of that British army himself joined with General Simpson in objecting to such an arrangement, which seemed to waste the Ninth Army's accumulation of bridging equipment even if the main strength of Simpson's army were left out of consideration, as well as to promise administrative and logistical troubles when the American army eventually crossed into British beachheads, Montgomery relented. Dempsey and Simpson wanted the assault area split around Xanten to give approximately equal frontage to both their armies. Montgomery's acquiescence was partial. He issued compromise instructions on February 4, still restricting the Ninth Army assault crossing to a single corps, but allowing the corps to cross under Ninth Army command, and agreeing that once the bridgehead was secure he would transfer Second Army bridge sites at Wesel to Simpson's control to hasten an American buildup beyond the river.

Meanwhile, rather inconsistently, Montgomery also importuned Eisenhower for an additional ten American divisions that he said he needed to guarantee the success of the great crossing. In effect, he was asking that Hodges's First Army again join Simpson's Ninth in his army group, and that all the American offensives to the southward be sacrificed accordingly. Eisenhower eventually said he would agree, but with a large proviso: that Bradley's 12th Army Group must move northward to take over command of the American armies in the crossing. On hearing this condition, Montgomery abruptly dropped the whole idea. He wanted more American troops only if he could submerge them in his own and a British command.

Still, it seemed certain that the field marshal and his countrymen would enjoy most of the glory. Before he left England on March 23 to witness Operation PLUNDER beginning that night, Prime Minister Churchill prerecorded a speech, to be released at the proper time, announcing to the world the British army's execution of the first modern assault crossing of the Rhine.

Crossing on the Run

General S. LeRoy Irwin of the 5th Division, XII Corps, called a conference of his principal subordinates for March 21, to discuss the imminent removal of the division from the line for rest, as the Saar-Palatinate campaign drew to a close. Before the meeting, however, General Eddy summoned Irwin to corps headquarters, and in consequence Irwin had a different and more exciting message for his unit commanders. General Patton wanted the 5th Division to make ready for a night assault crossing of the Rhine, perhaps as early as that very night.

The most likely area for a Third Army crossing was between Mainz and the beginning of the Rhine gorge at Bingen, for a crossing above Mainz would have to confront the Main River almost as soon as it was over the Rhine. Therefore Patton and his staff decided that the first crossing ought to take place above Mainz, where the Germans would not be expecting it. Earnest's 90th Division was to feint a crossing at Mainz; Irwin's division was to cross fifteen kilometers upstream, between Nierstein and Oppenheim.

The orders to Irwin originated in discussions between Bradley and Eisenhower, and then among Bradley, Patton, and Hodges, at Luxembourg City on March 19. With the Third and Seventh Armies about to attain Eisenhower's goal of closing to the Rhine all along the front, and with Montgomery's loss of interest in a northward shift of the First Army having clarified where Hodges's troops would fight, the Supreme Commander was ready at last to exploit the Remagen bridgehead. Hence his instructions through Bradley to Hodges to prepare for a breakout to the Lahn River and the Frankfurt-Kassel corridor. Thus the First Army would move into Germany by the very route Bradley had contemplated for months for both the First and Third Armies, to swing a pincer around the south of the Ruhr, and thence to mount a power drive eastward into Germany. The logic of his armies' locations permitted Bradley now to authorize Patton to head for Kassel as well, to converge upon Hodges there. At Luxembourg, Bradley asked Patton whether the Third Army was carrying close behind it the bridging equipment Patton had so carefully safeguarded from Devers's clutches during the Ardennes; if so, Patton might use it to take the Rhine on the run.

Even now, Bradley and his army commanders feared that unless they launched themselves toward Kassel immediately, Montgomery might yet contrive to divert the First Army northward as an adjunct to Operation PLUNDER. They had come to imagine SHAEF, if not Eisenhower himself, as virtually in Montgomery's pocket; life with Montgomery inevitably nourished paranoid delusions. The American commanders were still misreading Ike's acceptance of the priority of Montgomery's northern offensive as acquiescence in Montgomery's—and the British Chiefs of Staffs'—notion that the northern offensive should be the only one. Far from taking such a view, Eisenhower at last felt free to act according to both his strategic preconceptions and the promptings of his heart. If Montgomery wanted the First Army only if it came under British command, then he could not have it; even if Eisenhower had wanted to give Hodges's army to 21 Army Group, Marshall would never have allowed such a thing. So the road was clear toward a 12th Army Group invasion of Germany in the south, to supplement the 21 Army Group invasion in the north, and to provide the multiple guarantees against failure that Eisenhower always desired.

On March 19, Eisenhower left for a few days' rest in the South of France. While at leisure in Cannes, he decided firmly on following the directions set by the March 19 conferences, and on March 21 he telephoned Bull to issue a SHAEF directive. The operations of both Patton and Patch, the directive stated, "will be pushed vigorously with the object of establishing a firm bridgehead across the Rhine in the Frankfurt area from which an advance in strength can be made at a later date in the general direction of Kassel."[22]

In Bradley's instructions to Patton to cross the Rhine on the run, and even more in Patton's instructions to the XII Corps and the 5th Division, there was, naturally, a more immediate motive than the eventual power drive deep into Germany. They had read enough of Montgomery's manifestos about his imminent climactic offensive of the war to desire fondly to beat him across the Rhine.

They did not desire a fiasco, and even the Third Army required time to move its boats to the front, so as events turned out Irwin did not receive orders to cross on the night of March 21–22 after all. But on the morning of March 22, Eddy told Irwin that Patton insisted the crossing must occur during the coming night. Colonel Paul J. Black's 11th Infantry Regiment was to lead the assault at 10:00 P.M., its 3rd Battalion crossing at Nierstein, its 1st Battalion at Oppenheim. Five hundred assault boats would carry the first waves, but these boats would be followed promptly by LCVPs and dukws. Early waves would carry bulldozers and air compressors to begin at once to cut ramps for dukws and to prepare bridge and ferry sites. Some 7,500 engineers were to participate in the operation. Patton's crossing would be hasty; but he had turned his staff to thinking about it in detail at least three months earlier, and it would not be a fragile improvisation.

Thirteen artillery battalions were positioned to support the assault on call, but for the sake of surprise there would be no preliminary bombardment. The guns could be sited excellently on high ground commanding the grassy Hessian plain east of the river. The troops on the far side were expected to be fugitives of the Saar-Palatinate battles and still in a state of disorganization, along with oddments of the Volkssturm, convalescents, home security forces, and the like.

The Rhine at the crossing sites is about 300 to 400 meters wide. Unhappily, a bright moon almost at three-quarters shone down when the 11th Infantry's assault boats splashed into the water. Yet Company K, leading the 3rd Battalion, got across without stirring up resistance and promptly corralled seven surprised German soldiers on the east bank. Companies A and B, leading the 1st Battalion, were less lucky and began taking machine-gun fire about halfway across. They had to fight their way ashore. But it was not much of a fight; the 11th Infantry suffered only twenty casualties in the whole assault crossing. By midnight, the entire regiment was on the east bank and beginning to push inland.

Patton wanted the push to be rapid, both because the bridgehead was on low ground and therefore vulnerable, and because there was no good road network for exploitation short of Grossgerau, over ten kilometers inland. Although German artillery soon came into action, and the Luftwaffe sent twelve planes to bomb and strafe at daylight, the opposition continued off balance, confused, and weak. Thus the whole 5th Division was able to climb ashore by early afternoon, and the 90th Division began following before darkness. The LCVPs ferried tanks and tank destroyers, and the engineers opened a treadway bridge by late afternoon. The leading infantry battalions, fanning out inland, met no tanks, few heavy weapons, and few counterattacks. By night, the advance was only about two kilometers from Grossgerau, and Eddy decided to try to exploit with armor the next morning. Naturally, the waiting tanks were those of the 4th Armored Division, now under General Hoge, of the Remagen bridge, because Gaffey had moved up to a corps.

The prisoners hauled in from the ragtag German resistance belonged to that familiar but weary adversary, General Felber's Seventh Army. Felber knew the XII Corps all too well, and the unleashing of the 4th Armored would be just what he would expect; so it was not remarkable that he cranked up a fairly strong counterattack during the night to try to forestall the Shermans. The counterattackers were largely students from an officer candidate school at nearby Wiesbaden and therefore good soldiers. They infiltrated the American positions with skill, and the 5th Division required a busy night and part of the next morning to get rid of them. But the Germans were neither numerous enough nor well enough armed to pose a substantial threat.

Bradley had been finishing his breakfast on the morning of March 23 at the Château de Namur when Patton telephoned him: "Brad, don't tell anyone but I'm across."

"Well, I'll be damned—you mean across the Rhine?"

"Sure am, I sneaked a division over last night. But there are so few Krauts around there they don't know it yet. So don't make any announcement—we'll keep it a secret until we see how it goes."

A little later, at the 12th Army Group morning briefing, the Third Army reported: "Without benefit of aerial bombing, ground smoke, artillery preparation, and airborne assistance, the Third Army at 2200 hours, Thursday evening, March 22, crossed the Rhine River." The implied reference to Operation PLUNDER was highly pertinent, because as the day wore on, Patton had second thoughts about keeping silence lest Monty perform his show before the world learned that he had been upstaged. While the 5th Division was repelling Felber's officer candidates, Bradley decided the time was right for his public announcement; by now Patton was more than willing. American forces, Bradley told the press, were capable of crossing the Rhine without aerial bombardment or airborne assistance. In fact, on the night of March 22 the Third Army had done it.[23]

Montgomery's Mighty Crossing (II)

Even the signal to launch the northern crossing of the Rhine reasserted the national theme of so many of Montgomery's administrative arrangements for Operation PLUNDER: "Two if by sea"—that is to say, "The British are coming."[24]

Montgomery asked Winston Churchill during dinner on March 23 when British troops had last fought on German soil. Naturally, the Prime Minister knew: the Rocket Brigade, now O (Rocket) Battery, Royal Horse Artillery, had been attached to the Swedish army and saw action in the Battle of the Nations at Leipzig in 1813. Unfortunately, the battery was now in Marshal Alexander's armies in Italy and could not join in the crossing of the Rhine. The honor of the supposedly first assault crossing went to the 51st Highland Division of Horrocks's 30 Corps—the tough, stubborn Scots were Montgomery's favorites when it came to hard fighting.

Artillery fire from the west bank abruptly stepped up its intensity beginning at six in the evening, March 23, until at nine the Highlanders' assault waves launched their boats southeast of Rees. Within seven minutes they were ashore on the east bank. Opposition was minimal. The invaders were soon in the outskirts of Rees.

This was a preliminary, diversionary crossing. So was the crossing of the 1st Commando Brigade, two miles west of Wesel, an hour later. Also reaching the far shore with little trouble, the Commandos waited until Bomber Command gave Wesel a final pasting and then began moving into the devastated city.

The main artillery preparation began at 1:00 A.M., March 24. An hour later, the main British crossing commenced northwest of Xanten, spearheaded by the 15th Scottish Division of 12 Corps. The corps commander was Lieutenant General Sir Neil Ritchie, who had led the Eighth Army long ago in the CRUSADER battles of late 1941 but then had suffered the humiliations of Gazala and the loss of Tobruk in 1942; he had come to the desert army in the midst of CRUSADER and turned defeat into victory, and whatever had followed, it was fitting that Ritchie should be in on the kill.

The Ninth Army began crossing at the same hour.

In keeping with the scale of Montgomery's preparations, General Anderson's XVI Corps had been reinforced for the occasion to 120,000 men, virtually an army. The XII, XX, XV, and VI Corps each had commanded six divisions at various times in the Saar-Palatinate campaign, but none of them had ever received the increments in artillery and specialized troops that now swelled the five divisions of the XVI Corps. Beyond the regular corps artillery, Anderson had the 34th Field Artillery Brigade of thirteen battalions. He also had two antiaircraft artillery groups, a tank destroyer group of six battalions, six separate tank battalions, three engineer combat groups, Naval Unit No. 3 with the LCMs and LCVPs, a 4.2-inch mortar battalion, and a smoke generating battalion. The eleven battalions of the XIX Corps artillery would also join in the artillery support, giving Anderson fifty-four artillery battalions in all, and the neighboring XIII Corps artillery plus the guns of one division of that corps were also to fire in the artillery preparation and to answer calls for supporting fire.

General Eisenhower joined General Simpson in a church tower to watch as 2,070 American guns opened Anderson's attack. "Because the batteries were distributed on the flat plains on the western bank of the Rhine," the Supreme Commander recorded, "every flash could be seen."[25] For an hour, more than a thousand American shells a minute ranged across the Rhine, 65,261 rounds in all. Meanwhile 1,406 Eighth Air Force heavies were attacking Luftwaffe bases just to the east.

General Hobbs's workhorse 30th Division launched storm boats and double assault boats at 2:00 A.M., all three regiments in line—the 119th Infantry on the left, just southeast of the village of Büderich and the confluence of the Lippe River with the Rhine; the 117th in the center at Wallach; the 120th on the right at a bend northeast of Rheinberg. Montgomery's plan stipulated that the troops must cross in regular waves like an amphibious assault, the leading battalion of each regiment organized into four waves with two-minute intervals between waves, each assault battalion equipped with fifty-four fast storm boats, which were powered by 55-horsepower motors and carried seven men and a crew of two, and thirty double assault boats, which had 22-horsepower motors and carried forty men and a crew of three. The storm boats led off, followed by the slower assault boats. The navy landing craft would come with the later waves.

The river was 300 to 500 meters wide, with treacherous currents whose dangers might be enhanced if the enemy chose to manipulate dams on the eastern tributaries. Machine-gun tracers guided the first wave across. The artillery preparation had so subdued the Germans that only a few mortar shells fell among the men and boats as they prepared to launch, and the enemy hit nothing until two of the 119th Infantry's storm boats were struck when the first wave was well into the water, killing one man and wounding three. Everyone else reached the far shore safely. There were four- to five-meter dikes at various places on the east bank or some distance inland, and from one of these Company G of the 120th Infantry took some fire as it landed; but there were no casualties and nobody else came under infantry fire. The American guns had timed their preparation so well that their fire lifted only moments before the first wave touched down, signaling their shift to more distant targets with two rounds of white phosphorus.

Another veteran division that had been in the battle since Normandy, Wyche's 79th, began crossing farther southward an hour after the Old Hickory Division. The reason for the delay was that above the Rheinberg bend, the 79th was already several kilometers east of the 30th; the extra hour would give Hobbs's men a chance to begin coming abreast and would thus improve the flank security of both divisions. The 79th crossed with two regiments in line, the 315th on the left, the 313th on the right, toward the city of Dinslaken. Unlike Hobbs, Wyche arranged to launch his slower assault boats first, giving them a head start so the storm boats could catch up.

The method made little difference; again enemy fire was scattered and ineffective. But an earlier west wind had diminished so that fog and smoke hung low over the water, and some of the boats lost direction; one turned around and its men charged out in skirmish line only to discover they were back on the west bank facing other Americans.

The confusion was short-lived, and the 79th Division like the 30th soon had its assault battalions assembled and pressing inland. The two divisions together lost only thirty-one casualties while conquering Germany's historic defensive moat. So nearly perfect was the crossing that it was a matter of note when a 20-ton crane, hit by shell fragments, dropped an LCVP about the height of a two-story building, giving the occupants a scare and a bad jolt but nothing worse.

Ever good-natured, at least in repose, Eisenhower took pains when he described Montgomery's precautions in his memoirs to repeat that "The Rhine was a formidable obstacle, particularly so in its northern stretches," and to say that "We anticipated strong resistance, since we would achieve surprise only by the timing and strength of the assault."[26] In fact, intelligence did not anticipate particularly strong resistance; the G-2 estimates, which erred slightly on the side of caution, placed only 85,000 German troops in the whole 21 Army Group assault zone, including Volkssturm. The First Parachute Army commanded these troops. In its II Parachute Corps, opposite the British crossings, it had only 12,000 men. Its LXXXVI and LXIII Corps, which faced the American crossing sites and also, on the LXIII Corps front, reached all the way southward to Duisberg, had somewhat more men but on the whole lesser quality. To upset the conduct of the defense, Allied artillery fire badly wounded the First Parachute Army commander, General Schlemm, a few days before the crossings. General der Infanterie Günther Blumentritt, hastily brought down from command of the Twenty-fifth Army to the north, was just finding his way into his new job when the Allies assailed him.

Anderson's corps was to move eastward on a front some seventeen kilometers wide, bounded on the north by the Lippe. There were good roads only on the flanks; the consequent danger of a logistical bottleneck was one of the reasons why Dempsey as well as Simpson had tried to persuade Montgomery to widen the Ninth Army front to about Xanten, because there was an excellent highway network north of the Lippe. But Simpson would have to get along as best he could until Montgomery decided the British were secure enough to let him use their bridges at Wesel.

35: Eastward from the Rhine

BELIEVING after the failure of MARKET-GARDEN that the crossing of the Rhine must be a massive set-piece operation almost on the scale of NEPTUNE, Montgomery from the beginning planned to include another airborne effort. The first planning study for this effort, codenamed Operation VARSITY, was published as early as November 7, 1944. To participate in Montgomery's adventure, it seemed natural to General Brereton of the First Allied Airborne Army to designate once more to command the field force the headquarters of British 1 Airborne Corps, now under Lieutenant General R.N. Gale. Montgomery emphatically let it be known, however, that he wanted the XVIII Airborne Corps and Ridgway. He cited the superior signal communications—a sensitive subject after Arnhem—and combat experience of the XVIII Corps; the mention of superior combat experience probably implied Montgomery's appreciation by now of those qualities of combat leadership that Ridgway might have given to MARKET.

When General Marshall had urged Eisenhower to make the airborne phase of NEPTUNE a deep envelopment, dropping the airborne divisions as much as eighty kilometers inland, Eisenhower objected for the sound reason that once they were on the ground, airborne troops lacked both mobility and heavy weapons. "We must arrange all our operations," said Eisenhower, "so that no significant part of our forces can be isolated and defeated in detail. There must exist either the definite capacity of both forces to combine *tactically*, or the probability that each force can operate independently without danger of defeat."[1] Thus airborne troops should be propelled ahead of the ground forces only within a distance short enough to assure ground reinforcement before the exhaustion of the limited airborne capacity for independent survival. This rule, observed in Normandy, was later violated in MARKET-GARDEN with results tragic for the British 1st Airborne Division. Burned at Arnhem, Montgomery now returned to the rule with restrictions upon the airborne planners so severe that they cast doubt on the whole utility of Operation VARSITY.

"Commander-in-Chief, 21 Army Group," Ridgway was informed:

intended that airborne troops should be used in the operation in accordance with the following principles:

(a) They should be used concentrated and in strength.

(b) The area in which they were to operate should be within artillery range, at least, of medium artillery.

(c) Following from (b) the timing should be such that the airborne drop was immediately related to the main assault across the river.

(d) There should be a quick link-up between the ground and airborne troops.[2]

[647]

Correct as was point (d), its application in (b) and (c) suggested an airborne envelopment too shallow to lend to the ground advance assistance commensurate with the investment of men and resources in an airborne assault. Nevertheless, the planning proceeded. Within Montgomery's restrictions, his planning staff suggested, two airborne divisions might capture the high ground of the Diersfordterwald behind Wesel: ". . . in order to prevent the assaulting divisions being hemmed in on the far bank and to take enemy observation off the crossings, it would be most important that the Diersfordter Wald rise should be captured early. It seemed that it was here that airborne troops could most assist the crossing, and expedite the capture of Wesel."[3]

The restrictions appeared to threaten not only the very utility of the airborne drop but also the artillery preparation for the ground forces if, according to custom, the airborne troops dropped before the ground assault; obviously Montgomery's guns could not fire into drop zones already occupied by the airborne troops. Dempsey solved the artillery problem, at least, by proposing that custom be disregarded and the airborne assault follow the ground troops' crossing of the Rhine.

Thus Horrocks's, Ritchie's, and Anderson's leading battalions were already well on their way east from the river when at about 9:00 A.M., March 24, the drone of C-47 engines was heard overhead. Despite the restrictions, Montgomery had insisted that VARSITY be the largest single day's airborne operation of the war, exceeding even the first day of MARKET in numbers of troops, aircraft, and gliders. The American IX Troop Carrier Command, with 38 and 46 Groups of the RAF attached, carried 21,680 paratroopers and glidermen, 109 tons of ammunition, 695 vehicles, and 113 artillery pieces in 1,696 transport planes and 1,348 gliders. The troopers were the British 6th Airborne Division, out of combat since Normandy, and the American 17th Airborne, blooded in the Ardennes but making its first combat jump. Two hundred thirteen fighters from RAF Fighter Command and 676 of the Ninth Air Force provided escort to the target area. Nine hundred planes of 2nd TAF flew cover, escort, and patrol over the target area. To the east, 1,253 Eighth Air Force fighters guarded against interference from deeper within Germany. Two hundred forty Eighth Air Force Liberators dropped 582 tons of supplies in the wake of the landings.

Because there was a ground haze thickened by the smoke screen over the Rhine, the parachute drops were generally scattered and somewhat off target. But the gliders hit their marks almost perfectly, and the paratroopers were able to find their way to their objectives fairly promptly after they came down. The key to Diersfordt and its woods proved to be a defended castle, on the way to which the 3rd Battalion of the 507th Parachute Infantry was jumped by a couple of tanks. While a grenade persuaded the crew of one of the tanks to surrender, a 57mm. recoilless rifle knocked out the other, in the first successful combat use of this new weapon. The 17th Airborne had just received a shipment of 57s, which weighed only forty-five pounds and were fired from the shoulder; the troopers had also just received a shipment of 75mm. recoilless rifles, fired from a machine-gun tripod, issued to the antitank battalion, but weighing only 114 pounds, in contrast to the 3,400 pounds of the standard 75mm. gun.

Company C of the 507th not only cleared the castle but in the process captured 300 prisoners, including much of the command echelons of the LXXXVI Corps and the 84th Infantry Division. The Diersfordter Woods were well in hand by nightfall, and so were linkages between the airborne forces and the British ground troops. While seizing all their first day's geographical objectives, the two airborne divisions pretty well eliminated the 84th Division from the enemy order of battle. The 17th Airborne captured 2,000 prisoners, the 6th Airborne 1,500.

Nevertheless, the question of utility shadowed Operation VARSITY afterward as well as before. General Miley's 17th Airborne Division lost 159 killed, 522 wounded, and 840 missing on the first day (though 600 of the missing eventually reappeared). In contrast, the total first-day losses of the 30th and 79th Infantry Divisions were 41 killed, 450 wounded, and 7 missing. In addition, the IX Troop Carrier Command lost 41 killed, 153 wounded, and 163 missing, exclusive of its RAF attachments. VARSITY cost at least 44 transport aircraft and 50 gliders destroyed and 332 aircraft damaged, plus fifteen of the followup Liberators lost. The aerial losses were especially high because seventy-two C-46s had to be added to the dependable C-47s to complete the armada, and the C-46 proved exceptionally vulnerable to flak, twenty-two of the seventy-two going down and fourteen of those twenty-two bursting into flames as soon as they were hit. It is hard to discover a proportionate return, for VARSITY did not much hasten the Allied advance; the 30th Division on its own had already given the bridgehead as much depth as VARSITY added in the British sector.

The Battle of the Wesel Bridgehead

There were dikes and towns to be fought past, but the first major obstacle to Anderson's XVI Corps beyond the Rhine was likely to prove the two lines of the Ruhr-Wesel-Arnhem railroad. These tracks paralleled the river, the first line about six and the second about seven kilometers inland. The rail lines were mostly built on fill, with highways passing through culverts beneath them. They could offer good defensive positions, and the Germans retained enough strength and skill to take advantage of them. The 119th Infantry on the north flank of Hobbs's 30th Division met its first hard going at an underpass on the first railroad. The regiment could not push through until light tanks, ferried over the Rhine in LCMs, joined the battle. Similarly, an antitank gun in an underpass held up the 117th Infantry in the center, by frustrating efforts to fill a crater blocking the road. It took considerable time before artillery knocked out the gun. To the south, the 120th Infantry had to fight a respectable little battle for the town of Möllen astride the first rail line.

Wyche's 79th Division moved past the railroads more easily, partly because the division happened to strike the seam between the enemy's 180th Division and his Hamburg Division, and between the LXXXVI and LXIII Corps. Beyond the rail lines, the 315th Infantry began cleaning out the small city of Dinslaken, while the 313th turned southeast to create a flank defense along a canal flowing into the Rhine at Walsum.

Beyond the canal lay the industrial labyrinth of the Ruhr, and because the consistent intent of all Allied planners was to envelop that urban agglomeration before any entanglement in it, flank defense was the principal mission of Wyche's division. If the XVI Corps were to lead a 21 Army Group breakthrough, it was the Old Hickory Division that must carry the ball. By late afternoon of D-Day, a breakthrough appeared to be in the offing. After the fight at Möllen, Colonel Branner G. Purdue of the 120th Infantry appraised the opposition in front as weak enough to warrant an effort to thrust past the second railroad and on into open country beyond. Reinforced by medium tanks ferried across the Rhine, Purdue's 3rd Battalion led the way, soon pushing so far east that some of the 79th

Division artillery took it for a German concentration and fired on it. The battalion eventually halted for the night when it reached the limit of direct artillery support, over a kilometer beyond the Dinslaken-Wesel highway and almost ten kilometers east of the morning's crossing sites. General Hobbs promised to have a 105mm. artillery battalion up for support by the next morning, and he fulfilled his pledge, bringing the battalion across the Rhine on a treadway bridge that was opened at 4:00 P.M.

In quest of furthering the breakthrough and extending it into a breakout, on the morning of March 25 Hobbs also ordered the 120th and the 117th each to form a mobile task force built around attached tanks and tank destroyers, the 120th to press for Kirchhellen on the major highway leading from the town of Dorsten to the Ruhr, the 117th to head for Dorsten itself, on the Lippe-Seiten Canal. But by the time these composite task forces could get themselves organized and rolling, the day was well along; and then they did disappointingly little rolling. The limited road net of the Ninth Army zone, easily churned into mud and often traversing dense woods, helped make progress slow and cautious. As darkness approached, prisoner identifications explained stiffening resistance by revealing the arrival of an old adversary of Hobbs's men from the Mortain battle, the 60th Panzer Grenadier Regiment, the advance of the 116th Panzer Division. During the night the omens grew worse when the 117th Infantry captured prisoners from the 116th Panzers' other grenadier regiment, the 156th.

None of Hobbs's spearheads came near their objectives on the second day, and while everyone gained some ground on the third day, March 26, the hope of a quick breakout evaporated as the main body of the 116th Panzers' grenadiers and some of the tanks came into action. By March 27, command of the front opposite Hobbs had passed to General von Lüttwitz's XLVII Panzer Corps. The enemy thus provided flattering evidence that he regarded the XVI Corps as the most dangerous threat so far posed by Montgomery's crossings; but this was cold comfort to both Hobbs and Simpson, frustrated because a promising beginning had gone sour and, on Simpson's part, because the Ninth Army had plenty of surplus strength to break the 116th Panzer Division or anything else the enemy could offer, but no place to commit it. Simpson's narrow zone and the narrower road net were too constricting.

Late on March 26, Anderson's corps headquarters had ordered General Devine's 8th Armored Division committed through the 30th Division, but the prospects of its quickly prying open adequate maneuver space were not good. The 8th Armored simply aggravated road congestion and, as Simpson anticipated, failed to make a spectacular beginning when it struck Lüttwitz's defenses in the forests on March 28. North of the Lippe there were more and better roads, and in fact it was the Ninth Army engineers who built a treadway bridge, a pontoon bridge, and a Bailey bridge into this sector at Wesel, and were building a railroad bridge. (So much did Montgomery's big show demand American bridging and construction equipment that all bridge and road maintenance in rear of the Second Army had been turned over to the Ninth Army and would remain with the Americans until well into April.) But the British had gained ground beyond the Rhine so slowly farther downstream that they were doing most of their crossing on the Wesel bridges; so they insisted on full exercise of the prearranged schedule that gave them, until Montgomery considered his bridgehead fully secure, full use of the Wesel bridges for nineteen of every twenty-four hours, with only five hours for the Ninth Army. Anyway, such use as Simpson could make of the Wesel bridges led nowhere, because the British also controlled the roads north of the Lippe.

The best progress in the British sector was that of Ridgway's XVIII Airborne Corps, now assigned to drive along the north bank of the Lippe. The PLUNDER plans had called for Simpson to commit a second corps into the battle, McLain's XIX, north of the Lippe and into the southern part of the British bridgehead as soon as the British were ready to open the bridges and the roads to their allies. Doubting that the British would relinquish any rights-of-way very soon, Simpson proposed on March 27 to change the plan and to risk worsening the congestion in the existing Ninth Army sector by sending the XIX Corps across the Rhine through the XVI Corps. Only after the XIX was across the Rhine should it shift north of the Lippe, thence to swing around behind the stubborn opponents who were holding up the 30th Division.

Ridgway argued that his corps had not yet won quite enough ground north of the Lippe to make the scheme practical; the XVIII Corps zone was as congested as anybody's, if not worse, because of those Wesel bridges. Give him a few days, Ridgway asked, and his troopers ought to capture enough ground to afford elbow room for such a maneuver.

As usual, the general with the hand-grenade harness knew whereof he spoke. The previous day, the 6th Guards Armoured Brigade had been attached to his corps. On March 28, Ridgway improvised a mobile task force by having the troopers of the 513th Parachute Infantry climb aboard the Guards' Churchill tanks. This force promptly punched a hole in the enemy front big enough to permit a race of twenty-seven kilometers from north of Dorsten to Haltern. The forward plunge opened a defile through Haltern on the north shore of the Lippe. It also turned the north flank of the XLVII Panzer Corps and made further persistence by the 116th Panzer Division a hopeless enterprise. But the plunge also put Ridgway's men so far in advance of the rest of Montgomery's forces—the spearhead was forty kilometers beyond the Rhine—and so well fitted the plan that Simpson had advanced on March 27, that Simpson forthwith sent White's 2nd Armored Division of the XIX Corps into the XVI Corps area, thence to cross the Lippe and exploit through the Haltern defile.

Ridgway's gains also emboldened Marshal Montgomery to remove the administrative obstacles to Simpson's plan. Also on March 28, Montgomery announced that, beginning early on March 30, the roads east from Wesel would pass to the control of the Ninth Army. The following morning, March 31, the Ninth Army would take over the Wesel bridges, though the British would retain crossing rights for five hours each day. But with his breakout on the way, Simpson was not waiting for administrative niceties. Before Montgomery's new orders took effect, the 2nd Armored Division was hurrying out of Haltern late on March 29, to reach the Dortmund-Ems Canal about daylight on March 30. General Macon's 83rd Division was following aboard trucks borrowed from the XIX Corps artillery and miscellaneous vehicles borrowed from the enemy. Near the head of Macon's column, an expropriated German fire engine acquired a sign proclaiming, "Next Stop: Berlin." The German army seemed little able to contradict this message.

The Battle of the Rhine Gorge

"In the morning" of PLUNDER's D-Day, Prime Minister Churchill recorded, "Montgomery had arranged for me to witness from a hill-top amid rolling downland the great fly-in."[4] Churchill watched Operation VARSITY in the company of the Chief of the Imperial General Staff, and the next day in the company of Field Marshal Montgomery and General Simpson as well as the CIGS he crossed the Rhine. As the historian of United States naval operations remarks, Churchill "calls the boat a 'small launch' (by implication British)," but he actually crossed in an American LCM.[5] The Prime Minister also allowed his broadcast about the British army's making the first modern assault crossing of the Rhine to go out over the air.

No matter; this British self-satisfaction could now merely amuse Patton, who had not only beaten Monty across but seemed to be staging a new assault crossing of the Rhine almost every day.

It was in the American style of generalship, fostered by material plenty, always to have more than one string to one's strategic bow. The possible risks of so hastily prepared a crossing as Patton's of March 23, and of the necessity for his troops landed at Oppenheim to cross the Main as well as the Rhine, reinforced this predilection and led Patton as early as March 21 to order additional crossings to follow the XII Corps as soon as possible. The Third Army commander also wanted as many bridge sites as possible, to speed his subsequent advance. So both Middleton's VIII and Walker's XX Corps were to jump the Rhine downstream from Oppenheim.

For Middleton's crossing, Patton chose the gorge of the Rhine between Bingen and Koblenz, the river's surge through the Rhineland schist massif, the very stretch of dangerous water and forbidding terrain that SHAEF planners had virtually ruled out. The river cuts the massif—the Hünsruck Mountains on the west and the Taunus Mountains on the east—into cliffs 100 meters or more in height, with barely room for a road and railroad—only occasionally for a constricted town and terraced vineyards—between the Rhine and the rocks. In many places high stone walls directly flank the stream, built to reduce the persistent erosive effects of its swift current as it funnels through the canyon. Again, it was the very difficulties of the site that led Patton to choose it. The enemy would anticipate the Americans' crossing past the castles and the Lorelei rock of the Rhine gorge even less than he had expected them to take on the Main along with the Rhine.

Culin's 87th Division, which had occupied itself by taking Koblenz while the XII and XX Corps fought in the Saar-Palatinate, was to cross on March 25 on both sides of the bend at Boppard, a few kilometers upstream from Koblenz. Major General Thomas D. Finley's 89th Division, recently given its first combat experience when as part of the XII Corps it followed the 5th Division across the Moselle and guarded the 5th's right flank, was to cross the following morning about thirteen kilometers upstream, around St. Goar and the fabled Lorelei.

Patton's unlikely choice of crossing sites did not prevent the enemy from putting up a harder fight than he had upstream at Oppenheim. Perhaps the reason was that his defenders, the LXXXIX Corps, just transferred from the Seventh to the Fifteenth Army and built around the remains of the 276th Volksgrenadier Division, had fled to the east bank as much as a week before the crossings; they had had that much time to prepare. In any event, the Germans threw a hail of machine-gun, mortar, 20mm., and artillery fire onto the more northern of the 87th Division's two crossing sites just before the assault boats were scheduled to enter the water. It took the 347th Infantry almost an hour to recover and try again. Once in the river, many of the assault boats were snatched away by the current. So many disappeared, at least for the time being, that any prospect of an assault in orderly waves broke down and men crossed whenever an empty boat happened to return to the west shore. The leading companies of the 347th scratched out a small foothold, but in the afternoon the assistant division commander, Brigadier General John L. McKee, decided that reinforcement would have to take place by way of some more favorable crossing site.

Fortunately, the 345th Infantry upstream around the Boppard bend enjoyed better luck. It pushed over advance patrols which drew heavy fire, but somehow the enemy showed less interest in troubling its main force. The Rhine current gave less trouble than below. In the afternoon, the 347th's foothold downstream was reinforced by sending troops through the 345th.

Both bridgeheads found the going hard as they tried to push inland. The Germans had a good many multibarrel 20mm. antiaircraft mountings in the area. and the absence of prime movers for many of them did not prevent their proving harsh impediments to men struggling to climb the cliffs. General Finley of the 89th Division had been watching the fight, hoping that his division might cross through the 87th and spare itself an amphibious assault; but the congestion and slow progress on both sides of Boppard ruled that out.

Thus the 89th had to repeat on March 26 most of the 87th's experience of March 25—complete with German fire on the 354th Infantry's launching area before the assault boats got under way, and including the loss of many boats either permanently or temporarily to the current. Both the 354th Infantry at St. Goar and the 353rd upstream at Oberwesel established themselves so precariously on the far shore, and continued crossings to reinforce them remained so difficult, that in the afternoon Finley arranged to use the 345th Infantry crossing site, where a bridge was now ready, after all.

But the 276th Volksgrenadiers had not been one of the better German divisions three months earlier in the Ardennes, and since then they had absorbed painful punishment in the Eifel and the Palatinate; while the rest of the LXXXIX Corps was mostly inexperienced Volkssturm. About the same time the 89th Division began using the 345th Infantry's crossing, resistance crumbled at St. Goar and Oberwesel. As both of Finley's regiments on the east bank abruptly and surprisingly carried the cliffs, the Lorelei lured some of the infantrymen of the 354th to try to raise the Stars and Stripes atop the enchanted rock, which they contrived to do without shipwreck. Meanwhile on its second day the 87th Division had broken loose for an eight-kilometer gain. While Middleton had no armored division for exploitation, he ordered the 6th Cavalry Group to go into action next morning as a series of light armored task forces, the next best thing.

Middleton did not want his VIII Corps left behind in the surge into Germany, so he needed a means of picking up speed. The news had just arrived that the First Army's 9th Armored Division, striking from the Remagen bridgehead, was already across the Lahn over a captured bridge at Limburg east of the VIII Corps, while Eddy's exploitation to the south was now employing two armored divisions. And General Patch's Seventh Army had also crossed the Rhine.

Before he knew how severely the Saar-Palatinate battles would maul Patch's chief opponent, the German First Army, Eisenhower had offered the new 13th Airborne Division to assist Patch in crossing the Rhine with an aerial envelopment. Planning for an airborne operation led Patch's staff to propose crossing at Worms, because the hilly Odenwald to the east would offer a good protective shield for the paratroopers and glidermen against armor. When events outran the prospect of aerial envelopment—for an airborne attack could not be mounted before the end of March—the planners briefly considered the Speyer area for Patch's Rhine crossing; from here a plateau between the Odenwald and the Black Forest would offer a good invasion route eastward. Then Patton's Oppenheim crossing shifted the Seventh Army's attention quickly back to Worms, because crossings there would be within easy mutual supporting distance of Eddy's XII Corps bridgehead. In addition, crossings near the northern flank of Patch's zone would strike not the enemy's First Army but the yet worse battered German Seventh. Specifically, the Worms area was guarded by the German Seventh Army's XIII Corps, fugitives from Patton's envelopment in the Hunsrück, with only one reasonably strong division and two divisional fragments; part of the XIII Corps had already been diverted northward by the Third Army's Oppenheim assault. Patch therefore ordered Haislip's XV Corps to cross the Rhine at Worms, while Brooks's VI and Milburn's XXI Corps made contingency plans to cross around Speyer.

Haislip scheduled a two-division amphibious assault for the early morning of March 26, a few hours before the 89th Division would be crossing downstream. Frederick's 45th Division was to cross just north of Worms, O'Daniel's 3rd just to the south. As with Middleton's crossings, the Germans were alert enough to commence firing on the 3rd Division launching areas while engineers were only beginning to put the assault boats into the water. The crossing was therefore delayed while American guns pounded the German shore, after which O'Daniel's men experienced a relatively easy crossing. In the Thunderbird Division area, the Germans followed a different script, desisting from firing until the boats were in the river, then cutting loose to make Frederick's crossing costly. The 180th Infantry lost half the assault boats in its second and third waves. Once ashore, however, the 45th Division found itself fighting the 246th Volksgrenadier Division, a division only in name, and rapidly cracked the crust of resistance. O'Daniel's 3rd Division, in contrast, had to take on the one real division in the XIII Corps, the 559th Volksgrenadiers, who were supported by assault guns and mobile multigun 20mm. flakwagons; so the easy crossing gave way to a tough battle.

Both American divisions promptly had the help of DD tanks that crossed the Rhine under their own power. The engineers had a treadway and a pontoon bridge ready for the 3rd Division by the second morning and similar bridges for the 45th Division well along. By nightfall of the second day, Patch and Haislip judged a breakout imminent, and they ordered Roderick Allen's 12th Armored Division to go into action the next morning.

The Hammelburg Affair

The coup of crossing the Rhine on the run—with the especially delicious savor of making Monty's big show look slightly foolish—left Patton in exuberant spirits. He came to a meeting of Bradley's army commanders on March 26 looking "argumentative, as though he had captured some of the arrogance that was so conspicuous earlier in his career." In another two days, Major Hansen found him "riding higher than he ever has in all his career."[6] Through all his misfortunes, Patton had never learned to master good fortune with equanimity.

Patton's favorite division, the 4th Armored, had bypassed the city of Darmstadt on the afternoon of March 24 and headed northeast out of the Oppenheim bridgehead toward the Main, driving under moonlight well past midnight. Regretting now that they had not tried harder to take the Rhine bridge at Urmitz, the commanders and troopers of the 4th hoped to compensate by seizing a bridge over the Main. Early on March 25, CCA headed for Hanau, CCB for Aschaffenburg, both bridge sites. Still traveling fast and meeting few opponents, the two combat commands struck pay dirt.

A short distance upstream from Hanau, CCA found a structure much like the Urmitz bridge, a railroad bridge carrying an appendage for highway traffic. An enemy demolitions team tried to blow it in the tankers' faces, but the appendage did not fall. Quickly a company of armored infantry ran across. The bridge was in such poor shape that after a second infantry company used it, nothing else dared cross, and the two companies north of the Main had a hard time fending off counterattacks during the evening until the engineers completed a treadway bridge. Meanwhile, upstream at Aschaffenburg, CCB had enjoyed still better luck by taking a railroad bridge intact.

This stroke of good fortune in particular was too much for Patton. It tempted him to dispatch a task force to liberate an Allied officer prisoner-of-war stockade at Hammelburg, about sixty kilometers east-northeast. General MacArthur had recently liberated two prison camps in the Philippines and thereby touched off much fanfare; Patton is supposed to have said he would make MacArthur look like a piker. Among the prisoners at Hammelburg, as it turned out, was Lieutenant Colonel John K. Waters, Patton's son-in-law; it is probable that Patton had reason to suspect his presence in the camp, and this may have been at least a secondary motive.

Eddy, the corps commander involved, and Hoge, the division commander, both thought an excursion to Hammelburg would be an ill-advised eastward diversion from the main job of driving north-northeast to trap Germans and meet the First Army. The combination of their misgivings with Patton's insistence served, however, to compound the mistake, because Eddy decided to send not all of CCB but only a small armored task force. Both Hoge and the CCB commander, Creighton Abrams, feared the consequence would be the sacrifice of the force.

Task Force Baum—under Captain Abraham J. Baum, but with one of Patton's aides, Major Alexander Stiller, accompanying it—had 307 officers and men in ten medium and six light tanks, twenty-seven half-tracks, seven jeeps, three self-propelled 105mm. guns, and a "weasel" cargo carrier. The task force drove out from Aschaffenburg just after midnight, March 25–26. For the next several days Patton and his officers heard nothing of the expedition. Notwithstanding the confidence he exuded in his meetings with Bradley, Patton already felt "quite nervous all morning over the task force" by March 27, and by March 30 he was concluding, "I am afraid that this [expedition] was a bad guess, and that the column has been destroyed."[7] Later that day, German radio announced that the task force had indeed been captured or destroyed. On April 4, two officers who had been prisoners at Hammelburg reached the Third Army lines and told what had happened.

The task force began meeting German troops and vehicles, and losing some of its own tanks, during the first night. In the daylight hours of March 26, the Americans not only had to pause for additional fighting, but they were shadowed by a German liaison plane. Persevering nevertheless to the outskirts of Hammelburg, they collided there with an assault-gun battalion. They fought through to the PW camp, where the German commandant sent out one German and three American officers, including Colonel Waters, to negotiate with them. A nervous German soldier shot at the negotiating party, wounding Waters. Patton's son-in-law had to be returned to the compound for medical treatment.

Meanwhile Baum's tanks broke into the enclosure. After dark, the task force began its return journey, as many of the prisoners as possible crowding aboard its vehicles, others marching alongside. The procession quickly ran into a German ambush. The fighting did not go well for the task force, weary, outnumbered, and outgunned, and most of the prisoners decided to return to the stockade. Baum attempted to escape by a circuitous southward route, but he was intercepted and surrounded. Early in the morning of March 27 Baum told his men they must split up and try to find their way back to the American lines in small groups. Most of them probably were captured. During the following few days, fifteen members of the task force found their way back to safety, while nine were listed as definitely killed and thirty-two as wounded.

So the absence of simple good judgment as an underpinning to Patton's aggressive brilliance had produced another ugly incident, infinitely worse than the soldier slappings in its reckless sacrifice of life. Eisenhower tried to explain it to Marshall on April 15:

> . . . he sent off a little expedition on a wild goose chase in an effort to liberate some American prisoners. The upshot was that he got 25 prisoners back [who filtered into the American lines] and lost a full company of medium tanks and a platoon of light tanks. Foolishly, he then imposed censorship on the movement, meaning to lift it later, which he forgot to do. The story has now been released, and I hope the newspapers do not make too much of it. One bad, though Patton says accidental, feature of the affair was that his own son-in-law was one of the 25 released. [In fact, Waters was not released until April 6, when he was among seventy-five Americans still at Hammelburg as the 14th Armored Division overran it in the normal course of operations.] Patton is a problem child, but he is a great fighting leader in pursuit and exploitation.[8]

At least the decision to send only a small task force to Hammelburg freed the bulk of the 4th Armored to exploit its Main bridgeheads, continuing to press northward until by evening of March 28 the tanks had traveled another fifty kilometers and were almost at Giessen, to meet with the First Army and drive on to Kassel. Meanwhile, on the morning of March 26 Grow's 6th Armored Division had also joined Eddy's effort toward exploitation. By early afternoon Grow's CCA reached the Main at Sachsenhausen, a suburb of Frankfurt, and there found a bridge still standing. The Germans had tried to destroy the structure, and vehicles could not use it; but armored infantry quickly crossed, and during the night the advance of the 11th Infantry of Irwin's 5th Division arrived to help insure the latest bridgehead on the north bank.

When the Germans nevertheless proved recalcitrant about yielding Frankfurt, making liberal use of assault guns and the big stationary antiaircraft guns around its perimeter, the 6th Armored left the clearing of the city altogether to Irwin's infantry division and sideslipped west to jump the Main on March 28 at a bridgehead meanwhile established by the 90th Division between Frankfurt and Hanau. By nightfall Grow's armor was twenty-four kilometers north of the Main in a race to draw abreast of the 4th Armored.

Patton's remaining corps, Walker's XX, was now also across the Rhine. Patton had planned for Middleton's corps to send part of its strength southeast along the far bank of the Rhine to capture high ground overlooking Mainz, so Walker could then stage an easy crossing at Mainz. But the Oppenheim, Boppard, and St. Goar crossings convinced the army commander that Walker would need no such help in jumping the great river. Bradley's boast of March 23 that the Americans could cross virtually anywhere they pleased was receiving ample confirmation. Furthermore, the First Army spearhead across the Lahn at Limburg made Patton nervous; he feared Hodges's men might cut all the way across his front to Wiesbaden, only thirty kilometers from Limburg by a good highway. Leven Allen indeed called from Bradley's headquarters late on March 26 to ask Patton's permission for this very move. Patton felt obliged to consent, but obviously he desired no such embarrassment, and therefore no diversion of the VIII Corps from a plunge eastward. He ordered Walker to cross at Mainz without help from Middleton. He also ordered all three corps commanders to hasten toward Giessen.

Walker and Patton's chief of staff, Hobart Gay, worked out the details while Patton was busy arranging the Hammelburg jaunt. The 317th Infantry of McBride's 80th Division was to begin crossing at Mainz an hour after midnight of March 27–28. This crossing site would be so close to Eddy's expanding bridgehead, however, that there seemed no disadvantage and only gain in McBride's sending another regiment, the 319th, into the XII Corps bridgehead, thence to cross the Main at Hochheim and converge upon the 317th in the corner formed by the confluence of the Rhine and the Main. The plan would admirably fit the circumstance that the army retained enough bridging equipment for one more Rhine crossing but not two, but could spare enough for an additional Main crossing.

Patton had guessed wrong about Hammelburg, but he judged rightly that he could afford another assault crossing rather than a more indirect commitment of the XX Corps across the Rhine. A half-hour artillery preparation preceded the 317th Infantry's embarkation from the docks of the Mainz waterfront. German fire followed the assault boats across the river, but neither it nor two counterttacks on the opposite shore sufficed to kill anybody. On their first day east of the Rhine, the 317th and the followup 318th Infantry captured more than 900 prisoners in exchange for total casualties of five wounded. The 319th actually met slightly harder going by entering the XII Corps bridgehead but then having to cross the Main; it lost three killed, three missing, and sixteen wounded. In early afternoon, it linked hands with the 317th, and the Third Army's final bridgehead was firm.

La Revanche

As the Saar-Palatinate battles led swiftly into the American assault crossings of the Rhine, the French on the right of the 6th Army Group fretted because, all along their frontage on the Rhine, the West Wall fortifications frowned at them from the opposite shore. General de Gaulle feared that without a French assault across the Rhine there might be no French zone of occupation in postwar Germany, a dubious issue anyway. On March 29, de Gaulle therefore pressed General de Lattre to cross by any means and against any risks.

Anticipating his political chief, de Lattre had already appealed to Devers on March 27, pointing out that the American Seventh Army's crossing the previous day had occurred at the north edge of the 6th Army Group sector, and suggesting that Devers might consequently shift the interarmy boundary north to allow the French First Army to cross at Speyer. The affable and diplomatic Devers had more than ample good sense to head off another crisis like the Strasbourg affair when he smelled one brewing, and he readily agreed.

He did not set a date for the French crossing. De Lattre, however, anticipated that Patch's army might turn right from its Worms crossing and roll up the right bank of the Rhine. To forestall this possibility, the French commander ordered his II Corps to begin crossing in the early hours of March 31. On March 30, Devers inquired when the French would begin crossing. De Lattre replied he would begin before the next daylight. Devers approved.

Preparations were less complete than de Lattre thought. When the 3ème Division d'Infanterie Algérienne moved to cross at Speyer at 2:30 the next morning, they found only one assault boat awaiting them. The Algerians blandly proceeded to shuttle across the Rhine nevertheless, ten at a time. This invasion was evidently too miniature for the Germans to see it. By the time enemy guns at length began firing, some time after daylight, four more boats had been found, a whole company was across, and the Germans lacked the strength to drive the Algerians away.

Later in the morning the 2ème Division d'Infanterie Morocaine took to the water at Germersheim, complete with boats. Now alerted by an artillery preparation as well as the Algerian effort downstream, German small arms and mortars gave the Moroccans a hard time, sinking seventeen of twenty storm boats in the first wave. French artillery had to box in about thirty survivors until reinforcements could cross; but despite continuing heavy losses in the river, reinforcements did cross and this bridgehead was also firm by nightfall.

The next day French vehicles crossed on an American bridge at Mannheim. General Brooks's American VI Corps was now also east of the river, having crossed into the Worms bridgehead and moved south to Mannheim. On April 1 a French reconnaissance patrol ranging almost thirty kilometers east of the Rhine met part of General Morris's 10th Armored Division of Brooks's corps well within the French zone of advance. De Lattre felt confirmed in the wisdom of hastening the French crossing. Still suspicious of American intentions concerning the French role in the invasion of Germany, he hurried a third crossing at Leimersheim on April 2 and sent a fourth foray across at Strasbourg on April 15. By then, the condition of the enemy was such that the theme of the effort was almost completely the assurance of France's postwar prominence in Europe, rather than the destruction of German armies.

36: The Legions on the Rhine

FOR ALL the swiftness of the breaching of the Rhine barrier, the battles in the Eifel, the Saar, and the Palatinate and along the great river during March pushed American battle casualties for the month up from February's 39,400 to 53,200. In February, meanwhile, nonbattle casualties had run high, 52,100. For the last month of 1944 and the first three months of 1945, total American casualties had been 134,400 in December (77,700 battle casualties, 56,700 nonbattle), 136,700 in January (69,100 battle, 67,600 nonbattle), 91,500 in February, and 101,000 in March. Because the European Theater had turned in earnest to the conversion of rear-area soldiers into combat infantrymen only under the pressure of the German counteroffensive in December, and because the training for conversion took enough time to have produced few new riflemen before the crossing of the Rhine, the senior American commanders did not yet regard their replacement problem as solved even as their armies pushed eastward from the Rhine. They did not dare predict what sort of desperate defense Nazi fanaticism might yet muster. Victory itself proved also to strain their manpower resources, for the flocking into their lines of thousands of displaced persons, removed by the Germans from all over Europe to work the Nazis' factories, and the demands of military government to assure order as the armies rolled into the enemy's country drained whole regiments from the combat ranks.

Any gloomy forecasts still prevalent at the beginning of April seem in retrospect, of course, to have utterly lacked realism and perspective. But the American people and army had managed their manpower in a manner offering so thin a margin for error that, virtually to the last, there appeared cause for anxiety whether America had mobilized intensively enough to train enough combat soldiers to answer the command, *"Bayonets will be sharpened."* Employing a broad-front strategy to overwhelm the enemy by weight of resources all along the Western Front, the United States paradoxically had mobilized just enough resources to win through by a narrow margin. The one great German counteroffensive had taken the American command by surprise; how could they gamble that there would be no more?

Black Fighting Men

The division cupboard, it will be remembered, was bare. After the arrival of the 86th and 97th Divisions in the European Theater on March 3, no more divisions remained in the United States. The manpower problem thus had become altogether one of replacements—so much so that, to maintain the armored divisions already in action with a minimum of trained tank crews and functioning tanks, the theater command considered breaking up the last armored divisions to arrive, the 16th and 20th.

One of the most constricting shackles that the United States had bound around its own manpower resources was its neglect of the combat potential of the black 10 percent. When the numbers of black soldiers volunteering to retrain as combat infantrymen swelled to 4,562 by February, this very increment in a desperately needed resource went on creating additional embarrassment, so much was the army hobbled by its inheritance in the matter of race. By now, Eisenhower had clarified to his staff that his restating of General Lee's original circular meant that Negro volunteers should not be placed in white units in the same way as white replacements. But the Ground Forces Reinforcement (formerly Replacement) System was not equipped to train replacements except as individuals. Eisenhower's policy seemed to imply that the black volunteers would go to the existing black combat units, notably the 761st Tank Battalion and the 333rd Field Artillery Battalion. These units in fact needed replacements, the artillery battalion urgently; but the Ground Forces Reinforcement System was also unequipped to train replacements except as infantrymen.

Nevertheless, the GFRS had conscientiously organized black trainees as the 47th Reinforcement Battalion, 5th Retraining Regiment, at the 16th Reinforcement Depot at Compiègne; the blacks were learning to be infantrymen in spite of the mysteries about how they would be used. Lee remained intent "that we should afford the volunteers the full opportunity for infantry riflemen service. . . . To do otherwise would be breaking faith, in my opinion."[1] Accordingly, Lee forced himself into discussions of the issue once more in late January, and he wrested from Eisenhower a new opinion that "these colored riflemen reinforcements [should] have their training completed as members of Infantry rifle platoons" and then be made available as platoons to army commanders, who were to provide officers and NCOs.[2] Under this policy, the first 2,253 men, retrained by March 1, were organized into thirty-seven platoons, twenty-five of which went to the 12th Army Group and twelve to the 6th Army Group. Sixteen additional platoons were formed later, twelve going to Bradley and four to Devers. The policy notwithstanding, the GFRS remained geared to individual training, so platoon training for the blacks was minimal to nonexistent.

The 12th Army Group assigned its black platoons to divisions of the First Army in groups of three. It was impolitic to give them to Patton; he had already been unhappy when the 761st Tank Battalion came his way, because he fancied that black men did not have quick enough reflexes to drive tanks in battle. The First Army divisions receiving blacks usually assigned one platoon to a regiment, which then added a fourth rifle platoon to one of its companies. Naturally, the warmth of any division's welcome tended to be a function of its need for replacements. Most divisions fortunately gave the platoons additional training before sending them into combat. In Terry Allen's 104th Division, where the remarkable success of the division from the beginning rose out of Allen's mania for intense training, the assistant division commander remarked that it was only common sense that "we wanted to make sure they knew all the tricks of infantry fighting. . . . I watched those lads train and if ever men were in dead earnest, they were."[3] In the 1st Division, however, there was not much opportunity for additional training before the Rhineland campaign obliged the 16th and 26th Infantry Regiments to send their black platoons into action on March 12. The 18th Infantry committed its black platoon in the

Remagen bridgehead on March 18. "Over-eager and aggressive" at first, the new infantrymen learned quickly; the 26th Infantry's platoon, which had received no platoon training whatever, improved its rated combat efficiency from 30 percent to 80 percent in two weeks. The black platoons of the Big Red One fought with their regiments through the rest of the war, taking on every kind of assignment and performing to general satisfaction. The 78th Division received its black platoons when it was already in the Remagen bridgehead. They were the first black troops to fight east of the Rhine, and General Parker promptly said he wanted more such soldiers.

This sort of pattern became typical in the First Army. The blacks were eager to prove themselves; they were perhaps—and with good reason—a little more nervous than most troops in their first combat, but they surmounted their training deficiencies and forged both good combat and good disciplinary records. There was nothing exceptional about the intelligence and educational profiles of these black riflemen; they were simply a cross-section of the army's black soldiers, not a selection of the most promising. It became clear to any unbiased observer that blacks were a military resource of great potential. Yet the army remained slow to allow black infantrymen to advance beyond PFC.

In Allen's 104th Division, nevertheless, the new infantrymen proudly called themselves the "Black Timberwolves." In McBride's 80th, three of them used a captured Panzerfaust to knock out a 128mm. assault gun; the reward was a week in Paris, and thereafter, Bradley's headquarters heard, the 80th had many black soldiers calmly stalking the enemy's armored monsters with Panzerfäuste in hand.

In the 6th Army Group, the experience was less happy. Patch organized his first twelve black platoons into provisional companies and assigned them to the 12th Armored Division. The assignment was wrongheaded. That very day, the 12th Armored had managed to persuade army and army group to rid it of the 827th Tank Destroyer Battalion, a black outfit that had received inadequate training under inadequate officers and, thrown into combat during the Germans' January offensive in Alsace, had performed with predictable inadequacy. Expecting all black troops to be like the substandard 827th, the 12th Armored received its black infantry with unconcealed hostility and dismay. The black companies had received, of course, no company training at all, since they had barely received platoon training. They had no training as armored infantry, though they would now be obliged to fight as such, engaging in the tricky business of close support for tanks or of using close tank support. Here was a new performance of a tired old script written to guarantee fulfillment of prophecies that black soldiers would not fight well. The script had been followed with numerous black regiments in the Civil War, with the 92nd Division in World War I, to a considerable degree with the 827th Tank Destroyer Battalion. It prescribed putting black soldiers into units whose other members already felt sure that black men cannot be good soldiers, under white officers who already felt sure that black men cannot be good soldiers; thereupon blacks can only become the bad soldiers everybody expects. (Conversely, in World War I the regiments of the black 93rd Division had been distributed among French divisions whose officers and men did not pre-judge them as bad troops, so they made good records.)

By 1945, however, black aspirations were high enough that the script did not entirely play itself out. It is true that when General Benjamin Davis, Special Advisor and Coordinator to the Theater Commander on Negro Troops, visited Patch in April, the

Seventh Army commander complained that his black riflemen were not up to snuff as armored infantry. Patch also complained that they had not had company training, but in this he was telling Davis nothing new. Davis explained the limitations of the men's training. Furthermore, when Davis talked with battalion and company commanders he discovered a growing conviction that the black companies were good outfits after all. But he had to concede that the black soldiers themselves did not show the enthusiasm and high morale of their brothers in the First Army. This relative deflation also characterized the four platoons that had reached the Seventh Army late, on March 26, and were assigned as a provisional company of the 14th Armored Division, though they did not go to bat with quite so many strikes against them as the blacks in the 12th Armored.

When Devers saw Davis's report of his visit to the Seventh Army, he sent it to Patch with a notation that it would have been better to use the black soldiers in rifle platoons in an infantry division. By the time Patch prepared to take action on the recommendation, the war was over.

Unclogging the Replacement Pipeline

When the War Department and SHAEF both discovered in December that they were scraping the bottom of the white manpower barrel, and the SHAEF and 12th Army Group mission to Washington could not even reach an understanding with the War Department about the sources of their problems, General Marshall proposed to send a War Department manpower expert to Europe for a thorough survey of the situation. Eisenhower was somewhat defensive about his command's performance, but he had to welcome the visit and to agree that "Only a tough individual experienced in this particular kind of work can get maximum results quickly."[4]

The tough individual, Major General Lorenzo D. Gasser, had not yet departed from Washington when Marshall decided that more rank and still more toughness were required to make ETO shape up and comb its support areas completely in search of more combat troops. Gasser, Marshall cabled Eisenhower, "can only point the finger. The hatchet men must follow closely behind." For chief hatchet man, Marshall proposed Lieutenant General Ben Lear, General McNair's successor as head of the Army Ground Forces, whom Marshall described as "loyal, stern and drastic."[5] Once again, Eisenhower could only agree, and indeed he decided to appoint Lear deputy theater commander in charge of all manpower problems.

The sound assumption behind giving Lear so large a domain directly under the theater commander—in addition to coopting him—was that no small part of the problem of finding combat manpower had originated in the conflict of interest inherent in the dual capacity of General Lee's headquarters. Lee directed both the Communications Zone and the ETO command. Lee's staff in its ETOUSA capacity could hardly be disinterested about combing men from the rear areas that were also its major responsibility. Lear proved stern and drastic enough to triumph over the inevitable rearguard action by Lee's bureaucracy. For the remaining months of the war, Marshall and Eisenhower had their hatchet man to try to solve the replacement crisis.

The crisis and the shadow of Lear's coming had already spurred action that seemed drastic in terms of anything that had gone before; in the American army, nothing could have been more drastic than making combat soldiers of substantial numbers of black men. Pending a thorough survey of manpower utilization by Gasser and Lear, Lee assigned COMZ a quota of 21,000 men for infantry retraining for the first five weeks of 1945. The ETO command also directed General Spaatz to transfer 10,000 AAF men beginning in late January. The GFRS received orders to create infantry retraining facilities capable of accommodating 40,000 men, and to establish an officer training school to turn out 1,900 infantry officer replacements per month. Of the 1,900, 400 were to be officers retrained from other branches in a six- to eight-week course, the rest to come from an officer candidate school with a twelve-week course. Theater headquarters declared all physically qualified white enlisted men under age thirty-one and assigned to noncombat units eligible for infantry retraining. Those not to be chosen for retraining were key skilled specialists who were not in excess of minimum requirements and could not be replaced. Limited assignment men were to take over the jobs of the men called for retraining.

Retraining had produced only 1,325 infantrymen in November and 5,751 in December. By January and February the results were up to 7,685 and 8,193; and 13,600 men were in the process of retraining by the end of January, 33,400 by the end of February. But in late January the shortage of infantrymen reached 82,000 and appeared to be still growing. In February, the replacement system estimated that 90,000 replacements would be needed in each of the next three months, scarcely an inflated figure in terms of the total battle and nonbattle casualties of the early months of the new year. The War Department had relented enough to promise 44,000 men in May and 46,000 in June, higher estimates than earlier, but far from enough to remove the necessity for a much expanded ETO retraining program.

The 6th Army Group continued to suffer the worst manpower shortages early in 1945, because the Ardennes battle led SHAEF to order in early January that infantry riflemen replacements be allocated to the 12th and 6th Army Groups in the ratio of 8 to 1, armored replacements in the ratio of 10 to 1. Devers appealed by pointing to the enemy's Alsace counteroffensive; SHAEF responded by awarding him 3,000 men offered by the Mediterranean Theater, which had the effect of changing the infantry ratio to 5.7 to 1. But further appeals eventually led SHAEF to concede that it had still imposed an inequity, and for February it changed the allocation ratio to favor the 12th Army Group by only 3 to 1. This decision eased a strain that did much to account for Devers's operational difficulties in January and February, but the practical outcome was simply to spread the infantry shortage around.

In March, the expansion of the retraining centers began to pay off, producing 17,152 new infantrymen that month. This figure remained modest in relation to earlier estimates of need; but despite the increase of battle casualties in March over February, the prescient saw in the quality of German resistance promise of declining casualties in the coming months. Colonel Lyle T. Shannon, chief of the Theater Manpower Section under Lear, stated by the middle of March that there were enough infantry replacements already available to meet all existing, reported shortages. Nevertheless, the prevalent judgment continued to be pessimistic until in April General Spaatz asked for reconsideration of proposed diversions of AAF manpower to the infantry. The current ETO retraining schedule called for 55,180 COMZ men and 32,920 of Spaatz's men between February 1 and May 14, and for another 22,400 COMZ men and 10,500 AAF men between May 15 and June

15. Spaatz had enough influence that Lear answered his request with an order for yet another review of the whole retraining program. Then the weighing of the statistics in light of battlefield progress dissipated gloom at last.

Two weeks into April, the reappraisal showed that theater retraining efforts so far—due to produce 25,000 infantrymen by the end of the month—plus helpful War Department shipments from America, had produced an accumulation of 50,000 infantrymen in the replacement system beyond any reported shortages. Colonel Shannon's verdict of a month before was confirmed; the replacement problem was ending at last. By now there were openings for 20,000 in branches other than infantry; but even if infantry replacements were diverted to fill them, there would still be 30,000 available infantrymen. The 12th Army Group had already received about 5,000 infantry replacements to be used for military government and to guard prisoners of war, and Shannon thought 20,000 of the surplus could safely be directed to such purposes. One month after the first assault crossing of the Rhine, on April 21, Lear announced the suspension of withdrawals for infantry retraining.

A few lesser problems persisted. There was now a shortage of armored force enlisted men, which explained the consideration given to breaking up the 16th and 20th Armored Divisions. By March and April, the deficits in armor ranged from 3,000 to 5,000 men and were especially acute in tank crews. To step up the flow, the War Department said, would require diverting tanks from shipment to Europe so they could be used in training at home; infantry trainees would also have to be diverted to armor. The theater was unwilling to accept these consequences, so only patchwork solutions got under way. The First Army, for example, set up a training center to convert some of the recently desired infantry replacements into tank crewmen.

Nor was the shortage of infantry officer replacements remedied. The officer training and candidate schools created in the aftermath of the Ardennes were necessarily slower to produce graduates than the retraining centers for enlisted men. By late March, Lear was driven to abbreviate the officer candidate school course from twelve to eight weeks. Eisenhower repeated an appeal that had grown familiar, for an increase of direct commissions in the field for experienced and able NCOs. Earlier, officers awarding such commissions had risked losing the new officers from their units; now that deterrent was eliminated, though SHAEF still failed to encourage direct commissioning at a rate that would have brought a real easing of the shortage.

Nor did the passing of the acute crisis in quantity of infantry replacements resolve the long-range issue plaguing the American army's effort to maintain unit strength and integrity. Field commanders grumbled about the quality of the infantrymen turned out by the retraining program and reaching the combat units as they advanced from their Rhine bridgeheads. COMZ and AAF officers incorrigibly used the selection of men for infantry retraining as a means to slough off their misfits; the quality of the replacements showed it. Lear had recognized this temptation and tendency all along, of course, and he inveighed and pleaded against it; but he could not violate the chain of command to control who was selected. In late April he actually brought the Air Forces to confess their faults and apologize for hasty and improper selection, but the damage was done.

A further problem, moreover, was the inability of the theater replacement system to afford training as good as that given infantry trainees in the United States. This fault reflected the condition of the whole replacement apparatus as a neglected stepchild, unable to provide the individual soldiers caught in its pipelines with much beyond boredom and frustration.

Lear's successor in command of the Army Ground Forces had begun to bestow overdue thought on the fundamentals of the replacement system. The successor was General Joseph W. Stilwell, Vinegar Joe, who might have become a great combat commander had he not been condemned to waste most of the war entangled in the political coils of Kuomintang China, and who had an old infantryman's feeling for what assists or impedes the making of a good combat soldier. Stilwell started out in March with the modest—but in its implications profound—step of trying to assure that replacements were not shuttled around the world merely as lonely individuals. He proposed that the War Department dispatch infantry replacements in units of squads or platoons, and that it assign those units to specific divisions before their departure from the United States. Such a method would facilitate control, discipline, and training, Stilwell believed, during movement through the replacement system. More important, it would assign intact to combat units groups of men already trained to work with each other as a team.

For the usual bureaucratic kinds of reasons, the European Theater objected to specific unit assignments in advance. But the theater said it accepted the principle underlying Stilwell's proposal, and on March 10 it announced that all replacements would henceforth be organized into four-man groups. Three such groups would make a squad, four squads a platoon, and four platoons a company. Platoons and companies probably could not be assigned as units, and the replacemnt units would not be binding on the combat formations receiving them; but the theater promised every effort to maintain at least the four-man groups.

Stilwell moved on to the command of an army in the Pacific, and the war ended before much more could be done to improve replacement. Afterward, the army backed off again, toward even more emphasis on replacement by individuals and far less on maintaining the integrity of any sort of units. The backing off was of little benefit to the fighting capacities of the American army in Korea and Vietnam.

Pass the Ammunition

The supply of artillery ammunition remained a source of worry at least as long as manpower did. In February, the 12th Army Group complained that its receipts of ammunition failed to meet even the modest SHAEF standards of rounds per gun per day required to keep adequate supplies on hand—and the standards themselves were tailored to fit conditions of scarcity and rationing that had prevailed since NEPTUNE. Deficiencies were highest, as usual, in the heavy and long-range calibers: 89 percent in 4.5-inch gun ammunition, 39 percent in 240mm. howitzer ammunition, and 22 percent in 8-inch howitzer ammunition. Devers was to report similarly that for five weeks after the reduction of the Colmar pocket, the 6th Army Group had to restrict firing to about half the SHAEF maintenance rate to accumulate adequate stocks for the crossing of the Rhine. Both army groups continually reiterated that neither SHAEF nor War Department mainte-nance standards represented adequate guides for measuring need, because all existing standards derived from the curtailed firing imposed from the beginning of the campaign in Normandy. Standards for heavy artillery expenditure especially needed revision upward, because aerial observation to make accuracy possible at extreme ranges and improved tactical mobility for the big guns had brought about much more constant use of heavy calibers since June 6, 1944 than in any previous experience.

As usual, the southern armies suffered the shortages most acutely. The 6th Army Group was unable to persuade SHAEF that its ammunition allowances needed to be increased because of NORDWIND and the battle for the Colmar pocket, and thus Devers had to impose his approximately 50 percent cut in firing rates. In the 12th Army Group, the Ninth (which was administratively attached to Bradley though operationally with Montgomery), First, and Third Armies were assigned ammunition for February at rates of 45, 30, and 25 percent of the total army group supply, respectively. But the breaking of the discharge valves of the Roer dams forced the Ninth Army into inactivity for most of the month, while the Third Army went on slugging its way through the Eifel. Thus the imbalance between SHAEF's strategic priorities and the unwillingness of Eisenhower and Bradley to enforce those priorities went on aggravating supply problems.

Part of the problem was still its most fundamental feature, inadequate production schedules in the United States. Part remained a failure of the War Department and the European Theater to understand each other, Washington persistently overlooking the reminders that all experience with expenditure rates was misleading, because it was all based on severely rationed supplies. Part of the problem lay in the bookkeeping complexities of counting guns and supplies. Part lay in SHAEF's efforts to build its own reserves at the expense of the army groups and armies, as for example by attempting in mid-March to raise the stocks under its control from a seven- to a ten-day supply.

Happily, as with manpower, the accelerating disarray of the enemy when the Allied armies crossed the Rhine promised a resolution, if not of the underlying issues at least of the immediate difficulties. On March 22, as Patton prepared to cross the river, field force depots had on hand an average of fifteen days' supply of all major types of ammunition, with another forty-five days' supply in COMZ depots.

The Lines of Communication

With the opening of Antwerp at the end of November 1944, the main logistical base of the Allied armies as well as great numbers of service troops, locomotives, freight cars, and trucks shifted eastward. Beneficial and necessary as it was for the final campaigns, the shift produced a ripple effect of dislocations enough to make December another month of logistical crisis, even had there been no Ardennes counteroffensive.

The race across France and the conservative logistical planning that neglected to prepare for it had produced a dearth of intermediate bases between the ports of entry and the front. Until early February 1945, there was still so much congestion at the ports that more ships lay idle awaiting discharge than were actually being unloaded. Yet moving supplies out from the ports was a still slower process, impeded by the absence of intermediate depots to which to ship anything; so great quantities of matériel accumulated in all the port areas, not so much in port depots as in vast dumps, scattered about with no workable scheme for classifying and segregating different kinds of articles. When in December and January COMZ began a strenuous effort to move these stocks forward, they went indiscriminately without regard for the needs of the combat forces, to be dumped indiscriminately again at whatever depot would take them. High-priority items often disappeared in the confusion. To grasp what they needed, the armies still had to send their own agents roaming the rear areas on searching expeditions—the First Army ordnance officer alone had about 100 such agents scrounging for him. The armies still had to dispatch their own trucks expensively back and forth, as far as from the Third Army front in the Eifel to the Normandy beaches, to carry what their agents found.

Lieutenant General LeRoy Lutes, Director of Operations for the Army Service Forces—in effect chief of the logistical general staff—came to Europe at the beginning of December at Eisenhower's request to try to improve ETO supply. In part, Lutes served Eisenhower by confirming to Washington that the theater suffered genuine shortages, not only in ammunition but in tanks, general purpose vehicles, and tires among other material. In part, he served also by shaking up staff officers and unclogging channels of communication both inside and outside the theater. To hasten the flow of critical items from America to Europe, Lutes proposed an express shipping service using fast un-escorted vessels or small fast convoys. Lutes's superior, General Somervell, the chief of the Army Service Forces, approved the idea, and the result was the REX rapid express system inaugurated in late January for shipping critical items that could affect opera-tions. Similarly, Lutes proposed to the theater command an express rail service from the ports to forward depots to carry small quantities of urgently needed supplies, and the result was the "Toot Sweet Express," inaugurated January 21, offering thirty-six-hour service from Cherbourg through Paris to Namur and Verdun, and later a similar service to Liège and then Bad Kreuznach. In two months, Toot Sweet deliveries to advance depots averaged 305 tons a day. Meanwhile the ABC Haul, the only express truck route still functioning, offered fast truck transportation from Antwerp to the American armies, hauling 245,000 tons between the end of November and the end of March.

Lutes and Somervell, who followed Lutes to Europe in January, also pressed the forward movement of depots so supplies could be adequately sorted out and quickly delivered to support the coming push across the Rhine. It was hard for the service forces to press on with such tasks with as much urgency as they might have shown, because the SHAEF planners once again were as conservative in their predictions of need as they had been before the Normandy breakout. Assuming "optimistic conditions, with organized but weak enemy resistance,"[6] SHAEF still projected that the bridgehead beyond the Rhine would be only eighty kilometers deep north of the Ruhr and ninety-five kilometers deep to the south by May 15. SHAEF expected the armies to reach a line Lübeck-Magdeburg-Regensburg-Munich by mid-July. Lee's COMZ had learned enough from experience to plan for a rapid advance featuring an emergency marshaling of truck transport at the expense of port clearance and with a heavy drain on forward depots. Despite SHAEF's continual emphasis on its northern strategic priorities, COMZ also had the good sense to prepare flexible plans including simultaneous maximum-strength offensives from both north and south of the Ruhr. Lee's planners calculated the logistical apparatus could bear these various strains; once more, nevertheless, even their expansions of SHAEF's cautious plans failed to anticipate an advance as swift as the armies proved to achieve.

Armies and Leaders

As the armies crossed the Rhine at the end of March, there were 1,617,000 American soldiers in Bradley's, Devers's, and Montgomery's field forces on the Continent. Total American army forces in the European theater numbered 3,051,000 including 458,000 in the Army Air Forces—the latter almost equally divided now between those based in

England and those on the Continent—and 633,000 in the Communications Zone, along with those thousands who somehow were always coming and going between assignments. The total force of the Western Allies on the Continent numbered 2,553,000 men and women.

Montgomery's 21 Army Group commanded thirty divisions, including the 1st Canadian Corps, brought up from Italy with the 1st Canadian Division, the 5th Canadian Armoured Division, and the 1st Canadian Armoured Brigade. Simpson's Ninth Army counted twelve American divisions. In Devers's 6th Army Group there were another twelve American divisions in the Seventh Army and nine French divisions in de Lattre's army (which also commanded another two divisions not at the front, one holding the Italian border and one containing Germans in the estuary of the Gironde).

Bradley's 12th Army Group, soon to regain the Ninth Army, already commanded thirty-four divisions in three armies. Besides Hodges's First and Patton's Third, Bradley now had also the Fifteenth Army, initially to have been Truscott's, now under Gerow since Truscott had received the chance to head his old Fifth Army in Italy. For the first weeks of 1945, the Fifteenth had confined itself to staging and equipping units just arrived from America and to planning the occupation of Germany. Late in March it took command of the 66th Division containing the Brittany ports, and at the beginning of April it was about to relieve Bradley's other formations of occupation, patrolling, and mopping-up duties west of the Rhine.

With three airborne divisions currently not in the line assigned to the First Allied Airborne Army, Eisenhower commanded a total of ninety-one divisions, twenty-five of them armored, five airborne—slightly more than he had anticipated in January, thanks to the assignment to Europe of the last remaining divisions in the United States and the transfer of the Canadian 1st Corps. The draining away of Britain's manpower, the lingering traces of the American replacement shortage, and a few remaining matériel shortages notwithstanding, now truly the Supreme Commander might well apply a strategy of advance all along his broad front to annihilate the remaining enemy forces by sheer weight of resources. Since Eisenhower's cautious strategic assessments in January, the shifting of German forces eastward to meet the Soviet offensive and the entrapment and destruction of much of the remaining German strength in the West through the battles of envelopment in the Rhineland had left barely the skeleton of the Wehrmacht to confront the Allied hosts. German industry was nearly gone too, or at least cut off from the German forces by a ruptured transportation system; German food was nearly gone; and hundreds of German tanks and fighter planes stood motionless because Spaatz's petroleum campaign had at last been carried to almost total triumph.

The Allied armies occupied places bearing the names of famous German cities and towns but now only heaps of rubble. Seeking due credit for the wasteland they had created, the RAF and AAF asked the ground commanders to remind news reporters accompanying the armies that it was air power, not mere artillery, that had thus transformed the face of Germany.

German military skill and courage would surely rise up to wage a few more desperate battles; but the ease of the crossings of the Rhine had demonstrated that the broad-front versus single-front controversy had faded to irrelevance before the enemy's weakness. Eisenhower's legions could now pour forward almost everywhere. Strangely, they did not do so. At the moment of the most evident applicability of his and his country's favorite strategy, Eisenhower was to hold back a large share of his American armies from the advance, and thus very likely to delay the close of the war and shape the postwar balance of prestige if not of outright power to America's disadvantage.

37: The Ruhr

ALREADY the victors were claiming their laurels. The United States Senate had traditionally clung to a democratic chariness about awarding soldiers the rank of full
general. No United States soldier had held that rank until after the Civil War—only
Washington and Grant until then had been full lieutenant generals—and through the
whole of the nineteenth century only the great Union triumvirate of Grant, Sherman, and
Sheridan ever wore four stars, each as Commanding General of the Army after the Civil
War. The coming abandonment of such Old Republican restraint in favor of a dubious
late-twentieth-century inflation of military rank was perhaps foreshadowed in the series
of promotions to full general while the armies fought along the Rhine; but the magnitude
of the American hosts, the appropriateness of parity in rank with the British and other
Allies, and the triumphs already gained seemed to offer adequate warrant. The old
American conception of the meaning of a full general's rank struggled with newer
standards already invoked by the navy when General of the Army Eisenhower offered
advice on promotions to General of the Army Marshall:

> Only those persons occupying positions of very great responsibility and who have
> established a long record of good solid accomplishment therein should be given four
> star rank. I think your first list should be relatively small covering the men whose
> selection would be universally approved. Thereafter, at intervals, you could make a
> promotion occasionally as a special recognition for services along the line indicated
> above. You now have only Stilwell in four star grade. I believe the Navy already has
> [Harold R.] Stark, [Royal E.] Ingersoll, [William F.] Halsey, [Raymond A.]
> Spruance and possibly others and is now nominating four. In these circumstances
> you could make six or seven on your first list and be well on the conservative side
> considering the size of the Army.[1]

Eisenhower recommended Spaatz and Bradley for first promotion in his theater. He
hesitated about Devers, still the outsider to the Eisenhower circle, and thought he might
support Patton before Devers—though he eventually conceded that such an arrangement
would require moving Devers out of the theater and Patton to the 6th Army Group.
Marshall's list of promotions to full general began with Walter Krueger, an older man
than the European commanders and MacArthur's principal army subordinate, on March
5; Somervell on March 6; and Joseph T. McNarney, Alexander's American deputy in the
Mediterranean, on March 7. Eisenhower's views notwithstanding, Devers, the former
deputy supreme commander in the Mediterranean and before that Eisenhower's predecessor in command of the European Theater, received his fourth star on March 8.
MacArthur's air commander, George C. Kenney, followed on March 9; Mark Clark,

army group commander in Italy, on the 10th. Spaatz and Bradley received the reward Eisenhower desired for them on March 11 and 12, respectively. Eisenhower's army commanders would have to wait, but not for long.

Not long ago, the senior German commanders had enjoyed the awarding at their Führer's hands of a token of triumphant military command that American democracy was not yet willing to grant, the marshal's baton. Now the German field marshals' pride in their laurels had to yield to somber reflections on the old tradition—still alive, despite Marshal von Paulus's conduct at Stalingrad—that a German field marshal never surrenders. Their prospects were so hopeless, the might of the Allies so immeasurably superior to any tatters of the Wehrmacht, that to follow the marshals' last campaigns evokes a certain sadness, even when we recall the Nazi horrors inextricably entwined with the former glories of the German war machine.

Breakout from Remagen

The American First Army attacked out of the Remagen bridgehead on March 25. Bradley's orders to Hodges reflected the Supreme Commander's recent and gradual decision to grant the 12th Army Group's attack at least parity with that of 21 Army Group in the final assault upon the Reich. Collins's VII Corps on Hodges's left was to strike almost directly eastward with its left flank protected by the Sieg River, aiming for the road center at Altenkirchen and then for the crossings of the Dill River more than seventy kilometers beyond the Rhine. Van Fleet's III Corps in the center would also drive for the Dill but first would swing slightly southeast to shield the left flank of Huebner's V Corps. This corps on the army right was to press southeastward also, to link up with the Third Army on the Lahn River. Meeting around Limburg, the First and Third Armies together would drive northeast to Kassel. Thence the First Army was to turn north toward a meeting of the Ninth and an envelopment of the Ruhr. In the offing was a further First Army-Third Army eastward drive toward Leipzig and Dresden. For the Ninth Army, after the Ruhr envelopment might come—Berlin.

General von Zangen's German Fifteenth Army, trying to contain the Remagen bridgehead, still concentrated its main strength in the north, apparently expecting the Americans to attempt to cross the Sieg into the Ruhr. As the VII Corps attack opened, General Parker's 78th Division guarded against this German concentration along the stretch of the Sieg that the bridgehead had already attained, while Andrus's 1st Division moved out along the Sieg and Rose's 3rd Armored attacked through the 104th Division farther south. Enough of the Germans' northern concentration reached out across the path of this attack that Collins's men sometimes met hard going, especially where they collided with parts of the 11th Panzer Division and Panzer Lehr. Furthermore, the terrain was badly broken, and the Germans could lay on a wealth of heavy artillery from north of the Sieg. But the D-Day weather was clear, the fighter-bombers of IX TAC were out in force, and by noon the American armor had broken free.

Van Fleet's III Corps, with Craig's 9th Division on its left and Lauer's 99th on its right, met its strongest opposition on the 9th's northern flank, also because of the form of the German concentration. Craig had to fight the 9th Panzer Division through woods covering abrupt ravines and draws. The American 9th nevertheless gained over six kilometers on the first day, the 99th advanced about eight kilometers, and Van Fleet prepared to commit Hasbrouck's 7th Armored the next day.

Bradley and Hodges had planned initially that Van Fleet should carry the main burden of the drive to the Lahn and the meeting with Patton's army, Huebner merely shielding Van Fleet's right. But limited probing attacks in the final days before March 25 had revealed that the converse of relative German strength north of the bridgehead was special weakness to the south, in front of Huebner. Therefore Hodges redrew corps boundaries to assign Limburg to Huebner's V Corps. On the first day of the offensive, Leonard's 9th Armored Division fulfilled the expectations behind this change by advancing some thirteen kilometers to a road junction just north of Koblenz, whence the main highway runs east to Limburg. Robertson's 2nd Infantry Division on Leonard's right nearly kept pace with the armor.

Frustrated so long by Eisenhower's reluctance to exploit the bridgehead that the First Army had been so pleased with itself to take, the frustration aggravated by First Army's persistent sense that it should be first in everything and by an army headquarters dominated by the uncharismatic Kean or fitfully by the intolerant impatience of Hodges, the First Army could rejoice at last. Hodges's partisans could imagine by the close of March 25 that "The General is today showing the public that when it comes to using armor he is second to none." The First Army's hardest driver noted more soberly that the Third Army still reported faster rates of advance but was satisfied enough that he could use this circumstance as a jocular kind of goad: Collins reminded Rose that the 3rd Armored still fell short of the 4th Armored's reported twenty- or thirty-mile daily advances, to which "Rose's reply was that every time the 3rd Armd wanted to make a dash they found all the German available armor against them."[2]

The second day was even better: "Today our front really exploded."[3] This day, March 26, when to the south Patch's army began its Rhine crossings, and nearer at hand the VIII Corps of Patton's army crossed at St. Goar and began pushing out from Boppard toward Limburg, the V Corps resumed its drive toward the latter town against even lighter opposition—almost none at all. By midafternoon the 9th Armored's CCB had its foremost tip inside Limburg and found a bridge over the Lahn—the news that made Patton nervous about the prospect of a First Army plunge across his front to Wiesbaden.

But the First Army lacked Patton's good luck as well as his charisma. Something always went awry; Eisenhower would prevent the grasping of the full potential of Remagen, or—as happened now—only four tanks would cross a much-coveted bridge before the Germans blew it. So Leonard's CCB had to content itself with working dismounted armored infantrymen across the wreckage of the Limburg bridge to clear the town, while the armored drive awaited the building of a treadway bridge. During the wait, the 6th SS Mountain Division arrived from the Rhine front to strengthen a line around Limburg against Leonard's resumption of progress southeastward.

Yet it was too late in the war for the Germans to sour the First Army's fortunes very long. Before the SS troopers could anchor themselves, General Leonard had his treadway and Shermans were crossing the Lahn again. CCR ripped through the SS in the afternoon of March 27 and pressed forward fifteen kilometers to Idstein. This drive practically isolated the German LXXXIX Corps, whose 276th Volksgrenadier Division had been resisting the VIII Corps crossings at Boppard and St. Goar. Tatters of the LXXXIX Corps fought on for a few days in the wooded hills between Middleton's advance and the V Corps troops on the Limburg-Wiesbaden Autobahn. Some wandering SS men in search of trucks and gasoline captured an American field hospital; they conducted themselves properly, but a rumor spread that they had murdered the staff and raped the nurses, so the Americans proceeded to hunt down the remnants ruthlessly, killing some 500 of the last 1,300 ss troops in the area before the rest surrendered. The commander and headquarters of the 6th ss Mountain Division proved to be part of the final haul.

On March 28, the fourth day of the offensive, meanwhile, Leonard's CCR met elements of the 6th Cavalry Group of Middleton's VIII Corps at several points along the Autobahn, and even linked up farther south with McBride's 80th Division of Walker's XX Corps. These meetings of the First and Third Armies and the envelopment of the German LXXXIX Corps broke the last semblance of a continuous front between Army Groups B and G. General Bradley decided the time had come to turn the First Army northward for the larger envelopment of the great Ruhr industrial area and Army Group B within it. Meanwhile Patton would continue northeastward toward Kassel and guard Hodges's right flank and rear. On March 28, Bradley shifted boundaries and issued orders accordingly.

Abandoning hope of stemming Collins's and Van Fleet's progress, the enemy had already drawn most of his troops away from their front and north across the Sieg, apparently intending to make the Ruhr a vast fortress—and thus offering up all the more troops to be trapped by an envelopment of the Ruhr. With opposition peeling away before it, Rose's 3rd Armored Division reached out toward the rates of advance that Collins had chidingly held before it. Rose bypassed Altenkirchen on March 26 and despite a day of fog, rain, and no air support sent spearheads across the Dill at two places on March 27. Parts of Hasbrouck's 7th Armored of Van Fleet's corps raced ahead fifty kilometers on their first day in the battle, and Hasbrouck's spearhead also crossed the Dill on March 27. On the 28th, Collins's corps reached the cathedral and university town of Marburg on the upper Lahn, a medieval island spared from the strategic air forces' ocean of destruction. Van Fleet's corps charged to Giessen, fought a little battle for the Lahn crossings there, and won Hodges a box of cigars from Patton for beating out the Third Army. From these places, Bradley directed, the next day's march would turn north.

The Envelopment

Bradley's belated discovery of the satisfactions to be drawn from the completion of an envelopment had grown rapidly into an addiction. Savoring the envelopment battles of the Rhineland, he said as he shifted Hodges' direction toward a meeting with Simpson encircling the Ruhr: "I've got bags on my mind." "The General . . . is now after bags," his staff echoed.[4] Bags of surrounded prisoners, "the sack" as the GIs were to call the enveloped Ruhr, the classic Kesselschlacht that might have done much to shorten the war if Bradley had had bags on his mind when he helped allow German headquarters and cadres escape the Falaise pocket—the envelopment maneuver had come to dominate Bradley's strategy only when the disintegration of the German army drained entrapment of Wehrmacht divisions and corps of much of the meaning that a full completion of the Falaise-Argentan maneuver might have attained the previous summer. Record large bags of German prisoners tempted Bradley and his subordinates to seek ever higher records; but in the condition of the Wehrmacht, record bags of prisoners no longer signified so much. A better purpose might have been the most rapid possible advance to an objective whose psychological importance could have made its capture the signal for the immediate end of the war: perhaps such an objective was Berlin.

All through 1944, the strategy of the Western Allies had aimed ultimately at Eisenhower's "main prize," Berlin. The industrial importance of the Ruhr had made it throughout 1944 a major goal as well, the principal objective short of Berlin, the indispensable industrial nexus whose conquest would deprive Germany of the means to resist the final drive to Berlin. But when at the end of March 1945 Bradley was actually able to turn his troops to the envelopment of the Ruhr and of the German military forces within it, the Ruhr had lost much of the economic importance that hitherto made it an objective almost as magnetic as Berlin. Under Allied bombing, its steel production had fallen some 25 to 30 percent. Steel had always been the main contribution of the Ruhr to the German war machine, not finished munitions; the Ruhr had not built airplanes, had produced only one-tenth of Germany's tanks at its production peak, and only in the making of big guns had at all confirmed its reputation as a munitions center. With the Ruhr's crucial steel production already badly cut by the end of March 1945, it was still more pertinent to Allied planning that the air forces had almost separated the Ruhr factories from their markets. The air forces' Operation CLARION on February 22 had crippled eleven of the seventeen critical rail centers that connected the Ruhr with the rest of Germany. CLARION was the prelude to a systematic aerial effort through most of March to seal off the Ruhr both in preparation for Montgomery's crossing of the Rhine and to cancel the area's economic importance, particularly by wrecking all bridges and viaducts to the outside world. By March 24, bridge-busting had made the economic isolation of the Ruhr virtually complete, now that the Allied crossings had also put a final end to Nazi barge traffic on the Rhine.

Yet the image of the Ruhr as the great German workshop, along with the lure of bags of prisoners, still drew Bradley, and Eisenhower as well, toward the Ruhr as an objective overshadowing even Berlin. "Clearly Berlin is the main prize. There is no doubt whatsoever, in my mind, that we should concentrate our energies and resources on a rapid thrust to Berlin."[5] So Eisenhower had maintained in 1944. Now he allowed Bradley to concentrate energies and resources instead on the Ruhr, just when the Ninth Army's developing breakout from the Rhine made Berlin as well an imminently graspable prize.

Paderborn, created a bishopric by Charlemagne and more recently sacred not only in the annals of the Christian church but to the SS panzer forces as the nursery of their divisions, became Bradley's first target as the meeting place of the First and Ninth Armies to bind the noose around the Ruhr. In the Ninth Army, White's 2nd Armored Division had just been set in motion to exploit the breakthrough on the north bank of the Lippe into a breakout, and part of White's strength could turn rapidly upon the cathedral city at the source of the Lippe's tributary the Pader. In Hodges's army, Collins's VII Corps would make the main drive from its positions nearest Paderborn, while the III and V Corps wheeled northeast to shield it.

Orders filtered down the chain of command to Colonel Robert L. Howze, Jr., commander of Rose's 3rd Armored CCR. Late on March 28, Howze summoned Lieutenant Colonels Walter B. Richardson and Samuel M. Hogan and told Richardson to assemble a task force and lead it nonstop to Paderborn, still more than 100 kilometers away. Some of Bradley's urgent quest for bags had communicated itself to Howze, and he wanted the string drawn around the Ruhr quickly. "You mean—get to Paderborn in one day?" Richardson asked him.

"Tomorrow morning you leave for Paderborn. Just go like hell! Get the high ground at the Paderborn airport."[6]

Task Force Hogan would cover Richardson's left, moving slightly behind him. Task Force Welborn (Colonel John C. Welborn) would similarly cover his right. Richardson rose at four on the morning of March 29 and in a jeep personally reconnoitered three miles ahead to assure his troops' getting off to a fast start. The core of his task force was a medium tank battalion with three of the new Pershings. Continued overcast denied him air support, but through the day he proved to have all the strength he needed to plunge through roadblock after roadblock, and more often simply through bands of marching Germans dismayed and bewildered to meet the Americans deep in what they had thought were their rear areas. The day's worst impediment was some troopers' discovery of a champagne warehouse at Brilon. Some fifteen kilometers farther on, Richardson decided that the combination of exhaustion—his men had slept little since the start of the offensive out of the bridgehead—and inebriation demanded that he rest his men after all. Paderborn was now only twenty-five kilometers away, so the day's march seemed satisfactory even by post–March 25 standards, and a report that the SS panzer training center at Paderborn was not only still functioning but bristling with troops and armor also suggested caution.

The next morning proved the accuracy of the report. Overnight a German defensive line had sprung up, manned by SS panzer training students and equipped with Tigers and Panthers. Richardson with much difficulty bulled his way forward another fifteen kilometers, but then tanks and Panzerfäuste stopped him cold.

An effort to bypass the resistance produced tragedy. Task Force Welborn attempted to take a secondary road around to the right of Richardson's battle. About dusk, an ambush cut Welborn's column in two. In the rearward section of the column was the division commander, Maurice Rose, traveling in a jeep to take charge of the final assault on Paderborn. Rose had just radioed to his command post to send another task force to help against the accumulating resistance when four Tigers appeared coming up the road from behind. Rose and his party tried to race past the tanks in the gathering darkness, but one of them swerved and pinned the general's jeep against a tree. Rose, his aide, and his driver climbed out to surrender to a German soldier standing in the turret and wielding a burp gun. But as Rose reached either to unbuckle his pistol belt or take his pistol from its holster, the German shot him down. The aide and the driver escaped in the confusion. But the commander who had led the 3rd Armored into the foremost rank of the armored divisions was dead. Because he was a rabbi's son, some reports portrayed the killing as a deliberate atrocity; but an eventual investigation concluded Rose had fallen simply to an understandably nervous trigger-finger.

While the vanguard of the 3rd Armored column stalled against the sometimes nervous but often fervent resistance of the SS students, rumors also swelled up in the VII Corps throughout March 30 that a large concentration of enemy tanks and infantry was building up around Winterberg, southwest of Paderborn and almost directly west of Kassel. With this force the enemy reportedly intended to break out of the potential encirclement of the Ruhr. Terry Allen's 104th Division had its 414th Infantry riding along with the main body of the 3rd Armored while its other regiments followed close behind in an assortment of its own and borrowed vehicles and those of the attached tank, tank destroyer, and antiaircraft battalions. Allen responded to the rumors by ordering his troops to occupy the towns of Hallenberg, Medebach, and Brilon as well as secondary road junctions between them, to protect the armor's left flank and rear. As the reports steadily gained in verified substance, Hodges responded by ordering Van Fleet's III Corps to release its 9th Division to assist Collins the next day.

Meanwhile the 7th Armored of Van Fleet's corps drew almost abreast of the 3rd Armored during the course of March 30, capturing a dam at the east end of a reservoir called the Eder-See and several bridges over the reservoir and the Eder River below the dam. Leonard's 9th Armored Division of Huebner's V Corps also crossed the river downstream from the dam. With Van Fleet's and Huebner's infantry like Collins's traveling rapidly not far behind the armor, the drive toward Paderborn was well shielded against any German effort to assail it from the east, including the possible launching of a drive to meet with the concentration at Winterberg.

The warnings of March 30 materialized partially on the morning of the 31st, when Germans from the direction of Winterberg cut the Hallenberg-Medebach road in two places and compelled the 104th Division to fight to restore the route. The enemy pecked away at Allen's positions through the rest of the day, but the Germans never came in enough strength to create a serious danger; so either the warnings had exaggerated their strength, or for some reason they were hoarding it.

The resistance immediately south of Paderborn was a different matter, if anything growing stronger rather than weaker. Hodges appealed to Bradley to send General Harmon, former commander of the 2nd Armored, from command of the new XXII Corps to the 3rd Armored to assure experienced, aggressive divisional command for the climax at Paderborn, and Bradley prepared to comply. In addition, Collins directly called Simpson of the Ninth Army late in the day to see if he could drum up help from that source; such a step by Lightning Joe was eloquent testimony to the magnitude of the resistance. Collins said he had run into an ss hornets' nest that might sting him for days, and meanwhile prisoners were talking about a major effort to break out of the Ruhr pocket farther south. The whole Ruhr sack was in jeopardy.

Simpson told Collins that the 2nd Armored had moved out from Haltern and traveled all through the night of March 29–30, all through March 30, and all through the night of the 30th–31st; it had crossed the Dortmund-Ems Canal and a couple of major railroads and was in the process of cutting the Ruhr-Berlin Autobahn at Beckum. The VII Corps commander thereupon suggested that Simpson send a combat command of the 2nd Armored south into the First Army zone, heading for Lippstadt halfway between Beckum and Paderborn. Collins in turn would divert part of the 3rd Armored toward Lippstadt for a meeting there rather than at Paderborn, and the Ruhr encirclement would be complete despite the ss hornets' nest.

Simpson agreed. Early on Easter Sunday morning, April 1, General Hinds's CCB, 2nd Armored, turned toward Lippstadt. The combat command struck considerable numbers of enemy troops trying to flee the Ruhr before the American trap closed around them and willing to fight to keep their escape route open. Progress became so slow that the commander of the 3rd Battalion, 41st Armored Infantry in the van asked Hinds for reinforcements; but Hinds, not wanting to delay while more strength came up, told the battalion leader that "he was the reinforcements and to lay it on them."[7] General McLain, the XIX Corps commander, came forward to keep things moving, causing Hinds to commit his reserve—his own tank and armored car—to guard the corps chieftain.

Meanwhile Collins's conversation with Simpson had resulted also in sending a 3rd Armored task force under Lieutenant Colonel Matthew W. Kane, including some of the accompanying 414th Infantry, on a swing west from the Paderborn battle to look for the 2nd Armored. Artillery liaison planes of the two armored divisions could see the leading troops of both divisions by about noon. Not far into the afternoon, the First and Ninth Armies joined hands on the eastern edge of Lippstadt. With the circle closed in spite of their stout resistance, the defenders of Paderborn drew off late in the day, and the 3rd Armored rolled past the Romanesque cathedral of the ancient bishopric.

The Battle of the Ruhr Pocket

American intelligence estimated that 150,000 German soldiers were encircled in the Ruhr, in a pocket measuring some 50 by 120 kilometers. Field Marshal Model's Army Group B headquarters was inside. So were Generaloberst Josef Harpe's Fifth Panzer Army—Manteuffel had gone to the Eastern Front early in March—most of General von Zangen's Fifteenth Army, and two corps of the First Parachute Army.

The German effort to break the encirclement at Winterberg heated up again on April 1 even as the 2nd and 3rd Armored were closing the ring farther north. Before dawn, grenadiers and four tanks of the 3rd Panzer Grenadier Division hit the 415th Infantry at Medebach. Meanwhile the 9th Division's 39th Infantry attacking toward Winterberg out of Hallenberg collided with another force later diagnosed as intended for a breakout attempt, built around doughty old Panzer Lehr; but so much of the life had drained from the division that the GIs never realized they were contending with a counterattack. The 39th Infantry pushed into Winterberg itself the next day. By doing so it cut into the rear of the 3rd Panzer Grenadier Division and assured the failure of the grenadiers' brief infiltration of Medebach that morning—even if the 415th Infantry had not chased the Germans from Medebach directly, which it did, pursuing them closely into woods west of Medebach. Throughout its front the 415th's parent 104th Division "went about its business of clearing the heavy woods . . . and everywhere establishing road blocks and laying mines across a possible Boche effort to escape. The 4th Cavalry Group likewise cleared a few small villages and set up road blocks but only against the most bitter resistance."[8]

To the east around Kassel the Germans were trying to build up a new army, the Eleventh. The commander was General der Infanterie Otto Hitzfeld, who began with such remains of his previous command, the LXVII Corps, as had fled before the right wing of the First Army breakout from Remagen. Hitzfeld gathered several respectable units, principally the SS Ersatzbrigade Westfalen, formed from the trainees who had fought so well around Paderborn, and the 166th Infantry Division, just arrived from Denmark but already somewhat chewed up by the III Corps on Van Fleet's way to the Eder River. Yet the Eleventh Army fell far short of any strength that might have given the Americans concern about their ability to contain the Ruhr pocket.

The Germans could neither break out from the pocket nor expect to join hands with its defenders by thrusting from the east against the American divisions already forming the encirclement perimeter. If Berlin was "the main prize," as Eisenhower had maintained in 1944, the correct Allied strategy now would have appeared to be the containment of the pocket and of the bedraggled troops inside it with the minimum strength necessary for the task, while resuming with the overwhelming bulk of Eisenhower's forces the march east and to Berlin. The trapped German army group in the Ruhr could no longer substantially influence the course of the war through any counteroffensive initiatives of its own. The swift capture of Berlin might yet hasten the close of the war: if any one stroke could destroy the remaining authority of the Führer and of his insistence that the war proceed, that stroke was most likely to be the conquest of his capital. Toward Berlin White's 2nd Armored Division had already been rolling, with exhilarating speed, when the trouble at Paderborn pulled its CCB away southward.

Yet Bradley still feared that to emphasize Berlin as the main prize would hold the Ninth Army in 21 Army Group for a Montgomery offensive across the north German plain and award the final, crowning laurels to the insufferable British field marshal. Surely this consideration was not uppermost among Bradley's conscious motives; but in the face of strategic logic, Bradley persuaded Eisenhower to divert from the drive toward Berlin a huge slice of the American armies—eventually some eighteen divisions, drawn from the Ninth and First Army forces best positioned to strike toward Berlin—and to turn these divisions into the urban-industrial jungle of the Ruhr, a battleground long shunned in SHAEF planning, to grapple head on with German armies whose strategic significance was in fact essentially nil.

On April 2, the First Army and the Ninth—about to return to the 12th Army Group and sure to remain there if the main prize was the Ruhr instead of Berlin—established the Ruhr River as the dividing line between them. General Anderson's XVI Corps of Simpson's army already had Wyche's 79th, Baade's 35th, and Porter's 75th Divisions, from right to left beginning at the Rhine, pushing into the factories and cities of the Ruhr from the north. To meet Bradley's desires, Simpson also turned Twaddle's 95th Division and Devine's 8th Armored of McLain's XIX Corps against the northeastern circumference of the Ruhr, leaving McLain only the 2nd Armored and the 83rd Infantry Divisions with which to continue his drive eastward. South of the Ruhr River, Hodges sent Collins's VII and Huebner's V Corps on to the east; but Van Fleet's III Corps took over the attack on the southeastern side of the Ruhr circumference, and Ridgway's XVIII Airborne Corps headquarters was brought in to command against the Ruhr's southern edge. Van Fleet again had Craig's 9th Infantry, Hasbrouck's 7th Armored, and Lauer's 99th Infantry Divisions. Ridgway initially commanded Weaver's 8th Infantry Division and Parker's 78th. Four American corps thus would converge upon the German holdouts in the pocket. To lure German strength away from the perimeter, three divisions of Gerow's Fifteenth Army—Malony's 94th, Taylor's 101st Airborne, and Gavin's 82nd Airborne—were to patrol actively across the Rhine from the west bank into the Ruhr.

The First Army had the larger zone to clear, the rugged, forested Sauerland—a name suggesting the area's unpleasantness—along with the cities of Düsseldorf, Wuppertal, Hagen, Sollingen, and the eastern suburbs of Cologne. The Ninth Army faced the endless maze of factories and cities, each indistinguishable from the next, that had frightened SHAEF planners away from an assault on the Ruhr. Into the balance along with the overwhelming strength generously allotted by Bradley to the Ruhr went, however, the now unquestionable hopelessness of the enveloped garrison, to moderate the inherent difficulties of the battleground. As the Americans began to press inward against the perimeter, resistance proved spotty and unpredictable.

In some cities, white sheets hung everywhere to signify surrender. Essen and its famous Krupp works yielded without a struggle. Often it was the presence of SS troops that determined a fight instead of surrender. When battle erupted, SS men or formations like the 116th Panzer Division could still exploit factories and dwellings—or more accurately, the rubble left by the air forces—with tenacity and tactical skill to arouse the impatience of American soldiers who would rather have been moving eastward on Berlin. Until April 7, the skies remained overcast and the fighter-bombers could bring little of their invaluable assistance; even when the weather cleared, the congestion of the Ruhr pocket greatly limited the airplanes, especially north of the Ruhr River, because Americans and Germans were becoming indistinguishably intermingled.

Impatience prompted the commitment of still more American divisions—Miley's 17th Airborne on the north, Irwin's 5th Infantry on the east, Major General Harris M. Melasky's new 86th and Brigadier General Milton B. Halsey's new 97th on the south. Hodges entered his usual battle mood: on April 5, "The General has been extremely disappointed all day in the progress made by III Corps especially in the important road net area in the north part of our [First Army] sector and did some very plain speaking over the telephone tonight."[9] After another entire week of disappointing progress and further fulminations from army headquarters, the object of this wrath, General Van Fleet—who scarcely lacked aggressiveness—was driven to try putting the 7th Armored out in front of his corps, though neither the tactical circumstances nor the terrain warranted armored exploitation. In the event, the 7th Armored never cut loose from Van Fleet's infantry.

The 13th Armored Division, assigned to Ridgway's corps, succeeded even less in transforming battle into exploitation. Ridgway himself ordered Major General John B. Wogan of the armored division to destroy any Germans encountered, implying there should be none of the bypassing of knots of resistance characteristic of the usual armored exploitation. When Ridgway eventually changed his instructions on April 14 to encourage more conventional employment of the armored division and specifically a swift drive north along the right bank of the Rhine, Wogan almost immediately fell badly wounded at a roadblock while trying to get the effort under way. So there was delay again until General Millikin, the former commander of the III Corps, could arrive to take Wogan's place. To the extent that opportunity remained, Millikin was to prove himself an admirable leader of armor; but in the Ruhr, the situation never ripened for an armored breakout, and late in the day of Wogan's wounding the 8th Division's 13th Infantry pressed ahead of the armor to reach the Ruhr River southeast of Essen.

At the river, the soldiers of the 13th could call out to men of the 313th Infantry, 79th Division, XVI Corps, Ninth Army on the other side: the Ruhr pocket had been bisected. Ridgway knew that Field Marshal Model's headquarters was not far from his lines, and he had already sent a German-speaking aide with an appeal to surrender. Model had refused on the ground that his personal oath to Hitler bound to him to fight to the end, but the day after the meeting of the American armies on the Ruhr River, Ridgway tried again with a written appeal. "In the light of a soldier's honor," he pleaded, "for the reputation of the German Officer Corps, for the sake of your nation's future, lay down your arms at once. The German lives you will save are sorely needed to restore your people to their proper place in history." He pointed to the American R. E. Lee as a general whose honor was not dimmed but enhanced by surrender.[10] Model's chief of staff brought back the same answer as before, but then chose to stay with the Americans as a prisoner of war, and the pace of other surrenders, already accelerating in the past few days, became a rush after April 14.

General von Zangen of the Fifteenth Army had already surrendered to the 7th Armored Division on April 13. The last of Panzer Lehr surrendered to the 99th Division on April 15. Famous warriors such as Lüttwitz of the XLVII Panzer Corps and Bayerlein of the LIII Corps came into the American stockades. The 17th Airborne Division captured General Harpe of the Fifth Panzer Army as he tried to cross the Ruhr River toward the Netherlands. Thus generals and headquarters were at last caught up in a total collapse.

The final organized resistance in the Ruhr faded away on April 18. The intelligence estimate of 150,000 German troops in the pocket had proven far too conservative. The XVIII Corps alone took 160,000 prisoners. The total count rose to 317,000—including twenty-five generals and an admiral. In addition, the Americans liberated some 200,000 displaced persons from forced labor, as well as 5,639 Allied prisoners of war.

To the surprise of no German who knew him, and consistent with his replies to Ridgway, Model was not among the prisoners. Rumors soon circulated saying he had committed suicide, and eventually it was confirmed that on April 21, in a forest, he had done so by shooting himself. His aide, who testified to the event, buried him. After the war his son had the field marshal's body removed to a soldiers' cemetery in the Huertgen Forest.

Bradley rejoiced that he had taken a bigger bag than the Allies in Tunisia or the Russians at Stalingrad. The immediate cost to the Americans was 341 killed, 121 missing, and about 2,000 wounded in the Ninth Army, about three times Simpson's total in Hodges's army. Calculations of the full cost of the operation would have to include the reckoning that while eighteen divisions fought the two-week battle of the Ruhr pocket, only eight divisions remained to travel eastward north of the Harz Mountains on the most direct route to Berlin.

38: Berlin

O   N APRIL 3, the day before the formal reunification of the Ninth Army with the
12th Army Group, the First Army received with a certain disgruntlement Brad-
ley's distribution of objectives to the east: "This afternoon we received a proposed
tentative outline of Army boundaries which carry us up to our juncture with the
Russians. The general objective of the First Army is Leipzig; Ninth Army gets Berlin
. . . . We also, incidentally, get most of the Harz Mountains to clear and as both General
Hodges and General Kean remarked as the boundary was put on a map, 'We get no
Autobahns to travel on.'"[1]

On April 4, with Simpson again in his chain of command, Bradley ordered him to
attack eastward toward Magdeburg and thence to "exploit any opportunity for seizing a
bridgehead over the Elbe and be prepared to continue to advance on Berlin or to the
northeast."[2]

Simpson in turn instructed his staff that once the Ninth Army was on a phase line
along the Leine River, which he expected to reach in a matter of days, he planned "to get
an armored and an infantry division set up on the autobahn running just above Magdeburg on the Elbe to Potsdam, where we'll be ready to close in on Berlin."[3] White had
already instructed the 2nd Armored Division to prepare to "advance on Berlin generally
along the autobahn."[4] The word spread through the Ninth Army, aggravating the
impatience and restlessness of the formations consigned to the attack into the Ruhr,
stimulating to attack "with more spirit and energy than in any previous action" those
chosen to strike for Eisenhower's "main prize."[5]

The Decision of the Supreme Commander

The soldiers of the Ninth Army did not know, nor did General Simpson, nor even
Bradley, of a decision regarding Berlin that the Supreme Commander had taken a week
before, on March 28, or of a debate touched off by the decision and currently tearing at
the Anglo-American alliance.

Field Marshal Montgomery also wanted to capture Berlin. All his quests for the
narrow thrust into northern Germany aimed ultimately at a British procession through
the Brandenburg Gate. Late on March 27, just as the American stabs along the Lippe
seemed on the verge of opening 21 Army Group's breakout from the Rhine, Montgomery
signaled Eisenhower:

> Today I issued orders to Army commanders for the operations eastwards
> which are now about to begin. . . . My intention is to drive hard for the line of the
> Elbe using the Ninth and Second Armies. The right of the Ninth Army will be

directed on Magdeburg and the left of the Second Army on Hamburg. . . .

I have ordered Ninth and Second Armies to move their armoured and mobile forces forward at once to get through to the Elbe with utmost speed and drive. . . .

My tactical headquarters move to the northwest of Bonninghardt on Thursday, March 29. Thereafter . . . my headquarters will move to Wesel-Münster-Wiedenbrück-Herford-Hanover—thence by autobahn to Berlin, I hope.[6]

Evidently, Montgomery assumed he would retain the Ninth Army for his drive across Germany, though Eisenhower had never offered him such assurance; the Ninth had been promised to Montgomery only as far as the crossing of the Rhine. Just as evidently, Montgomery was taking it upon himself to decide the direction and scope of the offensive beyond the Rhine. In this, the message resembled others since Tunisia in which he had repeatedly tried to usurp the prerogatives of the higher command by blandly announcing his own plan of campaign without consultation. All of which is hardly to say that the plan itself was unsound; the pity was that Montgomery's self-centeredness had by now driven Bradley to an equal, though more insecure and defensive self-centeredness, which was in the process of sacrificing sound military judgment out of fear that Montgomery would seize the extended control over the Ninth Army that he claimed.

Bradley need not have been so fearful. Eisenhower's patience with the field marshal was also strained to the breaking point since the January 7 news conference and the latest effort to name Montgomery as Allied ground commander. When he read Montgomery's message, the Supreme Commander lost his temper. In his anger, indeed, he embarked on conduct as questionable, though on different grounds, as Bradley's concentration upon the strategic dead-end of the Ruhr.

Eisenhower read Montgomery's March 27 signal on the 28th, upon his return from Paris to the new SHAEF Forward headquarters in the red brick Collège Moderne et Technique de Garçons, École Supérieur de Commerce, at Reims. Also in his mail bag was a cable from General Marshall, which said:

> From the current operations report it looks like the German defense system in the west may break up. This would permit you to move a considerable number of divisions eastwards on a broad front. What are your views on . . . pushing U.S. forces rapidly forward on, say, the Nuremberg-Linz or Karlsruhe-Munich axis? The idea behind this is that rapid action might prevent the formation of any organized resistance areas. The mountainous country in the south is considered a possibility for one of these.
>
> One of the problems which arises from disintegrating German resistance is that of meeting the Russians. What are your ideas on control and coordination to prevent unfortunate instances and to sort out the two advancing forces? One possibility is an agreed line of demarcation. The arrangements we now have with the Russians appear quite inadequate for the situation you may face and it seems that steps ought to be initiated without delay to provide for the communication and liaison you will need with them during the period when your forces may be mopping up in close proximity or in contact with Russian forces.[7]

The convergence of Montgomery's and Marshall's messages prodded Eisenhower into crystallizing several decisions, which he stated in three cables composed during the afternoon of March 28. For one thing, he confirmed that, contrary to one of the

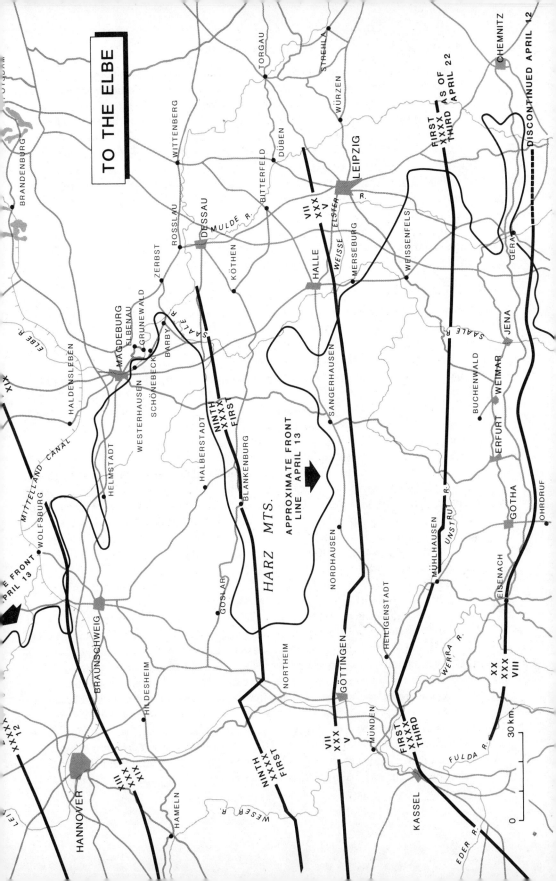

TO THE ELBE

APPROXIMATE FRONT
LINE APRIL 13

HARZ MTS.

BRANDENBURG

TORGAU
STREHLA
CHEMNITZ

WITTENBERG
WÜRZEN
LEIPZIG
FIRST XXXX AS OF THIRD APRIL 22
DISCONTINUED APRIL 12

BITTERFELD
DÜBEN
VII XXX V

ROSSLAU
DESSAU
MULDE R.
KÖTHEN
WEISSE ELSTER R.
HALLE
MERSEBURG
WEISSENFELS
GERA
JENA

MAGDEBURG
ELBENAU
GRUNEWALD
ZERBST
BARBY
SAALE R.
SANGERHAUSEN
SAALE R.
BUCHENWALD
WEIMAR
ERFURT

ELBE R.
HALDENSLEBEN
WESTERHAUSEN
SCHÖNEBECK
HALBERSTADT
NINTH XXXX FIRST
BLANKENBURG
GOTHA
OHRDRUF

HELMSTEDT
MITTELLAND CANAL
WOLFSBURG
GOSLAR
NORDHAUSEN
HEILIGENSTADT
MÜHLHAUSEN
UNSTRUT R.
EISENACH
WERRA R.

E FRONT
APRIL 13
BRAUNSCHWEIG
NORTHEIM
GÖTTINGEN
MÜNDEN
FULDA R.

XXXXX 12
HILDESHEIM
NINTH XXXX FIRST
VII XXX V
FIRST XXXX THIRD
XX XXX VIII
30 km.

HANNOVER
XIII XIX
HAMELN
WESER R.
KASSEL
EDER R.
0

XIX

LEIS

assumptions whereby Montgomery had essayed to shape events, once the Rhineland battles were completed with the junction of the First and Ninth Armies near Paderborn, the Ninth Army would return to Bradley's command.

This reincorporation of Simpson's army in the 12th Army Group would give Bradley the largest field command in American history, 1,300,000 troops in four armies, and would make Bradley's by far the strongest of Eisenhower's three army groups. More than that, the First Army's breakout from the Remagen bridgehead, the Third Army's crossings of the Rhine to the south and Patton's rapid exploitation across the Main, combined with the circumstance that it was the Ninth Army that was scoring the breakout from the 21 Army Group bridgehead east of the Rhine, put Bradley's forces in excellent position to drive on rapidly across Germany—provided, of course, that Bradley chose to do so. The geographic obstacles that hitherto stood in the way of the American armies, to deter Eisenhower and his planners from awarding the Americans the principal strategic roles, at last were behind them. The First and Third Armies had reached the Frankfurt-Kassel corridor and could drive on through good tank country with good highways between the Thüringerwald on the south and the Harz Mountains on the north to the Elbe. Across the Harz Mountains from the First Army, the Ninth Army faced a similar favorable corridor to the Elbe. And if Eisenhower had any longer needed convincing evidence that his American generals and armies were swifter to seize their opportunities than Montgomery and the British, the crossings of the Rhine thoroughly confirmed the superiority of Patton, Simpson, and Hodges and their American armies in bold improvisation and in designing and executing rapid advances led by armor. Eisenhower therefore decided to reverse his former strategic priorities. He would strike his major blow into Germany with the 12th Army Group, relegating 21 Army Group to the secondary task of protecting Bradley's left flank.

It is not least among the causes for criticizing Bradley's decision to commit eighteen divisions to mopping up the Ruhr that he thus weakened his punch into Germany at the very moment when Eisenhower for the first time gave him full freedom to punch hard. Yet Eisenhower participated in and accepted Bradley's decision, and he also set the stage for it with another of his lines of thought that crystallized on March 28. Eisenhower decided that the Western Allies no longer had much chance of capturing "the main prize," Berlin, anyway.

The Soviet offensive that had opened in January had carried the Red Army into a bridgehead west of the Oder River within fifty kilometers of the German capital. There, it was true, the Russians had paused again for the past month to bring up supplies and regroup. The closest Western troops nevertheless were still almost 450 kilometers from Berlin. The past September, when Eisenhower had called Berlin the main prize and his primary geographical objective after the Ruhr, he had recognized that the Soviets might get to Berlin first. As a substitute for a drive to Berlin in that eventuality, Eisenhower then had suggested a 12th Army Group offensive across central Germany to the Leipzig-Dresden industrial and urban complex, while 21 Army Group seized Hannover and the north German ports, and the 6th Army Group took the south German industrial cities. The Soviet shadow already falling across Berlin combined in late March with the fact that the center of gravity of Bradley's armies lay south of the Harz Mountains to focus Eisenhower's strategy not on Berlin but on Leipzig and Dresden. The Supreme Commander would shift the main weight of his offensive to Bradley's army group, but he would also shift the direction of the offensive to the south of Berlin.

This decision has often been interpreted as a shortsighted sacrifice of political advantage for the sake of military convenience. In fact it was a decision largely influenced by political considerations. It sacrificed for those considerations the possible military advantage of the rapid collapse of German resistance that might well follow the loss of Hitler's capital, and which an American offensive to Berlin could help assure in case the Soviets remained stalled between the Oder and the Brandenburg Gate.

The political considerations most relevant in Eisenhower's judgment were the zonal boundaries for postwar occupation of Germany already drawn up by the European Advisory Commission of the Allied powers meeting in London and approved by Roosevelt, Churchill, and Stalin at Yalta. In drawing the boundaries, the British had taken the lead. In November 1943, President Roosevelt had stated emphatically that American troops should race to be the first of the Allies to enter Berlin, and that the German capital should lie within the American postwar occupation zone. Thereafter, however, American diplomacy somehow had fallen into almost indolent passivity when occupation zones were discussed. The American representative to the European Advisory Commission received no adequate instructions, and well before the Yalta decisions Roosevelt had succumbed to illness and lethargy only fitfully broken. The occupation-zone boundaries drawn under these conditions placed Berlin 175 kilometers inside the Soviet zone. While Berlin nevertheless was to be an island of combined Allied occupation, the Western Allies would have access to it only by way of the Soviet zone. Thus, even if the Anglo-American armies might still have raced the Red Army into Berlin and won the race, their military success would make no difference in the political issue of the postwar status of Berlin. There might be a military advantage, but as Eisenhower saw it no political one.

The first of Eisenhower's three March 28 cables responded specifically to Marshall's injunction that something should be done soon to assure an orderly meeting between the Anglo-American and the Soviet armies in the interior of Germany; but in Eisenhower's mood of anger with Montgomery, this first cable responded in a strange and excessively peremptory manner. Marshall had requested Eisenhower's advice on the subject, not instant action. But without further consultation with Marshall or anyone else in Washington or London who might have been concerned with a move surely carrying political overtones, and with very little consultation among his own staff, Eisenhower acted instantly by contacting Josef Stalin.

Through the Allied Military Mission to Moscow, Eisenhower informed Stalin that after completing the encirclement and mopping up of the Ruhr, which he expected to accomplish by late April or earlier, he would send his main forces east on the Erfurt-Leipzig-Dresden axis. It was here that he hoped his armies would join hands with Stalin's. A secondary advance would seek another junction with the Soviets in the Regensburg-Linz area, to prevent any consolidation of resistance in the mountains of south Germany. By implication, the Anglo-American armies were not going to Berlin. Copies of the cable to Stalin went to the Combined Chiefs of Staff and the British Chiefs of Staff.

Eisenhower also sent a covering cable to Marshall, explaining the message to Stalin:

My views agree closely with your own [Eisenhower told the Chief of Staff], although I think the Leipzig-Dresden area is of primary importance. Besides offering the shortest route to present Russian positions, it would divide the German forces roughly in half and would overrun the one remaining industrial area in Germany to which also the high command headquarters and ministries are reported to be moving.

I also agree on the importance of forestalling the possibilities of the enemy forming organized resistance areas, and will make a drive toward Linz and Munich as soon as circumstances allow.

As regards control and coordination of our forces and the Russians . . . I am conscious of present shortcomings in this respect and would appreciate any help you can give me. I do not think we can tie ourselves down to a demarcation line but am approaching the Russians . . . with the suggestion that when our forces meet either side will withdraw to its own occupation zone at the request of the opposite side.[8]

Finally, in a dispatch whose curtness bespoke the effort required to bring his temper back under control, Eisenhower replied to Montgomery by informing him of the decision to return the Ninth Army to Bradley and by saying: "Bradley will be responsible for mopping up and occupying the Ruhr and with minimum delay will deliver his main thrust on the axis Erfurt-Leipzig-Dresden to join hands with the Russians.

"The mission of your army group will be to protect Bradley's northern flank. . . ."[9]

To be sure, pausing to mop up the Ruhr with a substantial portion of Bradley's force contributed no more to "forestalling the possibilities of the enemy forming organized resistance areas" farther east than it did to hurrying toward Berlin. So many debatable decisions lurked within Eisenhower's three cables that there is little wonder that controversy has swirled around them to this day.

The British Chiefs of Staff promptly protested both the manner and the substance of Eisenhower's decisions. They contended he had exceeded his powers as a military commander by his direct approach to the Soviet political leader, and that the southward shift of the main axis of advance into Germany was a strategic mistake and more, for it raised "issues which have a wider import than the destruction of the main enemy forces in Germany."[10] Needless to say, Field Marshal Montgomery urged on his friend Field Marshal Brooke in the COS's opposing the relegation of 21 Army Group to a secondary role. Prime Minister Churchill also forthwith supported his military chiefs with even more than his customary vigor, telephoning Eisenhower on March 29 to stress the political importance in Western prestige should the Anglo-American armies capture Berlin, especially as a balance to the imminent Russian taking of Vienna. (Privately, however, the Prime Minister chided his chiefs of staff for verging on politics themselves in their reference to "issues which have a wider import," and thus exposing themselves to an American riposte.)

The American Chiefs of Staff, in contrast, supported Eisenhower on every point. Particularly, they approved his strategy, concerning which they noted that his plan to fight the major battle while he had remained west of the Rhine and there to destroy as much as possible of the German army had proven altogether sound. Thus, they did not need to add, he had vindicated himself against the earlier British effort to compel a northern crossing of the Rhine before the American armies closed up to the river.

Unfortunately, this defense of Eisenhower's past strategy did not necessarily prove the soundness of his present plans.

In his own responses, the Supreme Commander defended his communicating with Stalin as proper in light of the Soviet marshal's capacity as commander of the Soviet armed forces; he held that his course was anticipated by the Yalta Conference approval of direct liaison between SHAEF and the Soviet General Staff via the Allied Military Mission to Moscow. Strategically, Eisenhower denied intending any basic change in plan: "I am still adhering to my old plan of launching . . . one main attack calculated to accomplish, in conjunction with the Russians, the destruction of the enemy armed forces." As for the strategic importance of Berlin, "through bombing as well as through partial transfer of German governmental offices, Berlin has lost much of its former military importance." As for Berlin's political importance, "I am the first to admit that a war is waged in pursuance of political aims, and if the Combined Chiefs of Staff should decide that the Allied effort to take Berlin outweighs purely military considerations in the theater, I would cheerfully readjust my plans and my thinking so as to carry out such an operation."[11]

With their decisions now conditioned by the American predominance in the Anglo-American armies in Europe, the Combined Chiefs of Staff did not compel Eisenhower to readjust. Still, his arguments were at least a trifle disingenuous. In terms of strategy, it was true that he had always planned to drive one major thrust into Germany; but his shift to the Leipzig-Dresden axis was hardly a mere modification of detail from his earlier emphasis on Berlin. And the roots of his own decision on Berlin were by no means "purely military." The decision was highly political.

To the Elbe

If General Bull was right about where Eisenhower's heart lay—and he no doubt was—then it seems possible that if the American armies' main weight had massed farther north, on the most direct route to Berlin, Eisenhower might have been more inclined to retain the northern drive as his primary effort and to thrust on to Berlin. To be sure, the Supreme Commander tried studiously to exclude national and personal considerations from his decisions; but it was also true that the prospect of Bradley's triumphal entry into Berlin would certainly have appealed to him more than Montgomery's, when his relations with the field marshal had deteriorated to the point that he communicated with him no more than he felt he must. As he later told Cornelius Ryan: "Montgomery had become so personal in his efforts to make sure that the Americans—and me, in particular—got no credit, that, in fact, we hardly had anything to do with the war, that I finally stopped talking to him."[12]

Of course, having Bradley in a position to mount the shortest thrust toward Berlin would not have changed the location of the Soviets, only fifty kilometers from the Reichs Chancellery. Yet if it had been the American armies that had marched on the Allied left from the crossing of the English Channel onward, and had thus been first to reach the Rhine, the past month's events suggested that the northern crossings would have been more prompt than they were under Montgomery's direction, and Eisenhower's armies might by the beginning of April have been considerably closer to Berlin, with better prospects of reaching it before the Soviets. There seemed to be no end to the tyranny imposed by those circumstances that had placed the British on the left and the Americans on the right all through the European campaign, persistently denying the opportunities for most rapid movement to the American armies that excelled their Allies in armored mobility.

And now Bradley's commitment of eighteen divisions to the Ruhr, so much a venture into a strategic dead end as to be scarcely explicable except by reference to fear that Montgomery would yet find a way to harness American armies to his chariot after all, had further compounded the problem of reaching Berlin with troops who possessed such mobility that they might outrace the Russians still.

But if Simpson and his soldiers could have their way, Americans might even now recapture the opportunity to be first in Berlin.

On April 7, when Eisenhower wrote to Marshall about his willingness to readjust his plans if the Combined Chiefs should decide that political considerations demanded it, the Supreme Commander also spoke of "the capture of Berlin . . . as something that we should do if feasible and practicable as we proceed on the general plan of (a) dividing the German forces by a major thrust in the middle, (b) anchoring our left firmly in the Lubeck area, and (c) attempting to disrupt any German effort to establish a fortress in the southern mountains."[13] Thus Eisenhower's new decisions had not yet ruled out Berlin absolutely—and the Ninth Army was moving fast to assure that American capture of Berlin would after all return to his plans.

Along an eighty-kilometer front, Gillem's XIII Corps on Simpson's left and McLain's XIX Corps on the right attacked first toward the Weser River. General Collier's CCA of White's 2nd Armored Division had potentially the most dangerous ground ahead of it, the Teutoburger Wald, a range of densely forested low hills arising between the north German and Westphalian plains northeastward from the Ruhr. The Teutoburger Wald was the historic German backstop to the Rhine as a barrier against invaders from the west, the region where in A.D. 9 the young Teutonic chief Arminius trapped and destroyed the XVII, XVIII, and XIX Legions of Publius Quintilius Varus to throw back the Roman frontier to the Rhine. The Roman army never again used the numbers of the three annihilated legions; but without superstition the American XIX Corps charged into the forest on Easter Sunday. General Collier divided CCA into three task forces to assault each of the three principal defiles through the hill mass. The entrapment of most of Army Group B in the Ruhr had opened a wide gap in front of the Ninth Army, between the elements of the First Parachute Army still resisting the British to the north and the Eleventh Army forming to oppose Hodges to the south. Nevertheless, the passes of the Teutoburger Wald gave so much natural assistance to makeshift oddments of German troops, and the forested terrain, much resembling the eastern Ardennes, was so unsuited to tanks, that on April 2 McLain attached the 119th Infantry of the 30th Division to CCA to help the armor fight its way clear.

Struggling through Augustdorf and toward Detmold against a mixture of SS men and almost equally determined Wehrmacht recruits, part of CCA came up against entrenchments built about the huge, metallic Hermannsdenkmal itself, the monument to Arminius, crowned with his giant statue, atop a particularly dominating crest. There the Germans paid homage to their ancestors by resisting apparently to the last man; but other garrisons also waited behind this one, and it was not until April 4 that CCA fought into Detmold.

The delay in the forest was a disappointment, and so was failure to find a bridge over the Weser. Yet such setbacks were hardly enough to quench the spirits of troops intent on reaching Berlin, and during the night of April 4–5 near Hameln the 119th Infantry crossed the river in boats against scattered small-arms fire to win a bridgehead for the 2nd Armored. The armor followed on an engineers' bridge during April 5. Hobbs's 30th Division, close behind White's, was held up for a time in an unusual battle in Hameln; there ss officers squeezed from some of the inhabitants the kind of citizens' resistance that Nazi propaganda had warned the Allies to expect but that almost nowhere else materialized. Remembering that the place was the Hamelin of the Pied Piper legend, Colonel Walter M. Johnson of the 117th Infantry commented, "This time we got the rats out with a slightly different kind of flute."[14] He meant the divisional artillery in particular, which turned the picturesque gingerbread houses into rubble. The Old Hickory Division quickly hurried on beyond the Weser in the wake of the 2nd Armored.

Farther north, Bolling's 84th Division of the XIII Corps was frustrated in its crossing efforts that day by enemy guns firing from a high ridge line that split the divisional sector, the Wesergebirge. So the Railsplitters shifted slightly to the south and resumed their part of the race beyond the Weser on April 6.

Also on April 6, the Germans reacted in the principal way still left to them. To deal with this Ninth Army wedge driving between OB West's principal remaining forces to the southward and the troops in northeast Holland and in front of 21 Army Group, the Germans shuffled headquarters again. Kesselring, practically cut off from his northern flank, ceded command of it to a new Oberbefehlshaber Nordwest, Generalfeldmarschall Ernst Busch, brought from the Eastern Front. There were now two Commanders in Chief in the West directly subordinate to OKW; but as with the Confederate States army at Bentonville in 1865, where there had been three full generals, four lieutenant generals, and twelve major generals to command 20,000 men, the inflation of the high command was merely another symptom of chaos growing uncontrollable.

The Ninth Army, of course, was indifferent to such puny machinations. In one day, White's 2nd Armored jumped the thirty kilometers between the Weser and the much smaller Leine River. At the Leine, the army had reached the army group's Hannover-Hildesheim phase line, and Bradley's instructions called for Simpson to pause so the First Army could come abreast in the main drive on Leipzig-Dresden. But as usual, there were opportunities too good for such instructions to be observed literally. With Hinds's CCB up alongside Collier's CCA again, General White of the 2nd Armored made sure of capturing several Leine bridges intact and drove on across the Innerste River near Hildesheim, some sixteen kilometers farther, before he paused the next day, April 7.

On April 8, while he was mainly resting and refitting as desired by army group headquarters, White was not too idle to secure a second crossing of the Innerste and a bridgehead over the Zweigcanal. That day the 84th Division of the XIII Corps also reached the Leine, and the Railsplitters crossed on a bridge held for them by the corps reconnaissance unit, the 11th Cavalry Group. General Bolling had been worried by the imminent prospect of his 84th's having to clear Hannover, before the war a city of 400,000 and likely to be strongly enough defended and a troublesome enough obstacle to delay him for days. At the Leine, however, besides the bridge the 84th found a German soldier who was carrying a detailed map of the Hannover defenses. Thus when word came from Bradley to Simpson on April 9 to move out again the next day, the Railsplitters were ready to bypass the main Hannover defenses, which faced south and southwest, and to conquer the rubble of the city from the north and northeast. They substantially completed the job in a single day, April 10.

That day the 2nd Armored's CCB covered over thirty kilometers, stopping a train whose engineer said he had not known the Americans were within eighty kilometers, and repeatedly scattering shoppers in towns where the trolleys were still running. CCA, encountering the urban industrial area of Braunschweig and Immendorf, had a harder time, not only because of the usual urban obstacles of blocked streets and rubble, but because it ran up against sixty-seven big antiaircraft guns grouped to protect the Hermann Göring Steel Works and able to fire against ground targets with devastating effect because the level terrain gave superb observation and fields of fire. Collier's men had to pause and arrange a flanking maneuver to capture the guns. They took them and the steel works by late evening, but the delay was to seem in retrospect a portent of further trouble.

For the present, however, it was only an annoying incident in an otherwise headlong advance. April 11 proved CCB's finest day of the war. Hinds's men and tanks attacked from around Schladen and Gross Dohren at 6:30 A.M. The left column early struck and destroyed an enemy truck column. The right column advanced farther without more than casual opposition, until it met a 1,700-man enemy marching column; but this obstacle also was quickly eliminated, by overawing the Germans into surrender. At Orschersleben, the left task force overran a defensive line and captured an airport with seventeen Fw 190s on the ground, while shooting two more German fighters out of the sky. As was happening often now, the lead platoon of the 82nd Reconnaissance Battalion ran off the eastern edge of its maps, and Colonel Merriam's adjutant had to hurry new ones up to the front; often the spearheads were following the tiny maps earlier issued to airmen to help them escape if they were shot down. In the afternoon, the 82nd Reconnaissance Battalion was slowed by a civilian traffic jam as it entered a shopping district in the western suburbs of Magdeburg. By evening, CCB's columns had covered ninety-two kilometers—some of their vehicles as much as 117 in actual road distance. A little after eight that evening, Colonel Paul A. Disney of the 67th Armored Regiment, commanding the right column of CCB, informed General White's headquarters: "We're on the Elbe."[15]

White had figured that from the Elbe, Berlin was only two more days away.

The Last River (I)

In twilight, at Schönebeck southeast of Magdeburg, Major James F. Hollingsworth led the advance of the 67th Armored Regiment across the last rise of ground before the Elbe and saw an intact highway bridge below him, German armored vehicles still using it to flee to the east bank. Hollingsworth immediately initiated the familiar ploy of using the gathering darkness to attach one of his tank companies to the tail of the retreating enemy armor as a means of getting on the bridge and controlling it before the enemy could destroy it.

The scheme almost worked. But some gun crews whose pieces were mounted on flat cars in a railroad yard spotted Hollingsworth's Shermans and sounded the alarm by opening fire on them. Then Hollingsworth's lead Sherman turned a corner to come upon a Panther already revolving its turret to take aim. Hollingsworth's gunner knocked out the Panther, but now it was, in Hollingsworth's words, "everyone . . . firing at everyone else. . . . the damnedest mess. Germans were hanging out of windows, either shooting at us with their *Panzerfäuste* or just dangling in death.''[16] His tanks blocked by stone walls and wrecked vehicles short of the bridge, Hollingsworth led an infantry charge but was wounded in the face and the left knee, and his column halted within fifteen meters of the bridge. Holding off the Americans through the night, the Germans blew the bridge at dawn on April 12.

So CCB had to find and capture a suitable assault crossing and bridging site. It spent the daylight hours of the 12th clearing the west bank south of Magdeburg and eventually choosing for the crossing an old wagon ferry site at Westerhausen. Meanwhile, division headquarters tried unsuccessfully to negotiate a surrender of Magdeburg and moved CCA to close off the city from the north and west, while CCR went into position southward to support CCB.

McLain's XIX Corps had more than one string to its bow—even if not as many strings as it might have without the Ruhr diversion. Macon's 83rd Infantry Division had gone on steadily enhancing the speed and firepower of its mobility by adding to its collection of American and German vehicles a menagerie of enemy tanks and reconnaissance vehicles, all promptly repainted with olive drab and the American white star, but still a weird enough assortment that correspondents called the division the "Rag Tag Circus." Macon's troops preferred the old, official division nickname, the Thunderbolt, which was not inapt, or to call themselves the 83rd Armored Division; for in friendly rivalry with the 2nd Armored they had just about kept pace with the Hell on Wheels Division—occasionally passing it—in the plunge toward Berlin. On April 12, while the 2nd Armored was struggling to clear the west shore of the Elbe from Westerhausen to Schönebeck, the 329th Infantry in the van of the 83rd reached the Elbe about ten kilometers upstream at Barby. The infantry fought a brisk engagement to clear defenders from the town and prepared to cross the Elbe the next day toward an east shore that gave little evidence of any enemy presence.

Nor was McLain's XIX Corps alone at the head of the Ninth Army on April 12. Oliver's 5th Armored Division of Gillem's XIII Corps had rolled on past the 84th Division while the Railsplitters were engaged in cleaning up Hannover, the armor aiming for an Elbe crossing at Tangermünde some fifteen kilometers downstream from Magdeburg. Oliver's advance entered Tangermünde about the same time the 83rd was reaching Barby, and also collided with an island of German defense able to put up at least a brief stout battle on the west shore. The tankers were about to call up artillery support when they met an American soldier who said he was an escaped prisoner of war, and who told them that about 500 prisoners were being held in the town. This news cancelled a bombardment. By the time the attackers had clawed their way street by street and house by house almost to the bridge—and the German garrison had passed the word that they were ready to surrender—the bridge blew up. Once more, the engineers had to hurry up boats and bridging equipment.

Concerned that the abrupt stiffening of resistance in the river towns might signal a last-gasp German effort to hold firm at the Elbe, both General White and General Hinds grew increasingly impatient throughout April 12. They determined they must allow not a minute more than was unavoidable for the enemy to build a cordon on the opposite shore. White ordered that as soon as the 2nd Armored had cleared a launching site at Westerhausen, isolated Magdeburg, and reassembled an assault force from the day's scattered fighting, Hinds was to begin crossing. White set 7:00 P.M. as H-Hour. It was not until nine that Hinds was actually able to bring together two battalions, the 1st and 3rd of the 41st Armored Infantry, and send their first wave eastward in dukws. But by eleven, the battalions were mostly beyond the Elbe. They were 100 kilometers from Potsdam, 125 from the center of Berlin. White telephoned Simpson: "We're across!"[17]

Yet the day's anxiety was well founded. In the Harz Mountains to the south and rear of the XIX Corps, knots of German resistance were growing disturbingly recalcitrant and aggressive against efforts to round them up. Too many of Simpson's and Hodges's divisions were still fighting in the Ruhr to spare much for this threat while hurrying anything to the Elbe and beyond at the same time. There were also reports of a new German Twelfth Army forming, with its mission the relief of the Harz and eventually of the Ruhr.

The 2nd Armored bridgehead immediately suffered further evidence of refreshed enemy resolution, which also proved in time to have its source in the enemy's Twelfth Army, headquartered on the east bank of the Elbe opposite Dessau not far upstream. The 3rd Battalion of the 119th Infantry had promptly followed the armored infantry across the Elbe and into the bridgehead, and the 2nd Armored Division's engineers had begun building a bridge before the two armored infantry battalions were altogether across. The river was too shallow for a vehicular ferry, so getting tanks to the east bank would have to depend on a treadway bridge. At first daylight of April 13, however, when the bridge was about half finished and enough pontons were ready to complete it, the enemy began laying a heavy and accurate artillery fire on the bridge and both adjacent banks. By the time the German guns paused about half an hour later, most of the pontons both in the river and on the bank had been wrecked.

The Americans brought up smoke pots for concealment, and American guns opened counterbattery fire. But the German artillery was soon in action again, and nothing available seemed able to squelch it. Largely, the Germans were using the heavy antiaircraft guns that formed a ring around Magdeburg, the same kinds of pieces that had caused trouble at the Hermann Göring Steel Works near Braunschweig. The 2nd Armored called on XIX TAC for help from fighter-bombers, but the race to the Elbe had carried the advance almost out of range of fighter airfields; no fighter-bombers appeared.

By about midday, the engineers nevertheless pushed the bridge to within twenty-five meters of the east shore. Then the Germans stepped up their bombardment again, and shells destroyed the eastern section of the bridge and mangled everything else. General White gave up. He ordered the three infantry battalions in the bridgehead to attack southward after nightfall, to capture a new crossing site about five kilometers upstream near the eastern end of the ruined Schönebeck bridge.

Before dawn on April 14, parts of the 3/41st Armored Infantry and the 3/119th Infantry entered the town of Elbenau, about three kilometers east of the river and shielding the proposed new crossing place, while parts of the 1/41st cleared the village of Grünewalde, and other elements of the three battalions dug in to anchor the flanks. The infantry had been under fire almost without respite since approaching the river on April 11, and they were dog-tired. Because there was no bridge, they had no tanks or antitank guns. About first light, while they were still establishing their positions, they trembled to hear the rumble and clatter of tank treads, and then they were hit by tanks, assault guns, and infantry fighting with a Nazi fanaticism that would have made the Führer proud. The German soldiers were young and obviously inexperienced, but military history is filled with instances wherein zeal compensates for a multitude of deficiencies, and this was one of them. Company L of the 119th became isolated in Elbenau and promptly the target of a systematic effort to destroy it altogether. By late morning, 2nd Armored headquarters had to report to the XIX Corps that it might already have lost the "3/41 AIR complete."[18] Frantic requests for air support again produced no help.

While some of the engineers tried once more to build a bridge, others were constructing a ferry to be anchored by a guide cable. The shallowness of the Elbe was a problem again. The first vehicle put on the ferry, about noon, was a bulldozer to shave the east bank for a landing site. As the bulldozer approached the far shore, German artillery broke the cable, and ferry and 'dozer went drifting downstream.

Except for Volkssturm and other local defense forces, the resistance came from a scratch formation whose soldiers were intended to be inspired by a historic name, Division Scharnhorst. The young men comprising the division, and their tanks and other equipment, came largely from army schools, especially officer training schools. This origin at least partially accounted for the fervor of their assaults; many a better cause would have paid dearly to enlist some of the desperate determination with which Division Scharnhorst's brave young men snatched at what might prove a final opportunity for glory by crumpling the 2nd Armored Division bridgehead back into the Elbe.

White's bridgehead was crumpling; but upstream, at Barby, no zealous young Nazis had yet reached the Elbe shores, and in the early afternoon of April 13 two battalions of the 83rd Division's 329th Infantry had crossed on an excursion "just like a Sunday afternoon picnic with no fire of any kind."[19] By nightfall the 295th Engineer Battalion and the 992nd Bridge Company had laid a treadway bridge to supplement the industrious ferries of the 308th Engineer Battalion, and the whole of the 329th Infantry was across along with the 331st, the 736th Tank Battalion, and the 643rd Tank Destroyer Battalion. Colonel Edwin B. Crabill of the 329th told his men, "You are on your way to Berlin."[20] On April 14, during the travail at Elbenau, the buildup at Barby went on unhindered except by four small counterattacks.

Flak Alley

Because Bradley chose to assault rather than contain the Ruhr pocket, only eight Allied divisions were pressing eastward north of the Harz Mountains on the most direct road to Berlin, while thirty-one American divisions, including the Seventh Army, moved at the same time toward the lesser objectives beckoning eastward south of the mountains.

When the III and XVIII Corps of Hodges's First Army turned around for the Battle of the Ruhr Pocket, Collins's VII and Huebner's V Corps resumed the march toward Leipzig and Dresden. To the Weser, Collins and Huebner experienced perhaps slightly harder going than the Ninth Army, because General Hitzfeld's Eleventh Army stood before them to provide the opposition. Collins's troops still had to finish off ss Ersatzbrigade Westfalen, the students, Panthers, and Tigers that had slipped eastward after halting the attack on Paderborn. Huebner's corps faced the best remaining old-line troops of the Eleventh Army, Hitzfeld's own LXVII Corps, the remnants of a half dozen or so infantry divisions. Major General Emil F. Reinhardt's new 69th Division, for example, leading the right wing of the V Corps, fought from April 5 to 7 to make its way through a triangle of wooded hills enclosed by the Fulda and Werra Rivers as they form the Weser.

Not that the Germans retained enough strength to do more than impose such delays sporadically. Robertson's 2nd Division on the V Corps left struck only weak scratch formations with which the Eleventh Army was trying to link the ss brigade and the LXVII Corps, and the Indian Head veterans swept these forces aside to cross the Weser in assault boats in the early darkness of April 6, the day the Ninth Army vanguard downstream was moving from the Weser to the Leine. Collins's leading division, the 3rd Armored, now under Brigadier General Doyle O. Hickey—the crisis at Paderborn having passed, Hodges was willing to let Harmon return to his corps—stalled again in front of ss Ersatzbrigade Westfalen long enough that the bridges were gone from its stretch of the Weser by the time the VII Corps arrived at the river. Therefore, on April 7 Collins crossed the advance of Terry Allen's 104th Division over the bridge built behind the 2nd Division. Other parts of the 104th and Andrus's 1st Division readily executed assault crossings before the end of the day.

On April 8, the 2nd Division pressed on across an intact bridge over the Leine and through the university town of Göttingen, which the Germans had declared an open city because it was filled with hospitalized soldiers. Reinhardt's 69th Division to the south jumped the Leine the same day, in assault boats. The Germans appeared to be withdrawing from Hodges's front into the Harz Mountains along the First Army-Ninth Army boundary, though on April 9 the 3rd Armored, hastening toward the Leine to bring Collins's spearhead abreast of Huebner's again, collided with a dozen Panthers and King Tigers that knocked out five Shermans. Collins turned the 1st Division into the Harz to clean out the incipient German refuge there.

As the 3rd Armored crossed the Leine at Northeim late on April 9, bringing Hodges's and Simpson's leading units all to the east bank of that stream, Bradley removed the restrictions that had detained the earlier arrivals. The Elbe flows farther eastward in the First Army zone than in front of Simpson, and except for the left wing of Collins's corps, Hodges's men were aiming first for its tributary the Mulde, just east of Leipzig. But organized resistance, such as it was, had so much fled into the Harz Mountains that despite the added distance to the Elbe even on Collins's front, by April 13 the 3rd Armored had spearheads across the Saale River northwest of Halle and was bearing down on the Elbe at Dessau.

Friday the 13th was the day, however, when events turned somewhat sour for the 2nd Armored Division around Magdeburg, and the First Army suffered similar misfortune. The day before, Leonard's 9th Armored Division, now leading Huebner's V Corps, had run into an even bigger concentration of heavy flak guns than those that had impeded the Ninth Army around Braunschweig and helped ruin the 2nd Armored's bridgebuilding on the Elbe. Somehow, word had never passed from the strategic air forces to the ground army that, in approaching Leipzig, Bradley's troops would strike "flak alley," perhaps as many as a thousand antiaircraft guns grouped in twelve- to thirty-six-gun batteries of 75mm. to 128mm. pieces.

Around Leipzig, these guns had the same sort of flat terrain for observation and aiming against ground attack that aided them against Simpson's advance. The 9th Armored lost nine tanks within the first few hours of tangling with them. On the 13th,

Huebner decided the 9th Armored had better back off from Weissenfels on the Saale, where it had stumbled into flak alley, to swing southeast away from Leipzig and reach the Mulde above the city. The infantry of the 2nd Division would take over the direct attack on Leipzig. Evidently the flak guns formed an arc around the city, but one of the most infuriating aspects of the situation was that it was to take three days before urgent requests for information about the guns' locations, filed by the 9th Armored on April 12, extracted an answer from the airmen.

When the First Army had swung northeast to Paderborn before turning some of its divisions more directly eastward, Patton's columns had raced out of their bridgeheads on the upper Rhine toward Kassel to shield Hodges's right flank. On March 28, the day Bradley shifted the direction of the Remagen breakout from east and southeast to northeast, the Third Army was already well placed to assume this role; for the 28th was the day when Hoge's 4th Armored exploited its Hanau bridgehead over the Main almost as far as Giessen, while Grow's 6th Armored crossed the Main into the 90th Division bridgehead west of Hanau and rumbled nearly twenty-five kilometers farther northward.

Because these northward plunges of the two armored divisions of Eddy's XII Corps were cutting across the eastward paths of both the XX and VIII Corps, Patton redistributed units and boundaries during March 28 to keep at least two of his corps in the action. He gave Walker of the XX Corps both the 6th Armored and Irwin's 5th Infantry Division, and ordered Eddy and Walker to drive northeast in tandem. Walker was to head straight for Kassel with the 6th Armored in the lead. Eddy, with the 4th Armored in the lead, was to drive through the northern part of the Fulda Gap, which separates the two hill masses called the Vogelsberg and the Hohe Rhön, and then turn more directly east. The next day Patton compensated Eddy for the loss of the 6th Armored by giving him Dager's 11th Armored, to drive straight through the Fulda Gap to the right of the 4th Armored.

Grow and Hoge were both still flowing into the hole between Army Groups B and G opened by the junction of the American First and Third Armies on the Lahn, and almost inevitable following the German debacle in the Palatinate produced by Eisenhower's insistence on destroying enemy forces west of the Rhine. Consequently, the two leading wedges of Patton's advance met only occasional roadblocks and virtually paraded through the Alsfeld area, where the local costume gave the brothers Grimm the title for their tale of Little Red Riding Hood. It was still true, however, that more substantial resistance usually lay in wait for somebody, and in this instance the victim was Dager's division. The 11th Armored had to push aside the north flank of the one corps of the German Seventh Army retaining a modicum of organization, the LXXXII; the relative respectability of this force could be explained by the fact that it had been passed on from the stronger German First Army to the south.

As recently as mid-March, Eisenhower had initiated planning for the largest airborne operation yet as the means of taking Kassel, with possibly one British and three American airborne divisions enveloping the place from the sky. Bradley had responded to the idea with his usual skepticism about airborne performances. When the assistant chief of staff of the First Airborne Army conferred with him and told him April 20 was the target date, Bradley gave assurance the ground attack would have the city by April 10; the ponderousness of airborne planning gave Bradley's skepticism a sound foundation. Bradley thought the C-47s could better be used for air supply of his advances into

Germany; he knew that his April 10 estimate was conservative. Grow's 6th Armored Division was within ten kilometers of Kassel by the evening of March 30, with a bridge across the Eder River. The next days, parts of the Germans' respectable 166th Infantry Division combined with the local defense forces to slow Grow's charge. Grow shifted direction to cross the Fulda River above Kassel on the night of March 31–April 1, leaving it to McBride's 80th Division to clear the city. The enemy made a house-to-house fight of it, but the 80th finished the job by April 4.

The Fulda River could have been a troublesome obstacle for Grow's armor, but by choosing to put their neighborhood eggs in the Kassel basket the Germans left themselves no adequate strength to realize the river's possibilities. When Grow's division won its bridgehead over the Fulda, Hoge's 4th Armored was almost at the Werra and Dager's 11th Armored could see the city of Fulda. Bradley thought the Third Army ought to pause in this vicinity to afford the First Army time to complete and assure the security of the encirclement of the Ruhr. Patton as usual could be depended on to produce a reason for not stopping; the 4th Armored had brought in a deserting German officer who said there was a major headquarters or communications center some fifty kilometers beyond the Werra in the town of Ohrdruf.

Almost as dependably, Bradley and Eisenhower gave Patton the green light to continue advancing as far as Ohrdruf. Hoge's CCA took the place on the afternoon of April 4. The source of the deserter's story proved to be a vast underground communications center that had been built for OKW during the Czech crisis of 1938. It had never been used, but workers had begun to renovate it as a possible retreat for Hitler just before the Americans arrived.

Ohrdruf also harbored the first concentration camp to be liberated by the Western Allies. It was a small camp compared with others soon to be discovered, but seeing its walking skeletons and piles of more than 3,000 naked, emaciated corpses caused Patton to vomit when he visited a few days later, and Eisenhower to comment that "The evidence of inhuman treatment, starvation, beating, and killing . . . was beyond the American mind to comprehend."[21] When the XX Corps took over the area, General Walker compelled the Ohrdruf burgomaster and his wife to view the camp; they went home and hanged themselves.

Obliged to pause elsewhere in deference to Bradley's Ruhr obsession, Patton took the opportunity to restore Middleton's VIII Corps to a sector of the front, inserting it between the XII and the XX. With spearheads at Mühlhausen, Gotha, Ohrdruf, and east of Meiningen, the Third Army was sixty kilometers or more in front of the First and Ninth Armies during the first days of April, because Hodges was busy with the Ruhr, and Simpson had taken longer to break out from his Rhine bridgehead. (Patton scoffed on April 5: "We never met any opposition because the bigger and better Germans fight Monty—he says so";[22] but the Ninth Army's hard contest before it could strike forward along the Lippe showed that for the present, at least, Monty's version of affairs carried a measure of truth.)

The outcome was that Bradley and Eisenhower held Patton in place longer than on any previous occasion except when there was a supply crisis. ("Whenever those two get together, they get timid."[23]) The Third Army was permitted no general advance again until April 10, when Hodges and Simpson had both drawn abreast. As part of the new Eisenhower strategy for the major offensive to cross central Germany toward Leipzig and

Dresden, Patton was next to move in tandem with Hodges on the First Army's right, aiming at Chemnitz. The rivers in Patton's front were less broad than those facing Hodges and Simpson, but the Third Army right would have to face the wooded ridges of the Thüringerwald. With this impediment in mind, Patton used part of his enforced leisure to send the 11th Armored Division southeast to the far side of the highest ridge, to find better terrain and also with an eye to a later southward turn by the whole army, a shift already well forecast in discussion with SHAEF and the 12th Army Group. Also during the pause, Grow's 6th Armored and Schmidt's 76th and McBride's 80th Infantry Divisions on the opposite flank around Mühlhausen absorbed a series of counterattacks from the German Eleventh Army. Believing that his customary constant aggressiveness was the key to his success, Patton had expected that the enemy would use the respite donated to him to muster some such riposte. Fortunately, the Germans proved able to husband only enough strength to regain a single village.

When Bradley at length gave the word "Go," Hoge's 4th and Grow's 6th Armored were promptly off to the races again. While the 80th Division cleared the city of Erfurt on April 11, the 4th Armored plunged thirteen kilometers farther eastward on the Autobahn south of the city, while the 6th Armored, driving into another vacuum, moved all of eighty kilometers, to cross the Saale River north of the old Napoleonic battleground of Jena. The next day, April 12, the 4th Armored practically caught up by bypassing the city of Jena and returning to the Autobahn some eight kilometers beyond it.

But, like Bradley's other two advancing armies at almost the same time, on April 12 the Third Army vanguard, the 6th Armored, found its headlong progress abruptly slowed, because it struck flak alley.

The Last River (II)

On that Thursday of impatience and frustration, the Supreme Commander visited the front. He flew from Reims to Bradley's latest tactical headquarters at Wiesbaden, then called on Hodges and Patton and their generals by Piper Cub. This was the day when Eisenhower saw the Ohrdruf concentration camp, and Patton also showed him an underground cache of gold reserves, art treasures, and jewelry that Earnest's 90th Division had discovered near Merkers. Returning with Bradley to Patton's command trailer, Eisenhower chose this occasion to inform Patton that he would enforce on his armies a stop-line in mid-Germany that would assure an orderly, peaceful meeting with the Russians.

In the interval since his March 28 cables to Stalin, Marshall and the Combined Chiefs, and Montgomery, Eisenhower had contributed to his American subordinates' impression that the 12th Army Group, the Ninth Army in particular, had an open road to Berlin. General Bolling of the 84th Division remembered, for example, that on a tour of the northern part of the army group on April 8, Eisenhower had asked him in Simpson's presence where he was going next. "Berlin," Bolling replied, "we're going to push on ahead, we have a clear go to Berlin and nothing can stop us." And Bolling recalled that Eisenhower replied: "Alex, keep going. I wish you all the luck in the world and don't let anybody stop you."[24]

However that may have been, by April 12 Eisenhower was explaining to Patton that, tactically, it was inadvisable for an American army to capture Berlin, that the city retained no tactical or strategic value, and that taking it would saddle the Americans with the care of thousands of Germans and displaced persons. Therefore, Bradley's northern divisions must stop short of Berlin. Similarly, in the southern area, Patton's army was to halt on the Mulde River fifteen kilometers west of Chemnitz, on a north-south line with the First Army on the lower Mulde and the Ninth Army on the Elbe around Magdeburg. Patton naturally objected: "Ike, I don't see how you figure that one. We had better take Berlin and quick, and on to the Oder."[25] But by this time Eisenhower had debated his decision more than enough with Churchill, and his mind was made up.

The slowing of his armies' advances by the flak guns and the enemy's new Twelfth Army on the Elbe happened to coincide in time with Eisenhower's enforcement of his decision to halt along the Elbe and the Mulde. These circumstances did not create the decision.

On the Ninth Army front, the loss of the ferry and the bulldozer convinced Genral Hinds that he could not hold the Grünewalde-Elbenau bridgehead. His division commander, General White, was already planning to cross part of the 2nd Armored through the 83rd Division bridgehead to the south at Barby. So White gave Hinds permission to act as he saw fit. About 1:30 P.M. on April 14 Hinds ordered the Grünewalde-Elbenau bridgehead evacuated.

The enemy's artillery had left him only three dukws to serve as ferries, and during the evacuation the number shrank to one. Still, the troops conducted an orderly withdrawal. American artillery fired a heavy barrage and laid down a smoke screen to help Company L of the 119th Infantry escape from the Elbenau cellars where it had hidden. XXIX TAC fighter-bombers with auxiliary fuel tanks rather than bombs arrived at last to strafe the Germans. By and large the evacuation was successful. Survivors continued straggling back during the night and into the next day; in the end the losses of the three battalions in the bridgehead were counted at 330, of whom only four were known to be dead and twenty wounded. About one company remained on the east bank protecting the ferry head in case there should be a renewed effort to use it.

At Barby, in contrast, there was every reason for optimism. "Truman Bridge. Gateway to Berlin over the Elbe. Courtesy 83d Thunderbolt Division. Constructed by 295 Engr. Bn., 992 Bridge Co.," declared an entrance sign at the treadway bridge. During April 14, CCR, 2nd Armored funneled into the bridgehead to help the Thunderbolt Division extend its conquests some eight more kilometers toward Berlin. The attached 320th Infantry of the 35th Division attacked across the Saale River into the angle formed by that stream and the Elbe to prepare the way for another Elbe bridge. The Ninth Army had a firm foothold beyond the Elbe.

Simpson's staff accordingly completed a plan "to enlarge the Elbe River bridgehead to include Potsdam."[26] On April 15 Simpson flew to Bradley's headquarters to propose the plan. Bradley listened carefully but said he would have to present the plan to Eisenhower. He telephoned the Supreme Commander, who also paid close attention.

Bradley later recalled that it was then that Eisenhower asked him the pertinent question that he records without a date in A Soldier's Story: "what I thought it might cost us to break through from the Elbe to Berlin." Bradley's estimate was 100,000 men. He said he was thinking not so much of the countryside between the Elbe and Berlin, though it was a humid lowland crisscrossed with streams and canals and it gave him pause. His main concern was for the fight he believed the Germans would wage inside their capital. The estimate remains astonishing nevertheless, compared with the lesser casualties of so fierce a battle as the Ardennes, and in the context of crumbling resistance all along the American front except for the temporary problem of the flak guns and the relatively small incident at the Grünewald bridgehead. The estimate is so completely astonishing, in fact, and so completely at odds with experience, that the only possible explanation must be that for whatever reason, fear that Montgomery would snatch the laurels or otherwise, Bradley simply did not want to go to Berlin.

If there was reason to expect even the slightest approximation of resistance in Berlin on the scale that Bradley forecast, then it should have followed that Berlin retained enough importance for the Germans that its capture might hasten the end of the war and retain considerable strategic importance after all. But Eisenhower did not want to capture Berlin either. Churchill had surely pressed too hard his efforts to change the Supreme Commander's mind. "PM is increasingly vexatious," Ike told Bradley. "He imagines himself to be a military tactician." Both Eisenhower and Bradley remained influenced also, not simply by military considerations as they professed, but by the political consideration of Berlin's location within the postwar Soviet zone: "A pretty stiff price to pay for a prestige objective," Bradley commented to Ike on his 100,000-casualties estimate, "especially when we've got to fall back and let the other fellow take over."

So the final words Simpson heard Bradley say to Ike to close the telephone conversation were: "All right, Ike. That's what I thought. I'll tell him." As the setback at Grünewalde did not determine Eisenhower's decision, neither did the success at Barby. The Anglo-American armies would not capture Berlin; the American army would not enter the sanctum of the military profession at Potsdam.[27]

The next night two Soviet army groups opened massive assaults toward the German capital.

"Yes I was terribly disappointed when the Ninth Army stopped at the Elbe River and our drive on Berlin was cancelled," Simpson wrote nearly twenty years later.

> My plan was to have the 2d Armored Division accompanied by an infantry division in trucks take off at night and push down the autobahn rapidly toward Berlin. With only 60 miles or less to go they could have reached Berlin by daylight the next morning. The remainder of the Army would have followed of course. My mistake was in not doing this more promptly immediately after we got across the Elbe.
>
> I was completely surprised and chagrined when Bradley ordered me to stop and withdraw back across the Elbe.
>
> I really believe that the Ninth Army could have captured Berlin with little loss well before the Russians reached the city.[28]

Bradley's mood was very different. At one point, Major Hansen recorded, Simpson had telephoned to say he expected to capture a bridge at Magdeburg intact. "I almost hoped the other fellow would destroy it," Bradley confessed—and then, Ninth Army "called me this afternoon to tell me they had—thank Gawd, there's no need to worry about a bridgehead there."[29]

39: The National Redoubt

To the extent that Eisenhower and Bradley could offer, then and later, a rational strategic argument—as distinguished from political reasons and inflated casualty estimates—for leaving Berlin to the Russians, their case rested on the German National Redoubt and the necessity to cut short its development lest the Nazis prolong the war for months or even years.

In September 1944, when the Western Allies had first dreamed that their armies were about to rush into Berlin, the Office of Strategic Services agency in Bern, Switzerland—the American intelligence listening-post closest to Germany—had warned of another center of Nazi authority and resistance besides the capital. In the mountains of the Salzkammergut on the old German-Austrian border, centering upon Hitler's mountain retreat at Berchtesgaden in the Obersalzberg, said Allen Dulles's Bern office of the OSS, the Nazis had begun preparing a redoubt whose subjugation could be difficult enough to extend the war as much as two years. Great stores of arms, ammunition, food, and fuel were being gathered; underground factories were carved from the mountain depths; elite, fanatical troops were earmarked to accompany the Führer and his lieutenants into almost impenetrable fastnesses whence to continue the war to the disintegration of the Grand Alliance and a Nazi recovery, or to Götterdämmerung.

On September 22, 1944, the Washington headquarters of the OSS similarly reported, in a detailed study of south Germany, that Nazi government agencies were being shifted to this mountain retreat and that the transfer was expected to accelerate as the Allied armies closed in on Berlin.

With Eisenhower's armies stalled at the West Wall, the Nazis did not need to retreat to the Salzkammergut in the autumn of 1944. During the autumn and winter, persisting reports of their preparation of an eventual National Redoubt were diluted in Allied headquarters by a considerable dose of skepticism. Yet Eisenhower believed by the spring of 1945 that "the strong possibility still existed that fanatical Nazis would attempt to establish themselves in the National Redoubt, and the early overrunning of that area remained important to us." Bradley's thoughts turned to the National Redoubt when his troops crossed the Rhine at Remagen. "Bradley believes," his aide, Major Hansen, recorded then, "and is convinced that we shall have to fight the Germans in the mountain fastnesses of southern Germany and there destroy the core of his SS units which are determined to carry on the battle." In early April, as Simpson's spearheads approached the Elbe and Bradley actually grew irritated at the thought of their capturing Elbe bridges, his irritation sprang in part from "the theory that the Germans, conforming to the Nazi intent to resist to the last man and the last village, will fall back into the Redoubt.

where with approximately twenty SS divisions supplied thru a system of underground factories and supported by aircraft from underground hangers [they] could presumably hold out for a year."[1]

General Strong, SHAEF G-2 and as shrewd an intelligence analyst as the Allies had, was among the skeptical; yet he pointed out that the Führer's purpose might be to create through a fighting, unconquered finale a legend of immortal Nazism, to plant the seeds from which his movement might some day rise up all over Germany again.

On March 10, 1945 the SHAEF Joint Intelligence Committee attempted a balanced assessment of the threat of the Redoubt but ended by tempering realism with pessimism. After the battles of annihilation insisted upon by Eisenhower west of the Rhine and the envelopment of the Ruhr, the committee predicted, "the German army in the West may well cease to exist as a cohesive force." Nevertheless, the Allies must still plan "on the assumption that some resistance may continue since there will be formations which may still be intact on the Southern part of the front. . . . At this stage, however, the enemy's forces are likely to be in such a state of confusion that resistance except by SS, panzer and parachute formations or guerilla groups will be negligible." The appropriate strategy must still take into account the potential represented by those remaining cohesive forces and by the geography of southern Germany:

> 8. There have been numerous reports that Hitler and the Nazi leaders, supported by SS units, young Nazi fanatics and Quislings, are planning to make a last stand in the so-called Redoubt in western Austria. . . . it is unlikely that large-scale preparations for organized military resistance are being made.
> 9. We should therefore be prepared to undertake operations in Southern Germany in order to overcome rapidly any organized resistance by the German armed forces or by guerilla movements which may have retreated to the inner zone and to this redoubt. . . .[2]

Later in the month, on March 25, the G-2 section of Patch's Seventh Army issued a "Study of the German National Redoubt" that breathed further life into Allied fears by concluding that there was hard evidence of Hitler's intention to stand finally in an Alpine Redoubt. Yet Patch's G-2 himself, Colonel William W. Quinn, whose lines to sources inside Germany were probably the best of any of the field army G-2s, believed many of the reports of active preparations were fanciful.

The next few days witnessed the Seventh Army's crossings of the Rhine and the virtual collapse of Army Group G in front of Patch's men. On March 31, Devers's 6th Army Group G-2, Brigadier General Eugene L. Harrison, seconded Quinn by remarking that if the enemy could not contain the Allied bridgeheads beyond the southern Rhine, he must already be too badly shattered to form a redoubt. The northern German armies, Harrison was sure, would be kept too fully occupied by the encirclement of the Ruhr to help Army Group G. The connection between Army Group G and the northern armies had already been broken anyway, the Germans were proving themselves incapable of restoring the breach, and they lacked the means to rebuild. In their Army Group G, their Seventh Army was foundering; their First Army at the least needed thorough refitting and was being beaten along the Rhine; and their Nineteenth Army, reduced practically to a training command after its loss of the Colmar pocket, had to defend a 100-mile front along the upper Rhine and could only withdraw or await envelopment. "The turn of

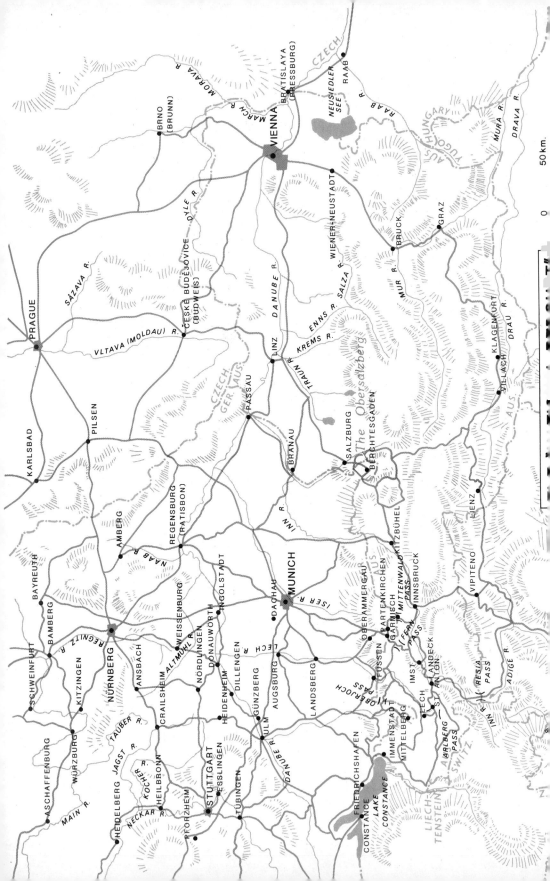

military events is effectively destroying the 'National Redoubt' for want of both territory and personnel."[3]

So Allied intelligence opinion was shifting away from fear of the Redoubt at the very time when Eisenhower and Bradley were making their crucial decisions affecting Berlin. SHAEF's Joint Intelligence Committee followed opinion from the field. On April 10, this body concluded: "There is no evidence to show that the strategy of the German High Command is being conducted with a view to occupying eventually the so-called National Redoubt." Of course, the JIC acknowledged, the Allied strategy of charging across central Germany to a meeting with the Russians and thus splitting the German forces would produce a natural tendency for part of the surviving armies to retreat southward. "Thus the National Redoubt would become occupied by selected remnants of the German Army from the Western and Eastern fronts and also the Italian front." But the Redoubt actually contained negligible industrial resources, lacked the agricultural means to support an increased population, and "It is clear . . . that the area is not one which could support large forces for any length of time even if, as is improbable, large quantities of supplies have been dumped."[4]

Still, on April 20 the SHAEF JIC reported further that as the Allied forces moved across central Germany toward the Soviets, "the enemy has tended to withdraw his forces to the south rather than to the north of the Allied wedge." Excluding eight divisions cut off in Holland, only thirteen German divisions now faced the Anglo-Americans from eastern Holland to Magdeburg, including the forces in Denmark. Another twenty-nine divisions confronted the Russians north of the Allied wedge. These troops might have as many as 500 tanks. South of the wedge, however, and including the divisions fighting the Russians as well as fourteen in Yugoslavia that would be difficult to extricate, the enemy retained 103 divisions. These included two-thirds of the SS divisions and three-fourths of the remaining armor in thirty panzer-type divisions, with possibly as many as 2,000 tanks. A retreat from Italy could add still more to the German strength in Austria and the Redoubt. Granting the weakness of many of the nominal German divisions, the high proportion of the enemy's remaining strength concentrated south of the wedge called for an Allied response aimed southward.[5] Thus, intelligence estimates concerning the National Redoubt remained a mixed and confusing bag to the last—or beyond their last major relevance, because, the turn to optimism among the G-2s earlier in April notwithstanding, Eisenhower and Bradley had already moved their armies as though the threat of the Redoubt merited a high strategic priority, higher than Berlin.

The Battle of the Neckar

The skepticism of Patch's and Devers's G-2s about the threat also notwithstanding, it would have seemed that once the Supreme Commander decided on a high strategic priority for destroying the enemy in the south, the 6th Army Group must carry a lion's share of the effort.

On March 31, accordingly, Devers sent his G-3, General Jenkins, to SHAEF to review with Eisenhower's staff the 6th Army Group's plan for its perhaps uncommonly important mission. Devers proposed to send the right wing of his Seventh Army attacking south and southeast behind the rear of most of the German First Army and all of the Nineteenth Army. Thus he would cut off the southern Germans from any withdrawal into the Redoubt. The French First Army would then drive south along the east bank of the Rhine to mop up the Germans.

Eisenhower's fear of the Redoubt might be acute enough to help divert him from Berlin as "the main prize," but the trouble with Devers's plan was that this fear was insufficient to persuade Eisenhower that Devers merited a role possibly approaching Bradley's in its conspicuousness. SHAEF rejected the plan and ordered instead that Devers should advance the Seventh Army as a right-flank guard for the 12th Army Group sweep across central Germany. Patch's troops should roll deep into Germany to the Nürnberg area. Only after completing this contribution to Bradley's security should they turn southeast to attack down the valley of the Danube to Linz in Austria, "to prevent consolidation of German resistance in the south."[6]

So much did Eisenhower's strategy in early April emphasize the offensive of his favored, Central Group of Armies rather than any help Devers could offer against the threat of the Redoubt, that Devers's army group received territorial responsibilities considerably disproportionate to its numbers. Because none of the Anglo-American commanders believed they could count on the French First Army as equivalent to an equal number of American divisions, SHAEF's and Devers's planners alike would impose most of the work of any 6th Army Group offensive on Patch. But the weakness of the French combined with the northeastward concentration of the 12th Army Group stretched the Seventh Army front to some 190 kilometers, more than twice the frontage of any of Bradley's armies. Devers and Patch, accommodating as usual, decided that the enemy's infirmities warranted their attacking nevertheless with all of Patch's corps and across the whole width of his front. In the sequel, the Seventh Army proved to be spread so thin that the Germans could still cause it exceptional trouble.

Patch's army was already attacking out of its Rhine bridgeheads when SHAEF decreed it must direct its offensive on Nürnberg. Frederick's 45th Division of Haislip's XV Corps moved out on March 28 across the railroad bridge just south of Aschaffenburg that had been captured by the 4th Armored Division of Patton's army—the bridge whence the Hammelburg raid had begun. Milburn's XXI Corps struck the same day through the Odenwald toward Würzburg. At the same time Brooks's VI Corps sallied from the Worms bridgehead to capture Mannheim and thence to turn southeast across the relatively open plateau called the Kreichgau Gate between the Odenwald and the Black Forest, heading for Heilbronn.

The XV Corps discovered that the enemy had lately shifted a division or so to oppose it and to contain the Aschaffenburg bridgehead. Together with Hitler Youth and another of those rare civilian risings such as the Ninth Army would encounter at Hameln, the reinforcements obliged the 157th Infantry of Frederick's division to wage a hard fight for the town of Aschaffenburg. But the rest of Haislip's corps moved instead into another near-vacuum, a gap opened between the German Seventh and First Armies because the former had shifted north in a vain effort to maintain contact with Army Group B. The woods were thick, the roads winding, and an occasional roadblock barred the way, but by April 3 Major General Albert Smith's 14th Armored Division was in Lohr beyond two additional crossings of the looping Main.

The XXI Corps received a little more resistance from the right wing of the enemy's First Army, but by March 31 Roderick Allen's 12th Armored Division had emerged from the Odenwald, and the next day it captured Generalleutnant Ralph Graf von Oriola, whose XIII Corps was crumbling before it. On April 1 and 2 an SS antiaircraft replacement regiment with a battalion of 88s forced a bitter contest for Königshofen, the scene of the first suppression of the Peasants' War in Martin Luther's time. By April 2, nevertheless, all three of Milburn's divisions were facing the loop of the Main that embraces Würzburg, and Blakeley's 4th Infantry Division won a crossing at the southern end of the loop, above the city.

It was the VI Corps that chiefly paid the penalty for the stretching of the Seventh Army front—the same fate that had befallen this corps in January. At first, Brooks's right and center advanced as readily as the XV and XXI Corps; but the left column of Morris's 10th Armored Division, moving through the southern fringe of the Odenwald to maintain contact with Milburn's corps, early encountered bothersome harassment from those old friends, the 17th SS Panzer Grenadier Division. By the time Brooks's corps approached the northward-facing arc formed by the Neckar River and its tributary the Jagst east of Heilbronn, clashes with stubborn SS panzer grenadiers were growing more widespread.

Early on April 4, the 3rd Battalion of the 398th Infantry in Burress's 100th Division crossed the Neckar in assault boats just below Heilbronn, but a counterattack isolated and captured two platoons and almost threw the rest of the Americans back into the stream. The crossing of the 2/397th in the afternoon permitted the bridgehead to hold, but barely. The next morning the 3/397th also crossed; but without tanks or direct heavy fire support the bridgehead could not expand enough to allow the engineers to build a bridge, and without a bridge General Burress could not cross tanks and artillery. The 1/397th meanwhile grasped another tiny bridgehead some three kilometers southward and closer to the center of Heilbronn; but it too provoked a reaction, uncommonly ferocious for this stage of the war, involving the harshly clanking arrival of four Tigers and the sharp crack of their 88s. On April 6, XII TAC eliminated two of the Tigers, but this small success was not decisive. The next day the engineers had nearly completed a treadway bridge into the southern bridgehead, when enemy artillery knocked it out.

Armored infantrymen of the 10th Armored fared no better in trying to advance a tiny bridgehead beyond the Jagst, and Brooks had to concede that the German First Army had somehow contrived to establish a genuine defensive front against him along the Neckar-Jagst crescent. Not only the 17th SS Panzer Grenadiers but the 2nd Mountain Division stiffened the usual hodgepodge of divisional fragments and Volkssturm, all under the command of an abruptly revitalized German XIII Corps. Brooks decided to deal with these unwonted developments by dint of a classic bold maneuver, a double envelopment. He sent the 10th Armored's CCB southwest along the Neckar in search of a bridge. The rest of Morris's division went southeast into the area between the Jagst and the Tauber Rivers, CCR to block any German foray across the Jagst, CCA to circle through Crailsheim and take the enemy's defensive arc from the rear, hoping to meet CCB to close the circle.

Starting out on April 5, CCA moved into Crailsheim late the next day, advancing against the customary scattered roadblocks. As the combat command pushed west from Crailsheim on April 7, however, it gradually stalled against growing resistance from entrenched infantry and antitank guns. CCR, following behind to protect CCA's line of communication, similarly found the path closing before it, as German soldiers emerged from flanking woods firing Panzerfäuste, and even the Luftwaffe mounted sporadic strikes. CCR was unable to push into Crailsheim. Meanwhile the garrison left by CCA in that city came under attack from an SS training battalion, and on April 8 the SS broke the garrison's defensive cordon. The main body of CCA was almost cut off.

Furthermore, CCB had found no bridge over the Neckar. Thereupon Morris turned CCB around to retrace CCA's route and bring it relief. His double envelopment scratched, Brooks lowered his sights for the remaining prong of his pincers, cancelling CCA's drive west toward Heilbronn for a shallower envelopment northwest from Crailsheim along the rear of the enemy's Jagst River line. This modest program promised to be difficult enough, for the Crailsheim garrison was barely fending off destruction at the hands of the SS. Sixty C-47s were called on to deliver supplies to CCA by landing on a captured airfield just outside Crailsheim. While they were on the field, the C-47s became the objects of further Luftwaffe attacks.

On April 10 C-47s flew another supply mission, while the arrival of CCB around Crailsheim greatly improved the security of ground communications. Nevertheless, the vanguard of CCA found that blown bridges were impeding even its limited envelopment, so the relevant commanders decided to restrict the 10th Armored's immediate task to a short stab northwest to make contact with Hibbs's 63rd Division fighting along the Jagst River. Together with the 100th Division, the 63rd had crossed the Jagst on April 5 and 6 but had achieved only the slowest progress against the rejuvenated German resistance. At Jagstfeld, where the Jagst and Neckar meet, the 63rd required an hour's artillery bombardment to soften a single factory enough to enter it, and then the Americans found the bodies of fifty-eight SS defenders inside.

CCA made contact with Hibbs's division before April 10 was over; but the salient the armor had driven into Crailsheim no longer seemed worth holding, and the 10th Armored retreated from Crailsheim the next night before the amazed eyes of German spectators, grown unaccustomed to even local victories. Once slow to take advantage of opportunities for envelopment, the American army now took it too much for granted that it could race through German positions and cut off bag after bag of prisoners. Between Heilbronn and Crailsheim the Americans essayed a double envelopment too lightly, without sufficient appraisal of the enemy First Army's ability to reinforce the Neckar-Jagst crescent. Now, the VI Corps reverted to frontal attacks.

At Heilbronn the battle had already come to that. On the morning of April 10, the engineers at length completed a treadway bridge into Burress's southern bridgehead, and a company of tanks and two platoons of tank destroyers crossed before German guns knocked the bridge out again about noon. Two days later the enemy artillery also wrecked a ponton ferry, just after it had carried across a few more tanks and tank destroyers. But with the help of the armor already on the south bank, the 100th Division linked its two Heilbronn bridgeheads soon afterward, and by April 12 the city was finally cleared. The battle was less bloody than it was frustrating; in nine days of fighting among Heilbronn's factories and railroad tracks, the Century Division lost eighty-five killed and about three times that number wounded. The division captured 1,500 prisoners.

General Brooks now made a last attempt at an envelopment along the Neckar-Jagst line by driving with the 63rd Division and part of the 10th Armored to meet the 100th east of Heilbronn in hopes of cutting off the 17th SS Panzer Grenadiers in the triangle formed by the two rivers. The pincers closed two days after the capture of Heilbronn, but without netting any considerable bag of panzer grenadiers.

The Battle of Nürnberg

The frustrations of the VI Corps did not prevent the XV and XXI Corps, stretched though they also were, from charging on deeper into Germany and fulfilling the Seventh Army's responsibility to protect the right flank of the 12th Army Group. In front of Haislip's and Milburn's corps, the German LXXXII and XIII ss Corps could still muster only sporadic efforts to take advantage of the Seventh Army's excessively broad front. CCB of Smith's 14th Armored Division liberated the remaining Hammelburg prisoners on April 6, including Patton's son-in-law, Colonel Waters; but most of the unwounded American prisoners had been marched away. On April 7 O'Daniel's 3rd and Frederick's 45th Divisions of Haislip's corps cleared the wooded hills of the Hohe Rhön to make possible a firm juncture with the Third Army's right flank in the Thüringerwald. Meanwhile General Harry Collins's 42nd Division of Milburn's corps, having completed a three-day battle to clear Würzburg, moved forward to reinforce Roderick Allen's 12th Armored in a final assault on Schweinfurt. Yet another improvised formation of German military students had been holding the 12th Armored at bay since April 5 outside this manufacturing center famous for the costly Eighth Air Force raids against its ball-bearing plants in August and October 1943. With the Rainbow Division on hand, the armor crossed the Main again to cut the principal highway southeast out of Schweinfurt, infantry circled north to block other escape routes, the 9th Bombardment Division administered a final aerial pasting, and Schweinfurt fell on April 11.

The XV and XXI Corps now had to turn southeast more directly toward Nürnberg to avoid colliding with the Third Army's eastward procession on the far side of the Thüringerwald. Because another of the events of April 11 was the Ninth Army's arrival at the Elbe, the 12th Army Group offensive through central and north-central Germany was now assured of about as much success as the Supreme Commander intended to permit it, and the American planners consequently directed their thoughts toward a more general southeasterly shift for the postponed business of dealing with the reputed National Redoubt. On April 15, SHAEF issued a new strategic directive, designed to make Patch's Nürnberg attack the foundation of a major southward and southeastward offensive, but also to bring Bradley's army group conspicuously onto the south German scene and into the completion of that offensive. Bradley was to hold the Ninth and First Armies along the Elbe and the Mulde but to turn a reinforced Third Army down the Danube into Austria to Salzburg. For this large-scale right turn, SHAEF moved the boundary between Bradley's and Devers's army groups west back to Würzburg and thence southeast to enter Austria midway between Munich and Salzburg. Thus Devers was to drive from Nürnberg into western Austria. While Bradley and Patton were assured much of whatever glory might lie in squelching the National Redoubt, Devers this time was dealt with not altogether ungenerously. At least he would no longer be overstretched—the width of his front was reduced by about eighty kilometers—and SHAEF offered him the First Airborne Army should he want it, while specifically giving him the new 13th Airborne Division for an airborne assault south of Stuttgart.

Meanwhile, the immediate consequence of the southward turn was to bring Patch's Seventh Army into the teeth of yet another uncommonly strong defensive position. By extricating most of the defenders of the Neckar-Jagst line, the German First Army had been able to assemble in front of Nürnberg some 15,000 men, twenty artillery battalions, and 200 tanks and assault guns, to supplement another flak alley of heavy antiaircraft guns, all commanded by the XIII ss Corps. On April 2 the Führer had sacked General Hausser of Army Group G for failing to contain the American and French upper Rhine bridgeheads. The new enemy army group commander, General der Infanterie Heinrich Schulz, another transfer from the Eastern Front, evidently hoped to buy time against the Americans' predictable new emphasis on the south both through a stout defense of Nürnberg and through another effort to close the gap on his right flank between the German First and Seventh Armies. Toward that gap Schulz began moving both the 17th ss Panzer Grenadier and the 2nd Mountain Divisions. Patch's attack hit Nürnberg before these still-respectable formations could make their way farther northeast, so Schulz had to settle for their joining the defense of the city. Finally, whatever the tactical considerations, a stout defense of Nürnberg was implicit in the aura of the city as a shrine to the Führer and the Nazi faith.

O'Daniel's 3rd and Frederick's 45th Divisions of Haislip's XV Corps paused to clear Bamberg on April 12 and 13, while the 106th Cavalry Group probed ahead along the Bamberg-Nürnberg highway. Covering the fifty kilometers from Bamberg to the outskirts of Nürnberg during the next two days, the 3rd Division was closing in on the city of Melanchthon and Dürer from the north by April 16, the 45th Division from the east and southeast. Meanwhile the Rainbow Division of Milburn's corps approached from the west. Haislip directed Albert Smith's 14th Armored Division on the XV Corps left to swing wide to the south to screen the attack against German reinforcement. Fortunately, the presence of the armor drew out from the city Gruppe Grafenwöhr, an improvised panzer force built around thirty-five tanks and the personnel of the Grafenwöhr panzer training center; the move gave Smith's tanks an opportunity to kill off a good slice of the defending armor, which the 14th Armored proceeded to do within two days.

The loss of Gruppe Grafenwöhr was scarcely enough, however, to dissuade the Nürnberg garrison from demanding a bruising fight for the city, all the more depressing to the Americans because they saw the war's outcome as assured and such persistently fanatical resistance as absurd. To have to die against such resistance in the final days would be still more absurd. Such reflections were generating a new caution among the American infantry now that there remained no incentive comparable to the race for Berlin. More than ever, the GIs preferred to let artillery and fighter-bombers clear their paths for them. Against Nürnberg, the American artillery worked overtime, and XII TAC's Mustangs flew in a constant stream overhead. The ring of flak guns nevertheless persisted for day after day in murderous reply; and once the Americans had scrambled past the guns they had to return to the deadly old game of house-to-house combat. From building to building and floor to floor, wily ss panzer grenadiers, mountain troops, and Luftwaffe men continually allowed Americans to work past them, only to pounce from the rear.

Not until April 19 did the veteran 30th Infantry Regiment of the Rock of the Marne Division seize the north gate of the medieval wall for the first opening into Old Nürnberg. The 7th Infantry joined in breaching the wall next day. The 3rd Division's remaining regiment, the 15th, grappled into the inner city against civilians as well as soldiers wielding grenade-throwers and Panzerfäuste. By late on April 20—Hitler's birthday—organized resistance had shrunk at last to about 200 Germans barricaded in a tunnel. These die-hards were pried out soon after midnight.

At least the battle brought the satisfaction of accomplishing the virtual destruction of the 17th ss Panzer Grenadier Division; the self-proclaimed heirs of the Peasants' War revolutionary Götz von Berlichingen had harried the Americans almost nonstop since Normandy, but they would do so no more. With this division and the equally mauled 2nd Mountain Division went any chance that General Schulz might reanchor the German First Army's right wing. Breaking loose from Nürnberg, the XV and XXI Corps found traveling the eighty remaining kilometers to the Danube little more than a route march.

Roderick Allen's 12th Armored Division of the XXI Corps was first to reach the great river of central and eastern Europe, crossing it over an intact bridge at Dillingen on April 22. Milburn's infantry and Haislip's corps arrived at the river on April 25.

Patton Turns Southward

The collapse of the right wing of the German First Army also left the old gap between that army and the enemy's Seventh Army yawning wider than ever for the American Third Army to plunge into it, as Patton turned toward Austria. For his and through him Bradley's part in the elimination of the National Redoubt, Patton was to be reinforced to fifteen divisions, including strength easily spared by the First and Ninth Armies as they settled down to await the Russians on the Mulde and the Elbe. For geographic convenience, Patton yielded Middleton's VIII Corps with five divisions to the First Army, to stand on the Mulde, while Hodges gave him Van Fleet's III Corps with six divisions, coming out of the Ruhr. In Middleton, Patton lost "the best tactician" among his corps commanders—the First Army regaining "our old favorite General Middleton"[7]—but for once Patton was willing to feel himself adequately compensated rather than persecuted.

He would have been less satisfied had he known that Bradley's caution about what might lie in wait in the National Redoubt extended so far that, had logistical complexities not prevented it, Bradley would have shifted "the First Army down behind the Third to use that army [the First] in his drive to the southeast and turn the campaign over to the deliberate direction of Hodges."[8] As it was, Patton met with both Bradley and Devers at Bradley's latest tactical headquarters at Wiesbaden on April 16 to thrash out the changes required by SHAEF's transfer of the main responsibility for the Redoubt from Devers to Bradley the day before. The Third Army came out favored yet again. The three generals agreed that rather than waste time relieving the Seventh Army divisions around Nürnberg which the SHAEF directive placed in the Third Army zone, these divisions should go about their business at Nürnberg and then by moving directly south let their advance carry them into their new boundaries; but as a supplementary decision, it was later confirmed that Smith's 14th Armored Division seemed so far east that it should be added to Patton's army, as part of the III Corps when Van Fleet came into line. Patch was eventually to get one of the new armored divisions in compensation.

So all the arrangements of which Patton was aware added to a mood of ebullience. Because of geography, he would not have been able to be the conqueror of Berlin no matter what Eisenhower decided about the German capital; he disagreed with Eisenhower's decision, but for his own army the new emphasis on the National Redoubt was better. If the Redoubt proved nonexistent—which Patton suspected—then another ancient capital might come within reach: Prague. Patton had seemed subdued for a few days after the Hammelburg affair, not so much because he recognized anything unseemly in the affair as because he feared another newspaper furor to reinjure his career; but the danger quickly passed, and as Major Hansen saw him, "he was robust again. 'What the hell,' he said [on April 13], 'with the President's death you could execute buggery in the streets and get no farther than the fourth page.' "[9]

Hammelburg had blown over so completely, in fact, that Patton could kick off the new campaign as a full general. He learned from the *Stars and Stripes* over breakfast on April 18 that President Truman had nominated him for his fourth star to rank from April 14. "While I am glad to be a full general, I would have appreciated it more had I been in the initial group, as I never had an ambition to be an also-ran."[10] That is, Hodges also became a full general, as of April 15. But the disappointment was small; Bradley's staff saw Patton once more as bursting with cocky self-assurance, "again a gorgeous Georgie with his enameled helmet, the brass buttoned battle jacket and his initialled gun at his hip with a long H. Upmann in his mouth."[11]

The Third Army moved out the day after Patton read about his impending promotion. By the time the III Corps formally entered the line on April 23, its newly acquired 14th Armored Division as well as Walker's XX Corps were within sixty-five kilometers of the Danube southeast of Nürnberg. The XII Corps was now under the veteran 5th Division commander General Irwin, because Eddy had yielded after prolonged resistance to medical relief forced by high blood pressure; by April 23 Irwin's corps was south of the Nürnberg-Pilsen highway. "The country here," Patton wrote his wife of the Fränkische Highland through which his troops moved, "is the most beautiful I have ever seen. All the trees are in bloom and there are yellow fields of mustard."[12] There were few hostile troops, but the moving columns still had to guard against the occasional roadblock or the ambush sprung against rear elements by bypassed Germans.

Though the latest shifting of commands had left the XX Corps without an armored division, Walker in the army center reached the Danube first, the 3rd Cavalry Group striking the river at Regensburg in the early afternoon of April 24. Three divisions of the III Corps on the army right—Smith's 14th Armored, Melasky's 86th, Lauer's 99th—arrived at the Danube on April 26; so did Paul's 26th Division of the XII Corps. Except in the XII Corps, which was to continue downstream between the Danube and the Czech border into Austria, crossings followed promptly. The XX Corps gratified Patton's sense of history by capturing the famous fortress of Ratisbon on the south bank on April 26. The next day, Van Fleet's corps collided with a pocket of resistance beyond the river southeast of Ingolstadt: Division Nibelungen, a youthful force much like the Division Scharnhorst that had troubled the 2nd Armored on the Elbe, and in fact originally intended for the German Twelfth Army and the defense of Berlin. But while Division Nibelungen entered battle nearly at full strength in manpower, it had only a few prewar tanks and no artillery, and within three days the III Corps destroyed it. With this force out of the way, Patton's army rolled on to find that increasingly the towns and cities as well as the countryside offered no resistance. White sheets hung everywhere in token of submission.

Troublesome Allies

Triumphs were accumulating rapidly enough, and with a few exceptions painlessly enough, that the Grand Alliance could afford an interlude of opéra bouffe. The Seventh

Army's turn southward practically restored Devers's original plan to cut the lines of communication of the German Nineteenth Army and the remnants of the First and isolate those forces in the Black Forest. Thus Devers directed Brooks's VI Corps on Patch's right to advance up the Neckar past Stuttgart to Tübingen, and thence south to Lake Constance and the Swiss border. The French First Army was then to sweep up the trapped Germans, with Brooks's troops giving such help as might be necessary.

While the VI Corps circled around Stuttgart—swiftly enough as usual that the promised airborne assistance was not required—General de Lattre's French army had the additional task of actually capturing the city; but Devers cautioned de Lattre not to move in too quickly lest the Nineteenth Army be frightened eastward to clutter the roads in front of Brooks and possibly to escape the trap. Devers also wanted the VI Corps to be able to move beyond Stuttgart rapidly and unimpeded because the corps was to be accompanied by a special intelligence mission, codenamed ALSOS, whose purpose was to investigate reported German nuclear experiments at Hechingen, eighty kilometers southwest of Stuttgart, and among other things to keep any nuclear information out of the hands of the French.

By this stage of the war, Devers cannot have been surprised when de Lattre turned out to have different ideas. When Devers issued his instructions on April 16, the French II Corps had already advanced out of its Rhine bridgeheads to capture the arc formed by the Enz River and the Neckar, and thus to advance within twenty kilometers of Stuttgart. On April 15, furthermore, the 5ème Division Blindée having charged up the right bank of the Rhine to a point opposite Strasbourg, the French I Corps crossed the river there and sent part of its strength straight east to split the Black Forest, while other elements drove up the Rhine to make additional penetrations of the Schwarzwald farther south. When de Lattre received his latest orders from Devers, he feared that it would be his own traps that would not close upon the Germans if he adhered to the instructions; so on April 17 he issued quite different orders for an immediate double envelopment of Stuttgart from the northwest and southwest and for another double envelopment of the area of the Black Forest lying south of Strasbourg. As de Lattre saw it, to wait for the Americans, who at this time were still more than thirty kilometers from Stuttgart, would be to acquiesce in a German escape both from Stuttgart and from the Black Forest.

On April 18 the French army defied Devers by plunging into the Seventh Army zone to capture Tübingen on their way to Stuttgart. The French maneuver split the LXIV Corps of the Nineteenth Army, but the threat of entrapment evidently provoked the bulk of the corps, north of Tübingen, to dig in its heels; for on April 19 and 20 the French sustained only slow and difficult progress north toward Stuttgart. This development restored the principal initiative to the Americans. While it was the VI Corps's 63rd and 100th Divisions that had barely been able to make headway on April 16–18, on April 19 the 10th Armored Division of Brooks's corps broke loose and advanced some fifty kilometers, circling east of Stuttgart. The next day the armor cut the Stuttgart-Ulm Autobahn at Kirchheim.

So despite the disorderly rivalry between French and Americans, a trap was about to close after all. The Germans now had only one main highway between Kirchheim and the French over which to extricate their LXXX as well as most of the LXIV Corps. The former, which had been defending north of Stuttgart, made a hasty and relatively successful withdrawal during the night of April 20–21; but the LXIV Corps was broken up and destroyed by combined American and French action, and its commander soon found himself a captive of the French.

The combination of a fait accompli with a substantial French victory persuaded Devers to shift the interarmy boundary to legitimate de Lattre's movements, though he continued to believe that adhering to orders would have produced a bigger bag of prisoners. The French had meanwhile pushed ahead of the ALSOS mission toward Hechingen, but the mission corrected this problem by hastening through and to the head of the French columns, bluffing their way past inquisitive French checkpoints, to reach Hechingen in time to be the first of the Allies into the research center.

On April 22 the French captured Stuttgart, which set the stage for yet another contretemps. So that French possession of this road center would not impede the Seventh Army's plunge into Austria, Devers had ordered that Patch's forces should have running rights over its main highways. The French army's habitual insubordination, plus the presence in the city of thousands of foreign laborers celebrating their liberation, including 20,000 Frenchmen, led Devers immediately upon Stuttgart's capture to transfer it to American control, effective April 23, as the only means of assuring Patch's running rights. De Lattre protested and reported the situation to General de Gaulle, who in turn ordered him to remain and set up a French military government. Stuttgart became a pawn in de Gaulle's effort to secure a French zone of occupation and a French share of the control machinery in postwar Germany. The only balm for Devers in this latest interallied crisis was that it swiftly became a political matter, the province of Eisenhower, the Combined Chiefs, and the highest interallied councils. As for Stuttgart, "Under the circumstances," Eisenhower told de Gaulle, "I must of course accept the situation, as I myself am unwilling to take any action which would reduce the effectiveness of the military effort against Germany. . . ."[13]

The more strictly military manifestations of French insubordination went on plaguing Devers with headaches enough. After capturing Stuttgart, according to Devers's orders, de Lattre was to concentrate on destroying what was left of the Nineteenth Army and clearing the Black Forest. Devers took pains to draw the interarmy boundaries in such a way that the French would have an avenue into Austria, to assuage another of de Gaulle's concerns. But this latter bow to French sensitivity did not suffice. In addition to his specified duties, de Lattre was intent on capturing yet another objective, which happened to lie within the Seventh Army zone. This was the famous imperial fortress of Ulm, on the Danube eighty kilometers southeast of Stuttgart, where the renaissance of French military power might appropriately reach a climax in the unfurling of the tricolor once more over the very battlements that Napoleon had conquered in 1805. The troubles residing in de Lattre's design included sending the 5ème Blindée directly into the path of the 10th Armored Division as the VI Corps drove to the Danube, with the Americans ignorant of the French approach and a collision therefore in the cards.

Morris's division reached the river at Ehingen, just west of Ulm, late on April 22. The next morning the French arrived. Luckily, the Americans immediately recognized their errant allies and no shots were exchanged. According to the French, Morris said: "Among tankers, we always understand each other."[14] Though Devers was near the limits of his patience and ordered an immediate French withdrawal, de Lattre's troops blandly drove on eastward to join the Americans in attacking and capturing Ulm the next day. The tricolor snapped in the breeze above the old fort.

Into the Redoubt

Each of the Seventh Army's three corps was bagging an average of more than 1,000 prisoners a day. "Push on and push hard," General Brooks ordered the VI Corps. "This is a pursuit, not an attack."[15] As O'Daniel's 3rd Division of the XXI Corps approached Augsburg, Blakeley's nearby 4th Division sent word early on April 27 implying that O'Daniel's famous ferocity should perhaps be restrained, for two industrialists had arrived at Blakeley's command post to try to arrange the surrender of the ancient Roman city. Some of Augsburg's ring of flak batteries were still firing, but others sprouted white pillowcases from their barrels, and O'Daniel ordered a moratorium on American artillery fire until the situation clarified itself.

The Augsburg commandant, Generalmajor Franz Fehn, evidently intended to fight, but his garrison was evaporating and anti-Nazi underground groups were rising up to take control of one part of the city after another. While the negotiations with the businessmen sputtered, O'Daniel moved his infantry into the streets. Thereupon a civilian patrol greeted the 3rd Battalion of the 15th Infantry and offered to lead its commander to General Fehn's bunker. The Americans went and gave Fehn five minutes to surrender. Displaying little regard for their acumen, or their knowledge of German, the general tried to telephone for ss reinforcements while within their earshot. A GI pulled the phone away. Fehn then submitted to being marched out a prisoner, to see a white flag flying from the fifteenth-century Benedictine abbey of St. Ulric, the highest point in the city, and other sheets and handkerchiefs of white fluttering everywhere.

Harry Collins's 42nd and Frederick's 45th Divisions, like virtually all the advancing infantry motorized with borrowed and captured vehicles, led the XV Corps toward Munich, Germany's third city after Berlin and Hamburg and a Nazi shrine at least as sacred as Nürnberg. Splinters of the 2nd Mountain Division and some ss troopers stood in the way, but these chastened adversaries contented themselves with a skillful retreat— except on April 29 at the Dachau concentration camp, where the vanguard of the Rainbow Division had to overpower some 300 of the ss before seeing the "Freight cars full of piled cadavers . . . bloody heaps at the rail car doors where weakened prisoners, trying to get out, were machine-gunned to death . . . rooms stacked almost to the ceiling high with tangled human bodies. . . ."[16]

Major General Orlando Ward's 20th Armored Division, whose commander had led the 1st Armored in North Africa, presently rolled out in front of Haislip's corps; but the divisions felt a rivalry to be first into Munich, and the 42nd and 45th stayed barely behind the armor. General Patch also inserted the 3rd Division into the XV Corps to join the attack on Munich by coming down the Autobahn and Highway 2 from Augsburg. Smith's 12th Armored Division of the XXI Corps joined up with an unauthorized entry into the race, barreling toward Munich from the southwest.

Rumors proclaimed that a series of revolts like those in Augsburg had broken out in Munich during the night of April 27, and once more a delegation of citizens turned up to try to arrange a surrender. The insurgents saved Munich's bridges over the Isar River and gave welcome guidance to the Americans as they began to prowl into the streets. But the

Nazis rallied to hold or restore their control of many neighborhoods, and the Americans met a decidedly mixed reception. The 3rd and 42nd Divisions pushed into the center of the city on May 3 amidst white flags and cheering crowds. The 45th Division struck an SS school and caserne and had to attack with its three regiments abreast. The 180th Infantry in the division center and its attached armor were stopped cold at a railroad underpass; the 179th Infantry on Frederick's left suffered the same experience at the Munich-Ingolstadt Autobahn; and because an overcast prevented air support, the infantry called down 240mm. howitzer barrages to open the way forward again. The final fight in the caserne was an ugly room-to-room brawl.

While the XV Corps alternately paraded and fought its way into Munich, the XXI Corps in Patch's center drew up to the Alpine peaks that bar the way from Augsburg across the Austrian frontier to the valley of the Inn River, searching for adequate roads through the barrier. The VI Corps on the right had a slightly better roadnet, albeit winding through narrow passes and across precipitous gorges. So Brooks's men had already cleared the Passion Play town of Oberammergau and the ski resort of Garmisch-Partenkirchen, and on April 29 the 10th Armored and 44th Divisions captured Füssen and crossed into Austria. SHAEF had just confirmed the southern armies' final assignments against the National Redoubt: the Third Army to take Salzburg, block the passes from Salzburg into the Austrian Tyrol, and meet the Russians inside Austria; the 6th Army Group to capture all the other routes into the Alps, seize the Landeck and Innsbruck areas of Austria, and seal the Brenner Pass.

Within his army group, Devers drew the boundary between Patch's and de Lattre's armies through the town of Höfen, south of Füssen, to give the Seventh Army the main route to Landeck, running from Füssen through the Fern Pass. Devers alerted de Lattre to be ready to advance on Landeck, however, if the Seventh Army should be delayed, and de Lattre responded characteristically by ordering his troops on Landeck forthwith. Only by reaching Landeck and from it the Resia Pass could the French find a route that could bring them to the Italian border and the honor of joining hands with the Allied troops in Italy, where the French army had contributed skillfully and bravely to the great Battle of Monte Cassino. Thus commenced another unauthorized French race with the Americans.

When he heard of de Lattre's precipitate move against Landeck, Devers signaled the complete exhaustion of his patience by changing the interarmy boundary to transfer even the difficult secondary route to that town, the Oberjoch Pass, from de Lattre to Patch. Irrepressible as ever, de Lattre resorted to a yet more difficult route, south from Immenstadt directly up and over the Arlberg massif to St. Anton and the Arlberg Pass. Such persistence almost deserved the prize it sought. An improvised French ski platoon, hastily equipped, emerged into the Arlberg Pass on May 6 after a forty-kilometer trek through white wilderness. But thereupon the platoon placed a telephone call to Landeck, and the American 44th Division answered the phone.

The two corps of the Third Army that had crossed the Danube were running slightly behind the Seventh Army, mainly because of the III Corps's late commitment and a spell of bad weather following. Both the III and XX Corps reached the Inn River where it forms the Austrian border around Hitler's birthplace, Braunau, on May 1; but because the bulk of Patton's infantry was still too far behind his armored spearheads for the Third Army to launch an immediate drive on Salzburg, Patton agreed that day to Devers's proposal that Salzburg be awarded to the Seventh Army. This change would allow Milburn's XXI Corps to solve the problem of penetrating its peculiarly difficult Alpine front by shifting east to the Munich-Salzburg Autobahn—a process that Milburn had already taken it upon himself to begin. Milburn could head from Rosenheim south to Kitzbühel and east to Berchtesgaden, while Haislip's XV Corps drew the assignment of capturing Salzburg itself. General Eisenhower had been worrying that German troops fleeing before Patton might slip through the Salzburg Pass into the Redoubt, so to hasten the closing of this route the Supreme Commander agreed to the enlargement of Devers's task at the expense of Bradley's.

Devers negotiated the changes by radio and telephone without normal security precautions. He felt sure there was no longer any need for such precautions. The principal remaining problems were unseasonable cold and occasional snow and the clogging of the roads by masses of German soldiers looking for somebody who would accept their surrender. The garrison commandant of Salzburg emerged from Mozart's city on the morning of May 4 for his own search of that kind, and he found General O'Daniel, who accepted his capitulation as a cold wind whipped across the Maytime snow.

During the previous night General Patch had cut in on a telephone conversation between Haislip and O'Daniel to assure them to feel free to capture Berchtesgaden if they could. Therefore the XV Corps immediately swung back into Germany over the Salzburg Pass, aiming for Hitler's aerie. Recent additions to Milburn's XXI Corps, Leclerc's 2ème Blindée and Taylor's 101st Airborne, were already well on their way toward the same destination from the opposite direction. "Everybody and his brother are trying to get into the town," remarked Seventh Army headquarters.[17] Motorized task forces of O'Daniel's division arrived first, followed quickly by Leclerc's armor and troopers of the 101st. The soldiers relished tearing down the Nazi banners, but their conquest of the Obersalzberg on the way to Berchtesgaden on May 4 had the more important significance of sealing the last Alpine pass and killing the last smidgeon of a possibility of an Alpine Redoubt.

The spectacle of American and French divisions falling all over each other in this campaign, so numerous were they in proportion to the roads and the resistance, makes the weight assigned the campaign into the Redoubt appear all the more incongruous in comparison with the weakness of the spearheads that Eisenhower and Bradley extended so tentatively toward an objective the Germans still considered worth defending, Berlin. The disproportion can be explained, if no longer really comprehended, by noting that the American high command cherished its belief in the chimera of the Redoubt practically to the end, all contrary evidence and reason notwithstanding. As late as April 26, Major Hansen was recording at Bradley's headquarters: "The general feels strongly on the necessity for speed in his attack to the southeast to prevent the German army from concentrating forces for a last ditch stand in the south. If we can effect our union [with the Russians coming through Vienna] through Austria, he will have only forty divisions of the 100 below our [more northerly] linkup with the Russians with which to defend his fortress." On April 29:

> The General persists in his contention that the German will run to the redoubt with what ss units he can salvage from the front.
>
> "After the redoubt is reduced, however," he says, "it is entirely likely that the fellows up in Denmark and in Norway will see the end and surrender to us."

Unless the German government capitulates, the General is convinced the redoubt campaign may be a relatively costly one for the troops to be cleared.

"We cannot simply contain this area," he explains to the [labor] union delegates today. "People must look at this realistically and though they may not like the necessity of going into those hills to clean out the German—we've got to do it. As long as anyone is fighting down in the Redoubt, the myth of Nazism will be with the German people."[18]

Those Americans who were inside the supposed Redoubt could readily see that no serious preparations had ever been made for a prolonged last resistance there. Some lesser Nazi figures had dreamt of a romantic last stand in the Alps. But the principal importance of this notion for the major leaders came from the discovery by Josef Goebbels, the propaganda minister, that the Western Allies apparently somehow believed in the existence of a National Redoubt. Goebbels therefore decided to nourish the belief to misguide the Anglo-American strategists. Since late 1944, Nazi agents had been diligently selling the myth of the Redoubt, to curiously eager buyers. At the end of April, Bradley told visiting Congressmen that the war might go on for another year[19]—yet he had balked against attacking the true symbolic rallying point of German resistance, the Prussian capital.

40: The Elbe, the Moldau, and the Brenner Pass

WITH THE help of the Combined Chiefs of Staff, General Eisenhower had labored into late April to win further assurance from the Red Army that the meeting of the Soviets with the Western Allies would not be an armed collision. The Russians had suffered numerous bloody encounters with their allies of the time when their troops met the Germans in Poland in 1939, but their distrustful reluctance to dispense the slightest information about their movements and intentions overshadowed this memory. On April 21, General Hodges spent much of the day on the telephone trying to learn from the 12th Army Group "the procedure to be used in making contact with and greeting our Allies now fast approaching from the east," and Bradley's headquarters in turn prodded SHAEF. " . . . the instructions were finally received which consisted of 'treat them nicely.'"[1] Eisenhower eventually wrung from the Soviets agreements that the armies should advance from both west and east until contact or an actual linkup occurred, that the Soviets would fire red rockets and the Western Allies green rockets as recognition signals, and that both should acquaint their troops with each other's vehicle markings. The Soviets were not responsive to Eisenhower's proposal for an exchange of liaison officers.

The sketchiness of the arrangements naturally reinforced Eisenhower's decision to halt his Central Group of Armies along the Elbe and its southward extension, the Mulde. He confirmed this decision in a message to the Soviet high command on April 23, adding that he would nevertheless be willing to push on to Dresden should the Soviets desire to halt on the Elbe instead of the Mulde. The Soviets declined to accept this latter offer.

Strehla

Hodges's First Army had clawed its way through flak alley around Leipzig during the middle days of April. While Leonard's 9th Armored Division of Huebner's V Corps swung south around the antiaircraft guns to reach the Mulde on April 15 and cross via two intact bridges to seize Colditz on April 16, Robertson's 2nd and Reinhardt's 69th Divisions fought their way into Leipzig itself. There was certainly no singleminded attempt made to defend the city—the chief of police offered to surrender and the bridges over the Weisse Elster remained intact—but April 18 and 19 had to be given over to hard street fighting before the garrison commandant surrendered the last hard-core defenders and the V Corps infantry moved on to join the armor at the Mulde. In Collins's VII Corps farther north, Hickey's 3rd Armored Division found that its road to the junction of the Mulde and the Elbe at Dessau led to a rendezvous with Divisions Scharnhorst and Ulrich von Hutton of the Germans' new Twelfth Army on April 14. The outcome was continual battle with the zealous young troops of those formations throughout the next ten days, climaxing in a two-day house-to-house fight for Dessau and another day's battle for an Elbe crossing at Rosslau. During April 16–19, Terry Allen's 104th Division was engaged in a similar struggle for the university city of Halle, before it could close up to the Mulde on the 3rd Armored's right.

To the southward in the Third Army, Hoge's 4th Armored Division of Walker's XX Corps had reached the Mulde on April 13, the day after Eisenhower told Patton he would have to halt along that river short of Chemnitz. By nightfall, the 4th Armored had discovered four intact bridges and created east-bank bridgeheads large enough to protect them. Middleton's VIII Corps, advancing without benefit of an armored division, arrived at the Mulde only on April 17.

When Eisenhower completed such meager signal arrangements as he could with the Soviets, on April 21, these advances had given him, along with the 83rd Division bridgehead over the Elbe at Barby, a series of footholds across the Mulde. They were occupied by that time by Reinhardt's 69th and Robertson's 2nd Divisions east and southeast of Leipzig, Grow's 6th Armored and Schmidt's 76th Divisions northwest of Chemnitz, and Culin's 87th and Major General Thomas D. Finley's 89th Divisions just west of Chemnitz. In the Ninth Army, White's 2nd Armored and Hobbs's 30th Divisions' battle for Magdeburg on April 17–18 failed to reach the Elbe before the Germans blew the remaining bridges—much to the relief of Bradley, who did not want to be pestered by additional pressures to push on toward such a target as Berlin.

Indeed, Eisenhower and Bradley were inclined to regard the existing bridgeheads as nuisances likely to produce trouble. On April 24 the Soviet command deigned to respond to Eisenhower's latest message by informing him that the Red Army was beginning an advance on Chemnitz that day. Air support for this drive, the Russians said, would have to bomb and strafe as far west as the Mulde south to Rochlitz, south of which place the Russian airplanes would be willing to observe a bomb line, running along a railroad from Rochlitz to Chemnitz and thence all the way to Prague. Eisenhower felt obliged to order his bridgeheads withdrawn from beyond the Mulde below Rochlitz. Outposts and small patrols might remain east of the river to protect bridges and make contact with the Russians, but the patrols were to range no more than five miles beyond the Mulde.

Fighter-bomber and artillery liaison pilots were now reporting numerous sightings of Russians east of the Elbe, though most of these reports were dubious if not assuredly in error. On the night of April 23–24, Colonel Charles M. Adams's 273rd Infantry of Reinhardt's 69th Division had sent a force beyond the Mulde east of Leipzig because the burgomaster of Wurzen offered to surrender his town, including thousands of Allied prisoners and hundreds of German soldiers. The following afternoon Colonel Adams ordered 1st Lieutenant Albert L. Kotzebue of Company G to lead a thirty-five-man patrol in jeeps as far as Kühren, a little over six kilometers eastward, to try to contact the Russians. Finding nothing at Kühren, Kotzebue secured permission to proceed another three miles, though this journey would put him about two miles in front of SHAEF's new limits. Later he received two messages instructing him to return before dark; but because it was already dark when the messages reached him, he ignored them.

The next morning Colonel Adams sent out two additional patrols, both with instructions to observe the five-mile limit. A fourth patrol set out from Wurzen under the 1st Battalion S-2, but simply to look for more Allied prisoners and surrendering Germans, not to seek out the Russians. One of the two patrols dispatched by Adams that morning was the only one that actually observed the five-mile restriction. Kotzebue meanwhile was heading toward the Elbe near Strehla, about twenty-eight kilometers southeast of Torgau.

In that neighborhood his patrol encountered a crowd of foreign laborers crowding around a horseman. The horseman was a Russian soldier. The time was 11:30 A.M. on April 25. The patrol continued forward to the Elbe, a little north of Strehla, where the Americans saw uniformed figures on the east bank. Kotzebue's men fired off green flares and received no answer, but they saw some of the figures begin walking toward the river. Lieutenant Kotzebue with five soldiers then commandeered a sailboat and crossed the Elbe. They were met by a Soviet major and two other Russians, one a photographer, and were soon joined by the lieutenant colonel commanding the 175th Rifle Regiment of the 50th Guards Infantry Division, 34th Army, First Ukrainian Front.

Before long, other American patrols made contact with the Soviets or, despite a mistake in radioing the map coordinates of the first meeting, joined Lieutenant Kotzebue. General Reinhardt's initial reaction to the news was one of fury that his troops had violated the five-mile restriction. Once he digested the fact that his division would be acclaimed for the first contact, he swallowed his anger and went forward to join in the exchanges of greetings.

To the Baltic Sea

Eisenhower had claimed to be responding to military considerations while remaining indifferent to political issues when he reached his decision not to go for Berlin. Not only was the Berlin decision less apolitical than the Supreme Commander pretended, however; in general, he and the other senior American generals were not at all so indifferent to the political purposes for which wars are waged as in self-deprecation they sometimes said they were. The Supreme Commander was altogether willing to adjust his operations to those political considerations that he judged appropriate. While restricting the 12th Army Group to the line of the Elbe and the Mulde, he strongly intended that 21 Army Group should advance beyond the Elbe, notwithstanding his sympathy for Bradley's resentments toward Montgomery. For as Eisenhower told Marshall two days after the meeting on the Elbe near Strehla: "The Prime Minister is finally waking up to one danger that I have been warning him about for some weeks, namely, the possibility that the Russians can reach Lubeck and the neck of the Danish Peninsula ahead of us. I have done everything humanly possible to support Montgomery and to urge him to an early attack across the Elbe to Lubeck." But Montgomery's pace was still such as to cause Eisenhower to worry about Denmark, so much that on the same day he took the unusual step of appealing to Field Marshal Brooke for help in hastening Montgomery forward.[2]

As early as March 28, when he had angered Montgomery by transferring Simpson's army to the 12th Army Group, Eisenhower had told Montgomery that he would return the Ninth Army if doing so became desirable to facilitate 21 Army Group's crossing of the Elbe. On March 31, he reiterated this offer to Montgomery, particularly because: "Manifestly, when the time comes, we must do everything possible to push across the Elbe [on Montgomery's front] without delay, drive to the coast at Lubeck and seal off the Danish peninsula."[3] When Montgomery appeared nevertheless to devote his principal energies not to getting on with the drive to Lübeck but to protesting the transfer of

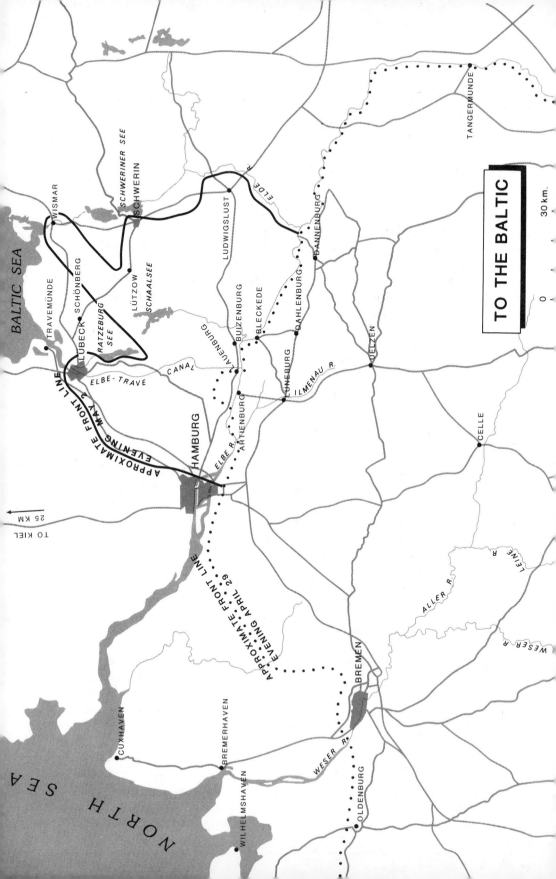

Simpson and Eisenhower's strategy in general, the Supreme Commander reminded him again on April 8 about protecting Denmark from the Soviets, while also informing him with unaccustomed coolness:

> You must not lose sight of the fact that during the advance to Leipzig you have the role of protecting Bradley's northern flank. It is not his role to protect your southern flank. My directive is quite clear on this point. Naturally, if Bradley is delayed, and you feel strong enough to push out ahead of him in the advance to the Elbe, this will be all to the good.[4]

Montgomery had the Canadian First Army attacking northward to reach the IJsselmeer and the North Sea, following which it was to clear the coast both westward and eastward, while the British Second Army strove to follow the Ninth Army out of the Wesel bridgehead and on to the Elbe.

Elusive Arnhem fell at last to the Canadian 1st Corps on April 14. The much-traveled General Blaskowitz, now OB Nederlander, used the German Twenty-fifth Army and the remnants of the First Parachute Army with his customary professional skill to compel the Canadians to work hard for the innumerable canal and river crossings on their way to the sea. As stubborn a defense as any at this stage of the war held off the right wing of the Canadian 2nd Corps from the Emden and Wilhelmshaven naval bases, but the left wing of the corps broke through to the North Sea within the northeast tip of the Netherlands on April 16. The 1st Corps arrived at the IJsselmeer two days later.

While the 2nd Corps then concentrated its efforts eastward as scheduled, the Allied command halted the 1st Corps drive to clear the remaining German pocket in the western Netherlands on April 22. This halt occurred in response to a threat from the German high commissioner in the Netherlands, Arthur Seyss-Inquart, that he would flood the countryside if the Canadians tried to force the principal remaining defenses, the Grebbe Line. On the other hand, if the Grebbe Line were not forced, he indicated he might be receptive to Allied proposals to feed the Dutch, who were on the verge of a famine brought on by embargoes that Seyss-Inquart had imposed to retaliate against labor slowdowns. So the Allies negotiated, hoping to achieve also a surrender of the Netherlands without further bloodshed. On this latter point, Seyss-Inquart remained stubborn until a general surrender developed elsewhere; but he permitted airdrops of food for the Dutch beginning April 20.

In the Second Army, meanwhile, the most rapid progress was achieved by 8 Corps, now under Lieutenant General E. H. Barker, on the British south flank next to the Ninth Army. On April 15, this corps ran into contingents of the German Twelfth Army that held it up in a four-day fight around Lüneburg, but on April 19 it reached the Elbe. Eisenhower found particular cause for anxiety in the progress of 12 Corps in Dempsey's center and 30 Corps on the left. Ritchie's corps did not arrive at the Elbe opposite Hamburg until April 23, while Horrocks's corps became entangled in Bremen for a week before clearing it on April 26. The defense of Bremen was stiffened by naval forces that still mustered good men, but Eisenhower judged that the British failed to keep pace with the Americans less because of the resistance of OB Nordwest's improvised Army Blumentritt than because their logistical system was inadequate to the challenge—and because Montgomery was not driving them hard enough.

This conclusion was exasperating, because on April 8 the Supreme Commander had asked Montgomery to specify the American help he would need to go to Lübeck, and he had followed up by sending Bradley to visit Montgomery with the same question. The field marshal had replied he would require nothing except a slight extension of Bradley's left flank. He needed no logistical or transport help whatever, said Montgomery, even to go all the way to Berlin. Unconvinced by this reply and dissatisfied by the British advance, Eisenhower himself went to see Montgomery on April 20. Now he was told that 21 Army Group needed part-time use of the railroad bridge built by American engineers at Wesel. Eisenhower immediately complied. Montgomery also acknowledged that he could use an American corps to assist in crossing the Elbe, so Eisenhower promptly sent him the 8th Infantry, 82nd Airborne, and 7th Armored Divisions under command of Ridgway's XVIII Airborne Corps. Eisenhower had actually earmarked the formations for this purpose for two weeks; the Ninth Army was to supply Ridgway's logistic and administrative support. Bradley, able to regard Montgomery with nothing but distrust and jealousy, naturally was not happy to lend the British "the best corps he has"[5] and feared another impediment to the prompt isolation of the formidable National Redoubt.

Here matters stood on April 27 when Eisenhower, worried because the Russians were breaking the German front around Stettin and appeared about to barrel toward Lübeck and Denmark, sent off his anxious dispatches to Marshall and Brooke and once more importuned Montgomery directly to make haste:

> All our plans have agreed on the tremendous importance of anchoring our flank on Lubeck as quickly as possible. I know that you fully appreciate the importance of this matter in the mind of the Prime Minister. I note in this morning's briefing that the front around Stettin is, as we anticipated, growing fluid. This re-emphasizes the need for rapidity. While I realize that you are straining every nerve to move as quickly as you can, I want you to let me know instantly if any slowness on the part of the U.S. corps assigned to your command might hold up your plans for a day or even an hour. I am informed here that additional logistic support promised your army group is fully forthcoming. This headquarters will do anything at all that is possible to help you insure the speed and the success of the operation.[6]

Montgomery, to be sure, was painstakingly constructing a plan. The plan called for crossing the Elbe on May 1. The enemy's deterioration and perhaps the prodding of higher authority persuaded him to the unwonted step of advancing the date to April 29. The plan called for Barker's 8 Corps to make the assault crossing and for Ritchie's 12 Corps and Ridgway's XVIII to cross into Barker's bridgeheads. Ritchie would then turn left to take Hamburg, while Barker hurried to the Baltic with Ridgway guarding his right and fanning eastward to meet the Russians.

When Ridgway first arrived on the Elbe, he brought the impression that the Germans on the opposite shore were "bruised and battered from years of hard pounding, but still full of fight."[7] Walking along the river bank, however, he drew no fire, and he promptly concluded that the enemy had grown too dispirited to repel a quick assault crossing in the XVIII Corps sector. Ridgway would not wait to cross through 8 Corps. The first of Ridgway's divisions to come north, the 8th, now under Brigadier General Bryant E. Moore, was already in the 8 Corps area planning to follow the British according to Montgomery's plan. But Gavin's 82nd Airborne command post was in Ridgway's sector, and all of the troopers from Gavin down were fuming because they had been called away from planning and training for the great adventure of the war, an airborne assault on Berlin. At least they might discharge their resentment upon the enemy. Gavin had only about two battalions of the 505th Parachute Infantry actually on hand; but to afford the paratroopers reasonably proper employment if not the climactic attack they had expected, and to capture the speed he knew was so essential, Ridgway began dispatching the 505th across the Elbe at Bleckede, ten kilometers above Lauenburg, at 1:00 A.M. on April 30. He promised Gavin four battalions of the 8th Division would be shifted quickly to give support.

There were spittings of unseasonable snow but only a few bursts of enemy small arms fire when the 505th put its boats into the water. Once the troopers had grasped a foothold on the far shore, German shelling opened the usual effort to prevent bridge-building. Gavin in fact thought it was the heaviest barrage he had ever faced. The engineers nevertheless had a 400-meter bridge complete before nightfall. With the news of April 30, Eisenhower felt sufficiently assured of what he could accomplish on his northern flank that he informed the Soviets he would advance beyond the Elbe to the approximate line Wismar-Schwerin-Dömitz.

However much the volume of enemy artillery impressed Gavin, resistance failed to generate enough consistency to threaten Ridgway's bridgehead before vehicles could cross. On May 1, Ridgway fed in the first four battalions of Moore's 8th Division, much of the 82nd, and the vanguard of Hasbrouck's 7th Armored, while his engineers completed a second bridge. His spearhead advanced some ten kilometers beyond the Elbe, and his left linked up with 8 Corps. That night German radio announced the death of Hitler. The implication was that he had died a hero's death in the defense of Berlin against the Bolsheviks, though in fact he had committed suicide on April 30. The concurrent announcement that Grossadmiral Karl Dönitz had inherited the Führer's powers could scarcely conceal from the German soldiers the imminence of the end, and resistance on May 2 became more sporadic and fainthearted than before. The 8th Division advanced more than seventy kilometers northeastward to capture Schwerin. The 11th Armoured Division of 8 Corps entered Lübeck without a fight. The British 6th Airborne Division, which had crossed the Elbe over an 8 Corps bridge but was then attached to Ridgway's corps, raced eighty-five kilometers to Wismar on the Baltic and fulfilled Eisenhower's object of sealing off Denmark. The Russians arrived about two hours later.

Czechoslovakia

In mid-April, Gillem's XIII Corps on the left flank of the Ninth Army had to turn parts of all its divisions northward to deal with Panzer Division von Clausewitz, another of the makeshift new German formations, but one equipped with about fifty tanks and able to create a nuisance when the Second Army's course toward Hamburg and Lübeck diverged enough from Simpson's eastward drive to open a gap between the XIII Corps and 8 Corps around Uelzen. Similarly, on the opposite flank of the Ninth Army, both Simpson and Hodges had to divert considerable strength between April 11 and 23 to cleaning out the Harz Mountains. In this forbidding massif, rising to over a thousand meters, as many as 70,000 troops of the German Eleventh Army used hills, defiles, forests, streams, and caves to force a last reprise of the kind of fighting the Americans had grown to loathe in the Huertgen Forest. Andrus's Big Red One waged its final battle of the war in the Harz, and the contest was as bitter as any the division had endured on its long road from OMAHA Beach. Hodges badgered Collins to force the 1st Division to pursue the fight with an intensity that Collins believed would entail a senseless loss of life; fortunately, being Collins, the corps commander could afford to hold Hodges off, proceeding at his own pace and thereby saving lives.

By the beginning of May, overwhelming material strength wielded now by battle-wise veterans had crushed most of the resistance in the Harz, and the rear areas of the Ninth and First Armies were substantially as quiet as the Elbe-Mulde front, where one round of ceremonial greetings after another marked new meetings with the Russians. SHAEF could begin the process of withdrawing Hodges's headquarters for a planned redeployment of the First Army to the Pacific.

As part of this process, Huebner's V Corps was transferred to the Third Army on May 4. Commencing April 28, this corps had already begun a shift to relieve the left flank of Irwin's XII Corps along the Czech frontier from the northwest corner of Czechoslova-kia to south of the latitude of Pilsen. This shift permitted the XII Corps to concentrate for a drive on Linz that would also set the stage for SHAEF's final offensive. To clear out the last remnants of resistance in the south, Eisenhower told the Soviets on April 30, his forces would either close generally to the Czech frontier or penetrate into Czechoslovakia as far as Karlsbad, Pilsen, and České Budějovice (Budweis). They would also drive into Austria past Linz, probably to the main north-south railroad east of Linz and thence along the valley of the Enna River.

Specifically, Patton's Third Army plan called for the V Corps to take Karlsbad and Pilsen, the XII Corps to take České Budějovice with its left while advancing its right along the north bank of the Danube to capture Linz, and Walker's XX Corps to move to the line of the Enna south of Linz. The addition of the V Corps gave Patton the largest army he had ever commanded—540,000 men—and Patton's hope was to use this strength not only to overrun the stated objectives but to become the conqueror bestriding at least one of the historic central European capitals, Prague. As for the troops, already weary of restrictions on their mingling with civilians in enemy Germany, "Now their battle cry," said Bradley, "is 'On to Czechoslovakia and fraternization.'"[8]

After the news of Hitler's death, resistance here as in the north became more spotty than ever. Walker's advance to the Enna was practically a motor march. He arrived there on May 4, to stop and await the Russians. The same day, Dager's 11th Armored Division of Irwin's corps approached Linz and received an offer of the city's surrender, provided the garrison be allowed to march east to fight the Soviets. The condition naturally had to be refused, but the next day the armor advanced effortlessly nevertheless into the city Hitler had planned to glorify as the metropolis closest to his birthplace. Farther north on the XII Corps front, Earnest's 90th Division on May 4 met a yet more welcome surrender delegation, the emissaries of those old antagonists General von Wietersheim and the 11th Panzer Division. Wietersheim demanded no unacceptable conditions, and so the last remains of an effective panzer division on the Western Front—the last ghost of the Blitzkrieg—faded into prisoner-of-war cages.

Also on May 4, Patton took an evening telephone call from Bradley, who said that Eisenhower had decided to proceed with the drive into Czechoslovakia. Patton re-sponded that he was ready to move the next morning. With Prague beckoning, he had seen to it that Earnest's 90th and Major General A. E. Brown's 5th Divisions and the 2nd

Cavalry Group had already begun the clearing of the frontier passes for a speedy entrance. The 90th completed opening the Regen Pass on May 5, and the next day Patton hastened his old favorite, the 4th Armored, through Earnest's infantry and forward to Pisek on a tributary of the Vltava—that is, the storied Moldau.

But that day, a Sunday, as he returned to his command post from church, Patton received another call from Bradley. The army group commander now indicated that Eisenhower's Karlsbad-Pilsen-Budweis line had to be the final goal. There was to be no patrolling more than five miles northeast of Pilsen. Prague was not to be touched.

The background was that on May 4, Eisenhower had suggested to the Soviets a possible American advance beyond Karlsbad-Pilsen-České Budějovice to the line of the Moldau and the Elbe. On behalf of the Soviet high command, General Alexei Antonov had replied promptly on May 5:

> In order to avoid a possible confusion of forces, the Soviet command asks General Eisenhower not to move the Allied forces in Czechoslovakia east of the originally intended line. . . . At the same time the Soviet command, to meet the wishes of General Eisenhower . . . stopped the advance of its own forces to the lower Elbe east of the line Wismar, Schwerin, Doemitz. We hope that General Eisenhower in turn will comply with our wishes relative the advances of his forces in Czechoslovakia.[9]

It was because Eisenhower did not want international complications, Bradley told Patton, that the halt order was coming through. Patton told Bradley and his diary that a great nation should let other people worry about complications. Furthermore, the people of Prague had risen to liberate their city, they were calling for and apparently in need of assistance, and they ought to be helped as quickly as possible. But Eisenhower could not ignore Antonov's implication of a quid pro quo for Denmark, even apart from the larger concern to avert pointless bloodshed that had guided his conduct toward the Soviets all along.

Surrender

Patch's Seventh Army had reached the passes of the Tyrol, and so narrow were they that the army front became restricted to two divisions. Brooks's VI Corps pushed McAuliffe's 103rd Division through the Mittenwald Pass which leads to Innsbruck. Dean's 44th Division battled from May 1 through 4 against recalcitrant Germans blocking the Fern Pass, before Austrian partisans showed the way along a flanking trail and thus allowed the 44th to occupy Landeck on May 5, to answer the French telephone call into the town the next day.

On the evening of May 3, while part of his division was struggling past roadblocks to reach the Austrian partisans who had taken over Innsbruck, McAuliffe sent his 411th Infantry Regiment, mounted on trucks, south through the night and a snowstorm, heading for the Brenner Pass. In the early morning of the eventful 4th of May, the 411th captured the town of Brenner without resistance. A mounted patrol continued moving and crossed the Italian border to Vipiteno. There at 10:51 A.M. the patrol met a similar reconnaissance force of the 338th Infantry Regiment, 88th Division, II Corps. The VI Corps of the Seventh Army had joined hands with the Fifth Army, whose commander, Lieutenant General Lucian K. Truscott, Jr., had led the VI Corps at Anzio and from the

DRAGOON beaches through the Rhône valley and almost to the German border. The armies of Italy were united with those of northwest Europe.

The German command in Italy had already surrendered to the Allied Mediterranean Command on April 29, effective at noon May 2. The surrender included areas into which Devers's 6th Army Group was already moving, the Austrian provinces of Vorarlberg, Tyrol, Salzburg, and part of Carinthia. On the day of the meeting at Vipiteno, the German Nineteenth Army and Army Group G separately opened surrender negotiations with the 6th Army Group. Army Group G now included the Twenty-fourth Army, which was an "army" for propaganda purposes only and in fact scarcely a division; but it happened to be facing the French First Army, so its command received an almost inevitable ultimatum from de Lattre that the French would continue attacking unless it surrendered separately to them. As events turned out, the simple dissolution of resistance denied the French the triumph of such a surrender ceremony.

The simple dissolution of resistance was occurring all over Germany, with German troops rushing to place themselves under the protection of the Western Allies before the Russians overran them, and the German command hardly able to keep pace as it tried to arrange capitulations more formal and, it hoped, more favorable. Amidst piecemeal surrenders of armies and army groups, the Dönitz government hoped particularly to arrange a separate surrender to the Western Allies that would afford almost all remaining German forces refuge within Eisenhower's lines. But Eisenhower insisted that any general surrender must take place on Eastern and Western Fronts simultaneously. When the Germans stalled, he threatened to seal his front against any further westward movement of German soldiers and civilians. This firm stand brought General Jodl to Eisenhower's schoolhouse headquarters at Reims, to sign the general German surrender at 2:41 A.M., May 7, effective at 11:01 P.M., May 8.

To the south, an American officer with a radio and two jeeps provided by General O'Daniel of the 3rd Division had set out into the Alpine fastnesses once thought to harbor the National Redoubt, there to establish communications between Army Group G and the 6th Army Group to speed the termination of all resistance in this rugged region where many knots of German soldiers had long since been operating practically on their own. The arrangement grew out of the completion of Devers's various surrender negotiations, particularly a conference with General Förtsch of the German First Army, representing General Schulz of Army Group G. In a sculptor's studio set amidst tall trees on the outskirts of Haar in Bavaria, General Haislip's XV Corps headquarters, Förtsch in the early afternoon of May 5 bowed from the waist to General Devers and introduced his staff, each rising and bowing when called on, to Devers and his staff and ranking subordinates, all seated. Förtsch maintained the cold, disinterested demeanor of his class and profession and sought to conduct the proceedings with businesslike dispatch.

Only in the closing moments did he betray a fleeting loss of self-control. Devers asked him whether he understood that the terms offered him were strictly those of an unconditional surrender and that at the will of the Allies all of Army Group G, including General Schulz and himself, General Förtsch, would become prisoners of war. Förtsch sat stiffly at attention for fully a minute without replying, while the muscles of his face worked convulsively. Then he bowed his head slightly and said: "I can assure you that no power is left at my disposal to prevent it."[10]

None remained anywhere in the ruins of the Third Reich.

Epilogue

T HE BREAKING of German power in northern Europe from the 6th of June 1944 to the 8th of May 1945 had cost 586,628 American casualties, among them 135,576 dead. The British, Canadians, French, and other Allies lost 179,666 in the campaign of France, the middle ground, and Germany, including about 60,000 dead. German losses in killed and wounded are not known with precision but probably equalled or somewhat exceeded those of the Allies.

To accomplish the defeat of Germany, Eisenhower commanded by the beginning of May 1945 over four and a half million troops, including ninety-one combat divisions of which sixty-one were American. From D-Day to V-E Day 5,412,219 Allied troops entered western Europe. They brought with them 970,044 vehicles and 18,292,310 tons of supplies. At the end, the Western Allies had some 28,000 combat aircraft, of which 14,845 were American.

The American army and air forces were overwhelmingly the preponderant force of the Western Allies, and still more did American tanks, trucks, guns, and equipment of all kinds dominate the Allied arsenal. With this American material preponderance, the campaign of France and Germany had become more and more an American campaign, shaped by the United States Army's concepts of strategy, operations, and tactics as well as fought on the Allied side mainly by American soldiers.

It was not only the greatest campaign in the history of the American army. In the campaign, the American army, nurtured as a constabulary force dealing with American Indians and Mexican irregulars, through most of its history not an instrument of its country's foreign policy and hardly a member of the universe of European armies, decisively entered a new historical era. The constabulary army from the periphery of the European world, having sought to transform itself for the purpose, fought and ultimately conquered what had been the mightiest of the European armies, indeed the army that had created the modern military profession. Victorious over the German army, the American army after V-E Day had to forsake altogether its former remoteness from the main currents of world military history to assume the central responsibility for the military defense of the West against a Red Army grown mightier than the Wehrmacht at its zenith.

Forsaking the habits of mind and organization shaped by a long history can never be easy for any human institution, and many of the difficulties of the United States in achieving security for itself and its Allies since 1945 have sprung from the abruptness with which the American army has had to remake itself from a domestic constabulary to an army of the classic European type writ staggeringly large, with missions and duties girdling the globe.

In major part, the difficulties of the campaign in Europe from D-Day to V-E Day in World War II sprang also from the abruptness with which the United States Army had to readjust the habits of its Indian-fighting past to engage in large-scale European war.

A history of fighting small-scale campaigns across vast geographic arenas had made the American army by 1940 an army whose essential, formative characteristic was mobility. It was true, nevertheless, that the army had never been quite so mobile as it might have in the days when its principal opponents were the light cavalry of the Plains Indians. Hollywood stereotypes to the contrary, most of the Old American Army had always been infantry, not cavalry. Robert M. Utley, historian of the Indian wars, has indeed made the point that the American army was always consciously enough comparing itself with European armies and preparing to engage some day in European-style war that it never adapted itself adequately in organization or doctrine for the highly mobile, tactically "irregular" wars with the Indians. "In examining the role of the frontier in nineteenth century military history . . .," says Utley, "we encounter a paradox. It is that the army's frontier employment unfitted it for orthodox war at the same time that the preoccupation with orthodox war unfitted it for its frontier mission."[1] The salient feature of the frontier experience of the American Indian-fighting army that limited its fitness for orthodox, European war even to the time of World War II was the frontier's elevation of mobility above the other military virtues, and particularly above the virtue of concentrated power.

Shaped by its heritage as a constabulary force for small wars, the American army entered upon the Second World War, and eventually upon the great campaign on France and Germany, as an army of mobility at the expense of power. The American army that raced across France in the summer of 1944 and across Germany in the spring of 1945 was the most mobile in the world, and in those races its mobility served it well. Its formation upon the principle of mobility and its lack of sustained combat power—either in reserves of men, or in armor and armament except for its artillery—did not serve it so well when it faced resolute and skillful enemies in strong defensive positions, as it did in the Bocage of Normandy in June and July 1944 and along the West Wall from September 1944 into February 1945. Then the limited capacity of the army to generate sustained combat power contributed to costly tactical deadlocks.

Because of another paradox of American military history, it was implicit in American strategy that the American army should encounter the tactical requirement for sustained combat power for which its history did not prepare it. The deadlocks of Normandy and the West Wall had their origins in no small degree in the American army's approach to war. The brief encounters with European-style war that had punctuated the army's long history as a frontier constabulary—the Civil War and the 1917–1918 participation in World War I—had convinced the army's leadership that victory in large-scale war depends on a strategy of direct confrontation with the enemy's main forces to destroy them. The preoccupation with orthodox war of which Utley speaks—a preoccupation with the study of European war in the American military school system, particularly at the influential Fort Leavenworth schools—nourished the same strategic dogma. As U. S. Grant had defeated the armies of the Confederacy through head-on assault by overwhelming strength to destroy them, so in any future great war the United States Army would seek the destruction of the enemy armed forces by similar means. To the extent that General John J. Pershing had been able to affect the strategy of World War I, he had applied Grant's strategy. This same line of strategic thought led in World War II to the American insistence on direct cross-Channel assault—and to the deadlocks of Normandy and the West Wall.

The paradoxical commitment to a power-drive strategy of head-on assault in an army shaped for mobility further contributed to prolonging the war by undermining the possible uses of mobility itself. Mobility might have been exploited to achieve rapid offensive concentrations—as it was used to achieve defensive and counterattacking concentrations in the Ardennes but was rarely employed offensively; an emphasis on concentration might seem an appropriate corollary of the American power-drive strategy, but instead American generals habitually preferred to advance on a broad front. Mobility might also have been exploited to translate breakthroughs attainable by means of concentration into breakouts sending fast-moving columns deep into the enemy's rear. Mobility was so used in COBRA and its aftermath, but COBRA was a rarity; when the front stabilized after COBRA and its follow-through across France, the Americans reverted to assaults on a broad front, not only strategically but operationally, within a single army as well as across the theater of war. A victim of the restabilized front, of the autumn deadlock on the West Wall, "P" Wood of the 4th Armored, addressed the causes of his own loss of his division and the larger issue of proper employment of mobility as well when he said: "And perhaps I had been too emphatic in my protests against linear employment of our forces, particularly armor, in frontal attacks all along the front instead of in deep thrusts in decisive directions."[2]

The failure to make use of the American army's mobility in ways that might best have complemented the power-drive strategy, the infrequency of bold concentration and exploitation in the manner of COBRA, the adherence to a broad-front strategy whether or not it was appropriate to the circumstances of a given time, all these features of American generalship in the campaign of France and Germany add up to unimaginative caution. American generalship by and large was competent but addicted to playing it safe. An argument can well be made for such generalship in the circumstances of the time. The resources of America and her Allies, and the engagement and destruction of so much of the Wehrmacht by the Red Army, assured that the war would not be lost. If the superior manpower and material resources of the Allies were bound to prevail in the long run, why take risks? But a bolder generalship might have shortened the war.

The disjuncture between a power-drive strategy aimed at confronting the enemy's main forces to destroy them, and an army designed not to generate sustained combat power but for mobility, suggests a more basic flaw in the American army and its generalship. The American army lacked a clear conception of war. It had resolved neither upon a doctrine of winning the war by way of the direct application of superior power, in the manner of U.S. Grant, nor upon a doctrine of winning by means of superior mobility and facility in maneuver, in the manner of the indirect approach of the British military critic B.H. Liddell Hart. In the end, the American army rumbled to victory because it had enough material resources to spare that it could exhaust the enemy's resources even without adequately focusing its own power for a decisive, head-on battle of annihilation, or exploiting its mobility in behalf of a consistent strategy of indirect approach.

The unresolved, ambivalent quality of the American army's very conception of war may well mirror the army's relative inexperience in large-scale war. Pitted against the German army, the United States Army suffered long from a relative absence of the finely honed professional skill of the Germans, officers and men, in every aspect of tactics and operations. In part because of American inexperience, in part because of unresolved inconsistencies in the American conception of war reverberating downward from the strategic to the tactical sphere—as in the lack of firepower in the assaults of the infantry platoons—the German army remained qualitatively superior to the American army, formation for formation, throughout far too many months of the American army's greatest campaign. In the end, it was its preponderance of material resources that carried its army through to victory in World War II. That preponderance, however, cannot be counted on again.

There is a British military aphorism that he who has not fought the Germans does not know war. The American army has fought the Germans twice; does it, at last, know war? Has it drawn from its experiences the clarity of conception and doctrine, the tactical and technical skill, that made the prowess of the Germans a byword and enabled the German army twice in the twentieth century to hold the world at bay? It is unlikely that our army will ever be called upon by American national policy to stand alone against the world as the Germans did. But the international military balance threatens us with dangerous and powerful forces, and we cannot afford a complacency drawn in part from past military victories, at least one of which—the victory in Europe in World War II—was more expensive and more often postponed than it might have been, because American military skills were not as formidable as they could have been.

Notes and Sources

Preface

1. Douglas Southall Freeman, *Lee's Lieutenants: A Study in Command* (3 vols., New York: Scribner's, 1942–1944), I, xxix–xxx.
2. In particular, Stephen E. Ambrose, *The Supreme Commander: The War Years of General Dwight D. Eisenhower* (Garden City: Doubleday, 1970); Forrest C. Pogue, *The Supreme Command (United States Army in World War II: The European Theater of Operations*, Washington: Office of the Chief of Military History, 1954).
3. Bradley to Eisenhower, 12 September 1944, p.3, National Archives (cited hereafter as NA), Record Group (hereafter RG) 331, Box 77, SHAEF.

Chapter One: The American Army

1. Hanson W. Baldwin, *Tiger Jack* (Ft. Collins, Colo.: Old Army Press, 1979), p.76.
2. Col. W.K. Naylor, Inf., "The Principles of War," Command Course No. 12, Army War College, 1922, Part I, Jan. 5, 1922, p.4, copy in Tasker H. Bliss Papers, Library of Congress, Box 277.
3. Lt. Col. Oliver Prescott Robinson, Infantry, *The Fundamentals of Military Strategy* (Washington: United States Infantry Assn., 1928), p.67.
4. FM 100–5, *Field Service Regulations (Tentative), Operations, 1939*, Par. 91, quoted in Captain Reuben E. Jenkins, Infantry, "Offensive Doctrine: Opening Phase of Battle," *Military Review*, XX (June 1940), 5.
5. Tasker H. Bliss, draft of article, Jan. 1923 (?), pp.1, 4–5, 6, Bliss Papers, Library of Congress, Box 274.
6. Lieutenant Commander H.H. Frost, USN, "National Strategy," United States Naval Institute *Proceedings*, LI (Aug. 1925), 1343–1390, quotations from pp.1348, 1351.
7. Naylor, "Principles of War," p.6.
8. Captain George J. Meyers, USN, *Strategy* (Washington: Byron S. Adams, 1928), pp.178, 74.
9. Course at the Army War College, 1926–1927, Command, Report of Committee No. 8, "Strategy of the World War," Date of Conference: Feb. 28, 1927, p.19, Army War College Collection, U.S. Army Military History Institute, Carlisle Barracks, Pa. (cited hereafter as USAMHI).
10. Robinson, *Fundamentals of Military Strategy*, pp.16, 75, 93.
11. FM 100–5, *1939*, Par. 413, quoted with comment in Jenkins, "Offensive Doctrine," p.16.
12. Wedemeyer quoted in Maurice Matloff and Edwin M. Snell, *Strategic Planning for Coalition Warfare, 1941–1942 (United States Army in World War II: The War Department*, Washington: Office of the Chief of Military History, 1953), p.61; Eisenhower diary note, Jan. 12, 1941, Alfred D. Chandler, Jr., ed., Stephen E. Ambrose, assoc. ed., et al., *The Papers of Dwight David Eisenhower: The War Years* (5 vols., Baltimore: Johns Hopkins Press, 1970), I, 66.

13. Review of *Paris, or the Future of War*, in *Review of Current Military Writings*, V (Oct.–Dec. 1925), 20.

My views on the strategic inheritance of the American army are more fully developed in Russell F. Weigley, *The American Way of War: A History of United States Military Strategy and Policy* (New York: Macmillan, 1973). For the failure of the Indian wars to prepare the army for either European or unconventional war, see the perceptive comments of Robert M. Utley, "The Contribution of the Frontier to the American Military Tradition," James P. Tate, ed., *The American Military on the Frontier: The Proceedings of the 7th Military History Symposium, United States Air Force Academy, 30 September–1 October 1976* (Washington: Office of Air Force History, Headquarters USAF, and United States Air Force Academy, 1978), pp. 3–13.

The deployment of the army between the world wars and the National Guard role in the early large-scale maneuvers are discussed in Jim Dan Hill, *The Minute Man in Peace and War: A History of the National Guard* (Harrisburg: Stackpole, 1964). The August 1940 and other maneuvers are examined in detail in Jean R. Moenk, *A History of Large-Scale Army Maneuvers in the United States, 1935–1964* (Fort Monroe, Va.: Headquarters United States Continental Army Command, 1969).

For the American adoption and adaptation of Fuller's principles of war, see Lt. Col. Charles Andrew Willoughby, *Maneuver in War* (Harrisburg: Military Service Publishing Co., 1939), pp.26–33.

Larry H. Addington, *The Blitzkrieg Era and the German General Staff, 1865–1941* (New Brunswick: Rutgers University Press, 1971) provides an introduction to German military thought in the age of Moltke and Schlieffen.

Chapter Two: Weapons and Divisions

1. Constance McLaughlin Green, Harry C. Thomson, and Peter C. Roots, *The Ordnance Department: Planning Munitions for War (United States Army in World War II: The Technical Services,* Washington: Office of the Chief of Military History, 1955), p.190.

2. *First United States Army, Report of Operations, 23 February–8 May 1945* (3 vols., Washington: Government Printing Office, 1946), I, 93.

3. James M. Gavin, *On to Berlin: Battles of an Airborne Commander, 1943–1946* (New York: Viking, 1978), p.52.

4. Kent Roberts Greenfield, Robert R. Palmer, and Bell I. Wiley, *The Organization of Ground Combat Troops (United States Army in World War II: The Army Ground Forces,* Washington: Historical Division, United States Army, 1947), p.236.

5. Ibid., pp.325, 334.

6. Ibid., p.325.

7. Ibid., p.326.

8. Omar N. Bradley, *A Soldier's Story* (New York: Holt, 1951), p.41.

9. Wesley Frank Craven and James Lea Cate, eds., *The Army Air Forces in World War II* (7 vols., Chicago: University of Chicago Press, 1948–1958), VI, *Men and Planes,* p.197.

10. Jean R. Moenk, *A History of Large-Scale Army Maneuvers in the United States, 1935–1964* (Fort Monroe, Va.: Headquarters United States Continental Army Command, 1969), pp.25, 39.

11. Greenfield et al., *The Organization of Ground Combat Troops,* p.316–317.

12. Major George C. Marshall, General Staff, "Profiting by War Experiences," *Infantry Journal,* XVIII (Jan. 1921), 34–37.

13. Chester B. Hansen Diaries, USAMHI, Sept. 5, 1944.

14. Apollo Edition, New York: Morrow, 1966. For the findings on the proportion of men who fired in combat, see especially pp.50–60.

15. Hansen Diaries, June 25, 1944. Hansen quoted an unnamed captain of the 12th Infantry.

16. Trevor N. Dupuy offers statistical evidence for these conclusions in his *A Genius for*

War: The German Army and General Staff, 1807–1945 (Englewood Cliffs: Prentice-Hall, 1977) and *Numbers, Predictions and War* (Indianapolis: Bobbs-Merrill, 1979). Whatever questions Dupuy's statistical method might raise, there is ample impressionistic evidence to confirm his conclusions.

17. War Cabinet, Chiefs of Staff Committee, "Operation 'OVERLORD,' Report and Appreciation with Appendices, 30th July, 1943," pp.ii–iii, National Archives, RG 331, Box 76, SHAEF.

18. Hansen Diaries, Aug. 12, 1944.

The National Defense Act of 1920, the legislative foundation for the army between the world wars, is in *United States Statutes at Large*, XLI, 759–812, and in Richard H. Kohn, ed., *Military Laws of the United States from the Civil War through the War Powers Act of 1973* (New York: Arno Press, 1979), original page numbers retained.

For American tank, tank destroyer, bazooka, and other weapons development, Green et al., *The Ordnance Department: Planning Munitions for War* is indispensable, one of the best of all studies of military technology.

For the mobilization and organization of ground combat troops, Greenfield et al., *The Organization of Ground Combat Troops* should be supplemented by its companion volume in *The Army Ground Forces* series of the official army history, Robert R. Palmer, Bell I. Wiley, and William R. Keast, *The Procurement and Training of Ground Combat Troops* (Washington: Historical Division, Department of the Army, 1948). On manpower and economic mobilization generally, see also Marvin A. Kreidberg and Merton G. Henry, *History of Military Mobilization in the United States Army, 1775–1945* (Washington: Department of the Army, 1955). Maurice Matloff analyzes "The 90-Division Gamble" in Kent Roberts Greenfield, ed., *Command Decisions* (Washington: Office of the Chief of Military History, 1960), pp.365–381.

On tanks and armored forces, foreign as well as American, see R.M. Ogorkiewicz, *Armoured Forces: A History of Armoured Forces and Their Vehicles* (New York: Arco, 1970) and Kenneth Macksey and John H. Batchelor, *Tanks: A History of the Armoured Fighting Vehicle* (New York: Ballantine, 1971). On German tanks, see F.M. von Senger und Etterlin, *German Tanks of World War II* (Harrisburg: Stackpole, 1969). On British armored forces, see B.H. Liddell Hart, *The Tanks: The History of the Royal Tank Regiment and Its Predecessors: Heavy Branch, Machine-Gun Corps, Tank Corps, and Royal Tank Corps, 1914–1945* (2 vols., New York: Praeger, 1959). On the evolution of American armored forces, see Mildred Harmon Gillie, *Forging the Thunderbolt: A History of the Development of the Armored Force* (Harrisburg: Military Service Publishing Co., 1947); Donald E. Houston, *Hell on Wheels: The 2d Armored Division* (San Rafael: Presidio, 1977); Mary Lee Stubbs and Stanley Russell Connor, *Armor-Cavalry, Part I: Regular Army and Army Reserve (Army Lineage Series*, Washington: Office of the Chief of Military History, 1969). Lieutenant General Jacob L. Devers, then commanding Headquarters European Theater of Operations, decided to retain the 2nd and 3rd Armored Divisions, which were in his theater, at the old Tables of Organization and Equipment "rather than make a change at this late date"; Devers to Major General A.C. Gillem, Jr., Commanding General, Headquarters Armored Command, 29 Nov. 1943, Gillem Papers, USAMHI, Box 2. For a critique of American armored organization, tanks, and tank gun power written at the close of the European campaign, see Gillem, then commanding the XIII Corps, to Major General C.L. Scott, Commanding Armored Center, 8 May 1945, Gillem Papers, USAMHI, Box 4.

For correctives to General McNair's interpretation of the use of armor in North Africa see Correlli Barnett, *The Desert Generals* (New York: Viking, 1961), especially pp.254, 263–266, 271–272; Ronald Lewin, *Rommel as Military Commander* (paperback, New York: Ballantine, 1970), especially pp.214, 222.

To enhance the mobility of American infantry, General Pershing recommended the triangular division in his Forwarding [of] Report of A.E.F. Superior Board on Organization and Tactics to the Secretary of War, June 16, 1920, especially pp.1–3, NA, RG 120,

Records of the American Expeditionary Forces, 1917–1923. Moenk's *History of Large-Scale Army Maneuvers* reviews the course of the concept through the late 1930s and early 1940s maneuvers.

On infantry tactics, see in addition to the field manuals of the time (many in the USAMHI collection): Jac Weller, *Weapons and Tactics: Hastings to Berlin* (New York: St. Martin's, 1966); Anthony Farrar-Hockley, *Infantry Tactics, 1939–1945* (London: Almark, 1976). For artillery, see John Batchelor and Ian Hogg, *Artillery* (New York: Ballantine, 1973) and Shelford Bidwell, *Artillery Tactics, 1939–1945* (London: Almark, 1976).

The evolution of German divisional organization to D-Day is outlined in Gordon A. Harrison, *Cross-Channel Attack (United States Army in World War II: The European Theater of Operations,* Washington: Office of the Chief of Military History, 1951), especially pp.236–241. Subsequent volumes of *The European Theater of Operations* series trace changes through the remainder of the war. On officer percentages and unit cohesion in the German and American armies, see Richard A. Gabriel and Paul L. Savage, *Crisis in Command: Mismanagement in the Army* (New York: Hill & Wang, 1978).

Chapter Three: The View of the Far Shore

1. Winston S. Churchill, *The Second World War* (6 vols., Boston: Houghton Mifflin, 1948–1953), II, *Their Finest Hour,* p.247.

2. Samuel Eliot Morison, *History of United States Naval Operations in World War II* (15 vols., Boston: Little, Brown, 1950–1962), XI, *The Invasion of France and Germany,* p.10; Marshall quoted the remark to Morison in 1956.

3. W.D. Puleston, *The Dardanelles Expedition: A Condensed Study* (Second Ed., Annapolis: United States Naval Institute, 1927), p. 168; Vice Admiral George C. Dyer, USN (Retired), "Naval Amphibious Landmarks," United States Naval Institute *Proceedings,* XCII, No. 8 (Aug. 1966), pp.55–56. A prominent American writer on tactics said: "Descents upon a hostile coast, if opposed, have a very small chance of success, particularly in modern times. It is true that the landing may be made, but getting away from the coast is the difficulty"; Col. William K. Naylor, *Principles of Strategy with Historical Illustrations* (Fort Leavenworth: General Service Schools Press, 1921), p.335.

4. *The Memoirs of Field-Marshal the Viscount Montgomery of Alamein* (Cleveland and New York: World, 1958), p.317.

5. Gordon A. Harrison, *Cross-Channel Attack (United States Army in World War II: The European Theater of Operations,* Washington: Office of the Chief of Military History, 1951), p.64.

6. Omar N. Bradley, *A Soldier's Story* (New York: Holt, 1951), p.239.

7. War Cabinet, Chiefs of Staff Committee, Operation "OVERLORD," Report and Appreciation with Appendices, 30th July, 1943, p.14, NA, RG 331, Box 76, SHAEF.

8. Charles H. Corlett, "One Man's Story, Some of It about War," ms. autobiography, Corlett Papers, USAMHI, p.232. Pp.229–236 review Corlett's concerns about amphibious preparations for D-Day, from Marshall's informing him that he was to go to Europe because of his amphibious experience through his various rebuffs in England.

9. Bradley, *Soldier's Story,* p.241; Montgomery, *Memoirs,* pp.218–219.

10. Bradley, *Soldier's Story,* p.241.

11. Operation "OVERLORD" Outline Plan, Covering Note by the British Chiefs of Staff, 10th Aug., 1943, p.2, NA, RG 331, Box 76, SHAEF; 21 Army Group/20721/g (Plans), 27 June 1944, Operation "LUCKY STRIKE," Appreciation of Possible Development of Operations, p.3, NA, RG 331, Box 68, SHAEF, 370.2 LUCKY STRIKE; Chester B. Hansen Diaries, USAMHI, July 23, 1944.

12. War Cabinet, Chiefs of Staff Committee, "Operation 'OVERLORD,' Report and Appreciation with Appendices, 30th July, 1943," p.10, NA, RG 331, Box 76, SHAEF.

13. Operation "RANKIN" "C"—Revision of Spheres of Responsibility, Memorandum by Chief of Staff to Supreme Commander (Designate), C.O.S. (43)786(0), 24th Dec., 1943, NA, RG 331, Box 114, SHAEF OC of S, SGS, Zones of Occupation—Germany, Vol. I.

14. "Synthesis of Experience in the Use of ULTRA Intelligence by U.S. Army Field Commands in the European Theatre of Operations," NA, RG 457, N.S.A. SRH-006, p.4.

15. Ibid., pp. 6, 4.

The development of Great Britain's Combined Operations and of the American involvement can be traced in "Administrative and Logistical History of the European Theater of Operations" (8 parts, CMH File No. 8–3, ACC No. 526/2–1, in files of Department of the Army, Center of Military History [hereafter cited as CMH], especially Part I, "The Special Observers (SPOBS) and the United States Army Forces in the British Isles"; Part V, "Survey of Allied Planning for Continental Operations"; and Part VI, "NEPTUNE: Training for and Mounting the Operation, and the Artificial Ports."

For the American army and amphibious war, see ibid., Part VI, I, 1–94. For the modern history of amphibious warfare, see Jeter A. Isely and Philip A. Crowl, *The U.S. Marines and Amphibious War: Its Theory and Practice in the Pacific* (Princeton: Princeton University Press, 1951) and, on the British side, L.E.H. Maund, *Assault from the Sea* (London: Methuen, 1949). For a British history of Combined Operations, see Bernard Fergusson, *The Watery Maze: The Story of Combined Operations* (New York: Holt, Rinehart & Winston, 1961).

There is much information on the development, production, and characteristics of landing ships and craft in L.F. Ellis, with G.R.G. Allen et al., *Victory in the West*, I, *The Battle of Normandy (History of the Second World War: United Kingdom Military Series*, London: H.M. Stationery Office, 1962), pp.511–517. There are diagrams of some types of craft as well as other useful data in Daniel E. Barbey, *MacArthur's Amphibious Navy: Seventh Amphibious Force Operations, 1943–1945* (Annapolis: United States Naval Institute, 1969), pp.359–363.

For the background of the selection of Eisenhower and Montgomery for their commands, see especially Forrest C. Pogue, *The Supreme Command (United States Army in World War II: The European Theater of Operations*, Washington: Office of the Chief of Military History, 1954). To supplement Pogue's study of Eisenhower and his headquarters, the best military biography of Eisenhower is Stephen E. Ambrose, *The Supreme Commander: The War Years of General Dwight D. Eisenhower* (Garden City: Doubleday, 1970). Eisenhower's war memoirs are his *Crusade in Europe* (Garden City: Doubleday, 1948). See also his *Report by the Supreme Commander to the Combined Chiefs of Staff on the Operations in Europe of the Allied Expeditionary Force, 6 June 1944 to 8 May 1945* (Washington: Government Printing Office, 1945). Part II of the "Administrative and Logistical History of the European Theater of Operations," CMH, concerns "Organization and Command in the European Theater of Operations." An informal view of Eisenhower's headquarters, selected from a larger manuscript diary but candid enough that the publication of some of its material caused Eisenhower considerable displeasure, is *My Three Years with Eisenhower: The Personal Diary of Captain Harry C. Butcher, USNR, Naval Aide to General Eisenhower, 1942 to 1945* (New York: Simon & Schuster, 1946).

In addition to Montgomery's *Memoirs*, see his *Normandy to the Baltic* (Boston: Houghton Mifflin, 1948). The better Montgomery biographies include Alun Chalfont, *Montgomery of Alamein* (New York: Atheneum, 1976) and Ronald Lewin, *Montgomery as Military Commander* (New York: Stein & Day, 1971). The view from Montgomery's headquarters is offered by his chief of staff, Sir Francis de Guingand, *Operation Victory* (London: Hodder & Stoughton, 1947) and *Generals at War* (London: Hodder & Stoughton, 1964); and by his chief operations officer, David Belchem, *All in the Day's March* (New York: Oxford University Press, 1978).

For COSSAC, see General Morgan's memoirs, *Overture to Overlord* (London: Hodder & Stoughton, 1950) and *Peace and War: A Soldier's Life* (London: Hodder & Stoughton, 1951).

The British preparations for OVERLORD are detailed in the official history, Ellis, *Victory in the West*, I, *The Battle of Normandy*.

On the French plan suggesting landings in Brittany and the Cotentin, see "Administrative and Logistical History of the European Theater of Operations,"CMH, Part V, "Survey of Allied Planning for Continental Operations" (2 vols.), I, 36–44.

On the German side, numerous records of field commands, though uneven in the amount of material that has survived, are available on microfilm from the National Archives. A collection of World War II military studies prepared by more than 200 German officers working under the direction of Colonel Harold A. Potter and then of Colonel Wilbur S. Nye is now in the National Archives; publication of a guide to and selection from these *World War II German Military Studies* is in preparation (14 vols., New York: Garland 1979–   ). For Hitler as supreme war lord, there are Felix Gilbert, ed., *Hitler Directs His War: The Secret Records of His Daily Military Conferences*, selected and annotated by Felix Gilbert (New York: Oxford University Press, 1950); Walter Hubatsch, *Hitlers Weisungen für die Kriegführung, 1939–1945* (Frankfurt am Main: Bernard & Graefe Verlag für Wehrwesen, 1962); H.R. Trevor-Roper, ed., *Hitler's War Directives, 1939–1945. Texts from Walter Hubatsch, Hitlers Weisungen für die Kriegführung, 1939-1945* (London: Sidgwick & Jackson, 1964). The war diary of the German supreme command is conveniently available: Helmuth Greiner, Percy Ernst Schramm, et al., eds., *Kriegstagebuch des Oberkommandos der Wehrmacht (Wehrmachtführungstabe), 1940–1945* (4 vols. in 7, Frankfurt am Main: Bernard & Graefe Verlag für Wehrwesen, 1961–1965), IV, Percy Ernst Schramm, ed., *1. Januar 1944–22 Mai 1945* (in 2 vols.).

Documents gathered by David Irving while preparing *The Trail of the Fox: The Search for the True Marshal Rommel* (New York: Dutton, 1977) and now part of the "Sammlung Irving" of the Institut für Zeitgeschichte in Munich are available on microfilm: *Selected Documents on the Life and Campaigns of Field Marshal Erwin Rommel* (11 reels, East Ardsley: EP Microform, 1978). Reel 3 includes material on German intelligence respecting the coming Allied invasion; Reel 11 includes Rommel's diary for 21 November 1943–22 February 1944 and the diary kept for him by Hauptmann Helmuth Lang in April–May 1944. Irving's book, however, has to be used with the caution suggested by Rommel's naval adviser in Friedrich Ruge, "*The Trail of the Fox:* A Comment," *Military Affairs*, XLIII (Oct. 1979), 158. See Ruge's own *Rommel in Normandy: A Reminiscence*, tr. Ursula R. Moessner (San Rafael: Presidio, 1979). Rommel's chief of staff, Hans Speidel, wrote *Invasion 1944: Rommel and the Normandy Campaign*, tr. Theo R. Crevenna (New York: Paperback Library, 1968). Rundstedt's operations officer, Generalleutnant Bodo Zimmerman, wrote "France, 1944," in Seymour Freidin and William Richardson, eds., *The Fatal Decisions* (New York: Sloane, 1956). See also Paul Carrel, *Invasion—They're Coming*, tr. E. Osers (New York: Dutton, 1963).

A consideration of the implications of D-Day's coinciding with various tidal conditions can be found in Naval Branch (British), 15 Sept. 1943, First Draft, Operation OVERLORD, "Pros and cons of 'D' day coinciding with Spring or Neap Tides," NA, RG 331, Box 76, SHAEF. It was the V Corps Breaching Plan, Underwater and Beach Obstacles, 17 March 1944, that commented on the likely "expensive" nature of passing the German obstacles; Harrison, *Cross-Channel Attack*, p.179.

On the obstacles and the German defenses in general, see Alan F. Wilt, *The Atlantic Wall: Hitler's Defenses in the West, 1941–1944* (Ames: Iowa State University Press, 1975).

For the V Corps, see *History V Corps June 6 '44* ([France]: 668th Engineer Topographic Co., 1945). For the 1st Division there is H.R. Knickerbocker, *Danger Forward: The Story of the First Division in World War II* (Sponsored by the Society of the First Division, Atlanta: Albert Love Enterprises, 1948); for the 29th Division, Joseph H. Ewing, *29 Let's Go! A History of the 29th Infantry Division in World War II* (Washington: Infantry Journal Press, 1948). For the VII Corps, there is the very brief *Mission Accomplished: The Story of the Campaigns of the VII Corps, United States Army in the War against Germany, 1944–1945* (Leipzig: J.J. Weber, 1945). For the 101st Airborne Division, see Leonard Rapport and Arthur Northwood, Jr., *Rendezvous with Destiny: A History of the 101st Airborne Division* (enl. and rev. ed., Greenville, Tenn.: 101st Airborne Division Association, 1965). For the 82nd Airborne, W. Forrest Dawson, ed., *Saga of the*

All American (Atlanta: Albert Love Enterprises, 1946) and Henry L. Covington, *A Fighting Heart: An Unofficial Story of the 82nd Airborne* (Fayetteville, N.C.: Privately printed, 1949).

There is no transcript of Montgomery's briefings on the OVERLORD plans at St. Paul's School on April 7 and May 15. Bradley's comments and Montgomery's notes are cited above. A folder in NA, RG 331, Box 38 concerns administrative arrangements for May 16, includes a guest list, and informs the researcher that 21 Army Group provided lunch and tea.

The Joint Operations Plan U.S. Forces for Operation OVERLORD—FUSAG [First United States Army Group]—Ninth Air Force—Western Naval Task Force, First Draft, 8 April 1944, is in NA, RG 331, Box 78, SHAEF OC of S, SGS Decimal File May 1943–Aug 1945 381 OVERLORD to 381/5 OVERLORD. A revision dated 8 May 1944 is in NA, RG 331, Box 85, Headquarters Twelfth Army Group, Special Staff, Adj. Gen. Section, Administrative Branch TS Decimal File 1943–45 370.2 NUTMEG to 370.2 OVERLORD FUSAG. The NEPTUNE Initial Joint Plan is in NA, RG 331, Box 84, Headquarters Twelfth Army Group, Special Staff, Adj. Gen. Section, Administrative Branch TS Decimal File 1943–45 370.2 NEPTUNE TUSA to Twenty-First Army Group Folder 370.2 OP "N" 21 AGp.

There were a few additional warnings about the Bocage from time to time. As early as 1940, SKYSCRAPER was a project of the Combined Commanders Planning Staff (British) to assess the resources required for a return to the Continent in northwest Europe in 1944, against opposition. "Administrative and Logistical History of the European Theater of Operations," Pt. V, I, 122. The SKYSCRAPER project mapped the poor tank country of the Bocage in contrast to the good tank country east of Bayeux (map, ibid., p.123). On July 15, 1943 General Morgan pointed out that "The best tank country lies between Caen and Bayeux, extending inland from the coast as far as Caumont and the Mont Pincon, subsequently expanding South-East and South-West"; War Cabinet, Chiefs of Staff Committee, Operation "OVERLORD," Report and Appreciation with Appendices, p.102, NA, RG 331, Box 76, SHAEF.

The discussion of ULTRA herein is based primarily on "Synthesis of Experience in the Use of ULTRA Intelligence by U.S. Army Field Commands in the European Theatre of Operations," NA, RG 457, N.S.A. SRH-006; and "Reports by U.S. Army ULTRA Representatives with Army Field Commands in the European Theatre of Operations," NA, RG 457, N.S.A. SRH-023. Adolph G. Rosengarten, Jr., ULTRA representative with the First Army, supplements his official report included in the latter collection with his "With Ultra from Omaha Beach to Weimar, Germany—A Personal View," *Military Affairs*, XLII (Oct. 1978), 127–132. Walter S. Dunn reviewed the first major releases of British ULTRA documents in "The Ultra Papers," ibid., pp.134–135. The first of three British volumes projected to present an official review in detail is F.H. Hinsley, with E.E. Thomas et al., *British Intelligence in the Second World War: Its Influence on Strategy and Operations*, I (New York: Cambridge University Press, 1979); this volume closes with June 1941. The best comprehensive secondary account so far is Ronald Lewin, *Ultra Goes to War: The First Account of World War II's Greatest Secret Based on Official Documents* (New York: McGraw-Hill, 1978). See also Martin Blumenson, "Will 'Ultra' Rewrite History?" *Army*, XXVIII, No. 8 (Aug. 1978), pp. 43–48; Gustav Bertrand, *Enigma, ou le plus grande enigme de la guerre, 1939–1945* (Paris: Plon, 1973); Harold C. Deutsch, "The Historical Impact of Revealing the ULTRA Secret," *Parameters: Journal of the US Army War College*, VII, No. 3 (1977), pp.16–32, and "The Influence of ULTRA on World War II," ibid., VIII, No. 4 (Dec. 1978), pp.2–15; Roger J. Spiller, "Assessing Ultra," *Military Review*, LIX, No. 8 (Aug. 1979), pp.13–23.

Chapter Four: By Air and by Sea

1. Alfred D. Chandler, Jr., ed., Stephen E. Ambrose, assoc. ed., et al., *The Papers of Dwight David Eisenhower: The War Years* (5 vols., Baltimore: Johns Hopkins University Press, 1970), III, 1820.

2. Wesley Frank Craven and James Lea Cate, eds., *The Army Air Forces in World War II* (7 vols., Chicago: University of Chicago Press, 1948–1958), III, *Europe: ARGUMENT to V-E Day, January 1944 to May 1945*, pp.161–162.

3. Gordon A. Harrison, *Cross-Channel Attack (United States Army in World War II: The European Theater of Operations*, Washington: Office of the Chief of Military History, 1951), p.224.

4. Craven and Cate, eds., *Army Air Forces*, III, 95.

5. Ibid., pp.100, 101.

6. Ibid., p.179, citing a United States Strategic Bombing Survey interview of May 19, 1945.

7. Forrest C. Pogue, *The Supreme Command (United States Army in World War II: The European Theater of Operations*, Washington: Office of the Chief of Military History, 1954), p.53.

8. Chester B. Hansen Diaries, USAMHI, June 1, 2, 1944.

9. Forrest C. Pogue, "D-Day—1944," in The Eisenhower Foundation, *D-Day: The Normandy Invasion in Retrospect* (Lawrence: University Press of Kansas, 1972), p.34.

10. Dwight D. Eisenhower, *Crusade in Europe* (Garden City: Doubleday, 1948), p.246.

11. Ibid.

12. Matthew B. Ridgway, as told to Harold H. Martin, *Soldier: The Memoirs of Matthew B. Ridgway* (New York: Harper, 1956), p.6.

The standard official account of the American aerial effort edited by Craven and Cate can be supplemented by General Lewis H. Brereton, *The Brereton Diaries: The War in the Air in the Pacific, Middle East, and Europe, 3 October 1941–8 May 1945;* Tedder's *With Prejudice: The Memoirs of Marshal of the Royal Air Force Lord Tedder* (London: Cassell, 1960) and *Air Power in War* (London: Hodder & Stoughton, 1948); the British official histories, Sir Charles Webster and Noble Frankland, *The Strategic Air Offensive against Germany, 1939–1945* (4 vols., *History of the Second World War: United Kingdom Military Series*, London: H.M. Stationery Office, 1961) and Denis Richards and Hilary St. George Saunders, *The Fight Is Won* (Vol. III, *The Royal Air Force, 1939–1945*, London: H.M. Stationery Office, 1954); Kenn G. Rust, *The 9th Air Force in World War II* (Rev. Ed., Fallbrook, Calif.: Aero Publishers, 1970); Milton Marx, *Ninth Air Force, USAAF* (Paris: Desfosses-Neogravures, 1945); *Time over Targets: The Story of the 9th Bombardment Division* (Paris: Desfosses-Neogravures, 1945); Ross E. Harlan, comp., *AAF Strikes* (323rd Bombardment Group) (N.p., 1945); *The History of a Bombing Outfit: The 386th Bomb Group* (St. Trond, Belgium: De Geneffe, 1945); Guy Ziegler, *Bridge Busters: The Story of the 394th Bomb Group* (New York: Ganis & Harris, 1949); Henry C. Beck, Jr., ed., *The 397th Bomb Group (M): Bridge-Busters* (Cleveland: Crane Howard, 1946); Bruce G. Ellison, ed., *Orange Tails: The Story of the 358th Fighter Group* (Chicago: Rogers Printing Co., 1945); *The Story of the 371st Fighter Group in the E.T.O.* (Baton Rouge: Army Navy Publishing Co., 1946); Andrew F. Wilson, ed., *Leap Off: 404th Fighter Group Combat History* (San Angelo, Texas: Newsfoto Publishing Co., 1946). For authoritative but brief overviews of the aerial preparation for invasion see Alfred Goldberg, "Air Campaign OVERLORD: To D-Day," with commentary by Alfred F. Hurley, in *D-Day: The Normandy Invasion in Retrospect*, pp.57–78.

On the Luftwaffe, see especially Cajus Bekker, *The Luftwaffe War Diaries*, tr. and ed. Frank Ziegler (Garden City: Doubleday, 1968); Werner Blumbach, *The Life and Death of the Luftwaffe*, tr. Robert Hale (New York: Coward-McCann, 1960); Adolf Galland, *The First and the Last: The Rise and Fall of the German Fighter Forces, 1938–1945*, tr. Mervyn Savill (New York: Ballantine, 1954).

American aircraft are described in detail in Ray Wagner, *American Combat Planes* (New Rev. Ed., Garden City: Doubleday, 1968). For Allied and enemy planes as well as American, see John W.R. Taylor, ed. and comp., *Combat Aircraft of the World from 1909 to the present* (New York: Putnam, 1969). The Messerschmitt Bf 109 and Bf 110 were thus abbreviated because they were originally produced by the Bayerische Flugzeugwerke; after July 1938, Messerschmitt designs were produced by Messerschmitt A.G., so the abbreviations of the later models are Me 163, Me 210, and so on.

Basil Collier recounts *The Battle of the V-Weapons* (New York: Morrow, 1965); see also his *The Defence of the United Kingdom (History of the Second World War: United Kingdom Military Series*, London: H.M. Stationery Office, 1957).

For the naval operations before and on D-Day, Admiral Morison's official history of *United States Naval Operations in World War II* (15 vols., Boston: Little, Brown, 1950–1962) is supplemented by his *The Two-Ocean War: A Short History of the United States Navy in World War II* (Boston: Little, Brown, 1963); the British official history, S.W. Roskill, *The War at Sea, 1939–1945* (3 vols., *History of the Second World War: United Kingdom Military Series*, London: H.M. Stationery Office, 1954–1961); Friedrich Ruge, "German Naval Operations on D-Day," in *D-Day: The Normandy Invasion in Retrospect*, pp.149–169; George M. Elsey, "Naval Aspects of Normandy in Retrospect," ibid., pp.170–177.

The crisis of the early June storm and Eisenhower's decision to proceed with June 6 as D-Day are described in all standard accounts, especially by Eisenhower himself in *Crusade in Europe* and by Pogue in *The Supreme Command*. On the responsibilities of planning the invasion and ordering that it begin, Eisenhower's chief of staff also wrote a useful account: Walter Bedell Smith, *Eisenhower's Six Great Decisions: Europe 1944–1945* (New York: Longmans, Green, 1956).

On the airborne assault, S.L.A. Marshall, *Night Drop: The American Airborne Invasion of Normandy* (Boston: Little, Brown, 1962) is one of the best battle accounts, thanks to Marshall's interviewing technique. See also Crookenden Napier, *Dropzone Normandy: The Story of the British and American Airborne Assault, D Day 1944* (New York: Scribner's, 1976). The D-Day drops are also chronicled in great detail in Gerard M. Devlin, *Paratrooper! The Saga of Parachute and Glider Combat Troops, 1914 to 1945* (New York: St. Martin's, 1978), including the story of the death of General Falley. In addition to Ridgway's and Gavin's memoirs and the airborne division histories already cited, see also James A. Huston, *Out of the Blue: U.S. Army Airborne Operations in World War II* (West Lafayette, Ind.: Purdue University Press, 1972); Huston emphasizes the evolution of airborne doctrine as well as combat operations. For troop carriers, see *Invaders: The Story of the 50th Troop Carrier Wing* (Paris: Desfosses-Neogravure, 1945) and *Ever First: The 53rd Troop Carrier Wing* (Paris: Desfosses-Neogravure, 1945).

Chapter Five: The Beach

1. Omar N. Bradley, *A Soldier's Story* (New York: Holt, 1951), p.270.
2. Chester B. Hansen Diaries, USAMHI, June 6, 1944, p.5.
3. Chester Wilmot, *The Struggle for Europe* (New York: Harper, 1952), p.259.
4. Gordon A. Harrison, *Cross-Channel Attack (United States Army in World War II: The European Theater of Operations*, Washington: Office of the Chief of Military History, 1951), p.320.
5. Bradley, *Soldier's Story*, p.271.
6. General Marshall to Admiral Ernest J. King, Nov. 4, 1943, in Forrest C. Pogue, *George C. Marshall: Organizer of Victory, 1943–1945* (New York: Viking, 1973), pp.276–277.
7. Harrison, *Cross-Channel Attack*, p.115.
8. Bradley, *Soldier's Story*, p.180.
9. Ibid., p.226.
10. Wilmot, *Struggle for Europe*, p.264.
11. Charles H. Taylor, *Omaha Beach (American Forces in Action*, Washington: Historical Division, War Department, 1945), p.71.
12. Cornelius Ryan, *The Longest Day* (paperback ed., New York: Popular Library, 1977), pp.288–289.
13. Samuel Eliot Morison, *History of United States Naval Operations in World War II* (15 vols., Boston: Little, Brown, 1950–1962), XI, *The Invasion of France and Germany, 1944–1945*, p.121.
14. Hansen Diaries, June 6, 1944, p.10.
15. Ibid., June 10, 1944.

Ryan's *The Longest Day* is the most vivid account of D-Day, based on interviews with participants. Another good popular account is David Howarth, *D-Day—The Sixth of June* (New York: McGraw-Hill, 1959). Among official histories, Harrison's *Cross-Channel Attack* should be supplemented by Taylor's *Omaha Beach* and R.G. Ruppenthal, *Utah Beach to Cherbourg (American Forces in Action*, Washington: Historical Division, Department of the Army, 1947). Morison's naval history, Craven and Cate's *Army Air Forces* cited in the preceding chapter, and the British official history, L.F. Ellis with G.R.G. Allen et al., *Victory in the West*, I, *The Battle of Normandy (History of the Second World War: United Kingdom Military Series*, London: H.M. Stationery Office, 1962) chronicle their respective forces. Ranger actions on D-Day are reviewed by Charles H. Taylor in *Small Unit Actions (American Forces in Action*, Washington: Historical Division, War Department, 1946). *Lightning Joe: An Autobiography* (Baton Rouge: Louisiana State University Press, 1979) tells J. Lawton Collins's story of UTAH Beach.

For Rommel's hearing that the Americans were the Allies' Italians, see David Irving, *The Trail of the Fox: The Search for the True Field Marshal Rommel* (New York: Dutton, 1977), p.266. Rommel's judgments of the Americans' fighting qualities and military skill remained complex and ambivalent from North Africa to Normandy. Of Kasserine he wrote: "Although it is true that the American troops could not yet be compared with the veteran troops of the Eighth Army, yet they made up for their lack of experience by their far better and more plentiful equipment and their tactically more flexible command. . . . The tactical conduct of the enemy's defense had been first class. They had recovered very quickly after the first shock." Erwin Rommel, *The Rommel Papers*, ed. B.H. Liddell Hart (New York: Harcourt Brace, 1953), p.407. As compared with the British, the remark about the Americans' tactical flexibility rings true.

Bradley's own memoirs remain the best portrait of him. There is also Charles Whiting's concise *Bradley* (New York: Ballantine, 1971). There is no biography of Hodges. The Chester Hansen Diaries offer the most rewarding informal glimpses of these generals and their staffs. The more formal diary kept for Major William C. Sylvan, aide to General Hodges, is less revealing but useful for its record of Hodges's activities and sometimes his attitudes; I have used a photocopy supplied by the National Archives. The sorts of doubts about Hodges that developed while he commanded the Third Army in training are outlined, by an observer admittedly close to Patton and not particularly well disposed toward Hodges, in Robert S. Allen, *Lucky Forward: The History of Patton's Third U.S. Army* (New York: Vanguard, 1947).

On the British specialized tanks, see Robin Higham, "Technology and D-Day," in The Eisenhower Foundation, *D-Day: The Normandy Invasion in Retrospect* (Lawrence: University Press of Kansas, 1971), pp.221–239; Ronald W. Clark, *The Boffins* (London: Phoenix House, 1962).

Chapter Six: Cherbourg and Caumont

1. Chester B. Hansen Diaries, USAMHI, June 6, 9, 1944. Hansen also observed the GIs on horseback, June 12, 1944.

2. Ibid., June 7, 1944.

3. Eisenhower to Marshall, July 5, 1944; Alfred D. Chandler, Jr., ed., Stephen E. Ambrose, assoc. ed., et al., *The Papers of Dwight David Eisenhower: The War Years* (5 vols., Baltimore: Johns Hopkins University Press, 1970), III, 1972.

4. Hansen Diaries, June 9, 1944.

5. Omar N. Bradley, *A Soldier's Story* (New York: Holt, 1951), p.301.

6. Chandler, ed., *Papers of Eisenhower*, III, 1972.

7. "Administrative and Logistical History of the European Theater of Operations," CMH, Pt. VI, "NEPTUNE: Training for and Mounting the Operation, and the Artificial Ports," I, iv.

8. Gordon A. Harrison, *Cross-Channel Attack (United States Army in World War II: The European Theater of Operations*, Washington: Office of the Chief of Military History, 1951), p.426.

9. Hansen Diaries, June 13, 1944.
10. Bradley, *Soldier's Story*, p.308.
11. Harrison, *Cross-Channel Attack*, p.430.
12. Chester Wilmot, *The Struggle for Europe* (New York: Harper, 1952), p.332.
13. Ibid., p.330.
14. Harrison, *Cross-Channel Attack*, p.441.
15. Ibid., p.372.
16. Wilmot, *Struggle for Europe*, p.310.
17. Hansen Diaries, June 14, 1944.

Harrison's *Cross-Channel Attack* remains the most detailed narrative of the Normandy campaign. For the campaign in the Cotentin, see R.G. Ruppenthal, *Utah Beach to Cherbourg (American Forces in Action*, Washington: Historical Division, Department of the Army, 1947) and J. Lawton Collins, *Lightning Joe: An Autobiography* (Baton Rouge: Louisiana State University Press, 1979). Unit histories contributing to this chapter include *Combat History of the Second Infantry Division in World War II* (Baton Rouge: Army Navy Publishing Co., 1946); Joseph B. Mittelman, *Eight Stars to Victory: A History of the Veteran Ninth US Infantry Division* (Columbus, Ohio: F.J. Heer Printing Co., 1948); and the very brief Joe I. Abrams, *A History of the 90th Division in World War II, 6 June 1944 to 9 May 1945* (Baton Rouge: Army Navy Publishing Co., 1946).

The MULBERRIES are described in detail in Roland G. Ruppenthal, *Logistical Support of the Armies*, I, *May 1941–September 1944 (United States Army in World War II: The European Theater of Operations*, Washington: Office of the Chief of Military History, 1953) and in "Administrative and Logistical History of the European Theater of Operations," Pt. VI.

On the force attained by the Great Storm, see Ruppenthal, *Logistical Support*, I, 413; Harrison, *Cross-Channel Attack*, p.426.

For the naval and aerial assaults on Cherbourg, see the official histories by Morison and edited by Craven and Cate, cited above. On Quesada and his command, there is *Achtung Jabos! The Story of the IX TAC* (Paris: Curial-Archereau, 1945). For Bradley's esteem for Quesada, see also Bradley to General H.H. Arnold, 7 July and 25 September 1944, Bradley Papers, USAMHI, Vol. III.

Ruppenthal's is the standard work on the Battle of the Buildup. Also basic is "Administrative and Logistical History of the European Theater of Operations," Pt. VII, "Opening and Operating Continental Ports."

On the Battle of Villers-Bocage and other British actions, see Ellis's *Battle of Normandy*, cited in Chapter Five; E. Belfield and H. Essame, *The Battle for Normandy* (London: Batsford, 1965); Wilmot, *Struggle for Europe* and *History of the 7th Armoured Division, June 1943–July 1945* (Germany: British Army of the Rhine, 1945).

The FORTITUDE deceptions are examined on the basis of the first reasonably full study of the documents in Charles Cruikshank, *Deception in World War II* (New York: Oxford University Press, 1980). There is a FORTITUDE file in NA, RG 331, Box 66, Headquarters Twelfth Army Group, Special Staff, Adj. General Section, Administrative Branch TS Decimal File 1943–45 370.2; it includes among other items a 12th Army Group evaluative report dated 20 November 1944 estimating that FORTITUDE "was responsible for containing a minimum of twenty enemy divisions in the Pas de Calais during the crucial first months of the invasion."

Chapter Seven: The Bocage

1. [SHAEF] G-3 Division, SHAEF/18008/Plans, 31 May 1944, "Post-'NEPTUNE' courses of action after capture of the lodgement area, Section II—Method of conducting the campaign," Tab A, p.1, NA, RG 331, Box 77, SHAEF, OVERLORD, Vol. I.
2. Ibid., "Discussion" (for first paragraph), Tab A, pp.2–3 (for second and third paragraphs).

3. PS-SHAEF (44)21(Final) 10th June, 1944, " 'NEPTUNE': Stabilisation of the 'NEPTUNE' Area," p.1, NA, RG 331, Box 77, SHAEF, OVERLORD, Vol. I. See also "The Administrative and Logistical History of the European Theater of Operations," CMH, Pt. V, "Survey of Allied Planning for Continental Operations" (2 vols.), II, 71–103; the quotation is from pp.102–103 of this account.

4. PS-SHAEF (44)21(Final) 10th June, 1944, pp.2, 3.

5. "Administrative and Logistical History," Pt. V, Vol. II, 84, for the custom of weekly planning cables. SHAEF, signed Eisenhower, to AGWAR for Joint Staff Planners, Ref. No. s-54384, 22 June 1944, NA, RG 331, Box 76, SHAEF, OVERLORD, Vol. I, for quotation.

6. Field Marshal the Viscount Montgomery of Alamein, *Normandy to the Baltic* (Boston: Houghton Mifflin, 1948), pp.19–21. This review of Montgomery's changing versions of his intentions follows Martin Blumenson, "Some Reflections on the Immediate Post-Assault Strategy," in The Eisenhower Foundation, *D-Day: The Normandy Invasion in Retrospect* (Lawrence: University Press of Kansas, 1971), pp.204–206.

7. *The Memoirs of Field-Marshal the Viscount Montgomery of Alamein* (Cleveland and New York: World, 1968), pp.227–228.

8. Field-Marshal Viscount Montgomery of Alamein, *A History of Warfare* (Cleveland and New York: World, 1968), p.525.

9. Chester Wilmot, *The Struggle for Europe* (New York: Harper, 1952), pp.339–340.

10. Alfred D. Chandler, Jr., ed., Stephen E. Ambrose, assoc. ed., et al., *The Papers of Dwight David Eisenhower: The War Years* (5 vols., Baltimore: Johns Hopkins Press, 1970), III, 1934.

11. Martin Blumenson, *Breakout and Pursuit (United States Army in World War II: The European Theater of Operations*, Washington: Office of the Chief of Military History, 1961), p.15.

12. Chandler, ed., *Papers of Eisenhower*, III, 1969.

13. 21 Army Group/20721/G(Plans), 27 June 1944, "Operation 'LUCKY STRIKE': Appreciation of Possible Development of Operations," p.1, NA, RG 331, Box 68, SHAEF, 370.2 LUCKY STRIKE.

14. Ibid., p.3.

15. Ibid., p.2.

16. Ibid., p.1.

17. Ibid., p.2.

18. Ibid., p.3.

19. Ibid., p.6.

20. Chester B. Hansen Diaries, USAMHI, June 30, 1944.

21. Ibid., June 10, 1944.

22. Ibid., June 18, 1944.

23. Bradley to Eisenhower, 29 June 1944, Bradley Papers, USAMHI, Correspondence with Famous Persons, Eisenhower File.

24. Ibid.

25. Frank James Price, *Troy H. Middleton: A Biography* (Baton Rouge: Louisiana State University Press, 1974), p.135.

26. Omar N. Bradley, *A Soldier's Story* (New York: Holt, 1951), p.30; Gen. Troy H. Middleton obituary, *New York Times*, Oct. 11, 1976, p.30.

27. Wilmot, *Struggle for Europe*, p.347, citing the testimony of Rundstedt's chief of staff, Generalmajor Günther Blumentritt.

28. *First United States Army Report of Operations, 20 October 1943–1 August 1944* (7 vols., Washington: Government Printing Office, 1944), I, 117.

29. Hansen Diaries, June 30, 1944.

30. *First U.S. Army Report, 20 October 1943–1 August 1944*, I, 121–122.

31. 21 Army Group/20721/G(Plans), 27 June 1944, "Operation 'LUCKY STRIKE,' " p.3; Hansen Diaries, July 23, 1944.

32. *First U.S. Army Report, 20 October 1943–1 August 1944*, I, 122.

33. Martin Blumenson, *The Patton Papers* (2 vols., Boston: Houghton Mifflin, 1972–1974), II, 521.

34. Charles B. MacDonald, *The Siegfried Line Campaign (United States Army in World War II: The European Theater of Operations*, Washington: Office of the Chief of Military History, 1963), p.269.

35. *First U.S. Army Report, 20 October 1943–1 August 1944*, I, 118, quoting unidentified officers.

36. Blumenson, *Breakout and Pursuit*, p.82.

37. Ibid., pp.84–85.

38. Hansen Diaries, June 14, 1944.

39. Blumenson, *Breakout and Pursuit*, p.103.

40. Ibid., p.111.

41. Ibid., p.140.

42. Chandler, ed., *Papers of Eisenhower*, III, 1982–1983.

43. *With Prejudice: The Memoirs of Marshal of the Royal Air Force Lord Tedder* (London: Cassell, 1960), p.557; Chandler, ed., *Papers of Eisenhower*, III, 1984.

44. Hansen Diaries, July 12, 1944.

45. Ibid., July 19, July 3, 1944 (the latter date for quoted description of Coningham).

46. Blumenson, *Breakout and Pursuit*, p.176.

The battles in the Bocage are recounted in greatest detail in Blumenson's *Breakout and Pursuit*. For a briefer but highly authoritative account, see the same author's *The Duel for France, 1944* (Boston: Houghton Mifflin, 1963). Major General H. Essame's *Normandy Bridgehead* (New York: Ballantine, 1970) is a concise review from a British perspective.

For the British actions around Caen, see again Ellis's *Battle of Normandy*, cited in Chapter Five, and Alexander McKee, *Caen: Anvil of Victory* (London: Souvenir Press, 1964).

General Middleton is portrayed largely from his own recollections, as well as from his papers, in Frank James Price's biography. For the VIII Corps see also *Anniversary Edition VIII Corps History* (VIII Corps, 1945). For the XIX Corps there is a brief overview, Frederick E. Pamp, *Normandy to the Elbe, XIX Corps* (N.p., 1946) and General Corlett's ms. autobiography at USAMHI. The 30th Division has one of the better divisional histories, Robert L. Hewitt, *Work Horse of the Western Front: The Story of the 30th Infantry Division* (Washington: Infantry Journal Press, 1946). Other pertinent unit histories include *The Cross of Lorraine: A Combat History of the 79th Infantry Division, June 1942–December 1945* (Baton Rouge: Army Navy Publishing Co., 1946); the attractively illustrated *Thunderbolt across Europe: A History of the 83d Infantry Division, 1942–1945* (Munich: F. Bruckmann K.G., n.d.); *Spearhead in the West, 1941–1945: The Third Armored Division* (Frankfurt am Main: Kunst und Wervedruck, 1945).

On the death of General Dollman, see David Irving, *The Trail of the Fox: The Search for the True Marshal Rommel* (New York: Dutton, 1977), pp.394–395.

For Bradley's preference for four infantry divisions plus an armored division in a corps, see Hansen Diaries, June 20, 1944. For disappointment with the 76mm. Sherman gun and General Brooks's suggestions, ibid., July 2, 1944.

On the battle of St. Lô, an excellent survey is *St. Lo, 7 July–19 July 1944 (American Forces in Action*, Washington: Historical Division, War Department, 1946). There is an especially effective and moving personal account: Charles R. Cawthorn, "July, 1944: St. Lô, " *American Heritage*, XXV, No. 4 (June 1974), 4–11, 82–88.

Chapter Eight: COBRA

1. Martin Blumenson, *Breakout and Pursuit (United States Army in World War II: The European Theater of Operations*, Washington: Office of the Chief of Military History, 1961), p.188, for the "massive stroke"; B.H. Liddell Hart, *History of the Second World War* (New York: Putnam, 1971), p.556, for the Dempsey quotation.

2. Alfred D. Chandler, Jr., ed., Stephen E. Ambrose, assoc. ed., et al., *The Papers of Dwight David Eisenhower: The War Years* (5 vols., Baltimore: Johns Hopkins Press, 1970),

III, 2003, for "the whole weight of air power" and p.2002, Eisenhower to Montgomery, July 13, 1944, for the Eisenhower quotation; Blumenson, *Breakout and Pursuit*, p.190, for Montgomery's promises.

3. Chester Wilmot, *The Struggle for Europe* (New York: Harper, 1952), p.361.

4. Chandler, ed., *Papers of Eisenhower*, III, 2020.

5. Ibid., p.2019.

6. Ibid.

7. Chester B. Hansen Diaries, USAMHI, June 18, 1944.

8. Major Kenneth W. Hechler, "VII Corps in Operation 'Cobra,' " CMH, p.18.

9. Hansen Diaries, July 19, 1944.

10. Blumenson, *Breakout and Pursuit*, p.218.

11. Hansen Diaries, July 19, 1944; Omar N. Bradley, *A Soldier's Story* (New York: Holt, 1951), p.332.

12. Hansen Diaries, July 19, 1944.

13. Ibid., July 24, 1944.

14. Ibid.

15. Bradley, *Soldier's Story*, p.347.

16. Hechler, "VII Corps in Operation 'Cobra,' " p.63. For "They've done it again," Bradley, *Soldier's Story*, p.248.

17. Bradley, *Soldier's Story*, p.358.

18. Hechler, "VII Corps in Operation 'Cobra,' " p.64.

19. Robert L. Hewitt, *Work Horse of the Western Front: The Story of the 30th Infantry Division* (Washington: Infantry Journal Press, 1946), p.37.

20. Hechler, "VII Corps in Operation 'Cobra,' " p. 67 for quotation; "Operations of 30th Infantry Division 24 Jul–1 Aug 1944 Operation COBRA," CMH, p.8.

21. Blumenson, *Breakout and Pursuit*, p.252.

22. Hechler, "VII Corps in Operation 'Cobra,' " p.133.

23. Martin Blumenson, *The Patton Papers* (2 vols., Boston: Houghton Mifflin, 1972–1974), II, 490. For Patton's offer to Eisenhower, Hansen Diaries, July 2, 1944.

24. Hechler, "VII Corps in Operation 'Cobra' " calls its Chapter VII, "VII Corps Loses the Race to Coutances," p.153.

25. Wesley Frank Craven and James Lea Cate, eds., *The Army Air Forces in World War II* (7 vols., Chicago: University of Chicago Press, 1948–1958), III, *Europe: ARGUMENT to V-E Day, January 1944 to May 1945*, p.242.

26. Hechler, "VII Corps in Operation 'Cobra,' " p.208.

27. Hansen Diaries, July 28, 1944.

28. Bradley to Eisenhower, 28 July 1944, Bradley Papers, USAMHI, Correspondence with Famous Persons, Eisenhower File.

29. Ibid.

30. Bradley, *Soldier's Story*, p.349.

31. Hansen Diaries, July 27, 1944.

32. Craven and Cate, eds., *Army Air Forces*, III, 235.

33. Hechler, "VII Corps in Operation 'Cobra,' " pp.16, 48.

34. Wilmot, *Struggle for Europe*, p.388.

35. Hansen Diaries, June 18, 1944. Bradley, *Soldier's Story*, p.337.

36. Craven and Cate, eds., *Army Air Forces*, III, 239–240.

37. Bradley to Arnold, 7 July, 25 September 1944, Bradley Papers, USAMHI, Vol. III. The preceding dialogue between airmen and ground soldiers is from Craven and Cate, eds., *Army Air Forces*, III, 240.

38. Bradley, *Soldier's Story*, p.338.

39. S/Sgt. Jose M. Topete, Major F. Ferriss, and Lt. Hollis Alpert, "Operations of V Corps: 'Cobra Operations,' 26 Jul–15 Aug 44," CMH, p.47.

The most persuasive discussions of Montgomery's intentions for GOODWOOD are by Liddell Hart, *History of the Second World War*, pp.552–556, and Martin Blumenson, "Some Reflections on the Immediate Post-Assault Strategy," The Eisenhower Foundation, *D-Day: The Normandy Invasion in Retrospect* (Lawrence: University Press of Kansas, 1971), pp.210–214. The editors of the *Papers of Eisenhower* offer a judicious summary of the issues and evidence, III, 2019–2020. Wilmot, *Struggle for Europe* is of course favorable to Montgomery's interpretation, as are both the British and the Canadian official histories, L.F. Ellis with G.R.G. Allen et al., *Victory in the West*, I, *The Battle of Normandy (History of the Second World War: United Kingdom Military Series*, London: H.M. Stationery Office, 1962) and C.P. Stacey, *The Victory Campaign (Official History of the Canadian Army in the Second World War*, III, Ottawa: Queen's Printer, 1960). Major General David Belchem, then head of Montgomery's Operations Staff, adopts a tone of downright grievance toward the Americans for hounding his chief, in *All in the Day's March* (New York: Oxford University Press, 1979). Also inclined to take Montgomery's part in the dispute with Eisenhower over GOODWOOD, though generally a critical work, is Ronald Lewin, *Montgomery as Military Commander* (New York: Stein & Day, 1971). Lewin nevertheless makes the interesting point that while there was "no prescription for a breakthrough" in the 21 Army Group instructions to the Second Army on July 15, Dempsey told him that this "was the only written order he received from Montgomery during the Normandy campaign—written 'for the record.' All other orders came to him by word of mouth in conversation or conference" (p.275).

There are good descriptions of the GOODWOOD attack in Ellis's and Stacey's works and a brief account in Wilmot's. For detail, there is John T. Sweet, *Mounting the Threat: The Battle of Bourguebus Ridge* (San Rafael: Presidio, 1978); the main title implies the overriding thesis.

The enthusiasm generated by the first demonstration of Sergeant Culin's hedgerow-breaking device to Bradley and Hodges is especially well conveyed by the William C. Sylvan Diary, photocopy supplied by National Archives, 14 July 1944, p.27.

The planning for COBRA can be followed in the memoirs of Bradley and Collins; in Blumenson, *Breakout and Pursuit*; and in Hechler, "VII Corps in Operation 'Cobra.' " For the execution, see also "Operations of the 30th Infantry Division 24 Jul–1 Aug 1944 Operation COBRA"; Hugh M. Cole, "VIII Corps Operations, 25–31 July 1944, 'Operation COBRA,' " also in CMH; Topete et al., "Operations of V Corps, 'Cobra Operations,' 26 Jul–15 Aug 44." Useful divisional histories are Hewitt, *Work Horse of the Western Front: The Story of the 30th Infantry Division*; Donald E. Houston, *Hell on Wheels: The 2d Armored Division* (San Rafael: Presidio, 1977); *Spearhead in the West, 1941–1945: The Third Armored Division* (Frankfurt am Main: Kunst und Wervedruck, 1945); Kenneth A. Koyen, *The 4th Armored Division from the Beach to Bastogne* (Munich: Herder Druck, 1945); Nat Frankel and Larry Smith, *Patton's Best: An Informal History of the 4th Armored Division* (New York: Hawthorn, 1978); Paul L. Bogen, *Combat Record of the Sixth Armored Division in the European Theater of Operations, 18 July 1944–8 May 1945* (Aschaffenburg: Steinbech Druck, 1945); *Combat History of the 6th Armored Division in the European Theater of Operations, 18 July 1944–8 May 1945* (Yadkinville, N.C.: Ripple Publishing Co., 1945).

On air-ground tactical cooperation, see Craven and Cate, eds., *Army Air Forces*, especially II, *Europe: TORCH to POINTBLANK, August 1942 to December 1943*, pp.137–145; III, 243–246; Kent Roberts Greenfield, *American Strategy in World War II: A Reconsideration* (Baltimore: Johns Hopkins University Press, 1963), pp.96–112; Christopher Chant, *Ground Attack* (London: Almark, 1976). There is a detailed account of the air support procedures later employed by the Ninth Army in Alvan C. Gillem to Commanding General, Ninth U.S. Army, 19 January 1945, Gillem Papers, USAMHI, Box 5.

Chapter Nine: The Crossroads South of Avranches

1. Chester B. Hansen Diaries, USAMHI, June 1, 1944.

2. Frank James Price, *Troy H. Middleton: A Biography* (Baton Rouge: Louisiana State University Press, 1974), p.184.

3. Hugh M. Cole, "VIII Corps Operations, 25–31 July 1944, Operation 'COBRA,' " CMH, p.62.

4. Ibid., p.62.

5. Martin Blumenson, *Breakout and Pursuit (United States Army in World War II: The European Theater of Operations*, Washington: Office of the Chief of Military History, 1961), p.432.

6. To Marshall, Aug. 2, 1944; Alfred D. Chandler, Jr., ed., Stephen E. Ambrose, assoc. ed., et al., *The Papers of Dwight David Eisenhower: The War Years* (5 vols., Baltimore: Johns Hopkins Press, 1970), IV, 2049.

7. Blumenson, *Breakout and Pursuit*, p.431.

8. Hansen Diaries, Aug. 6, 1944.

9. Martin Blumenson, *The Patton Papers* (2 vols., Boston: Houghton Mifflin, 1972–1974), II, 486, 482.

10. B.H. Liddell Hart, *History of the Second World War* (New York: Putnam, 1971), p.557n.

11. Quoted in Anthony Cave Brown, *Bodyguard of Lies* (New York: Harper & Row, 1975), p.777.

12. Price, *Middleton*, p.188.

13. Ibid.

14. Blumenson, *Breakout and Pursuit*, p.363.

15. Liddell Hart, *Second World War*, p.557n.

16. Blumenson, *Breakout and Pursuit*, p.367.

17. Ladislas Farago, *Patton: Ordeal and Triumph* (paperback, New York: Dell, 1970), p.447.

18. Blumenson, *Breakout and Pursuit*, p.351.

19. Reuben E. Jenkins to Colonel Robert M. Young, 28 January 1947, p.1, copy in Jenkins to MG Eugene A. Salet, 29 January 1967, Jenkins Papers, USAMHI.

20. Hansen Diaries, Aug. 2, 1944.

21. Ibid.; Blumenson, *Patton Papers*, II, 498.

22. Blumenson, *Breakout and Pursuit*, p.375.

23. Blumenson, *Patton Papers*, II, 502.

The statistics on Allied strength in France given at the beginning of this chapter are from SHAEF returns of July 29 as reported in Chester Wilmot, *The Struggle for Europe* (New York: Harper, 1952), p.388. To follow the Allied buildup, see Roland G. Ruppenthal, *Logistical Support of the Armies*, I, *May 1941–September 1944 (United States Army in World War II: The European Theater of Operations*, Washington: Office of the Chief of Military History, 1953), especially pp.449–458.

The rearrangements in the Allied and American command and the press furor associated with them are best outlined in Forrest C. Pogue, *The Supreme Command (United States Army in World War II: The European Theater of Operations*, Washington: Office of the Chief of Military History, 1954).

Patton presented his own account of his campaigns in *War as I Knew It* (Boston: Houghton Mifflin, 1947), but his judgments and prejudices are more candidly revealed in the excerpts from his diary and personal letters in Blumenson's *Patton Papers*. USAMHI now has a copy of the diary of Hobart Gay, Patton's deputy chief of staff and eventually chief of staff at Third Army headquarters. More informal views of Patton's headquarters are presented in Charles R. Codman, *Drive* (Boston: Little, Brown, 1957), based on the letters of Patton's aide to his wife, and in Robert S. Allen, *Lucky Forward: The History of Patton's Third U.S. Army* (New York: Vanguard, 1947).

The Brittany campaign is best detailed in Blumenson's *Breakout and Pursuit*. On "P" Wood there is Hanson W. Baldwin, *Tiger Jack* (Ft. Collins, Colo.: Old Army Press, 1979), based largely on Wood's unpublished memoirs.

Chapter Ten: The Short Envelopment

1. Martin Blumenson, *The Patton Papers* (2 vols., Boston: Houghton Mifflin, 1972–1974), II, 497.

2. Martin Blumenson, *Breakout and Pursuit (United States Army in World War II: The European Theater of Operations*, Washington: Office of the Chief of Military History, 1961), p.435, for first quotation; Ladislas Farago, *Patton: Ordeal and Triumph* (paperback, New York: Dell, 1970), p.509, for second quotation.

3. Farago, *Patton*, p.500.

4. Letter from Collins, 9 December 1945, quoted in Major Kenneth W. Hechler, "VII Corps in Operation 'Cobra,' " CMH, p.219.

5. Blumenson, *Patton Papers*, II, 503.

6. Chester B. Hansen Diaries, USAMHI, Jan. 29, 1945.

7. This aspect of ULTRA is especially commented upon by R.V. Jones, *The Wizard War: British Scientific Intelligence, 1939–1945* (New York: Coward, McCann & Geoghegan, 1978), p.204.

8. Hansen Diaries, Aug. 6, 1944.

9. Martin Blumenson, "General Bradley's Decision at Argentan (13 August 1944)," Kent Roberts Greenfield, ed., *Command Decisions* (Washington: Office of the Chief of Military History, 1960), p.406.

10. Memorandum, Patton to Major General Hugh J. Gaffey, 8 August 1944, copy in Hobart R. Gay Diary, USAMHI, 8 August 1944, p.447.

11. Blumenson, *Breakout and Pursuit*, p.494.

12. Omar N. Bradley, *A Soldier's Story* (New York: Holt, 1951), pp.375–376.

13. Blumenson, *Breakout and Pursuit*, p.487.

14. Blumenson, "Bradley's Decision at Argentan," p.406.

15. Hansen Diaries, Aug. 12, 1944.

16. Blumenson, *Patton Papers*, II, 506.

17. Bradley, *Soldier's Story*, p.376.

18. Ibid.

19. Chief of Staff, Third Army to Commanding General, XV Corps, 12 August 1944, copy in Gay Diary following p.457.

20. Farago, *Patton*, p.521.

21. Ibid.

22. Blumenson, *Patton Papers*, II, 508–509.

23. Bradley, *Soldier's Story*, p.377.

24. Ibid.

25. Ibid.

26. Ibid.

27. Hansen Diaries, March 28, 1945.

28. Blumenson, *Patton Papers*, II, 510.

29. Hansen Diaries, Aug. 14, 1944.

30. Ibid., June 10, 1944.

31. Interview with Gerow, 12 Sept. 1945, by Col. S.L.A. Marshall, copy in Hollis C. Alpert report on Chambois Gap, V Corps COBRA File, CMH, pp.1–2.

32. Gay Diary, 16 August 1944, p.465.

33. Alpert report, pp.11–13.

34. Charles Cawthorn, "Pursuit: Normandy, 1944: An Infantryman Remembers How It Was," *American Heritage*, XXIX, No. 2 (Feb./March 1978), p.80.

Blumenson, *Breakout and Pursuit* remains the basic account, to be supplemented on the question of the closing of the Falaise-Argentan envelopment by the same author's "General Bradley's Decision at Argentan (13 August 1944)," in Greenfield, ed., *Command Decisions*, pp.401–417. See also David Mason, *Breakout: Drive to the Seine* (New York: Ballantine, 1968); James Lucas and James Barker, *The Battle of Normandy: The Falaise Gap* (New York: Holmes & Meier, 1978); Eddy Florentin, *The Battle of the*

Falaise Gap, tr. Mervyn Savill (London: Elek Books, 1965). Unit histories in addition to those of participating units already cited include two of the 5th Armored Division: *The Victory Division in Europe: Story of the Fifth Armored Division* (Gotha: Engelhard-Reyersche Hofbuchdruckerei, 1945); 5th Armored Division Association, *Paths of Armor: Normandy, Northern France, Ardennes, Alsace, Rhineland, Central Europe* (Atlanta: Albert Love Enterprises, 1950).

Chester Wilmot, *The Struggle for Europe* (New York: Harper, 1952) has an especially good account of the Battle of Mont Pinçon, in addition to the customary controversial analysis of the campaign as a whole. For the Canadian army in the Falaise Gap, the official history is indispensable: C.P. Stacey, *The Victory Campaign (Official History of the Canadian Army in the Second World War*, III, Ottawa: Queen's Printer, 1960).

On ULTRA and the Battle of the Falaise Pocket, see Ronald Lewin, *Ultra Goes to War: The First Account of World War II's Greatest Secret Based on Official Documents* (New York: McGraw-Hill, 1978). This section of Lewin's book quotes directly from many of the relevant Enigma intercepts.

Chapter Eleven: The Riviera and the Rhône

1. Forrest C. Pogue, *The Supreme Command (United States Army in World War II: The European Theater of Operations*, Washington: Office of the Chief of Military History, 1954), p.220.

2. *The Seventh United States Army Report of Operations, France and Germany, 1944–1945* (3 vols., Heidelberg: Aloys Graf, 1946), I, 75.

3. Winston S. Churchill, *The Second World War* (6 vols., Boston: Houghton Mifflin, 1948–1953), V, *Closing the Ring*, p.488.

4. Wesley Frank Craven and James Lea Cate, eds., *The Army Air Forces in World War II* (7 vols., Chicago: University of Chicago Press, 1948–1958), III, *Europe: ARGUMENT to V-E Day, January 1944 to May 1945*, p.415.

5. Samuel Eliot Morison, *History of United States Naval Operations in World War II* (15 vols., Boston: Little, Brown, 1950–1962), XI, *The Invasion of France and Germany, 1944–1945*, p.249.

6. *Seventh Army Report*, I, 15.

7. Ibid., p.188.

8. Craven and Cate, eds., *Army Air Forces*, III, 434.

9. *Seventh Army Report*, I, 262.

10. Ibid., pp.265–266.

The volume *From the Riviera to the Rhine* in *United States Army in World War II* remains in preparation. In its absence, the basic account of the campaign in southern France is *The Seventh United States Army Report of Operations, France and Germany*. John Frayn Turner and Robert Jackson, *Destination Berchtesgaden: The Story of the United States Seventh Army in World War II* (New York: Scribner's, 1975) is concise to the point of being cryptic, sometimes even incomprehensible. DRAGOON is surveyed from a French perspective in Jacques Robichon, *The Second D-Day*, tr. Barbara Shuey (New York: Walker, 1969).

The best brief introduction to the controversy over the invasion of southern France is Maurice Matloff, "The ANVIL Decision: Crossroads of Strategy," Kent Roberts Greenfield, ed., *Command Decisions* (Washington: Office of the Chief of Military History, 1960), pp.383–400.

Général de Lattre de Tassigny, *Histoire de la Première Armée Française: Rhin et Danube* (Paris: Plon, 1947; Marshal de Lattre de Tassigny, *The History of the French First Army*, tr. Malcolm Barnes [London: Allen & Unwin, 1952]) tells the French army's story with characteristic verve and prejudice. General Lucian K. Truscott, Jr., wrote *Command Missions: A Personal Story* (New York: Dutton, 1954). The divisional history of the 3rd Infantry is among the better ones: Donald G. Taggart, ed., *History of the Third*

Infantry Division in World War II (Washington: Infantry Journal Press, 1947). See also *The Fighting Forty-Fifth: The Combat Report of an Infantry Division* (Baton Rouge: Army Navy Publishing Co., 1946). There is an amusing narrative of the airborne troops in DRAGOON, Robert H. Adleman and George Walton, *The Champagne Campaign* (Boston: Little, Brown, 1969).

For the role of ULTRA in the VI Corps's effort to close the trap at Montélimar, see "Synthesis of Experiences in the Use of ULTRA Intelligence by U.S. Army Field Commands in the European Theatre of Operations," NA, RG 457, N.S.A. SRH-006, p.26; "Reports by U.S. Army ULTRA Representatives with Army Field Commands in the European Theatre of Operations," NA, RG 457, N.S.A. SRH-023, Part I, Tab G, "Ultra and the U.S. Seventh Army, " p.A-1.

On the logistical importance of the southern French ports, see Morison, *United States Naval Operations*, XI, especially pp.291–292 (for the statistics on troops landed in August and September and by the end of the war); Roland G. Ruppenthal, *Logistical Support of the Army*, II, *September 1944–May 1945 (United States Army in World War II: The European Theater of Operations*, Washington: Office of the Chief of Military History, 1959), especially pp.117–125 (p.124 for the tonnage statistics).

Chapter Twelve: The Seine

1. Martin Blumenson, *The Patton Papers* (2 vols., Boston: Houghton Mifflin, 1972–1974), II, 510.

2. Ibid.

3. Chester B. Hansen Diaries, USAMHI, Aug. 24, 1944.

4. Blumenson, *Patton Papers*, II, 522.

5. Ibid.

6. Ibid., p.523.

7. Chester Wilmot, *The Struggle for Europe* (New York: Harper, 1952), p.427, for Hitler quotation; David Irving, *Hitler's War* (New York: Viking, 1977), p.572, for Jodl quotation.

8. Wilmot, *Struggle for Europe*, p.427.

9. Ladislas Farago, *Patton: Ordeal and Triumph* (paperback, New York: Dell, 1970), p.530.

10. Ibid., p.529.

11. B.H. Liddell Hart, *History of the Second World War* (New York: Putnam, 1971), p.567.

12. Bradley to Eisenhower, 10 September 1944, Bradley Papers, USAMHI, Correspondence with Famous Persons, Eisenhower File.

13. Hansen Diaries, Aug. 20, 1944.

14. Ibid., Aug. 22, 1944.

15. Blumenson, *Patton Papers*, II, 523.

16. Farago, *Patton*, p.536.

17. Martin Blumenson, *Breakout and Pursuit (United States Army in World War II: The European Theater of Operations*, Washington: Office of the Chief of Military History, 1961), p.598.

18. Omar N. Bradley, *A Soldier's Story* (New York: Holt, 1951), p.392.

Blumenson, *Breakout and Pursuit* remains the basic account. For the military geography of the campaign across France, a superbly useful book is Douglas W. Johnson, *Battlefields of the World War: Western and Southern Fronts: A Study in Military Geography* (1 vol. plus maps in slipcase, New York: Oxford University Press, 1921).

On the Third Army's aerial partners, see *Fly, Seek and Destroy: The Story of XIX TAC* (Paris: Desfosses-Neogravure, 1945).

On the liberation of Paris, the better works include Larry Collins and Dominique Lapierre, *Is Paris Burning?* (New York: Simon & Schuster, 1965); Adrien Dansett, *Histoire de la libération de Paris* (Paris: Fayard, 1946); and Willis Thornton, *The Liberation of Paris* (New York: Harcourt, Brace & World, 1962).

Chapter Thirteen: The Meuse

1. 21 Army Group/20721/G(Plans), 27 June 1944, "Operation 'LUCKY STRIKE': Appreciation of Possible Development of Operations," NA, RG 331, Box 68, SHAEF, 370.2 LUCKY STRIKE, pp.6 (main quotation), 3 ("force a crossing. . .").

2. Forrest C. Pogue, *The Supreme Command (United States Army in World War II: The European Theater of Operations*, Washington: Office of the Chief of Military History, 1954), p.53.

3. Chester B. Hansen Diaries, USAMHI, Aug. 18, 1954.

4. Martin Blumenson, *The Patton Papers* (2 vols., Boston: Houghton Mifflin, 1972–1974), II, 531.

5. Chester Wilmot, *The Struggle for Europe* (New York: Harper, 1952), p.458.

6. Pogue, *Supreme Command*, p.245.

7. Alfred D. Chandler, Jr., ed., Stephen E. Ambrose, assoc. ed., et al., *The Papers of Dwight David Eisenhower: The War Years* (5 vols., Baltimore: Johns Hopkins Press, 1970), III, 1933.

8. Ibid., p.1960.

9. Ibid., IV, 2087.

10. Ibid., p.2093.

11. *The Memoirs of Field-Marshal the Viscount Montgomery of Alamein* (Cleveland and New York: World, 1958), p.239.

12. Ibid.

13. Hansen Diaries, Aug. 28, 1944.

14. Ibid., Aug. 25, Sept. 1, 1944.

15. Ibid, Sept. 1, 1944.

16. Ladislas Farago, *Patton: Ordeal and Triumph* (paperback, New York: Dell, 1970), p.578.

17. Chandler, ed., *Papers of Eisenhower*, IV, 2116, 2122.

18. Hobart R. Gay Diary, USAMHI, Aug. 30, 1944, p.482a.

Pogue, *Supreme Command* offers the most judicious account of the possible axes of advance across northwest France into the Low Countries and Germany and of the considerations that shaped the Allied choices among them. For a basic assessment by SHAEF, see SHAEF/18008/Ops, "Post-'OVERLORD' Planning," 18 May 1944, NA, RG 331, Box 77, SHAEF, Vol. I.

On German casualties since D-Day see Pogue, *Supreme Command*, pp.247–248. On German rebuilding, ibid., pp.302–304; Charles B. MacDonald, *The Siegfried Line Campaign (United States Army in World War II: The European Theater of Operations*, Washington: Office of the Chief of Military History, 1963), pp.14–19; H.M. Cole, *The Lorraine Campaign (United States Army in World War II: The European Theater of Operations*, Washington: Historical Division, Department of the Army, 1950), pp.29–52, p.34 for figures on German tank production and distribution.

For Patton's shrewd intelligence chief, see his memoir, Oscar W. Koch with Robert G. Hays, *G-2: Intelligence for Patton* (Philadelphia: Whitmore, 1971).

On the CROSSBOW campaign and the resumption of the strategic bomber offensive, see the works on strategic bombing cited in Chapter Four and Basil Collier, *The Battle of the V-Weapons* (New York: Morrow, 1965).

The capacities of the Channel ports and Antwerp are described in detail in Roland G. Ruppenthal, *Logistical Support of the Armies*, II, *September 1944–May 1945 (United States Army in World War II: The European Theater of Operations*, Washington: Office of the Chief of Military History, 1959), pp.104–116.

For the number of tanks in the Third Army, see Cole, *Lorraine Campaign*, p.18.

Martin Blumenson, *Breakout and Pursuit (United States Army in World War II: The European Theater of Operations*, Washington: Office of the Chief of Military History, 1961) concludes with the final phase of the American pursuit across France, over the rivers and battlefields of World War I.

Chapter Fourteen: The Twin Tyrants: Logistics . . .

1. Roland G. Ruppenthal, *Logistical Support of the Armies*, I, *May 1941–September 1944 (United States Army in World War II: The European Theater of Operations*, Washington: Office of the Chief of Military History, 1953), p.551.

2. Ibid., p.564.

3. Chester B. Hansen Diaries, USAMHI, June 19, 1944.

4. Martin Blumenson, *Breakout and Pursuit (United States Army in World War II: The European Theater of Operations*, Washington: Office of the Chief of Military History, 1961), p.672.

5. Ibid., p.670.

6. Ibid., p.680.

7. Alfred D. Chandler, Jr., ed., Stephen E. Ambrose, assoc. ed., et al., *The Papers of Dwight David Eisenhower: The War Years* (5 vols., Baltimore: Johns Hopkins Press, 1970), IV, 2120–2121; *The Memoirs of Field-Marshal the Viscount Montgomery of Alamein* (Cleveland and New York: World, 1958), p.244 (italics not included in the latter version).

8. Chandler, ed., *Papers of Eisenhower*, IV, 2120. For the circumstances of Montgomery's receipt of the message, Montgomery, *Memoirs*, p.214; also Montgomery to Eisenhower, M-181, 9 September 1944, NA, RG 331, Box 77, SHAEF, Vol. I.

9. Montgomery, *Memoirs*, pp.245–246.

10. Chandler, ed., *Papers of Eisenhower*, IV, 2120.

11. Chester Wilmot, *The Struggle for Europe* (New York: Harper, 1952), p.489.

12. Montgomery, *Memoirs*, p.250.

13. Chandler, ed., *Papers of Eisenhower*, IV, 2136, for "a single knife-like and narrow thrust"; Dwight D. Eisenhower, *Crusade in Europe* (Garden City: Doubleday, 1948), p.306, for "pencillike thrust."

14. B.H. Liddell Hart, *History of the Second World War* (New York: Putnam, 1971), p.566.

15. Chandler, ed., *Papers of Eisenhower*, IV, 2125.

16. Eisenhower, *Crusade in Europe*, p.306.

17. S.L.A. Marshall, *Men against Fire: The Problem of Battle Command in Future War* (Apollo Edition, New York: Morrow, 1965), p.196. For Middleton's description of his infantry as "none too good," Blumenson, *Breakout and Pursuit*, p.644.

18. Blumenson, *Breakout and Pursuit*, p.649.

19. Martin Blumenson, *The Patton Papers* (2 vols., Boston: Houghton Mifflin, 1972–1974), II, 532.

20. Omar N. Bradley, *A Soldier's Story* (New York: Holt, 1951), p.367.

21. Hansen Diaries, Sept. 1, 1944.

For its basic information on logistical problems, this chapter relies on Ruppenthal's two volumes on *Logistical Support of the Armies*. Ruppenthal summarizes his conclusions in "Logistics and the Broad-Front Strategy," Kent Roberts Greenfield, ed., *Command Decisions* (Washington: Office of the Chief of Military History, 1960), pp.419–427. There is a wealth of data also in Joseph Bykofsky and Harold Larson, *The Transportation Corps: Operations Overseas (United States Army in World War II: The Technical Services*, Washington: Office of the Chief of Military History, 1957). The calculations of what might have been logistically possible are based on Martin van Creveld, *Supplying War: Logistics from Wallenstein to Patton* (Cambridge: Cambridge University Press, 1977).

Bradley discussed the issues of logistics and the broad-front advance in an unusual long letter to Eisenhower, 12 September 1944, NA, RG 331, Box 77, SHAEF, Vol. I. The logistical issues are also considered strongly in Stephen E. Ambrose, "Eisenhower as Commander: Single Thrust Versus Broad Front," Chandler, ed., *Papers of Eisenhower*, V, 39–48.

The Mons pocket merits more historical consideration than it has received. In addition to the official histories, there are brief accounts in J. Lawton Collins's *Lightning Joe: An Autobiography* (Baton Rouge: Louisiana State University Press, 1979) and

Charles H. Corlett's "One Man's Story, Some of It about War," USAMHI. See also *First United States Army Report of Operations, 1 August 1944–22 February 1945* (4 vols., Washington: Government Printing Office, 1946), I, 34–35.

The modest Lieutenant General Sir Brian Horrocks wrote ingratiating recollections, *A Full Life* (London: Collins, 1960), and with Eversley Belfield and H. Essame, *Corps Commander* (New York: Scribner's, 1977). The second volume of the British official history of the 1944–1945 Western Front begins with the advance into Belgium: L.F. Ellis with A.E. Warhurst, *Victory in the West*, II, *The Defeat of Germany (History of the Second World War, United Kingdom Military Series*, London: H.M. Stationery Office, 1968). For the capture of Antwerp, see also *Taurus Pursuant: A History of the 11th Armoured Division* (Germany: British Army of the Rhine, 1945).

For the Battle of Brest, see Blumenson, *Breakout and Pursuit;* Frank James Price, *Troy H. Middleton: A Biography* (Baton Rouge: Louisiana State University Press, 1974); Joseph H. Ewing, *29 Let's Go! A History of the 29th Infantry Division in World War II* (Washington: Infantry Journal Press, 1948).

Chapter Fifteen: . . . and Time

1. Alfred D. Chandler, Jr., ed., Stephen E. Ambrose, assoc. ed., et al., *The Papers of Dwight David Eisenhower: The War Years* (5 vols., Baltimore: Johns Hopkins Press, 1970), IV, 2133–2134.

2. Ibid., p.2164.

3. Chester B. Hansen Diaries, USAMHI, July 2, June 19, 1944.

4. Chandler, ed., *Papers of Eisenhower*, III, 1737–1738.

5. Charles B. MacDonald, *The Siegfried Line Campaign (United States Army in World War II: The European Theater of Operations*, Washington: Office of the Chief of Military History, 1963), p.133.

6. Ibid., p.134.

7. Chester Wilmot, *The Struggle for Europe* (New York: Harper, 1952), p.486.

8. B.H. Liddell Hart, *History of the Second World War* (New York: Putnam, 1971), p.559.

9. MacDonald, *Siegfried Line Campaign*, p.122.

10. Hansen Diaries, Sept. 12, 14, 1944.

11. Wilmot, *Struggle for Europe*, p.485.

12. Walter Goerlitz, *History of the German General Staff, 1657–1945*, tr. Brian Battershaw (New York: Praeger, 1953), p.335.

13. Hansen Diaries, Sept. 15, 1944.

14. First Army G-2 Estimate No. 28, 15 September 1944, in "Breaking the Siegfried Line," CMH, I, Chap. I, pp.9–13.

15. Hansen Diaries, Sept. 15, 1944.

There is a review of airborne activity and planning from D-Day onward in Brereton to Eisenhower, August 20, 1944, copy in Floyd Lavinius Parks Papers, USAMHI. Parks was chief of staff of the First Allied Airborne Army. His papers at USAMHI, including his diary, contain considerable information on the creation of the airborne army and the planning of MARKET-GARDEN. For further material concerning this planning, see the accounts of MARKET-GARDEN cited in the next chapter. On the skepticism of Eisenhower and Smith, see "Administrative and Logistical History of the European Theater of Operations," CMH, Pt. V, Vol. II, p.124.

The First Army's initial operations against the West Wall are detailed in MacDonald, *Siegfried Line Campaign*, and "Breaking the Siegfried Line," ms. in CMH.

Chapter Sixteen: Holland

1. Floyd Lavinius Parks Diary, USAMHI, 11 Sept. 1944, p.1, and 13 Sept. 1944, p.6.
2. Capt. John G. Westover, "The American Divisions in Operation Market," CMH, p.20.
3. Parks Diary, 19 Sept. 1944, pp.7–8.
4. Charles B. MacDonald, *The Siegfried Line Campaign (United States Army in World War II: The European Theater of Operations*, Washington: Office of the Chief of Military History, 1963), p.170.
5. Westover, "American Divisions in Market," p.29.
6. James M. Gavin, *On to Berlin: Battles of an Airborne Commander, 1943–1946* (New York: Viking, 1978), p.150.
7. Ibid., p.151.
8. MacDonald, *Siegfried Line Campaign*, p.163.
9. Gavin, *On to Berlin*, p.162.
10. MacDonald, *Siegfried Line Campaign*, p.168.
11. Gavin, *On to Berlin*, p.173.
12. Ibid., p.171.
13. Parks Diary, 20 September 1944, p.5.
14. T.J. McCarthy, "He Well Remembers 'A Bridge Too Far,' " Philadelphia *Sunday Bulletin*, July 24, 1977, Sec. 3, p.5.
15. Chester Wilmot, *The Struggle for Europe* (New York: Harper, 1952), p.512n.
16. Ibid., p.526.
17. Field Marshal the Viscount Montgomery of Alamein, *Normandy to the Baltic* (Boston: Houghton Mifflin, 1948), p.236.
18. Lewis H. Brereton, *The Brereton Diaries: The War in the Air in the Pacific, Middle East and Europe, 3 October 1941–8 May 1945* (New York: Morrow, 1946), pp.360–361.

MARKET-GARDEN has commanded more attention than any other battle of the 1944–1945 Western Front save the D-Day landings and the Ardennes. The published American official accounts are in MacDonald, *Siegfried Line Campaign* and John C. Warren, *Airborne Operations in World War II: European Theater* (Washington: Historical Division, U.S. Air Force, 1956). Also basic is Westover, "American Divisions in Operation Market," ms. in CMH. The most vivid book-length account is of course Cornelius Ryan, *A Bridge Too Far* (New York: Simon & Schuster, 1974). Also excellent is Christopher Hibbert, *The Battle of Arnhem* (London: Batsford, 1962).

Pertinent unit histories in addition to those of the 82nd and 101st Airborne cited in Chapter Three include *By Air to Battle: Official Account of the British Airborne Divisions* (London: H.M. Stationery Office, 1945); the Earl of Rosse and E.B. Hill, *The Story of the Guards Armoured Division* (London: Geoffrey Bles, 1956); and G.L. Derney, *The Guards Armoured Division* (London: Hutchinson, 1955).

First-hand accounts in addition to those by Gavin and Brereton include Horrocks's memoirs, cited in chapter 15; Ridgway's, cited in chapter 3; R.E. Urquhart with Wilfred Greatorex, *Arnhem* (New York: Norton, 1958); J.O.E. Vandeleur, *A Soldier's Story* (London: Gale & Polden, 1967); Stanislaw Sosabowski, *Freely I Served* (London: William Kimber, 1960).

For Browning's analysis of the reasons for the failure to hold Arnhem, as reported to First Airborne Army headquarters, see Parks Diary, 10 October 1944.

Chapter Seventeen: Attack in the Ardennes (I)

1. Charles B. MacDonald, *The Siegfried Line Campaign (United States Army in World War II: The European Theater of Operations*, Washington: Office of the Chief of Military History, 1963), p.56.

MacDonald's work is the basic account. See also *First United States Army Report of Operations, 1 August 1944–22 February 1945* (4 vols., Washington: Government Printing Office, 1946); "Breaking the Siegfried Line," ms. in CMH, I, chapter 6, "Breaking the Siegfried Line V Corps," and chapter 8, "Situation in September First U.S. Army."

Chapter Eighteen: Lorraine (I)

1. Capt. Harry A. Morris, 1st Lt. Chris G. Petrow, 2nd Lt. M. Ludden, and T/3 Weldon T. Patton, "The Capture of Metz," CMH, Chapter I, p.4.
2. H.M. Cole, *The Lorraine Campaign (United States Army in World War II: The European Theater of Operations*, Washington: Historical Division, Department of the Army, 1950), p.154.
3. A standard edition is William Balck, *Tactics, by Balck . . .*, tr. Walter Krueger (4th completely revised edition, 2 vols., Fort Leavenworth: U.S. Cavalry Association, 1911–1914).

The Morris et al. account is basic for events around Metz. For the entire campaign, see Cole, *Lorraine Campaign*. A richly detailed narrative of the Arnaville bridgehead battle is in Charles B. MacDonald and Sidney T. Mathews, *Three Battles: Arnaville, Altuzzo, and Schmidt (United States Army in World War II*, Washington: Office of the Chief of Military History, 1952).

The excellent Donald W. Johnson, *Battlefields of the World War: Western and Southern Fronts: A Study in Military Geography* (1 vol. plus maps in slipcase, New York: Oxford University Press, 1921) is especially good on the battlefields of Lorraine. For the battles of 1870, see Michael Howard, *The Franco-Prussian War: The German Invasion of France, 1870–1871* (New York: Macmillan, 1962).

USAMHI has a copy of a brief, 29-page study of the 4th Armored Division in *The Nancy Bridgehead* (Fort Knox, 1946). For the XII Corps there is George Dyer, *XII Corps: Spearhead of Patton's Army* (Baton Rouge: Military Press of Louisiana, 1947).

For the Allied right flank the principal narratives remain *The Seventh United States Army Report of Operations, France and Germany, 1944–1945* (3 vols., Heidelberg: Aloys Graf, 1946) and Général de Lattre de Tassigny, *Histoire de la Première Armée Française: Rhin et Danube* (Paris: Plon, 1947). On the activation of the 6th Army Group, see "Administrative and Logistical History of the European Theater of Operations," CMH, Pt. II, Vol. II, pp.229–231.

Chapter Nineteen: The Reich Frontiers

1. Alfred D. Chandler, Jr., ed., Stephen E. Ambrose, assoc. ed., et al., *The Papers of Dwight David Eisenhower: The War Years* (5 vols., Baltimore: Johns Hopkins University Press, 1970), IV, 2148; SHAEF G-3 Division (Forward), GCT 370–31/Plans, "Memorandum by Planning Staff: Advance into Germany after Occupation of the Ruhr," 24 Sept. 1944, NA, RG 331, Box 77, SHAEF, OC of S, SGS, Post-OVERLORD Planning, File No. 381, Vol. I.
2. Forrest C. Pogue, *The Supreme Command (United States Army in World War II: The European Theater of Operations*, Washington: Office of the Chief of Military History, 1954), pp.290–291, quotation from p.291.
3. Chandler, ed., *Papers of Eisenhower*, IV, 2164.
4. *The Memoirs of Field-Marshal the Viscount Montgomery of Alamein* (Cleveland and New York: World, 1958), pp.252–253.
5. Chester Wilmot, *The Struggle for Europe* (New York: Harper, 1952), pp.534,535.
6. Ibid., p.535.
7. Minutes of meeting held at SHAEF Forward, Sept. 22, 1944, quoted in Charles B. MacDonald, *The Siegfried Line Campaign (United States Army in World War II: The European Theater of Operations*, Washington: Office of the Chief of Military History, 1963), p.211.
8. Field Marshal the Viscount Montgomery of Alamein, *Normandy to the Baltic* (Boston: Houghton Mifflin, 1948), p.153.

9. MacDonald, *Siegfried Line Campaign*, p.204.

10. Chandler, ed., *Papers of Eisenhower*, IV, 2215.

11. Montgomery, *Memoirs*, p.254; Chandler, ed., *Papers of Eisenhower*, IV, 2216.

12. M532, 16–10–44, General Operational Situation and Directive, NA, RG 331, Box 77, SHAEF, Vol. II.

13. Charles H. Corlett, "One Man's Story, Some of It about War," USAMHI, p.277.

14. Ibid.

15. Ibid., p.278.

16. MacDonald, *Siegfried Line Campaign*, p.301.

17. Corlett, "One Man's Story," p.282.

18. William Walton, "The Battle of Hürtgen Forest: Gloomy German Woods Takes Its Place in U.S. History beside the Wilderness and the Argonne," *Life*, XVIII, No. 1 (Jan. 1, 1945), p.33.

MacDonald, *Siegfried Line Campaign* and "Breaking the Siegfried Line," 2 vols., CMH, remain the essential operational narratives.

On the battle to open Antwerp, there is R.H. Thompson, *The Eighty-five Days: The Story of the Battles of the Scheldt* (New York: Ballantine, 1957).

For the 104th Division, see Leo A. Hoegh and Howard J. Doyle, *Timberwolf Tracks: The History of the 104th Infantry Division, 1942–1945* (Washington: Infantry Journal Press, 1946). General Corlett's unpublished memoirs, USAMHI, consider the Battle of the Peel Marshes.

The buildup of American divisions is reviewed in Roland G. Ruppenthal, *Logistical Support of the Armies*, II, *September 1944–May 1945 (United States Army in World War II: The European Theater of Operations*, Washington: Office of the Chief of Military History, 1959).

Charles Whiting has recounted the battles of *Bloody Aachen* (London: Leo Cooper, 1976).

On the relief of Corlett, Bradley told Eisenhower that Hodges "requested the relief of General Corlett. . . . General Hodges stated that in his opinion General Corlett is not in good health and that he has shown signs of being tired." Bradley said that if after rest and a physical examination Corlett "completely regains his health, I would be glad to accept him as a Corps Commander later on." Bradley emphasized that "as far as I am concerned, the relief of General Corlett from command of the XIX Corps is done without prejudice and without reflection on his ability as a commander" (19 October 1944, Bradley Papers, USAMHI, Correspondence with Famous Persons, Eisenhower File). The William C. Sylvan Diary (copy secured from National Archives), however, reflects Hodges's growing irritation with Corlett, as on 14 October 1944, when in response to an appeal from Corlett for more troops and ammunition because the XIX Corps advance had been halted, Hodges "[f]or not the first time reminded him to obtain more troops and more ammunition was at the present time impossible" and commented sarcastically that "surely they [the XIX Corps] were not admitting that they could go no further or that 'as far as you are concerned the war is over' " (p.95).

Bradley's aide Major Hansen confirmed, on the other hand, that Bradley saw the relief as caused by health problems alone and recorded that on hearing the news, "Hobbs cried, thinking he had let Corlett down in the fulfillment of his mission. Ernie Harmon subsequently wrote a letter to the General [Bradley], telling the old man that his division had accomplished its mission as well as might be expected and that they were all highly pleased at Division level with the caliber of leadership offered by General Corlett in his capacity as corps commander" (Chester B. Hansen Diaries, USAMHI, Oct. 19, 1944).

For the Huertgen Forest, see Charles B. MacDonald, *The Battle of the Huertgen Forest* (Philadelphia: Lippincott, 1963) and, for the first battles, "Initial Attack on Schmidt, 6–16 October, 9th Division," Chapter 14 of "Breaking the Siegfried Line," I, and "V Corps Strikes at Schmidt," chapter 2 of Vol. II. MacDonald's detailed account of the 28th division's battle for Schmidt, November 2–8, is in Charles B. MacDonald and Sidney T. Mathews, *Three Battles: Arnaville, Altuzzo, Schmidt (United States Army in World War II*, Washington: Office of the Chief of Military History, 1952).

Chapter Twenty: Autumn Interlude

1. Ronald Lewin, *Rommel as Military Commander* (paperback, New York: Ballantine, 1968), p.217.

2. Wesley Frank Craven and James Lea Cate, eds., *The Army Air Forces in World War II* (7 vols., Chicago: University of Chicago Press, 1948–1958), III, *Europe: ARGUMENT to V-E Day, January 1944 to May 1945*, p.653.

3. Oct. 23, 1944; Forrest C. Pogue, *The Supreme Command (United States Army in World War II: The European Theater of Operations*, Washington: Office of the Chief of Military History, 1954), p.307.

4. Oct. 23, 1944; Alfred D. Chandler, Jr., ed., Stephen E. Ambrose, assoc. ed., et al., *The Papers of Dwight David Eisenhower: The War Years* (5 vols., Baltimore: Johns Hopkins University Press, 1970), IV, 2247.

5. Ibid., p.2248.

6. Omar N. Bradley, *A Soldier's Story* (New York: Holt, 1951), pp.440–441.

For the manpower and ammunition problems, see Roland G. Ruppenthal, *Logistical Support of the Armies*, II, *September 1944–May 1945 (United States Army in World War II: The European Theater of Operations*, Washington: Office of the Chief of Military History, 1959). On alterations in the Troop Basis during the course of the war, see Kent Roberts Greenfield, Robert R. Palmer, and Bell I. Wiley, *The Organization of Ground Combat Troops (United States Army in World War II: The Army Ground Forces*, Washington: Historical Division, United States Army, 1947). There is also much information on the replacement problem in Robert R. Palmer, Bell I. Wiley, and William R. Keast, *The Procurement and Training of Ground Combat Troops (United States Army in World War II: The Army Ground Forces*, Washington: Historical Division, Department of the Army, 1948). On ammunition, see also Henry C. Thomson and Lida Mayo, *The Ordnance Department: Procurement and Supply (United States Army in World War II: The Technical Services*, Washington: Office of the Chief of Military History, 1960) and Lida Mayo, *The Ordnance Department: On Beachhead and Battlefront (United States Army in World War II: The Technical Services*, Washington: Office of the Chief of Military History, 1968).

For the depleted strength of Union infantry regiments in the Gettysburg campaign, see Edwin B. Coddington, *The Gettysburg Campaign: A Study in Command* (New York: Scribner's, 1968), p.245.

On the proximity fuze, see Ralph B. Baldwin, *The Deadly Fuze: Secret Weapon of World War II* (San Rafael: Presidio, 1979), and for the development of the fuze, Constance McLaughlin Green, Henry C. Thomson, and Peter C. Roots, *The Ordnance Department: Planning Munitions for War (United States Army in World War II: The Technical Services*, Washington: Office of the Chief of Military History, 1955).

For the strategic bombing offensive, see in addition to Craven and Cate, eds., *Europe: ARGUMENT to V-E Day*, the British official history, Sir Charles Webster and Noble Frankland, *The Strategic Air Offensive against Germany* (4 vols., *History of the Second World War: United Kingdom Military Series*, London: H.M. Stationery Office, 1961) and two unofficial, critical British analyses: Anthony Verrier, *The Bomber Offensive* (New York: Macmillan, 1969) and Max Hastings, *Bomber Command* (New York: Dial, 1979). On the effects, David MacIsaac, ed., *The United States Strategic Bombing Survey* (10 vols., New York: Garland, 1976).

SHAEF responded to Marshall's urging of an inquiry into possible methods of hastening the end of the war with Office of the Deputy Supreme Commander, DSC/ TS.100, 25th October, 1944, "Notes on Air Policy to be Adopted with a View to Rapid Defeat of Germany," NA, RG 331, Box 77, SHAEF, Vol. II.

Chapter Twenty-One: Lorraine (II)

1. Omar N. Bradley, *A Soldier's Story* (New York: Holt, 1951), p.434.
2. Chester B. Hansen Diaries, USAMHI, Oct. 23, 1944.

3. H.M. Cole, *The Lorraine Campaign (United States Army in World War II: The European Theater of Operations*, Washington: Historical Division, Department of the Army, 1950), p.299.

4. E.C. Semple, *Influences of Geographic Environment* (New York: Russell & Russell, 1969; first published 1911), p.540.

5. Hansen Diaries, Oct. 11, 23, 1944.

6. Martin Blumenson, *The Patton Papers* (2 vols., Boston: Houghton Mifflin, 1972–1974), II, 588–589.

7. Captain Harry A. Morris, 1st Lt. Chris G. Petrow, 2nd Lt. M. Ludden, T/3 Weldon T. Patton, "The Capture of Metz," CMH, Chapter II, p.61.

8. Hobart R. Gay Diary, USAMHI, Oct. 4, 1944, p.522.

9. Ladislas Farago, *Patton: Ordeal and Triumph* (paperback, New York: Dell, 1970), p.634.

10. Hansen Diaries, Nov. 11, 1944.

11. Farago, *Patton*, p.643.

12. Blumenson, *Patton Papers*, II, 601.

13. Cole, *Lorraine Campaign*, p.482.

14. Blumenson, *Patton Papers*, pp.587, 586.

Cole, *Lorraine Campaign* and Morris et al., "Capture of Metz," CMH, are the basic narratives. The Hobart R. Gay Diary, also useful, reports on Oct. 9, p.526, Gay's termination of the attack on Driant, acting with Patton's authority, five days after Patton had insisted he could not allow an attack by the Third Army to fail.

See also George Dyer, *XII Corps: Spearhead of Patton's Army* (Baton Rouge: Military Press of Louisiana, 1947); *History of the 26th Yankee Division, 1917–1919, 1941–1945* (Salem, Mass.: Yankee Veterans Association, 1955); George M. Fuermann and Edward Cranz, *Ninety-Fifth Infantry Division History, 1918–1946* (Atlanta: Albert Love Enterprises, 1947).

Especially good on the Orscholz Switch Line and the surprise it occasioned is "Meeting the Saar-Moselle Switch Line," part of chapter 8, unpaged, of Morris et al., "Capture of Metz."

Chapter Twenty-Two: Alsace

1. Martin Blumenson, *The Patton Papers* (2 vols., Boston: Houghton Mifflin, 1972–1974), II, 576.

2. Chester B. Hansen Diaries, USAMHI, Nov. 24, 1944.

3. Blumenson, *Patton Papers*, II, 583.

The Seventh United States Army Report of Operations, France and Germany, 1944–1945 (3 vols., Heidelberg: Aloys Graf, 1946) remains the best account of American operations in the 6th Army Group and of the 2ème DB's operations while it was part of the Seventh Army. For the French, see Général de Lattre de Tassigny, *Histoire de la Première Armée Française* (Paris: Plon, 1947). H.M. Cole, *The Lorraine Campaign (United States Army in World War II: The European Theater of Operations*, Washington: Historical Division, Department of the Army, 1950) provides its usual skillful account when Third Army operations impinged on the Seventh Army's campaign, particularly in the battles of the 4th Armored Division against Panzer Lehr. The Michelin Green Guide to *Vosges-Alsace*, 1948 edition (Paris: Services de Tourisme Michelin) has interesting details on the entrance of the French First Army into Strasbourg.

Pertinent unit histories include *Combat History 44th Infantry Division, 1944–1945* (Atlanta: Albert Love Enterprises, 1946); Michael A. Bass, *The Story of the Century* (100th Division) (New York: Century Association, 1946); Ralph Mueller and Jerry Turk, *Report after Action: The Story of the 103rd Infantry Division* (Innsbruck: Wagner'sche Universitäts-Buchdruckerei, 1945).

Chapter Twenty-Three: Huertgen Forest and Roer Plain

1. Chester B. Hansen Diaries, USAMHI, Nov. 8 (first quotation), Nov. 14 (second and third quotations), 1944. For Bradley's tiredness, ibid., Oct. 9. For the mood of war weariness, Nov. 14.

2. Ibid., Nov. 8 (first quotation), Nov. 14 (second), Nov. 16 (third), 1944.

3. Ibid., Nov. 18, 1944. Though written on the third day of the attack, this entry reflects the impressions formed when detailed news of the first day reached 12th Army Group headquarters.

4. As stated in the present-day edition of FM 100–5, *Operations* (Washington: Headquarters, Department of the Army, 1976), p.4–3.

5. Charles B. MacDonald, *The Siegfried Line Campaign (United States Army in World War II: The European Theater of Operations*, Washington: Office of the Chief of Military History, 1963), p.488.

6. Cota to Gerhardt, July 1, 1963, Charles H. Gerhardt Papers, USAMHI. Despite the element of flattery in such a letter, Cota's character gives the phrase the ring of authenticity.

For the November offensive of the First and Ninth Armies, MacDonald, *Siegfried Line Campaign* and "Breaking the Siegfried Line" (2 vols., ms. in CMH), II, are the essential accounts. As usual, General Collins's memoirs should be consulted for VII Corps operations: J. Lawton Collins, *Lightning Joe: An Autobiography* (Baton Rouge: Louisiana State University Press, 1979). Charles B. MacDonald, *The Battle of the Huertgen Forest* (Philadelphia: Lippincott, 1963) continues its coverage of the nightmare war in the dark woods.

There is a reprint of the 104th Division's manual on the night attacks in which Terry Allen trained it to specialize: *Night Attack, 104th (Timberwolf) Division, 1944* (Fort Bliss: Air Defense School, 1969).

Mention of the Ninth Army's concise history of its actions is customarily accompanied by words of praise, and rightly so: *Conquer: The Story of Ninth Army, 1944–1945* (Washington: Infantry Journal Press, 1947). Furthermore, the operations of Simpson's army in the Roer and other campaigns are illuminated by two of the best of the division histories: Theodore Draper, *The 84th Infantry Division in the Battle of Germany, November 1944–May 1945* (New York: Viking, 1946) and Donald E. Houston, *Hell on Wheels: The 2d Armored Division* (San Rafael: Presidio, 1977). There is also Allen R. Mick, ed., *With the 102nd Infantry Division through Germany* (Washington: Infantry Journal Press, 1947). Much material about the XIII Corps, disguised as "X" Corps, can be found in postwar lectures by its commander, General Gillem, on the theme of corps command, in the Gillem Papers, USAMHI; e.g., "Action of a Corps," Lecture, Fort Benning, Ga., 3 March 1948, Box 13.

Eisenhower rated the principal generals in Europe on February 1, 1945, ranking Bradley and Spaatz equal and highest, Bedell Smith third, Patton fourth, Mark Clark fifth, Truscott sixth, Doolittle seventh, Gerow eighth, Collins ninth, Patch tenth, Hodges eleventh, and Simpson twelfth, among others. (It is noteworthy that Devers was ranked twenty-fourth, though with a comment that his "proper position . . . is not yet fully determined"); Alfred D. Chandler, Jr., ed., Stephen E. Ambrose, assoc. ed., et al., *The Papers of Dwight David Eisenhower: The War Years* (5 vols., Baltimore: Johns Hopkins Press, 1970), IV, 2466–2469, quotation from p.2469. Bradley had ranked the commanders at Eisenhower's request on December 1, 1944 (Bradley Papers, USAMHI, Correspondence with Famous Persons, Eisenhower File), as follows:

1. Smith, W.B.	7. Collins, J. Lawton
2. Spaatz, Carl A.	8. Gerow, L.T.
3. Hodges, C.H.	9. Clark, Mark W.
4. Quesada, Elwood R.	10. Bull, Harold R.
5. Truscott, L.K., Jr.	11. Gruenther, A.M.
6. Patton, George S., Jr.	12. Kean, W.B.

13. Allen, L.C.	23. Walker, W.H.
14. Middleton, Troy H.	24. Brooks, Edward H.
15. Patch, Alexander McC.	25. McLain, R.S.
16. Simpson, W.H.	26. Vandenberg, Hoyt S.
17. Doolittle, James H.	27. Littlejohn, R. McG.
18. Eddy, M.S.	28. Lee, John C.H.
19. Haislip, Wade H.	29. Huebner, C.R.
20. Corlett, Charles H.	30. Harmon, Ernest H.
21. Devers, Jacob L.	31. Ridgway, Matthew B.
22. Eaker, Ira C.	32. Van Fleet, J.A.

Regarding Eisenhower's ratings, however, by April 26, 1945, in a letter to Marshall on commanders who might go on to serve in the Pacific, for which Hodges had already been chosen, the Supreme Commander commended Bradley most highly and went on to say: "In Europe there are other men who have been thoroughly tested as high combat commanders, including Simpson, Patch, Patton, Gerow, Collins, Truscott, and others. Any one of these can successfully lead an army in combat in the toughest kind of conditions." *Papers of Eisenhower*, IV, 2647–2648, quotation from p.2648. The implication is that Simpson had risen in Eisenhower's ratings.

Chapter Twenty-Four: On the Eve of a Breakthrough

1. Charles B. MacDonald, *The Siegfried Line Campaign (United States Army in World War II: The European Theater of Operations*, Washington: Office of the Chief of Military History, 1963), p.326.

2. To Lieutenant General Thomas T. Handy, Deputy Chief of Staff of the Army, Dec. 5, 1944; Martin Blumenson, *The Patton Papers* (2 vols., Boston: Houghton Mifflin, 1972–1974), II, 587.

3. John S.D. Eisenhower, *The Bitter Woods* (New York: Putnam, 1969), p.173. Eisenhower prints the main text of the intelligence summary.

4. Dec. 1, 1944; Alfred D. Chandler, Jr., ed., Stephen E. Ambrose, assoc. ed., et al., *The Papers of Dwight David Eisenhower: The War Years* (5 vols., Baltimore: Johns Hopkins Press, 1970), IV, 2324.

5. Forrest C. Pogue, *The Supreme Command (United States Army in World War II: The European Theater of Operations*, Washington: Office of the Chief of Military History, 1954), p.312.

6. Dec. 2, 1944; Chandler, ed., *Papers of Eisenhower*, IV, 2326.

7. *The Memoirs of Field-Marshal the Viscount Montgomery of Alamein* (Cleveland and New York: World, 1958), pp.270–274, quotations from pp.270, 272. See also "Notes of Meeting at Maastricht on 7.12.1944 between S.A.C., Field Marshal Montgomery, General Bradley, and DISAC," DSC/TS.100/12, 8th December, 1944, NA, RG 331, Box 77, SHAEF, Vol. II.

8. Montgomery, *Memoirs*, p.274.

MacDonald, *Siegfried Line Campaign* and H.M. Cole, *The Lorraine Campaign (United States Army in World War II: The European Theater of Operations*, Washington: Historical Division, Department of the Army, 1950) remain the essential operational narratives for the First and Third Armies, respectively. See also "Breaking the Siegfried Line" (2 vols., ms. in CMH), II.

Conquer: The Story of Ninth Army, 1944–1945 (Washington: Infantry Journal Press, 1947) supplements MacDonald's *Siegfried Line Campaign* with one of the clearest concise descriptions of the Roer dams.

For divisions that fought for the Monschau corridor, see *Lightning: The History of the 78th Infantry Division* (Washington: Infantry Journal Press, 1947) and Walter E. Lauer, *Battle Babies: The Story of the 99th Infantry Division in World War II* (Baton Rouge: Military Press of Louisiana, 1951). Possibly the best personal narrative describing

combat experience in World War II written by an American begins with the late autumn
operations of the 2nd Infantry Division along the German-Luxembourg border: Charles
B. MacDonald, *Company Commander* (Washington: Infantry Journal Press, 1947).

On the relief of "P" Wood, see in addition to the Patton biographies Hanson W.
Baldwin, *Tiger Jack* (Ft. Collins, Colo.: Old Army Press, 1979); and for General Eddy's
belief that Wood's relief was necessary, Hobart R. Gay Diary, p.589, Nov. 1, 1944,
USAMHI.

Chapter Twenty-Five: The Breakthrough

1. Rosengarten, Memorandum for Colonel Telford W. Taylor, 21 May 1945, p.5, in
"Reports by U.S. Army ULTRA Representatives with Army Field Commands in the European
Theatre of Operations," NA, RG 457, N.S.A., SRH-023, Part I, Tab C.

2. Chester B. Hansen Diaries, USAMHI, Dec. 16, 1944.

3. John S.D. Eisenhower, *The Bitter Woods* (New York: Putnam, 1969), p.215.

4. Dwight D. Eisenhower, *Crusade in Europe* (Garden City: Doubleday, 1948), p.337.

5. J.S.D. Eisenhower, *Bitter Woods*, p.215, for quotation; also D.D. Eisenhower,
Crusade in Europe, pp.343–344; Omar N. Bradley, *A Soldier's Story* (New York: Holt, 1951),
p.465.

6. Forrest C. Pogue, *The Supreme Command (United States Army in World War II: The
European Theater of Operations*, Washington: Office of the Chief of Military History, 1954),
p.363.

7. Ibid., p.366.

8. Ibid., pp.366–369, quotations from pp.369, 368, 367, 366, 367, 368.

9. Rosengarten, Memorandum for Col. Taylor, 21 May 1945, p.5.

10. Pogue, *Supreme Command*, p.370.

11. Rosengarten, Memorandum for Col. Taylor, 21 May 1945, p.8.

12. Pogue, *Supreme Command*, p.365n, based on Strong to Pogue, 31 August 1951. On
the other hand, Strong gave a relatively optimistic assessment of the effect of constant Allied
attack in denying the enemy the opportunity to accumulate reserves; Office of the Assistant
Chief of Staff G-2 to Chief of Staff, G131/OI-A/091-3, 29th November, 1944, NA, RG 331, Box
114, SHAEF OC of S, Order of Battle Germany, Vol. I.

13. Bradley, *Soldier's Story*, p.459.

14. Ibid., pp.455, 447.

15. Ibid., p.455.

16. J.S.D. Eisenhower, *Bitter Woods*, pp.172–173.

17. Ibid., p.165.

18. Chester Wilmot, *The Struggle for Europe* (New York: Harper, 1952), especially
pp.612–614 on Bradley; John Strawson, *The Battle for the Ardennes* (London: Batsford, 1972),
especially pp.65–66, 115–119.

Around the Battle of the Ardennes has developed the richest literature of any battle
on the Western Front in World War II. The American official history is Hugh M. Cole,
*The Ardennes: Battle of the Bulge (United States Army in World War II: The European
Theater of Operations*, Washington: Office of the Chief of Military History, 1965). J.S.D.
Eisenhower's *The Bitter Woods* is another richly detailed account. Strawson's *Battle for the
Ardennes* is useful for a British perspective nevertheless bound by fairness to the Amer-
icans and for its fresh appraisals of commanders by an experienced general officer. Robert
E. Merriam, *Dark December* (Chicago: Ziff-Davis, 1947) offers the vividness of proximity
in time to the events it describes.

Other noteworthy general accounts of the battle include John Toland, *Battle: The
Story of the Bulge* (New York: Random House, 1959); Peter Elstob, *The Last Offensive:
The Full Story of the Battle of the Ardennes* (New York: Macmillan, 1971), another British
account; a French version, Jacques Nobécourt, *Le Dernier coup de dés de Hitler* (Paris:
Robert Laffort, 1967; *Hitler's Last Gamble: The Battle of the Bulge*, tr. R.H. Barry [New
York: Schocken, 1967]); and a number of German accounts: Hermann Jung, *Die
Ardennen-Offensive, 1944/45: Ein Beispiel für die Kriegführung Hitlers* (Zürich and Frank-

furt: Musterschmidt Göttingen, 1971); Heinz Kessler, *Der letzte Coup: Die Ardennenoffensive, 1944* (Berlin: Deutscher Militärverlag, 1966); Franz Kurowski, *Von den Ardennen zum Ruhrkessel: Das Ende an der Westfront* (Herford and Bonn: Maximilian-Verlag, 1965).

The tragic history of the 106th Division inspired the writing of one of the better divisional histories, R. Ernest Dupuy, *St. Vith: Lion in the Way: The 106th Infantry Division in World War II* (Washington: Infantry Journal Press, 1949).

Chapter Twenty-Six: The Doctrinal Response

1. Chester Wilmot, *The Struggle for Europe* (New York: Harper, 1952), p.575.
2. Hugh M. Cole, *The Ardennes: Battle of the Bulge (United States Army in World War II: The European Theater of Operations*, Washington: Office of the Chief of Military History, 1965), p.187.
3. LTC Adolph G. Rosengarten, Jr., Memorandum for Colonel Telford W. Taylor, 21 May 1945, p.5, in "Reports by U.S. Army ULTRA Representatives with Army Field Commands in the European Theatre of Operations," NA, RG 457, N.S.A., SRH-023, Part I, Tab C.
4. *The Battle at St. Vith, Belgium, 17–23 December 1944* ([Fort Knox, Ky.:] U.S. Army Armor School, [1963]), p.7.
5. Cole, *Ardennes*, p.395.
6. John S.D. Eisenhower, *The Bitter Woods* (New York: Putnam, 1969), p.286.
7. Ibid., p.299, for Clarke quotation; ibid., pp.300–301, or Cole, *Ardennes*, p.412, for Hasbrouck quotation.

The works on the Ardennes battle cited in chapter 25 remain pertinent. *The Battle at St. Vith* and Seventh Armored Division Association, *The Seventh Armored Division in the Battle of St. Vith* (Baltimore: E. John Schmitz & Sons, 1948) chronicle one of the critical defensive stands, while the defense of Bastogne has nourished a larger literature, including Fred MacKenzie, *The Men of Bastogne* (New York: McKay, 1968) and S.L.A. Marshall, *Bastogne: The First Eight Days* (Washington: Infantry Journal Press, 1946). Frank James Price, *Troy H. Middleton: A Biography* (Baton Rouge: Louisiana State University Press, 1974) recounts the trials of the VIII Corps and its headquarters. Matthew B. Ridgway, as told to Harold H. Martin, *Soldier: The Memoirs of Matthew B. Ridgway* (New York: Harper, 1956) and James M. Gavin, *On to Berlin: Battles of an Airborne Commander, 1943–1946* (New York: Viking, 1978) offer first-hand accounts of the XVIII Airborne Corps and, in Gavin's book, the defensive preparations and actions of the 82nd Airborne Division in particular.

Charles B. MacDonald, *Company Commander* (Washington: Infantry Journal Press, 1947) is excellent as usual in recapturing the atmosphere of the retreat of the 2nd Division to the Elsenborn Ridge. For General Robertson's wish for a 90mm. tank gun, see Cole, *Ardennes*, p.125.

On the Malmédy massacre, there is James J. Weingartner, *Crossroads of Death: The Story of the Malmédy Massacre and Trial* (Berkeley: University of California Press, 1973).

Chapter Twenty-Seven: The Precarious Balance

1. Chester B. Hansen Diaries, USAMHI, Dec. 19 (for descriptions of staff officers), 17 (for Bradley quotations), 1944.
2. SHAEF Main from Dickson and Strong to SHAEF Rear, Ref. No. S-71478, 19 Dec. 1944, NA, RG 331, Box 114, SHAEF SGS, German Counter Offensive, Vol. I.
3. Summary of JIC report 22 Dec., to SHAEF Main 27 Dec. 1944, Ref. No. 7550, NA, RG 331, Box 114, SHAEF SGS, German Counter Offensive, Vol. I.
4. Ibid.
5. From Headquarters COM Zone, ETO, signed Lee, Ref. No. EX-77284, 21 Dec. 1944, Intelligence appreciation No. 1, NA, RG 331, Box 114, SHAEF SGS, German Counter Offensive, Vol. I.

6. From Air Staff SHAEF, Ref. No. AI346, 21 Dec. 1944, NA, RG 331, Box 114, SHAEF SGS, German Counter Offensive, Vol. I.

7. Michelin Red Guide, *Benelux*, 1963 ed. (Paris: Pneu Michelin Services de Tourisme, 1963), p.124.

8. Hansen Diaries, Dec. 19, 1944.

9. Alfred D. Chandler, Jr., ed., Stephen E. Ambrose, assoc. ed., et al., *The Papers of Dwight David Eisenhower: The War Years* (5 vols., Baltimore: Johns Hopkins University Press, 1970), IV, 2355.

10. Ibid., p.2356.

11. Dwight D. Eisenhower, *Crusade in Europe* (Garden City: Doubleday, 1948), p.351.

12. Ibid., p.350.

13. Omar N. Bradley, *A Soldier's Story* (New York: Holt, 1951), p.470.

14. Martin Blumenson, *The Patton Papers* (2 vols., Boston: Houghton Mifflin, 1972–1974), II, 595.

15. Ibid., p.582.

16. Ladislas Farago, *Patton: Ordeal and Triumph* (paperback, New York: Dell, 1970), p.665.

17. Nov. 23, 1944; Oscar W. Koch, with Robert G. Hays, *G-2: Intelligence for Patton* (Philadelphia: Whitmore Publishing Co., 1971), p.82.

18. Farago, *Patton*, p.673.

19. Bradley, *Soldier's Story*, p.469.

20. D.D. Eisenhower, *Crusade in Europe*, p.350.

21. Ibid.; Eisenhower's words also appear in a dispatch to the Combined Chiefs of Staff, Dec. 19, 1944, Chandler, ed., *Papers of Eisenhower*, IV, 2358–2359.

22. Charles R. Codman, *Drive* (Boston: Little, Brown, 1957), p.232. Blumenson, *Patton Papers*, II, 599.

23. Ibid., p.600.

24. Kenneth Macksey, *Guderian: Creator of the Blitzkrieg* (New York: Stein & Day, 1976), pp.154, 124.

25. D.D. Eisenhower, *Crusade in Europe*, p.351.

26. Ibid., pp.351–352.

27. Chandler, ed., *Papers of Eisenhower*, IV, 2358. The text is of a message to the Combined Chiefs; p.2359n notes that a similar message went to Montgomery.

28. Ibid., p.2361.

29. Bradley, *Soldier's Story*, p.476.

30. Hansen Diaries, April 24, 1945.

31. *The Memoirs of Field-Marshal the Viscount Montgomery of Alamein* (Cleveland and New York: World, 1958), p.276.

32. Hugh M. Cole, *The Ardennes: Battle of the Bulge (United States Army in World War II: The European Theater of Operations*, Washington: Office of the Chief of Military History, 1965), p.557.

33. Chester Wilmot, *The Struggle for Europe* (New York: Harper, 1952), p.587n.

34. Bradley, *Soldier's Story*, p.477. Hansen Diaries, Dec. 19, 1944.

35. Montgomery, *Memoirs*, pp.275, 276. For "Christ come to cleanse the temple," Wilmot, *Struggle for Europe*, p.592.

36. Cole, *Ardennes*, p.413.

The previously cited accounts of the Ardennes continue to apply. For Peiper, see Robert Daley, "The Case of the SS Hero," *New York Times Magazine*, Nov. 7, 1976, pp.32–33, 102–111.

Chapter Twenty-Eight: The Battles of Christmastide

1. Michelin Red Guide, *Benelux*, 1963 edition (Paris: Pneu Michelin Services de Tourisme, 1963), p.61.

2. John S.D. Eisenhower, *The Bitter Woods* (New York: Putnam, 1969), pp.322–323.

3. Hugh M. Cole, *The Ardennes: Battle of the Bulge (United States Army in World War II: The European Theater of Operations*, Washington: Office of the Chief of Military History, 1965), p.472.

4. Ibid., p.475.

5. Ibid., p.480.

6. Omar N. Bradley, *A Soldier's Story* (New York: Holt, 1951), p.473.

7. Ladislas Farago, *Patton: Ordeal and Triumph* (paperback, New York: Dell, 1970), p.683.

8. J.S.D. Eisenhower, *Bitter Woods*, p.336, for "Drive like hell"; Nat Frankel and Larry Smith, *Patton's Best: An Informal History of the 4th Armored Division* (New York: Hawthorn, 1978), p.94.

9. SHAEF Main to EXFOR, 12th Army Group, 6th Army Group, Ref. No. S72069, 22 Dec. 1944, NA, RG 331, Box 114, SHAEF SGS, German Counter Offensive, Vol. I.

10. George S. Patton, Jr., *War as I Knew It* (Boston: Houghton Mifflin, 1947), p.342.

11. Cole, *Ardennes*, p.526.

12. Frankel and Smith, *Patton's Best*, p.95.

13. Martin Blumenson, *The Patton Papers* (2 vols., Boston: Houghton Mifflin, 1972–1974), II, 606.

14. EXFOR Main from Williams to SHAEF Main for GSI/G-2, Ref. No. GI-152, 24 Dec. 1944, NA, RG 133, Box 114, SHAEF SGS, German Counter Offensive, Vol. I.

15. Chester Wilmot, *The Struggle for Europe* (New York: Harper, 1952), p.597.

16. EXFOR Main from Neville to SHAEF Main PWD for McClure, Ref. No. PPW 88, 27 Dec. 1944, p.1, NA, RG 331, Box 114, SHAEF SGS, German Counter Offensive, Vol. I.

17. SHAEF Main from Strong to PWD SHAEF Rear for ELECTRA, Ref. No. S-72532, 26 Dec. 1944, NA, RG 331, Box 114, SHAEF SGS, German Counter Offensive, Vol. I.

18. Wilmot, *Struggle for Europe*, p.598.

19. J.S.D. Eisenhower, *Bitter Woods*, p.369.

20. Ibid., p.370.

The accounts of the Ardennes cited in chapter 26 remain pertinent. The uncommonly good divisional histories of the 2nd Armored and the 84th Infantry, cited in chapter 23, detail much of the fighting on the northwest flank of the German salient.

Chapter Twenty-Nine: Attack in the Ardennes (II)

1. Dec. 22, 1944; Alfred D. Chandler, Jr., ed., Stephen E. Ambrose, assoc. ed., et al., *The Papers of Dwight David Eisenhower: The War Years* (5 vols., Baltimore: Johns Hopkins Press, 1970), IV, 2369.

2. Ibid., pp.2361, 2362.

3. Dec. 23, 1944; ibid., pp.2374–2375.

4. Forrest C. Pogue, *The Supreme Command (United States Army in World War II: The European Theater of Operations*, Washington: Office of the Chief of Military History, 1954), p.382.

5. Chester B. Hansen Diaries, USAMHI, Dec. 25, 1944.

6. Arthur Bryant, *Triumph in the West: A History of the War Years Based on the Diaries of Field-Marshal Lord Alanbrooke, Chief of the Imperial General Staff* (Garden City: Doubleday, 1957), p.278.

7. Hugh M. Cole, *The Ardennes: Battle of the Bulge (United States Army in World War II: The European Theater of Operations*, Washington: Office of the Chief of Military History, 1965), p.610.

8. John S.D. Eisenhower, *The Bitter Woods* (New York: Putnam, 1969), p.379.

9. J.I.C. (44)512(0) (Revised Final), 27th Dec., 1944, War Cabinet Joint Intelligence Sub-Committee, "German Ability to Sustain the Present Counter-Offensive," pp.1, 4, NA, RG 331, Box 114, SHAEF SGS, German Counter Offensive, Vol. I.

10. EXFOR Main from Neville to SHAEF Main PWD for McClure, Ref. No. PPW 88, 27 Dec. 1944; EXFOR Main from Williams to SHAEF Main for GSI/G-2, Ref. No. GI-157, 27 Dec. 1944, both in NA, RG 331, Box 114, SHAEF SGS, German Counter Offensive, Vol. I.

11. *The Memoirs of Field-Marshal the Viscount Montgomery of Alamein* (Cleveland and New York: World, 1958), pp.284–285.

12. Pogue, *Supreme Command*, p.386.

13. Chandler, ed., *Papers of Eisenhower*, IV, 2387.

14. Montgomery, *Memoirs*, p.286.

15. Ibid., p.289.

16. Chandler, ed., *Papers of Eisenhower*, IV, 2388, 2364, 2370.

17. Ibid., pp.2384, 2388.

18. Montgomery, *Memoirs*, p.279.

19. Martin Blumenson, *The Patton Papers* (2 vols., Boston: Houghton Mifflin, 1972–1974), II, 615.

20. *On War*, Book One, Chaper Seven. Carl von Clausewitz, *On War*, tr. and ed. Michael Howard and Peter Paret (Princeton: Princeton University Press, 1976), p.119.

21. Chandler, ed., *Papers of Eisenhower*, IV, 2388.

22. EXFOR Main from Williams to SHAEF Main for GSI/G-2, Ref. No. GI-157, 27 Dec. 1944.

23. Dec. 19, 1944; Chandler, ed., *Papers of Eisenhower*, IV, 2359.

24. Devers to Eisenhower, Ref. No. B-22132, 31 Dec. 1944, p.2, NA, RG 331, Box 114, SHAEF SGS, German Counter Offensive, Vol. I.

25. Ibid.

26. Ibid., pp.2–3.

27. John Frayn Turner and Robert Jackson, *Destination Berchtesgaden: The Story of the United States Seventh Army in World War II* (New York: Scribner's, 1975), p.106.

28. Stephen E. Ambrose, *The Supreme Commander: The War Years of General Dwight D. Eisenhower* (Garden City: Doubleday, 1970), p. 577, from Air Marshal J.M. Robb's notes of Jan. 1 conference, Eisenhower Manuscripts, Eisenhower Library.

29. Dec. 25, 1944; Blumenson, *Patton Papers*, II, 606.

30. *The Seventh United States Army Report of Operations, France and Germany, 1944–1945* (3 vols., Heidelberg: Aloys Graf, 1946), II, 596, 598.

31. Blumenson, *Patton Papers*, II, 621–622.

32. Bradley, *Soldier's Story*, p.492.

33. Ibid., p.484.

34. Sir Francis de Guingand, *Operation Victory* (London: Hodder & Stoughton, 1947), p.434.

35. Montgomery, *Memoirs*, p.279.

36. Ibid., pp.280, 281; John Strawson, *The Battle for the Ardennes* (London: Batsford, 1972), pp.163, 173; Bradley, *Soldier's Story*, p.488.

37. *On War*, Book One, chapter 1. Howard & Paret edition, p.75. On Montgomery's efforts to read Clausewitz, see Field-Marshal Viscount Montgomery of Alamein, *A History of Warfare* (Cleveland: World, 1968), pp.20, 415.

38. George S. Patton, Jr., *War As I Knew It* (Boston: Houghton Mifflin, 1947), p.213.

39. Jan. 16, 1945; Blumenson, *Patton Papers*, II, 625.

40. Ibid., p.612.

The accounts of the Ardennes cited in chapter 26 also apply to this chapter. For the NORDWIND counteroffensive in Alsace *The Seventh United States Army Report of Operations* is the most detailed and useful account. For the 42nd Division, see Hugh C. Daley, ed., *42nd "Rainbow" Infantry Division: A Combat History of World War II* (Baton Rouge: Army Navy Publishing Co., 1946).

Chapter Thirty: "Inadequate Means"

1. The diary entry is dated Jan. 6, 1945, the letter to Stimson Jan. 10; Martin Blumenson, *The Patton Papers* (2 vols., Boston: Houghton Mifflin, 1972–1974), II, 616, 620.

2. Ulysses Lee, *The Employment of Negro Troops (United States Army in World War II: Special Studies*, Washington: Office of the Chief of Military History, 1966), p.689.

3. Ibid., p.690.

4. Stephen E. Ambrose, *The Supreme Commander: The War Years of General Dwight D. Eisenhower* (Garden City: Doubleday, 1970), p.560.

5. Lee, *Employment of Negro Troops*, pp.690–691, quotation from p.691.

6. Ibid., p.690.

7. Alfred D. Chandler, Jr., ed., Stephen E. Ambrose, assoc. ed., et al., *The Papers of Dwight David Eisenhower: The War Years* (5 vols., Baltimore: Johns Hopkins Press, 1970), IV, 2408–2409.

8. The remark was Colonel James Polk's; Blumenson, *Patton Papers*, II, 605.

9. "G-2 Special Summary Number 9 Dated 3 January," Ref. No. S-73566, NA, RG 331, Box 114, SHAEF SGS, German Counter Offensive, Vol. II.

10. William C. Sylvan Diary, copy obtained from NA, 1 Jan 1944 (actually 1945), p.156.

On issues of manpower and matériel, divisions and reinforcements, availability of ammunition and guns, the indispensable study remains Roland G. Ruppenthal, *Logistical Support of the Armies*, II, *September 1944–May 1945 (United States Army in World War II: The European Theater of Operations*, Washington: Office of the Chief of Military History, 1959). Lee, *Employment of Negro Troops* is the special authority on black reinforcements. On the problem of building a SHAEF reserve, see also "Administrative and Logistical History of the European Theater of Operations," CMH, especially Pt. V, Vol. II, pp.140–160.

The statistics on German strength in the West are from Chester Wilmot, *The Struggle for Europe* (New York: Harper, 1952), p.621. For the figures on German fighter production, see Wesley Frank Craven and James Lea Cate, eds., *The Army Air Forces in World War II* (7 vols., Chicago: University of Chicago Press, 1948–1958), III, *Europe: ARGUMENT to V-E Day*, p.658. For Luftwaffe sorties on December 17, ibid., p.687; the Luftwaffe flew only about 150 sorties on December 16, the first day of the Ardennes counteroffensive, its activity restricted both by the weather and by the desire to avoid early disclosure of the full force of the German effort (ibid.).

The figures on opposing strength in the Ardennes are drawn from Hugh M. Cole, *The Ardennes: Battle of the Bulge (United States Army in World War II: The European Theater of Operations*, Washington: Office of the Chief of Military History, 1965), p.650; on losses Dec. 16–Jan. 2, ibid., p.674; on losses Jan. 3–28 and German losses, Charles B. MacDonald, *The Last Offensive (United States Army in World War II: The European Theater of Operations*, Washington: Office of the Chief of Military History, 1973), p.53. Drew Middleton is quoted in Cole, *Ardennes*, p.675.

Chapter Thirty-One: The Eifel

1. Alfred D. Chandler, Jr., ed., Stephen E. Ambrose, assoc. ed., et al., *The Papers of Dwight David Eisenhower: The War Years* (5 vols., Baltimore: Johns Hopkins Press, 1970), IV, 2388 (for Dec. 31 directive), 2412–2414, quotations from pp.2413, 2414.

2. Forrest C. Pogue, *The Supreme Command (United States Army in World War II: The European Theater of Operations*, Washington: Office of the Chief of Military History, 1954), p.414; the quotation from Eisenhower appears also in Chandler, ed., *Papers of Eisenhower*, IV, 2463.

3. To Marshall, also Jan. 10, 1945; Chandler, ed., *Papers of Eisenhower*, IV, 2415.

4. To Marshall, Jan. 15, 1945; ibid., pp.2431–2432; to Montgomery, Jan. 17, 1945, ibid., p.2438.

5. To Montgomery, Bradley, Devers, and Brereton, Jan. 18, 1945; ibid., pp.2439–2440, quotation from p.2440.

6. Martin Blumenson, *The Patton Papers* (2 vols., Boston: Houghton Mifflin, 1972–1974), II, 628.

7. Ibid., p.629.

8. Ibid.

9. Charles B. MacDonald, *The Last Offensive (United States Army in World War II: The European Theater of Operations*, Washington: Office of the Chief of Military History, 1973), p.63.

10. Matthew B. Ridgway, as told to Harold H. Martin, *Soldier: The Memoirs of Matthew B. Ridgway* (New York: Harper, 1956), pp.127 (first quotation), 128.

11. William C. Sylvan Diary, copy obtained from NA, 1 Feb. 1945, p.182.

12. MacDonald, *Last Offensive*, pp.67–68.

13. George S.Patton, Jr., *War as I Knew It* (Boston: Houghton Mifflin, 1947), p.125.

14. Ibid., p.244.

15. In a letter to Mrs. Patton, Feb. 25, 1945; Blumenson, *Patton Papers*, II, 647–648.

16. Ibid., p.652.

MacDonald, *Last Offensive* is the basic narrative of the Eifel campaign. For the XVIII Airborne Corps in the campaign, see Ridgway, *Soldier*, and for the 82nd Airborne Division, James M. Gavin, *On to Berlin: Battles of an Airborne Commander, 1943–1946* (New York: Viking, 1978). For the 87th Division, there is *An Historical and Pictorial Review of the 87th Infantry Division in World War II, 1942–1945* (7 vols. bound in 1, Baton Rouge: Army Navy Publishing Co., 1946); for the 94th, Laurence G. Byrnes, ed., *History of the 94th Infantry Division in World War II* (Washington: Infantry Journal Press, 1948); for the 8th Armored, Charles R. Leach, *In Tornado's Wake: A History of the 8th Armored Division* (Chicago: Eighth Armored Division, Argus Press, 1956).

Chapter Thirty-Two: Two Tumors Excised

1. Alfred D. Chandler, Jr., ed., Stephen E. Ambrose, assoc. ed., et al., *The Papers of Dwight David Eisenhower: The War Years* (5 vols., Baltimore: Johns Hopkins Press, 1970), IV, 2431.

2. Forrest C. Pogue, *The Supreme Command (United States Army in World War II: The European Theater of Operations*, Washington: Office of the Chief of Military History, 1954), p.403.

3. James M. Gavin, *On to Berlin: Battles of an Airborne Commander, 1943–1946* (New York: Viking, 1978), p.261.

4. Chester B. Hansen Diaries, USAMHI, Feb. 11 and 12, 1945.

5. Gavin, *On to Berlin*, pp.232–233.

6. CG XIII Corps, 8 Feb. 1945, "Operation GRENADE," p.3, NA, RG 331, Box 67, Hdqrs. 12th Army Group, Special Staff, 370.2 GRENADE.

For the elimination of the Colmar pocket see *The Seventh United States Army Report of Operations, France and Germany, 1944–1945* (3 vols., Heidelberg: Aloys Graf, 1946). Devers's G-3, Brig. Gen. Reuben E. Jenkins, wrote for Devers an aide memoire on relations with the French, highly critical of those Allies, reviewing in detail the Jebsheim and Grussenheim battles; Jenkins to Devers, 24 Feb. 1946, Jenkins Papers, USAMHI, For the French perspective see of course Général de Lattre de Tassigny, *Histoire de la Première Armée Française: Rhin et Danube* (Paris: Plon, 1948).

Charles B. MacDonald, *The Last Offensive (United States Army in World War II: The European Theater of Operations*, Washington: Office of the Chief of Military History, 1973), recounts the fight for the Roer dams in detail. For the 78th Division, there is *Lightning: The History of the 78th Infantry Division* (Washington: Infantry Journal Press, 1947).

For the GRENADE preparations, see *Conquer: The Story of Ninth Army, 1944–1945* (Washington: Infantry Journal Press, 1947).

Chapter Thirty-Three: To the Rhine

1. 21 Army Group, General Situation, 21 Jan. 1945, p. 7, NA, RG 331, Box 77, SHAEF, Vol. III; Charles B. MacDonald, *The Last Offensive (United States Army in World War II: The*

European Theater of Operations, Washington: Office of the Chief of Military History, 1973), p.143.

2. Theodore Draper, *The 84th Infantry Division in the Battle of Germany, November 1944–May 1945* (New York: Viking, 1946), p.184.

3. Donald E. Houston, *Hell on Wheels: The 2d Armored Division* (San Rafael: Presidio, 1977), p.396.

4. Ibid.

5. For Bradley's characterization of the Ninth Army as "uncommonly normal," Omar N. Bradley, *A Soldier's Story* (New York: Holt, 1951), p.422; for Simpson's assurances about working with Montgomery, Simpson to Eisenhower, CPA 90378, 1 January 1945, NA, RG 331, Box 114, SHAEF OC of S, SGS, German Counter Offensive, Vol. I.

6. William C. Sylvan Diary, copy obtained from NA, 26 Feb. 1945, p.197; 27 Feb., p.199.

7. MacDonald, *Last Offensive*, p.202.

8. Bradley, *Soldier's Story*, p.509.

For GRENADE, there is the excellent history of Simpson's army, *Conquer: The Story of Ninth Army, 1944–1945* (Washington: Infantry Journal Press, 1947), supplemented by the equally excellent histories of the 84th Infantry and 2nd Armored Divisions cited above. For the XVI Corps, there is *History of the XVI Corps from Its Activation to the End of the War in Europe* (Washington: Infantry Journal Press, 1947); on the 102nd Division, Allen H. Mick, ed., *With the 102nd Infantry Division through Germany* (Washington: Infantry Journal Press, 1947).

For the statistics of German strength on the Eastern Front, see Chester Wilmot, *The Struggle for Europe* (New York: Harper, 1952), pp.617, 621–622, 624, 663–664.

On Operation VERITABLE, there is one of the best of the volumes of *Ballantine's Illustrated History of World War II:* Peter Elstob, *Battle of the Reichswald* (New York: Ballantine, 1970).

MacDonald, *Last Offensive* remains the basic narrative covering the Ninth, First, and Third Army operations described in this chapter. On the VII Corps in GRENADE, see J. Lawton Collins, *Lightning Joe: An Autobiography* (Baton Rouge: Louisiana State University Press, 1979).

Chapter Thirty-Four: The Crossing of the Rhine

1. Alfred D. Chandler, Jr., ed., Stephen E. Ambrose, assoc. ed., et al., *The Papers of Dwight David Eisenhower: The War Years* (5 vols., Baltimore: Johns Hopkins Press, 1970), IV, 2454.

2. Omar N. Bradley, *A Soldier's Story* (New York: Holt, 1951), p.513.

3. Chandler, ed., *Papers of Eisenhower*, IV, 2452.

4. [SHAEF] G-3 Division (Main), "Operations East of the Rhine," GCT/370–55/Plans, 12 Feb. 1945, pp.1, 4–5, 6, 3, 2, NA, RG 331, Box 94, SHAEF, 370.2 Operations & Reports; Bradley, *Soldier's Story*, p.513, for the characterization—by Bull—of Eisenhower's mind as "up north."

5. Winston S. Churchill, *The Second World War* (6 vols., Boston: Houghton Mifflin, 1948–1953), VI, *Triumph and Tragedy*, pp.408–410, 411–412.

6. William C. Sylvan Diary, copy obtained from NA, 5 March 1945, p.205.

7. Ibid., 7 March 1945, p.206.

8. Bradley, *Soldier's Story*, p.511.

9. Chester B. Hansen Diaries, USAMHI, March 7, 1945.

10. Bradley, *Soldier's Story*, p.511.

11. Hansen Diaries, March 7, 1945.

12. Ibid.

13. Martin Blumenson, *The Patton Papers* (2 vols., Boston: Houghton Mifflin, 1971–1974), II, 651.

14. Sylvan Diary, 15 March 1945, p. 213; 17 March, p.215.

15. 21 Army Group, General Situation, 21 Jan. 1945, p.1 NA, RG 331, Box 77, SHAEF, Vol. III.

16. Hq. 3d Inf. Div., Field Order Number 2, Operation "EARTHQUAKE," 13 March 1945, enclosed with [SHAEF] A.C. of S. G-3 to Chief of Staff, 17 March 1945, NA, RG 331, Box 77, SHAEF, Vol. III.

17. George S. Patton, Jr., *War As I Knew It* (Boston: Houghton Mifflin, 1947), pp.265–266.

18. Charles B. MacDonald, *The Last Offensive (United States Army in World War II: The European Theater of Operations*, Washington: Office of the Chief of Military History, 1973), p.258.

19. George F. Howe, *Northwest Africa: Seizing the Initiative in the West (United States Army in World War II: The Mediterranean Theater of Operations*, Washington: Office of the Chief of Military History, 1957), p.521.

20. *The Memoirs of Field-Marshal the Viscount Montgomery of Alamein* (Cleveland and New York: World, 1958), p.294.

21. W.G.F. Jackson, *The Battle for North Africa, 1940–43* (New York: Mason/Charter, 1975), pp.378, 380.

22. Chandler, ed., *Papers of Eisenhower*, IV, 2537.

23. Bradley, *Soldier's Story*, p.521.

24. MacDonald, *Last Offensive*, p.303.

25. Dwight D. Eisenhower, *Crusade in Europe* (Garden City: Doubleday, 1948), p.389.

26. Ibid., pp.388, 389.

Ken Hechler, *The Bridge at Remagen* (New York: Ballantine, 1957) grew out of the author's research for the Office of the Chief of Military History and is excellent. The Rhine crossings and particularly the capture of the Remagen bridge are reviewed, largely from interviews with participants, in John Toland, *The Last 100 Days* (New York: Random House, 1966). MacDonald, *Last Offensive* remains indispensable. For the Seventh Army battles, *The Seventh United States Army Report of Operations, France and Germany, 1944–1945* (3 vols., Heidelberg: Aloys Graf, 1946) continues as a richly detailed account. On the 11th Armored Division, see Hal D. Steward, *Thunderbolt* (Washington: 11th Armored Division Association, 1948); on the 14th Armored, Joseph Carter, *The History of the 14th Armored Division (World War II)* (Atlanta: Albert Love Enterprises, 1946).

The incident of Churchill's recalling the last British troops to fight in Germany is described in Montgomery, *Memoirs*, p.295.

Chapter Thirty-Five: Eastward from the Rhine

1. Alfred D. Chandler, Jr., ed., Stephen E. Ambrose, assoc. ed., et al., *The Papers of Dwight David Eisenhower: The War Years* (5 vols., Baltimore: Johns Hopkins Press, 1970), III, 1737.

2. CG FAAA, 31 Mar 45, "Narrative of Operation VARSITY, 31 March 1945," p.2, NA, RG 331, Box 95, SHAEF, 370.2 VARSITY.

3. Ibid.,

4. Winston S. Churchill, *The Second World War* (6 vols., Boston: Houghton Mifflin, 1948–1953), VI, *Triumph and Tragedy*, p.413.

5. Ibid., p.416; Samuel Eliot Morison, *History of United States Naval Operations in World War II* (15 vols., Boston: Little, Brown, 1950–1962), XI, *The Invasion of France and Germany*, p.322n.

6. Chester B. Hansen Diaries, USAMHI, March 26, 28, 1945.

7. Martin Blumenson, *The Patton Papers* (2 vols., Boston: Houghton Mifflin, 1972–1974), II, 666, 667.

8. Chandler, ed., *Papers of Eisenhower*, IV, 2617.

MacDonald, *Last Offensive*, cited in the preceding chapter, continues to offer a detailed review of the events of this chapter. As with all Ninth Army operations, *Conquer: The Story of Ninth Army, 1944–1945* (Washington: Infantry Journal Press, 1947) is indispensable. Matthew B. Ridgway, as told to Harold H. Martin, *Soldier: The Memoirs of Matthew B. Ridgway* (New York: Harper, 1956) recounts the airborne crossing of the Rhine. R.W. Thompson emphasizes British operations in *The Battle for the Rhineland* (London: Hutchinson, 1958). John Toland, *The Last 100 Days* (New York: Random House, 1966) contains a good account of the Hammelburg affair, which can be viewed with the sardonic humor of a 4th Armored Division soldier (though not a participant) in Nat Frankel and Larry Smith, *Patton's Best: An Informal History of the 4th Armored Division* (New York: Hawthorn, 1978).

Chapter Thirty-Six: The Legions on the Rhine

1. Ulysses Lee, *The Employment of Negro Troops (United States Army in World War II: Special Studies*, Washington: Office of the Chief of Military History, 1966), p.694.

2. Ibid. The words are General Lee's, transmitting Eisenhower's wishes to General Ben Lear.

3. Ibid., p.695.

4. Alfred D. Chandler, Jr., ed., Stephen E. Ambrose, assoc. ed., et al., *The Papers of Dwight David Eisenhower: The War Years* (5 vols., Baltimore: Johns Hopkins Press, 1970), IV, 2408.

5. Jan. 8, 1945; ibid., p.2411.

6. Roland G. Ruppenthal, *Logistical Support of the Armies*, II, *September 1944–May 1945 (United States Army in World War II: The European Theater of Operations*, Washington: Office of the Chief of Military History, 1959), p.377.

As usual, Ruppenthal, *Logistical Support of the Armies* offers the basic information on manpower and other resources. There is a table of battle and nonbattle casualties by months on II, 317.

On the replacement system, see also Robert R. Palmer and William R. Keast, "The Provision of Enlisted Replacements," in Robert R. Palmer, Bell I. Wiley, and William R. Keast, *The Procurement and Training of Ground Combat Troops (United States Army in World War II: The Army Ground Forces*, Washington: Historical Division, Department of the Army, 1948), pp.165–239.

Lee, *Employment of Negro Troops* gives the history of black soldiers. In *War as I Knew It* (Boston: Houghton Mifflin, 1947), p.160, Patton said of the black 761st Tank Battalion: "Individually they were good soldiers, but I expressed my belief at that time [when the battalion joined the Third Army], and have never found the necessity of changing it, that a colored soldier cannot think fast enough to fight in armor." For the Black Timberwolves, the black soldiers wielding Panzerfäuste, and other comments more favorable than Patton's, see Chester B. Hansen Diaries, USAMHI, April 13, 1945.

The statistics of Allied strength at the end of March are from a table in Ruppenthal, *Logistical Support*, II, 288, giving such information for each month of the campaign in northwest Europe. There is additional information on numbers of available divisions in Charles B. MacDonald, *The Last Offensive (United States Army in World War II: The European Theater of Operations*, Washington: Office of the Chief of Military History, 1973), pp.322–323.

Chapter Thirty-Seven: The Ruhr

1. Jan. 14, 1945; Alfred D. Chandler, Jr., ed., Stephen E. Ambrose, assoc. ed., et al., *The Papers of Dwight David Eisenhower: The War Year* (5 vols., Baltimore: Johns Hopkins Press, 1970), IV, 2426.

2. William C. Sylvan Diary, copy obtained from NA, 25 March 1945, p.211.

3. Ibid., 26 March 1945, p.211.

4. Chester B. Hansen Diaries, USAMHI, March 28, 1945.

5. To Montgomery, Bradley, and Devers, Sept. 15, 1944; Chandler, ed., *Papers of Eisenhower*, IV, 1957.

6. John Toland, *The Last 100 Days* (New York: Random House, 1966), p.309.

7. Donald E. Houston, *Hell on Wheels: The 2d Armored Division* (San Rafael: Presidio, 1977), p.405.

8. Sylvan Diary, 2 April 1945, p.216.

9. Ibid., 5 April 1945, p.218.

10. Matthew B. Ridgway, as told to Harold H. Martin, *Soldier: The Memoirs of Matthew B. Ridgway* (New York: Harper, 1956), p.140.

   Along with Charles B. MacDonald, *The Last Offensive (United States Army in World War II: The European Theater of Operations*, Washington: Office of the Chief of Military History, 1973) and Toland, *The Last 100 Days*, a detailed narrative of the Ruhr battles is to be found in Charles Whiting, *Battle of the Ruhr Pocket* (New York: Ballantine, 1970). From the German perspective, there is Franz Kurowski, *Von den Ardennen zum Ruhrkessel: Das Ende an der Westfront* (Herford and Bonn: Maximilian Verlag, 1965). For the closing of the pocket, Houston's history of the 2nd Armored Division should be supplemented by the history of the 3rd, *Spearhead in the West, 1941–1945: The Third Armored Division* (Frankfurt am Main: Kunst and Wervedruck, 1945). The latter, appropriately, is dedicated to General Maurice Rose.

   For Hodges's box of cigars from Patton, see Sylvan Diary, 27 March 1945, pp.212–213.

Chapter Thirty-Eight: Berlin

1. William C. Sylvan Diary, copy obtained from NA, 3 April 1945, p.217.

2. Charles B. MacDonald, *The Last Offensive (United States Army in World War II: The European Theater of Operations*, Washington: Office of the Chief of Military History, 1973), p.379.

3. Cornelius Ryan, *The Last Battle* (New York: Simon and Schuster, 1966), p.284.

4. Donald E. Houston, *Hell on Wheels: The 2d Armored Division* (San Rafael: Presidio, 1977), p.403.

5. Ibid.; for "main prize," see note 5, preceding chapter.

6. Ryan, *Last Battle*, pp.135–136.

7. Ibid., p.214 (first paragraph); Alfred D. Chandler, Jr., ed., Stephen E. Ambrose, assoc. ed., et al., *The Papers of Dwight David Eisenhower: The War Years* (5 vols., Baltimore: Johns Hopkins Press, 1970), IV, 2553 (complete second paragraph).

8. Chandler, ed., *Papers of Eisenhower*, IV, 2553.

9. Ibid., p.2552.

10. John Ehrman, *Grand Strategy*, VI (*History of the Second World War: United Kingdom Military Series*, London: H.M. Stationery Office, 1956), 135.

11. Chandler, ed., *Papers of Eisenhower*, IV, 2559 (first quotation, March 30, 1945); 2592 (other quotations, April 7, 1945).

12. Ryan, *Last Battle*, p.241.

13. Chandler, ed., *Papers of Eisenhower*, IV, 2592.

14. Ryan, *Last Battle*, p.292.

15. Houston, *Hell on Wheels*, p.417.

16. Ryan, *Last Battle*, p.309.

17. Ibid., p.315.

18. That is, the 3rd Battalion, 41st Armored Infantry Regiment; Houston, *Hell on Wheels*, p.420.

19. MacDonald, *Last Offensive*, p.387.

20. Ibid.

21. Martin Blumenson, *The Patton Papers* (2 vols., Boston: Houghton Mifflin, 1972–1974), II, 684.

22. Ibid., pp.679–680.

23. Ibid., p.679.

24. Ryan, *Last Battle*, p.292.

25. Blumenson, *Patton Papers*, II, 685.

26. MacDonald, *Last Offensive*, p.399.

27. Omar N. Bradley, *A Soldier's Story* (New York: Holt, 1951), p.535; Chester B. Hansen Diaries, USAMHI, April 12, 1945, for "PM is very vexatious"; MacDonald, *Last Offensive*, p.399, for Bradley's closing words heard by Simpson.

28. Simpson to Charles H. Gerhardt, Aug. 10, 1964, Gerhardt Papers, USAMHI. General Gillem of the XIII Corps not surprisingly retained similar conclusions:

... we arrived at the Elbe on the 12th of April. . . . I was some 48 miles from Berlin and in my very considerate judgment I could have been in Berlin before the Russians arrived for the simple reason that we did have advance parties on the Berlin side of the Elbe immediately. I would not say I had ordered this so as to proceed onto Berlin, but I had very aggressive commanders, who, very wise to get the far bank of any river when you arrived there, and specifically General Bolling I thought was a most able commander, one of the most able that I experienced during the war, and he had one of the leading divisions and I'm sure that Bolling had his people on the other side of the Elbe about the time we arrived on this date. It is my judgment that we could have been in Berlin ahead of the Russians because the distance was relatively nothing; that is, maybe a day and a half march the rates we were making, and German resistance was nonexistent. There was none. (Revised transcript of interview with Gen. Gillem conducted by Dr. Eugene Miller of Ursinus College early in 1972, Gillem Papers, USAMHI, Box 1.)

29. Hansen Diaries, April 19, 1945.

A concise discussion of the policy and strategy issues of the halt short of Berlin, sympathetic to Eisenhower, is Stephen E. Ambrose, *Eisenhower and Berlin, 1945: The Decision to Halt at the Elbe* (New York: Norton, 1967). The issues are also discussed in Ambrose's *The Supreme Commander: The War Years of General Dwight D. Eisenhower* (Garden City: Doubleday, 1970) and Forrest C. Pogue, *The Supreme Command (United States Army in World War II: The European Theater of Operations*, Washington: Office of the Chief of Military History, 1954). Much of Ryan, *Last Battle* and John Toland, *The Last 100 Days* (New York: Random House, 1966) concerns the Berlin question, treating Eisenhower's decision more critically; but on Ryan in particular, see also Ambrose's rejoinder, "Refighting the Last Battle: The Pitfalls of Popular History," *Wisconsin Magazine of History*, XLIX (Summer 1966), 294–301.

MacDonald, *Last Offensive* continues to offer the fullest account of operations. See also *Conquer: The Story of Ninth Army, 1944–1945* (Washington: Infantry Journal Press, 1947); Houston, *Hell on Wheels*; and *Thunderbolt across Europe: A History of the 83d Infantry Division* (Munich: F. Bruckmann Kg., [1945]).

Chapter Thirty-Nine: The National Redoubt

1. Dwight D. Eisenhower, *Crusade in Europe* (Garden City: Doubleday, 1948), p.415; Chester B. Hansen Diaries, USAMHI, March 9, April 7, 1945.

2. [SHAEF] Joint Intelligence Committee, JIC SHAEF(45)3(Final) 10 March 1945, "Ability of the German Army in the West to Continue the War," p.2, NA, RG 331, Box 114, SHAEF OC of S, SGS, German Plans and Operations, 381/1 Germany, Vol. I.

3. Charles B. MacDonald, *The Last Offensive (United States Army in World War II: The European Theater of Operations*, Washington: Office of the Chief of Military History, 1973), p.408.

4. JIC SHAEF(45)13(Final), 10 April 1945, "The National Redoubt," p.1, NA, RG 331, Box 114, SHAEF AC of S, SGS, German Plans and Operations, 381/1 Germany, Vol. I.

5. [SHAEF] Joint Intelligence Committee, JIC(45)17(Final), 20th April, 1945, "Disposition of German Forces after the Junction of the Allied and Russian Armies," quotation from p.1, NA, RG 331, Box 114, SHAEF AC of S, SGS, 381/2 Germany, Vol. II.

6. April 2, 1945; Alfred D. Chandler, Jr., ed., Stephen E. Ambrose, assoc. ed., et al., *The Papers of Dwight David Eisenhower: The War Years* (5 vols., Baltimore: Johns Hopkins University Press, 1970), IV, 2577.

7. From Hobart R. Gay Diary, April 5, 1947; Martin Blumenson, *The Patton Papers* (2 vols., Boston: Houghton Mifflin, 1972–1974), II, 680; William C. Sylvan Diary, copy obtained from NA, 16 April 1945, p.226.

8. Hansen Diaries, April 16, 1945.

9. Ibid., April 13, 1945.

10. Blumenson, *Patton Papers*, II, 690.

11. Hansen Diaries, April 16, 1945.

12. April 21, 1945; Blumenson, *Patton Papers*, II, 692.

13. MacDonald, *Last Offensive*, p.433.

14. Général de Lattre de Tassigny, *Histoire de la Première Armée Française: Rhin et Danube* (Paris: Plon, 1949), p.563.

15. John Frayn Turner and Robert Jackson, *Destination Berchtesgaden: The Story of the United States Seventh Army in World War II* (New York: Scribner's, 1975), p.169.

16. Ibid., p.173.

17. MacDonald, *Last Offensive*, p.442.

18. Hansen Diaries, April 26, 29, 1945.

19. Ibid., April 24, 1945.

Rodney G. Minott, *The Fortress That Never Was* (New York: Holt, Rinehart and Winston, 1964) deals with the National Redoubt. There is a judicious brief appraisal in L.F. Ellis with A.E. Warhurst, *Victory in the West*, II, *The Defeat of Germany (History of the Second World War: United Kingdom Military Series*, London: H.M. Stationery Office, 1968), pp.429–432. Joseph G. Persico, *Piercing the Reich: The Penetration of Nazi Germany by American Secret Agents during World War II* (New York: Viking, 1978) deals largely with efforts to discover the truth about the Redoubt.

MacDonald, *Last Offensive* details the operations reviewed in this chapter. For the Seventh Army's battles, see also *The United States Seventh Army Report of Operations, France and Germany, 1944–1945* (3 vols., Heidelberg: Aloys Graf, 1946). There is a brief manuscript history of "The Battle of the National Redoubt" by Devers's G-3, Brigadier General Reuben E. Jenkins, in the Jenkins Papers, USAMHI. One aspect of 6th Army Group operations is the subject of Boris T. Pask, *The ALSOS Mission* (New York: Award House, 1966).

Chapter Forty: The Elbe, the Moldau, and the Brenner Pass

1. William C. Sylvan Diary, copy obtained from NA, 21 April 1945, p.229.

2. Alfred D. Chandler, Jr., ed., Stephen E. Ambrose, assoc. ed., et al., *The Papers of Dwight David Eisenhower: The War Years* (5 vols., Baltimore: Johns Hopkins Press, 1970), IV, 2652 (for quotation), 2650–2651.

3. Ibid., p.2568.

4. Ibid., p.2594.

5. Chester B. Hansen Diaries, USAMHI, April 23, 1945.

6. Chandler, ed., *Papers of Eisenhower*, IV, 2649.

7. Matthew B. Ridgway, as told to Harold H. Martin, *Soldier: The Memoirs of Matthew B. Ridgway* (New York: Harper, 1956), p.142.

8. Hansen Diaries, April 16, 1945.

9. Chandler, ed., *Papers of Eisenhower*, IV, 2680.

10. Headquarters 6th Army Group, 7 May 1945, "Events Concerning Surrender of Army Group G, Army of the German Reich," quotation from p.2, Reuben E. Jenkins Papers, USAMHI.

MacDonald, *Last Offensive* and *Seventh United States Army Report of Operations*, both cited in the preceding chapter, continue to detail the military operations.

Epilogue

1. Robert M. Utley, "The Contribution of the Frontier to the American Military Tradition," James P. Tate, ed., *The American Military on the Frontier: The Proceedings of the 7th Military History Symposium, United States Air Force Academy, 30 September–1 October 1976* (Washington: Office of Air Force History, Headquarters USAF, and United States Air Force Academy, 1978), p.7.

2. Hanson W. Baldwin, *Tiger Jack* (Ft. Collins, Colo.: Old Army Press, 1979), p.100.

For Allied and German statistics of numbers and losses in the European campaign, see especially the Department of the Army's totals in Charles B. MacDonald, *The Last Offensive (United States Army in World War II: The European Theater of Operations*, Washington: Office of the Chief of Military History, 1973), pp.477–478.

Index